Labels
used in the Guid... F...ar...

disapproving	showing that the us... els disapprov... contempt
figurative	used before examples indicating non...eral or metaphorical usage
formal	usually used in serious or official, especially written, language
humorous	used with the intention of being funny
informal	used in a relaxed or unofficial context, especially in spoken English
ironic	used to mean the opposite of, or something very different from, the apparent meaning
less frequent	becoming less commonly used
offensive	used to address or refer to people in a very insulting way
old-fashioned	passing out of current use and seen as dated
old use	no longer in current use
rare	not often used
slang	very informal, mainly used in speech and sometimes restricted to a particular group of people
spoken	used only in spoken English
written	used only in written English

Noun and adjective types

[C]	countable noun, used in singular and plural forms with *is/are*, etc.; must have a determiner in the singular
[U]	uncountable noun, used in the singular only; can be used without a determiner
[C,U]	noun that can be countable or uncountable
[sing]	singular noun, agreeing with a singular verb
[pl]	plural noun, agreeing with a plural verb
[usually sing]	countable noun, usually singular
[usually pl]	countable noun, usually plural
[C+sing/pl *v*]	countable noun, used in both singular and plural forms but the singular form may also agree with a plural verb
[sing+sing/pl *v*]	singular noun, used with either a singular or plural verb
[not before *n*]	(of adjectives) not used before a noun
[only before *n*]	(of adjectives) only used before a noun
[usu before *n*]	(of adjectives or nouns) usually used before a noun

Verb types

[I]	intransitive
[T]	transitive

cul·ture /ˈkʌltʃə(r)/ *noun, verb*

■ *noun*

▸ **WAY OF LIFE 1** [U] the customs and beliefs, art, way of life and social organization of a particular country or group: *European / Islamic / African / American, etc.* **culture** ◇ *working-class culture* **2** [C] a country, group, etc. with its own beliefs, etc.: *The children are taught to respect different cultures.* ◇ *the effect of technology on traditional cultures*

▸ **ART / MUSIC / LITERATURE 3** [U] art, music, literature, etc., thought of as a group: *Venice is a beautiful city full of culture and history.* ◇ **popular culture** (= that is enjoyed by a lot of people) ◇ *the Minister for Culture*

▸ **BELIEFS / ATTITUDES 4** [C,U] the beliefs and attitudes about sth that people in a particular group or organization share: *The political cultures of the United States and Europe are very different.* ◇ *A culture of failure exists in some schools.* ◇ *company culture* ◇ *We are living in a consumer culture.*

▸ **GROWING / BREEDING 5** [U] (*technical*) the growing of plants or breeding of particular animals in order to get a particular substance or crop from them: *the culture of silkworms* (= for silk)

▸ **CELLS / BACTERIA 6** [C] (*biology, medical*) a group of cells or bacteria, especially one taken from a person or an animal and grown for medical or scientific study, or to produce food; the process of obtaining and growing these cells: *a culture of cells from the tumour* ◇ *Yogurt is made from active cultures.* ◇ *to do / take a throat culture*

■ *verb* [VN] (*biology, medical*) to grow a group of cells or bacteria for medical or scientific study

WORD ORIGIN

Middle English (denoting a cultivated piece of land): the noun from French *culture* or directly from Latin *cultura* meaning growing, cultivation; the verb from obsolete French *culturer* or medieval Latin *culturare*, both based on *colere*, to tend, cultivate. In late Middle English the sense was cultivation of the soil and from this early 16th century use came *cultivation* (*of the mind, faculties, or manners*); sense 3 dates from the early 19th century

cul·tured /ˈkʌltʃəd; *NAmE* -tʃərd/ *adj.* **1** (of people) well educated and able to understand and enjoy art, literature, etc. **SYN** CULTIVATED **2** (of cells or bacteria) grown for medical or scientific study **3** (of PEARLS) grown artificially

ˈculture shock *noun* [C,U] a feeling of confusion and anxiety that sb may feel when they live in or visit another country

ˈculture vulture *noun* (*humorous*) a person who is very interested in serious art, music, literature, etc.

Oxford Advanced Learner's Dictionary
Seventh edition, 2005

Oxford Guide to
British and American Culture
for learners of English

OXFORD
UNIVERSITY PRESS

OXFORD
UNIVERSITY PRESS

Great Clarendon Street, Oxford OX2 6DP

Oxford University Press is a department of the University of Oxford.
It furthers the University's objective of excellence in research, scholarship,
and education by publishing worldwide in

Oxford New York

Auckland Cape Town Dar es Salaam Hong Kong Karachi
Kuala Lumpur Madrid Melbourne Mexico City Nairobi
New Delhi Shanghai Taipei Toronto

With offices in

Argentina Austria Brazil Chile Czech Republic France Greece
Guatemala Hungary Italy Japan Poland Portugal Singapore
South Korea Switzerland Thailand Turkey Ukraine Vietnam

OXFORD and OXFORD ENGLISH are registered trade marks of
Oxford University Press in the UK and in certain other countries

ISBN-13: 978 0 19 431129 8
ISBN-10: 0 19 431129 5

Typeset by Data Standards Limited
Printed in China

ACKNOWLEDGEMENTS

Designer: Peter Burgess
Cover design: Philip Hargraves
Photographs and illustrations: Please see Acknowledgements on page viii
Maps: Phil Longford (British Empire, C14); others © Oxford University Press

ON THE COVER

From background to foreground: Mount Rushmore, Transport for London logo,
Stonehenge, New York taxi

Contents

Advisory Board

Key to entries

ba'roque *adj* in a highly decorated style of art that was fashionable in Europe in the 17th and early 18th centuries after developing in Italy. Examples of British baroque style include buildings designed by the architects *Wren and *Vanbrugh, and the music of *Purcell and *Handel
▶ **baroque** (*often* **the baroque**) *n* [U] the baroque style or baroque art.

,Battery 'Park /ˌbætəri/ a park at the southern end of *Manhattan (1) Island, New York, opposite the *Statue of Liberty. Boats take tourists, etc. from the park to the statue, *Ellis Island and *Staten Island.

▶ **beer**
In Britain, beer is the most popular alcoholic drink which is drunk in *pubs. Many people drink **bitter**, a brown-coloured beer. It is sold **on draught**, if it is drawn for each customer from a large container, usually a **keg** or **barrel**, or **bottled**.

Judge Roy 'Bean [1] /'biːn/ (1825–1903) a US judge of the *Wild West known as 'the hanging judge' because he ordered many people to be hanged. He called himself 'the only law west of the Pecos (river)'.

,Sean 'Bean [2] /ˌʃɔːn 'biːn/ (1959–) an English actor who is best known for his role in the *Lord of the Rings films and for playing Richard Sharpe in a series of television films (1993–97) about a soldier in the *Napoleonic Wars.

BMJ /ˌbiː em 'dʒeɪ/ ⇨ BRITISH MEDICAL JOURNAL.

the 'Beaufort scale /'bəʊfət; *AmE* 'boʊfərt/ *n* a scale for measuring wind speed, from 0 (calm) to 12 (hurricane).

,Buffy the 'Vampire ,Slayer /ˌbʌfi, 'væmpaɪə ˌsleɪə(r); *AmE* 'væmpaɪər ˌsleɪər/ (*also* 'Buffy) a US television series (1997–2003) about a teenage girl, Buffy Summers, played by Sarah Michelle Gellar (1977–), who has special abilities that help her to fight against vampires (= imaginary creatures in the form of dead people who suck the blood of living people), helped by her *high school friends.

the 'brat pack *n* [usually sing] (*informal*) a group of well-known or successful young people, especially actors, who enjoy being famous and sometimes behave badly: — *Tom Cruise was a member of the Hollywood brat pack.*

'bluegrass *n* [U] **1** a type of grass that is bluish-green in colour. It is common in parts of the US, especially *Kentucky, which is sometimes called the Bluegrass State.
2 a type of *country music of the southern US.

'billiards *n* [U] a game for two people, played by hitting three balls with long rods called *cues*, on a large table covered with cloth. The aim is to score points by hitting one ball against another or into one of six pockets around the table. Compare BAR BILLIARDS, POOL, SNOOKER.

'bar snack *n* [usually pl] (*BrE*) a light meal that can be bought and eaten in a pub. Bar snacks might include sandwiches, salads and pies. See also PLOUGHMAN'S LUNCH.

,Bob the 'Builder an animated (= using pictures on film which look as if they are moving) television series for young children.

66 Can we fix it? Yes, we can! 99
Bob's catchphrase

Acknowledgements

We are grateful to the following for permission to reproduce illustrations:

Alamy *C9, C11bl, C11tr,* Glenn Harper *C5bl,* Christopher Hill Photographic *C15l,* David Martin Hughes *C4r,* Rory Moore *C15r*

BBC *223r*

British Standards Institution *60l*

Corel *4t, 7tl, 7bl, 9r, 12r, 18r, 24l, 26r, 28r, 31b, 36l, 38l, 38r, 40r, 42t, 44b, 51l, 52t, 58l, 62l, 69r, 70l, 71l, 76l, 77l, 81r, 82l, 82b, 84r, 85l, 93r, 102tr, 103cl, 103r, 106r, 106t, 108r, 109l, 109r, 112r, 115b, 117l, 117r, 123r, 125r, 134l, 138cl, 138bl, 139r, 142l, 145l, 146l, 147l, 152l, 157l, 159l, 163b, 167b, 168b, 186b, 187r, 188r, 192r, 199l, 197l, 202l, 204r, 206l, 206r, 207l, 211l, 215c, 215b, 219r, 220l, 222r, 223r, 224l, 224r, 225l, 233l, 236r, 240r, 249r, 257l, 258r, 259l, 266l, 268l, 268r, 271l, 273l, 274bl, 276l, 281l, 282l, 283r, 285l, 287l, 294l, 298l, 309r, 313l, 317l, 318r, 321l, 325l, 326tl, 326cl, 331r, 338l, 346l, 347r, 348l, 350tr, 358l, 360l, 363l, 366r, 367l, 368l, 372r, 381t, 383l, 386l, 391l, 391r, 405b, 409r, 420l, 426l, 440br, 450l, 474b, 481cl, 481b, 482r, 503rt, 503br, 510l, 513r, 517l, 527r, 530l, 530tr, 530br, C2, C3, C4l, C6, C7, C8, C10r, C12, C13, C16, C17, C19, C21, C31l, cover images*

Corbis *C18tr, C28*

Digital Vision *504l, cover (taxi)*

Fotosearch *cover (Stonehenge)*

Greater London Authority *C10l*

Image Source *169b, 274tl, 301b, 469l*

iStockphoto *C26r*

Meccano™ Toys Ltd *295b*

Oxford University Press B Brecken *143c,* J M Dudley *102b, 350c, 440t,* R Judges *151b, 157l, 158b, 161l, 326c, 457r,* Martin Lonsdale/Hardlines *334l,* J Richards *31l,* Thomas-Photos Oxford *314l,* Michael Woods *3l, 279l, 281l, 317r, 422r, 441r,496l, 526r*

Photodisc Image *27l, 60r, 70r, 77tl, 82r, 83r, 87r, 162r, 163cl, 207b, 226l, 231r, 234l, 260l, 267r, 274r, 299l, 302b, 304l, 308l, 312l, 328r, 342l, 361l, 370l, 404l, 405l, 454r, 455r, 463r, 473l, 487r, 499l, 521, C11br, C18l, C22, C23, C24, C25, C27, C29, C30, C31r, cover (Mount Rushmore)*

Punchstock *C18br, C20, C26bl*

Queen's Awards Office *386l*

Scottish Parliament © Scottish Parliamentary Corporate Body 2004 *C5*

Transport for London *cover (logo)*

b = bottom   c = centre   l = left   r = right   t = top

A a

AA /ˌeɪ ˈeɪ/ **1** ⇨ ALCOHOLICS ANONYMOUS.
2 the AA (in Britain) an organization for drivers that provides help when their cars break down. The AA also offers other services, such as travel advice and insurance: *Are you in the AA?*

AAA[1] /ˌeɪ eɪ ˈeɪ, ˌθriː ˈeɪz/ ⇨ AMATEUR ATHLETIC ASSOCIATION.

AAA[2] /ˌeɪ eɪ ˈeɪ/ (*in full* the **American Automobile Association**) (*also* **Triple A**) an organization for US and Canadian drivers. It helps travellers to plan their trips and rescues drivers in emergencies on the road. It began in 1902 and now has about 44 million members.

A and P /ˌeɪ ənd ˈpiː/ (*in full* the **Great Atlantic and Pacific Tea Company**) a popular US supermarket with branches in all the states. It began in 1859 in New York City and became successful as one of the first companies to buy large numbers of items at a cheap rate and offer them for sale at low prices.

Hank ˈAaron /ˈeərən/ (1934–) a famous US *baseball player who hit more home runs (755) during his career than any other player. His popular name was 'Hammerin' Hank'. He played for 23 years (1954–74) with the Braves in *Milwaukee and then in *Atlanta. He was chosen for the Baseball *Hall of Fame in 1982.

AARP /ˌeɪ eɪ ɑː ˈpiː; *AmE* ɑːr/ (*in full* the **American Association of Retired Persons**) an organization in Washington, DC, for Americans who are at least 50 years old. It began in 1958 and offers its members medical insurance, a *credit union and other advantages. It publishes a monthly magazine and newspaper and produces two national radio series. It also tries to influence government policy in order to improve the lives of older people.

AAU /ˌeɪ eɪ ˈjuː/ ⇨ AMATEUR ATHLETIC UNION.

ABA /ˌeɪ biː ˈeɪ/ ⇨ AMERICAN BAR ASSOCIATION.

ˈAbbey a British bank with branches in many towns and cities. It was formerly the second largest building society in Britain, called the Abbey National, and became a bank in 1989, the first building society to do so. ⇨ note at BUILDING SOCIETIES.

ˈAbbotsford /ˈæbətsfəd; *AmE* ˈæbətsfɔːrd/ a large house near the river Tweed in Scotland for Walter *Scott in 1822–4. It was Scott's final home. The style of its architecture is like a romantic castle in one of his novels. It now contains some of his possessions and other Scottish historical objects.

George ˈAbbott /ˈæbət/ (1887–1995) a US writer of plays and director and producer of Broadway shows, mostly *musicals. He wrote nearly 50 plays, including *The Boys from Syracuse* (1938) based on The *Comedy of Errors* and *Damn Yankees* (1955). The George Abbott Theater on Broadway is named after him. He lived to be 108 and was still writing at the age of 100.

Abbott and Cosˈtello /ˌæbət, kɒsˈteləʊ/ the US comic actors **Bud Abbott** (1895–1974), who was thin and angry, and **Lou Costello** (1906–59), who was fat and funny. They were most popular as a team in films during the 1940s, making such successes as *Buck Privates* (1941) and *Abbott and Costello Meet Frankenstein* (1948).

ABC /ˌeɪ biː ˈsiː/ (*in full* the **American Broadcasting Company**) one of the original three major television networks in America. It began in 1943 as the 'Blue

Network' of six radio stations. Popular television shows on ABC have included *NYPD Blue* and *Roseanne*. ABC is now owned by the Walt *Disney Company. See also CBS, NBC.

the ˌabdiˈcation ˌcrisis *n* [sing] (in British history) a series of events in 1936, following King *Edward VIII's decision to marry a divorced American woman, Wallis *Simpson. It was thought that the British public would not accept a queen who had been divorced, and Edward was advised by the *Prime Minister to abdicate (= give up his position as king). The couple were married in France in 1937, and Edward's brother (as *George VI) became king in his place.

Aberˈdeen /ˌæbəˈdiːn; *AmE* ˌæbərˈdiːn/ a city and port in north-east Scotland. It is an important fishing port, and the main centre of the *North Sea gas and oil industries. Many of its buildings are made of granite, a hard grey stone, and for this reason it is often called the 'granite city'. It was the administrative centre of the former Grampian region until 1996, when it became its own *council area (officially called **Aberdeen City**).

Aberdeen ˈAngus /ˌæbədiːn ˈæŋgəs; *AmE* ˌæbərdiːn/ a breed of black cattle without horns, originally bred in Scotland. They are known for the quality of their meat.

Aberˈdonian /ˌæbəˈdəʊniən; *AmE* ˌæbərˈdəʊniən/ *n* a person from *Aberdeen.
▶ **Aberdonian** *adj* of or from Aberdeen.

A ˌbide With ˈMe a Christian hymn, written in the 18th century. It is sometimes sung at funerals, and English football supporters traditionally sing it at the *FA *Cup Final.

ˌaboˈlitionism *n* [U] the American campaign in the 1800s to free the slaves in the southern states. Its members were called **abolitionists**, and many hid slaves who were escaping on the *Underground Railroad. Famous abolitionists included the poet John Greenleaf *Whittier and the author Harriet Beecher *Stowe.

aˈbortion *n* [C, U] the deliberate ending of a pregnancy at an early stage. Abortion is the subject of strong public debate, especially in the US. Some people are in favour of abortion; called **pro-choice** supporters, they support a woman's right to choose whether to have a baby or not. On the opposite side are the **pro-life** campaigners, who believe in the **right to life** of the unborn child and think that abortion is wrong. In 1973 abortion during the first stages of pregnancy became legal all over the US through the *Supreme Court decision *Roe v Wade*. The US government has tried to change the laws about abortion, but the changes have been disputed by federal courts and the courts have supported a woman's right to abortion. In Britain the Abortion Act of 1967 made abortion legal. The Society for the Protection of Unborn Children (SPUC) was founded to campaign against the Act and is still an important pro-life organization in Britain today.

ˌAbsolutely ˈFabulous (*also informal* **AbFab**) a British television comedy series that began in 1992. It was written by Jennifer *Saunders, who also acted in it, together with Dawn *French. It is about two women in the fashion business, Patsy and Edina. They spend most of their time drinking, smoking and taking drugs, and arguing with Edina's daughter, who is very serious and disapproves of them.

'abstract ex'pressionism *n* [U] a style of painting that was developed in the 1940s by US artists such as Jackson *Pollock and Mark *Rothko. In their paintings they use shapes and colours to express their feelings instead of representing objects or scenes.
▶ **abstract expressionist** *n*, *adj*: *an abstract expressionist painting*.

ABTA /'æbtə/ (*in full* the **Association of British Travel Agents**) a British organization that protects the customers of travel agents, e.g. by giving people back the money for their tickets if the travel company goes bankrupt.

A'cademy Award *n* any of the famous *Oscar film awards. They are presented every March in *Los Angeles by the *Academy of Motion Picture Arts and Sciences. The awards were first presented in 1929 by Douglas *Fairbanks[1]. Winners receive a small metal statue, and the most important ones are for 'Best Actor', 'Best Actress', and 'Best Picture'. Walt *Disney has won the most Oscars (26), and the films winning the most (11) have been *Ben-Hur in 1959, *Titanic in 1998 and The *Lord of the Rings: The Return of the King in 2004.

the A'cademy of 'Motion ,Picture 'Arts and 'Sciences the US film organization in *Los Angeles that presents the *Academy Awards. It was created in 1927 by Louis B *Mayer and now has 6 000 members who are actors, directors, producers and technical workers. The Academy also decides on technical standards for the film industry.

the A'cademy of St 'Martin-in-the-'Fields a small British orchestra, formed in 1959 by Neville *Marriner. At first, it played only *baroque music, and all its concerts took place in the church of St Martin-in-the-Fields in *Trafalgar Square, London. Now it is one of London's most famous small orchestras, playing a wide variety of music.

ACAS /'eɪkæs/ (*in full* the **Advisory, Conciliation and Arbitration Service**) an independent British organization which brings together workers and their employers when the usual methods of dealing with arguments about pay and working conditions have failed. It was set up by the government in 1974: *Eventually ACAS was called in to mediate.*

'access course *n* (in Britain) an adult education course that prepares older students who do not have *A levels for study at a university or *college of higher education. ⇨ note at ADULT EDUCATION.

ac'cumulator /ə'kjuːmjəleɪtə(r)/ *n* (*BrE*) a form of betting on the results of sporting events, usually horse races. If the first bet is won, all the money won is bet on the second event, and all the money from that is bet on the third, etc. If all the bets are won, the person gambling can win a lot of money, but if one bet is lost, everything is lost.

Ace™ /eɪs/ *n* a US make of elastic bandage. It is often used by runners for muscle pain.

,Dean 'Acheson /'ætʃɪsn/ (1893–1971) a US diplomat. He directed the *Marshall Plan to help Europe after World War II and, as *Secretary of State under President *Truman, helped in 1949 to create the *North Atlantic Treaty Organization. He received a *Pulitzer Prize in 1970 for his book *Present at the Creation: My Years in the State Department*.

> 66 Great Britain has lost an empire and has not yet found a role. 99
> Dean Acheson 1962

'acid drop *n* (*BrE*) a type of hard sweet with a slightly bitter taste. Acid drops are often sold in paper bags by weight, and are popular with children.

,acid 'house *n* [U] a type of fast electronic pop music with few words (a form of *house) that first became popular in the US in the mid 1980s, and later in Britain. It was played especially at *raves or **acid house parties**, which were often held illegally in large buildings or outdoors, and where drugs such as Ecstasy were often used.

,acid 'jazz *n* [U] a type of dance music, popular in the 1990s. It is a mixture of *soul, *jazz and *hip hop styles. Groups such as Incognito and the Brand New Heavies are typical of the style, using jazz instruments, *rap singers and a fast rhythm.

,acid 'rock *n* [U] a type of *rock music that was popular in the 1960s when many groups and their audiences used acid (= a slang name for the drug LSD). US groups such as the *Grateful Dead and Jefferson Airplane were typical of this style. Their mysterious songs, played on electronic guitars, were much influenced by drugs.

ACLU /,eɪ si: el 'juː/ ⇨ AMERICAN CIVIL LIBERTIES UNION.

ACT /,eɪ si: 'tiː/ (*in full* **American College Test**) a standard test that a person must take to become a student at most American colleges. It tests knowledge of English, mathematics, sciences, and other subjects.

'Action Man™ *n* a toy in the form of a man, with different clothes and equipment that can be bought separately. When it was first sold in the 1960s as a doll for boys, Action Man was a soldier. Later, it was possible to dress the doll for other activities, including some sports. Some people in Britain have said that these toys should be forbidden because they encourage boys to be violent.

'Action on 'Smoking and 'Health ⇨ ASH.

'action ,painting *n* [U] a method of painting used by Jackson *Pollock and other *abstract expressionist artists. Instead of using a brush, the artist throws or pours paint onto the painting as a way of expressing unconscious feelings more directly.

Act of Parliament (in Britain) a new law which has been approved by *Parliament. After a *bill has been passed by the *House of Commons and the *House of Lords and it has received *royal assent, it becomes an Act of Parliament and therefore part of British law.

the ,Act of 'Settlement (in Britain) an *Act of Parliament in 1701, saying that the children of *James I's granddaughter Sophia would be the future kings and queens. The government made this law because the king at that time, *William III, had no children, and they wanted to stop the *Catholic *Stuarts from becoming kings and queens. Sophia was a *Protestant. She was married to the Elector (= a type of prince) of *Hanover. Their son became King *George I, the first king of the House of Hanover.

the ,Act of Su'premacy (in Britain) an *Act of Parliament in 1534 that made King *Henry VIII the head of the *Church of England. This left the Pope with no power in England.

the ,Act of 'Union (in Britain) either of two *Acts of Parliament. The first Act of Union, in 1707, officially joined England and Scotland as one kingdom, called Great Britain, ruled by the parliament in London. The second Act of Union, in 1800, added Ireland to this group of countries, which was then called the *United Kingdom of Great Britain and Ireland.

the ,Actors' 'Studio a school in New York for professional actors. It was begun in 1947 by Elia *Kazan, Robert Lewis, and Cheryl Crawford. It became the centre of *method acting under its artistic director Lee *Strasberg, and its many famous students included Marlon *Brando and Rod Steiger.

,Robert 'Adam /'ædəm/ (1728–92) a Scottish architect who, with his brother James (1730–94), started a new neoclassical style (= one influenced by the styles of ancient Greece and Rome) in British building and furniture design. They designed many famous houses, including *Kenwood House and the main building of *Edinburgh University.
▶ **Adam** adj [usually before noun] designed or influenced by Robert Adam: an Adam ceiling/fireplace.

Osterley Park designed by the Adam brothers

,Adam 'Bede /'bi:d/ the first novel (1859) by George *Eliot. Adam Bede, a carpenter in a village in the English *Midlands, falls in love with a beautiful young woman, but she has a tragic affair with another man. Later, Adam falls in love with and marries her cousin, a good, calm and religious person.

,Ansel 'Adams[1] /,ænsəl 'ædəmz/ (1902–85) a US photographer who took black and white photographs of the US South-West. One of his best-known books was Taos Pueblo (1930). He helped to create the department of photography at the *Museum of Modern Art in New York in 1940, and was director of the Sierra Club, an organization to protect nature, for 37 years.

,Douglas 'Adams[2] /'ædəmz/ (1952–2001) an English writer of comic science fiction. His best-known book is The *Hitch Hiker's Guide to the Galaxy.

,Gerry 'Adams[3] /'ædəmz/ (1948–) a Northern Ireland politician. He has been the President of *Sinn Fein since 1983. He was elected *MP for West *Belfast in 1983, 1987, 1997 and 2001 but did not take his seat in Parliament because he refused to recognize the authority of *Westminster(2) in Northern Ireland. He has been criticized for being involved with terrorists but he has played an important part in peace negotiations including those that led to the *Good Friday Agreement.

,John 'Adams[4] /'ædəmz/ (1735–1826) the second *President of the US after being the country's first Vice-President. He was a leader in forming the *Declaration of Independence. He was not a very popular president because of arguments within his government and problems in foreign relations, especially with France. He was the father of John Quincy *Adams.

'John 'Quincy 'Adams[5] (1767–1848) the sixth *President of the US. He was not a popular president because his government passed a tariff act (= a tax on imports). He had had more success earlier as *Secretary

of State, helping to write the *Monroe Doctrine and adding *Florida as a state. He was the son of John *Adams.

the ,Adam 'Smith 'Institute /'smɪθ/ a British organization formed in 1977 which gives economic advice to the British government, foreign governments and other groups. It is named after the 18th-century economist Adam *Smith, and shares many of his ideas (e.g. about the importance of reducing the extent to which the state is involved in social and commercial affairs). It was associated particularly with the *Conservative governments of the 1980s and 1990s in Britain.

ADAS /'eɪdæs/ ⇨ AGRICULTURAL DEVELOPMENT AND ADVISORY SERVICE.

,Jane 'Addams /'ædəmz/ (1860–1935) an American who worked to improve social conditions and shared the 1931 *Nobel Prize for peace. She and Ellen Gates Starr began the Hull House in *Chicago in 1889 to help poor people. From 1915 to 1929, Addams was President of the Women's International League for Peace and Freedom.

the 'Addams ,Family /'ædəmz/ a family of strange but funny cartoon characters who live in a large dark house and behave in an unusual way that suggests evil and death. They were created in 1935 in the *New Yorker magazine by Charles Addams. The characters were used for a popular television comedy series (1964–6) and two films (1991 and 1993).

,Joseph 'Addison /'ædɪsən/ (1672–1719) an English writer and poet who was also active in politics. With his friend Richard *Steele he started the *Spectator. He wrote many poems and a tragic play, Cato (1713), but he is remembered mainly for his essays in the *Spectator and the *Tatler, written in a simple, direct style.

A ,deste Fi'deles /æ,desteɪ fɪ'deɪleɪz/ the Latin title and first line of a popular Christmas *carol. The English version is called O Come, All Ye Faithful.

the ,Adi'rondack 'Mountains /,ædɪ'rɒndæk; AmE ,ædɪ'rɑːndæk/ (also the Adirondacks) a mountain range in the US state of New York, where the *Hudson River begins. Tourists are attracted to its lakes and forests, including the **Adirondack Forest Preserve**.

,Larry 'Adler /'ædlə(r)/ (1914–2001) a US musician who played the harmonica (= a small instrument held against the mouth). He moved to Britain in the 1950s. Several composers, including Malcolm *Arnold and Ralph *Vaughan Williams, wrote music specially for him. Adler wrote and played music for a number of films, including Genevieve (1953), A High Wind in Jamaica (1965) and My Life (1992).

the ,Admiral's 'Cup the prize given to the winner of a series of yacht races (= for boats with sails) held every two years off the south coast of England.

the 'Admiralty /'ædmərəlti/ **1** the British government department that was responsible for the Royal Navy until 1964, when it became part of the *Ministry of Defence.
2 the building in *Whitehall, London, that used to be the headquarters of the Admiralty. Now it is the headquarters of the *Civil Service.

,Admiralty 'Arch /,ædmərəlti/ a large, grand arch at the end of The *Mall in central London, England. It was built in 1906–10 in memory of Queen *Victoria and is next to the *Admiralty building. See p. 4.

▶ **adult education**

Adult education, sometimes called **continuing education**, includes courses of general interest at all levels, *vocational training for jobs in industry, and academic study for a degree.

In Britain most general interest courses are part-time and usually consist of **evening classes** held once a

Admiralty Arch

week at local colleges, schools and community centres. Some classes are also held during the day. Courses offered include both academic and recreational subjects, e.g. Spanish, local history, yoga and pottery. Students have to pay, but people who are unemployed may get a reduction or go free. Most classes are organized by *local education authorities or by the **Workers' Educational Association**. There are about 1500 centres for adult education in Britain. Some universities also have a **department of continuing education**, which runs courses and organizes residential summer schools.

Some people return to college as **mature students** and take full- or part-time training courses in a skill that will help them to get a job. The development of **open learning**, making it possible to study when it is convenient for the student, has increased the opportunities available to many people. This type of study was formerly restricted to book-based learning and **correspondence courses** but now includes courses on television, CD-ROM or the Internet, and **self-access courses** at language or computer centres.

Americans believe that education is important at all stages of life and should not stop when people get their first job. About 40% of adults take part in some kind of formal education. About half of them are trying to get qualifications and skills to help them with their jobs, the rest are taking recreational subjects for personal satisfaction. Schools and *community colleges arrange evening classes, and a **catalog** of courses is published by local boards of education.

Many US universities have a department of continuing education. State universities often allow anyone who wants to attend classes to do so, whether or not they are working towards a degree. Adults who never completed secondary school have a chance to take an **equivalency exam**, and if they pass they get a certificate saying that they have the same level of education as somebody who has finished *high school. See also OPEN UNIVERSITY.

'Advent (in the Christian religion) the first season of the Church year which begins with **Advent Sunday** and includes the four Sundays before *Christmas Day. It is called Advent, which means 'coming' in Latin, because it leads up to the feast celebrating the time when Jesus Christ came into the world.

'Advent ,calendar n a cardboard picture with tiny doors in it, given to children as a present for *Advent. They open one door for each day in the time before *Christmas from 1 December to 24 December. Behind each one is a picture, and sometimes a small gift.

▶ **advertising**

Most companies in Britain and the US have to work hard to **promote** and **market** their goods in order to sell them. Political parties, charities and other organizations also use advertising. Many pages in newspapers and magazines are filled with advertisements (also called **ads** or, in Britain, **adverts**), companies advertise on the Internet and there are also advertisements, usually called **commercials**, on radio and television.

Advertisements in newspapers and magazines are expensive and only the largest companies can afford to advertise their products in this way. Many organizations, however, use newspapers to advertise jobs and these are generally grouped together in the **jobs section**. Small companies, such as travel agents, advertise in the **classified ads** columns, where each advertisement consists of a few lines of text only. Shops and businesses, and individuals wanting to buy or sell second-hand household goods, advertise in local papers.

The wealthiest companies buy advertising time on television. There is no advertising on the *BBC, but programmes broadcast by US and British commercial stations are interrupted by a **commercial break** about every 15 minutes. Famous actors or singers sometimes **endorse** a particular product by appearing in advertisements for it. Some advertising **slogans** are known by everyone, e.g. 'Have a break – have a *Kit Kat.' Some advertisements are like very brief episodes of a story. Tobacco advertising is now banned (= forbidden) on radio and television in Britain and on television in the US. Advertisers have no influence over the people who make programmes, even if they help pay for them through sponsorship although there is an increasing amount of **product placement**, where firms pay for their products to be shown in films or television programmes. In the US some commercials are national, others are shown only in a particular area. National commercials are often fun to watch, but local ones have the reputation of being badly made. Some products are sold on smaller channels by an **infomercial**, a commercial that lasts half an hour or more and tries to look like an entertainment programme.

Other ways of advertising include displaying large posters on **hoardings** or **billboards** by the side of roads. **Flyers** (= small posters) advertising local events or special offers are given to people in the street. Restaurants advertise in theatre programmes, and shops advertise in their own magazines or on their shopping trolleys (*AmE* carts). Many companies advertise on the Internet.

The biggest US **ad agencies** have offices in New York on *Madison Avenue, so **Madison Avenue** has come to mean the advertising industry. In Britain, the advertising industry is controlled by the *Advertising Standards Authority and *Ofcom. All advertisements must be 'legal, decent, honest and truthful'. In the US the *Federal Communications Commission makes rules about advertising. Television and radio stations are required to do some **public service announcements** (= commercials that give information to the community) free of charge.

Many people are against advertising, partly because it adds to the cost of a product. People also say that the influence of advertising is too great, and that children especially want every product they see advertised. On the other hand, many people buy American newspapers on Sundays only because they advertise **special offers** and contain **coupons** (= pieces of paper enabling people to buy products at a reduced price).

the 'Advertising 'Standards Au'thority (*abbr* **ASA**) an independent organization which checks that advertisements do not lie or make false claims about a product. Anyone can ask the Advertising Standards Authority to investigate an advertisement. If there is a problem with it, the Authority may then tell the company to change or remove it.

the **Ad'visory, Con,cili'ation and Arbi'tration ,Service** ⇨ ACAS.

'advocate *n* [C] **1** (in England and Wales) any lawyer who presents a client's case in a court of law.
2 (in Scotland) a lawyer who has the right to speak in the higher courts of law. See also LORD ADVOCATE.

,Aesop's ,Fables /ˌiːsɒps 'feɪblz; *AmE* ˌiːsɑːps/ a collection of short stories about animals which behave in a human way. Each story teaches a moral lesson. They are said to be by a Greek called Aesop who lived in the 6th century BC, but many of them are much older than this. Well-known stories include *The *Tortoise and the Hare* and *The Fox and the Grapes*.

the **Aes'thetic ,Movement** a movement that developed in England in the late 1880s. It was based on the belief that art should exist as an independent idea, and not in order to support religion, the state, etc. This principle is most clearly expressed in the phrase 'art for art's sake'. The movement was influenced by the *Pre-Raphaelites and John *Ruskin. Its supporters included William *Morris, Oscar *Wilde and Aubrey *Beardsley. See also ARTS AND CRAFTS MOVEMENT.

the **AFC** /ˌeɪ ef 'siː/ ⇨ AMERICAN FOOTBALL CONFERENCE.

af,firmative 'action *n* [U] a US government policy requiring that minority groups and women should be favoured when people are being chosen for jobs or entry to college. Americans are divided about this practice and often say it is 'reverse discrimination'. It has existed since the 1960s, but the *Supreme Court has since decided against strict quotas (= numbers of people) and forcing affirmative action on private businesses. The more informal practice in Britain is sometimes known as 'positive discrimination'. See also EQUAL EMPLOYMENT OPPORTUNITY COMMISSION, EQUAL OPPORTUNITIES COMMISSION.

the **AFL-CIO** /ˌeɪ ef 'el ˌsiː aɪ 'əʊ/ (*in full* the **American Federation of Labor - Congress of Industrial Organizations**) the largest organization for workers in America, with 13 million members from 61 *trade unions. It was created in 1955 when the AFL and CIO joined together. It usually gives its powerful political support to the *Democratic Party.

the **AFN** /ˌeɪ ef 'en/ ⇨ AMERICAN FORCES NETWORK.

,African A'merican *n* a US name for black Americans descended from Africans, especially those descended from American slaves. The name has become more popular and politically correct (= avoiding language that may offend a particular group) than 'black'. About 12% of the US population are African Americans.
▶ **African American** *adj*.

,Afro-Carib'bean /ˌæfrəʊ kærɪ'biən/ *n* [C] (in Britain) a black person whose family comes from the *Caribbean.
▶ **Afro-Caribbean** *adj* of Afro-Caribbeans or their culture: *Afro-Caribbean music*.

AFTRA /'æftrə/ (*in full* the **American Federation of Television and Radio Artists**) a *trade union for US actors and other people working in television and radio. AFTRA works with the *Screen Actors Guild to gain better contracts and conditions of work for the members of both organizations.

'Aga™ /'ɑːgə/ *n* (*pl* **Agas**) a cooker that is made of solid iron. It has a traditional design, but is now very fashionable in Britain. Agas use coal, oil, gas or electricity and are usually left on once they have been lit. They can also be used to provide hot water and central heating. The phrase **Aga saga** is a humorous name for a novel about the lives of *middle-class British people.

,Age Con'cern a British charity that looks after the interests of old people by providing care and advice and working to influence government policy. It was begun in 1940.

,Agent 'Orange *n* [U] a poisonous chemical used by US soldiers during the Vietnam War to remove the leaves from forests so that they could see the enemy. It caused birth defects in many Vietnamese children, and after the war about 60 000 former US soldiers complained of illnesses.

the **,age of con'sent** *n* [sing] the age at which a young person can legally agree to have sex with someone. In Britain it is 16. The age of consent for men who want to have sex with other men was lowered from 18 in 2000. In the US the age of consent varies in different states, but it is usually between 16 and 18.

the **,age of di'scretion** *n* [sing] the age at which young people are considered able to deal with their own affairs, e.g. to own property, to make a contract with someone, or to make a will (= sign a document saying what will happen to their possessions when they die). The age of discretion in Britain is now 14. In the US it varies in different states.

the **,Age of En'lightenment** (*also* the **Age of Reason**) a period in Europe in the 18th century when many writers and thinkers began to question established beliefs, e.g. in the authority of kings or of the Church, in favour of reason and scientific proof. The idea developed that everyone was of equal value and had equal rights.

the **,age of 'steam** a phrase sometimes used to refer to the 18th and 19th centuries in Britain, when different types of steam engine were being invented and developed by people such as James *Watt and George *Stephenson. Steam engines were used as the power for factories, ships and trains. Some people in Britain speak of the age of steam with feelings of sadness because they imagine that life was more pleasant and relaxed then.

'Agincourt /'ædʒɪnkɔː(r)/ a battle fought in northern France in 1415, between the French and the English under King *Henry V. Though there were many more French soldiers, the English won and were then in a strong position to take much of France. Agincourt is especially remembered because it forms an important part of Shakespeare's play *Henry V.

the **,Agri'cultural De'velopment and Ad'visory ,Service** (*abbr* **ADAS**) a British company that carries out research in agriculture for the government and other customers and advises the government on policy.

Chri,stina Agui'lera /krɪˌstiːnə ægɪ'leərə; *AmE* ægɪ'lerə/ (1980–) a US pop singer who first became known in 1999 with her successful single *Genie in a Bottle*. She won a *Grammy for Best New Artist in 2000 and has won more awards in 2001 and in 2004 for the song *Beautiful*. Her albums include *Christina Aguilera* (1999) and *Stripped* (2002).

,Captain 'Ahab /'eɪhæb/ the main character in the novel *Moby-Dick by Herman *Melville. Captain Ahab, who hunts a white whale, is an example of a person who becomes crazy and puts others in danger by having only one aim in life.

▶ **aid**

Most aid (= money, food and equipment) is given to the world's poorest countries to help reduce poverty. Projects paid for by aid money are often aimed at improving local housing and water supply, agriculture, health and education. Training local people is a central part of many programmes. A lot of **aid money** comes from governments, but **development projects** are often run with the help of **non-governmental organizations** (**NGOs**), such as charities. Some charities, e.g. *Oxfam, the *Red Cross and the *Save the Children Fund, run their own aid programmes with money given by the general public. Additional emergency aid is given after natural disasters.

The British government gives over £3 000 million in aid each year to **developing countries**, especially those which belong to the *Commonwealth. British aid is distributed by the *Department for International Development. Some aid is given direct to individual countries; the rest is distributed through international organizations such as the *European Union, the *United Nations and the World Bank. Money is also invested in businesses in developing countries by the **Commonwealth Development Corporation**. Britain, together with other countries, is helping to reduce the debts of poorer countries and may under certain circumstances cancel debts from Commonwealth countries.

The US began giving foreign aid during *World War II, when the *Lend-Lease Act made it possible to give military equipment to foreign countries. After the war the US created the *Marshall Plan, a $15 billion programme to help European countries rebuild their economies. The US has continued to spend large amounts of money on foreign aid, but has been criticized for the way it decides who to help. In general, money goes to poor countries that are important to the US for commercial or military reasons. Formerly, the US gave money to countries in Africa, Asia and Latin America so that they would not accept money from the Soviet Union. *USAID distributes US foreign aid. In 2005 its budget was over $6 billion. Much of this was spent on US equipment, food and services to be sent abroad.

Two organizations are particularly concerned with training local people. In Britain *Voluntary Service Overseas arranges for skilled people to work abroad for a few years so that they can pass on their skills. They are paid at local rates by the government of the country they are working in. The *Peace Corps, a US government agency, does similar work but pays volunteers living expenses and gives them a small allowance.

'**Aintree** /'eɪntriː/ a course near *Liverpool, England, where horse races are held. The most famous of these is the *Grand National.

'**Air A'merica 'Radio** a US radio network which began broadcasting nationally in 2004 and expresses more liberal attitudes than many of the other, more conservative talk radio networks.

'**Airbus**™ /'eəbʌs; AmE 'erbʌs/ n (pl **-buses**) a type of passenger plane with a wide body. It is made by the European Aeronautic Defence and Space Company. The new A380 Airbus, the world's largest aircraft, which has been made in Britain, France, Germany and Spain, will start to carry passengers on commercial flights in 2006: We travelled on a Thai Airways Airbus.

'**Airedale** /'eədeɪl; AmE 'erdeɪl/ n (also **Airedale terrier**) a breed of dog, the largest of the English *terriers, originally bred in *Yorkshire. It has a black body and a yellowish-brown head and legs.

air force ⇨ note at ARMED FORCES.

,**Air Force 'One** the plane used by the US President. The first such plane was provided in 1944 for Franklin D *Roosevelt, but the first to be called Air Force One was the one provided for John F *Kennedy in 1961. The plane is now a US Air Force Boeing 747-200.

'**Air Miles**™ n [pl] a scheme to encourage air travel. People get points when they spend money on particular

goods, hotels, etc. which they can use to buy cheap flights: I've nearly got enough Air Miles for that trip to Florida.

'**Airstream**™ /'eəstriːm; AmE 'erstriːm/ a US company started in the 1920s by Wally Byam which makes trailers (= vehicles without an engine that can be pulled behind a car and which people can sleep in) which are known for their classic, rounded, silver design. Some people like to buy and restore old Airstreams and there is a club for owners called the Wally Byam Caravan Club International.

AKC /,eɪ keɪ 'siː/ ⇨ AMERICAN KENNEL CLUB.

,**Ala'bama** /,ælə'bæmə/ a southern US state, also called the Yellowhammer State, the Cotton State and the Heart of *Dixie. The capital city is *Montgomery and the largest city is *Birmingham. Important industries include the production of paper, textiles, chemicals and metals. It also has many agricultural products, including milk, wheat and cotton.

A'laddin /ə'lædɪn/ a poor young Chinese boy in a story in The *Arabian Nights. A magician (= a person who does magic tricks) asks him to go down into a deep cave full of gold and jewels, but to bring up only an old lamp. Aladdin will not give the magician the lamp until he helps him out of the cave, so the magician shuts him in. Aladdin discovers that when he rubs the lamp, a genie (= a spirit with magic powers) comes out of it. He uses the power of the genie to become rich, defeat the magician and marry a princess. The story of Aladdin is often performed as a *pantomime in Britain. The phrase an Aladdin's cave is sometimes used to mean a place full of wonderful things: The shop is a real Aladdin's cave of unusual gift ideas.

the 'Alamo /'æləməʊ/ the fort (now in *San Antonio, *Texas) where an army of about 4 000 Mexican soldiers killed all 187 Texans defending it in 1836. Davy *Crockett and James *Bowie died there. 'Remember the Alamo!' became a famous cry for Texas independence from Mexico. John *Wayne directed and acted in a film about the battle, The Alamo (1960).

A'laska /ə'læskə/ the largest and most northern state of the US, connected to the other states by the **Alaska Highway** through Canada. It is sometimes called 'the Last Frontier' and produces a lot of oil. The land was bought from Russia in 1867 and Alaska became the 49th state in 1959. The capital city is Juneau, and the largest city is *Anchorage, where 40% of the population live.

'**Albany** /'ɔːlbəni/ **1** the capital city of New York State, 145 miles/230 kilometres north of New York City. **2** (also **the Albany**) a very luxurious block of flats/apartments in *Mayfair that was built in the late 18th century.

,**Edward 'Albee** /'ɔːlbiː/ (1928–) a US writer of plays who became famous for Who's Afraid of Virginia Woolf? (1962). He later won the *Pulitzer Prize three times, for A Delicate Balance (1966), Seascape (1975) and Three Tall Women (1994).

,**Prince 'Albert** (1819–61) the husband (and also cousin) of Queen *Victoria. The son of a German *duke, Albert married Victoria in 1840, and in 1857 he was given the title of *Prince Consort. He took great interest in the arts, as well as business, science and technology, and was a strong influence behind the *Great Exhibition of 1851. Albert died suddenly when he was only 42, and the Queen wore black clothes for the next 40 years as a sign of her great sadness.

the ,Albert 'Dock /,ælbət/ part of the old port of *Liverpool, England, where many of the early *Victorian buildings have been made into restaurants and museums, including *Tate Liverpool.

the **Albert 'Hall** (*also* **the Royal Albert Hall**) a large round concert hall in west London, England, which holds 8 000 people. It was built in 1868–71 in memory of Prince *Albert. Various musical and sporting events take place in it, but it is best known as the concert hall where the *Proms are held.

the Albert Hall

the **Albert Me'morial** a monument opposite the *Albert Hall in London, England, built in the 1860s in memory of Prince *Albert.

Albert 'Square ⇨ EastEnders.

Albion /'ælbiən/ an ancient name for Britain or England. It may be connected with the Latin word *albus*, meaning 'white', and refer to the *white cliffs of Dover, often the first thing seen by anyone crossing the *English Channel to land in Britain. The word 'Albion' is now used only in poetry or in names, especially those of streets and football clubs. The expression *perfidious Albion*, meaning that England cannot be trusted, was often used by the French about the English in the time of Napoleon.

Madeleine 'Albright /'ɔːlbraɪt/ (1936–) the first woman US *Secretary of State (1997–2001). She was born in Czechoslovakia, but her family moved to the US in 1948. Albright was the US representative to the *United Nations for four years before becoming Secretary of State.

Alcatraz /'ælkətræz/ a small island with a famous prison on it in *San Francisco Bay, *California. The island was known as 'the Rock'. The prison was used from 1933 to 1963 for the country's most dangerous prisoners, including Al *Capone. It is now a popular tourist attraction.

Alcatraz

The **'Alchemist** a comedy play (1610) by Ben *Jonson about a man who pretends to be an alchemist (= a person who was thought to be able to turn ordinary metal into gold) in order to cheat people out of their money. Many people consider it to be Jonson's greatest play.

John 'Alcock /'ɔːlkɒk; *AmE* 'ɔːlkɑːk/ (1892–1919) an English pilot. In 1919 he and Arthur *Brown were the first people to fly across the Atlantic Ocean, from Newfoundland in Canada to the west coast of Ireland. Alcock was made a *knight in 1919.

Alcoholics A'nonymous (*abbr* **AA**) an international organization, begun in *Chicago in 1935, for alcoholics (= people who find it difficult not to drink too much alcohol) who are trying to stop drinking. They have regular meetings at which people help each other by talking about their problem.

'alcopop /'ælkəʊpɒp; *AmE* 'ælkoʊpɑːp/ *n* (*BrE*) a type of sweet alcoholic drink, usually sold in small bottles. Alcopops have been criticized in Britain because they are attractive to children, and some makes are now no longer sold.

Lou'isa 'May 'Alcott /'meɪ 'ɔːlkɒt; *AmE* 'ɔːlkɑːt/ (1832–88) the US author who wrote *Little Women*. She was also a nurse in the US Army during the American *Civil War and wrote about her experiences at the time.

the **Aldeburgh 'Festival** /,ɔːldbərə/ a music festival that takes place every summer in Aldeburgh, a small town in *Suffolk, England. The festival was created by Benjamin *Britten, who lived there.

'alderman *n* (*pl* **aldermen**) **1** (in the US) a local government officer, usually a member of a city council, responsible for part of the city.
2 (formerly in Britain) a senior member of a local council. The system of local government changed in 1974 in most of Britain, and the only aldermen left now are in the *City of London.

'Aldermaston /'ɔːldəmɑːstən; *AmE* 'ɔːldərmæstən/ a small town in Berkshire, England, close to an important nuclear weapons research centre. In the 1950s and 1960s and again in 2004 there were large organized marches from London to Aldermaston to protest against nuclear weapons.

'Alderney /'ɔːldəni; *AmE* 'ɔːldərni/ the furthest north of the *Channel Islands.

'Aldershot /'ɔːldəʃɒt; *AmE* 'ɔːldərʃɑːt/ a town in *Hampshire, England, which is one of the main centres for the army. People think of it as an army town.

'Buzz' 'Aldrin /,bʌz 'ɔːldrɪn/ (1930–) the second US astronaut to walk on the moon (15 minutes after Neil *Armstrong), in 1969.

the **Aldwych 'Theatre** /,ɔːldwɪtʃ/ a theatre in the *West End of London, famous for the **Aldwych farces**, comedy plays by Ben *Travers which were performed there in the 1920s and 1930s. It was the London home of the *Royal Shakespeare Company from 1960 to 1982.

the **A'leutian ,Islands** /ə'luːʃn/ about 150 islands spread over 1 200 miles/1 920 kilometres from the Alaskan Peninsula to Russia. About 8 000 people, mostly fishermen, live on the islands. See also Bering Strait. ⇨ note at Inuits.

'A ,level /'eɪ/ (*in full* **Advanced level**) *n* [U, C] (in Britain) a school leaving examination in a particular subject, normally taken in two parts at the age of 17 and 18 in England and Wales. Students usually take three or four subjects at the second level. This examination is needed for entrance to university: *She's got three A levels.* ◇ *I'm studying A level maths.* See also AS level, A2 level.

Ale'xander's 'Ragtime 'Band /,ælɪg'zɑːndəz; *AmE* ,ælɪg'zændərz/ the song that made Irving *Berlin famous. He wrote the quick, happy *ragtime tune in 1911. It was also sung in a 1938 film of the same name.

Alexandra 'Palace a large building in north London, England, surrounded by a park. It was first built for an

A

international exhibition in central London in 1862, and later moved. It is best known for having been the *BBC's main television centre when the first public broadcasts were made in the 1930s. Concerts and exhibitions are now held there.

The ˌAleˈxandria Quarˈtet /ˌælɪgˈzɑːndrɪə; *AmE* ˌælɪgˈzændrɪə/ a series of four novels by Lawrence *Durrell about the complicated love affairs of a group of friends in Alexandria, Egypt, in the 1930s. The four books are *Justine* (1957), *Balthazar* (1958), *Mountolive* (1958) and *Clea* (1960). The series forms Durrell's best-known work.

Mohamed Al-Fayed /məˌhæməd æl ˈfaɪəd/ (1927–) a businessman, born in Egypt, who owns a number of businesses in Britain including *Harrods and *Fulham Football Club. He was refused a British passport and now lives in Switzerland. His son, Dodi Al-Fayed (1955–1997), was killed in a car accident in Paris with *Diana, Princess of Wales.

ˌAlfred the ˈGreat (849–99) king of *Wessex (871–99). He is remembered for defending England against Danish attacks, for establishing the English navy, and for encouraging education and the use of the English language. There is a popular story of King Alfred and the cakes. After a battle he was hiding in a woman's house. Not knowing who he was, she told him to look after her cakes which were cooking by the fire, and then became very angry when he let them burn.

Hoˌratio ˈAlger /həˌreɪʃɪəʊ ˈældʒə(r)/ (1834–99) a US author of more than 100 books for boys. Most were about poor boys who became rich and successful by their hard work and good behaviour. Readers believed that these 'rags-to-riches' stories illustrated the opportunities for success in America.

the Alˈgonquin ˌRound ˈTable /ælˈgɒnkwɪn; *AmE* ælˈgɑːŋkwɪn/ the informal name for a group of Americans known for their humour. They met regularly in the 1920s and 1930s at the Algonquin Hotel in New York, and the group included the writers Dorothy *Parker and Robert Benchley. A film about the group, *Mrs Parker and the Vicious Circle* was made in 1994.

Muˌhammad ˈAli /məˌhæmɪd ˈɑːli, ɑːˈliː/ (1942–) a famous US boxer. He was the world heavyweight champion from 1964 to 1967 and from 1974 to 1978. His original name was Cassius Clay, but he changed this in 1964 after joining the *Black Muslims. He had a very strong and confident personality and wrote poetry about his victories. He has gradually become ill with a disease of the muscles.

> 66 I'm the greatest. 99
> Muhammad Ali

ˌAli ˈBaba /ˌæli ˈbɑːbɑː/ a character in an old Arabian story who hears some thieves say 'Open Sesame!', the magic words that open the door of the cave where they keep everything they have stolen. He steals their gold and they try to kill him, but he is saved by his servant Morgiana. The story is popular as a *pantomime in Britain.

ˌAlice in ˈWonderland a children's book (1865) by Lewis *Carroll. Its full title is *Alice's Adventures in Wonderland*. Alice, a young girl, dreams that she follows a white rabbit down its hole and has a series of adventures with imaginary creatures. Some of the characters, such as the *Mad Hatter and the *Cheshire Cat, are referred to in informal English expressions. There was a second book about Alice, *Through the Looking Glass*. A situation in which things happen that do not make any sense and are the opposite of what you would expect is

sometimes described as Alice in Wonderland: *The government's tax reform is pure Alice in Wonderland.*

ˌAli ˈG /ˌæli ˈdʒiː/ a comedy character played by the English comedian Sacha Baron Cohen (1970–). He first appeared in the British television series *The 11 O'Clock Show* in 1999 and later in *Da Ali G Show* in Britain and the US, and in the film *Ali G In Da House* (2002). He uses language, wears clothes and has attitudes which are typical of British black street culture in an extreme way which is funny. He is also very naive about the world outside his group of friends.

ˌAlka-ˈSeltzer™ /ˌælkə ˈseltsə(r)/ a medicine which is mixed with water to make a fizzy drink (= one containing many bubbles) that people take when they have indigestion (= stomach pain caused by difficulty in digesting food or drink): *Why don't you take an Alka-Seltzer?*

ˌall-Aˈmerican *n* a US player of a sport in college who is one of the best in the country. To be called an all-American, a player must be chosen for a national team, the best-known teams being for football and *basketball.
▶ **all-American** *adj* **1** of an American player who is one of the best in his or her sport: *an All-American quarterback on the All-American team.*
2 representing typical American characteristics, physical appearance, etc.: *an all-American boy.*

ˈAll-Bran™ *n* [U] a breakfast food made mainly of bran (= the outer skin of grain such as wheat, oats, etc.), which helps to make the bowels work properly. It is usually eaten with milk and sugar.

the ˌAlleˈgheny ˈMountains /ˌælɪˈgeɪni/ (*also* **the Alleghenies**) /ˌælɪˈgeɪniz/ a range of mountains that runs from south-west *Virginia to central *Pennsylvania. They are part of the central *Appalachian Mountains.

ˌGracie ˈAllen¹ /ˈælən/ (1906–64) a US comic actor who was married to and regularly acted with George *Burns. She played a humorous wife who mostly talked nonsense in their popular programmes on radio and television.

ˌWoody ˈAllen² /ˌwʊdi ˈælən/ (1935–) a US comic actor, director and writer of films. His films often make fun of the worries of modern life in big US cities. He has won three *Oscars, for writing and directing *Annie Hall* (1977), and for writing *Hannah and Her Sisters* (1986). His later films include *Husbands and Wives* (1992), *Sweet and Lowdown* (1999) and *Anything Else* (2003). In 1997 he married the adopted daughter of his former partner, the actor Mia *Farrow.

> 66 My one regret in life is that I am not somebody else. 99
> Woody Allen

the ˌAll ˈEngland Club (*in full* the **All England Lawn Tennis and Croquet Club**) the tennis club in *Wimbledon, London, where the famous tennis competition is held every year. It started as a *croquet club in 1868.

ˌEdward ˈAlleyn /ˈæleɪn/ (1566–1626) an English actor, famous for his performances in plays by *Marlowe, while his great rival Richard Burbage (c. 1567–1619) acted in Shakespeare's plays. He owned the *Rose Theatre, and provided the money to establish *Dulwich College.

ˈAll ˌHallows ˈEve /ˌhæləʊz/ ⇨ HALLOWEEN.

the Alˌliance and ˈLeicester /ˈlestə(r)/ a British bank with branches in many towns and cities. It used to be a *building society, and became a bank in 1997. In 1990 it took over the *Girobank.

A

the **Al'liance ˌParty** (*in full* the **Alliance Party of Northern Ireland**) a political party formed in Northern Ireland in 1970 by people who disagreed with the extreme views of both Catholics and Protestants. The party aims to end the *Troubles by uniting the moderate people from both sides.

the **'Allies** /'ælaɪz/ *n* [pl]   **1** the group of countries that fought together against Germany, Austria-Hungary, Turkey and Bulgaria in *World War I, including Britain, France, Italy, Russia, the US and the *Commonwealth countries.
2 the group of countries that fought together against Germany, Italy and Japan (the Axis powers) in *World War II. They included Britain, France, the US, the USSR and the *Commonwealth[1] countries.

'All 'My 'Children a popular US television *soap opera on *ABC which started in 1970 and is about the lives of a group of families in a suburb of *Philadelphia.

al'lotment /ə'lɒtmənt; *AmE* ə'lɑːtmənt/ *n* (in Britain) a small piece of land that a person can rent from the local *council for growing vegetables, flowers, etc. Allotments are usually grouped together in a large field in a town or city. In the 19th century and during the two world wars, many people used their allotments to feed their families. Working on an allotment is now a popular way of getting exercise.

ˌall points 'bulletin *n* ⇨ APB.

ˌAll 'Saints Day (*also* **All Hallows**) 1 November, when members of many Christian Churches traditionally say prayers to all the saints. The night before, known as All Hallows Eve, is now usually called *Halloween.

ˌAll 'Souls' Day 2 November, the special day in the *Catholic Church when people say prayers for people who have died.

ˌall-star 'game *n* (*AmE*) a game played between the best players in their sport. The 'all-stars' are often divided into teams that represent different sections of a league (= a group of sports clubs) or different parts of the country: *the NBA All-Star Game* ◇ *the East-West All-Star Game.*

'All's Well That 'Ends Well a comedy play by Shakespeare, written about 1603. Bertram is ordered by the king to marry Helena, who loves him, but under the bad influence of Parolles, he runs away to Florence. Helena follows him there, and tricks him into accepting her as his wife.

'All Things 'Bright and 'Beautiful a hymn (= a Christian religious song) sung especially by children. Many British and US people remember singing the first verse as children:

> 66 All things bright and beautiful,
> All creatures great and small.
> All things wise and wonderful,
> The Lord God made them all. 99

ˌAlly Mc'Beal /ˌæli mək'biːl/ a US sitcom (1997–2002) set in a law firm in *Boston in which Ally McBeal, a young lawyer played by Calista Flockhart, was the main character.

ˌAlly 'Pally /ˌæli 'pæli/ (*informal*) a popular name for *Alexandra Palace.

ˌalma 'mater *n* /ˌælmə 'mɑːtə(r)/ **1** (*also* **Alma Mater**) a person's old school or university. The words mean 'generous mother' in Latin. The *alma mater* is an especially important idea to Americans: *He's taking a post in the history department at his alma mater.* See also ALUMNI ASSOCIATION.
2 (in the US) the official song of a school, college or university.

'almshouse *n* (in Britain) a house provided by the Church or a charity for old poor people. Almshouses were mostly built between the 16th and 19th centuries by rich local men, often in a row and in a grand style. Many older British towns have almshouses.

almshouses at Polmear, Cornwall

ˌRobert 'Altman /'ɔːltmən / (1920–) a US film director. His films usually give a sad or funny picture of US life. They include *M*A*S*H (1970), *Nashville* (1975), *Short Cuts* (1995), based on stories by Raymond *Carver, and *Gosford Park* (2001) which is set in an English *country house.

'Altoids /'æltɔɪdz/ *n* [pl] sweets with a very strong mint flavour that are sold in small tins. They have been made in Britain since the 19th century and are especially popular in the US.

ˌAlton 'Towers /ˌɔːltən/ an amusement park near *Derby, England. It has some of the biggest rides in Britain.

a'lumni associˌation /ə'lʌmnaɪ/ *n* (in the US) an organization of people who have all been to a particular school or university. See also ALMA MATER.

AM /ˌeɪ 'em/ ⇨ ASSEMBLY MEMBER.

the AMA /ˌeɪ em 'eɪ/ ⇨ AMERICAN MEDICAL ASSOCIATION.

the ˌAmateur Ath'letic Associˌation (*also* the **AAA**, the **Three As**) the organization that controls amateur athletics in Britain. It began in 1880, when it was for men only, but in 1991 it combined with the Women's Amateur Athletic Association.

the Amateur Athletic Union (*abbr* the **AAU**) an organization that supports amateur sports in the US. It was established in 1888. Each year it gives the James E Sullivan Award to the Outstanding Amateur Athlete in the US.

ˌamateur dra'matics (*also informal* **am-dram**) *n* [U] the activity of people who perform plays, etc. as a hobby and not for money. It is very popular in Britain, where there are many amateur dramatics clubs, even in small towns and villages, and most schools and universities have them. They perform plays for local people, charging them a small amount in order to pay for the costumes, hall, etc. People who do amateur dramatics are often very enthusiastic, but not always very good actors.

Aˌmazing 'Grace /əˌmeɪzɪŋ 'ɡreɪs/ a popular 18th-century Christian hymn. It begins:

> 66 Amazing Grace, how sweet the sound
> That saved a wretch like me.
> I once was lost, but now am found,
> Was blind, but now I see. 99

'Amazon™ /'æməzən/ a company set up in 1995 to sell books through the Internet. It was one of the first large companies to sell goods in this way. Customers can order books, music, DVDs and other products online, often at lower prices than the prices in shops, and the goods are delivered to their homes. The US-based website was followed by services in the UK, France, Japan and other countries.

'Ambridge /'æmbrɪdʒ/ the village in the British radio programme *The *Archers* where all the main characters live. With its village hall, church, shop and pub it represents a safe, protected corner of England where the old social values still exist.

,am-'dram /,æm 'dræm/ ⇨ AMATEUR DRAMATICS.

a'mendment /ə'mendmənt/ *n* an addition or change to a law or official document. In the US the first ten amendments to the Constitution are called the *Bill of Rights. Each amendment to the US Constitution needs a two-thirds majority in each House and must be approved by 75% of the states.

,Ame'rasian /,æmə'reɪʒn/ *n* a person born to an American and an Asian. The word is mostly used for a child of a US soldier and an Asian woman. Many Amerasian children were born as a result of the *Vietnam War. Compare ASIAN AMERICAN.

A'merica a popular national song in the US, first sung in 1831. It has the same tune as the British *national anthem *God Save the Queen/King and begins with these lines:

> 66 My country, 'tis of thee,
> Sweet land of liberty,
> Of thee I sing. 99

▶ **America**

The **United States of America** is called by several different names, both by the people who live there and by people in other countries. These names include **the USA, the United States, the US, the States** and **America**. The official name, the United States of America, first appears in the *Declaration of Independence of 1776, when the country was called 'the thirteen united States of America'. *America* is widely used as a name for the US, though this seems unfair on all the other nations in **the Americas** (= the continents of North and South America). Songs like *America and **America the Beautiful* are about the US. Americans also use informal names like **the US of A** and **Stateside**, especially when they are out of the country. Other names, e.g. 'the land of the free', 'the land of liberty', 'God's country', 'the *melting pot' and 'the greatest nation on earth', show their pride in their country. People in Britain and America sometimes refer humorously to each other's countries as 'the other side of the pond', i.e. the other side of the Atlantic Ocean.

North America refers to a continent and region, and includes Canada and Mexico as well as the US. Between the US and South America is the region of **Central America**. Sometimes the countries of Central and South America are together referred to as **Latin America**.

America and the Americas are said to have been named after Amerigo *Vespucci, an Italian explorer who sailed to South America in 1499, visiting the area that later became known as Brazil, and also the *Bahamas. Vespucci believed that the land he had discovered was a new continent, not part of Asia as *Columbus had thought. By 1538, the famous map-maker Gerhardus Mercator was using the name 'America', the Latin form of Vespucci's name, for the **New World** (= North and South America, as opposed to Europe).

People from the US are called **Americans**, though British people may, rather rudely, call them 'Yanks'.

People from other countries in the Americas are called by national names derived from the name of their country, e.g. Canadians. The adjective used to describe things from the US is **American**. The US is always referred to in organizations such as the *American Legion and in expressions like 'the *American dream'. **US** is also used as an adjective, as in the US Olympic team. Official names of government organizations may use **United States**, e.g. the United States Military Academy.

the **A'merican A'cademy of Dra,matic 'Arts** a school for actors in New York City and, since 1974, in Los Angeles, California. It began in 1884 and is the oldest dramatic school in America.

the **A'merican Associ'ation of Re'tired ,Persons** ⇨ AARP.

the **A'merican 'Automobile Associ,ation** ⇨ AAA.

A,merican 'Bandstand a US television programme of pop music and dance. It started in Philadelphia and was broadcast nationally from 1952. For more than 40 years it was presented by Dick Clark, called 'the world's oldest teenager'.

the **A,merican 'Bar Associ,ation** (*abbr* **ABA**) a professional organization for US lawyers. It began in 1878 and has its main office in *Chicago. The ABA encourages legal standards, the study of law, and improvements in the US system of justice.

A,merican 'breakfast *n* a large morning meal in a hotel or restaurant in America. It usually includes several choices from such items as juice, cereal, eggs with ham or bacon, *pancakes, toast, and *hash browns or, in the southern states, *grits. Compare ENGLISH BREAKFAST.

the **A,merican 'Broadcasting ,Company** ⇨ ABC.

A,merican 'cheese *n* [U] a type of mild processed US cheese, similar to *Cheddar and yellow or orange in colour. It is often sold in separately wrapped slices.

the **A'merican ,Civil 'Liberties ,Union** (*abbr* the **ACLU**) a US organization that defends the rights of people under the US Constitution. It was involved in the legal case in 1954 that ended the system of separate schools for African Americans. The ACLU has sometimes been criticized for defending freedoms for everyone, as in 1978 when it supported the right of the Nazi Party in America to march. More recently it has opposed the introduction of prayers in public schools and, since *September 11, has fought against a reduction of civil rights in times of national emergency.

the **A'merican 'Civil 'War** ⇨ CIVIL WAR.

A,merican 'College Test ⇨ ACT.

the **A,merican 'dream** the belief of Americans that their country offers opportunities for a good and successful life. For minorities and people coming from abroad to live in America, the dream also includes freedom and equal rights.

the **A,merican 'eagle** the national symbol of the United States. It is also called the 'bald eagle', and it appears on the Great Seal of the United States and on coins. In its mouth, the eagle holds the words *e pluribus unum* (one out of many). It holds arrows (a symbol of war) in its left foot and an olive branch (a symbol of peace) in its right foot.

A,merican E'xpress™ (*abbr* **AmEx**) an international US company best known for its traveller's cheques (= cheques for various fixed amounts which can be exchanged for cash in foreign countries) and charge cards. Established in 1850, the company also now has the largest travel agency in the world and offers many financial services.

the **A,merican 'Football ,Conference** (*abbr* the **AFC**) one of the two divisions of the National Football League of professional football in the US. It has 15 teams, and the winner goes to the *Super Bowl to play the team that wins the *National Football Conference. See also NATIONAL FOOTBALL LEAGUE.

the **A'merican 'Forces 'Network** /'fɔːsɪz; *AmE* 'fɔːrsɪz/ (*abbr* **the AFN**) the television and radio stations run by the US armed forces for their members in foreign countries.

A,merican 'Gothic a painting (1930) by the US artist Grant Wood. It shows a farmer holding a pitchfork (= a farm implement with two or three sharp metal points) and standing next to a woman in front of a farm building. Both look sad, and the picture is often used for humorous advertisements.

A,merican 'Idol a very popular US television programme based on the idea of the British programme, *Pop Idol in which young people who want to be singers or entertainers have the chance to be chosen to perform on the programme in front of judges who select a group of the best. The worst performers in this first stage are often shown on the programme. In later programmes, which are filmed in *Hollywood members of the public can vote by phone for the person they think is best and the people with the most votes become the winners.

the **'War of A'merican Inde'pendence** the usual British name for the *American Revolution.

A,merican 'Indian *n* any of the native people of North and South America and the Caribbean, but especially North America. They lived in tribes until Europeans settling in America fought them and forced them to move west. Today many Indians still live on reservations (= land given and protected by the US government). The name for American Indians now preferred in the United States is *Native Americans.

the **A,merican 'Kennel Club** (*abbr* **the AKC**) a US organization that holds the official records relating to dog breeding in the US, proving that individual dogs are of a pure breed. It was established in 1884 and has more than 5000 local clubs which organize about 13000 dog shows each year. The AKC also encourages responsible dog ownership and has a service to find lost dogs and a Canine Health Foundation for research to improve the health of dogs. Compare KENNEL CLUB.

the **A'merican League** one of the two organizations of professional *baseball in the United States. It has 14 teams and the winning team plays the winner of the *National League in the *World Series.

the **A,merican 'Legion** the largest organization for former members of the US armed forces. It began in 1919 and now has about 3 million members. From its main office in *Indianapolis, Indiana, it supports benefits for former US soldiers, etc. and a strong national defence. Compare VETERANS OF FOREIGN WARS.

the **A,merican 'Medical Associ,ation** (*abbr* the **AMA**) the largest professional organization for US doctors. It began in 1847 and has its main office in *Chicago. The AMA supports high standards in medical education, research and work, and it has great political influence.

the **A'merican 'National 'Standards ,Institute** (*abbr* **the ANSI**) an organization that works to develop standards for measurements and products in the United States, and to help US businesses compete internationally. It began in 1918, and its members now include more than 1000 companies. Its main office is in New York.

the **A'merican plan** *n* [*sing*] (*AmE*) a system of hotel prices that includes the cost of a room, all meals and service. Compare EUROPEAN PLAN.

A,merican 'Psycho a novel (1991) by Bret Easton Ellis about a young man living in *Manhattan who is a psychopath (= a person suffering from a serious mental illness that causes them to behave in a violent way towards other people). The story was made into a popular film in 2000.

the **A,merican ,Revo'lution** (*BrE* **the War of American Independence**) a war between America and Britain (1775–1783) in which America became an independent nation. Britain had **colonies** (= places taken over by people from a foreign country) in North America from 1607 and in the 17th century the 13 colonies each had an **assembly** of representatives. After Britain passed a series of laws raising taxes and restricting trade, the assemblies wanted to decide what taxes they should pay rather than the British *Parliament and some colonists, called **patriots** began to want independence from Britain. After a number of events including the *Boston Massacre in 1770 and the *Boston Tea Party in 1773, the British tried to increase control over the colonies. Representatives of the colonies formed the *Continental Congress in 1774 and decided to form their own army. On 18 April 1775 when British soldiers near *Boston were looking for weapons hidden by the colonists, the soldiers met and the first shot of the war was fired. After the Battle of *Bunker Hill in 1775 when many British soldiers, known as *Redcoats, were killed, the Continental Congress suggested that Britain and America should make an agreement, but Britain refused and on 4 July 1776 members of the Congress signed the *Declaration of Independence. During the following years of fighting, the Americans received support from France and Spain. Finally, after seven years of war, Britain recognized the **United States of America** in 1783.

the **A'merican So'ciety for the Pre'vention of 'Cruelty to 'Animals** (*abbr* **the ASPCA**) a US charity that works to protect animals. It began in 1866 and is the oldest organization of this type in America. Its main offices are in New York.

the **A'merican So'ciety of Comp'osers, 'Authors and 'Publishers** (*abbr* **ASCAP**) an organization in America that protects the rights of writers of music. It collects money on behalf of its members from anyone who plays or sings in a professional performance.

the ***A'merican 'Standard 'Version*** (*abbr* the *ASV*) a new version by US scholars of the *King James Version of the Bible. It is sometimes called the *American Revised Version*. It was published in 1901 after its American authors had helped to write the *Revised Version* (1881–5) in England.

the **A,merican 'Stock Exchange** (*abbr* **AMEX**) a financial market that used to be the second largest in the US. It began in 1911 and is in the financial district of *New York. In recent times it has lost many members to the International Securities Exchange. See also NEW YORK STOCK EXCHANGE.

A,merica 'Online (*abbr* **AOL**) a US company, part of *Time Warner, which provides services that allow people to use the Internet, email and instant messaging (= a service which lets people communicate quickly using the Internet) using **AOL Instant Messenger** (**AIM**). It has customers around the world as well as in the US.

the **A,merica's 'Cup** an international sailing contest, first held in 1851. It is usually held every three or four years, and a US crew has won it every time except in 1983 when Australia won, in 1995 and 2000 when New Zealand won, and in 2003 when Switzerland won.

A

A'merica's 'Most 'Wanted a US television series started in 1987, which presents information about people who are wanted by the police for serious crimes, often people on the *FBI's **Ten Most Wanted list**. It asks viewers to telephone a special number if they have any information which might help to catch them. It also has information about missing people, especially children. Compare CRIMEWATCH.

A,merica the 'Beautiful a popular US song in praise of the country, written by Katharine Lee Bates in 1893. The first verse is:

> 66 O beautiful for spacious skies,
> For amber waves of grain,
> For purple mountain majesties
> Above the fruited plain.
> America! America!
> God shed His grace on thee,
> And crown thy good with brotherhood
> From sea to shining sea. 99

AmeriCorps a US organization for community service established in 1993. It has about 50 000 members of all ages active in over 1 200 communities. They help to build and repair homes, clean parks and other areas, prevent crime and take part in other projects. For this work, they receive money to attend college.

Ame'rindian n (old-fashioned) an *American Indian.
▶ **Amerindian** adj.

'Amex /'æmeks/ **1 AmEx** ⇨ AMERICAN EXPRESS.
2 AMEX ⇨ AMERICAN STOCK EXCHANGE.

'Amicus /'æmɪkəs/ one of the largest *trade unions in Britain with members in most industries. It was formed in 2001 when the AEEU (the Amalgamated Engineering and Electrical Union) joined with MSF (the Manufacturing, Science and Finance Union).

,Kingsley 'Amis¹ /,kɪŋzli 'eɪmɪs/ (1922–95) an English writer and poet. His most famous book is the comic novel Lucky Jim (1954). In 1986 he won the *Booker Prize with The Old Devils. Most of his novels are angry but humorous attacks on aspects of modern life. He was the father of Martin *Amis and was made a *knight in 1990.

,Martin 'Amis² /'eɪmɪs/ (1949–) an English writer and journalist. His novels include Dead Babies (1975), Money (1984), London Fields (1989), Time's Arrow (1991), The Information (1995) and Yellow Dog (2003). In 2000 he published an autobiography, Experience. He is the son of Kingsley *Amis.

the 'Amish /'ɑːmɪʃ/ a strict Christian group in America who were once part of the *Mennonites. They are mostly farmers in the states of Pennsylvania, Ohio and Indiana. Because of their many religious rules, they do not have cars, telephones or electricity, and they wear old-fashioned clothes. See also PENNSYLVANIA DUTCH(1).

,Amnesty Inter'national an international organization that works to help people who have been put in prison for their beliefs or because of their colour, race or religion (but only if these people do not believe in using violence). It is also opposed to torture and *capital punishment. It was established in Britain in 1961, and now has members in over 150 countries.

,Ampleforth 'College /,æmplfɔːθ; AmE ,æmplfɔːrθ/ a Roman Catholic *public school in *Yorkshire in the north of England. It was started in 1802.

'Amtrak™ /'æmtræk/ the public company, set up by *Congress in 1970, which runs trains for passengers in the US. Its formal name is the National Railroad Passenger Corporation. Only 1% of Americans using public transport travel by Amtrak. It has lost money every year and most of the network now has only one train a day.

'Amway™ /'æmweɪ/ a US company which employs people in more than 80 countries to sell its products in their spare time, often at special parties in their own homes. The things they sell include cosmetics (= beauty products) and cleaning products, and the more they sell the more money they are paid by the company.

,Ana'baptist /,ænə'bæptɪst/ n a member of any of several strict religious groups in the 16th century, during the *Reformation. They believed in following the Bible's teachings exactly, separating the Church from the State, and shared ownership of goods. They also believed that only adults should be baptized Their views were considered extreme by both *Protestants and *Catholics. They were strongest in Germany and the Netherlands, but later the movement spread to the US. They influenced the beliefs of the later *Baptist movement and of other groups such as the *Hutterites and the *Mennonites.

'Anacin™ /'ænæsɪn/ n [C, U] (in the US) a medicine taken to relieve minor pains, invented in 1918.

'Anadin™ /'ænædɪn/ n [C, U] the British name for the medicine called *Anacin in the US.

,Ana'sazi /,ænə'sɑːzi/ n (pl **Anasazis** or **Anasazi**) a member of an ancient Indian people of the southwestern US, the ancestors of the modern *Pueblo people. See also PRE-COLUMBIAN NORTH AMERICA.

'Anchorage /'æŋkərɪdʒ/ the largest city in *Alaska. It is a port in the southern part of the state. An earthquake badly damaged the city in 1964 and killed 131 people.

Anchorage

,ancient 'lights n [U] (in English law) the principle that you have the right to receive light through any window that has been there for 20 years or more. It may be used in cases where a person wants to build something in front of your house, etc.

The ,Ancient 'Mariner /'mærɪnə(r)/ (full title , **The Rime of the Ancient Mariner**) a long poem (1798) by Samuel Taylor *Coleridge. In it an old sailor tells a wedding guest how he once shot an albatross (= a large sea bird considered lucky by sailors). His friends hung the bird around his neck as a punishment. They all died of thirst, and he was left alive to tell his story to anyone who would listen. The best-known lines from the poem are these:

> 66 Water, water, everywhere
> Nor any drop to drink. 99

,ancient 'monument n (in Britain) a building or place officially protected by law from being damaged or destroyed. *Stonehenge is an example of an ancient monument. See also ENGLISH HERITAGE, LISTED BUILDING.

E'lizabeth 'Garrett 'Anderson[1] /'gærət 'ændəsən; AmE 'gærət 'ændərsən/ (1836–1917) the first British woman doctor, who fought for the right of other women to become doctors after struggling to get her own medical qualifications in 1865. Later she set up a hospital where women could be treated by women. In 1908 she also became the first woman *mayor of an English town.

Lindsay 'Anderson[2] /'ændəsən; AmE 'ændərsən/ (1923–94) an English theatre and film director. His film *If …* (1968) is a powerful comment on the British *public school system.

Marian 'Anderson[3] /'ændəsən; AmE 'ændərsən/ (1902–93) a US singer. In 1939 she was prevented from entering a hall to give a concert by the *Daughters of the American Revolution because she was black, so she gave a free concert from the steps of the *Lincoln Memorial. In 1955, she became the first black singer to perform at the *Metropolitan Opera in New York.

Sherwood 'Anderson[4] /ˌʃɜːwʊd 'ændəsən; AmE ˌʃɜːrwʊd 'ændərsən/ (1876–1941) a US writer. His most successful collection of short stories was *Winesburg, Ohio* (1919) about the dull life of a small town. His novels included *Poor White* (1920) and *Dark Laughter* (1925).

'Anderson ˌshelter /'ændəsən; AmE 'ændərsən/ n a hut made of metal that British people put up in their gardens during World War II. The huts were used for shelter when bombs were dropped during the *Blitz. They were named after the *Home Secretary in 1939–40, Sir John Anderson.

Mario An'dretti /ˌmæriəʊ æn'dreti/ (1940–) a US driver of racing cars, born in Italy. He has won the national championship of the United States Auto Club three times (1965–6 and 1969). He also won the Grand Prix championship in 1978 and the *Indianapolis 500 in 1969.

Prince 'Andrew[1] ⇨ YORK[3](1).

St 'Andrew[2] (1st century AD) the patron saint of Scotland. He was one of the 12 apostles, the brother of St Peter. He became the patron saint of the *Picts in the 8th century, when, it is thought, his bones were brought to a town on the east coast of Scotland, later called *St Andrews. According to tradition, he was killed in Greece on a cross in the shape of an X, and so this cross is on the Scottish flag. Andrew is also the patron saint of Greece and Russia.

Julie 'Andrews /'ændruːz/ (1935–) an English actor, best known for her film roles in *Mary Poppins* (1964), for which she won an *Oscar, and The *Sound of Music (1965). Because of these roles, people tend to see her as a healthy, cheerful, moral person, although she has played different roles in later films. She is married to the US film producer Blake *Edwards.

'Andrex™ /'ændreks/ a make of toilet paper. Its popular advertisements have often used a *Labrador puppy (= young dog).

Andy 'Capp™ /'kæp/ a humorous character in a British strip cartoon created by Reg Smythe (1917–1998) which appeared in the *Daily Mirror from 1957. The cartoon also appears in newspapers in the US. Andy Capp drinks a lot, is very lazy, and is unfair to his wife Flo. He always wears a flat cap, which was a traditional working man's piece of clothing, and has a cigarette hanging from his mouth.

'Anfield /'ænfiːld/ (also **Anfield Road**) the football ground of *Liverpool Football Club.

The ˌAngel, 'Islington /'ɪzlɪŋtən/ a busy place where several roads meet in Islington, an area of north London. It is called after a pub for travellers which existed there in the 17th century.

ˌAnge'leno /ˌændʒə'liːnəʊ; AmE ˌændʒə'liːnoʊ/ n (pl **-nos**) (AmE informal) a person who lives in Los Angeles.

'angel food cake (also **angel cake**) n a soft white cake with a light texture, made with sugar, flour and the white parts of eggs beaten until they are stiff.

ˌMaya 'Angelou /ˌmaɪə 'ændʒəluː/ (1928–) a US writer, singer and film director. Her best-known book is *I Know Why the Caged Bird Sings* (1970), a true story of her difficult but successful life. In 1997 she directed her first film for television, *Down in the Delta*.

'Anglepoise™ /'æŋglpɔɪz/ n a British make of lamp, used especially on a desk, that can be easily moved into different positions so that the light shines where it is needed. It was first designed in 1933 by George Carwadine (1887–1948).

'Anglesey /'æŋgəlsi/ a large island off the north-west coast of Wales, a part of *Gwynedd. It is joined to the mainland by both road and rail bridges, and passenger boats sail regularly between Holyhead on Anglesey and Ireland.

'Anglican n a member of one of the churches in the *Anglican Communion. In Britain these are the *Church of England, the *Church in Wales, the *Episcopal Church in Scotland, and the Church of Ireland. In the US, the Anglican Communion is represented by the *Protestant Episcopal Church. Many people in Britain call themselves Anglican, even if they never go to church. See also CHURCH OF SCOTLAND.
▶ **Anglican** adj.

the ˌAnglican Com'munion an organization consisting of the *Church of England and other churches in Britain and abroad that have historical links with the Church of England. Its leader is the *Archbishop of Canterbury. The *Episcopal Church of Scotland, the Church of Ireland, the *Church in Wales and the Episcopal Church in the US are all part of the Anglican Communion. There are also a number of large Anglican churches in Africa. There has been disagreement between members of the Anglican community in recent years especially about attitudes to homosexuality and whether women should be priests. Every ten years all the bishops of the Anglican Communion attend the *Lambeth Conference.

'angling /'æŋglɪŋ/ n [U] (BrE) the sport of fishing with a line and a hook, usually in rivers and lakes, etc. rather than in the sea. It is one of the most popular leisure activities in Britain. See also FLY-FISHING.

ˌAnglo-A'merican n an American, especially of the US, who is descended from an English family.
▶ **Anglo-American** adj involving Britain and America, especially the US: *the history of Anglo-American relations*.

ˌAnglo-Ca'tholicism n [U] a movement within the *Church of England that emphasizes its connections with the *Roman Catholic Church. **Anglo-Catholic** ideas were strongly expressed in the *Oxford Movement of the 1830s. When the Church of England started to accept women as priests in the 1990s some Anglo-Catholic priests who were opposed to this joined the Roman Catholic Church. See also ORDINATION OF WOMEN.

the ˌAnglo-Dutch 'Wars three wars fought by the English against the Dutch between 1652 and 1674, at a time when the two countries were competing strongly for trade around the world. One important result was that the town of *New Amsterdam was given to the English in 1667. They gave it the new name of New York.

the ˌAnglo-'Irish A'greement an agreement reached in 1985 between the UK and Ireland, allowing the Irish government to take part in discussions about Northern Ireland. See also GOOD FRIDAY AGREEMENT.

the **'Anglo-'Irish 'Treaty** the agreement that formally ended the *Troubles in Northern Ireland in 1921.

the **'Anglo-'Irish 'War** the formal name for the *Troubles in Northern Ireland between 1919 and 1921. It involved violent fighting between the *IRA and the *Black and Tans and was brought to an end by the *Anglo-Irish Treaty, which recognized the establishment of the independent republic of Ireland.

Anglo-'Saxon *n* **1** [C] an English person of the period between the time when the Romans left Britain in the 5th century AD and the *Norman Conquest in 1066. The name is formed from the names of two of the tribes that occupied England after the Romans left, the Angles and the *Saxons.
2 (*also* **Old English**) [U] the English language of the period before the *Norman Conquest. Compare MIDDLE ENGLISH.
3 [U] (*AmE*) the modern English language.
4 [C] a white person whose native language is English. See also WASP.
▶ **Anglo-Saxon** *adj.*

The **'Anglo-'Saxon 'Chronicle** an early history of England, written in *Old English. It ends in the 12th century, but mostly covers the period from the time when the Romans came to Britain until the *Norman Conquest in 1066.

angry young 'man *n* (*pl* **angry young men**) (*especially BrE*) a young person who strongly criticizes political and social institutions. The phrase was originally used by British newspapers in the late 1950s, after the success of the play *Look Back in Anger* by John *Osborne, to describe young British writers like Osborne, Kingsley *Amis and Alan Sillitoe.

animal 'crackers *n* [pl] small, sweet American biscuits shaped like different animals. They are sold in boxes and are popular with children.

Animal 'Farm a book (1945) by George *Orwell in which some farm animals start a revolution against the farmer but are betrayed by their leaders, the pigs, and suffer even more than before. *Animal Farm* is a satire on the Russian Revolution and the struggle for power between Stalin and Trotsky, represented by the pigs Napoleon and Snowball. The most often quoted and adapted line from the book is 'All animals are equal, but some animals are more equal than others.'.

the **'Animal Libe'ration 'Front** a British group, formed in the early 1970s, that believes in attacking any organization which they feel is cruel to animals. They use public protest and even violence to do this. For example, they sometimes steal animals that a company's scientists are doing experiments on, and damage the company's property. There are similar groups with the same name in the US. Compare ANIMALS, PRESSURE GROUPS.

▶ **animals**

The British and Americans are famous for being animal lovers, and many families have at least one *pet. People from other countries often think British and American people are sentimental about animals, and say that they fuss over them and treat them better than human beings.

At weekends people in Britain often visit **farm parks, safari parks** (= parks where people can drive close to lions, zebras etc.), **zoos, bird parks** and **sea life centres**. In the US there are zoos and **aquaria** (= large tanks of fish), which are educational, and also amusement parks with animals, like Busch Gardens and *Disney's Animal Kingdom.

Television programmes about animals are very popular. These range from factual programmes about wildlife to films starring fictional animals such as *Lassie and

*Tom and Jerry. Children are given cuddly toy animals and picture books. Children's literature has created many famous animal characters, such as *Black Beauty, *Brer Rabbit, *Pooh, and Ratty, Mole and Toad in *The *Wind in the Willows*. Many animals in books have their own distinctive character: lions are typically brave, foxes are cunning and cats are proud.

There are laws against cruelty to animals in Britain and the US. People give generously to animal charities such as the *RSPCA and the *ASPCA, and there are **animal hospitals** and **rescue centres** for injured and abandoned animals. Most are fairly modern, and many animals live in a large **enclosure** similar to their natural **habitat**, rather than in a cage. Often zoos keep only animals that cannot survive in the wild or were born **in captivity**. Some breed animals to put back into the wild and try to raise public awareness about the need for **conservation**.

Many people care about wild animals. People feed wild birds in the winter and some have a bird table in the garden. In the US the National Wildlife Federation (NWF) helps people to create their own 'backyard wildlife habitat'.

There are often campaigns to save species that are **endangered** (= that may become extinct), such as wolves and buffalo in the US, and red squirrels and hedgehogs in Britain. In rural areas people generally have much less romantic ideas about animals. In Britain *hunting foxes with dogs arouses hostile feelings, especially among people living in towns, but the law to ban it, which came into effect in 2005, is seen by many people living in the country as an attack on their way of life.

In Britain and the US many people are concerned about **animal rights**, especially the use of animals in scientific research and public pressure has forced many cosmetics manufacturers to stop testing products on animals. Several groups, including the *Animal Liberation Front and *PETA, strongly oppose **vivisection** (= the use of live animals in experiments) and **animal rights activists** organize protests at laboratories where animals are used. Sometimes people who work or invest in companies that own the laboratories are threatened.

Concerns about farming methods in which animals are fattened as quickly as possible in artificial conditions causes many people to become vegetarians or to buy only meat that is from animals that have lived in good conditions.

Jennifer 'Aniston /'ænɪstən; *AmE* ˌdʒɛnɪfər/ (1969–) a US actor best known for her role as Rachel in the popular television comedy series *Friends*. She has also appeared in a number of films, mostly comedies.

An'napolis /ə'næpəlɪs/ the capital city of the US state of *Maryland. The United States Naval Academy, where officers are trained, is there. The Academy is usually called Annapolis: *He's a senior at Annapolis.*

Princess 'Anne[1] (1950–) a British princess, the only daughter of Queen *Elizabeth II and Prince *Philip. She has a strong interest in horse riding, and represented Britain at the 1976 Olympic Games. She is also known for her work as the President of the *Save the Children Fund. In 1973 she married Captain Mark Phillips, and had two children, Peter (1977–) and Zara (1981–). In 1992 she was divorced, and in the same year she married Timothy Laurence (1955–), a Royal Navy Officer. She was given the title of *Princess Royal in 1987. ⇨ note at ROYAL FAMILY.

Queen 'Anne[2] (1665–1714) the queen of Britain from 1702 to 1714. She was the daughter of King *James II and the last of the House of *Stuart. None of her 18 children lived beyond the age of 11, so when she died, her

German cousin George from Hanover became King *George I. Queen Anne was the last British ruler to be able to prevent Parliament from passing a law by using her power to veto (= reject) it. See also QUEEN ANNE.

,**Anne of 'Cleves** /'kliːvz/ (1515–57) a German princess who in 1540 became the fourth wife of King *Henry VIII. They were divorced after six months.

,**Annie Get Your 'Gun** a US musical play (1946) by Irving *Berlin. It is a story about Annie *Oakley, and a film version was made in 1950. One of its songs, *There's No Business Like Show Business*, has a special meaning for entertainers.

,**Annie 'Hall** /'hɔːl/ a successful US film (1977), written and directed by Woody *Allen in which he acted with Diane *Keaton. It is a romantic comedy and won *Oscars for Best Picture, Best Director and Best Actress.

,**Annie 'Oakley** /'əʊkli; *AmE* 'oʊkli/ *n* (*AmE informal*) a free ticket or pass, e.g. for a theatre performance. It is called this because it has holes in it (so that it cannot be used again) and looks like one of the cards shot by Annie *Oakley as part of her act.

,**annual per'centage rate** *n* ⇨ APR.

,**annus hor'ribilis** /ˌænəs hʊˈriːbɪlɪs; *AmE* hɔːˈriːbɪlɪs/ *n* [sing] the Latin for 'horrible year'. Queen *Elizabeth II used this expression in a speech in 1992 to describe that year, when there was a serious fire at *Windsor Castle, the *Princess Royal got divorced, the Duke of *York(1) separated from his wife and the *Prince of Wales had marriage problems.

,**annus mi'rabilis** /ˌænəs mɪˈrɑːbɪlɪs/ *n* [sing] the Latin for 'remarkable year'. John *Dryden's poem *Annus Mirabilis* (1667) describes the year 1666 when the *Great Fire of London happened and the English defeated the Dutch: *That year was something of an annus mirabilis for British racing drivers.*

a,**nother 'place** an expression used in the *House of Commons to refer to the *House of Lords or in the House of Lords to refer to the House of Commons.

the **ANSI** /eɪ en es 'aɪ/ ⇨ AMERICAN NATIONAL STANDARDS INSTITUTE.

,**ante'bellum** /ˌæntiˈbeləm/ *adj* [only before noun] of the years before a war. The word is mainly used in the US to describe grand houses built in the southern states before the American *Civil War.

Susan B Anthony (Susan Brownell Anthony 1820–1906) a US teacher who was a leader of the campaign for women's right to vote. In 1869, she and Elizabeth Cady Stanton established the National Woman Suffrage Association. Anthony was its President from 1892 to 1900 and she also organized the International Council of Women in 1888. Her image is on the *Anthony dollar.

,**Anthony 'dollar** *n* a US dollar coin with the image of Susan B *Anthony on it. These coins were produced in memory of her between 1979 and 1981, and she is the first American woman to be honoured in this way. Some people like to collect and keep Anthony dollars.

An,**tigua and Bar'buda** /ænˌtiːgə, bɑːˈbjuːdə; *AmE* bɑːrˈbjuːdə/ a country consisting of three small islands in the Caribbean. Antigua and Barbuda were British colonies from the early 17th century until they became fully independent and a member of the *Commonwealth in 1981. Most of the country's population live on Antigua.
▶ **Antiguan** *adj*, *n*; **Barbudan** *adj*, *n*.

▶ **antiques**
Some people say that anything over 50 years old can be called an **antique**, while others say an antique must be over 100 years old. The term is usually applied to objects that are valuable because they are rare or are of high quality. In the US the word *antique* can also describe any

object that is old enough to be interesting and unusual, or was made by hand in the days before factories. Antiques include furniture, carpets, clocks, china, glass, silver, jewellery, embroidery, and even toys. Any extra information about an antique, such as the maker's bill or a **letter of provenance** (= a letter referring to an object's history and origin) increases its value. Other items that people may collect are called **collectables**. They may be of any age and include things like the picture cards that used to be given away in cigarette packets, metal signs and beer mats.

Many people in Britain are interested in antiques, even if they do not own any. Antique-collecting became especially popular in the late 1980s and 1990s, and towns such as *Warwick and Hungerford are famous for their **antique shops**. People also look in **junk shops** and **second-hand shops** in the hope of finding a bargain. **Antiques fairs** are held occasionally in hotels or conference centres. **Auction houses**, such as *Christie's and *Sotheby's, hold sales which are attended by members of the public and by **dealers**.

In the US antiques are especially popular with older people. Antiques can be bought in antique shops in large cities, in small shops in the country, in **flea markets** (= markets selling old and used goods cheaply) or at *garage sales. *New England is a popular area for **antique hunting** (*AmE also* **antiquing**), and many people spend weekends driving through small towns hoping to find something special. Antiques that originate in the US include *Shaker **furniture**, made in a very simple style. Some people are interested in **Americana**, objects associated with US history such as letters written by George *Washington, silver objects made by Paul *Revere, or early versions of the American flag.

The *Antiques Roadshow* has encouraged many people in Britain and the US to take an interest in antiques.

The ,**Antiques 'Roadshow** /'rəʊdʃəʊ; *AmE* 'roʊdʃoʊ/ a popular *BBC television programme in which members of the public bring interesting old possessions, e.g. furniture or pottery, for experts to examine and talk about their history and value. It began in 1979. A similar programme with the same name began on US television in 1996.

,**antisocial be'haviour ,order** ⇨ ASBO.

,**anti'trust legis,lation** /ˌæntiˈtrʌst/ *n* [U] laws introduced in the US to encourage competition in business. Their main aim has been to prevent or control monopolies (= companies which are so large that no others can compete with them). The most important early antitrust laws passed by the United States Congress were the Sherman Antitrust Act (1890) and the Clayton Antitrust Act (1914). See also TAFT-HARTLEY ACT.

the ,**Antonine 'Wall** /ˌæntənaɪn/ a wall built in 142 AD across southern Scotland during the reign of the Roman emperor Antoninus Pius. It was about 37 miles/59 kilometres long and was intended to replace *Hadrian's Wall further south as the northern frontier of the Roman Empire, but it had to be abandoned by 197 AD. Little of the wall now remains.

,**Antony and Cleo'patra** /kliːəˈpætrə/ a play (c. 1607) by William *Shakespeare about the true story of the great love between the Roman general Mark Antony and Cleopatra, the queen of Egypt. At the end, when Mark Antony has been defeated in battle, they both kill themselves, Antony by falling on his sword and Cleopatra by letting a poisonous snake bite her.

,**Any 'Questions?** a British radio programme in which members of the public can ask politicians and other well-known people for their opinions about issues that are in the news. It is broadcast every week from a different town, and has been running since 1948. People can also telephone the *BBC to give their response to what the politicians, etc. have said in a programme called *Any Answers?*. Since 1979 there has been a similar programme to *Any Questions?* on BBC television, called *Question Time*.

AOL /ˌeɪ əʊ 'el; *AmE* oʊ/ ⇨ AMERICA ONLINE.

AONB /ˌeɪ əʊ en 'biː; *AmE* oʊ/ (*in full* **Area of Outstanding Natural Beauty**) *n* an area of countryside in the UK which is protected because of its landscape or because it has important historical or cultural connections. There are 41 AONBs in England and Wales, 9 in Northern Ireland and 38 similar areas in Scotland which are called **National Scenic Areas**.

A1 ˌSteak 'Sauce™ /ˌeɪ wʌn ˌsteɪk 'sɔːs/ (*abbr* **A1**) a US popular brand of sauce which contains a mixture of spices and flavourings, is sold in tall bottles and is eaten especially with meat. The sauce was first made in 1824 and it now produced by *Kraft.

AP /ˌeɪ 'piː/ ⇨ ASSOCIATED PRESS.

A'pache /ə'pætʃi/ *n* (*pl* **Apaches** *or* **Apache**) a member of a *Native American group in the south-western US. In the late 19th century the Apaches, under such leaders as *Cochise and *Geronimo, were the last Native Americans to be defeated by the US Cavalry. Today many Apaches live on reservations (= areas of land given and protected by the US government) in the states of Arizona, Oklahoma and New Mexico.

APB /ˌeɪ piː 'biː/ (*in full* **all points bulletin**) *n* a US police radio message telling all officers on duty to look for a particular person: *There's an APB out for him.*

APEX (*also* **Apex**) /'eɪpeks/ (*in full* **advance purchase excursion**) a system that enables people to buy air or rail tickets more cheaply than normal if they buy them a certain time in advance.

APO /ˌeɪ piː 'əʊ; *AmE* ˌeɪ piː 'oʊ/ (*in full* **Army Post Office or Air Force Post Office**) the special post office system of the US Army. Mail can be sent between army bases in the US and abroad quickly and cheaply. Compare FPO.

the A'pollo ˌprogram /ə'pɒləʊ; *AmE* ə'pɑːloʊ/ the US space programme to put people on the moon. It was begun in 1961 by President John F *Kennedy and achieved its aim on 20 July 1969 when Neil *Armstrong and Buzz *Aldrin landed on the moon during the *Apollo 11* flight.

ˌAppa'lachia /ˌæpə'leɪʃə/ a region of the *Appalachian Mountains in the southern US. It includes parts of 13 states and is known for the poverty of its mostly white population in some areas. The local people are famous for their traditional arts.

the ˌAppa'lachian 'Mountains /ˌæpə'leɪʃn/ a range of mountains in eastern North America. It runs 1 800 miles/2 900 kilometres from Newfoundland in Canada to central Alabama in the US. This includes the region of *Appalachia and the *Allegheny Mountains, the *Great Smoky Mountains and the Blue Ridge Mountains. The Appalachian National Scenic Trail is the longest in the world with signs for hikers (= people walking for pleasure).

ap'peasement /ə'piːzmənt/ *n* [U] (*usually disapproving*) doing what somebody else wants you to do in order to keep them from attacking you. The word is used to describe the British government's policy of trying to remain on friendly terms with Hitler and Mussolini, despite their aggressive actions, before World War II. See also CHAMBERLAIN, MUNICH AGREEMENT.

'Apple™ (*BrE* **Apple Mac** /mæk/ (*informal* **Mac**) the popular name for the Macintosh computer produced by the US company Apple Computer, Inc, the first to use

icons (= symbols that represent programs or files) on the screen and a mouse. The company was started in 1976 by two engineers, Steven Jobs (1955–) and Steve Wozniak (1950–) and the name Macintosh was chosen by the designer Jef Raskin (1943–2005) because it was the name of his favourite apple. The company's main office is in *Silicon Valley, California.

'applejack /'æpldʒæk/ *n* [U] (*AmE*) a very strong alcoholic drink made from apples. It is stronger than cider. Compare SCRUMPY.

ˌapple 'pie *n* [U, C] a sweet dish popular in America and Britain. It is made with apples, sugar and spices cooked in pastry. The phrase *in apple-pie order* means 'in excellent or perfect order'. People say that something is *as American as apple pie* because it is a favourite dish in the US, often eaten with ice cream. Americans also say that nothing is better than *mom and apple pie*.

ˌJohnny 'Appleseed /'æplsiːd/ (1774–1845) the popular name for John Chapman, an American who planted apple seeds for 40 years in the Ohio River valley. He began planting in 1806, and his work made him an American legend. He had long hair and travelled around in torn clothes and without shoes.

ˌAppo'mattox 'Court House /æpə'mætəks/ a former small community in the US state of Virginia where the American *Civil War ended. General Robert E *Lee of the *Confederate States surrendered on 9 April 1865 to General Ulysses S *Grant in a private house. The area is now a national historical park.

ap'portionment /ə'pɔːʃnmənt; *AmE* ə'pɔːrʃnmənt/ *n* [C, U] (in the US) the way in which the number of seats (= places for members) is decided in a law-making assembly, especially the *House of Representatives, where the apportionment of seats is based on how many people live in each state: *a change in party rules to tie delegate apportionment more directly to primary election results.*

the Ap'prentice Boys' Pa'rade an occasion on 12 August every year when some of the Protestant citizens of Northern Ireland march through the streets of *Derry, in memory of the day in 1689 when the army of the Roman Catholic King *James II was forced to give up attacking the town. The march creates a lot of tension between Protestants and Catholics, and this sometimes leads to violence. See also ORANGEMEN.

ap'prenticeship *n* (in Britain) a system of training managed by the *Learning and Skills Council in which young people learn while working in a specific area of work to gain knowledge, skills and qualifications such as an *NVQ, or a *BTEC or *City and Guilds qualification in a that area.

APR /ˌeɪ piː 'ɑː(r)/ (*in full* **annual percentage rate**) *n* the rate of interest that you pay to an organization from which you borrow money in order to buy something. The APR can vary during the time the money is being paid back: *The APR on your credit card is 16.8% (variable).*

ˌApril 'Fool's Day (*also* **April Fools' Day**) 1 April, the day when people in many countries play tricks or jokes on each other. The victim of the joke is called the **April Fool**. A typical trick is to make somebody believe something that is not true, e.g. that the clocks have changed and everything is an hour later, or that the government has announced an election. Newspapers, television and radio stations often join in with imaginary news stories.

ˌApsley 'House /ˌæpsli/ a large elegant house near *Hyde Park(1) in London, sometimes called 'No 1, London'. It was built by Robert *Adam in the 18th century, and later belonged to the Duke of *Wellington. It is now the Wellington Museum.

The A,rabian 'Nights the name often given to the *Thousand and One Nights*, a collection of traditional stories from the Middle East, written in Arabic. Scheherazade marries a king who kills his wives after their first night together. She survives by telling him a different story every night. Many popular films, songs and *pantomimes are based on some of these stories, such as *Aladdin and *Sinbad the Sailor.

'Araldite™ /'ærəldaɪt/ n [U] a make of several types of very strong glue: *She mended the vase with Araldite.*

the 'Aran ,Islands /'ærən/ n [pl] a group of three islands off the west coast of Ireland.

,Aran 'jumper /,ærən/ (*also* **Aran sweater**) n a sweater (= a piece of clothing for the upper body) made of thick wool knitted in the traditional raised patterns of the *Aran Islands.

A'rapaho /ə'ræpəhəʊ; AmE ə'ræpəhoʊ/ n (pl **Arapahos** or **Arapaho**) a member of a Native American group. They lived on the *Great Plains, where they hunted buffalo. Today most Arapahos live on reservations (= areas of land given and protected by the US government) in Oklahoma and Wyoming, and earn money by renting their land for the discovery of oil and gas.

'Arbor Day /'ɑːbə; AmE 'ɑːrbər/ a special day in America when people plant trees. Each state chooses its own day, usually in the spring, but some southern states have it in the winter.

',Fatty' 'Arbuckle /'ɑːbʌkl; AmE 'ɑːrbʌkl/ (1887–1933) a US comic actor in silent films. He was one of the *Keystone Kops before becoming a star of popular films. In 1921 he was suspected of causing the death of an actress during a party. Although a court of law found him not guilty, his career was ruined.

arch'bishop n (in some Christian Churches) a *bishop of the highest rank, responsible for a large church district. In the *Church of England there are two archbishops, the *Archbishop of Canterbury and the *Archbishop of York, who both have a place in the *House of Lords. The *Archbishop of Westminster is the *Roman Catholic bishop of the highest rank in Britain. The title 'Your Grace' is used when talking to an archbishop and 'His Grace' when referring to one.

the Arch,bishop of 'Canterbury /'kæntəbəri; AmE 'kæntərberi/ the spiritual head of the *Church of England, who is also the *bishop of *Canterbury. His official title is 'Primate of All England'.

the Arch,bishop of 'Westminster /'westmɪnstə(r)/ the head of the *Roman Catholic Church in Britain.

the Arch,bishop of 'York /'jɔːk; AmE 'jɔːrk/ the second most senior religious leader of the *Church of England, who is also the *bishop of *York. His official title is 'Primate of England'. ⇨ note at CHURCH OF ENGLAND.

,Jeffrey 'Archer /'ɑːtʃə(r); AmE 'ɑːrtʃər/ (1940–) a former British *Conservative *Member of Parliament and a writer of best-selling novels about money, sex and power. In 1985 he became Deputy Chairman of the Conservative Party, but he had to leave the job in 1986 after a scandal reported in the *News of the World. He was made a *life peer in 1992, because of his loyalty to the Conservative party. He has often been in the newspapers and in court because of rumours about his sexual and financial affairs. He was in prison from 2001 to 2003 for perjury (= telling lies to a court of law).

The 'Archers /'ɑːtʃəz; AmE 'ɑːrtʃərz/ a popular British radio programme broadcast six days a week that presents a continuing story about the lives of ordinary people. The Archers are a family in the imaginary village of *Ambridge, a small farming community somewhere in the middle of England. The programme has been broadcast by the *BBC since 1951, longer than any other programme of its kind in the world. Many people try never to miss it: *Don't ring her up when she's listening to The Archers.*

the ,Forest of 'Arden /'ɑːdn; AmE 'ɑːrdn/ a large forest that once existed in *Warwickshire, England. Shakespeare's play *As You Like It is set in it.

,Edward ,Ardiz'zone /,ɑːdɪ'zəʊni; AmE ,ɑːrdɪ'zoʊni/ (1900–79) a British artist best known for his book illustrations, especially for children's books, some of which he also wrote.

'area code n (in the US) the first three numbers of a telephone number, usually shown in brackets. They identify the area of the country. Some states have one code but larger states and cities have several.

'Area of Out'standing 'Natural 'Beauty ⇨ AONB.

ARELS /'ærəlz/ a British organization of independent English language schools. Most British language schools that have been approved of officially by the *British Council are members of ARELS.

,Hannah 'Arendt /'ærənt; *also* 'eərənt/ (1906–75) a US political writer, philosopher and teacher born in Germany. She was Jewish and escaped from the Nazis by going in 1933 to Paris and in 1941 to the US. Her major books included *The Human Condition* (1958), *Eichmann in Jerusalem: A Report on the Banality of Evil* (1963) and *The Life of the Mind* (1977).

> **66** The sad truth is that most evil is done by people who never make up their minds to be good or evil. **99**
> Hannah Arendt

'Argos™ /'ɑːgɒs; AmE 'ɑːrgɑːs/ any of a chain of large shops in Britain selling electrical and other goods, usually at low prices. Only a small number of the goods on sale are displayed and people order in the shop from a catalogue containing illustrations of every item available.

▶ **the aristocracy**
British society still has quite a strong class system which is based on birth and social position. The upper class consists mainly of members of the aristocracy. The most senior are the *royal family and members of the *peerage. Next below them are *baronets. Baronets have hereditary titles (= ranks passed on in the family from one generation to the next) but, unlike some peers, are not allowed to sit in the *House of Lords. Below this there are various **orders of knighthood**.

*Knights are appointed by the king or queen. In *medieval times soldiers were made knights in recognition of military service for their local lord. Today, knighthoods and other *honours are announced at *New Year or on the king's or queen's birthday and are given in recognition of distinguished public service or achievement. New knights receive their title at a special ceremony, during which they kneel before the king or queen, who taps them once on each shoulder with a sword. Knights may put **Sir** (for men) or **Dame** (for women) before their first name, and are allowed to have their own **coat of arms** (= a family symbol, usually a design on a shield).

The oldest order of knighthood in England, which is also the oldest **order of chivalry** in Europe, is the *Order of the Garter. There are 25 Knights of the Garter, in addition to the king or queen and the *Prince of Wales. Other senior orders of knighthood include the *Order of the Thistle, the *Order of the

Bath, the *Order of the British Empire and the Royal Victorian Order. Letters after a person's name indicate which order he or she belongs to. Other knights are known as **knights bachelor**.

People who have an upper-class family background may be considered as part of the local aristocracy even if they do not have a title. They often have an upper-class accent and *Conservative social and political views and are referred to as **the county set**. Members of the aristocracy are sometimes described as 'blue-blooded', because in former times their veins showed blue through their skin which was pale from not having to work in the fields. They are also referred to informally as 'the upper crust', or more rudely as 'toffs'. Formerly, members of the aristocracy could command respect because of their noble birth. Nowadays, people are much more critical of those who inherit honours but who from their behaviour do not appear to deserve them.

The US has no formal aristocracy in that there are no families who have been given titles by the head of state. In fact, the *Constitution forbids an aristocracy, saying 'No title of nobility shall be granted by the United States.' Perhaps because of this, Americans are very interested in Britain's royal family and nobility. There is, however, respect for US families who, though they do not have titles, have wealth and a social position similar to the British aristocracy. Class in the US is, to a large extent, based on money, but some people have more respect for **old money** (= money, land, etc. that has belonged to a family for many years) than **new money** (= money that a person has earned by working). The *Boston Brahmins are the old, traditional families of *Boston and they, together with groups of old families from other parts of the US, make up a type of American aristocracy.

Ari'zona /ˌærɪˈzəʊnə; AmE ˌærɪˈzoʊnə/ a state in the south-western US, also known as the Grand Canyon State. Its capital and largest city is *Phoenix. Arizona's natural features include the *Grand Canyon, the *Painted Desert and the *Petrified Forest. It was the home of the *Apaches in the 19th century, and today Native Americans have 20 reservations (= areas of land given and protected by the US government) in the state. Its most important industry is manufacturing, especially of electrical and communication equipment. It also produces more than half of the country's copper.

'Arkansas /ˈɑːkənsɔː; AmE ˈɑːrkənsɔː/ a state in the central southern US, sometimes called the Land of Opportunity. Its capital and largest city is *Little Rock. The state's natural features include Hot Springs National Park and Buffalo National River. Its most important industries include the production of food and wood. See also ARKY.

the ˌArk 'Royal a British aircraft carrier (= a large ship with an area where aircraft can take off and land). There is a tradition in the *Royal Navy of naming important ships *Ark Royal*. The first one was a ship that fought the Spanish *Armada. Another famous *Ark Royal* was sunk in *World War II.

ˌRichard 'Arkwright /ˈɑːkraɪt; AmE ˈɑːrkraɪt/ (1732–92) an English businessman who invented a machine using water power for spinning cotton, which had been spun by hand until then. He built his own factory, and became one of the early leaders of the *Industrial Revolution. He was made a *knight in 1786.

'Arky /ˈɑːki; AmE ˈɑːrki/ n (informal) a person from *Arkansas.

'Arlington 'National 'Cemetery /ˈɑːlɪŋtən; AmE ˈɑːrlɪŋtən/ the most famous national cemetery in the US. It contains the *Tomb of the Unknown Soldier and

the grave of President John F *Kennedy. More than 160 000 Americans who were killed in wars are also buried there as well as politicians and other well-known people. It is in Arlington, Virginia, outside Washington, DC and was begun in 1864. In 1997 a Women in Military Service for America Memorial was put up at the entrance to the cemetery.

Arlington National Cemetery

ˌJohn 'Arlott /ˈɑːlət; AmE ˈɑːrlət/ (1914–91) a popular English *cricket commentator who described cricket matches on *BBC radio and television regularly from 1947 to 1980. Many people in Britain associated the sound of his voice with cricket, or with the summer in general.

the Ar'mada /ɑːˈmɑːdə; AmE ɑːrˈmɑːdə/ (also **the Spanish Armada**) n the group of 129 ships sent by Spain in 1588 to attack England. A group of British ships, led by Lord Howard of Effingham's *Ark Royal and Francis *Drake's *Revenge*, defeated the Armada in the *English Channel. It was the first sea battle in history involving large numbers of ships, and was seen by the English as a great victory. The word *armada* is now often used to mean any large group of ships: *A small armada of fishing boats blocked the port in protest against the new regulations.*

Ar'magh /ɑːˈmɑː; AmE ɑːrˈmɑː/ **1** one of the former *Six Counties of Ulster, in the southern part of Northern Ireland.
2 a town in the south of Northern Ireland. It is the religious centre of Northern Ireland and the Republic of Ireland, and has both a Roman Catholic and a Protestant *archbishop.

▶ the armed forces

The British armed forces, sometimes called the **services**, consist of the **Army**, the **Royal Navy** (**RN**), and the **Royal Air Force** (**RAF**). The Queen is **Commander-in-Chief** of all three services, but responsibility for their management lies with the **Ministry of Defence** (**MOD**), which is headed by the **Secretary of State for Defence**. The Army is the largest of the three services and the Royal Navy the smallest. The Navy is the service with the longest history and is sometimes known as the **senior service**. The regular forces are supported when necessary by the **regular reserves**, who are former members of the regular forces and **volunteer reserves**, people who train in their free time with the **Territorial Army**, the **Reserve Air Forces**, or the **Royal Navy Reserve**. In 1998 the government's **Strategic Defence Review** set out a plan of modernization of the armed forces and established a **Joint Rapid Reaction Force** which includes all three services.

In the US the President is **Commander-in Chief** of the armed forces and the **Secretary of Defense** is responsible for their management. The **Joint Chiefs of Staff** are the military leaders of the four services, the **Army**, **Navy**, **Air Force** and **Marine Corps**, which are supported when necessary by the reserve forces, the **US**

Army Reserve, the **National Guard** and the **Navy Reserve**. The Army is the service with the longest history. Four of its leaders became President: George Washington, Andrew Jackson, Ulysses S Grant and Dwight Eisenhower.

'Armistice Day 11 November, the anniversary of the end of *World War I, also called *Poppy Day. People used to stop what they were doing at 11 a.m. on Armistice Day and stand in silence for two minutes to remember the dead. After *World War II it was replaced by *Remembrance Sunday in Britain and *Veterans' Day in America.

ˌLance 'Armstrong[1] /ˌlɑːns 'ɑːmstrɒŋ; AmE ˌlæns 'ɑːrmstrɔːŋ/ (1971–) a US cyclist who recovered from cancer in 1996 and returned to the sport to have a very successful career, winning the **Tour de France** cycle race six times from 1999 to 2004.

ˌLouis 'Armstrong[2] /'ɑːmstrɒŋ; AmE 'ɑːrmstrɔːŋ/ (1900–71) a famous US *jazz musician and leader of a band. His popular name was 'Satchmo', a short form of 'Satchelmouth', because of his large mouth. He played the trumpet and sang with a rough voice. He appeared in more than 50 films and performed around the world as a special representative of the US *State Department. Many people think he was the greatest of all jazz musicians.

ˌNeil 'Armstrong[3] /'ɑːmstrɒŋ; AmE 'ɑːrmstrɔːŋ/ (1930–) the US astronaut who was the first man to walk on the moon, on 20 July 1969. He later taught at Cincinnati University in the 1970s. See also ALDRIN, APOLLO PROGRAM.

> **66** That's one small step for man, one giant leap for mankind. **99**
> Neil Armstrong when he stepped onto the moon

army ⇨ note at ARMED FORCES.

'Arnhem /'ɑːnəm; AmE 'ɑːrnəm/ a town in the Netherlands, on the River Rhine. A famous *World War II battle took place there in 1944, when Allied forces tried, and failed, to capture a bridge over the Rhine. Thousands of people were killed. The battle was the subject of the film *A Bridge Too Far*. See also ALLIES.

ˌBenedict 'Arnold[1] /ˌbenədɪkt 'ɑːnəld; AmE 'ɑːrnəld/ (1741–1801) an American general who betrayed his country in the *American Revolution. Although at first he fought bravely and won battles for the Americans, he tried in 1780 to give the fort at *West Point, which he commanded, to the British. He failed and escaped to London. His name is still used by Americans to mean somebody who betrays their country.

ˌMalcolm 'Arnold[2] /'ɑːnəld; AmE 'ɑːrnəld/ (1921–) a British composer who has written several symphonies, as well as music for ballets and films. He was made a *knight in 1993.

ˌMatthew 'Arnold[3] /'ɑːnəld; AmE 'ɑːrnəld/ (1822–88) an English poet and critic, son of Thomas *Arnold. He wrote several collections of poetry, and important essays about education and social and political life in Britain. His best-known poems are *Dover Beach* and *The Scholar-Gypsy*.

ˌThomas 'Arnold[4] /'ɑːnəld; AmE 'ɑːrnəld/ (1795–1842) headmaster of *Rugby School (1828–42). He introduced many changes that influenced the development of *public school(1) education in Britain. Matthew *Arnold was his son. See also TOM BROWN'S SCHOOLDAYS.

'Arsenal a *football club in North London. The name *Arsenal* and the *nickname of the club, 'the Gunners', come from the club's origin in the 1880s, when the players worked at the Royal Arsenal, the place where army

weapons were stored. The club has been quite successful in English and European competitions since the 1930s.

'Arsenic and 'Old 'Lace a humorous US play (1941) by Joseph Kasselring. The story is about two old women who murder their visitors. It had 1444 performances on Broadway and a film version was made in 1944. It is still regularly performed by amateur actors, especially in Britain.

ˌart 'deco /'dekəʊ; AmE 'dekoʊ/ (also **deco**) n [U] a style of art, design and architecture, popular in the 1920s and 1930s, using simple shapes, bright colours, and modern materials such as chrome and plastic. Many of New York's famous buildings are influenced by art deco: *I bought some art deco lamps in a local antique shop.*

the ˌArtful 'Dodger /'dɒdʒə(r); AmE 'dɑːdʒər/ a character in *Oliver Twist* by Charles *Dickens. He is a young thief who steals things from people's pockets, and is one of the group of thieves that Oliver joins.

▶ **art galleries and museums of art**
In Britain, works of art are displayed in art galleries and, especially outside London, in *museums. Shops that sell paintings are also called galleries. In the US public **art collections** are displayed in **art museums**, and a **gallery** is a place where people go to buy works of art.

Many galleries and museums in Britain and the US receive limited financial support from national or local government. Other money is raised through admission fees, although admission to many British museums is free, and the sale of postcards, calendars, etc. Some galleries obtain money through sponsorship. Many works of art are expensive and galleries can rarely buy them without organizing a public appeal or, in Britain, asking for money from the *National Art Collections Fund.

Visiting an art gallery is a popular leisure activity. Galleries and museums are friendlier places than they used to be. Many try to encourage children's interest in art by arranging school visits and many people make their first trip to an art museum with their school class.

The most popular galleries in Britain, all in London, are the *National Gallery, which receives over 4 million visitors a year, the *National Portrait Gallery, *Tate Britain and *Tate Modern. The *Royal Academy's Summer Exhibition of paintings sent in by the general public also receives a lot of visitors. Sculpture attracts less attention, and though the names of Henry *Moore and Barbara *Hepworth are known to many people, few could describe any of their works. Well-known galleries outside London include the *National Gallery of Scotland in Edinburgh and the Birmingham Museum and Art Gallery.

Important art museums in the US include the *Metropolitan Museum of Art, the *Museum of Modern Art and the *Guggenheim Museum, all in New York, and the *Smithsonian Institution in Washington, DC. Most US cities and many smaller towns have art museums.

Galleries sometimes **mount exhibitions** of the paintings of one artist, e.g. *Turner, that are brought together from all over the world. People are prepared to queue for a long time to see them. Many people admire **old masters**, famous works by great artists of the past, but have little interest in modern art. New works receive publicity in the media only when they are unusual or likely to shock people. Galleries and museums try to encourage a more positive attitude to modern art but many people remain doubtful. When the Tate displayed half a cow and its calf rotting in formaldehyde (= a chemical used to preserve it), the public criticized the artist, Damien *Hirst. There is usually controversy about the winners of the *Turner Prize

Some exhibitions bring together all kinds of art, not only paintings, from a particular time or country so that

A

A

people can learn about it. Exhibitions on subjects such as the Aztecs, *art nouveau and the art of Turkey attract large crowds.

'**art house** n (pl **houses**) (AmE) a small, usually independent cinema showing films which are made more for artistic reasons than for commercial profit: It makes a change to go to an art-house movie instead of another Hollywood blockbuster.

,**King 'Arthur** (5th or 6th century) a king of England who led the Britons in battles against the *Saxons. There are many stories about King Arthur, e.g. that he pulled his sword *Excalibur from a stone, and that he sat with his *knights at a *Round Table(1). Nobody knows if the stories are true, but they are very popular and have been used in poems, plays and films.
  ▸ **Arthurian** /ɑːˈθʊəriən; AmE ɑːrˈθjʊəriən/ adj.

▸ **Arthurian legend**

The legends of King *Arthur and the *Knights of the Round Table are familiar to many British people. They are the subject of several poems and stories of the *Middle Ages (11th-15th centuries), as well as of later novels, musical plays and films, and are a central part of British tradition and folklore. The most important **Arthurian** works include Sir Thomas *Malory's Le *Morte D'Arthur, a set of long prose romances (= stories of love and adventure) written in the 15th century, Alfred Lord *Tennyson's *Idylls of the King, a series of twelve poems dating from the 19th century and T H White's novel The Once and Future King (1958). The legends continue to be retold in new ways, for instance in the musical Camelot (1960) and the films The *Sword in the Stone and King Arthur (2004).

The real King Arthur lived in the late 5th and early 6th century. He was a warrior chief who fought against the *Anglo-Saxons and probably defeated them at the Battle of Badon. He is said to have died in the battle of Camlan. Stories about him were collected in the 12th century by the historian *Geoffrey of Monmouth. They were added to and developed by French writers such as Chrétien de Troyes, who wrote during the period 1170–90, and also became the centre of a group of legends in Germany. As a result, other characters such as *Lancelot, Tristram (Tristan) and Perceval (Parzival) became associated with Arthur and were included by Malory in Le Morte D'Arthur, the version of the legends which became most widely known in Britain.

The stories of Arthur and his knights celebrate the **age of chivalry**, when knights aimed to live according to the highest Christian principles. Their character and courage are tested by meetings with giants, dragons and sorcerers, and by their own human weakness, such as pride or forbidden love. The love affairs of Tristram and Isoud (Iseult) and Lancelot and Guinevere are part of the tradition of **courtly love** which was a central theme in European poetry of the Middle Ages.

According to legend, Arthur was born at *Tintagel in *Cornwall, the son of Uther Pendragon, King of all England. One version says that at a young age he was put under a spell by the magician *Merlin so that he grew up not knowing he was heir to the English throne. He became King at the age of 15 after he pulled the magic sword *Excalibur out of a stone when all the knights of the kingdom had failed to do so. Another version of the legend says that he received the sword from the *Lady of the Lake, and this fits in with the story that, as he was dying, he ordered the sword to be thrown back into the lake and it was caught by a hand that rose from the water. Arthur gathered round him the most worthy knights in the land, including Sir Lancelot, Lancelot's son Sir *Galahad, Sir Bedivere and Sir *Gawain, and

established his court at *Camelot. On Arthur's orders the knights all sat at the *Round Table, so nobody could sit at the head of the table and claim to be more important than the rest.

Arthur won many victories in battle and married the beautiful *Guinevere. Later, Arthur's half-sister, the sorceress Morgan le Fay, attempted to kill him, and Arthur's discovery of a love affair between his wife and Sir Lancelot further threatened his court. The knights went off in search of the *Holy Grail. Lancelot saw but failed to obtain it because he was not sufficiently pure, and it was eventually found by Sir Galahad. Arthur went to fight against Rome with Sir Gawain but while he was abroad, his nephew Mordred seized the kingdom and made Guinevere his prisoner. Arthur returned to England to defeat and kill Mordred at the battle of Camlan, but was himself seriously wounded. Morgan le Fay then appeared in a boat to take Arthur to *Avalon, the paradise of the *Celts. According to some versions Arthur and his knights now lie asleep underground, waiting for the day they are needed to wake and save England from danger.

Many people now visit Tintagel Castle high above the sea, the place where Arthur was born and later the home of Mark, the husband of Iseult, Tristram's lover. Several attempts have been made to identify where Arthur's Camelot was. Suggested sites include Caerleon in South Wales, Camelford and South Cadbury, both in Somerset, and *Winchester. *Glastonbury is said to be Avalon because in the 12th century some monks there claimed to have found the graves of Arthur and Guinevere.

the 'Articles of Con,fede'ration the first written American laws of government. The *thirteen colonies agreed to the articles in 1781 and used them until the US Constitution replaced them in 1789.

,**art nou'veau** /ˌɑː nuːˈvəʊ; AmE ˌɑːr nuːˈvoʊ/ n [U] a style of art, design and architecture, popular at the end of the 19th century. It uses long curving lines influenced by the shapes of leaves and flowers. The most famous British artists and designers working in this style were Aubrey *Beardsley and Charles Rennie *Mackintosh.

the ,Arts and 'Crafts ,Movement a social and artistic movement in Britain in the second half of the 19th century, led by William *Morris and John *Ruskin. Following the *Industrial Revolution, when more and more things were made by machines, the aim of the Arts and Crafts Movement was to make things such as furniture and silver objects by hand that were beautiful as well as useful.

'**Arts ,Council** n any of four organizations in Britain (one each for England, Scotland, Wales and Northern Ireland) that give government money to artistic projects with the aim of encouraging the arts and making them more popular. For example, if a theatre company receives money from the Arts Council, it may help the company to reduce the price of tickets.

the ASA /ˌeɪ es 'eɪ/ ⇨ ADVERTISING STANDARDS AUTHORITY.

ASBO /'æzbəʊ; AmE ˈæzboʊ/ (in full ,**antisocial be'haviour ,order**) n (in England and Wales) an official order, introduced in 1998, which can be given to someone telling them to stop doing something which is having a bad effect on the people living in an area, such as vandalism (= destroying or damaging property), harassment (= annoying or worrying people by saying or doing unpleasant things), causing a lot of noise etc. Anybody who breaks the conditions of the order can be charged with a criminal offence.

ASCAP /'æskæp/ ⇨ AMERICAN SOCIETY OF COMPOSERS, AUTHORS AND PUBLISHERS.

As'cension Day (*also* **Holy Thursday**) the 40th day after Easter, a Christian holy day celebrating the **Ascension** (= Christ's rising to heaven).

ASCII (*in full* **American Standard Code for Information Interchange**) a computer code using letters and numbers. It is used for storing information in computers and for exchanging information between computers: *If you save it as an ASCII file I should be able to read it on my computer.*

'Ascot /'æskət/ a course for horse races near *Windsor¹ in Berkshire, England. See also ROYAL ASCOT.

'Asda™ /'æzdə/ any of a chain of large supermarkets in Britain, selling food, clothes and household goods at low prices. Asda became part of *Wal-Mart in 1999.

ASH /æʃ/ (*in full* **Action on Smoking and Health**) a charity in Britain and other countries, set up in 1971, that campaigns to reduce smoking, mainly through advertisements showing the dangers of smoking and campaigning for laws to prevent smoking in public places.

Paddy Ashdown (1941–) a British politician, and the first leader of the *Liberal Democratic Party from 1988 to 1999. He was a *Member of Parliament until 2001. He was made a *knight in 2000 and a *life peer in 2001.

Arthur 'Ashe /æʃ/ (1943–93) a US *tennis player. He was the first African American to win the *US Open (1968) and *Wimbledon (1975). He became captain of the US *Davis Cup team in 1983.

the Ashes an imaginary prize that goes to the winner of each series of international *cricket matches between England and Australia. The name comes from a humorous newspaper article written when Australia beat England at cricket in 1882, saying that English cricket had died, that it would be cremated (= burnt after death), and that its ashes would be taken to Australia: *With this victory Australia have retained the Ashes.*

The 'Ash Grove a traditional Welsh song about a beautiful young woman who has died and is buried under a group of ash trees.

Laura 'Ashley ⇨ LAURA ASHLEY.

the Ash,molean Mu'seum /æʃ,məʊliən; *AmE* æʃ,məʊliən/ (*informal* **the Ashmolean**) a museum in *Oxford, England. It is the oldest public museum in Britain, and was opened by Elias Ashmole in 1683. It has important collections of paintings and archaeological objects such as ancient Greek sculptures and Roman coins.

Frederick 'Ashton /'æʃtən/ (1904–88) a British ballet dancer and choreographer. He was the first choreographer of the *Royal Ballet, and later its director (1963–70). His best-known ballets are *Façade*, *La Fille Mal Gardée* and *A Month in the Country*. He was made a *knight in 1962.

Ash 'Wednesday (in the Christian Church) the first day of *Lent. Traditionally, *Roman Catholics go to church on Ash Wednesday and their foreheads are marked with ashes as a sign that human bodies become dust. In the US this tradition is still widely followed. The ashes are not washed off but left to go away on their own. It is polite not to make a comment on the mark on a person's forehead.

Asian A'merican *n* an American who was born in an Asian country or who is descended from Asians. Asian Americans live mostly on the west coast of the US, and include Chinese, Japanese, Koreans and Vietnamese.
▶ **Asian-American** *adj.*

Asian 'Dub Foun,dation /'dʌb/ a British pop group, formed in 1994, who mix Asian music with *jungle, *dub and other styles. Their albums include *Facts and Fictions* (1995), *Rafi's Revenge* (1998) and *Enemy of the Enemy* (2003).

,Asian 'Times a British newspaper published every week, which contains articles on politics, culture, sport and other subjects of interest to people in Britain's Asian community. It first appeared in 1983.

,Isaac 'Asimov /'æzɪmɒf; *AmE* 'æzɪmɑːf/ (1920–92) a US writer of science fiction who invented the word 'robotics'. His books include *Foundation* (1951) and the short story collection *I, Robot* (1950).

,ask'Jeeves™ /'dʒiːvz/ (*also* **Ask.com**) a search engine (= a website which helps you to search for information on the Internet) started in 1997 which encourages users to type in questions rather than just keywords. The main web page uses a picture of the character Jeeves, the butler (= male servant) in the novels of P G *Wodehouse.

ASLEF /'æzlef/ (*in full* **the Associated Society of Locomotive Engineers and Firemen**) a British *trade union that represents train drivers and other rail transport workers. See also RMT.

AS level /,eɪ 'es ,levl/ (*in full* **Advanced Subsidiary level**) *n* [U, C] (in England and Wales) an exam usually taken in Year 12 of school or college (= the year before the final year) when students are aged 17. Together with *A2 level exams, AS levels form the *A level (Advanced level) qualification, which is needed for entrance to universities: *Students will normally take four or five AS subjects.* ◇ *She's doing an AS (level) in French.*

the ASPCA /,eɪ es piː siː 'eɪ/ ⇨ AMERICAN SOCIETY FOR THE PREVENTION OF CRUELTY TO ANIMALS.

'Aspen /'æspən/ a town that is famous as a centre for skiing, in the US state of Colorado. It is in the *Rocky Mountains and is often visited by rich and well-known people. It also has a cultural festival in the summer.

'Herbert 'Henry 'Asquith /'æskwɪθ/ (1852–1928) a British Liberal *prime minister (1908–16). His government introduced the first benefits of the *welfare state, such as *pensions for old people. He was also responsible for reducing the powers of the *House of Lords and for leading Britain into *World War I. He was made an *earl(1) in 1925.

As'say ,Office *n* (in Britain) any of the offices where gold, silver and platinum are tested and given *hallmarks (= small marks showing the quality of the metal). There are four such offices in Britain: in *London, *Birmingham, *Sheffield and *Edinburgh.

As,semblies of 'God the largest Pentecostal Church in the US. It began in 1914 and has more than a million members. They believe that illness can be cured by faith. The main office of the church is in Springfield, Missouri. See also PENTECOSTALIST.

As'sembly ,Member *n* (*abbr* **AM**) **1** a person elected to represent one of the 40 *constituencies or one of the five regions into which Wales is divided for the *Welsh Assembly. Each constituency elects one AM and each region elects four AMs. These elections are separate from general elections for the British *Parliament. They were first held in 1999 and take place every four years. **2** (*also* **Member of the Legislative Assembly** *abbr* **MLA**) a person elected to the *Northern Ireland Assembly. Six members are elected from each of 18 *constituencies. These elections are separate from elections for the British *Parliament. They were first held in 1998 and take place every four years. **3** any of the 25 elected members of the *London Assembly.

as,sisted 'area *n* (in Britain) a part of the country in which there are many unemployed people, and the government tries to encourage business and industry to employ more people, e.g. by lending money to com-

A

panies at low interest: *When the mines closed down the region was granted assisted area status.*

As,sociated 'Press (*abbr* **AP**) the oldest and largest US news service, with offices all over the world. Its members include newspapers and television and radio stations. They collect the news and AP sends it to all members. The service began in 1848 and is a non-profit company.

the As,soci'ation of 'British 'Travel ,Agents ⇨ ABTA.

the As,soci'ation of 'Recognized 'English 'Language Services ⇨ ARELS.

,Fred A'staire /əˈsteə(r); *AmE* əˈster/ (1899–1987) a US dancer, singer and actor. His many musical films included *Top Hat* (1935), *Easter Parade* (1948) and *Silk Stockings* (1957). He danced mostly with Ginger *Rogers but also with Audrey *Hepburn, Cyd Charisse and others.

,Aston 'Martin™ /ˌæstən ˈmɑːtɪn; *AmE* ˈmɑːrtɪn/ an expensive and fashionable British make of sports car. It is the make driven by James *Bond in several films.

,Aston Uni'versity /ˌæstən/ a university in *Birmingham, England, formed in 1966.

,Aston 'Villa /ˌæstən ˈvɪlə/ a *football club in *Birmingham, England, having its ground at Villa Park in the Aston area of the city. The club was very successful at the end of the 19th century, and in the 1970s and 80s, winning the *European Cup in 1982.

,Nancy 'Astor /ˈæstə(r)/ (1879–1964) a British politician, born in 1919 she became the first woman Member of Parliament in the *House of Commons.

A,stronomer 'Royal an honorary title given to an important British astronomer.

'Astroturf™ /ˈæstrəʊtɜːf; *AmE* ˈæstroʊtɜːrf/ *n* [U] a make of artificial grass used as a surface on which sports are played: *We can play football all year round now they've installed an Astroturf pitch.*

the *ASV* /ˌeɪ es ˈviː/ ⇨ AMERICAN STANDARD VERSION.

,As You 'Like It a comedy play (1599) by Shakespeare about the family and friends of a *duke who are forced to live in the Forest of *Arden when the duke's brother, Frederick, takes his land. Rosalind, the duke's daughter, disguises herself as a boy to be with the man she loves, Orlando. Her friend, Frederick's daughter, falls in love with Orlando's brother. They reveal who they really are, and the two couples get married. As well as the love story between the central characters, much of the comedy in the play comes from minor characters, including Touchstone and Jaques.

AT&T™ /ˌeɪ tiː ˈtiː/ (*in full* **American Telephone and Telegraph**) formerly the largest telephone and communications company in the US, providing many international services. It began in 1885 by running a telephone line from New York to *Philadelphia and was one of Americas's best-known companies until it was bought by SBC Communications in 2005.

ATF /ˌeɪ tiː ˈef/ ⇨ BUREAU OF ALCOHOL, TOBACCO, FIREARMS AND EXPLOSIVES.

the ,Athe'naeum /ˌæθɪˈniːəm/ a London club formed in 1824 for men in the fields of literature, art and science. It is named after an Ancient Greek temple where people met to discuss academic matters. ⇨ note at GENTLEMEN'S CLUBS.

,Chet 'Atkins¹ /ˌtʃet ˈætkɪnz/ (1924–2001) a US guitar player who helped to create the 'Nashville Sound'. In 1973, he was chosen for the Country Music *Hall of Fame. The Country Music Association named him 'Musician of the Year' nine times. See also NASHVILLE.

,Tommy 'Atkins² /ˈætkɪnz/ the name used by people to refer to the average British soldier in the 19th and early 20th centuries: *While the senior officers had comfortable beds, poor Tommy Atkins slept in the trenches.*

the 'Atkins ,Diet™ a weight loss programme developed by **Dr Robert Atkins** (1930–2003) which involves restricting the amount of carbohydrates, such as bread, pasta, etc., that you eat and replacing them with more protein and fat, such as meat, butter, etc. People who follow the diet are expected to lose weight because their body will burn more fat for energy. The diet has become very popular in the US and Britain and there are many Atkins books and food products available.

,Rowan 'Atkinson /ˌrəʊən ˈætkɪnsən; *AmE* ˌroʊən/ (1955–) an English comedy actor, well known for his ability to show amusing expressions on his face. He has acted in many popular films and television programmes, including *Blackadder* and *Mr Bean*.

At'lanta /ətˈlæntə/ the capital city of the US state of *Georgia. It is a major commercial centre for the southeastern US. Martin Luther *King led the *civil rights movement from Atlanta. The 1996 Olympic Games were also held there.

the At,lantic 'Charter /ətˌlæntɪk/ an agreement signed by Winston *Churchill, the British Prime Minister, and Franklin D *Roosevelt, the US President, in 1941 about the rights of nations and international relations. Its main purpose was to condemn the actions of Germany. In 1942 statements of the Atlantic Charter became part of the Declaration of the United Nations. See also WORLD WAR II.

At,lantic 'City /ətˌlæntɪk/ a city on the coast in the American state of *New Jersey. It is popular with tourists and contains many casinos (= gambling clubs) where people can gamble legally. The 'Miss America' competition is held there each year. The city has a famous Boardwalk (= a wide path made of wood) along the edge of the sea, and the names of some of its streets were used for the US version of the game *Monopoly*.

The At,lantic 'Monthly /ətˌlæntɪk ˈmʌnθli/ a US magazine known for its intelligent writing on culture and modern life. It is published in *Boston, where it began in 1857 as a 'journal of literature, politics, science, and the arts'. It became famous for its reports on the American *Civil War. Ernest *Hemingway sold his first short story to the magazine in 1927.

,Charles 'Atlas /ˈætləs/ (1894–1974) an American who had great success selling courses on how to develop muscles and a stronger body, using a method which he called 'dynamic tension'. The advertisements for his courses showed a thin man ('a seven-stone weakling') on the beach having sand kicked in his face by a strong man who was popular with the girls. Atlas's name is sometimes used to refer to somebody who is very strong.

,David 'Attenborough¹ /ˈætənbrə/ (1926–) an English television presenter and programme maker who has made many programmes about nature, including the series *Life on Earth*. He is well known for getting very close to the animals he films, and describing them in a voice that is very quiet but very enthusiastic. He was made a *knight in 1985. Richard *Attenborough is his brother.

,Richard 'Attenborough² /ˈætənbrə/ (1923–) an English film actor, producer and director. He has acted in many famous British films, including *Brighton Rock* (1947). His most successful film as director and producer was *Gandhi* (1982), which won eight *Oscars. He was made a *knight in 1976 and a *life peer in 1993. David *Attenborough is his brother.

at'tendance ,centre n (in Britain) a place where young people aged 17–21 are sent if they break the law but their crimes are not serious enough for them to be sent to a *young offender institution. They have to go to an attendance centre for a particular number of hours, usually in the evenings and at weekends: *He went to the youth court and got 24 hours at an attendance centre.*

,**Clement 'Attlee** /'ætli/ (1883–1967) a British *Labour politician who became Prime Minister (1945–51), defeating Winston *Churchill in the 1945 election. His government introduced the *National Health Service, nationalized important industries such as coal, gas, electricity and railways, and gave independence to India, Pakistan, Burma (now Myanmar) and Ceylon (now Sri Lanka).

At,torney 'General 1 the most senior legal officer in England, Wales and Northern Ireland. The Attorney General is a *Member of Parliament belonging to the party in power who advises the government on legal matters and represents it in law courts.
2 the head of the US *Department of Justice, who is chosen by the President to represent the government in legal matters.
3 the most senior legal officer in any state of the US.

A2 (level) /,eɪ 'tu:/ n [U, C] (in England and Wales) an exam usually taken in year 13 of school or college (= the final year) when students are aged 18. Students must first study a subject at *AS level before they can take an A2 exam. Together AS and A2 level exams form the *A level (Advanced level) qualification, which is needed for entrance to universities: *Students will normally take three A2 subjects.* ◇ *He's doing an A2 (level) in Maths.*

,**John 'Aubrey** /'ɔ:bri/ (1626–97) an English writer and archaeologist. He studied *Stonehenge and *Avebury and suggested the idea, which some people still believe today, that Stonehenge was built by *Druids. He is now mainly remembered for his book *Brief Lives*.

,**W H 'Auden** /'ɔ:dn/ (Wystan Hugh Auden 1907–73) an English poet who wrote poems of many different types, often using traditional forms of verse but with modern language. He also wrote the words for operas and a famous publicity film for the *Post Office. In the 1930s, when he wrote some of his best poems, he was a leading member of a group of left-wing writers. Many of his most famous poems are in the collection *Another Time* (1940). In 1946 he became a US citizen and his later poetry became more religious. His work has had a strong influence on later 20th–century poetry.

'**John 'James 'Audubon** /'ɔ:dəbən/ (1785–1851) a US naturalist, born in Haiti. He painted every bird that was then known in North America and collected over 1000 paintings in his book *Birds of America* (1827–38). See also AUDUBON SOCIETY.

the 'Audubon So,ciety /'ɔ:dəbən/ a non-profit US organization that works to protect birds and wild animals, and the places where they live and breed. The society began in 1905 and the main office is in New York City. It is named in memory of John James *Audubon.

the Au'gustan Age /ɔ:'gʌstən/ the period of English literature in the early 18th century, when writers such as *Swift and *Pope were active. The name comes from that of the Roman emperor Augustus, who ruled when Virgil, Horace and Ovid were writing, and suggests a classical period of elegant literature.

,**August Bank 'Holiday** (also **Summer Bank Holiday**) n [usually sing] (in England, Wales and Northern Ireland) a *bank holiday on the last Monday in August, when many people go to the coast, or to events such as the *Edinburgh Festival or the *Notting Hill Carnival: *We got stuck in the August Bank Holiday traffic on the way back.*

St Au'gustine /ɔ:'gʌstɪn/ (died 604) a Christian saint who was sent from Rome to England with 40 monks to teach Christianity to the *Anglo-Saxons. The king of *Kent, Ethelbert, was converted by him and became a Christian. Augustine built a church in his capital city, *Canterbury, and became the first *Archbishop of Canterbury.

,**Auld Lang 'Syne** /,ɔ:ld læŋ 'saɪn/ an old Scottish song about friendship and remembering good times in the past. The title means 'old long since'. Traditionally, people in Britain hold hands and sing it at midnight at a party on *New Year's Eve. It was already a traditional song when Robert *Burns wrote the version that most people sing now. Many people know the beginning of the song:

> 66 Should auld acquaintance be forgot,
> And never brought to min' (= mind)?
> Should auld acquaintance be forgot,
> And auld lang syne! 99

,**Auld 'Reekie** /,ɔ:ld 'ri:ki/ a popular name for *Edinburgh. It means 'old smoky' and refers to the smoke from the city's many chimneys.

,**Aunt Je'mima™** /dʒə'maɪmə/ the name of a US food product that is mixed with milk and eggs to make pancakes (= flat round cakes). The box originally had a picture of an African-American woman wearing a piece of material on her head like a servant. This came to be seen as offensive, and the name Aunt Jemima was sometimes used to mean an African-American woman who liked to serve white people. The picture was changed in the 1970s to show a modern African-American woman.

,**Aunt 'Sally** n (BrE) 1 a model of a person's head that people throw balls at to win prizes, usually at *fairs and other outdoor social events. The aim is to hit the head or knock it down.
2 a person or thing that everyone criticizes or laughs at: *His handling of the crisis has made him the Aunt Sally of politics.*

,**Jane 'Austen** /'ɒstɪn; AmE 'ɑ:stɪn/ (1775–1817) an English writer whose novels have had a strong influence on the development of English literature. In them she describes the personal relationships and social life of the English *upper middle class of her time with gentle humour. She herself never married. Her best-known books are *Sense and Sensibility* (1811), *Pride and Prejudice* (1813), *Emma* (1816) and *Persuasion* (1818). Many of her novels have been made into films.

,**Paul 'Auster** /'ɔ:stə(r); also 'ɒstə(r); AmE 'ɔ:stər, 'ɑ:stər/ (1947–) a US author of novels and poems who is best known for his collection of three detective stories, *The New York Trilogy* (1987). His later books include *The Music of Chance* (1990), and *Timbuktu* (1999). In 1999 he was responsible for The National Story Project on *NPR. Listeners from across the US sent in their own true stories and he selected the most interesting ones to read on the *Weekend All Things Considered* radio programme. He later published a collection of them in *I Thought my Father was God, and Other True Tales* (2001).

'**Austin¹** /'ɒstɪn; AmE 'ɔ:stɪn/ the capital city of the US state of *Texas, on the Colorado river.

'**Austin™²** /'ɒstɪn; AmE 'ɑ:stɪn/ n a popular make of British car, including the Austin Seven which was introduced in 1922 as the first small car. The company became part of *British Leyland in 1968 but the name *Austin* was still used on some British cars until the 1980s.

Au'stralia /ɒ'streɪliə; AmE ɔ:'streɪliə/ a large island country and continent in the south-west Pacific Ocean. Its capital city is Canberra and its official language is

English. The first inhabitants of Australia were the Aborigines, who now form only about 1.5% of the population. In 1770 the country was visited by Captain James *Cook, and in the 18th and 19th centuries it was used by the British as a place to send criminals. Many of Australia's present inhabitants are descended from British people. It is now independent from Britain, although it remains a member of the *Commonwealth. Most of the population live on or near the coast in the east and south of the country, and there are large areas in the west, north and centre of the country that have very few inhabitants. The climate is generally warm. Australian culture is popular in Britain. A number of Australian programmes, including *soap operas such as *Neighbours, appear regularly on British television. A popular informal name for Australia is 'Down Under'. See also BOTANY BAY.
▶ **Australian** adj, n.

the ˌAuthorized ˈVersion (abbr the AV) (also the **King James Version**) an English translation of the Bible that was ordered by King *James I for use in churches. It was first published in 1611 and became the main English version of the Bible. In the 20th century more modern translations were made, but many *Anglican churches continue to use the Authorized Version, and many people still prefer its old-fashioned language.

the ˈAutomobile Associˌation ⇨ AA(2).

ˌGene ˈAutry /ˈɔːtri/ (1907–98) a US actor and singer in *western films in the 1930s and 1940s. He was known as the 'singing cowboy' and made more than 90 films. His horse was called Champion. Autry also had a popular radio programme. His best-known songs included *Tumblin' Tumbleweeds* (1935) and *Rudolph the Red-Nosed Reindeer* (1950).

ˌautumn ˈstatement n a British government statement made every year in the autumn about the economy and the government's future economic plans: *The Chancellor announced in his autumn statement that he would lower income tax.*

AV /ˌeɪ ˈviː/ ⇨ AUTHORIZED VERSION.

ˈAvalon /ˈævəlɒn; AmE ˈævəlɑːn/ (in ancient Welsh stories) a beautiful island where dead heroes go. According to the legend (= story from ancient times) it is the place where King *Arthur's body was taken after his last battle. Some people believe Avalon to be in or near what is now *Glastonbury. The name is thought to mean 'land of apples'.

ˈAvebury /ˈeɪvbri/ a village in *Wiltshire, England, where there is an important prehistoric monument. This consists of *Silbury Hill and a circle of standing stones that is much larger than *Stonehenge. Avebury was made a *World Heritage Site in 1986.

Avebury

*The A*ˈvengers /əˈvendʒəz; AmE əˈvendʒərz/ a popular British television series, made in the 1960s, in which John Steed, an English *gentleman(3), and his friend Emma Peel, an expert in judo, had slightly comic adventures fighting crime. Many people remember *The Avengers* for Emma Peel's leather suits and Steed's bowler hat and rolled umbrella. A less successful film was made in 1998 with Ralph *Fiennes and Sean *Connery.

Aˈventis /əˈventɪs/ (also Aˌventis ˈPharma /ˈfɑːmə; AmE ˈfɑːrmə/) an international drugs company which provides the money for the **Aventis Prizes for Science Books**. The prizes, which started in 1988 and are judged by the *Royal Society, are given every year for general science books and science books for children.

ˌTex ˈAvery /ˌteks ˈeɪvəri/ (1918–80) a US cartoonist. He created the characters of *Daffy Duck (1937), *Bugs Bunny (1940) and Droopy (1943). He later joined *Hanna and Barbera for the television series *The *Flintstones*.

ˈAvis™ /ˈeɪvɪs/ a large car hire company with offices in many countries.

ˈAvon¹ /ˈeɪvn/ any of three rivers with the same name in south-west England. The longest of these flows through *Warwick and *Stratford-upon-Avon. Shakespeare, who was born at Stratford, is sometimes called the 'Bard of Avon'.

ˈAvon™² /ˈeɪvɒn; AmE ˈeɪvɑːn/ an international company selling beauty products, soap, etc. Avon representatives, usually women (called **Avon ladies**), sell these products by going to people's homes with them.

AWACS /ˈeɪwæks/ (in full **airborne warning and control system**) a US system of radar used in military planes to find and follow enemy planes and missiles. An AWACS plane can fly very high and for 10 hours without making a stop. It is easily recognized by the large disc above its wings.

Aˌway in a ˈManger a *carol sung especially by children at church services at *Christmas. The first verse is:

> 66 Away in a manger, no crib for a bed,
> The little Lord Jesus laid down his sweet head.
> The stars in the bright sky looked down where he lay,
> The little Lord Jesus asleep on the hay. 99

ˌRev W ˈAwdry /ˈɔːdri/ (Wilbert Awdry 1911–97) an English vicar (= *Church of England priest) and writer of children's books. He is best known for having created *Thomas, the Tank Engine*.

ˈAxminster /ˈæksmɪnstə(r)/ n [C, U] a type of thick carpet made by a special factory process so that it looks as if it has been made by hand. These carpets were originally made in Axminster, a town in *Devon, England: *The hall is carpeted in good-quality Axminster.*

ˌAlan ˈAyckbourn /ˈeɪkbɔːn; AmE ˈeɪkbɔːrn/ (1939–) an English writer of many plays for the theatre and television, well known for his cleverly written and often disturbing comedies about English *middle-class behaviour, including *Absurd Person Singular* (1973), *Absent Friends* (1975), *A Chorus of Disapproval* (1986) and the series of three plays called *The Norman Conquests* (1974). He usually gives the first performances of his plays in *Scarborough, where he is the artistic director of a theatre company. He was made a *knight in 1997.

> 66 Put three Englishmen on a desert island and within an hour they'll have invented a class system. 99
> Alan Ayckbourn

ˌA J ˈ**Ayer** /ˈeə(r); *AmE* ˈer/ (Alfred Jules Ayer 1910–89) a British philosopher. His best-known work, *Language, Truth and Logic* (1936), develops the philosophy of 'logical positivism', the idea that a statement only has meaning if it can be proved to be true or false. He was made a *knight in 1970.

ˈ**Ayrshire** /ˈeəʃə(r); *AmE* ˈerʃər/ **1** an administrative region in south-west Scotland made up of three *council areas: North Ayrshire, South Ayrshire and East Ayrshire. **2** *n* a brown and white breed of cow, originally bred in Ayrshire and now used in many countries for its milk.

B b

BA /ˌbiː ˈeɪ/ ⇨ BRITISH AIRWAYS.

BAA /ˌbiː eɪ ˈeɪ/ the company that owns and runs Britain's major airports.

Baa, Baa, 'Black Sheep an old children's song, which may refer to a tax put on wool in England in 1275. The full song is:

> 66 Baa, baa, black sheep,
> Have you any wool?
> Yes sir, yes sir,
> Three bags full.
> One for the master,
> And one for the dame,
> And one for the little boy
> Who lives down the lane. 99

the **'Baa-baas** /ˈbɑː bɑːz/ ⇨ BARBARIANS.

'Babbitt /ˈbæbɪt/ n (AmE) a man who is too satisfied with a narrow set of values and thinks mainly about possessions and making money. Babbitt is a character in a novel of that name by Sinclair *Lewis.

Babes in the 'Wood a traditional story about a boy and girl who go to live with their wicked uncle after their father dies. He pays two men to kill them, so that he can steal their property. However, one of the men feels sorry for the children, so he kills his partner and leaves them in a wood. They die and a bird covers them with leaves. Soon afterwards, the uncle's sons also die, and then he loses his property and dies himself, in prison. The story is often performed as a *pantomime, when it is given a happy ending.

the **'Baby Boom** the time between the end of *World War II and 1964 when an unusually large number of children were born in certain countries, including Britain and the US. People born in that time are often called **Baby Boomers**.

'Babycham™ /ˈbeɪbɪʃæm/ n [C, U] a British fizzy alcoholic drink made from pears. It is advertised with a picture of a small deer with a blue ribbon round its neck.

Baby 'Ruth™ a popular make of US chocolate bar that is filled with peanuts.

Lauren Ba'call /ˌlɔːrən bəˈkɔːl/ (1924–) a US actor well known for her deep voice. She was formerly married to Humphrey *Bogart, with whom she acted in several films, including The Big Sleep (1946) and Key Largo (1948). At the age of 72, she was nominated for an *Oscar as Best Supporting Actress for her role in The Mirror Has Two Faces (1996) and at 80 she starred in Birth (2004).

Burt 'Bacharach /ˌbɜːt ˈbækəræk; AmE ˌbɜːrt/ (1928–) a US composer of popular songs, often with Hal David as his partner. Their songs include Walk on By (1964) and Raindrops Keep Fallin' on My Head, which won an *Oscar in 1969.

'bachelor's degree n (formal) the first degree that you get when you study at a university. Bachelor's degrees include **Bachelor of Arts** (**BA**) and **Bachelor of Science** (**BSc**). Compare MASTER'S DEGREE.

back'bencher /bækˈbentʃə(r)/ n (in Britain) a *Member of Parliament who does not hold a senior position in the government or in the opposition. Backbenchers sit on the **backbenches**, the seats behind ministers or members of the *Shadow Cabinet. They are

expected to vote as the party *Whip tells them to: The government's announcement spread alarm among its own backbenchers. ⇨ note at PARLIAMENT.

the **'Backs** n [pl] the attractive area at the back of some of the colleges of *Cambridge University in England, between the colleges and the River Cam.

the Backs

back-to-'back n (BrE) a house that is part of a row and has its back against the back of a house in another row facing in the opposite direction. Back-to-back houses were built for workers in industrial towns in the nineteenth century.

back to 'basics a phrase used by politicians and others who are concerned about standards in education, government, public life, etc. to suggest that modern developments have made people forget what is important: Companies need to get back to basics: be honest, be frugal, be prepared.

Back to the 'Future a US comedy science fiction film (1985) that made a star of Michael J *Fox. He plays a boy in *high school who, helped by a funny scientist, travels back in time from 1985 to 1955 to meet his parents when they were young. Fox also appeared in Back to the Future II (1989), about a trip to the year 2015, and Back to the Future III (1990), in which he returns to the *Wild West of 1885. All three films were directed by Robert *Zemeckis.

Francis 'Bacon[1] /ˈbeɪkən/ (1561–1626) an English lawyer, politician and philosopher. He was very successful in his early career and became *Lord Chancellor to King *James I in 1618, but he was later accused of accepting money illegally and sent to prison. He was released after only four days, but never returned to public service. Bacon's books, including The Advancement of Learning (1605), show a scientific interest in the world which was new at that time.

   Since 1856 some people have claimed that Francis Bacon is the real author of the plays of William *Shakespeare, because they feel that Shakespeare's education and social background were not good enough to have produced such great literature.

Francis 'Bacon[2] /ˈbeɪkən/ (1909–92) an Irish painter who lived in England from 1928. He often painted people who were in pain or who were being treated in a cruel way, making their bodies look ugly and twisted in order to emphasize their pain. He destroyed any of his paintings that he was not satisfied with.

,Roger **'Bacon**[3] /'beɪkən/ (c. 1214–92) a Franciscan monk and philosopher who became known as 'Doctor Mirabilis', or 'the Admirable Doctor'. He was unusual for his time in regarding mathematics and science as very important. His writings show that he was particularly interested in chemistry, optics (= the scientific study of sight and light) and astrology, and he seems to have understood the possibilities of gunpowder (= an explosive powder), the telescope, glasses and flying. In 1278 his work was declared to be heretical (= opposed to religious beliefs) and he was put in prison until just before his death.

,**bacon and 'eggs** n [U] a dish consisting of fried or grilled slices of bacon and one or more fried eggs, eaten especially as part of a traditional English breakfast: *I had bacon and eggs for breakfast*.

'Bactine™ /'bækti:n/ n [U] a US product name for a substance that helps to prevent infection in small cuts and wounds. It can be bought without a doctor's prescription and is made by Miles Laboratories.

Lord ,**Baden-'Powell** /,beɪdn 'pəʊəl; *also* 'paʊəl; *AmE* 'poʊəl/ (Robert Stephenson Smyth Baden-Powell 1857–1951) a British soldier who became famous for defending the South African town of Mafeking in the *Boer War. He later left the army and started the Boy Scout organization (now called the *Scouts or the Scout Association) in 1908 and, with his sister Agnes, the Girl Guides (now called the *Guides or, in the US, the Girl Scouts) in 1910.

'badlands /'bædlændz/ n [pl] (*especially AmE*) a dry bare area of land with deep channels worn away by water. The **Badlands National Park** is in the US state of *South Dakota.

the Badlands National Park

'Badminton /'bædmɪntən/ (*also formal* the **Badminton Horse Trials**) a riding contest held every year on land around Badminton House, a large house near *Bath, England. Riders compete in riding across fields, water, etc., in jumping fences around a course, and in showing that their horses will obey them in various exercises. See also THREE-DAY EVENT.

,**BAE 'Systems** /,bi: eɪ i:/ the largest British aircraft company, making civil and military aircraft as well as weapons and space communication systems.

,**Joan 'Baez** /,dʒəʊn 'baɪez/ (1941–) a US singer who also plays the guitar and writes songs. She is known especially for her protest songs, her support for the *civil rights movement, and her strong, clear voice.

BAFTA /'bæftə/ (*in full* the **British Academy of Film and Television Arts**) a British organization which gives awards every year to film and television actors, producers, etc. It was formed in 1959. The BAFTA Interactive Entertainment Awards for websites, games, etc. were introduced in 1997. See also EMMY.

,Walter **'Bagehot** /'bædʒət/ (1826–77) an English economist and journalist, best remembered for his book *The English Constitution* (1867).

> 66 There is no method by which men can be both free and equal. 99
> Walter Bagehot

'bagel /'beɪgl/ n a hard bread roll in the shape of a ring which is cooked first in water and then baked. Bagels first became popular in New York City as a type of Jewish bread. They are often eaten there with cream cheese and smoked salmon. See also LOX.

'Baggies™ /'bægiz/ a US make of plastic bags for storing food in.

'bagpipes (*also informal* **pipes**) n [pl] a musical instrument played by blowing air into a bag held under the arm, and pressing it out through pipes. Similar instruments are played in many countries, including Ireland, but in Britain the bagpipes are mainly associated with Scotland. The sound they make is unusual, but their music is suitable both for dancing and for serious occasions such as funerals. A person who plays the bagpipes is called a *piper*: *the wail of the bagpipes*.

the Ba**'hamas** /bə'hɑːməz/ a group of about 700 small islands that form an independent state in the *West Indies. The two main islands are New Providence, where the capital city of Nassau is and where 75% of the population of 250 000 live, and Grand Bahama. The Bahamas is a member of the *Commonwealth, and its official language is English. It is very popular with tourists.
  ▶ Ba**'hamian** adj, n.

,David **'Bailey** /'beɪli/ (1938–) an English photographer who first became known for photographing actors and musicians in the 1960s. He is famous for his fashion photography and his pictures of famous people including members of the royal family. He has been married four times, including to the French actor Catherine Deneuve and the model Marie Helvin.

> 66 I never cared for fashion much. Amusing little seams and witty little pleats. It was the girls I liked. 99
> David Bailey

'bailiff /'beɪlɪf/ n **1** (in Britain) an officer who works for the county court. The bailiff's job is to make sure that the court's orders are obeyed. Bailiffs can come into a person's home to take goods in payment of a debt, to collect money owed for rent or taxes, to remove somebody who has no right to be there, etc. The police sometimes help them. There are also private companies of bailiffs, who have more limited powers. See also LAW ENFORCEMENT.
  2 (in the US) an official who keeps order in a court of law. **3** (especially in Britain) a person whose job is to look after land for its owner.

,Beryl **'Bainbridge** /'beɪnbrɪdʒ/ (1934–) an English writer of novels. Her books include *The Dressmaker* (1973), which was made into a film in 1989, *The Bottle Factory Outing* (1974), *Injury Time* (1977), which won the *Whitbread prize, and *An Awfully Big Adventure* (1989), also made into a film. Her later books have been based on real lives, *The Birthday Boys* (1991) on Captain *Scott's Antarctic expedition, *Every Man for Himself* (1996) about the *Titanic, *Master Georgie* (1998) about the *Crimean War and *According to Queeney* (2001) about Dr *Johnson. Her work has been shortlisted many times for the *Booker Prize. She was made a *dame(2) in 2000.

'John 'Logie 'Baird /'ləʊgi 'beəd; *AmE* 'loʊgi 'berd/ (1888–1946) a Scottish inventor who is remembered mainly for his work on early forms of television in the 1920s and 1930s. The *BBC began using Baird's system in 1929, but by 1937 Marconi-EMI had replaced his mechanical system by a much more efficient electronic one.

baked A'laska /ə'læskə/ n [C, U] a sweet dish consisting of cake and ice cream covered in meringue (= a mixture of egg whites and sugar) and cooked quickly in a very hot oven.

baked 'beans n [pl] **1** (in Britain) small white beans that are baked and sold in tins with tomato sauce, which gives them an orange colour: *I gave the children baked beans on toast for tea.* **2** ⇨ BOSTON BAKED BEANS.

'Bakelite™ /'beɪkəlaɪt/ n [U] a type of hard plastic that was widely used in the radio and electrical industry in the first half of the 20th century. It was invented by the Belgian-American chemist Leo Hendrik Baekeland: *an old Bakelite telephone.*

Janet 'Baker /'beɪkə(r)/ (1933–) an English singer who is well known for her performances of *baroque music as well as that of modern British composers, especially *Elgar and *Britten. She was made a *dame(2) in 1976.

Baker's 'Chocolate™ /ˌbeɪkəz; AmE ˌbeɪkərz/ n [U] a US make of chocolate mostly used for making cakes and sweets/candy. It is not very sweet and is sold in small squares. The original Baker's Chocolate Company started in 1780. It is now owned by *Kraft.

a ˌbaker's 'dozen a phrase meaning 13. It comes from the fact that in the past people who sold bread always added an extra loaf when somebody ordered a dozen (= 12) loaves, in case they might be punished for supplying too few.

'Baker Street /'beɪkə; AmE 'beɪkər/ a street in central London. It is perhaps best known as the place where Sherlock *Holmes, the detective created by Sir Arthur *Conan Doyle, lived. His address was number 221B Baker Street, which is now part of a bank. In the stories, Holmes sometimes uses a group of local children he calls the **Baker Street irregulars** to get information for him. See also DETECTIVE STORY.

Bakewell 'tart /ˌbeɪkwel/ n [C, U] an open pastry case filled with sponge cake flavoured with almonds over a layer of jam. It was originally made in Bakewell, a town in *Derbyshire, England.

'Bakke deˌcision /'bæki/ an important ruling made by the US *Supreme Court in 1978. A white man called Allan Bakke claimed that he had been illegally refused a job because of his colour. The Court decided that the employers had acted illegally in not offering him the job, but that employers did have a right to consider somebody's race when deciding whether to give them a job. See also AFFIRMATIVE ACTION.

Jim 'Bakker /'beɪkə(r)/ (1941–) an American religious leader who, with his wife Tammy Faye, had a popular national television programme. In 1989 he was sent to prison for 45 years for illegally taking money that people gave to support his work. He was released early from prison in 1994.

Bala'clava /ˌbælə'klɑːvə/ (*also* the Battle of Balaclava) a battle in the *Crimean War, fought in 1854 near the small town of Balaclava in the Ukraine. It is remembered for the *Charge of the Light Brigade, in which the British army suffered heavy losses.

bala'clava /ˌbælə'klɑːvə/ (*formal* balaclava helmet) n a woollen hat that fits closely over the head and neck, with an opening for the face. It was originally worn by soldiers in the *Crimean War.

George 'Balanchine /'bæləntʃiːn/ (1904–83) a US choreographer, born in Russia. After working with Diaghilev he went to the US and started the New York City Ballet.

bald 'eagle n ⇨ AMERICAN EAGLE.

James 'Baldwin¹ /'bɔːldwɪn/ (1924–87) a US writer of novels and plays. He had immediate success with his first novel *Go, Tell It On the Mountain* (1954), which, like much of his later work, deals with the condition of African Americans.

Stanley 'Baldwin² /'bɔːldwɪn/ (1867–1947) a British Conservative politician who was *Prime Minister three times in the 1920s and 1930s. His government created a law that defeated the *General Strike of 1926. He also dealt skilfully with the difficult matter of the abdication of King *Edward VIII. He was made an *earl(1) in 1937.

A J 'Balfour /'bælfə(r)/ (Arthur James Balfour 1848–1930) a British Conservative politician, the nephew of Lord *Salisbury. He was Prime Minister from 1902 to 1905 and Foreign Secretary from 1916 to 1919, during World War I. He was made an *earl in 1922.

the ˌBalfour Decla'ration /ˌbælfə; AmE ˌbælfər/ a letter of 2 November 1917 in which A J *Balfour, the British Foreign Secretary, wrote that the British government was in favour of establishing Palestine as a national home for the Jewish people. The other *Allies(1) soon said that they agreed with this.

Lucille 'Ball /ˌluːsiːl 'bɔːl/ (1911–89) a US comedy actor, especially on television where she was the star of the 1950s comedy series *I Love Lucy.* She received three *Emmy awards.

The **'Ballad of 'Reading 'Gaol** /'redɪŋ/ a long poem by Oscar *Wilde, written in 1898 after he had been in prison, about a fellow prisoner who is hanged and about the horror of prison life.

J G 'Ballard /'bælɑːd; AmE 'bælɑːrd/ (James Graham Ballard 1930–) a British author born in China who is best known for his science fiction novels and short stories, and for *Empire of the Sun* (1984), about a boy's experiences in a Japanese prison camp during *World War II. It was made into a film by Steven *Spielberg in 1988.

Bal'moral /bæl'mɒrəl; AmE bæl'mɔːrəl/ a castle near *Aberdeen, Scotland, which the British *royal family uses as a private holiday home every summer. It was built for Queen *Victoria in 1853–6.

Balmoral

'balti /'bɔːlti, 'bælti/ n [U, C] a type of hot and spicy food from *Pakistan that is popular in Britain. It is cooked and served in a round shallow dish also called a balti: *a balti house* (= a restaurant that serves balti meals) .

'Baltimore /'bɔːltəmɔː(r)/ the largest city in the US state of *Maryland. It is a busy port on the Atlantic Ocean and contains Fort McHenry which inspired Francis Scott Key to write The *Star-Spangled Banner. The famous Preakness horse race takes place in Baltimore.

'Bambi /'bæmbi/ a young deer in a 1923 children's story by Felix Salten and a Walt *Disney cartoon film (1942) of the same name. Bambi is a gentle and innocent animal whose mother dies in a forest fire. The film is remembered particularly for its sad moments.

'**Banbury** /'bænbri/ a town in the county of *Oxfordshire, England, once famous for its cakes. There is a stone cross in the town's centre, which is mentioned in the old children's *nursery rhyme *Ride a Cock-horse to Banbury Cross*.

'**Band Aid** a large group of pop stars brought together by Bob *Geldof in 1984 to help people without food in Ethiopia. The song that they recorded, *Do They Know It's Christmas?*, was bought by millions of people, and the profits were sent to Ethiopia. Twenty years later a new recording of the song was made and the profits sent to Sudan. See also LIVE AID.

'**Band-Aid**™ *n* [C, U] a US make of sticking plaster (= a strip of fabric that can be stuck to the skin to protect a small wound or cut), made by *Johnson & Johnson. They were first made in 1921 and are now so common that Americans use the name for any plaster/bandage.

,**bangers and** '**mash** *n* [U] (*BrE informal*) sausages and mashed potatoes (= boiled potatoes that have been crushed into a soft mass). The phrase is often used as an example of a simple, solid and very British meal: *I'd rather eat bangers and mash than an expensive meal in a French restaurant.*

,**Bangla'desh** /ˌbæŋglə'deʃ/ a country which was part of *Pakistan until it became an independent member of the *Commonwealth in 1971. Its capital city is Dhaka. About 250 000 people of Bangladeshi origin are now living in Britain.
▶ **Bangladeshi** *adj, n.*

,**bank 'holiday** *n* **1** (in Britain) an official public holiday (on a day other than Saturday or Sunday) when all banks and post offices are closed, as well as most factories and offices and some shops.
2 (in the US) a period when banks are closed to prevent a financial problem, usually with special instructions from the government.

the ,**Bank of** '**England** the central bank of the United Kingdom, in London. It is the official source of all paper money in Britain, it advises the government on financial matters, and it acts as banker to the government and to other banks. It was privately owned until 1946, when it came under government control. Since 1997 it has been responsible for deciding on the minimum lending rate.

,**Iain 'Banks**¹ /ˌiːən 'bæŋks/ (1954–) a Scottish author whose best-known novels include *The Wasp Factory* (1984), *The Crow Road* (1992) and *Dead Air* (2002). He also writes science fiction novels under the name **Iain M Banks**, including a series of books about a civilization called **the Culture**, which exists across many planets.

,**Joseph 'Banks**² /'bæŋks/ (1743–1820) an English naturalist who sailed with Captain *Cook on his first journey round the world. He discovered and collected many unknown plants, especially in Australia, and helped to start the famous collection of plants at *Kew Gardens. He was President of the *Royal Society for over 40 years and was made a *knight in 1781.

▶ **banks and banking**

In Britain, the **central bank**, which acts as banker for the state and commercial banks, is the *Bank of England. The Governor of the Bank of England advises the government on financial matters. The bank sets national interest rates (= the cost of borrowing money) and is responsible for issuing **banknotes**.

The main commercial banks, called **clearing banks** or **high-street banks**, are *NatWest, *Barclays, *Lloyds TSB and *HSBC. These are known as the 'big four' and have branches in most towns. Former *building soci-

eties that became banks in the mid 1990s, such as *Abbey and the *Halifax, now compete with them for customers. People can use a **current account** and. for savings, a **deposit account**.The high-street banks offer **bank loans** for individuals and small businesses. **Merchant banks** deal with company finance on a larger scale.

In the US there are thousands of banks. This is because banks are prevented by law from operating in more than one state. Some banks get round this rule by forming **holding companies** which own banks with the same names in different states. Unlike British banks, American banks are banks of **deposit** and **credit** and do not build up **capital**. Banking is dominated by large **money center** banks, such as *Chase, which raise money by dealing in the international money markets and lend it to businesses and other banks.

The US central bank is the *Federal Reserve Bank, often called the **Fed**. In addition to the national Fed in *Washington, DC, there are 12 regional ones. The Fed tells commercial banks how much money they must keep in reserve and decides what rate of interest to charge when lending them money. This affects the rate of interest the commercial banks charge their customers.

In the US people keep their accounts in commercial banks which must have a charter (= permission to operate) from the US or a state government. Each state decides whether to allow **branch banking**, i.e. to allow customers to do business at any branch of a bank, not just the one where they have their account. People also keep money in *savings and loans organizations. The most common accounts are **checking** and **savings** accounts.

'**Bankside** /'bæŋksaɪd/ an area on the south bank of the River *Thames in London, England. It is between Southwark Bridge and the area generally known as the *South Bank. It is where London's theatres were in the time of Shakespeare because they were not allowed in the city itself. Since the opening of *Tate Modern and the *Globe Theatre at the end of the twentieth century the area has become a popular place to visit and is linked to the *City of London by the Millennium Bridge, a new footbridge.

,**Roger 'Bannister** /'bænɪstə(r)/ (1929–) the first person to run a mile in under four minutes. He achieved this in 1954 while he was a medical student at *Oxford University. He later had an impressive medical career. He was made a *knight in 1975.

the ,**Battle of** '**Bannockburn** /'bænəkbɜːn; *AmE* 'bænəkbɜːrn/ a victory for the army of the Scottish king *Robert the Bruce over the army of the English king *Edward II in 1314. The battle was fought in central Scotland and it allowed Scotland to remain an independent country.

the '**Banqueting House** /'bæŋkwɪtɪŋ/ one of the most famous buildings in *Whitehall, London, designed by Inigo *Jones in 1622. Today it is used for formal social events.

'**Baptist** *n* a member of the largest group of Protestant Christians in the US, with over 38 million members around the world, including a small number in Britain. The group was formed in England in the early 17th century by people who disagreed with other Protestants about the ceremony of baptism. Baptists believe in putting a new member of the Church completely under water during baptism. They also believe that baptism should be for adults and not for children, because they think that children are not old enough to understand what the ceremony means.

B & Q™ /ˌbiː ənd ˈkjuː/ any of a chain of large shops in Britain where people can buy materials to decorate or repair their homes. The shops also sell tools, furniture, etc. for the garden. They are named after Richard Block and David Quayle, who started the company.

> 66 You can do it when you B and Q it. 99
> advertising slogan

the 'Bar (in Britain) the profession of *barrister. To be *called to the Bar* is to be received into the profession after *training for the Bar*. The Bar is governed by the *Bar Council. The head of the Bar of England and Wales and the Bar of Northern Ireland is called the *Attorney General, and the head of the Scottish Bar is called the Dean of Faculty.

Bar'bados /bɑːˈbeɪdɒs; *AmE* bɑːrˈbeɪdɑːs/ an island in the *Caribbean and an independent member of the *Commonwealth since 1966. Its capital city is Bridgetown.
▸ **Bar'badian** *adj, n.*

the 'Bar'barians /bɑːˈbeəriənz; *AmE* bɑːrˈberiənz/ (*also informal* **the Baa-baas**) a *Rugby Union team formed from many of the best players from Britain, France and the Commonwealth. It has no ground of its own but plays against English and Welsh clubs as well as games against foreign teams visiting Britain.

ˌSamuel 'Barber /ˈbɑːbə(r); *AmE* ˈbɑːrbər/ (1910–81) a US composer whose music is traditional in style. His best-known works are the *Adagio for Strings* (1936) and the opera *Vanessa* (1958).

the 'Barber Institute of 'Fine 'Arts /ˈbɑːbə(r); *AmE* ˈbɑːrbər/ an institution for the study of art history at the University of *Birmingham, England. Since it began in 1932 it has built up a fine collection of paintings from all periods.

'barbershop *n* [U] a type of singing performed by four men (or less often women) in close harmony, without instruments. It is especially popular in the US where many towns have **barbershop quartets**. Barbershop songs are often sentimental, and well-known favourites include *Sweet Adeline* (1903) and *Down by the Old Mill Stream* (1910).

the 'Barbican ˌCentre /ˈbɑːbɪkən; *AmE* ˈbɑːrbɪkən/ a large cultural centre in the **Barbican**, an area of modern buildings in the *City of London, north of *St Paul's Cathedral. The Centre includes a concert hall which is the home of the *London Symphony Orchestra, three cinemas, a theatre which was the London home of the *Royal Shakespeare Company until 2002, and a smaller theatre, an art gallery, a public library and two exhibition halls, as well as a conference hall, a bar and restaurants.

'Barbie doll™ /ˈbɑːbi; *AmE* ˈbɑːrbi/ *n* a child's toy doll in the form of an attractive young woman with a wide choice of fashionable clothes. In the US a woman who is attractive and well dressed but not intelligent is sometimes described as a Barbie doll.

ˌbar 'billiards *n* [U] (*BrE*) a game played mainly in *pubs on a small table. Players use cues (= long wooden rods) to try to hit balls into holes without knocking down the small wooden objects that stand in front of the holes. Compare BILLIARDS, POOL, SNOOKER.

ˌJohn ˌBarbi'rolli /ˌbɑːbiˈrɒli/ (1899–1970) an English musician and conductor whose family came originally from Italy. He was conductor of the *New York Philharmonic Orchestra from 1937 to 1943 and then conductor of the *Hallé Orchestra, Manchester, until his death. He was made a *knight in 1949.

'Barbour™ /ˈbɑːbə(r); *AmE* ˈbɑːrbər/ an English company that makes expensive coats of specially treated cotton that keeps out the rain and wind. Barbours are worn especially by people who live or spend time in the country, but they are also fashionable with city people. They are usually dark green in colour and often worn with green wellington boots. See also GREEN WELLY BRIGADE.

Bar'buda /bɑːˈbjuːdə; *AmE* bɑːrˈbjuːdə/ ⇨ ANTIGUA AND BARBUDA.

ˌBarchester 'Towers /ˌbɑːtʃestə / a novel (1857) by Anthony *Trollope. It is the second of his six *Barsetshire novels and is about a struggle for power among the people associated with the cathedral in Barchester, an imaginary town in England.

'Barclaycard /ˈbɑːklikɑːd/ the name of one of the most widely used British *credit cards and of the organization, owned by *Barclays Bank, from which these cards are available.

ˌBarclays 'Bank /ˌbɑːkliz; *AmE* ˌbɑːrkliz/ (*also* **Barclays**) one of the four main English banks. It was established in 1896 and has branches in most towns and cities in Britain.

the ˌBar 'Council (in Britain) the group of senior *barristers that governs the *Bar in England and Wales and the *Inns of Court. Its full name is the General Council of the Bar and of the Inns of Court.

bard /bɑːd; *AmE* bɑːrd/ *n* an old-fashioned word for a poet. Shakespeare is sometimes called the **Bard of Avon** after the river near his place of birth. The word is also used as the title of a poet who wins a competition at an *eisteddfod.

'Baring's Bank /ˈbeərɪŋ; *AmE* ˈberɪŋ/ the oldest merchant bank (= bank that lends money to large companies) in London, England. It stopped trading in 1995 after an employee, Nick Leeson, lost over £250 million while trading illegally in Singapore. The bank was bought by a Dutch company, ING, and began trading again. Leeson was sent to prison.

ˌPat 'Barker[1] /ˈbɑːkə(r); *AmE* ˈbɑːrkər/ (1943–) a British writer and historian who is best known for her three novels, *The Regeneration Trilogy*, set during *World War I: *Regeneration* (1991), *The Eye in the Door* (1993) and *The Ghost Road* for which she won the *Booker Prize in (1995). Her later novels include *Another World* (1998) and *Double Vision* (2003).

ˌRonnie 'Barker[2] /ˈbɑːkə(r); *AmE* ˈbɑːrkər/ (1929–) a popular English actor and comedian, especially on television. He is best known for *The Two Ronnies*, a regular show in which he appeared with Ronnie *Corbett, and *Porridge*, a comedy series about life in prison.

ˌSue 'Barker[3] /ˈbɑːkə(r); *AmE* ˈbɑːrkər/ (1956–) an English presenter of sports programmes on television, including *Grandstand (from 1994) and the quiz show *A* *Question of Sport (from 1997). She earlier had a successful career as a tennis player.

ˌbarley 'wine *n* [U] (*especially BrE*) a type of strong beer.

Bar'nardo's /bəˈnɑːdəʊz; *AmE* bərˈnɑːrdoʊz/ a British charity that helps children with social, physical or mental problems and their families. It began in 1870 when an Irish man, Dr Thomas Barnardo, started a home in London for poor children without parents and until the 1950s the charity ran many children's homes.

ˌBarnes & 'Noble™ /ˌbɑːnz, ˈnəʊbl; *AmE* ˌbɑːrnz, ˈnoʊbl/ a US chain of bookstores which opened its first store in 1917 in New York and in 2004 had 647 stores across the US. As well as books, the stores sell magazines, newspapers, music and DVDs, and many of them contain *Starbucks cafes. They also started selling books online in 1997.

P T 'Barnum /ˈbɑːnəm; AmE ˈbɑːrnəm/ (Phineas Taylor Barnum 1810–91) a US showman who was famous for his exaggerated claims. He owned a travelling circus, called the Greatest Show on Earth, and later joined his great rival J A Bailey to form Barnum and Bailey's Circus. His circus acts included *Tom Thumb and the elephant Jumbo.

'baron n a man who has the lowest rank in the British *peerage. He has the title 'Lord'. ⇨ note at PEERAGE.

'baroness n **1** (in Britain) a woman who has the rank of *baron and the title 'Lady' or sometimes 'Baroness'. **2** the wife of a *baron, having the title 'Lady'. ⇨ note at PEERAGE.

'baronet n (abbrs **Bart**, **Bt**) (in Britain) a man who has a rank of honour below a *peer but above a *knight. He has the title 'Sir' and his wife the title 'Lady': Sir Thomas Blank, Bart and Lady Blank.

ba'roque adj in a highly decorated style of art that was fashionable in Europe in the 17th and early 18th centuries after developing in Italy. Examples of British baroque style include buildings designed by the architects *Wren and *Vanbrugh, and the music of *Purcell and *Handel.
▶ **baroque** (often **the baroque**) n [U] the baroque style or baroque art.

Roseanne 'Barr /ˌrəʊzæn ˈbɑː(r); AmE ˌroʊzæn ˈbɑːr/ ⇨ ROSEANNE.

E'lizabeth 'Barrett 'Browning /ˈbærət ˈbraʊnɪŋ/ (born Elizabeth Barrett 1806–61) an English poet and the wife of Robert *Browning. Although her poetry was more popular than his during their life, she is now remembered more for the story of their secret love affair and marriage, which enabled her to escape from her harsh and selfish father to a new life in Italy.

J M 'Barrie /ˈbæri/ (James Matthew Barrie 1860–1937) a Scottish writer of plays and novels. His best-known works are the plays The Admirable Crichton (1902) and *Peter Pan (1904).

'barrister n (in England and Wales) a lawyer who has the right to represent people in the higher courts. The Scottish equivalent of a barrister is called an advocate. ⇨ note at LEGAL SYSTEM.

'barrow n (especially BrE) a large pile of earth built in ancient times to cover a grave. In Britain long barrows date mainly from the later *Stone Age (4000–2100 BC), and round barrows date from the *Bronze Age (2100–700 BC).

entrance sealed with
a large stone   earth and stones
                                        supporting
                                        stones

a long barrow

Charles 'Barry /ˈbæri/ (1795–1860) an English architect who designed the *Houses of Parliament(2) in London, built in the style of the *Gothic Revival. He was made a *knight in 1852.

'Barrymore a family of US stage and (later) film actors, Lionel (1878–1954), his sister Ethel (1879–1959), and his brother John (1882–1942). John was the grandfather of the actor Drew Barrymore (1975–).

'Barsetshire /ˈbɑːsɪtʃə(r)/ an imaginary English county in a series of six novels by Anthony *Trollope set in and around the cathedral city of Barchester.

'bar snack n [usually pl] (BrE) a light meal that can be bought and eaten in a pub. Bar snacks might include sandwiches, salads and pies. See also PLOUGHMAN'S LUNCH.

BART /bɑːt; AmE bɑːrt/ (in full **Bay Area Rapid Transit**) the underground transport system in the US city of *San Francisco. The trains also go across San Francisco Bay to *Oakland and *Berkeley.

Bart /bɑːt; AmE bɑːrt/ (also **Bt**) ⇨ BARONET.

John 'Barth /ˈbɑːθ; AmE ˈbɑːrθ/ (1930–) a US writer, formerly a teacher. His long and often complicated novels show the humorous aspect of modern life in the US. They include The Sot-Weed Factor (1960), Giles Goat-Boy (1966), and Tidewater Tales (1988).

Bartlett's Fam'iliar Quo'tations /ˈbɑːtləts; AmE ˈbɑːrtləts/ a popular US book of quotations (= passages from books, poems, plays, etc.). It was first published in 1855 by John Bartlett (1820–1905) and now contains more than 22 000 quotations.

Clara 'Barton /ˌkleərə ˈbɑːtn/ (1821–1912) a US nurse who started the American *Red Cross in 1881. She was its first president until 1904. Barton, who had earlier been a teacher, became a nurse for Union soldiers during the *Civil War and was known as 'the Angel of the Battlefield'.

Bart's /bɑːts; AmE bɑːrts/ the popular name for St Bartholomew's Hospital, a well-known teaching hospital in London, England. It has a long history going back to the 12th century. It is now a special hospital for cancer and heart disease.

▶ **baseball**

America's national sport, played mainly by men, which developed in the 19th century from the British games *rounders and *cricket. It is a popular sport to play and watch, with many families going to watch baseball games on a Sunday afternoon. Baseball has become an important part of US culture with many baseball terms becoming part of the language and it is the subject of songs, novels and films. Baseball shirts and caps have also become fashionable in many countries.

Baseball is played with long wooden **bats** and a small, hard ball, by two teams of nine players each. The **infield** has three **bases** (= bags filled with sand) and a **home plate** arranged in a **diamond**. The **pitcher**, who throws the ball to the **batter**, stands in the centre of the diamond. Each game lasts nine **innings** and in each inning the **visiting team** is first to **bat** (= hit the ball) while the **home team** plays defense. Players bat in turn but when a team has three **outs** it must let the other side bat. If a batter hits the ball and it is not caught in the air for an out, he runs to **first base**. If the ball is thrown to first base before he gets there, he is out and if not, he then tries to run to **second base**, **third base**

baseball

B

and back to home for a **run** while other players bat. The team that scores the most **runs** is the winner.

*Major League Baseball is organized into the *American League and the *National League and the season lasts from April to October. At the end of the season, the four best teams in each league play to decide which two teams will go forward to the *World Series. The New York *Yankees have won the World Series most times. Other well-known teams include the Boston Red Sox, the Cleveland Indians, the Detroit Tigers, the Chicago Cubs, the St Louis Cardinals, the Atlanta Braves and the Los Angeles Dodgers.

the 'Bash Street Kids /ˈbæʃ/ a group of children in the *Beano, a British *comic published every week. They are always playing tricks on their teacher and getting into trouble.

ˌbasic 'English n [U] a simple form of international English suggested by two *Cambridge University teachers in the 1920s. It used only 850 words and was intended for teachers and learners of English as a foreign language.

ˈˌCount 'Basie /ˌkaʊnt ˈbeɪsi/ (1904–84) a US *jazz musician. He formed his own orchestra in 1935, leading it from the piano. It became famous for its 'big band' sound.

ˌKim 'Basinger /ˈbæsɪndʒə(r)/ (1953–) a US actor who was a sex symbol in the 1980s. She became famous for the film 9½ Weeks (1985).

'Basin Street /ˈbeɪsn/ a street in the US city of *New Orleans which is especially associated with the playing of *jazz music. There is a well-known song called The Basin Street Blues.

▶ basketball

Basketball is the most popular sport played indoors in the US. It was invented in 1891 in Springfield, *Massachusetts, by Dr James Naismith. He used fruit baskets for the hoops and baskets, and a soccer ball. The first professional organization for male players was established in 1898, and the *NBA (**National Basketball Association**) was set up in 1949. Games are now played by rich basketball stars before huge audiences. The team seen most outside the US is the *Harlem Globetrotters. It is mainly an indoor sport but it is also played with just as much enthusiasm by young people on the streets of US cities.

Basketball is played by two teams of five players, but seven other players can be brought on to replace them during the game. The **court** is up to 94 feet/29.7 metres long and 50 feet/15 metres wide. At each end is a **hoop** (= a metal ring) 10 feet/3 metres above the floor. The hoop is attached to a backboard and has a net without a bottom hanging from it. Players score two points when they throw the ball through the hoop from an area near the basket, and three points if they are further away. The team that scores the most points wins. The most exciting score is a **slam dunk** when a tall player jumps up high and pushes the ball down through the hoop. The ball is moved between players by a **pass**, or a **dribble** if a player bounces it on the floor. Players are not allowed to push an opponent, but this often happens. When a **foul** is committed against a player, he or she can have one or two **free throws**, also called **foul shots**, that count one point each. If the **referee** calls five illegal plays on a player, he or she **fouls out** and cannot play the rest of the game.

The NBA teams play between November and June. The season ends when the best eight teams in the **Eastern Conference** and the best eight in the **Western Conference** compete to play in the **NBA Championship**. The Boston Celtics have won this most often, a total

of 16 times. The best team recently has been the Chicago Bulls, with six championships since 1991. Women players take part in the **American Basketball League** and the **Women's National Basketball Association** league. There is great interest in basketball at college level when 64 teams take part in the *NCAA (National Collegiate Athletic Association) Basketball Championships, called 'March Madness', in March each year. Basketball is also popular in *high schools.

NBA players are among the highest-paid sports people in the world. Michael *Jordan, the richest of all sports players, who played for the Chicago Bulls, earned more than $35 million in the 2003–4 season. Famous players in basketball history include Wilt 'the Stilt' *Chamberlain and Julius Erving. Together with many others, they are in the Basketball *Hall of Fame.

Basketball is also played in Britain, where there are national leagues for both men and women. But the sport receives less attention than in the US and, in contrast to the names of teams and players in football, the names of the leading basketball teams and players are unfamiliar to most people.

ˌSam 'Bass /ˈbæs/ (1851–78) a US outlaw (= criminal) who was called 'the Robin Hood of Texas'. He was a *cowboy before becoming an outlaw. In 1877, his gang stole $60 000 from a train in *Nebraska, the largest train robbery in history at that time. Bass died the following year after being shot.

ˌShirley 'Bassey /ˈbæsi/ (1937–) a British singer of popular music, born in Wales. She is famous for her strong voice and personality. Her most successful songs include Hey, Big Spender and the theme songs for two James *Bond films, Goldfinger (1964) and Diamonds are Forever (1971). She was made a *dame(2) in 2002.

BAT /ˌbiː ˈtiː/ (also **BAT Industries**) (in full **British American Tobacco**) a large company that makes cigarettes. Its brands include *Dunhill, *Lucky Strike, Rothmans and Peter Stuyvesant.

ˌH M 'Bateman /ˈbeɪtmən/ (Henry Mayo Bateman 1887–1970) a British cartoonist, born in Australia. His cartoons often show an embarrassed person who has just shocked everyone by accidentally breaking a rule of social behaviour.

ˌAlan 'Bates[1] /ˈbeɪts/ (1934–2003) an English actor in theatre, films and television. He appeared in the first theatre performance of *Look Back in Anger and his films include A Kind of Loving (1962), Women in Love (1969) and *Hamlet (1990).

ˌH E 'Bates[2] /ˈbeɪts/ (Herbert Ernest Bates 1905–74) an English writer of novels and short stories, many of which are about life in the English countryside. His best-known novel is The Darling Buds of May (1958).

ˌNorman 'Bates[3] /ˈbeɪts/ ⇨ PSYCHO.

Bath /bɑːθ; AmE bæθ/ a city in south-west England, famous for its healthy mineral water and hot springs, its ancient Roman baths and beautiful *Georgian buildings. The **Bath Festival** is a festival of classical music held every year in May and June. In 1987 Bath was one of the first places in Britain to become a *World Heritage Site.

ˌBath 'bun /ˌbɑːθ ; AmE ˌbæθ/ n a small round sweet cake that contains dried fruit and has crisp melted sugar on top. Bath buns were originally made in *Bath.

'bathing machine n a beach hut on wheels, used in the 18th and 19th centuries. People changed their clothes privately inside it and it was then pulled into the sea so that they could bathe from it.

ˌBath 'Oliver™ /ˌbɑːθ ˈɒlɪvə(r); AmE ˌbæθ ˈɑːlɪvər/ n a type of thin hard biscuit that is made without sugar and is eaten especially with cheese. It was invented in *Bath by Dr William Oliver (1695–1764), who wanted his patients to eat simple, healthy food.

'Batman /'bætmæn/ a character in US *comics, on television and in films who wears a costume like a bat (= a small animal like a mouse with wings), and has special powers of intelligence. With his friend Robin he spends his time helping ordinary people in trouble and fighting crime. He drives a vehicle called the **Batmobile** and is sometimes referred to as the 'caped crusader'. His regular enemies include the Penguin and the Joker.

'Battenberg /'bætnbɜːg; AmE 'bætnbɜːrg/ (also **Battenberg cake**) n [C, U] (BrE) a cake with a long square shape, covered with marzipan (= a soft mixture of almonds, sugar and eggs). When cut, each slice shows four squares of cake, two pink and two yellow.

Battersea 'Dog's Home /ˌbætəsiː; AmE ˌbætərsiː/ a temporary home for dogs and cats in Battersea, London. It finds new homes for dogs and cats whose owners do not want them, and returns lost pets to their owners.

Battersea 'Power Station /ˌbætəsiː; AmE ˌbætərsiː/ a very large building in Battersea, London, with four tall chimneys. It was built in 1937 to produce electricity for south London, but since it was closed down in the 1980s it has been completely empty, although there have been several plans to convert it.

Battery 'Park /ˌbætəri/ a park at the southern end of *Manhattan(1) Island, New York, opposite the *Statue of Liberty. Boats take tourists, etc. from the park to the statue, *Ellis Island and *Staten Island.

Battle 'Creek /ˌbætl 'kriːk/ a town in southern *Michigan, US, which is the centre of the breakfast cereal industry. The Kellogg Company has its main office there. See also KELLOGG'S.

The Battle Hymn of the Re'public an American religious song, written by Julia Ward *Howe for the North during the *Civil War. It is sung to the tune of John *Brown's Body. It was also used during marches for *civil rights in the 1960s and 1970s.

the **Battle of 'Britain** the fighting between British and German planes over the south of England in the autumn of 1940. It was a very important battle in *World War II, because the British prevented the Germans from controlling the skies over Britain and the English Channel, and so stopped the German army from invading Britain. The speech made by Winston *Churchill after the Battle of Britain is often quoted and the battle is remembered each year on **Battle of Britain Day** (15 September).

> 66 Never in the field of human conflict was so much owed by so many to so few. 99
> Winston Churchill

the **Battle of the At'lantic** /ət'læntɪk/ the long struggle for control of the Atlantic between the navies of Germany and the *Allies. The phrase can refer to this struggle in either of the two World Wars.

the **Battle of the 'Boyne** /'bɔɪn/ a victory in Ireland in 1690 for the English king *William III over the *Jacobite armies of the former King *James II. About 35 000 Protestants under William defeated about 25 000 Irish and French Catholics near the Boyne river. The event is celebrated by Protestants in Northern Ireland on 12 July every year.

the **Battle of the 'Bulge** /'bʌldʒ/ a strong but unsuccessful attack by German forces against the *Allies in southern Belgium in 1944. The word bulge means a swelling, so the phrase is also used in a humorous way

to mean a struggle to lose weight, e.g. by going on a diet: I'm fighting the battle of the bulge.

'battles See also AGINCOURT, ARNHEM, BALACLAVA, BANNOCKBURN, BLENHEIM, BOSWORTH FIELD, BULL RUN, BUNKER HILL, CHANCELLORSVILLE, CONCORD, COPENHAGEN, CRÉCY, CULLODEN, EDGEHILL, EL ALAMEIN, FLODDEN, GETTYSBURG, HASTINGS[1], LEXINGTON AND CONCORD, LITTLE BIGHORN, MARNE, MARSTON MOOR, MOBILE BAY, MONS, NASEBY, NILE, PASSCHENDAELE, PLASSEY, PRESTONPANS, SAN JACINTO, SARATOGA, SEDGEMOOR, SHILOH, SOMME, STAMFORD BRIDGE(1), TRAFALGAR, WATERLOO[2], WORCESTER[2], YPRES.

Nora 'Batty /'bæti/ a female character in the humorous *BBC television series *Last of the Summer Wine. People sometimes use her name to refer to a woman of middle age who is bad-tempered and rather ugly.

Bay 'City a popular name for *San Francisco.

the **Bayeux 'Tapestry** /ˌbaɪjɜː/ a finely decorated cloth wall covering made in the 11th century. It shows the events that led to the Battle of *Hastings (1066) between the *Normans under *William the Conqueror and the English under King *Harold II, and the death of King Harold. It is 74 yards/68 metres long and is kept in a museum at Bayeux in northern France.

Lilian 'Baylis /'beɪlɪs/ (1874–1937) an English theatre manager. She ran the *Old Vic, famous for its *Shakespeare productions, and *Sadler's Wells, the home of the companies that later became the *Royal Ballet and the *English National Opera.

the **Bay of 'Pigs** a bay on the south-west coast of Cuba, where in 1961 about 1 500 Cuban exiles, supported by the *CIA, landed in an attempt to end the rule of Fidel Castro. The attempt failed, causing great embarrassment to the US President John F *Kennedy and making Castro's position stronger than ever. See also CUBAN MISSILE CRISIS.

'Bayswater /'beɪzwɔːtə(r)/ a district in west London, England. It is between *Paddington and *Kensington Gardens and has many hotels.

'Baywatch /'beɪwɒtʃ; AmE 'beɪwɑːtʃ/ a popular US television series (1989–2001) about lifeguards (= people employed to rescue people who get into difficulty while swimming) on the coast of *California. People sometimes made fun of the series because they thought the actors were chosen more for their attractive bodies than because they could act well. One of the best known of these actors was Pamela Anderson (1967–).

Ba'zooka™ /bə'zuːkə/ n [U] a popular US make of bubble gum. Packets contain cards with pictures of baseball or other sports players on them, and these are collected and exchanged by young people. The older cards are becoming valuable. Bazooka was originally sold with a small *comic about a character called Bazooka Joe.

the **BBC** (in full the **British Broadcasting Corporation**) one of the main television and radio broadcasting organizations in Britain, paid for by the government since 1927 but free to choose the contents of its programmes. As well as several radio stations and its main television channels *BBC One and *BBC Two, the BBC also broadcasts on new digital channels, BBC Three with new drama and comedy and BBC Four for culture, arts and science, children's channels CBeebies and CBBC, as well as BBC News 24 and BBC Parliament. The head of the BBC has the title of 'director general'. ⇨ note at RADIO.

> 66 Nation shall speak peace unto nation. 99
> motto of the BBC

B

BBC 'English *n* [U] a form of English pronunciation that was traditionally associated with that used by *BBC news readers.

BBC One /ˌbiː biː ˈwʌn/ the main television channel of the *BBC. Its programmes are mostly of general interest, e.g. light entertainment, news, sport, films and children's programmes.

the **'BBC 'Philharmonic 'Orchestra** the *BBC's main orchestra in the north of England. It has a strong reputation for its performances of 20th-century British music, which can often be heard on *Radio 3.

the **ˌBBC 'Symphony ˌOrchestra** the *BBC's main orchestra, whose concerts are broadcast on *Radio 3. It is well known as the orchestra that plays at the *Last Night of the Proms.

BBC Two /ˌbiː biː si ˈtuː/ the second television channel of the *BBC. Some of its programmes are more serious than those of *BBC One and include plays, concerts and *Open University programmes.

ˌBBC 'World an international news programme broadcast by the *BBC on television 24 hours a day.

the **ˌBBC 'World 'Service** the service of English and foreign language radio programmes broadcast 24 hours a day to countries around the world by the *BBC from *Bush House in London. It began in 1932 and is highly regarded for its honesty and accuracy, especially in countries where broadcast news is controlled by the government.

BB gun /'biːbiː/ *n* (*AmE*) a long, light gun that uses air power to fire small round metal balls. BB guns are usually the first guns given to older children when they are learning to shoot. They use them to fire at targets and to shoot small animals.

the **'Beach Boys** a popular US pop group in the 1960s, many of whose songs were about enjoying life on the coast of *California, surfing and swimming in the sea. Their successes included the songs *I Get Around* (1964) and *Good Vibrations* (1966) and the album *Pet Sounds* (1966).

ˌBeachy 'Head /ˌbiːtʃi/ a high piece of land with steep white cliffs that sticks out into the sea on the south coast of England, between Eastbourne and *Brighton.

ˌBeacon 'Hill an old, fashionable area of *Boston, *Massachusetts, US, where many rich families and politicians live.

ˌJeremy 'Beadle /'biːdl/ (1948–) a British television entertainer who is famous for presenting programmes in which people were shown in embarrassing or ridiculous situations. The programmes often used videos made by members of the public.

ˌHMS 'Beagle /'biːgl/ the ship in which Charles *Darwin sailed to South America and the Galapagos Islands in 1831–6.

'Beaker People *n* [pl] people who came to Britain from the continent of Europe in the early *Bronze Age. They used beakers (= cups with wide mouths) for drinking, and many of these have been found in their burial places.

'Beale Street /'biːl/ a street in the US town of *Memphis, *Tennessee, famous for its African-American *blues music. There is a popular song called *The Beale Street Blues*.

ˌJudge Roy 'Bean¹ /'biːn/ (1825–1903) a US judge of the *Wild West known as 'the hanging judge' because he ordered many people to be hanged. He called himself 'the only law west of the Pecos (river)' and ran a careless and often humorous court of law in the town of Langtry, Texas.

ˌSean 'Bean² /ˌʃɔːn 'biːn/ (1959–) an English actor who is best known for his role in the *Lord of the Rings* films and for playing Richard Sharpe in a series of television films (1993–97) about a soldier in the *Napoleonic Wars, based on the novels by Bernard Cornwell.

the **'Beano** /'biːnəʊ; *AmE* 'biːnoʊ/ a popular British children's *comic which has been published every week since 1938. Its most famous character is *Dennis the Menace, a boy who, with his dog Gnasher, plays tricks on people. Other characters have included the *Bash Street Kids, Ivy the Terrible and Minnie the Minx.

'Bean Town a popular name for the US town of *Boston, *Massachusetts, because of its famous *Boston baked beans.

ˌJames 'Beard /'bɪəd; *AmE* 'bɪrd/ (1903–85) a well-known US cook and writer of books and newspaper articles on food and cooking. In 1945 he became the first person to present a programme about cooking on American national television.

ˌAubrey 'Beardsley /'bɪədzli; *AmE* 'bɪrdzli/ (1872–98) an English artist, best known for his book illustrations, mostly black and white, which were much influenced by the *Pre-Raphaelites and Japanese prints. His style, using long curved lines and a strong sense of visual design, was often openly erotic (= sexual) and considered shocking by many people. His best-known works are the illustrations for Oscar *Wilde's *Salome* and Thomas *Malory's *Morte d'Arthur*.

'bear ˌmarket /'beə; *AmE* 'ber/ *n* a situation at the stock exchange in which company share prices are falling rapidly. People who sell their shares, hoping to buy them back later at a lower price, are called **bears**. Compare BULL MARKET.

the **'Beastie Boys** /'biːsti/ a US *rock group formed in 1981. They perform mainly *rap music and their best-known record is *(You Gotta) Fight for your Right (to Party)*.

the **ˌBeast of 'Bodmin** /'bɒdmɪn; *AmE* 'bɑːdmɪn/ an animal that some people say they have seen on *Bodmin Moor in south-west England. Some think it is a big cat, such as a lion, that has escaped from a zoo. Other people think that there is no Beast of Bodmin, and that people have simply seen large dogs in the fog.

the **'beat geneˌration** *n* [sing+ sing/pl *v*] a group of young people in the 1950s and early 1960s, especially writers and artists, who rejected the social values of their time. They tried to find a different style of living, becoming interested in eastern religions and new forms of writing. The movement began in the US and included such writers as Jack *Kerouac and Allen *Ginsberg: *The hippies just carried on where the beat generation left off.*

ˌbeating the 'bounds an old custom, still kept in some parts of Britain, of marking the boundaries of a church *parish(1) by marching round them and hitting the ground, or certain boundary marks, with long sticks. The ceremony is performed once a year, usually on *Ascension Day or before *Easter.

ˌBeatle'mania /ˌbiːtl'meɪniə/ *n* [U] a word that was invented to describe the wild enthusiasm of the *Beatles' fans when they were very popular in the 1960s.

the **'Beatles** /'biːtlz/ an internationally famous British pop group whose members during their most successful period in the 1960s were John *Lennon, Paul *McCartney, George Harrison (1943–2001) and Ringo Starr (1940–). The group, sometimes called the 'Fab Four' in the press, all came from *Liverpool, England. Most of their songs were written by Lennon and McCartney. After their first great success with *Please Please Me* in 1963, their records were regularly No 1 hits in Britain and the US. In the late 1960s they became interested in eastern religions and drugs, and these influences appeared in their music. They separated in 1970 to follow individual careers. They have had more influence on the development of pop music than any other group. They also made several successful films.

,Cecil 'Beaton /'biːtn/ (1904–80) an English photographer and dress designer. He is best known for his photographs of famous people, especially the *royal family, and of fashion models, and for his costumes for films and the theatre. He was made a *knight in 1972.

,Warren 'Beatty /,wɒrən 'beɪti/ (1937–) a US film actor and director whose many films include *Bonnie and Clyde* (1967) and *McCabe and Mrs Miller* (1971). He received an *Oscar as 'Best Director' for *Reds* (1981). Beatty was famous for having affairs with many beautiful women until he married the actor Annette Bening in 1992. His sister is Shirley *MacLaine.

the 'Beaufort scale /'bəʊfət; AmE 'boʊfərt/ n a scale for measuring wind speed, from 0 (calm) to 12 (hurricane). It is named after the British admiral Sir Francis Beaufort (1774–1857), who invented it.

'Beaulieu /'bjuːli/ a village in *Hampshire, England, which many tourists visit to see the *National Motor Museum. The museum has examples of all the important cars and motorcycles ever made in Britain, as well as rare vehicles such as *Bluebird.

,Francis 'Beaumont /'bəʊmɒnt; AmE 'boʊmɑːnt/ (1584–1616) an English writer of plays, many of which he wrote with John *Fletcher. His best-known play is *The Knight of the Burning Pestle* (1607), which he probably wrote alone. He also helped Ben *Jonson to write several of his plays.

,Beauty and the 'Beast a traditional story about a young girl who manages to save a monster from a magic spell by her love. He turns into a handsome prince and they get married. The phrase *beauty and the beast* is sometimes used to describe partners when one of them is much more attractive than the other.

,Lord 'Beaverbrook /'biːvəbrʊk; AmE 'biːvərbrʊk/ (*born* William Maxwell Aitken 1874–1964) a British newspaper owner and politician. He was born in Canada, but settled in Britain and became a *Member of Parliament in 1910. He was a *Cabinet minister in both World Wars. He bought the *Daily Express* and the *Evening Standard* and started the *Sunday Express*. He used these newspapers to try to make various ideas popular, such as his desire to preserve the *British Empire.

'Beaver Scout (*also* **Beaver**) n a boy between six and eight years old who is a member of the most junior branch of the *Scouts.

,Beavis and 'Butt-head™ /,biːvɪs /, 'bʌthed/ a pair of US television cartoon characters who are very stupid and always behave in an unpleasant way.

'bebop /'biːbɒp; AmE 'biːbɑːp/ (*also* **bop**) n [U] a type of *jazz music that was especially popular in the 1940s and 1950s. It emphasizes the creative playing of individual musicians in small groups. Famous players include 'Dizzy' *Gillespie, Charlie 'Bird' *Parker and Thelonious *Monk. The music again became popular in the 1990s because of musicians like the trumpet player Wynton *Marsalis.

,Becher's 'Brook /,biːtʃəz 'brʊk; AmE ,biːtʃərz 'brʊk/ the most famous and one of the most difficult jumps on the *Grand National course, where many horses fall.

,Sidney 'Bechet /'beʃeɪ/ (1897–1959) a US *jazz musician who played the saxophone and the clarinet.

St ,Thomas 'Becket /'bekɪt/ (*also called* ,Thomas à 'Becket) (c. 1118–70) an English saint. He was a close friend of King *Henry II, who made him chancellor (= senior law official) and later *Archbishop of Canterbury,

hoping by doing this to be able to control the English Church. When Thomas resisted they quarrelled. According to tradition, Henry said, 'Who will rid me of this turbulent priest?' As a result four *knights murdered Becket in *Canterbury Cathedral, which became a place of pilgrimage where people travelled to show respect for the saint. His story was made into a play, *Murder in the Cathedral* (1935), by T S *Eliot.

,Margaret 'Beckett[1] /'bekɪt/ (1943–) a British *Labour politician. She became a *Member of Parliament in 1974 and held several important positions in the Labour *Shadow Cabinet. In 1998 she became *Leader of the House and in 2001 Secretary of State for Environment, Food and Rural Affairs.

,Samuel 'Beckett[2] /'bekɪt/ (1906–89) an Irish writer of plays, novels and poetry. He is best known for his plays, including *Waiting for Godot* (1952) and *Endgame* (1957). He settled in France early in his career and much of his work was written in French. He was given the *Nobel Prize for literature in 1969.

> 66 Nothing happens, nobody comes, nobody goes, it's awful. 99
> Estragon in *Waiting for Godot*

,David 'Beckham /'bekəm/ (1975–) an English footballer who played for *Manchester United (1992–2003) and has been captain of the England team since 2001. In 2003 he left Manchester United to play for Real Madrid. He married *Spice Girl Victoria Adams in 1999 and they are two of the most famous people in Britain.

'Bedales /'biːdeɪlz/ Britain's oldest boarding school (= a school where the pupils live) for boys and girls, in *Hampshire, England. It began as a school for boys in 1893 and started to take girls in 1898.

,bed and 'breakfast n 1 [U] a bed for the night and breakfast the next morning in a hotel, pub or private house, paid for as a single service by the guest: *It's £50 for bed and breakfast or £80 for bed, breakfast and evening meal.* 2 [C] a private house that provides bed and breakfast to paying guests. Bed and breakfasts are common throughout Britain and the US. They are cheaper than hotels and usually have a friendly atmosphere. In Britain they usually provide a cooked *English breakfast: *We went to Cornwall for a week and stayed in a funny little bed and breakfast.*

Bede /biːd/ (*also called* the ,Venerable 'Bede) (c. 673–735) an English monk and historian. At his monastery in *Jarrow in north-east England, he wrote many books, the most important of which, *Ecclesiastical History of the English People*, written in Latin, was the first serious work of English history.

'Bedfordshire /'bedfədʃə(r); AmE 'bedfərdʃər/ (*abbr* **Beds**) a county in southern central England. Its administrative centre is Bedford.

'Bedlam /'bedləm/ (formerly) a popular name for the Hospital of St Mary of Bethlehem in London. It was established as a priory (= a small Christian religious community) in 1274, and in the 14th century it became a place for mentally ill people, who were then called 'lunatics'. People used to come and watch the patients and be entertained by their disturbed condition. From this the word *bedlam* has come to mean a scene of noisy confusion: *The teacher's whistle could not be heard above the bedlam in the playground.*

'bedsit (*also* ,bed'sitter) n (in Britain) a flat consisting of one room, used for living and sleeping in. Bedsits are usually rooms in large old houses that have been divided into flats, and are mainly rented by people who live

B

alone, such as students. An area of a town where many houses have been made into bedsits is sometimes called **bedsit-land** or **bedsitter-land**: *He learned to cook in his first bedsit.*

the Beeb /biːb/ (*BrE*) an informal name for the *BBC.

Thomas 'Beecham /'biːtʃəm/ (1879–1961) an English conductor who established two of the great London orchestras, the *London Philharmonic and the *Royal Philharmonic, and helped to make the British music of his time, especially the music of his friend *Delius, more popular. He was also famous for making intelligent, funny and sometimes unkind remarks. He was made a *knight in 1916.

Beecham's 'pills™ /ˌbiːtʃəmz/ *n* [pl] a popular British medicine for minor illnesses like colds, headaches, etc. They were first produced in 1847 by the grandfather of Sir Thomas *Beecham. The medicine is also available in powder form, called **Beecham's powders**.

'beefeater *n* a popular name for a *Yeoman Warder of the *Tower of London.

the 'Bee Gees /'biː dʒiːz/ a British pop group consisting of three brothers, Barry, Robin and Maurice Gibb. Their most successful records have included *Massachusetts* (1967), *I've Gotta Get a Message to You* (1968), *How Deep is Your Love* (1977), *Night Fever* (1978) and *You Win Again* (1987). They also wrote and performed the music for the film *Saturday Night Fever* (1978). Maurice Gibb died in 2003.

a beefeater

▶ **beer**

In Britain, beer is the most popular alcoholic drink which is drunk in *pubs. Many people drink **bitter**, a brown-coloured beer. It is sold **on draught**, if it is drawn for each customer from a large container, usually a **keg** or **barrel**, or **bottled**, if it has been put in small bottles at a factory. Bottled beer is sometimes called **ale**. Bitter is usually drunk at room temperature. **Lager**, which is yellow in colour, has more gas in it and is usually drunk cold. Many pubs sell a selection of French, German and Australian lagers. **Stout** is a strong, dark brown beer which forms a thick white froth, or 'head', on top when poured into a glass. Two of the most popular makes are *Guinness and Murphy's. **Mild** is a sweeter, darker form of bitter but is less popular. **Shandy** is a mixture of beer and lemonade or ginger beer. Draught beer or lager is sold in **pints** or **half-pints**. Some people drink **low-alcohol** beers and lagers in order to reduce the risk of **drink-driving** (= driving a car while under the influence of alcohol), which is against the law. Many people like to drink **real ale**, beer that is made and stored in the traditional way, often made by smaller **breweries** (= companies that make beer). The interests of real ale drinkers are defended by *CAMRA, the Campaign for Real Ale, which publishes a list of real-ale pubs and campaigns to prevent small breweries closing.

The US **brewing** industry was begun by Germans who moved to the US, and so the typical US beer has always been like German beer, light in colour, similar to what the British call lager, although Americans do not use that word. Until the beginning of the 20th century there were many small, family-run breweries in the US, but then *Prohibition came into effect and it

became illegal to sell alcohol. By the time Prohibition was cancelled most of the small breweries had gone out of business. Today, most beer is produced by a few large breweries, all of whom make similar products. Recently, however, Americans have begun to appreciate different sorts of beer and many **microbreweries** have opened. These brew and serve high-quality beer made in traditional ways. This movement has even led some of the large breweries to return to traditional methods and materials. The microbrewery movement has been supported mostly by professional people with a high income but, in general, beer is seen as a drink for people with less money, or for informal occasions. People drink beer after playing sports or while watching them, but wine is considered more appropriate to drink with a meal.

Many makes of beer in the US are sold in both bottles and cans, though microbrewery beers come only in bottles. Restaurants always serve bottled beer. In some states beer can be sold in supermarkets, gas stations and local convenience stores (= shops that are open for many hours each day). In other states it can be sold only in specially licensed **liquor stores** or **bottle shops**. This can be confusing and even embarrassing for Americans when they travel to a different state, as well as for foreign visitors.

Max 'Beerbohm /'bɪəbəʊm; *AmE* 'bɪrboʊm/ (1872–1956) a British humorous writer who also drew caricatures (= exaggerated comic pictures) of well-known people in the artistic world. His best-known novel is *Zuleika Dobson* (1911), set in *Oxford during the 1890s. He was made a *knight in 1939.

'beer ˌgarden *n* **1** (in Britain) the garden of a pub where customers can sit in fine weather to eat the food and drink the beer, etc. that they have bought in the pub. **2** (in the US) a place where beer, etc. is served at outdoor events such as county fairs. ⇨ note at PUB.

'Beer Nuts™ *n* [pl] a product name for a popular US snack food (= one eaten quickly between meals). They are peanuts in their skins, treated to make them 'slightly sweet, slightly salty', according to the advertisements for them.

'beer tent *n* (*BrE*) a large tent, often open at one side, where drinks are served at an outdoor sporting event or entertainment such as a *cricket match.

'Beetle™ /'biːtl/ *n* the British name for the original Volkswagen small car with a rounded design. In the US it is also called the **bug**: *Her first car was a Beetle.*

Mrs 'Beeton /'biːtn/ (Isabella Mary Mayson Beeton 1836–65) the British writer of *the Book of Household Management* (1861), a famous book on cooking and running a household, which gives much information about 19th-century life in the home: *According to Mrs Beeton, we should cook it with cream.*

The ˌBeggar's 'Opera an opera (1728) by John *Gay, in which the songs are set to the popular tunes of the time. The main character is Macheath, a highwayman (= a person who robs travellers), and many of the other characters are criminals. The opera was written as a humorous comment on the dishonest government of the day. *The Threepenny Opera* (1928) by Bertolt Brecht and Kurt Weill was based on *The Beggar's Opera*.

Aphra 'Behn /ˌæfrə 'ben/ (1640–89) an English writer of plays, novels and poems. She was probably the first professional woman writer in England. Her best-known works include the play *The Rover* (1678) and the novel *Oroonoko* (1688), an attack on *slavery.

'Bix' 'Beiderbecke /ˌbɪks 'baɪdəbek; *AmE* 'baɪdərbek/ (Leon Bix Beiderbecke 1903–31) a US *jazz musician and composer who played the cornet (= a type of small trumpet) and the piano. He was chosen for the Jazz *Hall of Fame in 1962.

Harry Bela'fonte /belə'fɒnti; *AmE* belə'faːnti/ (1927–) a US singer and actor who became famous in the 1950s singing calypso songs (= West Indian songs in African rhythm, often about subjects of current interest). His most successful song was *The Banana Boat Song* (1956). He was a star of the film *Island in the Sun* (1957) and in 1960 he became the first African American to win an *Emmy award.

Bel'fast /bel'faːst, 'belfaːst; *AmE* bel'fæst, 'belfæst/ the capital city of Northern Ireland. Its main industries were making ships and aircraft, but the last ship was built in 2003 and the city has suffered greatly in recent times from unemployment and the *Troubles. Two streets are often mentioned in the news, the *Falls Road where mainly *Roman Catholic people live, and the *Shankhill Road, which is mainly *Protestant.

Bel'gravia /bel'greɪviə/ a fashionable and expensive area of London, near *Buckingham Palace and around Belgrave Square.

Be,lisha 'beacon /bə,liː'ʃə/ *n* (in Britain) a black and white post with an orange flashing light on top, marking a *zebra crossing. Belisha beacons are named after Leslie Hore-Belisha, the Minister of Transport when they were introduced.

Be'lize /be'liːz/ a country in Central America, on the Caribbean Sea, that used to be a British colony called **British Honduras**. It became independent and joined the *Commonwealth in 1981. Its main industries are sugar and wood production, and it has an important tourist industry.
▶ **Be'lizean** *adj, n.*

Ale'xander 'Graham 'Bell /'bel/ (1847–1922) a scientist and inventor who is best known for inventing the telephone. He was born in Scotland but from 1872 lived in the US, where he later started the **Bell Telephone Company** which became one of the largest companies in America.

'Bella /'belə/ a British magazine for women that contains articles on health, beauty, fashion, food and other subjects. It first appeared in 1987 and is published every week.

David 'Bellamy /'beləmi/ (1933–) a British scientist who appears regularly on television in programmes of popular science. He is particularly interested in the protection of the environment and in preserving wild life of all kinds.

La ,Belle 'Dame Sans Mer'ci /,bel 'dæm sɒ meə'siː; *AmE* mer'siː/ one of the best-known poems by John *Keats about a *knight who falls in love with a beautiful woman with magic powers. He dreams that he is with her in the countryside, but wakes up alone and sad.

Hilaire 'Belloc /,hɪleə 'belɒk; *AmE* ,hɪler 'belaːk/ (1870–1953) a British author, born in France. He wrote books of various different kinds, including biographies and travel books, but he is mainly remembered for his humorous poetry, especially *The Bad Child's Book Of Beasts* (1896) and *Cautionary Tales* (1907).

Saul 'Bellow /,sɔːl 'beləʊ; *AmE* 'beloʊ/ (1915–2005) a US writer of novels, born in Canada. His books often relate to his Jewish background and many are very humorous. They include *The Adventures of Augie March* (1953), *Herzog* (1964), *Humboldt's Gift* (1975) for which he won the *Pulitzer Prize, and *Ravelskin* (2000). He was given the *Nobel Prize for literature in 1976.

▶ **bells and bell-ringing**

Bells hung high in the towers of churches are rung to announce church services. In Britain the sound of church bells from a **belfry** is associated with Sunday mornings and with weddings. Bells throughout the country may also be rung at times of national celebration. Before minor services or to announce a funeral (= a service for a dead person), a single bell is usually sounded repeatedly for five or ten minutes. The blessing of the bread and wine at a Communion service may also be indicated by the sounding of a bell.

Churches usually have between 5 and 12 bells, which are rung by teams of **bell-ringers**. The ringers stand far below the bells and each pulls on a long rope attached to a bell in such a way that the bell swings over in a circle, causing the **clapper** inside the bell to strike the side. In a **peal** each of the bells is rung in turn, and the order in which they are rung changes according to a pattern. This is called **change-ringing**. Complicated tunes can be played and many **changes** have their own name, e.g. *Grandsire Triples* and *Oxford Treble Bob*.

Other types of institution also use bells: Great Tom, the big bell at Christ Church College, Oxford, is rung 101 times each night, indicating the original number of scholars at the college. The most famous bell in Britain is Big Ben, the large bell in the clock tower next to the *Houses of Parliament in London, which **chimes** the hours and is heard on radio and television.

Bell-ringing used to be a popular hobby though it is now sometimes necessary to use a recording of bells before church services because of a shortage of bell-ringers. Some people complain about the noise of bells but most people like the sound.

America's experience with bells did not begin well, since the nation's *Liberty Bell cracked in 1752. Bells are heard in churches and at colleges and universities. Some communities, especially in *New England, ring bells as a celebration. Bells are also used to announce the time, mostly using the eight notes of Big Ben.

There are very few traditional bell-ringers in the US. Instead, many institutions have **carillon bells**, a group of up to 70 bells controlled from a keyboard like that of an organ. Carillon bells can play tunes and simple harmonies. The 50 bells of the Allen & Perkins Carillon at Duke University in *North Carolina were first used to play songs in 1932. Other well-known carillons include the Sather Tower Carillon at the University of California at *Berkeley. Many of the bells in the US are imported from Britain.

the ,Belmont 'Stakes /,belmɒnt; *AmE* ,belmaːnt/ a horse race run at Belmont Park near New York City. It was first run in 1867 and is one of the races that form the US *triple crown. The horses in the race must be three years old.

'beltway *n* (*AmE*) a ring road (= a road built around a town to reduce traffic in the centre). The expression *inside the beltway* is used to describe affairs at the centre of *Washington politics.

,Ben & 'Jerry's™ a make of ice cream made by a company started in the US in 1978 by Ben Cohen (1951–) and Jerry Greenfield (1951–) and now owned by *Unilever. It became popular because of its new and unusual flavours and is now sold around the world.

the Bench the place where the judge sits in a court of law. It is also used to refer to the judge in a court, or to judges in general: *The prisoner was told to address his remarks to the Bench.*

'benefit so,ciety ⇨ FRIENDLY SOCIETY.

'Stephen 'Vincent Be'nét /bə'neɪ/ (1898–1943) a US writer of poems and novels. He received a *Pulitzer Prize for his best-known poem *John Brown's Body* (1928)

B

about the American Civil War. His brother, William Benét (1886–1950) was also a successful poet.

Ben'Gay™ /ben'geɪ/ *n* [U] a US make of ointment put on the body to help relieve pain in the muscles and joints. It can be bought without a doctor's prescription and is produced by Pfizer Inc.

Ben-'Hur /ˌben ˈhɜː(r)/ a novel (1880) by Lew *Wallace about the early days of Christianity. It has twice been made into a film. The second of these, made in 1959 with Charlton *Heston, won 11 *Oscars. The story is about Ben-Hur, a young Jew who meets Jesus and is converted to Christianity after many adventures.

Tony 'Benn /'ben/ (Anthony Wedgwood Benn 1925–) a British *Labour politician, famous for his left-wing views, who has had important positions in two Labour governments. He was a *Member of Parliament from 1950 to 2001. He is the son of a *viscount(1) and when his father died the title legally passed to him, so he was unable to continue in the *House of Commons. He refused to accept the title and started a campaign to introduce a law allowing people with such titles to give them up if they wished. The law was passed in 1963, and Benn returned to the House of Commons. He retired from Parliament as the longest serving Labour MP ever and continues to be active in politics especially in the anti-war movement. He has published diaries of his years in office and also has a new career as an entertainer performing round Britain in one-man shows such as *An Audience with Tony Benn*. His son Hilary Benn is a government minister.

Alan 'Bennett¹ /'benɪt/ (1934–) a writer and actor, well known for his humorous yet sympathetic plays, especially on television, about the lives of ordinary people. He first made his name in *Beyond the Fringe*. His best-known work includes the plays *Forty Years On* (1968), *Habeas Corpus* (1973), *A Question of Attribution* (1991) and *The History Boys* (2004) as well as the series of television monologues (= plays written for one character) called *Talking Heads* (1988 and 1998).

Arnold 'Bennett² /'benɪt/ (1867–1931) an English writer of novels, most of which are set in the *Potteries and describe the life of working people in great detail. His best-known works are *Anna of the Five Towns* (1902) and the *Clayhanger* series (1902–8).

Richard 'Rodney 'Bennett³ /'benɪt/ (1936–) an English composer, best known for his operas *The Mines of Sulphur* (1965) and *Victory* (1970) and for his music for several films. He was made a *knight in 1998.

Ben 'Nevis /ˌben ˈnevɪs/ a mountain in western Scotland which is 1343 metres/4406 feet high and is the highest mountain in the British Isles.

Jeremy 'Bentham /'ben-θəm; *also* 'bentəm/ (1748–1832) an English philosopher who believed that society's aim should be 'the greatest happiness for the greatest number' and argued that laws should be changed to produce this. His ideas had a great influence on 19th–century thought.
▶ **Benthamism** *n* [U] the philosophy of Jeremy Bentham.
Benthamite *n, adj.*

Ben Nevis

Bentley¹ /'bentli/ *n* an expensive make of car, formerly British. The company was sold to a German firm in 1998: *The chauffeur was waiting in the Bentley.*

a vintage Bentley

'Edmund 'Clerihew 'Bentley² /'klerɪhjuː 'bentli/ (1875–1956) an English journalist who wrote *detective stories and invented a form of comic verse with four lines, now called a **clerihew** after his middle name. Clerihews are usually about well-known people. A typical example is:

> **66** John Stuart Mill
> By a mighty effort of will
> Overcame his natural bonhomie
> And wrote 'Principles of Political Economy'. **99**

Bentley and 'Craig /ˌbentli, ˈkreɪg/ a famous British legal case. In 1952 two young men, Derek Bentley and Christopher Craig, were caught on a roof in south London by the police, who believed they were involved in a crime. Craig shot and killed a policeman after Bentley had shouted, 'Let him have it!' (which could mean either 'Give him the gun!' or 'Shoot him!'). Britain still had *capital punishment at the time, and Bentley, who was 19 but had a mental age of 11, was hanged. Craig, who was 16, was sent to prison. Bentley's family continued to argue that he should not have been executed, and in 1998 the *Court of Appeal finally pardoned him.

'Benzedrine™ /'benzədriːn/ *n* [U] (*also informal* **benny** [U, C]) a make of amphetamine (= a drug that makes people feel lively and excited) that is sometimes taken illegally. It was very popular with the *beat generation.

'Beowulf /'beɪəwʊlf/ a long poem in *Old English, probably written in the 8th century. It tells how the hero Beowulf kills two monsters and finally dies killing a third. It was the first major European poem that was not written in Latin or Greek.

Be'retta /bə'retə/ a make of small gun that is held in the hand. The Beretta company, which was started in Venice, Italy in 1526, makes many different kinds of guns used in the US.

John 'Berger /'bɜːdʒə(r); *AmE* 'bɜːrdʒər/ (1926–) an English writer and journalist, known for his left-wing views. Among his best-known works are *Ways of Seeing* (1972), a book about art and society, and the novel *G*, which won the *Booker Prize in 1972.

Ingrid 'Bergman /'bɜːgmən; *AmE* 'bɜːrgmən/ (1915–82) a Swedish actor who went to America and appeared in many *Hollywood films, including *Casablanca (1942). She did not work in the US for some time after she left her husband for the Italian film director Roberto Rossellini, and made many of her later films in Europe. She won *Oscars for *Gaslight* (1944), *Anastasia* (1956) and *Murder on the Orient Express* (1974).

the ,Bering 'Strait /ˌbeərɪŋ; *AmE* ˌberɪŋ/ the narrow passage of water between *Alaska and Russia. It connects the **Bering Sea**, the most northern part of the Pacific Ocean, with the Arctic Ocean. The Bering Strait and the Bering Sea are named after the Danish explorer Vitus Jonassen Bering (1681–1741).

'**Berkeley**¹ /'bɜːkli; *AmE* 'bɜːrkli/ a city on *San Francisco Bay in *California. It has the largest branch of the University of California. In the 1960s and 1970s protests by students at Berkeley influenced other student movements in America.

ˌBusby '**Berkeley**² /ˌbʌzbi 'bɜːkli; *AmE* 'bɜːrkli/ (1895–1976) a US film and stage director and choreographer. He is best remembered for his grand music and dance sequences involving many actors, in such films as *42nd Street* (1933).

ˌLennox '**Berkeley**³ /ˌlenəks 'bɑːkli; *AmE* 'bɑːrkli/ (1903–89) an English composer whose work was much influenced by Benjamin *Britten. He wrote a wide variety of music, but is best known for his chamber works (= music for a small orchestra) and some fine modern religious pieces. He was made a *knight in 1974.

ˌBerkeley '**Square** /ˌbɑːkli; *AmE* 'bɑːrkli/ a square in west central London that still has several of its original 18th-century buildings. It is mentioned in the song *A Nightingale Sang in Berkeley Square*, written in 1940 and still popular.

'**Berkshire** /'bɜːkʃə(r)/ (*also* **Royal Berkshire**) (*abbr* **Berks**) a county in southern England, west of London. It is one of the oldest counties.

the '**Berkshires** /'bɜːkʃəz/ (*also* the **Berkshire Hills**) a range of hills in the western part of the US state of *Massachusetts. It is an area of beautiful woods that are popular with tourists.

ˌMilton '**Berle** /ˌmɪltən 'bɜːl; *AmE* 'bɜːrl/ (1908–2002) a US comedian known as 'Mister Television'. He became the first national television star in the 1950s with his programme *Texaco Star Theater*.

ˌIrving **Ber'lin**¹ /ˌɜːvɪŋ bɜː'lɪn; *AmE* ˌɜːrvɪŋ bɜːr'lɪn/ (1888–1989) a US writer of popular songs, born in Russia. Although he had little technical skill, he wrote over 100 songs. Many of his greatest successes, like *White Christmas* (1942), were written for *Hollywood films. He also wrote *God Bless America* (1918).

ˌIˌsaiah **Ber'lin**² /aɪˌzaɪə bɜː'lɪn; *AmE* bɜːr'lɪn/ (1909–97) a British writer and philosopher, born in Russia. He was made a *knight in 1957 and a member of the *Order of Merit in 1971.

'**Bermondsey** /'bɜːmənzi/ a traditionally *working-class area of south-east London, on the south bank of the *Thames near *Tower Bridge, where formerly many people worked in the docks, loading and unloading ships. The character of the area has changed and the old dock buildings have been developed as expensive flats, restaurants, etc.

Ber'**muda** /bə'mjuːdə; *AmE* bər'mjuːdə/ a British dependency in the west Atlantic, consisting of a large number of small islands. It has an important tourist industry. The capital city is Hamilton.
▶ **Bermudian** *adj, n.*

Ber,muda '**shorts** /bəˌmjuːdə; *AmE* bərˌmjuːdə/ (*also* **Bermudas**) *n* [*pl*] short trousers, often with a colourful design, that reach down to just above the knees.

the Berˌmuda '**Triangle** /bəˌmjuːdə; *AmE* bərˌmjuːdə/ an area of the Atlantic Ocean between *Bermuda and *Florida that is thought to be dangerous because of the number of ships and planes that have disappeared there in a mysterious way.

ˌElmer '**Bernstein**¹ /ˌelmə 'bɜːnstaɪn/ (1922–2004) a US composer, especially of music for films. He received an *Oscar for *Thoroughly Modern Millie* (1967) and his

other successes include *The Magnificent Seven* (1960), *To Kill A Mockingbird* (1962), *The Age of Innocence* (1993) and *Far from Heaven* (2002).

ˌLeonard '**Bernstein**² (1918–90) a US conductor, composer and piano player. He wrote several popular *musicals. The most successful was *West Side Story* (1957) which became a film in 1961. He also wrote more serious works for orchestras and choirs.

ˌ'**Yogi**' '**Berra** /ˌjəʊgi 'berə; *AmE* ˌjoʊgi/ (1925–) a US baseball player and manager. He played in 14 *World Series. He is famous for saying things which make no sense or use language in a ridiculous way, e.g. 'No wonder nobody comes here – it's too crowded.'

> 66 It ain't over till it's over. 99
> Yogi Berra

ˌ'**Chuck**' '**Berry**¹ /ˌtʃʌk 'beri/ (1926–) a US *rock and roll singer and writer of songs whose style has influenced many other musicians, including the *Beatles and Bob *Dylan.

ˌHalle '**Berry**² /ˌhæli 'beri/ (1966–) a US actor who in 2002 became the first African American woman to win an *Oscar for her part in (*Monster's Ball*). Her other films include *X-Men* (2000), *Die Another Day* (2002) and *Catwoman* (2004).

ˌBertram '**Mills** /ˌbɜːtrəm 'mɪlz; *AmE* ˌbɜːrtrəm/ a popular British circus which regularly travelled round the country between 1920 and 1966. One of its most famous attractions was Coco the clown.

ˌBeryl the '**Peril** /ˌberəl/ a character in a British children's *comic, *The *Dandy*. She often gets into trouble.

ˌHenry '**Bessemer** /'besɪmə(r)/ (1813–98) an English engineer and inventor, best known for inventing the **Bessemer process**, a way of making steel by blowing air through melted iron to remove the other substances from it. He was made a *knight in 1879.

Best /best/ a British magazine for women that contains articles on health, fashion, sex, food and other subjects. It first appeared in 1987 and is published every week.

ˌGeorge '**Best** /'best/ (1946–) a football player from Northern Ireland who played for *Manchester United (1963–73) and Northern Ireland. He was a skilful and exciting attacking player, and many people think that he was one of the best players of all time.

ˌBethnal '**Green** /ˌbeθnəl/ an area of east London, at the centre of the *East End. It was once a traditional *cockney area but it is now the home of one of the largest Bengali communities in Britain.

ˌJohn '**Betjeman** /'betʃəmən/ (1906–84) an English poet who wrote humorous popular verse about ordinary people and social situations. He was also well known for his interest in *Victorian(1) architecture and his campaigns to preserve Victorian buildings. His best-known work is *Summoned by Bells* (1960), a long poem about his own life. He was made a *knight in 1969 and *Poet Laureate in 1972.

'*Better* ˌ*Homes* and '*Gardens* a US magazine that gives advice on how to decorate homes and create beautiful gardens. It also includes articles about food, health and other information for families.

ˌBetty '**Boop**™ /'buːp/ a popular US cartoon character created by Max Fleischer. She was often shown wearing a very short skirt. The cartoon began in 1915 and was based on Helen Kane, who was called the 'boop-a-doop' singer.

ˌBetty '**Crocker**™ /'krɒkə(r); *AmE* 'krɑːkər/ the name of an imaginary woman used since 1922 for popular US books on cooking. *Betty Crocker's Cookie Book* was published in 2003. Several Betty Crocker food products are also made by the General Mills Company.

A,neurin 'Bevan /ə,naɪrɪn 'bevn/ (1897–1960) a British *Labour politician, born in Wales. He started work as a coal miner before becoming a trade unionist and politician. As minister of health (1945–51) he was responsible for introducing the *National Health Service. He was well known for his left-wing views and for his skill as a public speaker.

> 66 This island is made mainly of coal and surrounded by fish. Only an organizing genius could produce a shortage of coal and fish at the same time. 99
>
> Aneurin Bevan in 1945

the 'Beveridge Re,port /'bevərɪdʒ/ a report about social conditions in Britain produced in 1942 by a committee led by the economist William Beveridge (1879–1963). It led to the post-war development of the *welfare state.

The ,Beverly 'Hillbillies /,bevəli 'hɪlbɪliz; AmE ,bevərli/ a successful US comedy television programme in the 1960s. It was about a poor family who become rich and go to live in fashionable *Beverly Hills. The characters were Jed Clampett, 'Granny' Moses, Jethro Bodine and Elly May Clampett.

,Beverly 'Hills /,bevəli; AmE ,bevərli/ a fashionable town in the US state of *California. It is surrounded by *Los Angeles but is not part of it. It is expensive and many people living there are film stars. Its most famous street for shopping is *Rodeo Drive.

,Ernest 'Bevin /'bevɪn/ (1881–1951) a British *trade union leader and *Labour politician. He established the *TGWU and became its leader. During *World War II he was minister of labour and national service. Later, as foreign secretary (1945–51), he played an important part in creating *NATO.

'Bevin boys /'bevɪn/ n [pl] (informal) the young British men who were sent to work in coal mines instead of joining the armed forces during *World War II, when Ernest *Bevin was minister of labour and national service.

,Thomas 'Bewick /'bjuːɪk/ (1753–1828) an English artist who worked mainly in book illustrations. He brought a new realistic style to the art of engraving (= cutting designs on metal, and then printing from it). He is especially famous for his pictures of animals and birds. His best-known works are A General History of Quadrupeds (1790) and the History of British Birds in two volumes (1797–1804).

Be'yoncé /bɪ'ɒnseɪ; AmE bɪ'ɑːnseɪ/ (Beyoncé Knowles 1981–) a US pop singer and actor. Beyoncé was a singer and songwriter with the pop group **Destiny's Child** before becoming a solo singer. She won five *Grammys for her first solo album Dangerously in Love (2003).

Be,yond the 'Fringe a British satirical comedy show, written and performed by Alan *Bennett, Peter *Cook, Jonathan *Miller and Dudley *Moore. It was first performed at the *Edinburgh Festival in 1960, and then moved to the *West End and *Broadway. It had a strong influence on later British comedy.

the BFI /,biː ef 'aɪ/ (in full the **British Film Institute**) an organization established in 1933 to encourage people to make films in Britain. It has a large collection of films, film scripts and books about films and also runs the *National Film Theatre.

Bhs /,biː eɪtʃ 'es/ any of a group of shops in Britain selling clothes and goods for the home, such as lights, curtains, etc. The name was changed from British Home Stores in 1986.

the 'Bible Belt a name sometimes used to describe the US *Deep South and parts of the Midwest because many people there are *Protestants who follow the words of the Bible very closely.

,Ambrose 'Bierce /,æmbrəʊz 'bɪəs; AmE ,æmbroʊz 'bɪrs/ (1842–c. 1914) a US journalist who wrote realistic but satirical short stories. They were collected in In the Midst of Life (1892). He also wrote a humorous dictionary, The Devil's Dictionary (1906). Bierce disappeared in Mexico in 1914 and was never found.

the ,Big 'Apple (AmE informal) a popular name for New York City. The name was first used by *jazz musicians to mean the 'big time', or success.

the ,Big Bad 'Wolf a frightening wolf that appears in several children's stories, e.g. *Little Red Riding Hood. In the story of the *Three Little Pigs the pigs sing the popular children's song Who's Afraid of the Big Bad Wolf? when the wolf threatens to blow their houses down. The phrase 'big bad wolf' is sometimes used to describe a person who is regarded as a dangerous enemy.

'big band a large band of musicians playing *jazz and other forms of dance music. Big bands were especially popular in the 1940s and produced what was called the **big band sound**. The most famous were led by Glenn *Miller, Benny *Goodman, 'Duke' *Ellington, 'Count' *Basie, and Jimmy and Tommy *Dorsey.

,Big 'Bang (informal) (in Britain) the name given to the introduction of important changes to the *London Stock Exchange rules in 1986, when some controls were removed and new ways of trading allowed.

,Big 'Ben the bell in the clock tower of the British *Houses of Parliament(2). Its sound is well known because it has often been used in films, and it is used on British television and radio to introduce news broadcasts. Many people think wrongly that Big Ben is the name of the clock, or of the tower itself.

the ,big 'board (AmE informal) a popular name for the *New York Stock Exchange because of its large sign showing the prices of shares in companies.

the tower of Big Ben

,Big 'Brother a character in George *Orwell's *Nineteen Eighty-Four. He is the ruler of the state, who watches people all the time and controls everything they do, allowing them no freedom. Heads of state or government departments who act in this way are sometimes referred to as 'Big Brother': They are putting these Big Brother surveillance cameras up all over the place. See also REALITY TV.

the ,big 'C /'siː/ an informal name for cancer.

,big 'daddy (AmE informal) a man who is powerful, important or rich, or all of these. He is usually a man who acts like a father to people who work for him or depend on him. Big Daddy is the name of the frightening head of the family in the play Cat on a Hot Tin Roof (1955) by Tennessee *Williams.

,Big 'Easy (AmE informal) a popular name for the American city of *New Orleans because of the relaxed atmosphere there.

'Bigfoot /'bɪɡfʊt/ n (pl **Bigfeet**) ⇨ SASQUATCH.

The ‚**Big** '**Issue** a British magazine, started in 1991. It is sold on the street by homeless people, who are allowed to keep most of the money they make from selling it. It consists mainly of news of the music, films, plays, etc. that are on in the area where it is sold, as well as articles about homelessness and unemployment. The aim is for homeless people to earn money without begging, and to inform other people about their situation.

‚**Big** '**Mac**™ *n* a type of hamburger made by *McDonalds which contains more meat than their standard hamburgers.

‚**Big Man on** '**Campus** (*abbr* **BMOC**) (*AmE informal*) a successful, usually popular, male student at a college or university. He is often the president of the Student Government Association or a well-known football or *basketball player.

‚**Big** '**Muddy** /'mʌdi/ (*AmE informal*) **1** the *Mississippi River.
2 a name for Vietnam used by US soldiers who fought there.

‚**big** '**stick** *n* [sing] the use of military or political power to influence or threaten other countries. The phrase was made popular by President Theodore *Roosevelt, who said that the US government should 'speak softly and carry a big stick'.

‚**Big** '**Sur** /'sɜː(r)/ a town on the coast of *California 100 miles/160 kilometres south of *San Francisco. The area is famous for its high cliffs and grand scenery. The writer Henry *Miller lived in Big Sur and the actor Orson *Welles had a small house there.

‚**Sergeant** '**Bilko** /'bɪlkəʊ; *AmE* 'bɪlkoʊ/ the main character in a US comedy television series (1955–9), *You'll Never Get Rich*, later called *Sergeant Bilko* and then *The Phil Silvers Show*. Ernie Bilko, played by Phil Silvers, is an army sergeant who talks fast and is dishonest but has great charm and usually tricks his senior officers.

The '**Bill** /'bɪl/ a British television series that has been shown since 1983, about the officers of a police station in an imaginary area of London. It is very realistic in the way it shows the problems faced by the police in British cities. *The Bill* and *the Old Bill* are British slang names for the police.

bill *n* **1** (in Britain) a written proposal for a new law, which must be discussed in the *House of Commons and the *House of Lords before it can become a law: *Thousands of people marched through London to protest against the Criminal Justice Bill.* ⇨ note at ACT OF PARLIAMENT.
2 (in the US) a proposal for a new law which must be discussed either in the *House of Representatives or the *Senate. If enough people vote for it there, it is discussed in *Congress, and if it is passed it goes to the President, who decides whether or not it should become a law.

'**Billboard** /'bɪlbɔːd/ a US magazine about the music industry. Each week it publishes lists ('the charts') of the most popular single songs, albums, videos and Hits of the Web.

'**billiards** *n* [U] a game for two people, played by hitting three balls with long rods called *cues*, on a large table covered with cloth. The aim is to score points by hitting one ball against another in a particular way, or into one of the six pockets around the table. Compare BAR BILLIARDS, POOL, SNOOKER.

'**Billingsgate** /'bɪlɪŋzgeɪt/ a famous old London fish market that used to be on the north bank of the *Thames in the *City. It was well known for the bad language of the people who worked there. In 1982 it was moved to the Isle of Dogs, an area of London's *Docklands.

▶ the **Bill of Rights**
The Bill of Rights is the name given to two different documents.

In the US the Bill of Rights consists of the first ten **amendments**, or changes, to the US *Constitution. All of the amendments were agreed in 1791, two years after the Constitution was signed. They give Americans rights which are now considered basic, but which were unusual at the time. The government cannot limit these rights.

Some of the amendments apply to all Americans. The First Amendment promises *freedom of religion and also **free speech** and *freedom of the press, which means that ordinary people and journalists can speak or write what they want, without restriction by the government. The Second Amendment, which gives people the right to own guns, is now the subject of much debate. The Fourth Amendment says that people cannot be arrested and their houses may not be searched, unless the police have a good reason for doing so. The Ninth and Tenth Amendments say that people and states have other rights beside those mentioned in the Constitution, but that the US government has only the powers that are listed there.

Other amendments give rights to people who are accused of a crime. The Fifth Amendment says that people do not have to give evidence against themselves. Somebody who wants to use this right says, '**I plead the Fifth**' or '**I take the Fifth**', and this is often thought to mean that they are afraid to answer questions in case they get into trouble. The Sixth Amendment promises that people who have been accused of a crime will get a trial quickly. In fact, US courts are so busy that people often have to wait a long time, but the government cannot make them wait longer than necessary. The Seventh Amendment gives people who are accused of a serious crime the right to have their case heard by a jury, so that 12 ordinary citizens, not just a judge, decide whether they are innocent or guilty. The Eighth Amendment says that people who are found guilty of a crime cannot be given 'cruel and unusual punishments'. There has been a lot of discussion about exactly what this means. This amendment was once used as an argument against *capital punishment but it was decided later that the death sentence was not a cruel and unusual punishment.

In Britain the Bill of Rights is the informal name of the Act Declaring the Rights and Liberties of the Subject, which was passed by *Parliament in 1689. This Act dealt with the relationship between the king or queen and Parliament, not with the rights of individuals. The earlier Declaration of Right had greatly reduced the power of the king or queen, and the new Act helped make Britain a *constitutional monarchy, in which real power lies with Parliament, not with the monarch. The Act also prevented a *Roman Catholic from becoming king or queen.

‚**Billy the** '**Kid** (1859–81) the popular name for William H Bonney, also known as William Wright, a US outlaw (= criminal) in the *Wild West. By the age of 12 he had murdered a man, and by 18 had killed 21 more. Bonney was shot dead by Sheriff Pat *Garrett. He was later turned into a romantic character in *dime novels and films, such as *Billy the Kid* (1930), *The Kid from Texas* (1950) and *Pat Garrett and Billy the Kid* (1973). Aaron *Copland wrote the music for the ballet *Billy the Kid* (1938).

'**bingo** /'bɪŋgəʊ/ *n* [U] a game of chance for any number of players. Each player is given a card with numbers on it. Players mark their cards as numbers are called out, and the first person to have all their numbers called wins a prize or an amount of money. In Britain it used to be thought of as a game for older people but is now popular

B

also with the young. In the 1970s many large buildings such as cinemas were converted into **bingo halls**. It was traditional to have special names for numbers as they were read out. For example, 66 was 'clickety-click' and 88 was 'two fat ladies'. Now the numbers are produced by a computer and the old names are rarely used.

'**Birds Eye™** /'bɜːdz aɪ; *AmE* 'bɜːrdz aɪ/ a US make of frozen food sold in many countries. It is named after Clarence Birdseye (1886–1956) who in the 1920s developed a method of freezing fresh fish quickly to preserve the flavour.

Lord ˌBirken'head / ˌbɜːkən'hed; *AmE* ˌbɜːrkən'hed/ (*born* Frederick Edwin Smith 1872–1930) a British lawyer and *Conservative politician who was well known for the humorous things he said. He was *Attorney General (1915–18) and then *Lord Chancellor (1919–22), when he improved the laws of land and property.

'**Birmingham** /'bɜːmɪŋəm; *AmE* 'bɜːrmɪŋəm, 'bɜːrmɪŋhæm/ **1** an industrial city in the *West Midlands of England. It is the second largest city in Britain. Since the late 18th century it has been well known as a centre for business and engineering. In the late 20th century it began to be known also as a centre for the arts. Much of the architecture in the city centre was destroyed in order to build roads in the 1950s and 1960s.
2 the largest city in the US state of *Alabama, sometimes called 'the Magic City'. It is a centre of iron and steel production, which is why it was named after Birmingham, England. In the 1960s it was the scene of many protests by *African Americans and other members of the *civil rights movement, some of which led to fighting in the streets. Martin Luther *King was arrested there in 1963 and wrote his *Letter from the Birmingham Jail* to explain why he did not obey unfair laws.

The ˌBirmingham ˌPost /ˌbɜːmɪŋəm; *AmE* 'bɜːrmɪŋəm/ an English daily newspaper for the Birmingham area, first published in 1857. It is the main newspaper of the *Midlands.

the ˌBirmingham 'Six /ˌbɜːmɪŋəm; *AmE* 'bɜːrmɪŋəm/ six Irishmen who were sent to prison for life in England for putting *IRA bombs in two *pubs in *Birmingham, England, in 1974. The bombs had killed 21 people, but the six men protested that they were innocent. In the 1980s new scientific tests proved that the evidence against them was not reliable, and that the police had changed their notes. In 1991 the Six were set free. The police officers responsible for their being sent to prison were never punished. This was one of several cases at around the same time that made the British public doubt the honesty of the police, particularly when dealing with Irish or black people. See also BRIDGEWATER, GUILDFORD FOUR, TOTTENHAM THREE.

ˌ**Birnam 'Wood** /ˌbɜːnəm; *AmE* ˌbɜːrnəm/ a wood in central Scotland. In *Shakespeare's play *Macbeth*, the witches tell Macbeth that he will not be defeated until Birnam Wood comes to Dunsinane. Later, Macduff's army hide themselves behind branches cut from the wood as they advance to attack Macbeth's castle at Dunsinane, so it appears as though the wood is moving.

ˌ**Val 'Biro** /'baɪrəʊ; *AmE* 'baɪrəʊ/ (1921–) a British writer and illustrator, born in Hungary. He is best known for his series of books for children about Gumdrop, an old car based on Biro's own 1926 *Austin². The *Gumdrop* books have been translated into many languages.

ˌ**Birthday 'Honours** (in Britain) the honorary titles and other awards given to people by the queen on her

Val Biro's Austin

*Official Birthday each year: *She got an OBE in the Birthday Honours List*. Compare NEW YEAR HONOURS. ⇨ note at HONOURS.

▶ **birthdays**
Birthdays are especially important to the very young and the very old. On their birthday, people receive **birthday cards** and **birthday presents** from their family and friends. Children's cards often have a large number on them showing how old they are. Cards for adults have pictures of flowers or scenery, or humorous or rude cartoons. Inside there is usually a simple greeting, such as 'Happy Birthday' or 'Many Happy Returns of the Day'. Children expect to receive a special birthday present from their parents. As they get older, many expect larger, more expensive presents, such as a music system or a television.

In the US, children who have their birthdays during the school year take a cake to school and have a small party with their class. In Britain children sometimes get **bumped** by their friends (= lifted off the ground horizontally and put down again sharply), the same number of times as their age. Some US parents have the custom of **spanking** their child, once for each year of their age.

Many younger children invite their friends to a **birthday party** at their home. Balloons are often tied to the gate of the house where the party is being held. Children wear their **party clothes** and take a present. They play **party games** such as 'pin the tail on the donkey' or 'musical chairs'. Sometimes parents arrange for an entertainer such as a magician to visit the house. After the games there is a special tea with a **birthday cake**. The cake is covered with sugar icing (*AmE* frosting), and has small candles on top, the same number of candles as the child's age. As the cake is carried into the room with the candles lit, everyone sings '*Happy Birthday To You!*' and then the **birthday boy** or **birthday girl** tries to blow out all the candles with one breath and makes a secret wish.

In the US the 16th birthday is called **sweet sixteen**. In many states it is the age at which a person can get a US driver's licence, and some wealthier parents give their children a car as a present. At 18, in Britain and in the US, young people become adults and many have a big party. In most parts of the US 21 is the age at which people can drink alcohol legally. In Britain people celebrate 21st birthdays less than when 21 was the age at which they became adults.

Many adults dislike getting older and a few lie about their age, saying they are younger than they really are. But in general older people are now much more willing to tell others their age. You may see a sign by the side of a road saying: 'Dave Ellis 40 today!', put there by Dave's friends. At about 65 people retire, and those who have reached this age are called 'senior citizens'. Few people live to be 100, so a 100th birthday is very special. In Britain people reaching this age may receive a card containing a printed message from the Queen.

The ˌBirth of a ˈNation a US silent film (1915) by D W *Griffith. It tells the story of the American *Civil War and the period of *Reconstruction after it. Although it was a great success and influenced later films, it made the *Ku Klux Klan seem good, and there was violence in several US cities when it was shown.

ˌHarrison ˈBirtwistle /ˌhærɪsən ˈbɜːtwɪsl; *AmE* ˈbɜːrtwɪsl/ (1934–) an English composer who has written classical music for large and small orchestras, and is well known for his music for the theatre and opera. He has been responsible for the music at the *National Theatre since 1975. His operas include *Punch and Judy* (1967) and *Sir Gawain and the Green Knight* (1991). He was made a *knight in 1988.

ˈbishop *n* a senior priest in the Anglican, Roman Catholic, Episcopal or Eastern Orthodox churches. Bishops are in charge of the work of other priests in a diocese (= a city or district). On ceremonial occasions a bishop wears a tall pointed hat, called a *mitre*, and carries a long decorated stick, or *staff*. When talked about, a bishop has the title 'the Right Reverend' or, in the Roman Catholic Church, 'the Most Reverend'. A bishop is usually addressed as 'Your Grace'. In Britain some senior bishops are members of the *House of Lords. In 1989, the first female bishop was appointed, in the Episcopal Church of the United States. In the Anglican church, women cannot be bishops or archbishops.

ˈBisquick™ /ˈbɪskwɪk/ *n* [U] a US make of biscuit (= a type of bread roll) mixture with which it is possible to cook biscuits quickly. It is made by General Mills.

ˈBisto™ /ˈbɪstəʊ; *AmE* ˈbɪstoʊ/ *n* [U] a British make of gravy powder which has been sold since 1910. Bisto is well known for the advertisement in which two children, called the Bisto kids, are seen enjoying the smell of a pie cooked with Bisto in it, and saying 'Ah, Bisto!'

ˈbitter *n* [U] (*BrE*) a type of strong *draught beer with a bitter taste. ⇨ note at BEER.

ˌCilla ˈBlack /ˈblæk/ (1943–) a well-known English singer of the 1960s, born in *Liverpool. She later became the presenter of several popular entertainment shows on British television, including *Blind Date* and *Surprise, Surprise*. She is known for her cheerful and friendly personality.

ˈBlackadder /ˈblækædə(r)/ the main character, played by Rowan *Atkinson, in several *BBC comedy television series. Each series was set in a different historical period, the last one being during *World War I. The other character best remembered from *Blackadder* is Baldrick, Blackadder's dirty servant, who remains loyal to his master although he is often badly treated.

> **❝** I have a cunning plan. **❞**
> Baldrick's most famous line

the ˌBlack and ˈTans (*disapproving*) a name for the extra police force sent from England to Ireland in 1920, during the *Troubles, to help the police there against *Sinn Fein. As there were not enough police uniforms,

they were given a mixture of police and army clothing: dark green caps and tan (= light brown) uniforms. The name 'Black and Tans' was also a reference to their cruel methods, as it was the name of a pack of dogs used for hunting in County Limerick.

the ˌBlack and White ˈMinstrels a British group of men and women who sang and danced on the stage and in a popular *BBC television show (1958–78). The men often had black make-up on their faces. This type of entertainment had been popular in 19th–century America, and Al *Jolson had used similar make-up in his films in the 1930s, but by 1978 this had become unacceptable to audiences and the show never returned to television.

ˈBlackbeard /ˈblækbɪəd; *AmE* ˈblækbɪrd/ (*died* 1718) the name by which the English pirate (= a sailor who attacks other ships and steals from them) Edward Teach was known. He was active in the *Caribbean and along the eastern coast of North America during 1717 and 1718, until he was killed during a battle at sea with two ships of the English navy.

ˌBlack ˈBeauty a black horse which is the main character in a novel (1877) of the same name written for children by Anna Sewell (1820–78). The story is about the horse's experiences with a series of different owners. There have been several films and television programmes made of it.

ˌblack ˈbottom *n* [sing] a lively dance popular in America in the 1920s. It involved a lot of movement of the hips.

the ˈBlack ˌCountry a large industrial area in Britain whose centre is the town of Dudley in the *Midlands. Mining and the black smoke from heavy industry gave the area its name.

the ˌBlack ˈDeath the name given to the major outbreak in Europe in 1348–51 of bubonic plague (= a serious disease spread from rats by fleas). People with the disease coughed up blood and got large painful black spots on their bodies, and usually died. It is thought that the Black Death killed about one third of the population of Europe. See also GREAT PLAGUE.

▶ Black English

The forms of English spoken by black and white Americans have always been different. At one time, the speech of white Americans was believed to be correct, and that of *African Americans to be wrong. More recently, the way African Americans speak has been treated with more respect. Black English is considered to be a dialect. It is called **Black English Vernacular** (**BEV**) or **African-American Vernacular English** (**AAVE**). The study of Black English has been called **Ebonics**. Not all African Americans speak BEV, and some only speak it when talking to other African Americans. There are variations within Black English, and some forms overlap with regional dialects of American English.

Black English developed at the time when black people were brought as slaves to the US. They came from different parts of Africa and spoke different languages, so they used **pidgin**, a method of communication based on their own languages and English, in order to talk to each other. Over time, this developed into a **Creole** (= a language that has developed from a European and an African language). Black English developed further as a result of contact with other American English dialects, but since African Americans traditionally led very separate lives from white Americans, differences in language have remained.

There are many differences between BEV and standard English in vocabulary, grammar and pronunciation, although many Black English words have become stand-

B

ard English. Black English contains many words from West Africa, e.g. *yam* for 'sweet potato' and *tote* for 'carry'. There are a lot of *slang expressions: for instance, the word *bad* may be used to mean its opposite, 'good', and *cool* and *hot* can both mean 'excellent'. Differences of grammar include sometimes leaving out the verb 'to be', and the use of several negatives in one sentence. Inflected endings for plural and possessive forms are often omitted. The 'l' is left out of words like *help* and *self* which are pronounced /hep/ and /sef/. Consonant groups may be reduced, e.g. *desk* is said as /des/ and *test* as /tes/. A final or middle 'r' is not pronounced. Words like *this* and *that* are pronounced with a /d/ instead of /ð/ sound, as /dɪs/ and /dæt/. Words with two syllables usually have heavy stress on the first syllable.

BEV has influenced the language of white Americans, and has much in common with the way white people from the *South speak. *Homies*, a word first used by African Americans to refer to people from their own neighbourhood, is now used as an informal word for 'friends' by some white Americans. Features of pronunciation are also shared by African Americans and southern white Americans.

Special features of Black English include **the dozens** (= verbal insults towards an opponent's family), **sounding** (= having verbal contests), **shucking** and **jiving** (= deceiving white people) and **rapping** (= language used for seduction and in the words of songs). These are based on traditions brought from Africa.

There has been much debate in the US about the use of BEV in schools. Some people believe that BEV is not as good as other forms of English, and should not be used in school. This is linked to an idea that speaking Black English is a sign of ignorance and lack of education. Although the number of people who think this way is decreasing, they still have influence. BEV had first to be taken account of in schools as a result of the *civil rights protests of the 1960s. Some people now believe that students learn best if they use a language they know well, and that teachers who respect BEV are more likely to help African-American students learn. Others say African Americans need to speak the form of English used by white people if they are to find jobs and succeed, and that schools should help them.

In Britain the term *Black English* is used to refer to the English of West Indian communities, and is the dialect used by immigrants to Britain from the *Caribbean in the 1950s. The children of these immigrants, and their children, often now use a regional British dialect or speak a modified version of their parents' Creole, or switch between the two.

black-eyed 'pea *n* [usually pl] (*AmE*) (*BrE* **cowpea**, **black-eyed bean**) a small white bean with a black spot on it, eaten a lot in the US. A dish called **hopping John** (black-eyed peas and rice) is eaten in the southern US states on *New Year's Day because it is thought to bring good luck in the new year.

'Blackfoot /'blækfʊt/ *n* (*pl* **Blackfeet** *or* **Blackfoot**) a member of a Native American tribe. They had this name because they wore black moccasins (= shoes made of soft leather). They grew tobacco and had more horses than most tribes. Today many of their people live on reservations (= land given and protected by the government) in the state of *Montana and in Canada in the province of Alberta.

'Black ,Forest 'gateau *n* [U, C] (*pl* **gateaux**) a rich chocolate cake with cherries and cream in the middle of it. In Britain it often used to be eaten in restaurants as the sweet course of a meal.

Black'heath /blæk'hiːθ/ an area of open land in south-east London, England. It was the place where

people gathered to support Wat *Tyler in 1381 and Jack *Cade in 1450, and where they greeted King *Henry VII after the Battle of *Agincourt and King *Charles II at the *Restoration. The name Blackheath is now most commonly used to refer to the area where people live, around the open land.

the ,Black 'Hills a US mountain range in western *South Dakota and eastern *Wyoming. They are covered with forests which look dark from a distance, and this explains their name. The mountains contain many minerals, including gold. The highest part is Harney Peak (7242 feet/2209 metres). Mount *Rushmore is also there.

the 'Black Hole of Cal'cutta /kæl'kʌtə/ the name later given to the tiny room in Calcutta (Kolkata), India, in which 146 British prisoners, including one woman, were put by the Indian leader who captured them on 20 June 1756. The next morning only 22 men and the woman were still alive, though some Indian sources of information say that far fewer people were involved. People sometimes talk about a small dark room without fresh air as being 'like the Black Hole of Calcutta'.

,Black 'Magic™ *n* [U] a popular British make of dark chocolates, sold in a black box: *Get her some Black Magic.*

,Black 'Monday Monday 19 October 1987, when prices on stock exchanges all over the world suddenly began to fall. Over the next four days the Financial Times Index in London fell by 25%, and the *Dow-Jones Index in New York fell by 33%. See also FINANCIAL TIMES INDICES. Compare BLACK TUESDAY.

the ,Black 'Mountains a range of mountains in the *Brecon Beacons in south Wales.

,Black 'Muslim *n* a member of an organization of African Americans, formed in 1930, who want their own separate nation within the US. They believe in the religion of Islam and are officially named the Nation of Islam. Well-known members have included *Malcolm X and Muhammad *Ali. A new group, the Lost-Found Nation of Islam, was organized in 1977 by Louis *Farrakhan, who later became leader of the Nation of Islam. See also BLACK PANTHERS, BLACK POWER.

,Black 'Panther *n* a member of the Black Panther Party, an organization of *African Americans with extreme views, formed in 1966. They supported legal action and even violence to gain better conditions for black people. One of the leaders was Eldridge *Cleaver. See also BLACK MUSLIM, BLACK POWER.

'Blackpool /'blækpuːl/ a town on the coast of *Lancashire in north-west England. In the past it was a popular holiday place for workers in the Lancashire cotton mills. Its famous beach is 7 miles/11 kilometres long, and the town offers a lot of entertainment. The **Blackpool Tower** is a famous landmark in the area. It was built in 1894 out of metal, like the Eiffel Tower in Paris, and is 520 feet/158 metres high. Blackpool is also famous for the **Blackpool Illuminations**, an event in the

Blackpool

autumn when the Tower and the streets are lit up every night for several weeks with thousands of coloured lights.

,**black 'power** *n* [U] a movement among *African Americans in the 1960s and 1970s which supported the rights and political power of black people. The expression was used officially by the *Black Panthers. A **black power salute** was made by holding up a fist. See also BLACK MUSLIMS.

the ,Black 'Prince (1330–76) the name by which Prince Edward, the eldest son of King *Edward III of England, is usually known, though the reason for the name is not known. He showed that he was an excellent soldier at the Battle of *Crécy when he was only 16. He died before his father, so his son Richard became the next king.

,**black 'pudding** (*especially BrE*) (*AmE also* **blood sausage**) *n* [U, C] a type of large dark sausage made from dried pig's blood, fat and grain and cooked by boiling or frying. In Britain, it is associated with the North of England, where it is a popular dish.

,**Black 'Rod** (*in full* **Gentleman Usher of the Black Rod**) an official who is responsible for keeping order in the British *House of Lords. He is known to the public because he has an important part in the ceremony of the *State Opening of Parliament. When he goes to the *House of Commons to call its members to the *House of Lords to hear the *Queen's Speech, they close the door and he has to knock three times with his rod (a black stick) and announce who he is. They let him in and he gives the message that 'The Queen commands the presence of the honourable House.' Then they all go to the House of Lords. This ceremony started after 1642, when King *Charles I tried to arrest five Members of Parliament in the House of Commons. It shows that the queen or king has no right to interfere in the business of the House of Commons.

'**blackshirt** /'blækʃɜːt; *AmE* 'blækʃɜːrt/ *n* [*usually pl*] the name people gave to any member of the British Union of Fascists, a political party started by Oswald *Mosley in 1932. Members wore black uniforms, like the members of other Fascist parties in Europe. In 1936, after a lot of disturbances in Jewish areas of London, the wearing of uniforms by political groups was made illegal under a new Public Order Act.

,**Black 'Tuesday** (in the US) the name given to 29 October 1929, the day on which the *New York Stock Exchange lost $9 billion. It was the beginning of the *Great Depression. When another large loss occurred on 19 October 1987, the day was called Black Monday.

,**black 'velvet** *n* [C, U] an alcoholic drink made by mixing *stout and champagne.

the ,Black 'Watch the popular name for the *Royal Highland Regiment in the British army, given to them because of the dark *tartan that they wear.

,**Black 'Wednesday** Wednesday 14 September 1992, when the British *Chancellor of the Exchequer raised interest rates by 5% in one day and spent billions of pounds in an unsuccessful attempt to improve the value of the British currency within the *exchange-rate mechanism.

,**Tony 'Blair** /'bleə(r); *AmE* 'bler/ (1953–) a British *Labour politician who became *Prime Minister after the election of 1 May 1997, with a very large Labour majority in Parliament. After becoming the leader of the Labour Party in 1994, he had made major changes to its organization, calling it *New Labour. He got rid of the old image of Labour as a party controlled by the trade unions, and one which rejected the idea of individuals getting more private wealth, having more personal

choices about education, health care, etc. In 2001 his government was elected for a second term of office.

The 'Blair 'Witch 'Project a 1999 horror film about three students who go into the woods to investigate the story of the **Blair Witch**, but who are attacked and killed by something which is never seen. The whole film is made using video cameras as if it were a film shot by the three characters and so tells the story from their point of view. The film cost very little to make and was very successful.

,**Eubie 'Blake**[1] /ˌjubi 'bleɪk/ (1883–1983) a US piano player and composer. Both his parents had been slaves. He began playing *ragtime music and continued performing on stage until he was 99 years old. His successful songs include *I'm Just Wild About Harry* (used by President *Truman as his political song) and *Memories of You*. Blake received the *Presidential Medal of Freedom in 1981.

,**Quentin 'Blake**[2] /ˌkwentɪn 'bleɪk/ (1932–) a British cartoonist, illustrator and author who has written and illustrated many books for children. He is especially well known for his illustrations for books by Roald *Dahl. His style of drawing uses untidy ink drawings with patches of colour. He became the first UK Children's Laureate (= a title given every two years to honour an important writer or illustrator of children's literature) in 1999.

,**William 'Blake**[3] /'bleɪk/ (1757–1827) an English artist and poet who from childhood claimed to have visions (= religious experiences like dreams) and talk to beings from heaven. He had a very personal style, full of religious symbols. He produced 'illuminated books' of his work, containing his poems and paintings to illustrate them, done by hand. The most famous of these is *Songs of Innocence and of Experience* (1794). His best-known poems are *Jerusalem* (1804) and *The Tyger*. He was very poor all his life, and is buried in London in a common grave. The biggest collection of his paintings is in *Tate Britain.

,**Art 'Blakey** /ˌɑːt 'bleɪki; *AmE* ˌɑːrt/ (1919–90) (*also called* **Abdulla Ibn Buhaina**) a US *jazz musician who played the drums. From 1954 he led a small group, the Jazz Messengers, and one of their most successful records was *Buhaina's Delight* (1961). He was chosen for the Jazz *Hall of Fame in 1981.

the 'Blarney Stone /'blɑːni; *AmE* 'blɑːrni/ a famous stone on the outside wall of Blarney Castle in County Cork, Ireland. It is supposed to give any person who kisses it the ability to speak well and skilfully, and the power to persuade people.

,**Bleak 'House** a novel (1853) by Charles *Dickens in which he attacks the ridiculous procedures of English law at the time. One of the many colourful characters in the book is Mrs Jellyby, an old woman who is concerned for the welfare of poor people in foreign countries and offers them help, but ignores the needs of the people around her, including her own children.

'**Blenheim** /'blenɪm/ **1** (*also the ,Battle of 'Blenheim**) a battle fought in 1704 near the small town of Blindheim in Bavaria, at which the British, led by the first Duke of *Marlborough, defeated the army of the French king Louis XIV.
2 (*also ,Blenheim 'Palace**) a grand house in large grounds near *Oxford, England, the home of the Duke of *Marlborough. It was designed by Sir John *Vanbrugh between 1705 and 1724. Sir Winston *Churchill was born there in 1874. It was made a *World Heritage Site in 1987.

'**Captain 'William 'Bligh** /'blaɪ/ (1754–1817) an officer in the British navy who is remembered because his men turned against him when he was the captain of a ship called *HMS *Bounty* in the Pacific Ocean in 1789. Bligh was put in an open boat with 18 of his men and a few supplies. They reached land seven weeks later. In 1805 Bligh became the Governor of New South Wales in Australia, and in 1808 the soldiers there also turned against him, putting him in prison for two years. He was not blamed by the British government, however, and was made an admiral in 1811. See also MUTINY ON THE BOUNTY.

ˌColonel 'Blimp /'blɪmp / n [usually sing] a man who is very traditional in his attitudes and values, especially one who believes that Britain is best and who will not accept any change. Originally, Colonel Blimp was a cartoon character created by David Low (1891–1963) in the 1930s. He was an old, bald, fat man who had been an army officer. He was not very intelligent and considered his own opinions to be more important than anyone else's: *The club is full of retired military officers of the Colonel Blimp type.*

ˌBlind 'Date a popular British television programme shown on ITV (1985–2003) in which a person chooses a member of the opposite sex and they spend a few days together before coming back on the programme to tell the audience what they think about each other. It was presented by Cilla *Black and was based on an earlier US television programme called *The Dating Game* (1963–74).

ˌblind man's 'buff (*AmE also* **blindman's bluff**) *n* [U] a children's game, played at parties, in which a player whose eyes have been covered tries to catch and identify the other players. ⇨ note at TOYS AND GAMES.

ˌArthur 'Bliss /'blɪs/ (1891–1975) an English composer. He studied under *Holst and *Vaughan Williams at the *Royal College of Music, and went on to write a wide variety of music, including ballets and film music. He was made a *knight in 1950, and *Master of the Queen's Music in 1953.

the 'Blitz the period of intense bomb attacks by German planes on British cities in *World War II.

ˌJoe 'Bloggs ⇨ JOE BLOGGS.

'Blondie¹ /'blɒndi; *AmE* 'blɑːndi/ a US pop group, formed in 1974, whose singer is Deborah Harry. Their most successful records include *Heart of Glass* (1978), *Call Me* (1980), *The Tide Is High* (1980) and, more recently, *Good Boys* (2004).

'*Blondie*² /'blɒndi; *AmE* 'blɑːndi/ a popular US *comic strip which first appeared in 1930. The main characters are clever Blondie and her often confused husband, Dagwood Bumstead. The characters have also been used for radio and television programmes and for a series of films.

the ˌBloodless Revo'lution the events in Britain in 1688 when the *Roman Catholic *James II was removed as king and replaced by his daughter *Mary and her husband *William III (William of Orange). So many of James's *Protestant officers joined William's side that there was no fighting, and James escaped to France with his family. These events are also called the **Glorious Revolution** because *constitutional monarchy was introduced at the same time.

ˌblood 'sausage ⇨ BLACK PUDDING.

the ˌBloody As'sizes /ə'saɪzɪz/ a series of assizes (= courts of law) in the west of England in 1685 at which Judge *Jeffreys condemned 300 people to death, and 1000 to be sent as slaves to America, for supporting the Duke of *Monmouth against King *James II.

ˌBloody 'Mary 1 a *nickname for the British queen *Mary I because of the many people who were killed for religious reasons when she was queen.
2 (*also* **bloody mary**) *n* a drink consisting of vodka (= a

strong, colourless, alcoholic drink) and tomato juice, often with *Worcester sauce.

ˌBloody 'Sunday the day (30 January 1972) when British soldiers shot and killed 13 people taking part in a march in *Derry, Northern Ireland, to protest against the government putting its political opponents in jail. This event, and the fact that the soldiers were not punished, caused more violence in Northern Ireland, and this led to *direct rule.

the ˌBloody 'Tower the name given to one of the towers of the *Tower of London, built in the 14th century, the place where the *Princes in the Tower were kept prisoner and probably murdered in the late 15th century.

ˌOrlando 'Bloom /ɔː'lændəʊ 'bluːm; *AmE* ɔːr'lændoʊ/ (1977–) an English actor who is best known for playing Legolas in the *Lord of the Rings films. He has also acted in *Black Hawk Down* (2001), *Pirates of the Caribbean* (2003) and *Troy* (2004).

'Bloomingdale's /'bluːmɪŋdeɪlz/ a large, expensive department store in New York City. It began in 1872 and is known for selling high-quality clothes and furniture. Bloomingdale's also has stores in many other US cities.

'Bloomsbury /'bluːmzbri/ an area of central London, England. The *British Museum and the main buildings of *London University are in Bloomsbury, and many famous people have lived there, including the *Bloomsbury Group.

the 'Bloomsbury Group /'bluːmzbri/ a group of artists and writers who met regularly as friends in *Bloomsbury, London, in the early 20th century. They rejected *Victorian(2) attitudes and believed in art, friendship and social progress. They included many of the leading figures of the time, such as Virginia *Woolf, E M *Forster, Maynard *Keynes and Lytton *Strachey.

BLT /ˌbiː el 'tiː/ an abbreviation for bacon, lettuce and tomato, a popular mixture of food used for filling *sandwiches in Britain and the US.

ˌblue 'badge *n* (in Britain) a blue card with a picture of a wheelchair which can be displayed in the window of a car. It shows that someone is officially recognized as a disabled person and is allowed to park in certain places where other people may not park.

'*Bluebird* /'bluːbɜːd; *AmE* 'bluːbɜːrd/ the name of any one of a series of very fast cars and boats that were built and driven by Malcolm *Campbell and his son Donald *Campbell to travel at faster speeds than anybody had ever gone before.

'blue book *n* 1 (in Britain) an official report published by Parliament, usually from a government committee or a *Royal Commission. It is bound in a blue cover. Compare WHITE PAPER.
2 (in the US) a book that gives details of people who have an important position in society.

The '*Blue Boy* a famous painting (1779) by Thomas *Gainsborough. It is one of his best-known works, and is a portrait of a boy dressed in blue.

ˌBlue 'Cross 1 the largest private health insurance company in the US. It was formed in 1929 and in 1982 joined with its rival Blue Shield, which began in 1917. The main office of the Blue Cross and Blue Shield Association is in *Chicago.
2 the Blue Cross a British charity organization that treats sick animals.

ˌblue 'ensign /ˌbluː 'ensən/ *n* a blue flag with a *Union Jack in the top left quarter. It is displayed on ships to show that they are being used by the British government. Compare RED ENSIGN, WHITE ENSIGN.

'bluegrass n [U] **1** a type of grass that is bluish-green in colour. It is common in parts of the US, especially *Kentucky, which is sometimes called the Bluegrass State.
2 a type of *country music of the southern US. It has fast strong rhythms and is played on instruments with strings, especially guitars, violins and banjos.

'blue law n [often pl] (*AmE*) a law that forbids business and certain other activities, such as dancing or sport, on Sundays. Blue laws were first introduced in colonial *New England and were originally printed on blue paper. Now they vary widely in different parts of the US. Although many shops open on Sundays, they often do not sell alcohol on that day because of a blue law.

,**Blue 'Peter** a British children's television programme broadcast by the *BBC since 1958. It is well known for teaching children how to make things from objects that they can find at home, and for organizing events to collect money for charities.

,**blue 'plaque** n any of the round blue notices that are attached to the front walls of houses, especially in London, to show that a famous person once lived there.

,**Blue 'Riband** /'rɪbənd/ the title given to the ship that crosses the Atlantic in the fastest time. The last ship that held the title was the *United States* in 1952. The phrase *blue riband* or *blue ribbon* is also used to refer to anything that is the best in its field: *The Cheltenham Gold Cup is one of racing's blue riband events.*

the 'blues n [U+sing/pl v] a type of US *jazz music with a slow, sad sound. *African Americans created it in the southern states to express the sadness of their experience. The music developed into *rhythm and blues and then *rock and roll and *soul.

,**Blue Tail 'Fly** a lively American song sometimes called 'Jimmy Crack Corn'. It was written before the American *Civil War by Daniel Emmett who also wrote *Dixie*. It became popular among slaves, because it was about the death of an owner of slaves.

,**David 'Blunkett** /'blʌnkɪt/ (1947–) a British *Labour politician. He became a *Member of Parliament in 1987 after being the leader of Sheffield city council. He was *Education Secretary (1997–2001) and then *Home Secretary until 2004 when he resigned after politically embarrassing publicity related to his sexual relationship with a married woman. David Blunkett has been blind since birth.

,**Anthony 'Blunt** /'blʌnt/ (1907–83) a British spy who gave British secrets to the Soviet Union. He was a member of the group called the *Cambridge spies, which also included *Burgess², *Maclean² and *Philby. He was a successful art historian, working for the Queen, who made him a *knight. When in 1979 it was discovered that he was a spy, his knighthood was taken away from him.

Blur /blɜː(r)/ a British pop group, one of the most popular of the *Britpop groups of the 1990s. Their most successful albums include *Parklife* (1994), *The Great Escape* (1995) and *Think Tank* (2003).

,**Enid 'Blyton** /ˌiːnɪd 'blaɪtn/ (1897–1968) a very successful English writer of children's books. She wrote over 700 books, including the *Famous Five, Secret Seven and *Noddy series, which are still very popular with children.

the BMA /ˌbiː em 'eɪ/ (*in full* the **British Medical Association**) a professional association like a *trade union that represents British doctors. It also organizes discussions on medical and moral questions, and acts as a *pressure group: *The BMA has called for an inquiry into the sale of human organs for transplants.*

BMJ /ˌbiː em 'dʒeɪ/ ⇨ BRITISH MEDICAL JOURNAL.

BMOC /ˌbiː em əʊ 'siː:; *AmE* oʊ/ ⇨ BIG MAN ON CAMPUS.

BMX /ˌbiː em 'eks/ (*in full* **bicycle motocross**) n
1 [C] a type of strong bicycle with small wheels, designed for riding on rough ground. They are popular with young people, who use them to perform jumps and other tricks.
2 [U] the sport of riding or racing BMX bicycles on rough ground.

,**B'nai 'B'rith** /ˌbəneɪ 'brɪθ/ n the oldest and largest Jewish organization in the world with associations in many countries. It began in 1843 in New York and has its main office in Washington, DC. It is a cultural, social and educational organization that supports hospitals and gives help after disasters. In 1913 it created the Anti-Defamation League to fight unfair treatment of Jews and others. B'nai B'rith means 'Sons of the Covenant'.

BNFL /ˌbiː en ef 'el/ (*in full* **British Nuclear Fuels**) an international company that produces nuclear fuel and processes nuclear waste so that it can be used again. It is based at *Sellafield in north-west England.

BNP /ˌbiː en 'piː/ ⇨ BRITISH NATIONAL PARTY.

,**Boadi'cea** /ˌbəʊədɪ'siːə; *AmE* ˌboʊədɪ'siːə/ ⇨ BOUDICCA.

,**Chris 'Boardman** /'bɔːdmən; *AmE* 'bɔːrdmən/ (1969–) an English cyclist who won a gold medal at the 1992 Olympic Games on a new design of bicycle that looked very different from the traditional style. He also took part in the Tour de France bicycle race.

the 'Boat Race a race that takes place each year on the River *Thames in west London, England, between rowing teams from the universities of *Oxford and *Cambridge. Unlike other sports contests between the two universities, it is seen as a national event and is watched by many people on television. The first Boat Race was in 1829.

,**Bobby 'Shafto** /'ʃæftəʊ; *AmE* 'ʃæftoʊ/ an old children's song, which may have been sung in support of Robert Shafto, a candidate in the British general election in 1761. Many British people know the first verse:

> 66 Bobby Shafto's gone to sea,
> Silver buckles at his knee,
> He'll come back and marry me,
> Bonny Bobby Shafto! 99

,**Bob the 'Builder** an animated (= using pictures on film which look as if they are moving) television series for young children about Bob, a builder, his friends and the people who live near him. The programmes were first shown on *BBC television and are now shown in over 30 countries in different languages.

> 66 Can we fix it? Yes, we can! 99
> Bob's catchphrase

'Boca ,burger /'bəʊkə; *AmE* 'boʊkə/ n a US make of burger made without meat. Boca burgers are made from soya and flavoured to taste like beef, chicken, etc.

the ,Bodleian 'Library /ˌbɒdliən; *AmE* ˌbɑːdliən/ the main library of *Oxford University. It has one of the largest collections in the world of books and papers, many of them written by hand. It is one of the six *copyright libraries in the British Isles.

,**Bodmin 'Moor** /ˌbɒdmɪn; *AmE* ˌbɑːdmɪn/ a moor in *Cornwall, England.

the 'Body Shop any of a chain of shops selling products for cleaning and caring for the skin and hair. The shops are well known for only selling natural products that have not been tested on animals. The business was started in Britain by Anita *Roddick, and there are now shops in many countries around the world: *She gets all her make-up and stuff from the Body Shop.*

'Boeing /'bəʊɪŋ; *AmE* 'boʊɪŋ/ a US company that makes aircraft. Its well-known passenger planes include the Boeing 707, Boeing *737 and Boeing *747 (the 'jumbo jet'). In 1997 it joined other companies to create a satellite for the *Internet. William Boeing (1881–1956) began the company in 1917, and its main offices are in *Seattle.

the ‚Boer 'War /ˌbɔː(r)/ (*BrE*) (*also* **the South African War**) a war (1899–1902) between the British and the Boers, Dutch farmers who had settled in southern Africa. The Boers had established two independent republics (Transvaal and Orange Free State) in what is now *South Africa, and the British wanted to control the whole region. The British won, but only after much bitter fighting.

‚Dirk 'Bogarde /'bəʊɡɑːd; *AmE* 'boʊɡɑːrd/ (1920–99) an English actor who first became well known in the 1950s in a series of British comedy films about medical students, and later worked in more serious films, many of them in Europe, such as *The Damned* (1969) and *Death in Venice* (1971). He also wrote an autobiography and several novels. He was made a *knight in 1992.

‚Humphrey 'Bogart /'bəʊɡɑːt; *AmE* 'boʊɡɑːrt/ (1899–1957) a US film actor. His popular name was Bogey. He often played tough, world-weary characters. His successful films include *The *Maltese Falcon* (1941), *Casablanca* (1942) and *The African Queen* (1951) for which he received his only *Oscar. He was married to Lauren *Bacall, and they made several films together.

> 66 Here's looking at you, kid. 99
> Humphrey Bogart in *Casablanca*

‚Peter Bog'danovich /bɒɡ'dænəvɪtʃ; *AmE* bɑːɡ-'dænəvɪtʃ/ (1939–) a US film director and actor, born in New York. His most famous film is *The Last Picture Show* (1971) which won two *Oscars. His other films include a sequel, *Texasville* (1990), *Paper Moon* (1973), *Daisy Miller* (1974) and in 1992 a version of Michael *Frayn's stage play *Noises Off.*

'Bogside /'bɒɡsaɪd; *AmE* 'bɔːɡsaɪd/ an area of *Derry(1), Northern Ireland, where mainly *Roman Catholic people live. There have been many violent incidents between the two religious communities there during the *Troubles.

The ‚Bold and the 'Beautiful a *soap opera shown on *CBS in the US and also shown in many other countries. It started in 1997 and is about the lives of several rich and powerful families in *Los Angeles, especially about their romances and rivalries.

‚Anne Bo'leyn /bə'lɪn/ (1507–36) the second wife of King *Henry VIII and the mother of Queen *Elizabeth I. Her marriage to Henry against the wishes of the Pope led to England's break from the *Roman Catholic Church and the start of the *Church of England. However, when she failed to produce a son, Henry lost interest in her. She was accused of having affairs with other men, and her head was cut off.

‚Robert 'Bolt /'bəʊlt; *AmE* 'boʊlt/ (1924–95) an English writer of plays and films. He first achieved fame with his play about Thomas *More, *A Man for All Seasons* (1960). He also wrote the script for the film *Lawrence of Arabia* (1962). Two of his film scripts won *Oscars: *Dr Zhivago* (1965) and *A Man for All Seasons* (1967).

‚bombay 'mix /ˌbɒmbeɪ; *AmE* ˌbɑːmbeɪ/ *n* [U] a cold snack which is a mixture of nuts, lentils (= small green, orange or brown seeds) and small pieces of fried noodle (= a long thin strip of pasta) covered in spices, often

served in Britain in Indian restaurants while people are waiting for their meal and in bars.

Bo'nanza a popular *western series on US television between 1959 and 1972. It was about a father and his three sons living on the Ponderosa Ranch in the *Wild West.

‚Edward 'Bond[1] /'bɒnd; *AmE* 'bɑːnd/ (1934–) an English writer of plays. Many people were shocked by the violence in his early plays, and his *Early Morning* (1968) was the last play to be banned in the UK by the *Lord Chamberlain. His other works include *Lear* (1971) and *The Sea* (1973).

‚James 'Bond[2] /'bɒnd; *AmE* 'bɑːnd/ the main character in a series of novels by Ian *Fleming. James Bond is a daring and attractive British secret agent, who is also known as '007'. The first James Bond book was *Casino Royale* (1953). Many of the books have been made into exciting and often humorous adventure films.

'Bond Street /'bɒnd; *AmE* 'bɑːnd/ a street in the *West End of London, England, known for its expensive shops and art galleries.

▶ **Bonfire Night**

British people celebrate Bonfire Night every year on 5 November in memory of a famous event in British history, the *Gunpowder Plot. On 5 November 1605 a group of *Roman Catholics planned to blow up the *Houses of Parliament while King *James I was inside. On the evening before, one of them, Guy *Fawkes, was caught in the cellars with gunpowder (= an explosive), and the plot was discovered. He and all the other conspirators were put to death. Bonfire Night is sometimes called **Guy Fawkes Night**.

Originally, Bonfire Night was celebrated as a victory for *Protestants over Catholics, but the festival is now enjoyed by everyone. Some children make a **guy**, a figure of a man made of old clothes stuffed with newspaper or straw to represent Guy Fawkes. The guy is then burned on top of a **bonfire** on Bonfire Night. A few days before, children take their guy into the street and ask for a 'penny for the guy', money for **fireworks** (= small packets of explosives which, when lit, make a bang or send a shower of coloured light into the air). Only adults are legally allowed to buy fireworks.

Some people hold private **bonfire parties** in their gardens, while others attend larger public events organized by local councils or charities. Chestnuts or potatoes are often put in the bonfire so that they will cook as it burns. Fireworks such as Roman candles, Catherine wheels (*AmE* pinwheels), bangers and rockets are put in the ground and are let off one by one. Children hold lighted sparklers (= metal sticks covered in a hard chemical substance that burns brightly when lit) in their hands and wave them around to make patterns. Unfortunately, there are sometimes accidents involving fireworks and there are now restrictions on the type of fireworks that can be used by the general public.

The events of 5 November 1605 are celebrated in a nursery rhyme:

> 66 Please to remember,
> The fifth of November,
> Gunpowder, treason and plot. 99

‚Chris 'Bonington /'bɒnɪŋtən; *AmE* 'bɑːnɪŋtən/ (1934–) an English mountaineer who led a team of British climbers up Mount Everest in 1975 and again in 1985 and 1997. He was made a *knight in 1996.

‚Bonnie and 'Clyde /ˌbɒni, 'klaɪd; *AmE* ˌbɑːni/ a pair of young US criminals, **Bonnie Parker** (1911–34) and **Clyde Barrow** (1909–34). They met in 1932 and robbed

Booker Prize Winners

B

banks and murdered 12 people in the south-western US before being shot dead by police in *Louisiana. Their story was made romantic in the film *Bonnie and Clyde* (1967) with Faye Dunaway and Warren *Beatty in the main parts.

Bonny Prince 'Charlie (1720–88) the popular name of Prince Charles Edward Stuart, also sometimes called the *Young Pretender. His father was the son of *James II, the king of England, Scotland and Ireland, and Charles therefore believed that his father should be king. Many people in Scotland supported the Stuarts, and in 1745 Charles led a Scottish army against King *George II. After some successes, Charles's army was defeated at the battle of *Culloden. He then spent five months hiding from government soldiers in Scotland before escaping to France. He never returned to Britain. See also SKYE, MACDONALD.

'Bono /'bɒnəʊ; *AmE* 'bɑːnoʊ/ (Paul David Hewson 1960–) an Irish rock singer, the lead singer with the rock band U2. He has been involved in political issues such as Third-World debt (= money owed by poor countries) and the problem of AIDS in Africa. In 2002, he set up an organization called **DATA** (Debt, Trade, AIDS in Africa) to raise awareness about these issues.

'boogie /'buːgi/ (*also* **boogie-woogie**) /ˌbuːgi 'wuːgi/ *n* [U] a type of US *blues music with a strong beat, played on the piano. It was especially popular in the 1930s. Musicians who helped to make it popular included 'Cow Cow' Davenport and 'Pine Top' Smith, who recorded *Pine Top's Boogie-Woogie* in 1928. The 'boogie-woogie' was also an early name for the *jitterbug dance.

the **'Booker Prize** /'bʊkə; *AmE* 'bʊkər/ (*also* the **Man Booker Prize**) a prize that is given each autumn for the best novel by a citizen of the Commonwealth or the Republic of Ireland published that year. New judges are chosen each year and include famous critics, writers and academics. The prize was first given by Booker, a large food company, in 1968. Since 2002 the Man Group has provided the money for the prize, which is £50 000. In 2004 a second Booker Prize was announced, the Man Booker International Prize of £60 000, given once every two years for the best novel available in English by an author from any country in the world.

the **'Book of ,Common 'Prayer** the name of the prayer book most commonly used in the *Church of England. It was first published in 1549, with a new version appearing in 1622. The beauty of its language is widely admired, but many people now prefer the modern *Alternative Service Book*.

the **,Book of 'Kells** /'kelz/ a copy of the four Gospels of the Bible made in the 8th century at a religious community in the town of Kells in Ireland. It has many beautiful illustrations, and can be seen in the library of Trinity College, *Dublin.

the **,Book of the 'Month Club** a US company that sells books at reduced prices through the post. It began in 1926 and now offers a catalogue of books on the *Internet.

George 'Boole /'buːl/ (1815–64) an English mathematician who invented a type of mathematical logic known as **Boolean algebra**. This in its simplest form became the language of computers.

Daniel 'Boone¹ /'buːn/ (1734–1820) a famous American *frontiersman. He crossed the *Appalachian Mountains to explore and help in settling land that became *Kentucky. He fought the Native Americans and was twice captured by them. Later he was elected a representative to the Kentucky government. He became an American legend and is even mentioned in *Byron's poem *Don Juan*.

Pat 'Boone² /'buːn/ (1934–) a US singer and actor who was especially popular in the late 1950s. He began with *rock and roll songs, such as *Ain't That a Shame* (1955). He was attractive to many people because he was religious and did not behave badly. In 1997, however, he changed his image at the age of 62 and recorded the *heavy metal album *No More Mr Nice Guy*.

John 'Boorman /'bɔːmən; *AmE* 'bɔːrmən/ (1933–) an English film director. After working in television in Britain, he moved to the US to make *Point Blank* in 1967. His best-known films since then have included *Deliverance* (1972), *Excalibur* (1981), *The General* (1998), and *In My Country* (2005).

John Wilkes 'Booth /wɪlks 'buːð/ (1838–65) the US actor who shot and killed President Abraham *Lincoln on 14 April 1865 in Ford's Theater, Washington, DC, while the President was watching a play. Booth had sympathy for the *Confederate States and was angry at their defeat by Lincoln's government. After shooting the President, he jumped onto the stage and broke his leg but escaped. He was later found in a barn and died when he either shot himself or was shot.

B

,**Boot 'Hill** (*AmE informal*) a humorous name for a cemetery in the *Wild West. One of the best known is at
*Tombstone, *Arizona. The name comes from the idea
that many people were buried in the boots they were
wearing when they were killed.

,**Betty 'Boothroyd** /'buːθrɔɪd/ (1929–) a British
*Labour politician who in 1992 became the first woman
to be elected *Speaker of the *House of Commons. She
was made a *life peer in 2000.

Boots /buːts/ a company with shops in almost every
town in Britain. The shops sell medicines and many
other items for personal use, as well as some food.

,**Bo-'peep** ⇨ LITTLE BO-PEEP.

,**Lizzy 'Borden** /'bɔːdn; *AmE* 'bɔːrdn/ (1860–1927) an
American woman who was accused of murdering her
rich father and stepmother with an axe on 4 August
1892. Her trial was a famous event. She was judged to be
innocent, but many people still believed her guilty. Her
name is remembered in a popular children's rhyme that
begins:

> 66 Lizzy Borden took an axe
> And gave her mother forty whacks.
> And when she saw what she had done,
> She gave her father forty one. 99

'**Borders**[1] /'bɔːdəz; *AmE* 'bɔːrdərz/ ⇨ SCOTTISH
BORDERS.

'**Borders**™[2] /'bɔːdəz; *AmE* 'bɔːrdərz/ a US chain of
bookstores which opened its first store in *Michigan in
1971 and in 2004 had around 420 stores across the US
and 35 stores in other countries including the UK. As well
as books, the stores sell magazines, newspapers, music
and DVDs, and many of them contain *Starbucks cafes.
The company works together with *Amazon to sell
books online.

'**borough** *n* a district, town or part of a large city that
has some powers of local government. London,
England, has 32 boroughs, which make up the area
known as *Greater London. The five boroughs of New
York City are *Manhattan(1), *Brooklyn, *Queens, the
*Bronx and *Staten Island. See also LOCAL GOVERN-
MENT.

the '**Borscht Belt** /'bɔːʃt; *AmE* 'bɔːrʃt/ (*also* the
'**Borscht ,circuit**) (*AmE humorous*) a holiday area in
the *Catskill Mountains in New York State. It was known
especially in the 1950s and 1960s for attracting Jewish
visitors and many American Jewish entertainers began
their careers there. Borscht is a soup that is popular with
Jewish people.

'**Borstal** /'bɔːstl; *AmE* 'bɔːrstl/ *n* [C, U] a British prison
school for young offenders (= people who commit
crimes) which opened in 1902 in Borstal, Kent. Similar
institutions became known as 'borstals', and later as
'detention centres'. They are now called *young
offender institutions.

'**Boston** /'bɒstən; *AmE* 'bɑːstən/ the capital and largest
city in the US state of *Massachusetts. It is a major port
and cultural centre, having nearly 50 colleges and universities. It also has the oldest underground railway in
the US. Boston was settled in 1630 and played an important part in the *American Revolution. It became a centre
for Irish immigrants in the second half of the 19th century. International runners compete each year in the
Boston Marathon race, first run in 1897. See also
BOSTON MASSACRE, BOSTON TEA PARTY.

'**Boston ,baked 'beans** /'bɒstən; *AmE* 'bɑːstən/ (*also*
baked beans) *n* [pl] (in the US) white haricot beans
baked with pork and brown sugar or molasses (= a dark,

sweet, thick liquid obtained from sugar). They were originally popular in *Boston, US.

,**Boston 'Brahmin** /,bɒstən 'brɑːmɪn; *AmE* ,bɑːstən/
n (*AmE*) a member of one of the old families with high
social and cultural status in *Boston, US. The Brahmins
have traditionally lived in the city's best area, *Beacon
Hill, and had the most money and power. This has slowly
changed as Boston has become larger and new groups
have become more rich and powerful.

the ,**Boston 'Massacre** /,bɒstən; *AmE* ,bɑːstən/ an
incident on 5 March 1770 when British soldiers shot at
American colonists and killed five of them. It was called
a *massacre* (= the killing of many people) to increase hatred for the British, and was one of the events that led to
the *American Revolution.

the ,**Boston 'Pops** /,bɒstən; *AmE* ,bɑːstən/ a US
orchestra that plays popular classical and other music.
Its musicians are members of the Boston Symphony
Orchestra.

the ,**Boston 'Strangler** /,bɒstən; *AmE* bɑːstən/ the
name given by newspapers, etc. to Albert DeSalvo, a US
man who attacked and killed 13 women in *Boston,
Massachusetts, between 1962 and 1964. He killed the
women by strangling them (= squeezing their throat
tightly). He was sent to prison for his crimes and was
killed by another prisoner.

the ,**Boston 'Stump** /,bɒstən; *AmE* ,bɑːstən/ the
popular name for the very tall 15th–century church
tower in the English town of Boston, *Lincolnshire. The
tower can be seen easily from the sea and this was helpful to sailors when Boston was an important port. The
US city of *Boston is named after this port because many
of the *Pilgrim Fathers began their journey from there in
1608.

the ,**Boston 'Tea ,Party** /,bɒstən; *AmE* ,bɑːstən/ an
incident in American history. It occurred on 16 December
1773, two years before the *American Revolution. In
order to protest about the British tax on tea, a group of
Americans dressed as Indians went onto three British
ships in *Boston harbour and threw 342 large boxes of
tea into the sea.

,**James 'Boswell** /'bɒzwel; *AmE* 'bɑːzwel/ (1740–95) a
Scottish writer. He is best known for his book about his
famous friend Dr *Johnson, *The Life of Samuel Johnson*
(1791), and for his personal diaries, which were discovered in the 1920s.

the '**Battle of 'Bosworth 'Field** /'bɒzwəθ; *AmE*
'bɑːzwərθ/ the last battle (1485) in the *Wars of the
Roses. It was fought near Market Bosworth in
Leicestershire between King *Richard III of England and
Henry Tudor. Richard died in the battle and Henry
became King *Henry VII. There is a dramatic version of
the battle at the end of Shakespeare's play *Richard III*.

,**Botany 'Bay** /,bɒtəni; *AmE* ,bɑːtəni/ the place on the
east coast of Australia where Captain *Cook landed in
1770. The British government decided in 1787 to send
criminals there from British prisons. After that the name
Botany Bay was often used to mean any place in
Australia where criminals were sent from Britain.

,**Ian 'Botham** /'bəʊθəm; *AmE* 'boʊθəm/ (1955–) an
English cricket player who played for England between
1977 and 1992, including a short period as captain. He
was one of the most successful players of all time, both
as a batsman and as a bowler. He has also raised a lot of
money for charity and often appears on television.

the ,**Earl of 'Bothwell** /'bɒθwel; *AmE* 'bɑːθwel/
(*c.* 1536–78) the third husband of *Mary, Queen of Scots.
He was probably involved with her in the murder of her
second husband, the Earl of *Darnley, in 1567. When
they got married three months after the murder, they

were forced to leave the country and finally became prisoners until their deaths. Bothwell died in prison in Denmark.

Bot'swana /bɒt'swɑːnə; *AmE* bɑːt'swɑːnə/ a country in southern Africa and an independent member of the Commonwealth since 1966. Its capital city is Gaborone.

'**Bottom** /'bɒtəm; *AmE* 'bɑːtəm/ a comic character in Shakespeare's play *A *Midsummer Night's Dream*. For most of the play, Bottom has the head of an ass because of a magic trick played by *Oberon.

'**Boudicca** /'buːdɪkə/ (*also* **Boadicea**) (*died* AD 62) the queen of the *Iceni tribe of eastern Britain when it was part of the Roman Empire. She led the Iceni against the Romans and destroyed several of their camps. When she was defeated she killed herself. She is often shown in pictures driving a chariot (= an open carriage pulled by a horse) with blades attached to the wheels.

Adrian '**Boult** /'bəʊlt; *AmE* 'boʊlt/ (1889–1983) an English conductor who worked with many orchestras, including the Birmingham Symphony Orchestra (1924–30), the *BBC Symphony Orchestra (1931–50) and the *London Philharmonic Orchestra (1951–7). He was made a *knight in 1937.

the '**Boulting** ˌ**brothers** /'bəʊltɪŋ; *AmE* 'boʊltɪŋ/ **John Boulting** (1913–85) and **Roy Boulting** (1913–2001), twin brothers who produced films together. Their films, mostly about life in Britain in the years after *World War II, include *Brighton Rock* (1947), *Lucky Jim (1957) and *I'm All Right Jack* (1959).

the '**Boundary Com**ˌ**missions** the four British government organizations (one each for England, Scotland, Wales and Northern Ireland) which decide the boundaries of *constituencies. They recommend changes to the boundaries so that the average population of constituencies (about 70 000) remains the same in spite of population movements.

ˌHMS '**Bounty** (*also* **The Bounty**) a British ship on which a famous mutiny took place in 1789. The ship was returning from Tahiti in the Pacific Ocean when one of the officers, Fletcher *Christian, led the crew against their harsh captain, William *Bligh. Captain Bligh and some men who supported him were left in a small open boat while Christian and the crew returned on *HMS Bounty* to Tahiti and then settled in the *Pitcairn Islands. See also MUTINY ON THE BOUNTY.

replica of the HMS Bounty

'**Bounty**™ *n* a chocolate bar with sweet coconut inside, sold in Britain.

'**bourbon** /'bɜːbən; *AmE* 'bɜːbən/ *n* [U, C] a type of American whisky made with maize/corn and rye.

'**Bournemouth** /'bɔːnməθ/ a town on the south coast of England, in *Dorset. Many British people go there on holiday, and it is also a place where many foreign students of English go to study. The **Bournemouth Symphony Orchestra** is well known for encouraging young British composers.

'**Bournville** /'bɔːnvɪl; *AmE* 'bɔːrnvɪl/ a suburb of Birmingham, England. It was built by the brothers George and Richard Cadbury to provide houses for the workers at the chocolate factory which they opened there in 1879. The Cadburys were *Quakers and believed that social problems were often the result of bad homes.

The houses at Bournville were well designed, with gardens, and they had an important influence on the planning of other suburbs in Britain. See also CADBURY SCHWEPPES.

'**Bovril**™ /'bɒvrɪl; *AmE* 'bɑːvrɪl/ *n* [U] a dark brown substance that tastes of beef. It is sold in jars, especially in Britain, and can be mixed with hot water to make a drink, added to food to give it a stronger taste of meat, or spread on bread.

ˌClara '**Bow** /ˌklærə 'bəʊ; *AmE* 'boʊ/ (1905–65) a US actor known as the 'It Girl'. She was in both silent and talking films and usually played a lively *flapper of the *Roaring Twenties. Her best films included *Wings* (1927) and *It* (1927), from which she got her special name. 'It' means the quality that makes women attractive to men.

ˌBow '**Bells** /ˌbəʊ; *AmE* ˌboʊ/ the bells of the church of St Mary-le-Bow in the *East End of London, England. Traditionally, a true *cockney is somebody who was born within the sound of Bow Bells. The bells are also important in the story of Dick *Whittington. See also ORANGES AND LEMONS.

the '**Bowery** /'baʊəri/ an area of south-east *Manhattan(1) in New York City. Until the 1990s it was known as a poor area with many homeless people but also as a centre for young musicians. One of the streets there is also called the Bowery.

the '**Bow Group** /'bəʊ; *AmE* 'boʊ/ a political group within the *Conservative Party. It was started in 1951 by young Conservatives who wanted to encourage new ideas in the party, including a freer economy and independence for the countries in the *British Empire. The group publishes a magazine called *Crossbow*. Compare MONDAY CLUB.

ˌDavid '**Bowie**[1] /'bəʊi; *AmE* 'boʊi/ (1947–) an English pop singer, writer of songs, and actor. He is especially known for introducing fresh combinations of music and images, and for the characters that he has created. These have included Major Tom, in his first hit song *Space Oddity* (1969), and Ziggy Stardust in songs and performances in the 1970s. Through the character of Ziggy, Bowie has also acted in plays and films. His recent albums include *Heathen* (2002) and *Reality* (2003).

> 66 We have created a child who will be so exposed to the media that he will be lost to his parents by the time he is 12. 99
> David Bowie, 1972

ˌJames '**Bowie**[2] /'buːi/ (*c.* 1796–1836) a famous American *frontiersman and soldier. The large, heavy knife called a **bowie knife** was named after him. He was killed at the *Alamo with Davy *Crockett.

'**bowl game** (*also* **bowl**) *n* (*AmE*) a US college football game played in December or January at the end of the football season. The best teams meet in several bowl games (so called because the stadiums in which they are played are bowl-shaped). The most famous are the *Rose Bowl in Pasadena, *California, the Sugar Bowl in *New Orleans, the Orange Bowl in *Miami and the Cotton Bowl in *Dallas.

bowls *n* [U] a game, played on a smooth grass area called a **bowling green**, in which two to eight players take turns to roll large black balls as near as possible to a small white ball. The balls are heavier on one side so they travel in a curve. Bowls has been popular in Britain for about 600 years and there is a famous story from 1588 about Sir Francis *Drake and a game of bowls. According to the story, he was told during the game that the Spanish *Armada was coming, but he said, 'There is time to win this game and beat the Spaniards, too.' Bowls is now usually played by older people.

bowls

'Bow Street /'bəʊ; AmE 'boʊ/ the main police court in London, which was in the street of this name until the early 1990s. It is now at *Charing Cross. When Henry *Fielding was a magistrate at Bow Street in the 1740s, he formed the **Bow Street Runners**, a group of people trained to catch thieves. This was the first step towards the creation of the *Metropolitan Police in 1829.

'Boxing Day (in Britain) 26 December, the day after *Christmas Day. It is a *bank holiday. Traditionally it was the day when people gave **Christmas boxes** (small gifts of money) to their employees or servants. Now most people relax, digest the food and drink of the day before, and perhaps visit friends or relatives.

Robert 'Boyle /'bɔɪl/ (1627–91) a British scientist whose experiments and the way he wrote about them were ahead of his time. Before chemical elements were discovered, he suggested a theory of atoms, saying that things were made of 'corpuscles'. He is best remembered for **Boyle's Law**, which explains the relationship between the pressure and volume of gases.

the 'Boys' Brigade a British Christian organization for boys. It was set up in 1883 with the aim of teaching boys discipline and respect for themselves and others.

Boy 'Scouts of A'merica (abbr **BSA**) the US branch of the *Scouts. It was formed in 1910 and was based on the British organization. The US Scouts have kept the traditional camps and skills and also learn about different careers. The main groups are Cub Scouts (7 to 10), Boy Scouts (11 to 17) and Venturers (14 to 20). See also EAGLE SCOUT.

Boy's Own 'Paper a British magazine of adventure stories for boys that was published from 1879 to 1967. British people sometimes use the phrase Boy's Own to describe brave or exciting things that people have done: His escape from the rebels' camp was pure Boy's Own stuff.

Boz /bɒz; AmE bɑːz/ a name used by Charles *Dickens instead of his own name for some of his early work.

BP /ˌbiː 'piː/ (in full **British Petroleum**) a large international company which produces oil, petrol/gasoline, gas, and chemicals. It owns many petrol stations in Britain, and is the largest producer of *North Sea gas and oil.

Lady 'Bracknell /'bræknəl/ a character in Oscar *Wilde's play The *Importance of Being Earnest. She is a severe *upper-class Englishwoman who speaks some of Wilde's most humorous lines. Jack, the main character, is in love with her daughter.

> ❝ To lose one parent, Mr Worthing, may be regarded as a misfortune; to lose both looks like carelessness. ❞
> Lady Bracknell

Malcolm 'Bradbury[1] /'brædbri/ (1932–2000) an English writer and university teacher who wrote mainly comic novels about university life. His best-known book, The History Man (1975), was made into a television series in 1981. He was made a *knight in 2000.

Ray 'Bradbury[2] /'brædbri/ (1920–) a US science fiction writer who first became known for his novel The Martian Chronicles 1950. His best-known books include *Fahrenheit 451, The October Country (1955), Dandelion Wine (1957) and Something Wicked This Way Comes (1962).

'Bradford[1] /'brædfəd; AmE 'brædfərd/ an industrial city in *Yorkshire, England. Since the Middle Ages it has been an important centre for the wool trade and for textile production. It now has a large Asian community and is the home of the *National Museum of Photography, Film and Television.

Barbara 'Taylor 'Bradford[2] /'teɪlə 'brædfəd; AmE 'teɪlər 'brædfərd/ (1933–) one of the world's most popular writers of fiction. By 2004 her books had sold 63 million copies. The stories are usually about modern, successful women who fall in love. They include A Woman of Substance (1979), and Power of a Woman (1997). Bradford was born in England, where she was a journalist, and now lives in the US.

Omar 'Bradley /ˌəʊmɑː 'brædli; AmE ˌoʊmɑːr/ (1893–1981) a US general in *World War II. He led the Allied forces at Normandy on *D-Day in 1944 and into Germany. He then became the first Chairman of the *Joint Chiefs of Staff from 1949 to 1953. Bradley was named General of the Army in 1950. He won many medals including the *Presidential Medal of Freedom.

'Bradshaw /'brædʃɔː/ an informal name for Bradshaw's Railway Guide, a book published each year from 1839 to 1961 giving details of all the railway services in Britain.

Anne 'Bradstreet /'brædstriːt/ (1612–72) an American writer of poems, born in England. She is considered to be one of the first true American poets. Her first book of poems, The Tenth Muse Lately Sprung Up in America (1650), was published in England without her knowledge. Her later poems describe daily life and her love of her family and home.

Melvyn 'Bragg /ˌmelvɪn 'bræg/ (1939–) an English writer and presenter of television and radio programmes. He is best known for presenting The *South Bank Show, in which he introduced the British television audience to serious art, literature, drama, etc. He has also written several novels, mostly set in the *Lake District. He was made a *life peer in 1998.

Dennis 'Brain /'breɪn/ (1921–57) an English musician who played the French horn and the German double horn. He was considered one of the greatest players of these instruments. His best-known recordings are of Mozart's music.

John 'Braine /'breɪn/ (1922–86) an English writer of realistic novels, the best known of which is *Room at the Top (1957). He is usually considered one of the *angry young men.

Brain of 'Britain a British radio quiz programme which has been broadcast regularly on the *BBC since 1967. The winner of each series of programmes is named Brain of Britain for that year: You don't need to be Brain of Britain to see what's going on.

The **'Brains Trust** a *BBC radio programme in the
1940s which became a television programme in the
1950s. In it a group of well-known intellectuals discussed
a wide range of topics.

'Bramley /'bræmli/ (*also* **Bramley apple**, **Bramley's
seedling**) n a type of large green apple that is suitable
for cooking rather than for eating raw. Bramleys are
especially popular in Britain.

ₗ**Kenneth 'Branagh** /'brænə/ (1960–) a British actor
and director who has worked successfully both in the
theatre and in films. He is especially well known for his
versions of Shakespeare's plays. He was married to
Emma *Thompson and they appeared together in several films. His best-known films (as both actor and director) include *Henry V (1989), *Much Ado About Nothing
(1993), *Hamlet (1997) and Love's Labour's Lost (2000).

ₗ**Branch Da'vidians** /də'vɪdiənz/ a US religious
group, based in Waco, *Texas,which believed that Christ
would soon return to earth. Their leader was David
*Koresh. In 1993 members of the group killed four US
government officers who were trying to enter their
building. The building was then surrounded for 51 days
until the Branch Davidians began a fire in which 82 of
them died, including 33 British people.

ₗ**Max 'Brand** /'brænd/ (1892–1944) a popular US writer
of novels about the *Wild West. He also created the character of Dr Kildare for several books and then wrote a
series of Dr Kildare films.

ₗ**Marlon 'Brando** /ˌmɑːlən 'brændəʊ; *AmE* ˌmɑːrlən
'brændoʊ/ (1924–2004) a US actor known for playing
strong and sometimes violent characters. He began on
the stage in *A Streetcar Named Desire* (1947) and acted in
the film version four years later. He received *Oscars as
Best Actor for *On the Waterfront* (1954) and *The Godfather*
(1973).

ₗ**Brand's 'Hatch** /ˌbrændz 'hætʃ/ a motor racing track
in *Kent, England, where many *British Grand Prix
races took place until 1986.

ₗ**Bill 'Brandt** /'brænt/ (1904–83) a German photographer who worked mainly in Britain after 1931. He is
well known for his photographs showing the contrasts
between the lives of the different English social classes
in the 1930s, and for his nudes.

ₗ**brandy 'butter** n [U] (*BrE*) a thick sauce made by mixing brandy, butter and sugar. It is traditionally served
with Christmas pudding.

ₗ**Richard 'Branson** /'brænsn/ (1950–) an English businessman who became very rich through the successful
*Virgin companies he created. He set up the Virgin
record company in 1970 and sold it to Thorn-EMI in 1992.
In 1984 he started the airline Virgin Atlantic and his company Virgin Trains runs many trains in Britain. He is also
well known for being the first person to cross the
Atlantic (1987) and the Pacific (1991) by balloon. He was
made a *knight in 2000.

ₗ**Branston 'Pickle**™ /ˌbrænstən/ n [U] a make of
pickle (= a mixture of fruit and vegetables preserved in
vinegar) which is popular in Britain. It is usually eaten
with cold meat or cheese. A phrase often used in advertising it is 'Bring on the Branston'.

ₗ**brass 'band** n a band that plays mainly brass instruments such as trumpets, trombones and tubas. In Britain
brass bands are traditionally associated with northern
England, where many bands were started by groups of
workers in a particular factory or coal mine.

'Brasso™ /'brɑːsəʊ; *AmE* 'bræsoʊ/ n [U] a British make
of polish for cleaning things made of brass.

'brass ˌrubbing n [U] the British hobby of making copies of church brasses. These are large flat pieces of decor-

ated brass which have been put in the walls and floors of
churches in memory of dead people. Most brasses were
put into churches from the 13th century to the 17th century, and usually have designs cut into them representing the dead person. People make their own copies by
covering the brass with paper and rubbing the paper
with coloured chalk or wax.

the 'brat pack n [usually sing] (*informal*) a group of
well-known or successful young people, especially
actors, who enjoy being famous and sometimes behave
badly: *Tom Cruise was a member of the Hollywood brat
pack.*

ₗ**Wernher von 'Braun** ⇨ von BRAUN.

'Braveheart /'breɪvhɑːt; *AmE* 'breɪvhɑːrt/ a film
(1995) about the Scottish hero William *Wallace, played
by Mel *Gibson. It won four *Oscars.

Brave New 'World a novel (1932) by Aldous *Huxley.
It is set in the future, when there have been many scientific advances but people have no personal freedom.
People sometimes use the phrase *brave new world* to
refer to present societies like this, or to refer humorously
to something new and unknown: *I'm a bit sceptical about
the brave new world of community policing promised by
the government.*

ₗ**Angela Bra'zil** /brə'zɪl/ (1868–1947) an English writer
of books for girls, mainly set in girls' boarding schools.

ₗ**bread-and-butter 'pudding** n [U] (*BrE*) a traditional British sweet dish, made of slices of bread and
butter mixed with raisins and sugar and baked in a mixture of milk and eggs.

ₗ**bread 'sauce** n [U] (*BrE*) a sauce made with milk,
onion, breadcrumbs and spices. It is usually served hot
with chicken or turkey.

ₗ**breakfast 'television** n [U] (*BrE*) television programmes shown early in the morning. The most popular
breakfast television programmes in Britain are *Breakfast
News*, a serious news programme on *BBC One, and
GMTV, a mixture of news and interviews with people
such as television actors and sports stars on *ITV. The
phrase 'breakfast television' is not used in the US, where
television all through the day has been common for
much longer.

ₗ**Julian 'Bream** /'briːm/ (1933–) an English musician,
well known for playing classical music on the guitar and
the lute, an ancient instrument like a guitar. Composers
such as *Britten and *Walton wrote music especially for
him.

the ˌBrecon 'Beacons /ˌbrekən 'biːkənz/ an area of
mountains in south Wales. It is popular with tourists
who like walking and enjoying the attractive scenery.

ₗ**Rory 'Bremner** /'bremnə(r)/ (1961–) an English entertainer who makes fun of well-known people, especially
politicians, by copying the way they behave and speak.
He frequently appears on television and is known for his
political satire.

ₗ**St 'Brendan** (c. 485–c. 578) an Irish monk who travelled
around Ireland and Scotland. According to legends he
was also the first European to sail to America. In 1977 a
group of people sailed from Ireland to America in a leather boat like the ones used in the 6th century, to prove
that it was possible.

'William J 'Brennan'Junior /'brenən/ (William
Joseph Brennan 1906–97) a US Supreme Court judge
(1956–90) who was known for his liberal views and for
his strong support for personal freedom and the rights of
minorities. In 1990 he was responsible for a court decision which stated that the government could not stop
people who insulted or destroyed the US flag, because
that would restrict their freedom.

Brer 'Rabbit /ˌbreə; *AmE* ˌbrer/ the main animal character in the *Uncle Remus books by the US writer Joel Chandler Harris. 'Brer' is how some people in the southern US say 'brother'.

the **'Brethren** ⇨ PLYMOUTH BRETHREN.

Bretton 'Woods /ˌbretn/ a holiday town in the White Mountains in the US state of *New Hampshire. The *International Monetary Fund and the World Bank were created in 1944 during an international financial meeting held there.

'Brewer's 'Dictionary of 'Phrase and 'Fable /'bruːəz; *AmE* 'bruːərz/ (*also* **Brewer**) a dictionary that gives information about and the origins of many English words and phrases by referring to history, religion, art, etc. It was first published in 1870 and the original author was Dr E Cobham Brewer. It has been regularly revised and there are versions dealing with areas such as film and politics: *Look it up in Brewer.*

'brewpub /'bruːpʌb/ *n* (*AmE*) a bar that sells beer made in its own small brewery called a **microbrewery**. Brewpubs first became popular in the US in the 1980s as a reaction to the fact that most beer was made by very large companies and there was little variety.

Brideshead Re'visited /ˌbraɪdzhed/ a novel (1945) by Evelyn *Waugh. It is the story of an Oxford student who becomes involved with a rich but tragic Catholic family in England. The family's large country home is called Brideshead. The book was made into a very successful television series in the 1980s. The British public enjoyed watching how the *upper classes of a period in the past dressed, spoke and behaved towards each other, and the series influenced fashions and other television programmes.

the **Bridge of 'Sighs** **1** an attractive old bridge over the river Cam in *Cambridge, England. It belongs to St John's College, part of Cambridge University, and looks like the famous Bridge of Sighs in Venice.
2 a similar bridge between two buildings of Hertford College, part of *Oxford University. It is built across a street, not a river.

Jim 'Bridger /'brɪdʒə(r)/ (1804–81) a *mountain man in the American West who discovered the *Great Salt Lake in 1824. He trapped animals and sold their furs, and worked for the army as a scout (= a person who goes first to watch for danger). He began the town of Fort Bridger in *Wyoming. One of his friends said Bridger had 'little fear of God and none of the devil'.

Robert 'Bridges /'brɪdʒɪz/ (1844–1930) an English poet, best known for his short poems. He was more popular during his life than he is now and was made *Poet Laureate in 1913.

Carl 'Bridgewater /'brɪdʒwɔːtə(r)/ (1965–78) a British child who was murdered in 1978. He was delivering newspapers to a farm and was shot by thieves who were robbing the house. Four men were arrested and sent to prison because one of them, Patrick Molloy, admitted the murder to a policeman who has since been proved dishonest. Molloy died in prison. The others, who became known as the **Bridgewater Three**, protested that they were innocent. In 1996 they were set free. See also BIRMINGHAM SIX, GUILDFORD FOUR, TOTTENHAM THREE.

Brief En'counter a British film (1945) made by David *Lean, based on a play by Noel *Coward. It is about a married woman and a doctor who meet in a railway station and fall in love. After a short relationship they decide to separate, although they love each other. The film is well known for its beautiful photography and for the typically British *middle-class way the couple don't show strong emotions.

Brief 'Lives a book written in the 17th century by John *Aubrey. It consists of the stories of the lives of famous people from that time. Each person's story is short but full of interesting information, and written in a relaxed, amusing style.

Raymond 'Briggs /'brɪgz/ (1934–) an English writer and illustrator of children's books, mostly in *comic strip form. His original characters and strong, clear illustrations show great understanding of children's imagination. *The *Snowman* and *Fungus the Bogeyman* (1977) are among British children's favourites. Another book, *When the Wind Blows* (1982), is a warning about nuclear weapons. Some of his books have been made into successful cartoon films.

'Brighton /'braɪtn/ a large town on the coast of *East Sussex in southern England. In the 18th century it became a fashionable place for people to swim, and it is still a popular place for people to spend their holidays. Its well-known buildings include the *Royal Pavilion and the Palace Pier, and it is also famous for its *Regency architecture. The Grand Hotel was the scene of the **Brighton bombing** in 1984, when five people died after the *IRA tried to kill members of the *Conservative government who were in Brighton for the party conference. See also BRIGHTON CAR RALLY.

the **Brighton 'car ˌrally** /ˌbraɪtn/ (*also* the **Brighton run**, the **London to Brighton Veteran Car Run**) *n* an event in which many veteran cars (= ones made before 1905) drive from London to *Brighton, England. It takes place in November every year and is an important social event for the owners of the old cars. Many people go to Brighton to watch them arrive. Recently, other groups of car owners have organized their own London-to-Brighton runs at different times of the year.

Brighton Pa'vilion /ˌbraɪtn/ ⇨ ROYAL PAVILION.

bright young 'things *n* [pl] (*sometimes disapproving often ironic*) a phrase originally used to describe certain rich young people in the 1920s who went to many parties and behaved in a way that older people found shocking. The phrase is now used to refer to any group of clever, ambitious young people: *The club was full of TV researchers and politicians' assistants, all bright young things on their way up.*

'Brillo pad™ /'brɪləʊ; *AmE* 'brɪloʊ/ *n* a British product for cleaning kitchen pans, etc., consisting of a pad of very fine wire with soap inside: *His hair was thick and wiry like a Brillo pad.*

Brink's 'Mat /ˌbrɪŋks 'mæt/ a British company, the owner of a building for storing valuable things at *Heathrow Airport. In 1983 thieves stole gold worth £26 million from the building. At that time it was Britain's largest robbery. The police spent many years investigating the crime, but it is still not certain that they have caught all the criminals. A lot of the money was never found and there have been nine murders of people who were connected with the crime. It is one of those crimes, like the *Great Train Robbery, that the British public and press like to talk about.

'Bristol /'brɪstl/ a large port and industrial city in southwest England, on the river *Avon. It was an important port in the slave trade in the 17th and 18th centuries. In the 1990s local pop groups such as *Massive Attack and *Portishead became famous all over the world and their style of music, trip hop, is sometimes called the 'Bristol sound'.

the **Bristol 'Channel** a long area of water between south-west England and the south coast of Wales. The *Severn and *Avon rivers flow into it.

Bristol 'Cream™ /ˌbrɪstl/ *n* [U, C] a type of rich,
sweet sherry sold by *Harvey's. It is one of the best-
known sherries in Britain, and bottles of it are often
given as presents, e.g. at Christmas.

Bristol Old 'Vic /ˌbrɪstl, 'vɪk/ a British theatre com-
pany. It was formed in 1946 as a branch of the London
*Old Vic and has been based since then at the Theatre
Royal, Bristol, Britain's oldest theatre in continuous use.

▶ **Britain and the US**

The relationship between Britain and the US has always
been a close one. Like all close relationships it has had
difficult times. The US was first a British colony, but
between 1775 and 1783 the US fought a war to become
independent. The US fought the British again in the *War
of 1812.

In general, however, the two countries have felt closer
to each other than to any other country, and their foreign
policies have shown this. During *World War I and
*World War II, and more recently in the *Gulf War and
the Iraq War, Britain and the US supported each other.
When the US looks for foreign support, Britain is usually
the first country to come forward and it is sometimes
called 'the 51st state of the union'.

But the **special relationship** that developed after
1945 is not explained only by shared political interests.
An important reason for the friendship is that the
people of the two countries are very similar. They
share the same language and enjoy each other's literature, films and television. Many Americans have
British ancestors, or relatives still living in Britain.
The US government and political system is based on
Britain's, and there are many Anglo-American businesses operating on both sides of the Atlantic. In
Britain some people are worried about the extent of
US influence, and there is some jealousy of its current
power.

The special relationship was strong in the early 1980s
when Margaret *Thatcher was Prime Minister in Britain
and Ronald *Reagan was President of the US. Since
*September 11 the support given by Britain under Tony
*Blair for US actions in Afghanistan and Iraq has led to
problems at home and with Britain's partners in the
*European Union.

Bri'tannia¹ /brɪ'tænjə/ a figure of a woman representing Britain on many coins. She is shown sitting down
wearing a helmet and holding a trident (= a long
weapon with three points). Britannia was the Roman
name for Britain. See also RULE, BRITANNIA!.

Bri'tannia² /brɪ'tænjə/ the last British *royal yacht. Its
permanent home is now in the port of Leith, in
*Edinburgh, where it has been turned into a tourist
attraction.

the **Bri'tannia ˌRoyal 'Naval ˌCollege** /brɪ-
'tænjə/ (*also* the **Royal Naval College**) a military college in *Dartmouth, south-west England, where people
train to be officers in the *Royal Navy.

'Britart /'brɪtɑːt; *AmE* 'brɪtɑːrt/ a type of art created by
a group of young British artists, including Damien
*Hirst, Tracey *Emin and the Chapman Brothers, espe-
cially during the 1990s. Britart caused controversy
because it does not follow traditional styles and, as well
as paintings and sculptures, includes collections of
objects and things designed to shock people. It has been
particularly supported by Charles *Saatchi and has been
shown in the Saatchi Gallery in London since 2003.

the **'Brit Awards** /'brɪt/ a ceremony at which pop
groups and singers are given prizes such as 'best album'
or 'best breakthrough artist' of the year. It has taken
place in London every year since 1977 and many people
watch it on television.

the **ˌBritish A'cademy** a society of leading academic
people in Britain that was established in 1901 to encourage the study of history, philosophy and language. It is
responsible for deciding which university research projects should receive money from the government. Its full
name is the National Academy for the Humanities and
Social Sciences. Compare ROYAL SOCIETY.

the **'British A'cademy of 'Film and 'Television 'Arts** ⇨ BAFTA.

ˌBritish 'Airways (*abbr* **BA**) Britain's largest airline.
The company was owned by the state until 1987. In
recent years it has lost business while low-cost airlines
such as *Ryanair and Easyjet have grown.

'British A'merican To,bacco ⇨ BAT.

the **'British As,soci'ation** (*also* the **British
Association for the Advancement of Science**) a
British organization established in 1831 to encourage
people to be interested in science. It organizes talks and
exhibitions and publishes small books. It aims particularly to encourage science in schools.

the **'British 'Board of 'Film Classifi,cation** the
organization that decides which films and videos are
suitable to be seen by people of different ages in Britain.
See also FILM CERTIFICATE.

the **ˌBritish 'Broadcasting Corpo,ration**
⇨ BBC.

▶ the **British Constitution**

Britain is a **constitutional monarchy**: it is ruled by a
king or queen who accepts the advice of *Parliament. It
is also a **parliamentary democracy**, a country whose
government is controlled by a parliament that has been
elected by the people. The highest positions in government are taken by elected *Members of Parliament, also
called MPs. The king or queen now has little real power.

The principles and procedures by which Britain is governed have developed over many centuries. They are not
written down in a single document that can be referred
to in a dispute. The British Constitution is made up of
statute law (= laws agreed by Parliament), **common
law** (= judges' decisions made in court and then written
down) and **conventions** (= rules and practices that
people cannot be forced to obey but which are considered necessary for efficient government). The
Constitution can be altered by *Acts of Parliament, or
by general agreement.

Similarly, there is no single document that lists people's
rights. Some rights have been formally recognized by
Parliament through laws, e.g. the right of a person not
to be discriminated against (= treated differently)
because of his or her sex. The Human Rights Act 1998
made all the rights established in the European
Convention on Human Rights part of British law. It is generally understood that these rights are part of the
Constitution.

A government department, the *Department for
Constitutional Affairs, was set up in 2003 with responsibility for the areas of government where there are constitutional changes, for example the reforms in the *House
of Lords and relations with the *Scottish Parliament and
the *Welsh Assembly.

the **ˌBritish 'Council** a British government organization that was set up in 1934 to develop a better understanding of Britain, British culture and the English language in other countries. It has libraries and cultural
centres in many countries, and organizes films, exhibitions, visits by British writers and artists, student
exchanges and language lessons.

the **ˌBritish 'Empire** the countries ruled by Britain
starting in the late 15th century until a peak around 1920
when the British Empire included around a quarter of

the world's population. British **colonies** (= places taken over by a foreign country and settled by people from that place) included parts of North America, islands in the *West Indies, *India, *Australia, *New Zealand and several countries in Africa. Many of them became colonies at a time when several European countries, including Britain, France, Spain and the Netherlands, were competing for trade around the world and for new sources of raw materials. Most of these colonies became independent during the 20th century, when it was generally recognized that it was not morally acceptable to take over other countries and exploit them, and many colonies had growing nationalist movements for independence. Through the *Commonwealth many of the countries still have political and economic links with Britain. Perhaps the most important and lasting cultural influence of the British Empire has been the spread of the English language which is still either an official language or taught as a second language in many countries.

the ˌBritish Expe'ditionary Force /ekspə-ˈdɪʃənri/ (abbr the **BEF**) the name used for the first groups of British soldiers sent to fight on the continent of Europe in both *World War I and *World War II.

the ˌBritish 'Film ˌInstitute ⇨ BFI.

ˌBritish 'Gas the largest company supplying gas to homes and businesses in Britain, part of Centrica which supplies gas in many countries. It used to be a nationalized industry but was sold to private owners in 1986.

the 'British ˌGrand 'Prix **1** an international motor race for very fast cars that takes place every year at *Silverstone. It is one of a series of races around the world at this level. The driver who wins most points in the series in a particular year becomes the world champion.
2 an important international motorcycle race that takes place in England every year at Donington Park, near Derby.

ˌBritish 'Home Stores ⇨ BHS.

the ˌBritish 'Isles the name for the group of islands that includes Great Britain, Ireland and all the smaller islands around them, including the *Shetland Islands, the *Isle of Man and the *Channel Islands. Compare GREAT BRITAIN, UNITED KINGDOM.

the ˌBritish 'Legion (also the **Royal British Legion**) a charity organization that helps former members of the British armed forces by giving them money and other things that they may need, and by providing clubs where they can meet. Most British towns have a **British Legion Club**. The charity collects most of its money on *Poppy Day.

ˌBritish 'Leyland /'leɪlənd/ a large British company that made cars, buses and lorries/trucks in the 1970s and 80s. It was formed in 1968 when several large companies including *Austin, *Morris, *Rover and *Jaguar combined, but continued to use the original names for the cars they produced. The company was losing money in the 1970s and was nationalized and then in the 1980s it was separated into smaller companies and sold to private owners.

the ˌBritish 'Library the national library of Britain and the most important of the *copyright libraries. It used to be part of the *British Museum but in the 1990s a new library was built near *St. Pancras station in London. It is built in the shape of a ship. Although it is much larger than the old library, it is still not big enough for all the books and documents that need to be kept. The newspaper collection is in North London and there is another reading room at Boston Spa in the north of England.

the ˌBritish 'Lions n (also the **Lions**) [pl] a *Rugby Union team consisting of the best players from England, Ireland, Scotland and Wales. The team is chosen to play on tours abroad.

the ˌBritish 'Medical Associ'ation ⇨ BMA.

The ˌBritish 'Medical Journal (abbr The **BMJ**) a British magazine, the official magazine of the *British Medical Association, which contains news and information about medicine and matters of interest to doctors. It first appeared in 1857 and is published every week.

the ˌBritish Mu'seum the national museum of Britain, established in 1753. The main building is in *Bloomsbury, London, and includes the famous reading room, a large round room that used to be part of the *British Library. When the new library building was opened, the inner court that contained the reading room was redesigned by Norman *Foster. Many well-known writers have studied and written their books there. The museum has one of the world's finest collections of art and ancient objects, including the *Elgin marbles and the *Rosetta Stone.

the ˌBritish 'National ˌParty (abbr the **BNP**) a small, extreme right-wing British political party that was formed in 1982. Its members are mostly white people who have a strong fear or dislike of other races. It has no *Members of Parliament, but in 2004 had 17 members elected as local councillors in England. See also NATIONAL FRONT.

ˌBritish 'Nuclear 'Fuels ⇨ BNFL.

the ˌBritish 'Open (also the **Open**) the British Open Golf Championship, the most important golf contest in Britain, which takes place once a year at one of several British golf courses. It is the oldest international golf event in the world, and both professional and amateur players take part.

ˌBritish 'Rail the company, owned by the state, which ran the rail transport system in Britain until the 1990s, when it was separated into several smaller companies and sold to private owners. See also NETWORK RAIL.

the ˌBritish 'Raj ⇨ RAJ.

ˌBritish 'Sky 'Broadcasting ⇨ BSkyB.

the ˌBritish 'Standards Insti'tution ⇨ BSI.

ˌBritish 'Summer Time n (abbr **BST**) [U] the time shown on clocks, etc. in Britain from March to October each year. It is one hour ahead of *GMT, giving an hour more light each evening.

ˌBritish U'nited 'Provident As,soci'ation ⇨ BUPA.

'Briton n **1** (also informal, sometimes disapproving **Brit**) a British person: More and more Britons are travelling abroad now.
2 (also **Ancient Briton**) one of the Celtic people who lived in Britain before the Romans arrived. ⇨ note at CELTS.

'Britpop /'brɪtpɒp; AmE 'brɪtpɑːp/ n [U] a type of pop music played in the 1990s by white British groups such as *Blur, *Oasis and *Pulp. They were influenced by British groups from the 1960s like the *Beatles and the Kinks, and play short, simple songs with strong tunes and words full of clever humour.

ˌBenjamin 'Britten /'brɪtn/ (1913–76) a composer who wrote some of the best and most popular British classical music of the 20th century. His best-known music was written for voices, including the operas Peter Grimes (1945) and Billy Budd (1951). Many of his pieces were written to be sung by his friend Peter *Pears, and many others were written for children. He lived the second half of his life in Aldeburgh, and established the music

festival there. He was made a *life peer in 1976. See also
ALDEBURGH FESTIVAL.

'Brixton /'brɪkstən/ a district of south London,
England. It is well known as one of the most multicultural parts of London, with large communities of *Afro-
Caribbean people, and smaller communities from many
European, African, and Asian countries. In the early
1980s there were violent protests on the streets of
Brixton, called the **Brixton riots**, against the lack of jobs
and houses, and the prejudice of some members of the
police against people of other races. As a result the government spent money on improving the houses, the
sports centre and the opportunities for young people in
Brixton.

Broadcasting 'House the main building of the
*BBC, in central London. It contains most of the BBC's
administrative offices, and many studios where radio
programmes are made.

'Broadmoor /'brɔːdmɔː(r)/ a hospital in Berkshire,
southern England, for people who are mentally ill. It is
well known to British people as a place to which criminals are sent if they cannot go to an ordinary prison
because of mental illness: *He was sent to Broadmoor in
1985 and may never be released.*

the **'Broads** /'brɔːdz/ (*also* the **Norfolk Broads**) *n*
[pl] a *national park in *East Anglia, England, where
there are many small lakes connected to each other by
rivers and canals. It is a very popular area for people
who go on holiday/vacation in boats.

'broadsheet *n* (in Britain) a newspaper with large
pages. The more serious newspapers such as The
*Guardian, The *Independent and The *Times are often
referred to as 'the broadsheets', although they all publish
at least part of the paper in *tabloid format.

▶ **Broadway**
Broadway is the name of a street in New York that is
closely associated with the theatre and is often used to
mean US theatre in general. The street runs the whole
length of *Manhattan, but its 36 theatres are in the
Theater District between West 41st Street and West
57th Street. The most famous are between 44th and 45th
Streets, near *Times Square. This part is called the
*Great White Way because of its many bright lights. The
first theatres were built there in 1894 and New York's subway system was extended north shortly afterwards to
help audiences get to them. Other theatres in New York,
usually smaller, are said to be **off-Broadway**, and there
are even **off-off-Broadway** theatres, which are less commercial.

Before the rise of the film industry, Broadway was the
place where actors could become famous. Broadway's
best years were in the 1920s when there were about 80
theatres. Most of the longest-running plays on Broadway
have been *musicals such as *South Pacific, *Guys and
Dolls, *My Fair Lady and A *Chorus Line. Andrew *Lloyd
Webber's *Cats, which closed in 2000, had the longest
run with 7485 performances. Serious plays that have
won *Tony awards include *Death of a Salesman, *Long
Day's Journey into Night and *Who's Afraid of Virginia
Woolf? Famous actors who have appeared on Broadway
include Dustin *Hoffman, Robert *Redford, Elizabeth
*Taylor, Liza *Minnelli and, from Britain, Vanessa
*Redgrave, Jeremy *Irons, Maggie *Smith and Ralph
*Fiennes.

Since the early 1970s the high cost of producing plays
has forced many theatres to close or to become cinemas/
movie theaters, and Broadway is not as important as it
once was. It has had fewer successful new plays and has
tried to attract audiences with **revivals** or with successful British productions. A bad **review** by the drama
critic of the *New York Times can close a play. Paul

Simon's $11-million musical, *The Capeman*, for
instance, ran for only two months after bad reviews.
Broadway has attracted larger audiences with musicals such as *Chicago* and *The Producers*, but most new
avant-garde (= experimental) works are produced off-
Broadway, or off-off-Broadway in the **lofts** (= old warehouses) of *SoHo.

'Broadwood /'brɔːdwʊd/ a British company that has
produced pianos since 1728, and became famous by making one for Beethoven in 1817. Some people consider
Broadwoods the best pianos in the world.

'Brobdingnag /'brɒbdɪŋnæg; *AmE* 'brɑːbdɪŋnæg/ an
imaginary country visited by Gulliver in Jonathan
*Swift's *Gulliver's Travels. The people there are much
bigger than Gulliver, and they are disgusted by his
descriptions of life in Europe.

Tom 'Brokaw (1940–) a US journalist who presented
the *NBC Nightly News*, one of the most watched television
programmes in the US, from 1982 until 2004. He began
his career with *NBC in 1973 as their journalist for the
*White House, and also presented the *Today show
(1976–81). He also writes for television and has written a
number of books. Compare RATHER, JENNINGS.

Brompton 'Oratory /ˌbrɒmptən; *AmE* 'brɑːmptən/
a large *Roman Catholic church in central London,
England, built in the late 19th century in the highly decorated *baroque style. It was London's main Catholic
church until *Westminster Cathedral was built.

Edgar 'Bronfman Jr /ˌedgə 'brɒnfmən; *AmE* ˌedgər
'brɑːnfmən/ (1955–) a Canadian businessman who is the
head of Seagram, a large corporation. He started by
working in the film and music industries and he joined
Seagram, his father's business, in 1982. He has been
responsible for changing the business from being mainly
a maker of alcoholic drinks, to becoming involved in the
entertainment industry by buying businesses such as
Universal film studios and Polygram Records.

the **'Brontë ,sisters** /'brɒnteɪ; *AmE* 'brɑːnteɪ/
Charlotte Brontë (1816–55), **Emily Brontë** (1818–48) and
Anne Brontë (1820–49), three British writers who lived
most of their lives in *Haworth, a small village in
*Yorkshire, England, where their father was the local
*Anglican priest. They began to write poetry and novels
when they were very young, creating imaginary worlds
when they were alone in the Yorkshire countryside. They
died before their best-known books, including
Charlotte's *Jane Eyre, Emily's *Wuthering Heights and
Anne's *Tenant of Wildfell Hall (1848), became the famous
works of English literature that they are today.

the **'Bronx** /'brɒŋks; *AmE* 'brɑːŋks/ one of the five
*boroughs of New York City, north of *Harlem. In the
past it had a reputation as a poor area with a lot of crime
and drug dealing in its southern part but its image has
improved. It contains Yankee Stadium, the New York
Botanical Garden and the Bronx Zoo. See also YANKEES.

Bronx 'cheer /ˌbrɒŋks; *AmE* ˌbrɑːŋks/ *n* (*AmE informal*) a rude noise made by sticking out the tongue and
blowing, sometimes directed at a rival team in *baseball
or some other sport. It is also called a raspberry.

▶ **Bronze Age Britain**
In Britain the *Stone Age changed slowly into the Bronze
Age from about 2100 BC. Metal started to be used for the
first time instead of stone to make tools. The skill to
make things with metal may have been brought to
Britain soon after 2000 BC by the Beaker Folk who were
named after the bell-shaped beakers (= cups with wide
mouths) found in their tombs. Copper was used at first,
then bronze, a mixture of copper and tin. Tools were
made by pouring the metal into a mould. In the latter

part of the Bronze Age most **settlements** (= villages) had their own **smiths** or skilled craftsmen.

Bronze Age people built the impressive **stone circles** still to be seen at *Stonehenge and other places. The double circle of **standing stones** at Stonehenge dates from about 2100 BC. Several pairs of stones still have a large, thick horizontal stone across the top of them. The upright sandstone boulders, called *sarsens*, are thought to have been dug from the ground about 20 miles/32 kilometres away, but the smaller blue-coloured stones laid across the top come from Wales. It is not known whether they were transported by people using rollers or whether they were left near the site of Stonehenge by glaciers during the Ice Age. In either case, many people would have been involved in building the monument. Stonehenge now attracts a lot of visitors and is a source of wonder and pride. Some people believe that it has a special religious or astronomical meaning and was originally used to calculate when the seasons began and ended.

On *Dartmoor many **stone rows** extend in lines for distances up to two miles/3 kilometres. There are few traces of Bronze Age houses, though **pounds** (= areas surrounded by stone walls) on the edge of the moor may have contained groups of houses.

In the Bronze Age important people were buried in round *barrows (= piles of earth) made near the top of a hill. Over 20 000 round barrows are known. There was usually only one person buried in each, together with metal goods and pottery.

In about 500 BC iron began to be used instead of bronze for making tools, and the period after this became known as the Iron Age. Compare IRON AGE BRITAIN.

ˌPeter ˈ**Brook** /ˈbrʊk/ (1925–) a British theatre director who became famous in the 1960s and 1970s for presenting plays in new and interesting ways. In 1970 he moved to France and set up an experimental theatre company in Paris which became internationally famous for its new versions of works such as the ancient Indian story *The Mahabharata*.

ˌRupert ˈ**Brooke** /ˈbrʊk/ (1887–1915) an English poet who fought and died in *World War I. His best-known poems are about the war, such as *The Soldier* (1915), which includes the famous lines:

> 66 If I should die, think only this of me:
> That there's some corner of a foreign field
> That is forever England. 99

ˈ**Brooklyn** /ˈbrʊklɪn/ one of the five *boroughs of New York City, south of *Manhattan(1) and connected to it by the *Brooklyn Bridge. It is an industrial port, but the area in it called **Brooklyn Heights** is one of the most beautiful in the city. Atlantic Avenue in Brooklyn is famous for its Middle Eastern restaurants and shops.

the Brooklyn Bridge

the ˌ**Brooklyn** ˈ**Bridge** /ˌbrʊklɪn/ the bridge over the East River in New York City that connects *Manhattan(1) with *Brooklyn. It was opened in 1883 and has a length of 1595 feet/486 metres. The expression *selling the Brooklyn Bridge* to somebody means tricking them in a deal.

ˌ**Brookly'nese** /ˌbrʊklɪˈniːz/ *n* [U] the pronunciation and words used by many people living in *Brooklyn in New York City. 'You' becomes 'youse', 'them' is 'dem' and 'thirty-third' is 'toidy-toid'. This way of speaking is also heard in other parts of the city, so many Americans believe that all people from New York speak Brooklynese.

Aˌnita ˈ**Brookner** /ˈbrʊknə(r)/ (1928–) an English writer who had a successful career writing about the history of art before she began writing novels in the 1980s. She writes with intelligence and humour about *middle-class people. Her best-known book, *Hotel du Lac* (1984), won the *Booker Prize. Her more recent work includes *The Bay of Angels* (2001), and *The Rules of Engagement* (2003).

ˌGarth ˈ**Brooks**[1] /ˌɡɑːθ ˈbrʊks; *AmE* ˌɡɑːrθ/ (1956–) a US singer of *country music who has sold more albums than any other. His shows on stage are exciting, with Brooks sometimes 'flying' on wires over the audience as he sings. His album *No Fences* sold 13 million copies. He won *Grammy awards for *Ropin' the Wind* (1991) and *In Another's Eyes* (1998).

ˌMel ˈ**Brooks**[2] /ˌmel ˈbrʊks/ (1926–) a US comic actor who also directs, writes and produces films. He is known for his wild humour. He began in the 1950s as a television writer for Sid *Caesar. His films have included *The Producers* (1968), for which he won an *Oscar, the comic *western *Blazing Saddles* (1973), *Young Frankenstein* (1974), and *Robin Hood: Men in Tights* (1993). In 2001 a *Broadway musical was based on *The Producers* and won 12 *Tony awards. Brooks is married to the actor Anne Bancroft.

ˈ**Brookside** /ˈbrʊksaɪd/ a British television *soap opera about the lives of a group of families living on the same street in *Liverpool. It was broadcast from 1982 until 2003 by *Channel Four and was one of the most serious soap operas, dealing with subjects such as death, disability, drugs and child abuse.

ˌDavid ˈ**Broome** /ˈbruːm/ (1940–) the most successful British showjumper (= a person who rides horses over difficult barriers as a sport) of all time. His many successes included gold medals in the world championships (1970 and 1978) and bronze medals at the Olympic Games (1960 and 1968).

ˈArthur ˈWhitten ˈ**Brown**[1] /ˈwɪtn ˈbraʊn/ (1886–1948) a Scottish pilot. In 1919 he and John *Alcock were the first people to fly across the Atlantic Ocean, from Newfoundland in Canada to the west coast of Ireland. Brown was made a *knight in 1919.

ˌ'Capa'bility' ˈ**Brown**[2] /ˈbraʊn/ (real name Lancelot Brown 1716–83) a British gardener and architect who designed the gardens of many great houses and parks, including *Blenheim Palace and *Chatsworth. He is famous for designing gardens to look natural rather than formal. He was known as 'Capability' Brown because he told people that their gardens had 'great capabilities', meaning that they were capable of being greatly improved in design.

ˌCharlie ˈ**Brown**[3] /ˈbraʊn/ the main character in the US *comic strip *Peanuts*. He is a child who has bad luck with the important things in life (such as baseball), worries that his friends do not respect him and is too shy to speak to the girl he loves.

'Ford 'Madox 'Brown⁴ /'fɔːd 'mædəks 'braʊn; AmE 'fɔːrd/ (1821–93) a British artist. He was a friend of the *Pre-Raphaelites and his style of painting was similar to theirs. His best-known works are The *Last of England (1852–5) and Work (1852–65), which is full of realistic details.

Gordon 'Brown⁵ /'braʊn/ (1951–) a British *Labour politician. He became a *Member of Parliament in 1983 and held several important positions in the Labour *Shadow Cabinet before becoming *Chancellor of the Exchequer in the Labour government of 1997.

'Helen 'Gurley 'Brown⁶ /'ɡɜːli 'braʊn; AmE 'ɡɜːrli/ (1922–) a US writer and journalist. She became editor of the magazine *Cosmopolitan in 1965 and changed it from a general magazine into one for women with articles about 'the new woman', love and sex. Although she was criticized for this, Cosmopolitan became more popular and other women's magazines copied it. Brown also wrote the books Sex and the Single Girl (1962) and Having It All (1982).

James 'Brown⁷ /'braʊn/ (1928–) a US singer and writer of *soul music. He is known for his great energy on stage. He received *Grammy awards for the songs Papa's Got A Brand New Bag (1965) and Living in America (1986). He spent some time in prison (1988–91) for violence and having a gun.

Jim 'Brown⁸ /'braʊn/ (1936–) a US football player and actor. He played for the Cleveland Browns, and scored more touchdowns (= taking the ball across the opponents' line) during his career (1957–66) than any player had ever done. He was chosen for the Pro Football *Hall of Fame in 1971. His films include The Dirty Dozen (1967).

John 'Brown⁹ /'braʊn/ (1800–59) an American abolitionist (= a person who campaigns against slavery). On 16 October 1859 he led a group of his supporters to occupy a building containing military weapons in Harpers Ferry, Virginia. He was captured, put on trial and hanged. During the American Civil War, northern soldiers sang a song called John Brown's Body to the tune of The *Battle Hymn of the Republic. It is still sung in the US and contains the lines:

> 66 John Brown's body lies a-mouldering in the grave, But his soul goes marching on. 99

the Brown 'Bomber the popular US name for the heavyweight boxer Joe Louis (1914–81).

'Brownie (also Brownie Guide) n a member of the junior branch of the *Guides, for girls between the ages of 7 and 11. Many British girls join their local group of Brownies. Each group is led by a woman who is called Brown Owl, and there are regular group meetings at which the girls play games and learn to do useful things. In the US Brownies are called Brownie Girl Scouts and are between 6 and 8 years old.

Robert 'Browning /'braʊnɪŋ/ (1812–89) an English poet. His early work was written to be performed in the theatre, and most of his poetry is easy to read, but full of meaning. In 1846 he secretly married Elizabeth Barrett and they went to live in Italy. They were friends of many other important British writers, including *Carlyle and *Tennyson. Browning is probably best remembered for his poems The Pied Piper of Hamelin (1842) and Home Thoughts from Abroad (1845).

'Brown v 'Board of Edu'cation a law case in 1954 which was held after a school for white children in Topeka, *Kansas, refused to accept a black girl called Linda Brown. The case led to a decision of the US *Supreme Court that made *segregation in public schools illegal. The decision ended the idea of 'separate but equal' schools for whites and *African Americans,

and encouraged the *civil rights movement. Compare PLESSY V FERGUSON.

Dave 'Brubeck /'bruːbek/ (1920–) a US *jazz musician who plays the piano and writes music. He became famous in the 1950s leading his Dave Brubeck Quartet. They were the first to sell over a million copies of a record that used only jazz musical instruments, Take Five (1959).

Lenny 'Bruce¹ /'bruːs/ (1926–66) a US performer of comedy who used rude language and told jokes about subjects that are usually avoided, such as sex, religion and race. He was sent to prison for this in 1961 and two years later was refused permission to enter Britain. He died after taking too much of the drug heroin. His story was told in the film Lenny (1974) with Dustin *Hoffman as Bruce.

Robert the 'Bruce² ⇨ ROBERT THE BRUCE.

Brum /brʌm/ (BrE) an informal name for *Birmingham, England, used especially by people living there. See also BRUMMIE.

Beau 'Brummel /ˌbəʊ 'brʌməl; AmE ˌboʊ/ (real name George Bryan Brummel 1778–1840) the best-known dandy (= man who cares very much about the way he looks) in British history. He was a friend of the *Prince of Wales and his choice of clothes had a strong influence on the fashions of the *Regency period.

'Brummie /'brʌmi/ n (BrE informal) a person who lives in or comes from *Birmingham, England.
▶ Brummie adj (BrE informal) of or from Birmingham: She had lost her Brummie accent.

'Brunei /'bruːnaɪ/ a small country in south-east Asia, on the north coast of Borneo. It has been influenced and protected by Britain since 1888, and became a member of the *Commonwealth in 1984. It produces large amounts of oil and gas, and its ruler, the Sultan of Brunei, is one of the richest people in the world.
▶ Bru'neian adj, n.

'Isambard 'Kingdom Bru'nel /'ɪzəmbɑːd 'kɪŋdəm bruː'nel; AmE 'ɪzəmbɑːrd/ (1806–69) an English engineer, famous for his ambitious designs for ships, bridges and railways. He designed the *Clifton Suspension Bridge and the largest ships that had ever been built at the time, including the Great Western, the first steamship designed to cross the Atlantic.

Frank 'Bruno /'bruːnəʊ; AmE 'bruːnoʊ/ (1961–) an English boxer. He became the European heavyweight champion in 1985, and the world heavyweight champion in 1995. After losing to Mike *Tyson a year later, he retired from boxing. His easy humour and natural good nature made him a popular television personality and he appeared in *pantomimes in the 1990s.

'William 'Jennings 'Bryan /'dʒenɪŋz 'braɪən/ (1860–1925) a US politician known for his great skill as a public speaker. His famous 'Cross of Gold' speech in 1896 supported the idea that US coins should be made of silver. Bryan was very religious and at the *Scopes trial he spoke against the teaching of evolution. He was the US *Secretary of State from 1913 to 1915.

'Brylcreem™ /'brɪlkriːm/ n [U] a make of hair cream used mainly by men to fix their hair in a particular style. It was fashionable in the 1950s, and is now used mainly by older men, or by people who want to copy the hair styles of the 1950s.

Bill 'Bryson /'braɪsn/ (1951–) a US writer, best known for his humorous travel books. He lived in England from 1977 to 1997 and then moved to *New England. His books include The Lost Continent (1989), about his visits to small US towns, Neither Here Nor There (1991), about his travels in Europe, Made in America (1994), about American English, Notes from a Small Island (1995), about Britain, *A Walk in the Woods* (1998), about his walk along the Appalachian Trail and *Down Under* (2000), about Australia, as well as *I'm a Stranger here Myself* (2000), *A Short History of Nearly Everything* (2004) and *Bryson's dictionary of Troublesome Words* (2004).

> **❝** I come from Des Moines. Somebody had to. **❞**
> *The Lost Continent*

BSA /ˌbiː es 'eɪ/ **1** (*in full* **Birmingham Small Arms**) a British company that produces motorcycles. It originally made weapons but began making motorcycles in the early 20th century. In the middle of the 20th century BSA motorcycles were popular all around the world, but by the 1960s they were less successful than Japanese ones, and no more were made after 1971. There is now a British company that makes BSA hand-built motorcycles. **2** ⇨ BOY SCOUTS OF AMERICA.

BSE /ˌbiː es 'iː/ (*in full* **bovine 'spongiform en,cepha'lopathy**) /'spʌndʒɪfɔːm enˌsefə'lɒpəθi; AmE 'spʌndʒɪfɔːrm enˌsefə'lɑːpəθi/ (*also informal* **mad cow disease**) *n* [U] a disease that affects the brains of cows and kills them. In the 1980s many British cows were found to have the disease, and thousands of them were destroyed. Scientists believe it is caused by feeding the cows with parts of sheep that had a similar disease (called *scrapie*), and that people can catch another similar disease, Creutzfeldt-Jakob disease (CJD), by eating the meat of cows with BSE. For a time in the 1990s many people stopped eating British beef, and many countries refused to import it.

BSI /ˌbiː es 'aɪ/ (*in full* **the British Standards Institution**) the organization responsible for establishing standards for goods produced in Britain, such as clothes, tools and containers. It is also responsible for making sure that things such as electrical goods are not dangerous. Goods that have been tested by BSI and found acceptable are given a label in the shape of a heart, called a **Kitemark**. Since 1998 the BSI Group has provided services in standards and testing in over 100 countries.

Kitemark

BSkyB /ˌbiːskaɪ'biː/ (*in full* **British Sky Broadcasting**) (*also* **Sky**) a company formed in 1990 that uses satellites to broadcast television programmes. It is partly owned by Rupert *Murdoch's News International company, and was formed by joining British Satellite Broadcasting and *Sky TV. People in Britain can receive the programmes by paying for the service and using a small satellite dish (= a device for receiving signals from a satellite) which is usually fixed to the outside of their homes. Programmes include films, sport and news. Some sports events can only be seen on BSkyB.

BST /ˌbiː es 'tiː/ ⇨ BRITISH SUMMER TIME.

BT /ˌbiː 'tiː/ the largest telephone company in Britain. The British telephone service used to be run by the *Post Office but in 1984 it was sold to private owners as a company called British Telecom. It was the first of Britain's public services to become a private company. In 1991 it changed its name to BT. Compare CABLE AND WIRELESS.

BTEC /'biːtek/ (*in full* **the Business and Technology Education Council**) a British organization, part of Edexcel, that runs courses and awards qualifications at various levels in a wide range of areas relating to work, such as business, design, engineering and public administration. BTEC courses are offered by schools, colleges and universities.

,bubble and 'squeak *n* [U] (*BrE*) a British dish consisting of potatoes and cabbage that have already been cooked. They are mixed together and fried. It is a way of using food that is left from an earlier meal. Its name comes from the noise it makes as it is being fried.

'bubblegum *n* [U] (*informal disapproving*) a very simple type of pop or rock music made for children and young teenagers. It was especially popular in America and Britain in the 1960s and 1970s. The name comes from a type of chewing gum that can be blown into bubbles and is popular with children.

'Bubbles a painting (1886) by *Millais of his young grandson blowing soap bubbles. It is especially well known in Britain because it was bought by Pears, a soap company, who used it in their advertisements.

,John 'Buchan /'bʌkn/ (1875–1940) a Scottish writer and politician, best known for his adventure stories, many of which involved the character Richard Hannay, including *The Thirty-Nine Steps* (1915). He was made a *baron in 1935, and was Governor General of Canada from 1935 to 1940.

,Pearl S 'Buck /'bʌk/ (Pearl Sydenstricker Buck 1892–1973) a US author who won the 1938 *Nobel Prize for Literature. She wrote mainly about China, where she lived for many years as a Christian teacher. It was the subject of her best-known novel, *The Good Earth*, for which she received the 1932 *Pulitzer Prize. Her other books include *East Wind; West Wind* (1930), *A House Divided* (1935) and *Dragon Seed* (1942).

,Buck 'House (*BrE often ironic*) an informal name for *Buckingham Palace: *We stayed at Thomas's place. It isn't exactly Buck House, but it's comfortable enough.*

,Buckingham 'Palace /ˌbʌkɪŋəm/ the official home of the British *royal family in central London. It is a very large house, originally built in 1703 for the Duke of Buckingham, though the part that can be seen from the road was built in 1913. Many tourists stand outside the Palace to watch the ceremony of *Changing the Guard, and since 1993 parts of the house have been opened to the public in the summer.

Buckingham Palace

'Buckinghamshire /'bʌkɪŋəmʃə(r)/ (*abbr* **Bucks**) a county in central southern England. Its main town and administrative centre is Aylesbury.

,Buck's 'Fizz *n* [U, C] (*BrE*) a drink consisting of champagne mixed with orange juice. It is usually drunk at special events such as weddings or important parties. It is named after Buck's, a London club.

▶ the **budget**

To people in Britain the budget means an announcement made each year by the *Chancellor of the Exchequer, the minister in charge of finance, about the government's plans concerning **taxation** and **public spending** (= money to be spent by the government).

Budget Day is in March each year. A **pre-budget report** each autumn is given to introduce ideas on which the following year's budget will be based.

On Budget Day the Chancellor explains in a long speech to the *House of Commons the financial policy of the *Treasury, plans for government spending, and how the money for this will be raised through taxation. There is then a debate on the budget, which lasts for several days, followed by a vote to accept or reject it. The contents of the budget speech are kept secret until the last moment, and any leak of information is a serious embarrassment. The speech is broadcast on national radio and television and is much discussed by financial and political experts. Photographs of the Chancellor on Budget Day usually show him holding up the red leather case in which the speech is contained. The word *budget* originally meant a small leather bag.

Many people fear budget changes, because they usually mean tax increases rather than reductions, particularly on alcohol, tobacco and petrol. Some of these increases become effective immediately and car drivers may rush to buy petrol just before the budget. Budgets announced close to general elections usually contain fewer tax increases to avoid making the government unpopular.

In the US the budget is a document describing how much money the government expects to have, and how it will use that money. *Congress spends a lot of time discussing how much money each part of the government needs. Each member of Congress tries to make sure that as much money as possible will be spent in the area he or she represents. This is called **pork-barrel politics**, and money spent to benefit a particular place is called **pork**. When Congress has decided on a budget the President considers it. In the past the President had to approve or veto the whole budget, but now he has a **line-item veto** and can veto an individual item. The *Office of Management and Budget helps prepare the budget and checks how the money is spent.

The US budget includes **revenues** (= sources of money) and **spending**. The government's largest source of money is *income tax. Since the government's revenues are smaller than its spending, the US has a **budget deficit**. Individual states also make budgets, and the laws of a particular state may say that it must not have a deficit.

Budweiser™ /ˈbʌdwaɪzə(r)/ (*informal* **Bud**) *n* [U, C] a US beer produced by the Anheuser-Busch Company.

Buffalo 'Bill the popular name of William Cody (1846–1917), an American *frontiersman and (later) entertainer. He killed many buffalo to provide meat for workers on the Kansas Pacific Railroad. He was also a rider for the *Pony Express in 1860. Ned *Buntline made him famous by writing stories about his life in his *dime novels. In the 1870s Buffalo Bill organized his own Wild West Show to entertain audiences in the US and Europe.

Buffy the 'Vampire ,Slayer /ˌbʌfi, ˈvæmpaɪə ˌsleɪə(r); *AmE* ˈvæmpaɪər ˌsleɪər/ (*also* **Buffy**) a US television series (1997–2003) about a teenage girl, Buffy Summers, played by Sarah Michelle Gellar (1977–), who has special abilities that help her to fight against vampires (= imaginary creatures in the form of dead people who suck the blood of living people), helped by her

*high school friends. The shows are a mix of horror, romance, fight scenes and elements of comedy.

Bugs 'Bunny™ /ˌbʌgz/ an American rabbit cartoon character. He was created in 1940 by Tex *Avery for *Warner Brothers. Bugs likes carrots (= long orange vegetables) and always tricks the hunter Elmer Fudd. In 1997 he became the first cartoon character to appear on a US stamp.

> **66** What's up, doc? **99**
> Bugs Bunny catchphrase

Buick™ /ˈbjuːɪk/ *n* a US make of car produced by *General Motors.

▶ **building societies and savings and loan associations**

Building societies are British financial institutions that give *mortgages (= a type of loan) to people to help them buy a house. They also offer a range of **savings accounts** for those who want to save money. In the US savings and loan associations provide a similar service. Mortgages are paid for from the interest paid by people borrowing money and from money placed by the public in savings accounts, which is then invested by the society at a profit.

Traditionally, building societies operated as **mutual organizations** which shared profits with their members. The first building societies had a few members who paid subscriptions towards their own home. When homes had been built for all of them the societies were closed. In the 19th century hundreds of permanent societies were created throughout Britain. Names such as The Coventry Building Society showed their local origins. People investing money in these societies did so in order to obtain interest on their savings, not necessarily because they wanted a loan for a house. Many building societies later joined together to form larger, national organizations, each with hundreds of **branches**.

In the 1980s and 1990s, building societies had to compete for customers with banks, which also offered mortgages, and they began to offer banking facilities themselves. After 1986, many of the larger building societies including the *Abbey, the Halifax and the Woolwich became banks. This meant that they could offer a full range of banking services. The country's largest surviving building society, the Nationwide, decided not to become a bank because it believed that it could defend customers' interests more effectively as a building society.

In the US savings and loan associations, also called **S & Ls** or **thrifts**, were created for people who wanted to get a mortgage or save money. Originally, they operated under different rules from banks and had limits on the services they could provide. In the 1980s, as in Britain, the rules changed and now S & Ls and banks offer similar kinds of accounts.

In the late 1980s S & Ls got a bad reputation when many failed. This was partly because they had taken risks in investing money in an attempt to compete with banks, and partly because many were dishonestly run. The US government gave back to people the money they had invested, but many Americans still associate S & Ls with this problem. The S & Ls that exist now are run under tighter controls and are regarded as safe places to keep money.

James 'Bulger /ˈbʊldʒə(r)/ (1990–3) a boy who was murdered in *Merseyside, England, when he was two years old. The murder was particularly shocking because he was killed by two boys who were only ten years old and were the youngest people to be found guilty of murder in Britain for 250 years.

the ˌbulldog ˈbreed *n*
[sing+ sing/pl *v*] a phrase used to refer to British people in general, and especially to British soldiers. The bulldog, a strong British dog with a large head and short thick neck and legs, is traditionally used to represent qualities that some people liked to think were typically British, such as courage, loyalty and determination. See also JOHN BULL.

a bulldog

ˌBulldog ˈDrummond /ˈdrʌmənd/ a character in a series of novels by the English writer 'Sapper' (Herman Cyril McNeile 1888–1937). He is a former British soldier who becomes a secret agent. He is not very attractive or intelligent but he has the qualities of the *bulldog breed such as courage and loyalty. The books were very popular in the first half of the 20th century, and many were made into films.

ˈbull ˌmarket *n* a situation at the stock exchange in which the prices of shares are rising and people known as **bulls** buy shares in order to make a profit by selling them later at a higher price.

the ˈBull Ring a large shopping centre in *Birmingham, England. It was first built in the 1960s on an old market where bulls used to be sold. For some people it represents a mistake of 20th–century architecture, destroying historical areas and replacing them with buildings that have no interesting features or beauty. It was itself replaced by a new shopping centre in 2003.

the ˈBattles of ˌBull ˈRun (*also* **Maˈnassas**) /məˈnæsəs/ two battles of the American *Civil War, both won by the South. They were fought near Bull Run Creek at Manassas Junction, *Virginia. The first, on 21 July 1861, was the first major battle of the war. The second was on 29–30 August 1862. The area can now be visited in the Manassas National Battlefield Park. See also JACKSON⁹.

ˈbullying /ˈbʊliɪŋ/ *n* [U] a problem that is common in schools where some children use their strength or important positions to hurt or frighten smaller or weaker children. The people who do this are called **bullies**. There are many books about British schools that describe how bullies make other children unhappy in this way. The most famous bully in English literature is *Flashman in *Tom Brown's Schooldays*.

Bundt™ pan *n* a US type of heavy metal pan in the shape of a ring, made by Nordic Ware. Bundt pans are used mostly to shape and bake cakes but also for bread and salads.

ˈbungalow *n* a small house in which all the rooms are on ground level. Many old people live in bungalows because there are no stairs to climb. In Britain, especially in the 1920s, large groups of bungalows were often built together on the edges of towns, or in places where people go to live when they have retired from work, such as the south coast. People who don't like bungalows sometimes describe this as 'bunglaloid growth'. The word *bungalow* comes from the Hindi name for an old type of house built for Europeans in Bengal.

ˌArchie ˈBunker /ˈbʌŋkə(r)/ the main character in the popular US television comedy series *All in the Family* (1971–6). He is often bad-tempered and has very old-fashioned opinions, especially about people of a different race or social class to his own. The series aimed to make fun of the typical attitudes of white *working-class Americans. The character of Bunker was copied from the British television character Alf *Garnett.

the ˈBattle of ˌBunker ˈHill /ˌbʌŋkə; *AmE* ˌbʌŋkər/ the first major battle of the *American Revolution. It is named wrongly because the battle was actually fought on Breed's Hill. It was on 17 June 1775 near *Boston. Although the British won, the Americans were encouraged because they fought well and killed many British soldiers until they had used all their bullets.

ˌBilly ˈBunter /ˈbʌntə(r)/ the main character in a series of children's stories by Frank Richards. He is a greedy fat boy at a British *public school called Greyfriars who often gets into trouble. There have been several television series based on the Bunter stories.

ˌNed ˈBuntline /ˈbʌntlaɪn/ (1823–86) a US writer of cheap novels of action and adventure. He wrote more than 400 of these, many of them based on his own experiences, and created *Buntline's Own*, a magazine containing similar stories. His style was later copied by writers of *dime novels.

ˌJohn ˈBunyan¹ /ˈbʌnjən/ (1628–88) an English writer of religious books, who also made religious speeches in public places. He fought on the side of *Parliament in the *English Civil War and later spent 11 years in prison for making *Nonconformist religious speeches. While in prison, he began his most famous book, *The *Pilgrim's Progress*.

ˌPaul ˈBunyan² /ˈbʌnjən/ a character in American legends. He is said to be a very large and strong lumberjack (= a person whose job is cutting down trees). He has a blue ox called Babe. Wild stories were told about him. In one of these the British navy built seven ships with the wood from his baby bed. Another said that Babe was so big that a new iron mine had to be opened each time he needed shoes.

BUPA™ /ˈbuːpə/ (*in full* **British United Provident Association**) a British company that sells insurance to people who want to have private medical treatment instead of using the *National Health Service. It also owns several private hospitals: *I had the operation on BUPA*.

ˈBurberry™ /ˈbɜːbəri; *AmE* ˈbɜːrbəri/ *n* a British make of raincoat that is well known for being expensive and of very good quality: *He was wearing a grey Burberry and carried an umbrella*.

ˌJulie ˈBurchill /ˈbɜːtʃɪl; *AmE* ˈbɜːrtʃɪl/ (1959–) an English journalist who began writing about *punk(1) music for *New Musical Express in the 1970s. She has written articles about a wide range of subjects for different newspapers and magazines, and became well known for saying things that people find shocking or annoying. She has also written novels and an autobiography, *I Knew I Was Right* (1998).

ˌBureau of ˈAlcohol, Toˈbacco, ˈFirearms and Exˈplosives (*abbr* **ATF**) the division of the US Department of Justice that is responsible for laws relating to alcohol, tobacco, guns and explosives. The Bureau was established in 1972 as part of the *Department of the Treasury and was moved to the *Department of Justice in 2003.

ˌWarren ˈBurger /ˈbɜːgə(r); *AmE* ˈbɜːrgər/ (1907–95) a Chief Justice of the US *Supreme Court for longer than any other in the 20th century (1969–86). He was appointed by President Richard *Nixon, but the Supreme Court under him ordered Nixon to give his telephone tapes relating to *Watergate to the House Judiciary Committee.

'Burger King a well-known group of restaurants selling hamburgers and other types of *fast food. The group began in the US in 1954 and now has more than 11000 restaurants around the world. Its most famous hamburger is called the Whopper.

,Anthony **'Burgess**[1] /'bɜːdʒɪs; AmE 'bɜːrdʒɪs/ (1917–93) an English writer, best known for his novel *A Clockwork Orange* (1962). He wrote many different types of novel, including *Earthly Powers* (1980), a description of the main events of the 20th century from the point of view of an imaginary character. He also wrote books and newspaper articles about literature and music, and several pieces of classical music.

,Guy **'Burgess**[2] /'bɜːdʒɪs; AmE 'bɜːrdʒɪs/ (1911–63) a British spy who sold government secrets to the former Soviet Union. He was one of the famous *Cambridge spies and escaped to Moscow with Donald *Maclean in 1951.

,Lord **'Burghley** /'bɜːli; AmE 'bɜːrli/ (William Cecil 1520–98) a British politician. He was one of the most important members of Queen *Elizabeth I's government, working as *Secretary of State (1558–72) and Lord Treasurer (1572–98). He was responsible for making England a strong military and economic power. He was also responsible for many grand buildings, including *Burghley House. He was made a *knight in 1551 and a *baron in 1571.

,Burghley **'House** /,bɜːli; AmE 'bɜːrli/ a large and grand house near Peterborough in eastern England, built in the *Elizabethan style in the 16th century. The inside of the house was decorated in the *baroque style 100 years later, and in the 18th century the gardens were designed by 'Capability' *Brown. Each autumn an important *three-day event, the **Burghley Horse Trials**, takes place in the grounds.

,Edmund **'Burke** /bɜːk; AmE 'bɜːrk/ (1729–97) a British *Whig(1) politician and writer, born in Ireland. He was a *Member of Parliament (1765–94) but is best remembered for speaking and writing in favour of American independence and the rights of Irish Catholics. In his best-known book, *Reflections of the Revolution in France* (1790), he argued against the more extreme acts of the French Revolution.

,Burke and **'Hare** /,bɜːk, 'heə(r); AmE ,bɜːrk/ two Irish criminals who lived in *Edinburgh in the early 19th century. They stole bodies from graves and sold them to medical students for their experiments. They also killed people in order to sell their bodies, but they are best known to most British people as grave robbers.

'Burke's 'Landed 'Gentry /'bɜːks 'lændɪd; AmE 'bɜːrks/ a book published regularly in Britain that gives details of many families with high social positions who own land in Britain but do not belong to the aristocracy. Compare BURKE'S PEERAGE.

,Burke's **'Peerage** /,bɜːks; AmE ,bɜːrks/ a book published regularly in Britain that gives details and short family histories of the members of the British aristocracy and other people with titles. Its full title is *Burke's Peerage, Baronetage and Knightage*. Compare DEBRETT. ⇨ note at PEERAGE.

bur'lesque (also **burlesk**) n [U, C] (AmE) a type of stage variety show once very popular in the US and now becoming so again. It began as family entertainment in the 1860s with singers, dancers, performers of comedy, etc. It started to include striptease (= women taking their clothes off) in the 1920s when films began to reduce the audiences. Performers who began in burlesque included W C *Fields, Fanny Brice and Al *Jolson.

,Burlington **'House** /,bɜːlɪŋtən 'haʊs; AmE ,bɜːrlɪŋtən/ a large building in *Piccadilly, London, that is the home of the *Royal Academy. It consists of four buildings combined to form a square. The main part was built in the 17th century and the other three sides were added in the 19th century for other artistic and scientific organizations.

the ,Burma **'railway** /,bɜːmə; AmE ,bɜːrmə/ a railway built by the Japanese in Burma during *World War II. They used prisoners of war to build the railway, and many of them died. The film, *Bridge on the River Kwai* (1957), is about a group of British prisoners who have to build a bridge for the railway.

'Burma Shave™ /'bɜːmə; AmE 'bɜːrmə/ a US make of cream used on the face when shaving. Between 1926 and 1963 the Burma-Vita Company advertised it on a series of small signs along roads. Each sign in a group had a few words printed on it, and the whole group, read in sequence, formed a short humorous poem. At one time, there were 35000 of these. One was:

> 66 Noah had whiskers
> In the ark
> But he wouldn't get by
> On a bench
> In the park.
> Burma-Shave. 99

'Edward 'Burne-'Jones /'bɜːn 'dʒəʊnz; AmE 'bɜːrn 'dʒoʊnz/ (1833–98) an English *Pre-Raphaelite painter. He was influenced by Dante Gabriel *Rossetti and painted many scenes from old legends. He also created designs for his friend William *Morris. He was made a *baronet in 1894.

'Frances 'Hodgson Bur'nett /'hɒdʒsən bɜː'net; AmE 'hɑːdʒsən bɜːr'net/ (1849–1924) a US writer, born in Britain. She is best remembered for her children's books, especially *Little Lord Fauntleroy* and *The Secret Garden* (1911).

,George **'Burns**[1] /'bɜːnz; AmE 'bɜːrnz/ (1896–1996) a US comedian who continued to perform until he was nearly 100. He was known for his large cigar, slow talk and humorous singing. He joined his wife, Gracie Allen (1906–64), on stage, in films and on radio and television. He received an *Oscar as 'Best Supporting Actor' for *The Sunshine Boys* (1975) and played God in *Oh, God!* (1977) and two later films.

,Robert **'Burns**[2] /'bɜːnz; AmE 'bɜːrnz/ (1759–96) a Scottish poet, often referred to as Robbie (or Rabbie) Burns. He wrote many poems and songs in English, and in the dialect of Lowland Scotland, about love, the countryside, the life of working people, and his love of Scotland. He is regarded as Scotland's national poet and his poems and songs, such as *Tam o' Shanter* and *Auld Lang Syne*, are widely known.

'Burns Night /'bɜːnz; AmE 'bɜːrnz/ 25 January, the birthday of Robert *Burns. It is celebrated every year in Scotland, and by Scottish people all around the world, in an evening of music, poetry, food and drink. People drink *whisky and eat typical Scottish food such as *haggis while *bagpipes music is played and some of Burns's most popular poems are read aloud.

the **'Burrell Col,lection** /'bʌrəl / a very large collection of paintings, sculptures and works of decorative art that was given to the city of *Glasgow by Sir William Burrell, a local businessman, in 1944. In 1983 it was moved to the **Burrell Gallery**, a new museum built especially for the collection.

'Edgar 'Rice 'Burroughs[1] /'raɪs 'bʌrəʊz; AmE 'bʌroʊz/ (1875–1950) a US writer who created the character of *Tarzan. The first book in the series was *Tarzan of the Apes* (1914) and 23 more followed. Many Tarzan films have been made. Burroughs also wrote science fiction novels, including *The Gods of Mars* (1913).

William 'Burroughs² /'bʌrəʊz; *AmE* 'bʌroʊz/ (1914–97) a US writer of the *beat generation. His experiences as a homosexual and drug user are often reflected in his books. His best-known novel is *The Naked Lunch* (1959).

'Burton¹ /'bɜːtn; *AmE* 'bɜːrtn/ any of a group of British *high-street shops selling men's clothes. There are Burton shops in many British towns.

Richard 'Burton² /'bɜːtn; *AmE* 'bɜːrtn/ (1821–90) an English writer and explorer. He travelled to India, Arabia and several African countries, and learnt many languages so that he could talk to local people and write about their cultures and traditions. He is also well known for his translation of *The *Arabian Nights*. He was made a *knight in 1886.

Richard 'Burton³ /'bɜːtn; *AmE* 'bɜːrtn/ (1925–84) a Welsh actor. He first became famous for his performances of Shakespearian roles in the theatre, and in the 1960s and 1970s he acted in many major British and US films. He was also well known for his relationship with Elizabeth *Taylor. They were married and divorced twice, and acted in several successful films together, including *Cleopatra* and *Who's Afraid of Virginia Woolf?*.

Robert 'Burton⁴ /'bɜːtn; *AmE* 'bɜːrtn/ (1577–1640) an English academic at *Oxford University who is best known for writing *The Anatomy of Melancholy* (1621), a study of depression, its history and effects.

bus *n* a large vehicle carrying passengers along a fixed route with places for stopping on the way. London still has a few traditional double-deckers (= buses with two floors) where passengers get on and off through the open platform at the back, and a conductor walks around inside the bus selling tickets. Modern buses have no conductor. Passengers pay the driver when they get on. The door is at the front, and only opens at official bus stops.

Buses used for long distances or tours are often called *coaches* in Britain but not in the US. Yellow school buses are a tradition in the US and parts of Britain.

Matt 'Busby /'bʌzbi/ (1909–94) a British football player and manager. He was a successful player for *Manchester City and *Liverpool in the 1930s but is best remembered as the manager of *Manchester United (1945–69). Several members of the team died in a plane crash in 1958 and Busby introduced many new young players, who were called the **Busby babes**. They became the most successful team in England, winning the *European Cup in 1968. Busby was made a *knight in 1968.

George 'Bush¹ /'bʊʃ/ (1924–) the 41st US *President (1989–93) and a member of the *Republican Party. He was twice the Vice-President under Ronald *Reagan (1981–89). Bush was popular after the *Gulf War was won in 1991, but lost support during America's later economic problems. He was defeated by Bill *Clinton in the election of 1992. His son, George W Bush, became President in 2001.

> 66 What's wrong with being a boring kind of guy? 99
> George Bush, 1988

George W 'Bush² /'bʊʃ/ (George Walker Bush 1946–) the 43rd US *President, from 2001. He is the son of the 41st President George *Bush and is also known by the nickname 'Dubya'. He is a member of the *Republican Party and was previously the governor of *Texas. The 2000 election for President, between Bush and the *Democratic Party candidate Al *Gore, was very close

and the votes had to be counted again. The US *Supreme Court ruled that Bush had won. He became very popular in the United States after the attack on the *World Trade Center in New York on September 11th 2001. He is well known for his *neoconservative politics and for using the phrase 'axis of evil' about the countries the United States government considers to be a danger to world peace. His decision to invade Iraq in 2003 was opposed by many of America's allies. He defeated John *Kerry in the presidential election in 2004. Bush is famous for his strange use of English grammar and vocabulary and his lack of logic in speeches. Some people like to collect these 'Bushisms'.

> 66 I am mindful not only of preserving executive powers for myself, but for predecessors as well. 99
> a Bushism

Bush 'House /ˌbʊʃ/ the main centre of the *BBC World Service. It is a large building in central London containing the administrative offices and the studios where World Service programmes are recorded.

the 'Business and Tech'nology Edu'cation Council ⇒ BTEC.

'busking /'bʌskɪŋ/ *n* [U] (*BrE informal*) a way of earning money by entertaining people in a public place, usually by playing music. In Britain, some places, such as *Covent Garden in London, have special areas for **buskers** to perform in and buskers also perform in London's *Underground stations.

'bus pass *n* (*BrE*) (in Britain) a special ticket that allows a *senior citizen to travel more cheaply or, in some cities, free on a bus. If you say that somebody has got their bus pass, it is a humorous way of saying that they have become a senior citizen.

Darcey 'Bussell /ˌdɑːsi 'bʌsl; *AmE* ˌdɑːrsi/ (1969–) an English dancer. She became Principal Ballerina of the *Royal Ballet in 1989.

'bussing (*AmE also* **busing**) /'bʌsɪŋ/ *n* [U] (in the US) the system of transporting children in buses from their homes to schools in a different area, in order to achieve a greater mixture of races in schools. Usually African American children travel to schools in white areas. This began in 1954 and was approved by the US *Supreme Court in 1971. Many white parents moved out of cities to avoid bussing.

R A ('Rab') 'Butler¹ /ˌræb 'bʌtlə(r)/ (Richard Austen Butler 1902–82) an English *Conservative politician who held every important position in government except that of *prime minister. He is sometimes described as 'the best Prime Minister we never had'. He was *Chancellor of the Exchequer (1951–5), *Home Secretary (1957–62), and *Foreign Secretary (1963–4). Most people expected him to follow *Macmillan as Prime Minister, but Macmillan preferred Sir Alec *Douglas-Home. Butler was made a *life peer in 1965.

Rhett 'Butler² /ˌret 'bʌtlə(r)/ one of the main characters in the novel *Gone with the Wind. Clark *Gable played the role in the 1939 film version. Butler marries Scarlett *O'Hara but leaves her at the end.

> 66 Frankly, my dear, I don't give a damn! 99
> Rhett Butler's final words to Scarlett

Samuel 'Butler³ /'bʌtlə(r)/ (1835–1902) an English writer who escaped from his extremely religious English family to become a farmer in New Zealand. He wrote about this experience in his novel *The Way of All Flesh* (1903). His other famous book, *Erewhon*, makes fun of religion and other human ideas.

'Butlin's /'bʌtlɪnz/ any of a group of British holiday centres, formerly called 'holiday camps', where families can sleep, eat and be entertained without leaving the centre. The first one was opened in Skegness, on the east coast of England, in 1936 by Billy Butlin (1899–1980). They were very popular in the 1950s before travel abroad became cheap, and they still attract many British families who want to enjoy a wide range of entertainments that are not too expensive: *It's a glorified holiday camp, a sort of Butlin's of the Caribbean.*

'Buttons /'bʌtnz/ a character in the *pantomime *Cinderella*. He is Cinderella's friend, and usually wears a suit with many buttons.

A S 'Byatt /ˌeɪ es 'baɪət/ (Antonia Susan Byatt 1936–) an English writer and university teacher of English literature. Her novels contain many references to other works of literature. She won the *Booker Prize for her novel *Possession* (1990). The author Margaret *Drabble is her sister.

'by-e‚lection *n* (in Britain) the election of a single *Member of Parliament to the *House of Commons at any time other than a general election, usually when another MP has died or resigned. See also CHILTERN HUNDREDS.

'by-law (also **bye-law**) *n* **1** (in Britain) a law made by a local authority, such as a town *council, which only applies in that area, rather than a law made by the central government.
2 (in the US) a rule made by a particular organization, such as a club or company, which only applies to the members of that organization.

John 'Byng /'bɪŋ/ (1704–57) a British admiral who was tried by a military court and shot for failing to protect some British soldiers when they were being attacked. The French writer Voltaire referred to Byng's death in his humorous book *Candide*. He said that in England they liked to kill an admiral occasionally 'to encourage the others'. This phrase, (in French *pour encourager les autres*) is still often used in written and spoken English.

Richard E 'Byrd¹ /'bɜːd; *AmE* 'bɜːrd/ (Richard Evelyn Byrd 1888–1957) a US explorer and navy pilot. In 1926, he and Floyd Bennett made the first flight over the North Pole. Byrd also flew over the South Pole in 1929 and went on several journeys to Antarctica.

William 'Byrd² /'bɜːd; *AmE* 'bɜːrd/ (1543–1623) an English composer, known for his religious music. He was a student of Thomas *Tallis, and one of the greatest musicians of the *Tudor(1) period. Although he was a *Roman Catholic, he also wrote many pieces of music for the *Church of England.

Lord 'Byron /'baɪrən/ (George Gordon Byron 1788–1824) an English poet whose life is as well known as his poetry. He had love affairs with many women, including Lady Caroline Lamb, and probably had a child by his half-sister (= sister by a different mother). He was a leading figure in the *Romantic Movement and himself lived the life of a romantic hero, often unhappy about a love affair and angry about the unfair political and social situations he saw around him. His work, including *Childe Harold's Pilgrimage* (1812–18) and *Don Juan* (1818–20), often expresses the same feelings. Rejected by British society, he spent much of his life abroad and died helping the Greeks in their struggle against Turkish rule.

> **❝** Mad, bad and dangerous to know. **❞**
> Lady Caroline Lamb's description of Byron

By'ronic /baɪˈrɒnɪk; *AmE* baɪˈrɑːnɪk/ *adj* of or typical of Lord *Byron, considered especially as a romantic figure: *He spent a year wandering around Europe in a melancholy, almost Byronic sort of way.*

B

C c

the CAA /ˌsiː eɪ 'eɪ/ ⇨ CIVIL AVIATION AUTHORITY.

the CAB /ˌsiː eɪ 'biː/ ⇨ CITIZENS ADVICE BUREAU.

▶ **the Cabinet**

In Britain, the Cabinet is a committee responsible for deciding government policy and for coordinating the work of government *departments. It consists of about 20 *ministers chosen by the *Prime Minister and meets for a few hours each week at *Downing Street. Its members are bound by oath not to talk about the meetings. Reports are sent to government departments but these give only summaries of the topics discussed and decisions taken. They do not mention who agreed or disagreed. The principle of **collective responsibility** means that the Cabinet acts unanimously (= all together), even if some ministers do not agree. When a policy has been decided, each minister is expected to support it publicly or resign. In recent years, prime ministers have changed the members of their Cabinet quite often in Cabinet **reshuffles**. Some members are dropped, new ones are brought in, and the rest are given new departmental responsibilities.

The leader of the main opposition party forms a **shadow cabinet** of **shadow ministers**, each with a particular area of responsibility, so that there is a team ready to take over immediately if the party in power should be defeated.

Committees are appointed by the Cabinet to examine issues in more detail than the Cabinet has time for. Members of these committees are not necessarily politicians. The *Cabinet Office led by the Secretary to the Cabinet, the most senior *civil servant in Britain, prepares agendas for Cabinet meetings and committees.

In the US the Cabinet consists of the heads of the 15 departments that make up the **executive branch** of the *federal government. Each president appoints the department heads, called **secretaries**, from his or her own party, and they give advice on policy. Since the Cabinet was not established by the *Constitution, the President can add, remove or combine departments, and can decide when to ask the Cabinet for advice, and whether or not to follow it.

State governments are usually organized in a similar way to the national government, and most have a cabinet.

the 'Cabinet ˌOffice a British government department that is responsible for the administrative work of the *Cabinet, and for managing the *Civil Service.

ˌCable and 'Wireless a large international telecommunications company. Its British company is the second largest telecommunications company in Britain after *BT.

ˌCable 'News ˌNetwork ⇨ CNN.

ˌJohn 'Cabot /'kæbət/ born (c. 1450–c. 1498) an Italian explorer who was born Giovanni Caboto. With his son Sebastian he sailed across the Atlantic in 1498 on behalf of the English king, *Henry VII, and reached North America (which he thought was China) before *Columbus.

ˌMother Ca'brini /kə'briːni/ (1850–1917) the first US citizen to become a Roman Catholic saint. She was born Francesca Cabrini in Lombardy, Italy. She became a nun, began the Missionary Sisters of the Sacred Heart and

went to the US in 1889 to continue her work. She was named a saint in 1946.

ˌCadbury 'Schweppes /ˌkædbri 'ʃweps/ a large British food and drinks company. It was formed in 1969 when Cadbury's, Britain's leading chocolate producer, combined with Schweppes, which makes soft drinks (= drinks containing no alcohol) such as tonic water and lemonade.

ˌJack 'Cade /'keɪd/ (died 1450) the leader in 1450 of a violent protest in *Kent, England, against *Henry VI's high taxes and bad government. His army defeated the royal forces and entered London. After receiving certain promises, Cade's army went back to their homes but Cade himself was later caught and killed.

'Cadillac™ /'kædɪlæk/ n a large and expensive US make of car. Owning a Cadillac is seen by many Americans as a sign of wealth and success. Cadillacs were first produced in 1903 in *Detroit by the Cadillac Motor Car Company and are now made by *General Motors.

'Caedmon /'kædmən/ (7th century) the first English poet. According to *Bede, he worked for a monastery, looking after the cows. One day he woke up after having a dream and was able to write religious poetry in English. Only a small part of his work survives.

Caer'narfon /kə'nɑːvn; AmE kər'nɑːrvn/ a town in *Gwynedd, Wales. It is famous for its 13th–century castle. At a ceremony there in 1969, Prince *Charles became officially the *Prince of Wales.

Caer'philly /keə'fɪli; AmE ker'fɪli/ n [U] a type of mild white cheese, originally made in Caerphilly, a town in the south-east of Wales.

ˌJulius 'Caesar¹ ⇨ JULIUS CAESAR.

ˌSid 'Caesar² /'siːzə(r)/ (1922–) a very popular comedian on early US television. His programme was *Your Show of Shows* (1950–55) with Imogene Coca, and Caesar won two *Emmy awards. The show's writers included Woody *Allen, Neil *Simon, and Mel *Brooks.

ˌCaesar 'salad /ˌsiːzə; AmE ˌsiːzər/ n [C, U] an American cold dish made mainly with lettuce, cheese and eggs. It was created about 1903 by an Italian-American cook in *Chicago, who named it after Julius Caesar.

the ˌCafé 'Royal a famous restaurant in *Regent Street, London, England. In the 19th century it was a fashionable place for artists and writers to meet.

CAFOD /'kæfɒd; AmE 'kæfɑːd/ (in full **Catholic Agency for Overseas Development**) a charity organization run by the *Roman Catholic Church in Britain. Its aims are to help development projects in poor countries, and to educate people in Britain about these countries.

ˌJohn 'Cage¹ /'keɪdʒ/ (1912–1992) a US composer of music who was an important influence on other composers. He used ordinary noises and a 'prepared piano' with items attached to its strings to produce different sounds. His works include the silent *Four Minutes 33 Seconds* (1952), during which a person sits at a closed piano for that length of time without making a sound.

ˌNicolas 'Cage² /'keɪdʒ/ (1964–) a US film actor who won an *Oscar and *Golden Globe Award for his part in

Leaving Las Vegas (1995). His uncle is the director Francis Ford *Coppola. Cage's other films include *Raising Arizona* (1987), *Wild at Heart* (1990), *The Rock* (1996), *Con Air* (1997), *Adaptation* (2002) and *The Weather Man* (2005).

James 'Cagney /'kægni/ (1899–1986) a US film actor who usually played tough characters and criminals, as in the films *The Public Enemy* (1931) and *Angels with Dirty Faces* (1938). He won his *Oscar, however, as a dancer and singer in *Yankee Doodle Dandy* (1942).

Cagney and 'Lacey /,kægni, 'leɪsi/ a popular US television series in the 1980s about the work and private lives of two women police detectives, played by Tyne Daly and Sharon Gless, who both won *Emmy awards for their performances. See also DETECTIVE STORY.

Sammy 'Cahn /'kɑːn/ (1913–93) a US writer of songs, especially for films. He won *Oscars for *Three Coins in the Fountain* (1954), *All the Way* (1957) and *High Hopes* (1959). Many of his songs were sung by Frank *Sinatra.

Michael 'Caine /'keɪn/ (1933–) an English film actor, well known for his *cockney accent. He became famous in the 1960s when he was the main actor in films such as *The Ipcress File* (1965), *Alfie* (1966) and *Get Carter* (1971). Since then he has acted in over 100 British and US films and has won *Oscars for *Hannah and her Sisters* (1986) and *Cider House Rules* (2000). He was made a *knight in 2000.

> 66 My career must be slipping. This is the first time I've been available to pick up an award. 99
> Michael Caine at the Golden Globe awards, 1999

the 'Cairngorms /'keəngɔːmz; AmE 'kerngɔːrmz/ a mountain range in central Scotland which is popular for climbing, walking and skiing. A valuable stone, called **cairngorm**, is found in the mountains.

cairn 'terrier /,keən / (also **cairn**) n a small breed of *terrier with rough hair, originally bred in Scotland for hunting.

'Cajun /'keɪdʒən/ n a member of the people in the US state of *Louisiana who are descended from French Canadians called Acadians. They moved to Louisiana after the British forced them in 1755 to leave Acadia (Nova Scotia) in Canada. They speak a form of French, and are known for their lively music and hot, spicy food. Compare CREOLE.
▶ **Cajun** adj: a Cajun restaurant.

'Calais /'kæleɪ/ a town in northern France. It is the nearest port to England, across the *English Channel from *Dover. It was captured by the British in 1347 during the *Hundred Years War, and remained a British town in France until 1558. Now it is the main port for passenger ships from Dover, and many British people go there to buy things such as alcohol and cigarettes, which have lower tax in France than in Britain: a day trip to Calais.

Ca,lamity 'Jane (c. 1852–1903) the popular name of Martha Jane Burke, a woman who became famous in America's *Wild West for her skill at riding and shooting. She dressed like a man and said she would bring calamity (= great harm) to anyone who made her angry or tried to love her. She was well known in Deadwood, South Dakota, in the 1870s and was a friend or lover of Wild Bill *Hickok.

the Cal,cutta 'Cup /kæl,kʌtə/ the prize given to the winner of a *Rugby Union match played once a year between the teams of England and Scotland.

Ale,xander 'Calder /'kɔːldə(r)/ (1898–1976) a US sculptor. He is well known for his many large outdoor sculptures, and for inventing the mobile, a type of sculpture

consisting of different parts that move freely, usually hanging on wires.

the ,Cale'donian Ca'nal /,kælɪ'dəʊniən; AmE ,kælɪ'dəʊniən/ a system of canals and lakes, including *Loch Ness, that crosses Scotland from the Atlantic Ocean to the *North Sea. It was built in the 18th century for industrial and business transport, but is now used mainly by tourists.

▶ the calendar

Britain and the US follow the Gregorian calendar, which replaced the Roman Julian calendar in 1752. The year is divided into 12 months, with 30 or 31 days in each month, except February, which has 28 days. An extra day is added to February every fourth year, called a **leap year**, to keep the calendar in time with the moon. A well-known verse helps people remember how many days there are in each month:

Thirty days hath September,
April, June and November.
All the rest have thirty-one,
Excepting February alone,
Which hath twenty-eight days clear,
and twenty-nine in each leap year.

The **calendar year** starts on 1 January, *New Year's Day. The number of each year (2003, 2004, etc.) represents the number of years that have passed since the birth of Jesus Christ. The year 2000 marked the end of the second millennium (= a period of 1000 years) since Christ was born. The years before Christ are described as **BC** (= before Christ), e.g. 55 BC or **BCE** (= before the Common Era). The abbreviations **AD** (Latin *Anno Domini*, meaning 'in the year of the Lord') or **CE** (= Common Era) are put before or after the date for the years after Christ's birth, e.g. AD 44 or 44 AD, but they are not used with years after about 200 AD. Some cultural and religious groups use different calendars: the year 2000 in the Gregorian calendar began during the year 5760 in the Jewish calendar, 1420 in the Islamic calendar and 1921 in the Hindu calendar.

The **academic year** used by schools and colleges in Britain runs from September to July, with short holidays at *Christmas and in the spring and a long summer vacation. In the US the academic year runs from August or September to May or June. Many business companies have a **financial year** (= a period of accounting) that runs from April to the following March. The **tax year** in the US is the same as the calendar year but the tax year in Britain begins on 5 April. The reason is that in *medieval times the calendar year began on 25 March, not 1 January. When the Gregorian Calendar was introduced, an adjustment was needed and 11 days were removed from September 1752. To avoid being accused of collecting a full year's taxes in a short year, the government extended the end of the tax year 1752–3 to 4 April.

Many festivals are celebrated during the year. Christmas and Easter are the main Christian festivals. Jews remember Passover and Yom Kippur. Ramadan, a month of fasting, and Eid ul-Fitr are celebrated by Muslims. Diwali, the Hindu festival of light, takes place in October or November, and the Chinese celebrate their new year in January or February. Special occasions such as *Bonfire Night in Britain and *Thanksgiving in the US are enjoyed by almost everyone.

,Cali'fornia /,kælɪ'fɔːniə; AmE ,kælɪ'fɔːrniə/ a US state on the Pacific Ocean, also called the Golden State. California has the largest population of all the states. Its largest city is *Los Angeles and the capital is Sacramento. It is known for *Hollywood, *Disneyland, *Silicon Valley and for its agricultural and wine products. Its history has included the *Gold Rush of 1849 and

C

the *San Francisco earthquake of 1906. Ronald *Reagan was the governor of California from 1966 to 1974. Arnold *Schwarzenegger was elected governor in 2003.

,James 'Callaghan (1912–2005) a British *Labour politician and *Prime Minister (1976–9). During his time as Prime Minister there were many strikes in Britain, including the *winter of discontent, and Labour lost the next general election. Callaghan was made a *life peer in 1987.

> 66 There are times, perhaps once every thirty years, when there is a sea change in politics. It then does not matter what you say or what you do. There is a shift in what the public wants and what it approves of. I suspect there is now such a sea change – and it is for Mrs Thatcher. 99
>
> James Callaghan, 1979

Ma,ria 'Callas /'kæləs/ (1923–77) a US opera singer, with Greek parents. Her strong voice and personality helped to make opera more popular in the US. She had a long romantic friendship with Aristotle Onassis, who later married Jackie *Kennedy. Callas is remembered as one of the greatest singers of the 20th century.

'Cambria /'kæmbriə/ a poetic name for Wales. Originally it was the Latin name for Wales. Now it is used mainly in company names and the names of pubs, hotels, etc.: *Cambria Magazine*.

'Cambrian /'kæmbriən/ adj 1 of the first period of the Palaeozoic era (= 570–510 million years ago). This period is called Cambrian, from *Cambria*, the Latin name for Wales, because it was first identified by a scientist studying rocks in Wales.
2 relating to Wales.

'Cambridge /'keɪmbrɪdʒ/ 1 the main city and administrative centre of *Cambridgeshire, England, on the River Cam. It is famous for its university, the second oldest in Britain, and is visited by many tourists. ⇨ note at OXBRIDGE.
2 a city in the US state of *Massachusetts, across the Charles River from *Boston. It is famous for its universities, *Harvard and the *Massachusetts Institute of Technology.

the ,Cambridge Cer'tificate /,keɪmbrɪdʒ/ any of three qualifications in English for speakers of other languages who are successful in examinations set by *Cambridge University. The full names are the First Certificate in English, the Certificate in Advanced English and the Certificate of Proficiency in English.

the ,Cambridge 'Footlights /,keɪmbrɪdʒ/ a club for students at *Cambridge University which performs regular comedy shows. Many famous British comedians, including several members of *Monty Python's Flying Circus*, were originally members of the Cambridge Footlights.

'Cambridgeshire /'keɪmbrɪdʒʃə(r)/ (abbr Cambs) a county in south-east England. Its administrative centre is *Cambridge.

the ,Cambridge 'spies /,keɪmbrɪdʒ/ n [pl] a group of British spies who gave British secrets to the Soviet Union. They were at *Cambridge University together in the 1930s, and believed that Communism was the only way of fighting Fascism. People first knew about the group when two of them, Guy *Burgess and Donald *Maclean, went to live in the Soviet Union in 1951. A third man, Kim *Philby, joined them in 1963, and in 1979 the fourth man was named as Anthony *Blunt. John Cairncross was named as a fifth member of the group in 1991.

,Cambridge Uni'versity /,keɪmbrɪdʒ/ Britain's second oldest university, in the city of *Cambridge in eastern England. It has a high reputation for academic achievement. The university consists of a number of independent colleges, the oldest of which is Peterhouse (established 1284). Other famous colleges include Corpus Christi, King's, Magdalene, Queens' and Trinity. Most take both male and female students. Among the university's famous buildings are *King's College chapel, the *Bridge of Sighs and the Fitzwilliam Museum. Since the 19th century the university has been a major centre of scientific research, particularly at the *Cavendish Laboratory. See also BACKS, TRIPOS. Compare OXFORD UNIVERSITY. ⇨ note at OXBRIDGE.

'Cambridge Uni'versity 'Press /'keɪmbrɪdʒ/ a publishing company belonging to *Cambridge University. Its offices are in *Cambridge, England, and it produces mainly educational books. It started printing in 1534, and is the oldest printing company in the world.

'Camden /'kæmdən/ (also ,Camden 'Town) an area of north London, England. It was once a *working-class area but is now a fashionable place to live. It has a lively market which is particularly popular with young tourists.

the ,Camden 'Town Group /,kæmdən/ a group of British artists based in London in the early 20th century, including Walter *Sickert and Augustus *John. They organized exhibitions together of their paintings of the ordinary scenes, objects and people of London.

'Camel™ /'kæml/ n a US make of cigarette produced by the R J Reynolds Tobacco Company. It was one of the first popular cigarettes in the US and a well-known advertisement included the line, 'I'd walk a mile for a Camel.'

'Camelot /'kæmələt; AmE 'kæmələːt/ 1 according to tradition, the wonderful and magic place where King *Arthur lived with his family and the *Knights of the Round Table. Some people believe Camelot was in what is now *Winchester(1). Others think it was in *Somerset, *Cornwall or Caerleon in south-east Wales.
2 the name of the company that runs Britain's *National Lottery.
3 a name that was associated with the presidency of John F *Kennedy, used to describe the atmosphere of the *White House at the time. After Kennedy was killed his wife quoted the lines from a song in the musical *Camelot* which she said was her husband's favourite:

> 66 Don't let it be forgot,
> That once there was a spot
> For one brief shining moment
> That was known as Camelot. 99

the Cam'paign for 'Nuclear Dis'armament ⇨ CND.

the Cam'paign for ,Real 'Ale ⇨ CAMRA.

the Cam'paign to Pro'tect ,Rural 'England (abbr CPRE) a *pressure group that aims to preserve the English countryside in its natural state and prevent people from building on the land.

,Alastair 'Campbell[1] /,ælɪsteə 'kæmbl; AmE ,ælɪstər/ (1957–) a British journalist who worked for Tony *Blair from 1994 until 2003, as a senior political adviser, press secretary and Director of Communications and Strategy. He was famous for the way he controlled the media on behalf of the Labour government. He left his job after he was involved in the events that led to the *Hutton Inquiry and returned to work for the Labour Party's election campaign in 2005.

ˌDonald **'Campbell**[2] /ˈkæmbl/ (1921–67) an English
sports driver whose aim was to travel faster than anybody had ever done before. In the 1950s and 1960s he
held the world records for speed on land and water. He
died in 1967 when his boat *Bluebird crashed while he
was trying to break another speed record. Malcolm
*Campbell was his father.

ˌGlen **'Campbell**[3] /ˈkæmbl/ (1936–) a US singer of
*country music. He received *Emmy awards for the
song *Gentle on My Mind* (1967) and the album *By the Time
I Get to Phoenix* (1968). His other successes include
Rhinestone Cowboy (1975).

ˌMalcolm **'Campbell**[4] /ˈkæmbl/ (1885–1948) a British
motor racing driver who held the world records for
speed on land and water in the 1920s and 1930s. Many of
his cars and boats were called *Bluebird and his son
Donald continued this tradition. He was made a *knight
in 1931.

ˌNaomi **'Campbell**[5] /ˌneɪəmi ˈkæmbl/ (1970–) an
English fashion model whose photographs appear in
magazines and advertisements all over the world. She
was the first black model to appear on the front of
*Vogue and *Time Magazine.

'Mrs 'Patrick **'Campbell**[6] /ˈkæmbl/ (1865–1940) an
English actor who was well known for her intelligent
and humorous remarks. Her name before her marriage
to Patrick Campbell was Beatrice Tanner. Her best-
known role was as Eliza in George Bernard *Shaw's
*Pygmalion.

ˌCampbell's **'soups**™ /ˌkæmblz/ a range of soups
produced by the US Campbell Soup Company and usually sold in cans. They were first made in 1897 and were
advertised for a long time by two children with round
faces called the Campbell Kids. The company's main
office is in Camden, New Jersey, and it also now makes
frozen dinners, chocolates and many other food products. See also WARHOL.

ˌCamp **'David** the special home, office and camp for the
US President in the Catoctin Mountains in the state of
*Maryland. It was called Shangri-La when first used in
1942 by President Franklin D *Roosevelt but in 1953
President *Eisenhower named it after his grandson
David. Meetings there in 1978 led to the **Camp David
Agreement** for peace between Egypt and Israel.
Compare CHEQUERS.

ˌEdmund **'Campion** /ˈkæmpiən/ (1540–81) an English
Catholic martyr (= a person who is killed because of
their religious beliefs) in the time of Queen *Elizabeth I.
He joined the Jesuits, a branch of the *Roman Catholic
Church, and performed secret religious services for
Catholics in Britain. He was caught and hanged for trea-
son. The Pope made him a saint in 1970.

ˌCamptown **'Races** /ˌkæmptaʊn/ a popular old US
song. It was written by Stephen *Foster in 1850 and has
the line of nonsense, 'Oh dee doo dah day'.

CAMRA /ˈkæmrə/ (*in full* **the Campaign for Real
Ale**) a British organization whose aim is to support beer
companies that produce traditional beer, and to encourage people to drink it. It was started in the 1970s by a
group of people who felt that beer made in industrial
processes by large companies was losing its flavour.
CAMRA publishes books about beer and pubs, and organizes beer festivals. ⇨ note at BEER.

'Canada /ˈkænədə/ a large country in the northern half
of North America. The parts of the country away from
the coasts have very cold winters, and much of the land
is covered with forests and lakes. Canada was formerly
owned by Britain and France, and is now an independent member of the *Commonwealth. Its capital city is
Ottawa, and its official languages are English and

French. Today there are still some tensions between
English and French speakers, especially in Quebec,
where many French speakers wish to form a separate
country. See also CABOT, HUDSON'S BAY COMPANY,
WOLFE.
▶ **Canadian** *adj, n.*

'Canada-U,nited 'States ,Free 'Trade
A,greement a 1989 agreement to end barriers to
trade between the US and Canada. It received the
approval of the US Congress in 1991 and the following
year Mexico was included in the new *North American
Free Trade Agreement.

▶**canals**

a narrow boat

Britain's canals (= man-
made channels of water
for boats to travel along)
were built in the late 18th
and early 19th centuries,
at the start of the
*Industrial Revolution.
They provided a cheap
and convenient means of
transport for heavy goods,
especially between the
mining and industrial
centres of the Midlands
and north-west England.
Coal, grain, clay and other
materials were transported on **narrow boats**, also called
barges, that were pulled along by horses walking along
a **towpath** beside the canal. Many miles of channel had
to be dug, with some sections passing through tunnels or
over **aqueducts**. Hundreds of **locks** were built to enable
boats to go up or down a hill. A **flight** (= series) of 20 or
30 locks was needed on some steep sections.

In the US canals were used for a short period to transport goods to areas where there were no large rivers. The
most famous, the *Erie Canal in New York State, ran
from Buffalo on Lake *Erie to Albany on the *Hudson
River and connected New York City with *Ohio,
*Michigan and *Pennsylvania. Mules, not horses, were
used to pull the barges. The growth of the railway in the
1840s soon took business away from the canals, but the
canal system played an important role in expanding
trade and encouraging people to move west.

After the railways were built, many canals were filled
in. In Britain especially, canals that still exist have
become popular with people wanting a quiet country
holiday away from traffic. Old narrow boats have been
fitted with motors and converted to provide attractive
holiday accommodation. Speed is restricted on canals
so the pace is slow and restful. Some locks are operated
by **lock-keepers**, but many are **worked** (= opened and
closed) by people on the boats. Going through a flight
of locks is seen as part of the fun. At night, people
moor their boats at the side of the canal. Canals are
also popular with fishermen, and with walkers using
the towpath. Many pubs are built beside canals and
attract people enjoying a canal holiday or having a
day out.

In Britain, some people live in narrow boats and stay
most of the time on a particular stretch of canal. These
houseboats are often painted in bright colours, with
pictures of flowers on the side. On the flat roof there
are sometimes traditional jugs and pots painted with
similar designs.

Ca,nary **'Wharf** part of the *Docklands area of east
London, England, where modern offices were built in
the 1980s. The **Canary Wharf tower**, where several
newspapers have their offices, is the highest building in

C

Britain. Many offices in Canary Wharf were damaged when an *IRA bomb exploded there in 1996.

Canary Wharf

,**Cancer Re,search U'K** /juː ˈkeɪ/ a British organization that does research into the causes of cancer and tries to find new treatments for it. It receives its money from donations from the public and is one of the largest *charities in Britain. It was formed in 2002 when the Imperial Cancer Research Fund joined with the Cancer Research Campaign.

,**Candid 'Camera** a television programme that was popular in Britain and the US in the 1950s and 1960s. It showed members of the public who had been secretly filmed in funny or embarrassing situations. At the end of each section the person being filmed was told, 'Smile, you're on *Candid Camera!*'

,**George 'Canning** /ˈkænɪŋ/ (1770–1827) a British *Tory prime minister (1827). He died soon after becoming Prime Minister, and is better remembered for his period as *Foreign Secretary (1822–7), when he gave British support to many independence movements in Europe and South America. He is also well known for fighting a duel with his rival, Lord *Castlereagh.

'**Canterbury** /ˈkæntəbri; AmE ˈkæntərbri/ a city in *Kent, England, with many fine old buildings, including the famous cathedral, the central church of the *Church of England. It became a special place for Christians to visit after Thomas *Becket was killed there in 1170. It is now a popular tourist centre. Canterbury Cathedral was made a *World Heritage Site in 1988. See also ARCHBISHOP OF CANTERBURY. ⇨ note at CHURCH OF ENGLAND.

The ,**Canterbury 'Tales** /ˌkæntəbri; AmE ˌkæntərbri/ a long poem by Geoffrey *Chaucer, begun in 1387. It consists of the stories told by a varied group of pilgrims, people travelling from London to *Canterbury to show respect for St Thomas *Becket. It is one of the first great poems in English, and some of the stories are well known for referring to sex in humorous ways.

,**Eddie 'Cantor** /ˈkæntə(r)/ (1892–1964) a US comedian and singer who performed in films and on stage, radio and television. He was known for his cheerful personality, big eyes and high voice. He began in 1917 with the *Ziegfeld Follies and his best-known songs were *Making Whoopee* and *If You Knew Susie*. In 1956 he received a special *Oscar.

Ca'nute /kəˈnjuːt/ (also **Cnut**) (c. 994–1035) a king of England (1017–35) who was born in Denmark and was also king of Denmark and Norway. He is best remembered for the story of how he proved to his companions that not everything in the world obeyed him. He took them to the sea and ordered it to stop rising, but it continued to rise. Canute's name is now sometimes used when describing somebody who foolishly tries to do

something impossible: *He was the King Canute of Parliament, trying to turn back the tide of reform.*

CAP /ˌsiː eɪ ˈpiː/ ⇨ COMMON AGRICULTURAL POLICY.

,**Cape Ca'naveral** /kəˈnævərəl/ the US base in *Florida on the Atlantic coast where spacecraft and rockets are launched by *NASA. It has been used for this since 1947 and was named **Cape Kennedy** between 1963 and 1973.

,**Cape 'Cod** /ˈkɒd; AmE ˈkɑːd/ a summer holiday area in the US state of *Massachusetts, on the Atlantic coast. The most popular towns are Hyannis and Provincetown. Cape Cod is also known for growing cranberries (= red berries eaten especially at Thanksgiving). The *Pilgrim Fathers landed there in 1620.

Cape Cod

the ,**caped cru'sader** ⇨ BATMAN.

,**capital 'gains tax** *n* [C, U] (*abbr* **CGT**) (in Britain) a tax on the profits people make from selling investments (= things in which they have invested money), such as shares or property.

▶ **capital punishment**

Capital punishment is the legal killing of a person for a crime they have been proved in a court of law to have committed. In the US the **death penalty** is used in 38 states. In 1972 the *Supreme Court decided that it was 'cruel and unusual punishment', which the *Constitution does not allow, and it became illegal until 1976, when the Court changed its mind.

Each state decides what methods of **execution** (= killing) will be used. This is usually a **lethal injection** (= an injection of a poisonous chemical) but other methods used include the **electric chair** (= a chair which sends a strong electric current through the prisoner's body), and, rarely, **hanging**, a **firing squad** (= a group of soldiers who shoot the prisoner), and the **gas chamber** (= a room that is filled with poisonous gas when the prisoner is inside).

In the US the death penalty is passed on people found guilty of murder. Since 1976 over 900 people have been executed. Most people who receive the **death sentence** appeal to higher courts, and the sentence may be changed. The legal system moves slowly, so that a long time passes between the sentence being given and the execution taking place. The result is that there are about 3500 prisoners **on death row**, i.e. waiting to be executed. The state governor can give a **stay of execution** (= a delay so that the prisoner has time to appeal to another court) or a **pardon**. This can happen at any time until the execution takes place.

Another reason why many death sentences are not carried out is that there is strong opposition to capital punishment. People argue that it is immoral and that if a mistake is made it cannot be put right. They also say that the death penalty does not prevent people from committing murder. Another strong argument is that more African Americans who are found guilty of murder are sentenced to death than other racial groups and this is unfair.

In Britain the death penalty for murder was abolished in 1965, but it can still be passed on anyone found guilty of treason (= crimes against the state). Some British people think that the death penalty should be brought back for crimes such as terrorism (= the use of violence for political aims) or the murder of a police officer, but Parliament has voted several times against this. In former times about 200 crimes were **capital offences**, punishable by **hanging**. The wooden **gallows** or **gibbet** on which criminals were hanged can still be seen in some places. Many criminals were hanged in public at *Tyburn in London, and later at *Newgate prison. Traitors were **hanged, drawn and quartered**, i.e. hanged on the gallows, then taken down whilst still alive and their intestines cut out. Their heads were cut off and their bodies cut into four pieces.

ˌ**Capital 'Radio** a commercial radio station in London, England, which plays pop music and has advertisements. The company that owns it also owns several other local radio stations in southern England and **Capital Gold**, a station that plays pop music of the 1960s, 1970s and 1980s.

the ˈ**Capitol** /ˈkæpɪtl/ the building where the US Congress meets, on *Capitol Hill in Washington, DC. The *Senate meets in the north side and the *House of Representatives in the south side. The building was begun in 1793, burnt by the British army in 1814 and built again in 1863.

the Capitol

ˌ**Capitol 'Hill** /ˌkæpɪtl/ **1** the hill in Washington, DC, on which the US *Capitol stands.
2 (also **the Hill**) (informal) the US Congress: Capitol Hill decided to lower taxes.

ˌ**Al Ca'pone** /kəˈpəʊn/ (1898–1947) a powerful leader of organized crime in *Chicago, during the period of *Prohibition. His nickname was Scarface. He had seven rival criminals murdered in the *St Valentine's Day Massacre, but the police could not find enough evidence on which to arrest him. He was finally sent to prison in 1931 for not paying enough income tax.

ˌ**Truman Ca'pote** /ˌtruːmən kəˈpəʊti; AmE kəˈpoʊti/ (1924–84) a US writer. His best-known works are Breakfast at Tiffany's (1958) and the 'non-fiction novel' In Cold Blood (1966). Film versions were made of both books. Capote became popular with members of New York society but was later rejected after writing unpleasant things about them.

ˌ**Frank 'Capra** /ˈkæprə/ (1897–1991) a US film director known especially for his comedies. His best films show

an ordinary, good person fighting against evil people in business or government. Capra received *Oscars for It Happened One Night (1934), Mr Deeds Goes to Town (1936) and You Can't Take It With You (1938).

ˌ**Jennifer Capri'ati** /ˌkæpriˈɑːti/ (1976–) a US tennis player. She had a lot of success while still very young but was then arrested for stealing and possessing drugs. She stopped playing tennis seriously in 1994 but returned in 1996. Her experience is often seen as an example of the pressures of professional sport on young players.

ˌ**Captain 'Beefheart** /ˈbiːfhɑːt; AmE ˈbiːfhɑːrt/ (1941–) a US *rock musician with a harsh voice who also played the saxophone and who had a great influence on *punk(1) rock music. He was born Don Van Vliet and began his recording career in 1964. Albums recorded by him and his Magic Band included Safe as Milk (1967), Trout Mask Replica (1969) and Ice Cream for Crow (1982). Captain Beefheart himself gave up performing in 1982 to become a painter.

ˌ**Captain 'Hook** a character in J M *Barrie's play *Peter Pan. He is the leader of the pirates and has a metal hook instead of one of his hands.

ˌ**Captain Kanga'roo** a US children's television programme. It began in 1953 and continued for nearly 30 years, longer than any other programme of its kind. It won an *Emmy award in 1978.

ˌ**Captain 'Kidd** /ˈkɪd/ ⇨ KIDD.

ˌ**Captain 'Marvel** a US comic book character. He began in 1940 in Whiz Comics and has also appeared in Marvel Comics and DC Comics. He was an ordinary man who changed into a 'super hero' by saying 'Shazam'. Other characters were Mary Marvel and Captain Marvel, Junior. The stories had unusual titles, such as 'The Mad Master of the Murder Maze'. ⇨ note at COMICS AND COMIC STRIPS.

ˌ**car 'boot sale** n (BrE) an informal market, often in a field, where people sell things from the backs of their cars or from tables. People usually sell books, clothes, children's toys, etc. which they no longer want, but some people use the sales to sell stolen goods or illegally copied music, videos or computer programs. Car boot sales are very popular in Britain and take place regularly in many parts of the country: The tools didn't cost much – I got them at a car boot sale.. Compare GARAGE SALE.

ˌ**cardboard 'city** n a place in a city where many people with nowhere to live sleep, often using pieces of cardboard as beds or shelters.

ˈ**Cardiff** /ˈkɑːdɪf; AmE ˈkɑːrdɪf/ the capital city of Wales, in the south-east of the country. It is an important industrial city and port, and a major cultural centre. It is governed by a unitary authority.

ˌ**Lord 'Cardigan** /ˈkɑːdɪgən; AmE ˈkɑːrdɪgən/ (James Brudenell 1797–1868) a British army officer, well known for leading the *Charge of the Light Brigade during the *Crimean War.

CARE /ˈkeə(r); AmE ˈker/ (in full the **Cooperative for American Relief Everywhere**) a private US charity. It was established as the Cooperative for American Remittances to Europe in 1945, to help Europeans after the *World War II by sending **CARE packages** of food and other items. Today these are sent to refugees (= people forced from their homes by war or other events) and people who have survived natural disasters. The phrase 'CARE package' is sometimes also used in a humorous way to mean a parcel of items sent by US parents to children who are away from home.

ˌ**care in the com'munity** n [U] (in Britain) the policy of taking people out of institutions such as special hospitals for the mentally ill, and letting them live in their own homes with some help from the local social ser-

C

vices. Care in the community, which started in the 1980s, has been criticized when some of the people involved have been unable to look after themselves, and when former patients have committed crimes such as murder.

,George 'Carey /'keəri; *AmE* 'keri/ (1935–) the *Archbishop of Canterbury from 1991 to 2002. During his time as archbishop, Britain's first women priests were ordained. He was made a *life peer in 2002.

the ,Carib'bean /,kærə'bi:ən, kə'rɪbiən/ the area of the Caribbean Sea, to the east of Central America, that includes islands such as Cuba, Jamaica, Puerto Rico, Trinidad, Tobago and Barbados. Many of these islands, sometimes called the **West Indies**, are members of the British *Commonwealth. Most of the people living in the Caribbean are descended from African slaves taken there by people from Britain and other European countries in the 16th and 17th centuries. Since the 1950s, many people from these islands have come to live and work in Britain, and refer to themselves as **West Indians** or **Afro-Caribbeans**.

,*Caribbean* '*Times* /,kærɪbi:ən/ a British newspaper, published every week, which contains articles on politics, culture, sport and other subjects of interest to people in Britain's African-Caribbean community. It first appeared in 1981.

'Carling™ /'kɑːlɪŋ; *AmE* 'kɑːrlɪŋ/ *n* [U] a British make of lager, a type of pale light *beer. A series of amusing advertisements for Carling Black Label appeared in the 1980s and 1990s. They showed a man doing something very unusual or surprising, usually requiring special skill or strength, and somebody else saying, 'I bet *he* drinks Carling Black Label.'

,Will 'Carling /'kɑːlɪŋ; *AmE* 'kɑːrlɪŋ/ (1965–) a British *Rugby Union player who played for the *Harlequins club and was captain of the England team during one of their most successful periods (1988–96). His troubled private life received a lot of publicity.

Car'lisle /kɑː'laɪl; *AmE* kɑːr'laɪl/ a city in *Cumbria, England. It has been a border town between England and Scotland since the time when the Romans were in Britain, and as a result it has an interesting military history and many fine buildings.

,Carlsbad 'Caverns /,kɑːlzbæd; *AmE* ,kɑːrlzbæd/ a series of beautiful underground caves in the US state of *New Mexico. They were discovered in 1901 and are more than 40 miles/64 kilometres long. The **Carlsbad Caverns National Park** was made a *World Heritage Site in 1995.

the 'Carlton Club /'kɑːltən; *AmE* 'kɑːrltən/ a club in London, England, which is closely connected with the *Conservative Party. It was established by the *Tories in 1832. In 1922 the *1922 Committee was formed there.

,Carlton House 'Terrace /,kɑːltən; *AmE* ,kɑːrltən/ a fashionable street of large houses in central London, England, near *St James's Park. It contains the official home of the *Foreign Secretary.

,Thomas Car'lyle /kɑː'laɪl; *AmE* kɑːr'laɪl/ (1795–1881) a Scottish writer of books and essays about history and philosophy, who attacked the social injustice that resulted from the *Industrial Revolution. His best-known work is *The French Revolution* (1837). He was also famous for his public talks.

'Carmel /'kɑːmel; *AmE* 'kɑːrmel/ (*in full* **Carmel-by-the-Sea**) a small US town on the coast of central *California. Many rich people live there and it is a popular holiday town. The actor Clint *Eastwood was *mayor of Carmel from 1986 to 1988.

,Hoagy 'Carmichael¹ /,həʊgi 'kɑːmaɪkl; *AmE* ,hoʊgi 'kɑːrmaɪkl/ (1899–1981) a US song writer, piano player and singer. His songs are usually slow and beautiful.

The best known is *Stardust* (1927) and others include *Lazy River* (1931) and *In the Cool, Cool, Cool of the Evening* (1951) which won an *Oscar. Carmichael was chosen for the Songwriters' *Hall of Fame in 1971.

,Stokely 'Carmichael² /,stəʊkli 'kɑːmaɪkl; *AmE* ,stoʊkli 'kɑːrmaɪkl/ (1941–98) an African American leader of the 1960s who introduced the idea of 'black power'. He led the *Student Nonviolent Coordinating Committee in 1966 and was later a member of the *Black Panthers. In 1969 he moved to Guinea and changed his name to Kwame Toure.

'Carnaby Street /'kɑːnəbi; *AmE* 'kɑːrnəbi/ a small street in central London, England, which was famous in the 1960s for its shops selling fashionable clothes: *In the 60s all the pop stars came to Carnaby Street. Now it's full of tourists buying souvenirs.*

,Andrew Car'negie¹ /kɑː'neɪgi; *AmE* kɑːr'neɪgi/ (1835–1919) a rich American who gave about $350 million to help good projects. He was born in Scotland and made his wealth in the steel industry. He gave money to organizations working for world peace and to build many libraries and other buildings, such as *Carnegie Hall.

,Dale 'Carnegie² /kɑː'neɪgi; *AmE* kɑːr'neɪgi/ (1888–1955) a US author and public speaker. He is best known for his book *How to Win Friends and Influence People* (1936), a guide on how to achieve success in life. It is still in print and is probably the most successful book of its kind ever written. Carnegie also wrote *How to Stop Worrying and Start Living* (1948), and established the Carnegie Institute for Effective Speaking and Human Relations.

Car,negie 'Hall /,kɑːnəgi; *AmE* ,kɑːrnəgi/ a large concert hall in New York, used for all types of music. When it first opened in 1891 it was called the Music Hall, but in 1898 it was named after Andrew *Carnegie. Performers there have included Yehudi *Menuhin and *the Beatles. There were plans to destroy it in the late 1950s but a campaign by well-known musicians saved it.

the Car,negie 'Medal /kɑː,neɪgi; *AmE* kɑːr,neɪgi/ **1** (in Britain) an award for the best children's book published each year, made by the Library Association and named after Andrew *Carnegie. The first book to win the award was Arthur *Ransome's *Pigeon Post* (1936). **2** (in the US) a medal given to citizens of the US and Canada who risk or lose their lives trying to save someone's life. The award was started in 1904 by Andrew *Carnegie who provided money for a fund to help winners who suffered as a result of their action and to help the survivors of those who lost their lives.

,Anthony 'Caro /'kɑːrəʊ; *AmE* 'kɑːroʊ/ (1924–) an English sculptor, well known for his large abstract sculptures of brightly painted metal. He was one of the first artists to leave his finished works on the floor, instead of putting them on a stand. He was made a *knight in 1987.

▶ **carols and carol singing**

Carols are traditional songs that are sung just before *Christmas. Many of them celebrate the birth of Jesus Christ.

Carols were first sung in the 14th century. They were popular songs with a lively tune, and contained references to the celebrations and feeling of goodwill associated with Christmas, as well as to Christ's birth. One of the oldest printed carols, dating from 1521, is the *Boar's Head Carol*, which was sung in Queen's College, *Oxford as Christmas lunch was carried in. Other traditional carols that are thought to have originated at this time include *God Rest You Merry, Gentlemen* and *While Shepherds Watched Their Flocks by Night*.

In England during the 16th century, the *Puritans tried to stop people singing carols, but the words continued to be handed down from one generation to the next. In the 19th century many of these carols were collected and printed. Some tunes were taken from *folk songs, others were specially written. Many of the most popular carols heard today date from this time. They include *O Come, All Ye Faithful, *Hark! the Herald Angels Sing, *Good King Wenceslas, *Away in a Manger and *O Little Town of Bethlehem.

Traditional carols are very popular in Britain and America, but children also like more modern songs, such as *Rudolph, the Red-nosed Reindeer, about how a reindeer's bright red nose lights the way for *Santa Claus to take toys to children during a storm, and Frosty the Snowman, which tells the story of a figure made of snow who comes to life.

In the 19th century groups of **carol singers**, called *waits*, used to gather in the streets to play and sing for local people, who thanked them by offering drinks or mince pies (= small round pies containing dried fruit, apples and sugar). This custom became known as **was-sailing** and still continues in Britain, with people meeting to sing carols in most town and village centres. Any money that is collected is given to charity. Some singers walk from street to street, singing carols outside each house. In the US door-to-door carol singing is not common, except in a few small communities. Families sing carols when they decorate the Christmas tree.

Carols are also sung in churches and, in Britain, in schools, in special Christmas services. One of the most famous **carol services** is the *Festival of Nine Lessons and Carols, which is performed at *King's College, Cambridge, and broadcast on *BBC radio on Christmas Eve.

'carpet,bagger n (disapproving) **1** (AmE old use) a politician from the north who became active in the southern US after the American *Civil War in order to take advantage of the political situation there.

2 (especially AmE) any politician who hopes for success in an area where he or she is not known.

Jim 'Carrey / 'kæri / (1962–) a US comic actor, born in Canada. His best-known film is Ace Ventura: Pet Detective (1994). He was paid $20 million to act in Cable Guy (1997), the most ever paid to a comic actor at the time.

Lewis 'Carroll /'kærəl/ (1832–98) an English writer, best known for his children's books *Alice in Wonderland and *Through the Looking Glass. He also wrote nonsense verse. He taught mathematics at *Oxford University. His real name was Charles Dodgson.

Carry 'On film n any in a series of popular British comedy films made mostly in the 1960s and 1970s with the same group of actors, including Sid James, Kenneth *Williams and Hattie Jacques. The films had titles like Carry On Nurse and Carry On up the Khyber, and were full of rude jokes about sex and parts of the body.

Edward 'Carson[1] /'kɑːsn; AmE 'kɑːrsn/ (1854–1935) an Irish politician and lawyer, well known as the lawyer who questioned Oscar *Wilde at his trial in 1895. He was against *Home Rule in Ireland, and led the Northern Irish opposition to it. He was made a *knight in 1900 and a *life peer in 1921.

Johnny 'Carson[2] /'kɑːsn; AmE 'kɑːrsn/ (1925–2005) a US television star who presented The *Tonight Show for 30 years from 1962 to 1992. He was known for his friendly personality and easy style. Each programme was introduced with the words 'Here's Johnny!'.

Kit 'Carson[3] /'kɑːsn; AmE 'kɑːrsn/ (1809–68) a US explorer, guide and army officer in the American *Wild West. He was an Indian agent (= a government official dealing with Native Americans) in 1853 and was in the

Union army during the *Civil War. Carson City, *Nevada, is named after him.

Rachel 'Carson[4] / 'kɑːsn; AmE 'kɑːrsn/ (1907–64) a US scientist and author. Her book Silent Spring (1963), about the threat to animals from farm chemicals, helped to change the way such chemicals are used. She also wrote The Sea Around Us (1951).

Willie 'Carson[5] /'kɑːsn; AmE 'kɑːrsn/ (1942–) a British jockey, born in Scotland. He is one of the most successful jockeys of all time, winning most of the important British races. He retired from racing in 1997.

'car tax (also **road tax**) n [U, C] (in Britain) tax paid by the owners of motor vehicles. People who pay the tax receive a **tax disc** (also called a **road fund licence**) which they must display, usually in a corner of the front window of their vehicle. It is illegal to have a vehicle on a public road without a tax disc.

Angela 'Carter[1] /'kɑːtə(r); AmE 'kɑːrtər/ (1940–92) an English writer of fiction. She was especially known for describing magical or impossible situations in a realistic way. Her best-known novels are Nights at the Circus (1984) and Wise Children (1991). She also wrote the film The Company of Wolves (1984), which was based on one of her stories.

Jimmy 'Carter[2] /'kɑːtə(r); AmE 'kɑːrtər/ (1924–) the 39th US *President (1977–81), a member of the *Democratic Party and known for his strong moral principles. He arranged for the *Camp David peace agreement in 1979 between Egypt and Israel. In the same year, an attempt to rescue Americans being held as hostages in Iran was a failure and he lost the following election to Ronald *Reagan. He has since represented the US in international situations. In 1982 he started the **Carter Center**, an international human rights organization. He received the *Nobel Prize for peace in 2002.

Nick 'Carter[3] /'kɑːtə(r); AmE 'kɑːrtər/ a US detective character in more than 500 *dime novels, a magazine, radio and television series, and films. He was created in 1886 by John Russell Coryell and Ormond G Smith, and the later stories were by many different writers.

the 'Carter ,Family /'kɑːtə; AmE 'kɑːrtər/ a US family of *folk music singers. The original Carter Family performed from 1927 to 1941 and included A P Carter, his wife Sara and his brother's wife Maybelle. Their successful songs included Wabash Cannonball and Will the Circle Be Unbroken? 'Mother' Maybelle later formed a second Carter Family with her three daughters. In 1970 the original Carter Family was the first group chosen for the Country Music *Hall of Fame.

Barbara 'Cartland /'kɑːtlənd; AmE 'kɑːrtlənd/ (1900–2000) an English writer of popular romantic fiction. She wrote over 700 books, and sold over a billion copies. She was also well known for encouraging people to eat healthy food, and wearing very colourful (especially pink) dresses. She was made a *dame(2) in 1991.

Raymond 'Carver /'kɑːvə(r); AmE 'kɑːrvər/ (1938–88) a US writer of short stories and poetry. He used short, simple sentences and wrote about poor American workers. His works were collected in several books, including Cathedral (1983) and Ultramarine (1985). See also ALTMAN.

Casa'blanca /ˌkæsə'blæŋkə/ a popular romantic film (1942) set in the North African town of Casablanca during World War II, with Humphrey *Bogart and Ingrid *Bergman. The film includes the song As Time Goes By. It won three *Oscars, including 'Best Picture'.

> 66 Play it again, Sam. 99
> a famous misquote from Casablanca

Ca'scades /kæ'skeɪdz/ a mountain range that runs from northern *California in the US to British Columbia in Canada. The range includes Mount *Rainier and Mount *St Helens.

,**Casey at the 'Bat** /,keɪsi/ a popular US poem (1888) by Ernest Lawrence Thayer, about a great baseball player who fails. Casey has a chance to win the game but he strikes out (= fails to hit the ball three times and is dismissed). The poem ends:

> 66 And somewhere men are laughing, and somewhere children shout;
> But there is no joy in Mudville – Mighty Casey has struck out. 99

,**Casey 'Jones** /,keɪsi 'dʒəʊnz/ a popular US song about a brave railway engineer called John Luther ('Casey') Jones (1864–1900). When the train he was driving was about to crash, Jones stayed on it to slow it down. The passengers survived the crash but Jones was killed. The song has the lines:

> 66 Casey said just before he died,
> 'There's two more roads that I'd like to ride.'
> The fireman said what could they be?
> 'The Southern Pacific and the Sante Fe.' 99

,**Johnny 'Cash** /'kæʃ/ (1932–2003) a US singer and writer of *country music. He was called 'The Man in Black' because he often wore black clothes. His successful songs include *I Walk the Line* (1956) and *A Boy Named Sue* (1969). He received many *Grammy awards, including one in 1994 for the album *American Recordings*. His wife June Carter was also a country music singer as is his daughter Roseanne.

,**cash for 'questions** (in Britain) the name given to events in 1996 when some *Conservative *Members of Parliament were accused of accepting money from business people in order to ask questions for them in *Parliament. The 'cash for questions affair' was one of the reasons why the *Conservatives were so badly defeated in the 1997 general election.

,**Mary Cas'satt** /kə'sæt/ (1844–1926) a US artist known especially for her paintings of mothers and children. She worked mostly in France, where she was a student of Degas and became a member of the Impressionist group. One of her most famous paintings is *Woman Bathing* (1891).

,**Butch 'Cassidy¹** /,bʊtʃ 'kæsədi/ (1869–c. 1908) the leader of a group of criminals in the American *Wild West called the 'Wild Bunch' or the 'Hole-in-the-Wall Gang'. Another member of the group was Harry Longbaugh, also called the 'Sundance Kid'. They robbed trains in *Wyoming. Both Cassidy and Longbaugh disappeared to Bolivia and may have died there. Their story was told in the 1969 film *Butch Cassidy and the Sundance Kid* with Paul *Newman and Robert *Redford.

,**Hopalong 'Cassidy²** /,hɒpəlɒŋ 'kæsədi; *AmE* ,hɑːpəlɔːŋ/ a character in a series of US Western books, films and television programmes. He was created by the writer Clarence E Mulford and used in 26 books written between 1912 and 1956. William Boyd (1898–1972) played him in 66 films, beginning in 1935. Hopalong, also called 'Hoppy' by his friends, wore black and was very polite.

,**Hugh 'Casson** /'kæsn/ (1910–1999) an English architect and artist. He was the director of architecture for the *Festival of Britain and has designed several important buildings. He has also published books of his drawings, and was President of the *Royal Academy (1976–84). He was made a *knight in 1952.

,**Barbara 'Castle** /'kɑːsl; *AmE* 'kæsl/ (1911–2002) a British *Labour politician. She was a government minister in the 1960s and 1970s and the leader of the Labour group in the *European Parliament (1979–89). She was made a *life peer in 1990.

,**Castle 'Howard** /'haʊəd; *AmE* 'haʊərd/ a large and grand house in *Yorkshire, England, designed by *Vanbrugh and *Hawksmoor in the early 18th century. It is well known for its *baroque style and decoration.

,**Lord 'Castlereagh** / 'kɑːslreɪ; *AmE* 'kæslreɪ/ (born Robert Stewart 1769–1822) a British *Tory politician who was responsible for the *Act of Union with Ireland (1800). In 1809 he fought a duel with his rival, Canning, and left the government. He returned as *Foreign Secretary (1812–22). After the *Napoleonic Wars he tried to keep the balance of power between European states.

▶ **castles**

Thick walls and strong towers are characteristic features of Britain's castles. When built, they were solid buildings with few comforts, designed for the defence of a town or region. About 1200 castles were built in the 11th and 12th centuries, but the grandest were built in *Edward I's reign (1272–1307). These include the castles of *Caernarfon, Conwy and *Harlech, all in Wales, which were built by Edward after he defeated the Welsh leader Llewelyn ap Gruffydd. Many Scottish castles were built between the 13th and 17th centuries. They were **tower houses**, square buildings five or six floors high with small towers on top.

Few castles are now lived in. Some are museums and contain valuable old furniture and weapons; others are ruins. Many are open to the public and are popular tourist attractions.

The site for a castle was very important. It needed to be on top of a hill or steep cliff, and to have a reliable source of water. The earliest **fortifications**, dating from the 9th century, consisted of earthen **ramparts** (= high banks of soil) and a **stockade** (= wooden fence).

In the 11th century, the *Normans built **motte and bailey** castles. On top of a **motte**, a steep bank of earth, they built a wooden tower surrounded by a **palisade** (= fence). Around this was a **bailey** (= courtyard) which was surrounded by another palisade and a ditch. Later, wooden towers were replaced with stone towers, called **keeps**. The tower contained accommodation for people living in the castle, a **great hall** where they ate meals, and often a **dungeon**, a room under the ground where prisoners could be kept. The Great Tower at the *Tower of London, begun in 1078, is one of the earliest stone keeps.

In the 13th century, wooden fences were replaced by long, high **curtain walls** made of stone, with **battlements** (= a wall with gaps in it at intervals) along the top. Walls might be 10 feet/3 metres thick. Towers often projected outwards at the base so that people attacking could easily be seen from above.

Many castles had a strong **gatehouse** or a **moat** (= a deep, wide channel of water) which was crossed by a **drawbridge** that was raised and lowered by chains operated from inside the gatehouse. There was also a thick door and a **portcullis**, heavy metal grating that slid down to block the entrance.

The main method of attacking a castle was to fill the moat with stones and to attack the walls with **battering rams** (= heavy wooden beams). Stones and balls of fire were thrown into the castle by **siege engines**. Attackers also dug tunnels under the walls. Defenders shot arrows from the battlements or through **slit windows** (= very narrow openings), or poured hot oil onto the attackers. In later times **cannon** were used. If the castle was strong and could not be captured, the attackers would **besiege** it until the defenders had no more food and were forced to surrender.

'Casualty a popular British television *soap opera, set in a hospital. It has been broadcast regularly by the *BBC since 1986.

Catcher in the 'Rye a US novel (1951) by J D *Salinger. The story is about Holden Caulfield, a young man who runs away from school and finds the adult world to be false and unfair. The book was very popular with students in the 1950s, and is widely regarded as a major novel about the problems of growing up.

Catch-22 /ˌkætʃ twentiˈtuː/ a comic but serious US novel (1961) about the madness of war. It was written by Joseph Heller (1923–1999), and a film version was made in 1970. The story is about a US Air Force pilot during World War II. He hates the war and tries to avoid having to fly planes. The book was a great success with US students in the 1960s. The expression *Catch-22* has now entered the English language, meaning an unpleasant situation from which you cannot escape because you need to do one thing before doing a second, and you cannot do the second thing before doing the first: *We're in a Catch-22 situation.*

> **66** There was only one catch and that was Catch-22, which specified that a concern for one's own safety in the face of dangers that were real and immediate was the process of a rational mind … Orr would be crazy to fly more missions and sane if he didn't, but if he was sane he had to fly them. If he flew them he was crazy and didn't have to; but if he didn't want to he was sane and had to. **99**

Willa 'Cather /ˌwɪlə ˈkæðə(r)/; *also* ˈkæθə(r)/ (1876–1947) a US writer of novels, short stories and poetry. She began as a teacher and journalist. Her stories were often about the US West. She won the *Pulitzer Prize for *One of Ours* (1922) and for *Death Comes for the Archbishop* (1927).

Catherine of 'Aragon /ˈærəgən/ (1485–1536) a Spanish princess who in 1509 became the first wife of King *Henry VIII of England. They had six children, all of whom died soon after being born except for *Mary I. Henry wanted a son to be the next king, and had the marriage annulled in 1533. The Pope did not agree with this, and the *Reformation was a result of the divorce.

'Catholic ⇨ ROMAN CATHOLIC.

the 'Catholic 'Agency for 'Overseas De'velopment ⇨ CAFOD.

the 'Catholic 'Herald a British religious newspaper, published once a week. Most of the writing is about *Roman Catholic matters, but the newspaper is independent, and often disagrees with the ideas of the Church.

Cathy Come 'Home a British television play about a young mother who has nowhere to live. It was directed by Ken Loach and first broadcast by the *BBC in 1966. It had a strong effect on the British public, who did not know about the problems of homelessness until they saw it.

Cats a musical show (1981) by Andrew *Lloyd Webber, based on *Old Possum's Book of Practical Cats*, a book of poems by T S *Eliot. It has been very successful in many cities around the world and has been shown in London and New York longer than any other musical show in history.

the 'Catskill 'Mountains /ˈkætskɪl/ (*also* **the Catskills**) a range of low mountains in the US in southeast New York State. They are part of the *Appalachian Mountains and a popular holiday region. See also BORSCHT BELT.

'catsup /ˈkætsʌp/ ⇨ KETCHUP.

CATV /ˌsiː eɪ tiː ˈviː/ (*in full* **Community Antenna Television**) the oldest US company supplying cable television. It serves areas that cannot receive normal signals or receive them badly. The name is still sometimes used for all cable television.

▶ **caucus**

In US politics the word *caucus* is used to refer to several different types of meeting, usually held by a group of people in private.

Leaders and important people in political parties may hold a caucus in order to choose and agree privately on candidates for public office. Until the early 1800s, caucuses decided who would be candidates for President. Now, they mostly choose candidates for local offices. Candidates for important positions are openly elected by party members through elections.

A *caucus* can also refer to a meeting of the members of each party in *Congress or in a state legislature (= government) to decide what political action the party will take. In a majority party a caucus also decides which people will hold important positions, e.g. be in charge of committees. In Congress the word *conference* is sometimes used instead of *caucus*.

More generally, *caucus* can be used to describe any private meeting of politicians to decide something between themselves. Americans have a strong belief that political processes and institutions should be public and open, and so the word *caucus*, since it refers to a secret and private activity, is often used in a negative or disapproving way.

Holden 'Caulfield /ˌhəʊldən ˈkɔːlfiːld; *AmE* ˌhoʊldən/ ⇨ CATCHER IN THE RYE.

Steve 'Cauthen /ˈkɔːθən/ (1960–) a US jockey. He moved to Britain in 1979 and became the first person to win both the *Kentucky Derby (1978) and the British *Derby (1985 and 1987) He retired from racing in 1993.

Cava'lier *n* [often pl] a supporter of King *Charles I in the *English Civil War. The name Cavaliers, which originally meant soldiers on horses, was first used by their enemies, the *Roundheads, to show their disapproval of the Cavaliers' enthusiasm for war: *The children play war games like Roundheads and Cavaliers in the playground.*

Edith 'Cavell /ˈkævl/ (1865–1915) an English nurse who became a national heroine in *World War I. From the *Red Cross hospital where she worked in Belgium she helped many Allied soldiers to escape to Holland, before she was caught and shot by the Germans.

the 'Cavendish La,boratory /ˈkævəndɪʃ/ a centre for scientific experiments in *Cambridge, England. Since it was set up in 1871 many famous discoveries have been made there, including parts of the atom and the structure of DNA (= the substance in the human body that passes from parents to children and makes it possible to identify every individual human being).

the 'Cavern Club a nightclub in *Liverpool, England. It is famous as the place where the *Beatles first performed in the early 1960s.

William 'Caxton /ˈkækstən/ (c. 1422–91) the man who set up the first printing firm in Britain. He printed his first book in 1474. By printing books in English, Caxton had a strong influence on the spelling and development of the language. Many of the books he published were French stories which he translated himself.

the 'Cayman ,Islands /ˈkeɪmən/ a group of three islands in the *Caribbean Sea, north-west of *Jamaica. The islands were a British colony from the 17th century until they became independent in 1962, when they voted to remain under British control. Their main industries are banking and tourism.

CB /ˌsiː ˈbiː/ ⇨ CITIZEN'S BAND.

the **CBI** /ˌsiː biː ˈaɪ/ (*in full* the **Confederation of British Industry**) the employers' organization in Britain, started in 1965 and paid for by member companies. It aims to keep the government and the public informed about the needs and problems of industry.

CBS /ˌsiː biː ˈes/ (*in full* **Columbia Broadcasting System**) one of the original three US national broadcasting companies. It began as a national radio company in 1927 and added television in the 1950s. The company also has branches in the recording and entertainment business. Compare ABC, NBC.

the **CBSO** /ˌsiː biː es ˈəʊ; *AmE* ˌsiː biː es ˈoʊ/ ⇨ CITY OF BIRMINGHAM SYMPHONY ORCHESTRA.

CDC /ˌsiː diː ˈsiː/ ⇨ CENTERS FOR DISEASE CONTROL AND PREVENTION.

CDT /ˌsiː diː ˈtiː/ ⇨ CENTRAL DAYLIGHT TIME.

ˌRobert ˈCecil /ˈsesl/ (1563–1612) a British politician who became Queen *Elizabeth I's most important minister after the death of his father, Lord *Burghley. He was made a *knight in 1591 and *Secretary of State in 1596. He remained an important politician when *James I became king.

ˈCeefax™ /ˈsiːfæks/ *n* [U] a British television information service provided by the *BBC. It offers many different types of information, e.g. weather reports, sports results and financial news, and the information is shown without sound on special channels: *According to Ceefax there are road works causing delays on the M6 near Preston.* See also TELETEXT.

ˈCeltic /ˈseltɪk/ a Scottish football team, based in *Glasgow. Traditionally, Celtic's supporters are from Glasgow's *Roman Catholic community, and their rivals, *Rangers, are supported by the *Protestants. Celtic and Rangers are the two most successful teams in the history of Scottish football. In 1967 Celtic became the first British team to win the *European Cup.

ˌCeltic ˈcross /ˌkeltɪk/ *n* a version of the Christian symbol of the cross, found mainly in Britain. It has a circle at the point where the two parts cross. The most famous crosses of this type are the ancient carved stone crosses found in Ireland.

the ˌCeltic ˈfringe /ˌkeltɪk/ *n* [sing] (*sometimes disapproving*) a name for the parts of Britain where many people are descended from *Celts, such as Scotland, Ireland, Wales and *Cornwall. The phrase is used mainly by people in England, who feel that they have a different way of life.

a Celtic cross

ˌCeltic ˈtwilight /ˌkeltɪk/ *n* [U] (*sometimes ironic*) the romantic and mysterious atmosphere that many people associate with the Irish people and their literature, including their belief in fairies, ghosts, etc. *The Celtic Twilight* is the title of a collection of stories (1893) by W B *Yeats.

the **Celts** /kelts/ a group of people whose influence spread to Britain and Ireland from Austria and Switzerland in the late *Bronze Age and *Iron Age. **Celtic culture** became established in Britain and continued during the Roman occupation. In the south and east it combined with Roman culture, but remained separate in Scotland, Ireland and parts of Wales and south-west England. Celtic society was organized in tribes, each of which had a king or chief and was then divided into warriors and noblemen, **druids** (= learned people) such as doctors, priests and craftsmen, and ordinary people. Different forms of the Celtic language developed including *Gaelic in Scotland and Ireland, and the Welsh and Cornish languages which are similar to Breton, the Celtic language of north-west France. The Celts are best known for their art, including the bronze objects, such as swords, brooches and mirrors which have been found buried with the dead. These objects had elaborate designs engraved on the metal or created with enamel (= a hard, coloured substance like glass). The Celtic tradition is also known for decorating texts from the Bible such as the *Book of Kells and the *Lindisfarne Gospels and for its gold and silver jewellery designs from the 7th and 8th centuries. Celtic stone crosses from the 8th to 10th centuries can still be seen in Scotland, Ireland, Wales and Cornwall.

the ˈCenotaph a stone monument in the middle of *Whitehall, London, built in memory of the members of the armed forces who died in the two *World Wars. Every year, on *Remembrance Sunday, the Queen and the leaders of the main political parties place wreaths (= arrangements of flowers) there as part of a special ceremony. The word *cenotaph* means 'empty tomb'.

ˈCENTCOM /ˈsentkɒm; *AmE* ˈsentkɑːm/ ⇨ UNITED STATES CENTRAL COMMAND.

ˈCenter Parcs a number of holiday villages in the UK and Europe operated by a Dutch company which opened its first centre in the UK in 1987. The accommodation is in small houses in the countryside, usually in a forest. There are cafes, restaurants and other facilities, and many sports and activities especially for families, usually including a large covered area with swimming pools surrounded by trees.

ˈCenters for Diˈsease Conˌtrol and Preˈvention (*abbr* **CDC**) the US government office in *Atlanta, *Georgia, that works to protect Americans from infectious and other diseases. It counts the numbers of cases, does medical research and sends out health information to the public. CDC was established in 1946 and is part of the US Department of Health and Human Services.

the ˌCentral ˈCriminal Court ⇨ OLD BAILEY.

ˌCentral ˈDaylight Time (*abbr* **CDT**) (in the US) the time used between early April and late October in the central states. It is an hour earlier than *Central Standard Time.

the ˌCentral Inˈtelligence ˌAgency ⇨ CIA.

ˌCentral ˈPark the large park in the middle of *Manhattan(1) in New York City. It is very popular but is known to be a dangerous place at night. Concerts are given on the Sheep Meadow in the summer. The park also contains *Cleopatra's Needle and a zoo.

the ˈCentral ˌSchool of ˈSpeech and ˈDrama a school for actors in central London. As well as being one of Britain's most important drama schools, it also trains speech therapists (= people who help those with speaking problems).

Central Park

Central 'Standard Time (*abbr* **CST**) (*also* **Central Time**) (in the US) the time used between late October and early April in the central states. It is six hours earlier than *Greenwich Mean Time.

Centre 'Point a tall office building at the end of *Oxford Street in central London, England. It was built in the 1960s but remained empty for several years. In the 1970s some people occupied it to protest against such a large building staying empty when so many people in London had nowhere to live. It is now a *listed building. A charity in central London for people without homes is also called Centre Point.

the Ceremony of the 'Keys a ceremony that takes place at 10 p.m. every night at the *Tower of London, when a *beefeater closes the gates, exchanges secret passwords with a guard, and gives him the keys.

the Cerne 'Giant /,sɜːn; *AmE* ,sɜːrn/ a very large figure of a naked man holding a heavy stick as a weapon, cut in ancient times in the side of a hill near Cerne Abbas in Dorset, England. The ground is chalk, so the figure appears white against the green grass.

the Cerne Giant

CGT /,siː dʒiː 'tiː/ ⇨ CAPITAL GAINS TAX.

'chain gang *n* (especially in the US) a group of prisoners who are made to work together joined by chains on their legs. The practice was considered cruel and was stopped in the 1960s, but it began again in 1996 in *Alabama and then in *Arizona and *Florida.

'Challenger /'tʃælɪndʒə(r)/ the name of the US space shuttle (= spacecraft that can be used again) which exploded in the air on 28 January 1986 and killed all seven astronauts in it. This disaster was seen on television by millions of people and resulted in flights with astronauts being stopped for two years. There were other *Challenger* spacecraft.

Austen 'Chamberlain[1] /,ɒstɪn 'tʃeɪmbəlɪn; *AmE* ,ɔːstɪn 'tʃeɪmbərlɪn/ (1863–1937) a British *Conservative politician and son of Joseph *Chamberlain. He was the leader of the Conservative Party (1921–2) and *Foreign Secretary (1924–9). He was given the *Nobel Prize for peace in 1925 for his work on fixing Germany's borders after *World War I.

Joseph 'Chamberlain[2] /'tʃeɪmbəlɪn; *AmE* 'tʃeɪmbərlɪn/ (1836–1914) a British *Liberal politician. He first became well known as the *mayor(1) of *Birmingham, where he was responsible for many improvements to the city's houses and services. He became a Member of Parliament in 1876, and was soon a *Cabinet minister. He left the Cabinet in 1886 because he disagreed with *Gladstone's policy of *Home Rule for Ireland.

Neville 'Chamberlain[3] /,nevɪl 'tʃeɪmbəlɪn; *AmE* 'tʃeɪmbərlɪn/ (1869–1940) a British *Conservative *prime minister (1937–40) and son of Joseph *Chamberlain. He is mainly remembered for his policy of *appeasement. He signed the *Munich Agreement in 1938, trying to avoid a war against Germany and Italy, but said that Britain would defend Poland if Germany attacked it. This led to the start of *World War II. He left the government soon after Britain entered the war, when British forces were defeated in Norway.

> **66** This is the second time in our history that there has come back from Germany to Downing Street peace with honour. I believe it is peace for our time. **99**
>
> Neville Chamberlain, September 1938

Wilt 'Chamberlain[4] /,wɪlt 'tʃeɪmbəlɪn; *AmE* 'tʃeɪmbərlɪn/ (1936–1999) a famous US *basketball player. His popular name was 'Wilt the Stilt' because he was very tall and thin. Stilts are poles used for walking high above the ground. Chamberlain played for the University of Kansas and then was a professional from 1959 to 1973 with teams in *Philadelphia, *San Francisco and *Los Angeles. During his professional career he scored 31 419 points, and he was chosen for the Basketball *Hall of Fame in 1978.

'Chamberlain's Men /'tʃeɪmbəlɪnz; *AmE* 'tʃeɪmbərlɪnz/ the most famous company of actors in *Elizabethan England. *Shakespeare joined them in 1594, and wrote most of his plays for the company.

chamber of 'commerce *n* an organization of local business people in a particular town or city formed to encourage, protect and improve their businesses.

the Chamber of 'Horrors a special part of *Madame Tussaud's waxworks museum in London, containing wax models of famous criminals and murder scenes: *His kitchen looked like something out of the Chamber of Horrors.*

champion 'jockey *n* (in Britain) the jockey who has won the most horse races in a season. There are two champion jockeys each year, the one who wins the most steeplechases (= races with jumps) in the winter, and the one who wins the most flat races (= ones without jumps) in the summer.

the 'Championship the second most important group of football teams in England, consisting of the top 24 teams in the *Football League. The top three teams in the Championship at the end of each season move up into the *Premiership for the following season. ⇨ note at FOOTBALL – BRITISH STYLE.

Charlie 'Chan /'tʃæn/ an American Chinese detective character in books, in films and on television, who regularly solved crimes which the police had failed to solve. He was created in 1925 by the author Earl Derr Biggers who based him on the real detective Chang Apana. More than 40 films were made with different actors playing

Chan, including Peter *Ustinov in 1980. Chan was very polite and was often helped by his 'Number One Son'. See also DETECTIVE STORY.

'Chancellor n **1** ⇨ CHANCELLOR OF THE EXCHEQUER.
2 (in Britain) the official head of a university. Chancellor is an honorary title. Compare VICE CHANCELLOR.
3 (in the US) the title of the head of some universities. Compare VICE CHANCELLOR. See also LORD CHANCELLOR.

the 'Chancellor of the 'Duchy of 'Lancaster /'læŋkəstə(r)/ a British *Cabinet minister who has almost no official duties, and so is free to work on any special jobs chosen by the *Prime Minister. The title remains from the 15th century, when the royal family came from *Lancashire(1), and owned land there.

the ˌChancellor of the 'Exchequer (also **the Chancellor**) the British government minister who is responsible for financial affairs. The Chancellor decides the government's economic policy with the *Prime Minister and makes decisions about taxes and government spending.

the ˌBattle of 'Chancellorsville /'tʃɑːnsələzvɪl; AmE 'tʃɑːnsələrzvɪl/ a major battle (1–5 May 1863) fought in *Virginia during the American *Civil War. The South, led by Robert E *Lee and Thomas 'Stonewall' *Jackson, defeated a large northern army. More than 30 000 soldiers died in the battle, including Jackson himself.

'Chancery Diˌvision (also **Chancery**) (in Britain) the section of the *High Court of Justice which deals mainly with commercial cases such as company law, patents (= official documents that give people the right to make, use or sell an invention, and stop other people from copying them) and bankruptcy. ⇨ note at LEGAL SYSTEM.

ˌRaymond 'Chandler /'tʃɑːndlə(r)/ (1888–1959) a US writer of crime novels. He created the tough detective character Philip *Marlowe who appears in several books, including *The Big Sleep* (1939). Chandler also wrote several films, including *Double Indemnity* (1944). See also DETECTIVE STORY.

ˌLon 'Chaney /ˌlɒn 'tʃeɪni; AmE ˌlɑːn/ (1883–1930) a US actor in silent films who often played ugly and frightening characters. He was known as the 'Man of a Thousand Faces' because he used make-up to change his appearance in many different parts. His best films include *The Hunchback of Notre Dame* (1923) and *The Phantom of the Opera* (1925). His son, Lon Chaney Junior (1906–73), also played similar characters in films.

'Changing the 'Guard a traditional and formal ceremony that takes place in London, England, when one set of soldiers guarding a royal building replaces another on duty. It takes place every day in summer, and every two days in winter outside *Buckingham Palace and outside the *Horse Guards(1) building on *Whitehall, and is very popular with tourists.

the 'Channel ⇨ ENGLISH CHANNEL.

ˌChannel 'Four a British commercial terrestrial television station that started broadcasting in 1982 and can be seen all over Britain, except Wales, which has *S4C. It is paid for by selling its advertising time. It broadcasts many cultural and educational programmes, as well as documentaries (= films presenting facts about real life) and programmes for minorities. Until 2002 Channel Four was also an important producer of British films with its business, Film Four.

the 'Channel ˌIslands n [pl] a group of islands in the *English Channel near the north-western coast of France. They have belonged to Britain since the *Normans arrived in the 11th century, although they are not officially part of the *United Kingdom. Each island has its own parliament and laws. The main islands are *Jersey(1), *Guernsey, *Alderney and *Sark. They are popular with British tourists because of their pleasant climate. They are also popular with people who want to invest money or avoid British taxes, since their taxes are lower than in Britain.

the ˌChannel 'Tunnel (also informal **the Chunnel**) a rail tunnel under the *English Channel between England and France. There had been proposals for a tunnel since the 19th century, but political and practical problems prevented any progress being made until the 1980s. It was opened in 1994 and is managed by *Eurotunnel, which also operates a train service through the tunnel for cars and trucks. Other trains using the tunnel include the *Eurostar passenger trains: *Cross-Channel ferry prices are lower than ever, thanks to competition from the Channel Tunnel.*

'chapel n **1** (in Britain) a place where *Nonconformists have their Christian religious services.
2 a part of a church or cathedral which has its own altar and is used for private prayer.
3 (BrE) a small building or room in a hospital, prison, school, cemetery, etc. that is used for Christian worship.
▶ **chapel** adj [not before noun] (old-fashioned) (in England and Wales) belonging to a *Nonconformist group: *Were your family church* (= *Anglican) or chapel?*

ˌchapel of 'rest n (BrE) a room in an undertaker's offices where dead bodies are kept before the funeral. Although called a chapel, it is not a religious place.

ˌCharlie 'Chaplin /'tʃæplɪn/ (1889–1977) an English film actor and director who did most of his work in the US. Most people consider him the greatest comic actor of the silent cinema. He appeared in many of his films as the best-known character he created, a poor man with a small round hat, a small moustache and trousers and shoes that are too big for him, causing him to walk in a funny way. He made many short comic films, such as *The Kid* (1921), and several longer films, such as *City Lights* (1931), *The Gold Rush* (1935) and *Modern Times* (1936), which combined comedy with social and political comments. He was made a *knight in 1975.

'Chap Stick™ n a stick of a substance like soft wax which is put on the lips to make them less sore or to protect them from the sun. Chap Sticks were first made in the US more than 100 years ago, and they are now available in various flavours.

the ˌCharge of the 'Light Brigade a famous attack by British cavalry (= soldiers on horses) during the *Crimean War in 1854. An order was understood wrongly, and the soldiers, armed only with swords, were sent into a valley with heavy guns on both sides of them. 247 out of 637 men were killed. The event is remembered as an outstanding example of bad military leadership and the blind courage of soldiers obeying orders. It is described in a famous poem by *Tennyson:

> 66 'Forward the Light Brigade!'
> Was there a man dismay'd?
> Not tho' the soldier knew
> Some one had blunder'd:
> Theirs not to make reply,
> Theirs not to reason why,
> Theirs but to do and die,
> Into the valley of Death
> Rode the six hundred. 99
> *The Charge of the Light Brigade*

ˌCharing 'Cross /ˌtʃærɪŋ/ an area of central London, England, where *Whitehall joins *Trafalgar Square. Its name comes from one of the stone crosses left at each place where the body of Queen *Eleanor of Castile spent a night on its way to be buried at *Westminster Abbey in 1290. The original cross was close to what is now Charing Cross Station, one of London's main train stations, for trains to and from south and south-east England, which also has a station on the *London Underground. A copy of the cross stands in front of the station. Charing Cross is considered to be the exact centre of London when measuring distances to other towns.

ˌ**Charing Cross 'Road** /ˌtʃærɪŋ/ a street in central London, England, which is famous for its second-hand bookshops. Many of London's most important shops selling new books are also on Charing Cross Road.

ˌ**Chariots of 'Fire** a film (1981) about the 1924 Olympic Games, in which Harold Abrahams, a British runner, won the gold medal for the 100 metres race. The film won several *Oscars and was very popular in Britain. Its title is a phrase from the poem *_Jerusalem_ by William *Blake.

▶ **charities**

Charities are independent organizations that help the poor, the homeless, children, old people and animals. They are involved with human rights, education, medical research and conservation of the environment. Many of them began in the time before governments provided any social services, when poor people had to turn to charitable organizations for help. Charities rely on money given by the public, and on help from volunteers in fund-raising and carrying out their activities.

In 2003 there were about 187 000 charities in Britain, with a total income of £30 billion. The charity with the highest income was *Cancer Research UK. Many charities that are now well known throughout the world, such as *Oxfam and *Amnesty International, began in Britain. Americans are also enthusiastic supporters of charities. In 2002 they gave over $240 billion. The *Salvation Army received the most money.

In Britain organizations qualify for **charitable status** if they are established for the 'public good'. Many charities ask well-known people, including members of the royal family, to become their **patrons**. Charities do not pay tax on the money they receive, but they are not allowed to make a profit.

Charities in Britain are not allowed to take part in political activity, so some set up a separate *pressure group which campaigns on related issues. The *Charity Commission keeps a list of charities and advises them. Well-known charities working in Britain include Oxfam, the British Heart Foundation, which pays for research into heart disease, *Barnardo's, *Age Concern, *Help the Aged and *Shelter

In the US religious organizations receive most money from the public, followed by those concerned with social services, education and health. Well-known charities include the Salvation Army, the *Red Cross, the *United Negro College Fund, which helps *African Americans get an education, and the American Cancer Society. Local charities operate shelters for the homeless and soup kitchens where poor people can eat free.

A lot of the work done by charities in the US, such as caring for the poor or providing education, is done in other countries by the government. Americans have a strong belief that, if possible, private groups, not the government, should do this work.

The traditional method of raising money is to organize a **flag day**. Volunteers stand in busy streets asking members of the public to put money in a **collecting tin**. In exchange, they are given a paper sticker, formerly a small paper flag with a pin through it, with the charity's name on it. This is sometimes called 'tin-rattling'. The *British Legion's flag day, called *Poppy Day, has become a feature of British life.

Nearly every town in Britain has several **charity shops**. These are run by volunteer staff and sell second-hand clothes, books and household goods at low prices in aid of charity. Some shops, e.g. Oxfam shops, also sell goods made by people who are benefiting from the charity's work. At *Christmas, people often buy **charity cards**, cards sold in aid of charity. Charity shops (_AmE_ **thrift shops**) are less common in the US, but include shops run by the Salvation Army and *Goodwill.

In recent years, the **telethon** has proved an effective method of fund-raising. During an evening of popular television programmes, television stars ask the public to telephone and **pledge** (= promise) money to the charities involved. The *Comic Relief evening in Britain and the muscular dystrophy telethon in the US are the most famous. Other fund-raising activities include **fêtes** (= outdoor sales of craftwork, plants, etc.) and **jumble sales** (= sales of second-hand goods). Sponsored walks, cycle rides, even parachute jumps, where people agree to give money to a person completing a task, are also popular. At Christmas or *Thanksgiving, schools and churches organize collections of food, called **food drives** in the US, for old people and the poor.

An important source of funds for charities in Britain is the *National Lottery, which gives a proportion of its income to 'good causes'.

In both Britain and the US many workers have money taken from their pay and sent to charity. This is called **payroll giving**. Some companies in the US hold **fund-raising drives**, in which different parts of the company compete to see which of them **pledges** the most money. The *United Way, a national organization that collects money to give to small local charities, benefits from this. As in Britain, many people leave money to charity in their will. It is also common, when somebody dies, for the family to ask people to send a contribution to a charity instead of sending flowers to the funeral.

the 'Charity Com,mission the British organization responsible for controlling all the charities in Britain. It is made up of five **Charity Commissioners**, who keep a list of all the charities, check that they are run properly, and make decisions about new groups that apply to become charities.

ˌ**Prince 'Charles**[1] (1948–) the present *Prince of Wales. He is the first son of Queen *Elizabeth II and the heir to the throne (= is expected to become the next British king). In 1981 he married Lady Diana Spencer, who became *Diana, Princess of Wales. They had two children but separated in 1992. In 2005 he married Camilla *Parker-Bowles with whom he had had a sexual relationship for many years. She became Duchess of *Cornwall when they married. Prince Charles is well known for his interest in architecture, in particular his dislike of modern architecture, and his concern for the environment. He is also a keen painter and has written a children's book, _The Old Man of Lochnagar_ (1980). ⇨ note at ROYAL FAMILY.

ˌ**Ray 'Charles**[2] (1930–2004) a blind US singer who wrote songs and played the piano. He recorded many kinds of music, including the *blues, *country music, *gospel and *jazz. His best-known songs include _I've Got a Woman_ (1955) and _Georgia on My Mind_ (1960). Charles received 19 *Grammy awards, eight of them in 2005 after his death, including those for _Hit the Road Jack_ (1961), _A Song for You_ (1963) and _Crying Time_ (1966), _Genius Loves Company_ (2005) and _Here We Go Again_ (2005).

Charles I /ˌtʃɑːlz ðə ˈfɜːst; AmE ˌtʃɑːrlz/ (1600–49) king of England, Scotland and Ireland (1625–49). He often disagreed with *Parliament, and in 1629 he stopped it meeting and tried to rule the country without it until 1640, when he needed Parliament to help raise money for a war against Scotland. The *Long Parliament refused to help him, and this led to the *English Civil War. Charles was arrested in 1647 and two years later he was killed by having his head cut off.

Charles II /ˌtʃɑːlz ðə ˈsekənd; AmE ˌtʃɑːrlz/ (1630–85) king of England, Scotland and Ireland (1660–85). He was the son of *Charles I. He spent most of the *English Civil War living abroad until *Parliament invited him to return to be king after the death of Oliver *Cromwell. He enjoyed the pleasures of life and was well known for having affairs with many women, including Nell *Gwyn. See also RESTORATION.

'Charleston /ˈtʃɑːlstən; AmE ˈtʃɑːrlstən/ **1** a beautiful US city on the coast of *South Carolina. The American *Civil War began here in 1861 when the South captured *Fort Sumter.
2 the Charleston n [sing] a lively dance, popular in the 1920s. It was named after the city of Charleston.

ˌCharley's 'Aunt /ˌtʃɑːliz; AmE ˌtʃɑːrliz/ a British comedy play (1892) by Brandon Thomas (1856–1914) which is still often performed, especially by amateur actors. It is about a man who pretends to be his friend's rich aunt from Brazil. Amusing and ridiculous things happen when the real aunt arrives.

ˌCharlie 'Brown ⇒ PEANUTS.

ˌBobby 'Charlton¹ /ˈtʃɑːltən; AmE ˈtʃɑːrltən/ (1937–2004) an English football player who played for *Manchester United (1954–73) and England. He scored 49 goals for England, more than any other player. He is best remembered for the exciting goals he scored by kicking the ball very hard from a long distance outside the goal area. He was made a *knight in 1994.

ˌJack 'Charlton² /ˈtʃɑːltən; AmE ˈtʃɑːrltən/ (1935–) an English football player who played for Leeds United (1952–73) and England. He often played in the England defence in the same team as his younger brother Bobby *Charlton. He later became a successful football manager, taking the Republic of Ireland team to the final rounds of the World Cup in 1990 and 1994.

'Charmin™ /ˈʃɑːmɪn; AmE ˈʃɑːrmɪn/ n [U] the name of a range of US paper products made by *Procter and Gamble. For many years television advertisements for soft Charmin toilet paper showed Mr Whipple, a supermarket employee, telling customers: 'Please don't squeeze the Charmin!'

'Charterhouse /ˈtʃɑːtəhaʊs; AmE ˈtʃɑːrtərhaʊs/ (also **Charterhouse School**) a British *public school which was built in 1611 at a place in London where a Carthusian monastery used to be. The pupils are still called **Carthusians**. In 1872 it moved to new buildings in *Surrey. It was a school for boys only until 1972, when girls were allowed into the *sixth form.

'charter school (in the US) a school which receives money from the state but which operates separately from the state system with its own aims and often its own way of teaching. Charter schools often specialize in teaching children with special education needs.

'Chartist /ˈtʃɑːtɪst; AmE ˈtʃɑːrtɪst/ n [usually pl] a member of a group of people in Britain in the 1830s and 1840s who supported the *People's Charter*. This document demanded improvements to the political system, such as the right to vote for all adult men, the right to vote in secret, and the right to become a Member of Parliament without owning land. Over three million people signed the Charter, and some Chartists took part in political vio-

lence, but most of the changes they demanded were not made until much later.

the charts n [pl] a list of pop music which changes regularly to show which song is selling the most copies.

'Chartwell /ˈtʃɑːtwel; AmE ˈtʃɑːrtwel/ a large house in *Kent, England, where Winston *Churchill lived from 1922 until he died. The house and gardens, which contain many objects from his life, are now open to the public as a museum.

Chase one of largest banks in the US, operating in many states. It used to have its main office in Manhattan, New York, where its history goes back over 200 years. It is now part of the JPMorgan Chase company and has its headquarters in Chicago and Delaware.

'Chatham¹ /ˈtʃætəm/ a town in *Kent, England, on the River *Medway. *Henry VIII established a royal dockyard for building ships there, and some of Britain's most important military ships were built there until 1984, when the dockyard became a museum.

the ˌEarl of 'Chatham² /ˈtʃætəm/ (William Pitt, also called Pitt the Elder 1708–78) a British *Whig(1) *Prime Minister (1756–61 and 1766–86) who was called the Great Commoner because he was so popular in the country. He was also known as a great speaker in *Parliament, and successfully led Britain in the *Seven Years War against France. See also PITT.

'chat show (BrE) (also especially AmE **talk show**) n a television or radio programme in which people, especially famous people, are invited to talk in an informal way about various topics.

'Chatsworth /ˈtʃætswəθ; AmE ˈtʃætswərθ/ a large and grand house in *Derbyshire, England, built in the 17th century. It is now open to the public, and attracts many tourists. Its beautiful gardens were originally designed by 'Capability' *Brown and Joseph Paxton (1801–65).

ˌChatta'nooga /ˌtʃætəˈnuːgə/ a US city in the state of *Tennessee. It is on the Tennessee River and next to Lookout Mountain. During the American *Civil War, Union soldiers climbed the mountain to defeat the Southern army at the Battle of Chattanooga (1863). The city is also well known because of the song *Chattanooga Choo Choo*.

ˌLady 'Chatterley /ˈtʃætəli; AmE ˈtʃætərli/ ⇒ LADY CHATTERLEY'S LOVER.

ˌThomas 'Chatterton /ˈtʃætətən; AmE ˈtʃætərtən/ (1752–70) an English poet. He wrote poetry in an old-fashioned style, and pretended it was the work of a 15th–century priest called Thomas Rowley, who never existed. In 1770 he came to London to produce an opera he had written. He was not very successful, and killed himself at the age of 17. His poetry and his death influenced the Romantic poets and the *Pre-Raphaelites and Chatterton is the subject of a novel of the same name published in 1987 by Peter Ackroyd. See also ROMANTICISM.

ˌGeoffrey 'Chaucer /ˈtʃɔːsə(r)/ (c. 1343–1400) an English poet. He is often called 'the father of English poetry' because he was the first major poet to write in English rather than Latin or French. His best-known work is The *Canterbury Tales*.

Céˌsar 'Chávez /ˌseɪˌzɑː ˈtʃɑːvez; AmE seɪˌzɑːr/ (1927–93) a Mexican-American trade union leader. In 1962, he organized the United Farm Workers Association. He also led several strikes which resulted in better pay and conditions for workers picking fruit and vegetables.

ˌ'Chubby' 'Checker /ˌtʃʌbi ˈtʃekə(r)/ (1941–) a US singer who was popular in the 1960s. He is mainly remembered for *The Twist* (1960) which created a craze (= something that is suddenly very popular or fashionable) for the dance of that name. He was born Ernest Evans and chose his new name as a humorous variation of the name Fats *Domino. (A checker and a domino are pieces used in different board games.).

'**Checkers** /'tʃekəz; *AmE* 'tʃekərz/ the name of a dog that belonged to Richard *Nixon. Nixon was accused of accepting money illegally when he was a candidate for Vice-President in 1952. He made an emotional speech on television and said the only gift he had accepted was his dog. This **Checkers speech** was a great success and made Nixon more popular. He was elected with President *Eisenhower.

,**Checkpoint 'Charlie** an official place at which people crossed the border between East Berlin and West Berlin during the time when the city was divided. It was opened in 1961. Checkpoint Charlie was moved in 1990 to a museum, and this was seen as a symbol of the end of the *Cold War.

,**checks and 'balances** a phrase that expresses one of the basic principles of government in the US. It means a system in which each branch of government has a certain amount of control over the other branches, creating a balance of power. For example, the *President can veto (= reject) laws passed by *Congress, but Congress can overcome this veto and even investigate the President and dismiss him from his job.

'**Cheddar** /'tʃedə(r)/ (*also* **Cheddar cheese**) *n* [U] a type of firm yellow cheese, originally made in Cheddar, a small town in *Somerset, England. It is Britain's best-known cheese, and is now made in many other countries. Most Cheddar has a mild flavour, but **farmhouse Cheddar**, which is still made in the traditional way, can be very strong.

,**Cheddar 'Gorge** /,tʃedə; *AmE* ,tʃedər/ a long deep valley in *Somerset, England. It is known for its attractive scenery and many caves in the cliffs around the valley, where people lived in prehistoric times.

'**Cheerios**™ /'tʃɪəriəʊz/ *n* [pl] a popular US cereal made of oats, usually eaten with milk at breakfast. Each piece is round with a hole in the middle.

Cheers a popular US comedy television programme of the 1980s and 1990s. It involved characters in a bar in *Boston and won several *Emmy awards.

,**John 'Cheever** /'tʃiːvə(r)/ (1912–82) a US author. His books are often about the private problems of families who seem to be successful. They include *The Wapshot Chronicle* (1957), *The Wapshot Scandal* (1964) and *Falconer* (1977). He also wrote short stories, many of which appeared in *The *New Yorker. Some were collected in *The Stories of John Cheever* (1978), which received the *Pulitzer Prize and other awards.

,**chef's 'salad** *n* a US salad that contains meat, lettuce and sometimes eggs, cheese or potatoes. A chef's salad is often large and eaten as a meal in itself.

'**Chelsea** /'tʃelsi/ **1** a district of London, England, on the north bank of the *Thames west of *Westminster(1). In the 19th and early 20th centuries many artists lived there and it had a reputation as an artistic area. Now it is one of the most fashionable and expensive parts of London to live in.
2 an English football club, based in *Fulham(1), West London, which has been successful in Britain and Europe at various times since the 1950s.

The ,**Chelsea 'Arts Club** /,tʃelsi/ a London club which was established in 1891 by a group of artists living in *Chelsea including *Whistler. It was well known for the **Chelsea Arts Ball**, a party held every year from 1910 to 1958 at the *Albert Hall, for which art students in London made special costumes and decorations.

the ,**Chelsea 'Flower Show** /,tʃelsi/ an exhibition of flowers, plants and garden design that takes place every year in the gardens of the *Chelsea Hospital, London. It is the most important garden exhibition in Britain, and a major social event.

,**Chelsea 'Hospital** /,tʃelsi/ (*also* **Chelsea Royal Hospital**) a large building in *Chelsea, London, built in the 1680s by *Charles II as a home for 440 old or injured soldiers, who became known as the *Chelsea Pensioners. It was designed by Christopher *Wren.

,**Chelsea 'Pensioner** /,tʃelsi/ *n* [often pl] any of the former soldiers who live at *Chelsea Hospital, London. They can often be seen in the *Chelsea area wearing their traditional uniform, long red coats in summer and long blue coats in winter.

Chelsea Pensioners

,**Chelsea 'Physic Garden** /,tʃelsi 'fɪzɪk/ one of Britain's oldest botanical gardens, where plants and trees are grown for scientific study. It was established in 1673 in *Chelsea, London. It is still used mainly for scientific research and education, though it is open to the public in the summer.

'**Cheltenham** /'tʃeltnəm/ a town in *Gloucestershire, England. In the 18th century it was an important spa town, where people came to drink the spring water for their health. Now it is well known for its elegant architecture and the two **Cheltenham Festivals**. The music festival takes place every summer and is an important event in modern British music. The literature festival takes place every autumn, and attracts writers and visitors from all over Britain.

the '**Cheltenham ,Gold 'Cup** /'tʃeltnəm/ a horse race with jumps that takes place in March each year in *Cheltenham. It is one of the most famous British races, and many people gamble on it.

'**Cheltenham 'Ladies' 'College** /'tʃeltnəm/ one of the best-known British *public schools for girls, established in *Cheltenham in 1853.

The '**Chemical ,Brothers** a British pop group, formed in 1992 and known for their electronic dance music. The group's best-known albums include *Exit Planet Dust* (1995), *Dig Your Own Hole* (1997) and *Surrender* (1999).

,**Dick 'Cheney** /'tʃeɪni/ (Richard Bruce Cheney 1941–) a US politician and businessman and Vice-President of the US under George W *Bush from 2001. He was first elected to the *House of Representatives in 1978 and served as Secretary of Defense under George H W *Bush from 1989 to 1993. He was also the head of a large energy services company, Halliburton, from 1995 to 2000.

'**Chequers** /'tʃekəz; *AmE* 'tʃekərz/ a large house in the country in *Buckinghamshire, England, built in the 16th century. It is the official country home of the British *prime minister. Compare DOWNING STREET.

Cher /ʃeə(r); *AmE* ʃer/ (1946–) a US singer and actor. Her original name was Cherilyn Sarkisian La Piere. She was married to the singer Sonny Bono and, as Sonny and Cher, they made a number of successful records, including *I've Got You, Babe* (1965) and *The Beat Goes On* (1967). Cher won a *Grammy award for *Believe* (1998) and an *Oscar for her part in the film *Moonstruck* (1987). Her other films have included *Silkwood* (1983) and, for television, *If These Walls Could Talk* (1996).

'Cherokee /'tʃerəki:/ n (pl **Cherokees** or **Cherokee**) a member of a *Native American people who lived by farming and trading. Their language was written in 1826 by *Sequoyah, and they had a form of government called the **Cherokee Nation**. The US government moved them in 1838 from *Georgia to *Oklahoma, and many died on the journey, called the *Trail of Tears. Some Cherokees still live in the eastern US in the *Great Smoky Mountains.

'Cheshire¹ /'tʃeʃə(r)/ (abbr **Ches**) a county in north-west England. Its administrative centre is *Chester.

Leonard 'Cheshire² /'tʃeʃə(r)/ (1917–92) a British pilot, well known for his courage in *World War II. He took part in many dangerous flights and was given the *Victoria Cross. After the war he set up the first of the **Cheshire Homes**, large houses where people can be cared for when they are very sick and not likely to get better. There are now many Cheshire Homes around the world. Cheshire himself was made a *life peer in 1991.

the ,Cheshire 'Cat /,tʃeʃə; AmE ,tʃeʃər/ a character in Lewis *Carroll's novel *Alice in Wonderland. It is a cat that disappears, leaving only its smile behind. If a person is described as smiling *like a Cheshire cat*, it means that they have a broad, fixed smile: *He just sat there, grinning like a Cheshire cat and saying nothing.*

Cheshire 'cheese /,tʃeʃə; AmE ,tʃeʃər/ (also **Cheshire**) n [U] a type of mild white cheese that breaks easily into small pieces. It was originally made in Cheshire, a county in north-west England.

'Chester /'tʃestə(r)/ a city in Cheshire, north-west England, and its administrative centre. It was an important military centre in *Roman Britain, and is best known now for its 15th– and 16th–century buildings and for the city wall, originally built all round the town to protect it from attack, which still stands.

,G K 'Chesterton /'tʃestətən; AmE 'tʃestərtən/ (Gilbert Keith Chesterton 1874–1936) an English writer of essays, novels and poetry. He is best remembered for his short stories about *Father Brown, a *Roman Catholic priest who solves *detective mysteries.

,Albert Che'valier /ʃə'vælieɪ/ (1861–1923) a British *music-hall(1) entertainer, well known for singing *cockney songs, including *My Old Dutch*.

the 'Cheviots /'tʃeviəts/ (also the **Cheviot Hills**) a range of hills that forms part of the border between England and Scotland. **Cheviot sheep**, which were originally bred there, are famous for the quality of their wool.

'Chevrolet™ /'ʃevrəleɪ/ (also informal **Chevy**) a well-known US make of car produced by *General Motors since 1915. It was first made in 1911 by Louis Chevrolet and William Durant. One successful advertisement for it

the Cheviot Hills

included the phrase 'See the USA in your Chevrolet.' It is a large car and therefore a favourite with US families. See also CORVETTE.

Chex™ /tʃeks/ n [U] the name of a range of US breakfast cereals, made by General Mills Inc. Different varieties are made with corn, rice and wheat.

Che'yenne /ʃaɪ'en/ (pl **Cheyennes** or **Cheyenne**) a member of a *Native American people of the *Great Plains. They had wars against other Native American groups and helped the *Sioux to defeat General *Custer at the Battle of *Little Bighorn. They were then forced to live on reservations (= land given and protected by the US government) in *Oklahoma and *Montana.

Chi'antishire /ki'æntiʃə(r)/ (BrE ironic) a humorous name for Tuscany, an area of Italy which is very fashionable among rich British people. Many British people live there, and many more spend their summer holidays there. Chianti is the name of a wine produced in Tuscany: *They've invited us to stay at their villa in Chiantishire.*

Chi'cago /ʃɪ'kɑ:gəʊ; AmE ʃɪ'kɑ:goʊ/ the third largest US city. It is in the state of *Illinois on Lake *Michigan and is sometimes called the 'Windy City'. It had the world's first *skyscrapers, and the *Sears Tower is the tallest building in the US. Chicago is the centre of the American *Middle West and its O'Hare airport is the busiest airport in the world. The *El train runs

Chicago

around the business district, called the *Loop. During *Prohibition, Chicago was known for its gangsters (= criminals), especially Al *Capone.

the Chi,cago 'Seven /ʃɪ,kɑ:gəʊ ; AmE ʃɪ,kɑ:goʊ/ a group of seven people who protested violently against the *Vietnam War in Chicago during the 1968 *Democratic Party convention (= national meeting to select a candidate for President). Their leaders were Abbie Hoffman and Jerry Rubin. They were arrested and put on trial, and five of them, including Hoffman and Rubin, were found guilty. A judge later said that the trial had been unfair, and they did not go to prison.

Chi'cana /tʃɪ'kɑ:nə/ n (pl **Chicanas**) a female Mexican American. See also CHICANO.

Chi'cano /tʃɪ'kɑ:nəʊ; AmE tʃɪ'kɑ:noʊ/ n (pl **Chicanos**) a Mexican American, i.e. a Mexican person now living in the US or an American descended from Mexicans. The word Chicano was originally a name used by others as an insult but is now the name preferred by Mexican Americans.

'Chichester¹ /'tʃɪtʃɪstə(r)/ the main town of *West Sussex, England. It is known for its 18th–century architecture and for the **Chichester Festival**, a theatre festival that takes place every summer.

the Festival Theatre, Chichester

C

,Francis **'Chichester²** /'tʃɪtʃɪstə(r)/ (1901–72) an English yachtsman. In 1960 he won the first race across the Atlantic for people sailing alone in yachts. He is best remembered for sailing alone round the world at the age of 65 in 1966–7. He was made a *knight in 1967.

,**Chick-fil-'A™** /,tʃɪkfil'eɪ/ any of a group of fast-food restaurants in the US that sell many types of chicken dishes and especially chicken sandwiches. The first restaurant opened in a shopping mall in *Atlanta in 1967 and many of the restaurants are in shopping malls.

,**Chief E'xecutive** *n* the US President in his position as head of government.

,**Chief 'Joseph** ⇨ JOSEPH.

,**Chief of 'Air Staff** *n* the officer in charge of the *Royal Air Force.

,**Chief of De'fence Staff** *n* the military officer in charge of all of Britain's armed forces.

,**Chief of 'Naval Staff** *n* the officer in charge of the *Royal Navy.

,**Chief 'Rabbi** /'ræbaɪ/ *n* the main Jewish religious leader in a particular country. The British Chief Rabbi is usually considered a representative of all the Jews in Britain, although he is only officially responsible for the Orthodox branch of the Jewish religion. There is no Chief Rabbi in the US.

the ,**Chief 'Secretary to the 'Treasury** *n* the title of a member of the British *Cabinet who works under the *Chancellor of the Exchequer and is in control of the money the state spends on health, education, etc.

,**Chief 'Whip** *n* (in Britain) a member of a political party who is in charge of the other *Whips in the party. The Chief Whips are among the most powerful people in *Parliament, with responsibilities for keeping discipline among the party's *MPs, making sure that they go to debates, and advising them how to vote.

'**child ,benefit** *n* [U] (in Britain) payments made weekly by the government to the parents of all children under 16. Child benefit is also paid for older children if they are still at school.

,*Childe **'Harold's 'Pilgrimage*** /,tʃaɪld/ a long poem (1812–18) by Lord *Byron. It tells the story of a young Englishman travelling through several European countries, and of the romantic ideas and historical events that these places make him think of. It is one of Byron's best-known poems, and describes many of his own feelings and experiences.

'**ChildLine** /'tʃaɪldlaɪn/ a British charity started in 1986 that provides a special telephone service for children to call for advice and help with their problems. It is aimed especially at children who are being treated violently or sexually abused by adults. See also RANTZEN.

,**Children in 'Need** a British charity, set up by the *BBC. Once a year it organizes a special evening of television and radio entertainment to persuade people to send money, which it then gives to other children's charities in Britain.

'*Children's **Hour*** a *BBC radio programme for children that was broadcast in Britain early every evening from 1922 to 1964. It was very popular in the years before children's television.

the ,**Child Sup'port ,Agency** (*abbr* **the CSA**) the British government department that is responsible for finding parents, usually divorced fathers, who do not live with their children, and making them pay the other parent regular amounts of money to look after the children.

the ,**Chiltern 'Hundreds** /,tʃɪltən; *AmE* ,tʃɪltərn/ an administrative region that used to exist in *Buckinghamshire, England. British *Members of Parliament are not allowed to resign during the course of a *Parliament, but the person with the traditional job of looking after the Chiltern Hundreds is not allowed to be an *Member of Parliament, so any MP who wishes to resign can *apply for the Chiltern Hundreds* as a way of leaving parliament. A *hundred* was formerly a division of a county in England, so called because it contained roughly one hundred families.

the '**Chilterns** /'tʃɪltənz; *AmE* 'tʃɪltərnz/ (*also* **the Chiltern Hills**) a range of hills in southern England, between *London and *Oxford, well known for their attractive scenery. It is a fashionable and expensive area to live in, and is protected as an *Area of Outstanding Natural Beauty.

'**Chinatown** /'tʃaɪnətaʊn/ *n* [U, C, usually sing] the area of a city where many Chinese people live and where there are Chinese shops, restaurants, etc. In cities such as *San Francisco, New York and London the Chinatown street signs are in Chinese as well as English.

Chinatown

,**Chinese 'whispers** /,tʃaɪniːz/ *n* [U] a game in which one person in a circle of people whispers a message (= says it very quietly) to the next person, who whispers it to the next, and so on until it comes back to the first person. The words have usually changed completely on their way around the circle, and this makes everyone laugh: *It's like Chinese whispers in the office at the moment — all sorts of rumours are going around.*

chin'oiserie /ˌʃiːnˈwæzəri/ *n* [U] the copying of Chinese designs in furniture or decoration. It became very popular in 17th-century Europe. Well-known examples of chinoiserie are the *willow pattern on plates, etc. and, on a larger scale, the Banqueting Hall and Music Room at the *Royal Pavilion in Brighton, England.

'**Chippawa** (*also* **Chippaway**) ⇨ OJIBWA.

'**Chippendale¹** /'tʃɪpəndeɪl/ *n* [U] a style of 18th-century furniture, based on the designs of Thomas *Chippendale. His book of designs, *The Gentleman and Cabinet-Maker's Director* (1754), spread the English rococo (= highly decorated) style to furniture makers outside Britain. A lot of the furniture made in America between 1755 and 1790 became known as Chippendale: *a set of Chippendale chairs*.

,**Thomas 'Chippendale²** /'tʃɪpəndeɪl/ (1718–79) an English designer of strong but elegant furniture, often with flowing lines and carved decoration. Chippendale's work influenced many others, including George *Hepplewhite and Thomas *Sheraton. His son, also called Thomas, continued his business until 1813.

the '**Chippendales** /'tʃɪpəndeɪlz/ a group of male entertainers. They are good-looking young men with attractive bodies who do stage shows in which they take most of their clothes off. Their audiences consist mainly of women. The group started in the US, but now there are British Chippendales too: *My brothers seem to think they're Glasgow's answer to the Chippendales!*

Chips A'hoy!™ a popular US make of chocolate-chip cookies (= sweet biscuits with small pieces of chocolate in them). They have been made since 1963 by *Nabisco.

the **Chisholm 'Trail** /ˌtʃɪzəm/ (in the American West) a route along which cows were driven to eastern markets in the late 19th century. It was also called 'the long drive'. About two million cattle went along the Trail, from south *Texas to Abilene, *Kansas, where they were put on trains to *Chicago. It was named after Jesse Chisholm (1806–68), a scout (= a person who goes ahead to check the route and look for dangers).

'Choctaw /'tʃɒktɔː; *AmE* 'tʃɑːktɔː/ *n* (*pl* **Choctaws** or **Choctaw**) a member of a peaceful *Native American people. They were farmers who lived mostly in an area that became the state of *Mississippi. They were moved west by the US government in 1832 and most of them now live in *Oklahoma.

Noam 'Chomsky /ˌnəʊəm 'tʃɒmski; *AmE* ˌnoʊəm 'tʃɑːmski/ (1927–) a US linguist (= expert on language). In his theory of 'transformational generative grammar' he developed the idea that language and the understanding of grammar result from an ability that everyone has when they are born. He explained this in his book *Syntactic Structures* (1957). Chomsky is also interested in politics and has strongly criticized US government policy in books such as *What Uncle Sam Really Wants* (1992), *Rogue States* (2000), *9–11* (2001), and *Hegemony or Survival* (2003).

'Chopsticks a simple, cheerful piano tune for one or two players. Even people who have never properly learnt to play the piano often know how to play *Chopsticks*.

A 'Chorus Line a very successful US musical play (1975) and film (1985) about dancers trying to get a part in a *Broadway show. The play won a *Pulitzer Prize and a *Tony Award. The music was written by Marvin Hamlisch and the words by Edward Kleban. The show ran for 6137 performances on Broadway between 1975 and 1990, at that time more than any other show in history. A film with the same name was made in 1985.

'chowder *n* [U] a thick US soup usually made with fish, potatoes, onions and other vegetables. Clam chowder, made with a type of shellfish, is especially popular in *New England.

'christening *n* a ceremony at which a baby is named and becomes a member of the Christian Church. The priest baptizes the child by putting water from the font (= a special bowl) on the child's head and gives it a name. Promises are made on behalf of the child by its godparents. A christening is a special occasion for a family, although fewer people have one now than in the past. The baby wears a special dress, or **christening robe**, and receives **christening presents**, which are often things made of silver.

'Christian¹ the main character in *The *Pilgrim's Progress* by John *Bunyan.

Fletcher 'Christian² /ˌfletʃə 'krɪstʃən; *AmE* ˌfletʃər/ (*c.* 1764–*c.* 1794) the leader of the mutiny on *HMS *Bounty against Captain *Bligh, who had originally been his close friend. Christian took the *Bounty* to Tahiti, and later moved on with some of the other sailors and some Tahitians to the *Pitcairn Islands.

Christian 'Aid a British charity supported by most of the Churches in Britain. It was established in 1949 and provides help and money all over the world, especially in poorer countries.

Christian Coa'lition of A'merica a US conservative political organization which supports traditional ideas about family life, is against *abortion (= the deliberate ending of a pregnancy at an early stage) and encourages Christian ideas in education.

***Christian 'Science 'Monitor** a national US newspaper published every day from Monday to Friday by the *Christian Scientists. It was started in 1908.

Christian 'Scientist *n* a person who believes in **Christian Science**, a form of Christianity started by Mary Baker *Eddy in *Boston, US, in 1879. She said that the mind is the only thing that is real, that the physical world is just an illusion (= false idea), and that suffering and death can be overcome by prayer alone. Christian Scientists do not take medicine or go into hospital, but talk to a **Christian Science Practitioner** who helps them deal with their illness. They have no priests, and their services are very simple, consisting of readings from the Bible and the works of Mary Baker Eddy, religious songs, and accounts of people who have been cured.

Agatha 'Christie¹ /ˌægəθə 'krɪsti/ (1890–1976) one of the most successful English authors of *detective stories. Her 67 books and 16 plays have been translated into many different languages. They include *The Mysterious Affair at Styles* (1920), *The Murder of Roger Ackroyd* (1926), *Murder on the Orient Express* (1934), *Death on the Nile* (1937) and *A Murder is Announced* (1950). She created the detectives Hercule *Poirot and Miss *Marple. Agatha Christie's play *The *Mousetrap* has been running in the *West End continuously since 1952. Christie also wrote under the name of Mary Westmacott. She was made a *dame(2) in 1971.

Linford 'Christie² /ˌlɪnfəd 'krɪsti/ (1960–) one of Britain's finest athletes. He won the gold medal for the 100 metres race at the Olympic Games in Barcelona in 1992, and was also world, Commonwealth and European champion at this distance.

'Christie's /'krɪstiz/ a well-known firm of London auctioneers, with a branch also in New York. It was started by James Christie in London in 1776 and now deals mainly with paintings, sculpture, furniture, etc. Its full name is Christie, Manson and Woods. See also SOTHEBY'S.

'Christmas the Christian celebration of the birth of Jesus Christ which takes place on 25 December. Before Christmas, in the UK and US, people send **Christmas cards** to their friends and family showing traditional Christmas symbols such as *Santa Claus, angels, holly and snowmen. Shops are decorated for Christmas from September and in the weeks before Christmas people do their **Christmas shopping**, buying **Christmas presents** for friends and family. In schools in Britain at the end of the Christmas term children often sing carols, decorate **Christingle oranges** and perform a **nativity play** representing the birth of Christ which parents are invited to watch. A few days before Christmas, families decorate a **Christmas tree**, a fir tree covered in lights and colourful decorations, in their home. Many people go to **midnight mass** in church on **Christmas Eve**. Young children believe that Santa Claus will bring them presents during the night and they usually wake up to find a **stocking**, a long sock filled with small presents, by their bed. Presents

Christmas dinner

wrapped in coloured paper are put under the Christmas tree and on **Christmas morning** many families open their presents together. Families try to get together at Christmas and celebrate with special food. In Britain people eat **mince pies** and **Christmas cake**, and in the US they make **Christmas cookies**. They share a special meal, **Christmas dinner**, which in Britain usually consists of roast turkey or goose and vegetables, followed by **Christmas pudding**, a rich pudding made with dried fruit that is served with brandy burning on it and eaten with **brandy butter**. People pull paper **crackers** which make a loud bang and contain paper hats, jokes and small toys. On the day after Christmas, called **Boxing Day** in Britain, many sporting events take place, and in the US large shops begin their sales. See also CAROLS AND CAROL SINGING.

a nativity play

A ˌ**Christmas** ˈ**Carol** a short novel (1843) by Charles *Dickens. It is about Ebenezer *Scrooge, a mean old man, who on the night before Christmas sees ghosts of Christmasses past, present and future. He realizes that he has been very unpleasant to people and that no one likes him. He immediately changes and sends gifts to his poor employee, Bob Cratchit, and to Cratchit's family, including his little lame son, *Tiny Tim.

ˌ**Christopher** ˈ**Robin** a small boy who is the main character in the books of A A *Milne, including the *Winnie-the-Pooh stories. He was based on the author's only son, Christopher Robin Milne.

ˌ**Christ's** ˈ**Hospital** an English independent school for boys and girls, started by King *Edward VI in 1533 to help poor children in London. Later it split into two schools, one for boys and one for girls, but since 1985 it has been a single school for both again, in Horsham, *Sussex. Christ's Hospital is sometimes called 'the Blue-Coat School', because of the traditional long blue coats sometimes worn by the boys as part of their uniform.

ˈ**Chrysler** /ˈkraɪzlə(r)/ n a large US car made by the Chrysler Corporation, a company begun by Walter Chrysler (1875–1940) in 1925 and joined with the German car company Daimler-Benz in 1998 to form DaimlerChrysler. Popular Chrysler models have included the New Yorker, the Le Baron and the PT Cruiser.

the ˈ**Chrysler** ˌ**Building** /ˈkraɪzlə; AmE ˈkraɪzlər/ a skyscraper (= very tall building) on East 42nd Street in New York. It was completed in 1930 and was then the tallest building in the world. Its design has been greatly admired.

Chubb™ /tʃʌb/ n a type of lock that is especially difficult to open without a key. It is named after Charles Chubb, the Englishman who invented it in 1818.

the ˈ**Chunnel** /ˈtʃʌnl/ (informal) a name, used mainly in the press, for the *Channel Tunnel.

the ˌ**Church** ˈ**Army** a Christian organization within the *Church of England, that gives help to people who need it, such as the poor, the old and the homeless. It was started by Wilson Carlile in London in 1882. Compare SALVATION ARMY.

the ˌ**Church Com'missioners** an organization set up by the British government in 1948 to deal with the money and lands of the *Church of England. It is based in London.

▶ **churches and cathedrals**
In Britain churches are landmarks in every town and village. Their tower or spire (= a cone-shaped structure on top of a small tower) can often be seen from far away. Churches are used for worship by the *Church of England, *Roman Catholics and other groups, while some *Nonconformist Churches use chapels or halls. The church and **church hall**, a building used for meetings and *Sunday School, were formerly the centre of the community. Now, far fewer people attend church and this has resulted in some churches being closed or used for other purposes such as housing.

Cathedrals may belong to either the Church of England or the Roman Catholic Church. Many cathedrals were built as part of a monastery, for example *Durham was started in the 11th century by Benedictine monks. Some of these cathedrals are called **minsters**, e.g. *York Minster, and they were originally centres for teaching Christianity. St Chad's in Birmingham dates from the middle of the 19th century and was the first Roman Catholic cathedral built in England since the Reformation. A cathedral is the headquarters of a *bishop or *archbishop. Canterbury Cathedral is the headquarters of the *Archbishop of Canterbury, who is head of the Church of England.

Many people visit churches and cathedrals to admire their architecture. In Britain churches are usually built of stone, with a **tower** or **spire** at the west end. *Bells are placed high up in the tower and rung by long ropes before services. In villages the church is approached through a gate, sometimes a **lychgate** (= a gate with a roof over it), which leads into the **churchyard** where people are buried. The main entrance is usually on the south side. The church **porch** has a noticeboard and often a seat in it. Cathedrals are large churches, usually built in the shape of a long cross with a central tower. Older cathedrals are often in a quiet grassy **cathedral close**.

The earliest stone churches date from the *Anglo-Saxon period (6th-11th centuries). *Norman churches, from the 11th and 12th centuries, are massive structures. Rounded arches over doorways and windows are a distinctive feature of Norman architecture. Examples of Norman cathedrals are those at Durham and Ely. The English *Gothic style of the 13th-15th centuries is characterized by pointed arches and increasingly ornate designs for the vault. Windows were tall and narrow in the *Early English period (13th century), and later, in the *Decorated period, had tracery (= lace-like patterns) at the top. In the *Perpendicular period (15th century), they were greatly increased in size and filled with **stained glass** (= small pieces of coloured glass in a lead frame) showing pictures of saints. Ceilings with elaborate **fan vaults** (= curved strips of stone spreading out from a point, with patterns between them) are supported by **flying buttresses** that lean at an angle from the wall and form an arch. Salisbury Cathedral is a characteristic Early English building. Exeter Cathedral dates mainly from the Decorated period and Gloucester Cathedral with its fan vaults is typical of the Perpendicular period.

Some later buildings, such as *St Paul's Cathedral designed by Christopher *Wren, are more like classical temples, with a central dome and spire added. Wren and James Gibbs, designer of *St Martin-in-the-Fields,

C

influenced architects in America: Christ Church in *Philadelphia is a copy of St Martin. But the modern Coventry Cathedral, designed by Basil Spence in the 1950s, is a hall-like church with narrow stained-glass windows.

In the US the earliest churches were one-room buildings made of wood that were used also as schools. Most communities now have several churches in varying styles. Some are made of stone in order to look like old English churches, some are small, plain buildings made of brick or wood, and others are modern buildings with glass walls. **Storefront churches** are found in shopping streets and look like shops/stores.

ˌCaryl 'Churchill[1] /ˌkærəl 'tʃɜːtʃɪl; AmE 'tʃɜːrtʃɪl/ (1938–) an English writer of stage plays who is known for her plays about *feminism and her use of methods which are not realistic. Her plays include *Cloud Nine* (1979), *Top Girls* (1982) and *The Skriker* (1994).

ˌWinston 'Churchill[2] /ˌwɪnstən 'tʃɜːtʃɪl; AmE 'tʃɜːrtʃɪl/ (1874–1965) a politician who is remembered as one of Britain's greatest statesmen. He was the son of the *Conservative politician Lord Randolph Churchill and his American wife Jennie. As a young man he served as a soldier in India and Egypt, and as a journalist in South Africa. He was a *Member of Parliament from 1900 to 1965, for five different *constituencies. He started as a *Conservative, changed to the *Liberal Party in 1904 and back to the Conservative Party in 1925 Between 1906 and 1929 he held many important positions in government, but went against the general feeling of his day in opposing Hitler's moves to increase Germany's supplies of weapons. When Neville *Chamberlain was forced to resign in 1940, Churchill became Prime Minister and Minister of Defence. His radio speeches during *World War II gave the British people a strong determination to win the war, especially at times of great crisis. The Conservative Party, led by Churchill, lost the election of 1945, but he became Prime Minister again from 1951 to 1955 when he retired, aged 80. He was made a *knight in 1953, the same year in which he won the *Nobel Prize for literature. Churchill was also a skilled painter. He was famous for smoking a large cigar, and making a *V-sign for 'victory'. He was often referred to simply as 'Winnie' and is remembered with great affection in both Britain and the US. In 1963 Congress made him an honorary US citizen. See also BATTLE OF BRITAIN.

> **❝** I have nothing to offer but blood, toil, tears and sweat **❞**
> Winston Churchill on becoming Prime Minister

the ˌChurch in 'Wales /'weɪlz/ the Welsh branch of the *Church of England. It became the main Welsh Church in the 16th century, although in the 18th and 19th centuries the majority of people in Wales left it and joined *Nonconformist Churches such as the *Baptists and the *Methodists. The Church in Wales is now a 'disestablished' church, i.e. the British king or queen is no longer its Supreme Governor and it has no connections with the British State.

the ˌChurch 'Missionary Soˌciety a *Church of England organization that sends missionaries all over the world to teach people about Christianity. It was started in 1799.

the ˌChurch of 'England the official *Protestant church in England, which became independent of the *Roman Catholic Church in the 16th century at the time of *Henry VIII. The king or queen is the **Supreme Governor** of the English, or **Anglican**, Church and it is led by the *Archbishop of Canterbury and governed by the *General Synod of bishops, clergy and laity (= ordinary church members). England is divided into 13 000 **parishes**, each based around a parish church and with a **vicar** or **rector** in charge. Parishes are grouped into 43 **dioceses** each led by a **bishop**. Church of England priests are allowed to marry and members of the clergy usually wear a white circular collar, informally called a **dog collar**. Services are given in English, the most important of them being **Holy Communion**, often just called **Communion**, at which people **take Communion** (= share bread and wine in memory of Christ). People become members of the Church at a *christening ceremony. Later, when they are old enough to understand the Church's teachings, they are **confirmed** and are allowed to take Communion. Many people are christened but are not confirmed and do not go to church regularly, but they use the church at important times in their lives such as when they get married or when members of their family die.

the 'Church of 'Jesus 'Christ of 'Latter-Day 'Saints /'læta deɪ; AmE 'læta deɪ/ the official name of the Church to which *Mormons belong. It is more correct to call Mormons 'latter-day saints'. 'Latter-day' means 'recent' or 'modern', because Mormons believe that the Church did not survive in the form that Jesus intended and was started again by Joseph *Smith in 1830. 'Saint' here means, as in the Bible, 'a member of Jesus Christ's church'.

the ˌChurch of 'Scotland the official Church in Scotland, started by John *Knox and Andrew Melville in 1560, and officially accepted in 1690. It does not have *bishops like the *Church of England, and the members of its clergy are called *ministers*, rather than *priests*. Both men and women can be ministers. The churches of the Church of Scotland are run by a minister and a group of senior church members called *elders*. This system is known as *Presbyterianism. See also EPISCOPAL CHURCH, FREE CHURCH OF SCOTLAND, MODERATOR OF THE CHURCH OF SCOTLAND.

ˌchurch'warden /tʃɜːtʃ'wɔːdn/ n (in the *Church of England) either of two elected officials in every *parish(1) who are responsible for church money and property.

ˌChutes and 'Ladders™ n [U] (AmE) a children's game played on a special board with pictures of chutes and ladders on it. Players move their pieces up the ladders to go forward and down the chutes to go back. Compare SNAKES AND LADDERS.

the CIA /ˌsiː aɪ 'eɪ/ (in full the **Central Intelligence Agency**) the US government organization that gathers information and does research on foreign governments and operations. In the 1960s it changed its methods of operating, after being criticized in the US for trying to influence or remove foreign governments. It was established in 1947 and is based in Langley, *Virginia. It publishes the *CIA World Factbook* every year, which gives information about all the countries in the world.

the CID /ˌsiː aɪ 'diː/ (in full the **Criminal Investigation Department**) (in Britain) the branch of a police force that is responsible for solving crimes. It often has a number of **specialist units** to investigate particular types of crimes, for example a *Fraud Squad or Child Protection Unit. See also FLYING SQUAD, SPECIAL BRANCH.

ˌCinde'rella /ˌsɪndə'relə/ a traditional story about a young girl called Cinderella who has to work very hard for her stepmother (= the woman who married her father after her mother died) and her two ugly older sisters. One day the sisters go to a ball (= a grand event at which people dance) at the royal palace, and Cinderella wishes she could go too. Suddenly her fairy godmother appears and says, 'You *shall* go to the ball!' She uses her magic powers to produce a wonderful dress and glass slippers (= shoes) for Cinderella, and makes a coach and horses for her from a pumpkin and four white mice. But she warns Cinderella that she must leave the ball at midnight. Cinderella is so beautiful that the prince dances with her all the time, but at midnight she suddenly runs from the palace, leaving one of her glass slippers behind. The prince sends his servants all over the country to find her by trying the slipper on every young woman's foot. When at last they find Cinderella the prince marries her.

The story of Cinderella is a favourite one for British *pantomimes. The Ugly Sisters are played by men dressed as women. The prince is called Prince Charming and is played by a woman, Cinderella (or 'Cinders') has a male friend called *Buttons who works with her and secretly loves her. The word *Cinderella* is also used to refer to things that have not been given enough attention in the past: *The railways are the Cinderella of public transport services.*

the ˌCinque ˈPorts /ˌsɪŋk/ a group of towns on the south-east coast of England that had the responsibility of protecting the coast and providing most of the English navy from the 11th to the 14th centuries. 'Cinque' is an old French word meaning 'five'. The original five towns were Dover, Hastings, Hythe, Romney and Sandwich. Later Rye and Winchelsea were added to the group.

ˌcircle the ˈwagons a call of warning in the American *Wild West, used by people travelling together in a line of wagons. When they were in a dangerous situation, such as an attack by *Native Americans, they formed a circle with the wagons as a protective barrier. The expression is now sometimes used in a humorous way when problems occur.

the ˈCitadel /ˈsɪtədəl/ a well-known US military college in *Charleston, *South Carolina. It began in 1842. The Citadel refused to have women students until pressure from the US government forced them to accept the first ones in 1996.

ˌCitizen ˈKane /ˈkeɪn/ a US film (1941), which many people think is one of the best ever made. Orson *Welles wrote, produced and directed it and played the main character. He received an *Oscar for 'Best Screenplay'. The story was based on the life of the rich US newspaper owner William Randolph *Hearst, who tried to stop it being filmed. It showed Kane as a rich but immoral person who becomes sad and lonely in his old age.

the ˌCitizens Adˈvice ˌBureau (*abbr* **CAB**) a British organization with offices in many towns to which people can go for free advice about the law, money problems, the government services available to help them, etc. The Citizens Advice Bureau is mostly paid for by local authorities. It started in 1939, when people needed information about the arrangements that had to be made during World War II.

ˈCitizens' Band (*abbr* **CB**) a radio system used for communicating over short distances, especially by drivers of lorries and cars. It first became popular in the US in the 1970s as a way of exchanging warnings about traffic problems and police. It was illegal in Britain until 1981. CB users give themselves unusual radio names, such as 'Hound Dog' and 'Sweet Mama'.

the ˌCitizen's ˈCharter a social programme introduced by the British Prime Minister John *Major in 1991. Its aim was to improve the standard of public services and to make government departments explain their actions more clearly to the public.

▶ **the City**

The business and financial centre of London is called **the City** or **the City of London**. It covers an area in east central London north of the River Thames, between Blackfriars Bridge and *Tower Bridge. It is only about one square mile/2.5 square kilometres in size and is often referred to as **the Square Mile**.

Many financial institutions have their head offices in the City, including the *Bank of England in Threadneedle Street, the *London Stock Exchange in Old Broad Street and *Lloyd's of London in Lime Street. Many banks, insurance companies and **stockbrokers** (= companies that buy and sell shares for others) have been in the City many years. When journalists talk about 'the City' they are usually not referring to the place but to the people involved in business and commerce, as in: *The City had been expecting poor results from the company.* (Compare WALL STREET.)

In the City old and new buildings stand next to each other. The most famous older buildings include *St Paul's Cathedral, the *Guildhall and the *Mansion House, where the *Lord Mayor of London lives. Tower 42, which is 600 feet/183 metres high, and the *Swiss Re Tower, nicknamed 'the Gherkin', are two of the City's more recent landmarks. The *Barbican Centre includes an art gallery, a theatre and a concert hall, as well as flats/apartments.

Few people live in the City and at night the population is about 7000. During the day it rises to about half a million, as business people commute to the City by car, bus and train. In the past the traditional image of the **City gent** was of a businessman in a dark suit and bowler hat, carrying a briefcase and a newspaper or an umbrella. The expression *She's something in the City* means 'She has an important job with a bank or firm of stockbrokers', and suggests wealth and high social status.

the City

the ˈCity and ˈGuilds ˈInstitute a British organization that gives qualifications in technical subjects and in skills that require practical ability, such as hairdressing or travel and tourism. It was started in 1878: *She's doing her City and Guilds* (= the City and Guilds Institute course) *in customer service.*

ˌCity ˈHall an unusual round glass building near *Tower Bridge in London, built in 2002 for the administrative offices of the *Mayor of London, the *London Assembly and the *Greater London Authority.

the ˈCity of ˈBirmingham ˈSymphony ˌOrchestra /ˈbɜːmɪŋəm; *AmE* ˈbɜːrmɪŋəm/ (*abbr* **CBSO**) the orchestra of the city of *Birmingham, in England, which was started in 1920 and now has an international reputation. Simon *Rattle was its conductor for many years.

ˌCity Techˈnology ˌCollege *n* (*abbr* **CTC**) (in Britain) a type of secondary school in a town or city that puts a special emphasis on teaching mathematics, technology and science. It has no connection with the *Local Education Authority, getting its money directly from the government and from business companies. The first City

Technology College opened in 1988 near *Birmingham, and there are now 12 of them.

the ‚Civic 'Trust a British organization that aims to preserve and improve the environment, for example by giving awards to good modern architecture and supporting nearly 900 local civic societies. It was started in 1957.

the ‚Civil Avi'ation Au‚thority (*abbr* **the CAA**) (in Britain) an organization that controls how airlines and air transport companies operate and deal with customers. In the past it also controlled air traffic in Britain, but since 2001 this responsibility has been carried out by the *National Air Traffic Services, an independent company that the CAA regulates. Compare FAA.

the 'Civil List (in Britain) the amount of money that parliament agrees to give every year to the king or queen to meet official expenses, such as allowances for other members of the Royal Family and wages for the *royal household. See also PRIVY PURSE.

the Civil Rights Act of 1964 /ˌsɪvl 'raɪts ækt əv 'naɪntiːn sɪksti 'fɔː(r)/ the US law that forced the southern states to allow *African Americans to enter restaurants, hotels, etc. which had been reserved for white people only, and to end the practice of having separate areas for black and white people in theatres, train stations, buses, etc. The act was mostly the result of the *civil rights movement and was strongly supported by President Lyndon *Johnson. It was followed the next year by the *Voting Rights Act.

the ‚civil 'rights ‚movement (in the US) the national campaign by *African Americans for equal rights, especially in the 1950s and 1960s. The campaign included boycotts (= refusals to buy particular products), the actions of *freedom riders, and in 1963 a march to Washington led by Martin Luther *King. It succeeded in causing the introduction of *affirmative action. The *Civil Rights Act of 1964 and the *Voting Rights Act of 1965 were also introduced as a result of the civil rights movement, which has helped to change the attitudes of many white Americans.

▶ **the Civil Service**

British **civil servants** are servants of the **Crown**, which in practice means the government. Responsibility for the Civil Service is divided between the *Cabinet Office and the *Treasury. The Prime Minister is Minister for the Civil Service.

Some civil servants work in government *departments. They are expected to work with a government formed by any political party and to remain fair and impartial, whatever their personal opinions. A change of government, or the appointment of a new minister in charge of a department, does not involve a change of its civil servants. This is very useful to ministers who are new to an area of responsibility and have little time to learn about it. The most senior civil servant in a department is called the **Permanent Secretary**.

Ministers are not allowed to ask civil servants to do work that is intended to promote a political party. In the past ministers relied almost entirely on the advice of their civil servants when making decisions and the power that senior civil servants had over politicians has been humorously shown in the television series *Yes, Minister. Now, party politics and pressure from *Members of Parliament and commercial organizations may have greater influence on decision-making.

Most civil servants are not directly involved in government. They have technical or administrative jobs outside London, e.g. calculating and collecting taxes, paying *social security benefits or running *Jobcentre Plus offices. In 2002 there were about 500 000 civil servants, 80 per cent of whom were employed outside London.

The Civil Service Commissioners are responsible for employing new staff and for ensuring that recruitment methods are fair.

In the US civil servants are government employees who are chosen on the basis of ability and experience, not political favour. The US Civil Service was created so that government employees would not lose their jobs every time a new president was elected. Although the President can appoint people to important jobs, the majority of the three million government employees are civil servants. People wanting a government job take the **Civil Service Exam**. Civil servants are expected to be loyal to the government, and not to any political party. Some people believe that, because it is difficult to dismiss civil servants, they do not work very hard or efficiently. Each individual state also has its own civil service which works in a similar way.

the ‚Civil 'War (*BrE* **the American Civil War**) a war fought between the northern and southern states of America from 1861–65. In the 19th century, an increasing number of people mostly from the industrial northern states, called **abolitionists**, wanted to make *slavery illegal, but the more agricultural southern states wanted the right for each state to decide whether to keep slavery or not. Southern states also wanted individual states to have more power than the US *federal government and many became **secessionists**, believing that southern states should **secede from the Union** (= become independent from the US). In 1860, Abraham *Lincoln became President and although he was against slavery, he said that he would not end it. The southern states did not believe this and eleven states left the Union and formed the *Confederate States of America, often called the **Confederacy**, with Jefferson *Davis as its President and its capital in *Richmond, Virginia. On 12 April 1861 the **Confederate Army** attacked *Fort Sumter, which was in the Confederate state of South Carolina but still occupied by the **Union Army,** and the Civil War began. Over the next four years, the Union army tried to take control of the South. After the battle of *Gettysburg in 1863, President Lincoln made the famous *Gettysburg Address about democracy. The same year he issued the *Emancipation Proclamation which made slavery illegal, but only in the Confederacy. Slaves played an important part in the war, giving information to Union soldiers and also serving in the Union army. In the South especially, people suffered greatly during the war and had little to eat. On 9 April 1865, when the South could fight no more, General Robert E *Lee surrendered to General Ulysses S *Grant at *Appomattox Court House in Virginia. After the war, many Southerners still had very bad feelings towards the North and did not want to end slavery. On 14 April 1865, an actor who supported the South, John Wilkes *Booth, shot and killed President Lincoln at Ford's Theatre in Washington. Many southern cities had been destroyed during the war and the economy ruined, and there followed a long, difficult period of **Reconstruction**. Compare ENGLISH CIVIL WAR.

'clambake /'klæmbeɪk/ *n* (*AmE*) (especially in *New England) a party held outdoors, often on a beach, at which people bake and eat clams (= a type of sea creature in a shell) and other food. The clams, etc. are usually baked on hot stones in a hole in the ground.

‚Tom 'Clancy /'klænsi/ (1947–) a popular US writer of novels about spies and military operations by the US government. Many have Jack Ryan of the *CIA as the main character. Clancy's books are known for their technical details. They include *The Hunt for Red October* (1984), *Patriot Games* (1987), *Clear and Present Danger* (1989), *Executive Orders* (1996) and *Battle Ready* (2004). Several have been made into films.

▶ clans

A clan is a Scottish social group whose members usually claim to be descended from the same family. In the 11th century, tribes living in Scotland divided into small clans that settled round lochs (= lakes) and glens (= valleys), and on the islands. Among the most powerful were the Campbells and the MacGregors of Argyll, the MacLeods and the MacDonalds of the Western Isles, the MacKays of Caithness and the Stewarts of Appin. The **chief** of each clan had complete authority. **Clansmen** were known by the name of their father, and this was shown by the prefix *Mac-* added to the father's name. Many Scottish surnames begin with *Mac-*. Clan membership did not in fact depend on sharing the same name, and many clan members were not related to the chief, but were admitted to the clan as loyal supporters.

The clans often fought one another. The most famous argument was between the Campbells and the MacDonalds. After *William III became king in 1688, many clans joined the *Jacobites who supported the former *Roman Catholic king, *James II. When William ordered all the clans to swear allegiance (= swear that they would be loyal) to himself, the MacDonalds of *Glencoe failed to do so. The Campbells were sent to punish them, resulting in the Massacre of Glencoe (1692), in which many MacDonalds were murdered.

The clans fought together with the Jacobites against the English in 1715 and again, under *Bonny Prince Charlie, in 1745, but they were finally defeated at the Battle of *Culloden (1746). Many clansmen were killed or put in prison. Shortly afterwards, the *Highland Clearances, in which the crofts (= small farms) of many Scots were destroyed by the landowners to make way for sheep farming, further reduced the influence of the clans.

After Culloden, the clans were forbidden to wear *tartan because it was thought to be a symbol of the desire for an independent Scotland. A tartan **kilt** (= man's knee-length pleated skirt) was an important part of a clansman's traditional clothing, but individual tartan patterns were not associated with a particular clan until *Victorian times. Today, Scotsmen generally only wear kilts on special occasions.

Clans are still important in Scotland, especially in the *Highlands. Many people outside Scotland, especially in the US, also take pride in having Scottish ancestors and being members of a clan.

ˌClapham ˈJunction /ˌklæpəm/ a railway station in south London, England. It is the busiest station in Britain, with over 2200 trains passing through it each day. Thirty-five people were killed in a train crash there in 1988. People sometimes use 'Clapham Junction' to describe a place that is crowded and busy: *We've got builders in this week and the house is like Clapham Junction.*

the man on the ˌClapham ˈomnibus /ˌklæpəm/ (*BrE*) a phrase like *the man in the street*, which means the average ordinary English person (of either sex). The phrase has been in use since the 1890s when the word 'bus' was already replacing 'omnibus'. The choice of the bus from Clapham, an area of south-west London, has no special meaning; it is just a typical bus from a fairly ordinary place: *What will the man on the Clapham omnibus think of this new tax?*

ˌEric ˈClapton /ˈklæptən/ (1945–) an English *rock musician and singer known for his great skill on the guitar. He played with The Yardbirds (1963–65) and with Cream (1966–68), one of the first heavy rock bands. Since then he has recorded many successful songs with other bands and alone. He won *Grammy awards for *Tears in Heaven* (1992), the album *Unplugged* (1992) and *Change the World* (1997) and he was chosen for the Rock and Roll *Hall of Fame in 2000.

ˌJohn ˈClare /ˈkleə(r); *AmE* ˈkler/ (1793–1864) an English poet who wrote poems about the English countryside, including *Shepherd's Calendar* (1827). He was a farm worker for much of his life but he became mentally ill and spent the last part of his life in an institution, where he continued to write poetry.

ˌClarence ˈHouse /ˌklærəns/ a large house in London, England, next to *St James's Palace. It was built in 1829 for the Duke of Clarence (later King *William IV). It was the home of the *Queen Mother(2) from 1953 to 2003 and then became the London home of Prince *Charles.

the ˌEarl of ˈClarendon /ˈklærəndən/ (*born* Edward Hyde 1609–74) an English politician and historian who was the chief adviser of King *Charles II. He was *Lord Chancellor from 1660 to 1667 when he lost his influence over the king and had to leave the country. He then wrote his *Life* and the *History of the Rebellion and Civil Wars in England*.

ˈClaridge's /ˈklærɪdʒɪz/ a famous hotel in *Mayfair in the *West End of London, England. It has been fashionable since the early 1800s among rich people, including various kings and queens. The present building was opened in 1898.

ˌAlan ˈClark¹ /ˈklɑːk; *AmE* ˈklɑːrk/ (1928–1999) a British politician who was also known for his sexual adventures. His father was Kenneth *Clark. He was a member of Margaret *Thatcher's government and came to the public's attention through the *Matrix Churchill affair and through his diary of the Thatcher years, which was very successful when it was published in 1993.

> 66 There are no true friends in politics. We are all sharks circling, and waiting, for traces of blood to appear in the water. 99
> from Alan Clark's diary

ˌKenneth ˈClark² /; *AmE* ˈklɑːrk/ (1903–83) an expert on the history of art who wrote many books. He is best known for his very successful television series and book *Civilisation* (1969) about the history of Western European art and culture. He was made a *knight in 1938 and a *life peer in 1969.

ˌArthur C ˈClarke¹ /ˈklɑːk; *AmE* ˈklɑːrk/ (Arthur Charles Clarke 1917–) an English writer of science-fiction novels and books about space travel. He is best known for the very successful Stanley *Kubrick film *2001: A Space Odyssey* (1968) which was made from his story *The Sentinel* (1951). Clarke has lived for many years in Sri Lanka. He was made a *knight in 1998.

> 66 I don't believe in astrology. I'm a Sagittarius and we're sceptical. 99
> Arthur C. Clarke

ˌCharles ˈClarke² /ˈklɑːk; *AmE* ˈklɑːrk/ (1950–) a British *Labour politician, who has been a *Member of Parliament since 1997. He became the *Secretary of State for Education and Skills in 2002 and *Home Secretary in 2004.

ˌKenneth ˈClarke³ /ˈklɑːk; *AmE* ˈklɑːrk/ (1940–) a British politician in the *Conservative Party. He was *Secretary of State for health (1988–90) and for education (1990–92). He became *Home Secretary in 1992 and was *Chancellor of the Exchequer 1993–97.

Clarks™ /klɑːks; *AmE* klɑːrks/ the name of a British company that makes and sells shoes, or any of the shops owned by the company. Clarks are well known for making children's shoes in several widths.

The Clash /klæʃ/ a British *punk group (1976–85). Their best-known songs included *White Riot* (1977), *Tommy Gun* (1978) and *Should I Stay or Should I Go?* (1982 and 1992).

class A 'drug /ˌklɑːs eɪ; AmE ˌklæs/ n an illegal drug which is on a list of the strongest, most harmful drugs and which carries a heavy penalty for anyone caught with the drug or selling it. Class A drugs include heroin, cocaine and LSD.

Classic FM /ˌklæsɪk ˌef 'em/ a British national commercial radio station, begun in 1992, which broadcasts popular classical music.

Clause 4 /ˌklɔːz 'fɔː(r)/ (in Britain) a part of the original constitution of the *Labour Party. It states that the Party will try to increase the number of nationalized industries. Many members of the Labour Party no longer believe this is a good idea, but others were angry when it was dropped in 1994.

Clause 28 /ˌklɔːz twenti'eɪt/ (in British law) section 28 of the Local Government Act (1988), which makes it illegal for local government authorities to present homosexuality in a favourable way. There was strong opposition to this law when it was introduced.

Cassius 'Clay /ˌkæsiəs 'kleɪ/ ⇨ ALI.

the 'Clean 'Air Act (in Britain) any of a series of laws passed between 1956 and 1968 with the aim of making the air cleaner, especially by forbidding in certain areas the burning of any fuel that produces smoke. Before the first Clean Air Act of 1956, a mixture of smoke from coal fires and damp winter air produced the famous London smog (= smoke mixed with fog), which in some years caused the deaths of thousands of people.

the 'Clearances ⇨ HIGHLAND CLEARANCES.

'clear and 'present 'danger the expression used by the US Supreme Court to indicate a situation in which complete freedom of speech is not a person's legal right. No one has a right to say something that would cause a clear (= obvious) and present (= immediate) danger to other people. As an example, the freedom of speech protected by the *First Amendment does not allow a person to shout 'Fire' in a crowded theatre.

'Clear ˌChannel (*also* **Clear Channel Communications**) a US media company started in 1972 which owns over 1 200 radio stations and 30 television stations in the US, as well as advertising and entertainment companies in the US and many other countries.

'clearing bank n (BrE) a bank that is a member of a **clearing house**, an organization that arranges for payments to be made between customers of different banks. There is a single clearing house for all cheques paid in Britain called the Cheque and Credit Clearing Company. Members of the company are able to provide cheque books and other services to their customers at a lower cost than other banks, which have to arrange for a clearing bank to handle cheques on their behalf. The UK clearing banks include *Barclays Bank, *Lloyds TSB, *HSBC, and *NatWest.

Eldridge 'Cleaver /ˌeldrɪdʒ 'kliːvə(r)/ (1935–98) an African-American leader and writer in the 1960s. After being in prison for several crimes, he joined the *Black Panthers and collected his writings in *Soul on Ice* (1968). After more trouble with the police, he went to Cuba and Algeria, but then returned to the US as a 'born-again' Christian.

John 'Cleese /'kliːz/ (1939–) a popular English comedy actor and writer. He became famous through two very successful television series, *Monty Python's Flying Circus* and *Fawlty Towers*, both of which are widely remembered in Britain. He has also appeared in several

films, including *The Life of Brian* (1978) and *A Fish Called Wanda* (1988). He has also written several books, including *Families and How to Survive Them* (1984) and *Life and How to Survive It* (1989).

Samuel 'Clemens /'klemənz/ ⇨ TWAIN.

'Clementine /'kleməntaɪn/ a popular old US song about Clementine, a girl who drowns. It is usually sung with a false sadness that makes it humorous. It includes the lines:

> 66 Oh my darling, oh my darling,
> Oh my darling, Clementine;
> You are lost and gone forever,
> Dreadful sorry, Clementine. 99

Cleo'patra /ˌkliːə'pætrə/ a US film (1963), directed by Joseph L Mankiewicz. Elizabeth *Taylor played the part of the Egyptian queen Cleopatra and Richard *Burton played her lover Mark Antony. These actors also had a romantic relationship and later married. *Cleopatra* cost $44 million to make and was at the time the most expensive film ever made.

Cleopatra's Needle /ˌkliːə.pætrəz/ the popular name of either of two ancient stone obelisks (= tall stone columns with four sides and pointed tops), originally from Egypt, one of which stands on the bank of the River Thames in London and the other in *Central Park, New York.

'clerihew /'klerɪhjuː/ n ⇨ BENTLEY.

'Cleveland[1] /'kliːvlənd/ **1** the second largest city in the US state of *Ohio. It is on Lake *Erie and is a major port. John D *Rockefeller began *Standard Oil there in 1870. Cleveland was the first large US city to have an *African-American *mayor.
2 a former county in north-east England, formed in 1974 from parts of Durham and North Yorkshire. Its administrative centre was Middlesbrough.

Grover 'Cleveland[2] /ˌgrəʊvə 'kliːvlənd; AmE ˌgrəʊvər/ (1837–1908) a US *Democratic Party politician who was also *President for two separate periods (1885–9 and 1893–7). He was known for his honest government, but the country had economic problems while he was President.

Van 'Cliburn /ˌvæn 'klaɪbɜːn; AmE 'klaɪbɜːrn/ (1934–) a US piano player of classical music. He first became famous in 1958 when he won the International Tchaikovsky Competition in Moscow, the first time it had been won by somebody who was not Russian.

Max 'Clifford /'klɪfəd; AmE 'klɪfərd/ (1943–) an English publicist (= a person whose job is to make something known to the public) who often acts for people who want to sell their story, especially stories involving famous people, to the *tabloid newspapers.

the ˌClifton Su'spension Bridge /ˌklɪftən/ a very high road bridge over the river *Avon near *Bristol in the west of England. It was designed by Isambard Kingdom *Brunel, and when it was completed in 1864 it was the longest and highest bridge in the world. Many people have killed themselves by jumping off the bridge.

Patsy 'Cline /ˌpætsi 'klaɪn/ (1932–63) a US singer of *country music. Her most popular songs were *I Fall to Pieces* (1961) and *Crazy* (1961). She was killed in a plane crash. The film *Sweet Dreams* (1985) is the story of her life.

Bill 'Clinton[1] /'klɪntən/ (1946–) the 42nd US *President (1992–2001). He is a *Democrat and was previously the governor of *Arkansas. The US economy improved under Clinton, and the *North American Free Trade Agreement was signed. His successes in helping to achieve world peace included the *Camp David

Agreement for the Near East and the Dayton Agreement to end the war in Bosnia and Herzegovina. In 1998 President Clinton admitted that he had had a sexual relationship with Monica Lewinsky, who was working in the *White House, after denying it earlier. He was impeached (= charged with acting illegally) for lying under oath and obstructing justice, but the United States Senate judged him not guilty. See also IMPEACHMENT, WHITEWATER AFFAIR.

> 66 It depends on what the meaning of 'is' is. 99
> Bill Clinton in videotaped evidence to the grand jury in 1998

,George 'Clinton[2] /'klɪntən/ (1940–) a US singer who also produces records and helped to establish funk music in the 1970s. With his group, Funkadelic, he produced such successful albums as *Funkadelic* (1970) and *One Nation Under a Groove* (1978). At the same time he sang with the group Parliament, which together with Fundakelic and other individuals formed a family of musicians known as P-Funk.

,Hillary 'Clinton[3] /'klɪntən/ (Hillary Rodham Clinton 1947–) a senator for New York State since 2000. Her husband is the former US president Bill *Clinton, and she is the first *First Lady to be elected to the *United States Senate. As a *Democrat Senator, she strongly supports policies that aim to improve the lives of families and children. When she was the First Lady she got involved in many political issues, especially health and education. She is also known for her support of women's rights and human rights. Before going into politics she had a very successful career as a lawyer. In 1997, she wrote the bestselling book *It Takes a Village: and Other Lessons Children Teach Us* and in 2003 she published her memoirs under the title *Living History*.

,Robert 'Clive /'klaɪv/ (1725–74) an English soldier and administrator. He is also known as 'Clive of India' because he played a major part in making India part of the *British Empire. While working for the *East India Company, he fought against the French and broke their power in India. Then at the battle of *Plassey (1757) Clive defeated the ruler of the Indian state of Bengal and replaced him with a ruler who allowed the British to govern Bengal through him. This was the beginning of a system that later spread through most of India.

A ,Clockwork 'Orange a novel (1962) by Anthony *Burgess which was made into a film by Stanley *Kubrick in 1971. The story is set in the future and is about a young man, Alex, who loves violence and the music of Beethoven. The characters all speak a future version of English invented by the author.

clog *n* [usually pl] a shoe made of wood or partly of wood. In traditional **clog dancing** the dancers' clogs were used to beat a rhythm on the floor. This type of dancing was popular in Ireland and northern England and later influenced tap-dancing in the US. Charlie *Chaplin's first performance as a child in England was a clog dance.

,George 'Clooney /'kluːni/ (1961–) a US actor. He first became famous playing the doctor Doug Ross in the television medical series *ER. His films include *One Fine Day* (1996), *Batman and Robin* (1997) in which he plays *Batman, *Out of Sight* (1998) and *O Brother, Where Art Thou?* (2000). In 2003 he protested against the planned US invasion of Iraq.

,Glenn 'Close /ˌglen 'kləʊs/ (1947–) a US actor best known for her film roles as a dangerous woman in *Fatal Attraction* (1987) and *Dangerous Liaisons* (1988). Her other films include *The World According to Garp* (1982), *Reversal of Fortune* (1990) and *Air Force One* (1997). Close has also had a successful stage career. She has won three

*Tony awards as Best Actress for *The Real Thing* (1984), *Death and the Maiden* (1992) and *Sunset Boulevard* (1995).

,**closed 'shop** *n* a factory, business, etc. whose employees must be members of a particular trade union. Closed shops were made illegal in Britain in the 1980s. In the US they were made illegal by the *Taft-Hartley Act of 1947, but they became legal again in 1951: *support for the closed shop* (= the practice of having closed shops) ◊ *a closed-shop agreement*. ⇨ note at TRADE UNION.

'**close season** (*BrE*) (*AmE* **closed season**) *n* [usually sing] a time of the year when it is illegal to kill certain animals, birds and fish because they are breeding. Most of these times are during the spring and summer, but for some fish they are during the winter.

,**clotted 'cream** /ˌklɒtɪd; *AmE* ˌklɑːtɪd/ *n* [U] (*especially BrE*) thick cream that is made by slowly heating milk and taking the solid layers of cream that form on the top. It is common in the south-west of England where the cows produce milk with a lot of cream in it. Clotted cream is often eaten with jam on *scones or with fruit such as strawberries. See also CREAM TEA.

,Brian 'Clough /'klʌf/ (1935–2004) an English football player and team manager. While he was manager of *Nottingham Forest (1975–93), the club won the *Football League, the League Cup four times and the European Cup twice.

▶ clubs and societies

Many people in Britain and the US belong to at least one club or society. *Club* is often used to refer to a group of people who regularly meet together socially or take part in sports. Most young people's groups are called *clubs*. A *society* is usually concerned with a special interest, e.g. birdwatching or local history, and sends newsletters or magazines to its members. National societies, such as the *Royal Society for the Protection of Birds, usually have local **branches**.

Social clubs have a bar where members can sit and talk to each other. Members of the upper class or business people may belong to a *gentlemen's club. Most of these are in London and even today only some of them allow women to be members. They are places to relax in, but also to make business contacts and take clients. *Freemasonary attracts business and professional men who may join a lodge (= branch) in their home town. Masons are sometimes accused of giving unfair advantages to other Masons in business, etc.

Some clubs combine social events with community service. Members of the *Rotary Club, the *Round Table, the *Kiwanis and the *Lions Club are usually professional or business people. In the US these organizations are called **service clubs**. Some are open only to men. They hold events to raise money for good causes, e.g. to provide scholarships for university students or to raise money for a hospital.

In Britain, **working men's clubs** were set up for men doing manual jobs. The clubs offer a range of entertainment, such as comedians or *darts matches, as well as a bar. In recent years some clubs have decided to admit women. In the US there are clubs based on ethnic origin, religion or military background. For example, the *Knights of Columbus is a club for *Roman Catholic men. People who have served in the armed forces join the *Veterans of Foreign Wars or the *American Legion. The *British Legion is a similar organization for former British servicemen.

In Britain, the *Women's Institute and the Townswomen's Guild began with the aim of improving women's education. Both now organize social and cultural activities.

Nightclubs, often called simply **clubs**, are places where mainly young people meet to drink and dance.

They charge **admission fees** rather than a subscription. Fees are higher at weekends and in large cities, especially London.

Many **sports clubs** hold parties and arrange social events, as well as providing facilities for various sports. *Golf clubs are often expensive to join, and there is often a long waiting list. Other sports clubs include those for squash, tennis, cricket, bowls, snooker and cycling. Many clubs own their own sports ground and **clubhouse** with a bar. Most towns also have gyms or fitness clubs. In Britain, **sports and social clubs** are run by some big companies for their employees and in the US most sports clubs are associated with companies. *Softball and *basketball teams play against teams from other companies in the same city.

Country clubs are found in green areas near cities all over the US. They offer sports like swimming, golf and tennis, and hold dances and other social events in the restaurants and bars. The oldest and most famous country club was established in Brookline, Massachusetts in 1882.

Many Americans belong to the **alumni club** of the college or university they attended. Members take part in social activities and raise money for the university.

Some students join **Greek societies**, societies named with Greek letters, e.g. Alpha Epsilon Pi. **Fraternities** are for men, and **sororities** are for women. Most Greek societies are social organizations and their members, who usually come from rich families, live in a fraternity or sorority house. After they leave university, many members continue to be active in the organization. There are also **honor societies** for outstanding students, which also have Greek letters in their names. *Phi Beta Kappa is the most famous of these. Some are for students in a particular subject, for example Psi Chi is for students in psychology. In Britain, schools, colleges and universities have societies for former students, often called **old boys'** or **old girls' associations**.

In most towns there are local societies for many interests, including singing, drama, film, folk music, archaeology, natural and local history and photography. Local branches of national societies, such as the *National Trust in Britain and the *Audubon Society in the US, organize events in their area. Only a small proportion of members attend local events, and most people join these societies because they support their aims.

Clubs are an important feature of school life, especially in the US. They include clubs for science, drama and music, as well as language clubs. Outside school, children can join a local **youth club**, *Scouts or *Girl Guides, or another youth organization.

'Cluedo™ /ˈkluːdəʊ; AmE ˈkluːdoʊ/ (AmE **Clue™**) a board game in which each player is one of the characters in a murder mystery and tries to discover who committed the murder, with what instrument and where.

the 'Clyde /ˈklaɪd/ a river in south-west Scotland, flowing through *Glasgow and into the *Irish Sea. It is 106 miles/170 kilometres long. There were once shipyards (= places where ships are built) along its banks but this industry has now almost disappeared in Britain.

the ˌClydesdale 'Bank /ˌklaɪdzdeɪl/ one of the three main Scottish banks. It started in 1838 and has its head office in *Glasgow, which is in Clydesdale, the broad valley of the river *Clyde.

CND /ˌsiː en 'diː/ (in full **the Campaign for Nuclear Disarmament**) a British organization started in 1958 to protest against nuclear weapons. It was originally best known for organizing the *Aldermaston marches in the 1960s, but it became very active again in the 1980s organizing concerts, marches and other events to protest against US nuclear bases in Britain, in particular the

cruise missile bases at *Greenham Common and RAF Molesworth.

CNN /ˌsiː en 'en/ (in full **Cable News Network**) a US television company owned by *Time Warner that broadcasts news and special information programmes all round the world by satellite, 24 hours a day. It was begun in 1980 by Ted *Turner and is based in *Atlanta, Georgia.

▶ **coal mining**

Coal was very important in the economic development of Britain. It was used as fuel in the factories built during the *Industrial Revolution and continued to be important until the 1980s. The main **coalfields** were in northeast England, the north Midlands and the valleys of south Wales, especially the *Rhondda Valley. Towns and villages grew around the **collieries** or **pits** (= coal mines) and were dominated by the **pithead** where the lifting machinery was, and by large black **slag heaps** (= piles of waste material). Poor conditions and low pay led to a long history of industrial trouble and caused miners to play a leading role in the development of the *trade union movement.

In 1913 Britain produced 292 million tons of coal and employed over a million miners. In 1947, when the mines were nationalized (= brought under government control), there were still about 1000 collieries and 700 000 miners. Increased use of *North Sea oil and gas in the 1970s led to a lower demand for coal. Coal gas was replaced by natural gas. By the mid 1980s there were only 160 collieries and 200 000 miners. Fear of further job losses led to the long and violent *miners' strike of 1984–5. In the 1990s there were more **pit closures**. Coal mining has almost completely ended in south Wales. In mining communities throughout Britain thousands of former miners have struggled to find new jobs. Collieries were returned to private ownership in 1994, and most coal now produced in Britain is sold to the electricity-generating industry. In 2003 just over 11 000 people were employed in mining.

Coal mining is important in the US. In 1988 the US produced nearly a fifth of the world's coal. Most is mined in the *Appalachian Mountains. Modern mining techniques used in *West Virginia have removed whole mountain tops and destroyed large areas of forest. Coal is used especially in the electricity-generating industry and in the manufacture of steel. In 2002 the US coal mining industry employed about 110 000 workers.

ˌKurt 'Cobain /ˌkɜːt 'kəʊbeɪn; AmE ˌkɜːrt 'koʊbeɪn/ (1967–94) a US singer and writer of *rock music, married to the singer Courtney Love. He played the guitar and was the leader of the *grunge(1) band *Nirvana. Cobain had problems with drugs and shot himself.

ˌJohn 'Cobb /ˈkɒb; AmE ˈkɑːb/ (1899–1952) an English driver who held the world speed record on land from 1947 until 1964 when the record was broken by Donald *Campbell. Cobb died trying to break the water speed record on *Loch Ness in Scotland.

ˌWilliam 'Cobbett /ˈkɒbɪt; AmE ˈkɑːbɪt/ (1763–1835) an English political journalist who became a leader of the movement towards modern democracy in Britain. He published most of his work in his own magazine *Political Register*, which also contained summaries of debates in Parliament and later developed into the modern *Hansard. His frequent attacks on authority often got him into trouble, including two years in prison. He was the son of a farmer and he is best known today for his book *Rural Rides* (1830) which describes life in the English countryside and the conditions of poor farm workers before the *Reform Act of 1832.

'cobbler n **1** a fruit pie with thick pastry on top. It is usually served in a bowl.

2 a cold drink made with wine, *whisky or rum, lemon or other fruit, sugar and ice.
3 (*old-fashioned*) a person who repairs shoes.

ˌRichard **'Cobden** /'kɒbdən; *AmE* 'kɑːbdən/ (1804–65) an English politician who, with John Bright, led the argument in the *House of Commons against the *Corn Laws and in favour of *free trade. He also campaigned for state education and against the *Crimean War.

ˌCoca-'Cola™ (*also informal* **Coke™**) *n* [C, U] a sweet fizzy drink (= one containing many bubbles). It was invented in 1886 by Dr John S Pemberton, a pharmacist (= a person trained to prepare medicines) in *Atlanta, who said it would cure feelings of sickness in the stomach or the head. Coca-Cola was originally made with cocaine, but this was replaced by caffeine in 1906. It is sold in cans and bottles and is bought more than any other product in the world.

Co'chise /kəʊ'tʃiːs; *AmE* koʊ'tʃiːs/ (c. 1823–74) a leader of the *Apache people. In 1861 he began to lead about 200 Apaches in attacks on US soldiers in *Arizona, but in 1871 he agreed to live with his people on a reservation (= land given and protected by the US government).

ˌEddie **'Cochran** /'kɒkrən; *AmE* 'kɑːkrən/ (1938–60) a US singer of *rock and roll music whose career began in 1956. He played the guitar, and his most popular songs were *C'mon Everybody* (1958) and *Summertime Blues* (1958). He died in a car crash. Cochran had recorded *Three Steps to Heaven* (1960) just before his death.

ˌcock-a-'leekie /ˌkɒk ə 'liːki; *AmE* ˌkɑːk ə 'liːki/ *n* [U] a Scottish soup made from chicken boiled with vegetables, including leeks.

ˌJoe **'Cocker** /'kɒkə(r); *AmE* 'kɑːkər/ (1944–) an English pop singer with a very rough voice. His most successful record was *With a Little Help from my Friends* (1968). He won an *Oscar for *Up Where We Belong* in the film *An Officer and a Gentleman* (1982).

ˌcocker **'spaniel** (*also* **cocker**) *n* a small dog with thick golden-brown hair and long ears.

'cockney *n* **1** [C] a person born in the *East End of London, England. Traditionally, a true cockney was somebody born within the sound of *Bow Bells, but the word is often used of any Londoner who speaks with a local accent. Cockneys are thought of as quick, cheerful people with a good sense of humour.
2 [U] the type of English that is spoken by cockneys. One famous feature of cockney is its use of *rhyming slang.
▸ **cockney** *adj* of, belonging to or typical of the cockneys or their way of speaking: *a cockney accent/woman* ◇ *cockney humour* ◇ *She's always cheeky and full of jokes – a true cockney sparrow* (= person).

ˌJohn **'Cockroft** /'kɒkrɒft; *AmE* 'kɑːkrɑːft/ (1897–1967) the English scientist who, with Ernest Walton, succeeded in splitting the atom at the *Cavendish Laboratory in 1932. He was later closely involved with Britain's nuclear energy programme and was the first director of the research centre at *Harwell. He was made a *knight in 1948 and he and Walton shared the *Nobel Prize for physics in 1951.

ˌWilliam **'Cody** /'kəʊdi; *AmE* 'koʊdi/ ⇨ BUFFALO BILL.

Seˌbastian **'Coe** /'kəʊ; *AmE* 'koʊ/ (1956–) a successful English athlete and later a politician. He broke three world records in 1979 and won the 1500 metres race in the Olympic Games in 1980 and 1984. When he retired in 1990 to start a career in politics, he had broken a total of twelve world records. He was a *Conservative *MP from 1992 to 1997. He was made a *life peer in 2000.

the **'Coen ˌbrothers** /'kəʊɪn; *AmE* 'koʊɪn/ two US film directors, brothers **Joel Coen** (1954–) and **Ethan Coen** (1957–), who have worked together on a number of successful films which are often quite unusual and not in the style of other popular US films. Their films include *Barton Fink* (1991), *Fargo* (1996), *The Big Lebowski* (1998) and *O Brother, Where Art Thou?* (2000).

ˌCoeur de **'Lion** /ˌkɜː də 'liːɒn; *AmE* ˌkɜːr ˌliːɑːn/ ⇨ RICHARD I.

'coffee cake /'kɒfi keɪk; *AmE* 'kɑːfi keɪk/ *n* (*AmE*) **1** [C] any of several types of cake or sweet bread often served with coffee. The cakes usually contain nuts and raisins and are covered with melted sugar.
2 [C, U] (*BrE*) a cake flavoured with coffee or with a coffee-flavoured filling.

ˌGeorge M **'Cohan** /'kəʊhæn; *AmE* 'koʊhæn/ (George Michael Cohan 1878–1942) a US actor and writer of musical plays that praised America. His best-known songs include *Give My Regards to Broadway* (1904), *You're A Grand Old Flag* (1904) and the *World War I song *Over There* (1917) for which he received a special medal from *Congress. The film *Yankee Doodle Dandy* (1942) was the story of his life, with James *Cagney playing Cohan.

COI Com,muni'cations /ˌsiː əʊ ˌaɪ/ (*abbr* **COI**) a British government department that writes and publishes information and advertising for the government and other public service organizations.

Coke™ ⇨ COCA-COLA.

col'cannon /kɒl'kænən; *AmE* kɑːl'kænən/ *n* [U] an Irish dish made with potatoes and cabbage which are boiled and then mixed with butter.

'Colchester /'kəʊltʃəstə(r); *AmE* 'koʊltʃestər/ a town in *Essex, England. It is probably the oldest town in Britain and was one of the richest towns in *Roman Britain. It has a castle built by the *Normans in the 11th century, and some good museums.

'Cold 'Comfort 'Farm a humorous novel (1932) by the English author Stella Gibbons (1902–89), about a lonely farm and the strange people who live there. It is a parody (= a work that copies the style of another in order to be amusing) of the 'earthy' novels influenced by *Hardy and *Lawrence that were fashionable in the 1920s.

ˌcold **'duck** *n* [U] (*AmE*) a drink made by mixing red wine and champagne, sometimes with lemon juice and sugar added.

'Coldplay /'kəʊldpleɪ; *AmE* 'koʊldpleɪ/ a British pop group formed in the mid 1990s with three members including the lead singer Chris *Martin. Their first album *Parachutes* (2000) won a number of music awards including two *Brit Awards and a *Grammy. Their second album *A Rush of Blood to the Head* (2002) also won three *Grammys.

the ˌColdstream **'Guards** /ˌkəʊldstriːm; *AmE* ˌkoʊldstriːm/ the second regiment of *Foot Guards, the personal guards of the British king or queen. It was formed in 1650 and is one of the oldest and most respected regiments in the British army.

the Coldstream Guards

C

the ˌCold 'War n [sing] the political conflict between the capitalist countries of the West (the US and western Europe) and the Communist countries of the East (the Soviet Union and eastern Europe) that began after *World War II. Both sides had large military forces which were kept ready for war, and threatened each other with nuclear weapons. They also tried to find out each other's secrets using spies. There was no actual fighting, except where the US and the Soviet Union supported different sides in conflicts such as the *Korean War. The Cold War ended in the early 1990s after the Soviet Union had begun to break up, and agreements were made to reduce military forces on both sides. See also CUBAN MISSILE CRISIS, NORTH ATLANTIC TREATY ORGANIZATION.

ˌNat 'King' 'Cole /'kəʊl; AmE 'koʊl/ (1919–65) a US singer, especially of love songs, with a soft and pleasant voice. He was also an excellent piano player. He was the first *African American to have a programme on radio (1948–9) and television (1956–7). His most successful songs included Mona Lisa (1950) and Rambling Rose (1962). His daughter, Natalie Cole (1949–), is a singer who received a *Grammy award for Unforgettable (1991), in which she added her voice to her father's old recording.

ˌDavid 'Coleman /'kəʊlmən; AmE 'koʊlmən/ (1926–) a British sports commentator well known for his great enthusiasm, especially on the *BBC television programmes *Grandstand and Sportsnight. He also presented the BBC television quiz show A *Question of Sport for many years. See also COLEMANBALLS.

'Colemanballs /'kəʊlmənbɔːlz; AmE 'koʊlmənbɔːlz/ n [pl] (BrE) the funny or ridiculous things that people, especially sports commentators such as David *Coleman, sometimes say by mistake when they are speaking fast and excitedly. The word was invented by the magazine *Private Eye as the title of its regular list of the funniest examples.

> 66 He just can't believe what isn't happening to him! 99
> David Coleman

'Samuel 'Taylor 'Coleridge /'teɪlə 'kəʊlərɪdʒ; AmE 'teɪlər 'koʊlərɪdʒ/ (1772–1834) an English poet. One of his most famous poems is The *Ancient Mariner. This was published in Lyrical Ballads (1798), a collection of poems by Coleridge and William *Wordsworth which marked the beginning of *Romanticism in Britain. His other well-known poem is *Kubla Khan, which was written under the influence of the drug opium.

ˌColgate-Palm'olive™ /ˌkəʊlgeɪt pɑːm'ɒlɪv; AmE ˌkoʊlgeɪt pɑːm'ɑːlɪv/ a US company, started in 1806 in New York City, that makes Colgate toothpaste, Palmolive soap and other household products. It introduced toothpaste in tubes in 1896.

the ˌColi'seum /ˌkɒlə'siːəm; AmE ˌkɑːlə'siːəm/ the largest theatre in the *West End of London, England, and the home of the *English National Opera.

the ˌCollege of 'Arms (also the ˌCollege of 'Heralds) an organization in London that is responsible for giving coats of arms (= designs with special symbols) to families and institutions in England and Wales. It was formed in the 15th century and its head is the Earl Marshal, who is responsible for organizing state ceremonies in Britain.

'college of 'further edu'cation (also CFE) n (BrE) a college for students over the age of 16, providing courses that lead to *A levels, *GNVQs and other qualifications. Many further education courses prepare people for jobs. ⇨ note at FURTHER EDUCATION.

'college of 'higher edu'cation n (BrE) a college that provides courses mostly at university level. Many of them provide training for people who want to be teachers.

ˌJackie 'Collins¹ /'kɒlɪnz; AmE 'kɑːlɪnz/ (1941–) an English writer of popular novels, often about rich people. She lives in *Hollywood and is the sister of Joan *Collins.

ˌJoan 'Collins² /'kɒlɪnz; AmE 'kɑːlɪnz/ (1933–) an English actor who has been in many films but is best known for playing the part of Alexis in the US television series *Dynasty.

ˌJudy 'Collins³ /'kɒlɪnz; AmE 'kɑːlɪnz/ (1939–) a US singer and writer of *folk music. She has a very clear voice. In the 1960s she protested against the *Vietnam War and supported the *civil rights movement. Her most successful songs include Amazing Grace (1970) and Send in the Clowns (1975). She has also written a novel, Shameless (1995). President *Clinton named his daughter Chelsea, after Judy Collins's song Chelsea Morning (1972).

ˌMichael 'Collins⁴ /'kɒlɪnz; AmE 'kɑːlɪnz/ (1890–1922) a leader in the fight against British rule in Ireland. He fought in the *Easter Rising in Dublin in 1916, joined *Sinn Fein and helped to form the *Irish Republican Army. After taking part in the creation of the Irish Free State in 1921, he commanded the Irish Free State forces and was head of the state for ten days before being killed by Irishmen who disagreed with him.

ˌWilkie 'Collins⁵ /ˌwɪlki 'kɒlɪnz; AmE 'kɑːlɪnz/ (1824–89) an English writer of novels. His most famous novels are The Woman in White (1860) and The *Moonstone (1868), which is regarded as the first real *detective novel in English.

ˌColonel 'Bogey /'bəʊgi; AmE 'boʊgi/ a march tune which was written at the beginning of World War I and remained popular during World War II. It was later used in the film The Bridge on the River Kwai.

ˌColonel 'Sanders ⇨ SANDERS.

ˌColo'rado /ˌkɒlə'rɑːdəʊ; AmE ˌkɑːlə'rædoʊ/ a western US state, also called the Centennial State because it became a state 100 years after the *Declaration of Independence. Its capital and largest city is *Denver. It is popular with tourists and is famous for *Aspen and other towns in the *Rocky Mountains where people ski. The state's history includes the discovery of gold in 1858 and the cultural influences of *Native Americans and Mexicans. See also PIKE'S PEAK.

the ˌColorado 'River /ˌkɒlərɑːdəʊ; AmE ˌkɑːlərædoʊ/ 1 a major US river that runs through the *Grand Canyon. It begins in the *Rocky Mountains in northern *Colorado and flows 1450 miles/2333 kilometres to the Gulf of California. For 90 miles/145 kilometres it is in Mexico. See also HOOVER DAM.
2 a US river in *Texas that flows 894 miles/1438 kilometres from the north-western part of the state to the *Gulf of Mexico.

'colour ˌsupplement n (BrE) a magazine, printed all or partly in colour, that is part of a newspaper, especially a Saturday or Sunday newspaper. The phrase is also used to describe something that looks like an advertisement in a colour supplement. For example, a colour supplement kitchen is very smart, modern and well equipped.

ˌSamuel 'Colt /'kəʊlt; AmE 'koʊlt/ (1814–62) an American who invented the revolver (= gun with a container for bullets that turns) in 1835. It was sometimes called the Colt 'six shooter' because it could hold six bullets. Another name for it was the 'Great Equalizer'. It was first used by the US Army in the *Mexican War. Colt built the world's largest gun factory in 1855 at Hartford, *Connecticut, where the Colt company is still based.

,**John Col'trane** /kɒl'treɪn; AmE kɔːl'treɪn/ (1926–67) a US *jazz musician who played the saxophone. He became well known in the Miles *Davis Quintet in the 1950s and then formed his own group in 1960. He helped to develop 'free jazz'. One of his best recordings was *Giant Steps* (1959). He was chosen for the Jazz *Hall of Fame in 1965.

,**St Co'lumba** /kə'lʌmbə/ (c. 521–97) an early Christian missionary (= person sent to teach religion to others) from Ireland who went to live on the island of *Iona off the west coast of Scotland, and from there brought the Christian religion to Scotland.

Co'lumbia /kə'lʌmbiə/ the first US space shuttle (= spacecraft that can be used again). Its first flight was in 1981 with two astronauts, John Young and Robert Crippen. By 1996 Columbia had made 20 flights and that year made the longest one (more than 405 hours). In 2003 all seven of its crew members died when the space shuttle exploded as it was returning to earth.

the **Co,lumbia 'Broadcasting ,System** /kə,lʌm-biə/ ⇨ CBS.

Co,lumbia 'Pictures /kə,lʌmbiə/ a large *Hollywood film company, producing films for cinema and television. It was established in 1924 and its first big success was *It Happened One Night* (1934). Others have included *Easy Rider* (1969), *Taxi Driver* (1976) and *Ghandi* (1982). The company was bought by the *Coca-Cola company in 1982, which sold it to Sony in 1989.

Co,lumbia Uni'versity /kə,lʌmbiə/ (also **Columbia**) a large private university in New York City. It was established in 1754 as King's College and became Columbia University in 1896. It has a high reputation for training students to become doctors, lawyers and journalists. See also IVY LEAGUE.

Co'lumbo /kə'lʌmbəʊ; AmE kə'lʌmboʊ/ a US television series (1971–93) in which the main character is Lieutenant Columbo (whose first name was never revealed), played by Peter Falk. Columbo is a *Los Angeles police detective who wears an untidy old coat and drives an old car. See also DETECTIVE STORY.

,**Christopher Co'lumbus** /kə'lʌmbəs/ (1451–1506) the Italian explorer who was the first European to discover America, in 1492. He had persuaded King Ferdinand and Queen Isabella of Spain to pay for his attempt to find a new route to Asia by crossing the Atlantic Ocean. When he arrived at one of the Caribbean islands, he thought he had found the coast of Asia and continued to believe this for the rest of his life. He made three more journeys to America, but because they were not commercially successful he lost favour and died in poverty.

Co'lumbus Day /kə'lʌmbəs/ a US holiday that celebrates the discovery of America by Christopher *Columbus. It is sometimes also called Discovery Day. It is the second Monday in October in most states. The day was first celebrated in 1792 in New York City.

Co'manche /kə'mæntʃi/ n (pl **Comanche** or **Comanches**) a member of a *Native American people of the *Great Plains in the south-western US. They are related to the *Shoshone people. The Comanches were excellent riders who fought hard and kept white people out of western *Texas until the 1870s. Most now live in western *Oklahoma.

,**Come 'Dancing** a popular British television programme in which couples and teams competed in ballroom dancing competitions. It ended in 1996 and a new show called *Strictly Come Dancing* replaced it in 2004.

The ,**Comedy of 'Errors** the first of *Shakespeare's comedy plays (c. 1593). It is about a pair of twins (= chil-dren of the same mother born at the same time), both called Antipholus, who employ another pair of twins, both called Dromio. None of the twins know of their twin brothers because they were separated at birth, so there is great confusion when they all come by chance to the same city. See also GEORGE ABBOTT.

'**Comet**[1] /'kɒmɪt; AmE 'kɑːmət/ the world's first commercial jet plane, operated by BOAC (British Overseas Airways Corporation) from 1952. Comets were almost twice as fast as earlier planes, but three of them crashed in 1953–54 because of problems in the metal from which they were made. They stopped flying until 1958 when an improved type of Comet offered the first jet service across the Atlantic.

'**Comet™**[2] /'kɒmɪt; AmE 'kɑːmət/ any of a chain of large shops found in many towns in Britain. They sell household electrical goods such as televisions and cookers.

,**Comic Re'lief** a British charity organization that was started by a group of comedy actors to raise money for poor people and people with special disadvantages. Once every two years in March there are comedy programmes on television in which the actors and presenters ask people to send money for various charities. On the same day, also called *Red Nose Day, people buy and wear red noses and do silly or amusing things to raise money.

the '**comics** ⇨ FUNNIES.

▶ **comics and comic strips**

A *comic* in the US means a **comic strip** or **strip cartoon**. *Comic strips* are a series of small drawings, called **frames**, with words that tell a story. Most US newspapers contain comic strips that are read by both adults and children. On weekdays they are usually four frames long, printed in black and white. On Sundays they are longer and in colour. Comic strips are also popular in British newspapers. Some can be found on the *Internet.

Most comic strips make jokes about the characters in them and the things that happen to them. For instance, in the *Peanuts* strips (1950–2000) many of the jokes are about Charlie *Brown, who has very bad luck, and his friend Lucy, who is unkind to him. In *Calvin and Hobbes* (1985–1995), the humour comes from the relationship between a boy and his imaginary friend, a toy tiger. Comic strips in British newspapers include *Andy Capp* and *The Perishers*. In the US, *Dilbert is about life in the office while *Doonesbury* comments on political situations through its characters. Most newspapers also print single frames that comment humorously on politicians and other people in the news.

In Britain a *comic* is a picture magazine, usually for children. Comics contain short stories written as comic strips, and sometimes also competitions and articles. Some parents do not approve of comics, but others argue that they encourage children to read. Popular children's comics include *Beano, *Dandy, and *2000 AD*, which features mainly science fiction stories. Comics for very young children are often based on popular television programmes, such as *Thomas and Friends* (which features *Thomas the Tank Engine) and *Bob the Builder*. Adult comics, such as *Viz*, are usually very rude.

Some of the characters in *Beano* and *Dandy* have not changed much over the years and now look old-fashioned. Teachers, for instance, still wear mortar boards (= stiff black hats with a square top), though real teachers stopped wearing them long ago. Many of the most popular comics appear in the form of books, called **annuals**, around Christmas each year.

Comic books are similar to comics. Each book has a set of characters who have adventures. Many of the characters, such as *Spider-Man, *Superman and

Wonder Woman, have powers that ordinary people do not have.

Pictures of the most famous characters from comic strips and comic books are used on a range of products. For instance, Gnasher and *Snoopy, a character from the *Peanuts* strip, are printed on bed covers, T-shirts, lunch boxes and birthday cards.

,**coming of 'age** n [usually sing] a person's 18th birthday, when they become legally an adult. At 18, a person can also vote in elections and get married without the agreement of their parents (though in Scotland people can get married at 16 without such agreement). The 21st birthday might also be thought of as a coming of age, especially in some US states where people are not allowed to buy alcohol until the age of 21. This was also the legal coming of age in Britain until the law was changed in 1969.

,*Coming through the 'Rye* the title of a well-known Scottish song. The words were written by the Scottish poet Robert *Burns.

the **Com'mandos** a British military unit. They are part of the *Royal Marines and are specially trained to make quick attacks on difficult targets inside enemy areas. The word *commando* is also used to mean soldiers of this type in other countries.

the **Com'mission for 'Racial E'quality** (*abbr* the **CRE**) a British government organization formed by the *Race Relations Act of 1976 to make sure that people of all races receive equal opportunities from employers, schools, etc.

the **Com'mission on ,Civil 'Rights** an independent US government organization which works to achieve equal rights for all Americans. It investigates complaints, informs the President and *Congress, and sends information to the public. An original Commission was established by the Civil Rights Act of 1957 and the present one by the Civil Rights Act of 1983.

the **Com'mittee on 'Standards in 'Public 'Life** a committee set up by the British government in 1994 to examine standards of behaviour among people such as *Members of Parliament who have a responsibility to the public to behave in an honest and respectable way. It was first led by Lord Nolan and was also called the Nolan Committee.

com'mittee stage n [sing] (*BrE*) the stage between the second and third reading of a *bill(1) in the *Houses of Parliament(1). At this stage the bill is closely examined by a small committee of *MPs.

the ,**Common Agri'cultural ,Policy** (*abbr* the **CAP**) the policy introduced in 1962 by the European Community, now the *European Union, to protect European farmers. Under the system, farmers were paid even if they produced food that was not needed. Too much food was produced as a result, and this was given names such as the 'butter mountain' and the 'wine lake'. This great waste of money caused much argument about how to improve the system, and in the 1980s some changes were made. One of the solutions (called set-aside) was to pay farmers not to produce food in some of their fields. When ten new members joined the EU in 2004 further changes were introduced to reduce the CAP budget.

,**Common 'Entrance** the entrance examination for British *public schools. Children whose parents want them to go to a public school take this examination at the age of 10 or 12, often at a *preparatory school(1).

'**common land** n [U] (in Britain) land that belongs to or may be used by the whole community, especially in a village. Most areas of common land have been used for keeping sheep or cows on or for other purposes for many centuries. With the 'enclosures' of the 18th and 19th centuries much common land was taken by private owners but the remaining areas have been protected by law since 1852.

,**common 'law** n [U] (in England) law which has developed from old customs and from past decisions made by judges, i.e. not created by Parliament. A **common law wife/husband** is a person with whom a man or woman has lived for some time as a wife or husband, although the couple are not legally married. Such relationships are recognized by the law in some countries but not in the UK.

the ,**Common 'Market** an old name for the *European Union.

the '**Commonwealth**[1] an association of 53 independent nations and several British dependencies (= countries controlled by another country) most of which used to be part of the *British Empire. The **British Commonwealth of Nations** was set up in 1931 and has been known simply as the **Commonwealth** since 1949. Members of the Commonwealth have special links with the UK and with each other and agree to work together towards world peace, the encouragement of trade, the defence of democracy and improvements in human rights, health and education. It also encourages joint cultural and sporting events, particularly the *Commonwealth Games. The British king or queen is the head of the Commonwealth and the senior official is the **Secretary-General**. Donald McKinnon, from New Zealand, has been the Secretary-General since 2000. A meeting of heads of government of all Commonwealth countries called the **Commonwealth Conference** takes place every two years and is organized by the **Commonwealth Secretariat** which is based in London. The second Monday in March is celebrated in many member countries as *Commonwealth Day.

the '**Commonwealth**[2] a period (1649–60) in English history when the country was governed without a king or queen. For the first four years after the death of King *Charles I, the country was governed by the *House of Commons. Then in 1653 the army gave power to Oliver *Cromwell with the title of Lord Protector. The years 1653–9 are therefore known as the *Protectorate. The Commonwealth ended with the *Restoration of King *Charles II.

the ,**Commonwealth 'Conference** a meeting of the *prime ministers of all the countries in the *Commonwealth, which takes place every two years.

'**Commonwealth Day** a public holiday in some parts of the *Commonwealth (but not Britain), celebrated every year on Queen *Elizabeth II's *Official Birthday. Until 1966 it was celebrated on Queen *Victoria's birthday (24 May). Before 1958 it was called Empire Day.

the ,**Commonwealth 'Games** a sports contest for competitors from *Commonwealth countries. It has taken place every four years since the first Games in Hamilton, Canada, in 1930. The event was called the British Empire Games until 1970.

the ,**Commonwealth 'Institute** the educational and cultural centre of the *Commonwealth. The Institute organizes events and exhibitions aimed especially at young people. Its present building in London, England, was opened in 1962.

the '**Communist 'Party of 'Britain** a very small political party whose members believe that the ideas of Karl Marx should form the basis of government in Britain. The party was formed in 1920 but never achieved more than two seats in *Parliament.

the '**Communist 'Party of the ,United 'States of A'merica** (*abbr* the **CPUSA**) a small US political

Members of the Commonwealth

Nation	Year Joined	Nation	Year Joined	Nation	Year Joined
Antigua and	1981	Jamaica	1962	St Lucia	1979
Barbuda		Kenya	1963	St Vincent and	1979
Australia	1931	Kiribati	1979	the Grenadines	
Bahamas	1973	Lesotho	1966	Samoa	1970
Bangladesh	1972	Malawi	1964	Seychelles	1976
Barbados	1966	Malaysia	1957	Sierra Leone	1961
Belize	1981	Maldives	1982	Singapore	1965
Botswana	1966	Malta	1964	Solomon Islands	1978
Brunei	1984	Mauritius	1968	South Africa	1931–61,1994
Darussalam		Mozambique	1995	Sri Lanka	1948
Cameroon	1995	Namibia	1990	Swaziland	1968
Canada	1931	Nauru*	1968	Tanzania	1961
Cyprus	1961	New Zealand	1931	Tonga	1970
Dominica	1978	Nigeria	1960	Trinidad and	1962
Fiji	1970–87, 1997		(suspended 1995–9)	Tobago	
Gambia	1965	Pakistan	1947–72, 1989	Tuvalu*	1978
Ghana	1957		(suspended 1999–04)	Uganda	1962
Grenada	1974	Papua New	1975	United Kingdom	1931
Guyana	1966	Guinea		Vanuatu	1980
India	1947	St Kitts and Nevis	1983	Zambia	1964

* special member, not entitled to attend Commonwealth Conferences

party which believes in the principles of Communism. It was established in 1921 and was called the Workers' Party of America before it changed to the present name in 1929. *Congress took away many of its rights in 1954, but the party began open activities again in 1966. Its newspaper is called *People's Weekly World*.

the com'munity charge (*also informal* **the poll tax**) *n* [sing] (in Britain) a local tax introduced by the *Conservative government in 1990 to replace the *rates. It was very unpopular because poor people had to pay the same as rich people. There were serious protests, and many people refused to pay the tax. It was replaced in 1993 by the *council tax.

com'munity ,college *n* (in the US) a junior college for local students in a particular area. There is an emphasis on practical career courses, and many adult students attend. Community colleges usually receive money from the local government.

com,munity 'policing /pəˈliːsɪŋ/ *n* [U] a system for developing trust and understanding between the people who live in a particular area and the local police, in order to reduce crime in that area. The system involves regular contact between the public and individual police officers and members of the public cooperate with the police to prevent crime and antisocial behaviour.

com,munity 'service *n* [U] (in Britain) work done for no pay in a local community, such as helping old people or repairing community buildings. People can do community service through various local organizations. Many young people do it as part of the *Duke of Edinburgh's Award scheme. Some types of community service are also performed as a punishment for small crimes following a **community service order** from a court: *He was given a 150-hour community service order.*

▶**commuting**
Commuting is the practice of travelling a long distance to a town or city to work each day, and then travelling home again in the evening. The word *commuting* comes from **commutation ticket**, a US rail ticket for repeated journeys, called a **season ticket** in Britain. Regular travellers are called **commuters**.

The US has many commuters. A few, mostly on the East Coast, commute by train or subway, but most depend on the car. Some leave home very early to avoid the traffic jams, and sleep in their cars until their office opens. Many people accept a long trip to work so that they can live in quiet **bedroom communities** away from the city, but another reason is '**white flight**'. In the 1960s most cities began to desegregate their schools, so that there were no longer separate schools for white and black children. Many white families did not want to send their children to desegregated schools, so they moved to the suburbs, which have their own schools, and where, for various reasons, few black people live.

Millions of people in Britain commute by car or train. Some spend two or three hours a day travelling, so that they and their families can live in **suburbia** or in the countryside. Cities are surrounded by **commuter belts**. Part of the commuter belt around London is called the **stockbroker belt** because it contains houses where rich business people live. Some places are **dormitory towns**, because people sleep there but take little part in local activities.

Most commuters travel to and from work at the same time, causing the morning and evening **rush hours**, when buses and trains are crowded and there are **traffic jams** on the roads. Commuters on trains rarely talk to each other and spend their journey reading, sleeping or using their mobile phones. Increasing numbers of people now work at home some days of the week, linked to their offices by computer, a practice called **telecommuting**.

Cities in both Britain and the US are trying to reduce the number of cars coming into town each day. Some companies encourage **car pooling** (called **car sharing** in Britain), an arrangement for people who live and work near each other to travel together. Some US cities have a public service that helps such people to contact each other, and traffic lanes are reserved for car-pool vehicles. But cars and petrol/gas are cheap in the US, and many people prefer to drive alone because it gives them more freedom. Many cities have **park-and-ride** schemes, car parks on the edge of the city from which buses take drivers into the centre. In Britain in 2003 a scheme called *congestion charging was introduced in

London to make people who drive in the city centre pay a **congestion charge**.

Perry 'Como /ˌperi ˈkəʊməʊ; *AmE* ˈkoʊmoʊ/ (1912–2001) a US singer of popular songs. He had a very relaxed style and pleasant voice. Most of his successful records were made in the 1950s when *The Perry Como Show* was on television. They include *No Other Love* (1953) and *Catch A Falling Star* (1958), for which he received a *Grammy award.

▶ **companies**

There are several types of business company in Britain. A **statutory company** is set up by an *Act of Parliament. Many former statutory companies that were managed by the government, such as those responsible for Britain's railway system and coal industry, have now been privatized (= sold and made into privately-run companies operating for profit), because these are thought to be more efficient.

Most commercial businesses in Britain are **registered companies**. Lists of these are kept by the Registrar of Companies, and company information and accounts are kept at *Companies House. Registered companies may be either **private companies** or **public companies**. Private companies have a limited number of **shareholders** (or **members**), and their shares are not available to the general public. Shares in public companies can be bought and sold by the public on the stock exchange.

A **limited company**, sometimes called a **limited liability company**, can be either private or public. The liability (= responsibility) of shareholders for any losses is limited to the value of their shares. Private limited companies have the letters **Ltd** after their name. A **public limited company** (**plc**) must offer its shares for sale to the public. Most large companies in Britain, such as *BT and *Marks & Spencer, are public limited companies. A special type of limited company, the **company limited by guarantee**, is used especially for charities. Rather than buy shares, its members promise to pay for a share of debts if it fails.

Most businesses in the US are **corporations**, which are similar to British limited companies. People who invest money in them are liable for (= risk losing) only the amount they have invested. Some corporations sell their shares on the stock exchange, but others do not. Small corporations, e.g. family businesses, may be called **close corporations**. Corporations often have the letters **inc.** (short for 'incorporated') after their name. The laws about how corporations are formed and should operate vary from state to state.

In both Britain and the US, professional businesses like law firms are often **partnerships**, which consist of two or more people who own a business and are together responsible for its debts. In a **limited partnership** 'general partners' run the business and take responsibility for debts while 'limited partners' only invest money.

A **sole proprietorship** is run by one person only. Many small businesses in the US operate in this way because the rules are much simpler than those for corporations. Sole proprietorships do not have limited liability. If the name of the business is not the same as the name of the person who runs it, the letters **d.b.a.** are used, short for **doing business as**, e.g. Ted Smith, d.b.a. Ted's Book Store.

Companies 'House the building in Cardiff, Wales, where records of companies in England and Wales are kept. Companies must send certain information to Companies House, and most of this information is available to the public. There is an office in Edinburgh for companies in Scotland.

Com,panion of 'Honour *n* (*pl* **Companions of Honour**) any of the 65 members of a British *order of chivalry which was started by King *George V in 1917. This honour is given to men and women who have performed a special service of national importance, often in politics or the arts. Members receive no title with the honour but may place the letters **CH** after their name.

the **'Company** an informal name for the *CIA.

the **,Compe'tition Com'mission** an independent organization set up by the British government in 1999 to replace the Monopolies and Mergers Commission. Its job is to prevent unfair trading when single companies have so great a share of the supply of particular goods or services in Britain that there is little or no competition. The Commission investigates cases in which one company takes over another or when two companies join together, when asked to do so by another organization, usually the *Office of Fair Trading. It then takes any action it considers necessary.

,compre'hensive school (*also informal* **comprehensive**) *n* (in Britain) a large state secondary school for boys and girls of all abilities aged 11 or over. Comprehensive schools were introduced in the 1960s to replace the system of dividing children between more academic *grammar schools and less academic *secondary modern schools.

'Arthur 'Conan 'Doyle /ˈkəʊnən ˈdɔɪl; *AmE* ˈkoʊnən *also* ˈkɒnən; *AmE* ˈkɑːnən/ (1859–1930) a Scottish writer. He is best known as the creator of the famous detective Sherlock *Holmes, but he also wrote historical novels and science fiction. He began his working life as a doctor but gave this up after the success of his first Holmes story, *A Study in Scarlet* (1887). He was made a *knight in 1902. See also DETECTIVE STORY.

'Concord /ˈkɒŋkɔːd; *AmE* ˈkɑːŋkɔːrd/ a small town in the US state of *Massachusetts about 12 miles/19 kilometres north-west of *Boston. The Battle of Concord was the second battle of the *American Revolution. The town is remarkable for the number of famous writers who lived there, including Nathaniel *Hawthorne, Ralph Waldo *Emerson, Henry David *Thoreau and Louisa May *Alcott. See also LEXINGTON AND CONCORD.

'Concorde /ˈkɒŋkɔːd; *AmE* ˈkɑːŋkɔːrd/ the first passenger plane to fly faster than the speed of sound. It was designed and built by the British and the French together, and its first test flight was in 1969. The plane was in service from 1976 to 2003. It flew between London and Paris and New York, and between London and *Barbados. Flying on Concorde was expensive, so most people regarded it as a very special experience. After a crash in 2000 which killed everybody on board, passenger numbers were low and flights in the twelve remaining planes ended: *He was on Concorde's last ever flight.*

,Cone'stoga ,wagon /ˌkɒnəˈstəʊgə; *AmE* ˌkɒnəˈstoʊgə/ (*also* **Conestoga**) *n* a large *covered wagon used by Americans who moved west between 1725 and 1850. The wagons were first made in the Conestoga Valley of eastern *Pennsylvania.

,Coney 'Island /ˌkəʊni; *AmE* ˌkoʊni/ a famous beach and amusement park of south *Brooklyn in New York City. It is not an island. The beach has been popular since 1881 and is often very crowded. The *hot dog was invented there, and so is sometimes called a 'coney'.

the **Con,federate 'States** (*also* **the Con'federacy**) the 11 southern states that left the US in 1861 to form a new nation. This caused the American *Civil War. The President of the Confederate States was Jefferson *Davis and their capital city was first *Montgomery,

*Alabama, and later *Richmond, *Virginia. The Confederate States, in their order of leaving the Union, were *South Carolina, *Mississippi, *Florida, Alabama, *Georgia, *Louisiana, *Texas, Virginia, *Arkansas, *Tennessee and *North Carolina.

the Con͵fede'ration of 'British 'Industry
⇨ CBI.

con'gestion ͵charging *n* [U] a system where drivers are charged for driving into the centre of a city as a way of reducing traffic and pollution. Congestion charging was introduced in central London in 2003. Drivers must pay before they enter the congestion charging zone, which is marked by the letter C painted in white on a red circle on the road.

͵Congre'gationalist /͵kɒŋgrɪ'geɪʃnəlɪst; *AmE* ͵kɑːŋgrɪ'geɪʃnəlɪst/ *n* a member of the **Congregational Church**, which is one of the *Protestant branches of the Christian Church and has its origins in 16th–century England. It spread to America in the early 17th century with the first English settlers, the *Pilgrim Fathers, who came from a group of Congregationalists. Congregationalists were also known as Independents because of their belief that each local group should be independent of any central control. They had most influence during the *Puritan period in England when the country was ruled by one of their members, Oliver *Cromwell. English and Welsh Congregationalists have now joined with the *Presbyterians to form a new Church, the *United Reformed Church.

Congress one of the three branches of the US federal government, the **legislative branch**. Congress is **bicameral**, i.e. it has two **houses**, the *Senate and the *House of Representatives. The main job of Congress is making laws. Before a new law can be made, both houses have to pass it, and it must then have the approval of the President. In a system of government based on a series of **checks and balances**, the two houses of Congress act as a check on each other, as well as together forming a check on the powers of the **executive branch**, especially the President. ⇨ note at FEDERAL GOVERNMENT.

͵Congress 'House the headquarters of the British *Trades Union Congress in London, England.

the Con͵gressional Gold 'Medal
the highest award given by *Congress to US civilians. It is presented to men and women who have done something special for the nation. The first was given to George *Washington in 1776, and the singer Frank *Sinatra received the 258th award in 1998. Others who have received it include John *Wayne, Bob *Hope, Walt *Disney, George and Ira *Gershwin, Irving *Berlin, Marian *Anderson and Aaron *Copland.

the Con͵gressional 'Medal of 'Honor
(*also* the **Medal of Honor**) the highest military award in the US. It was established in 1862 and is given by the US *Congress for special personal courage. A total of 125 were given in *World War I, 433 in *World War II, 131 in the *Korean War and 239 in the *Vietnam War. Compare PURPLE HEART.

the Con͵gressional 'Record
a printed record, published every day, of all the speeches and votes in the US *Congress. It has been published since 1873 by the Government Printing Office. Members of Congress can add extra comments or even newspaper articles in the 'Extensions of Remarks' section at the end. Compare HANSARD.

the 'Congress of 'Racial E'quality
(*abbr* **CORE**) a US organization that supports equal rights for *African Americans by peaceful actions. It was established in 1942 in *Chicago by James Farmer. It became well known in

the 1960s for encouraging African Americans to vote and for leading *freedom riders into the southern states.

͵William 'Congreve /'kɒŋgriːv; *AmE* 'kɑːŋgriːv/ (1670–1729) an English writer of plays, which are fine examples of *Restoration comedy. His best-known play is *The Way of the World* (1700).

͵Coniston 'Water /͵kɒnɪstən; *AmE* ͵kɑːnɪstən/ a long, narrow lake in the English *Lake District, famous as the place where Malcolm *Campbell and Donald *Campbell achieved the highest speeds on water in their boats called *Bluebird. At the northern end of the lake there is a mountain called Coniston Old Man.

Con'necticut /kə'netɪkət/ a small US state forming part of *New England. It was one of the 13 original states. Its nickname is the Constitution State and the state song is *Yankee Doodle. Connecticut has many industries but also large forests. The capital city is Hartford, which is the centre for US insurance companies. Its largest city is Bridgeport. Many people living in south-western Connecticut travel to work each day in New York City. See also YALE UNIVERSITY.

͵Sean 'Connery /'kɒnəri; *AmE* 'kɑːnəri/ (1930–) a Scottish actor who is best known for his role as James *Bond in many of the Bond films, including the first one, *Dr No* (1962). He has made many other films, including *The Name of the Rose* (1986), *The Russia House* (1990), *Rising Sun* (1993) and *The Rock* (1996). He was over 60 years old when the readers of a popular women's magazine voted him the world's sexiest man (= the man most attractive to women). He was made a *knight in 2000.

'Harry 'Connick 'Jr /'kɒnɪk; *AmE* 'kɑːnɪk/ (1967–) a US singer and actor. His best-known song is *It Had to Be You* and his albums have included *When Harry Met Sally* (1989) and *To See You* (1997). His films include *Memphis Belle* (1990), *Independence Day* (1996) and *Hope Floats* (1998).

͵Billy 'Connolly¹ /'kɒnəli; *AmE* 'kɑːnəli/ (1942–) a Scottish comedian and actor, known for his rude stories and jokes, which he tells in a strong Scottish accent. He is sometimes called the 'Big Yin' (which means the 'big one') because of his size and loud voice. In 1997 he played Queen *Victoria's servant John Brown in the film *Mrs Brown*.

͵Cyril 'Connolly² /'kɒnəli; *AmE* 'kɑːnəli/ (1903–74) an English author and literary critic. His best-known book is *The Rock Pool* (1935), a novel about artists living in the south of France. He started a literary magazine called *Horizon*, through which his ideas influenced many writers between 1930 and 1950.

> ❝ There is no more sombre enemy of good art than the pram in the hall. ❞
> Cyril Connnolly

͵Jimmy 'Connors /'kɒnəz; *AmE* 'kɑːnərz/ (1952–) a US tennis player. He won the *US Open five times between 1974 and 1983, and *Wimbledon in 1974 and 1982. He was known for his great enthusiasm while playing but also for his bad temper and behaviour. In 1998 he was chosen for the International Tennis *Hall of Fame.

the 'Conqueror
⇨ WILLIAM I.

the 'Conquest
(*also* the **Norman Conquest**) the events of 1066, the most famous date in English history, when the *Normans defeated the English and took control of England. William, Duke of Normandy, landed with his army at Pevensey in south-east England and defeated the English under King *Harold II at the Battle of *Hastings. King Harold was killed, and William became King *William I of England. By 1070, the

Normans had firm control of the whole country. See also
BAYEUX TAPESTRY.

,Joseph 'Conrad /'kɒnræd; AmE 'kɑːnræd/ (1857–
1924) a British novelist who was born Teodor Josef
Konrad Korzeniowski in a part of Poland under Russian
rule. He left home at 17 to go to sea and, after many
adventures, he joined the crew of a British ship. He
changed his name and became a British citizen in 1886.
He used his experiences around the world as the background to many of his novels, such as *Lord Jim, *Heart
of Darkness and Nostromo (1904). He is considered by
many people to be one of the greatest novelists in the
English language.

,Shirley 'Conran¹ /'kɒnrən; AmE 'kɑːnrən/ (1932–) an
English designer, journalist and author, formerly married to Terence *Conran. Her books include Superwoman
(1982) and Action Woman (1979).

> 66 Life is too short to stuff a mushroom. 99
> Shirley Conran

,Terence 'Conran² /'kɒnrən; AmE 'kɑːnrən/ (1931–)
an English designer and businessman who started the
*Habitat chain of furniture shops in 1964. The influence
of his style on modern furniture increased as his shops
spread throughout Britain and then to the US and
France. Conran also owns several restaurants. He was
made a *knight in 1983.

'consequences n [U] (BrE) a game in which each
player writes the first line of a story on a piece of paper
and then passes it to the next player who writes the second line, and so on. Each player folds the paper so that
the next player cannot see what is already written. The
result is a number of crazy and often funny stories. The
stories follow a pattern that always begins with the
names of two people and ends with the sentence 'And
the consequence was…'

,conser'vation ,area n (in Britain) an area of special
natural or historical value which is protected by law
from new building or other changes that would damage
its character.

the Con'servative ,Party (also the Conservatives,
the Tories) one of the main British political parties. It
developed from the old Tory Party in the 1830s and is
still sometimes called by this name. It is a right-wing
party, supporting capitalism and free enterprise (= an
economic system in which there is open competition in
business and trade, and no government control). It
formed the government in Britain from 1979 to 1997, during which time its leaders were Margaret *Thatcher and
then John *Major. Michael *Howard became party
leader in 2003.
▶ Conservative (also Tory) n a member or supporter
of the Conservative Party.
Conservative (also Tory) adj.

,John 'Constable /'kʌnstəbl/ (1776–1837) an English
painter who is considered to be one of the greatest
English landscape artists. He often painted scenes from
the countryside of *East Anglia, especially along the
River Stour, an area that is now described in tourist
advertisements as Constable Country. One of the most
famous of these paintings is The *Hay Wain. A large collection of his work was given by his daughter to the
*Victoria and Albert Museum in London.

con'stituency n one of the 659 administrative districts
into which Britain is divided for the purpose of electing
*Members of Parliament, or one of the 87 larger div-
isions for electing *Euro-MPs. ⇨ note at ELECTIONS.

the 'US,S Consti'tution a famous US Navy ship. Its
popular name is 'Old Ironsides' because bullets could not
pierce its strong oak sides. It was completed in 1797 in
*Boston and used in the *War of 1812. When the ship
was old there were plans to destroy it, but Oliver
Wendell *Holmes's poem Old Ironsides (1828) created
strong public feeling against the decision and it was
saved. The Constitution has been open to the public in
Boston since 1934. In 1997 it sailed for the first time in 116
years, to celebrate its 200th birthday.

the ,Consti'tution (in the US) the document which
sets out the system of government and how it works.
The Constitution was created after the *American
Revolution when leaders from each state held a meeting
called the Constitutional Convention to agree on a
document describing the new system of government
and limiting its powers, which was signed in 1789. This
established the three branches of government: the
legislative branch which consists of *Congress, the judicial branch which is the *Supreme Court and lower
courts created by Congress and the executive branch
which consists of the *president, vice-president and government departments. The Constitution contains details
about the responsibilities of each branch and who can be
elected to Congress. It says that the US government is
responsible for protecting individual states. Since 1789
there have been 27 amendments (= changes) to the
Constitution including the *Bill of Rights (1791) which
promised citizens a number of rights such as the right to
free speech and freedom of religion. There is sometimes
disagreement about how to interpret the Constitution,
some people believing that it is better to follow exactly
what the Constitution says and others that it is necessary
to consider what the intention of each part was and how
that relates to the situation today. The Supreme Court
can decide that a law is unconstitutional so that it cannot be used any more.

,consti'tutional 'monarchy n a country that is governed by a king or queen within laws which limit his or
her power. Britain is governed in this way, with the
Queen (or King) as head of state and with *Parliament
and the elected government holding almost all the real
power. This system began to develop slowly in the 17th
century, when the *Bill of Rights became law, and then
developed more quickly after the *Reform Act of 1832.

the Con,sumer 'Price ,Index (AmE the
Consumer Prices Index) (abbr the CPI) a measurement of average prices of goods and services which
people buy in a country. It is calculated by looking at the
average price of a range of things which an average person might buy each month and shows general movements in prices. In the US it is used as the basis for
changes in social security benefit payments. In the UK it
is the name used for the Harmonized Index of Consumer
Prices, the index used in all countries of the *EU so that
inflation rates of member states can be compared. The
CPI is used by the *Treasury for the inflation target each
year but social security benefits in Britain are increased
on the basis of the older *Retail Price Index.

Con,sumer Re'ports a US magazine, published each
month, which tests products and writes about their quality and value. It is published by the independent
Consumers Union that does not make a profit. There are
no advertisements in the magazine. Compare WHICH?.

,continental 'breakfast n a light breakfast of the
type eaten in some European countries, including
Britain. The phrase is used mainly by hotels and restaurants and not by people in their own homes. A continental breakfast consists typically of bread rolls or croissants
with butter and jam, and coffee to drink. Compare
AMERICAN BREAKFAST, ENGLISH BREAKFAST.

the ,Continental 'Congress the first governing
body (1774–89) of the *thirteen colonies which later

became the US. It met in *Philadelphia. The First Continental Congress was in 1774 and made demands for more rights from Britain. The Second Continental Congress began in 1775 and passed the *Declaration of Independence and the *Articles of Confederation.

the ˌConti'nental Di'vide (also **the Great Divide**) the range of *Rocky Mountains in North America. It is called this because it divides the flow of rivers on the continent, some going east and others going west.

conˌtinuing edu'cation (AmE also **continued education**) n [U] education at any time during a person's adult life. In Britain it is usually provided by *Local Education Authorities and includes a great variety of courses in many different places. Courses are usually part-time and often take place in the evenings. They include cultural subjects, training in new technology, and skills for people with special needs. Many colleges and universities, especially in the US, have a department for adult education, often called the School (or Department) of Continuing Education.

ˌBeryl 'Cook¹ /'kʊk/ (1926–) an English artist who paints humorous pictures of ordinary British people doing everyday things. In 2004 a cartoon series of her characters called *Bosom Pals* was shown on BBC television: *She sent me a Beryl Cook postcard of two fat ladies hanging out their washing.*

ˌCaptain 'Cook² /'kʊk/ (James Cook 1728–79) an English sailor and explorer who made three journeys by sea to the Pacific Ocean. He was the first European to arrive on the east coast of Australia. He drew maps of the coasts of Australia, New Zealand and New Guinea. He was also the first European to arrive at *Hawaii, where he was killed in a fight with the local people.

ˌPeter 'Cook³ /'kʊk/ (1937–95) an English comedy actor and writer who first became famous in the stage show *Beyond the Fringe* in the 1960s. He is best remembered for his performances with Dudley *Moore as Dud and Pete, two men who think that they are being philosophical, but are talking nonsense. He helped to start the magazine *Private Eye*, and remained one of its main owners until his death. A collection of his comic work called *Tragically, I was an Only Twin* was published in 2002.

ˌRobin 'Cook⁴ /'kʊk/ (1946–) a British *Labour politician. He became a *Member of Parliament in 1983 and held several important positions in the Labour *Shadow Cabinet before becoming *Foreign Secretary (1997–2001). He became *Leader of the House of Commons but resigned in protest against the invasion of Iraq in 2003.

ˌThomas 'Cook⁵ /'kʊk/ (1808–92) an English travel agent who set up the world's first package tours (= holidays for which hotels, meals, etc. are organized in advance) after hiring a train to take people to a meeting of the *temperance movement. **Thomas Cook** is now one of the world's largest travel companies: *They had a little of the local currency and a few Thomas Cook traveller's cheques.*

ˌAlistair 'Cooke¹ /'kʊk/ (1908–2004) a US broadcaster and journalist, born in Britain. He was well known for his *BBC radio series *Letter from America*, in which he described US life to the British. The series ran from 1946 until his death. He wrote and presented a very successful television series on American history called *Alistair Cooke's America* (1973). He also appeared on US television to talk about British life, and to introduce British plays in the *Masterpiece Theater series.

ˌSam 'Cooke² /'kʊk/ (1935–64) a US singer and writer of *soul music. His best-known song was *You Send Me* (1957). Cooke was killed by a woman who was judged innocent because she was defending herself from him.

ˈCookham /'kʊkəm/ a village on the river *Thames, west of London, England, where Stanley *Spencer lived and set some of his best-known paintings, such as *Christ Preaching at Cookham Regatta.*

ˌCatherine 'Cookson /'kʊksən/ (1906–98) an English writer of romantic novels about life in the north-east of England. She was one of Britain's most popular authors, and was made a *dame(2) in 1993.

ˌCool Bri'tannia /brɪ'tænjə/ (informal) a phrase used to describe Britain, showing approval of the British pop groups, artists and fashions of the late 1990s. It became a popular phrase partly because it sounds like *Rule, Britannia!*, a well-known song.

ˌCalvin 'Coolidge /ˌkælvɪn 'kuːlɪdʒ/ (1872–1933) the 30th US *President (1923–9). He was known for his honesty and called 'Silent Cal' because he used few words when speaking. He was a *Republican(1), and had previously been Governor of *Massachusetts (1919–20) and US Vice-President (1921–3). The US economy did well under Coolidge, and he signed the *Kellogg Pact to encourage international peace.

the 'Co-op (in Britain) a shop run by the *Co-operative Group. There is a Co-op in most British towns and cities. It can be either a *corner shop, a supermarket or a department store selling food, furniture, electrical goods and household products: *I bought it at the local Co-op.* See also CO-OPERATIVE MOVEMENT.

'Cooper¹ /'kuːpə(r)/ a British company that made successful racing cars in the 1950s and 1960s. It is best known for the Mini Cooper, a sports car version of the original *Mini.

ˌGary 'Cooper² /'kuːpə(r)/ (1901–62) a US film actor who is best remembered for his roles in *westerns as a strong, silent hero. These included *High Noon* (1952) for which he received an *Oscar. He received another for playing a soldier in *Sergeant York* (1940). He also had comic roles, as in *Mr Deeds Goes to Town* (1936). Cooper was given a special Oscar in 1961.

ˌHenry 'Cooper³ /'kuːpə(r)/ (1934–) a popular English boxer who was twice the British heavyweight champion (1959–69 and 1970–71). He is remembered in Britain for having knocked down Muhammad *Ali, although he lost the contest and never became world champion. He was made a *knight in 2000.

'James 'Fenimore 'Cooper⁴ /'fenɪmɔː 'kuːpə(r); AmE 'fenɪmɔːr 'kuːpər/ (1789–1851) the first major US writer of novels. He wrote mostly about *frontiersmen and Native Americans. His best-known books include *The *Last of the Mohicans* (1826) and *The Deerslayer* (1841). He also wrote novels about sailors and histories of the US Navy.

ˌTommy 'Cooper⁵ /'kuːpə(r)/ (1921–84) an English comedian who performed magic tricks as part of his act. He was well known for wearing a fez (= a small red traditional Turkish hat) and saying 'Just like that' when his tricks went wrong, as they often did.

the Co'operative for 'American Re'lief 'Everywhere ⇒ CARE.

the Co-ˌoperative 'Group (also **the Co-op**) a company set up in 1863 by members of the *Co-operative Movement to produce and buy goods, and sell them in special shops. It now has supermarkets all over Britain, and several other businesses, including its own bank, the **Co-operative Bank**, and insurance services. Members still receive a share of the profits. It changed its name from The Co-operative Wholesale Society in 2001.

the Co-'operative ˌMovement an international movement that aims to encourage people to produce, buy and sell things together, and to share the profits. The movement started in northern England in the 19th

C

century when poor working people started giving regular small amounts of money so that, as a group, they could buy food, clothes, etc. for less than a single person could. Some members worked for the Movement making these goods.

Coors™ /kʊəz; AmE kʊrz/ an expensive US beer produced by the Adolph Coors Company of *Denver, *Colorado. It is advertised as special because it is made with water from the *Rocky Mountains. The company also makes many other products, including Killian's Irish Brown Ale.

ˌWendy ˈCope /ˈkəʊp; AmE ˈkoʊp/ (1945–) a British poet who is best known for her humorous poems about everyday life. Her books of poetry include *Making Cocoa for Kingsley Amis* (1986), *Serious Concerns* (1992) and *If I Don't Know* (2001). She has also written books for children.

the ˌBattle of Copenˈhagen /ˌkəʊpənˈheɪgən; AmE koʊpənˈheɪgən/ a sea battle (1801) between the navies of Britain and Denmark during the *Napoleonic Wars. *Nelson was in charge of a group of ships attacking the Danish ships in Copenhagen harbour. It is a well-known story in Britain that Nelson was sent a signal ordering him to leave the battle, but he put his telescope to his blind eye and said that he could not see the signal. His ships stayed where they were, and won the battle.

ˌAaron ˈCopland /ˌeərən ˈkəʊplənd; AmE ˌerən ˈkoʊplənd/ (1900–1990) a US composer of modern classical music, much of which uses traditional folk songs. His best-known works include the ballets *Appalachian Spring* (1944), for which he won the *Pulitzer Prize, and *Billy the Kid* (1939). He also wrote music for eight films and received an *Oscar for *The Heiress* (1949).

ˌDavid ˈCopperfield¹ ⇨ DAVID COPPERFIELD.

ˌDavid ˈCopperfield² /ˈkɒpəfiːld; AmE ˈkɑːpərfiːld/ (1956–) a US magician who does magic tricks on a grand scale. He has made the *Statue of Liberty 'disappear' and has 'walked through' the Great Wall of China.

ˈFrancis ˈFord ˈCoppola¹ /ˈfɔːd ˈkɒpələ; AmE ˈfɔːrd ˈkɑːpələ/ (1939–) an American writer, film producer and director. He is best known for three films about the same criminal family, *The *Godfather Parts I—III* (1972, 1974, 1990). He received three *Oscars for these and another for writing *Patton* (1970). He directed the expensive *Apocalypse Now* (1984) about the *Vietnam War and produced *Mary Shelley's Frankenstein* (1994). Coppola is the uncle of the actor Nicholas *Cage and the father of the director Sofia *Coppola.

Soˌfia ˈCoppola² /səˌfiːə ˈkɒpələ; AmE ˈkɑːpələ/ (1971–) an American who writes, produces and directs films. She received an *Oscar for writing *Lost in Translation* (2003). She is the daughter of Francis Ford *Coppola.

ˈcopyright ˌlibrary n any of six libraries in the British Isles that have the right to receive a free copy of any work published in Britain or Ireland. They are the *British Library, the *Bodleian Library, the *Cambridge University Library, the national libraries of Scotland and Wales and Trinity College Library, *Dublin.

"Gentleman 'Jim' ˈCorbett¹ /ˈkɔːbɪt; AmE ˈkɔːrbɪt/ (1866–1933) a US boxer. He became World Heavyweight Champion (1892–7) when he defeated John L *Sullivan in the first contest fought with gloves and under the *Queensberry Rules. He lost his title to Bob Fitzsimmons in the first filmed fight, and then became an actor. He was born James John Corbett and was called 'Gentleman Jim' because of his elegant manner.

ˌRonnie ˈCorbett² /ˈkɔːbɪt; AmE ˈkɔːrbɪt/ (1930–) a British comedian, best known as the very small partner of the much larger Ronnie *Barker in the *BBC television series *The Two Ronnies*.

CORE /kɔː(r)/ ⇨ CONGRESS OF RACIAL EQUALITY.

ˈcorgi n (pl **-gis**) a breed of small dog with smooth hair, a long body and short legs, originally bred in Wales. Corgis are well known in Britain because Queen *Elizabeth II keeps them as pets.

a corgi

ˌCorioˈlanus /ˌkɒrɪə-ˈleɪnəs; AmE ˌkɔːrɪəˈleɪnəs/ a play (c. 1608) by *Shakespeare about Caius Martius Coriolanus, a successful military leader in ancient Rome. He is sent away from Rome because he is too proud, and joins the enemy, bringing an army to attack Rome. The Romans send his mother, wife and son to persuade him not to attack, and Caius Martius is killed by the enemy.

ˌRoger ˈCorman /ˈkɔːmən; AmE ˈkɔːrmən/ (1926–) a US director of horror and crime films. He is best known for directing several films based on stories by Edgar Allan *Poe. These include *The Pit and the Pendulum* (1961) and *The Raven* (1963). Corman's other films include *Bloody Mama* (1969), *Frankenstein Unbound* (1990) and *Little Shop of Horrors* (1960) which he made in two days and one night.

the ˈCorn Belt the popular name for the US states of the Midwest, the area that grows most of the nation's corn. The main corn states are *Iowa, *Illinois and *Indiana.

ˈcorn ˌcircle ⇨ CROP CIRCLE.

ˈcorn ˌdolly n (BrE) a small figure made from pieces of wheat or dried grass twisted together. Originally corn dollies were made as symbols for the gathering of crops, but now they are mostly for decoration.

ˌcorner ˈshop (AmE **corner store**) n a small shop, often on a street corner, that sells food, drinks, cigarettes and small household goods, and usually stays open later than other shops. In Britain many corner shops are run by families of Indian or Pakistani origin: *I'm just going down to the corner shop for some milk.*

corn dollies

Corˈnetto™ /kɔːˈnetəʊ; AmE kɔːrˈnetoʊ/ n (pl **-ttos**) a type of ice cream, made by *Unilever, that is popular in Britain. It is a long piece of biscuit in the shape of a cone, filled with ice cream of different flavours, chocolate and nuts. The television advertisement shows a couple in a gondola in Venice hearing a song 'Just one Cornetto' sung to the tune of the Italian song 'O Sole Mio'.

ˈcornhusk doll /ˈkɔːnhʌsk; AmE ˈkɔːrnhʌsk/ n (AmE) a children's toy traditionally made by *Native Americans from the outer leaves covering maize/corn. The leaves are woven into the shape of a person and dressed as a girl or boy.

ˈCorning Ware™ /ˈkɔːnɪŋ; AmE ˈkɔːrnɪŋ/ n [U] a US make of ceramic (= hard clay) dishes used for baking food in. They have been made since 1958 by Corning Inc, which also makes Pyrex glass bowls, glass for computer screens, etc.

'Cornish /'kɔːnɪʃ; *AmE* 'kɔːrnɪʃ/ *n* [U] the *Celtic language that used to be spoken in *Cornwall, England. There are no people left who speak it as their first language, but there is a political party, Mebyon Kernow ('Sons of Cornwall'), that tries to encourage its use.

ˌCornish 'pasty /ˌkɔːnɪʃ 'pæsti; *AmE* ˌkɔːrnɪʃ/ *n* (*pl* **pasties**) a small pie, traditionally made in *Cornwall, in the shape of a half circle containing meat and vegetables which can be eaten hot or cold.

the 'Corn Laws *n* [pl] a set of British laws, first introduced in the Middle Ages, which controlled the import and export of grain in order to protect the price of British wheat. They were unpopular in the 19th century when there was a shortage of wheat and the laws were keeping the prices high. Many Members of Parliament owned agricultural land and made large profits from these high prices. In 1846, under pressure from the Anti-Corn Law League, the government changed the laws.

'corn pone /pəʊn; *AmE* poʊn/ *n* [C, U] (*AmE*) a simple type of bread made of maize/corn, especially in the southern US. Each is baked or fried as a small piece ('pone') shaped like a slightly flat lemon. It is sometimes called by other names, including 'hoe cake', 'johnny cake' and 'ash cake'.

'Cornwall¹ /'kɔːnwɔːl; *AmE* 'kɔːrnwɔːl/ a region at the south-west tip of England. It forms a county together with the *Scilly Isles. It used to produce a lot of tin, but there are now very few tin mines left. Its scenery, sandy beaches and mild climate now make it popular with tourists. The administrative centre is Truro.
▶ **'Cornish** *adj*.

a tin mine, Cornwall

the ˌDuchess of 'Cornwall² /'kɔːnwɔːl; *AmE* 'kɔːrnwɔːl/ the title given to *Camilla Parker-Bowles after her marriage to the *Prince of Wales in 2005.

the ˌDuke of 'Cornwall³ /'kɔːnwɔːl; *AmE* 'kɔːrnwɔːl/ another title of the *Prince of Wales, who owns land in the county of *Cornwall in south-west England. See also DUCHY OF CORNWALL. ⇨ note at ARISTOCRACY, ROYAL FAMILY.

ˌLord 'Charles Corn'wallis /kɔːnˈwɒlɪs ; *AmE* kɔːrnˈwɑːlɪs / (1738–1805) a general in charge of British forces during the *American Revolution. When he admitted defeat to George *Washington at the Battle of *Yorktown the war was ended. Cornwallis was later made Governor General of India.

the ˌCoro'nation the ceremony that takes place at *Westminster Abbey when a new British king or queen is crowned. After a religious ceremony, they are given the crown and other items that represent power and wealth, and become officially king or queen. The Coronation is always marked by a public holiday and celebrations all over the country. Since the coronation of Queen Victoria coronation mugs have been made as souvenirs and some people like to collect them: *Edward VIII coronation mugs are very rare because the coronation did not take place.*

a 1953 Wedgwood coronation mug designed by Eric Ravilious

the ˌCoronation 'Chair a special chair in *Westminster Abbey where the king or queen sits during the *Coronation ceremony. It was made for King *Edward I and used to have the *Stone of Scone under it.

the Coronation Chair

ˌCoro'nation Street a British television *soap opera about the lives of the people who live in Coronation Street, a street in a typical *working-class area of *Manchester. It is one of Britain's most popular programmes and one of the world's oldest soap operas. It started in 1960, and since 1989 has been broadcast three times a week: *He thinks northerners all speak like Coronation Street characters.*

ˌcorpo'ration tax (*AmE* **corporation income tax**) *n* [U] a tax paid by companies on their profits. British companies pay between 19% and 30% corporation tax, depending on the size of their profits. In the US different rates are charged in each state.

Cor'vette /kɔːˈvet; *AmE* kɔːrˈvet/ (*also informal* **Vette**) *n* a low, fast US sports car produced by the *Chevrolet section of *General Motors. It was first sold in 1953, and one of its most popular models was the Stingray. There are hundreds of clubs of Corvette owners, and the National Corvette Museum opened in 1994 in Bowling Green, *Kentucky.

ˌCosa 'Nostra /ˌkəʊzə 'nɒstrə; *AmE* ˌkoʊzə 'nɑːstrə/ another name for the US *Mafia(1). *Cosa nostra* is Italian for 'our thing'.

ˌBill 'Cosby /'kɒzbi; *AmE* 'kɑːzbi/ (1937–) a US comic actor known for his easy style. He is one of the most highly paid performers on US television. The two most successful series in which he has appeared are *I Spy* (1965–68) and *The Cosby Show* (1984–92). He has received several *Emmy awards and also written a successful book, *Fatherhood* (1986). His son Ennis was murdered in 1997 in *Los Angeles.

ˌCosmo'politan (*also* **Cosmo** /'kɒzməʊ; *AmE* -moʊ/) a magazine for young women, published each month in the US and Britain. It first appeared in 1972 and was one of the first women's magazines to discuss sex. It still contains many articles about sex, but many people now find its views old-fashioned.

the ˌCosta del 'Crime /ˌkɒstə del 'kraɪm; *AmE* ˌkɑːstə/ a humorous name, often used by British *tabloid newspapers, for the Costa del Sol, part of the Mediterranean coast of southern Spain. It is a popular area with British tourists, and it is well known that British criminals used to go to live there before the British and Spanish governments agreed to send each other's criminals back for trial.

'Costco /'kɒstkəʊ; *AmE* 'kɑːstkoʊ/ a US company that owns warehouses where people who become Costco members can buy goods in large quantities at very low prices. The first warehouse opened in *Seattle in 1983.

ˌLou Co'stello /kɒˈsteləʊ; *AmE* kɑːˈsteloʊ/ ⇨ ABBOTT AND COSTELLO.

,Kevin **'Costner** /'kɒstnə(r); *AmE* 'kɑːstnər/ (1955–) a US actor who also directs films. He usually plays characters who are serious and morally good. His films have included *Field of Dreams* (1989) about *baseball, *Dances with Wolves* (1990) about *Native Americans, for which he won an *Oscar as Best Director, *Robin Hood: Prince of Thieves* (1991), *Waterworld* (1995), *The Postman* (1997), *Thirteen Days* (2001) about the *Cuban missile crisis and *Open Range* (2003).

the **'Cotswolds** /'kɒtswəʊldz; *AmE* 'kɑːtswoʊldz/ a range of hills in south-west England. It was once a major centre for sheep farming and the wool trade. Now it is a popular tourist area, famous for its beautiful scenery and pretty towns. Many houses in the area are built with the local **Cotswold stone**, which has an attractive pale greyish-yellow colour: *We've rented a cottage in the Cotswolds for the summer.*

,cottage **'loaf** *n* (*pl* **loaves**) (*BrE*) a type of traditional British bread consisting of a large round loaf baked with a smaller round piece on top.

,cottage **'pie** ⇨ SHEPHERD'S PIE.

'cotton *n* [U] a type of cloth made from a plant and used for making clothes. In the 19th century the cotton industry made the north-west of England one of the richest areas in the world. The cotton arrived at the port of *Liverpool, was made into clothes in factories in *Lancashire, and the clothes could be sent to other countries from Liverpool. The new inventions of the *Industrial Revolution meant that the Lancashire factories could produce cotton goods and sell them around the world at lower prices than local goods. In the 20th century many other countries developed their own cotton industries, and most of the Lancashire factories closed.

In the US, the production of cotton was greatly improved after Eli *Whitney invented the **cotton gin** (= a machine for separating the seeds of a cotton plant from the cotton). The economy of the *South was strongly based on cotton in the 19th century, and this led to the *Civil War because the cotton plantations (= large farms) kept slaves. When the boll weevil insects destroyed many cotton fields in the early 20th century, Southern farmers began to grow other crops.

the **'Cotton Belt** a popular name for the southern US states, in which most of the country's cotton is grown. The 10 cotton states are *Alabama, *Arkansas, *Georgia, *Louisiana, *Mississippi, *North Carolina, *Oklahoma, *South Carolina, *Tennessee and *Texas.

the **'Cotton Club** a famous US *jazz club in *Harlem, New York City. Its best years were in the late 1920s when 'Duke' *Ellington and his band played there. Most of the performers at the club were black but only white people were allowed in the audience. The club provided the idea for the film *The Cotton Club* (1984), directed by Francis Ford *Coppola.

'council *n* [C+sing/pl *v*] (in Britain) a group of people elected to form the local government of an area. Councils represent counties, towns, or parts of a large city. They make local laws and are responsible for roads, parks, cultural services, *council houses, etc.: *The neighbours made so much noise he complained to the council.* ⇨ note at LOCAL GOVERNMENT.
▶ **councillor** *n* a person who is a member of a council.

'council ,area *n* an administrative area in Scotland. From 1975 until 1995, Scotland was divided into nine **regions**, which operated in a similar way to *counties. Each region had two levels of local government: an upper level consisting of a single regional council, and a lower level made up of a number of smaller district councils. The regions were replaced in 1996 by a **single-tier** (= one-level) system in which there are 32 **council areas**, each with a single council in charge. Some of the

council areas, for example *Highland, cover a wide geographical area, while others consist of single cities, for example *Glasgow City and the City of *Edinburgh. Compare UNITARY AUTHORITY.

'council house *n* (in Britain) a house provided by a local council at a low rent. Council houses and **council flats** are mainly rented by people with lower incomes. The first ones were built after *World War I. They are often on **council estates**, areas with many houses or flats/apartments. Council houses and flats can still be rented, but many are now privately owned since people were given the right to buy the home they were renting from the council in 1980.

the **,Council of 'Europe** an organization that aims to protect human rights and encourage European countries to work together in areas such as culture, education, sport, health, crime and the environment. It is based in Strasbourg, France, and has 45 European countries as its members. It is responsible for the *European Court of Human Rights.

the **,Council of the ,European 'Union** the most powerful organization of the *European Union, consisting of one government minister from each *European Union member country. Governments can send different ministers to the Council, depending on the subject being discussed. It is based in Brussels and is responsible for most EU decisions.

'council tax *n* [C, U] (in Britain) a local tax paid by every household, according to the value of their house or flat/apartment. It replaced the *poll tax, a tax paid by every adult, in 1993. Council Tax Benefit is given to people who have a low income to help them pay the tax: *This year's council tax bills will be the highest ever.*

'Countdown a popular British television show (1982–) in which competitors play games with words and numbers. It is presented by Richard Whiteley and Carol *Vorderman, and was the first programme to be shown on *Channel Four. It is broadcast every afternoon except Saturday and Sunday.

▶ **counties**

Britain is divided into small administrative regions, many of which are called **counties**. Three regions, the counties of *Essex and *Kent and the region of *Sussex (which includes the counties of East and West Sussex), have the same names and cover almost the same areas as three of the former *Anglo-Saxon kingdoms. Other counties, e.g. *Dorset, are probably based on areas where particular tribes once lived.

Counties were previously called **shires**. The original shires were the counties of the English *Midlands and the word became part of their name, e.g. *Northamptonshire. Administrative and legal affairs were dealt with by shire courts presided over by shire-reeves, later called sheriffs. Many shires were divided into smaller districts called **hundreds**. The large former county of *Yorkshire was until 1974 divided into **ridings**, North Riding, East Riding and West Riding, named after the three divisions of the 9th century *Viking kingdom of *York.

The families of people who own land in the **shire counties**, are sometimes described as **county**, as in *a county family* and *She's very county*, or are said to belong to the **county set**. Such people have a high social status and are thought to have a way of life that is typical of the *upper class.

Counties were for a long time the basis for *local government. Since 1972 there have been many changes to their boundaries and names, and to the structure of local government. Most recently, *unitary authorities have been created throughout Wales and in many places in England, and a similar system of *council areas introduced in Scotland. The main difference is that counties have two tiers (= levels) of local government, at county and at district level, and unitary authorities and council areas have only one level. Some towns that were previously part of counties, e.g. *Southampton, are now separate unitary authorities. Many people are confused by all the changes and continue to use the old county names. People do not like to have changes forced upon them, and in 1974 local people were unhappy when the small county of *Rutland was abolished and became part of *Leicestershire. In 1996, when they had the opportunity to change, the people of Rutland chose to have their own separate unitary authority.

In the US most states are divided into counties, which are the largest units of local government. There are over 3000 counties in the US; Delaware has just three, while Texas has 254. *Connecticut and *Rhode Island have none. In *Louisiana, similar units of local government are called **parishes**, and in *Alaska they are called **boroughs**. In some urban areas, such as *Philadelphia and *Boston, the city takes up almost the entire county.

the ¦Country 'Code (in Britain) a set of rules to prevent people from harming the environment when they are in the countryside. They must keep dogs under control, for example, and leave no rubbish/garbage behind.

¦country 'house *n* (in Britain) a large house in the countryside which is surrounded by large gardens and is often owned by a rich or important family. Many country houses are now open to the public to visit and many are owned by the *National Trust. Some of the most famous English country houses include *Chatsworth in *Derbyshire and *Blenheim Palace near *Oxford.

¦Country 'Life a British magazine, published every week, about houses, gardens, country sports and social life in the country. Many people associate it with rich people who own large houses in the country. It was first published in 1897.

'country ¦music (*also* **country and western music**) *n* [U] a type of popular American music that combines the traditional music of the US West and the South. These two types included *cowboy songs and *hillbilly music. There are more US radio stations playing country music than for any other type of music. The home of country music is *Nashville, *Tennessee, with its *Grand Ole Opry. See also BLUEGRASS, ROCKABILLY.

¦country 'park *n* (in Britain) any of the areas of countryside that have been preserved by the *Countryside Agency for the public to enjoy. Many of them have picnic areas and nature trails (= special paths where people can see interesting animals and plants).

▶ **the countryside**

The countryside of Britain is well known for its beauty and many contrasts: its bare mountains and moorland, its lakes, rivers and woods, and its long, often wild coastline. Many of the most beautiful areas are *national parks and are protected from development. When British people think of the countryside they think of farmland, as well as open spaces. They imagine cows or sheep in green fields enclosed by hedges or stone walls, and fields of wheat and barley. Most farmland is privately owned but is crossed by a network of *public footpaths.

Many people associate the countryside with peace and relaxation. They spend their free time walking or cycling there, or go to the country for a picnic or a pub lunch. In summer people go to fruit farms and pick strawberries and other fruit. Only a few people who live in the country work on farms. Many commute to work in towns. Many others dream of living in the country, where they believe they would have a better and healthier lifestyle.

The countryside faces many threats. Some are associated with modern farming practices, and the use of chemicals harmful to plants and wildlife. Land is also needed for new houses. The *green belt, an area of land around many cities, is under increasing pressure. Plans to build new roads are strongly opposed by organizations trying to protect the countryside. Protesters set up camps to prevent, or at least delay, the building work.

America has many areas of wild and beautiful scenery, and there are many areas, especially in the West in states like *Montana and *Wyoming, where few people live. In the *New England states, such as *Vermont and *New Hampshire, it is common to see small farms surrounded by hills and green areas. In *Ohio, *Indiana, *Illinois and other Midwestern states, fields of corn or wheat reach to the horizon and there are many miles between towns.

Only about 20% of Americans live outside cities and towns. Life may be difficult for people who live in the country. Services like hospitals and schools may be further away and going shopping can mean driving long distances. Some people even have to drive from their homes to the main road where their mail is left in a box. In spite of the disadvantages, many people who live in the country say that they like the safe, clean, attractive environment. But their children often move to a town or city as soon as they can.

As in Britain, Americans like to go out to the country at weekends. Some people go on camping or fishing trips, others go hiking in national parks.

the 'Countryside ¦Agency the British government organization responsible for preserving the countryside in England. It encourages local authorities to provide parks, and sets up and runs *national parks and *country parks. Scotland and Wales have their own organizations, **Scottish Natural Heritage** and the **Countryside Commission for Wales**.

the 'Countryside Al'liance a British political organization formed in 1998 which campaigns for people living in country areas. It is best known for its campaign against the law banning fox hunting (= a sport in which foxes are hunted by dogs and by people on horses) but it also campaigns on issues which affect farmers and against the closing of services such as post offices in country areas.

the ¦county 'championship /ˈtʃæmpiənʃɪp/ *n* (in Britain) a *cricket competition that takes place each year between teams representing *counties. **County cricket** matches last four days each and the championship is considered the most important British cricket competition. The **county champions** are the team that wins. Compare ONE-DAY CRICKET.

¦county 'court *n* **1** (in England and Wales) a local court of law for minor civil cases (= ones concerned with the private rights of citizens rather than crimes), e.g. disputes about the ownership of land. Such cases are dealt with by a judge without a jury. See also CROWN COURT. **2** (in some US states) a court of law in a county, where small civil cases or criminal cases are dealt with. See also MAGISTRATES' COURT. ⇨ note at LEGAL SYSTEM.

¦County 'Durham /ˈdʌrəm/ the county of *Durham in north-east England. Its administrative centre is the city of *Durham.

¦County 'Hall a large building in London, on the south bank of the *Thames opposite the *Houses of Parliament(2). It was the main offices of the local government of London until the *Greater London Council was abolished in 1986. It was then sold to a private company. There are now two hotels in the building, a restaurant and a gallery of modern British art owned by Charles *Saatchi.

C

county 'school n (in Britain) a school that is run by the *LEA of a particular county. Compare VOLUNTARY SCHOOL.

county 'town (AmE **county seat**) n the main town of a county, where its local government and administration is based.

the ,Courtauld 'Institute /ˌkɔːtəʊld; AmE ˌkɔːrtoʊld/ an art gallery in *Somerset House, London, England, especially famous for its collection of Impressionist paintings. Donations by Viscount Lee of Fareham (1868–1947) and Samuel Courtauld (1876–1947), the founder of a large textile company in Britain, led to the founding of the Institute. It is also part of *London University, where people study the history of art and architecture.

'courtesy ,title n (in Britain) any title used by a relative of a member of the *peerage which is not legally valid but is given as a form of politeness, especially to the sons and daughters of *dukes and *earls.

the ,Court of Ap'peal the highest court of law in England and Wales, apart from the *House of Lords. If somebody is found guilty in a court of law, they may apply for their case to be considered again at the Court of Appeal. ⇨ note at LEGAL SYSTEM.

the ,Court of 'Session the highest civil (= not criminal) court of law in Scotland, apart from the *House of Lords. If somebody is found guilty in a *sheriff court, they may apply for their case to be considered again at the Court of Session.

the ,Court of St 'James's /snt ˈdʒeɪmzɪz/ the official name for the British royal court. Ambassadors in Britain are officially called ambassadors to the Court of St James's.

Coutts /kuːts/ a very old British bank, with mainly very rich customers. Queen *Elizabeth II has an account there. It is now owned by the *Royal Bank of Scotland.

'Covenanter /ˈkʌvənəntə(r)/ n any of a group of 17th–century Scottish *Presbyterians who supported two **Covenants** (1638 and 1643). These were formal statements defending *Presbyterianism and protesting against the religious policies of *Charles I, who wanted to set up a Scottish Church with bishops, like the *Church of England. The Covenanters supported *Parliament in the *English Civil War.

,Covent 'Garden /ˌkɒvənt; AmE ˌkɑːvənt/ **1** a fashionable area in central London, England, that used to be London's main market for flowers, fruit and vegetables. In 1974 the market moved to *New Covent Garden and the market square was filled with small shops and restaurants. It is a popular area with tourists, and the street performers who come to entertain them: We spent all day shopping and sitting around in cafes in Covent Garden. **2** another name for the *Royal Opera House, which is next to the former Covent Garden market. The original flower market building, called the Floral Hall, is now part of the opera house: We've got two tickets for La Traviata at Covent Garden.

'Coventry /ˈkɒvəntri; AmE ˈkɑːvəntri/ an industrial city in the English *Midlands, where cars have been made since the end of the 19th century. Many of its buildings were destroyed by bombs in *World War II, including its cathedral. A new cathedral designed by Basil Spence was built next to the ruins of the old one after the war.

Coventry Cathedral

,covered 'wagon n a form of transport used by American pioneers (= people moving west to settle there). The wagons were covered with canvas (= rough cloth) supported by iron hoops. Groups of horses usually pulled the wagons, but sometimes mules or oxen were used.

,Cow and 'Gate™ a company that produces milk products and food for babies.

,Noel 'Coward /ˈkaʊəd; AmE ˈkaʊərd/ (1899–1973) an English writer and actor, well known for his elegant appearance and intelligent humour. He wrote several successful plays, including The Vortex (1924), Hay Fever (1925) and Private Lives (1930), and film scripts such as *Brief Encounter (1945). He was also well known for writing and performing comic and romantic songs, such as Mad Dogs and Englishmen. He was made a *knight in 1970.

'cowboy n **1** (also informal **'cowpoke** /ˈkaʊpəʊk; AmE ˈkaʊpoʊk/ **'cowpuncher** /ˈkaʊpʌntʃə(r)/) a man who looks after cattle in the US West. He usually rides a horse to move and control them. Cowboys were especially important during the late 19th century, when they were needed to drive cattle over long distances. They were given a good public image in books and *westerns, and Americans greatly admire their tough outdoor life and independent spirit. They still exist in the western US, and some compete in *rodeos. See also COWBOYS AND INDIANS. **2** (BrE informal disapproving) a dishonest or careless person in business, especially one who has no qualifications: The men who repaired the roof were just a bunch of cowboys.

,cowboys and 'Indians n [U] a children's game in which some children pretend to be *cowboys and others pretend to be Indians (Native Americans). They have imaginary fights, sometimes wearing special clothes, based on what they have seen in *westerns: The kids were playing cowboys and Indians in the back garden.

Cowes Week

Cowes /kaʊz/ a port on the *Isle of Wight. Once a year a series of international yacht races takes place there, called **Cowes Week**. This is an important social event, and is usually attended by members of the *royal family.

,**Abraham 'Cowley** /ˌeɪbrəhæm 'kaʊli/ (1618–67) an English doctor and writer of poems, and one of the first members of the *Royal Society. His most popular work is *The Mistress*, a collection of love poems.

,**William 'Cowper** /'kuːpə(r)/ (1731–1800) an English poet whose work is simpler and more natural than most 18th–century English poetry. He was very unhappy for most of his life, and much of his work is sad. His best-known works are hymns, such as *God Moves in a Mysterious Way*.

'**Cox's ,orange 'pippin** /'kɒksɪz; AmE 'kɑːksɪz/ (also **Cox**) n (pl **Coxes**) a type of English apple with a sweet flavour and greenish-yellow and red skin. Many people think it is the best apple for eating.

the CPI /ˌsiː piː 'aɪ/ ⇨ CONSUMER PRICE INDEX.

the CPRE /ˌsiː piː ɑːr 'iː/ ⇨ CAMPAIGN TO PROTECT RURAL ENGLAND.

the CPS /ˌsiː piː 'es/ ⇨ CROWN PROSECUTION SERVICE.

the CPUSA /ˌsiː piː ˌjuː es 'eɪ/ ⇨ COMMUNIST PARTY OF THE UNITED STATES OF AMERICA.

,**cracker-barrel phi'losophy** n (AmE informal) honest, simple or direct opinions such as those expressed during a friendly conversation or argument. The phrase was originally used for discussions around the large barrel of crackers (= thin, dry biscuits) once kept in most large US food shops.

'**Cracker Jack™** a sticky US sweet/candy, popular with children, made of caramel, popcorn and peanuts. It is sold in a box that contains a small gift.

,**Steve 'Cram** /'kræm/ (1960–) an English runner who won many races in the 1980s. In 1985 he held the world records for running 1500 metres, 2000 metres and one mile.

,**Stephen 'Crane¹** /'kreɪn/ (1871–1900) a US journalist who wrote poems and realistic novels. His most famous novel is *The Red Badge of Courage* (1895) about a frightened soldier who finds courage in the *American Civil War. Crane went to live in England in 1897 but died three years later at the age of 28.

,**Walter 'Crane²** /'kreɪn/ (1845–1915) an English artist and member of the *Arts and Crafts Movement. His colourful book illustrations had a strong influence on the development of children's books.

,**Thomas 'Cranmer** /'krænmə(r)/ (1489–1556) the first *Anglican *Archbishop of Canterbury. He was influenced by the ideas of Martin Luther, and supported King *Henry VIII over the ending of his marriage to *Catherine of Aragon and in establishing the *Church of England. He was responsible for the *Book of Common Prayer and had a strong influence on the *Reformation. He was killed by burning when the *Roman Catholic *Mary I became Queen.

'**Cranwell** /'krænwel/ a military college in *Lincolnshire, where people are trained to be officers in the *RAF.

,**Crate & 'Barrel™** a US group of shops which started in 1962 and sells furniture and other things for the home which are simple and modern in design.

,**Joan 'Crawford¹** /'krɔːfəd; AmE 'krɔːfərd/ (1908–77) a US film actor who was a *Hollywood star for more than 40 years. She won an *Oscar for *Mildred Pierce* (1945) and acted with Bette *Davis in *Whatever Happened to Baby Jane?* (1962). Her daughter Christina wrote a book, *Mommie Dearest* (1978), which attacked Crawford

as a mother, and there was a film version in 1981 in which Faye Dunaway played Crawford.

,**Michael 'Crawford²** /'krɔːfəd; AmE 'krɔːfərd/ (1942–) an English comedy actor, especially on television where he played the part of Frank Spencer in *Some Mothers Do 'Ave 'Em* (1973–8). He later had international success in musical stage shows, especially *Barnum* (1981) and *The Phantom of the Opera* (1986).

Cray'ola™ /kreɪ'əʊlə; AmE kreɪ'oʊlə/ a US make of crayons (= coloured pencils or sticks of soft coloured chalk or wax) which have been popular with children for many years and are sold in boxes of different sizes in many countries. Binney & Smith of Easton, *Pennsylvania, have produced them since 1903.

the 'Crazy Gang a group of British comedians who first gave a *music-hall(1) show together in 1932, and continued to perform as a team for the next 30 years. See also FLANAGAN.

'**Crazy Horse** (c. 1849–77) a *Native American leader of the *Sioux people. In 1876 he and *Sitting Bull defeated General *Custer and his soldiers at the Battle of *Little Bighorn. He was captured and put in prison the following year, and was killed while trying to escape. A large **Crazy Horse Memorial**, showing him riding a horse, is being carved into Thunderhead Mountain in *South Dakota.

the CRE /ˌsiː ɑːr ˌiː/ ⇨ COMMISSION FOR RACIAL EQUALITY.

,**cream 'cracker** (also **cracker**) n a thin, hard, dry biscuit, usually square, which is often eaten with cheese at the end of a meal.

,**Cream of 'Wheat™** n [U] a US wheat cereal which is cooked and eaten hot. It was first produced in 1893 and is now made by *Kraft.

,**cream 'puff** n a type of cake made of very light pastry filled with cream or custard.

,**cream 'soda** n [U, C] (especially AmE) a sweet fizzy drink, flavoured with vanilla: *a glass of cream soda*.

,**cream 'tea** n (BrE) an afternoon meal consisting of tea and *scones (= small cakes made with flour, fat and milk) eaten with *clotted cream and jam. Cream teas are traditional in *Devon and *Cornwall and are now popular with visitors and tourists throughout Britain.

the ,Battle of 'Crécy /'kresi/ a battle fought in 1346 near the small town of Crécy in northern France. The army of the English king *Edward III defeated the much larger French army, mainly because the English soldiers were armed with longbows.

▶ **credit cards**

Credit cards are increasingly used instead of cash or cheques to pay for goods and services. When the **card-holder** is present, e.g. in a shop, the card is **swiped** and a bill is printed. The cardholder has to sign the bill or key their **PIN** (**personal identification number**) into a special machine. Purchases by credit card can also be made by mail, over the telephone or on the *Internet. Credit cards can be used to get money from a cash dispenser. Cards linked to organizations such as **Visa** and **MasterCard** can be used in many countries. People with very good **credit ratings**, i.e. who earn a good salary and have no debts, may get a **gold card** with a higher **credit limit**. Credit card holders receive a monthly **statement** of all their purchases and must pay part of the bill. They are charged interest on the amount they do not pay.

The term *credit card* is sometimes used to include **charge cards**, but the whole amount owed on a charge card account must be paid each month. One of the most famous charge cards is *American Express. Some people have an **affinity card**, a credit card that is linked to a charity. Each time the card is used the card company pays a small amount of money to the charity. Credit cards from shops, called **store cards** or sometimes charge cards, can usually be used only in branches of the shop concerned. **Debit cards** or **banker's cards**, such as **Maestro**, can be used to pay for goods but the whole amount is automatically deducted from the user's bank account within a few days.

Most Americans have a variety of **plastic money**, including Visa and MasterCard (often more than one of each), American Express and *Diners Club, as well as store cards. People decide which cards to have depending on the way they plan to use them. For example, some cards are free but have a high rate of interest, called the **annual percentage rate** or **APR**; others have an **annual fee**, but charge lower interest rates, and so are good for people who do not pay the whole bill every month.

'credit ,union (*also* **co-operative credit union**) *n* (*AmE*) a type of US co-operative bank. Members buy shares, and the bank lends money to them at a low rate. Most credit unions are for people who work together, as in a hospital or a university, or who live in an area, such as a state.

Cree /kriː/ *n* (*pl* **Crees** *or* **Cree**) a member of a *Native American people. They were hunters, originally from Canada where most Crees still live, but one group moved south to land that is now the US state of *Montana.

Creek /kriːk/ *n* (*pl* **Creeks** *or* **Creek**) a member of a *Native American people. They were mostly farmers, originally in the states of *Alabama and *Georgia. They were one of the *Five Civilized Tribes. Under their leader *Tecumseh they were defeated by General Andrew *Jackson at the Battle of Horseshoe Bend (1814) in Alabama. They were then moved to the West. Many now live in the state of *Oklahoma.

'Creole /'kriːəʊl; *AmE* 'kriːoʊl/ *n* **1** [C] (in the US) a person descended from French or Spanish people who settled in the southern states, especially around *New Orleans. Creoles speak a mixed language of their own and are known for their spicy food.
2 [U] the language of the Creoles. Compare CAJUN.

Crewe /kruː/ a town in *Cheshire, England, which became an important railway junction (= a place where several lines meet) during the 19th century.

,Michael 'Crichton /'kraɪtən/ (1942–) a popular US writer of novels and films, mostly involving science and medicine. His books include *The Andromeda Strain* (1969), *Jurassic Park* (1990), *The Lost World* (1995) and *Timeline* (1999), all of which he adapted for films.

,Francis 'Crick /'krɪk/ (1916–2004) an English scientist. His work with James *Watson at the *Cavendish Laboratory led to the discovery of the structure of DNA in 1953. Crick, Watson and Maurice Wilkins shared the *Nobel Prize for this work in 1962. Crick's later career involved work on the visual system and the brain, and he published a book, *The Astonishing Hypothesis*, on this subject in 1994. He became a member of the *Order of Merit in 1992.

▶ **cricket**

a summer sport played in England and some other *Commonwealth countries between two teams of 11 players on a grass **pitch**. In England, it is played between April and September at many levels, from informal games on the beach to matches between schools, villages and professional sides representing a county. Players traditionally play wearing white, although this is now being replaced in some competitions by coloured clothing.

Cricket is a complicated game played with wooden **bats** and a leather ball. Each team **bats** (= hits the ball) for an **innings**, trying to score **runs**, while the other team **bowls** (= throws the ball) and **fields** (= tries to catch or stop the ball after it has been hit). Their aim is to get the **batsman out** for as few runs as possible. Two batsmen are **in** (= on the pitch) at the same time, each defending a **wicket** (= three upright wooden posts with two short pieces of wood resting on top of them) which the **bowler** tries to hit. Each bowler in turn **bowls an over** (= throws the ball six times from the same end of the pitch). The two wickets are 22 yards apart and runs are scored when the batsmen run between them after they have hit the ball. A batsman can also score four runs if he hits the ball over the **boundary** (= a line round the edge of the pitch) or six runs if it goes over the boundary before it hits the ground. A batsman can be out for a variety of reasons and an innings usually ends when all but one of the batting team are out.

Matches may last for several days, though **one-day** and **limited-over** matches are popular. In England and Wales, 18 counties compete each year in two divisions in the *county championship. They also compete in the Twenty20 Cup, a series of limited-over matches in which each team bowls 20 overs, which started in 2003. The English national team plays **test matches** against other national sides including Australia, New Zealand, South Africa, India, Pakistan and the West Indies and in the **Cricket World Cup** which takes place every four years. England and Australia also compete for the *Ashes, a series of 5-day test matches.

cricket

the Cri,mean 'War /kraɪˌmiːən/ a war fought by Britain, France and Turkey against Russia between 1853 and 1856 in the Crimea, a part of the Ukraine. Russia wanted power over Turkey, and Britain and France wanted to end Russia's power in the Black Sea. Most of the military action was around Sebastopol, the Russian navy base. It was the first war during which the European public were able to follow events as they happened, because of the invention of the telegraph (= a device for sending messages along wires by the use of electric current). See also CHARGE OF THE LIGHT BRIGADE, NIGHTINGALE.

'Crimewatch /'kraɪmwɒtʃ; *AmE* 'kraɪmwɑːtʃ/ a British television programme on *BBC One. It describes serious crimes that the police need help with and often shows films of actors copying a crime to help witnesses remember what they saw. Members of the public are asked to call the programme if they have any information about the crimes. *Crimewatch* began in 1984.

the 'Criminal In,vesti'gation De,partment ⇨ CID.

the 'Criminal 'Justice and ,Public 'Order Act a British law passed in 1994 dealing with a number of social and legal issues. It gave the police new powers to prevent people gathering in large groups, especially *New Age travellers and people attending outdoor *rave parties. It also introduced new laws to deal with terrorism, and allowed *secure training centres to be established for children who repeatedly break the law. The Act was opposed by many people who thought it gave the police too much power and restricted people's freedom unfairly.

,Dr 'Crippen /'krɪpən/ (Hawley Harvey Crippen 1862–1910) a US doctor who came to London in 1896. He fell in love with his secretary Ethel le Neve, murdered his wife and hid her body in the cellar of his house. Crippen and Ethel tried to escape on a ship to New York, with Ethel dressed as a boy, but the captain became suspicious and used the ship's radio to tell the British police. Crippen was hanged for the murder, but Ethel was found not guilty and lived until 1967.

,Stafford 'Cripps /,stæfəd 'krɪps; AmE ,stæfərd/ (1889–1952) a British *Labour politician who is best remembered for his policy of 'austerity' after *World War II, when as *Chancellor of the Exchequer he kept a tight control over Britain's economy. He was the nephew of Beatrice *Webb, and was made a *knight in 1930.

'Crisco™ /'krɪskəʊ; AmE 'krɪskoʊ/ a US make of vegetable shortening (= fat used to make pastry crisp). It is mostly used for making cakes, sweet biscuits, etc. It was first sold in 1911.

'Crisis /'kraɪsɪs/ a British charity that began in 1972. Each year it uses empty buildings in large cities to give homeless people shelter, food and clothing in the time around Christmas.

,Davy 'Crockett /,deɪvi 'krɒkɪt; AmE 'krɑːkɪt/ (1786–1836) a famous American *frontiersman from *Tennessee. He was also a soldier with General Andrew *Jackson and a politician, being elected to the US *Congress (1827–31 and 1833–5). He was killed at the *Alamo. Many stories are told of his life. Walt *Disney made a television series about him in the 1950s and the film *Davy Crockett* (1955).

'Crockford's /'krɒkfədz; AmE 'krɑːkfərdz/ (Crockford's Clerical Directory) a book that gives details of all living *Anglican priests and ministers of the Church in Britain. It is published every two years and was first published in 1860.

'Crock-pot™ /'krɒk pɒt; AmE 'krɑːk pɑːt/ n a US make of electric pot that cooks food slowly at a low temperature.

croft n (BrE) (in Scotland) a small farm, especially, in the past, a rented house with a small piece of land and the right to graze animals on land shared with other crofters (= people who farm a croft).

a crofter's house

,Richmal 'Crompton /,rɪtʃməl 'krɒmptən; AmE 'krɑːmptən/ (1890–1969) an English author who wrote the *William books as well as novels for adults.

,Oliver 'Cromwell¹ /'krɒmwel; AmE 'krɑːmwel/ (1599–1658) an English general and politician who for a short time ruled England, Scotland and Ireland. Cromwell was a *Puritan who began his political career as the *Member of Parliament for Huntingdon in 1628. When the *English Civil War started in 1642, he gathered soldiers in his area to fight for *Parliament and soon became the leader of the *New Model Army and the greatest soldier in England. He was one of those who signed the

statue of Oliver Cromwell at Westminster

death warrant of King *Charles I in 1649. As a leader of the *Commonwealth, he was responsible for the cruel treatment of those who were opposed to the *Puritans in Ireland and Scotland. In 1653 Cromwell dismissed Parliament and became the *Lord Protector of England, Scotland and Ireland, with almost the same power as a king. He was offered the crown, but refused it. In 1658, he died of malaria and was buried in *Westminster Abbey. Cromwell's son Richard took his place as Lord Protector for a short time after his death, but he did not have his father's gifts as a leader, and in 1660 *Charles II became king and the *Restoration. Oliver Cromwell's body was dug up and his head was put on a pole on the roof of one of the buildings in *Westminster(1) for 24 years.

Cromwell is also remembered for a famous remark he made to the artist Peter Lely (1618–80). People often say that something or somebody should be shown *warts and all*, meaning that faults or unpleasant features should not be left out.

> 66 Mr Lely, I desire you would use all your skill to paint my picture truly like me, and not flatter me at all; but remark all these roughnesses, pimples, warts, and everything as you see me, otherwise I will never pay a farthing for it. 99
> Oliver Cromwell

,Thomas 'Cromwell² /'krɒmwel; AmE 'krɑːmwel/ (c. 1485–1540) the chief minister to King *Henry VIII during the 1530s. After the fall of Thomas *Wolsey, Cromwell arranged the king's divorce from *Catherine of Aragon and later organized the *Dissolution of the Monasteries. In 1540, Cromwell was made the Earl of Essex, but four months later the King accused him of treason and had his head cut off. Cromwell said at his execution that he died a Catholic.

,Walter 'Cronkite /'krɒŋkaɪt; AmE 'krɑːŋkaɪt/ (1916–) a US television journalist who presented the national CBS Evening News programme from 1962 to 1981. He ended each programme by saying, 'And that's the way it is.' Cronkite was known for his honesty and in 1973 was chosen as the 'Most Trusted Man in America'.

'crop ,circle (also corn circle) n [often pl] an area in a field where parts of the crop have been made flat. The area is round or in other shapes and patterns. Crop circles began to appear in Britain in the 1980s. Some people think that they are made by beings from other planets or by unusual winds, while others think that they are made by local people as a joke.

'croquet /'krəʊkeɪ/ n [U] a game played on grass in which the players hit balls through a series of hoops, using a mallet (= a wooden hammer with a long handle). Croquet became popular among the *upper classes in Britain in the 1850s, and is still often regarded as an upper-class game today. The All England Croquet Club began at *Wimbledon in 1868. The four countries where croquet is most played (Britain, Australia, New Zealand and the US) compete every three or four years for the MacRobertson Shield.

Bing 'Crosby /ˌbɪŋ 'krɒzbi; AmE 'krɑːzbi/ (1904–77) a US singer and film actor, known for his fine voice and relaxed style. His recording of White Christmas (1942) was the most popular Christmas song ever recorded. He won an *Oscar for the film Going My Way (1944) and made a series of seven comedy films (1940–47) with Bob *Hope, all with 'road' in the title, including Road to Morocco (1942).

Crosse and 'Blackwell /ˌkrɒs, 'blækwel; AmE ˌkrɔːs/ a British company now owned by Premier International Foods that makes a lot of different food products.

▶ **crosswords**

Crosswords, or **crossword puzzles**, first appeared in the US in the early 20th century. Today, many people in the US and in Britain regularly **do crosswords**, sometimes on the bus or train on their way to work. Most newspapers and magazines contain at least one crossword and there are often prizes for people who send in the correct **solution**. Books of crosswords are also popular.

Solving a crossword involves answering a set of **clues**. The answers are words or phrases which fit together in a patterned grid. The clues are usually numbered and listed as **across** and **down**, according to whether the answer reads across the grid or from top to bottom.

There are two basic types of crossword, called in Britain **quick crosswords** and **cryptic crosswords**. In quick crosswords the clues are usually definitions of the answers. This is much the most common type of crossword in the US, where the grids are usually a lot bigger and contain many more words. These crosswords are not necessarily easy, and the one in the Sunday issue of the *New York Times is considered very difficult.

Cryptic crosswords, which began in Britain and are much more popular there than in any other country, have clues which contain both a definition of the answer and a word puzzle involving the letters in it. One common type of word puzzle is an **anagram**, in which the letters of the answer word are rearranged in the clue to form another word or phrase. For example, CARTHORSE and SHORT RACE are both anagrams of the word ORCHESTRA.

Crow[1] /krəʊ; AmE kroʊ/ n (pl **Crows** or **Crow**) a member of a *Native American people who lived on land that is now *Montana and *Wyoming. They were hunters and grew tobacco. They helped the US Army against the *Sioux people. Most Crows now live on a reservation (= land given and protected by the US government) in southern Montana.

Sheryl 'Crow[2] /ˌʃerəl 'krəʊ; AmE 'kroʊ/ (1963–) a US singer who also writes songs. Her first album was Tuesday Night Music Club (1994), and that year she won three *Grammy awards, one as Best New Artist and two for the song All I Wanna Do. She has also received Grammy awards for the song If It Makes You Happy (1996), the album The Globe Sessions (1998) and the songs Sweet Child O' Mine (1999), There Goes the Neighbourhood (2000) and Steve McQueen (2002).

Russell 'Crowe /ˌrʌsl 'krəʊ; AmE 'kroʊ/ (1964–) a film actor born in New Zealand who grew up in Australia. He won an *Oscar for his part in Gladiator (2000) and his other films include A Beautiful Mind (2001) and Master and Commander (2003).

the 'Crown n [sing] (in Britain) the power and authority of the State, as represented by the King or Queen. It is used in phrases such as *Crown Estate, although most things are now the responsibility of the government rather than the King or Queen. ⇨ note at BRITISH CONSTITUTION.

Crown 'Agent a member of an organization, started in 1833 by the British government, which provides financial and commercial services for foreign governments and international organizations. Crown agents are professional people appointed by the government. Their full official title is Crown Agents for Overseas Governments and Administrations, which in 1997 became a private company as part of the Crown Agents Foundation.

Crown 'Colony ⇨ OVERSEAS TERRITORY.

Crown 'Court n (in England and Wales) a local court in larger towns and cities where serious criminal cases are tried by a judge and jury. Cases may come to the Crown Court when a magistrates' court decides that they are too serious for it to deal with. If a decision of the Crown Court is questioned, the case goes to the *Court of Appeal. See also COUNTY COURT. ⇨ note at LEGAL SYSTEM.

Crown De'pendency n a term applied to either of two places close to the British mainland: the *Channel Islands and the *Isle of Man. These have their own governments, which make decisions about the law, police, education and other matters, but rely on the British *Crown for their defence and foreign policy. Compare OVERSEAS TERRITORY.

Crown 'Derby /'dɑːbi; AmE 'dɑːrbi/ n [U] a type of china (= fine pottery) made in *Derby, England, in the 18th and 19th centuries. Objects made of Crown Derby are marked with a crown over the letter D.

the ˌCrown E'state all the lands owned by the British King or Queen and the money that is made from them. In 1760, King *George III gave up the monarch's rights to these in return for the *Civil List, a payment made to the King or Queen every year by Parliament. As a result the money from the Crown Estate, which is managed by the **Crown Estate Commissioners**, is now collected by the government on behalf of the British people. In 2003 the lands and property were worth more than £4 billion and the income from them was about £170 million.

crown green 'bowls n [U] a form of the game of *bowls that is played on an area of grass with a slightly raised centre, instead of on a flat surface. It is played especially in the north of England.

the ˌCrown 'Jewels the jewels and other precious objects worn or carried by the British King or Queen on official occasions. They are kept for the public to see in the *Tower of London and include several crowns, sceptres (= a decorated rod carried as a symbol of power) and swords. Only two small items are from before 1660, as the original Crown Jewels were destroyed during the *Commonwealth under Oliver *Cromwell. See also KOHINOOR.

the ˌCrown Prose'cution ˌService (abbr **the CPS**) an independent organization started in 1986 that decides whether a person should be charged with a crime in a court of law in England or Wales. Before 1986, the police made this decision themselves. The person in charge of the Crown Prosecution Service is the *Director of Public Prosecutions.

the ˌ**Crucible** ˈ**Theatre** /ˌkruːsɪbl/ a theatre, opened in 1971, in *Sheffield, England. As well as showing plays, the theatre is well known as the place where major *snooker competitions are held.

Crufts /krʌfts/ the most important dog show in Britain, held for four days every year at the *National Exhibition Centre in *Birmingham. It is run by the *Kennel Club. The show is named after Charles Cruft, who started it in London in 1886: *One of her dogs was Best of Breed at Crufts in 2004.*

ˌ**George** ˈ**Cruickshank** /ˈkrʊkʃæŋk/ (1792–1878) an English artist who was famous for his political cartoons. He also drew illustrations for the books of many famous authors, including Charles *Dickens and Walter *Scott.

ˌ**Tom** ˈ**Cruise** /ˈkruːz/ (1962–) a US actor. He won *Golden Globe Awards for *Born on the Fourth of July* (1990), *Jerry Maguire* (1996) and *Magnolia* (2000). He is probably best known for playing a US Navy pilot in *Top Gun* (1986). His other films have included *Mission Impossible* (1996) and *Eyes Wide Shut* (1999) in which he appeared with Nicole *Kidman, to whom he was married until 2001.

the **Cru'sades** a series of military expeditions between the 11th and 14th centuries, in which armies from the Christian countries of Europe tried to get back the Holy Land (= the area that is now Israel, Palestine, Jordan and Egypt) from the Muslims. The soldiers who took part in the Crusades were called **Crusaders**. The best known British Crusader was King *Richard I. The Crusades achieved very little, but as a result of them new ideas were exchanged, trade was improved, and new goods such as sugar and cotton came to Europe for the first time.

Cruse /kruːz/ a British charity formed in 1959 that gives help and advice to people when a relative or friend has died. Its full name is Cruse – Bereavement Care.

ˌ**Crystal** ˈ**Palace** **1 the Crystal Palace** a very large building made of glass and metal, designed in nine days by Joseph Paxton (1801–65) for the *Great Exhibition of 1851. It took six months to put up in *Hyde Park in London. After the Exhibition, it was taken to a new park in south London. In 1936 it burned down. Its name was given to it by the humorous magazine *Punch.
2 a football club in south London: *He plays for Crystal Palace.*
3 a stadium where sports contests are held in south London.

the **CSA** /ˌsiː es ˈeɪ/ ⇨ CHILD SUPPORT AGENCY.

CSI: ˈCrime Scene Investiˌgation /ˌsiː es ˈaɪ/ a US television drama series on *CBS, which has been shown in other countries, about a team of scientists who use scientific techniques to investigate and solve serious crimes, especially murders. The original series is set in *Las Vegas and two other series have also been created set in *Miami and New York.

CST /ˌsiː es ˈtiː/ ⇨ CENTRAL STANDARD TIME.

CTC /ˌsiː tiː ˈsiː/ ⇨ CITY TECHNOLOGY COLLEGE.

the ˌ**Cuban** ˈ**missile** ˌ**crisis** /ˌkjuːbən/ a dangerous political situation that developed in 1962 between the US and USSR. President *Kennedy became aware that there were Soviet nuclear weapons in Cuba and sent the US Navy to stop Soviet ships from bringing more. It seemed possible that there would be a nuclear war between the two countries, but the Soviet leader Nikita Khrushchev ordered the Russian ships to turn back and later removed all of the weapons.

ˈ**Cub Scout** (*also* **Cub**) *n* a member of the junior branch of the *Scouts, for boys aged between 8 and 10 in Britain and 7 and 10 in the US. Since 1992 girls have been able to join the British Cub Scouts, but only in areas where the

local group has agreed to accept them. In Britain the adult in charge of a group (or 'pack') of Cubs is known as *Akela*, from a character in *The *Jungle Book.*

ˌ**George** ˈ**Cukor** /ˈkjuːkɔː(r)/ (1899–1983) a US film director. He is best remembered for his film comedies, including *The Philadelphia Story* (1940), *Pat and Mike* (1952) and *My Fair Lady* (1964), for which he received an *Oscar.

the ˈ**Cullinan** ˌ**diamond** /ˈkʌlɪnən/ the largest diamond ever found, weighing about 620 grams. It was named after Thomas Cullinan, the head of the Transvaal mine in which it was found in 1905. Two years later the Transvaal government bought it for one million dollars and presented it to King *Edward VII. It was then cut into nine large stones and 96 small ones and used in the *Crown Jewels.

the ˌ**Battle of Culˈloden** /kəˈlɒdn/ a battle (1746) fought on Culloden Moor near Inverness in Scotland between the mainly English soldiers led by the Duke of *Cumberland (the second son of King *George II) and the Scottish army of Charles Edward *Stuart (*Bonny Prince Charlie). Charles was defeated and most of his soldiers were killed. Culloden was the last battle to be fought in Britain, and it brought the *Jacobite rebellions to an end.

ˈ**culture shock** *n* [U] a feeling of confusion and anxiety that someone experiences when they visit or go to live in a place with a very different culture, especially a different country, where they do not know how to behave and what is appropriate and what is not: *Nothing could have prepared me for the culture shock I experienced when I first arrived in New York.*

ˈ**Cumberland**[1] /ˈkʌmbələnd; *AmE* ˈkʌmbərlənd/ a former county in north-west England. In 1974 it was joined with *Westmorland and part of *Lancashire(1) to form *Cumbria.

the ˌ**Duke of** ˈ**Cumberland**[2] /ˈkʌmbələnd; *AmE* ˈkʌmbərlənd/ (1721–65) an English general, the second son of King *George II. He defeated the Scottish army at the Battle of *Culloden and then treated them so severely that he was given the nickname 'Butcher Cumberland'.

the ˌ**Cumberland** ˈ**Gap** /ˌkʌmbələnd; *AmE* ˈkʌmbərlənd/ a way through the Cumberland Mountains between the US states of *Virginia and *Kentucky. It was used by Daniel *Boone and the early settlers of Kentucky.

ˌ**Cumberland** ˈ**sausage** /ˌkʌmbələnd; *AmE* ˈkʌmbərlənd/ *n* [U, C] a very long, spicy pork sausage traditionally made in the north of England. It is usually twisted into a spiral before cooking.

ˈ**Cumbria** /ˈkʌmbriə/ a county in north-west England, on the border with Scotland. It consists of the former counties of *Cumberland and *Westmorland and part of *Lancashire. It contains the *Lake District and *Scafell Pike, the highest mountain in England.

ˌ**cum** ˈ**laude** /ˌkʊm ˈlaʊdeɪ/ (in the US) the Latin expression, meaning 'with praise', used to indicate a high academic achievement of a college or university student who has completed his or her studies. It is the lowest of the three highest grades and is shown on the diploma (= document awarded for completing a course of study). Compare MAGNA CUM LAUDE, SUMMA CUM LAUDE.

ˌ**E E** ˈ**Cummings** /ˌiː iː ˈkʌmɪŋz/ (Edward Estlin Cummings 1894–1962) a US writer of poetry and novels. His poems contain highly original language and were often printed in an unusual style, e.g. using only small letters. He often wrote about himself as 'i' and signed his name 'e.e.cummings'. His poetry collections include

C

Tulips and Chimneys (1923). His best-known novel is *The Enormous Room* (1922).

,Samuel **Cu'nard** /kju:'nɑːd; *AmE* kju:'nɑːrd/ (1787–1865) a Canadian ship owner who in 1839 started a service carrying passengers across the Atlantic between Britain and North America. The journey then took about two weeks. The company became known as the **Cunard Line** and had many famous ships, among them the *Mauretania* and the *Lusitania* from 1907, the *Queen Mary* (1936), the *Queen Elizabeth* (1940) and the *QE2* (1967).

'**cupcake** /'kʌpkeɪk/ *n* a small cake baked in a paper container shaped like a cup, often with icing/frosting (= mixture of sugar, egg white, flavours, etc.) on top.

the ,**Cup 'Final** an important football event in England every year. The two teams that remain after playing in the *FA Cup competition play against each other in the Cup Final. There is a separate Scottish Cup Final.

,**curate's 'egg** *n* [sing] a thing that is partly good and partly bad. The phrase comes from a cartoon in the British magazine *Punch* in 1895, in which a nervous young curate (= priest) is having breakfast with a *bishop. The bishop says 'I'm afraid you've got a bad egg there' and the curate, not wanting to upset the bishop, replies, 'Oh no, my Lord! … Parts of it are excellent!': *Their investment plan shows the familiar curate's egg pattern of some bits doing well and others doing badly.*

Ed,wina '**Currie** /ed,wi:nə 'kʌri/ (1946–) a former British *Conservative politician who is known for saying what she thinks in a very direct way. A famous example was when in 1988 as a health minister she said that most eggs produced in Britain at the time were infected with salmonella (= a germ that can cause food poisoning). Currie has also written some novels.

,**Currier and 'Ives** /,kʌriər ənd 'aɪvz/ a US company (1835–1907) that produced more than 7000 different coloured lithographs (= prints made from metal plates) of US life in the 19th century. The pictures are still popular and often used on greetings cards.

'**Currys** /'kʌriz/ (in Britain) a chain of shops that sell electrical goods: *You can buy it at your local Currys.*

,Tony '**Curtis** /'kɜːtɪs; *AmE* 'kɜːrtɪs/ (1925–) a US film actor who has appeared in a wide variety of films, including *Some Like It Hot* (1959) and *The Boston Strangler* (1968). His former wife Janet Leigh (1927–2004) was also a film actor, as is their daughter Jamie Lee Curtis (1958–).

the ,**Curtis 'Cup** /,kɜːtɪs; *AmE* ,kɜːrtɪs/ a women's golf competition held every two years, in which the British and Irish play against the USA. It was started by two sisters, Margaret and Harriet Curtis, in 1932. See also WALKER CUP.

,Lord '**Curzon** /'kɜːzən; *AmE* 'kɜːrzən/ (George Nathaniel Curzon 1859–1925) a British diplomat and politician. He became Viceroy of India at the age of only 39. Later (1919–24) he was *Foreign Secretary. Curzon had a strong personality and many people thought he was too proud. There was a popular rhyme about him:

❝ My name is George Nathaniel Curzon, I am a most superior person. ❞

'**custard** *n* [U] (*especially BrE*) a thick yellow liquid that is eaten hot or cold with various sweet dishes. It is made with milk, eggs, flour and sugar. It can also be bought in tins, or as a powder that is mixed with milk. Some British people associate custard with school meals: *For pudding we had apple crumble with lumpy custard.*

'**General ,George 'Custer** /kʌstə(r)/ (1839–76) a US general who first became famous for his wild courage

fighting for the *Union during the American *Civil War. He was proud of his appearance and his long fair hair. From 1868, he fought the *Cheyenne and the *Sioux, until he and all his soldiers were killed by them at the Battle of *Little Bighorn. This battle is sometimes called **Custer's Last Stand**.

customary measure *n* [U] a system of weights and measures used in the US which is similar to the British *imperial system.

,**Customs and 'Excise** /,kʌstəmz ənd 'eksaɪz/ (*also formal* **Her Majesty's Customs and Excise**) the British government department responsible for collecting **customs duties**, taxes charged on imports from outside the European Union, and **excise duties**, taxes charged on certain types of goods, such as wine and beer, petrol and tobacco products. The Department of Customs and Excise also collects *VAT, a tax charged on the price of many goods and services in Britain, and works to prevent banned goods such as some drugs being imported into Britain: *A large quantity of drugs has been seized by Customs and Excise officials today.*

the ,**Cutty 'Sark** /,kʌti 'sɑːk; *AmE* 'sɑːrk/ a famous British sailing ship, built in 1869, which carried tea from China and then, after 1879, wool from Australia. From 1895 until 1922, the *Cutty Sark* was owned by the Portuguese, and then she became a training ship for British sailors. Since 1957 she has been open to visitors at *Greenwich. Her name comes from the 'cutty sark' (short shirt) worn by one of the witches in the poem *Tam o' Shanter* by Robert *Burns.

the *Cutty Sark*

the **CWU** /,si: dʌblju: 'ju:/ (*in full* the **Communication Workers Union**) a British *trade union for workers in the *Post Office, *BT and similar organizations. It was formed in 1920.

the '**Cybermen** /'saɪbəmen; *AmE* 'saɪbərmen/ *n* [pl] ⇨ DOCTOR WHO.

'**Cyclone**™ /'saɪkləʊn; *AmE* 'saɪkloʊn/ *n* a US type of fence made of connected steel links. Cyclone fences are especially strong and often used to protect people's homes.

'**Cymbeline** /'sɪmbəli:n/ a play (*c.* 1610) by William *Shakespeare. It tells how the love of a faithful wife, Imogen, survives a series of terrible experiences, and the play ends happily. Cymbeline, Imogen's father, is based on Cunobelin, a British king of the 1st century.

'**Cymru** /'kʌmri/ the Welsh word for 'Wales'. See also PLAID CYMRU.

'**Cyprus** /'saɪprəs/ an island in the Mediterranean Sea which became a colony of Britain in 1914. Because there has been a lot of tension between the Greek and Turkish communities on the island, United Nations soldiers have been there since 1964 to keep the peace.
▶ **Cypriot** /'sɪpriət/ *adj*, *n*.

D d

DA /ˌdiː ˈeɪ/ ⇨ DISTRICT ATTORNEY.

ˌDad's ˈArmy a popular *BBC television comedy series (1968–77) about an inefficient group of soldiers in the *Home Guard whose job is to defend Warmington-on-Sea, an imaginary village on the south coast of England, during *World War II. The phrase 'dad's army' is now sometimes used in British English to refer to any group of old soldiers.

ˈdaffodil n a tall yellow flower that comes out in Britain between February and April. Since the early 20th century the daffodil has been one of the national emblems of Wales, and many Welsh people wear the flowers on their clothes on *St David's Day. See also LEEK.

ˈDaffodils a famous poem (1807, revised in 1815) by William *Wordsworth. It is remembered by older British people as a poem studied at school, and is considered to be a typical example of *Romantic poetry. Its first lines are:

> 66 I wandered lonely as a cloud
> That floats on high o'er vales and hills,
> When all at once I saw a crowd,
> A host, of golden daffodils;
> Beside the lake, beneath the trees,
> Fluttering and dancing in the breeze. 99

ˌDaffy ˈDuck™ /ˌdæfi/ a character in the *Looney Tunes* and *Merry Melodies* cartoon series. He first appeared in 1937. Daffy behaves in a crazy way and spits when he says the 's' sound. See also AVERY.

ˈDagwood /ˈdægwʊd/ **1** a character in the US strip cartoon *Blondie*. Dagwood Bumstead is the rich, lazy husband of Blondie. He makes and eats very large sandwiches.
2 (also **Dagwood sandwich**) n (AmE humorous) a large sandwich filled with a variety of meat, cheese, etc.

ˌRoald ˈDahl /ˌrəʊəld ˈdɑːl; AmE ˌroʊəld/ (1916–90) a British author best known for his very popular children's books. These include *James and the Giant Peach* (1962), *Charlie and the Chocolate Factory* (1964), *The BFG* (1982) and *Matilda* (1988), all of which have been made into films. Dahl is one of the most popular children's authors ever, though some adults are worried by the cruel aspects of many of his stories. He was born in Wales, of Norwegian parents.

the ˌDaily Exˈpress ⇨ EXPRESS.

the ˌDaily ˈMail (informal **the Mail**) one of Britain's national daily newspapers, started in 1896 by Alfred *Harmsworth, who later became Lord *Northcliffe. It presents political views that are generally right-wing. It has a *tabloid format (= size of page) and is considered to be part of the 'popular press', not one of the 'quality papers': *Could you get me a copy of the Daily Mail?* See also MAIL ON SUNDAY.

the ˌDaily ˈMirror the former name for the *Mirror* newspaper.

the ˌDaily ˈNews a New York *tabloid newspaper, established in 1919 and known as 'New York's Hometown Paper'. It is the best-selling New York paper.

the ˌDaily ˈSport one of Britain's national daily *tabloid newspapers, started in 1988. It mainly includes articles about sport and sex, and has a lot of pictures.

the ˌDaily ˈStar (informal **the Star**) one of Britain's daily *tabloid newspapers. It was started in 1978 as a paper for the North but became a national newspaper the following year.

the ˌDaily ˈTelegraph (informal **the Telegraph**) one of Britain's national daily newspapers, started in 1855. It is traditionally right-wing in its views and supports the *Conservative Party, though it sometimes criticizes its policies. The *Daily Telegraph* is considered to be one of the 'quality papers' and to be especially good in its writing about sport: *She writes for The Daily Telegraph.* See also SUNDAY TELEGRAPH.

the ˌDaily ˈWorker ⇨ MORNING STAR.

ˈDaimler™ /ˈdeɪmlə(r)/ n an expensive make of car formerly produced in *Coventry, England. The company was formed in 1896 and was named after the German designer of the original engine, Gottfried Daimler. Daimlers are typically associated with *upper-class people in Britain, and with the British royal family, who have owned several. In 1960 the company was sold to *Jaguar, which continued to use the name on some of its more expensive cars. A separate German company, Daimler-Benz, joined with *Chrysler in 1998 to form DaimlerChrysler.

ˌDairy ˈQueen™ (abbr **DQ**) a large group of US *fast food restaurants that sell soft ice cream, milkshakes, hamburgers, pizzas, etc. The first Dairy Queen opened in *Illinois in 1940 and there are now Dairy Queens in many countries. They are especially popular with young people.

Daˈkota /dəˈkəʊtə; AmE dəˈkoʊtə/ n the British name for a US aircraft, the Douglas DC 3. About 11 000 were built between 1935 and 1946. They were popular with airlines, and a military version was built during *World War II.

the Daˈkotas /dəˈkəʊtəz; AmE dəˈkoʊtəz/ the US states of *North Dakota and *South Dakota. The original **Dakota Territory** (1861–89) included these states, most of *Montana and *Wyoming, and a small part of *Nebraska. It was named after a Native American people, also called the *Sioux.

ˈDalek /ˈdɑːlek/ n a strange and frightening metal creature in the British television series *Doctor Who. The Daleks are Doctor Who's enemies. When they shoot at people they say, 'Exterminate, exterminate!' in harsh electronic voices. They helped to make the series popular, especially with children.

ˌArthur ˈDaley¹ /ˈdeɪli/ a character in the British *ITV television series *Minder* (1979–1994). A Londoner who sells used cars and other goods, he is always interested in making money, not necessarily in an honest way, but is usually unsuccessful. He employs a 'minder', Terry, to protect him. His name is often used to refer to someone like this. Some of the expressions Arthur Daley uses have also become part of the language. For example, he sometimes describes a business deal as 'a nice little earner', meaning that it will make him a lot of money easily. He also talks about his wife (who is never seen) as ''er indoors': *The law will make things difficult for the Arthur Daleys of this world.*

ˌRichard J ˈDaley² /ˈdeɪli/ (Richard Joseph Daley 1902–76) the mayor of *Chicago from 1955 to 1976, well known for his strong methods. In 1968 he ordered the Chicago police to attack a group of demonstrators (= people taking part in a public protest) and this was embarrassing to the *Democratic Party which was meeting there to choose a candidate for President. Daley's son, Richard M Daley (1942–), was elected mayor of Chicago in 1989.

,Kenny **'Dalglish** /dæl'gliːʃ/ (1951–) a Scottish football player and club manager. He played for *Celtic (1970–77), for *Liverpool, where he was also manager (1977–90), and for Scotland more times than any other player, between 1971 and 1986. He was manager at the English club Blackburn Rovers between 1991 and 1996, and at Newcastle United from 1997 to 1998.

'Dallas /'dæləs/ the third largest city in the US state of *Texas. It was established in 1856 and is now a major business centre. President *Kennedy was murdered there in 1963. ⇨ note at FOOTBALL – AMERICAN STYLE.

'Dallas /'dæləs/ a popular US television series (1978–88) which has been shown in many countries. The stories were about rich people in the oil industry and their love of money and sex. The main characters were the Ewing family who owned the Southfork ranch (= large farm).

,Hugh **'Dalton** /'dɔːltən/ (1887–1962) a British *Labour politician who became *Chancellor of the Exchequer in 1945. He had to resign in 1947 because he had given some information to a journalist before he had told the *House of Commons. He soon returned to politics, however, and was made a *life peer in 1960.

dame *n* **1** (*also* **pantomime dame**) one of the main characters in a British *pantomime. The dame is an ugly old woman who has a strong comic role, and is almost always played by a man.
2 (*also* **Dame**) (in Britain) the title of a woman who has been given the *OBE or any of certain other awards by the King or Queen: *Dame Judi Dench ◊ She was made a dame in the Birthday Honours List.* ⇨ note at HONOURS.

,Dame Com**'mander** (in Britain) the title of a woman who has been given one of a particular set of honours by the King or Queen. Compare KNIGHT COMMANDER. ⇨ note at HONOURS.

,Dame **'Edna** ⇨ EVERAGE.

,Dame Grand **'Cross** (in Britain) the title of a woman who has been given one of a particular set of honours by the King or Queen. Compare KNIGHT GRAND CROSS. ⇨ note at HONOURS.

,dancehall **'reggae** ⇨ RAGGA.

the **'Dance ,Theater of 'Harlem** /'hɑːləm; *AmE* 'hɑːrləm/ a US dance group with mostly *African American dancers. It was established in 1971 in *Harlem in New York by Arthur Mitchell (1934–), the first African American principal artist in the New York City Ballet, and has performed many works by George *Balanchine.

A **'Dance to the 'Music of 'Time** a sequence of twelve novels by the English author Anthony Powell (1905–2000), published between 1951 and 1975. The novels present a broad picture of the British upper and middle classes during those years and are known for their very large range of characters, including the very ambitious Kenneth Widmerpool. A television version of the series was broadcast in 1997.

'Dance Um,brella a festival of modern dance which started in 1978 and takes place every year in *London with performances by contemporary dance companies from around the world.

,Dan **'Dare** /'deə(r); *AmE* 'der/ a popular character in the British boys' *comic *Eagle*. Colonel Dan Dare was the 'Pilot of the Future', a traveller in space. His main enemy was the Mekon, a small green space creature with a big head.

,Dandie **'Dinmont** /,dændi 'dɪnmənt/ *n* [C] a type of *terrier with short legs, a long body and tail, and long ears. Its hair is greyish or yellowish. Dandie Dinmonts came originally from Scotland and are named after a Scottish character in a novel by Walter *Scott.

,**D&'T** /,diː ən 'tiː/ (*in full* **Design and Technology**) a subject taught in British secondary schools. In it, pupils learn how to design and make things, usually in metal or wood.

The **'Dandy** /'dændi/ a popular British weekly *comic for children, first published in 1937. One of its most popular characters is *Desperate Dan.

'Danegeld /'deɪngeld/ *n* [U] a land tax that was introduced in *Anglo-Saxon England in 991 in order to raise money to pay the *Danes not to attack southern England. The payments of Danegeld only delayed the attack until 1013 when the Danish king Sweyn I brought England under Danish control. The tax was introduced again by the *Normans in the 11th century to pay for national defence.

'Danelaw /'deɪnlɔː/ the part of north-eastern England that was ruled by the *Danes from 878 until the whole of England came under Danish rule in 1013. The line between Danelaw and the rest of *Anglo-Saxon England ran roughly between London and *Chester. Many places in the north-east of England still have Danish names. For example, Denby means Dane Village, and Thorpe in names like Middlethorpe means farm.

the Danes /deɪnz/ *n* [pl] the name used in English history for those *Vikings who attacked and settled in the eastern and northern parts of England in the 9th century, and whose kings ruled the whole of England from 1013 to 1042.

,Paul **'Daniels** /'dænjəlz/ (1938–) a popular English television entertainer best known for his magic tricks on *The Paul Daniels Magic Show* and his catchphrase 'You'll like this - not a lot, but you'll like it.'

,Danish **'pastry** /,deɪnɪʃ/ (*especially AmE* **Danish**) *n* a sweet cake, round and flat in shape, made with rich pastry and fruit, nuts, cheese, etc.

,John **'Dankworth** /'dæŋkwɜːθ; *AmE* 'dæŋkwɜːrθ/ (1927–) an English saxophone player, writer of *jazz music and leader of his own jazz orchestra. In 1985 he became the Pops Music Director of the *London Symphony Orchestra. He is married to the jazz singer Cleo *Laine.

DA-notice /,diː 'eɪ nəʊtɪs; *AmE* noʊtɪs/ *n* an official notice from the British government advising the press not to publish certain information because it would harm the country if it were to be made public. The 'DA' in 'DA-notice' stands for 'Defence Advisory'. Until 1993 they were called **D-Notices**.

,Darby and **'Joan** /,dɑːbi; *AmE* ,dɑːrbi/ a typical old couple who are happily married. The names come from an 18th–century poem about such a couple. In Britain, **Darby and Joan clubs** are social clubs for old people, usually run by charity workers.

the ,Darda**'nelles** /,dɑːdə'nelz; *AmE* ,dɑːrdə'nelz/ the narrow piece of water that separates European Turkey from Asian Turkey. In 1915 Australian and New Zealand soldiers landed in *Gallipoli on the western shore of the Dardanelles to attack Turkey, which had entered the war on Germany's side. At the same time, British ships tried to fight their way through the Dardanelles in order to get supplies to southern Russia. Both attacks failed and more than 200 000 men were killed.

the ,dark **'lady of the 'sonnets** the woman to whom *Shakespeare wrote most of his last *sonnets. Her identity is not known but many guesses have been made about it. She is described as dark because of the colour of her skin and hair and because of the dark thoughts and feelings of guilt that she caused.

The 'Darkness a British *rock group whose first song, *I Believe in a Thing Called Love*, and the album which it was from, *Permission to Land* (2003) both went to number one in the UK music charts.

ˌAlistair **'Darling**[1] /ˌælɪsteə 'dɑːlɪŋ; *AmE* ˌælɪstər 'dɑːrlɪŋ/ (1953–) a British *Labour politician, who has been a *Member of Parliament representing *Edinburgh since 1987. He became the *Secretary of State for Transport in 2002 and also the *Secretary of State for Scotland, representing Scotland at Westminster, in 2003.

ˌGrace **'Darling**[2] /'dɑːlɪŋ; *AmE* 'dɑːrlɪŋ/ (1815–42) an English woman who helped her father, a lighthouse keeper, to rescue nine sailors during a storm off the coast of *Northumberland in 1838. Her name is still remembered in that part of Britain, and her father's boat is now in a museum in the village of Bamburgh, where she was born.

ˌLord **'Darnley** /'dɑːnli; *AmE* 'dɑːrnli/ (Henry Stuart 1545–67) the second husband of *Mary, Queen of Scots, and the father of King *James I of England (James VI of Scotland). Darnley is best known for his murder of Mary's secretary, David Rizzio, in 1566. Darnley was himself murdered the following year, probably by the Earl of *Bothwell, who then took Darnley's place as Mary's third husband.

ˌClarence **'Darrow** /'dærəʊ; *AmE* 'dæroʊ/ (1857–1938) a US lawyer who became famous for defending people on trial. These included *Leopold and Loeb and John T Scopes, the teacher who was taken to court for teaching the theory of evolution to his students. See also SCOPES TRIAL.

ˌDarth **'Vader** /ˌdɑːθ 'veɪdə(r); *AmE* ˌdɑːrθ 'veɪdər/ an evil and frightening character in the *Star Wars films. He breathes loudly and has a black costume and a black protective covering over his face and head.

'Dartington /'dɑːtɪŋtən; *AmE* 'dɑːrtɪŋtən/ a centre for arts and country crafts in and around Dartington Hall, a large 14th-century house in Devon in south-west England. It was started in the 1920s. Until 1987 there was also a school there, which was known for its freedom and new ideas on methods of education. Since 1991 a 10-day festival of literature has been held there every year.

'Dartmoor /'dɑːtmɔː(r); *AmE* 'dɑːrtmɔːr/ a wild, open and hilly part of *Devon in south-west England, 365 square miles/945 square kilometres in area. It is a *national park and a popular place for walking and horse riding. **Dartmoor ponies** are small, dark brown horses with long hair that live wild on Dartmoor. Parts of Dartmoor are also used for military exercises. **Dartmoor prison** is a men's prison in the middle of Dartmoor, well known because it is difficult to escape from.

Dartmoor ponies

'Dartmouth /'dɑːtməθ; *AmE* 'dɑːrtməθ/ an old port in Devon, south-west England, and now a popular place for people who enjoy sailing. The *Britannia Royal Naval College at Dartmouth trains people to become officers in the British *Royal Navy.

▶ **darts**

Darts is a popular indoor game, often played in British *pubs and *working men's clubs. Players throw small steel **darts** with feathers or plastic flights attached to one end at a round **dartboard** fixed to a wall. The dartboard is divided into 20 numbered areas, each of which has a particular score, and an outer, middle and inner ring. Double points are scored if a dart lands in the outer ring around the edge of the board and treble points if it lands in the inner ring. If a dart lands in the small centre circle, called the **bullseye**, 50 points are scored.

Two or four players play against each other. They take turns to throw three darts each at the board, standing behind a line on the floor called the **oche** (pronounced /'ɒki/). Each player starts with 301, or sometimes 501, and scores are deducted from this. The game is won when one of the players reduces their score to zero. The last throw must land in the outer ring or in the bull's-eye.

The game is thought to have developed out of archery several hundred years ago and is said to have been played by the *Pilgrim Fathers on the *Mayflower. Today, pubs have teams that play in local darts leagues and a few players have been able to turn professional. Major darts matches are sometimes shown on television, including the Lakeside World Darts Championship which is held every year in Surrey.

In the US darts is a popular game in bars. The teams sometimes have humorous names, such as The Good, The Bad, The Ugly, and The Flying Syringes. US **dart teams** are organized into leagues that play for money. Competitions include the Bluebonnet Classic and the Treasure Island Open.

ˌCharles **'Darwin** /'dɑːwɪn; *AmE* 'dɑːrwɪn/ (1809–82) the English naturalist who developed the theory of evolution by natural selection. As a young man he spent five years on a British ship, *HMS *Beagle*, visiting coasts and islands in the southern part of the world. The different types of animals and plants that he found, especially on the Galapagos Islands in the Pacific, led him to believe that living things develop differently in different places over long periods of time. At that time, most western people believed that all things were created by God in seven days. Darwin returned to England in 1836 and spent the next 23 years collecting evidence to support his theory. When he published *On the Origin of Species by Means of Natural Selection* (1859) it caused much argument and anger because it seemed to disagree with the story of creation in the Bible. Most people now accept the main points of Darwin's theory, and many see it and the Bible as two ways of saying the same thing, but others, especially in the US, interpret the Bible account literally and believe that only **creationism**, also called **creation science**, should be taught in schools.

▶ **Darwinian** *adj* of or relating to the theories of Charles Darwin.

Darwinism *n* [U] Charles Darwin's theory of evolution.

the ˌ**Data Pro'tection Act** a British law which limits the use of personal information stored in computers. Organizations that keep this kind of information about other people must inform the *Information Commissioner's Office. They must make sure that the information is accurate and they may use it only for specific purposes. The law also gives people the right to see most of the information that is kept about them in this way and to have any mistakes corrected.

D

'Daughters of the A'merican Revo'lution a US organization for women who are descended from people who fought or helped in the *American Revolution. The group was established in 1890. It is very conservative and supports anything it believes is good for America.

E,lizabeth 'David¹ /'deɪvɪd/ (1913–92) an English writer of cookery books, especially about French and Italian cooking. She had an influence on cooking in Britain from the 1950s onwards.

,St 'David² (c. 520–600) the patron saint of Wales. Little is known about him except that he started several religious houses in Wales and he lived in the place now called *St David's. *St David's Day (1 March) is Wales's national day.

,David 'Copperfield /'kɒpəfiːld; AmE 'kɑːpərfiːld/ a novel (1850) by Charles *Dickens. David, a boy in *Victorian England, is sent to London for a life of hard work and poverty. He becomes a successful writer, but marries a childish woman, Dora, without realizing that another woman, Agnes, really loves him. Agnes's father is cheated out of his money by his employee, Uriah *Heep, but in the end they are saved by David's friend Mr *Micawber. Dora dies, and David marries Agnes. The novel is partly based on Dickens's own life.

'Peter 'Maxwell 'Davies /'mækswel 'deɪvɪs/ (1934–) an English composer of modern classical music, known mostly for his chamber music and operas, which include The Lighthouse (1979). He was made a *knight in 1987.

The ,Da 'Vinci Code /,də 'vɪntʃi kəʊd; AmE koʊd/ a novel by US writer Dan Brown which was first published in 2003. It is about a murder which is connected with a secret code in the paintings of Leonardo Da Vinci, and the attempts of a university professor to solve the mystery. The book became a best-seller across the world.

,Bette 'Davis¹ /,beti 'deɪvɪs/ (1908–89) a US film actor for more than 50 years. She was famous for playing strong emotional parts and for smoking a lot. She received *Oscars for Dangerous (1935) and Jezebel (1938). Her other films included All About Eve (1950) and Whatever Happened to Baby Jane? (1962).

,Colin 'Davis² /'deɪvɪs/ (1927–) an English conductor who worked with the *English National Opera in the 1960s and at the *Royal Opera House in the 1970s and 1980s. He has also conducted the Boston Symphony Orchestra and has been the main conductor of the *London Symphony Orchestra since 1995. He was made a *knight in 1980.

,Jefferson 'Davis³ /,dʒefəsən 'deɪvɪs; AmE ,dʒefərsən/ (1808–89) the only President of the *Confederate States (1861–5). He had earlier been a US Senator and Secretary of War. After the South lost the American *Civil War, Davis was kept in prison by the US government for two years before being released without a trial.

,Joe 'Davis⁴ /'deɪvɪs/ (1901–78) an English *snooker player who won the World Professional Championship fifteen times in a row: every year from 1927 until 1940, and in 1946 when the competition started again after the Second World War. His younger brother, Fred Davis (1913–1998) won the same competition eight times between 1948 and 1956. Joe Davis was also the first player to achieve on television the maximum score in a single game of 147.

,Miles 'Davis⁵ /'deɪvɪs/ (1926–91) a US trumpet player who led a *jazz band. He played with Charlie 'Bird' *Parker in the 1930s, then helped to develop *bebop in the 1940s, 'cool' jazz in the 1950s (with John *Coltrane in his group) and modern jazz with an electronic trumpet in the 1960s.

'Sammy 'Davis 'Jr⁶ /'deɪvɪs/ (1925–90) an *African American singer, dancer and actor. He was known for his

energy and cheerful manner on stage. His successes included the film Porgy and Bess (1959), the *Broadway show Golden Boy (1964) and the song Candy Man (1972).

,Steve 'Davis⁷ /'deɪvɪs/ (1957–) an English *snooker player who has won more titles than any other player in the world. In the 1980s he won the World Professional Championship six times. He is not related to the first holder of the world title, Joe *Davis.

the ,Davis 'Cup an international tennis competition for teams of men representing different countries, or the cup which is presented every year to the country whose team wins this competition. It began in 1900 and is named after Dwight F Davis, who gave the cup.

,Emily 'Davison /'deɪvɪsən/ (1872–1913) an English *suffragette who died when she threw herself in front of the king's horse during the *Derby as a protest. She had been involved in the campaign for votes for women for eight years, and had been in prison several times for protests that included throwing stones and causing fires. After her death, her body was carried through London by 2000 *suffragettes.

,Humphrey 'Davy /'deɪvi/ (1778–1829) an English chemist who was one of the first scientists to make use of electricity to break chemical compounds into their separate elements. Between 1807 and 1808 he discovered six chemical elements, including calcium, potassium and sodium. However, he is better known for a practical invention that saved many lives: the **Davy lamp**, a safe lamp for use in coal mines. This was widely used in mines until it was replaced by the electric lamp in the 20th century.

'Davy 'Jones's 'locker /'deɪvi 'dʒəʊnzɪz; AmE 'dʒoʊnzɪz/ (informal often humorous) the bottom of the sea, as the place where people who have died at sea lie dead. Davy Jones was a name used by sailors in the 18th century for the evil spirit of the sea: The crew ended up in Davy Jones's locker.

,Richard 'Dawkins /'dɔːkɪnz/ (1941–) an English scientist at *Oxford University who is best known for his books about evolution (= the process by which animals and plants develop from earlier, simpler forms). These include The Selfish Gene (1976), The Blind Watchmaker (1987) and Unweaving the Rainbow (1998).

,Doris 'Day /'deɪ/ (1924–) a US singer and actor known for her healthy and happy image. She made several popular film comedies with Rock *Hudson, including Pillow Talk (1959). Her songs included Whatever Will Be, Will Be (Que Sera Sera) (1956), which won an *Oscar.

'Cecil 'Day-'Lewis¹ /'deɪ 'luːɪs/ (1904–72) an English poet and author, born in Ireland. In the 1930s he was a member of the left-wing group of poets led by W H *Auden. He also wrote detective stories under the name Nicholas Blake. He was made *Poet Laureate in 1968.

'Daniel 'Day-'Lewis² /'deɪ 'luːɪs/ (1958–) an English actor who became well known in 1985 for his parts in the films My Beautiful Laundrette and A Room with a View. He won an *Oscar for his performance in My Left Foot (1989). His other films include The Unbearable Lightness of Being (1987), The Last of the Mohicans (1992), The Age of Innocence (1993), The Crucible (1996) and Gangs of New York (2002). He is the son of Cecil *Day-Lewis and is married to the artist and film director, Rebecca Miller.

,daylight 'saving time n (also ,daylight 'savings time) (abbr **DST**) [U] the time shown on clocks in some countries during the spring and summer months which is one hour ahead of the standard time and is used in order to make best use of the hours of daylight. In the US, the clocks are changed to daylight saving time (they **go forward**) on the first Sunday in April and **go back** on the last Sunday in October. In the UK, *British

Summer Time starts on the last Sunday in March and the clocks go back on the last Sunday in October.

‚Days of Our ˈLives a popular US television *soap opera on *NBC which started in 1965. The show is set in the imaginary village of Salem and is about the lives of the people who live there. It has won several *Emmy awards.

Daytona 500 /deɪˌtəʊnə faɪv ˈhʌndrəd; AmE deɪˌtoʊnə/ a race held each year in Daytona Beach, *Florida for stock cars (= ordinary cars fitted with very powerful engines). Compare INDIANAPOLIS 500.

Daytona Beach

DC /ˌdiː ˈsiː/ ⇨ DISTRICT OF COLUMBIA.

the DCA /ˌdiː siː ˈeɪ/ ⇨ DEPARTMENT FOR CONSTITUTIONAL AFFAIRS.

the DCMS /ˌdiː siː em ˈes/ ⇨ DEPARTMENT FOR CULTURE, MEDIA AND SPORT.

ˈD-Day /ˈdiː deɪ/ **1** 6 June 1944, the day on which the *Allies landed in Normandy, northern France, during *World War II. They were led by General *Eisenhower, and defeated the German forces defending the beaches. The secret name of the landings was ‘Overlord’. They are often also called the *Normandy landings. The ‘D’ is short for ‘day’. In the First World War H-hour was used for the time of a planned attack. See also MULBERRY HARBOURS.

2 a date on which something important is planned to happen: *As D-Day approached we still weren’t ready to move house.*

DDC /ˌdiː diː ˈsiː/ ⇨ DEWEY DECIMAL CLASSIFICATION.

DEA /ˌdiː iː ˈeɪ/ ⇨ DRUG ENFORCEMENT ADMINISTRATION.

the ˌdead ˈparrot sketch a widely remembered and very funny sketch (= short comic play) from *Monty Python’s Flying Circus* on British television. John *Cleese plays a man who goes into a pet shop to complain about a parrot (= a large colourful bird) which he has just bought there. Although the bird is obviously dead, the pet shop owner, played by Michael *Palin, argues that it is just ‘resting’, while Cleese tries harder and harder to prove that it is dead.

ˈˌDizzy’ ˈDean[1] /ˌdɪzi ˈdiːn/ (Jay Hanna Dean 1911–74) a famous US baseball pitcher (= player who throws the ball to be hit). He was chosen for the National Baseball *Hall of Fame in 1953. His best years (1930–37) were with the St Louis Cardinals. He was named the Most Valuable Player in 1934.

the ˌForest of ˈDean[2] ⇨ FOREST OF DEAN.

ˌJames ˈDean[3] /ˈdiːn/ (1931–55) a US actor who has come to represent the popular image of a young person resisting authority. He appeared in only three films, *East of Eden* (1955), *Rebel Without a Cause* (1955) and *Giant* (1956), before being killed in a car accident when *Giant*

was almost finished. Posters of him are still popular, especially with young people.

ˌdean’s ˈlist n a list produced each year at most US colleges and universities of students who have achieved the highest grades in their courses of study. The list is published in local newspapers. A dean is an administrative officer at a school or college.

ˌDear ˈAbby /ˈæbi/ a regular newspaper column, appearing in several US newspapers, which answers readers’ questions about love and family problems. It began in 1956 and is written by Abigail Van Buren (real name Jeanne Phillips) and was started by her mother, Pauline Phillips.

ˌDear ˈJohn ˌletter (also **Dear John**) n (AmE informal) a letter sent by a woman to a man to say that she wants to stop their relationship. This is usually because she now loves someone else.

ˌDeath of a ˈSalesman a play (1949) by Arthur *Miller that won the *Pulitzer Prize. It is about an ordinary man, Willie Loman, who kills himself because his life has been a failure. A film version was made in 1951.

ˌDeath ˈValley a desert covering part of the US states of *California and *Nevada. It is the lowest land in the western hemisphere, being 282 feet/86 metres below sea level, with very high temperatures (up to 50° Celsius). The desert was a source of the mineral borax in the late 19th century. In 1933, the area became the **Death Valley National Monument**.

Death Valley

ˈDebenhams™ /ˈdebənəmz/ any one of a chain of large shops in Britain. Each shop has various departments selling mainly clothes and household goods.

ˈdebit card n a small plastic card which is given by banks to their customers to enable them to pay for things without having to write a cheque. When somebody uses a debit card, money is taken directly from their bank account. ⇨ note at CREDIT CARDS.

ˌEdward de ˈBono /də ˈbəʊnəʊ; AmE də ˈboʊnoʊ/ (1933–) a British doctor and psychologist who wrote *The Use of Lateral Thinking* (1967). This explained how to solve problems by thinking round them instead of thinking directly about them. Since then the phrase *lateral thinking* has become part of the English language.

Deˈbrett /dəˈbret/ (also **Deˈbrett’s** /dəˈbrets/) the popular name for *Debrett’s Peerage and Baronetage*, a book containing lists and information about the *royal family, the *peerage and other people in Britain who hold titles of rank. The name is also used to refer to other books from the same publisher, such as a guide to polite social behaviour. Compare BURKE’S PEERAGE.

ˌEugene V ˈDebs /ˈdebz/ (Eugene Victor Debs 1855–1926) a US socialist politician and trade union leader. In 1893 he established the American Railway Union. He helped organize the Social Democratic Party of America in 1897 and was its candidate for US president five times from 1900 to 1920, even while in prison for opposing the government’s decision to enter *World War I.

ˈDecca™ /ˈdekə/ an international record company which was formed in Britain in 1929 and became the second largest record group in the world after *EMI. Decca was bought by Polygram in 1980.

D

D

decimali'zation n [U] the change of the British currency to the present decimal system of 100 pence to the pound, which happened on 15 February 1971. Before that date, the pound was divided into 20 shillings with 12 pence in each shilling.

the **Decla'ration of Inde'pendence** the document in which the *thirteen colonies declared that they were independent of Britain and stated the principles of the new government in America. One of its most famous sentences is this: 'We hold these truths to be self-evident: that all men are created equal; that they are endowed by their creator with certain inalienable rights; that among these are life, liberty, and the pursuit of happiness.' The document was mostly written by Thomas *Jefferson and received the approval of the *Continental Congress on 4 July 1776. Those signing it included Benjamin *Franklin, John *Adams and John *Hancock. ⇨ INDEPENDENCE DAY.

De,cline and 'Fall the first novel by the English writer Evelyn *Waugh. It was written in 1928 and is about the comic troubles of a quiet young man who has to leave *Oxford University and gets a job at a very bad *public school. The rich mother of one of his pupils brings him into her social circle and he gets put in prison, before finally returning to his religious studies at Oxford. The novel was an immediate success and established Waugh's career as a writer of satire.

The De'cline and 'Fall of the ,Roman 'Empire a historical work in six books (1776–88) written by the English historian Edward *Gibbon. It covers the history of Europe from Rome in the first century AD to the fall of Constantinople in 1453. Its full title is The History of the Decline and Fall of the Roman Empire, but it is usually referred to simply as Gibbon's Decline and Fall.

'Decorated style a style of *Gothic architecture that was common in England from about 1290 to about 1350. Its main feature was the ornamental stone carving around windows and doors. This style replaced the simple *Early English style and was followed by the *Perpendicular style.

Deep 'Blue the name of a computer program that plays chess. In one second, it can analyse 100 million possible positions on the board. It was invented in 1985 by two students at Carnegie Mellon University in the US and developed at *IBM. In 1989 Garry Kasparov, the World Chess Champion, defeated the computer in two matches. The program was later improved and in 1997 it defeated Kasparov in a match of six games.

the **Deep 'South** (often disapproving) the most southern states of the south-east US: *Alabama, *Florida, *Georgia, *Louisiana, *Mississippi, *South Carolina and eastern *Texas. They are among the states that once had slaves and left the *Union during the American *Civil War. They still have racial problems and the people there are mostly conservative in their politics and religion.

Deep 'Throat the humorous name taken from the title of a sex film and used by two *Washington Post journalists, Carl Bernstein and Bob Woodward, to refer to the person who gave them a lot of information about *Watergate. They never revealed the person's real name.

The 'Deer ,Hunter a US film (1978), directed by Michael Cimino, which received three *Oscars, including the one for 'Best Picture'. The story is about a group of friends who hunt deer together and later join the US forces fighting in Vietnam, where they have terrible experiences.

the **De,fence of the 'Realm Act** (abbr **DORA**) a law introduced by the British government in 1914 to give special powers to the authorities in Ireland. At that time, after the beginning of the war between Britain and Germany, the British government feared a revolution in Ireland with German support. After the *Easter Rising (1917) against British rule in Ireland, the Act was used to arrest and put in prison many people who had supported the rising.

De,fender of the 'Faith a title used by all kings and queens of England since the 16th century. The abbreviation of the title's Latin form, Fidei Defensor, is FD or FID DEF, and this appears on every British coin. The title was first given to King *Henry VIII by Pope Leo X after Henry's defence of the *Roman Catholic faith against the teachings of Martin Luther. But the title was taken away when England left the Roman Catholic Church. King Henry then asked the English *Parliament to give him the same title with a different meaning: defender of the *Church of England.

,Daniel De'foe /dɪˈfəʊ; AmE dɪˈfoʊ/ (1660–1731) an English writer who is considered to be the first English writer of novels. His most famous novel, *Robinson Crusoe (1719), was followed by *Moll Flanders (1722), A Journal of the Plague Year (1722) set during the *Great Plague of London, and Roxana (1724). For most of his life Defoe worked as a political journalist, and he did not begin writing his novels until he was nearly 60.

'Defra /ˈdefrə/ ⇨ DEPARTMENT FOR ENVIRONMENT, FOOD AND RURAL AFFAIRS.

,Ellen De'Generes /dəˈdʒenərəz/ (1958–) a US actor and comedian who is best known for her television comedy series, Ellen (1994–98) and as the presenter of a daytime television talk show, The Ellen DeGeneres Show. She is also known as a supporter of gay (= homosexual) rights.

,Geoffrey de 'Havilland /də ˈhævələnd/ (1882–1965) a British aircraft designer whose company produced many of Britain's best-known aircraft. He started the company after designing planes in *World War I, and it produced the Mosquito fighter plane during *World War II and then the *Comet, the world's first passenger jet plane. He was made a *knight in 1944. His company is now part of *BAE Systems.

,Len 'Deighton /ˈdeɪtn/ (1929–) an English writer of novels, especially spy stories (= ones about people employed to find out secret information). These include The Ipcress File (1962) and Funeral in Berlin (1964), which were both made into films. Deighton has also written war novels, such as Bomber (1970), and a history of *World War II, Blood Tears and Folly (1996), as well as several cookery books which he illustrated himself.

,Willem de 'Kooning /ˌwɪləm də ˈkuːnɪŋ/ (1904–97) a US artist, born in the Netherlands. He went to the US in 1926 and soon became a leader in the *abstract expressionism movement. He painted large pictures with bright colours and great energy. He was also interested in painting the human form, as in his series Woman I–V (1952–3). See also ACTION PAINTING.

,Walter de la 'Mare /də lɑː ˈmeə(r); AmE də lɑː ˈmer/ (1873–1956) an English writer of poems, novels and short stories for adults and children. His best-known works are the poems Songs of Childhood (1902), The Listeners (1912), Peacock Pie (1913) and the novel Memoirs of a Midget (1921).

'Delaware /ˈdeləweə(r); AmE ˈdeləwer/ a small eastern state in the US, named after a *Native American people. Its capital city is Dover and its largest city is Wilmington. The northern part of the state is industrial, with a large chemical industry, and the southern part agricultural. Delaware was one of the original *thirteen colonies and is sometimes called the First State because it was the first to accept the US *Constitution.

'Del Boy /'del/ the nickname of Derek Trotter, a character played by the English actor David *Jason in the *BBC television comedy series *Only Fools and Horses*. Del Boy makes a living by selling things like cheap watches and is not completely honest, but he is friendly, cheerful and warm-hearted.

Frederick 'Delius /'di:liəs/ (1862–1934) an English composer who wrote operas, works for the orchestra, and songs. His parents were originally from Germany, and Delius himself spent much of his adult life in France, but his work often celebrated his love of the English countryside. Two of his best-known works are the opera *A Village Romeo and Juliet* (1907) and the short piece for orchestra *On Hearing the First Cuckoo in Spring* (1912).

Del 'Monte /ˌdel 'mɒnteɪ; AmE 'mɑːnteɪ/ a US company known for selling fruit and vegetables in cans, and fruit juice. Its best-known advertising character is the 'Man from Del Monte' who visits farmers to judge whether their fruit is good enough to be sold by the company.

'Delta Force /'deltə/ (Special Forces Operational Detachment Delta) a special unit in the US Army that fights against terrorists and guerrillas. Its base is at Fort Bragg, *North Carolina, and it has been active in Vietnam, Iran, Afghanistan and Iraq. Delta Force was organized like the British *SAS, and many of its members have trained with that unit.

Agnes De 'Mille[1] /də 'mɪl/ (1905–93) a US dancer and choreographer. She created a new type of dance for *Broadway musical shows when she combined ballet with popular music for *Oklahoma!* (1943) and later for *Carousel* (1945) and *Paint Your Wagon* (1951). Her ballets included *Black Ritual* (1940) and *Fall River Legend* (1948). In the early part of her career she danced in London with the *Rambert Ballet Company. Her uncle was Cecil B *De Mille.

66 The truest expression of a people is in its dances and its music. Bodies never lie. 99
Agnes de Mille

Cecil B De 'Mille[2] /də 'mɪl/ (Cecil Blount De Mille 1881–1959) a US film director and producer. He had a strong personality and was famous for making actors do exactly what he wanted. He is remembered for directing expensive films on a large scale, including *Samson and Delilah* (1949) and (twice) *The Ten Commandments* (1923 and 1956).

'Democrat *n* a member or supporter of the *Democratic Party of the US.

the ˌDemo'cratic ˌParty (*also* **the 'Democrats**) one of the two major political parties in the US. Compared with their rivals, the *Republican Party, the Democrats are more liberal and have strong support from minorities and the trade/labor unions. The party began in 1792 as the **Democratic Republican Party**. Democratic Presidents have included Thomas *Jefferson, Andrew *Jackson, Woodrow *Wilson, Franklin D *Roosevelt, Harry S *Truman, John F *Kennedy, Jimmy *Carter and Bill *Clinton. The traditional symbol for the party is the donkey.

'Demos /'demɒs; AmE 'demɑːs/ an independent British think tank (= a group of experts who provide advice and ideas on political, social or economic issues) which started in 1993 and is seen as being close to the *Labour Party and Tony *Blair.

Jack 'Dempsey /'dempsi/ (1895–1983) a US boxer who was the World Heavyweight Champion from 1919 to 1926. His popular name was the 'Manassa Mauler' because he was from Manassa, *Colorado, and mauled

his opponents (= treated them very roughly). Dempsey was involved in the famous 'long count' when he knocked down Gene *Tunney in a 1927 fight. The referee delayed before he began counting. Tunney got up just before he had counted to ten and went on to win the fight.

66 Tall men come down to my height when I hit 'em in the body. 99
Jack Dempsey

D

De'nali /dəˈnɑːli/ a US national park in *Alaska which includes Mount *McKinley, the highest mountain in North America. Denali is the local Native American name for the mountain. The park has glaciers (= masses of ice) and many wild animals, including bears and moose.

Judi 'Dench /ˌdʒuːdi 'dentʃ/ (1934–) an English actor who has played many leading roles in the plays of Shakespeare, especially with the *Royal Shakespeare Company. She has also appeared in several television series and films, including *A Room with a View* (1986), *Mrs Brown* (1997), in which she played the part of Queen *Victoria, and *Iris* (2001), in which she played Iris *Murdoch. She received an *Oscar for *Shakespeare in Love* (1999). She was made a *dame(2) in 1988.

'Denglish /'deŋglɪʃ/ *n* [U] (*humorous*) language which is a mixture of English and German. It is often used in advertisements in Germany, where English words and phrases appear, sometimes used in a way which is different from standard English.

Robert De 'Niro /də 'nɪərəʊ; AmE də 'nɪroʊ/ (1945–) a US film actor known for his intense style of acting in a wide range of parts. He won *Oscars for *The Godfather Part II* (1974) and *Raging Bull* (1979). His other work includes the Martin *Scorsese films *Mean Streets* (1973), *Taxi Driver* (1976) and *New York New York* (1977).

Dennis the 'Menace   **1** a character in the British *comic *The *Beano*. He is a small boy with untidy hair who is always playing tricks on people and getting into trouble. He has a dog called Gnasher that regularly bites people.
2 a US cartoon character created in the early 1950s. He is a small boy who behaves badly and especially annoys his neighbour, Mr Wilson. Dennis has also appeared in a television series (1959–63) and a film (1993).

'Denny's /'deniz/ any of a chain of *fast-food restaurants in the US. In 1994 the company was accused in a class action (= a type of law case that is started by a group of people who have the same problem) of refusing to serve *African Americans and was made to pay $54 million as a result. Denny's now serves everyone and even produced humorous advertisements in 1997 which said that its food is so good that even African Americans eat there.

'Denver /'denvə(r)/ the capital and largest city of the US state of *Colorado. It is close to the *Rocky Mountains, and its popular name is the 'Mile High City'. Many people moved to the city in the 1870s and 1880s to work in the local gold and silver mines. In 1995 the city opened the largest airport in North America.

Denver 'boot /ˌdenvə; AmE ˌdenvər/ *n* (AmE) a heavy metal device for attaching to the wheel of a car that is illegally parked, so that it cannot be driven away. The driver must wait for somebody to remove it and usually has to pay for this to be done. *Denver was one of the first US cities to introduce the device. In British English it is called a wheel clamp.

deoch an 'doris /ˌdɒx ən 'dɒrɪs; AmE ˌdɑːx ən 'dɑːrɪs/ *n* a *Gaelic phrase from Scotland which means *a* *drink at the door*, i.e. a drink given to a guest before leaving.

the **De'partment for Consti'tutional Af'fairs** the British government department responsible for the law and for people's rights to be treated fairly and to elect their government freely. Its aims are to improve the justice system and the way the government of the country is organized, for example, by establishing a *supreme court to replace the *Law Lords. The *Scotland Office and the *Wales Office are part of this department. It replaced the Lord Chancellor's Department in 2003.

the **De'partment for 'Culture, 'Media and 'Sport** (*abbr* the **DCMS**) a British government department which is responsible for issues connected with cultural and sporting activities and which helps to develop the tourist, arts and leisure industries. It is responsible for policy in relation to the *National Lottery.

the **De'partment for Edu'cation and 'Skills** (*abbr* the **DfES**) the British government department responsible for all levels of education and for job training in England. (The *Scottish Executive deals with these responsibilities in Scotland and the *Welsh Assembly in Wales.).

the **De'partment for En'vironment, 'Food and 'Rural Af'fairs** (*abbr* **Defra**) the British government department in charge of the environment, farming and food production. It replaced the Ministry of Agriculture, Fisheries and Food in 2001.

the **De'partment for Inter'national De'velopment** (*abbr* **DFID**) a British government department that gives help to poorer countries by sending money, food, equipment, etc. ⇨ note at AID.

the **,Department for 'Transport** (*abbr* **DfT**) the British government department responsible for road, rail, sea and air transport, including the building of new roads.

the **De'partment for 'Work and 'Pensions** (*abbr* the **DWP**) the British government department responsible for paying regular amounts of money from the state to people who are retired, ill or very poor, or who have young children.

the **De,partment of 'Agriculture** the US government department that helps farmers and controls agricultural practices. It is in charge of research into such problems as plant diseases and better ways to use the land. The Department also helps the public through programmes such as its approval marks on meat and information concerning food safety.

the **De,partment of 'Commerce** the US government department in charge of trade within the country and with other nations. Its divisions include the Economic Development Administration, the Minority Business Development Agency, the Patent and Trademark Office and the Bureau of Industry and Security.

the **De,partment of De'fense** (*abbr* the **DOD**) the US government department in charge of the country's military forces. It is the government's largest department and receives the most money. The Secretary of Defense is never a military person. The Secretary's assistants include the military *Joint Chiefs of Staff and three who are not in the armed forces, the Secretary of the Army, the Secretary of the Navy and the Secretary of the Air Force.

the **De,partment of Edu'cation** the US government department that establishes policies for the country's schools and is in charge of national programmes for education, including financial help.

the **De,partment of 'Energy** (*abbr* the **DOE**) the US government department that plans and controls the development of the country's energy resources. It is particularly concerned with ways of saving energy resources and of producing more energy. It does research into the dangers of nuclear power and also is in charge of the US nuclear weapons programme.

the **De,partment of 'Health** (*abbr* **DH**) the British government department responsible for health. Its main duty is to manage the *National Health Service, and it is also in charge of social services to old people, children, the mentally ill and others in need, though decisions on spending in these areas are made by local authorities.

the **De,partment of 'Health and 'Human 'Services** (*abbr* the **HHS**) the US government department responsible for national health programmes and the Social Services Administration.

the **De'partment of 'Homeland Se'curity** (*abbr* **DHS**) the US government department created in 2002 to protect the country from terrorist attack. The department provides advice on security to the government and to private companies, and prepares for emergency situations. It also includes border control and immigration services, the *United States Coast Guard and the *Secret Service.

the **De,partment of 'Housing and 'Urban De'velopment** (*abbr* **HUD**) the US government department in charge of financial programmes to build houses and to help people buy their own homes. It provides insurance for mortgages and helps pay for houses for poor and old people. It also plans the development of cities.

the **De,partment of 'Justice** the US government department responsible for making sure that national laws are obeyed. It is also in charge of the country's prisons and the *Bureau of Alcohol, Tobacco, Firearms and Explosives. The Department represents the government in legal cases and gives advice on legal matters to the *President. See also ATTORNEY GENERAL.

the **De,partment of 'Labor** the US government department responsible for national laws concerning workers. This includes working conditions, such as safety and the hours worked, as well as the pay workers receive. It is also in charge of job training programmes.

the **De,partment of the In'terior** (*abbr* the **DOI**) the US government department responsible for protecting the country's environment. Its divisions include the National Park Service, the Bureau of Land Management, the Fish and Wildlife Service and the Geological Survey. It is also in charge of government programmes for *Native Americans.

the **De,partment of the 'Treasury** the US government department responsible for national policies to do with money, including the collection of taxes through its *Internal Revenue Service division. Other divisions include the US Mint and the Alcohol and Tobacco Tax and Trade Bureau.

the **De'partment of 'Trade and 'Industry** (*abbr* the **DTI**) the British government department responsible for trade policy, research and development in industry, and company law.

the **De,partment of Transpor'tation** the US government department in charge of national policy on transport. Its divisions include the *Federal Aviation Administration, the Federal Highway Administration and the National Highway Traffic Safety Administration.

the **De'partment of 'Veterans Af'fairs** (*abbr* the **VA**) the US government department in charge of assistance for Americans who have served in the armed forces and for their families. This includes programmes that help to pay for education and houses, and payments after death or serious injury caused by military service. The Department also runs special hospitals.

▶ **departments of government**

The government of the United Kingdom, formally called **Her Majesty's Government**, consists of a group of **ministers** led by the *prime minister. Ministers are attached to specialist **departments** which carry out government policy. **Ministers of the Crown**, the most senior ministers, are appointed by the queen or king on the recommendation of the prime minister. Other ministers are appointed directly by the prime minister. All ministers sit in *Parliament, most of them in the *House of Commons.

The senior minister in each department is generally called the **Secretary of State**, e.g. the Secretary of State for Health. The minister in charge of the *Foreign and Commonwealth Office is called the *Foreign Secretary. The *Home Secretary is in charge of the *Home Office. The finance minister is known as the *Chancellor of the Exchequer and is head of the *Treasury. Ministers in charge of departments are usually members of the *Cabinet. The prime minister may also appoint a **Minister without Portfolio** (= without departmental responsibilities) to take on special duties.

A Secretary of State is usually supported by several **Ministers of State**, who each have a specific area of responsibility, and **Parliamentary Under-Secretaries of State**, often called **junior ministers**.

Departments are run by *civil servants who are not allowed to show favour to any political party. Unlike ministers, they do not have to leave their jobs when the government changes. Many departments are assisted by special groups that give advice and do research. A change of government does not necessarily affect the number and general organization of departments. A new government may, however, create new departments or change the structure of existing ones.

Some departments, e.g. the *Ministry of Defence, have responsibility for the whole of the United Kingdom. Others cover only part and the *Scottish Parliament and the *Welsh Assembly have responsibility for the corresponding areas in Scotland and Wales. (⇨ note at DEVOLUTION.)

The leader of the main opposition party appoints a **shadow cabinet** of **shadow ministers**. Each is responsible for speaking about an area of government.

In the US the *federal government has 15 departments. These, together with the *president and various government **agencies**, make up the **executive branch** of the government and are responsible for its day-to-day operation.

The people in charge of government departments are called **secretaries**. For example, the *Department of Agriculture is led by the Secretary of Agriculture. The head of the *State Department, the department that deals with US foreign policy, is called the *Secretary of State. The President decides who will be the head of each department. Not all secretaries are well known: many people know the name of the Secretary of State, but few know the name of the Secretary of Agriculture.

Most of the people working in US government departments are civil servants whose jobs do not depend on political influence. In this way each department has a base of employees with a lot of knowledge and experience, whose careers last longer than a single political administration. Departments may be reorganized according to what issues seem important at a particular time but this kind of change does not happen very often.

The heads of departments form a group called the *Cabinet, which meets regularly with the President.

The President is not required to accept their advice, but may choose to do so.

de,pendent 'territory ⇨ OVERSEAS TERRITORY.

,Johnny 'Depp /'dep/ (1963–) a US actor who often plays strange characters. He began his career as a member of The Kids pop group and now plays with the P band. His films include *A Nightmare on Elm Street* (1984), *Edward Scissorhands* (1990), *What's Eating Gilbert Grape?* (1993), *Fear and Loathing in Las Vegas* (1998), *Sleepy Hollow* (1999), *Blow* (2001) and *Pirates of the Caribbean: the Curse of the Black Pearl* (2003).

the De'pression ⇨ GREAT DEPRESSION.

,De Pro'fundis /,deɪ prə'fʊndiːs/ a long letter written by Oscar *Wilde in 1897 and published in 1905. It was written to his lover, Lord Alfred *Douglas, when Wilde was in prison. The Latin title means *from the depths*, and the serious tone of the letter makes a strong contrast with the clever humour of his earlier works.

,Thomas De 'Quincey /də 'kwɪnsi/ (1785–1859) an English writer who regularly took the drug opium and described its effects on him in his best-known book, *Confessions of an English Opium-Eater* (1821). He was a friend of the poets *Wordsworth and *Coleridge.

'Derby¹ /'dɑːbi; *AmE* 'dɑːrbi/ a city in central England famous for its fine *Crown Derby china and for the *Rolls-Royce cars, aircraft engines and other engineering products made there.

the 'Derby² /'dɑːbi; *AmE* 'dɑːrbi/ a famous English horse race without jumps which is run every year at Epsom, near London, in May or June. Although **Derby Day** is always a Wednesday, the race is attended by large crowds, and there is a holiday atmosphere. The Derby was first run in 1780 and takes its name from the 12th *earl(1) of Derby, who was one of the original organizers of the event. A painting called *The Derby Day* (1858) by William Frith (1819–1909), now in *Tate Britain, is famous as a picture of *Victorian life. Compare KENTUCKY DERBY.

'Derbyshire /'dɑːbiʃə(r); *AmE* 'dɑːrbiʃər/ a county in north central England. It contains the *Peak District national park. Its administrative centre is the town of Matlock.

'derringer /'derɪndʒə(r)/ *n* a small US hand gun. It was invented in 1825 by Henry Deringer and was popular in the *Wild West because a person could hide it easily, even in the hand. Derringers are still popular today and often kept by Americans in their homes for protection.

'Derry /'deri/ the second largest city in Northern Ireland. In 1611 the *Roman Catholic city of Derry, a port on the north coast, was settled by large numbers of *Protestants from England who gave it the new name of *Londonderry(1). This was the city's name until 1984 when it was officially changed back to Derry.

'Derwentwater /'dɜːwəntwɔːtə(r); *AmE* 'dɜːrwəntwɔːtər/ one of the most beautiful lakes in the English *Lake District. The lake is surrounded by hills and mountains and has several small islands.

'Desert ,Island 'Discs a popular *BBC radio programme in which famous people are asked to choose the eight records they would most like to have with them if they were alone on an island. It has been broadcast regularly since the 1940s.

,Desert 'Rat *n* [usually pl] (*informal*) a soldier in the British 7th Armoured Division, which fought in North Africa in *World War II. The Desert Rats were later among the soldiers sent to Kuwait in 1991 during the *Gulf War and to Iraq in 2003.

'Operation ,Desert 'Shield the name used for the military operation in which international armed forces, including British and US troops, were sent to protect Saudi Arabia after Iraq attacked Kuwait in 1990. The operation developed into the *Gulf War.

'Operation ,Desert 'Storm the name used for the military operation in which international armed forces, including British and US troops, attacked Iraq in the *Gulf War. It began on 16 January 1991 and lasted 100 days.

the De'sign ,Council a British organization set up in 1944 to improve design in British industry. Its offices are in *Covent Garden, London.

,Des 'Moines /ˌdə 'mɔɪn/ the capital and largest city of the US state of *Iowa. It began as Fort Des Moines in 1843 and developed into a centre of the *Corn Belt. The city also grew because of coal mines in the area. It was named after the Des Moines River which runs through it.

,Desperate 'Dan a character in the British children's *comic, The *Dandy. He is a very strong *cowboy with a big jaw who is not very intelligent but has a gentle nature. His favourite meal is 'cow pie'.

,Desperate 'Housewives a very successful American television series shown on *ABC and in Britain on *ITV about the lives of four women in a road in the suburbs called Wisteria Lane. A fifth woman, a friend of the other four, has just killed herself when the series begins and her voice is heard commenting on the events in the road after her death. The series won two *Golden Globe Awards in 2005.

de'tective ,story (also **de'tective ,novel**) n a story in which there is a murder or other crime and a detective who tries to solve it. The best-known British writers of detective stories include Arthur *Conan Doyle, Agatha *Christie and Ruth *Rendell. The older type of British detective story is often set in a large country house, and typically includes the discovery of a murder at the beginning, a small group of characters who are all suspected of having committed the murder, and a surprising solution at the end. In the US, detective stories more often involve the police or the adventures of a 'private eye' (= private detective), and are often more violent and realistic. Famous US writers of such stories include Dashiell *Hammett, Raymond *Chandler and Elmore *Leonard. Detective stories are also known as 'detective fiction' or 'crime fiction' and informally as 'whodunnits' (or 'whodunits').

De'troit /dɪ'trɔɪt/ **1** the largest city in the US state of *Michigan. It began in 1701 as a French trading post. It is on the Detroit River and connected by a bridge to Windsor, Canada. Detroit is the centre of the US car industry and often has many unemployed workers because of the increase in imports of foreign cars. It also has a music industry and produces salt from local mines, steel and chemicals. See also MOTOWN.
2 n [U] the US car industry: Detroit's fight against foreign brands.

'Dettol™ /'detɒl; AmE 'detɑːl/ n [U] a strong liquid for killing bacteria, used especially for treating skin problems such as cuts, stings and spots.

,Eamon de Va'lera /ˌeɪmən də vəˈleərə; AmE də vəˈlerə/ (1882–1975) an Irish political leader, born in the US. He was put in prison by the British on various occasions and took part in the *Easter Rising against the British in 1916. He was leader of the *Sinn Fein party from 1917 until 1926 when he formed the *Fianna Fáil party. He directed the talks with Britain which led to southern Ireland's independence from Britain in 1921. He was Taoiseach (*Prime Minister of the Irish republic) three times and its President from 1959 to 1973.

Ni,nette de 'Valois /ˌniːnet də 'vælwɑː/ (1898–2001) the stage name of Edris Stannus, an Irish dancer and

choreographer who had a great influence on the development of British ballet. After appearing in London and Paris in the early 1920s, she opened a ballet school in London with Lilian *Baylis. In 1931, she started the Vic-Wells ballet, which performed at *Sadler's Wells and later became the *Royal Ballet, which she directed until 1963. Among her works are The Rake's Progress (1935) and Checkmate (1937) with music by Arthur *Bliss. She was made a *dame(2) in 1951.

,devil's 'food cake n [C, U] a rich chocolate cake, often made for birthday parties.

,devils on 'horseback n [pl] **1** (BrE) a dish made with prunes wrapped in bacon and then cooked, usually served at the end of a meal or at a party.
2 (AmE) a dish made with oysters wrapped in bacon and then cooked and served on toast with a spicy sauce, usually before a meal.

,Danny De'Vito /də'viːtəʊ; AmE də'viːtoʊ/ (1944–) a US comic actor who also directs and produces films. DeVito, who is short and fat, played the loud character Louis in the television series Taxi (1978–83). His film roles include being the twin brother of Arnold *Schwarzenegger in Twins (1987) and the evil Penguin in Batman Returns (1992). He has also directed the films The War of the Roses (1989) and Matilda (1996).

▶ **devolution**

Devolution involves the transfer of political power from a central government to a regional government. In the United Kingdom, this process took place in Scotland, Wales and Northern Ireland in the late 1990s. Scotland and Wales, mainly through their **nationalist** parties, the *Scottish National Party and *Plaid Cymru, had both demanded to have power **devolved** from the *Parliament of the United Kingdom to their own **political assemblies**. Both parties had only a few MPs in the British parliament.

Scotland has for a long time had its own system of law and a lot of control over its affairs, and until 1999 the Secretary of State at the **Scottish Office** had wide powers. Wales had always been concerned about its cultural as well as its political identity. The *Welsh language is spoken in many homes, especially in the western half of the country, and it is taught in schools. Until 1999 the **Welsh Office** in Cardiff had responsibilities for the local economy, education and social welfare.

Northern Ireland had its own parliament from 1921 until 1972, when the British government closed it and established *direct rule from London. In 1998 a new *Northern Ireland Assembly was set up as part of the peace process agreed between Irish politicians and the British government.

In 1997 Tony *Blair's government held a **referendum** in Scotland and Wales on the issue of devolution. A large majority of Scottish people and a small majority of Welsh people voted in favour of it.

The *Scottish Parliament started work in Edinburgh in 1999. It consists of 129 **MSPs** (*Members of the Scottish Parliament). 56 of them are elected by *proportional representation. It is led by a *First Minister who is chosen by the Parliament and who chooses the other members of the *Scottish Executive (the group within the parliament that is responsible for deciding its policies). It has the power to raise or lower the basic rate of income tax, and to make laws affecting Scotland in areas including education, health, transport, local government, justice, agriculture and the environment.

The *Welsh Assembly was opened in *Cardiff in 1999. It consists of 60 **AMs** (*Assembly Members). 20 of them are elected by *proportional representation. The Welsh Assembly has less power than the Scottish Parliament.

It cannot make its own laws or raise taxes, but it has the power to develop and carry out policies affecting Wales in areas including education, culture, health, agriculture, the environment, tourism and the Welsh language. It is led by a *First Minister who is chosen by the Assembly and who chooses the other Assembly Ministers to make up a *cabinet.

Matters affecting Scotland and Wales that are outside the control of the Scottish Parliament and the Welsh Assembly, including foreign affairs, defence and social security, are the responsibility of the *Scotland Office and the *Wales Office. These offices replaced the Scottish Office and the Welsh Office, and are part of the *Department for Constitutional Affairs.

Scotland and Wales still have MPs in the British parliament in London, and people may be members of both parliaments, though some people think it is wrong that Scottish and Welsh MPs continue to discuss English affairs in the British parliament.

In 2002 the government published its plans to hold referendums to decide whether there should be **regional assemblies** in parts of England where research showed that there was interest in devolved government. There were plans to hold referendums in three areas: the North East, the North West, and *Yorkshire and Humberside but when the first referendum was held in 2004 in the North East, a large majority voted against having a regional assembly. See also WEST LOTHIAN QUESTION.

ˈ**Devon** /ˈdevən/ (*also* **Devonshire** /ˈdevənʃə(r)/) a county in south-west England. With two national parks, *Dartmoor and *Exmoor, and two coasts, north and south, it is a popular area for holidays. The administrative centre is *Exeter.

ˌ**Donald** ˈ**Dewar** /ˈdjuːə(r)/ (1937–2000) a British *Labour politician. He became *Secretary of State for Scotland in 1997 and then *First Minister of the Scottish Parliament.

the ˌ**Dewey** ˈ**decimal** ˌ**classification** /ˌdjuːi; *AmE* ˌduːi/ (*also* **the Dewey System**) (*abbr* **DDC**) the most commonly used system for organizing books in public libraries. It was invented by Melvil Dewey (1851–1931), a US librarian. Dewey gave every subject a number between 0 and 999. Every book in a library is given one of these numbers so that books on a particular subject are easy to find. New subjects have been added to Dewey's original list by using decimal numbers, e.g. 331.1, 331.2, etc.

DFC /ˌdiː ef ˈsiː/ ⇨ DISTINGUISHED FLYING CROSS.

the **DfES** /ˌdiː ef iː ˈes/ ⇨ DEPARTMENT FOR EDUCATION AND SKILLS.

DFID /ˌdiː ef aɪ ˈdiː/ ⇨ DEPARTMENT FOR INTERNATIONAL DEVELOPMENT.

DFM /ˌdiː ef ˈem/ ⇨ DISTINGUISHED FLYING MEDAL.

DfT /ˌdiː ef ˈtiː/ ⇨ DEPARTMENT FOR TRANSPORT.

DH /ˌdiː ˈeɪtʃ/ ⇨ DEPARTMENT OF HEALTH.

DHS /ˌdiː eɪtʃ ˈes/ ⇨ DEPARTMENT OF HOMELAND SECURITY.

ˈ**Jack "Legs' Diamond** /ˈdaɪəmənd/ (1896–1931) a US leader of a crime organization in New York in the 1920s. He was called 'Legs' because, when young, he was a fast runner and could run away quickly after stealing something. During *Prohibition, he sold illegal alcohol and drugs. He killed a number of other criminal leaders but was himself murdered after he opposed a powerful one, 'Dutch' Schultz.

the ˌ**Diamond** ˈ**Sculls** a rowing race for single sculls (= boats rowed by a single person) that takes place every

year at *Henley in early July. The first of these races was in 1844 and it is now the most important international contest of its type.

Diˈana, ˈPrincess of ˈWales (*also* **Princess Diana**) (1961–1997) the former wife of Prince *Charles and the mother of Prince William and Prince Henry (Harry). Her name before she married was Lady Diana Spencer. The Spencer family are descended from the English kings *Charles II and *James II, and Diana's father was the 8th Earl Spencer. She was married to Prince Charles in 1981 and soon became

Princess Diana

the most popular member of the *royal family, often referred to informally as Di. However, the marriage failed and in 1992 the prince and princess separated. Although Princess Diana gave up her public duties and was divorced in 1996, she continued some of her work with charities and she remained an object of intense interest to the press and the public. She died in a car accident in Paris while trying to escape from photographers, and her funeral, like her wedding, was watched by almost a fifth of the world's population.

> **66** I'd like to be a queen in people's hearts but I don't see myself being Queen of this country. **99**
> Princess Diana in a television interview, 1995

the **Diˌana ˈFountain** (*also* the **Diana, Princess of Wales Fountain**) a fountain in the shape of a large oval stream of flowing water, in *Hyde Park in *London opened in 2004 as a memorial (= something built in order to remind people of a famous person who has died) to *Diana, Princess of Wales.

The ˈ**Diary of a ˌCountry ˈParson** the diary of James *Woodforde (1740–1803), which was published in five volumes (1924–31) more than a hundred years after his death. It describes Woodforde's life as a parson (= priest) in the country village of Weston Longeville in *Norfolk, and is full of enthusiasm for the ordinary pleasures of life, especially food.

The ˌ**Diary of a ˈNobody** the diary of Mr Charles *Pooter published in London in 1892. Pooter was not a real person; the diary was written by George and Weedon *Grossmith as a comic story of life in *suburbia and the type of person who lives there. It begins when the good but boring Mr Pooter and his wife move into their new house. Pooter describes the pleasures of home improvements, small polite parties, his fear of social embarrassment and his many other small pleasures, problems and accidents.

Leoˌnardo DiˈCaprio /liːəˌnɑːdəʊ dɪˈkæpriəʊ; *AmE* liːəˌnɑːrdoʊ dɪˈkæprioʊ/ (1974–) a US actor who became an international star after his performance in the film *Titanic* (1998). He has a German mother and an Italian father. His other films include *This Boy's Life* (1993), *The Man in the Iron Mask* (1998), *The Beach* (2000) and *The Aviator* (2004), a film about the life of Howard *Hughes.

ˌ**Charles ˈDickens** /ˈdɪkɪnz/ (1812–70) an English writer of novels who combined great writing with the ability to write popular stories full of interesting characters, such as *Scrooge, *Fagin and the *Artful Dodger. His many books are mostly about life in *Victorian(1) England and often describe the harsh conditions in which poor people lived. His early novels, which include *Pickwick Papers* and *Oliver Twist*, were written in parts for magazines published each week or each month. His later books include *David Copperfield*, A *Tale of Two Cities* and *Great Expectations*.

Emily 'Dickinson (1830–86) an American poet whose work has had a strong influence on modern poetry. Her poems were often about religion and death, and they contain impressive images. She wrote nearly 1800 of them, but only seven were published during her life. Dickinson spent the last half of her life alone in her home in Amherst, *Massachusetts, writing secretly.

> 66 Because I could not stop for Death
> He kindly stopped for me 99
> Emily Dickinson *The Chariot*

Dick 'Tracy /'treɪsi/ a US comic strip about a police detective (= a member of the police who solves crimes). It began in 1931 and is still published. Tracy has a famous square chin and has fought criminals with colourful names such as Mumbles, Flattop and the Mole. There have been radio and television versions and several films, including *Dick Tracy* (1990) with Warren *Beatty.

A **'Dictionary of 'Modern 'English 'Usage** a guide to the rules of good written British English, written by Henry Fowler (1858–1933). It was first published in 1926 and became one of the standard reference books on the English language. It is often referred to as *Modern English Usage*, or simply 'Fowler': *Look it up in Fowler.*

The **'Dictionary of 'National 'Biography** (abbr the **DNB**) a book in many volumes containing the life stories of famous British people from the earliest historical period to the present time. It is published by the *Oxford University Press and was first completed in 1900. A new DNB, the *Oxford Dictionary of National Biography*, was published in print and online in 2004.

Bo 'Diddley /ˌbəʊ 'dɪdli; AmE ˌboʊ/ (1928–) a US singer and writer of *rock music and the *blues. He also plays the guitar. The titles of his songs often include his own name, e.g. *Hey Bo Diddley* (1955). His music influenced the *Rolling Stones who have recorded several of his songs.

Dido and 'Aeneas /ˌdaɪdəʊ, ɪˈniːəs; AmE ˌdaɪdoʊ/ the first English opera (1689). It was composed by Henry *Purcell with words by the Irish poet Nahum Tate. The story is based on *The Aeneid* by the Roman poet Virgil.

'ˌBabe' 'Didrikson /'dɪdrɪksn/ (Mildred Didrikson 1913–56) an American woman who was famous in many sports, including *baseball, *basketball, *golf and *tennis. She has been called 'the greatest woman athlete in history'. In the 1932 Olympic Games she won the javelin and 80-metre hurdles race with world records. In 1938 Didrikson married George Zaharias, a wrestler, and began competing as 'Babe' Zaharias. She began playing professional golf in 1947 and won the US Women's Open three times.

Marˌlene 'Dietrich /mɑːˌleɪnə 'diːtrɪx; AmE mɑːrˈleɪnə/ (1901–92) a US film actress and singer, born in Germany. She was known for her deep voice and beautiful legs. She first became famous in Germany in *The Blue Angel* (1930), directed by Josef von Sternberg. They both went to *Hollywood where he directed her in such films as *Blonde Venus* (1932) and *The Scarlet Empress* (1934). Her later films included *Witness for the Prosecution* (1957) and *Judgment at Nuremberg* (1961).

Dieu et mon 'droit /ˌdjɜː eɪ mɒn 'drwɑː; AmE mɑːn/ a French phrase meaning *God and my right* which has

been the motto of the English kings and queens since the 14th century.

'Dilbert™ /'dɪlbət; AmE 'dɪlbərt/ a US cartoon character created in 1989 by Scott Adams. Dilbert is an electrical engineer who works with computers in an office. He is polite and honest but often confused by the company's policies. The *Dilbert* cartoon makes fun of boring and stupid office jobs. It now appears in over 2000 newspapers around the world and a television series began in 1998.

John 'Dillinger /'dɪlɪndʒə(r)/ (1903–34) a US criminal who killed 16 people and robbed 20 banks in the *Midwest during the *Great Depression. The *FBI named him 'Public Enemy Number One'. Although he was violent, many Americans regarded Dillinger as an exciting person. He was killed by FBI men in *Chicago as he was leaving a cinema.

Joe Di'Maggio /dɪˈmædʒiəʊ; AmE dɪˈmædʒioʊ/ (1914–1999) one of America's most famous *baseball players. His popular name was 'Joltin' Joe'. He played for the New York *Yankees (1936–51) and helped them to win nine *World Series. He was named *Most Valuable Player in the *American League three times and was chosen for the Baseball *Hall of Fame in 1955. DiMaggio married the actor Marilyn *Monroe in 1954 but the marriage lasted only nine months.

David 'Dimbleby¹ /'dɪmblbi/ (1938–) a British television broadcaster who presents the *BBC's political programmes *Panorama and *Question Time, and programmes on national occasions, such as royal weddings and funerals.

Jonathan 'Dimbleby² /'dɪmblbi/ (1944–) a British radio and television broadcaster who presents the weekly *BBC radio programme *Any Questions?.

'dime ˌnovel n (in the US) a type of cheap novel popular in the late 19th century and again from the 1920s to the 1940s. The writing in dime novels was often bad, but the action was fast. The original ones were usually about American *frontiersmen, such as *Buffalo Bill, and soldiers in US wars. The later ones were often about love, crime or horror.

Jim 'Dine /'daɪn/ (1935–) a leading US artist in the *pop art movement. He used ordinary objects that he found and attached to his paintings. He also created art 'happenings' (events and performances). Dine's recent work has been more traditional in style.

'Diners Club™ /'daɪnəz/ the international company, started in the US, that operates **Diners Club cards**, also known as **Diners cards**. These are charge cards, which allow members of the Diners Club to pay for things using their card and settle their account at the end of each month.

'dinkie (also **dinky**) n (pl **-ies**) (informal humorous) one of a couple who have a lot of money to spend because both partners work and they have no children. The word was formed from the first letters of 'double income, no kids'.

David 'Dinkins /'dɪŋkɪnz/ (1927–) the first *African American to be elected *mayor of New York (1990–94). He is from the *Democratic Party. Dinkins was politically moderate and tried to bring people together. He was unable to solve the city's financial and racial problems, however, and was defeated in the next election by Rudolph Giuliani of the *Republican Party.

'Dinky Toy ™ /'dɪŋki/ (also **Dinky**) n a British make of small toy vehicle. Dinky Toys were made from the 1930s until 1980 and included a wide range of model cars and other vehicles. Old Dinky Toys are now collected by adults as a hobby and can cost hundreds of pounds.

'dinner *n* [C, U] the main meal of the day, eaten either at midday or in the evening. In Britain the word 'dinner' is used differently according to a person's social class or the place they come from. A **dinner party** is a private social occasion in the evening, to which guests are invited for dinner. Compare TEA(2). ⇨ note at MEALS.

,DipH'E /ˌdɪpeɪtʃˈiː/ ⇨ DIPLOMA OF HIGHER EDUCATION.

'Diplock court *n* a special court of law in Northern Ireland for people accused of terrorist offences. Diplock courts were set up in 1972 under the British judge Lord Diplock (1907–85) when the normal system of trial by jury had become difficult because jury members were being threatened and even murdered. In Diplock courts, each case is heard by a single judge. The absence of a jury has been criticized as unfair, although the accused person has certain extra rights in these courts.

Di'ploma of 'Higher Edu'cation *n* (*abbr* **DipHE**) (in Britain) one of the qualifications that can be obtained from a British *college of higher education. A Diploma is higher than a Certificate but below a degree.

the ,Diplo'matic ,Service the department of the British *Civil Service that provides staff to work in British embassies around the world for the *Foreign and Commonwealth Office.

Di'rector of 'Public Prose'cutions (*abbr* the **DPP**) the head of the *Crown Prosecution Service, which is responsible in England and Wales for deciding whether a case should be tried in a court of law. He or she is appointed by the *Attorney General.

di,rect 'rule *n* [U] the government of Northern Ireland by the British Parliament instead of by Stormont, the Northern Irish Parliament in *Belfast. Direct rule began in 1972 and ended in 1999 when a new *Northern Ireland Assembly was elected, but started again in 2003 when the Assembly was suspended for the first time.

Di,recT'V /daɪˌrektiːˈviː/ a satellite television service started in 1994 which broadcasts digital satellite television in the US.

,Dire 'Straits a British pop group formed in 1977. Their best-known albums were *Dire Straits* (1978) and *Brothers in Arms* (1985), which was the most successful album of all time in Britain and sold more than 25 million copies worldwide.

,Dirty 'Den /'den/ the *nickname of Dennis Watts, a sometimes dishonest character in the British television *soap opera *Eastenders*.

,Dirty 'Harry a US film (1971), directed by Don Siegel, about a tough *San Francisco police detective called Harry Callahan. The film was very popular because people felt threatened by the increase of violent crime in the US. Clint *Eastwood played Harry in this and later films, including *Magnum Force* (1973), *The Enforcer* (1976) and *Sudden Impact* (1983).

> 66 Go ahead, make my day. 99
> Dirty Harry in *Sudden Impact*

the *Dis'covery* the name of two famous British ships. The first was the ship in which Henry *Hudson sailed in 1610 to Hudson Bay, which he had discovered the previous year. The second *Discovery* was the ship in which Captain *Scott sailed on his first journey to the Antarctic (1901–4). This ship became a museum on the River *Thames in London until it was moved to the River *Tay in *Dundee, Scotland, where it was built.

the *Discovery*

the Dis'covery Channel a major US cable television channel, which offers programmes on history, technology, nature and adventure.

Dis'gusted, ,Tunbridge 'Wells /ˌtʌnbrɪdʒ ˈwelz/ (*BrE*) a humorous name for an angry *middle-class older person who writes strong letters of complaint to newspapers about modern behaviour. The name comes from the signature that such a person might put at the end of the letter instead of writing his or her name. *Tunbridge Wells is a town in *Kent where many retired people live and a typical resident is considered to be a retired army officer.

'Disney /'dɪzni/ ⇨ WALT DISNEY COMPANY.

,Walt 'Disney /ˌwɒlt ˈdɪzni; *AmE* ˌwɑːlt/ (1901–66) a US producer of films, especially cartoons. He created *Mickey Mouse and *Donald Duck, and made the first long cartoon films, which included *Snow White and the Seven Dwarfs* (1937), *Fantasia* (1940) and *Bambi* (1942). He also produced many successful nature films, the first of which was *The Living Desert* (1953), and films with live actors, such as *Treasure Island* (1950) and *Mary Poppins* (1964). Disney won 26 *Oscars for his work and people remember him as one of the greatest producers of family entertainment. He also had a television programme and created *Disneyland.

> 66 Fancy being remembered around the world for the invention of a mouse! 99
> Walt Disney

'Disneyland™ /'dɪznilænd/ the original US amusement park opened by Walt *Disney in 1955 at Anaheim, *California. It is divided into different 'lands' such as Adventureland, Frontierland and Tomorrowland, and also has hotels, restaurants and theatres. Similar parks built later are *Disney World in 1971, Tokyo Disneyland in 1983 and Disneyland Paris (Euro Disney) in 1992.

'Disney World /'dɪzni/ the popular name for Walt Disney World™, the famous US amusement park near *Orlando, *Florida. It was opened in 1971 and is much larger than *Disneyland although it has similar features, such as live Disney characters, Main Street USA, Frontierland and Adventureland. It is the largest entertainment area in the world (about twice the size of *Manhattan(1)) and is being continuously developed. It includes Disney's newer attractions Magic Kingdom, Animal Kingdom, the EPCOT Center and the Disney-MGM Studios.

di'spatch box *n* **1** (in British political life) a red leather case in which important papers are delivered to senior government ministers. It is traditional for the *Chancellor of the Exchequer to hold his dispatch box up in the air for photographers and tourists to see when he comes out of his house in *Downing Street before going to the *House of Commons to make his speech about the *budget each year.
2 [usually sing] either of the two wooden boxes which are permanently kept near the *mace on the table

D

between the two front rows of seats in the *House of Commons. Government and Opposition ministers stand beside the dispatch box on either side of the table when speaking: *The Prime Minister made a lengthy statement from the dispatch box.*

'Disprin™ /'dɪsprɪn/ n [C, U] a mild medicine for relieving pain, such as headaches, etc. It is sold in tablets which can be dissolved in water.

Benjamin Dis'raeli /dɪz'reɪli/ (1804–81) a British *Conservative politician who was twice *Prime Minister (1868 and 1874–80). He also wrote a number of popular novels which showed his interest in social change. He became leader of the *Conservative Party in 1846 and created its modern central organization. As Prime Minister, he increased Britain's influence abroad and he bought half of the Suez Canal for Britain. He also introduced improvements in housing for poor people in the cities and increased the number of people who could vote at elections. He became a close friend of Queen *Victoria, and she made him an *earl (Earl of Beaconsfield) in 1876.

> 66 There are three kinds of lies: lies, damned lies and statistics. 99
> Benjamin Disraeli

the ,Disso'lution of the 'Monasteries the destruction or sale of buildings and land belonging to religious communities in England by King *Henry VIII (between 1536 and 1541) after he became head of the *Church of England. Henry wanted to make the Church less powerful and he needed money. Many people in England at the time felt that the Church was too rich and wasted its great wealth, so Henry had little difficulty in taking the Church's wealth for himself, although many fine old buildings were destroyed. See also REFORMATION.

the Di,stinguished 'Flying Cross (abbr the **DFC**) a medal for brave actions in battle which is given to officers in the British *Royal Air Force.

the Di,stinguished 'Flying Medal (abbr the **DFM**) a medal for brave actions in battle which is given to men below officer rank in the British *Royal Air Force.

the Di,stinguished 'Service Cross (abbr the **DSC**) n a British medal for brave actions, given to officers in the *Royal Navy since 1914 and in the *merchant navy (= the country's commercial ships) since 1942.

the Di,stinguished 'Service Order n (abbr the **DSO**) a British medal for brave actions, given since 1886 to officers in the *Royal Navy and the Army and now also to officers in the *Royal Air Force and the *merchant navy (= the country's commercial ships).

,district at'torney n (AmE) (abbr **DA**) a lawyer in a particular district who is responsible for bringing legal charges against people. He or she represents a state government or the US government. Successful district attorneys often become politicians. Compare CROWN PROSECUTION SERVICE.

,district 'council n (in Britain) the *local government for a district, which may be a town, part of a large city or part of a county. The members of a district council are elected for four years by the people living in the district and are responsible for local services such as local roads, buses, parks and libraries.

,District of Co'lumbia /kəlʌmbiə/ (abbr **DC**) the district of the US capital city of *Washington, DC. The city covers all of the land. It is on the east side of the *Potomac River and belongs to the US government. It was established by *Congress in 1790 and contains many government buildings. The land was originally

given by the states of *Virginia and *Maryland, though Virginia later took back its gift. People who live in the district were not allowed to vote for US President until 1961.

the di'vine 'right of 'kings n [sing] the idea that kings and queens are given their right to rule by God and that therefore nobody should question that right. The last king in Britain to rule completely according to this belief was *Charles I. After the *English Civil War the idea was gradually replaced by *constitutional monarchy.

'Dixie /'dɪksi/ (also **'Dixieland** /'dɪksilænd/) an informal US name for the south-eastern states. It came from the song *Dixie but has never been fully explained. It may refer to the imaginary *Mason-Dixon line that separates the North from the South.

'Dixie /'dɪksi/ the battle song of the *Confederate States. It was written in 1859 in New York as *Dixie's Land by Daniel Emmett, who was later upset that it became the 'Confederate national anthem'. *Dixie was, however, a favourite song of Abraham *Lincoln. It begins

> 66 I wish I was in the land of cotton,
> Old times there are not forgotten;
> Look away, look away, look away,
> Dixie land! 99

the 'Dixiecrats /'dɪksikræts/ (in US politics), the popular name for the States' Rights Party, a 'third party' that competed in the 1948 election for US President against the *Democratic Party and *Republican Party. It was formed to support *states' rights. The candidate was J Strom *Thurmond, who won five states in the *South with 39 votes in the *Electoral College.

'Dixie Cup™ n a US make of small paper cup. People usually buy a quantity of them in a plastic container which can be kept in the kitchen or bathroom.

'Dixieland /'dɪksilænd/ **1** (also **,Dixieland 'jazz** /,dɪksilænd/) n [U] a type of US *jazz music played by a small band. It has a strong, happy rhythm, and the musicians also play individually during a song. Dixieland began in the South at the end of the 19th century and is still popular, especially in *New Orleans. The best known Dixieland song is *When the Saints Go Marching In.* **2** ⇨ DIXIE.

'Dixons™ /'dɪksnz/ any of a group of shops in Britain that sell electronic equipment such as televisions, cameras and computers. The group, which also owns *Currys, is the largest group of this type in Britain.

DIY /,di: aɪ 'waɪ/ (in full **do-it-yourself**) n [U] (especially BrE) repairing, painting, improving or adding to your own house without the help of professional workmen. This is one of the most popular free-time activities in Britain and almost every town has at least one large DIY shop, where all the necessary materials and equipment are sold.

DLR /,di: el 'a:(r)/ ⇨ DOCKLANDS LIGHT RAILWAY.

DMs /,di: 'emz/ ⇨ DOC MARTENS.

the DNB /,di: en 'bi:/ ⇨ DICTIONARY OF NATIONAL BIOGRAPHY.

'Dockers™ /'dɒkəz; AmE 'dɑ:kərz/ a popular US make of trousers/pants. They are made of cotton, often khaki (= a strong cloth of a brownish yellow colour) by the Levi Strauss Company. Styles include long and short lengths and golf trousers. Compare LEVI'S.

'Docklands /'dɒkləndz; AmE 'dɑ:kləndz/ an area of houses and offices in east London, England, on the north side of the River *Thames where London's commercial docks used to be. The old docks were too shallow for large modern ships and this had become a poor area, so the London Docklands *Urban Development Corporation was set up by the government in 1979 to develop it. The project had many problems, but the area now has a new life and includes one of Europe's tallest buildings, the *Canary Wharf tower. However, some people have criticized the development because only rich people and yuppies (= successful young professional people) have enough money to buy the expensive new Docklands houses. See also DOCKLANDS LIGHT RAILWAY.

the ˌ**Docklands** ˈ**Light** ˈ**Railway** /ˈdɒkləndz; AmE ˈdɑːkləndz/ (abbr **DLR**) a system of light trains used for public transport in the London *Docklands which started operating in 1987. The trains are controlled by computer and travel above ground, often high up on raised lines. Many of its stations are linked to the *London Underground.

ˌ**Doc** ˈ**Martens** /ˌdɒk ˈmɑːtɪnz; AmE ˌdɑːk ˈmɑːrtnz/ ⇨ DR MARTENS.

Doctor In some entries the word **Doctor** is replaced by the abbreviation, **Dr**, e.g. **Dr Scholl's**, **Dr Seuss**. This is the usual written abbreviation in British English. In American English the form **Dr.** is always used.

ˈ**doctorate** n the highest type of university degree, e.g. a PhD (Doctor of Philosophy). Someone with a doctorate has the title of 'Doctor' and can write 'Dr' before their name. Doctorates are sometimes given as an honour, e.g. to politicians.

ˌ**Doctor** ˈ**Dolittle** /ˈduːlɪtl/ the main character in a series of children's books by the English author Hugh Lofting (1886–1947). Dr Dolittle is an expert in animal languages and has many animal friends who he defends against humans when necessary. One is a strange animal called a Push-me-pull-you, with a head at each end of its body. The doctor first appeared in The Story of Doctor Dolittle (1920).

ˌ**Doctor** ˈ**Faustus** /ˈfaʊstəs/ one of the greatest plays of Christopher *Marlowe, written in about 1590. Its full title is The Tragical History of Dr Faustus. It is about a man who has studied all sciences and arts and finds nothing more in the world to study, so he turns to magic. He sells his soul to the Devil in return for 24 years of power and pleasure. He enjoys his 24 years but is finally dragged away by the Devil.

ˌ**Doctor** ˈ**Foster** /ˈfɒstə(r); AmE ˈfɑstər/ a character in a short children's poem from the mid 19th century. Nobody knows whether the doctor was a real person or not. These are the words of the poem:

> 66 Doctor Foster went to Gloucester
> In a shower of rain.
> He stepped in a puddle
> Right up to his middle,
> And never went there again. 99

ˌE L ˈ**Doctorow** /ˈdɒktərəʊ; AmE ˈdɑːktəroʊ/ (Edgar Laurence Doctorow 1931–) a US writer of novels in which fiction is combined with historical facts. His books include Ragtime (1975) and Billy Bathgate (1989).

ˌ**Doctor** ˈ**Who** /ˈhuː/ a *BBC television science-fiction series made for older children and also popular with many adults. The main character was Doctor Who himself, who travelled through time and space in a machine called the *Tardis. In his adventures he had to fight many strange enemies, including the *Daleks and the Cybermen. It was shown from 1963 to 1989 and a new series was announced in 2004.

DOD ⇨ DEPARTMENT OF DEFENSE.

ˌKen ˈ**Dodd** /ˈdɒd; AmE ˈdɑːd/ (1931–) an English comedian and singer from *Liverpool with untidy hair and

big teeth that stick out. His type of comedy continues many of the old traditions of the *music-hall.

Dodge™ /dɒdʒ; AmE dɑːdʒ/ a make of US car produced by the Chrysler Corporation.

ˌ**Dodge** ˈ**City** /ˌdɒdʒ; AmE ˌdɑːdʒ/ a city in the US state of *Kansas. Originally called Buffalo City, it was important in the 19th century as a centre for cattle at the end of the *Santa Fe Trail. At that time it had a reputation for violence and was known as 'the wickedest little city in America'. See also EARP.

ˌ**Charles** ˈ**Lutwidge** ˈ**Dodgson** /ˈlʌtwɪdʒ ˈdɒdʒsn; AmE ˈdɑːdʒsn/ (1832–98) the real name of the English children's author Lewis *Carroll.

ˌ**Samuel** ˈ**Dodsworth** /ˈdɒdswɔːθ; AmE ˈdɑːdswɜːrθ/ a character in the novel Dodsworth (1929) by Sinclair *Lewis. Dodsworth has retired from his job and travels to Europe with his wife. Lewis uses him to show the different values and behaviour of Americans and Europeans. He is also seen as an example of a typical rich man who cannot communicate well with his wife.

the **DOE** /ˌdiː əʊ ˈiː; AmE oʊ/ ⇨ DEPARTMENT OF ENERGY.

ˈ**Dog Chow**™ n [U] a popular US make of dry dog food, made by Purina. The company also makes Puppy Chow, Cat Chow and Kitten Chow.

ˈ**Doggett's** ˈ**Coat and** ˈ**Badge** /ˈdɒgɪts; AmE ˈdɑːgɪts/ a rowing race that has been held every year since 1715 on the River *Thames between *London Bridge and *Chelsea. The winner receives a red coat in 18th-century style and a silver badge. It was started by the Irish comedian Thomas Doggett (c. 1670–1721), and is the oldest regular sporting contest in Britain.

ˈ**doggy bag** n a paper or plastic bag provided by a restaurant at the end of a meal for customers who want to take home any of their food that they have not eaten. This is normal practice in the US but not in Britain, where children are sometimes given doggy bags after a birthday party.

the **DOI** /ˌdiː əʊ ˈaɪ; AmE oʊ/ ⇨ DEPARTMENT OF THE INTERIOR.

ˌ**do-it-your**ˈ**self** ⇨ DIY.

ˈ**Dolby**™ n [U] /ˈdɒlbi; AmE ˈdɑːlbi/ an electronic system that reduces noise to improve the sound of tape recordings, films, etc. It was invented in London by Ray Dolby (1933–), a recording engineer born in the US: The new cinema has a Dolby sound system.

ˌ**Anton** ˈ**Dolin** /ˌæntɒn ˈdɒlɪn; AmE ˌæntɑːn ˈdɔːlɪn/ (1904–83) an English dancer and choreographer. He began his career with Diaghilev's Ballets Russes in Paris and later formed several ballet companies with Alicia Markova, including the one which became the *English National Ballet. He was made a *knight in 1981.

ˌ**Richard** ˈ**Doll** /ˈdɒl; AmE ˈdɑːl/ (1912–) an English scientist whose research first found a definite link between smoking and lung cancer. He worked for the *Medical Research Council and was a professor at *Oxford University. He was made a *knight in 1971.

ˈ**Dolly** the name given to a sheep bred by British scientists in 1997. The sheep was a clone (= an exact copy) of another sheep, and was the first clone to be made by using cells taken from another adult animal. Many people think that the technology of cloning will lead to important new benefits for farming, medicine and other areas of life. Others are worried because they think the technology will not be used wisely, or that clones of people might be created. Dolly died in 2003.

ˈ**dolly** ˌ**mixtures** n [pl] (BrE) small brightly coloured sweets, bought especially by children.

the **'Domesday Book** /ˈduːmzdeɪ/ a written record of the ownership and value of land in England in 1086. It was made for *William the Conqueror in order to calculate the size and value of the king's property and the tax value of other land in the country. The book is of great historical importance because it tells us a lot about England at that time. It can be seen at the *Public Record Office in London: *Their house is mentioned in the Domesday Book.*

Domi'nica /ˌdɒmɪˈniːkə; AmE ˌdɑːmɪˈniːkə/ an island with many mountains in the eastern *Caribbean which has been a member of the *Commonwealth since it became independent in 1978. It has a population of about 70 000 and its capital city is Roseau.
▶ **Dominican** adj, n.

'Fats' Domino /ˌfæts ˈdɒmɪnəʊ; AmE ˈdɑːmɪnoʊ/ (born Antoine Domino 1928–) a US *rock musician who plays the piano and sings in a happy, easy style. He was especially popular in the 1950s, when his most successful songs included *Ain't That A Shame* (1955) and *Blueberry Hill* (1956). Domino was chosen in 1986 for the Rock and Roll *Hall of Fame.

Domino's 'Pizza /ˌdɒmɪnəʊz; AmE ˌdɑːmɪnoʊz/ the largest company in the world delivering pizzas to people's homes. It was started in 1960 and by 2004 it had more than 7 000 shops in the US and in over 50 other countries. The company's policy is not to charge for its pizzas if they are delivered late or the customer is not satisfied.

Donald 'Duck a popular cartoon character created by Walt *Disney. Donald first appeared in *The Wise Little Hen* (1934). He is a lively and sometimes bad-tempered duck, with a voice that is difficult to understand. He has a female friend called Daisy, and three young nephews, Huey, Dewey and Louie. Compare MICKEY MOUSE, BUGS BUNNY.

Liam 'Donaldson /ˌliːəm ˈdɒnəldsn; AmE ˈdɑːnəldsn/ (1949–) a doctor who has been the **Chief Medical Officer**, the most senior medical expert, for the *Department of Health in England since 1999. He was made a *knight in 2002.

'Doncaster /ˈdɒŋkəstə(r); AmE ˈdɑːŋkəstər/ an industrial town in south *Yorkshire in the north of England. It is famous for the *St Leger, a horse race that has been run there every year since 1776.

The 'Dong with a 'Luminous 'Nose /ˈdɒŋ wɪð ə ˈluːmɪnəs ˈnəʊz; AmE ˈdɑŋ, noʊz/ a nonsense poem (1877) by Edward *Lear about an imaginary creature with a light on his nose to help him search at night for his lost love, a 'Jumbly Girl' with blue hands and green hair.

'donkey ˌderby n a race on donkeys, usually ridden by children on the beach or at a *fête.

John 'Donne /ˈdʌn/ (c. 1572–1631) an English poet who is now regarded as the greatest of the *metaphysical poets. In his youth he was a law student, soldier, drinker, lover and writer of love poems which are famous for their original and surprising comparisons. In one, for example, he compares a woman to a newly discovered continent: 'Oh, my America! my new-found land!' In 1615 he became an *Anglican priest, and six years later Dean of *St Paul's Cathedral. He became famous as a religious speaker and writer, putting the same powerful emotion and intellect into his religious poetry as he had put into his love poems.

E,liza 'Doolittle¹ /ˈduːlɪtl/ a character in *Pygmalion*, a comedy play by George Bernard *Shaw, and in *My Fair Lady*, the musical comedy based on it. She is a London *flower girl(2) with a strong *cockney accent who is taught by a language expert, Professor Henry Higgins, to speak like an *upper-class woman.

ˌHilda 'Doolittle² /ˈduːlɪtl/ (1886–1961) a US poet who also wrote plays, novels and children's stories. She usually wrote as 'H D'. From 1911 to 1937 she lived in Europe, where she was influenced by Ezra *Pound and married the poet Richard Aldington in 1913. Her collections of poetry include *Sea Garden* (1916) and *The Walls Do Not Fall* (1944).

'Doonesbury /ˈduːnzbri/ a US *comic strip by Gary Trudeau (1948–) which appears in many newspapers and which won the *Pulitzer Prize in 1975. It is well known for its liberal comments about American politics and society and often makes fun of politicians. Characters include Michael Doonesbury who runs a computer business with his family, Mark Slackmeyer, an openly homosexual radio commentator and Zonker Harris the *hippy.

The Doors /dɔːz; AmE dɔːrz/ a US *rock group formed in 1965. The singer was Jim *Morrison. He and the band were regularly in trouble for bad behaviour, and their songs were criticized for emphasizing drugs and sex. These included *Light My Fire* (1967) and *Touch Me* (1969). After Morrison died, the band continued into the early 1980s. Their story was told in the film *The Doors* (1991).

'doo-wop /ˈduː wɒp; AmE ˈduː wɑːp/ n [U] an *African-American style of singing popular in the 1950s. It involved groups singing in harmony, and nonsense phrases like 'doo-wop' and 'sha-boom' regularly repeated. Early doo-wop groups included the Drifters and the Platters.

DORA /ˈdɔːrə/ ⇨ DEFENCE OF THE REALM ACT.

'Dorchester¹ /ˈdɔːtʃəstə(r); AmE ˈdɔːrtʃəstər/ a town in *Dorset in southern England with a long history. Nearby *Maiden Castle was occupied at least 4 000 years ago, and there was a Roman town, Durnovaria, where Dorchester now stands. In the 19th century, the *Tolpuddle Martyrs were put on trial in Dorchester and the author Thomas *Hardy was born there. In his novels the town is called Casterbridge.

the 'Dorchester² /ˈdɔːtʃəstə(r); AmE ˈdɔːrtʃəstər/ a well-known expensive hotel in London's *Park Lane. It first opened in 1931.

Do'ritos™ /dəˈriːtəʊz; AmE dəˈriːtoʊz/ n [pl] a crisp US snack food (= one eaten quickly between meals) made from corn and sold in various spicy flavours.

'Dorset /ˈdɔːsɪt/ a county on the coast of south-west England. Its administrative centre is *Dorchester. The author Thomas *Hardy set many of his stories in Dorset.

'Tommy and 'Jimmy 'Dorsey /ˈdɔːsi; AmE ˈdɔːrsi/ two American brothers who, together and separately, led a number of popular dance bands in the 1930s and 1940s. Tommy played the trombone and Jimmy played the clarinet. They appeared together in the film *The Fabulous Dorseys* (1947).

ˌJohn Dos 'Passos /dɒs ˈpæsɒs; AmE dɑːs ˈpæsɑːs/ (1896–1970) a US author who wrote about the problems of 20th-century American life. He is best known for *USA*, a series of three related novels called *42nd Parallel* (1930), *1919* (1932) and *The Big Money* (1936). Dos Passos used fictional characters and real events in describing the failures of modern society.

ˌDotheboys 'Hall /ˌduːðəbɔɪz/ ⇨ NICHOLAS NICKLEBY.

ˌAbner 'Doubleday /ˌæbnə ˈdʌbldeɪ; AmE ˌæbnər/ (1819–93) a US general in the American *Civil War. He was in *Fort Sumter when it was attacked by the South. According to a story that is probably not true, he invented the game of baseball (in 1839).

Double 'Gloucester /ˈglɒstə(r); AmE ˈglɑstər/ n [U] a type of hard English cheese first made in *Gloucestershire. It is orange in colour and has a mild taste.

double-'header n (AmE) (in baseball) two games played on the same day, usually by the same two teams, with a short interval between them. Double-headers are traditionally played on Sundays.

double 'jeopardy n [U] (in US law) putting somebody on trial or punishing them for something for which they have already been tried or punished. This is not allowed under the *Fifth Amendment of the US *Constitution: *He claimed the trial placed the men in double jeopardy.*

'Douglas[1] /ˈdʌgləs/ the capital of the *Isle of Man in the *Irish Sea. It is a port, mainly for boats from *Liverpool, and a holiday town. See also TYNWALD.

Kirk 'Douglas[2] /ˈdʌgləs/ (1916–) a US film actor well known for playing tough characters. His films include *Lust for Life* (1956), *Gunfight at the O.K. Corral* (1957) and *Spartacus* (1960). In 1990 Douglas received the Lifetime Achievement Award from the American Film Institute and in 1996 a special *Oscar for his 50 years in films. He has also written the story of his life and several novels. His son is the actor Michael *Douglas.

Lord 'Alfred 'Douglas[3] /ˈdʌgləs/ (1870–1945) the young English aristocrat who was Oscar *Wilde's lover when Wilde was arrested and sent to prison for homosexuality, which was illegal at that time. The long letter that Wilde wrote in prison, published later as *De Profundis* (1897), was addressed to Douglas.

Michael 'Douglas[4] /ˈdʌgləs/ (1944–) a US film actor well known for playing strong, emotional characters. He received an *Oscar for his role as the tough financial expert Gordon Gecko in *Wall Street* (1987). His other films have included *Fatal Attraction* (1987), *The War of the Roses* (1989), *Basic Instinct* (1992) and *The Game* (1997). He married Catherine *Zeta-Jones in 2000. He is the son of the actor Kirk *Douglas.

> 66 Lunch is for wimps. 99
> Gordon Gecko

Stephen 'Douglas[5] /ˈdʌgləs/ (1813–61) a US politician who defeated Abraham *Lincoln in 1858 for the US *Senate but lost to him in the 1860 election for US *President. The Lincoln-Douglas debates are famous in US history. Douglas's *Kansas-Nebraska Act allowed new states to choose whether they wanted slaves. He had the popular name of the 'Little Giant'.

Alec 'Douglas-'Home /ˈdʌgləs ˈhjuːm/ (1903–95) a British *Conservative politician and *Prime Minister (1963–4). He was an *MP when he became Lord Home on the death of his father in 1951 and moved to the *House of Lords. But in 1963 he gave up his title so that he could return to the *House of Commons as Sir Alec Douglas-Home and become Prime Minister. In 1974 he was made a *life peer and returned to the House of Lords as Lord Home.

Frederick Douglass /ˈdʌgləs/ (1817–95) a US slave who escaped in 1838, wrote the story of his life as a slave and later went to England, where friends gave him enough money to return to America and buy his freedom. He became the leading *African American working to end the system of *slavery and was the US government's representative to Haiti from 1889 to 1891. He also established the *North Star* newspaper in Rochester, New York.

Dove 'Cottage /ˌdʌv/ a house in the village of *Grasmere in the English *Lake District where the poet William *Wordsworth lived with his sister Dorothy from 1799 to 1808, after which it became the home of another poet, Thomas *De Quincey.

'Dover /ˈdəʊvə(r); AmE ˈdoʊvər/ a port in *Kent, southeast England, and the nearest English town to France. The part of the *Channel between Dover and Calais (called the **Strait of Dover**) is 21 miles/34 kilometres wide and is one of the busiest sea routes in the world. The high *white cliffs of Dover, which can be seen from a distance, have a special meaning to British people returning home by this route. Dover has a long history. It was a town in Roman times, and its castle, which was the administrative centre of the *Cinque Ports, was an important part of the country's defences.

Anthony 'Dowell /ˈdaʊl/ (1943–) the director of the British *Royal Ballet (1988–2001). He joined the Royal Ballet as a dancer in 1961 and often danced with Antoinette Sibley in roles created for them by Frederick *Ashton. In the 1970s he also worked with the American Ballet Theatre in New York. He was made a *knight in 1995.

the 'Dow-Jones 'Average /ˌdaʊ dʒəʊnz; AmE ˌdaʊ dʒoʊnz/ (also the **'Dow-Jones 'Index**, also informal **the Dow**) any of several numbers produced on each day of trade by the *New York Stock Exchange. They each represent the total average price of the shares of certain specific companies. The Dow began in 1884 and is used to measure the strength of the US stock market. The numbers are in points, not dollars. Four separate averages are given, and the most important is the **Dow-Jones Industrial Average**, based on 30 major companies. Compare FINANCIAL TIMES INDICES.

John 'Dowland /ˈdaʊlənd/ (c. 1562–1626) an English composer of songs and music, mainly for the lute, an ancient instrument like a guitar. He worked at various royal courts in Europe before entering the service of King *James I. His best-known work is *Lachrimae* (1604).

'Downing Street /ˈdaʊnɪŋ/ a short street in *Westminster(1), London, which contains the official London home of the British *Prime Minister at Number 10. In fact, the words 'Downing Street' and '*Number Ten' are often used to mean the Prime Minister's office or the British government. In the same street is the official home of the *Chancellor of the Exchequer at Number 11 and the office of the Chief *Whip at Number 12. The street was built in about 1680 by an *MP, George Downing: *Downing Street has just issued a statement denying the rumours.*

the 'Downing Street ˌDecla'ration /ˈdaʊnɪŋ/ a statement about Northern Ireland made by the British and Irish *prime ministers, John *Major and Albert Reynolds, in London in December 1993. The Declaration tried to push forward the peace process in Northern Ireland by offering something to all the opposing groups. For the first time the British government agreed to include *Sinn Fein in discussions if they and the *IRA promised not to use violence in future. In the following year the IRA stopped their bombing campaign, but refused to make any promises about the use of violence.

Down in the 'Valley a US *folk song about a man who asks a woman if she loves him. Kurt *Weill wrote an opera (1948) with the same name, based on the song. It begins:

> 66 Down in the valley, the valley so low,
> Hang your head over, hear the winds blow.
> Hear the winds blow, Dear, hear the winds blow.
> Hang your head over, hear the winds blow. 99

the Downs the general name for a number of ranges of low chalk hills, covered with grass but no trees, in southern England. The different ranges have different names, including the North Downs, the *South Downs and the Berkshire Downs.

,**Downside 'School** /ˌdaʊnsaɪd/ an English *Roman Catholic *public school(1) for boys (and, from 2005, girls) at Downside, near *Bath. The school was started in France in 1606 because at that time Roman Catholic schools were not allowed in England. However, the school moved to England after the French Revolution and has been at Downside since 1814. Its history is therefore similar to that of *Ampleforth College.

'**Downtown** /'daʊntaʊn/ **1** the area of *Manhattan(1) in New York City that is south of 34th Street. It includes *Wall Street, the *Chase Bank, *Greenwich Village and *SoHo. Compare UPTOWN(1).

2 '**downtown** n [U] (AmE) the central business area of any large town or city.

▶ **down'town** adj, adv (AmE) to or in the centre of a large town or city, especially the main business area: a downtown store ◊ Let's go downtown and see a movie.

'**Arthur 'Conan 'Doyle** ⇨ CONAN DOYLE.

'**Richard 'D'Oyly 'Carte** /'dɔɪli 'kɑːt; AmE 'kɑːrt/ (1844–1901) the man who brought W S *Gilbert and Sir Arthur *Sullivan together to write their very successful series of operas, called the *Savoy Operas because they were performed after 1881 at D'Oyly Carte's new Savoy Theatre in London. D'Oyly Carte also built the *Savoy Hotel.

DPP /ˌdiː piː 'piː/ ⇨ DIRECTOR OF PUBLIC PROSECUTIONS.

DQ ⇨ DAIRY QUEEN.

,**Margaret 'Drabble** /'dræbl/ (1939–) an English writer, famous for novels about life in England and its political, economic and social changes from her first novel, A Summer Birdcage (1964) to The Seven Sisters (2002). She also writes non-fiction (= books about real facts, people and events), drama and short stories and has won several awards and literary prizes. She is the editor of the Oxford Companion to English Literature. She is married to the writer and biographer Michael Holroyd and her older sister is the writer A S *Byatt.

'**Dracula** /'drækjələ/ a character in many horror films who is a vampire (= a dead person who comes alive at night to suck the blood of living people). He was created by the Irish writer Bram Stoker (1847–1912) in his novel Dracula (1897).

the **draft** n [sing] (AmE) the US government's Selective Service system, in which young people were required by law to serve in the armed forces. It was replaced in 1973 by a system in which people may join the forces only if they wish to. However, young men must still add their names to the **draft list** when they are 18, in case of a future military emergency. People who tried to avoid the draft, especially during the *Vietnam War, were known as **draft dodgers**. ⇨ note at NATIONAL SERVICE.

'**Dragnet** /'drægnet/ a US television police series in the early 1950s and again in the 1960s on *NBC. It received three *Emmy awards (1952–4). Jack Webb wrote and produced it and played the main character, Sergeant Joe Friday. Dragnet had earlier been a radio series, and was based on cases of the Los Angeles Police Department. It was the first US programme of its type to be shown on British television (in 1955). There have been two later Dragnet series (1967–70 and 2003–4) and a film was made in 1987.

,**Francis 'Drake** /'dreɪk/ (c. 1540–96) an English sailor who fought against the Spanish and was the first Englishman to sail around the world. After a career attacking and robbing Spanish ships in the *Caribbean, he was given five ships by Queen *Elizabeth I to sail around the world, attacking Spanish ships along the

way. When he returned three years later (1580) in the only surviving ship, the *Golden Hind, Queen Elizabeth made him a *knight.

In 1587 the Spanish were preparing to attack England, but Drake led a surprise attack on the port of Cadiz and burnt the Spanish ships. When the Spanish attack, known as the *Armada, finally came in 1588, Drake was one of the leaders who defeated it. There is a popular story that he was playing *bowls when the Armada was first seen and that he calmly finished his game before turning his attention to the enemy.

Dram'buie™ /dræm'bjuːi/ n [U, C] a very strong alcoholic drink made from Scotch *whisky and drunk in a small glass, usually after a meal. The name comes from a *Gaelic phrase meaning 'the drink that pleases'.

'**Drano**™ /'dreɪnəʊ; AmE 'dreɪnoʊ/ n [U] a US chemical used for dissolving substances that block pipes, especially in the kitchen and the bathroom. It is available as a liquid or in the form of crystals, and is made by the SC Johnson Company.

'**draught beer** (AmE **draft beer**) n [C, U] beer that is stored in and served from a large container, usually a barrel. Many people who have a lot about beer think draught beer is better than beer sold in bottles or tins: They do some good draught beers at the local pub. ⇨ note at BEER.

,**Dr 'Dre** /ˌdɒktə 'dreɪ; AmE ˌdɑːktər/ (Andre Young 1965–) an influential US *hip hop and *rap artist and music producer. Dr Dre has made a number of his own records including The Chronic (1992) and 2001 (1999) and has worked with other rap artists including *Snoop (Doggy) Dogg, Tupac *Shakur, *Eminem and *50 Cent.

The ,**Dream of Ge'rontius** /dʒəˈrɒntiəs; AmE dʒəˈrɑːntiəs/ a religious poem (1865) by Cardinal *Newman which was made into a musical work for voices and orchestra by Edward *Elgar in 1900.

DreamWorks SKG /ˌdriːmwɜːks es keɪ 'dʒiː; AmE ˌdriːmwɜːrks/ a US film company established in *Hollywood in 1994 by Steven *Spielberg, Jeffrey Katzenberg and David Geffen. Its films have included The Peacemaker (1997), The Lost World: Jurassic Park (1997), American Beauty (1999), Shrek (2001) and Shrek 2 (2004).

the ,**Dred 'Scott Case** /ˌdred 'skɒt; AmE 'skɑːt/ (also the ,**Dred 'Scott de,cision**) a US *Supreme Court decision in 1857 that a slave was not a citizen and could not begin a legal case against anyone. Dred Scott was a slave who wanted a court to say he was free because his owner took him to a free state. The Supreme Court also decided that *Congress had no power to prevent *slavery in new states. The case divided the nation and led indirectly to the *Civil War.

,**Theodore 'Dreiser** /'draɪsə(r)/ (1871–1945) a US writer of novels and short stories, which were often about poor people with unhappy lives. He was opposed to the idea of the *American dream of success. His best-known books were Sister Carrie (1900) and An American Tragedy (1925), both of which were made into films.

,**Nancy 'Drew** /'druː/ the main character in a series of US children's books written by Carolyn Keene, a name used by several writers, including Mildred Augustine Wirt. Nancy is a young amateur detective who solves mysteries. The series began in 1929 with The Secret of the Old Clock and is still being published. By 2004 over 200 million copies had been sold. There have been film and television series as well as computer games. See also DETECTIVE STORY.

'**drive-in** n [C] (especially AmE) a service that people can use or enjoy without leaving their cars. The idea began in the US with cinemas in 1933 and was followed there by restaurants and banks that serve customers in their cars outside.

▸ **drive-in** adj [only before noun]: a drive-in movie theater/bank.

'Driver and 'Vehicle 'Licensing ˌAgency
⇨ DVLA.

▸ driving
Americans have long had a 'love affair' with the automobile (also car), and are surprised when they meet somebody who cannot drive. In 2001 around 88% of the people aged 15 or older were drivers and only 8% of households had no vehicle available for regular use. American life is arranged so that people can do most things from their cars. There are **drive-in** banks, post offices, restaurants, movie theatres and even some churches.

In Britain around 70% of the population had driving licences in 2003, and 72% of household had access to a car. As in the US, many people prefer to use their car rather than public transport, because it is more convenient and because they like to be independent. In order to reduce pollution the government tries, not very successfully, to discourage car ownership by making driving expensive. In particular, it puts a heavy tax on petrol and regularly increases the annual **road tax**.

To many people the make and quality of their car reflects their status in society, and it is important to them to get a smart new car every few years. In Britain since 2001 the **registration number** of a car shows the place and date of registration but older **number plates** can be used and a **personalized number plate** (= a registration number that spells out the owner's name or initials) may also suggest status. Many people prefer to buy a small, economical car, or get a second-hand one. Cars in the US are often larger than those in Britain and though petrol/gas is cheaper, insurance is expensive. In the US car **license plates**, commonly called **tags**, are given by the states. New ones must be bought every two or three years, or when a driver moves to another state. The states use the plates to advertise themselves: *Alabama plates say 'The heart of Dixie' and have a small heart on them, and *Illinois has 'The land of Lincoln'.

In Britain, before a person can get a **driving licence** they must pass an official **driving test**, which includes a written test of the *Highway Code and a practical driving exam. Only people aged 17 or over are allowed to drive. **Learner drivers** who have a **provisional driving licence** must display an **L-plate**, a large red 'L', on their car, and be supervised by a qualified driver. The US has no national **driver's license** (AmE), but instead licences are issued by each state. Most require written tests, an eye test and a short practical test. The minimum age for getting a licence is normally 16, although some states will issue a **learner's permit** to drivers as young as 14. Many states now apply a system of **graduated licenses** in which young drivers are first required to have an **intermediate license** for a period of time before being given a **full license**. An intermediate licence may, for example, prevent driving alone at particular times of the day or require the driver to take special classes if they drive badly. Americans have to get a new driver's licence if they move to another state. US licences have on them a picture of the holder and are important as a means of identity.

In Britain people drive on the left and in the US they drive on the right. Generally British and US drivers are relatively careful and courteous but there is dangerous driving. In the US there were over 42000 deaths due to **traffic accidents** in 2003. About 40% of these accidents were caused by drivers who had drunk alcohol. **Drink-driving** (AmE **driving under the influence** or **driving while intoxicated**) (= driving a car after drinking alcohol) is also a serious problem in Britain. In some British towns special cameras have been set up to catch drivers who go too fast. In the US the main job of state **highway patrols** is to prevent **speeding**.

Many drivers belong to a motoring organization in case their car breaks down. In Britain the main ones are the *AA (Automobile Association) and the *RAC (Royal Automobile Club), and in the US the largest is the *American Automobile Association.

ˌDr 'Jekyll and ˌMr 'Hyde /'dʒekl, 'haɪd/ a novel
(1886) by the Scottish author Robert Louis *Stevenson. It is about a doctor who is interested in the good and evil parts of human nature and invents a drug that can separate them. When he tries the drug himself, he temporarily becomes an evil version of himself, Mr Hyde. His further experiments lead to disaster because he finds it more and more difficult to return to his original self. There have been several film versions of the story.

ˌDr 'Martens™ /'mɑːtɪnz; AmE 'mɑːrtnz/ (informal
Doc Martens) n (abbr **DMs**) a popular British make of strong shoes and boots. A special feature of them is a 'cushion of air' under the foot to make them more comfortable to wear. DMs were part of the uniform of the *skinheads in the 1960s and the *punks in the late 1970s, after which they became more widely fashionable.

'drop scone (also **Scotch pancake**) n (BrE) a small flat
cake eaten at *tea(2) with butter and jam. It is made from a mixture of flour, eggs and milk dropped in small amounts onto a hot pan. It is more like a small thick *pancake than a *scone.

ˌDr 'Pepper™ /'pepə(r)/ a popular US sweet fizzy drink
(= one containing many bubbles). It was created and first sold in 1885 by a chemist in Waco, *Texas.

ˌDr 'Scholl's™ /'ʃɒlz; AmE 'ʃɑːlz/ a type of open shoes
with wooden soles and leather straps invented by Dr William Scholl in 1961 and originally sold mainly in medical shops. They are now regarded as fashionable and sold in shoe shops.

ˌDr 'Seuss /'suːs/ the name used by the US writer and
artist Theodor Seuss Geisel (1904–91) for his popular series of children's books. They are long, funny poems that have been praised as a good way to teach children to read. They include Horton Hears a Who (1954), How the Grinch Stole Christmas (1957) and The Cat in the Hat (1957). Several were made into television cartoon films.

the ˌDrug En'forcement Admini'stration (abbr the DEA) an organization
established in 1973 to see that US drug laws are obeyed. It is part of the US Department of Justice. The DEA especially tries to stop drugs entering the country. It works closely with the *FBI, which was given a similar task in 1982, and with the US Customs Service and the *United States Coast Guard.

▸ drugs
The problem of **drug abuse**, the use of drugs for pleasure, is common in Britain and the US, especially among young people, but using drugs is illegal in both countries. Most teenagers try drugs before they leave school, and many of them use drugs regularly. There is also concern that younger children are being offered drugs. Drugs are much more widely available today than they were 20 years ago and can be easily obtained from **pushers** on the streets, in schools, at nightclubs and elsewhere.

Many different drugs are available, each known by a variety of slang names. They include **amphetamines** (**uppers** or **speed**), **barbiturates** (**barbs** or **downers**), **cannabis** (**marijuana**, **dope**, **grass**, **pot** or **weed**), cocaine (**coke**, **crack**, **ice** or **snow**), **heroin** (**junk** or **smack**), **LSD** (**acid**), and also **benzodiazepines** which are sometimes prescribed by doctors as **tranquillizers**. Other drugs include **mescaline**, **methadone**, **morphine**, **nitrates** (**poppers**) and **phencyclidine** (**angel dust** or **PCP**). Some children experiment with **glue-sniffing** (= breathing in the gas given off by strong glue). One of the most fashionable drugs of the 1990s was **MDMA**, better known as **Ecstasy** or **E**. Using Ecstasy has led to several highly publicized accidental deaths.

Many people are concerned about the problems associated with drug-taking. The main worry is that using drugs often leads to **addiction**, poor health, and even death. Reflecting public concern, the courts have taken a tough attitude towards pushers and **drugs barons**, the people who supply drugs to the pushers. **Addicts** are less severely punished but are encouraged to get medical treatment and attend **rehabilitation centres**.

Drug-taking is blamed for a lot of crimes, as **addicts** sometimes steal in order to get money to buy drugs. Also, criminal organizations that sell drugs use violence to prevent others selling them. In the 1980s these problems caused the US government to begin the **War on Drugs** and it set up the **Office of National Drug Control Policy** in 1988. But not everyone supports the programme: many young people say that they can use drugs without becoming addicted. They also say that it is wrong for alcohol, also an addictive drug, to be legal, while the drugs they enjoy are not. In Britain there have been many campaigns to try to reduce drug use, and in 1998 the government appointed a **drugs czar** to lead the fight against drugs.

There are often calls in both Britain and the US for **soft drugs**, the less harmful drugs such as cannabis, to be made legal, but this is resisted by many experts on the grounds that people taking them are likely to go on eventually to **hard drugs**, the more dangerous drugs such as heroin. People who want drug-taking to be legalized say that making tougher laws against using drugs has not worked, and that many of the problems associated with drugs would be solved if it were legal to use them. For instance, the government would be able to control the supply of drugs, and their quality and price. Criminal organizations would no longer be involved, and that would help reduce violence. The government could put a tax on drugs, as is the case with tobacco and alcohol, and the money could be used to help pay for medical treatment for people who become addicted. But many people are worried by the increasing use of drugs and do not believe that legalizing them is a solution. In Britain, the possession of cannabis was made a less serious crime in 2004.

'Druid a priest in the religion of the ancient *Celts in Britain, France and Ireland. This religion was destroyed by the Romans in France and Britain but continued in Scotland and Ireland until Christianity replaced it. Today some people who want to bring this ancient religion back to life call themselves Druids. They sometimes try to hold ceremonies at *Stonehenge.

‚drum 'n' 'bass *n* [U] a type of pop music that developed from *jungle in Britain in the mid 1990s, with the same very fast drum beats, loud bass and electronic sound effects.

‚Drury 'Lane /‚drʊəri; *AmE* ‚drʊri/ a street in central London, near *Covent Garden, which contains the *Theatre Royal.

‚John 'Dryden /'draɪdn/ (1631–1700) an English poet and writer of plays. He was made *Poet Laureate by King *Charles II in 1668, and most of his poems are about national events of his time. *Absalom and Achitophel*

(1681), for example, is about the Duke of *Monmouth's attempt to become king. His best-remembered play is *All For Love*, a new version of Shakespeare's *Anthony and Cleopatra*.

DSC /‚di: es 'si:/ ⇨ DISTINGUISHED SERVICE CROSS.

DSO /‚di: es 'əʊ; *AmE* 'oʊ/ ⇨ DISTINGUISHED SERVICE ORDER.

DTI /‚di: ti: 'aɪ/ ⇨ DEPARTMENT OF TRADE AND INDUSTRY.

dub /dʌb/ *n* [U] a type of *reggae music. In dub recordings emphasis is given to drum and bass sounds. There are usually few words, and unusual sound effects are often added. Dub records are often remixes of existing reggae songs.

'Dublin /'dʌblɪn/ the capital city of the Republic of Ireland, situated on its east coast on the River Liffey. Dublin was the scene of the 1916 *Easter Rising against the British, who ruled Ireland from Dublin's 13th–century castle until the south of Ireland became an independent state in 1922. Many great writers and poets have come from Dublin, including Jonathan *Swift, Oscar *Wilde, George Bernard *Shaw, W B *Yeats and James *Joyce.

‚W E B Du 'Bois /du: 'bɔɪs/ (William Edward Burghardt Du Bois 1868–1963) a US writer who helped to establish the *NAACP. His books include *The Souls of Black Folk* (1903), and he was the editor of the NAACP magazine *Crisis* (1910–34). He was the first African American to receive a PhD degree from *Harvard University and taught economics and history at Atlanta University (1897–1910 and 1932–44). In 1961 Du Bois became a Communist and moved to Ghana, where he died.

Du'buque /də'bjʊk/ a US town on the *Mississippi River in the state of *Iowa. It is sometimes referred to as the typical example of a small, boring US community. A writer in the *New Yorker* once said that it was not the magazine for 'the old lady from Dubuque'.

The ‚Duchess of 'Malfi /'mælfi/ a play (1613) by the English writer John *Webster about a woman who marries against the wishes of her two powerful and cruel brothers. It is a dark story of evil and guilt, expressed in great poetry. All the main characters die in the end.

the ‚Duchy of 'Cornwall /'kɔːnwəl; *AmE* 'kɔːrnwəl/ the areas of land in the English county of *Cornwall owned by the Duke of Cornwall. These were first given by King *Edward III to his eldest son Edward the *Black Prince in 1337. Since then the Duchy has always passed to the eldest son of the King or Queen.

the ‚Duchy of 'Lancaster /'læŋkəstə(r)/ the areas of land, mainly in the English county of *Lancashire(1), which have been owned by the King or Queen since 1399 and which now provide the money for the payments from the *Privy Purse each year.

'duct tape *n* [U] (*AmE*) a strong type of tape used for repairing many things. It keeps out water and was originally designed to repair ducts (= tubes carrying wires, liquids, etc.).

'dude ranch *n* (in the western US) a ranch (= large farm) which is used as a holiday centre. Visitors can ride horses, do ranch work and camp outdoors. A *dude* is a person from a city, especially from the eastern US states.

‚due 'process of 'law *n* [U] a legal right in the US. The *Fifth Amendment to the US *Constitution states that a person cannot be 'deprived of life, liberty or property without due process of law'. This includes a fair trial and informing people of their rights if they are suspected of a crime. Due process is an important part of the US legal system and is used by the US *Supreme Court to declare some laws 'unconstitutional'.

'Duesenberg /'du:zənbɜ:g; AmE 'du:zənbɜ:rg/ n a large, fast and expensive car made in the US between 1920 and 1937 during the *Jazz Age. Its popular name was a 'Duesie', and Americans still use the informal word 'doozy' or 'doozie' to mean something that is special. It was the first US car to win the Grand Prix at Le Mans, France, in 1921.

duke n a member of the British *peerage with the highest rank. The wife of a duke is called a **duchess**. Dukes who are members of the royal family are known as **royal dukes** and include the Duke of *Cornwall, the Duke of *Edinburgh and the Duke of *York. The land owned by a duke is called a **duchy**. ⇨ note at ARISTOCRACY.

the ¸Duke of 'Cornwall ⇨ CORNWALL².

the ¸Duke of 'Edinburgh ⇨ EDINBURGH².

the ¸Duke of 'Edinburgh's A'ward a programme of activities for young people between the ages of 14 and 24. It was started in Britain in 1956 by the *Duke of Edinburgh and others. The Award has become international and is known by different names in some countries, such as the **Congressional Award** in the US. Young people choose a personal interest to develop and also do community service and outdoor activities. Awards for achievement are given at three levels: bronze, silver and gold. The Award scheme is operated mainly by schools and youth organizations.

'John 'Foster 'Dulles /'fɒstə 'dʌlɪs; AmE 'fɑstər/ (1888–1959) a US lawyer who became *Secretary of State (1953–9) under President *Eisenhower. He developed a US foreign policy that was strongly opposed to the USSR and to Communism, which he considered to be morally evil.

'Dulux™ /'dju:lʌks/ a British company that makes paint. Its advertisements use an *Old English sheepdog, which people now sometimes call a 'Dulux dog': the Dulux range of gloss paints ◇ a tin of Dulux.

¸Dulwich 'College /¸dʌlɪdʒ/ a large *public school for boys in Dulwich, an area of south-east London. It was started in 1619 by the actor Edward *Alleyn. The writer P G *Wodehouse was a student there.

¸Daphne du 'Maurier¹ /dju: 'mɒrieɪ; AmE dju: 'mɔ:rieɪ/ (1907–89) a popular English writer of exciting and romantic novels set in the south-west of England. Films of her most famous novel, Rebecca (1938), and one of her short stories, The Birds (1952), were made by Alfred *Hitchcock.

¸George du 'Maurier² /dju: 'mɒrieɪ; AmE dju: 'mɔ:rieɪ/ (1834–96) a cartoonist and writer of novels, the son of English and French parents. He is best known for his cartoons (= humorous drawings) in *Punch about the social life of rich people. His novels were also very successful, and the name of one of his characters, *Svengali in the novel Trilby, has become part of the English language. He was the grandfather of Daphne *du Maurier.

¸Dum¸barton 'Oaks /dʌm¸bɑ:tn; AmE dʌm¸bɑ:rtn/ a large house in the Georgetown area of *Washington, DC, in which the **Dumbarton Oaks Conference** was held in 1944 to discuss the idea of forming the *United Nations. The four countries with representatives at the conference were the US, Britain, the USSR and China.

Dum'fries /dʌm'fri:s/ a town in south-west Scotland, sometimes called 'Queen of the South'. It is the administrative centre of the Scottish *council area of **Dumfries and Galloway**. Robert *Burns is buried there.

'Dumpster™ /'dʌmpstə(r)/ n a US make of very large metal container for rubbish, left in the street or near a place where there is building work. **Dumpster diving** is taking things, including food, from these containers,

often as a way of protesting about excess and waste in modern society.

¸Dun and 'Bradstreet /¸dʌn, 'brædstri:t/ a US company that is the largest source of business information in the world. It publishes several books each year and regular news about the financial situation and organization of companies. In 2002, it could provide information on 83 million companies in 214 countries. The company's main office is in Wilton, *Connecticut.

Dun'blane /dʌn'bleɪn/ a town in central Scotland. In March 1996 a local man called Thomas Hamilton shot and killed 16 children and a teacher in a Dunblane *nursery school, before killing himself. Public feeling was so great that by the middle of 1997 the British government had passed a law making it illegal to own most types of handgun: the Dunblane massacre.

¸Isadora 'Duncan /¸ɪzədɔ:rə 'dʌŋkən/ (1878–1927) a US dancer who helped to develop modern dance. She was influenced especially by ancient Greek art and often danced in bare feet, wearing a loose tunic. She worked mostly in Europe, and started schools of dance in Berlin, Moscow, Vienna and Salzburg. Her life was very tragic: her Russian husband killed himself, her children were killed in a car accident, and she herself died when her long shawl became caught in the wheel of her car and strangled her.

¸Duncan 'Hines™ /¸dʌŋkən 'haɪnz/ a name for a US range of mixtures for baking different types of cakes. They are produced by Aurora Foods and were named after a US food expert who used to travel around the country finding and recommending the best restaurants.

Dun'dee /dʌn'di:/ a large city in Scotland on the Firth of Tay. It is an important port. Dundee is known for its marmalade (= jam made with oranges and similar fruit) and as a centre for making cloth. Since 1996 it has been governed as a *council area (officially called **Dundee City**).

Dun'dee cake /dʌn'di:/ n [C, U] (especially BrE) a large rich cake containing dried fruit and usually decorated on the top with almonds.

¸Dunge'ness /¸dʌndʒə'nes/ a place on the coast of *Kent in England where there are two nuclear power stations. The artist Derek *Jarman created a garden there that is kept as a work of art.

'Dunhill™ /'dʌnhɪl/ a British company that makes tobacco products, men's clothes, leather goods and gifts.

¸Dunkin' 'Donuts™ /¸dʌŋkɪn 'dəʊnʌts; AmE 'doʊnʌts/ the largest group of shops in the world selling doughnuts (= small, sweet, ring-shaped cakes) and coffee. They also sell other baked products. In 2004, there were more than 5 000 Dunkin' Donuts shops in 31 countries. The US company began in 1950, and its main office is in Randolph, *Massachusetts.

Dun'kirk /dʌn'kɜ:k; AmE dʌn'kɜ:rk/ a port in northern France. During *World War II about 220 ships of the *Royal Navy and 660 small private boats sailed across the *Channel between 26 May and 4 June 1940 to bring back to England many British, French and Belgian soldiers who were trapped in Dunkirk by the advancing German army. More than 330 000 soldiers were rescued, and the expression the Dunkirk spirit is now sometimes used in referring to occasions when people show great determination and courage in a difficult situation: The Prime Minister praised the Dunkirk spirit shown by the organizers of the event.

'Dunlop /'dʌnlɒp; AmE 'dʌnlɑ:p/ **1** a British company that makes tyres and other rubber goods. It is named after John Dunlop, the Scottish inventor of the pneumatic tyre (= one that contains a rubber tube filled with air).

2 a soft cheese similar to *Cheddar, first made at Dunlop in *Ayrshire, Scotland.

the ˌDunmow ˈFlitch /ˌdʌnməʊ ˈflɪtʃ; AmE ˌdʌnmoʊ/ a very large piece of bacon which is regularly given in the *Essex village of Great Dunmow as a prize to a man and woman who can prove that, after being married for at least a year and a day, they have never once wished that they were not married. The ceremony is at least 600 years old, and is mentioned by *Chaucer in *The *Canterbury Tales*. Now it is regarded as just a bit of fun.

ˌDunnet ˈHead /ˌdʌnɪt/ a place in Scotland which is the most northern part of the British mainland. The most northern point in the whole of Britain, including its islands, is a rock called Muckle Flugga, a mile off the coast of the island of Unst in the *Shetland Islands. See also JOHN O'GROATS.

the DUP /ˌdiː juː ˈpiː/ (in full the **Democratic Unionist Party**) ⇒ ULSTER DEMOCRATIC UNIONIST PARTY.

ˈDuPont /ˈduːpɒnt; AmE ˈduːpɑːnt/ a large US chemical company. It also sells petroleum, fibres, plastics and other products. It began in 1802 as a small family company producing gunpowder (= an explosive powder) in Wilmington, Delaware, and the main office is still there.

ˈDuracell™ /ˈdjʊərəsel; AmE ˈdjʊrəsel/ a company that makes batteries. Duracell batteries are said to last longer than most others.

ˌJimmy **Duˈrante** /djʊˈrænti/ (1893–1980) a US comic actor and singer with a harsh voice who was called 'Schnozzola' because of his large nose. He was a star of *vaudeville, radio and television, and ended each show by saying 'Goodnight, Mrs Calabash, wherever you are,' although he never revealed who she was. Durante also appeared in many films.

ˈDurex™ /ˈdjʊəreks; AmE ˈdjʊreks/ n (pl **Durex** or **Durexes**) (in Britain) a make of rubber contraceptive worn on the penis (= male sex organ) during sex: *a packet of Durex.*

ˈDurham /ˈdʌrəm/ **1** (abbr **Dur**) (also ˌ**County** ˈ**Durham**) a county in north-east England that used to be a major centre of coal mining, shipbuilding and steel-making.
2 (also ˌ**Durham** ˈ**City**) a city in the county of Durham and its administrative centre. It has a castle, now a college of the University of Durham, and a beautiful *Norman cathedral, one of the best examples of *Romanesque architecture in Europe. Durham Castle and Durham Cathedral were made a *World Heritage Site in 1986.

Durham Cathedral

the ˈDurham ˈMiners' ˈGala /ˈdʌrəm, ˈgeɪlə/ an occasion every year when the miners of *Durham, England, parade through the streets of the town. There are colourful displays, traditional *brass bands, etc. The procession is led by leading members of the *Labour Party and of the *NUM. It is held on the second Saturday in July.

ˌMark ˈDurkan /ˈdɜːkən; AmE ˈdɜːrkən/ (1960–) a politician in Northern Ireland who has been the leader of the *Social Democratic and Labour Party (SDLP) since 2001 and was the Deputy *First Minister in the *Northern Ireland Executive from 2001 until it was suspended in 2002.

ˌGerald ˈDurrell[1] /ˈdʌrəl/ (1925–95) an English zoologist (= person who studies animals) and author of books about his life studying and collecting animals. These include *My Family and Other Animals* (1956) and *A Zoo in my Luggage* (1960). He was the younger brother of Lawrence *Durrell.

ˌLawrence ˈDurrell[2] /ˈdʌrəl/ (1912–90) an English author and poet, best known for his sequence of four novels *The *Alexandria Quartet*. Born in India, Durrell lived most of his life in the eastern Mediterranean, where many of his books are set. He was the older brother of Gerald *Durrell.

the ˈDust Bowl an area in the western central US where there were terrible dust storms in the 1930s. These were caused by strong winds blowing the dry earth off the fields, and they made it difficult to grow crops. Many farmers became poor and moved with their families to other areas. This was especially bad because it happened during the *Great Depression. See also GRAPES OF WRATH.

ˈDustbuster™ /ˈdʌstbʌstə(r)/ n a US make of small vacuum cleaner (= a machine that sucks up dust, dirt, etc.), held in the hand. It is used especially to clean in people's homes and inside cars. It has been made since 1978 by the Black and Decker Corporation who developed it from technology needed for the spacecraft of the *Apollo program.

ˌDutch ˈelm disease n [U] a disease that kills elm trees. It is caused by a fungus carried by a type of insect. It seriously affected elm trees in Britain in the 1970s and 1980s, killing about 20 million of them.

DVLA /ˌdiː viː el ˈeɪ/ (in full **Driver and Vehicle Licensing Agency**) a British government agency responsible for collecting road tax and sending people their driving licences and vehicle licences. It is in *Swansea, Wales.

ˌAndrea ˈDworkin /ˌændriə ˈdwɔːkɪn; AmE ˈdwɔːrkɪn/ (1946–2005) an extreme US feminist (= person who believes strongly that women should have the same rights and opportunities as men). She has written many books expressing her views, including *Pornography: Men Possessing Women* (1981), *Intercourse* (1987) and *Life and Death* (1997).

the DWP /ˌdiː ˈdʌbljuː ˈpiː/ ⇒ DEPARTMENT FOR WORK AND PENSIONS.

ˌAnthony van ˈDyck /væn ˈdaɪk/ (1599–1641) a Dutch portrait painter who went to live in London in 1632. He was immediately made a *knight and became the official painter for the court of King *Charles I. One of his most famous paintings is of the king on his horse. His style of painting had a great influence on later British artists, including *Gainsborough.

D'ye ˌKen John ˈPeel? /djə ˌken, ˈpiːl/ a popular British song written in about 1829 by John Graves, a friend of a farmer called John Peel who for fifty years had a pack of hunting dogs in *Cumberland. It is sung to an old folk tune, *Bonnie Annie*.

ˌBob ˈDylan /ˈdɪlən/ (1941–) a famous US singer and writer of *folk *rock music, whose unusual voice and sometimes mysterious way of life made him even more popular. His songs of political and social protest greatly influenced young people in the 1960s. They include *Blowin' in the Wind* (1963) and *The Times They Are A-Changin'* (1964). Among his other successful songs are *Mr Tambourine Man* (1965), *Lay Lady Lay* (1969) and *Knocking on Heaven's Door* (1973). Recent albums include *Time Out of Mind* (1997) and *Love and Theft* (2001). He received an *Oscar for the song *Things have Changed* in 2001.

'**Dynasty** /'dɪnəsti/ a US television *soap opera (1981–89) which was also shown in many countries round the world. It was about the Carringtons, a rich family in the oil business in *Denver. The actors included Joan *Collins as Alexis Carrington and John Forsythe as her former husband, Blake Carrington.

,**James 'Dyson** /'daɪsn/ (1947–) an English designer and inventor who developed a vacuum cleaner (= an electrical machine that sucks up dirt and dust from floors) which works without a bag and is therefore more efficient. Called the Dyson, it was first made in Japan and is now a best-selling make of vacuum cleaner in many countries.

E e

'Eagle a British *comic for boys started in 1950 by a priest, Marcus Morris. Its most famous character was *Dan Dare. *Eagle* stopped being published in 1969, and was later published in a different form (1982–93).

'Eagle Scout a boy who has achieved the highest rank in the *Boy Scouts of America and can wear the **Eagle Scout** badge.

the ˌEaling 'comedies /ˌiːlɪŋ/ the comedy films produced between 1948 and 1950 by the **Ealing Studios** in west London, England. They are famous for being well written and for their clever stories. They include *Kind Hearts and Coronets* (1949), *The Lavender Hill Mob* (1951) and *Passport to Pimlico* (1949).

Aˌmelia 'Earhart /əˌmiːliə 'eəhɑːt; *AmE* 'erhɑːrt/ (1898–1937) a US pilot who in 1932 became the first woman to fly across the Atlantic alone. She and Fred Noonan, another pilot, disappeared in their plane somewhere in the Pacific while trying to fly around the world. What happened to them is still a mystery. In 1997 Linda Finch successfully flew around the world using Earhart's route and the same model of plane that she flew in.

earl *n* **1** a member of the British *peerage, with a rank above a *viscount(1) and below a *marquess. The wife of an earl, or a woman with a similar rank, is called a *countess*.
2 a *courtesy title given to the eldest son of a *duke or *marquess. ⇨ note at ARISTOCRACY.

ˌEarl 'Grey *n* [U] a popular type of Chinese tea with the flavour of the herb bergamot. It was introduced into Britain by Earl Grey (1764–1845), an English political leader, after he received some as a gift from the Chinese: *a cup of Earl Grey*.

ˌEarl's 'Court **1** a large exhibition hall in west London, England, in which many important events are held, e.g. the *Ideal Home Exhibition and the *Royal Tournament: *events at Earl's Court*.
2 an area of west London, part of the *borough of *Kensington, where there are many small hotels.

ˌEarly 'English an early style of *Gothic architecture which developed in England in the 13th century. Its main characteristics are tall narrow pointed windows without decorative stonework, and thick walls. The cathedrals of *Salisbury and *Wells are typical examples of the Early English style. See also DECORATED STYLE.

the ˌEarly 'Learning ˌCentre a company with shops in many British towns, selling things that help young children to learn about numbers, letters, materials, etc. in an interesting and exciting way.

ˌWyatt 'Earp /ˌwaɪət 'ɜːp; *AmE* 'ɜːrp/ (1848–1929) a US law officer in the *Wild West, first in Wichita and then in *Dodge City. He is best remembered for being involved in the gun fight at the *OK Corral in *Tombstone in 1881. The story of this and of Earp's life have been told in many books and films, and in a television series in the 1950s and 1960s.

'Earth, 'Wind and 'Fire a US *jazz funk group who were especially popular in the 1970s. Their album *That's the Way of the World* (1975) included the song *Shining Star*, which won a *Grammy award. Other albums included *I Am* (1979) and *Let's Groove* (1981). The group split up in 1984 but came together again in 1987. They

were chosen for the Rock and Roll *Hall of Fame in 2000.

ˌEast 'Anglia /ˈæŋgliə/ a region of eastern England that includes *Norfolk, *Suffolk and parts of *Cambridgeshire and *Essex. The landscape is flat and it is an agricultural area, producing a lot of grain.

the ˌEast 'End an area to the east of the *City of London, from the *Tower of London along the north bank of the River *Thames. It contains most of the old docks, where many of the local people used to work. The people living in the East End were mostly poor but well known for their friendly and lively nature. With recent new housing developments, the character of the area has completely changed. See also COCKNEY, DOCKLANDS. Compare WEST END.
▶ **East Ender** *n* a person living in the East End.

ˌEast'Enders /ˌiːst'endəz; *AmE* -'endərz/ a popular British *soap opera on *BBC One. It is about the lives of the people who live in Albert Square in the *borough of Walford, an imaginary place in the *East End of London. Its best-known families are the Fowlers and the Mitchells and the local pub is the Queen Vic.

▶ **Easter**

Easter is a holiday in late March or early April, the first Sunday after the first full moon after 21 March. Many people spend it with their family or have a short holiday/vacation. It is also an important Christian festival. **Easter Sunday**, the day of the Resurrection, is the end of *Lent and the most important date in the Christian year. Many people who do not go to church at other times go on Easter Sunday. It was once common for people to wear new clothes to church on this day. Women wore new hats, called **Easter bonnets**. Today, people sometimes make elaborately decorated Easter bonnets for fun. A few people send **Easter cards** with religious symbols on them or pictures of small chickens, lambs, rabbits and spring flowers, all traditionally associated with Easter.

The Friday before Easter Sunday is called *Good Friday and is remembered as the day Christ was crucified (= hanged on a cross to die). On Good Friday many people eat **hot cross buns** (= fruit buns decorated with a simple cross). The Monday after Easter is called **Easter Monday**. In Britain, Good Friday and Easter Monday are both *bank holidays. In the US, each company decides for itself whether to close or remain open on those days.

Children look forward to Easter Sunday because they are given chocolate **Easter eggs**. These are also popular with adults and millions are sold in the weeks before Easter. Many are packed in coloured foil in brightly-coloured boxes decorated with pictures of cartoon characters. Others are decorated with sugar flowers and wrapped in clear paper tied with a ribbon. Some shops write the person's name on the egg with icing (*AmE* frosting). Inside each egg are sweets or chocolates. Smaller eggs with a sweet cream inside are also popular. Eggs represent new life and the start of spring, and children sometimes colour the shells of real eggs at home. In some parts of Britain Easter is a time for traditional events such as *egg-rolling.

When American children wake up on Easter morning, they hope that the **Easter Bunny** has been. The Easter

Bunny is an imaginary rabbit, and parents tell their children that it goes from house to house while they are sleeping. The Easter Bunny brings an **Easter basket** with chocolate eggs and other sweet things, or hides in the house small plastic eggs filled with sweets or little presents. When they wake up all the children run about trying to find the eggs. The Easter Bunny also often brings chocolate in the shape of a rabbit. In Britain some families now organize an Easter egg hunt, and people buy chocolate rabbits as well as eggs.

Eastern 'Daylight Time (*abbr* **EDT**) (in the US) the time used between early April and late October in the eastern states. It is an hour earlier than *Eastern Standard Time.

the ,Eastern E'stablishment (*sometimes disapproving*) the people and institutions in the north-eastern US that have traditionally had great economic and political power in the country. These include the old, rich families in cities like *Boston, *Philadelphia and New York, and institutions like the *Ivy League and the *New York Stock Exchange.

Eastern 'Eye a UK newspaper for people from an Asian background living in Britain. It contains news stories, sport and entertainment news from India, Pakistan, Sri Lanka and Bangladesh, and from Asian communities in the UK.

Eastern 'Standard Time (*abbr* **EST**) (*also* **Eastern Time**) (in the US) the time used between late October and early April in the eastern states. It is five hours earlier than *Greenwich Mean Time.

the ,Easter 'Rising the rebellion in Dublin against British rule, which took place at Easter in 1916. An announcement was made that an independent Irish Republic was read out in front of the main post office. 450 people were killed in the four days of fighting, including 64 of the rebels. Several leaders of the rebellion were later executed. See also ANGLO-IRISH WAR.

the ,East 'India ,Company /'ɪndɪə/ an English company started in 1600 to develop trade in the **East Indies** (= the islands off the south-east coast of Asia, including Java and Borneo). By the 18th century it had its own army and political service, and was responsible for the administration of parts of India. In the early 19th century the company founded the modern *Singapore, which became a British colony in 1826. The East India Company continued to increase its power in India, but after the *Indian Mutiny in 1858 the British government took over its work there, and the company ceased to exist.

George 'Eastman /'iːstmən/ (1854–1932) the American who invented a camera small enough to carry and film in a flexible roll. He started a company in 1888 that later became the Eastman Kodak Company. His *Kodak box camera was first sold in 1888 and the Brownie camera in 1900. This made photography available to many ordinary people for the first time.

East of 'Eden a novel (1952) by the US author John *Steinbeck. It is about a farmer and his family in the Salinas Valley of *California during the early years of the 20th century. A film version (1955) used mostly the second half of the book, in which one of the farmer's sons discovers that his mother owns a brothel. This was James *Dean's first major role.

the ,East 'Side the area in New York City between *Fifth Avenue and the East River. See also LOWER EAST SIDE.

East 'Sussex /'sʌsɪks/ a county in south-east England, formed in 1974 from part of *Sussex. Its administrative centre is Lewes.

Clint 'Eastwood /'iːstwʊd/ (1930–) a US film actor who also directs and produces films. He began in tele-

vision but then became internationally famous through a series of *spaghetti westerns, including *A Fistful of Dollars* (1964). He often plays strong and good but violent characters, as in *Dirty Harry* (1971). He won an *Oscar in 1992 for directing the Western *Unforgiven* and a special Oscar in 1995. His more recent films include *The Bridges of Madison County* (1995), *Absolute Power* (1997) and, as director, *Mystic River* (2003).

,Easy 'Rider a 1969 US film. It was especially popular with young people, because it showed the freedom from responsibility that many of them wanted in the 1960s. It made stars of Jack *Nicholson, Peter *Fonda and Dennis Hopper (who directed it). The story is about *hippies riding their motorcycles from *Los Angeles to *New Orleans.

'eBay™ /'iːbeɪ/ a popular auction (= selling things to the person who offers the most money for them) website through which people buy and sell all kinds of goods on the Internet. It was started in the US in 1995 by Pierre Omidyar and Jeff Skoll and by 2004 it had nearly 100 million users around the world.

E'bonics /eˈbɒnɪks; *AmE* eˈbɑːnɪks/ *n* [U] the type of English spoken by many *African Americans. Language teachers call it African American Vernacular English (AAVE). It became a political issue in 1996 when school officials in *Oakland, *California, recognized it as a special language and accepted it in students' written work. Some other schools did the same, but by 1998 many had stopped doing so because of the need for students to speak and write standard English in order to get the best jobs. Compare ENGLISH-ONLY MOVEMENT.

'Ebony /'ebəni/ a US magazine of general interest with many photographs, which is mostly for and about *African Americans. It was first published in Chicago in 1945 by John H. Johnson.

EC /ˌiː 'siː/ ⇨ EUROPEAN COMMUNITY.

'Eccles cake /'eklz/ *n* a small round cake made of pastry covered with sugar, and filled with currants (= dried grapes). They were originally made in Eccles, in *Lancashire (now *Greater Manchester).

ECG'D ⇨ EXPORT CREDITS GUARANTEE DEPARTMENT.

Eco'nomic and 'Monetary 'Union (*also* **European Monetary Union**) (*abbr* **EMU**) the idea that there should be completely free movement of people, goods and money between the countries of the *European Union. From 1 January 1993 many controls on the movement of goods and people between the EU countries were removed. There is now a European Central Bank and a single European currency, the *euro, was introduced in 2002 in 12 EU countries.

The E'conomist a British political and economic newspaper that is published every week. It was started in 1843.

Pat 'Eddery /'edəri/ (1952–) an Irish flat-racing jockey who has been the British champion eleven times since 1973. In 1990 he rode more than 200 winners in one season, the first time this had been done since Gordon *Richards did it in 1947.

'Mary 'Baker 'Eddy /'beɪkə(r) 'edi/ (1821–1910) the American woman who in 1879 began the Church of Christ, Scientist. She first presented her idea that religious belief can cure illness in her book *Science and Health* (1875). She also began the *Christian Science Monitor* newspaper in 1908. See also CHRISTIAN SCIENTIST.

the ,Eddystone 'lighthouse /ˌedɪstəʊn; *AmE* ˌedɪstoʊn/ a lighthouse (= tower containing a strong light to warn or guide ships) on a rock in the *English Channel about 9 miles/14 kilometres from the coast of *Cornwall. It rises 133 feet/41 metres above the water and can be seen for 17 miles/28 kilometres. There has been a lighthouse there since 1696.

,Anthony 'Eden /ˈiːdn/ (1897–1977) a *Conservative politician who had a long career, mostly in foreign affairs, and became *Prime Minister in 1955 when Winston *Churchill retired. The following year the *Suez Crisis occurred, and in January 1957 Eden resigned. He was made a *knight in 1954 and an *earl(1) in 1961.

the 'Eden ,Project /ˈiːdn/ a large area in *Cornwall, England which contains plants from all over the world, some growing outside and others in two very large transparent domes called **biomes**. The project opened in 2001 and has become very popular with visitors. It aims especially to show people the natural resources which come from plants and their importance to people's lives.

'Edgbaston an area of *Birmingham, England, where there is an international cricket ground with the same name. Birmingham University is also in Edgbaston.

the ,Battle of 'Edge'hill /edʒˈhɪl/ the first important battle of the *English Civil War, fought in *Warwickshire in 1642. Neither side really won.

'Edinburgh¹ /ˈedɪnbrə/ the capital city of Scotland and a popular tourist centre. It has a famous castle, the *Scottish Parliament, a zoo, two universities and many museums and art galleries. Other famous features of the city include the *Royal Mile and *Princes Street. In the 18th century Edinburgh was known as 'the Athens of the north'. The name *Edinburgh* means 'Edwin's fort'. The city was made a *World Heritage Site in 1995. Since 1996 it has been governed as a *unitary authority (officially called **City of Edinburgh**). See also AULD REEKIE, DUKE OF EDINBURGH, EDINBURGH FESTIVAL.

Edinburgh Castle

the ,Duke of 'Edinburgh² /ˈedɪnbrə/ (1921–) the title by which Prince *Philip, the husband of Queen *Elizabeth II, is usually known. His father was Prince Andrew of Greece and his mother was Princess Alice of Battenberg, sister of Lord *Mountbatten. He was educated in Britain and was in the *Royal Navy in *World War II. In 1947 he married Princess Elizabeth, who later became Queen Elizabeth II. Among his many interests are British industry, projects for young people, wild animals and various sports.

the Duke of Edinburgh

the ,Edinburgh 'Festival /ˈedɪnbrə/ a festival of music and drama that has been held in *Edinburgh for three weeks every summer since 1947. The shows and concerts include hundreds that are not part of the official Festival. These are known as **the Edinburgh Fringe**, and are now considered as important as the Festival itself because of the many new and exciting ideas they contain.

,Edinburgh 'rock /ˌedɪnbrə/ n [U] a sweet in the form of short sticks of sugar, like chalk in texture and tasting of peppermint or lemon, sold in different colours. It was first made in *Edinburgh in 1822.

,Thomas 'Edison /ˈedɪsn/ (1847–1931) a famous US inventor. His inventions included a machine for reproducing sound, the electric light bulb and the 'kinescopic camera', later used in cinemas. He produced the first talking films in 1912.

> 66 Genius is one per cent inspiration, ninety nine per cent perspiration. 99
> Thomas Edison

,St 'Edmund (849–870) a king of *East Anglia, a region of eastern England, who was killed fighting the Danes. It was known all over Europe that he was very holy, and his shrine at Bury St Edmunds in *Suffolk was famous.

'Edsel™ /ˈedsəl/ a Ford car model that was a famous failure. It was named after the son of Henry *Ford. Fewer than 100 000 were sold from 1957 to 1960. It became a popular US joke, and other unsuccessful products are still sometimes referred to in a humorous way as Edsels.

EDT /ˌiː diː ˈtiː/ ⇨ EASTERN DAYLIGHT TIME.

,Prince 'Edward ⇨ WESSEX.

Edward I /ˌedwəd ðə ˈfɜːst; AmE ˌedwərd, ˈfɜːrst/ (1239–1307) the king of England from 1272 to 1307, the eldest son of *Henry III. He spent a lot of time trying to control Wales and Scotland, fighting, among others, William *Wallace and *Robert the Bruce. As a result he was called the 'Hammer of the Scots'. In 1296 he brought the *Stone of Scone to England. Although he was the first *Norman king of England called Edward, there were two King Edwards before the *Conquest.

Edward II /ˌedwəd ðə ˈsekənd; AmE ˌedwərd/ (1284–1327) the king of England from 1307 to 1327, the son of *Edward I and the first *Prince of Wales. He took his armies to Scotland, but was defeated at the Battle of *Bannockburn (1314) by *Robert the Bruce. He was a weak king who upset the English *barons, and in 1327 his son *Edward III replaced him. Later that year he was murdered.

Edward III /ˌedwəd ðə ˈθɜːd; AmE ˌedwərd, ˈθɜːrd/ (1312–77) the king of England from 1327 to 1377, the son of *Edward II. He had continuing problems with the Scots, but he had some success in his attempts to become the king of France, for example at the battles of *Crécy (1346) and Poitiers (1355). After his death his grandson became the king of England as *Richard II, because his son Edward, the *Black Prince, had died the year before. See also HUNDRED YEARS WAR.

Edward IV /ˌedwəd ðə ˈfɔːθ; AmE ˌedwərd, ˈfɔːrθ/ (1442–83) the king of England from 1461 to 1470 and from 1471 to 1483. He was the son of Richard, Duke of *York³. In 1461 his army defeated the soldiers of *Henry VI of the House of *Lancaster. Edward had the support of the powerful Earl of Warwick, known as Warwick the Kingmaker, to whom he was related, but in 1470 he lost this support and also for a short time his throne (to *Henry VI). After the defeat of Warwick and Henry in 1471, England had a period of great stability under Edward, who encouraged the development of art, music, etc. as well as the new science of printing. See also WARS OF THE ROSES.

Edward V /ˌedwəd ðə ˈfɪfθ; AmE ˌedwərd/ (1470–83) the king of England for three months in 1483, a son of *Edward IV. It is generally believed that his uncle, who took the throne by force to become King *Richard III, murdered Edward V and his younger brother. See also PRINCES IN THE TOWER.

Edward VI /ˌedwəd ðə ˈsɪksθ; *AmE* ˌedwərd/ (1537–53) the king of England from 1547 to 1553. He was the son of King *Henry VIII and his third wife Jane *Seymour, and the half-brother (= brother by a different mother) of *Mary I and *Elizabeth I. He became king at the age of ten, so other people, called *regents* governed on his behalf. One of them persuaded him to change his will, giving the throne to Lady Jane *Grey, but the plan failed and Mary became queen when Edward died. During this period, with Edward's support, England became much more strongly Protestant, so that Mary was unable to change it back to Catholicism.

Edward VII /ˌedwəd ðə ˈsevənθ; *AmE* ˌedwərd/ (1841–1910) the king of Great Britain and Ireland from 1901 to 1910, the son of Queen *Victoria and Prince *Albert. He was the *Prince of Wales for most of his life, while his mother ruled. Victoria did not let him play much part in state affairs, so he spent most of his time at social events, such as parties, horse racing, etc. When she died in 1901, he became a popular king. His reign was a period of peace and economic success before *World War I.

Edward VIII /ˌedwəd ði ˈeɪtθ; *AmE* ˌedwərd/ (1894–1972) the eldest son of King *George V. He became the king of Great Britain and Ireland when his father died in January 1936, but never had the crown officially placed on his head. He had fallen in love with Mrs *Simpson, an American who was divorced, and it was not acceptable at that time that he should marry her and remain king. So in December 1936 he abdicated (= gave up his position as king) and his brother became King *George VI, giving Edward the title of Duke of *Windsor. Edward married Mrs Simpson in June 1937, and they lived in France for many years. See also ABDICATION CRISIS.

Ed'wardian /edˈwɔːdiən; *AmE* edˈwɔːrdiən/ *n* a person who lived during the time of King *Edward VII.
▶ **Edwardian** *adj* of the time of King *Edward VII, especially in relation to the fashions and social customs of that period: *an Edwardian house* ◇ *the Edwardian era*.

ˌBlake **'Edwards**[1] /ˌbleɪk ˈedwədz; *AmE* ˈedwərdz/ (1922–) an American who directs, writes and produces films. He became well known for the series of *Pink Panther* comedy films which he wrote and directed. He also directed *Breakfast at Tiffany's* (1961) and *Victor/Victoria* (1982) in which his wife Julie *Andrews appeared. He received a special *Oscar in 2003 for his work.

ˌGareth **'Edwards**[2] /ˈedwədz; *AmE* ˈedwərdz/ (1947–) a Welsh *Rugby player who was made captain of Wales before he was 21. He played 63 matches for Wales. He helped the teams of *Cardiff, Wales and the *British Lions to win many victories.

ˌJohn **'Edwards**[3] /ˈedwədz; *AmE* ˈedwərdz/ (1953–) a US *Senator from *North Carolina who tried to become the *Democratic Party's candidate to run for President in 2003. He was not successful, but became the candidate for Vice-President with John *Kerry in 2004.

ˌJonathan **'Edwards**[4] /ˈedwədz; *AmE* ˈedwərdz/ (1703–58) a US clergyman whose powerful sermons (= religious talks) on the power of God helped to create a major religious movement, called the Great Awakening, in *New England (1734–5). Edwards became President of the College of New Jersey (now *Princeton University) in 1757.

ˌEdward the Con'fessor /ˌedwəd ðə kənˈfesə(r); *AmE* ˌedwərd/ (c. 1003–66) the king of England from 1042 to 1066, a son of *Ethelred the Unready. He was considered a very holy man, and in 1161 the Pope made

him a saint and gave him the title of 'Confessor'. However, he does not seem to have been very interested in government, and there was great confusion when he died over who had been promised the throne of England. His brother-in-law *Harold Godwin became king, but was soon removed by William of Normandy in the *Norman Conquest of 1066.

the tomb of Edward the Confessor in Westminster Abbey

the EEA /ˌiː iː iː ˈeɪ/ ⇨ EUROPEAN ECONOMIC AREA.

EEC /ˌiː iː ˈsiː/ ⇨ EUROPEAN ECONOMIC COMMUNITY.

ˈEeny ˈMeeny ˈMiney ˈMo /ˈiːni ˈmiːni ˈmaɪni ˈməʊ; *AmE* ˈmoʊ/ a children's rhyme used for choosing a person or thing. The child saying the rhyme points to each person or thing in turn on each beat of the rhyme and the person or thing pointed to on the last 'mo' is chosen. Different words are sometimes used instead of *tigger* and *hollers*. The words are:

> 66 Eeny meeny miney mo,
> Catch a tigger (= tiger) by his toe;
> If he hollers (= shouts), let him go,
> Eeny meeny miney mo. 99

EEOC /ˌiː iː iː əʊ ˈsiː; *AmE* oʊ/ ⇨ EQUAL EMPLOYMENT OPPORTUNITY COMMISSION.

ˈEeyore /ˈiːɔː(r)/ the donkey in the *Winnie-the-Pooh* books by A A *Milne. He is always complaining about things in a very sad way. His name comes from the sound a donkey makes.

Egg™ /eg/ a British company started in 1998 which provides financial services through the Internet, including credit cards, savings accounts, loans, investments and insurance. It is the largest bank that operates only on the Internet.

ˌegg-and-'spoon race *n* a race in which each runner has to carry an egg on a spoon without dropping it. Egg-and-spoon races are especially popular with children, and often run at school *sports days.

ˈeggnog (*BrE* also ˈegg-flip) *n* [C, U] a drink made with beaten eggs, milk, sugar, nutmeg (= a type of spice) and usually alcohol (often rum or *whisky). In the US it is traditionally drunk at Christmas and sometimes New Year.

ˈegg-rolling *n* [U] a traditional *Easter custom in northern England, Scotland, Northern Ireland and the *Isle of Man. Each person taking part rolls a hard-boiled egg down a slope, and if it is not damaged at the bottom they will be lucky in various ways. Egg-rolling was introduced into the US in 1877 by Dolly Madison, the wife of President James *Madison. It was originally done at Easter on *Capitol Hill in *Washington, DC, and later in the grounds of the *White House(1), where it still happens every year, except in time of war. It also takes place in many local communities.

ˌeggs ˈBenedict /ˈbenədɪkt/ *n* [U] a US dish of ham on toast or an English *muffin, with poached eggs on top, covered with a rich sauce.

the ˌEighth ˈArmy a branch of the British army, formed to fight in North Africa during *World War II. After 1942 it was led by Field Marshal *Montgomery, and took part in the battles at El Alamein and Tobruk in north Africa. It later fought in Italy. Compare DESERT RAT.

800 number /eɪt ˈhʌndrəd nʌmbə(r)/ (*also* **888 number** /ˌeɪt eɪt ˈeɪt nʌmbə(r)/) *n* (in the US) a telephone number beginning with 800 or 888, which can be called free of charge. They are provided by companies so that customers can telephone them to order their products, etc. In Britain such free numbers begin with 0800. Compare FREEFONE.

ˌAlbert ˈEinstein /ˈaɪnstaɪn/ (1879–1955) a physicist, born in Germany, who was possibly the greatest scientist of the 20th century. In 1905 he published his theory of relativity. This led to the equation giving the relationship between mass and energy, $E=mc^2$, which is the basis of atomic energy. Einstein suggested how it could be used for making weapons, but after *World War II he spoke publicly against nuclear weapons. By 1917, he had become famous all over the world. He was given the Nobel Prize for physics in 1921. When Hitler came to power, Einstein, who was Jewish, went to live in the US, becoming a US citizen in 1940. In 1933 he wrote a book called *Why War?* with Sigmund Freud. He became a professor at *Princeton University in 1934, and he spent the rest of his life looking, without success, for a theory that combined those of gravitation and electromagnetism. In 1952 he was offered the presidency (= the position of president) of the state of Israel, but did not accept it.

ˈEire /ˈeərə; *AmE* ˈerə/ the official name for Ireland between 1937 and 1949, when it became the Republic of Ireland. The name Eire is still sometimes used outside Ireland.

ˌDwight D ˈEisenhower /ˌdwaɪt diː ˈaɪznhaʊə(r)/ (Dwight David Eisenhower 1890–1969) the 34th *President of the US (1953–61) and a famous general. His popular name was Ike. He was the Supreme Commander of the Allied Forces in *World War II and directed the *Allies' plans for *D-Day. As a *Republican(1), Eisenhower was strongly against Communism but he ended the *Korean War. He is also remembered for sending US soldiers into *Little Rock, *Arkansas, to protect *African American children in white schools. He was a popular president, known for his friendly smile and mild manner.

eiˈsteddfod /aɪˈsteðvɒd; *AmE* aɪˈsteðvɑːd/ *n* any of several cultural events held every year in Wales at which there are competitions for poets (called **bards**) and musicians. The biggest of these is the Royal National Eisteddfod of Wales. Eisteddfods started in the 12th century. The word *eisteddfod* means 'chairing', from the custom of putting the winning bard in a special chair. Compare LLANGOLLEN.

the El /el/ the popular name for the elevated (= raised) railway in *Chicago. It was built in 1897 by Charles Tyson Yerkes. The city's central business district is called the *Loop because the railway makes a loop around the area.

ˌEleanor of ˈAquitaine /ˈækwɪteɪn/ (1122–1204) a queen of France from 1137 until 1152, when it was officially declared that her marriage to King Louis VII was not valid. Soon afterwards Eleanor married Henry of Anjou, who in 1154 became King *Henry II of England. She supported their sons when they fought against Henry in 1173, and was put in prison until 1189. Henry died in that year and their son Richard then became King

*Richard I. Eleanor was a remarkable woman who led her own soldiers on the second *Crusade.

ˌEleanor of Caˈstile /kæˈstiːl/ (*c.* 1245–90) the Spanish wife of King *Edward I of England. When she died, the king placed nine crosses along the route of her funeral procession, and three still survive at *Northampton, Geddington and Waltham Cross. Another was at *Charing Cross in London.

▶ **elections**

In Britain, a **general election** takes place at least every five years, when the **electorate** (= all the people in the country who can vote) vote for the 659 *Members of Parliament or **MPs** in the *House of Commons. Each MP represents a **constituency**, which is an area of the country with a roughly equal number of people (about 90 000 people) and is expected to be interested in the affairs of the constituency and to represent the interests of local people. If an MP dies or resigns, a *by-election is held in the constituency he or she represented. Before an election one person is chosen by each of the main political parties to be their **candidate**. **Independent candidates**, who do not belong to a political party, can also **stand for election**. Each candidate has to leave a **deposit** of £500 with the *returning officer, the person responsible for managing the election, which is returned to them if they win more than 5% of the votes, otherwise they **lose their deposit**. Before an election, candidates campaign for support in their constituency and local **party workers** spend their time **canvassing**, going from house to house to ask people about how they intend to vote. At the national level the parties spend a lot of money on advertising and media coverage. They cannot buy television time, but each party is allowed a number of strictly timed *party political broadcasts.

Anyone over the age of 18 has the right to vote at elections, provided they are on the **electoral register** (= list of adults in a constituency). Voting is not compulsory. The **turnout** (= number of people who vote) in recent general elections has been about 60%, although in the past 75% was more usual. On the day of the election, called **polling day**, voters go to a **polling station**, often in a local school or church hall, and are given a **ballot paper**. The ballot paper lists all the candidates for that constituency and the parties they represent. The voter goes into a **polling booth**, where nobody can see what he or she is writing, and puts a cross next to the name of one candidate only. After **the polls** close, the ballot papers are taken to a central place to be counted. **Counting** usually takes place on the same day as the election, continuing late into the night if necessary. If the number of votes for two candidates is very close, they can demand a **recount**. Only the candidate who gets the most votes in each constituency is elected. This system is called *first past the post. The winning party, which forms the next **government**, is the one that wins most **seats** in Parliament (= has the most MPs).

In the US, elections are held regularly for *President of the US, for both houses of *Congress and for state and local government offices. Candidates usually **run for office** with the support of one of the two main political parties, the *Republicans or the *Democrats, although anyone wanting to run as an **independent** can organize a **petition** and ask people to sign it. Some people also run as *write-in candidates: they ask voters to add their name to the ballot when they vote. A large amount of money is spent on election campaigning, where candidates try to achieve **name recognition** (= making their names widely known) by advertising on television, in newspapers and on posters. They take part in **debates** and hold **rallies** where they give speeches and go round **'pressing the flesh'**, shaking hands with as many voters as possible.

Only a person over 35 who was born in the US can **run for President**. Presidential elections are held every four years and early in election year, the political parties choose their candidates through a series of *primary elections held in each state. As these **races** take place it gradually becomes clear which candidates are the strongest and in the summer each party holds a **convention** to make the final choice of candidates for President and Vice-President. In November, the people go to vote and although the President is said to be directly elected, the official vote is made by an *electoral college. Each state has a certain number of **electors** in the college based on the state's population. All the electors from a state must vote for the candidate who got the most votes in the state, and the candidate with at least 270 votes out of 538 becomes President. After the election, the new President goes to Washington for the **inauguration** on 20 January, and takes the **oath of office**.

Americans over the age of 18 have the right to vote, but only about half of them take part in presidential elections and **voter turnout** for other elections is even lower. On election day, voters go to polling stations where they first have to sign their name in a book that lists all the voters in the **precinct** (= area) and then **cast a vote**. Some states use computerized voting systems and in others voters pull down a metal lever beside the name of the person they want to vote for which operates a mechanical counter. It is possible to select all the candidates from one party, which is called **voting a straight ticket**, but many voters choose candidates from both parties and **vote a split ticket**. Journalists and **pollsters** are allowed to ask people how they voted and these **exit polls** help to predict election results. However, the results of exit polls may not be announced until polling stations everywhere have closed, in case they influence the result.

the E,lectoral 'College the system for electing the US *President and Vice-President. People do not vote directly for them. In each state, they vote for 'electors', who vote for a particular candidate. All the electoral votes of a state go to one candidate. It is therefore possible for the President to be elected without getting a majority of the US people's votes. Many Americans think that the system is old-fashioned and should be changed.

the E,lectoral Re'form So,ciety a group formed in 1884 to work for a change in the way British elections are decided, and to persuade Parliament that a system of *proportional representation should be used. Through its company, Electoral Reform Services, it helps organizations with elections and ballots.

e,lectoral 'register (*also* **e,lectoral 'roll**) *n* [usually sing] (in Britain) the official list of all the people in a particular *constituency who have the right to vote in general and local elections.

the e,lectric 'chair *n* [usually sing] a chair used in certain US states for executing criminals who have been condemned to death. The person is held in the chair by straps and killed with a powerful electric current. The electric chair was first used in 1890, at Auburn Prison in New York State, and is still used in six states.

'Elegy 'Written in a 'Country 'Church Yard ⇨ GRAY'S ELEGY.

,ele'mentary school (*informal* **grade school**) *n* (in US education) the lowest school at which children receive formal teaching, from the age of six. This usually lasts for six or eight years. Elementary schools normally also have a kindergarten for children aged five.

the ,Elephant and 'Castle the name of a place where several major roads meet in London, south of the River *Thames. It was the name of an inn (= a pub) that once stood there.

the e,leven-'plus *n* an examination that used to be taken in England and Wales at the age of 11 in order to decide whether a child would go on to a *grammar school or a *secondary modern school. It was stopped almost everywhere when *comprehensive schools were introduced by most *Local Education Authorities in the late 1960s: *I failed my eleven-plus.*

,Edward 'Elgar /'elgɑ:(r)/ (1857–1934) an English composer. His *Enigma Variations* (1899) and The *Dream of Gerontius* (1900) established him as the leading figure in British music at the time. One of the tunes from his *Pomp and Circumstance* marches was turned into the song *Land of Hope and Glory* (1902), which is now always sung at the last night of the *Proms. Elgar's work encouraged people to take more interest in English music. He was made a *knight in 1904.

the ,Elgin 'marbles /,elgɪn/ a set of marble sculptures of the 5th century BC from the outside of the Parthenon in Athens which are now in the *British Museum. They were bought in 1801 by Lord Elgin from the Turkish authorities who were governing Greece at that time. Elgin sold them to the British government in 1816. The Greek government has asked Britain to return them to Greece many times.

the 'Elim ,Pente'costal 'Church /'i:lɪm/ one of the two main Pentecostal Churches in Britain. Many of its members are of West Indian origin. See also PENTECOSTALIST.

,George 'Eliot[1] /'eliət/ (1819–80) the man's name that the English author Mary Ann Evans used on her books. Her works include *Adam Bede, The *Mill on the Floss, Silas Marner* (1861), *Middlemarch* and *Daniel Deronda* (1876). Her books give a remarkable picture of Victorian social and domestic life. She was unusual for her time in living for many years with a man, George Henry Lewes, without getting married. He died in 1878 and shortly before her own death she married a man 20 years younger than her.

,T S 'Eliot[2] /'eliət/ (Thomas Stearns Eliot 1888–1965) a British poet, writer of plays, and literary critic, born in the US. Ezra *Pound encouraged him to live in England, where from 1914 he made his home. Eliot's poems have had a great influence on other poets, particularly The *Waste Land* and *Four Quartets*. One of his most important new ideas was to use the natural rhythms of speech in his poetry. His best-known plays are *Murder in the Cathedral* (1935) and *The Cocktail Party* (1951). In 1948 he was given the *Nobel Prize for literature.

Elizabeth I /ɪ,lɪzəbəθ ðə 'fɜːst; AmE 'fɜːrst/ (1533–1603) the queen of England and Ireland from 1558, after the death of her sister *Mary I. She is regarded as one of England's greatest rulers. The daughter of King *Henry VIII and Anne *Boleyn, Elizabeth was an extremely strong and clever woman who controlled the difficult political and religious situation of the time with great skill. During her reign the country's economy grew very strong, the arts were very active, and England became firmly Protestant and confident in world affairs. However, Elizabeth is often seen as a very lonely figure and is known as the 'Virgin Queen' because she never married, although she is thought to have had sexual relationships with the Earl of *Leicester and the Earl of *Essex. See also ARMADA, MARY QUEEN OF SCOTS. See p. 142.

E

> 66 I know I have the body of a weak and feeble woman, but I have the heart and stomach of a King, and of a King of England, too. 99
> Elizabeth I

Elizabeth II /ɪˌlɪzəbəθ ðə 'sekənd/ (1926–) the queen of the United Kingdom since 1952. She is the daughter of King *George VI and his wife Queen Elizabeth. She had one sister, Princess *Margaret. In 1947 she married Prince Philip of Greece, who had just been made the Duke of *Edinburgh, in *Westminster Abbey. Her father died in 1952 and Elizabeth was crowned on 2 June 1953. She is a respected and well-loved

Queen Elizabeth II

monarch with a great interest in the *Commonwealth. The Queen and Prince Philip have four children, Charles, Anne, Andrew, and Edward. ⇨ note at ROYAL FAMILY.

E,liza'bethan n a person who lived during the time of Queen *Elizabeth I. People of the time of *Elizabeth II are sometimes called the 'New Elizabethans'.
▶ **Elizabethan** adj of a style of architecture used during the time of *Elizabeth I. Its features included large windows, wooden panels on the walls, and decorative effects in plaster. Houses in the Elizabethan style are often in the shape of an E or an H. *Longleat House is a good example.

Queen E'lizabeth, the Queen 'Mother /ɪˈlɪzəbəθ ðə ˌkwiːn ˈmʌðə(r)/ ⇨ QUEEN MOTHER(2).

the Elks /elks/ a US organization for men, started in 1868 and now international. Its full name is the Benevolent and Protective Order of Elks. Members are called Elks, and they have meetings in **Elk Lodges**. In 2004 the organization had 1.1 million members.

Elle /el/ a magazine for women, published each month and aimed especially at readers who are interested in fashion and socially aware. It first appeared in France in 1985 but there are now versions published in Britain, the US and other countries.

',Duke' 'Ellington /'elɪŋtən/ (1899–1974) a US *jazz musician who played the piano and wrote music for the band he led. The band became well known at the *Cotton Club in *Harlem and played a concert at *Carnegie Hall (1943). Ellington wrote more than 2000 pieces, including Mood Indigo (1930), It Don't Mean a Thing If It Ain't Got That Swing (1932) and Sophisticated Lady (1933). He received the *Presidential Medal of Freedom in 1969.

,Bret ,Easton 'Ellis (1964–) a US writer whose novels about modern life in America include Less Than Zero (1985), The Rules of Attraction (1987) and *American Psycho (1991), which have all been made into films.

'Ellis ,Island /'elɪs/ a small island off *Manhattan(1) which was the official place of entry to the US for most immigrants between 1891 and 1943. About 20 million people entered the US there, but it was called the 'island of tears' because some were refused entry. In 1990 it became the Ellis Island Museum of Immigration.

,Ralph 'Ellison /'elɪsn/ (1914–94) a US author who is best known for his novel Invisible Man (1952), which won the *National Book Award. It tells, with sadness and

humour, the story of an African American's search for identity in a white world.

,Elmer 'Gantry /'gæntri/ a novel (1927) by Sinclair *Lewis. Elmer Gantry is a successful preacher who holds religious meetings in the *Middle West, but does many of the bad things he warns people not to do. The book turned some Americans against this type of preacher but made others angry at the author. In a 1960 film version, Burt *Lancaster played Gantry and won an *Oscar.

,Elmer's 'glue™ /ˌelməz; AmE ˌelmərz/ n [U] a US make of white glue which for many years has been a standard item in the art classes of American schools.

'Elsinore /'elsɪnɔː(r)/ ⇨ HAMLET.

,Elstree 'Studios /ˌelstriː/ a place in north London where many films have been made, including the *Indiana Jones films and *Star Wars. The studios began producing films in the 1920s.

,Ben 'Elton /'eltən/ (1962–) an English comedian and writer of humorous books, plays and television shows, including *Blackadder and the *Queen musical We Will Rock You. He has also appeared regularly in his own shows on television.

'Ely /'iːli/ a town in *Cambridgeshire, England, with a famous cathedral. In the past, the town was on an island in the *Fens called the **Isle of Ely**, from which *Hereward the Wake fought the *Normans.

the E,manci'pation Act the British law of 1829 which made it possible for Roman Catholics to hold public positions, including being *Members of Parliament, for the first time since 1678.

the E,manci'pation Procla'mation the statement made by President Abraham *Lincoln on 1 January 1863 that all slaves in the *Confederate States were 'forever free'. It had no actual power to make them free, but people talk about Lincoln 'freeing the slaves' because of this proclamation (= announcement). It helped the North in the American *Civil War as well, by allowing black people to serve in the army and navy, and by changing the war into a fight against *slavery, which caused many people in England and France to give their support to the North. The Proclamation led in 1865 to the Thirteenth Amendment to the American *Constitution, which officially ended slavery in all parts of the US.

the Em'bankment (in full the **Victoria Embankment**) a street that runs along the north bank of the River *Thames in central London.

▶ **emblems**

Emblems, **logos** and other **symbols** are widely used as a simple way of identifying countries, states, organizations, companies and sports teams.

Emblems of Great Britain include the figure of *Britannia, a woman in long robes carrying a shield with a *Union Jack pattern. Each country within the United Kingdom has a national emblem, as well as its own flag. England's official emblem is a **red rose**. Red and white roses were chosen as emblems during the *Wars of the Roses. Afterwards, the two were combined in the *Tudor rose. Other emblems include a **bulldog**, often wearing a Union Jack waistcoat, and *John Bull, an old-fashioned, fat country gentleman. Wales has two plants, the *leek and the *daffodil, and the *Welsh dragon as its emblems, and also uses the figure of a Welsh woman dressed in traditional costume. Welsh people often wear a daffodil on St *David's Day. Scotland has the **thistle** (= a prickly weed) as its official emblem, but a *tartan pattern is used on many products made in Scotland. The national symbol of Northern Ireland is the *Red Hand of Ulster, which appears on its flag. The *shamrock and *harp are also associated with Ireland and the shamrock is the emblem of the Republic of Ireland.

Members of the British *royal family and the aristocracy have **coats of arms**. The *royal arms are placed behind judges and magistrates in law courts as a symbol of authority. Below the arms is the **motto** *Dieu et mon droit*, French for 'God and my right'. Some commercial organizations whose products have royal approval are granted special permission to show the royal arms on their products.

The best-known emblem of the British government is the **portcullis** (= a barred, chained gate) that appears on official government papers. The *Great Seal of the United States, which appears on US money and government documents, shows a *bald eagle, a very large bird which is itself a symbol of the US, and the Latin motto *e pluribus unum* which refers to the fact that the US is one country made up from many individual states.

Each US state has a variety of emblems, including animals and plants which are commonly found in that state. For example, *Michigan has a state bird (the robin), a state fish (the trout), a state flower (the apple blossom), a state insect (the dragonfly) and a state stone (the Petoskey stone). These symbols may appear on the state flag and on official documents.

Most commercial organizations, charities, political parties, sports clubs, etc. have an emblem that they put on flags, notepaper, badges and vehicles, sometimes together with their initials. These emblems are often so well known that there is no need for the organization's name to be added. They may involve a picture that suggests the name, e.g. a picture of an apple for *Apple computers, or the name written in a particular way. Such commercial emblems can be very valuable and may be registered as **trademarks**, to prevent anyone else using them.

red rose　　leek　daffodil　　thistle　　shamrock

the ˌEmerald ˈIsle a name for Ireland, referring to the strong green colour of its countryside.

ˌEmeril ˈLive /ˌemərɪl/ a popular US television show about cooking which is presented by Emeril Lagasse, a chef who also owns restaurants, many of them in *New Orleans. He is known for his *Creole and *Cajun recipes. He is famous for saying 'Bam!' or 'Kick it up a notch' when adding spices to food.

ˈRalph ˈWaldo ˈEmerson /ˈrælf ˈwɔːldəʊ ˈeməsn; AmE ˈwɑːldoʊ ˈemərsn/ (1803–82) a US writer of essays and poems. He greatly influenced religion and philosophy, especially with his idea of Transcendentalism, which said that God's nature was in every person and thing. After being a Unitarian minister (= church leader) in *New England, he settled in 1834 in *Concord, *Massachusetts, where he worked closely with Henry David *Thoreau and others. Emerson's essay *Nature* (1836) explained Transcendentalism as the unity of nature.

EMI /ˌiː em ˈaɪ/ (in full **Electric and Musical Industries**) a large international music company started in 1931 when two other companies joined together. The new company included many of the most famous recording labels, such as Columbia, *HMV and Parlophone, and the recording studios at Abbey Road in London.

ˌTracey ˈEmin /ˈemɪn/ (1963–) an English artist, part of the *Britart movement, many of whose works are about

her own life. Her best-known work, which was part of the *Turner Prize exhibition in 1999, is *My Bed*, an untidy bed and various objects such as dirty clothes, cigarette packets etc.

Emiˈnem (1972–) a US *rap artist (real name Marshall Mathers III) who is well known for the strong opinions, strong language and violence in his songs and is often criticized for this, but his albums *Slim Shady* (1999) and *Marshall Mathers* (2000) were extremely successful. The film *8 Mile* (2002), in which he plays the main character, is partly based on his life story.

ˌeminent doˈmain *n* [U] (in US law) the right of the government to take private property for public use. The Fifth Amendment to the US Constitution states that 'just compensation' (= fair payment) must be given to the owner when this happens. Eminent domain is used, for example, when houses must be destroyed to build a new motorway/freeway.

ˌEminent Vicˈtorians a book (1918) by Lytton *Strachey about the lives of four famous *Victorians. It was important because, with his other books, it changed the art of biography, by giving real opinions instead of simply praise.

ˈEmma a novel (1816) by Jane *Austen. The main character, a young woman called Miss Emma Woodhouse, believes that she knows what is best for everyone around her, particularly her friend Harriet Smith. Emma realizes how foolish she has been when Harriet seems to be falling in love with the man Emma herself loves. In the end both women marry happily.

ˈEmmerdale /ˈemədeɪl; AmE ˈemərdeɪl/ a popular British *soap opera on *ITV. It is about the people who live in an imaginary *Yorkshire village called Emmerdale.

ˈEmmy /ˈemi/ *n* (*pl* **Emmys**) a US television award in the form of a small statue about the size of an *Oscar. Emmys are given each year by the Academy of Television Arts and Sciences to the best shows and actors. This began in 1949 and so many are now presented that there are two separate ceremonies. The word Emmy comes from 'immy', an informal name for 'image orthicon tube', a kind of television camera tube. Compare ACADEMY AWARD.

the ˌEmpire ˈState ˌBuilding an office building in *Manhattan(1), New York City, which for over 40 years after it was built (in 1931) was the tallest in the world. It is 1250 feet/381 metres high and has 102 floors. See also KING KONG.

the EMS /ˌiː em ˈes/ ⇨ EUROPEAN MONETARY SYSTEM.

EMU /ˌiː em ˈjuː/ *Economic and Monetary Union

the *Enˌcycloˈpaedia Briˈtannica /ɪnˌsaɪkləˈpiːdiə brɪˈtænɪkə/ the most famous encyclopedia in English, printed in many volumes and regularly revised. It was begun in 1768 by a 'society of Gentlemen in Scotland' and has been mostly American since 1928. It was owned for many years by William Benton in Chicago and sold directly to the public by a door-to-door sales force. In 1996 it was bought by Jacob Safra. Since 1994 electronic versions have been available.

The *Enˌcycloˈpedia Aˌmeriˈcana /ɪnˌsaɪkləˈpiːdiə əˌmeriˈkɑːnə/ a large US encyclopedia, regularly revised. The first edition, in 13 volumes (1827–33), was created by Francis Lieber (1798–1972), a German teacher of politics who settled in the US in 1827. The modern edition contains 45000 articles and is also published online.

Enˈdeavor¹ the name of a US space shuttle (= spacecraft that can be used again) used by *NASA. It first flew in 1992 and was used by astronauts in 1993 to repair the *Hubble Space Telescope.

The En'deavour² the first ship which Captain *Cook commanded, from 1768 to 1771.

'Harry 'Enfield /'enfi:ld/ (1961–) an English comedian who appears regularly on television. He makes fun of stupid or unpleasant people by appearing as a range of exaggerated characters, such as Tim Nice-but-Dim and Wayne Slob.

the 'England and 'Wales 'Cricket Board the organization that governs the sport of cricket in England and Wales, based at *Lord's in London. ⇨ note at CRICKET.

'England ex'pects the first words of a famous signal sent by Admiral *Nelson to the ships he commanded, before the Battle of *Trafalgar in 1805. The full signal was 'England expects that every man will do his duty.' The phrase 'England expects' is sometimes used in a humorous way today: *England expects nothing less than a win in today's match.*

'English 'breakfast *n* a large breakfast consisting of fruit juice, cereal, a cooked dish (usually bacon and eggs, sometimes with sausages, mushrooms and tomatoes), toast with butter and jam, and tea or coffee. Few British people eat so much for breakfast at home but many enjoy 'a full English breakfast' when staying in a hotel. Compare CONTINENTAL BREAKFAST.

the 'English 'Channel (*also* the Channel) the area of sea between southern England and northern France. Although it is so narrow at one point (20 miles/32 kilometres) that some people can swim across it and on a clear day it is possible to see *Calais from *Dover, it has always formed a physical and cultural barrier between Britain and the rest of Europe. The first person to swim the Channel was Captain Matthew Webb (1848–83) in 1875 and in 1926 an American, Gertrude Ederle, became the first woman to do so. See also CHANNEL TUNNEL.

the 'English 'Civil 'War a war (1642–51) between the King of England, *Charles I, and his parliament. Its causes were both political and religious. It divided the people of England and caused great suffering. Charles I's soldiers (the *Cavaliers) were defeated by those of Parliament (the *Roundheads) at the battles of *Marston Moor (1644) and *Naseby (1645). The Roundhead soldiers were very well organized, in the *New Model Army, under Thomas *Fairfax and Oliver *Cromwell. Charles I was held prisoner for more than two years, and was then executed, in January 1649. The *Commonwealth was declared and Oliver Cromwell ruled as 'Protector'. The Commonwealth did not last long after Cromwell's death, however, and in 1660 Charles's son took his place as King *Charles II at the *Restoration.

the 'English di'sease an expression that has been used by people in Europe about various different aspects of English life. In the 1960s and 1970s it meant the poor productivity of English factories and the many strikes by workers. In the 1980s it was used to refer to the bad behaviour of English football supporters, and more recently nostalgia (= preferring to look back to the past) has been described as the English disease.

'English 'Heritage another name for the Historic Buildings and Monuments Commission for England, a government organization started in 1984 to look after historically important places and buildings in England. It encourages people to visit these places to understand and enjoy their history. *Stonehenge is one example of an English Heritage site. English Heritage also has responsibility for *listed buildings in England. Compare NATIONAL TRUST, WORLD HERITAGE SITE.

the 'English 'National 'Ballet a ballet company started in 1950 by Alicia Markova and Anton *Dolin. It was first called Festival Ballet, and from 1969 to 1989 the London Festival Ballet. It performs both traditional and modern pieces at many theatres around Britain.

the 'English 'National 'Opera (*abbr* the ENO) an opera company started in London in 1931, and known until 1974 as Sadler's Wells Opera. It performs operas in English and has often taken them on tour to different parts of England and to other countries. See also COLISEUM.

'English 'Nature a British government organization established in 1991 to protect wild animals, plants and natural features in England, and to identify *sites of special scientific interest.

'English-'Only 'Movement a campaign by some US groups to make English the official language of the country. It is mainly supported by two organizations, English First and U.S. English. An English Language Amendment to the American *Constitution was introduced in *Congress in 1981, but it has never been approved. However, 27 states have passed their own official English-Only laws.

The 'English 'Patient a popular and successful film (1996), directed by Anthony Minghella. It is set mainly in *World War II, and is about a dying Hungarian man who remembers a love affair he had with an English woman. The film was based on a book of the same name (1991) by Michael Ondaatje (1943–), and won seven *Oscars. The main actors are Ralph Fiennes, Juliette Binoche and Kristin Scott Thomas.

'English 'rose *n* [usually sing] an expression that people sometimes use to describe any lovely young English woman who looks attractive in a traditional way and has a sweet nature: *She is best known for playing English rose roles.*

'English 'setter *n* a British breed of large dog with a long, soft coat, usually black and white or brown and white. It is sometimes used in hunting birds.

the 'English-Speaking 'Union (*abbr* the ESU) an independent organization started in 1918. At first its aim was to help the peoples of Britain and the US to become closer, but it was soon decided to include people of other countries where English is spoken. The English-Speaking Union organizes social events, lectures, etc., and helps young people to travel and study.

the 'English 'Stage 'Company an English theatre company started in 1956 to perform modern plays by new young writers. One of its first plays was *Look Back in Anger by John *Osborne. The company has its base at the *Royal Court Theatre in London.

The E'nigma Vari'ations the name usually given to a popular piece of music by Edward *Elgar called *Variations on an Original Theme*, written in 1899. An enigma is a mystery, and Elgar said that the music had a secret connection with another well-known tune, though no one has discovered for certain which tune it is. Some people think it may be *Auld Lang Syne*, while others argue that it is *Rule, Britannia!*. The *Variations* also contained another mystery, as each of the 13 parts was intended to represent one of Elgar's friends, but there were clues to them and they have all been identified.

ENO /ˌiː en 'əʊ; *AmE* 'oʊ/ ⇨ ENGLISH NATIONAL OPERA.

E'nola 'Gay /eˌnəʊlə 'geɪ; *AmE* eˌnoʊlə/ the name of the US plane that dropped the first atomic bomb on Hiroshima in 1945 at the end of *World War II.

'Enron /'enrɒn; *AmE* 'enrɑːn/ (*in full* Enron Corporation) a US energy trading company that was started in 1985 as a gas pipeline company based in *Houston. Under the leadership of Kenneth Lay it grew to become one of the largest companies in the US and the largest energy trading company in the world. In 2001 its collapse as a result of fraud within the company became the second largest business failure there has ever been. Dishonest accounting practices had allowed it to declare profits which did not exist.

ENSA /'ensə/ (*in full* **the Entertainments National Service Association**) an organization that provided concerts and other forms of entertainment for British soldiers serving abroad during *World War II, and for workers in Britain.

the Entente Cordi'ale /ˌɒntɒnt kɔːdi'ɑːl; *AmE* ˌɑːntɑːnt kɔːrdi'ɑːl/ the friendly understanding reached between the British and French governments in 1904, mainly about issues relating to their colonies around the world.

'enterprise zone *n* (in Britain) an area where the government encourages companies to open new offices and factories, for example by offering them money and tax advantages. Enterprise zones are usually city areas which have serious economic problems and where more jobs are badly needed.

the En'vironment Agency a British government organization that is responsible for protecting and improving the environment in England and Wales. It controls pollution and manages water resources and flood defence. There is a separate organization for Scotland **The Scottish Environment Protection Agency**.

En,vironmental 'Health Officer *n* (in Britain) a person who is trained in the ways that the environment can affect people's health. Environmental Health Officers work mainly for local authorities, examining places where food is prepared, checking the safety of places of work, teaching children about their health, helping people who are disturbed by noise made by their neighbours, etc.

the En,vironmental Pro'tection Agency (*abbr* **the EPA**) a US government organization that establishes rules and standards for protecting the environment, e.g. against pollution. It was started in 1970.

E111 /ˌiː wʌn ɪ'levn/ *n* an official form that you need if you are from one of the countries in the European Economic Area and you want to get emergency medical treatment during a visit to another one of these countries. It covers treatment received from the public health services, not private treatment.

EPA /ˌiː piː 'eɪ/ ⇨ ENVIRONMENTAL PROTECTION AGENCY.

'EPCOT™ /'epkɒt; *AmE* 'epkɑːt/ (*in full* **Experimental Prototype Community of Tomorrow**) a popular *Disney attraction in Lake Buenavista, *Florida, near *Disney World. It opened in 1982. It was originally planned that people would live there in an experimental community of the future but after Walt Disney's death the idea was dropped. Visitors can see and work the machines of the future. Epcot displays new ideas in communication, energy and transport and is the most educational of the Disney theme parks.

EPCOT

the E,piscopal 'Church (*also* **the Protestant Episcopal Church**) the US Church that is part of the *Anglican Communion. It separated from the *Church

of England during the *American Revolution. It has the reputation of having many rich and socially important people as members. A member of the church is called an **Episcopalian**.

the E,piscopal ,Church in 'Scotland the *Anglican church in Scotland, established in the 16th century. It has fewer members than the Scottish national Church, the *Church of Scotland.

,e 'pluribus 'unum /ˌeɪ 'plʊərɪbəs 'uːnəm; *AmE* 'plʊrɪbəs/ a Latin phrase, meaning 'one from many', which was chosen for the *Continental Congress when a single country was created from the *thirteen colonies. The phrase appears on the *Great Seal(2) of the United States and on many US coins.

,Epping 'Forest /ˌepɪŋ/ a large forest in *Essex, just north of London, which is a popular place for walking, riding, etc.

'Epsom /'epsəm/ a town in *Surrey, England, which is famous as a place where horse races are run. The most famous Epsom races are the *Derby and the *Oaks.

,Jacob 'Epstein /'epstaɪn/ (1880–1959) a sculptor who was born in New York and from 1905 lived mainly in England. His works include *Christ in Majesty* in *Coventry Cathedral. In 1954 Epstein was made a *knight.

the 'Equal Em'ployment Oppor'tunity Com,mission (*abbr* **the EEOC**) the US government organization that investigates unfair employment practices. It was established by the *Civil Rights Act of 1964. The Commission uses laws that forbid prejudice by employers against a person's race, sex, age, religion or country of origin. It can do this by taking employers to a court of law. Compare EQUAL OPPORTUNITIES COMMISSION.

the ,Equal Oppor'tunities Com,mission a British government organization, started in 1975, which encourages companies, colleges, etc. to give the same opportunities to men and women. It also tries to make sure that men and women receive the same pay for the same work. It has the power to enforce (= force people to obey) parts of the *Sex Discrimination Act and the *Equal Pay Act.

the ,Equal 'Pay Act a British law (1970) which says that men and women should receive the same pay for the same work or work of equal value.

the ,Equal 'Rights A,mendment /əˌmendmənt/ (*abbr* **the ERA**) a proposal for an *amendment to the US *Constitution which would give women equal rights with men. The proposal began in *Congress in 1923 and was finally passed in 1972. A total of 38 of the 50 states had to give their approval by 1982 for it to become law, but only 35 did, so it failed.

'Equity 1 the trade union to which most professional actors in Britain belong. Any actor who wants to act for pay must have an **Equity card** to show that he or she is a member.
2 (*also* **Actors' Equity Association**) a US trade union for actors who work in the theatre. Compare AFTRA, SCREEN ACTORS GUILD.

ER /ˌiː 'ɑː(r)/ a US television medical series that began in 1994. ER is the abbreviation for Emergency Room, and the programme is set in a *Chicago teaching hospital. It is the most popular series in the US and by 2004 had won 21 *Emmy awards, including one for 'Outstanding Drama Series' in 1996.

The ERA /ˌiː ɑːr 'eɪ/ ⇨ EQUAL RIGHTS AMENDMENT.

E'rector Set™ /ɪ'rektə; *AmE* ɪ'rektər/ a US make of children's toy which consists of a set of long, flat pieces of metal, nuts, bolts and screws, etc. which are used to build mechanical models. It was invented in 1913 by A C Gilbert. Compare MECCANO™.

'Erewhon /'eriwɒn; *AmE* 'eriwɑːn/ a novel (1872) by Samuel *Butler about an imaginary place called Erewhon. It is an attack on British attitudes of the time towards religion, science, the law, etc., using satire. The word 'Erewhon' is made up of the letters of the word 'nowhere'.

ˌLake 'Erie /'ɪəri; *AmE* 'ɪri/ one of the *Great Lakes on the border between the US and Canada, named after the Eriez, a *Native American people. It has an area of 9 907 square miles/25 667 square kilometres. It is linked to Lake *Huron and Lake *Ontario. Cities on Lake Erie include Buffalo, *Cleveland and Toledo. See also ERIE CANAL.

the ˌErie Ca'nal /ˌɪəri; *AmE* ˌɪri/ a US canal completed in 1825. It was built to connect Lake *Erie with the *Hudson River, so that goods from New York City could be sent by water to the states in the *Midwest. The canal was 365 miles/585 kilometres long. The New York State Barge Canal replaced it in 1918 and goes along some of the old route.

the ERM /ˌiː aːr 'em/ (*in full* **the exchange-rate mechanism**) an agreement reached between member countries of the *European Union in 1979 to stop their currencies changing too much in value in relation to each other. Britain joined the ERM in 1990, but left it in September 1992 after the pound fell below the lowest level allowed. See also BLACK WEDNESDAY.

'Ermine Street /'ɜːmɪn; *AmE* 'ɜːrmɪn/ the name given to one of the main Roman roads in Britain, from London to *York.

'Ernie /'ɜːni; *AmE* 'ɜːrni/ the computer that chooses the numbers of winning *Premium Bonds. Its name is made up of the first letters of the words 'electronic random number indicator equipment'.

'Eros /'ɪərɒs; *AmE* 'ɪrɑːs/ the popular name for the statue of a figure with wings that stands in the centre of *Piccadilly Circus in London, a place where people often arrange to meet. Eros was the Greek god of love, often represented as a boy with wings and a bow and arrow. However, the figure on the statue was not meant to represent him, but the idea of Christian charity.

Eros

ESA /ˌiː es 'eɪ/ ⇒ EUROPEAN SPACE AGENCY.

Eskimo *n* ⇒ note at INUITS.

ESPN /ˌiː es piː 'en/ a US cable television sports network that shows US and international sports events and certain other special programmes. It began as a local television channel in *Connecticut in 1979 and is now owned by *ABC.

Esq /ɪsk/ (especially in Britain) the short form of the word 'Esquire', sometimes still written after a man's name on an envelope instead of 'Mr' before it, e.g. 'Charles Lewis, Esq'. This used to be the polite way to address a letter written to a man, but it is now very old-fashioned. Most people now write 'Mr Charles Lewis' or simply 'Charles Lewis'.

E'squire /ɪ'skwaɪə(r)/ a magazine for men aged between about 20 and 40. It contains articles on topics such as sport, fashion and business. It has published work by writers such as Ernest *Hemingway, F Scott

*Fitzgerald, Tom *Wolfe and Norman *Mailer. It began in the US in 1933 and one of its best-known features was the series of drawings of attractive girls done by Alberto Vargas (1896–1983). It has been published in Britain since 1991.

'Essex¹ /'esɪks/ a county in eastern England. Its administrative centre is Chelmsford.

the ˌEarl of 'Essex² /'esɪks/ (Robert Devereux, second Earl of Essex 1566–1601) an English soldier born to an important family who was for some years a favourite of Queen *Elizabeth I and may have had a sexual relationship with her. In 1601 he tried without success to make the people of London turn against Elizabeth. He was condemned to death and had his head cut off.

'Essex girl /'esɪks/ *n* (*BrE humorous disapproving*) the name used especially in jokes, etc. to refer to a type of young English woman who is rather stupid, dresses badly, talks in a loud and unpleasant way, and is very willing to have sex: *The men at the bar started telling Essex girl jokes*.

'Esso /'esəʊ; *AmE* 'esoʊ/ the original name of the US oil company *ExxonMobil, and the name still used by the branches of the company outside the US, e.g. in Britain.

EST /ˌiː es 'tiː/ ⇒ EASTERN STANDARD TIME.

the E'stablishment *n* [sing] (*especially BrE usually disapproving*) the group of powerful people who influence or control policies, ideas, taste, etc. and usually support what has traditionally been accepted: *The members were drawn from the ranks of the Establishment.* ◇ *The defence establishment in Washington and London.*

the E'stablishment Clause the article in the *First Amendment to the American *Constitution which created the separation of Church and State in the US by forbidding the government to establish a state religion. The US Supreme Court used it in 1962 for a decision that stopped prayers in schools, and this upset many US Christians. However, 'In God We Trust' is still the *National Motto and is on US coins.

e'state tax *n* [C, U] in the US, a tax charged by the federal government on the value of the money and property of somebody who has died. Many people, especially *Republicans, refer to it as the **death tax** and want to have it stopped. Compare INHERITANCE TAX.

ˌEstée 'Lauder ⇒ LAUDER.

ˌEstuary 'English *n* [U] (*sometimes disapproving*) a type of spoken English, especially common among younger people in Britain, that combines standard English and *cockney. It began in the area around the estuary of the River *Thames (= the wide part of the river where it joins the sea).

the ESU /ˌiː es 'juː/ ⇒ ENGLISH-SPEAKING UNION.

ET /ˌiː 'tiː/ a film (1992) directed and produced by Steven *Spielberg. ET is an 'extraterrestrial' (= a visitor from space) who has been left on earth by mistake. Three children protect him until he can return to his planet. The film was then the most successful ever made and won several *Oscars.

Eˌternal 'Father, ˌStrong to 'Save the title and first line of a Christian hymn written in 1860 by William Whiting. It is especially associated with sailors, as it asks God to help 'those in peril on the sea'. It is the official hymn of the US Navy.

ˌEthelred the Un'ready /ˌeθəlred ði ʌn'redi/ (*c.* 969–1016) the king of England from 978–1016. His name 'the Unready' comes from an old English word and means that he received bad advice. During his rule the *Danes attacked England repeatedly, and after his death the Dane *Canute became king of England.

'Eton /'iːtn/ (*also formal* ˌEton **'College**) an English
*public school(1) for boys near *Windsor(1) in Berkshire,
started in 1440 by King *Henry VI. Its students are
mainly from rich families, and many of Britain's public
figures were educated there. Its former students are
known as **Old Etonians**. There is a strong sense of competition between Eton and *Harrow, another boys' public school: *Princes William and Harry were sent to Eton.*

'E-type™ /'iː taɪp/ n a make of sports car produced in
Britain by *Jaguar between 1961 and 1975. People who
drove an E-type were considered to be very modern and
successful.

an E-type Jaguar

EU /ˌiː 'juː/ ⇨ EUROPEAN UNION.

EURATOM /jʊər'ætəm; *AmE* jʊr'ætəm/ ⇨ EUROPEAN
ATOMIC ENERGY COMMUNITY.

'euro /jʊərəʊ; *AmE* 'jʊroʊ/ n (*pl* **euro** or **euros**) the unit
of currency of a number of countries within the
*European Union. It came into existence on 1 January
1999 but coins and paper money were only issued from 1
January 2002. Three of the member states, Denmark,
Sweden and the UK, did not introduce the euro. The
British government decided to wait before joining it. See
also ECONOMIC AND MONETARY UNION.

'Euro-MP /'jʊərəʊ em piː; *AmE* 'jʊroʊ/ n (*informal*) a
*Member of the European Parliament.

**the 'European A'tomic 'Energy
Com,munity** (*abbr* **EURATOM**) an organization
started in 1957 with the aim of developing the use of
nuclear energy within the *European Community and
ensuring that member countries have a supply of nuclear
fuels. Euratom has no control over nuclear materials
that are used for military purposes.

the ˌEuropean Com'mission one of the main institutions of the *European Union. It consists of 25 members (*European Commissioners) who make proposals
for new laws, deal with the administrative work of the
European Union and make sure that agreements are
kept. It is based in Brussels.

ˌEuropean Com'missioner n any of 25 members of
the *European Commission. They are appointed for five
years, and each Commissioner is in charge of a particular
department such as Transport or Agriculture.

the ˌEuropean Com'munity (*abbr* **the EC**) the former name (1967–1993) of the *European Union.

the 'European 'Court of 'Human 'Rights the
court of law of the *Council of Europe, started in 1950
and based in Strasbourg, France. It decides whether the
agreed Convention for the Protection of Human Rights
and Fundamental Freedoms has not been obeyed.
Compare EUROPEAN COURT OF JUSTICE.

the 'European 'Court of 'Justice (*also* **the Court
of Justice of the European Communities**) the
court of law of the *European Union since 1958. Its base

is in Luxembourg, with judges from each of the member
countries. It interprets EU law and decides when individual member countries have broken that law. Compare
EUROPEAN COURT OF HUMAN RIGHTS.

the ˌEuropean 'Economic ˌArea (*abbr* **the EEA**) a
free-trade area created in 1994 that includes the countries of the *European Union together with Iceland,
Norway and Liechtenstein.

the ˌEuropean Eco'nomic Com'munity (*abbr*
the EEC) a former organization, started in 1957, to
encourage trade within Europe. In Britain it was also
known as the *Common Market. It became a part of the
*European Community (now the *European Union) in
1967.

the ˌEuropean 'Monetary ˌSystem (*abbr* **the
EMS**) a system, started in 1979, to help the member
countries of the *European Union to keep a steady economic balance in Europe before the introduction of the
*ERM.

'European 'Monetary 'Union ⇨ ECONOMIC AND
MONETARY UNION.

the ˌEuropean 'Parliament the parliament of the
*European Union. Between 1958 and 1979, its members
were chosen from the parliaments of the member countries, but they are now directly elected every five years
by the people in those countries. Its base is in Strasbourg
in northern France, but its committees meet in Brussels
and its administrative department is in Luxembourg. See
also MEMBER OF THE EUROPEAN PARLIAMENT.

Euro'pean plan n [sing] (*AmE*) a system of charging
for a hotel room only, without meals. Compare
AMERICAN PLAN.

the ˌEuropean 'Space ˌAgency (*abbr* **ESA**) an
organization of European countries, including Britain,
for research into space technology, started in 1975. Its
base is in Paris. It has worked with *NASA on many projects.

the ˌEuropean 'Union (*abbr* **the EU**) an organization
of European states, based in Brussels, which aims to
encourage closer cooperation between the members,
especially in the areas of economic policy, trade and
travel between member countries. The **European
Economic Community** (**EEC**) was established under the
Treaty of Rome in 1957 and in 1967 joined two other
European organizations to become the **European
Community** (**EC**). Britain joined the EC, often referred to
in Britain at the time as the **Common Market**, in 1973. In
1992 the *Maastricht **Treaty** made changes to the Treaty
of Rome and established the **European Union** (**EU**). The
number of member states has gradually increased and in
2004 ten new countries, mainly from eastern Europe,
joined the EU bringing the total to 25, with two more
due to join in 2007. EU institutions include the
*European Commission, which puts forward proposals
and carries out decisions of the Council of Ministers and
the *European Parliament, which meets in Strasbourg,
and has 732 members, called *MEPs, representing the
member states. The single European currency became
an official currency in 1999 and in 2002, 12 European
countries, not including Britain, started to use *euro
coins and bank notes. In Britain some politicians are
pro-European and are in favour of closer links with the
EU, but there are also the **Euro-sceptics**, especially the
United Kingdom Independence Party (*UKIP), who
believe that the EU has too much control over British
affairs.

ˌEuro-'sceptic /ˌjʊərəʊ 'skeptɪk; *AmE* ˌjʊroʊ 'skeptɪk/
n a person, especially a politician, who is not enthusiastic about increasing the powers of the European
Union: *a group of Euro-sceptic Conservative backbenchers.*

'Eurostar™ /'jʊərəʊstɑː(r); AmE 'jʊroʊstɑːr/ a train that takes people through the *Channel Tunnel between Britain and France or Belgium: *the Eurostar service to Lille*. See also EUROTUNNEL.

'Eurotunnel™ /'jʊərəʊtʌnl; AmE 'jʊroʊtʌnl/ a company formed in 1986 that built and now manages the *Channel Tunnel. It also operates a shuttle train service that takes cars, trucks and their passengers between England and France. Its shares are traded on the London, Paris and Brussels stock exchanges. Compare EUROSTAR.

the **ˌEuroviˈsion ˈSong ˌContest** /ˌjʊərəʊvɪʒn; AmE ˌjʊroʊvɪʒn/ a competition, taking place every year, in which a singers or groups of singers from many European countries sing songs specially written for the occasion. Groups of judges from each country then choose the winner by a system of points. Many people criticize the quality of the songs, but the contest is watched on television by millions all over Europe. It started in 1956 with 10 countries taking part, and there are now 36. Britain has won five times.

Euˈrythmics /jʊəˈrɪðmɪks/ a British pop group formed in 1980, whose successful songs include *Sweet Dreams* (1983) and *There Must Be An Angel* (1985). The group's singer, Annie Lennox, began a career as a singer on her own in 1992.

'Euston /'juːstən/ (also **Euston Station**) a major train station in north London for trains to and from the *Midlands, northern England and Scotland. It also has a station on the *London Underground.

ˌevanˈgelical n a member of a Protestant Christian movement who believes that people come to God through their own faith and by reading the Bible, and that Christians should bring others to God. There are many different evangelical Churches in the US, where they greatly increased in the 1970s. They include the Evangelical Free Church of America and the Evangelical Covenant Church.
▶ **evangelical** adj.

eˈvangelist n a Protestant Christian who travels to different places and holds religious meetings to persuade people to become Christians or better Christians. See also TELEVANGELIST.

ˌChris ˈEvans¹ /'evnz/ (1966–) an English radio and television presenter who first became well known when he introduced the morning television programme *The Big Breakfast* from 1992, and *Don't Forget Your Toothbrush* on *Channel Four. He is very popular with young people, though his behaviour and remarks sometimes shock people and he has lost several jobs because he failed to come to work.

ˌEdith ˈEvans² /'evnz/ (1888–1976) an English actor who appeared in a wide variety of plays and films and continued acting until she was over 80. Her most famous role was as Lady *Bracknell in Oscar *Wilde's *The *Importance of Being Earnest*. She was made a *dame(2) in 1946.

ˌWalker ˈEvans³ /ˌwɔːkər 'evnz/ (1903–75) a US photographer. His best-known photographs were of poor people in the southern states during the *Great Depression. These were published in *American Photographs* (1938) and *Let Us Now Praise Famous Men* (1941).

ˌJohn ˈEvelyn /'iːvlɪn/ (1620–1706) an English writer and traveller, best known for his diary, which was first published in 1818. This tells us a lot about his busy life and many interests. He spent a lot of time at court, was one of the original members of the *Royal Society, and was active in the building of *St Paul's Cathedral after the *Great Fire of London. He was also a close friend of Samuel *Pepys.

the **ˌEvening ˈStandard** (informal **the Standard**) London's only evening newspaper, started in 1827. It has stories on both local and national issues and has a *colour supplement, called *ES Magazine*. It is owned by the publishers of the *Daily Mail.

ˌEdna ˈEverage /'evərɪdʒ/ a popular female character created and played on stage and television by the male Australian comedian Barry *Humphries. 'Dame' Edna Everage is a middle-aged housewife from Melbourne, Australia, who wears wildly unusual clothes and many different pairs of glasses. She behaves as though she is an international star and is rude to everyone in a loud and funny way.

> 66 Hello, possums. 99
> Dame Edna Everage's usual greeting

ˌEveˈready™ /ˌevəˈredi / an international company that makes electrical batteries. The main names of its products are Eveready and Energizer, and its most popular advertising character is a toy rabbit which is driven by a battery and plays a drum.

the **ˈEverglades** /'evəgleɪdz; AmE 'evərgleɪdz/ a large, low, wet region in the southern part of the US state of *Florida. Some *Seminole *Native Americans still live there. There are alligators and many varieties of birds and snakes there. Its area is about 5000 square miles/12 950 square kilometres. Dry weather has recently damaged parts of the Everglades, and there is concern about the region's future. The **Everglades National Park** was created in 1947 and made a *World Heritage Site in 1979.

the **ˈEvers ˌbrothers** /'evəz; AmE 'evərz/ two *African American brothers who led the US *civil rights movement in the state of *Mississippi. **Medgar Evers** (1925–63) was the first Mississippi Field Secretary for the *NAACP and was murdered in 1963. It took 31 years before the person who killed him was sent to prison. **Charles Evers** (1922–) took his brother's NAACP job and then in 1969 became the first African American *mayor of Fayette, *Mississippi. He published his autobiography, *Have No Fear*, in 1997.

ˌChris ˈEvert /'evət; AmE 'evərt/ (1954–) a US tennis player who won *Wimbledon three times (1974, 1976 and 1981), the *US Open(2) six times (1975–8, 1980 and 1982), and the French Open seven times (1974–5, 1979–80, 1983, 1985–6). She was married to the English tennis player John Lloyd for several years and was then known as Chris Evert Lloyd.

'Everton /'evətən; AmE 'evərtən/ one of the two major football clubs in *Liverpool, England. Its ground is called Goodison Park: *Everton won the match 3–1*.

▶ **exams**

Greater emphasis is placed on examination results in Britain than in many other countries. Most universities and employers still rely mainly on exam results for evidence of a person's academic ability.

Children in England and Wales complete **National Curriculum Tests**, (still often called by their former name, **standard assessment tasks** or **SATs**) at ages 7, 11 and 14 as part of the *National Curriculum. These tests are set nationally and results can be compared across the country. In some areas children take an *eleven-plus exam to decide where they will go for their secondary education.

In secondary schools exams are usually held at the end of each school year to assess students' progress. The most important exams are the national *GCSE exams that children take at 16. Schools are free to choose which of several **examination boards** they use to set and mark GCSE exams. Exams are marked on a seven-point scale, A to G, with an additional grade, A*, being awarded to those who reach the highest standard and U for 'unclassified'. Final grades are also based on **continuous assessment**, i.e. marks gained for essays and project work during the course, as well as on a student's performance in the exam. Many students take GCSE exams in seven or eight subjects, sometimes more.

Students who do well in their GCSEs usually go on to take *A level exams two years later. Most study four or five subjects at AS level in the first year and then three at A2 level in the second year. They must achieve reasonably high grades in order to be offered a place at university.

In Scotland students sit *Scottish Certificate of Education exams which, at **Standard Grade**, are the equivalent of GCSEs. The highest grade is 1. A year later students take the higher grade, **Highers**. After a further year some students take **Advanced Highers**.

At university students work towards a **degree**, and most courses end in a series of exams called **finals**. Many take an **honours degree** which is awarded in one of several **classes**. The highest class is a first. The second class is often split between upper second and lower second (a 2:1 and a 2:2), and below that is the third class. If a student does not meet the standard for an honours degree, he or she may be awarded a **pass degree**.

In the US there are no national exams like those in Britain. Students at school and university usually take one or more exams as part of their **grade assessment** (= a mark from A to E or F showing how well they have done) for each class. At colleges and universities these exams are often called **midterms** or **finals**, and during the year students have exams in all or most of their classes.

People who wish to study at a US university usually have to take one or more of several **standardized tests**. Students going to university for the first time may take the *SAT (**Scholastic Aptitude Test**) or the *ACT (**American College Test**). People who want to do a higher degree may take the *GRE (**Graduate Record Examination**), *LSAT (**Law School Admission Test**) or *MCAT (**Medical College Admission Test**), depending on what they want to study. Students from other countries must usually show a knowledge of English and the most common test for this purpose is the *TOEFL (**Test of English as a Foreign Language**). Standardized tests often do not test how much people know about a subject, but how strong their skills are in areas like reading and solving problems. People do not pass or fail but instead each college or university decides on the lowest score it will accept. Test scores are never the only factor to be considered in deciding whether to offer a place to a student.

Some professions require people to pass special exams before they are qualified to practise. Lawyers in the US, for example, must pass the **bar exam** in the state in which they wish to work, to show that they know the laws of that state.

Ex'calibur /eks'kælɪbə(r)/ the magic sword of King *Arthur. As a boy, he pulled it from a stone when no one else could move it. At the end of his life he told one of his men to throw it into a lake, where it was caught by the hand of the *Lady of the Lake coming out of the water. According to another version of the story Arthur also received Excalibur from the Lady of the Lake.

Ex,change and 'Mart /'mɑːt; *AmE* 'mɑːrt/ a British magazine that consists entirely of advertisements, mostly put in by individual people or small businesses. It is published every week and was started in 1868.

the **'exchange-rate ,mechanism** ⇨ ERM.

the **Ex'chequer 1** (formerly) the British government department in charge of public money. This is now the responsibility of the *Treasury. See also CHANCELLOR OF THE EXCHEQUER.
2 the account at the *Bank of England into which taxes are paid: *It contributed £1.5 billion to the Exchequer.*

the **e'xecutive branch** *n* [sing] the division of the US government under the President, who is called the Chief Executive. It carries out the decisions of *Congress, because the American *Constitution says the President must 'take care that the laws be faithfully executed'. The executive branch includes the Vice-President, the President's Cabinet, ambassadors (= senior government representatives in foreign countries), all departments (such as the Department of State and Department of Defense) and many other smaller government organizations. ⇨ note at FEDERAL GOVERNMENT.

e,xecutive 'privilege *n* [U] the right of the US President to keep official information from *Congress or special investigations, in order to protect important discussions. President *Nixon used this during *Watergate, but the *Supreme Court decided that some items, such as tapes of telephone calls, were not protected. The last president to have total executive privilege was *Eisenhower.

'Exeter /'eksɪtə(r)/ a city in south-west England. It is the administrative centre of the county of *Devon.

'Exmoor /'eksmɔː(r)/ an area of moorland (= high land that is not cultivated) in *Somerset and *Devon in England. It is a *national park 265 square miles/686 square kilometres in extent. The **Exmoor pony** is a small but strong breed of horse, originally from Exmoor and often trained for children to ride.

ex'pat /eks'pæt/ *n* (*informal, sometimes disapproving*) a person living outside their own country (a short form of *expatriate*). Many people in Britain think of typical British expats as people who live an easy relaxed life in some warm country, meeting each other often for drinks and other social events, and having little contact with local people.

Explorer I /ɪk,splɔːrə 'wʌn; *AmE* ɪk'splɔːrər/ the first US artificial satellite in space. It was sent up on 31 January 1958 from *Cape Canaveral, *Florida, by the US Army. *Explorer I*, which weighed 30 pounds/13.5 kilograms, discovered the Van Allen radiation belt. Several other *Explorers* were later sent up to study radiation and 'wind' from the sun.

the **'Export 'Credits Guaran'tee De,partment** (*abbr* ECGD) a British government department that provides insurance for British companies when they sell their goods abroad. The department pays companies for their goods, for example, if their foreign customers do not pay them.

the ***Ex'press*** one of Britain's national daily newspapers, started in 1900 by Arthur Pearson and bought in 1914 by Lord *Beaverbrook. It is a *tabloid, formerly called the *Daily Express*, and its political views are generally right-wing.

ex'pressway *n* (*AmE*) a road for faster travel through cities, with two lanes (= sections for single lines of traffic) in each direction, divided in the middle. Traffic can only enter and leave at certain special places. Other roads cross expressways on bridges or pass under them through tunnels. Compare INTERSTATE, MOTORWAY. ⇨ note at ROADS AND ROAD SIGNS.

E

'ExxonMobil™ /'eksɒn'məʊbl; *AmE* 'eksɑːn'moʊbl/ the largest oil company in the world. Exxon was formed in 1999 when the Exxon and Mobil companies were joined together. It sells its fuel and other products under a number of different brand names, including Exxon, Esso and Mobil. Worries about the company's activities in relation to the environment led to the StopE$$o campaign by environmental groups. See also EXXON VALDEZ.

,Exxon Val'dez /,eksɒn væl'diːz; *AmE* ,eksɑːn/ the ship owned by the Exxon company that caused the worst oil disaster in US history. It was badly damaged when it hit rocks off the coast of *Alaska in March 1989 and lost more than 10 million gallons/40 million litres of oil into the sea. This killed many birds and animals and ruined the shores.

,Richard 'Eyre /'eə(r); *AmE* 'er/ (1943–) an English theatre, film and television director. His work includes the films *The Ploughman's Lunch* (1983), *Iris* (2001) and successful stage productions of *Guys and Dolls* (1982) and *Richard III* (1990). He was the director of the *National Theatre from 1988 to 1997, and has published *National Service* (2003), a diary of those years, as well as *Changing Stages* (2000), a guide to twentieth century British theatre. He was made a *knight in 1997.

F f

FA /ˌef ˈeɪ/ ⇨ FOOTBALL ASSOCIATION.

the FAA /ˌef eɪ ˈeɪ/ (*in full* **the Federal Aviation Administration**) the US government organization that controls air transport. This includes air traffic, aircraft safety and noise, and standards for pilots and airports. The FAA is part of the US Department of Transportation. It was established in 1958.

the 'Fabian So,ciety /ˈfeɪbiən/ a British political organization that was formed in 1884 with the aim of gradually changing Britain into a socialist society. Many famous left-wing politicians and writers have been members, including George Bernard *Shaw. The Fabian Society was one of the groups responsible for creating the *Labour Party. It still has many important members, but its influence on the Labour Party is not as strong as it used to be.

,Face The 'Nation a US television news programme on *CBS which has been running since 1954. The programme, broadcast every Sunday, consists of interviews and discussions with politicians, experts and other people connected with current political issues. It has been presented by Bob Schieffer (1937–) since 1991.

the 'Factory Acts *n* [pl] a series of British laws concerning safety and working conditions in factories. During the *Industrial Revolution British factories were dangerous places to work in, and in most of them even young children had to work for long hours. People working for social change fought hard campaigns to force the government to make these laws. The most important Factory Acts were those passed in the first half of the 19th century. They limited the number of hours that children could work, and made it illegal to employ very young children.

the ,FA 'Cup /ˌef eɪ/ (*in full* the **Football Association Challenge Cup**) an English football competition that takes place every year. Teams from the *Premiership and the *Football League take part, as well as teams which are not professional and not part of the league. The winner of each match goes into the next round and the team that loses no longer takes part. It is England's oldest football competition, and one of the most important. It is often very exciting when teams from small towns play against famous teams from the Premiership. The winner of the FA Cup each year enters one of the major European competitions in the following season. See also CUP FINAL. ⇨ note at FOOTBALL – BRITISH STYLE.

The ,Faerie 'Queene /ˌfeəri ˈkwiːn; *AmE* ˌferi/ a long poem (1590–6) by Edmund *Spenser. It was written in praise of Queen *Elizabeth I and its imaginary characters and events represent moral values. It is Spenser's best-known poem. The style of writing had a strong influence on the development of English poetry, and the pattern of rhymes in each verse was used by many later poets.

'Fagin /ˈfeɪɡɪn/ a character in Charles *Dickens's novel, *Oliver Twist*. He is an ugly, evil old man who receives stolen goods and controls the group of young thieves that Oliver joins.

,Fahrenheit 45'1 a science fiction novel (1953) by the American writer Ray *Bradbury about a world in which books are officially forbidden. The book was written during the *McCarthy[2] era and it is about many of the issues about *freedom of speech which were raised at that time. A film of the book was made in 1966.

,Fahrenheit 9/'11 a documentary film (2004) made by Michael *Moore which looks in a critical way at the government of George W *Bush and his **War on Terrorism** policies since the *9/11 terrorist attacks in *New York and *Washington. The film made more money than any other documentary film in the US when it was shown in cinemas.

,Douglas 'Fairbanks[1] /ˈfeəbæŋks; *AmE* ˈferbæŋks/ (1883–1939) one of the most popular stars of US silent adventure films and one of the people who established *United Artists. He was married to the actor Mary *Pickford. His films included *The Mark of Zorro* (1920) and *Robin Hood* (1922). He made a few films with sound that were not great successes. After he died, Fairbanks was awarded an *Oscar for his life's work in films. His son Douglas was also a film actor.

,Douglas 'Fairbanks[2] /ˈfeəbæŋks; *AmE* ˈferbæŋks/ (1909–2000) a US actor, the son of Douglas *Fairbanks[1] and usually called Douglas Fairbanks Junior. His films include *The Prisoner of Zenda* (1937), *Gunga Din* (1939) and *Ghost Story* (1981). He was in the US Navy during the *World War II and won many medals. He settled in London in the early 1950s and produced films and television shows. Fairbanks was married to the actor Joan *Crawford.

the ,Fair 'Deal the name used by US President Harry S *Truman in 1949 for his domestic (= national) programme. *Congress passed much of it, which continued the *New Deal(1) programme of President Franklin D *Roosevelt. The Fair Deal brought improvements in employment, education, *civil rights, health services and many other areas.

,Thomas 'Fairfax /ˈfeəfæks; *AmE* ˈferfæks/ (1612–71) an English soldier, the most important general on the side of *Parliament in the *English Civil War. He was responsible for forming the *New Model Army and was its first leader. He was made a *knight in 1640 and a *baron in 1648.

'Fair Isle *n* [U] a style of knitting clothes using different colours and designs which are repeated in rows. It was originally developed on Fair Isle, one of the *Shetland Islands: *She was knitting a Fair Isle sweater.*

a Fair Isle sweater

▶ **fairs**

Some British fairs, such as St Giles Fair in *Oxford and the Goose Fair in *Nottingham, date back hundreds of years. They are travelling fairs that occupy part of a town centre for a few days each year. The people who run the fairs usually live in caravans. Originally, animals were sold at these fairs and people could change employers there. The Appleby Horse Fair in *Cumbria still has animals, but most fairs now consist only of **fairground rides** and **amusements** such as rifle ranges where people shoot to win prizes. They are especially popular with children and young people and some holiday towns, for example Blackpool, have permanent **fairgrounds**. In modern times a number of **theme parks**, such as *Alton Towers, have also been developed, in which the rides are based on particular ideas or themes.

Some fairs in the US also have long histories. **State and county fairs** held at the end of summer were important in the days when transport was limited and most Americans were farmers living far from the nearest town. They provided an opportunity to see friends, buy supplies and look at the latest farm equipment. People entered their best animals in competitions and afterwards sold them. Today there are also competitions for crops, e.g. the sweetest corn, and for home crafts like baking and sewing. The winner of the first prize gets a **blue ribbon**. In Britain, competitions like these take place at **village horticultural shows** and **agricultural shows**, such as the *Royal Show. Many Americans who are not farmers go to fairs for other kinds of entertainment. There is a **midway**, a large area with different kinds of rides and games, and an area where ice cream, pies and candy (*BrE* sweets) are sold. The US also has permanent **amusement parks** or theme parks, which have rides like those at British fairs.

Fairs and amusement parks in Britain and the US typically include rides such as **merry-go-rounds** or **carousels**, **shooting galleries**, where people can win small prizes by shooting at targets, and stalls selling traditional food such as **candy floss** (*AmE* **cotton candy**; pink spun sugar on a stick), **toffee apples** (*AmE* **candy apples**; apples coated in a boiled sugar mixture) and **hot dogs** (= sausages in bread rolls). Many have a **Ferris wheel**, also called a **big wheel**, **bumper cars** (*BrE* also **dodgems**; small cars in which people crash into each other), a **helter-skelter** (= a tall, circular slide), and a **roller coaster** or **big dipper** (= a steep track on which people ride in special cars). There is often a 'dark ride' or **ghost train** (= a ride in the dark past things that jump out or make a frightening noise).

In Britain and the US other events are sometimes called fairs. At **craft fairs** (*AmE* **arts and crafts fairs**) people sell things they have made, e.g. pottery, jewellery, candles and leather goods. But **trade fairs** are large events

a fairground ride

where business companies show their products and make new contacts.

Fairy 'Liquid™ *n* [U] a British make of liquid soap used for washing dishes, etc. It is often advertised as being 'kind to your hands'.

Nick 'Faldo /ˈfældəʊ; *AmE* ˈfældoʊ/ (1957–) an English golfer. In the early 1990s he was one of the most successful golfers in the world, winning many major competitions including the *British Open three times (1987, 1990 and 1992) and the *US Masters Tournament three times (1989, 1990 and 1996).

the 'Falkland ˌIslands /ˈfɔːlklənd/ (*also* **the 'Falklands** /ˈfɔːlkləndz/) a group of small islands in the south Atlantic Ocean. A few British people live there, mainly as sheep farmers. The islands belong to Britain, but they are claimed by Argentina, where they are called the Malvinas. See also FALKLANDS WAR.

the ˌFalklands 'War /ˌfɔːlkləndz/ a war between Britain and Argentina that took place in the *Falkland Islands in 1982. The two countries had disagreed about who the islands belonged to since the early 19th century, and when Argentinian armed forces moved there in 1982, Britain declared war. Less than two months later, British forces captured the islands again. Nearly 1000 soldiers were killed.

the ˌFalls 'Road /ˌfɔːlz/ a street in *Belfast, Northern Ireland. It is in a *Roman Catholic area of the town and is known for the many violent conflicts that have taken place there between Catholics and *Protestants during the *Troubles.

'falsely 'shouting 'fire in a 'crowded 'theater the example used in 1919 by the US Supreme Court judge Oliver Wendell *Holmes to show that in certain circumstances free speech should be limited, although he greatly supported free speech.

> 66 The most stringent protection of free speech would not protect a man in falsely shouting fire in a theater and causing a panic. 99
> Oliver Wendell Holmes

Sir John 'Falstaff /ˈfɔːlstɑːf; *AmE* ˈfɔːlstæf/ a character who appears in three of *Shakespeare's plays, *Henry IV Parts 1 and 2, and The *Merry Wives of Windsor. He is fat, greedy, dishonest, often drunk, but always humorous and entertaining. He is one of Shakespeare's most popular characters, best known as the friend of young Prince Hal in *Henry IV Part 1.

ˌJerry 'Falwell /ˈfɔːlwel/ (1933–) the US *evangelist who established the Moral Majority 1979–1989 to try to persuade politicians to follow conservative policies on issues such as *abortion and homosexuality. The group worked to elect Ronald *Reagan as President. Falwell has a church and national television programme in Lynchburg, *Virginia, and started the Liberty Baptist College (now the Liberty University) there in 1971. See also TELEVANGELIST.

the 'Family Diˌvision one of the three parts of the English *High Court of Justice. The Family Division deals with matters such as divorces, disagreements about who keeps the children when parents separate, and medical cases. Compare CHANCERY DIVISION, QUEEN'S BENCH. ⇨ note at LEGAL SYSTEM.

the ˌFamily 'Law Act a British *Act of Parliament (1996) dealing with subjects such as divorce and domestic violence (= violence between a husband and wife).

the ˌFamous 'Five™ the main characters in a series of children's books by Enid *Blyton. They are four children and a dog who have exciting adventures, often preventing criminals from doing evil things. Although written between 1942 and 1963, the books are still popular with British children.

ˌFaneuil ˈHall /ˌfænəl/ a building in *Boston, *Massachusetts, which is called the 'Cradle of Liberty'. It was built in 1742 and again in 1763 after a fire. The ground floor was used for an indoor market and there was a large room upstairs for meetings. People met there to plan the *American Revolution. It is still used as a market and meeting place today.

ˌFanny ˈHill /ˌfæni/ a novel (1749) by John Cleland (1707–89) about the sexual adventures of a young woman in 18th–century London. Its original title was *Memoirs of a Woman of Pleasure*. The book was banned in Britain when a company tried to publish it in 1963, and became very popular when it was finally published in 1970.

Fanˈtasia /fænˈteɪziə/ a film made by Walt *Disney in 1940. It uses cartoon characters, including *Mickey Mouse, to illustrate classical music. Although many people felt that this was not an appropriate way to present serious music, the film has remained popular with the public ever since and is still shown in cinemas today.

FAO /ˌef eɪ ˈəʊ; *AmE* ˈoʊ/ ⇨ FOOD AND AGRICULTURE ORGANIZATION.

ˌF A O ˈSchwarz /ˌef eɪ əʊ ˈʃwɔːts; *AmE* oʊ, ˈʃwɔːrts/ a famous toy shop/store in Manhattan, New York City. It is one of the largest in the world.

ˌMichael ˈFaraday /ˈfærədeɪ/ (1791–1867) an English scientist. His family was very poor and he had to teach himself about science, before becoming the assistant of Humphrey *Davy. His early work was in chemistry, but his most famous work was in physics. He discovered electromagnetic induction, the condition under which a magnet can produce electricity. This led to the development of the electric dynamo and motor. His discoveries in the field of electrolysis are still known as **Faraday's Laws**.

the ˌFarewell Adˈdress the speech made by President George *Washington to the US people when he retired. It was not spoken publicly by Washington but published in the *American Daily Advertiser*, a *Philadelphia newspaper, on 19 September 1796. Alexander *Hamilton helped Washington to write the speech, in which he told the nation to have 'as little political connection as possible' with other countries, and also warned about the dangers of political parties because they divide the people.

ˈFar from the ˈMadding ˈCrowd /ˈmædɪŋ/ a novel (1874) by Thomas *Hardy. It is a love story about a farm worker, Gabriel Oak, and the woman who owns the farm where he works. He wants to marry her but she has relationships with several other men who seem more exciting to her. In the end she agrees to marry Gabriel.

ˌFarley's ˈRusks™ /ˌfɑːliz; *AmE* fɑːrliz/ n [pl] a British make of hard, dry biscuits for babies. They are often dissolved in milk before eating.

ˌFannie ˈFarmer /ˌfæni ˈfɑːmə(r); *AmE* ˈfɑːrmər/ (1857–1915) a US writer of books on cooking which have been popular for more than a century. Her *Boston Cooking School Cook Book* (1896) was the first one to use standard measurements and instructions. It developed into *Fanny Farmer's Cookbook* which is still sold today. Compare BEETON.

ˌFarmer ˈGeorge a popular name for King *George III in the drawings of the political cartoonist James *Gillray. His pictures showing the king as a rude, uneducated farmer were very popular at the time, and many people referred to the king as Farmer George. George is now often thought of as a typical name for any farmer.

ˈfarmers' ˌmarket n a market where local farmers and other producers of food, flowers, etc. sell their produce directly to customers. Markets are often held in the open air on one day a week. They have become very popular in the US and in Britain because many people like to buy food from small local producers, partly because of environmental worries about transporting food from thousands of miles away and also because they like to support producers in their own area. In the US some farmers' markets are wholesale markets where, for example, fruit growers in *California sell to firms from the north-eastern states.

the ˌFarnborough ˈAir Show /ˈfɑːnbrə; *AmE* ˌfɑːrnbrə/ an international exhibition of aircraft that takes place every two years in Farnborough, southern England. Companies show new aircraft to their customers at the show, which is open to the public, and there are flying displays by groups such as the *Red Arrows.

the ˈFarne ˌIslands /ˈfɑːn; *AmE* ˈfɑːrn/ a group of small islands off the coast of north-east England. Nobody lives there, and the many birds and seals (= large sea animals) that go there are protected by law. The islands are perhaps best known because Grace *Darling lived in a lighthouse (= a tower containing a strong light to warn or guide ships) on one of them.

ˌLouis ˈFarrakhan /ˌluːɪs ˈfærəkæn/ (1934–) the African American leader since 1977 of the Nation of Islam, the *Black Muslim organization. Farrakhan has been criticized as a person who hates white people and Jews.

ˌJames T ˈFarrell /ˈfærəl/ (James Thomas Farrell 1904–79) a US writer of novels, short stories and poems. His realistic novels were about the Irish in the poor section of *Chicago. He wrote three novels between 1932 and 1935 about the character Studs *Lonigan and five between 1936 and 1953 about Danny O'Neill. His collected poems were published in 1965.

ˌMia ˈFarrow /ˌmiːə ˈfærəʊ; *AmE* ˈfæroʊ/ (1945–) a US film actor, formerly married to Frank *Sinatra and then André *Previn. Her films include *Rosemary's Baby* (1968), *The Great Gatsby* (1974) and *Hannah and Her Sisters* (1986), one of several she made with Woody *Allen, with whom she had a relationship until 1992.

The ˌFar ˈSide the general name for one or more of the cartoons drawn by the US artist Gary Larson (1950–). He is known for his unusual humour, which includes cows, dogs and other animals talking and acting like humans. Larson stopped drawing the cartoons in 1995, but the old ones still appear in newspapers and books and on cards, calendars, etc.

the ˌFar ˈWest the most western states of the US. This usually means those on the Pacific Ocean (*California, *Oregon and *Washington), but some Americans say the Far West begins with the *Rocky Mountain States.

ˌfast ˈfood n [U] hot food such as hamburgers, fried chicken, etc., that is served quickly in restaurants and often taken away to be eaten in the street: *fast food chains like McDonald's*.

the ˈFastnet Race /ˈfɑːstnet; *AmE* ˈfæstnet/ a race for sailing boats that takes place every two years. The boats start at *Cowes on the *Isle of Wight and sail to Fastnet Rock, off south-west Ireland, and back to *Plymouth in south-west England. It is one of the most famous races in the sailing world, and the final event of the *Admiral's Cup.

the ˈFast Show a popular and successful *BBC comedy show (1994–2000) with many different characters in short scenes. It was known for its many catchphrases.

,**Father 'Brown** the main character in a series of stories by G K *Chesterton. He is a *Roman Catholic priest who solves *detective mysteries.

,**Father 'Christmas** ⇨ note at SANTA CLAUS.

,**father of the 'chapel** *n* (in the past) the title of the person in charge of a branch of any of several British *trade unions. Some unions in the printing industry called their branches chapels.

,**Father of the Consti'tution** the popular US name for James *Madison, a leading member of the group who planned and wrote the American *Constitution. He also later suggested the *amendments to the Constitution which formed the *Bill of Rights.

the ,**Father of the 'House** the title given to the *Member of Parliament who has been a member of the *House of Commons for the longest time without interruption, and to the peer who has been a member of the *House of Lords for the longest time.

'**Father's Day** the third Sunday in June, when it is traditional for people to give cards and sometimes presents to their fathers. In Britain it is not regarded as being as important as *Mother's Day, and many British people ignore the tradition, which began in America in the 20th century.

,**Fathers 4 'Justice** /ˌfɑːðəz fə; *AmE* ˌfɑːðərz fər/ (*abbr* **F4J**) a British *pressure group formed in 2003 which campaigns against what its members believe is unfair treatment of divorced and separated fathers by the family courts in relation to fathers' rights to spend time with their children. Their actions have received a lot of publicity and include climbing the walls of the *Royal Courts of Justice and *Buckingham Palace dressed as *Batman and throwing purple coloured flour at the prime minister in the *House of Commons. They have also held demonstrations outside the homes of judges who work in the family courts.

,**William 'Faulkner** /ˈfɔːknə(r)/ (1897–1962) one of the most important US writers of novels and short stories in the 20th century. He won the *Nobel Prize for literature in 1949. He wrote about people in the imaginary Yoknapatawpha County in the state of *Mississippi. Most of his stories are about families that were once rich and powerful but have lost their wealth. The writing is excellent but complicated, and many people find it difficult to read. The novels include *The Sound and the Fury* (1929), *A Fable* (1954) and *The Reivers* (1962). The last two won the *Pulitzer Prize.

,**Guy 'Fawkes** /ˈfɔːks/ (1570–1606) one of the people involved in the *Gunpowder Plot to blow up the British *Houses of Parliament(2). He is the most famous of the conspirators (= people involved in the plan) because he was caught with the gunpowder (= explosive powder), tortured until he gave the names of the others, and later killed. There is a tradition in Britain of burning 'guys' representing him every year on *Guy Fawkes Night.

,**Fawlty 'Towers** /ˌfɔːlti/ a British comedy television series made in the 1970s and still regularly repeated. The programmes are set in a hotel called Fawlty Towers, where things are always going wrong. The owner, Basil Fawlty, played by John *Cleese, always makes the situation worse in his wild and amusing attempts to hide the problem: *The food was awful and the service was straight out of Fawlty Towers.*

the **FBI** /ˌef biː ˈaɪ/ (*in full* the **Federal Bureau of Investigation**) a US government police organization that investigates national crimes. It is also responsible for the safety of the country from international enemies. It publishes a '10 Most Wanted List' of the most dangerous criminals. The FBI, which is part of the US Department of Justice, was created in 1908 as the Bureau of Investigation, and took its present name in 1935. See also HOOVER[2].

the **FCC** /ˌef siː ˈsiː/ (*in full* the **Federal Communications Commission**) an independent US government organization, created in 1934, which makes decisions about communications. This includes the use of television, radio, wires and satellites. The FCC gives stations their licences and the wave ranges on which they can broadcast. It also puts pressure on stations to avoid offensive programmes.

the **FDA** /ˌef diː ˈeɪ/ (*in full* the **Food and Drug Administration**) a US government organization, started in 1928, that establishes standards for food and drugs and tests their safety. It also stops the false advertising of such products. It is part of the Department of Health and Human Services.

FDIC /ˌef diː aɪ ˈsiː/ (*in full* **Federal Deposit Insurance Corporation**) an independent US government organization that provides insurance for bank accounts. It was created in 1933, and all *Federal Reserve Banks are covered by its insurance. If a bank fails, the FDIC can give each customer up to $100 000. Since 1989 it has also controlled the Savings Association Insurance Fund after *savings and loan associations failed in the 1980s.

FDR /ˌef diː ˈɑː(r)/ ⇨ ROOSEVELT[2].

the **Fed** /fed/ ⇨ FEDERAL RESERVE SYSTEM.

the ,**Federal Avi'ation Admini,stration** ⇨ FAA.

the '**Federal 'Bureau of Investi'gation** ⇨ FBI.

the ,**Federal Communi'cations Com'mission** ⇨ FCC.

the '**Federal De'posit In'surance Corpo,ration** ⇨ FDIC.

,**Federal Ex'press** ⇨ FEDEX.

,**federal 'government** (in the US) the system of government as defined in the *Constitution which is based on the **separation of powers** among three branches: the **executive**, the **legislative** and the **judicial**. This system provides a series of *checks and balances because each branch is able to limit the power of the others. The **executive** branch consists of the *President and Vice-President, based in the *White House in Washington, DC, and government departments and agencies. The President can approve or stop laws proposed by *Congress, appoints senior officials, such as heads of government departments and federal judges, and is also Commander-in-Chief of the military forces. There are 15 government departments, the heads of which make up the *Cabinet which meets regularly to discuss current affairs and advise the President. The **legislative** branch is the *Congress which is made up of the two **houses**, the *Senate and the *House of Representatives which both meet in the *Capitol Building in Washington, DC. The main job of Congress is to make laws, but its other responsibilities include establishing federal courts, setting taxes and, if necessary, declaring war. The President and members of Congress are chosen in separate elections. The Senate has 100 members, two from each state, both of whom represent the whole state and are elected for six years. The House of Representatives has 435 members, who are elected every two years. The number of members from each state depends on the population of the state, with larger states divided into **districts**, each with one representative. The **judicial** branch of government has three levels: the *Supreme Court, 13 courts of appeal and many federal district courts. The Supreme Court has nine members, called **justices** who are chosen by the President and headed by the **Chief Justice**. The Supreme Court has the power to influence the law through a process called **judicial review**.

the **Federal 'Housing Admini,stration** (*abbr* the **FHA**) the US government organization that was started in 1934 to provide houses for poor families and minority groups. The FHA insures *mortgages and is part of the Department of Housing and Urban Development.

the **'Federal In'surance Contri'butions Act** (*abbr* **FICA**) the US law by which money is automatically taken from an employee's regular pay as a tax for *social security.

The **Federalist 'Papers** a collection of American essays published as a series in newspapers in 1787–8. Their aim was to persuade citizens in New York State to support the proposal for the American *Constitution. The papers give a complete explanation of the US system of government. They were signed 'Publius' and written mostly by Alexander *Hamilton, James *Madison and John Jay.

the **'Federalist ,Party** the first real political party in the US. It was established in 1789 by Alexander *Hamilton and included John *Adams, the only *president elected by the party. The **Federalists** held power for six years (1794–1800), creating a strong central government. They favoured friendship with Britain and opposed the *War of 1812. They lost power as a national party in 1816 after Hamilton and Adams became enemies.

'Federal Re'serve 'Bank *n* any of the 12 banks in different regions of the US that are part of the *Federal Reserve System.

the **,Federal Re'serve ,System** (*also* the **Federal Reserve**) (*abbr* the **FRS**) (*also informal* the **Fed**) the central bank system of the United States that controls the supply of money and therefore the nation's economy. It was established by the Federal Reserve Act of 1913. Its *Federal Reserve Banks deal with commercial banks in their regions. All national banks must join the system and state banks, *savings and loan associations and *credit unions may join with the Fed's approval. The system is directed by seven people appointed by the US *President, and their chairman is extremely powerful. Alan Greenspan (1926–) has had this job since 1987.

the **,Federal 'Trade Com,mission** ⇨ FTC.

,Fed'Ex /ˌfedˈeks/ (*in full* **Federal Express**) a US group of companies which are best known for their mail delivery services, delivering more than three million parcels around the world every day. The company began in 1973 and its main office is in *Memphis, *Tennessee

66 Absolutely, positively whatever it takes 99
FedEx advertising slogan

▶ **feelings**

British and American people are similar in many ways, but in **expressing feelings** they have little in common. Americans believe, at least in principle, that it is better to share what they think and feel. Relatives and friends are expected to say, 'I love you', 'I care for you', or 'I'm glad to have a friend like you.' When people are upset they cry, even in a public place. It is even considered good to show you are angry, to **let it all out** and say what you feel. **Bottling it up inside** is thought only to make matters worse.

In contrast to this is the traditional **British reserve**, a national tendency to avoid showing strong emotion of any kind. Many visitors to Britain think that because the British do not express their feelings easily they are cold and uncaring. **Keeping a stiff upper lip**, not showing or talking about your feelings, was formerly thought to be a sign of strong character, and people

who revealed their feelings were thought to be weak or bad-mannered. This attitude is far less common today and people are now encouraged to show or talk about their feelings.

Most British men, and some women, are embarrassed to be seen crying in public. People are also embarrassed when they see somebody crying, and do not know whether it is better to pretend they have not noticed or to try and comfort them. Women are more likely to respond than men and will put their arm round the person or touch their shoulder. Many people now show feelings of affection in public. Women sometimes kiss each other on the cheek as a greeting and people may greet or say goodbye to each other with a hug. Lovers hold hands in public, and sometimes embrace and kiss each other. Some British people are embarrassed about showing anger. If somebody starts to complain in public, e.g. about being kept waiting in a restaurant, people around them may pretend not to hear and avoid getting involved.

When British people are part of a crowd they are less worried about expressing their emotions. Football crowds sing and they cheer when their side scores a goal. Players hug each other when they score. Even cricket supporters, who in the past had a reputation for being much quieter, cheer as well as giving the traditional polite applause.

,Felix the 'Cat™ a US cartoon character created in the early 1920s by Otto Messmer. Felix is a black-and-white cat who has big eyes and is innocent and happy. He first appeared in silent films in 1921. Charles *Lindbergh carried a Felix doll for good luck during his famous flight over the Atlantic. There are now Felix comics and a Felix television series.

'Fellow of the ,Royal So'ciety (*abbr* **FRS**) the title of a member of the *Royal Society. People are usually made members after doing some original scientific work: *Sir John Randall FRS* ◊ *She was elected FRS in 2003.*

▶ **feminism**

The issue of **equality** for women in British society first attracted national attention in the early 20th century, when the *suffragettes won for women the right to vote. In the 1960s **feminism** (= the belief that women and men are equal in abilities and should have equal rights and opportunities) became the subject of intense debate when the *women's lib movement encouraged women to reject their traditional supporting role and to demand equal status and equal rights with men in areas such as employment and pay.

Since then, the **gender gap** between the sexes has been reduced. The *Equal Pay Act of 1970, for instance, made it illegal for women to be paid less than men for doing the same work, and in 1975 the *Sex Discrimination Act aimed to prevent either sex having an unfair advantage when applying for jobs. In the same year the *Equal Opportunities Commission was set up to help people claim their rights to equal treatment and to publish research and statistics to show where improvements in opportunities for women need to be made. Women now have much better employment opportunities than formerly, though they still tend to get less well-paid jobs than men, and very few are appointed to top jobs in industry.

Many people believe that there is still a long way to go before women are treated as equals in employment. In education, however, girl's and women's opportunities have improved rapidly and in public employment there are policies to increase the proportion of women employed, which is still very low at senior levels.

In the US the movement that is often called the 'first wave of feminism' began in the mid 1800s. Susan B

*Anthony worked for the right to vote, Margaret Sanger wanted to provide women with the means of contraception so that they could decide whether or not to have children, and Elizabeth Blackwell, who had to fight for the chance to become a doctor, wanted women to have greater opportunities to study. Many **feminists** were interested in other social issues.

The second wave of feminism began in the 1960s. Women like Betty *Friedan and Gloria Steinem became associated with the fight to get equal rights and opportunities for women under the law. An important issue was the *Equal Rights Amendment (**ERA**), which was intended to change the *Constitution. Although the ERA was not passed there was progress in other areas. It became illegal for employers, schools, clubs, etc. to **discriminate** against women. But women still find it hard to advance beyond a certain point in their careers, the so-called **glass ceiling** that prevents them from having high-level jobs. Many women also face the problem of the **second shift**, i.e. the household chores.

In the 1980s feminism became less popular in the US and there was less interest in solving the remaining problems, such as the fact that most women still earn much less than men. But American women have more opportunities than anyone thought possible 40 years ago. One of the biggest changes is in how people think. Although there is still discrimination, the principle that it should not exist is widely accepted.

Feminism has brought about many changes in the English language. Many words for job titles that included 'man' have been replaced, for example 'police officer' is used instead of 'policeman' and 'chair' or 'chairperson' for 'chairman'. 'He' is now rarely used to refer to a person when the person could be either a man or woman. Instead **he/she**, or sometimes (s)**he**, is preferred. The title **Ms** is used for women instead of 'Miss' or 'Mrs', since, like 'Mr', it does not show whether a person is married or not.

'Fenian /'fi:niən/ n a member of a revolutionary organization formed in the 1850s in the US and Ireland. Its aim was to end British rule in Ireland. The Fenians were involved in the *Easter Rising in 1916, and in forming the *IRA in 1919. Some people, especially *Protestants in Northern Ireland, use the word 'Fenian' as an offensive way of referring to a *Roman Catholic.

the Fens an area of low wet land in eastern England between *Lincoln and *Cambridge. Much of the land used to be covered by the sea, and it contains many drains and sluices (= sliding gates to control the flow of water) to prevent floods. It is a very rich agricultural area.

Edna 'Ferber /'fɜ:bə(r); AmE 'fɜ:rbər/ (1887–1968) a US writer of novels, short stories and plays. Her long novels often tell stories spread over many years. So Big (1924), about rich families in *Chicago, won the *Pulitzer Prize, Giant (1952) was about *Texas, and *Show Boat (1926), about a Southern family, became a successful *Broadway musical play. All three were made into films. Ferber also wrote plays with George Kaufmann, including Dinner at Eight (1932).

Alex 'Ferguson[1] /'fɜ:gəsn; AmE 'fɜ:rgəsn/ (1941–) a Scottish *football manager. He turned *Aberdeen into the most successful club in Scotland in the 1980s. In 1986 he moved to *Manchester United, and made it the most successful English club. He was made a knight in 1999.

Niall Ferguson[2] /,naɪəl 'fɜ:gəsn; AmE 'fɜ:rgəsn/ (1964–) a British historian who is particularly interested in modern imperialism (= when one powerful country has power over other countries). His books include

Colossus: the Rise and Fall of the American Empire (2004) and Empire: How Britain Made the Modern World (2003).

Sarah 'Ferguson[3] /'fɜ:gəsn; AmE 'fɜ:rgəsn/ (also informal **Fergie**) (1959–) the English woman who became the Duchess of York when she married Prince *Andrew in 1986. She was well known for her informal and lively behaviour, which some people did not think was suitable for a member of the *royal family. She separated from Prince Andrew in 1992, and in the 1990s started writing children's books and appearing on US television programmes.

Fer'managh /fə'mænə; AmE fər'mænə/ one of the historical *Six Counties of Northern Ireland. It is now a *local-government district.

Geraldine Fer'raro /fə'rɑːrəʊ/ (1935–) a lawyer and congresswoman who was the only woman to be a candidate for US Vice-President for a major political party. The *Democratic Party chose her to join Walter Mondale in the 1984 election, but they lost to Ronald *Reagan and George *Bush.

Kathleen 'Ferrier /,kæθli:n 'feriə(r)/ (1912–53) an English singer who performed the leading roles in many operas. She was also known for singing classical song cycles (= sets of songs) and English *folk songs.

the Festival 'Hall ⇨ ROYAL FESTIVAL HALL.

the Festival of 'Britain an event consisting of exhibitions and celebrations that took place on the *South Bank of the Thames in London in 1951. The aim of the festival was to celebrate 100 years since the *Great Exhibition, and to show Britain's economic and technical progress after *World War II. It was the first time that the South Bank was used as a centre for the arts. Similar celebrations took place in other parts of Britain.

'Festival of 'Nine 'Lessons and 'Carols a Christian service that takes place in many British churches just before *Christmas. People sing *carols and appropriate sections of the Bible are read aloud.

▶ **festivals**

Many branches of the arts hold festivals each year in towns and cities throughout Britain and the US. Some of the larger festivals last several weeks and include music, drama, art and literature. People travel a long way to hear the top international performers that such festivals attract. Smaller festivals concentrate on one art form, such as poetry. Because the US is so large, most of its festivals are local, although a few famous ones, such as the *Monterey Jazz Festival in California, attract people from around the world. Americans most like summer festivals where they can enjoy art, music and food outdoors.

Many festivals try to obtain sponsorship money from local businesses to help cover the costs. In the US events are relatively cheap so the entire family can spend the day out. In Britain, however, tickets may be expensive. This tends to restrict the number and type of people who go to the main festivals, and many **festival-goers** are middle-aged, middle-class professional people. This in turn can affect the type of music or drama that the organizers put on.

Some festivals, such as the *Edinburgh Festival, have been running for many years. A special feature of the Edinburgh Festival is the *Fringe. Fringe events are usually avant-garde and attract a wide audience. They also get a lot of attention from the critics, and this can help the careers of younger performers. In Wales, several *eisteddfods celebrate Welsh culture and include competitions for composers and artists. In the US the *Carmel Performing Arts Festival in California offers a range of music, dance, theatre, stories and poetry.

Many festivals concentrate on music. In Britain, the *Aldeburgh Festival was founded by Benjamin *Britten. The most famous British music festival, however, is the *Proms, held each summer at the *Royal Albert Hall in London. Concerts contain a mixture of old favourites and new, specially commissioned pieces. Classical music is less popular in the US, but several festivals offer a mixture of concerts and classes, e.g. the *Aspen Music Festival.

Festivals of rock and pop music are often huge informal open-air events attended by thousands of people, many of whom camp overnight in a nearby field. The biggest rock festivals in Britain include *Glastonbury, *Reading and the Download festival, Donnington. There are huge numbers of festivals every year across the US for different types of music. These include **Rock Fests**, for example the one held near Cadott, Wisconsin and the Southwest Louisiana Zydeco Music Festival which celebrates the music (and *Cajun food) of Black French and *Creole peoples. The Beale Street Music Festival in *Memphis and the W C Handy Blues and Barbecue Festival in Henderson, *Kentucky, celebrate the *blues.

Film festivals are especially popular in the US. The best-known is the *Sundance Film Festival in *Utah. The Hollywood Film Festival attracts big stars, but America's mix of people from different races and cultures has led to many smaller events such as the Boston Jewish Film Festival and the Los Angeles Asian-Pacific Film Festival. The main event in Britain is the *London Film Festival, run by the *BFI (British Film Institute). There is also the Celtic Film and Television Festival, which promotes Celtic languages and cultures and takes place in a different town each year in *Cornwall, Ireland, Scotland, Wales or Brittany.

Fewer people generally attend literature festivals, but in the US the annual Tennessee Williams/New Orleans Literary Festival has become a major event. It includes performances of Williams's plays and a walking tour of 'Williams's New Orleans'. The Dodge Poetry Festival is held every two years in New Jersey. In Britain the town of *Hay-on-Wye has a literary festival, and *Stratford-upon-Avon has a poetry festival every summer.

In the US the most common festivals are arts, or arts and crafts, festivals. For example, the Utah Arts Festival mixes art with music, theatre and cooking.

fête /feɪt/ n (BrE) (in Britain) an outdoor event that takes place in the summer. Fêtes usually consist of sports, children's games and competitions, with people selling things that they have made, such as jam and cakes. They are often used to raise money for a local charity, church or school. In small towns they are important social events. Similar events in the US are usually called *bazaars*. Church and Christmas bazaars are traditional.

at a fête

Fettes 'College /ˌfetɪz/ a *public school(1) in *Edinburgh, Scotland. It was established in 1870 as a school for boys, and began to take girls in 1980. It is one of the best-known public schools in Scotland.

▸**feudalism**

Feudalism is a social system that was introduced to England by the *Normans in the 11th century and lasted throughout much of the *medieval period (1066–1485).

Under the Normans, English society was divided into a pyramid-like structure with the king at the top, below him the **barons**, then less powerful local **lords**, and finally the **peasants**. An area of land owned by a lord was called a **manor** and this was the basic farm unit. Lords gave peasants several long strips of their land to grow crops in a system known as *strip-farming. In exchange, peasants had to promise loyalty to the lord and do military service when required. **Villeins** or **serfs** had a lower status than peasants and had to work a specified number of days on the lord's land. In 1086 a detailed survey of land was carried out in every village in order to decide its ownership and value, and the information was recorded in the *Domesday Book.

The feudal system started to break down in the 12th century, when the king and the barons began to rely on professional soldiers instead of peasant armies. Instead of doing military service peasants paid **dues** (= money) for working their land. By the end of the 14th century many peasants had bought their land and become the yeomen (= small farmers). The system of holding land with permission from the local lord finally ended in England in 1661, though not until 1914 in Scotland.

The influence of feudalism can still be seen in modern British land law and in the British class system.

Richard 'Feynman /'faɪnmən/ (1918–88) a US physicist who began the first research into quantum electrodynamics. He shared the 1965 *Nobel Prize for physics for his work in this field. His 'Feynman diagrams' help to explain the behaviour of substances and light. During *World War II, Feynman worked on the *Manhattan Project. In 1986, he was a member of the committee that investigated the explosion of the *Challenger* spacecraft.

the Ffe,stiniog 'Railway /fe,stɪnɪɒg; AmE fe,stɪnɑːg/ a small railway line in north-west Wales which was used in the 19th century to carry slate (= a type of smooth grey stone used for covering roofs) down the Vale of Ffestiniog to the coast. The scenery is very beautiful and in the late 20th century the old steam trains were brought back into use as a tourist attraction.

the FHA /ˌef eɪtʃ 'eɪ/ ⇨ FEDERAL HOUSING ADMINISTRATION.

Fianna 'Fáil /ˌfiːənə 'fɔɪl/ an Irish political party, formed in 1926 by Eamon *de Valera and others who believed that the whole of Ireland should become one republic. It is one of the two main parties in the Republic of Ireland, and has been in power for most of the 20th century. Compare FINE GAEL.

FICA /'faɪkə/ ⇨ FEDERAL INSURANCE CONTRIBUTIONS ACT.

FID DEF /ˌfɪd 'def/ (also **FD**) an abbreviation of the Latin phrase *Fidei Defensor*, which means 'Defender of the Faith', a title originally given to *Henry VIII by the Pope for defending the *Roman Catholic religion. When he created the *Church of England he kept the title, referring to the new religion. The phrase appears on most British coins.

Fiddler on the 'Roof a musical play that ran for 3 242 performances on *Broadway (1964–72). It won several *Tony Awards. The story is about the difficult life of a poor Jewish father in a Ukrainian village before the

Russian Revolution. The songs include *If I Were a Rich Man*.

The Field a British magazine, published every month since 1853, which contains articles about farming and the countryside, and in particular about horses and country sports such as shooting and fishing. Many people associate it with rich people who own land in the country.

'**field hockey** ⇨ note at HOCKEY.

Henry '**Fielding** /'fiːldɪŋ/ (1707–54) an English writer. In the 1730s he wrote political plays that made fun of the government, until the government became more strict about censoring (= removing or changing offensive parts in) plays. He then began writing novels. His most famous work, *Tom Jones, has a long and complicated story and presents a strong, clear picture of English society at the time. It had an important influence on the development of the English novel. Fielding became a *Justice of the Peace in 1748 and was responsible for forming the *Bow Street Runners.

the '**Field of ,Cloth of 'Gold** an event that took place near Calais in northern France in the summer of 1520 when the English king *Henry VIII met the French king Francis I. The meeting became famous for the beautiful tents the two kings stayed in, the grand meals they ate, and the sports that took place to mark the occasion.

W C '**Fields** /'fiːldz/ (William Claude Fields 1879–1946) a US comic actor well known for his humorous remarks. He had a large nose and the characters he played often drank a lot of alcohol and hated children and dogs. He was in the Ziegfeld Follies on *Broadway (1915–21) and often on radio. His films, some of which he wrote, include *My Little Chickadee* (1940) with Mae *West, *The Bank Dick* (1940) and *Never Give a Sucker an Even Break* (1941).

> 66 If at first you don't succeed, try, try again. Then quit. No use being a damn fool about it. 99
> W C Fields

▶ **field sports**

The main field sports are **hunting**, **shooting** and **fishing**. They are often also called **blood sports** because they involve killing animals. In Britain all three sports were traditionally associated with the upper classes, although today they all, especially fishing, attract a much wider group of people.

fox-hunting

Fox-hunting, usually called just 'hunting' in Britain, was until recently the most common form of hunting. A pack of specially trained dogs (called **foxhounds**) chase after and kill a fox while a group of people follow on horseback, traditionally wearing **pink** (= red jackets) and blowing **horns**. Fox-hunting was once a popular subject for painting and some English country *pubs display sets of prints. Fox-hunting, together with **stag-hunting** (= the hunting of male deer), **hare-coursing**, in which greyhounds chase after a **hare** (= a type of rabbit) are now illegal, as are other blood sports such as badger-baiting and cockfighting.

The ban on hunting was an important political issue in Britain. Many people believe hunting is cruel and should be stopped, but some people living in the country see the ban as an attack on their way of life. The ban finally came into effect in 2005. Organizations opposed to hunting with dogs include the *League Against Cruel Sports and the RSPCA (*Royal Society for the Prevention of Cruelty to Animals). The main organization in favour is the *Countryside Alliance.

Shooting **game birds**, such as pheasant and grouse, is a sport mainly of the upper and middle classes. Grouse shooting begins each year on 12 August, the *Glorious Twelfth, and takes place mainly in Scotland. The hunters often employ **beaters** to drive the birds towards their guns. Those who object to shooting at live birds for sport do **clay-pigeon shooting** (= shooting at clay discs fired into the air).

Fishing, often called **angling**, is a very popular sport and there are many angling clubs. Three main types angling take place: *fly-fishing, **coarse fishing** and **sea fishing**. Fly-fishing, which is expensive, is fishing for salmon, trout and other fish in fast-flowing rivers, using specially disguised hooks. Coarse fishing in rivers and lakes for fish other than salmon and trout, most of which are thrown back after being caught, is more widely popular. On the coast people may fish with a **rod and line** from a boat or from the shore.

artificial flies used for fly-fishing

The US probably has more hunting organizations than any other country. This is mainly because of two strong traditions: the *Constitution gives all Americans the right to own guns, and Americans have always hunted animals for food. The first Europeans who settled America hunted deer, bear, foxes, turkeys and ducks to survive, and many Americans still eat what they shoot. For these reasons, hunting is a sport for all classes and many people own **hunting rifles**. Americans do not use the name *field sports*. Instead they say **outdoor sports** or, because that can include camping, walking and boating, simply **hunting and fishing**. **Bird hunting** is often used instead of *shooting*, because that can also mean shooting at targets made of wood. People who enjoy these sports buy magazines like *Field & Stream* and *American Rifleman*. There are also many television programmes about hunting and fishing.

Many other Americans are against hunting, but animal rights groups have little power against organizations like the *National Rifle Association, which has more than 4 million members, and other politically active groups that support hunting and fishing. Conservation organizations like the Colorado Wildlife Coalition also use their influence to protect the rights of people to hunt and fish.

The first US hunting club, the Gloucester Fox Hunting Club, was established in 1766 in *Philadelphia. Fox-hunting now only takes place in a few eastern states where it is associated with the upper class and has little opposition. Americans generally hunt deer, elk, bear, antelope, mountain lion, raccoon and wild birds. Hunting licences may cost only $10 for one day's fishing but rise to $135 for a general hunting and fishing licence and $250 for hunting and **trapping** (= catching live animals). The **US Fish and Wildlife Service** is in charge of fishing and hunting laws. States have their own wildlife departments and sometimes both national and state permission is needed to hunt.

Fishing is the most popular outdoor sport in America. Freshwater (= river) fish caught in the US include trout, bass and salmon. Saltwater (= sea) fish include flounder, mackerel, shark, snapper and tuna.

ˌRalph ˈFiennes[1] (1962–) an English film and theatre actor. His films include *Schindler's List (1993), *The English Patient* (1996), *The End of the Affair* (1999) and *Sunshine* (2000). He comes from an artistic family of six children. His younger brother, Joseph Fiennes, is also an actor, and his sister Martha directed him in the film *Onegin* (1999).

ˌRanulph ˈFiennes[2] /ˌrænəlf ˈfaɪnz/ (full name Ranulph Twisleton-Wykeham-Fiennes 1944–) an English explorer. He is well known for his trips to the North and South Poles. In 1993 he and Michael Stroud became the first people to walk across Antarctica without help. He was made a *knight in 1993.

Fife a *council area (= administrative region) of eastern central Scotland. Its administrative centre is the town of Glenrothes.

the Fifˈteen (*also* **the '15 Rebellion**) an attempt in 1715 by the *Jacobite supporters of James *Stuart to defeat the forces of the House of *Hanover and make James king. By the time James arrived from France, the Jacobites had lost two important battles. James returned to France and the rebellion soon ended.

the ˌFifth Aˈmendment /əˈmendmənt/ one of the *amendments to the American *Constitution which is part of the *Bill of Rights. It states that people need not say anything against themselves in a court of law. However, when people 'take the Fifth' or 'plead the Fifth' in court, some people believe it is because they are guilty. The Fifth Amendment also protects individuals from *double jeopardy and requires *due process of law and fair payments in cases of *eminent domain.

ˌFifth ˈAvenue a New York street famous for its expensive shops and department stores, especially between 47th Street and 59th Street. These include Saks Fifth Avenue, Bergdorf Goodman, *Tiffany's and *F A O Schwarz. Also on Fifth Avenue are the *Empire State Building, *St Patrick's Cathedral, *Central Park, the *Metropolitan Museum of Art and the *Guggenheim Museum. The avenue divides the *East Side and *West Side of *Manhattan(1). On 17 March each year, the central line along it is painted green for the *St Patrick's Day parade.

the ˌFifth of ˈNovember ⇨ BONFIRE NIGHT.

50 Cent /ˌfɪdi ˈsent/ (Curtis Jackson 1976–) a US *rap artist from New York. He grew up in *Queens, heavily involved in drugs and crime, and his records are often about crime and violence. His records include *Guess Who's Back?* (2002) and *Get Rich or Die Tryin'* (2003).

The ˌFighting Téméˈraire /teməˈreə(r); *AmE* teməˈrer/ a famous painting (1838) by J M W *Turner. It is a picture of the *Téméraire*, an old military sailing ship, being pulled up the *Thames by a steamship, on its way to being destroyed. The subject of ships on the river and the colourful London sky are typical of Turner.

ˈFiji /ˈfiːdʒiː/ a country in the southern Pacific Ocean, consisting of over 800 islands. The capital city is Suva, and the country's economy is based mainly on agriculture, fishing and tourism. Fiji, formerly a part of the *British Empire, became independent in 1970. In 1987 the armed forces took over the country, and Fiji left the *Commonwealth, though it has since joined it again. In 2000 the Prime Minster and members of the government were imprisoned when there was a failed attempt to take over the country.

▸ **Fijian** *adj, n.*

ˈfilm cerˌtificate (*BrE*) (*AmE* **ˈmovie ˌrating**) *n* a label that is put on films and videos, stating who can watch them legally. In Britain, the *British Board of Film Classification places films and videos in one of five groups, U (Universal) for films which can be seen by anybody, PG (Parental Guidance) for films which may disturb young children, 12A for films where a child under 12 must be with an adult, 15 where no one under 15 may see the film or buy the video, and 18 which only adults may see.

In the US, a film is given one of six labels by the Code and Rating Administration of the Motion Picture Association of America. These are: G for general audiences, PG for 'parental guidance' (meaning that parents decide whether to let their children see the film), PG-13 for parental guidance for children under 13, R for 'restricted' (which means that children under 17 can only see the film with a parent or guardian (= an adult legally responsible for a child), and NC-17 ('no-one 17 and under') for films which may only be seen by adults. The ratings are the same for videos of the films.

ˈFilofax™ /ˈfaɪləʊfæks/ *n* a book (sometimes called a 'personal organizer') in which people can write down addresses, appointments and other information, with loose pages that can be taken out or added.

the Fiˌnancial ˈServices Auˌthority (*abbr* **the FSA**) an independent organization set up in 1997 to control the UK financial services industry, including banks, insurance companies, credit card companies, etc. It is paid for by the industry itself and its job is to encourage good business practices, protect customers, deal with complaints and reduce financial crime.

The Fiˌnancial ˈTimes (*abbr The FT*) Britain's most important financial newspaper. It is published every day except Sunday, and has a lot of news about companies and stocks and shares. It is read mainly by business people and people who invest money in the financial markets. It is printed on pink paper and is sometimes called the 'pink 'un'. The Saturday paper has a colour magazine.

> “ No FT, no comment ”
> Financial Times advertising slogan

Fiˈnancial ˈTimes ˈIndices *n* [pl] different lists of share prices on the *London Stock Exchange that are published every day in *The *Financial Times*. They are used to show general trends in the British financial markets. The oldest of these is the **Financial Times Ordinary Share Index**, or **FT Index**, a list of the average prices of 30 industrial shares. The best known is the *FTSE 100, also called the *Footsie, which gives the share values of the 100 largest British companies traded on the London Stock Exchange. The newspaper also publishes the **FT-Actuaries All-Share Index**, based on a wider range of share prices and giving the values of the top 250 and the top 350 shares in Britain.

ˌFine ˈGael /ˌfɪnə ˈgeɪl/ an Irish political party. It is one of the two main parties in the Republic of Ireland and is usually considered the more conservative. In 1985 the Fine Gael government signed the *Anglo-Irish

Agreement with the British government. Compare
FIANNA FÁIL.

Fingal's 'Cave /ˌfɪŋglz/ a large cave on the island of
*Staffa in the *Hebrides, Scotland. It is well known for
its large rock columns. Many poets and musicians have
visited the cave and written about it, but it is best known
as the subject of Mendelssohn's *Hebrides Overture* (1832),
which is also known as *Fingal's Cave*.

Huckleberry 'Finn /ˌhʌklberi 'fɪn/ a character created
by Mark *Twain for his novel *The Adventures of Tom
Sawyer* (1876), who he then made the main character in
The Adventures of Huckleberry Finn (1885). Huckleberry,
called Huck by his friends, is not educated but is an independent and happy boy. The second book is considered
one of the greatest American novels. It is about Huck's
trip down the *Mississippi River with a slave called Jim
who has escaped.

> 66 But I reckon I got to light out for the territory
> ahead of the rest, because Aunt Sally she's going to
> adopt me and sivilize me, and I can't stand it. I been
> there before. 99
> the end of *The Adventures of Huckleberry Finn*

Finnegans 'Wake /ˌfɪnɪgənz/ a novel (1922) by James
*Joyce. It describes in great detail one day in the lives
and thoughts of a Dublin man, his wife and friends, and
contains many references to history, mythology (=
ancient stories) and literature. It was Joyce's last novel,
and is well known for being difficult to read. It is a long
book, written in an experimental style. Joyce made up
his own grammar, and many of the words are invented
or borrowed from other languages. The book was originally published in Paris and was not published in Britain
until 1936.

Albert 'Finney[1] /'fɪni/ (1936–) an English actor. He has
been successful in the theatre and in films since the
1960s, when he became well known for playing young
*working-class northern men, such as the main roles in
Billy Liar (1959) and *Saturday Night and Sunday Morning*
(1960).

Tom 'Finney[2] /'fɪni/ (1922–) a British footballer who
played for Preston North End (1937–59) and 76 times for
England. He was considered one of the greatest attacking players of his time and was made a *knight in 1998.

the ,Fire of 'London (also the ,Great 'Fire) a very
large fire which lasted for two days in 1666 and destroyed many parts of London, including the old *St
Paul's Cathedral. Many people remember that it is said
to have started in a street called Pudding Lane and finished in another called Pie Corner.

fireside 'chats n [pl] the series of informal radio
broadcasts that President Franklin D *Roosevelt made in
1932 to explain his *New Deal(1) and the decisions of his
government. He was the first president to use radio to
talk directly to the people. He called them 'my fellow
Americans' and spoke as if he was talking with friends.

the ,First A'mendment /əˈmendmənt/ the first
*amendment to the American *Constitution and part of
the *Bill of Rights. It protects a person's freedom of religion (in the *Establishment Clause) as well as freedom
of speech, the freedom of the press and the right to
gather together in peaceful groups. It is often used by
journalists to protect their sources and by the Supreme
Court to explain why it cannot restrict offensive communications.

first-class 'cricket n [U] the type of *cricket in which
it takes three days or more to play a match. In Britain,
first-class cricket refers to the *county championship
and to international matches.

the ,First 'Folio the first collection of *Shakespeare's
plays to be published. It consists of 36 plays and was
published in 1623 by two actors who had worked with
Shakespeare. Some of the individual plays had already
been published, and were called *quartos*, but many of
them contained mistakes. The First Folio is considered
the first true and genuine written version of the plays.
Copies of it are rare and very valuable.

first-'footing n [U] the Scottish tradition of waiting for
a new person to enter a house at *New Year before the
celebrations can begin. Many people enjoy first-footing
in Scotland by going to other people's houses.
Traditionally, they take a piece of coal for the fire, some
*whisky to drink, and sometimes something to eat.

the ,First 'Lady (in the US) the wife of the *President
or the wife of a state governor. The President's family is
also referred to as the **First Family**.

,First 'Minister the leader of one of the regional governments in the United Kingdom: the *Northern Ireland
Assembly, the *Scottish Parliament or the *Welsh
Assembly. The First Minister is chosen by the Parliament
or Assembly, and is usually the leader of the party with
the largest number of members. In Scotland and
Northern Ireland, the First Minister selects an Executive,
a group of ministers within the Parliament or Assembly
that is responsible for deciding its policy and managing
the work of its departments. The Welsh Assembly, which
has less power, has no Executive, but the First Minister
selects a group of Assembly Ministers to make up a *cabinet. In Northern Ireland the First Minister works with a
Deputy First Minister from an opposition party, so that
the leaders of the main *Unionist and Nationalist parties
can work together as a team, representing both communities.

,first past the 'post a phrase describing the British
election system, in which the person with the highest
number of votes is the winner, even if they only have one
vote more than the person who comes second. In the
same way, the party with the most *MPs wins the election, even if they only have one more MP than the second party. Many people, particularly those in smaller
parties, think that this system is unfair, and demand
*proportional representation. ⇨ note at ELECTIONS.

,first 'reading n **1** (in Britain) the first time that a
*bill(1) is discussed in the *House of Commons. Bills are
formally announced at the first reading, and discussed
in more detail in the *second reading and the *third
reading.
2 (in the US) the introduction of a *bill(2) in the *House
of Representatives or the *Senate, usually by reading
out its name or number.

'first school n (*BrE*) a type of *primary school in some
parts of Britain for children between five and eight years
old. At the age of eight or nine they go on to a *middle
school.

,Colin 'Firth /'fɜːθ; *AmE* 'fɜːrθ/ (1960–) an English actor
who is most famous for playing the roles of Mr Darcy in a
*BBC film of *Pride and Prejudice* in 1995 and Mark Darcy
in two *Bridget Jones* films.

,Bobby 'Fischer /'fɪʃə(r)/ (1943–) a US chess player who
became the youngest world champion when he defeated
the Russian Boris Spassky in 1972. Fischer then stopped
playing publicly and in 1975 he lost his title when he
refused to play Anatoly Karpov. In 1992 he began again
and defeated Spassky in Belgrade, but he has rarely competed since then.

fish and 'chips n [U] a traditional British dish. It consists of fish (usually cod, plaice or haddock) which is
covered in batter (= a mixture of flour and milk) and fried
in deep fat. This is served with chips (= long thin pieces

of fried potato). People usually buy it at a **fish and chip shop** and take it away wrapped in paper: *I didn't have time to cook anything so I went to the fish and chip shop.*

a fish and chip shop

'Fishbourne /'fɪʃbɔːn; *AmE* 'fɪʃbɔːrn/ the place near *Chichester in southern England where in 1960 parts of a large Roman building were found under the ground. It was probably built by the Romans in the 1st century for the leader of a local tribe. Much of it has been destroyed, but it is still possible to see that it was a very important house. It is open to the public. ⇨ note at ROMAN BRITAIN.

,Fisherman's 'Friends™ *n* [pl] a British make of sweet that is small and hard and tastes very strong. Many people suck them when they have a cold or a cough because they help to clear the nose and throat.

,Edward Fitz'gerald¹ /fɪts'dʒerəld/ (1809–83) an English writer and translator, best known for his English translation of the *Rubáiyát of Omar Khayyám*, a popular collection of 12th-century Persian poetry.

,Ella Fitz'gerald² /fɪts'dʒerəld/ (1918–96) a US singer of *jazz and popular songs. She had a clear, strong voice and was called 'the first lady of song'. She performed regularly with 'Duke' *Ellington, 'Count' *Basie and Louis *Armstrong, and later recorded many songs by George *Gershwin and Cole *Porter.

,F Scott Fitz'gerald³ /skɒt fɪts'dʒerəld; *AmE* skɑt/ (Francis Scott Key Fitzgerald 1896–1940) a US writer of novels and short stories about the *Jazz Age, a name he invented. The life of fun and immoral behaviour led by many rich people in those years are described in his best-known novel, *The *Great Gatsby*. Fitzgerald and his wife Zelda (1901–48) lived a wild life themselves. She developed a mental illness, and he drank too much alcohol, experiences he used in *Tender is the Night* (1934). In 1936 Fitzgerald moved to Hollywood to write films. His last novel, *The Last Tycoon*, was not finished when he died.

> 66 Let me tell you about the very rich. They are different from you and me.
>
> Yes, they have more money. 99
>
> remark made by Scott Fitzgerald to Hemingway and Hemingway's reply

,Mrs Fitz'herbert /fɪts'hɜːbət; *AmE* fɪts'hɜːbərt/ (Maria Anne Fitzherbert 1756–1837) the first wife of the British king *George IV. They were married secretly in 1785, before George became king, but the marriage was illegal because it did not have the king's official permission. Mrs Fitzherbert was a *Roman Catholic, and under British law a prince who married a Catholic could not become king.

Five a British commercial terrestrial television station that started broadcasting in 1997 as Channel Five and can be seen in most of Britain. It broadcasts mainly popular programmes such as games, comedies and films.

,five-and-'ten (*also* ,five-and-'ten-cent 'store, ,five-and-'dime, 'dime store) *n* (*AmE old use*) a type of large shop/store in the US selling cheap goods. The first of them were opened in 1879 by F W *Woolworth and for many years they sold everything at a price of either five cents or ten cents. The last 400 five-and-tens in the US closed in 1997.

the 'Five 'Civilized 'Tribes the name used to refer to five groups of Native American people in the *South: the *Cherokee, *Choctaw, Chickasaw, *Creek and *Seminole. The tribes were forced to leave their own lands and settle in the *Indian Territory, even though it was thought that they could be trusted because they had developed their own versions of the American *Constitution and US laws.

the ,Five 'Nations ⇨ IROQUOIS LEAGUE.

fives *n* [U] a British game in which two or four players hit a small hard ball with their hands against any of three walls. The aim is to make the ball bounce in such a way that the next player makes a mistake. It is a game typically played at *public schools such as *Eton and *Rugby, which each have their own particular versions of the game.

the ,Five 'Towns *n* [pl] five former towns in the *Potteries region of the English *Midlands. The towns were Tunstall, Burslem, Hanley, Stoke-upon-Trent and Longton. They were close to each other and were important centres of the pottery industry from the 17th century until, in 1910, they joined together as one town, *Stoke-on-Trent. The Five Towns became well known as the setting for the novels of Arnold *Bennett.

'Flag Day (in the US) 14 June, when people fly the US flag. It is the anniversary of the day in 1777 when the *Continental Congress passed a law making the *Stars and Stripes the official American flag.

,Bud 'Flanagan /'flænəgən/ (1896–1968) a British *music-hall(1) singer and comedian who was a member of the *Crazy Gang. He and his partner Chesney Allen became famous during *World War II as Flanagan and Allen and made several successful films and records. Their best-known song is *Underneath the Arches*.

,Flanders and 'Swann /,flɑːndəz, 'swɒn; *AmE* ,flɑːndərz, 'swɑːn/ a pair of English entertainers, **Michael Flanders** (1922–75) and **Donald Swann** (1923–94), who wrote and performed many humorous songs together. Flanders wrote the words and sang, and Swann wrote the music and played the piano.

,Flanders 'fields /,flɑːndəz; *AmE* ,flɑːndərz/ *n* [pl] a phrase used to refer to the areas of north-east France and Belgium where many soldiers died and were buried in *World War I. The phrase comes from a poem, *In Flanders Fields* (1915) by John McCrae, which contains the lines:

> 66 In Flanders fields the poppies blow
> Between the crosses, row on row,
> That mark our place. 99

'flapper *n* a fashionable and lively young woman of the 1920s. The typical flapper wore short skirts, had short hair, drank alcohol, and enjoyed smoking and dancing. At the time many people thought flappers were immoral, but they are now often regarded as the first modern, independent women.

Harry 'Flashman /'flæʃmən/ a character in *Tom Brown's Schooldays*. He is a cruel older boy who is unkind to Tom and the other young boys. In the 20th century George MacDonald Fraser wrote a series of novels about Flashman's adventures as an adult. See also BULLYING.

the ˌFlat ˈEarth Soˌciety an organization whose members claim that the earth is flat, and refuse to believe in modern science. The society was established in America and has branches in Britain. Its members are called **flat-earthers**, and the expression is sometimes used to describe people who refuse to believe something that is clearly true.

ˌFlatford ˈMill /ˌflætfəd; AmE ˌflætfərd/ a painting (1817) by John *Constable of a water mill (= a building by a river that uses the water to turn a wheel and operate machinery) on the river Stour in south-east England. It is one of Constable's most famous paintings, and in 1928 the actual mill was given to the nation to be preserved in memory of the artist.

the ˈFlatiron ˌBuilding /ˈflætaɪən; AmE ˈflætaɪərn/ a tall, thin office building that was New York's first *skyscraper. It was built in 1902 on *Fifth Avenue. The building has one thick end and one narrow, sharp end. It has 22 floors and is 285 feet/87 metres tall. When it was completed, people said it was so tall it might fall over. It still stands today. A *flatiron* is an old-fashioned iron for pressing clothes.

the ˌFleet ˈAir Arm the branch of the British *Royal Navy responsible for aircraft. Most of its planes are based on aircraft carriers, but some are also based on land. Compare RAF.

ˈFleet Street a street in central London, between the *City and the *West End, where most of Britain's major newspapers used to have their main offices. In the 1980s most of the newspapers moved to new buildings in other parts of London to use new printing technology, but 'Fleet Street' is still used to mean 'the British press': *Their election defeat took Fleet Street by surprise.*

ˌFleetwood ˈMac /ˌfliːtwʊd ˈmæk/ a British pop group, formed in 1967, which plays a mixture of *rock and *blues. The group's best-known songs include *Don't Stop* (1977) and *Little Lies* (1987). It was chosen for the Rock and Roll *Hall of Fame in 1998. Its recent album *Say You Will* appeared in 2003.

ˌAlexander ˈFleming¹ /ˈflemɪŋ/ (1881–1955) a Scottish scientist who became well known for discovering penicillin, the first antibiotic that successfully killed bacteria and cured infections. He was made a *knight in 1944, and in 1945 shared the *Nobel Prize for medicine with two colleagues who helped him to develop the use of penicillin.

ˌIan ˈFleming² /ˈflemɪŋ/ (1908–64) an English writer, best known for creating the world's most famous secret agent, James *Bond. Fleming had some experience of the work of secret agents when he worked for the intelligence department of the *Royal Navy during *World War II. He used that experience, and his love of technology and foreign travel, to write his series of James Bond novels, which were later made into successful films.

ˌJohn ˈFletcher /ˈfletʃə(r)/ (1579–1625) an English writer of plays, many of which he wrote with Francis *Beaumont. He also worked with Ben *Jonson and possibly *Shakespeare.

ˌflexible ˈfriend n (BrE informal ironic) a humorous way of referring to a *credit card after the phrase was used in British television advertisements for the former Access card in the 1980s.

ˌRussell ˈFlint /ˈflɪnt/ (1880–1969) a Scottish painter, well known for his watercolours, especially landscapes (= pictures of the countryside) and pictures of women with few clothes on. Many British people have copies of these in their homes. Flint was made a *knight in 1947.

The ˈFlintstones /ˈflɪntstəʊnz; AmE ˈflɪntstoʊnz/ a US comedy cartoon television series (1960–66) about a prehistoric family. The humour comes from the way they behave like modern Americans, using pieces of stone and wood as if they were cars, telephones, etc. There was a new series in the 1970s, and a film version of *The Flintstones*, with real actors, appeared in 1994.

ˈFlodden /ˈflɒdn; AmE ˈflɑːdn/ a battle which took place in 1513 between the armies of England and Scotland on a hill in *Northumberland, near the border between the two countries. The English won the battle, and more than 10 000 Scots were killed, including their king, James IV.

ˈFlo-Jo /ˈfləʊ dʒəʊ; AmE ˈfloʊ dʒoʊ/ the popular name for the US runner Florence Griffith *Joyner.

ˈfloor ˌleader n a leader of the *Democratic Party or the *Republican Party in the US *Congress. There are four floor leaders because each of the two main parties chooses its own floor leader in both the *Senate and *House of Representatives. The floor leader of the party that has a majority is called the *majority leader and that of the other party the *minority leader. Their job is to speak for their party and work to pass their bills.

ˈFlora™ /ˈflɔːrə/ n [U] a British make of margarine (= a substance like butter, but usually made from vegetable oil). Flora is advertised as a healthy type of margarine.

ˈFlorida /ˈflɒrɪdə; AmE ˈflɔːrɪdə/ the most southern state in the US. It is internationally famous for its hot weather and white beaches. Florida's popular name is 'the Sunshine State'. It forms a long, flat area of land in the south-east between the Atlantic Ocean and the *Gulf of Mexico. The largest city is *Jacksonville and the capital city is Tallahassee. Florida was discovered in 1513 by Juan *Ponce de León of Spain. Agriculture, manufacturing and tourism are all important to the state's economy. Its attractions include *Disney World, *Cape Canaveral, *Miami Beach, the *Everglades and the *Florida Keys.

the ˌFlorida ˈKeys /ˌflɒrɪdə ; AmE ˌflɔːrɪdə/ a line of about 20 islands to the west of the southern end of *Florida. The islands are connected by the world's longest road over water, the Overseas Highway, that runs 160 miles/256 kilometres. The best-known Keys are *Key West and Key Largo. The islands are popular with tourists and people who like fishing.

the Overseas Highway, Florida Keys

ˈflower ˌchildren (also ˈflower ˌpeople) n [pl] young people in many countries in the 1960s who believed in peace and love, and were against war. They carried flowers or wore them in their hair as a symbol of their beliefs. They were part of the *hippie movement, and took part in many peaceful protests against wars, especially the *Vietnam War. See also FLOWER POWER.

'flower girl n **1** (*AmE*) a very young girl who walks behind the bride at a wedding and holds flowers or throws flower petals. She is usually a member of the family of one of the people who are being married. **2** (*BrE*) (especially in the past) a woman or girl who sells flowers in the street: *Shaw's play about Eliza Doolittle, the cockney flower girl.*

Flower of 'Scotland /'skɒtlənd; *AmE* 'skɑːtlənd/ a song that was performed in the 1960s by the Corries, a Scottish pop group. In the 1980s it became the traditional song sung by Scottish supporters at international *football and *Rugby games.

'flower ˌpower n [U] the beliefs of the *flower children in the 1960s that peace and love were more important than military and commercial activities, and that if enough people shared their ideas, wars would stop and the world would be a better place.

'ˌPretty Boy' 'Floyd /ˌprɪti bɔɪ 'flɔɪd/ (Charles Arthur Floyd 1901–34) a US criminal who robbed banks in the Midwest during the *Great Depression and was for a time *Public Enemy Number One. Some Americans admired him because he gave money to poor people, but he also murdered about ten men, including two *FBI officers. He was finally killed by the FBI in a field in Ohio.

'fly-ˌfishing n [U] the sport of fishing in rivers or lakes using artificial flies of various types at the end of the line instead of live bait such as worms. The flies float on, or move just under, the surface of the water instead of sinking like worms, and are attractive to salmon and trout. Fly-fishing requires a lot of skill, and it is considered a higher-class sport than using live bait.

fly-fishing

the ˌFlying 'Scotsman /'skɒtsmən; *AmE* 'skɑːtsmən/ a British steam railway engine, built in 1923, which was the fastest of its kind for many years. It was used mainly on trains travelling between London and Edinburgh, until 1963. It is now owned by the National Railway Museum and is still driven on special journeys for people who are interested in old trains.

the Flying Scotsman

the 'Flying Squad a department of the British *Metropolitan Police that deals with serious crimes, especially armed robbery. The name indicates that the department's officers are ready to move quickly to the scene of a crime. It used to be known informally as 'the Sweeney': *The Met's Flying Squad were one step ahead of the gang.*

ˌErrol 'Flynn /ˌerəl 'flɪn/ (1909–59) an Australian actor who became famous as the strong and handsome hero of many *Hollywood adventure films. He is particularly remembered for roles that required him to run, jump, fight, etc., such as *The Adventures of Robin Hood* (1938). Flynn was also famous for his many affairs with women.

ˌMichael 'Foale /'fəʊl; *AmE* 'foʊl/ (1957–) a US astronaut, born in Britain. In 1997 he travelled on the space shuttle (= spacecraft that can be used again) *Atlantis* to join the Russian space station Mir, where he spent 145 days before returning to earth. He has spent over 374 days in space, the US record.

ˌFoggy 'Bottom an area of low land in *Washington, DC, by the *Potomac River, on which the US *State Department buildings are situated. The name is also used to refer to the *State Department itself, and journalists often joke that this is a good name for the Department, because the information it gives them is 'foggy', i.e. not clear.

the FOIA /ˌef əʊ aɪ 'eɪ; *AmE* oʊ/ ⇨ FREEDOM OF INFORMATION ACT.

▶ folk dancing

Folk dances are traditional dances in which everyone can take part. They are danced to folk tunes and have sequences of **steps** that are repeated several times. Dances are performed by pairs of dancers often arranged in **sets** (= groups of six or eight people). Dancers move up and down the set and change partners. The dancing is often very fast. A **caller** usually **calls** the steps during the dance. In England folk dances are now danced mainly by people who belong to a **country dancing** club, or at **barn dances** held in a village hall.

Many English villages have *morris dancing teams. Morris dancing is usually performed on *village greens or outside country *pubs on *May Day and throughout the summer. The dancers dress in white and wear sets of small bells at the knee. Dances consist of a series of jumps and hops. As they dance the dancers often wave handkerchiefs in the air. In some dances they carry a stick which they strike against that of their partner. Themes of the dances include death and rebirth in nature. In some dances mythological characters like the *Green Man appear. Sometimes dancers paint their faces black, perhaps reflecting the possible origin of Morris dancing in Moorish dance. The music is provided by a fiddle (= violin) or accordion.

Another variety of English folk dance, also performed on May Day, is *maypole dancing. Children often take part. Each dancer holds the end of a long ribbon, which is attached to the top of a brightly painted maypole. The ribbons are woven round the maypole as the dancers dance round each other. Some towns have their own folk dance: for example, the **Furry Dance**, or **Floral Dance**, is danced through the streets of Helston in Cornwall.

Scottish dances are usually danced to the music of the *bagpipes or a fiddle at a **ceilidh** (= an evening of dancing, music and, formerly, storytelling). Traditionally they are performed in Scottish national dress, with men wearing kilts and women in plain dresses. Some people go to **Scottish dancing** classes as a hobby. The best-known Scottish dance is the *Highland fling, which is usually performed by one man alone. The **sword dance** is performed by one or two dancers over two crossed swords. Popular dances for groups of people are the **Gay Gordons** and the **Eightsome Reel**.

Ireland has a similar ceilidh tradition. In **Irish dancing** the dancers do not move the upper part of their body. In recent years there has been greater interest in Irish folk dancing resulting from the success of *Riverdance* stage show in 1994. In Irish **clog dancing**, the dancers wear clogs (= heavy wooden shoes) with which they strike the floor.

*Line dancing, which comes from the US, is also popular in Britain. In the US itself there are folk dances from many different countries, brought by people when they settled there. But the best-known kind of folk dancing is **square dancing**, which has its origins in various dances from Britain. Square dancing was an important part of social life in the days when people were moving west. On Saturday evenings people would gather in a barn for a dance. As in English country dancing there was a caller, and the dancers danced to the music of a fiddle. Most square dances start and finish with couples standing in a square, but some, like the **Virginia Reel**, involve people standing in two lines. American children still learn square dancing, but very few adults now do it.

'folk museum *n* a museum that displays interesting or historical objects that were part of the local people's everyday lives, such as clothes and tools. Many British towns and cities have folk museums. Similar museums exist in the US but they are not often called folk museums.

▶ **folk music and songs**

Traditional British folk music has many different forms, including songs and **ballads**. Many **folk songs** relate to the lives of ordinary people in past centuries; others tell of famous love stories or celebrate nature. The verses may be sung by one voice alone, with the choruses sung by everyone present. Some folk songs are learned at school and are familiar to everyone, for example *Greensleeves, The *Ash Grove, *Green Grow the Rushes O and *Auld Lang Syne, which is always sung at *New Year. In Wales and Ireland a *harp may sometimes be used to accompany the singing, but most songs are now accompanied by a guitar or piano.

A lot of instrumental folk music comes from Scotland and Ireland and ranges from laments on the *bagpipes to lively dance tunes. Most dance music is traditionally played on the fiddle (= violin). Irish folk bands usually have flutes, tin whistles, string instruments, pipes and a bodhrán (= an Irish drum).

American folk music was created by the combination of many folk styles brought to America by immigrants. Music helped keep alive the traditions and memories of people's former homes. From the late 19th century many songs and tunes that had been passed down orally were collected together and written down. In America more than 10 000 old songs were collected by John and Alan Lomax, and in Britain Cecil Sharp (1859–1924) collected both songs and *folk dances. Such collections influenced major works by composers such as *Vaughan Williams and *Britten. Dvořák used American folk music in his symphony *From the New World* (1893), as did *Copland in *Appalachian Spring* (1944).

In the US the *Carter Family helped make folk music popular again in the 1920s. By the 1950s the recording industry had made folk music commercially successful. This interest in folk music also led to **folk clubs** being established all over the US.

In the 1960s other styles developed, including the *bluegrass of Bill Monroe and the *country music of Hank *Williams. The most important was *folk rock which combined traditional folk music with features of rock and pop. The US created urban folk music

which used the problems of cities as subjects for folk songs. By the 1960s, folk music was being used to encourage social change and it became the music of *hippies and the *civil rights movement. A new generation of singer-songwriters emerged, including Joan *Baez, Bob *Dylan, Richard Thompson and Dick Gaughan. **Folk festivals** were popular. In 1963, just before the *Vietnam War, performers at the Newport, Rhode Island, festival included Bob *Dylan, Pete *Seeger, and Peter, Paul and Mary. They attacked the prejudices of society and the violence of war in songs such as *Blowin' in the Wind, The Times They Are a Changin'* and *If I Had a Hammer*.

Folk music is still very popular. In Britain folk festivals are held regularly at Cropredy near *Banbury, and at *Warwick and *Cambridge. Many towns still have a folk club for amateur singers and musicians, which meets regularly in a local *pub.

'folk rock *n* [U] a type of *rock music in which groups with electric instruments perform traditional folk songs with a strong beat, sometimes also using traditional instruments such as flutes and violins. Folk rock was popular in Britain and America in the 1960s and 1970s. Many folk-rock songs by singers such as Bob *Dylan contained social and political comments about life in that period, such as protests against the *Vietnam War. Popular folk-rock groups in Britain have included Fairport Convention, Steeleye Span and Pentangle. See also FOLK MUSIC AND SONGS.

follow-my-'leader (*AmE* **follow-the-leader**) *n* [U] a children's game in which one player is the 'leader' and the others must do exactly what the leader does, such as jumping, holding out their hands, etc. The phrase is sometimes used to refer to people who do what they are told to do without thinking about it: *She warned investors that playing follow-the-leader gets you nowhere.*

Henry 'Fonda¹ /'fɒndə; *AmE* 'fɑːndə/ (1905–82) a US actor who often played calm, honest characters. He was a *Hollywood star for more than 40 years in over 100 films, but won only one *Oscar, for his last film, *On Golden Pond* (1981). His other successes included *The *Grapes of Wrath* (1940) and *Twelve Angry Men* (1957). He was the father of the actors Jane *Fonda and Peter *Fonda.

Jane 'Fonda² /'fɒndə; *AmE* 'fɑːndə/ (1937–) a US actor also known for her strong political opinions and her successful video of physical exercises for keeping fit. She won *Oscars for *Klute* (1971) and *Coming Home* (1978). Her other films include *Barbarella* (1968) and *On Golden Pond* (1981), the only film she made with her father Henry *Fonda. Fonda was once called 'Hanoi Jane' because of her long campaign against the *Vietnam War. She was married to Ted *Turner until 2001.

Peter 'Fonda³ /'fɒndə; *AmE* 'fɑːndə/ (1939–) a US actor and director who is the son of Henry *Fonda and the brother of Jane *Fonda. His daughter Bridget Fonda (1964–) is also an actor. He became well known with the film *Easy Rider* but others, such as *Futureworld* (1976) and *The Hired Hand* (1971), were less successful. In 1997 he made *Ulee's Gold* about a man who keeps bees, as Fonda's own father did.

F-1 'visa /ˌef wʌn/ *n* an official US government document that a person from another country must have in order to enter the US as a student. Compare M-1 VISA.

Margot Fon'teyn /ˌmɑːgəʊ fɒnˈteɪn; *AmE* 'mɑːrgoʊ fɑːnˈteɪn/ (1919–91) a British ballet dancer who became internationally famous for the natural way in which she expressed emotions in her dancing. She is best remembered for her performances with Rudolf Nureyev in the ballets directed by Frederick *Ashton in the 1960s.

the 'Food and 'Drug Admini'stration ⇨ FDA.

The **'Food ˌProgramme** a *BBC radio programme about food. As well as discussing different dishes and styles of cooking, it also investigates the relationships between food and health, for example reporting on the dangers of some chemicals that are added to food. It has been broadcast regularly since 1979.

'food stamp *n* [usually pl] (in the US) originally a small piece of printed paper, now a debit card, that can be used to get food in shops. The government gives food stamps to people who are unemployed and have very little money: *Families receiving food stamps will not be affected by the cuts.*

the **ˌFood 'Standards Agency** (*abbr* the **FSA**) the British government organization responsible for food safety. It was set up in 2001.

ˌMichael **'Foot** /'fʊt/ (1913–) a British *Labour politician. He was *Secretary of State for employment (1974–6), *Leader of the House of Commons (1976–9) and leader of the Labour Party from 1980 to 1983, when Labour lost a general election. He is well known for his left-wing views such as his opposition to nuclear weapons, but he is respected by both sides of British politics as a thinker, speaker and writer.

the **ˌFootball Associˌation** (*abbr* the **FA**) a British organization that was established in 1863 to decide the rules of the game of *football. It controls the way game is played in England and is responsible for all English international football. It tries to encourage the playing of football by men, women and children and organizes several competitions each year, most importantly the *FA Cup. Its members include representatives from the different professional and non-professional football leagues.

the **ˌFootball 'League** a British *football competition in which each team in a particular division plays every other team twice. At the end of the season, the team with the most points is the champion of the division. The League was established in 1888 because the *Football Association did not allow professionals to enter its competitions. It was the major competition in English football until the top clubs left to form the FA *Premiership in 1992.

▶ **football – American style**

Football is one of the major sports in the US. In Britain and elsewhere the game is often called **American football** to distinguish it from soccer. American football developed from the games of football and *Rugby. There is a lot of dangerous play, so **helmets** and thick **pads** must be worn. Each game has **cheerleaders** and bands of musicians that march on the field between the **halves** of the game. Whole families go to watch games, and there is almost no violence from supporters. Many games are shown live on US television. British television now also shows some games. In US *high schools, colleges and universities, football games are the centre of many social events, such as *homecoming.

The game is played by two teams of 11 players each, with different players used for **defense**, **offense** and **kicks**. The field is 100 yards/91.5 metres long and 53 yards 1 foot/49 metres wide. It is sometimes called a **gridiron** because the lines across it that mark every 10 yards/9 metres make it look like the metal tray on which meat is grilled or broiled. At each end of the field there is an extra 10 yards/9 metres, called the **end zone**, with a **goal post** in the shaped of an 'H'. The ball is oval-shaped and sometimes called a **pigskin** because the balls were formerly made from pig's skin.

A team scores when its players send the ball down the field and across the opponent's **goal line** for a **touchdown** of seven points. They can then add a **point after touchdown** (**PAT**) if they kick the ball through the goal posts. A team can get three points if the ball is kicked between the goal posts without a touchdown, and two points if their defense stops the opponents in their own end zone.

The team with the ball must move it 10 yards/9 metres in four **downs** (= separate actions). This is done from behind **linemen** who face the defense's linemen. An action begins when the **quarterback** takes the ball from between the legs of the **center** and runs with it, hands it to another runner or **passes** (= throws) it to another player. Between actions, the team with the ball has a **huddle** so the quarterback can tell them what to do next. If 10 yards/9 metres are not made in 4 downs, the team must **punt** (= kick the ball to the other team). The defense can also get the ball by an **interception** (= a catch of the opponent's pass) or a **fumble** (= a ball accidentally dropped).

The **National Football League** (**NFL**) has 32 professional teams. Six teams in the *American Football Conference and six in the *National Football Conference play against each other to decide the two that will meet in the *Super Bowl. The Dallas Cowboys have won it the most (eight times), followed by the Denver Broncos (six times). Other well-known teams include the Green Bay Packers, the Pittsburgh Steelers and San Francisco 49ers.

The best college teams play in **bowl games**, e.g. the *Rose Bowl, Sugar Bowl, Orange Bowl and Cotton Bowl. The best college players are chosen as *All-Americans. Famous professional players almost always play in college teams first. They have included Jim *Brown[8], Jim *Thorpe[2], O J *Simpson[1] and Joe *Montana[2].

▶ **football – British style**

Football is the most popular sport in Britain, particularly amongst men. It is played by boys in most schools. Most towns have an amateur football team which plays in a **minor league**. Football is also the most popular **spectator sport** in Britain. Many people go to see their favourite professional team playing **at home**, and some go to **away matches**. Many more people watch football on television.

The rules of football are relatively simple: two teams of 11 players try to get a round ball into the opposing team's **goal** and to prevent their opponents from scoring. The ball may be kicked or **headed**, but never handled, except by the **goalkeepers**. The *Football Association was founded in 1863 to decide the rules of football and the resulting game became known formally as **association football**. It is sometimes also called **soccer**. Many of today's leading **clubs** were established shortly afterwards.

Most professional clubs represent large cities, or parts of London. They include *Everton, Liverpool, *Manchester United, *Arsenal, *Chelsea and *Tottenham Hotspur. The most famous Scottish clubs include *Rangers and *Celtic. In 1992 football was reorganized so that the best 20 teams in England and Wales play in the *Premiership, while 70 other teams play in three **divisions**, run by the *Football League. There is a *Scottish Premier League and three divisions run by the Scottish Football League. At the end of each season, the top few teams in each division are **promoted** and the bottom teams are **relegated**. As well as the *Premiership, the main competitions are the *FA Cup and the **League Cup**. A few of the most successful sides have won **the Double**, both titles in the same year. The biggest clubs are now run as major businesses, and top players earn large salaries. They are frequently **transferred** between clubs for millions of pounds. Many foreign stars also now play for British teams.

F

England, Wales, Scotland and Northern Ireland all have their own national sides. England won the World Cup in 1966, when its stars included Bobby *Charlton[1], Bobby *Moore[1] and Geoff Hurst.

An increase in **football hooliganism** in the 1970s and 1980s frightened many people away from football matches. English fans got a bad reputation in Europe and football violence became known as 'the English disease'. Disasters such as that at *Hillsborough, in which many people died, also discouraged people from going to matches. Formerly, football grounds had **terraces**, where supporters stood packed close together, and **stands** containing rows of seats which were more expensive. These grounds have now almost all been replaced by **all-seater stadiums**, but people complain about the rising cost of tickets. Many clubs have their own **fanzine** (= a magazine about the club written and published by the fans). Some supporters also buy a copy of their team's **strip** (= shorts and shirt in team colours).

This type of football is known in the US as soccer to distinguish it from the American game. Enthusiasm increased after 1994 when the World Cup was played for the first time in the US. In 1999 the US won the Women's World Cup. In 1996 **Major League Soccer** (**MLS**) was established, and teams compete for the **MLS Cup**. Students in colleges and universities also play soccer in three *NCAA divisions. The nation's oldest tournament is the US Open Cup. About 18 million American children now play regularly, and the expression *soccer mom* (= a mother who spends a lot of time taking her children to sporting activities) has entered the language.

'**Foot Guards** *n* [pl] (in Britain) five infantry regiments (= groups of soldiers who fight on foot) whose historical duty has been to protect the king or queen. They are the *Grenadier Guards, the *Coldstream Guards, the *Scots Guards, the Irish Guards and the *Welsh Guards. They are considered the best soldiers of their kind in the British Army.

the '**Footsie** /'fʊtsi/ an informal name for the *FTSE 100-Share Index. It is the best known of the *Financial Times Share Indices, giving the share values of the 100 largest British companies every day. It is used to indicate the state of the British financial markets: *The Footsie closed three points higher today at 4750.*

Forbes /'fɔːbz; *AmE* 'fɔːrbz/ a US business magazine, started in 1917, containing news stories and articles about world business and finance. It is best known for its lists of the most successful companies and the richest people, such as the **Forbes 500**, a list of the 500 most successful American companies, which is published each year.

'**Ford 'Madox 'Ford**[1] /'fɔːd 'mædəks 'fɔːd; *AmE* 'fɔːrd/ (1873–1939) an English writer. He wrote many novels, poems and critical studies (= books judging the qualities of works of literature, etc.), and worked with Joseph *Conrad on two novels, *The Inheritors* (1901) and *Romance* (1903). His best-known novels, *The Good Soldier* (1915) and the series of four *World War I novels together called *Parade's End* (1924–8), give a picture of the English *upper classes in changing times.

,**Gerald 'Ford**[2] /'fɔːd; *AmE* 'fɔːrd/ (1913–) the 38th US *President. He was a *Republican(1) who was Vice-President under Richard *Nixon and replaced him in 1974, after *Watergate. Ford was criticized for giving Nixon a pardon (= official notice forgiving somebody) for Watergate. Ford could not change the poor economic condition of the US at that time, and he lost the next election in 1976 to Jimmy *Carter.

,**Harrison 'Ford**[3] /ˌhærɪsn 'fɔːd; *AmE* 'fɔːrd/ (1942–) a US actor whose films have earned more money (almost $6 billion) than those of any other actor. The National Association of Theater Owners named him 'Star of the Century' in 1994, and in 1997 readers of *Empire* film magazine voted him Britain's favourite film star of all time. Ford often plays strong, calm characters, especially in adventure films. He first became well known as Han Solo in the *Star Wars films and as Indiana *Jones. His other films have included *Witness* (1985), *The *Fugitive* (1993) and *Air Force One* (1997), in which he played a US president.

,**Henry 'Ford**[4] /'fɔːd; *AmE* 'fɔːrd/ (1863–1947) the American who created the Ford car and changed the motor industry by introducing new ways of making cars in great numbers. He began the *Ford Motor Company in 1903 and five years later produced the first *Model T. He became very rich and successful, and established the international *Ford Foundation.

> **❝** Any customer can have a car painted any colour that he wants so long as it is black. **❞**
> Henry Ford on the Model T Ford

,**John 'Ford**[5] /'fɔːd; *AmE* 'fɔːrd/ (1586–c. 1639) an English writer of plays and poems. His writing is well known for its strong descriptions of sadness and despair (= loss of hope). His best-known play is *'Tis Pity She's a Whore* (1633).

,**John 'Ford**[6] /'fɔːd; *AmE* 'fɔːrd/ (1895–1973) a US film director, especially of *westerns. He received four *Oscars, for *The Informer* (1935), *The *Grapes of Wrath* (1940), *How Green was my Valley* (1941) and *The Quiet Man* (1953). Ford made about 125 films, many of them with his favourite actor, John *Wayne.

,**Richard 'Ford**[7] /'fɔːd; *AmE* 'fɔːrd/ (1944–) a US author who won the *PEN/Faulkner Award for Fiction and the *Pulitzer Prize for his novel *Independence Day* (1995). His other books include *The Sportswriter* (1986) and several collections of short stories.

the '**Ford Foun,dation** /'fɔːd; *AmE* 'fɔːrd/ one of the world's largest public trusts (= organizations providing money for projects that help society). It was established in the US in 1936 by Henry *Ford and his son Edsel Ford for the state of *Michigan, and in 1950 it became a national and international organization. By 1997, it had given or lent over $8 billion, especially to projects for democracy, world peace and justice, education and the arts, science and communication. The Foundation also helped to establish the US *Public Broadcasting Service.

the ,**Ford 'Motor Company** /,fɔːd; *AmE* ,fɔːrd/ a large US company that makes cars. It was established in *Detroit in 1903 by Henry *Ford and had a major influence on the way cars were made. It introduced the world's first moving production line and started using standard types of parts. This reduced production times and costs, allowing Ford to sell cars to more people at lower prices. By the end of 1913, 50% of cars in the US were Fords. The first *Model T was sold in 1908. The company has produced the Lincoln since 1922 and the Mercury since 1938. It became the owner of *Aston Martin in 1993 and has bought *Jaguar, *Land Rover, Volvo Cars, and a share of Mazda. It also owns the *Hertz Corporation, the world's largest company that rents cars. The Ford Motor Company had produced 300 million vehicles by 2003.

the ,**Foreign and 'Commonwealth ,Office** the British government department responsible for relations with other countries. The Foreign Office and the Commonwealth Office used to be two different departments. They were joined together in 1968, but many people still refer to it as the Foreign Office. Compare HOME OFFICE.

the **Foreign Re'lations Com,mittee** *(full title* **Senate Committee on Foreign Relations***)* a committee of the US *Senate that studies the American government's policy towards other countries, and offers advice and criticism.

the **Foreign 'Secretary** *(full title* **Secretary of State for Foreign and Commonwealth Affairs***)* the British government minister in charge of the *Foreign and Commonwealth Office. It is one of the most important jobs in the government. The Foreign Secretary represents Britain at many international meetings, and discusses foreign policy with the *Prime Minister.

the **'Foreign ,Service** all the officials who work in US embassies and consulates in other countries.

,George 'Foreman /'fɔːmən; *AmE* 'fɔːrmən/ (1949–) a US boxer who became the oldest heavyweight champion ever in 1994 at the age of 45 when he beat Michael Moorer. The next year, his title was taken away from him when he refused to fight Tony Tucker. Foreman was also champion from 1973 to 1974 and won a gold medal at the 1968 Olympics. He is now famous for advertising products, especially the **George Foreman Grill**.

,C S 'Forester /'fɒrɪstə(r)/ (Cecil Scott Forester 1899–1966) an English writer, best known for his historical novels about life in the *Royal Navy. He created the famous character Horatio *Hornblower, and wrote 12 novels about his adventures at sea during the *Napoleonic Wars.

,Forest 'Lawn a large US cemetery in Glendale, *California, near *Los Angeles. Its full name is Forest Lawn Memorial Park. Many *Hollywood stars are buried there. Copies of several famous British churches have also been built among the graves.

the **,Forest of 'Arden** /'ɑːdən; *AmE* 'ɑːrdən/ ⇨ ARDEN.

the **,Forest of 'Dean** /'diːn/ a forest in south-west England containing many very old oak and beech trees. In 1938 it became Britain's first *forest park.

,forest 'park *n* *(BrE)* an area of British forest that has been made into a park for the public to enjoy. Like *national parks, forest parks are usually large areas of attractive country with marked paths and special areas for camping.

the **'Forestry Com,mission** /'fɒrɪstri; *AmE* 'fɔːrɪstri/ a British government organization that manages the forests that are owned by the state. It is responsible for cutting down old trees, planting new ones, controlling diseases, and managing the *forest parks. It also gives help and advice to private owners of forest land.

For 'He's a 'Jolly Good 'Fellow a song that people sing to praise somebody who has done something that they admire. If the person is a woman, they sing *For She's a Jolly Good Fellow*. The song is usually sung without being planned or prepared, and the person is sometimes carried on the shoulders of the people singing. The words are:

> 66 For he's a jolly good fellow,
> For he's a jolly good fellow,
> For he's a jolly good fellow,
> And so say all of us. 99

▶ **formal and informal dress**

In general, people in Britain and the US dress fairly informally. Many wear **casual clothes** most of the time, not just when they are at home or on holiday. Men and women wear *jeans or cords (= corduroy trousers) with a shirt or T-shirt and a sweater to go shopping, meet friends, go to a pub or bar, or take their children out. Older people are more likely to dress more smartly, with women wearing a dress or skirt and blouse, and men a shirt, jacket and trousers, when they go out. In summer younger people may wear shorts (= short trousers/pants), but some people think they are only appropriate on the beach.

Most people **dress up** (= put on smart clothes) to go to a party or club. Some restaurants will not let in people who are wearing jeans. Most people do not now dress up to go to the theatre. Young people are most interested in following *fashion and regularly buy new clothes.

Men wear **lounge suits**, and women wear suits or dresses, for formal occasions like funerals or interviews for jobs. Some wear suits or smart clothes every day because their employer expects it or because they think it makes them look more professional. In London many people who work in the *City wear **pinstripe suits** made of dark cloth with narrow grey vertical lines. Most people prefer casual, comfortable clothes for work but some companies do not like people wearing jeans. Employees in banks and some shops often have uniforms.

For formal occasions during the day, such as a wedding, men may wear **morning dress**. This includes a jacket with long 'tails' at the back, dark grey trousers and a grey top hat. Women wear a smart dress and often a hat. For very formal events in the evening, men may wear **evening dress**, also called **white tie**, which consists of a black tailcoat, black trousers, a white waistcoat, white shirt and white bow tie. Women usually wear a long evening dress or ball gown. Usually for formal evening events men wear **black tie/tuxedo**, consisting of a black dinner jacket, black trousers and a black bow tie.

,Milos 'Forman /,miːlɒs 'fɔːmən; *AmE* ,miːlɑːs 'fɔːrmən/ (1932–) a US film director who was born in Czechoslovakia and moved to America in 1968. He won *Oscars for *One Flew Over the Cuckoo's Nest* (1975) and *Amadeus* (1983). His other films include *The Fireman's Ball* (1967), *Ragtime* (1980) and *Man on the Moon* (1999) about the comedian Andy Kaufman.

,George 'Formby /'fɔːmbi; *AmE* 'fɔːrmbi/ (1904–61) an English singer and comedy actor from *Lancashire. He began his career in *music-hall(1) and later made many successful films. He always played a slightly silly character with a strong northern accent and a big smile, and sang songs with sexual double meanings while playing the ukulele, an instrument like a small guitar.

'Formula the word used to indicate different classes of cars that take part in international Grand Prix motor races. Formula One is the fastest class, Formula Two the second fastest, etc. The cars are built specially for these races, and the class that they are in is decided by factors

Formula One racing

such as the size of the engine and the weight of the car. Compare INDYCAR RACING.

Forrest 'Gump /ˌfɒrɪst 'gʌmp; AmE ˌfɔːrɪst/ a US comedy film (1994), directed by Robert *Zemeckis, which won several *Oscars including Best Picture, Best Actor and Best Director. In its first year, it earned the third largest amount of any film ever ($330 million). Tom *Hanks plays Forrest, a mentally slow man who becomes successful because he speaks the truth. The film was especially popular because it showed that honesty and a simple life can bring happiness.

> 66 My momma always said life was like a box of chocolates … you never know what you're gonna get. 99
> Forrest Gump

E M 'Forster /'fɔːstə(r); AmE 'fɔːrstər/ (Edward Morgan Forster 1879–1970) an English writer of novels, short stories and essays. He is best known for his novels, which examine themes of understanding and friendship among the English *upper middle classes and satirize the behaviour of the English when travelling abroad. His best-known works include *A Room with a View* (1908), *Howards End* (1910) and *A *Passage to India* (1924).

The 'Forsyte ˌSaga /'fɔːsaɪt; AmE 'fɔːrsaɪt/ a series of novels by John *Galsworthy, written between 1906 and 1921. They tell the story of Soames Forsyte, a lawyer, and his family from the 1880s to the 1920s. At the beginning they build a house in London, but after 40 years of difficult and complicated relationships there is nobody living in the house. Successful television series of the story were made in the 1960s and in 2002.

Bruce 'Forsyth¹ /'fɔːsaɪθ; AmE 'fɔːrsaɪθ/ (1928–) an English comedian and television presenter. He is best known for presenting game shows in which members of the public play games and win prizes. He is also known for introducing his shows by saying, 'Nice to see you, to see you … nice.' Another phrase he often uses is 'Didn't he (or she) do well?'.

Frederick For'syth² /fɔːˈsaɪθ; AmE fɔːrˈsaɪθ/ (1938–) an English journalist and writer of novels about international crime and politics, well known for their realistic details and exciting stories. They include *The Day of the Jackal* (1971) and *The Odessa File* (1972), both of which have been made into successful films.

Forth /fɔːθ; AmE fɔːrθ/ a river that flows through central Scotland into the *North Sea. The long wide area of water where the Forth flows into the sea is called the **Firth of Forth**, and is well known for the *Forth Bridges.

the ˌForth 'Bridge /ˌfɔːθ; AmE ˌfɔːrθ/ **1** (also **Forth Rail Bridge**) a railway bridge over the Firth of *Forth near *Edinburgh. It was built in 1890 and is considered one of the greatest engineering achievements of its period. Most British people know the story that it is always being painted, because when the painters have finished painting it from one end to the other, it is necessary to start at the beginning again: *Tidying up after the children is like painting the Forth Bridge.*

the Forth Rail Bridge

2 a road bridge that was built beside the Forth Rail Bridge in 1964. It is a suspension bridge (= a bridge hanging from cables supported by towers at each end) and one of the longest of its kind in the world.

Fort 'Knox /'nɒks; AmE 'nɑːks/ a military area in the state of *Kentucky where the US government keeps the nation's gold, in the US Gold Bullion Depository. It is famous for being impossible to enter because it has thick steel doors and is extremely well guarded: *Our security system is so complicated it's like trying to get into Fort Knox.*

ˌFortnum and 'Mason /ˌfɔːtnəm, 'meɪsn; AmE ˌfɔːrtnəm/ a large shop in *Piccadilly, London, which also contains a restaurant. It began in 1707 and is famous for selling expensive and unusual food, and for its hampers (= large boxes or baskets containing several different types of food and drink). The shop is considered one of the smartest in London and is very popular with tourists.

Fort 'Sumter /'sʌmtə(r)/ the US fort on a small island in the harbour of *Charleston, *South Carolina, where the *Civil War began. Soldiers from South Carolina, led by General Beauregard, shot at the fort with cannons (= large heavy guns) on 12 April 1861, and it surrendered the next day. The Union forces did not capture it again until 1865. Fort Sumter is now open to the public as a museum.

Fort ˌTiconde'roga /ˌtɪkɒndəˈrəʊgə; AmE ˌtɪkɑːndəˈroʊgə/ an American fort built as Fort Carillon by the French in 1755 in north-east New York State. British forces captured it in 1759 in the *French and Indian War, and named it Fort Ticonderoga. During the *American Revolution, it was captured in 1775 by the Green Mountain Boys led by Benedict *Arnold and Ethan Allen, but the British under General John Burgoyne took it again in 1777. It is now a museum.

the Fortune 500 /ˌfɔːtʃuːn faɪv 'hʌndrəd; AmE ˌfɔːrtjuːn/ a list showing the sales and profits of the 500 largest US companies which has been published each year since 1955 in the American business magazine *Fortune*. Companies want to be included because being a **Fortune 500 company** shows their importance.

Fort 'William /'wɪljəm/ a town in the southern *Highlands of Scotland. It takes its name from a fort built in 1655 and destroyed in 1866. It is now an important tourist centre.

Fort 'Worth /'wɜːθ; AmE 'wɜːrθ/ a city in the US state of *Texas. It is very close to *Dallas, and the Dallas-Fort Worth Airport is one of the largest in the world. Fort Worth contains the Texas Christian University, the Kimball Art Museum and the Cattleman's Museum, and its opera house and orchestra are well known. It is a centre for the oil, gas, electronics and aircraft industries. It was settled in 1843 and soon became the last stop for cattle being moved to *Kansas.

the ˌForty-'Five (also **the '45 Rebellion**) the second attempt by the Scottish *Jacobites to defeat the English and make the *Stuarts the kings of England and Scotland. This attempt, led by *Bonny Prince Charlie in 1745, was successful at first. The English forces were defeated at *Prestonpans and the Jacobites moved into England. They soon had to return to Scotland, however, and were finally defeated at *Culloden. See also FIFTEEN.

ˌforty-'niner *n* **1** any of the people who went to *California to look for gold during the *Gold Rush of 1849.
2 the Forty-Niners [pl] the popular name for the *San Francisco professional football team.

42nd Street /ˌfɔːtiˈsekənd striːt/ a *Hollywood musical film (1933) directed by Lloyd Bacon, with dances designed by Busby *Berkeley. A stage version opened on *Broadway in 1980. The film is about a Broadway producer whose musical star breaks an ankle. He has to use an unknown actor, but she is a great success. The title refers to a street in *Manhattan, New York City, in the heart of the city's theatre district.

the ˌ**Fosbury ˈflop** /ˌfɒzbri; *AmE* ˌfɑːzbri/ (in sport) a way of doing the high jump. The person jumps backwards over the bar with the legs following the upper body. It is named after the US athlete Dick Fosbury (1947–) who first used this method at the 1968 Olympics and won a gold medal. It is now widely used by other athletes.

ˌ**Bob ˈFosse** /ˈfɒsi; *AmE* ˈfɑːsi/ (1927–87) a US film director who won an *Oscar for *Cabaret* (1972). He began on *Broadway as a dancer and choreographer and won nine *Tony awards. He directed and designed the dances for the films *Sweet Charity* (1969) and *All That Jazz* (1979) (which was based on his own life). In 1999 *Fosse*, a Broadway musical based on his best works won three Tony awards.

ˌ**Fosse ˈWay** (*also* **the Fosse Way**) /ˌfɒs; *AmE* ˌfɑːs/ a Roman road which crosses southern England from *Lincoln in the east to *Exeter in the south-west.

ˌ**Jodie ˈFoster**[1] /ˌdʒəʊdi ˈfɒstə(r); *AmE* ˈfɑːstər/ (1962–) a US actor who has won *Oscars for *The Accused* (1988) and *Silence of the Lambs* (1991). She was a child actor who became famous in *Taxi Driver* (1976). Her more recent films have included *Sommersby* (1993), *Contact* (1997) and *Panic Room* (2002), and she also directed *Home for the Holidays* (1995). She established her own production company, Egg Pictures, in 1990. When John Hinckley shot President Ronald *Reagan in 1981, he said he did it to impress Foster, because he loved her.

the court at the British Museum

ˌ**Norman ˈFoster**[2] /ˈfɒstə(r); *AmE* ˈfɑːstər/ (1935–) an English architect. He is well known for his 'high-tech' style (= using metal and glass to show the structure of a building instead of hiding it). His most famous buildings include the Sainsbury Centre for Visual Arts (1979) near Norwich, England, the Hong Kong and Shanghai Bank (1986) in Hong Kong, *Stansted Airport (1991), the new German Parliament (1999), the glass-covered court at the *British Museum (2000), the *Swiss Re Tower (2004) and the world's highest bridge in Millau, France (2005). He was made a *knight in 1990 and a *life peer in 1999.

ˌ**Stephen ˈFoster**[3] /ˈfɒstə(r); *AmE* ˈfɑːstər/ (1826–1864) a US writer of almost 200 popular songs, most of them about the US South. They are sometimes called *folk songs because they are so simple. Most were for musical shows performed by white entertainers with words representing the speech of African Americans at that time. They include *Oh! Susanna*, *Old Folks at Home*, *Camptown Races*, *My Old Kentucky Home*, *Beautiful Dreamer* and *Old Black Joe*. Foster himself only visited the South once.

the ˌ**Founding ˈFathers** /ˌfaʊndɪŋ/ *n* [pl] the Americans who established the form of the US government at the Federal Constitutional Convention in *Philadelphia (1787) when they created and signed the American *Constitution. The best-known Founding Fathers were George *Washington, Thomas *Jefferson, Benjamin *Franklin, Alexander *Hamilton, John *Adams and James *Madison.

the ˌ**Fountain of ˈYouth** (in old stories) a spring of water that is believed to give youth to anyone who drinks it. In 1513, the Spanish explorer Juan *Ponce de León searched for it in America in an area that is now the state of *Florida. The city of Saint Augustine in that state has a 'Fountain of Youth' for tourists which, it is claimed, might have been the one he searched for.

ˌ**Fountains ˈAbbey** /ˌfaʊntənz/ a ruined abbey near Ripon in north-east England. It was built in 1132 and destroyed in the 16th century during the *Dissolution of the Monasteries. Many people visit the ruins, which have been well preserved in attractive countryside. They were made a *World Heritage Site in 1986.

ˌ**Four ˈCorners** the place in the US where the states of *Arizona, *New Mexico, *Colorado and *Utah meet and the area round it. It is the only place in the US where four states meet.

the ˌ**Four ˈFreedoms** four types of freedom that US President Franklin D *Roosevelt said were worth fighting for. They are freedom of speech and expression, freedom of worship, freedom from want (= the lack of basic needs) and freedom from fear. He said this during his *State of the Union Address to *Congress on 6 January 1941 nearly a year before the US entered *World War II. After the war, the Four Freedoms were included in the *United Nations Charter (= statement of the rights of people).

the ˌ**Four ˈHundred** the popular US name for members of high society in New York City. Other US cities also now use the expression. The origin of the term is thought to be a list of guests invited to a social event in New York City in 1892 that was reduced to the 400 most important people, because the person inviting them had a ballroom that could only hold that number.

ˌ**Four Quarˈtets** a group of four poems by T S *Eliot, *Burnt Norton* (1935), *East Coker* (1940), *The Dry Salvages* (1941) and *Little Gidding* (1942). The poems contain Christian religious messages, and deal with themes such as time, nature, history and human experience. The titles refer to places that had a special meaning in Eliot's life or his Christian beliefs.

F

the ˌFourteen ˈPoints the 14 aims of the US at the end of *World War I, as presented by President Woodrow *Wilson to *Congress on 8 January 1918. They included a reduction in military weapons, freedom of the seas, free international trade and several land agreements, such as establishing an independent Poland. The Fourteen Points were used in preparing the *Treaty of Versailles. The League of Nations was based on the last of them, which called for a general 'association of nations'.

the ˌFourteenth Aˈmendment /ə'mendmənt/ an *amendment to the American *Constitution, allowing former slaves to become US citizens. It also gave all Americans the right to *due process of law and to equal protection by the law. It was passed by *Congress in 1866 and received the approval of the states two years later.

the ˌFourth of Juˈly (also **Independence Day**) the official US holiday on 4 July that celebrates the nation's independence. On that day in 1776, the *Continental Congress gave its approval to the *Declaration of Independence. The day is celebrated with fireworks, outdoor meals, processions, flags and speeches.

ˌFour ˈWeddings and a ˈFuneral a British comedy film (1994) in which Hugh *Grant plays a young man who falls in love with an American woman at a friend's wedding. They continue to meet at other weddings and social events, and although she marries somebody else, they are together at the end of the film.

John ˈFowles /'faʊlz/ (1926–) an English writer who has written successful novels in a wide range of styles, four of which have been made into films. These include *The Collector* (1963), a psychological crime novel, and *The Magus* (1966), a complicated and mysterious story about a young man on a Greek island. Fowles's best-known work is probably *The French Lieutenant's Woman* (1969) and the film, with a screenplay by Harold *Pinter, appeared in 1981.

ˈCharles ˈJames ˈFox¹ /'fɒks; AmE 'fɑːks/ (1749–1806) an English *Whig(1) politician. For most of his career he was the *Leader of the Opposition, while *Pitt was *Prime Minister. He was a friend of the *Prince Regent and a supporter of ideas that shocked people at the time, such as the French Revolution, American independence and the ending of the slave trade. ⇨ note at SLAVERY.

ˌGeorge ˈFox² /'fɒks; AmE 'fɑːks/ (1624–91) an English Christian religious leader. He established the *Society of Friends (the *Quakers) in the 1650s, after spending much of his life travelling and telling people about his belief that people should find God inside themselves. He was often put in prison for his beliefs.

ˌMichael J ˈFox³ /'fɒks; AmE 'fɑːks/ (1961–) a *Hollywood actor, born in Canada. He was in the US television comedy series *Family Ties* (1982–9) before he became an international star in *Back to the Future, Parts 1, 2 and 3* (1985, 1989 and 1990). His later films have included *Doc Hollywood* (1991), *The American President* (1995) and *Mars Attacks!* (1996). He also appeared in the popular television comedy series *Spin City* (1996–2002). His book *Lucky Man* (2002) describes living with Parkinson's disease, the illness which caused him to give up acting.

ˈFoxe's ˈBook of ˈMartyrs /'fɒksɪz ; AmE 'fɑːksɪz / (also ˈActs and ˈMonuments of these ˈLatter and ˈPerilous ˈDays) a book (1554) written by John Foxe (1516–87). It describes the deaths of the many British *Protestants who were killed because of their religious beliefs when the Catholic *Mary I was queen. The book, with its frightening descriptions and illustrations, influenced many British people against *Roman Catholics.

ˌFox ˈNews ˌChannel a US television company, started in 1996, that broadcasts news programmes 24 hours a day by cable and satellite in the US and around the world.

ˈFoyle's /'fɔɪlz/ one of the largest bookshops in the world, on *Charing Cross Road, central London, England. It was first established by the brothers William and Gilbert Foyle in 1906.

ˌA J ˈFoyt /'fɔɪt/ (Anthony Joseph Foyt 1935–) a US driver of racing cars who has had great success in *IndyCar racing. He has won the *Indy 500 four times (1961, 1964, 1967 and 1977), a record shared only by Al *Unser. Foyt has been the US Auto Club Champion seven times.

FPA /ˌef piː ˈeɪ/ (formerly **the Family Planning Association**) a British organization that gives people free advice about contraception (= ways of preventing a woman from becoming pregnant), and often gives people free contraceptives.

FPO /ˌef piː ˈəʊ; AmE 'oʊ/ (in full **Fleet Post Office**) the special post office system of the US Navy. Mail can be sent between navy bases and to ships quickly and at a reduced cost.

ˌJohn ˈFrancome /'fræŋkəm/ (1952–) an English jockey. He was the most successful *National Hunt jockey in the early 1980s, and became *champion jockey seven times before retiring in 1985, when he became a television presenter. He has also written 15 novels.

ˈfranglais /'frɒŋgleɪ; AmE 'frɑːŋgleɪ/ n [U] **1** the use of English words in French, from the French words *français* (French) and *anglais* (English). Many French people do not like franglais phrases such as 'le weekend' or 'le fair play' because they think that they are making the French language less pure.
2 (humorous) language which is a mixture of French and English that sounds funny: *'C'est pas une good news,' he said in his best franglais.*

ˌRobert ˈFrank /'fræŋk/ (1924–) a photographer who was born in Switzerland but has lived and worked in the US since 1947. He worked for fashion magazines and has produced many books of photographs, the best known of which is *The Americans* (1958). He has also worked in film and video.

ˌAl ˈFranken /ˌæl 'fræŋkən/ (1951–) a US comedian, writer and political activist, best known for his political satire and his performances on *Saturday Night Live*.

ˈFrankenstein /'fræŋkənstaɪn/ a novel (1818) by Mary *Shelley. It is the story of a Swiss scientist, Dr Frankenstein, who makes a living creature from parts of dead bodies. It is like a man, but stronger, and although it is gentle at first, it later attacks Frankenstein and kills his brother. There have been many films based on the story and variations of it: *Everybody was dressed up as a ghost, a vampire or Frankenstein's monster.* See also KARLOFF.

ˌFelix ˈFrankfurter /'fræŋkfɜːtə(r); AmE 'fræŋkfɜːrtər/ (1882–1965) a US *Supreme Court judge (1939–62), born in Austria. He believed in 'judicial restraint', the idea that judges should not try to influence government policies through their decisions in courts of law. He helped to establish the *American Civil Liberties Union, taught at the Law School of *Harvard University (1914–39) and advised Presidents Woodrow *Wilson and Franklin D *Roosevelt. He received the *Presidential Medal of Freedom in 1963.

ˌFrankie and ˈJohnny an old US ballad about a woman who murders her lover and is hanged for the crime. In the story, Frankie sees Johnny with Alice Pry in a *Memphis hotel and shoots him three times. Most verses end with the line 'He was her man but he done her wrong'.

A,retha 'Franklin[1] /əˌriːθə ˈfræŋklɪn/ (1942–) a US singer who has been called 'Lady Soul' and the 'Queen of Soul'. She won a *Grammy award every year from 1967 to 1974 and by 1997 had received 16, more than any other woman performer. Her best-known songs are *I Say a Little Prayer* (1967) and *Respect* (1968). In 1987 she was chosen for the *Rock and Roll *Hall of Fame.

,Benjamin 'Franklin[2] /ˈfræŋklɪn/ (1706–90) one of America's most famous *Founding Fathers. He was a wise and clever political leader, writer and printer, and a scientist who invented many things. Franklin helped to write the *Declaration of Independence, which he signed, and later the American *Constitution. In 1776 he went to France and persuaded the French to send money and military forces for the *American Revolution. Franklin proved that lightning is electricity by flying a kite in a storm, and his inventions included the Franklin Stove. He also published *Poor Richard's Almanack* (1732–57).

> **66** In this world nothing is certain but death and taxes. **99**
> Benjamin Franklin

,Rosalind 'Franklin[3] /ˌrɒzəlɪnd ˈfræŋklɪn; *AmE* ˌrɑːzəlɪnd/ (1920–1958) a British scientist who played an important part in the discovery of the structure of DNA (= the chemical in the cells of plants and animals which carries genetic information). Some of her research was used by James *Watson, Francis *Crick and Maurice Wilkins who won the *Nobel Prize for their work on DNA.

,Franz 'Ferdinand /ˌfrænts ˈfɜːdɪnænd, ˌfrænz; *AmE* ˈfɜːrdɪnænd/ a Scottish rock band formed in 2001 whose first album, *Franz Ferdinand*, won the *Mercury Music Prize in 2004. In the 2005 *Brit Awards they were named best British rock act and best British group.

'Frasier /ˈfreɪʒə(r)/ a US television comedy series (1993–2004) on *NBC. It won 31 *Emmy awards for the best comedy, more than any other show. The main character, Frasier Crane, is a psychologist who presents a radio advice programme. He first appeared as a character in the television comedy *Cheers*.

fra'ternity *n* a social organization for male students or for male and female students at many US colleges and universities. The members usually live in a house together and are called Greeks, because each fraternity takes as its name two or three Greek letters, such as Lambda Delta Chi. Fraternities do charity work but are sometimes criticized for their wild parties. See also PHI BETA KAPPA. Compare SORORITY.

the 'Fraud Squad a special department in a British police force that investigates people who make money by deceiving other people: *The manager of the company is being questioned by Fraud Squad detectives.* Compare SERIOUS FRAUD OFFICE.

,Michael 'Frayn /ˈfreɪn/ (1933–) an English writer of novels and plays who began his career as a journalist. Among his best-known works are the plays *Noises Off* (1982), *Copenhagen* (1998) and *Democracy* (2003). His novels include *A Landing on the Sun* (1991), *Headlong* (1999) and *Spies* (2002).

,James 'Frazer /ˈfreɪzə(r)/ (1854–1941) a Scottish anthropologist. He is best known for writing *The Golden Bough*, a study of many customs and religions. He had an important influence on the development of the science of anthropology in Britain, although most anthropolo-

gists now disagree with his ideas on the progress of human beliefs.

,Free 'Church *n* any Christian religious group in Britain that is not part of the *Church of England or the *Roman Catholic Church. Such groups include the *Presbyterians, the *Baptists and the *Methodists. Many people think of Free Church members as living strictly according to the rules of their church, for example not drinking alcohol and not working on Sundays. Compare NONCONFORMIST.

the ,Free Church of 'Scotland /ˈskɒtlənd; *AmE* ˈskɑːtlənd/ a large group of Scottish Protestants who left the *Church of Scotland in 1843 and established their own branch of the Christian religion because they did not agree with the way the Church of Scotland chose its priests. In 1929 most members of the Free Church joined the Church of Scotland again. Some members, especially in the *Highlands, remained independent, and they are often called the **Wee Frees**. (*Wee* is a Scottish word meaning small).

▶ **freedom and rights**

Many of the rights of US citizens are laid down in the *Constitution and the first ten *amendments to it, which are together called the *Bill of Rights. The Constitution was written in the late 1700s to explain not only how the US government would work, but also what limits there would be on its power. At that time, people were beginning to believe that the rights of individuals were important, and that the government was the main threat to those rights. Limiting the *federal government's power was also seen as necessary to protect the rights of states within the United States.

Britain does not have a written constitution or legal document describing the rights of individuals but for British people freedom to live without interference from government is important. Proposals to introduce **identity cards** for everyone are always resisted and people often talk about the **nanny state** when they feel the government is interfering in their lives.

In Britain and the US the most basic rights include **freedom of expression** (= freedom to say or write what you think), **freedom of choice** (= freedom to make decisions about your own life) and **freedom of worship** (= freedom to practise any religion).

Freedom of expression does not imply complete freedom for people to say what they like. In the US the *First Amendment protects freedom of speech and of the press but the courts, especially the *Supreme Court, decide how it should be applied. For instance, a newspaper is not allowed to print something bad about a person that is known not to be true: this is **libel**. The courts do not practise **prior restraint**, i.e. they cannot stop a newspaper from printing something, but they can punish the newspaper afterwards. However, in a few cases, e.g. when national security is involved, the courts may order newspapers not to print a report.

The right to free speech in the US has not always been respected. In the 1950s, when *McCarthyism was at its height, people who were suspected of being Communists were called before *Congress to answer questions. People who used their right to free speech and said they believed in Communism, or who *took the fifth, i.e. used their right under the *Fifth Amendment not to give evidence against themselves, often lost their jobs or went to prison.

In Britain until 1968 all plays had to be approved by the Lord Chamberlain before they could be performed in theatres. **Censorship** of the press ended in the 1960s. Newspapers are expected to behave responsibly and members of the public have the right to complain

F

about what is published in the press to the *Press Complaints Commission.

The **right of equal opportunity** (= the right to be treated the same as others, regardless of race, sex, etc.) is enforced in Britain through the *Race Relations Acts and the *Sex Discrimination Act. In the US the *civil rights movement of the 1960s influenced the making of new laws to protect the rights of minority groups, especially *African Americans. In 1972 an *Equal Rights Amendment, which would have given women the same rights and opportunities as men, failed to get the support of enough states to be passed. Later, however, several laws were passed making it illegal to discriminate against women.

People in Britain and the US have a much valued **right to privacy**. The US and British *Freedom of Information Acts and the British *Data Protection Act allow a person access to information held about them and the opportunity to correct it if it is wrong.

In the US several amendments to the Constitution deal specifically with the rights of people suspected or accused of a crime. In Britain, a person detained by the police has a right (*habeas corpus) to be released if not charged within 24 hours. As in the US, people also have the **right to remain silent**. The police are heavily criticized if these rights are **infringed**.

In the US an individual's right to own weapons continues to cause disagreement. When this right was included in the Second Amendment, America had just finished fighting for independence. Since the US did not want to keep a permanent army, its defence in the case of future attacks depended on ordinary people having weapons. Many people believe that, since the US now has a professional army, individuals do not need guns, and that the interpretation of the amendment should take account of the modern situation. But others want to keep the right to have weapons and resist any changes to the law.

ˌfreedom of asˈsembly n [U] the right to have public meetings. This right became part of US law under the *First Amendment. In Britain, people are generally free to have public meetings and this freedom is now protected by the European Convention on European Rights.

ˌfreedom of inforˈmation n [U] the right to see any information that is held by the government. Both the US and UK have a *Freedom of Information Act that allows people to see certain information held by the government. In Britain, the government can keep some information secret under the *Official Secrets Act, *DA-notices and the *thirty-year rule.

the ˌFreedom of Inforˈmation Act 1 (abbr the **FOI Act**) in the UK (except Scotland) a law that gives people the right to ask a public authority or organization whether they have any information on a particular subject, and if so, to obtain it. The authority or organization must reply to a request within 20 days but may refuse to provide information in some circumstances, for example where it could harm national security (= the protection of the nation and its interests). The law also requires public institutions to actively follow a program of publishing the information that they hold. It was passed in 2000 but only came into effect in 2005. A separate but similar law applies in Scotland. Compare DATA PROTECTION ACT, OFFICIAL SECRETS ACT.
2 (abbr the **FOIA**) in the US, a law that allows anyone to ask to see information kept by the government on a person or an organization. Such requests must be in writing and name specific documents. The law was passed in 1966 and strengthened in 1974, and journalists have often used it. Some personal files and information relating to national security are not included under the law. Individual states have similar laws.

ˌfreedom of reˈligion n [U] the right to choose which religion to belong to, or to belong to no religion. This right became part of American law under the *First Amendment. In Britain, religious freedom was achieved gradually through a series of laws from the 17th century to the 19th century.

ˌfreedom of ˈspeech n [U] the right to express any opinions in public. This right became part of American law under the *First Amendment. If the opinions expressed are false or damage a person's reputation, however, that person can take legal action under US law. In Britain, people are free to express most opinions, but it is against the law to express some ideas, e.g. ideas that aim to cause racial hatred.

the ˌfreedom of the ˈcity n [U] an honour that a particular city gives to people. It is usually given to a famous person by the city that they live in or were born in, or to a person who has done some good work for a city. It is a historical title, and does not give the person any special rights. In the US, a person who is given the freedom of the city is also given a large key as a symbol of the honour. For this reason the honour is commonly called **the keys to the city**.

ˌfreedom of the ˈpress n [U] the right to publish news and opinions in the press without the government removing any of the information. This right became part of American law under the *First Amendment. In Britain the press is free to publish most types of information but the government can prevent newspapers and broadcasters from reporting some stories by using the *Official Secrets Act or *DA-notices.

ˈfreedom ˌriders n [pl] (AmE) groups of both black and white people from the northern US who in 1961 rode together in buses in the *Deep South as a protest against *segregation on public transport there. The first 'freedom rides' were organized by the *Congress of Racial Equality. The freedom riders were often attacked by angry crowds, but in November that year the Interstate Commerce Commission legally ended segregation on buses.

ˈFreefone™ /ˈfriːfəʊn; AmE ˈfriːfoʊn/ (in Britain) a special service provided by *BT which allows people to make free telephone calls to a company or organization. Freefone numbers begin with 0800. They are usually used by businesses to give people information or to sell their products on the telephone: To place your order call Freefone 0800 567891.. Compare 800 NUMBER.

ˈfree house n (in Britain) a pub that is not controlled by a particular beer company and is able to choose which makes of beer it sells. Compare TIED HOUSE(1). ⇨ note at BEER.

▶**Freemasonry**

Freemasons, often called **Masons**, are members of a secret society for men, the **Free and Accepted Masons**, which is based on brotherly love, faith in the Supreme Being (= God) and good works.

Freemasonry, or **Masonry**, developed in Britain from *medieval **guilds** (= trade associations) of **masons** (= craftsmen) who travelled round the country. There was a guild for each craft. Its members were highly skilled master craftsmen and journeymen (= trained workers). Titles given to modern Masons reflect these origins. New members are admitted as **apprentices** and may go on to the higher rank of **fellowcraft** or **journeyman**, and finally **master mason**. Tools traditionally used by stonemasons are still used in the society's ceremonies.

During the 17th century the guilds became popular with rich gentlemen who gradually took them over. They developed into secret societies whose religious beliefs and practices provoked the hostility of many, including the *Roman Catholic Church. In 1717 the **Grand Lodge** was founded in London and became the most important branch of the society with authority over other branches or lodges. The Grand Lodge of Scotland was founded in 1736. There are about 8600 lodges in Britain, each in the charge of a **master**, with a total of about 320 000 Masons, and further branches in the US, Canada and other countries.

Most Masons today belong to the professional and middle classes and are lawyers, *civil servants, businessmen, etc., though members of the aristocracy and the royal family have also been Masons. The present Duke of *Kent is **Grand Master** of the Grand Lodge. In Britain, new members are only admitted at the invitation of existing Masons and have to go through a special **initiation** ceremony in which they promise not to tell anyone else the secrets of the society. It is commonly believed that they also learn special signs and words, and the Masons' **handshake**, which they can use in public to identify themselves to other Masons. In the US some of the details of Masonic practices are different: for example, people who wish to become Masons must ask to join, because Masons are not allowed to invite others to become Masons.

In Britain, because Masons keep their affairs secret, Freemasonry has often been viewed with suspicion. Many people believe that Masons in positions of power give other members of the society an unfair advantage. Masons themselves deny such practices and emphasize the social and charitable aspects of the movement. In the US there is a more tolerant attitude to Freemasonry. Perhaps the best known Freemasons in the US are a group called **Shriners**. Shriners are well known for their circuses which are held every year to raise money for charity work, including hospitals that the Shriners run.

Many other social clubs in the US which call themselves **fraternal organizations** have titles and ceremonies that are based on those of the Masons.

ˌfree 'paper n a free local newspaper that is delivered to people's homes every week. Most British and US towns and cities have free papers, which contain mostly advertisements and some local news. Some people dislike receiving them and ask for them not to be delivered to their homes.

'Freepost /'fri:pəʊst; AmE 'fri:poʊst/ (in Britain) a special service provided by the *Post Office that allows people to post letters without a stamp to a company or organization by using 'Freepost' in the address. The company that receives the letter pays the cost.

ˌfree 'trade n [U] a system in which trade can take place between different countries without the payment of special taxes or other charges. After the end of the *Corn Laws in the 19th century Britain was in favour of free trade, but during the *Depression there were special charges on imports to protect local industry. In the second half of the 20th century Britain joined free-trade organizations such as EFTA, (the European Free Trade Association) and the *European Union.

During its history, the US has generally tried to protect its industries with charges on imports. Since *World War I, however, it has supported free trade, and in 1994 it began operating *NAFTA with Canada and Mexico.

'freeway n the name used in the western US for a road for fast travel, with a limited number of places where drivers can join or leave it. ⇨ note at ROADS AND ROAD SIGNS.

ˌDawn 'French /'frentʃ/ (1957–) an English comedy actor best known for appearing with Jennifer *Saunders in the television comedy series *French and Saunders. She has also appeared in other television comedy series,

including *Murder Most Horrid* (from 1991), *The *Vicar of Dibley* (from 1994) and *Wild West* (from 2003).

the ˌFrench and ˌIndian ˌWar the part of the *Seven Years' War that was fought in America (1754–63). After a series of battles, the British forces defeated the French and Indians (*Native Americans), and the Treaty of Paris (1763) gave Britain all of Canada and much of the *Louisiana region, which reached nearly to Canada. George *Washington was one of the British military leaders, and this war gave Americans the experience they needed to fight the *American Revolution.

ˌFrench and ˌSaunders /ˌfrentʃ, 'sɔːndəz; AmE 'sɔːndərz/ a series of popular British comedy television programmes written and performed by Dawn *French and Jennifer *Saunders in the 1980s and 1990s. The programmes consisted of several short plays that made fun of modern life, films and other television programmes.

the ˌFrench ˌQuarter the old district of *New Orleans, *Louisiana. Local people sometimes call it the Vieux Carré (Old Square). It is next to the *Mississippi River and includes Bourbon Street, Rampart Street, Jackson Square and the French Market. The area is popular with tourists for its *jazz music, good food and buildings of Spanish and French architecture with decorative iron balconies.

'Fresno /'freznəʊ; AmE 'freznoʊ/ a city in the US state of *California. It is an international agricultural centre and produces many farm products, including grapes, wine, cotton, tomatoes and fruit. It also has oil and gas wells.

ˌLucian 'Freud /ˌluːsiən 'frɔɪd/ (1922–) a British artist, born in Germany. He is well known for his harshly realistic paintings of people including lovers, friends and members of his family. He has also painted portraits of famous people including the Queen and Kate *Moss. Freud is the grandson of the Austrian psychiatrist Sigmund Freud.

'Friars Club /'fraɪəz; AmE 'fraɪərz/ a US club for people in the entertainment business. There are several around the country, but the most famous are in New York and *Los Angeles. They hold regular 'Stag Roasts', often on television, in which film or television stars sit among friends who make speeches with humorous insults about them.

ˌFriar 'Tuck /ˌfraɪə 'tʌk; AmE ˌfraɪər/ one of *Robin Hood's group of outlaws (= people who have broken the law and must hide to avoid being caught). According to the legend, he was a fat friar (= member of a Christian religious community) who enjoyed eating and drinking.

'Friday (also ˌMan 'Friday) a character in Daniel *Defoe's novel *Robinson Crusoe. He becomes Crusoe's faithful servant after Crusoe saves him from being eaten by cannibals. The phrase *Man Friday* or *Girl Friday* is sometimes used to describe an assistant who does many different jobs in an office.

ˌBetty 'Friedan /'friːdən/ (1921–) a US writer and feminist (= a person who believes strongly that women should have the same rights and opportunities as men). She began the *National Organization for Women in 1966 and was its President until 1970. Her book *The Feminine Mystique* (1963) was an important influence on the *women's lib movement. Friedan later wrote *The Second Stage* (1981) and *The Fountain of Age* (1993).

ˌMilton 'Friedman /ˌmɪltən 'friːdmən/ (1912–) a US economist who received the 1976 *Nobel Prize for Economic Science. He supports monetarism, the belief that a nation's economy is mostly affected by the control of the supply of money by its government. Friedman advised Presidents *Nixon and *Reagan. He wrote *Capitalism and Freedom* (1962) and *Free to Choose* (1980), and taught at the University of Chicago from 1946 to 1977.

> 66 There's no such thing as a free lunch. 99
> Milton Friedman

'Friendly So,ciety (*also* **Provident Society**) (*BrE*) (*AmE* **benefit society**) *n* an association whose members regularly pay small amounts of money so that they can be cared for when they are ill or old. Friendly Societies first became common in Britain in the 18th century, and there are still several thousand of them in Britain and the US which operate as non-profit savings associations.

Friends a popular US television comedy series (1994–2004) about six close friends in New York. The characters are Monica, Rachel, Phoebe, Chandler, Ross and Joey. The stories are about the joys and problems of love, work and friendships.

> 66 How you doin'? 99
> Joey in *Friends*

'Friends' 'Meeting House (*also* **meeting house**) *n* a building where *Quakers have their religious meetings. Many Friends' Meeting Houses are also used for other functions such as public talks.

the ,Friends of the 'Earth an international *pressure group which began in the US in 1969 and aims to persuade people, companies and governments to do less damage to the environment. It has many members in 70 countries, and organizes a wide range of activities, from international campaigns to protect tropical forests to local communities' demands for clean water.

,Friends Reu'nited /,ri:ju:'naɪtɪd/ a UK company set up in 1999 which provides a website to help people find out about and contact old school friends. People can add their name and some details about their life to the website under the name of the school they attended as a child and they can look at the information of other people and contact them by email through the website. Millions of people use the service to find not only school friends but also family members, colleagues, etc.

Frigidaire™ /,frɪdʒɪ'deə(r)/ *n* a US make of refrigerator. There are also Frigidaire washing machines, dishwashers and other electrical household products.

the Fringe /frɪndʒ/ the performances at the *Edinburgh Festival that are not part of the official programme. These performances are usually more experimental than the official events, and are usually organized by small groups of people who are not well known, though some become famous after performing at the Fringe. See also BEYOND THE FRINGE.

E,lisabeth 'Frink /'frɪŋk/ (1930–93) an English artist, well known for her sculptures in bronze, especially of the male figure and of birds and horses. She was made a *dame(2) in 1982.

,Frito-'Lay™ /,fri:təʊ leɪ; *AmE* ,fri:toʊ/ a US company, owned by PepsiCo, that makes a range of small potato and corn food products. They include Fritos, Doritos, Ruffles and Lay's.

From ,Here to E'ternity a novel (1951) by the US author James Jones (1921–77) about army life in *Pearl Harbor before the Japanese attack. It was made into a 1953 film which won *Oscars for Best Picture, Best Director (Fred *Zinnemann), Best Supporting Actress (Donna Reed) and Best Supporting Actor (Frank *Sinatra). The film is remembered especially because of a scene in which two of its other stars, Deborah Kerr and Burt *Lancaster, make love in the waves on a beach. This was regarded as rather shocking at the time.

'frontiersman /'frʌntɪəzmən/ *n* (*pl* **frontiersmen**) a man who enters wild, unknown land or settles on the edge of it. In America, such people moved west in the 18th and 19th centuries and helped to increase the size of the United States. Famous frontiersmen include Davy *Crockett, Daniel *Boone, Kit *Carson and *Buffalo Bill.

,David 'Frost¹ /'frɒst; *AmE* 'frɑːst/ (1939–) an English television presenter. He first became famous during the 1960s when he presented the comedy news programme *That Was The Week That Was. Since the 1960s he has had great success as a television journalist on both British and US television. His Sunday morning interview programme *Breakfast with Frost* has been on British television since 1992. He was made a *knight in 1993.

,Robert 'Frost² /'frɒst; *AmE* 'frɑːst/ (1874–1963) a US poet who won four *Pulitzer Prizes. He is best known for his poems about the countryside. From 1912 to 1915 Frost lived in England where he wrote *A Boy's Will* (1913). He then settled in the US state of *New Hampshire and wrote about *New England. His books of poetry include *A Witness Tree* (1942) and *In the Clearing* (1962). His best-known poems are *Mending Wall* and *Stopping by Woods on a Snowy Evening*. At the age of 87, Frost read his poem *A Gift Outright* at the 1962 inauguration of John F *Kennedy (= the ceremony at which he was formally made President).

> 66 Two roads diverged in a wood, and I –
> I took the one less travelled by,
> And that has made all the difference. 99
> Robert Frost *The Road Not Taken*

'Frosties™ /'frɒstiz; *AmE* 'frɑːstiz/ a well-known breakfast food, made by *Kellogg's and called Frosted Flakes in the US. It consists of small flat pieces of corn covered in sugar, and is eaten with milk. Its most famous advertising character is Tony the Tiger, who says, 'They're Gr-r-r-eat!'.

FRS /,ef ɑːr 'es/ **1** ⇨ FEDERAL RESERVE SYSTEM. **2** ⇨ FELLOW OF THE ROYAL SOCIETY.

,Fruit and 'Nut *n* [U] a popular British chocolate bar containing raisins and nuts, made by *Cadbury Schweppes: *Do you want a piece of Fruit and Nut?*

'fruit gum *n* [usually pl] (*BrE*) a small round British sweet/candy like a hard piece of jelly. Fruit gums are usually sold in a roll and have different fruit colours and flavours. They are especially popular with children. Many people remember the phrase used in advertisements, 'Don't forget the fruit gums, mum!'.

,Fruit of the 'Loom™ a US company that makes mainly cotton sports clothes and underwear.

,C B 'Fry¹ /'fraɪ/ (Charles Burgess Fry 1872–1956) one of the greatest English sportsmen of all time. He represented England in international *cricket, *football and athletics. He held the world record for the long jump for 21 years, and was the first person in the history of cricket to score 100 runs (= points) six times in a row.

,Christopher 'Fry² /'fraɪ/ (1907–) an English writer of plays in a form of poetry that is full of humour and rich language. They include *The Lady's Not For Burning* (1948) and *Venus Observed* (1950).

E,lizabeth 'Fry³ /'fraɪ/ (1780–1845) an English *Quaker who led many campaigns to improve the conditions of people in prison, especially women.

,Stephen 'Fry[4] /'fraɪ/ (1957–) an English actor and writer who wrote and appeared in several British comedy television programmes in the 1980s and 1990s, often with Hugh Laurie as his partner. They became famous in 1989 with their own *BBC comedy series, *A Bit of Fry and Laurie*. Fry has also acted in films and written several novels, including *The Liar* (1991) and he directed the film *Bright Young Things* (2003), an adaptation of Evelyn *Waugh's novel *Vile Bodies*.

the FSA /,ef es 'eɪ/ **1** ⇨ FINANCIAL SERVICES AUTHORITY.
2 ⇨ FOOD STANDARDS AGENCY.

The FT /ef ti:/ ⇨ FINANCIAL TIMES.

the FTC /,ef ti: 'si:/ (*in full* **the Federal Trade Commission**) an independent US government organization created in 1914 to protect free competition in business. It uses *antitrust legislation to prevent monopolies (= companies which are so large that no others can compete with them). It investigates unfair business practices and has the legal power to stop them and to take companies to a court of law. The FTC also controls labels on products and tries to stop false advertisements. Compare OFFICE OF FAIR TRADING.

FTSE 100-Share Index /,ef ti: es 'i: wʌn 'hʌndrəd 'ʃeər ,ɪndeks/ ⇨ FOOTSIE.

The 'Fugitive /ˈ a popular US television series (1963–7) on *ABC which told the story of an innocent man, played by David Janssen, who is condemned to death for the murder of his wife, but escapes to find the person who killed her. The final show, in which the criminal is found, had the largest television audience in the 1960s. There was a film version in 1993, with Harrison *Ford in the main part.

,Francis Fuku'yama /,frɑːnsɪs fukuˈjɑːmə; *AmE* ˌfrænsɪs fukuˈjæmə/ (1955–) a US political economist who is best known for his controversial book, *The End of History and The Last Man* (1992).

> 66 What we may be witnessing is not just the end of the Cold War but the end of history as such. 99
> Francis Fukuyama

'Fulbright ,scholarship /'fʊlbraɪt/ *n* any of a number of US scholarships (= awards of money for study) given for exchanges between US and foreign universities and colleges. Those who receive them are called **Fulbright scholars** and include students and teachers. The programme was established by the Fulbright Act (1946) of Senator J William Fulbright (1905–95), and it first used money from the sale of old US military equipment. More than 250 000 scholarships had been awarded by 2004.

'Fulham /'fʊləm/ **1** a district of west London on the north bank of the *Thames, west of *Chelsea, consisting mainly of houses. Since the 1980s it has been a fashionable area to live in.
2 a football club whose ground is in the district of Fulham.

,Fulham 'Palace /,fʊləm/ a large and grand house in *Fulham(1), London, built in the 16th century. It is the official home of the *Bishop of London.

'R ,Buckminster 'Fuller /'ɑː ˌbʌkmɪnstə 'fʊlə(r); *AmE* 'ɑːr ˌbʌkmɪnstər 'fʊlər/ (Richard Buckminster Fuller 1895–1983) a US engineer and inventor of devices and buildings that made the most efficient use of materials. His best-known inventions include the geodesic dome and the Dymaxion House. Fuller also created the idea of 'Spaceship Earth' which imagines all people on earth as travellers together through space. He was awarded the *Presidential Medal of Freedom in 1983.

The ,Full 'Monty /'mɒnti; *AmE* 'mɑːnti/ a very successful British film (1997) about a group of unemployed men from *Sheffield in the north of England who get jobs as strippers (= performers who take their clothes off in front of an audience as a form of entertainment) because they cannot find any other work. It won an *Oscar for its music and a musical of the same name opened on *Broadway in 2000. *The full monty* is an informal phrase in British English meaning 'absolutely everything'.

Dr ,Fu Man'chu /,fu: mæn'tʃuː/ the main character in a series of novels by the British crime writer Sax Rohmer (c. 1883–1959), some of which were made into films in the 1930s and the 1960s. Dr Fu Manchu is an extremely clever criminal with a long moustache with ends that hang down, and long hair tied together at the back. In the films he was shown as Chinese.

,funda'mentalism /,fʌndə'mentəlɪzəm/ *n* [U] the belief, especially among some Protestant Christian groups in the US South and Midwest, that all statements in the Bible are true. **Fundamentalists** do not accept the theory of evolution. In recent years, the political Moral Majority led by Jerry *Falwell was based on fundamentalism. Compare EVANGELICAL, PENTECOSTALIST. See also SCOPES TRIAL.

funk ⇨ JAZZ FUNK.

the 'funnies /'fʌniz/ (*also* **the 'funny ,papers**, **the 'funny ,pages**, **the 'comics**) *n* [pl] (*AmE*) the section of a newspaper containing *comic strips. US Sunday newspapers print colour sections with longer comic strips. Most are funny, like *Peanuts*, but some tell adventure or crime stories, like *Dick Tracy*. The funnies have been a US tradition since the early 20th century.

the 'Furry Dance /'fɜːri/ a traditional event that takes place in May each year in Helston, a small town in *Cornwall, England. People dance through the streets and into some of the houses.

▶ further education

Further education in Britain means education after *GCSE and *GNVQ exams taken around the age of 16. It includes courses of study leading to *A levels which students take at their school or **sixth-form college**. Some students go straight to a *college of further education which offers a wider range of full- and part-time courses. Further education also includes training for professional qualifications in nursing, accountancy and management, and in fields such as art and music. The term *higher education* is used in Britain and the US to refer to degree courses at universities.

In the US *further education* usually means any other education after secondary school. It can mean study at college, or any study towards a professional qualification, and it can have a meaning similar to that of *adult education or **continuing education**, i.e. something that people do after completing their main education, often for personal interest and satisfaction.

Many students in Britain take *vocational training courses in fields such as building, engineering, hairdressing or secretarial skills. Colleges of further education offer courses leading to *NVQs and other certificates and diplomas. **Work-related courses** are designed with advice from industry, with the aim of producing students who will have the skills employers require. On longer courses students may do **placements** (*AmE* **internships**) (= periods of work) lasting several months with companies. On other courses, called **sandwich courses**, students divide their time between periods of paid work and periods of study. A common arrangement is for students to get **day release** from their work to attend college one or two days a week over several years. Some students do a formal **apprenticeship**, learning their skills on the job and attending college part-time.

The British government is keen to persuade more young people to remain in education as long as possible in order to build up a more highly skilled, better educated workforce. About 3.9 million people take part-time further education courses, while another 1.1 million are full-time students.

'**fusion** *n* [U] **1** a type of music that is a mixture of different styles, especially *rock and *jazz. It was popular in the 1970s when groups such as Weather Report and jazz musicians such as Miles *Davis made several fusion records.
2 cooking that is a mixture of European and Asian styles.

G g

,Clark 'Gable /'geɪbl/ (1901–60) a US film actor who was especially famous in the 1930s and 1940s. He was sometimes referred to as the 'King of Hollywood'. His best-known role was as Rhett *Butler in *Gone with the Wind. Gable won an *Oscar for his part in the comedy *It Happened One Night, and his other films included *Mutiny on the Bounty (1935) and The Misfits (1960) with Marilyn *Monroe.

,Peter 'Gabriel /'geɪbriəl/ (1950–) an English pop singer and writer. In the early 1970s he sang with the *rock group Genesis, but in 1975 he left the group to record and perform alone. In the 1980s he became interested in music from other cultures and established *WOMAD (World of Music, Arts and Dance).

the ,Gadsden 'Purchase /,gædzdən/ an area in the south-west US that was bought from Mexico for $10 million in 1853. It was 29 640 square miles/76 768 square kilometres and became part of the later states of *Arizona and *New Mexico. The agreement to buy the land was made by James Gadsden (1788–1858), the US ambassador in Mexico.

'Gaelic n [U] the *Celtic languages spoken in Ireland and Scotland. In Scotland Scottish Gaelic is spoken by around 58 000 people (1.2 per cent of the population), mainly in the *Highlands and on the west coast. Many more people speak Irish (also called Irish Gaelic), which is taught in schools in Ireland as one of the country's two official languages.

,Gaelic 'football n [U] a sport played by two teams of 15 players each. They play with a round ball that can be kicked, punched or bounced, but not carried. Points are scored either by kicking the ball into a net or by kicking it over the net between two tall posts. It is a popular game in Ireland, where it developed, and in some American cities.

the 'Gaiety Girls n [pl] the women who sang and danced in musical comedies at the Gaiety Theatre in London, England, in the 1890s. They were well known for their beauty, and many of them married members of the *peerage.

,Thomas 'Gainsborough /'geɪnzbrə/ (1727–88) an English artist. He was influenced by Dutch artists such as Rubens and Van Dyck, and became famous for his landscapes (= pictures of the countryside) and his portraits, usually of members of the *aristocracy. He often combined both skills and painted his portraits with outdoor country backgrounds, representing the effects of light on people's clothes or on trees, etc. His best-known paintings are probably The *Blue Boy and Mr and Mrs Andrews.

'Galahad /'gæləhæd/ (also Sir Galahad) one of the *knights of King *Arthur's *Round Table(1). According to the legend he was the most innocent and morally good of all the knights, and because of this he succeeded in finding the *Holy Grail. Sometimes people are humorously called Sir Galahad if they have been very kind or polite to somebody: He did his Sir Galahad act and helped her with her luggage.

'Galaxy™ /'gæləksi/ n [C, U] a popular British make of chocolate bar.

'John 'Kenneth Gal'braith /gæl'breɪθ/ (1908–) a US economist, born in Canada. He advised President John F *Kennedy and was the US ambassador in India (1961–63). Galbraith has said that governments should spend more to help poor and unemployed people. He has criticized the power of international companies and the desire for continuous economic growth. His books include The Affluent Society (1958), The Anatomy of Power (1983) and A Short History of Financial Euphoria (1990).

,John Galli'ano /gæli'ɑːnəʊ; AmE gæli'ɑːnoʊ/ (1961–) a British fashion designer, born in *Gibraltar. He has been successful in both Britain and France.

Gal'lipoli /gə'lɪpəli/ a peninsula (= an area of land almost surrounded by water) in Turkey, which the armed forces of the *Allies tried to capture during *World War I. The Allies, including many soldiers from Australia and New Zealand, landed at Gallipoli but failed to capture the peninsula. More than 200 000 Allied soldiers died there.

,George 'Galloway /'gæləweɪ/ (1954–) a British politician who became the *Member of Parliament for an area of *Glasgow in Scotland in 1992. He was a member of the *Labour Party but was forced to leave in 2003 because of his strong views against the war in Iraq. He formed a new political party, *Respect - The Unity Coalition in 2004.

'Gallup poll™ /'gæləp/ n a way of estimating the public opinion in a country by selecting a group of people that represents the whole country and asking them questions. Gallup polls are often used in predicting the results of elections. They are named after G H Gallup, the US statistician (= expert on analysing information from numbers) who invented them. Compare MORI.

,John 'Galsworthy /'gɔːlzwɜːði; AmE 'gɔːlzwɜːrði/ (1867–1933) an English writer of novels and plays. He wrote several successful plays that examine social and moral themes, including Strife (1909), about a strike, and Justice (1910), a criticism of the prison system, but he is best known for his series of novels The *Forsyte Saga. He was given the *Nobel Prize for literature in 1932.

,James 'Galway¹ /'gɔːlweɪ/ (1939–) a Northern Irish musician who plays the flute. As well as playing and recording classical music with some of the world's leading orchestras, he performs as a soloist and played for the soundtrack of the *Lord of the Rings films. He was made a *knight in 2001.

'Gambia /'gæmbiə/ (also the Gambia) a country in West Africa where the official language is English. It is a long narrow country, on each bank of the Gambia river, surrounded by Senegal. Gambia was formed when Britain and France both had empires in the region, and could not agree on who should own this land. In the 19th century Britain took the banks of the river, and France the rest of the country. Gambia became independent in 1965, and is a member of the *Commonwealth. It now has an important tourist industry and many British people go there on holiday/vacation, especially in the winter. The capital city is Banjul.
▶ Gambian adj, n.

,Michael 'Gambon /'gæmbən/ (1940–) an English actor, born in Ireland. He has acted in many successful plays and films, but is best known for playing the main character in The Singing Detective (1986), a British television series by Dennis *Potter, and Dumbledore in the third *Harry Potter film (2004). Gambon was made a *knight in 1998.

'Game Boy™ *n* an electronic device with a small computer screen that can be held in the hand. It is used for playing computer games with special cartriges (= sealed cases) that fit it. Game Boys are especially popular with children.

the 'Gaming Board for ,Great 'Britain the government organization that controls gambling in Britain. People or companies who want to run casinos (= gambling clubs), lotteries, *bingo or gambling machines must have a licence from the Gaming Board. Plans for changes to the laws on gambling announced by the Government in 2003 include the replacement of the Gaming Board by a new Gambling Commission.

g and t /,dʒiː ən 'tiː/ *n* (*informal*) an abbreviation of gin and tonic, a popular alcoholic drink. In Britain, many people think of it as a drink for older *middle-class people.

▶ **gangs**

In US history gangs are often associated with the Wild West, the western part of the US during the period when people were beginning to move there. People like Jesse *James became famous for leading gangs which committed crimes like robbing banks. People involved in organized crime, particularly during the 1920s and 1930s, were called **gangsters**. The word *gang* is no longer used to refer to the group known as the *Mafia, though members of the Mafia are often involved in **gangland killings**. Gangs involved in organized criminal activity were less of a problem in Britain, though in the 1960s the *Kray twins ran a gang in the *East End of London and **triads**, gangs similar to the Mafia, operate in some Chinese communities in Britain. Criminal gangs involved in **human trafficking**, bringing people to the UK illegally and making them work for very little pay are an increasing problem.

In Britain and the US *gang* now usually means a **street gang**, a group of young people in an **inner city** area. Gangs have their own parts of the city and keep other gangs out of them. They may show which parts of the city they control by **tagging**, spraying paint in particular designs on the walls in the area. People who belong to such gangs are called **gang members**. Crimes commonly associated with street gangs include selling *drugs and, in the US, **drive-by shootings**, when they shoot a member of another gang while driving past, often injuring other people at the same time. In Britain gun crime related to rival gangs is increasing. In Britain in the 1960s and 1970s gangs of **skinheads** caused fear among ethnic minority groups, and in recent years Asian and West Indian gangs have been established in places such as Birmingham and Manchester. Many of these gangs were formed originally to defend the local community, but then became involved in criminal activity. There are also football gangs, groups of supporters who attack rival fans at big matches.

The Gap /ɡæp/ any of a group of fashionable US clothes shops. The first was opened in *San Francisco in 1969 and sold only *jeans. The company later started developing its own range of clothes and opened shops in several other countries, including Britain, where they are called simply Gap.

'garage *n* [U] a type of dance music with strong, fast rhythms that became popular in nightclubs in America and Britain in the 1990s.

'garage sale *n* (*especially AmE*) a sale of family possessions that are old or no longer wanted, usually held in or in front of the garage of a private house. People often have a garage sale before they move to a new house.

,Greta 'Garbo /,ɡretə 'ɡɑːbəʊ; *AmE* 'ɡɑːrboʊ/ (1905–90) a Swedish actor who moved to the US in 1925. Her beauty and acting skills made her one of the first famous *Hollywood stars, in silent as well as talking films. She is well known for avoiding the public and for retiring in 1941 to live a life alone in New York. Her films include *Queen Christina* (1933) and *Anna Karenina* (1935).

> 66 I want to be alone. 99
> Greta Garbo

,garden 'city *n* one of several British towns built in the first half of the 20th century, including **Letchworth** and **Welwyn Garden City**. They were planned to encourage ordinary people to move from crowded cities and to give them a better standard of living, and consist of simple, modern houses, shops and businesses surrounded by gardens, trees and parks. The garden city movement was started by **Sir Ebenezer Howard** and was followed by the idea of *new towns in the second half of the 20th century.

,Gardeners' 'Question Time a popular British radio programme, broadcast once a week on *BBC *Radio 4 since 1947. It is recorded in different towns around the country, where local people ask a group of experts for advice about looking after their gardens.

,Gardeners' 'World a British television programme, broadcast on *BBC Two since 1968. It is filmed in a real garden, and usually gives advice on how to grow different types of flowers and plants.

the ,garden of 'England a popular name for *Kent, a county in south-east England. Many different types of fruit and vegetables are grown there and in the past it was famous for the number of fruit trees.

▶ **gardens and yards**

Most British people prefer to live in a house rather than a flat and one of the reasons for this is that houses usually have gardens. The garden is surrounded by a fence or hedge and is a place where people can be outside and yet private.

If a house has a front and back garden, the front is likely to be formal and decorative, with a **lawn** (= an area of grass) or fancy paving and **flower borders**. The back garden usually also has a lawn and **flower beds**, and sometimes a vegetable plot or fruit trees. There is often a **bird table** (= a raised platform on which food is put for birds) and a **shed** in which garden tools are kept.

Many British people spend quite a lot of money on their gardens and even the smallest may contain a variety of flowers and shrubs. In spring some people fix **window boxes** containing bulbs or other plants on their window sills, or attach a **hanging basket** on the wall near the front door.

Some houses have only a very small paved back garden, called a **patio**. People often decorate it with plants in **tubs**, or in pots or baskets fixed to the wall and many see the garden as an extension of their home.

In the US the area of grass in front of and behind most houses is called a **yard**. The word *garden* is used only for the areas where flowers and vegetables grow. Yards usually consist of a lawn and trees, flowers and bushes. Many backyards have swings, slides or climbing frames for children. There may also be a patio or a **deck** (= a wooden platform attached to the house) where chairs and tables are kept in the summer. Garden decorations include **bird feeders** (= containers of food for birds) and lamps so that people can use the yard after dark.

G

During warm weather, Americans spend a lot of time in their yards, especially the backyard. Children play there and often have small pools or **sand boxes**. People like to eat outside and prepare meals on a **barbecue**.

For British many people gardening is a *hobby and they take great pride in their gardens. Some towns and villages have competitions for the best-kept small garden. Keen gardeners may have a **greenhouse** in which to grow more delicate plants. People with a small garden, or no garden at all, can rent a piece of land, called an *allotment, from the local council. Most people grow vegetables on their allotments.

There are **garden centres** near most towns, selling everything a gardener might need, from flowerpots to fish ponds as well as a huge range of plants.

Keen gardeners can join a local **horticultural society** and take part in annual competitions and shows. National events such as the *Royal Horticultural Society Show and the *Chelsea Flower Show in London attract many visitors. Thousands more people listen to radio shows such as *Gardeners' Question Time, in which a panel of experts offer solutions to gardening problems. On television, *Gardeners' World is equally popular.

Although a smaller proportion of Americans enjoy gardening, it is increasingly popular and almost half of the retired population garden. People work to make the yard a pleasant place to sit. Modern garden design, with the garden as an extension of the living space in the house, was developed in California.

The British interest in gardening affects the appearance of whole towns. Public parks and traffic roundabouts often have bright displays of flowers in summer and public buildings have window boxes and hanging baskets. Towns and villages enter for the annual *Britain in Bloom* competition.

At *weekends Many British people like to visit famous gardens, such as that at Stowe near Banbury, developed by William *Kent and 'Capability' *Brown in the 18th century. Other popular attractions include Vita *Sackville-West's gardens at Sissinghurst, and the garden and **glasshouses** of the Royal Botanic Gardens at *Kew. Every summer the National Gardens Scheme publishes a booklet listing private gardens belonging to enthusiastic gardeners which are open to the public on a particular day. Visitors like to look around and get ideas for their own gardens.

In the US parks and other public green spaces usually have paths for people to walk along, large areas of grass where children can play, and trees and flowers. There are some formal gardens in the US, and, as in Britain, many universities have botanical gardens which are used for research and teaching. Famous American gardens include Longwood in *Pennsylvania and the Huntington Botanical Gardens in *California.

'John 'Eliot 'Gardiner /'eliət 'gɑːdnə(r); AmE 'gɑːrdnər/ (1943–) an English conductor. He is best known for his performances of early music. He formed the Monteverdi Choir in 1968, the English Baroque Soloists in 1978 and the ORR (Orchestre Révolutionnaire et Romantique) in 1990. He was made a *knight in 1998.

¸Ava 'Gardner¹ /ˌeɪvə 'gɑːdnə(r); AmE 'gɑːrdnər/ (1922–90) a US film actor who was once called 'the most beautiful woman in the world'. She was especially successful in the 1950s and 1960s. Her films included *Mogambo* (1953), *Bhowani Junction* (1956), *On The Beach* (1959) and *The Night of the Iguana* (1964).

'Erle 'Stanley 'Gardner² /'ɜːl, 'gɑːdnə(r); AmE 'ɜːrl, 'gɑːrdnər/ (1889–1970) a US author of over 140 crime novels and short stories. His best-known character was Perry *Mason but he also wrote a series of novels about District Attorney Doug Selby.

'Garfield™¹ /'gɑːfiːld; AmE 'gɑːrfiːld/ a character in humorous cartoons by Jim Davis that appear in more than 2000 newspapers. Garfield is a cat that eats lasagne (= a type of pasta). There was a film *Garfield* in 2004 and there have also been many cartoon film versions.

¸James A 'Garfield² /'gɑːfiːld; AmE 'gɑːrfiːld/ (James Abram Garfield 1831–81) the 20th US *President, and a member of the *Republican Party. He had been a US Army general in the *Civil War. Four months after becoming President he was shot by a disappointed person who had wanted a government job.

¸Art 'Garfunkel /ˌɑːt 'gɑːfʌŋkl; AmE ˌɑːrt 'gɑːrfʌŋkl/ ⇨ SIMON AND GARFUNKEL.

¸Gari'baldi /ˌgærɪ'bɔːldi/ (also **Garibaldi biscuit**) n (BrE) a type of flat dry biscuit containing currants (= dried grapes). The humorous name for Garibaldis is 'squashed fly biscuits'.

G

¸Judy 'Garland /'gɑːlənd; AmE 'gɑːrlənd/ (1922–69) a US singer and actor. She began her acting career as a child actor at *MGM. She became famous as Dorothy in *The Wizard of Oz* (1939), in which she sang her best-known song, *Somewhere Over the Rainbow*. Her other films include *Meet Me in St Louis* (1944), *A Star is Born* (1954) and *Judgment at Nuremberg* (1961). Garland had problems with drugs, and she died accidentally after taking too many. The singer and actor Liza *Minnelli is her daughter.

¸Alf 'Garnett /'gɑːnɪt; AmE 'gɑːrnɪt/ a character played by the actor Warren Mitchell in the *BBC television series *Till Death Us Do Part* (1966–74). He is an *East Ender with extreme right-wing opinions. He loves the *royal family and hates foreigners, black people and socialists, especially his son-in-law.

¸Pat 'Garrett /'gærət/ (1850–1908) a sheriff (= law officer) in the American *Wild West, who arrested his former friend, the criminal *Billy the Kid, in 1880. When he escaped, Garrett chased him for months and finally shot him at Fort Sumter, *New Mexico, on 4 July 1881.

¸David 'Garrick /'gærɪk/ (1717–79) an English actor. He changed the way plays were performed in Britain by introducing a more natural style of acting. His versions of Shakespeare's characters made Shakespeare popular again in the 18th century, and made Garrick the most famous actor of the period. He was also a theatre manager, and introduced many improvements to the way plays were shown.

the 'Garrick Club /'gærɪk/ a club in Garrick Street in central London, England. It was established in 1831 as a club for 'actors and men of refinement', and named after David *Garrick. Today its members are mainly actors, journalists and lawyers. In 1992 they voted to continue the ban on women as members.

¸Marcus 'Garvey /ˌmɑːkəs 'gɑːvi; AmE ˌmɑːrkəs 'gɑːrvi/ (1887–1940) a US leader of the campaign for *African-American rights, born in Jamaica. After moving to the US in 1916 he began the Universal Negro Improvement Association. He also began a 'Back to Africa' campaign to encourage African Americans to move to Africa and establish a new nation there. In 1925 Garvey was sent to prison for illegal use of money. He was sent back to Jamaica and finally settled in Britain.

¸Paul 'Gascoigne /'gæskɔɪn/ (also informal **Gazza**) (1967–) an English football player. In the 1980s and 1990s he played for Newcastle United, *Tottenham Hotspur, Glasgow *Rangers, the Italian club Lazio, and England. At his best he was regarded as one of the most skilful English players of his time.

¸Mrs 'Gaskell /'gæskl/ (Elizabeth Gaskell 1810–65) an English writer of novels. Most of these are set in the north-west of England, including *Cranford* (1853), which is set in Knutsford, the town near *Manchester where she lived, and *Mary Barton* (1848), which is about the social conditions of *working-class people in Manchester. She also wrote a biography of her friend Charlotte *Brontë, published in 1857.

,**Bill 'Gates** /'geɪts/ (1955–) the US businessman who, with Paul Allen, started the *Microsoft Corporation when he was only 19. He is thought to be the richest person in the world. In 2000 Gates and his wife started the Bill and Melinda Gates Foundation which has about $27 million and gives money to educational and health projects.

'Gatorade™ /'geɪtəreɪd/ a US drink intended for people who play a lot of sport. It replaces liquids in the body rapidly and adds carbohydrates. It was invented in 1965 at the University of Florida for its football team, who are called the Gators. It is now produced by *PepsiCo.

'Gatwick /'gætwɪk/ a major international airport, 27 miles/43kilometres south of London. It is Britain's second largest airport. Compare HEATHROW.

'gaudy /'gɔːdi/ *n* the name used in some colleges at the universities of *Oxford and *Cambridge for the special dinner for former students that takes place each year.

Sir **'Gawain and the ,Green 'Knight** /'gɑːweɪn/ a long English poem written in the 14th century by an unknown author. It is about Sir Gawain, a *knight at the court of King *Arthur, who is told to perform various tasks by the mysterious Green Knight as a test of his faith. The poem is admired for its fine language and is regarded as one of the greatest poems of the period. Some people think it was written to celebrate the *Order of the Garter. See also BIRTWISTLE.

,**John 'Gay** /'geɪ/ (1685–1732) an English writer of poems and plays. Most of his work was satirical, and his greatest success, *The *Beggar's Opera*, was banned from British theatres. He was a friend of Alexander *Pope and wrote the words for *Handel's *Acis and Galatea*.

,**Marvin 'Gaye** /,mɑːvɪn 'geɪ; AmE ,mɑːrvɪn/ (1939–84) a US singer and writer of *soul music who was one of the stars of the *Motown(2) group. His best-known songs include *How Sweet It Is* (1964), *Ain't that Peculiar* (1965) and *I Heard It Through the Grapevine* (1968). Gaye was killed when his father shot him during an argument.

the ,Gay 'Gordons /'gɔːdnz; AmE 'gɔːrdnz/ *n* [sing] a lively traditional Scottish dance for several couples.

,**Gay 'Times** Britain's largest magazine for homosexuals, published once a month since 1984. It used to be called *Gay News*, but changed its name when *Gay News* went bankrupt after losing a case in a court of law against Mary *Whitehouse, who found some of the writing offensive.

'Gazza /'gæzə/ ⇨ GASCOIGNE.

GB plate /,dʒiː 'biː/ *n* a white sign with the letters GB on it in black, attached to the back of a car to show that the car is from Great Britain. Many British people attach GB plates to their cars when they take them to other countries, although they are not required by law in the *European Union.

GCHQ /,dʒiː siː eɪtʃ 'kjuː/ (*in full* **Government Communications Headquarters**) a British government centre in *Cheltenham, England, responsible to the *Foreign Secretary. It was set up after *World War II to gather information that is important for national security and to protect government communications.

GCSE /,dʒiː siː es 'iː/ (*in full* **General Certificate of Secondary Education**) *n* (in England, Wales and Northern Ireland) a school examination in any one of several subjects. Most students take GCSEs at the end of

their fifth year of secondary school, around the age of 16. They are taken by students of all abilities, but those who want to continue studying for *A levels need to pass a certain number of GCSEs at a particular level.

GE /,dʒiː 'iː/ ⇨ GENERAL ELECTRIC.

the 'Geffrye Mu,seum /'dʒefri/ a museum of furniture in east London, England. Most of the museum consists of a series of rooms, each one showing what an ordinary English home would look like in various periods between 1600 and the present day.

,**Lou 'Gehrig** /'geriɡ/ (1903–41) a famous US *baseball player for the New York Yankees team. Gehrig was called 'the iron man' because he once played 2130 games in a row, a record that was not broken until 56 years later. He died of a disease of the muscles which is now often called **Lou Gehrig's disease**. See also RUTH.

the G8 /,dʒiː 'eɪt/ (*in full* **the Group of Eight**) eight of the richest industrial countries in the world: Britain, Canada, France, Germany, Italy, Japan, Russia and the US. Politicians from these countries have regular meetings, usually to discuss economic problems and policies. Before Russia joined the group in 1998 it was know as the **G7** ('Group of Seven'):: *The Prime Minister is urging the heads of the other G8 countries to come to an agreement.*

,**Bob 'Geldof** /'geldɒf; AmE 'geldɔːf/ (1951–) an Irish pop singer who was the singer of the *punk(1) group the Boomtown Rats in the 1970s. In 1984 he heard about the lack of food in Ethiopia and brought together some of Britain's most famous pop stars to form a group called *Band Aid. Their record, *Do They Know It's Christmas?*, raised millions of pounds for Ethiopia. In 1985 even more money was raised when Geldof organized the *Live Aid concerts. He was made an honorary *knight by the British government in 1986.

the 'Gemini ,program a series of US space flights (1963–66) with two men in each. During the Gemini flights astronauts made space 'walks' and brought two spacecraft together in space for the first time. This was a preparation for the *Apollo program, and one of the Gemini astronauts was Neil *Armstrong, the first man on the moon.

▶ **General American English**

General American English (GAE) is a term for the standard English of the US, though few Americans have heard of the name. GAE includes grammar and vocabulary as well as pronunciation. It can be compared in some respects to standard British English spoken with an RP (*Received Pronunciation) accent. GAE can be used as a standard of comparison for examining other **dialects** and **accents**, though it does not imply that they are inferior or wrong.

GAE is especially common in the Midwestern part of the US, although speakers of GAE can be found all over the country. It is also the form of American English that it is often heard on news programmes on national television. An important difference between GAE and standard English spoken with an RP accent is that GAE is connected more closely with certain geographical regions of the US than with a particular social class.

Sometimes, the term *General American* is used to refer only to a form of American pronunciation that does not have a strong regional accent.

the ,General As'sembly the main body of the *United Nations. It includes representatives of all the member nations of the UN, who discuss the problems of the world, including peace, human rights and health. They also give approval to the UN *budget. Each nation has one vote, and there must be a two-thirds approval on all important issues before any action can be taken.

G

the 'General As'sembly of the 'Church of 'Scotland /'skɒtlənd; AmE 'skɑtlənd/ the group of
people governing the *Church of Scotland. It consists of ministers (= priests) and other officials who are elected by members of the Church. It is responsible for important decisions affecting the Church.

ˌGeneral E'lectric (abbr GE) a US company that pro-
duces electrical products and aircraft engines, and owns *NBC and *Universal. It is the largest company in the world and was formed in 1892 when Thomas *Edison's company, Edison General Electric, joined with Thomson-Houston Electric. It is the only one of the 12 original companies on the *Dow-Jones Industrial Average that still remains. It broadcast the first dramatic play on television in 1928, and Ronald *Reagan presented The General Electric Theater on television in the 1950s.

the ˌGeneral E'lectric ˌCompany ⇨ MARCONI.

ˌGeneral 'Hospital a popular US television *soap
opera on *ABC, set in a hospital. It began in 1963 and has won four *Emmy awards as the Best Daytime Drama Series (1981, 1984, 1994 and 1996).

the 'General 'Medical 'Council (abbr the GMC) a
professional organization in Britain, started in 1858, which keeps a register (= an official list of names) of qualified doctors. It encourages good standards in medicine and deals with doctors who have not behaved in a professional way. If necessary, it can remove a doctor from the register so that they cannot continue to work as a doctor.

ˌGeneral 'Motors (abbr GM) the US car company that
is the largest in the world, based in *Detroit. It produces the *Chevrolet, Oldsmobile, *Cadillac, *Buick, *Pontiac, Saab, Hummer and Daewoo brands and owns a share in Fiat and Suzuki. GM brands in Europe also include Opel and Vauxhall. The company was established in 1908 by William Durant. It is often said that 'what is good for General Motors is good for the USA'.

'General 'National Vo'cational Qualifi'cation ⇨ GNVQ.

the ˌGeneral 'Post Office ⇨ GPO.

ˌgeneral prac'titioner ⇨ GP.

the ˌGeneral 'Strike a strike by workers in all of
Britain's important industries, including public transport, that took place in 1926. The coal miners were on strike because the owners of the mines wanted them to work for less money, and the *TUC advised all its members to go on strike in support of the miners. Over three million people joined the strike, which lasted for nine days until the TUC accepted a new offer for the miners. The miners did not accept the offer and stayed on strike for six months. The strike had a great effect on people's attitudes in Britain. Many people were happy to see that workers could act together to improve their conditions, while others were afraid that it could lead to a revolution.

the ˌGeneral 'Synod the group of people governing
the *Church of England. It consists of three levels: *bishops, clergy and laity (= members of the Church who are not priests). The *Archbishop of Canterbury and the *Archbishop of York are in charge of the Synod, which is responsible for important decisions affecting the Church, such as educational policy, choosing the clergy and the care of church buildings. It meets twice a year.

Generation X /'eks/ (informal Gen X) a generation of
people in North America born in the 1960s and 1970s, whose parents were born during the *Baby Boom, who are characterized as well educated, but who feel that they do not want to be part of modern society and are not interested in social status, jobs or money. The term was made popular by a book by Douglas Coupland Generation X: Tales from an Accelerated Culture (1991) and the attitudes of **Generation Xers** are seen in popular culture in people such as Kurt *Cobain and the films of Quentin *Tarantino.

'Genesis /'dʒenəsɪs/ a British pop group, formed in
1967, whose albums included Foxtrot (1972), Selling England by the Pound (1973), Duke (1980) and We Can't Dance (1991). Two of its members, Phil Collins and Peter *Gabriel, have also had successful careers outside the group.

geˌnetically 'modified (abbr GM) (of a plant) with
*genes that have been changed by science so that it grows in a different way, is stronger or can produce more food. Some companies, for example *Monsanto, are working on changing the structure of plants that are grown as food using new technology called **biotechnology** or **genetic engineering**. An example is changing the genes of a type of grain so that it will not be destroyed when farmers spray the crop with pesticides (= chemicals for killing insects which eat crops) or herbicides (= chemicals for killing plants). There has been a lot of discussion in the media about **GMOs** (genetically modified organisms). Some scientists, food companies and governments argue that it can help to feed the world's growing population, especially in poor countries. Others argue that genetically modified food may be harmful and that GM crops may affect other crops grown nearby. Public opposition has led some supermarkets in Britain not to sell food that contains genetically modified ingredients and EU governments have passed laws about labelling so that consumers can know whether the food they buy contains GM ingredients or not.

'gentleman n (pl gentlemen) 1 a formal or polite
way of referring to a man. A common way to begin a speech, for example, is 'Ladies and gentlemen, …':
There's a gentleman waiting to see you.
2 (old-fashioned) a man who is kind and polite and behaves well: He behaved like a perfect gentleman.
3 (in Britain, especially in the past) a man who belonged to the gentry, a social class of people who were wealthy and did not need to work.

ˌGentleman 'Jim ⇨ CORBETT.

ˌgentleman's 'gentleman n (old-fashioned) a rich
man's personal servant.

▶ gentlemen's clubs

The **gentlemen's club** is a British institution. Gentlemen's clubs are comfortable, private places with bars, a restaurant, a library and sometimes bedrooms. They attract as members businessmen, politicians and others from the *upper class and the *Establishment. Members use their club as a place to meet friends or take business contacts. Most are situated in London's *West End and many have large impressive buildings.

Membership is expensive and at most clubs is restricted to men, though the *Reform Club has had women members since the 1960s. Generally, women and other non-members are not allowed inside clubs except as guests of a member, and women are allowed only in certain rooms. Members must obey rules about dress and behaviour. People wanting to be members may have to wait a long time before they are admitted to the most popular clubs, and will only be allowed to join if an existing member **seconds** (= supports) them. Any member may object to membership being offered to a particular person by **blackballing** (= voting against) him.

Gentlemen's clubs developed in the mid 18th century. Men had previously met socially and to discuss business in coffee houses where coffee, tea and chocolate, all new drinks in Britain at the time, were available. *White's, the oldest London club, developed from a chocolate house. Some coffee houses, like the later clubs, were linked with particular professions. For instance, Lloyd's coffee house was associated with shipping and later became *Lloyd's of London. In the 18th century clubs were mainly used for drinking and gambling but later attracted members who shared more serious interests. People interested in science and literature joined the *Athenaeum, politicians went to the Reform, the *Carlton Club or Brooks's, and theatre people joined the *Garrick.

Today, the gentlemen's club suggests to many people an old-fashioned world based on class, where snobbery and prejudice still survive. There is now less interest among younger business people in joining clubs and several have had to close.

In the US there are not many institutions like the gentlemen's club. Private universities like *Harvard have *alumni associations for people who have studied there, and being a member of such clubs is associated with wealth and social status. The club building of the Harvard Club has in many ways the atmosphere of an English gentlemen's club.

Geoffrey of 'Monmouth /'mɒnməθ; AmE 'mɑːnməθ/ (c. 1100–54) a Welsh *bishop and writer. He wrote Historia Regum Britanniae, a history of the kings of Britain before the arrival of the *Anglo-Saxons. It tells the stories of the kings in *Shakespeare's plays, such as Lear and Cymbeline, but it is best known as the main source of all the legends about King *Arthur.

'Geordie /'dʒɔːdi; AmE 'dʒɔːrdi/ n (BrE informal) a person from the *Newcastle area of north-east England. Geordies are well known in Britain for their friendly nature and sense of humour and for their accent, which is very different from standard English.

▶ **Geordie** adj: She has a strong Geordie accent.

St 'George the national saint of England. Many people believe he was a Christian martyr (= a person who is killed because of their religious beliefs) in the third century. According to the legend, he killed a dragon to save a woman. He is often shown in pictures fighting the dragon.

George I /,dʒɔːdʒ ðə 'fɜːst; AmE ,dʒɔːrdʒ, 'fɜːrst/ (1660–1727) king of Great Britain and Ireland (1714–27). He was the first of the *Hanoverian kings and came to Britain from Germany on the death of Queen *Anne. He was not popular in Britain, mainly because he did not learn to speak English, and because he arrived with two German lovers who were not liked by the British people. He did not get involved in British politics, leaving most decisions to the *Cabinet, which became much more important during his time as king.

George II /,dʒɔːdʒ ðə 'sekənd; AmE ,dʒɔːrdʒ/ (1683–1760) king of Great Britain and Ireland (1727–60). He was the only son of *George I and, like his father, was not very interested in the government of Britain, allowing the development of the *constitutional monarchy. He was, however, interested in the army, and fought against the French in the War of the Austrian Succession (1740–48). He was the last British king to lead his army into a battle.

George III /,dʒɔːdʒ ðə 'θɜːd; AmE ,dʒɔːrdʒ, 'θɜːrd/ (1738–1820) king of Great Britain and Ireland (1760–1820). He was the grandson of King *George II. He was very interested in the government of Britain, and worked closely with *prime ministers such as Lord North and William *Pitt. He was strongly opposed to American independence, and was blamed by the public for losing the war of the *American Revolution. He suffered from

illness for some periods of his life and in 1811 he became so ill that his son was made *Prince Regent.

George IV /,dʒɔːdʒ ðə 'fɔːθ; AmE ,dʒɔːrdʒ, 'fɔːrθ/ (1762–1830) king of Great Britain and Ireland (1820–30). Before becoming king, he ruled as *Prince Regent because his father *George III was ill. He had many lovers and shocked many people by the way he lived, spending a lot of time eating, drinking and gambling.

George V /,dʒɔːdʒ ðə 'fɪfθ; AmE ,dʒɔːrdʒ/ (1865–1936) king of Great Britain and Northern Ireland (1910–36). He was the son of *Edward VII. He became popular with the British people for supporting the British armed forces in *World War I. In 1917 he dropped all his German titles and changed the family name from *Saxe-Coburg-Gotha to *Windsor1(2).

George VI /,dʒɔːdʒ ðə 'sɪksθ; AmE ,dʒɔːrdʒ/ (1895–1952) king of Great Britain and Northern Ireland (1936–52). He was the second son of *George V and became king after the abdication of his brother *Edward VIII. He was greatly admired by the British people during *World War II for staying in London when it was being bombed. He was the last British king to be called 'emperor' and the first head of the *Commonwealth of Nations.

the ,George 'Cross the highest award given to British civilians for doing something very brave, such as risking danger to help other people. It is a silver medal in the shape of a cross. The George Cross is not given to many people, and is considered a great honour. It was introduced by King *George VI in 1940.

the ,George 'Medal an award given to British civilians for doing something brave. It is a round silver medal. The George Medal is considered a great honour, though not as great as the *George Cross. The two awards were introduced at the same time.

'Georgetown /'dʒɔːdʒtaʊn; AmE 'dʒɔːrdʒtaʊn/ a fashionable and expensive district of *Washington, DC. It is on the *Potomac River and is the oldest area of the city. Georgetown University, one of the best in the country, was established in 1789 and has around 12 000 students.

the ,George 'Washington Bridge /'wɒʃɪŋtən; AmE 'wɑːʃɪŋtən/ a large US suspension bridge (= a bridge hanging from steel cables supported by towers at each end) across the *Hudson River from *Manhattan(1) in New York City to Fort Lee, *New Jersey. It is a 'double-decker', with one road above the other, and the length of the main section is 3500 feet/1067 metres. The bridge was completed in 1931.

'Georgia /'dʒɔːdʒə; AmE 'dʒɔːrdʒə/ a US state in the *Deep South. It was named after King *George II of Great Britain and was one of the 13 original American states. It later joined the *Confederate States. Georgia's popular names are the Peach State and the Empire State of the South. Its capital and largest city is *Atlanta. Important products of the state include paper, textiles, cotton, tobacco and peaches.

'Georgian /'dʒɔːdʒən; AmE 'dʒɔːrdʒən/ adj of the period of the British kings *George I, II and III, most of the 18th century and the beginning of the 19th century. British architecture, furniture and silver of this period are considered particularly attractive. Many British towns and cities have areas of simple but elegant Georgian houses. Some people also refer to the time of *George IV as Georgian, while others call it *Regency: a four-storey Georgian house.

the ,Georgian 'poets /,dʒɔːdʒən; AmE 'dʒɔːrdʒən/ n [pl] a group of British poets who wrote and published poems together in the early part of the 20th century, when *George V was king. The group included Rupert *Brooke, Walter *de la Mare, A E *Housman and John

*Masefield. They were influenced by *Wordsworth and wrote many poems about nature and country life.

Georgie 'Porgie /ˌdʒɔːdʒi 'pɔːdʒi; AmE ˌdʒɔːrdʒi 'pɔːrdʒi/ a boy in an old *nursery rhyme with these words:

> 66 Georgie Porgie, pudding and pie,
> Kissed the girls and made them cry;
> When the boys came out to play,
> Georgie Porgie ran away. 99

Richard 'Gere /'ɡɪə(r)/ (1949–) a US film actor. His films have included *American Gigolo* (1980), *An Officer and a Gentleman* (1982), *Pretty Woman* (1990), *Primal Fear* (1996) and *Chicago* (2002). Gere has been active in the campaign in support of the people of Tibet and their religious leader, the Dalai Lama.

Ge'ronimo /dʒə'rɒnɪməʊ; AmE dʒə'rɑːnɪmoʊ/ (c. 1829–1909) an *Apache who led his people in *Arizona against the US Army and the white people who settled there. After fighting for ten years (1876–86), Geronimo surrendered and finally settled in *Oklahoma as a farmer. In *World War II US military paratroopers used to shout his name as they jumped from their planes, to give themselves courage. Today, people often do this when jumping from a high place or doing something dangerous.

> 66 Once I moved about like wind. Now I surrender to you and that is all. 99
> Geronimo

George 'Gershwin /'ɡɜːʃwɪn; AmE 'ɡɜːrʃwɪn/ (1898–1937) a US composer who wrote many popular songs. He also wrote serious music in which he introduced elements of *jazz and other forms of popular music. His best-known works include *Rhapsody in Blue* (1924) and the *African-American opera *Porgy and Bess* (1935). He also wrote several musical comedy shows, including *Lady Be Good* (1924), *Strike up the Band* (1927) and *Of Thee I Sing* (1931), which won a *Pulitzer Prize. George Gershwin's brother Ira (1896–1983) wrote the words for many of his songs.

Ricky Ger'vais /ˌrɪki dʒɜː'veɪz; AmE dʒɜːr'veɪz/ (1961–) an English actor, writer and comedian who is best known for playing the character David Brent, an office manager, in the television comedy series *The Office* (2000–2003). The series was written and directed by Ricky Gervais and Stephen Merchant.

▶ gestures

Some gestures are used by all British and American people. Many are appropriate only in informal situations; others are considered rude and some have several different meanings, depending on the context.

People **nod** (= move the head gently down and up) to indicate 'yes'. Sometimes people nod repeatedly during a conversation to show that they agree with the speaker. Nodding at somebody can indicate that it is their turn to do something. You can also nod towards somebody or something instead of pointing with your finger. Nodding to somebody while you are talking to someone else shows that you have noticed them.

Shaking the head from side to side means 'no' but can also mean disbelief, amusement or annoyance depending on the expression on the face.

Thumbs up is a gesture showing approval or success. It is usually made with the thumb of only one hand. The thumb points straight up while the fingers are curled into the palm. The gesture is used to tell somebody that they can go ahead and do something, or to indicate that the person making the gesture has suc-ceeded in something. To **give somebody the thumbs up** is to give them permission to do something. **Thumbs down** is a similar gesture but the thumb points down towards the ground. It is used by somebody to indicate they have failed to do or get something.

People **thumb a lift** (= try to get a ride in a passing vehicle) by holding their arm out with the thumb up and slightly forward. **Twiddling your thumbs** (= holding the hands loosely and letting the thumbs rub gently against each other) suggests boredom or impatience. The phrase is often used metaphorically to mean 'having nothing to do'.

Pointing with the forefinger (= first finger) at somebody or something shows which person or thing you want or are talking about. But in both Britain and the US it is considered rude to point at people.

People can indicate that they think somebody is mad by pointing one finger at the side of their forehead and turning it. If you hold two fingers at the side of your head like a gun you are pretending to shoot yourself for doing something silly. A finger held to the lips indicates 'Sh!' (= Be quiet!). If you **pinch your nose** you are indicating that there is a bad smell. If a child holds its thumb to its nose, with the fingers spread out and waving, they are making an insulting gesture called **cocking a snook**. American children move one forefinger down at right angles to the other to indicate somebody has done something bad.

Fingers crossed is a wish for good luck. The index finger is crossed over the forefinger of the same hand. In Britain people give a **V-sign** by holding the index finger and forefinger apart like a V and curling the other fingers and the thumb into the palm. If the palm is held outwards the sign means 'victory' if the palm is turned inwards the gesture is rude and offensive. In the US people use the V-sign with the palm outwards to mean 'peace' but the rude version is not used. **Giving somebody the finger** (= holding the middle finger straight up and curling the other fingers into the palm) is used instead.

Drumming your fingers, i.e. tapping them repeatedly on a desk or table, suggests impatience. **Scratching your head** suggests you are not sure what to do. These gestures may also be a sign that a person is nervous.

When somebody **waves**, one arm is raised and bent slightly and the wrist is shaken. You wave when saying goodbye to somebody or as a greeting. In Britain children sometimes wave to trains, hoping that the driver will wave back. In the US children hold up their fist and move it down when a truck approaches, hoping the driver will sound the horn.

People **beckon** somebody to come over by holding the hand with the palm up and the fingers curled loosely in, and moving the hand or just the forefinger backwards and forwards. If the person is further away the forearm is also moved.

Lifting the arm is used to attract attention. In schools teachers say 'Hands up' when they ask a question, so that all the children get a chance to answer. Sometimes a vote can be taken by **a show of hands**, i.e. asking people who agree to **raise their hands**, and then, after they have lowered them, asking those who disagree to do the same. Adults also lift their arm to attract the attention of a waiter or a taxi driver. In Britain people stop a bus by holding one arm out at right angles while facing towards the bus.

If you stand with your hands on your hips it can suggest anger or defiance. If you **clench your fist** (= make the hand into a tight ball) you are angry.

G

People **clap their hands** to show they are pleased about something. After a concert, play, etc. they clap repeatedly to show they enjoyed it.

Shrugging your shoulders shows impatience or lack of interest. It can also be used to indicate that you do not mind which of several things is chosen.

People sometimes **tap their feet** (usually only one foot) on the floor in time to music, but more often the gesture shows that they feel impatient. Children sometimes **stamp their feet** when they are angry.

Winking at somebody suggest a shared secret or is used as a private signal. **Raising the eyebrows** with the eyes wide open, or **blinking** (= closing and opening both eyes very quickly) several times, expresses surprise, shock, or sometimes disapproval. The phrase *eyebrows were raised* is often used to say that people were surprised or disapproved.

Frowning may suggest concentration, but is often a sign of disapproval or annoyance. **Wrinkling the nose** (= moving it up and to one side) suggests there is a bad smell.

Children **stick their tongues out** to show they do not like somebody, but this is rude. **Pursing the lips**, making them very small and tight, is something people may do if they are concentrating hard. Sometimes, however, it shows a person is angry but trying hard to control their anger.

,**J Paul 'Getty**[1] /'geti/ (Jean Paul Getty 1892–1976) a US businessman who was one of the richest men in the world. He became President of the Getty Oil Company in 1947 and was estimated to be worth more than $1 billion by 1968. He collected art and in 1954 established the J Paul Getty Museum which is now in Los Angeles, *California. He settled in Britain in the early 1950s.

'**John Paul 'Getty 'Junior**[2] /'geti/ (1932–2003) the son of J Paul Getty, who lived in Britain and gave over £140 million to cultural causes. He was very interested in *cricket and had a valuable collection of books. He was made a *knight in 1987 and became a British citizen in 1997.

the ,**Battle of 'Gettysburg** /'getɪzbɜːɡ; AmE 'getɪzbɜːrg/ a major battle (1–3 July 1863) during the American *Civil War which helped the US to win the war. More soldiers died than in any other battle in US history. It was fought in Gettysburg, *Pennsylvania, between the southern forces under General Robert E *Lee and the US soldiers led by General George Mead. Over 40 000 men on both sides were killed or wounded, and the battle ended as a major victory for the North.

the ,**Gettysburg Ad'dress** /,getɪzbɜːɡ; AmE 'getɪzbɜːrg/ a short but very famous speech by US President Abraham *Lincoln on 19 November 1863 during the *Civil War. He was at the military cemetery at Gettysburg, *Pennsylvania, four months after the Battle of *Gettysburg. The speech consisted of only ten sentences, and Lincoln thought it was a 'flat failure' and would soon be forgotten. He said that the US was 'conceived in liberty and dedicated to the proposition that all men are created equal' and that 'government of the people, by the people, for the people shall not perish from the earth'.

,**Stan 'Getz** /'gets/ (1927–91) a US *jazz musician who played the saxophone. He was a leader of the 'West Coast Cool' type of jazz, and his successes included *Early Autumn* (1948), *The Girl from Ipanema* (1963) and *I Remember You* (1991). Getz played with Benny *Goodman, Woody Herman and other famous bands. He received three *Emmy awards (1962, 1964 and 1991) and was chosen for the Jazz *Hall of Fame in 1986.

'**Ghana** /'gɑːnə/ a country in West Africa. It was part of the *British Empire from 1874, when it was called the Gold Coast, until 1957, when it was one of the first African countries to become independent. It is a member of the *Commonwealth, and many Ghanaian people now live in Britain. The capital city is Accra.
▶ **Gha'naian** /gɑːˈneɪən/ adj, n.

,**Ghirar'delli** /ˌɡɪrɑːˈdeli; AmE ˌɡɪrɑːrˈdeli/ a firm that makes high-quality chocolate in *San Francisco. It was started in 1852 by Domingo Ghirardelli and its most famous products are its chocolate squares. Ghirardelli Square in San Francisco is the site of the original factory.

the '**Ghost Dance** a *Native American dance and religion that started among the *Paiute people in western *Nevada about 1870. The religion was based on a dance which lasted five days and which Native Americans believed would help them to get back their land. The *Sioux danced the Ghost Dance before the battle of *Wounded Knee. During the battle they wore 'ghost shirts' which they believed would stop bullets.

GI /,dʒiː ˈaɪ/ (also ,**GI 'Joe**) n a name for a US soldier, used especially in *World War II. It came originally from the letters 'GI' (meaning 'government issue') stamped on military equipment.

the ,**Giant's 'Causeway** a group of several thousand columns of rock on the north-east coast of Northern Ireland. Most of the columns have five or six flat sides. According to the legend, it is one end of a road built by a giant across the sea to the island of *Staffa, where there is a similar group of rocks. It is an important tourist attraction and was made a *World Heritage Site in 1986.

,**Edward 'Gibbon** /'gɪbən/ (1737–94) an English historian and *Member of Parliament who spent much of his life writing his main work, *The *Decline and Fall of the Roman Empire*. He is regarded as one of the major thinkers and writers of the *Age of Enlightenment in Britain.

,**Grinling 'Gibbons**[1] /,grɪnlɪŋ 'gɪbənz/ (1648–1721) an English sculptor. He is best known for his realistic decorative wood carvings, some of which can be seen in *St Paul's Cathedral in London.

Or,**lando 'Gibbons**[2] /ɔː ˌlændəʊ 'gɪbənz; AmE ɔːrˌlændoʊ/ (1583–1625) an English composer and musician. He was the greatest player of keyboard instruments of his time, and wrote many pieces of music for the *Church of England which are still used today.

the '**GI ,Bill of 'Rights** (also the **GI Bill**) a US law passed in 1944 to give financial help to members of the armed forces when they returned from *World War II. This included money given to help pay for homes and education. By 1947, about 4 million people had benefited from the law. It now helps anyone leaving the US armed forces.

Gi'braltar /dʒɪˈbrɔːltə(r)/ a large rock at the western end of the Mediterranean Sea, connected to the south coast of Spain. There is a small town and a large military base on Gibraltar, which is owned by Britain but claimed by Spain. It used to be an important centre for the *Royal Navy and the *RAF, guarding the area where the Mediterranean flows into the Atlantic, but many of the armed forces have left Gibraltar, and tourism is becoming a more important industry. Many monkeys, called Barbary apes, live on the Rock of Gibraltar, and there is a legend that the British will leave Gibraltar when the monkeys die or stop living there.

,**Mel 'Gibson** /,mel 'gɪbsn/ (1956–) a *Hollywood film star. He was born in the US but grew up in Australia from the age of 12. His best-known films include the *Mad Max* series in the 1980s, the *Lethal Weapon* series in the 1980s and 1990s, *Braveheart* (1995), which he also directed and which won two *Oscars, and *The Passion of the Christ* (2004), which he produced and directed.

Gideon 'Bible /ˌgɪdiən/ n a copy of the Bible that has been left in a room in a hotel, hospital, etc. by the **Gideons**, a US Christian organization. They put Bibles in rooms in many countries around the world hoping that people will read them and learn about Christianity.

John 'Gielgud /'giːlgʊd/ (1904–2000) an English actor. He was well known for his fine voice. He first became famous for his stage performances in *Shakespeare plays with Laurence *Olivier in the 1930s, playing characters such as Romeo and Hamlet. He was also successful in comedy plays, and appeared in many films. He is considered one of the greatest actors of the 20th century. He was made a *knight in 1953.

Ryan 'Giggs /ˌraɪən 'gɪgz/ (1973–) a Welsh footballer who has played for *Manchester United and Wales since the early 1990s. He plays attacking football in the middle of the field or along the edges, and is well known as one of the most skilful players in Britain.

GI 'Joe™ /ˌdʒiː aɪ/ (in the US) a popular children's toy in the form of a small figure with moving arms and legs which can be dressed in different military uniforms. GI Joe was first sold in 1964 and since then other GI Joe products, including a television cartoon series, have also been created. The advertising slogan for the toys is ' GI Joe — A Real American Hero!'. Compare ACTION MAN.

W S 'Gilbert /'gɪlbət; AmE 'gɪlbərt/ (William Schwenk Gilbert 1836–1911) an English writer of comedy plays and the words for comic operas. He is best known for the comic operas he wrote with Arthur *Sullivan, which show his skill at writing humorous songs and making fun of British life and politics. **Gilbert and Sullivan** wrote 14 popular comic operas (sometimes called the *Savoy Operas), including The *Mikado and The *Pirates of Penzance. They are still performed regularly in Britain and are a popular choice by amateur groups. See also LEIGH.

Gilbert and 'George Gilbert Proesch (1943–) and George Passmore (1942–), two English performance artists (= artists who include themselves and their activities in a particular style of visual art). Gilbert was born in Italy and studied in Austria and Germany. In the 1960s and 1970s they presented themselves as works of art by covering their bodies with paint or powder to look like sculptures. Their film *Gordon's Makes Us Drunk* shows them drinking *Gordon's gin. They are well known for producing large photographs of themselves, often referring to themes of sex and politics, which many people found shocking. They are usually seen wearing matching business suits.

Giles /dʒaɪlz/ (Carl Ronald Giles 1916–95) an English cartoonist. His cartoons showed a large family which was always in a state of disorder. They were published in the *Daily Express from the 1940s.

Eric 'Gill /'gɪl/ (1882–1940) an English artist. He is well known for his sculptures, especially his bas-reliefs (= sculptures in which the design sticks out only slightly from its background) such as his *Stations of the Cross* (1914–18) in *Westminster Cathedral and the carving of *Prospero and Ariel on the front of the *BBC building. He was a calligrapher (= someone who practises beautiful handwriting that you do with a special pen or brush) and also created several new typefaces (= styles for printing letters in books, magazines, etc.), of which the most famous is Gill Sans.

'Dizzy' Gil'lespie /ˌdɪzi gɪ'lespi/ (1917–93) a US *jazz musician who invented the name *bebop and helped to develop that type of music. He played the trumpet in a wide range of groups and wrote several successful pieces, including *Hot House* (1941) and *Groovin' High* (1944). He was chosen for the Jazz *Hall of Fame in 1960.

James 'Gillray /'gɪlreɪ/ (1757–1815) an English caricaturist (= an artist who makes people appear ridiculous by exaggerating their characteristics). He often made fun of the government and the royal family and had a strong influence on the development of political cartoons in Britain. See also FARMER GEORGE.

Gary 'Gilmore /'gɪlmɔː(r)/ (1940–77) a US criminal who was executed for murder in January 1977. He is mainly remembered because he chose to be shot by a firing squad, as a condemned person is allowed to do in the state of *Utah, though no one else has chosen this form of death since.

'Gingerbread a British charity that offers help and advice to people who are bringing up their children alone.

Newt 'Gingrich /ˌnjuːt 'gɪŋgrɪtʃ/ (1943–) a US *Republican(1) politician. He was *Speaker of the House of Representatives from 1995 to 1999, when he resigned from the post. He is well known for his right-wing views, e.g. that Americans should pay less tax and that unemployed people should be given less money by the state. In 1995 he disagreed with President *Clinton about how to spend the government's money that year, and their disagreement led to many government departments closing temporarily because they did not have any money. In 1997 the House Ethics Committee found that Gingrich had used tax laws wrongly and lied to the committee and he was fined $300 000. Since leaving office he has opposed the *Bush administration's strategy in Iraq.

Gin 'Lane a drawing (1751) by William *Hogarth. It is a shocking picture of people in a London street who are too drunk to care about their homes or families. Gin, a strong alcoholic drink, was very popular at the time because of its low price, and many people in London were drinking too much of it.

Allen 'Ginsberg /'gɪnzbɜːg; AmE 'gɪnzbɜːrg/ (1926–97) a US poet of the *beat generation of the 1950s who was also closely associated with the *hippies of the 1960s. He supported illegal drugs and the rights of homosexuals, and protested against the *Vietnam War. Ginsberg's collections of poems included *Howl* (1956) which criticized American values, and *Kaddish and Other Poems* (1961).

gin 'sling n a drink that is of a mixture of gin, sugar, water and lemon or lime juice, served with ice. Many people think of it as a typical drink of British people in tropical countries at the time of the *British Empire.

the ˌGirl 'Guides ⇨ GUIDE.

ˌGirl 'Scout n a member of the Girl Scouts of the USA, an organization for girls similar to the *Boy Scouts of America. It was established in 1912 and had about 3.7 million members in 2003. The main groups of Girl Scouts are Daisy Girl Scouts (for ages 5 to 6), Brownie Girl Scouts (6 to 8), Junior Girl Scouts (8 to 11), Cadette Girl Scouts (11 to 14) and Senior Girl Scouts (14 to 17). Compare GUIDE.

'Girobank /'dʒaɪrəʊbæŋk; AmE 'dʒaɪroʊbæŋk/ a British bank that has its branches in post offices. It used to belong to the *Post Office but it was sold in 1990 to the *Alliance and Leicester. Many people use the Girobank because they find it more convenient to use their local post office than to go to a bank.

ˌLillian 'Gish /'gɪʃ/ (1893–1993) a US actor in silent and sound films, and on the stage. She was small and delicate, but her acting career lasted for nearly 90 years. She and her sister Dorothy Gish (1898–1968) were favourite actors of D W *Griffith, and Lillian became internationally famous in his *Birth of a Nation* (1915). Her 'talkies' (= films with sound) included *Night of the Hunter* (1955) and her last, *The Whales of August* (1987). She received a special *Oscar in 1971.

Rudy Giuli'ani /ˈruːdi dʒuːliˈɑːni/ (1944–) the mayor of New York City from 1994 to 2001. He was best known for his strong policies to reduce crime in the city, known as 'zero tolerance'. He became very popular because of his actions after the *9/11 attacks on the city.

the GLA /ˌdʒiː el ˈeɪ/ ⇨ GREATER LONDON AUTHORITY.

'Gladiators a popular British television programme (1992–1999) in which members of the public took part in a series of difficult physical contests against the Gladiators, a group of very strong men and women with colourful names like Scorpio, Wolf and Cobra. Some of the Gladiators became stars and appeared in other television programmes. A similar programme on US television, called *American Gladiators*, ran from 1989 to 1997.

William 'Gladstone /ˈɡlædstən/ (1809–98) an English *Liberal politician who was *Prime Minister four times (1868–74, 1880–85, 1886 and 1892–4). He began as a *Tory *MP but left to form the Liberal Party, becoming its leader in 1867. He and his rival *Disraeli were the leading figures in British politics for over 30 years. Gladstone was responsible for many improvements to life in Britain: he made voting secret, gave the right to vote to most men (but not women), and gave all children the right to an education. He also believed that the countries in the *British Empire should govern themselves and that Ireland should have *home rule(1), but he died before these aims could be achieved.

Glamis 'Castle /ˌɡlɑːmz/ a castle in Scotland, north of *Dundee. It was built in the 17th century and was the family home of the *Queen Mother(2).

Gla'morgan /ɡləˈmɔːɡən; *AmE* ɡləˈmɔːrɡən/ a region and former administrative county of south-east Wales. Its cities and many of its towns and their surrounding areas are now governed by separate *unitary authorities: *Cardiff, *Swansea, Bridgend, Caerphilly and Merthyr Tydfil. The northern part has many mountains and until the 1980s, was known especially for its coal, iron and steel industries. The southern part, now governed by the Vale of Glamorgan unitary authority, is known for its agriculture and beautiful coastline. Glamorgan County Cricket Club, whose ground is in Cardiff, is the only Welsh club in the *county championship.

'Glamour a US women's magazine published by Condé Nast. It began in 1939 and now describes itself as 'the largest fashion, beauty and health magazine in the world'. It also has articles about other interests of women, such as business, politics, travel, food and relationships. There has been a British version of the magazine since 2001.

'Glasgow /ˈɡlɑːzɡəʊ; *AmE* ˈɡlæzɡoʊ/ an industrial city in south-west Scotland. It is Scotland's largest city and a major port. It used to be an important centre for shipbuilding, and when this and several other industries closed down in the late 20th century it became well known for problems connected with unemployment, drugs and crime. Glasgow has many interesting and attractive buildings, as well as important schools, universities and museums, and in the 1990s it developed into a major centre for culture, the arts and education. In 1990 it was named European City of Culture and in 2003 was European Capital of Sport. Since 1996 it has been governed as a *council area (officially called **Glasgow City**). See also GLASGOW SCHOOL.

the 'Glasgow Boys /ˈɡlɑːzɡəʊ; *AmE* ˈɡlæzɡoʊ/ a group of artists from *Glasgow, Scotland, who became known at the end of the 19th century (c. 1870–1895) for a new style of painting which was less traditional than the style of the time. Their paintings were often of ordinary people and outdoor scenes. The group included the artists Joseph Crawhill (1861–1913), Sir James Guthrie (1859–1930), George Henry (1858–1943) and E.A.Hornel (1864–1933).

the 'Glasgow 'Herald /ˌɡlɑːzɡəʊ; *AmE* ˈɡlæzɡoʊ/ a Scottish daily newspaper. It is read mainly in the Glasgow area and the west of Scotland. It is one of Scotland's two main newspapers. Compare SCOTSMAN.

the 'Glasgow School /ˈɡlɑːzɡəʊ; *AmE* ˈɡlæzɡoʊ/ a group of architects and designers who had been students at the Glasgow School of Art in the late 19th century. Their *art nouveau style had a strong influence on European architecture and design. The best-known members of the Glasgow School were Charles Rennie *Mackintosh and Margaret Macdonald, who was his wife.

Philip 'Glass /ˈɡlɑːs; *AmE* ɡlæs/ (1937–) a US composer. He is well known for developing a 'minimal' style of music based on repeated rhythms with slight changes of pattern. His best-known work is the opera *Einstein on the Beach* (1976), the first of a trilogy that also includes *Akhnaten* and *Satygraha*. He wrote the music for the films *The Hours* (2002) and *The Fog of War* (2003). He has been a Buddhist since 1972.

'Glastonbury /ˈɡlæstənbəri/ a town in south-west England. According to legend, *Joseph of Arimathea went there with the *Holy Grail. Another story states that King *Arthur and Queen *Guinevere are buried there, and that Glastonbury was originally *Avalon. Today it is famous for the **Glastonbury Festival**, a very large pop concert that takes place in fields outside the town every summer.

Glas'wegian /ɡlæzˈwiːdʒn/ *n* a person who comes from or lives in *Glasgow.
▶ **Glaswegian** *adj*: *He still has a strong Glaswegian accent.*

'Glaxo'Smith'Kline /ˈɡlæksəʊ; *AmE* ˈɡlæksoʊ/ (*also* **Glaxo**) (*abbr* **GSK**) a large British company that produces many different types of drugs and medicines. It employs over 100 000 people worldwide.

the GLC /ˌdʒiː el ˈsiː/ (*in full* **the Greater London Council**) the local authority that was in control of *Greater London from 1965 to 1983. In the 1980s Margaret *Thatcher found the GLC and its leader, Ken *Livingstone, too left-wing, and changed the system of local government so that each *borough was responsible for itself. No single authority was then responsible for the whole of Greater London until the election of the *London Assembly in 2000.

Glen'coe /ɡlenˈkəʊ; *AmE* ɡlenˈkoʊ/ a valley in the Scottish *Highlands. In 1692 it was the scene of the **Glencoe Massacre**. About 40 members of the MacDonald *clan were killed by members of the Campbell clan and the soldiers of the English king,

Glencoe

*William III. The MacDonalds were killed because they had supported the first *Jacobite rebellion and had been slow to recognize *William and Mary as king and queen.

Owen Glen'dower /ˌəʊɪn glenˈdaʊə(r)/ (c. 1355– c. 1417) a Welsh military and political leader who led the Welsh forces resisting the English king *Henry IV in Wales. He had his own parliament in 1404 and was the last Welsh person to have the title of *Prince of Wales. He was defeated in battle by the son of Henry IV, who also claimed the title of Prince of Wales, but he was never captured. Many people know of him as a character in *Shakespeare's play *Henry IV.

Glen'eagles /glenˈiːglz/ a pair of famous golf courses (called the King's course and the Queen's course) belonging to a hotel in central Scotland. In 1977 the leaders of the *Commonwealth governments met there to sign the **Gleneagles Principle**, in which they agreed to have no contact in sport with South Africa because of the political situation there at the time.

Glen'fiddich™ /glenˈfɪdɪk/ n [U, C] a famous make of malt *whisky which is produced in Glenfiddich, a village in north-east Scotland.

glen'garry /glenˈgæri/ n a type of Scottish cap, usually made of wool with a *tartan design. Glengarries have no brim (= flat edge around the bottom) and often have ribbons (= narrow strips of cloth) hanging at the back. They are worn by some regiments of Scottish soldiers.

John 'Glenn /ˈglen/ (1921–) a US astronaut and politician. He joined the *NASA *Mercury program in 1958 and was the first American to complete an orbit (= circular path in space) of the earth, in the spacecraft *Friendship 7*. Glenn left NASA two years later and was elected a Senator from *Ohio for the *Democratic Party until 1998. He twice tried but failed to become the Democratic candidate for US *President. In 1998 he again took part in a space flight, at the age of 77.

the Globe /gləʊb; *AmE* gloʊb/ the theatre in London where *Shakespeare's most famous plays were first performed. It was built in 1599 by the actor Richard Burbage on the south bank of the *Thames. It was a round, open-air building with a roof over the stage. It had three levels of seats and an area in front of the stage where some of the audience could stand. It was closed by the *Puritans in 1642. An exact copy of the Globe was built in the 1990s and Shakespeare's plays are again performed there. Compare ROSE THEATRE.

the Glorious Revo'lution ⇨ BLOODLESS REVOLUTION.

the Glorious 'Twelfth 1 12 August, the first day of the season for shooting grouse (= a fat bird which is shot for sport and food) in Britain. Grouse shooting, especially on the Scottish moors, is very popular with rich people in Britain.
2 12 July, the anniversary of the *Battle of the Boyne, which is celebrated by many Protestants in Northern Ireland. See also ORANGEMAN.

'Gloucester /ˈglɒstə(r)/ *AmE* ˈglɑːstər/ a city in south-west England, on the river *Severn. It was established as a Roman military camp in the first century. Its cathedral has fine examples of *Norman and *Perpendicular architecture. See also DOUBLE GLOUCESTER.

'Gloucestershire /ˈglɒstəʃə(r)/ *AmE* ˈglɑːstərʃər/ (*abbr* **Glos**) a county in south-west England, on the border with Wales. It contains part of the *Cotswolds. The administrative centre is *Gloucester.

'Glyndebourne /ˈglaɪndbɔːn/ *AmE* ˈglaɪndbɔːrn/ a large, grand house near *Brighton in southern England which is well known for the opera festival that takes place there every summer. A theatre was built in the garden for the first festival in 1934 and was replaced by a larger theatre in 1994. The Glyndebourne opera is one of the important social events of the English summer. The gardens are beautiful, and many members of the audience take their own picnic and eat it on the lawn during the interval. The **Glyndebourne Touring Opera** (the GTO) travels in the autumn to many cities in Britain and provides an opportunity for young singers to sing major roles.

Glyndebourne

GM /ˌdʒiː ˈem/ **1** ⇨ GENERAL MOTORS.
2 (*BrE*) ⇨ GENETICALLY MODIFIED.

G-man /ˈdʒiː mæn/ n (pl **G-men**) (*AmE old-fashioned informal*) a man working for the *FBI. The word is an abbreviation of 'government man'.

GMAT /ˈdʒiːmæt/ (*in full* **Graduate Management Admissions Test**) (in US *graduate schools) a standard test that students must take in order to be accepted to study for a degree in Business Administration.

the GMB /ˌdʒiː em ˈbiː/ (*in full* in full **the General, Municipal and Boilermakers Union**) one of the largest British *trade unions, formed in 1989 when two large trade unions combined. In 2004, as a protest against government policies, the GMB voted not to give money to the *Labour Party for its election campaign but to give money only to Labour *MPs whose views the union supported.

the GMC /ˌdʒiː em ˈsiː/ ⇨ GENERAL MEDICAL COUNCIL.

GMT /ˌdʒiː em ˈtiː/ (*in full* **Greenwich Mean Time**) the time of day on the line of 0° longitude (= a straight line between the North Pole and the South Pole), which goes through *Greenwich (also called the Greenwich Meridian Line). It is the official time in Britain from October to March. Different time zones in other parts of the world are usually described with reference to GMT: *New York is five hours behind GMT so it's early morning there now.* Compare BRITISH SUMMER TIME. See also ROYAL OBSERVATORY.

GMTV /ˌdʒiː em ti ˈviː/ a British *breakfast television show on *ITV. It is a mixture of news and interviews with people such as actors and sports stars. It started in 1993 and it is broadcast every day from 6 a.m. to 9.25 a.m.

GNT /ˌdʒiː en ˈtiː/ ⇨ GOOD NEWS BIBLE.

GNVQ /ˌdʒiː en viː ˈkjuː/ (*in full* **General National Vocational Qualification**) n a type of qualification introduced in 1992 in England, Wales and Northern Ireland. It is designed to prepare students in schools and colleges to do certain jobs, and is offered in subjects such as business, tourism and computer skills. They are gradually being replaced by *GCSEs and other qualifications. ⇨ note at VOCATIONAL TRAINING. See also NVQ.

'gobstopper /'gɒbstɒpə(r); AmE 'gɑːbstɑːpər/ n (BrE informal) a large hard round sweet. Many gobstoppers change colour as they are sucked. They are popular with children. The name comes from gob, a British *slang word for 'mouth'.

,**God Bless A'merica** a song praising America that was written by Irving *Berlin in 1919. It became the 'unofficial national anthem' for the US during World War II, when Kate *Smith regularly sang it and it was frequently sung after *September 11. Some Americans still want it to replace The *Star-Spangled Banner.

The '**Godfather** a successful novel (1969) by Mario Puzo about the *Mafia(1). 'Godfather' is a popular name for a Mafia leader. A 1972 film of the story, directed by Francis Ford *Coppola, won the *Oscar for Best Picture. An Oscar also went to Marlon *Brando who played the Mafia leader Don Corleone, though Brando refused the award as a protest against the treatment of *Native Americans. Al *Pacino played his son Michael, and was the star of two later films by Coppola which continued the story, The Godfather II (1974) and The Godfather III (1990). The three films won a total of 9 Oscars.

,**Lady Go'diva** /gə'daɪvə/ (11th century) the wife of an *earl(1) of *Mercia. According to legend, she asked her husband to lower the taxes on the people of *Coventry and he said that he would do so if she rode her horse naked through the town. She did this, and the taxes were lowered. See also PEEPING TOM.

,**God 'Rest You ,Merry, 'Gentlemen** a popular *carol sung at *Christmas.

,**God Save the 'Queen** the British *national anthem. It is not known who wrote the words or the music, but it was already a traditional song in the 18th century. When the country has a king, the word 'Queen' is replaced by 'King'. The song has several verses, but usually only the first verse is sung:

> 66 God save our gracious Queen,
> Long live our noble Queen,
> God save the Queen.
> Send her victorious,
> Happy and glorious,
> Long to reign over us;
> God save the Queen. 99

'**God's ,country** an expression used to describe a beautiful and greatly loved land. Americans use it to mean the US or regions of the country, especially the open areas of the western states.

,**Bernard 'Goetz** /gɜːts/ (1948–) a man who in 1984 shot and wounded four *African American teenagers on a New York underground train after one of them asked for $5. He became known as the Subway Vigilante and there was major debate in the US over whether ordinary people should be allowed to use such violence to defend themselves. Goetz was sent to prison for 8½ years, but only for illegally having a gun. In 1996, he was taken to a court of law by one of the young men he had injured, and the jury decided that Goetz must pay him $43 million.

the **Gog,magog 'Hills** /gɒg,meɪgɒg; AmE gɑːg,meɪgɑːg/ an area of low hills south of *Cambridge in England that is popular with walkers and cyclists.

,**Rube 'Goldberg**[1] /ˌruːb 'gəʊldbɜːg; AmE 'goʊldbɜːrg/ (1883–1970) a US cartoonist who drew complicated, ridiculous machines performing tasks that could be done more easily without them. The phrase 'Rube Goldberg' is still used to describe any complicated

machine or plan with many parts. Goldberg was also a political cartoonist and won the *Pulitzer Prize in 1948 for his work. Competitions are sometimes held in the US to see who can build machines of the type that Goldberg was famous for. Compare HEATH ROBINSON.

,**Whoopi 'Goldberg**[2] /ˌwʊpi 'gəʊldbɜːg; AmE 'goʊldbɜːrg/ (1955–) a US actor who usually makes comedy films. She won a *Golden Globe Award for a serious role in her first film, The Color Purple (1985), and received an *Oscar for Ghost (1990). Her later films include Sister Act (1992) and The Associate (1996).

,**Gold 'Blend**™ n [U] a make of instant coffee. It is made by *Nescafé. Many people in Britain remember a series of television advertisements for the coffee in the 1990s in which a man and a woman gradually fell in love while drinking or talking about Gold Blend.

the ,Golden 'Gate 'Bridge

the famous US bridge that connects *San Francisco with Marin County, *California, to the north. It is the second longest US suspension bridge (= bridge hanging from cables supported by towers at each end). It is orange, not gold, in colour and crosses the Golden Gate, the water between San Francisco Bay and the Pacific Ocean. It was completed in 1937, and the length of the central section is 4 200 feet/1 281 metres. The bridge takes four years to paint, and the work of painting it never stops. Compare FORTH BRIDGE.

the Golden Gate Bridge

,**Golden 'Globe A,ward** n any of several film and television awards given at a special ceremony each year since 1944 by the Hollywood Foreign Press Association. Compare OSCAR, EMMY.

the ,**Golden 'Hind** ⇨ DRAKE.

The ,**Golden 'Treasury** a book (1861) of English poetry. The poems were chosen by Francis Turner *Palgrave with some help from Lord *Tennyson. It had an important influence on future collections of poems, and on what the British public considered to be great poetry. Later editions were larger and the book is still published today.

,**Golden 'Wonder**™ a popular British make of potato crisps/chips (= very thin slices of fried potato sold in small bags, often with salt or other flavours).

'**Goldilocks and the ,Three 'Bears** /'gəʊldɪlɒks; AmE 'goʊldɪlɑːks/ a popular children's story. Goldilocks, a young girl with golden curly hair, goes to a house where three bears live (Mother Bear, Father Bear and Baby Bear). The bears are not at home, and Goldilocks eats some of their *porridge and tries all their beds before going to sleep in one of them. The bears return, see that someone has been there, and say 'Who's been eating my porridge?' and 'Who's been sleeping in my bed?' until they find her and she escapes. The story is often used as the basis for a *pantomime in Britain.

,**William 'Golding** /'gəʊldɪŋ; AmE 'goʊldɪŋ/ (1911–93) an English writer of novels. He is best known for his first novel, The *Lord of the Flies (1954). Like many of his other works, it is concerned with human cruelty. He won the *Booker Prize for the novel Rites of Passage (1980), and the *Nobel Prize for literature in 1983. He was made a *knight in 1988.

the '**Gold Rush** the rapid movement of about 40 000 people to the US state of *California in 1848–9 after gold was discovered there. They were called *forty-niners.

The gold rush later spread to *Canada and *Alaska. See also CHAPLIN, JEANS. Compare KLONDIKE.

ˌOliver 'Goldsmith /'gəʊldsmɪθ; AmE 'goʊldsmɪθ/ (c. 1730–74) an Irish writer of plays, novels and poetry. His best-known works are the play *She Stoops to Conquer and the novel The *Vicar of Wakefield. He was a close friend of Samuel *Johnson and one of the group of writers living in 18th–century London known as the Club.

ˌSamuel 'Goldwyn /'gəʊldwɪn; AmE 'goʊldwɪn/ (1882–1974) a US film producer, born in Poland. In 1916 he established Goldwyn Pictures, which later became part of *Metro-Goldwyn-Mayer. He received an *Oscar for The Best Years of Our Lives (1946), and his other films included *Wuthering Heights (1939), *Guys and Dolls (1955) and Porgy and Bess (1959). Goldwyn was famous for his strange and sometimes comic use of English.

> 66 Gentlemen, include me out. 99
> Sam Goldwyn

▶ **golf**
Golf was first developed in Scotland in the 15th century but is now played all round the world by both professional and amateur players.

The aim of golf is to hit a small ball from a **tee** (= a flat area of grass) into a hole on a **green** (= a very finely cut area of grass), which may be up to 600 yards/550 metres away, using as few **shots** (= hits) as possible. Most **golf courses** consist of 18 **holes**. To make play more difficult they are often hilly and have various natural and man-made hazards such as lakes, bunkers (= pits filled with sand), and **rough**, long grass or trees on either side of the **fairway**.

Each player has their own ball and several different types of **club** (**woods**, **irons** and a **putter**) with which to hit it. The club chosen depends on the type of shot the player needs to make. In professional tournaments players have a **caddie** to carry the bag of clubs from one hole to the next and to advise them on their play. Players try to finish each hole in a given number of shots, which is known as **par**. If they use one shot less than par they score a **birdie**; if they use two shots less they score an **eagle**; if they use three shots under par they score an **albatross**. If they manage to get the ball into the hole in a single shot they can claim a **hole in one**. If they use a shot more than par they score a **bogey**. A **handicap** is an advantage given to weaker players which is expressed as a number related to the number of shots above par. Professional golfers have a handicap of zero. At the end of a **round** (= all 18 holes), the player with the lowest score is the winner. Professional matches may consist of several rounds. The result sometimes depends on the total number of shots players have taken (**stroke play**), or else on the number of individual holes each player has won (**match play**).

Golf began as a sport of the upper classes and in Britain it continues to attract mainly people in business and the professions. The game is quite expensive to play and membership of the most popular **golf clubs** may cost a lot of money. The most famous British clubs include the *Royal and Ancient at *St Andrews, where the first official rules of golf were agreed in 1754, *Muirfield and *Wentworth. Golf may have been taken to America by people from Scotland in the 17th century, but the first permanent club was not established there until 1888, in Yonkers, New York.

There are four important international competitions for professional golfers, known as the **majors**, three of them held in the US. The *Masters Tournament is always held at Augusta, Georgia. The others are the *US Open and the **US PGA Championship**. The *British Open is regarded as the world's top golf tournament. US and European teams also compete every two years in the *Ryder Cup. The major US competitions for women include the **US Women's Open** and the **LPGA Women's Championship**. Amateur events include the *Walker Cup and the *Curtis Cup. Television has helped to increase the popularity of the game, and many new golf courses have been created.

Many people who do not play golf enjoy a game of **crazy golf** (AmE **miniature golf**) in a local park. The idea is to hit a golf ball round a small grass and concrete course of nine holes, through tunnels, over bridges, round small pools, etc. Others enjoy **putting**, a miniature form of golf on a small grassy course.

ˌE H 'Gombrich /'gɒmbrɪtʃ; AmE 'gɑːmbrɪtʃ/ (Ernst Hans Gombrich 1909–2001) a British art historian, born in Austria. He wrote several important books about art, including Art and Illusion (1960) and The Story of Art (1950), which has sold more than four million copies. He was made a *knight in 1972.

The ˌGondo'liers /ˌgɒndə'lɪəz/ a comic opera (1889) by *Gilbert and *Sullivan[1]. It is set in Venice, Italy, where a gondolier (= a person who takes people on a boat through the canals of Venice) is believed to be the prince of an imaginary country. A local aristocrat wants his daughter to marry the prince, but she loves a servant called Luiz. In the end, it is discovered that Luiz is the real prince.

ˌGone with the 'Wind a popular US novel (1936) by Margaret Mitchell that won the *Pulitzer Prize. In 1939 it was made into one of the most successful films ever made, winning 10 *Oscars. The story is set in the state of *Georgia and follows the troubled love affair between Scarlett *O'Hara, and Rhett *Butler, during the *Civil War, which changes their lives.

> 66 Frankly, my dear, I don't give a damn. 99
> from Gone with the Wind

Alberto 'Gonzales /gɒn'zaːlɪz; AmE gaːn'zaːlɪz/ (1955–) a lawyer and politician, born in *Texas of Mexican parents, who became US *Attorney General in 2005. He worked as adviser to George W *Bush when he was governor of *Texas and was appointed by President Bush as White House Counsel in 2001. His legal advice to the President in relation to many issues, including the treatment of prisoners in *Guantánamo Bay, was the subject of controversy and his appointment as Attorney General was opposed by many.

ˌJane 'Goodall /'gʊdɔːl/ (1934–) a British scientist, who became famous for her study of chimpanzees. She discovered that these animals use tools. Before her studies, people thought that only humans understood how to make and use tools with their hands. At the age of 23, she met Dr Louis Leakey on a trip to Africa and became his assistant. Then she went to Gombe National Park in Tanzania in 1960. She lived and worked there studying how chimpanzees live. She has won many prizes for her work and in 1977 she started the Jane Goodall Institute for Wildlife Research, Education and Conservation.

ˌGoodbye Mr 'Chips /'tʃɪps/ a novel (1934) by James Hilton. It is the story of a lonely teacher at an English *public school whose students make fun of him. Later, after he has married a beautiful woman, they respect him. The book was made into two successful British films, in 1939 and in 1969.

ˌGoodˌbye to All 'That a book (1929) by Robert *Graves about the early part of his life. It describes his experiences at *public school(1), at *Oxford University, and as a soldier in *World War I, and explains why he decided to leave England for the rest of his life.

The ‚Good Com'panions a novel (1929) by J B *Priestley. It is Priestley's best-known novel, and tells the story of three people from different parts of England who set up a small theatre company together.

The ‚Good 'Food Guide a book giving information about many restaurants in Britain, and the writers' opinions about the quality of the food they offer. It is published every year by the *Consumers' Association, and contains comments by members of the public.

‚Good 'Friday the Friday before *Easter. In the Christian religion it represents the day on which Christ died. It is a *bank holiday in Britain. In the US, part of Good Friday is an official holiday in certain states. See also HOT CROSS BUN.

the ‚Good 'Friday A‚greement an agreement reached on *Good Friday 1998 between Irish political leaders and the British government. The aim of the agreement was to end the violence of the *Troubles in Northern Ireland and establish new Irish political institutions, including a new *Northern Ireland Assembly in *Belfast. Other parts of the agreement concerned the release of prisoners and the giving up of weapons. The agreement was the result of talks led by the US Senator George Mitchell between *Unionist and *Republican groups, and was signed by politicians including Gerry *Adams, David *Trimble, John *Hume, Mo *Mowlam and Tony *Blair. Most of the people of Northern Ireland and the Irish Republic supported the agreement in a vote held in May 1998.

‚Good 'Housekeeping a magazine containing articles about homes, family, health, food and fashion. It is published once a month in different versions in America and Britain and was first published in the US in 1885 and in Britain in 1922.

‚Good King 'Wenceslas /'wensəslæs/ a Christmas *carol. Most people in Britain and the US know the first lines of the song:

> 66 Good King Wenceslas looked out
> On the feast of Stephen,
> When the snow lay round about,
> Deep and crisp and even. 99

The 'Good Life a British comedy television series which was popular in the 1970s. It is about a couple who decide to convert their suburban house into a farm where they grow all their own food, make their own clothes, etc.

‚Benny 'Goodman /'gʊdmən/ (1909–86) a US musician who played the clarinet and led a successful dance band in the 1930s and 1940s. He was called the 'King of Swing', and one of his hits was *Stompin' at the Savoy* (1936). Goodman was the first white band leader to use *African American musicians. In 1938, his band played the first *jazz concert in *Carnegie Hall. He also played classical music written for him by Aaron *Copland, Béla Bartók and others.

‚Good 'Neighbor ‚Policy a friendly policy created by President Franklin D *Roosevelt for US dealings with Latin America, which was signed in 1933. It encouraged good relations between the US and the other nations, and gave US financial support for programmes for agriculture, health, education and business.

The ‚Good 'News Bible (abbr **GNT**) a modern version of the Bible in simple English, published in 1976 by the American Bible Society and revised in 1992. The 'good news' is from the word 'gospel', which means 'good message'. Since 2001 it has also been called the *Good News Translation*.

‚good old 'boy n (AmE informal) an expression used by white men in the southern US states to refer to a man they like and welcome into their group. He is usually a friendly person who has an easy manner and enjoys typically male activities.

The 'Good Old Days a British television series (1953–1983) consisting of old-fashioned *music-hall(1) performances. The programmes were broadcast from a real music-hall, with members of the audience dressed in Victorian costume.

‚Goodwill 'Industries a major US charity, begun in 1910 by Edgar Helms, a *Methodist minister. It operates in the US and in many other countries to provide training and employment for people who have physical or mental problems or who have committed crimes, etc. It collects money by asking people to give clothing and household items which are then sold in over 1900 Goodwill shops.

‚Goodwin 'Sands /‚gʊdwɪn/ a group of dangerous banks of sand just below the surface of the sea in the *English Channel near *Dover. Many ships have been damaged and sunk there. According to legend, they used to be an island belonging to an *earl(1) called Godwin which was washed away by the sea.

‚Goodwood 'House /‚gʊdwʊd/ a *stately home near *Chichester in southern England. It was first built in the 17th century, and rebuilt in the late 18th century. It contains valuable pieces of furniture and works of art, especially from 18th-century France. It is best known for the horse races that take place near the house. The five-day race meeting that takes place in July each year is called 'Glorious Goodwood' and the racecourse is often described as the most beautiful in the world.

'Goodyear /'gʊdjɪə(r)/ (in full **the Goodyear Tyre and Rubber Company**) a large US company, established in 1898 and based in Alcron, *Ohio, which produces and sells tyres and other rubber products in many countries around the world. The company is also well known for its airships called blimps (= aircraft like large balloons filled with gas lighter than air and driven by engines). These regularly fly with television cameras over sports events.

'Google™ /'guːgl/ a very popular Internet search engine (= a website which helps you to search for information on the Internet). The US company which runs it, Google Inc, was started in 1998 by Larry Page (1973–) and Sergey Brin (1973–). The name comes from *googol*, meaning the number one followed by 100 zeros.

The 'Goon Show /'guːn/ a British comedy radio programme, broadcast by the *BBC in the 1950s. It consisted of jokes, songs and situations that were full of surprising and ridiculous humour, and had an important influence on the development of British comedy. The actors and writers, Michael Bentine (1922–97), Spike *Milligan, Harry *Secombe and Peter *Sellers, were called the **Goons**.

'Goosebumps /'guːsbʌmps/ the title of a popular series of books for children by the US author R L Stine. They are horror stories, but are often humorous as well. Versions of the stories have appeared on children's television in Britain and the US.

GOP /'dʒiː əʊ 'piː; AmE oʊ/ (in full **Grand Old Party**) a popular name for the US *Republican Party.

the 'Gorbals /'gɔːblz; AmE 'gɔːrblz/ a district of south *Glasgow. It used to be known for its slums (= streets of old buildings in a poor, dirty condition) but much of the area was rebuilt in the late 20th century.

‚General 'Gordon /'gɔːdn; AmE 'gɔːrdn/ (Charles George Gordon 1833–85) an English military leader. He became known as 'Chinese Gordon' after defeating a

G

rebellion against British rule in China in 1863. He was killed in a small military camp in Khartoum, Sudan, after resisting attacks from Sudanese forces for ten months.

Gordon 'Bennett! /ˌɡɔːdn ˈbenɪt; AmE ˈɡɔːrdn/ (BrE informal) a rather old-fashioned phrase used to express surprise or shock. The original Mr Bennett was a 19th-century US newspaper owner, James Gordon Bennett Junior, who was famous for his extravagant lifestyle and his support of sporting events. He also provided the money for *Stanley's journey to Africa to look for David *Livingstone. He lived for many years in Paris, where he started the *International Herald Tribune.

the **Gordon 'riots** /ˌɡɔːdn; AmE ˈɡɔːrdn/ n [pl] a series of violent disturbances that lasted for a week in 1780 in London, England, the most serious riots ever to occur in Britain. They started when a large group of people, led by Lord Gordon (1751–93), went to the *House of Commons to protest against the *Emancipation Act. They also attacked the *Bank of England and *Newgate prison, allowing prisoners to escape and cause more damage. The riots are described in Charles *Dickens's novel Barnaby Rudge.

'Gordon's™ /ˈɡɔːdnz; AmE ˈɡɔːrdnz/ a British company that has produced a popular make of gin called Gordon's Original Dry London gin since 1769. Since 1908 it has been sold in green bottles in Britain and exported in clear bottles.

'Gordonstoun /ˈɡɔːdnstən; AmE ˈɡɔːrdnstən/ a *public school(1) in north-east Scotland, established in 1934 by a German, Dr Kurt Hahn. It is well known for the importance it gives to developing students' physical as well as academic abilities. Several members of the British *royal family have been students there.

Al 'Gore /ˈɡɔː(r)/ (1948–) the 45th Vice-President of the US (1993–2001). Gore was the *Democratic Party candidate for President in 2000 when George W. *Bush was elected but the result was very close and there is still controversy about the counting of the votes in *Florida.

Antony 'Gormley /ˈɡɔːmli; AmE ˈɡɔːrmli/ (1950–) an English sculptor.He is best known for his sculptures of people and figures, especially The Angel of the North near Gateshead in north-east England, the largest sculpture in Britain.

'gospel music (also gospel) n [U] Christian religious music that is sung in a *blues style, especially by *African Americans. Mahalia *Jackson was a famous gospel singer, and Aretha *Franklin was strongly influenced by gospel music. Compare SOUL.

'Gotcha! /ˈɡɒtʃə; AmE ˈɡɑːtʃə/ a humorous way of writing the phrase 'I've got you!', which a person says when they have found or caught somebody, or when they win an argument. Many people were shocked when it was used as the headline of the *Sun newspaper with a picture of an Argentinian ship after it had been hit during the *Falklands War.

'Gotham /ˈɡɒθəm; AmE ˈɡɑːθəm/ a popular name for New York City, first used by Washington *Irving. It comes from the name of an English village whose inhabitants were known to be very stupid.

'Gothic adj of a style of architecture that was common in Western Europe from the 12th to the 16th centuries. Gothic buildings can be recognized by their tall pointed arches and tall narrow windows and columns. Many British churches and cathedrals were built in this style. Compare PERPENDICULAR, DECORATED STYLE.

Gothic 'novel n any of a class of English novels dealing with frightening or magic subjects. Most Gothic novels are set in ruined castles or large old houses with ghosts, and were written in the late 18th and early 19th centuries. The style was made popular by Horace *Walpole's The Castle of Otranto (1764), and influenced writers such as Mary *Shelley and Edgar Allan *Poe, as well as 20th-century horror stories and horror films.

the **Gothic Re'vival** the return to a *Gothic style in British architecture that occurred between the middle of the 18th century and the middle of the 19th century. Many British churches were built in the new Gothic style, also called **neo-Gothic**, and are often more highly decorated than older Gothic churches. The style was also used for buildings such as hotels, railway stations and government buildings, including the *Houses of Parliament(2). See also PUGIN, SCOTT.

Stephen Jay 'Gould /ˈɡuːld/ (1941–2002) a US palaeontologist (= person who studies the remains of animals and plants in rock as a guide to the history of life on earth). He is well known for his theory of 'punctuated equilibrium', which explains evolution (= the development of life forms) that takes place in short periods of rapid change separated by long periods without change. He wrote many popular books and articles about the history of life on earth.

government 'health warning n (in Britain) a warning that must by law appear on all tobacco products and advertisements for them, to show that they are considered harmful to health. They may also appear on other products such as mobile phones.

the **Gower Pe'ninsula** /ˌɡaʊə; AmE ˌɡaʊər/ a peninsula (= an area of land almost surrounded by water) on the south coast of Wales, near *Swansea. It is well known for its attractive scenery and for the many remains of prehistoric people and animals that have been found there.

GP /ˌdʒiː ˈpiː/ (in full **general practitioner**) n (in Britain) a doctor who treats all types of illnesses within a community, sometimes called a **family doctor**. They can write prescriptions (= instructions that allow people to buy medicines), and may recommend that a person goes to see a specialist in a particular disease. Patients are usually treated at the doctor's surgery, and may also be visited at home. GPs are employed by the *National Health Service but they may also have some *private patients.

GPA /ˌdʒiː piː ˈeɪ/ ⇨ GRADE POINT AVERAGE.

the **GPMU** /ˌdʒiː piː em ˈjuː/ (in full **the 'Graphical, 'Paper and 'Media Union**) a trade union in Britain and Ireland, mainly representing workers in the printing, paper and design industries. It was formed in 1991 and is the world's largest media union.

the **GPO** /ˌdʒiː piː ˈəʊ; AmE ˈoʊ/ **1** (in full **the General Post Office**) the former name for the British organization of post office services. In 1969 its name was changed to the *Post Office, but some people still refer to it as the GPO. See also ROYAL MAIL, POST OFFICE.
2 (in full **the Government Printing Office**) the organization that is responsible for publishing federal government documents in the US, including new laws. Its head is called the Public Printer and is chosen by the President. The first Public Printer was Benjamin *Franklin.

GQ /ˌdʒiː ˈkjuː/ a magazine for men that contains articles on fashion, sport, sex, health and other subjects. The letters 'GQ' stand for 'Gentlemen's Quarterly'. It is published every month and first appeared in the US in 1957. The British edition first appeared in 1988.

W G 'Grace /ˈɡreɪs/ (William Gilbert Grace 1848–1915) an English cricketer, equally successful as a batsman and as a bowler, who played for *Gloucestershire and England from the 1860s to the beginning of the 20th century. He was one of the greatest cricket players of all time.

G

Grace and 'Favour ˌresidence *n* a house or flat/apartment owned by the British king or queen, in which people are invited to live without paying any rent. Among the best-known are the ones in *Kensington Palace and *Windsor Castle.

'Graceland /'greɪslənd/ the large house in *Memphis, *Tennessee, where Elvis *Presley lived and died. It is now a popular museum. Each year many thousands of fans gather there on 16 August, the anniversary of his death.

ˌMichael 'Grade /'greɪd/ (1943–) a British television executive who has worked for the *BBC and *Channel Four. He became chairman of the *BBC in 2004.

'grade point ˌaverage *n* (*abbr* **GPA**) (*AmE*) an average academic score for a student in a US *high school, college or university. The highest grade A receives 4 points, B is 3, C is 2, D is 1 and F is 0. Points received during an academic period of weeks or months are added together and the average calculated. A high GPA helps a high school student to get into a good college or university. High points received at a college or university can result in a student being named on the *dean's list and other honours. Students with low GPAs can be dismissed.

The 'Graduate a US comedy film (1967) about an older woman who has sex with a young man who then realizes he loves her daughter. The film made a star of Dustin *Hoffman, and Mike Nichols won an *Oscar for directing it. *Simon and Garfunkel wrote the music, including the song *Mrs Robinson*.

'Graduate 'Management Ad'missions Test ⇨ GMAT.

the ˌGraduate 'Record Exami ˌnation ⇨ GRE.

'graduate school *n* (in the US) the department of a university or college for studies after the first degree. Students must do well in the *Graduate Record Examination to be accepted. Graduate school degrees include the *master's degree and PhD.

ˌBilly 'Graham¹ /'greɪəm/ (1918–) a US *evangelist and minister in the Southern Baptist Church. He has led large religious meetings in many countries around the world. During these 'Crusades for Christ', Graham asks people to come forward and give their lives to Christ, and millions have done so.

ˌKatherine 'Graham² /'greɪəm/ (1917–2001) a US newspaper owner who was one of America's most powerful women. She published the *Washington Post* from 1968 to 1978 (during the time it discovered *Watergate), and controlled The Washington Post Company which owns *Newsweek* magazine. Graham won a *Pulitzer Prize in 1998 for her book about her life, *Personal History*.

ˌMartha 'Graham³ /'greɪəm/ (1894–1991) a US dancer and choreographer who helped to develop modern dance. She began her own dance company in 1929 and designed more than 160 works including *Appalachian Spring* (1944) and *Seraphic Dialogue* (1955). Graham received the *Presidential Medal of Freedom in 1976.

'graham ˌcracker /'greɪəm/ *n* (*AmE*) a small, square, slightly sweet biscuit made with wholemeal flour. Graham crackers are often given to children as a healthier alternative to cookies. They are named after Sylvester Graham (1794–1851), an American who encouraged people to eat healthy foods.

ˌKenneth 'Grahame /'greɪəm/ (1852–1932) a Scottish writer of children's books. He is best known for writing *The *Wind in the Willows*, which was based on bedtime stories he told to his son.

the Grail /greɪl/ ⇨ HOLY GRAIL.

ˌPercy 'Grainger /'greɪndʒə(r)/ (1882–1961) an Australian composer and pianist who lived most of his life in Britain and the US. He is best known for collecting and arranging English *folk music.

'grammar school *n* (in Britain) a type of secondary school at which more academic subjects are studied than at *secondary modern or *comprehensive schools. Most British towns used to have at least one grammar school, which children could enter only if they passed an examination at the age of eleven. Many people thought that this system was unfair, and by the end of the 20th century most local education authorities had changed to the comprehensive system. Some of Britain's older grammar schools became *independent schools.

'Grammy /'græmi/ *n* any of the awards for special achievements in the recording industry presented each year since 1958 by the US National Academy of Recording Arts and Sciences. The name comes from the small model of a gramophone (= an old-fashioned machine for playing records) that is given to each winner.

the 'Grampians /'græmpiənz/ (*also* the ˌGrampian 'Mountains** /ˌgræmpiən/) *n* [pl] a range of mountains in central Scotland that includes the *Cairngorms and Ben Nevis. They are popular with mountain climbers and hill walkers, and with people who like to shoot grouse (= birds that are shot for sport and food).

the ˌGrand 'Canyon an extremely large gorge (= a valley with steep sides) in the US state of *Arizona which is a major tourist attraction. The Canyon was created by the Colorado River and is about 1 mile/1.6 kilometres deep, 200 miles/320 kilometres long and 4–18 miles/6–29 kilometres) wide. It has colourful layers of rock, the oldest of which are about 2 billion years old. **Grand Canyon National Park** was opened in 1919 and was made a *World Heritage Site in 1979.

'Grand 'Central 'Station (*also* **'Grand 'Central 'Terminal**) the best-known railway station in the US. It is on East 42nd Street in New York and was completed in 1913. The main area is very large, and the trains enter and leave the station on 67 tracks, arranged on two levels. The station is often very crowded: *You can't move in there – it's like Grand Central Station!*

Grand Central Station

'Grand 'Coulee 'Dam /'ku:li/ a large dam on the Columbia River in the US state of *Washington. It was completed in 1942 and made larger in the 1980s. It was built to produce electricity from water power. The dam is 550 feet/168 metres high and 4 173 feet/1 273 metres long. It holds back the waters of Franklin D Roosevelt Lake, one of the largest US reservoirs (= places where water is stored for use).

the ˌGrand 'Lodge the leading organization in British *Freemasonry, established in London in 1717. Many members of the British *royal family have been Grand Masters (= leaders) of the Grand Lodge.

,**Grandma 'Moses** /'məʊzɪz; *AmE* 'moʊzəs/ (1860–1961) the popular name for the US painter Anna Mary Robertson Moses. She was a farmer's wife who did not paint until the age of 76 and then produced more than 1 200 works. Her colourful paintings are in the primitive style and show the countryside where she had lived in New York State and *Virginia. Her last paintings were done at the age of 101.

the ,**Grand 'National** (*also informal* **the National**) the most famous and important horse race in Britain. It is a very long race, with many high fences for the horses to jump over, and it takes place every year in March or April at *Aintree, near *Liverpool. Many British people bet on the Grand National, even if they do not usually gamble on horse races.

The '**Grand Old ,Duke of 'York** /'jɔːk; *AmE* 'jɔːrk/ a British *nursery rhyme about the Duke of York, a soldier who was the second son of *George III. It is sometimes quoted when somebody cannot decide what to do. The first verse is:

> 66 Oh the Grand old Duke of York
> He had ten thousand men,
> He marched them up to the top of the hill
> And he marched them down again. 99

,**Grand Old 'Man** *n* [usually sing] (*sometimes humorous*) a title used to describe a man who has been involved in a particular activity for a long time at a high level. It was originally used to refer to William *Gladstone, who spent many years in politics and was *Prime Minister four times: *He is very much the Grand Old Man of Canadian literature.*

The ,**Grand Ole 'Opry** /əʊl 'ɒpri; *AmE* oʊl 'ɔːpri/ (*also informal* **The Opry**) a US radio programme that has broadcast *country music from *Nashville, *Tennessee, on Saturday nights since 1925. It has been running longer than any other radio programme in the world and all the most famous country singers and musicians have appeared on it.

the '**Grand 'Order of 'Water Rats** a British organization whose members are entertainers. They organize events to raise money for charity, including an annual ball each November.

,**grand 'slam** *n* **1** (in tennis and golf) a victory for a single player in all of the four most important competitions in a particular year (which are sometimes called **grand slam events**).
2 (in Rugby Union) a situation in which one country beats all five others in the *Six Nations Tournament.
3 (in baseball) a home run that is hit when three players are on the bases, so that four players each score a run (= point).
4 (in certain card games) a situation in which one player wins all 13 tricks (= rounds of cards) in a single game.

'**Grandstand** a popular *BBC sports television programme. It is broadcast on Saturday and Sunday afternoons and usually consists of some sports events shown as they happen, and recordings and reports of other events.

the ,**Grand 'Tour** *n* (especially in the 18th century) a tour of Europe that was regarded as part of the education of a wealthy young man. The tour sometimes took several years, and usually included visits to Paris, the Alps, Florence and Rome.

the '**Grand 'Union Ca'nal** a canal that links London with *Birmingham and *Leicester. It is the longest canal

in Britain, and used to be an important route for goods between the *Midlands and the south of England.

the ,**Grand 'Wizard** ⇨ KU KLUX KLAN.

,**Grange 'Hill** a British children's television programme in the 1970s and 1980s. It was set in a school in London, and was more realistic than many children's programmes, dealing with problems such as *bullying.

Gra'nita /grə'niːtə/ a restaurant in Islington, *London which became famous as the place where Tony *Blair and Gordon *Brown made an agreement in 1994 about who would lead the *Labour Party. The restaurant closed in 2003.

,**Granny 'Smith** *n* a type of apple with a green skin and hard sweet flesh. Granny Smiths are very popular in Britain.

gra'nola *n* [U] (*AmE*) a US breakfast food that is a mixture of whole grains, fruits, seeds and nuts (called *muesli* in British English). It is eaten in a bowl with milk and sometimes sugar.

,**Cary 'Grant**[1] /ˌkeəri 'grɑːnt; *AmE* ˌkeri 'grænt/ (1904–86) a US film actor, born in England. He was known for his easy charm in romantic and comedy parts. His films included *The Philadelphia Story* (1940), *To Catch a Thief* (1955), *Indiscreet* (1958) and *North by Northwest* (1959). He received a special *Oscar in 1969.

,**Hugh 'Grant**[2] /'grɑːnt; *AmE* 'grænt/ (1960–) an English actor who is known for playing typically English men in romantic comedy films. His films include *Four Weddings and a Funeral* (1994), *Notting Hill* (1999), *Bridget Jones' Diary* (2001) and *Love Actually* (2003).

U,**lysses S 'Grant**[3] /juː,lɪsɪːz, 'grɑːnt; *AmE* 'grænt/ (Ulysses Simpson Grant 1822–85) the general who commanded the US Army during the *Civil War and later became the 18th *President of the US (1869–77). His greatest Civil War victory was at *Vicksburg, *Mississippi, and he accepted the surrender of Robert E *Lee at *Appomattox Court House. Grant was a *Republican. He was not a successful president because he failed to stop the illegal actions of friends he appointed. His two volumes of *Personal Memoirs* (1885–6) are among the best military books ever written.

'**Granta** /'grɑːntə; *AmE* 'græntə/ **1** the local name for the river Cam as it flows through *Cambridge, England. Compare ISIS.
2 a British publishing company which is best known as the publisher of *Granta*, a literary magazine of new writing including short stories, poems, and parts of novels and travel books. *Granta* began as a *Cambridge University student magazine, but is now sold in many countries.

'**Grantchester** /'grɑːntʃestə(r); *AmE* 'græntʃestər/ a village near *Cambridge, England. It is well known because of a famous poem, *The Old Vicarage, Grantchester*, by Rupert *Brooke, who stayed there in 1910.

,**Grant's 'Tomb** /ˌgrɑːnts; *AmE* ˌgrænts/ the impressive stone building in which US President Ulysses S *Grant and his wife are buried, in Riverside Park, New York City. It was designed by John Duncan and completed in 1897. Its official name since 1958 has been the General Grant National Memorial.

'**Grape Nuts**™ *n* [U] a breakfast food consisting of crisp pieces of cooked wheat, usually eaten with milk. It is made by the US Kraft Foods company and is also sold in Britain.

The ,**Grapes of 'Wrath** a novel (1939) by the US writer John *Steinbeck which won the *Pulitzer Prize. It tells the story of the Joad family, whose farm is ruined in the *Dust Bowl, and their journey to the 'promised land' of

G

California. It is a sad story about the lack of government support for poor people. A film version in 1940 was directed by John *Ford[6], with Henry *Fonda as Tom Joad, the head of the family. The title of the book is a phrase from The *Battle Hymn of the Republic.

'Grasmere /'grɑːsmɪə(r); AmE 'græsmɪr/ a village in the English *Lake District where William *Wordsworth lived for much of his life, and where the *Lake Poets used to meet. Wordsworth's house, *Dove Cottage, and the churchyard where he is buried are popular with tourists. The village is by a small lake, also called Grasmere.

The ,Grateful 'Dead a US *rock band that formed in 1965 in *San Francisco. They were known for their many stage performances and their willingness to change songs each time they played them. Their successful albums included Grateful Dead (1967) and American Beauty (1970). Their leader, Jerry Garcia (1942–96), died at a drug treatment centre in California. In 1998 three other original members of the group formed a new group called The Other Ones.

'Grauman's 'Chinese 'Theater /'grɔːmənz 'tʃaɪniːz/ the original name of a famous *Hollywood cinema, now called Mann's Chinese Theater, which was built in 1927 by Sid Grauman and designed like a Chinese pagoda (= religious building). Near its entrance there is a place where well-known film stars leave images of their hands or feet by pressing them into wet cement which then dries.

,Robert 'Graves /'greɪvz/ (1895–1985) an English writer. He wrote many books of poetry, books about literature, and novels. He is now best known for his historical novels set in ancient Rome, I, Claudius (1934) and Claudius the God (1934), which were made into a *BBC television series in 1976, The Long Weekend (1940), a social history of Great Britain from 1918 to 1939, and his autobiography *Goodbye to All That (1929) about his experiences in the First World War. After fighting in *World War I, Graves left Britain and lived most of his life in Majorca.

,Thomas 'Gray /'greɪ/ (1716–1771) an English poet, best known for his *Elegy Written in a Country Church Yard. He was a friend of Horace *Walpole. The few poems that he wrote had a strong influence on the development of the *Romantic Movement.

> 66 Where ignorance is bliss
> 'Tis folly to be wise. 99
> Thomas Gray On a Distant Prospect of Eton College

,Gray's A'natomy /,greɪz/ the name by which Anatomy, Descriptive and Surgical is commonly known. It is a book consisting of descriptions and illustrations of the human body, first written in 1858 by Henry Gray, an English doctor. Many revised editions have been published and it is still used by many medical students in Britain.

,Gray's 'Elegy /,greɪz/ the name most people use to refer to the poem called Elegy written in a Country Church Yard (1751) by Thomas *Gray. It describes life in the country and the dignity of man, and was an early influence on the writers of the *Romantic Movement.

> 66 The curfew tolls the knell of parting day,
> The lowing herd wind slowly o'er the lea,
> The ploughman homeward plods his weary way,
> And leaves the world to darkness and to me. 99

GRE /,dʒiː ɑːr 'iː/ (in full **Graduate Record Examination**) a standard US examination taken to enter an American *graduate school.

Grease /griːs/ a US musical play about the love affairs of young people, especially Danny and Sandy, in a *high school in the early days of *rock and roll. The title refers to the hair oil used by the boys. In the successful film version (1978) John *Travolta and Olivia Newton-John played the main parts. Grease 2 (1982) with different actors was less successful.

the 'Great A'merican 'Desert the area of desert in the south-west US and northern Mexico. It runs from southern *California north into *Idaho and *Oregon and east to the *Rocky Mountains. It includes the *Mojave Desert and the *Painted Desert.

the 'great A'merican 'novel any novel that is regarded as having successfully represented an important time in US history or one that tells a story that is typical of America. Many US writers have tried to write such a book and The Great American Novel is the title of novels by William Carlos Williams (1923) and Philip *Roth (1973). Books that are considered to deserve to be called 'the great American novel' include *Huckleberry Finn, *Gone with the Wind and The *Grapes of Wrath.

▶ **Great Britain**

Great Britain is, strictly, a geographical area consisting of the large island which is divided into England, Wales and Scotland. It is often called **Britain**. The name Great Britain was first used in a political sense after the *Act of Union of Scotland with England and Wales in 1707.

The British Isles describes the geographical area of Great Britain, all of Ireland (including the independent Republic of Ireland), and all the many smaller offshore islands, including the *Orkney Islands and the *Scilly Isles. It has a total area of 121 544 square miles/314 798 square kilometres.

The United Kingdom of Great Britain and Northern Ireland, called for short **the United Kingdom** or **the UK**, refers to the political state that includes the countries of England, Wales, Scotland and Northern Ireland. It does not include the *Isle of Man or the *Channel Islands, which are **Crown dependencies**. The United Kingdom was formed in 1801 when the Irish parliament was joined with the parliament for England, Wales and Scotland in London, and the whole of the British Isles became a single state. However, in 1922 the south of Ireland became the Irish Free State and, in 1949, a completely independent republic.

The names Great Britain and United Kingdom are now often used informally to mean the same thing. There are older names for parts of the United Kingdom, but these are found mostly in literature. *Britannia is the name the Romans gave to their province which covered most of England. *Albion was the original Roman name for England, **Caledonia** their name for Scotland, **Cambria** for Wales and **Hibernia** for Ireland. The people of the United Kingdom are **British** and have British nationality. As a group they are usually referred to as **the British**, rather than as **Britons**, though this name is used in the media. **Ancient Britons** were the people who lived in Britain before the Romans came. Only people who come from England can be called **English**. People from Ireland are **Irish**, people from Wales **Welsh**, and people from Scotland **Scots** or **Scottish**, and they do not like being called English. The term **the Brits** is only used informally, often humorously. Many people from Scotland, Wales and Northern Ireland have stronger feelings of loyalty towards their own country than they do to the United Kingdom. British people who have come originally from Asia, Africa or the West Indies may also feel two sets of loyalties.

the **Great 'Britain** a large steamship, designed by
*Brunel and built in 1843. It was the first of the large pas-
senger ships that travelled regularly between Europe
and America.

the **Great De'pression** (*also* **the Depression**) the
period of severe economic failure in most countries of
the world that lasted from 1929 until *World War II. It
began in the US when the *New York Stock Exchange
fell on 29 October 1929, known as *Black Tuesday. Many
businesses and banks failed and millions of people lost
their jobs. President Franklin D *Roosevelt improved the
situation with his *New Deal(1) policy, but the Great
Depression was only ended by industrial production for
the war.

the **Great Di'vide** ⇨ CONTINENTAL DIVIDE.

Greater 'London /'lʌndən/ the area covered by the
32 *boroughs of London. It was established as a local
government area in the 1960s when parts of the *counties closest to London became parts of London. It is a
very large area, covering 610 square miles/1580 square
kilometres, with a population of around 7.2 million. See
also LONDON ASSEMBLY.

the **Greater London Authority** (*abbr* **the GLA**)
the local authority that is responsible for *Greater
London. It is made up of an elected *Mayor of London,
the separately elected *London Assembly, and about
500 staff to help the Mayor and Assembly in their duties.
From 1983 to 2000 there was no single authority responsible for London; each *borough was responsible for
itself. In 2000 the GLA was created to fulfil the needs of
London as a whole and to work with the boroughs in
areas such as transport, planning, economic development, the environment, police, fire and emergency services, culture and health. See also GLC, LIVINGSTONE.

the **Greater London 'Council** /lʌndən/ ⇨ GLC.

Greater 'Manchester /'mæntʃɪstə(r)/ a *metropolitan county in north-west England consisting of
*Manchester and parts of the towns and counties that
surround it.

the **Great Exhi'bition** an exhibition of products
from many countries around the world that took place in
London in 1851. It was the world's first international
trade fair (= a large event where companies display
their products in order to increase sales) and the
*Crystal Palace was built for it.

Great Expec'tations a novel (1861) by Charles
*Dickens. It is the story of a young man, Pip, who helped
a prisoner to escape when he was a boy. Later, the man
sends him money, but Pip thinks that it comes from the
family of Estella, the girl he loves. He moves to London,
expecting to become rich and to marry Estella. He is
cruel to the people who looked after him as a child,
because he is ashamed of their poverty, but when the
money stops coming, and Estella marries somebody
else, he goes back to them and learns to be a better person.

the **Great Fire of 'London** ⇨ FIRE OF LONDON.

The **Great 'Gatsby** /'gætsbi/ a novel (1925) by the US
writer F Scott *Fitzgerald. The story is about Jay Gatsby,
a man who has become very rich through illegal activities, and his attempts to win back his former lover Daisy
Buchanan. The book is regarded as one of the best
descriptions of the lives of rich, lazy people in the *Jazz
Age. There have been three film versions.

the **Great 'Glen** (*also* **Glen 'More** /'mɔː(r)/) a long
valley running across the *Highlands of Scotland from
the west coast near *Fort William to the east coast near
Inverness. Loch *Ness fills part of the valley.

the **Great 'Lakes** a group of five large lakes along the
central and eastern border between the US and Canada.

They are connected and have a total area of 95 170
square miles/246 490 square kilometres, the largest area
of fresh water in the world. They are Lake *Superior,
Lake *Michigan (completely in the US), Lake *Huron,
Lake *Erie and Lake *Ontario. Ships use them to travel
between the Atlantic Ocean and cities like *Chicago and
Duluth, *Minnesota.

the **Great North 'Road** the name of the old road
between London and *Edinburgh. It used to be the main
road north from London, before it was replaced in the
20th century by *motorways. Some parts of the A1 road
are still referred to as the Great North Road.

Great 'Ormond Street /'ɔːmənd; *AmE* 'ɔːrmənd/ a
street in central London which contains the Hospital for
Sick Children, which most people call the Great Ormond
Street Hospital. It is the best-known children's hospital
in Britain. Charities often collect money for it and part of
the profits from all sales and performances of *Peter Pan
go to the hospital: *She was transferred to Great Ormond
Street for a life-saving operation.*

the **Great 'Plague** the serious and widespread attack
of bubonic plague (= a disease causing fever, swellings
and death) in London in 1664–5, when about one fifth of
the population died. The disease was spread by the fleas
(= insects that feed on blood) from rats and killed over
70 000 people. Most British people know about the
plague from pictures, stories and films in which bodies
are collected each morning in the streets. See also
BLACK DEATH.

the **Great 'Plains** a large area of the west central US
where the land is high and flat. It includes the 10 *Plains
States, stretching about 400 miles/644 kilometres east
from the *Rocky Mountains, and from Canada to southern *Texas. It was the home of the *Plains Indians and is
also called the *Wheat Belt of America, although dry
weather in the 1930s turned the southern part into the
*Dust Bowl.

Greats /greɪts/ **1** the second part of the four-year
undergraduate course at *Oxford University in Greek
and Latin, including the Greek and Latin languages and
the literature, history and philosophy of ancient Greece
and Rome.
2 the final examinations in this course.

the **Great Salt 'Lake** a large shallow lake in the US
state of *Utah whose water is more salty than sea water.
It is the largest lake in North America, about 72
miles/116 kilometres long and 30 miles/48 kilometres
wide. Industry takes salt and other minerals from it. Five
miles south-east of the lake is *Salt Lake City. To the
west is the Great Salt Lake Desert with the Bonneville
Salt Flats where drivers have established the highest
speeds on land.

the **Great 'Seal 1** the state seal (= a tool for putting a
design in wax on a document to show that it is official) of
the United Kingdom. It is kept by the *Lord Chancellor
and used on documents of national importance.
2 the national seal of the US. It is kept by the *Secretary
of State and used on documents of national importance.

the **Great 'Smoky 'Mountains** (*also* **the Great
Smokies**) a beautiful part of the *Appalachian
Mountains that separates *Tennessee from *North
Carolina. It gets its name from the thin clouds like smoke
which often cover the valleys. The highest point is
Clingman's Dome (6 642 feet/2 026 metres). Most of the
area is within the **Great Smoky Mountains National
Park** which was established in 1934 and was made a
*World Heritage Site in 1983.

the **Great So'ciety** a phrase used by US President
Lyndon *Johnson in 1964 to explain what his new social
and economic programmes could achieve. He wanted to

G

create a society in which all Americans were equal and there was no poverty. As part of this aim, Johnson's government created the *Medicare and *Medicaid medical programmes, the Head Start educational programme for poor children and the US Department of Housing and Urban Development. It also passed the *Voting Rights Act.

the ˌGreat 'Spirit (in the religions of many *Native American peoples) the father god who created everything.

The ˌGreat 'Train ˌRobbery a 10-minute US silent film (1903) which has been called 'the first real movie', because it was the first to tell a story. It is a *western about criminals who rob a train and then celebrate in town. It was made by the Edison Company and was the main attraction in nickelodeons for several years.

the ˌGreat 'Train ˌRobbery a robbery that took place in southern England in 1963. A group of men attacked a mail train and stole £2.6 million. It is Britain's most famous robbery because little of the stolen money was ever found. Most of the robbers were caught and sent to prison, but one of them, Ronald Biggs, escaped from prison but returned there in 2001.

'Great Uni'versal 'Stores the former name for *GUS.

the ˌGreat 'War (old-fashioned) World War I.

the ˌGreat White 'Fleet a group of 16 US war ships sent on a tour around the world for 15 months (1907–9) by President Theodore *Roosevelt. His main aim was to show foreign countries, especially possible enemies, how powerful the US was.

ˌgreat white 'hope n (AmE) any white boxer who was thought to have a chance of beating Jack *Johnson, who was the first *African American heavyweight champion. The Great White Hope was a film (1970) based on Johnson's life. The expression is still sometimes used in the sport of boxing today, but usually in a humorous way.

the ˌGreat White 'Way a popular name for the theatre district of *Broadway in New York, because of the many bright lights outside the theatres.

ˌKate 'Greenaway¹ /'griːnəweɪ/ (1846–1901) an artist who drew pictures for children's books. She developed her own style of drawing children, usually playing, dressed in early 19th–century clothes. The **Kate Greenaway Medal** is a prize given every year for the best illustrated book for children published in that year.

ˌPeter 'Greenaway² /'griːnəweɪ/ (1942–) an English film director who makes artistic and sometimes controversial films. His best-known films include Drowning by Numbers (1988), The Cook, The Thief, His Wife and Her Lover (1989), Prospero's Books (1991) and The Pillow Book (1996).

ˌgreen 'belt n [C, U] an area of countryside around a town. In Britain, building is strictly controlled in green belts to make sure that towns do not become too big and that there is some countryside for the people from the towns to enjoy. There are often strong protests when people are given permission to build on this land. In the US, a green belt is usually a nature area protected by a town or city. It is often a large park, with paths where people can walk. The town of Greenbelt, Maryland, was one of several created in this way in the 1930s as part of the *New Deal(1) programme of President Franklin D *Roosevelt: The council rejected plans for a housing development on green belt land.

the ˌGreen 'Berets the popular name for the US Army Special Forces because of the green caps they wear. They fought a lot in the tropical forests of Vietnam during the

*Vietnam War. The Green Berets (1968), with John *Wayne, was a film about that war.

ˌgreen 'card n **1** (in the US) an official document required by people who come from other countries to work in the US.
2 (in Britain) a green document provided by British insurance companies to show that a person is insured to drive in other countries.

the ˌGreen Cross 'Code a set of rules, first published in 1971, for teaching children how to cross roads safely in Britain.

ˌGraham 'Greene /'griːn/ (1904–91) an English writer of novels. He became a *Roman Catholic in 1926, and many of his books, such as The *Power and the Glory, have strong moral or religious themes. He travelled to many different parts of the world and many of his books are set in tropical countries. He divided his books into 'entertainments', such as Our Man in Havana (1958), and more serious novels, such as The Heart of the Matter (1948) and The Quiet American (1955). Greene also wrote plays, travel books, essays and scripts for films, such as The *Third Man.

ˌGreene 'King /ˌgriːn/ an English company based in *Suffolk that makes beer and owns more than 2 000 *pubs. Its beers include **Greene King IPA, Abbot Ale, Old Speckled Hen** and **Ruddles County.**

ˌSusan 'Greenfield /'griːnfiːld/ (1950–) an English scientist, writer and broadcaster who is particularly interested in illnesses which affect the brain, such as Alzheimer's disease, and the relationship between the brain and the mind. She has been the director of the *Royal Institution of Great Britain since 1998. She was made a *life peer in 2001.

ˌGreen 'Giant™ a name used on its products by a company that sells vegetables, either fresh or frozen or in cans. It was founded in Minnesota in 1903. The advertisements describe the food as coming from 'the valley of the jolly Green Giant'. A giant is a creature in stories with a human form but very great size and strength.

ˌgreen 'goddess n the *nickname for a British military fire engine (= vehicle carrying equipment for putting out fires), which is green in colour. Green goddesses are used for fighting fires when the normal services for doing this are not available, e.g. during a strike.

ˌGreen Grow the 'Rushes O an old English *folk song in which the line 'Green grow the rushes O' is repeated in every verse. Each verse names a number of people or things, mostly connected with the Bible, and repeats all the things named in the previous verses. The song is sometimes sung by children in British schools.

ˌGreenham 'Common /ˌgriːnəm/ a military air base in southern England. In the 1980s when the British government agreed to keep US nuclear missiles there, a large group of women set up a camp around it to protest against the weapons. Many of the women were arrested several times, but they usually returned to the camp. Some stayed there until the weapons were taken away in 1991: She was one of the original Greenham Common women.

ˌGreen 'Man n [usually sing] **1** a figure of a person that has a green light shining through it at traffic lights in Britain. The green man lights up when the traffic has stopped, to show people that it is safe to cross the road. **2** an image of a man surrounded by green plants, trees, etc. In Britain it is an old symbol of fertility (= the ability of people to have children, trees to produce fruit and the soil to produce crops). The Green Man is a common name for a pub.

the 'Green ˌParty 1 a British political party that aims to protect the environment. It is against the use of nuclear power and other forms of industry and transport that it considers harmful. It was formed in 1973 as the Ecology Party, and changed its name to the Green Party in 1985. In 2005 the party had two *MEPs, two members of the *London Assembly, seven *MSPs and 61 councillors, but no *MPs in the *House of Commons.

2 (also **the Green Party of the United States**) a US political party formed in 1996 as the Association of State Green Parties. It changed its name to the Green Party of the United States in 2001. It aims to protect the environment and supports social justice. The party has a number of elected representatives across the US at all levels of politics. One of its best-known supporters is Ralph *Nader.

'**Greenpeace** /'gri:npi:s/ a large international *pressure group that aims to protect the environment. Its members are well known for taking direct action and putting their own lives in danger in order to stop people from harming the environment. For example, they often go out in small boats to stop people from killing whales or throwing poisonous material into the sea. See also RAINBOW WARRIOR.

'*Greensleeves* /'gri:nsli:vz/ a famous English song that has been popular since the 16th century. Its gentle tune has been arranged in many different musical styles. In the song a man sings sadly that he loves a woman, Lady Greensleeves, but she does not return his love. Some people believe that it was written by *Henry VIII, but there is no evidence for this.

‚Alan '**Greenspan** /'gri:nspæn/ (1926–) a US economist, the chairman of the *Federal Reserve from 1987 until 2006. He has a very important influence on US economic policy and the financial markets.

the ‚**green** '**welly bri‚gade** /'weli/ n [sing+ sing/pl v] (BrE humorous disapproving) a *nickname for *upper-class and *upper-middle-class British people who live in or like to visit the countryside. The name comes from the green wellington boots (= rubber boots) that such people often wear: *There was a showjumping competition in the village and the green welly brigade were out in force.*

'**Greenwich** /'grenɪtʃ/ a district of south-east London, on the south bank of the *Thames, with many attractive old buildings and parks. The original *Royal Observatory was built there in the 17th century. Its buildings now form part of the *National Maritime Museum. The *Millennium Dome was built in Greenwich as the main centre for Britain's celebrations for the year 2000. Maritime Greenwich was made a *World Heritage Site in 1997.

‚**Greenwich** '**Mean Time** /‚grenɪtʃ/ ⇨ GMT.

‚**Greenwich** '**Village**
/‚grenɪtʃ/ (also **the Village**) a district of *Manhattan(1) where many artists, writers and students live and meet in the galleries, cafes, bars and clubs. It was associated with the *beat generation. In 1969 the *Stonewall riots took place there. See also VILLAGE VOICE.

Greenwich Village

Ger‚maine '**Greer** / dʒ3:‚meɪn 'gri:ə(r); AmE dʒ3:r‚meɪn 'gri:ər/ (1939–) an Australian writer, broadcaster and professor of English who has lived mainly in Britain since the 1960s. She became internationally famous as a feminist (= a person who believes strongly that women should have the same rights and opportunities as men) after writing *The Female Eunuch* (1970), one of the most popular feminist books of the time. She has written many other books about sexual politics, art history and *Shakespeare.

▶ **greetings cards**

Specialist greetings card shops, newsagents and department stores sell millions of cards every year to help people celebrate important events in the lives of their friends and family. Most people send *birthday **cards**. They also send cards to celebrate engagements, weddings, births, moving to a new house and retirement from work, to wish somebody good luck, or to express sympathy when somebody has died. In addition, there are cards for *Christmas and *Easter, and other religious festivals.

Most greetings cards are folded and have a picture on the front and a verse or message inside. There are also many cards that are blank inside so that people can write their own message. Other cards say things like 'just because I was thinking about you', and are for people to send when there is no special occasion. There are also many postcards printed with simple pictures and messages such as 'Miss you' or 'Write to me'. Some cards show famous paintings, others have country scenes, flowers, animals, etc. on them. Children's birthday cards often have a number for the child's age, and sometimes a badge (AmE button). Many cards for adults have cartoons or rude jokes about getting old, or humour with a strong sexual content.

The most popular time to send cards is at Christmas. **Christmas cards** often have pictures of *Santa Claus, reindeer, robins and snow on them, as well as scenes from the story of Christ's birth. Many families send over 100 Christmas cards each year. People send cards to neighbours or people they work with, as well as to friends they see less often. Sending a Christmas card is a way of keeping in touch with friends and family members who live far away. Many people like to send **charity cards**, cards sold in aid of a charity, because they want to do some good for others at Christmas time. Business companies send cards to their main customers, and some have cards specially printed.

Some special days are thought to have been invented by greetings card manufacturers in order to increase their profits, e.g. **Father's Day**, when children are expected to send a card to their father, and **Grandparents' Day**. *Mother's Day is a much older festival which has its origins in the Christian Church. Another important date is *St Valentine's Day, when people send cards to the person they love, sometimes without signing them, or signing them with phrases like 'from a secret admirer'. In the US, children give small Valentine's Day cards to everyone in their school class.

Gre'nada /grə'neɪdə/ a country consisting of the island of Grenada and a group of smaller islands in the *Caribbean. It has been an independent state and a member of the *Commonwealth since 1974. In 1983, after the *Prime Minister had been killed, Grenada was attacked and taken over by US armed forces, who set up a new government. Many people around the world protested against the US action.
▶ **Grenadian** adj, n.

the ‚**Grenadier** '**Guards** /‚grenədɪə; AmE ‚grenədɪr/ one of the oldest and best-known regiments in the British army. It was the first regiment of *Foot Guards.

‚Joyce '**Grenfell** /'grenfəl/ (1910–79) an English entertainer who wrote and performed humorous songs and spoken pieces in which she made fun of different types of English women. She also appeared in many British films and television programmes.

Gretna 'Green /ˌgretnə/ a village just north of the border between England and Scotland. It is famous as the place where English couples traditionally ran away to get married, usually without their parents' permission, which they would have needed to be married in England. The Scottish laws concerning marriage were much less strict, and many couples were married by the Gretna Green blacksmith (= a person whose job is making things out of iron). These marriages were made illegal in Scotland in 1940.

Lady Jane 'Grey[1] /ˈgreɪ/ (1537–54) queen of England for nine days in 1553. She was a great-granddaughter of *Henry VII and a *Protestant. She was 15 years old when the Duke of Northumberland persuaded her to marry his son and persuaded the king, *Edward VI, to name her as the next queen instead of his *Roman Catholic sister, *Mary I. Jane became queen when Edward died, but was soon put in prison by supporters of Mary, and was later killed in the *Tower of London.

Zane 'Grey[2] /ˌzeɪn ˈgreɪ/ (1872–1939) a US author of *western novels which have sold millions of copies. They include *The Last of the Plainsmen* (1908) and his most famous, *Riders of the Purple Sage* (1912).

Greyhound 'bus n any of the buses of the Greyhound Lines Company, the largest US bus company operating between towns and cities. It was established in 1914 and took its present name in 1930 because the buses were painted grey and had a smooth design. They have become part of US life, and one *country music song has the title *Thank God and Greyhound She's Gone*.

the ˌGreyhound 'Derby one of the most important races in Britain for greyhounds (= thin dogs that can run very fast). It took place once a year at *White City until 1984, when it was moved to *Wimbledon. Many people bet on the race.

'greyhound ˌracing n [U] a popular sport in Britain in which greyhounds (= thin dogs that can run very fast) race around a circular track chasing an imitation hare. People make bets on the races, and refer to the sport informally as 'the dogs'. The two most important British races are the Greyhound Derby and the Grand National. The sport is also found in the US but is less popular there than in Britain.

D W 'Griffith /ˈgrɪfɪθ/ (David Wark Griffith 1875–1948) the leading US director of silent films. He is remembered especially for making films on a large scale, using grand scenery and many actors. These included *The *Birth of a Nation* (1915), *Intolerance* (1916) and *Broken Blossoms* (1919). In 1919 Griffith, together with Mary *Pickford[1], Douglas *Fairbanks[1] and Charlie *Chaplin, established the independent film production company *United Artists. He later made two sound films, and received a special *Oscar in 1936.

Joseph Gri'maldi /grɪˈmɔːldi/ (1779–1837) an English comedy actor who is regarded as the first British clown. He invented the style that is now typical of clowns in many countries, wearing strange, brightly-coloured clothes and white make-up on his face. Many clowns are still called 'Joey' after him.

'gringo /ˈgrɪŋgəʊ; AmE ˈgrɪŋgoʊ/ n (pl **-os**) (informal often offensive) a foreigner in a Latin-American country. The word is used especially by Mexicans to refer to people from the US.

John 'Grisham /ˈgrɪʃəm/ (1955–) a US author of popular novels about lawyers. He was formerly a lawyer in a small town in *Mississippi. His books, many of which have become films, include *A Time to Kill* (1988), *The Firm* (1989), *The Chamber* (1994), *The Partner* (1997) and

The Last Juror (2004). Grisham, a member of the *Democratic Party, was also elected to the Mississippi State Legislature (1983–90).

Virgil 'Grissom /ˌvɜːdʒɪl ˈgrɪsəm; AmE ˌvɜːrdʒɪl/ (1926–67) the second US astronaut to be sent into space (1961), and the first to make two space flights. He was killed with two other astronauts, Roger Chaffee and Edward White, in the Apollo 1 spacecraft when it was destroyed by fire during a test on the ground. See also APOLLO PROGRAM.

grits /grɪts/ n [U] (AmE) corn which has been partly crushed and then boiled. It is usually eaten warm, with butter, as part of breakfast in the southern US states. Compare HOMINY.

George and 'Weedon 'Grossmith /ˈwiːdn ˈgrəʊsmɪθ; AmE ˈgroʊsmɪθ/ two English brothers (1847–1912 and 1854–1919), best known for writing *The *Diary of a Nobody*. Weedon also illustrated the book.

> **❝** I left the room with silent dignity but caught my foot in the mat. **❞**
> from *The Diary of a Nobody*

Grosvenor 'Square /ˌgrəʊvnə; AmE ˈgroʊvnər/ a large square in central London, England. The US embassy is on one side of the square, and people have traditionally gone there to protest against US actions which they disapprove of, such as the *Vietnam War or the invasion of *Grenada.

'Groundhog Day (in the US) 2 February. According to tradition, if the groundhog (= a small animal that lives under the ground) comes out of its hole after its winter sleep on that day and sees its own shadow, it is frightened by it and goes back down into its hole. This means that there will be six more weeks of winter. If it sees no shadow, it is a sign that there will be an early spring. In many US communities people watch for the appearance of a groundhog on Groundhog Day. The best-known of these places is Punxsutawney, *Pennsylvania, where the groundhog is always called Phil. An event that is repeated without changing is sometimes called a Groundhog Day after the film/movie *Groundhog Day* (1993) about a man who lives the same day many times: *The Government lost the vote then and it can expect a Groundhog Day next time.*

Ground 'Zero ⇨ WORLD TRADE CENTER.

Grove /grəʊv; AmE groʊv/ (full name , **The 'New Grove 'Dictionary of 'Music and 'Musicians**) a large British dictionary in many volumes containing information about most types of serious music and musicians. It was originally written by George Grove (1820–1900). New editions have been published throughout the 20th century.

'Growmore /ˈgrəʊmɔː(r)/ n [U] a substance that people put on their gardens to make plants grow better.

'Grub Street the former name of a street in London, England, which became famous as a place where you could find someone to write short books or articles on anything at all, though the quality would not be very good. The phrase 'Grub Street' is now used to refer to journalists and other writers who produce work of poor quality, simply to earn money: *a piece that shows all the worst aspects of Grub Street journalism.*

grunge /grʌndʒ/ n [U] **1** (also **grunge rock**) a relaxed style of *rock music, with a harsh guitar sound. It was especially popular in the early 1990s. **2** a fashion associated with grunge music. It included untidy hair and torn clothes, especially *jeans.

GSK ⇨ GLAXOSMITHKLINE.

Guam /gwɑːm/ an independent US territory in the western Pacific Ocean. It is the largest and most southern of the Mariana Islands. Guam is popular with tourists, and there are large US Air Force and Navy bases there. In 1944, during *World War II, US forces landed in Guam and defeated the Japanese who occupied it. In 1997, a Boeing 747 plane of Korean Air crashed there and 225 people in it were killed.

Guan,tánamo 'Bay /gwɑːnˌtɑːnəməʊ; AmE gwɑːnˌtɑːnəmoʊ/ a bay in Cuba where there is a US Navy base. The sailors call it 'Gitmo'. The base has been there since 1903. Since the attack on the *World Trade Center people suspected of being terrorists have been kept there as prisoners.

The 'Guardian one of Britain's national newspapers. When it started in 1821 in *Manchester it was only published once a week, but since 1855 it has been published every day except Sunday. Until 1959 it was called The *Manchester Guardian*. The paper's political views are left-wing and it is regarded as one of the 'quality newspapers'.

the ,Guardian 'Angels a US organization of young people who work to protect people from crime in large US cities. They do not have weapons, and the police work with them. Members wear red caps, and shirts with 'Dare to Care' printed on them. The Guardian Angels formed in New York in 1979 to prevent crime on the underground trains. There are now groups in many other countries.

'Guardian ,reader n an educated *middle-class British person who is thought to be typical of the kind of people who regularly read The *Guardian* newspaper: *It's a policy that is sure to be popular among Guardian readers, if no one else.*

the 'Guards Di,vision the infantry division (= soldiers who fight on foot) in the British army. It consists of the *Coldstream Guards, the *Grenadier Guards, the *Irish Guards, the *Scots Guards, and the *Welsh Guards.

'Guards ,regiment n any of the regiments in the *Guards Division of the British army or in the *Household Cavalry.

'Guernsey /'gɜːnzi; AmE 'gɜːrnzi/ the second largest of the *Channel Islands. It is famous for its milk products, as a tourist centre, and as a place where the people pay very little tax. Its capital is St Peter Port. **Guernsey cattle** are a breed of cows that produce very rich milk.

the 'Guggenheim Mu,seum /'gʊgənhaɪm/ a museum of modern art in New York, built with money given by Solomon R Guggenheim (1861–1949), a rich businessman. The unusual circular building was designed by Frank Lloyd *Wright and opened in 1959. It is sometimes called the 'giant snail'.

the Guggenheim Museum

Guide n a member of the **Guides Association**, especially one aged between 10 and 14. This organization for girls (formerly called the Girl Guides Association) was started in 1910 as an equivalent to the *Scouts (formerly called the Boy Scouts). It encourages practical skills and a helpful attitude to other people. In Britain, Guides are divided into four groups: Rainbows (aged 5 to 7), Brownies (aged 7 to 10), Guides (aged 10 to 14), and the Senior Section, consisting of Rangers Guides and Young Leaders (aged 14 to 25). Adult helpers in the Guides Association are called **Guiders**. Compare GIRL SCOUT.

'Guide Dogs for the 'Blind Associ,ation a British charity, started in 1933, which trains dogs to lead blind people. The equivalent US organization is the Guide Dog Foundation for the Blind, established in 1946.

The ,Guiding 'Light the oldest US television *soap opera. It began as a radio series in 1936 and moved to television in 1952. It has won several *Emmy awards. Actors who appeared in *The Guiding Light* before they became famous include James Earl Jones, Cicely Tyson and Christopher Walken.

the ,Guildford 'Four /ˌgɪlfəd; AmE ˌgɪlfərd/ four Irishmen who spent 18 years in prison because a court of law said they were members of the *IRA and found them guilty of putting bombs in pubs in Guildford and Woolwich, London, in 1974. They were released in 1989, when it was discovered that the police had made changes to their notes after questioning the four men. This was one of several similar cases at about this time which damaged the reputation of the British police and public confidence in them. See also BIRMINGHAM SIX, TOTTENHAM THREE.

the 'Guildhall /'gɪldhɔːl/ the building that serves as the town hall (= local government offices) for the City of London. Grand meals and other events take place there on important occasions. The original building of 1411 was mostly destroyed in the *Fire of London (1666), and the one built in its place was badly damaged by bombs in *World War II. See also MANSION HOUSE.

'Guinevere /'gwɪnəvɪə(r)/ the wife of King *Arthur, who became the lover of *Lancelot, Arthur's friend and his best *knight.

'Guinness™¹ /'gɪnɪs/ n [U, C] a type of stout (= dark strong beer) first made in Dublin in 1759 by the Guinness company. It is very popular in Ireland, the only place where it was made until 1936: *A pint of Guinness, please.*

,Alec 'Guinness² /'gɪnɪs/ (1914–2000) an English actor who appeared in a wide variety of plays and films. Some of his best-remembered films were *Ealing comedies, including *Kind Hearts and Coronets* (1949), in which he played eight parts, both male and female. He won an *Oscar in 1957 for his part in *The Bridge on the River Kwai*. He also took the part of George Smiley in two television series based on novels by John *Le Carré, and played Obi-Wan Kenobi in *Star Wars. He was made a *knight in 1959.

'Guinness 'World 'Records /'gɪnɪs/ a book, published every year, which gives all the records achieved in a very wide range of fields and activities. For example, the names of the oldest, tallest, richest and fastest people in the world are all given. The book was first published in 1955 as *The Guinness Book of Records* and is now so popular that it is available in nearly 40 languages. People sometimes talk of doing something that has never been done before just to 'get into' (= have their names mentioned in) the book.

the ,Gulf of 'Mexico /'meksɪkəʊ; AmE 'meksɪkoʊ/ part of the western Atlantic Ocean between the southeast coast of the US, Mexico and Cuba. At its northern edge are the US **Gulf States** of *Florida, *Alabama,

*Mississippi, *Louisiana and *Texas. The Gulf has wide white beaches that attract many tourists, but it is also an area of hurricanes (= violent storms with strong winds). The **Gulf Stream** is a current of warm water that flows from the Gulf of Mexico across the Atlantic to north-west Europe, affecting the climate there.

the ,Gulf 'War a war from 15 January to 28 February 1991 between Iraq and the United Nations Security Forces, which included British and US soldiers. The war started after Saddam Hussein had refused to take his soldiers out of Kuwait, which they had occupied in August 1990. The UN troops forced the Iraqi army out of Kuwait and destroyed many of their military weapons, but not before the Iraqis had set fire to many Kuwaiti oil wells, causing great damage to the environment. See also DESERT SHIELD, DESERT STORM.

,Gulf 'War ,Syndrome n [U] a disease that has affected many of the soldiers who fought in the *Gulf War in 1991, though its cause is not fully known. Those with the disease feel very weak and tired all the time. Some people believe that it is connected with the use during the war of chemicals or depleted uranium (= a type of heavy, slightly radioactive metal, sometimes used in ammunition and armour). But the governments of Britain and America were for a long time not willing to accept that this is the case, or even that such a disease exists.

,Gulliver's 'Travels /ˌgʌlɪvəz; AmE ˌgʌlɪvərz/ a novel (1726) by Jonathan *Swift in which he attacked the British attitudes of his time towards religion, science, the law, etc., using satire. Lemuel Gulliver, an English traveller, visits strange lands, including *Lilliput, where the people are all tiny, *Brobdingnag, where the people are all giants, and the country of the *Houyhnhnms and the *Yahoos, where the horses are wise and the humans are stupid and cruel. The story has always been very popular with both adults and children.

'gumbo /'gʌmbəʊ; AmE 'gʌmboʊ/ n [U, C] a traditional *Cajun dish. It is a thick, often spicy soup made with okra (= a type of vegetable with long green seed cases), tomatoes, vegetables and usually fish, but sometimes meat.

,Gunga 'Din /ˌgʌngə 'dɪn/ a poem (1892) by Rudyard *Kipling. It is written in the language of an ordinary British soldier praising a Hindu who carries water for the British Army in India and dies taking water to a wounded soldier during a battle. Many people know the last line of the poem:

66 You're a better man than I am, Gunga Din. 99

'gun ,laws n [pl] laws passed to restrict the sale of guns and to control their use. In the US many people feel strongly that ordinary people should not be allowed to own guns because of the large number of violent crimes in which they are used. Others argue that this would be against the US *Constitution which says that everyone has the 'right to bear arms'. The *National Rifle Association has opposed all gun laws, but in 1993 *Congress passed the 'Brady Bill' restricting the sale and use of some types of guns. In Britain, *Parliament passed a law in 1997 that forbids the ownership of handguns. See also DUNBLANE.

,Sally 'Gunnell /'gʌnl/ (1966–) an English athlete who was the first woman to hold the world, Olympic, *Commonwealth and European titles in the women's 400-metre hurdles race all at the same time.

the 'Gunpowder Plot a secret plan by a group of Roman Catholics to blow up the *Houses of Parliament and kill King *James I in 1605. They put gunpowder (= an explosive powder) in the cellars before the open-

ing of Parliament by the King on 5 November. The plan was discovered before the gunpowder could be exploded, and one of the group, Guy Fawkes, was arrested and forced to give the names of the others. His name has remained the only one most people know, although he was not the leader of the group. Every year, before the opening of Parliament, the cellars are searched in a special ceremony. ➪ note at BONFIRE NIGHT.

'Gunsmoke /'gʌnsməʊk; AmE 'gʌnsmoʊk/ a successful US television *western series (1955–75), the longest ever made. It developed strong characters and did not emphasize violence. The stories were set in *Dodge City and were about Marshal Matt Dillon, played by James Arness. Other characters included Miss Kitty, Chester and 'Doc'.

,Guns N''Roses /ˌgʌnz ən 'rəʊzɪz/ a US *hard rock band, formed in 1986. They were especially popular until the mid 1990s and became known for the violent words of some of their songs. Their albums have included *Appetite for Destruction* (1987) and *Use Your Illusion I* and *II* (1991). The singer, Axl Rose, is the only remaining original member of the band.

GUS /ˌgʌs/ a large British company, formerly called Great Universal Stores, which was originally a business selling goods through mail order catalogues (= books sent to people's homes showing items that can be ordered by post). Its businesses are now *Argos, *Burberry and Experian, which provides information to businesses worldwide.

,Woody 'Guthrie /ˌwʊdi 'gʌθri/ (1912–67) a famous US folk singer who played the guitar and wrote more than 1000 songs. Many of his songs were written during the *Great Depression and were protests against poverty and war, but he also wrote many happy songs, including *This Land is Your Land* and *So Long, It's Been Good to Know Ya*. Guthrie was a major influence on popular musicians in the 1960s, especially Bob *Dylan and his own son, Arlo Guthrie.

Guy'ana /gaɪ'ænə/ a country on the north-east coast of South America, formerly called British Guiana. It was a British colony from 1796 until it became independent in 1966, since when it has been a member of the *Commonwealth. Guyana's official language is English and the capital city is Georgetown. More than half its population are descended from Indian workers brought in for the sugar industry after *slavery was ended there in 1838.

▶ ,Guya'nese /ˌgaɪə'niːz/ adj, n (pl **Guyanese**).

,Guy 'Fawkes Night /'fɔːks/ ➪ note at BONFIRE NIGHT.

,Guys and 'Dolls a *Broadway comedy musical play (1950), based on stories by Damon *Runyon. It is about some New York criminals and the attempts of a woman in the *Salvation Army to convert them to Christianity. The songs in the show include *Luck Be A Lady* and *Sit Down, You're Rocking the Boat*. Marlon *Brando and Frank *Sinatra appeared in the later film version (1955).

,Guy's 'Hospital (also informal **Guy's**) a leading *teaching hospital in south London, England. It was started in 1721 by Thomas Guy, a man who had made a lot of money printing and selling books. John *Keats was at Guy's medical school in 1816. Guy's is now part of an NHS hospital trust with *St Thomas's Hospital.

Gwent /gwent/ an administrative county of south Wales from 1974 to 1996, when it was divided between a number of *unitary authorities. The word Gwent is still used in the names of many institutions of south Wales, for example the Royal Gwent Hospital in Newport.

,**Nell 'Gwyn** /'gwɪn/ (1650–87) an English actor who was the lover of King *Charles II for many years. She came from a poor background and could not read or write, but she had two of Charles's sons. She is thought of as a lively, cheerful and attractive woman who at one time sold oranges in the theatre at *Covent Garden.

'**Gwynedd** /'gwɪnəð/ a county of north Wales, governed by a *unitary authority. Its administrative centre is *Caernarfon.

▶ Gypsies

Gypsies are a people scattered through many countries. The name *Gypsy* comes from the word 'Egyptian' because Gypsies were once thought to have come from Egypt. Some people now believe that they originally came from India. In the US Gypsies are called **Roma**, and in Britain they are known as **Romanies** or **travellers**, although the name travellers is more often used for Irish travellers, a group in Britain who, like Gypsies, do not live in settled communities but travel about from place to place living in caravans. The traditional language of the Gypsies is **Romany**, and new words are made up from Romany elements rather than borrowed from English.

Roma or Romanies, like many other minority groups, have a strong sense of pride in their identity. In Britain, they are sometimes treated with fear and suspicion by the rest of the population and are often forced to move on from places where they stop.

Gypsies usually make money by selling new and second-hand goods. Some collect and sell scrap metal, while others do agricultural work. A few make a living from entertainment and singing. The women are known for selling clothes pegs, 'lucky' white heather or bunches of flowers. Many meet each year at the Appleby Horse Fair in Cumbria.

Gypsies have always been associated with **fortune-telling**. They can be found at fairgrounds predicting people's future by reading their palms (= examining their hands) or looking into a crystal ball. Because of the mystery associated with their origins and their magical powers, Gypsies have a popular romantic image that conflicts with the reality of families living on dirty caravan sites and being moved on by council officials or the police. Americans have little contact with Gypsies and think of the Roma only as exciting, mysterious people who wear brightly coloured clothes and gold jewellery and have unusual powers. The romantic image was taken up by the US striptease artist, Rose Havoc, who called herself Gypsy Rose *Lee on stage. In Britain a character called Mystic Meg used to appear on television each week, dressed in strange clothes and with an extravagant air of mystery, to predict the winners of the *National Lottery.

'**Gypsy 'Rose 'Lee** ⇨ LEE.

H h

,Häagen-'Dazs™ /,heɪgən 'dɑːs/ a US make of ice cream which is sold in many countries around the world, often through its own shops.

,habeas 'corpus /,heɪbiəs 'kɔːpəs; AmE 'kɔːrpəs/ n a writ (= legal order) saying that a particular person who is being held by the police or in prison must be brought before a court of law so that the court can decide whether he or she is being held legally. Habeas corpus is one of the most important ways of protecting people's personal freedom. It formally became a part of the law in Britain in 1679. US procedure is also based on the Act of 1679. Article 1 of the American *Constitution says that a person's right to get a writ of habeas corpus can never be taken away except in cases of rebellion or invasion. 'Habeas corpus' is part of the Latin phrase *Habeas corpus ad subjiciendum*, which means 'You should have the body brought before the judge.'

'Habitat /'hæbɪtæt/ a group of shops selling furniture and other things for the home like cushions, china and lamps. It was started in Britain in 1964 by Terence *Conran, with some shops opening later in the US and France. It was especially successful in the 1960s and 1970s when it was one of the first companies to sell original designs of furniture, etc. that many people could afford.

,Zaha Ha'did /,zɑːhə hæ'diːd/ (1950–) a British architect, born in Iraq, whose designs for buildings have won many international awards. They are often very unusual and many of them have not been built. Built designs include the Rosenthal Center for Contemporary Art in *Cincinnati, a building for the Vitra furniture company in Germany and the Hoenheim North tram station in Strasbourg, France.

,Hadrian's 'Wall /,heɪdriənz/ a wall in northern England built between 122 and 127 AD by the Roman emperor Hadrian, from Wallsend on the River *Tyne to Bowness on the *Solway Firth. It was the northern border of the Roman Empire, from which the Romans could keep back the *Picts. It was a major achievement, 73 miles/ 120 kilometres long and 16 feet/4.9 metres high, with forts (= strong military buildings for defence) every mile along its length. Long sections of the wall still remain, and thousands of tourists visit it every year. It was made a *World Heritage Site in 1987. See also ANTONINE WALL.

Hadrian's Wall

,Rider 'Haggard /,raɪdə 'hægəd; AmE ,raɪdər 'hægərd/ (1856–1925) an English writer of exciting adventure stories. The best-known of these, *King Solomon's Mines* (1885) and *She* (1887), are set in southern Africa, where Haggard worked for many years. He was made a *knight in 1912.

'haggis /'hægɪs/ n [C, U] a famous Scottish dish made mainly from a sheep's or calf's (= young cow's) heart, lungs and liver and boiled in a bag made from part of a sheep's stomach. Haggis is traditionally eaten by the Scots on *Burns Night.

,William 'Hague /'heɪg/ (1961–) an English *Conservative politician. He became a *Member of Parliament in 1989 and Secretary of State for Wales in 1995. In 1997, following the *Labour Party's victory in the general election, he replaced John *Major as leader of the Conservative Party. He resigned as leader after losing the general election in 2001.

,Earl 'Haig /'heɪg/ (born Douglas Haig 1861–1928) a British soldier who commanded the British Army in France during *World War I. After the war he helped to start the *Royal British Legion and organized *Poppy Day. He was made an *earl(1) in 1919.

,Haight-'Ashbury /,heɪt 'æʃbri/ a small area of *San Francisco that became famous in the 1960s for the many *hippies who lived there. Haight-Ashbury is two miles west of the business district of San Francisco and east of Golden Gate Park. It has beautiful Victorian houses and interesting shops.

,Hail to the 'Chief the official song for welcoming the US *President. It is a march played by a band when he enters a room or an outdoor area for an official event. It was first played in 1815 to celebrate both the birthday of George *Washington and the end of the *War of 1812. The music was written about 1812 by James Sanderson, an Englishman, and the words are by Sir Walter *Scott.

,Peter 'Hain /'heɪn/ (1950–) a British *Labour politician, born in Kenya. He became a *Member of Parliament in 1991. He was Minister for Europe from 2001 to 2002 and has been the *Secretary of State for Wales since 2002 and also the *Leader of the House of Commons and the *Lord Privy Seal since 2003. He was first a member of the *Liberal party and was an active campaigner against apartheid (= the political system in South Africa in which only white people had full political rights) and campaigned to prevent South African all-white sports teams playing in Britain.

***Hair** a 'rock musical' play (1967) about *hippies. It opened in New York and a year later in London. It was criticized (and attracted audiences) because in one scene the actors were naked and because the characters were against the *Vietnam War and thought that drugs were fun. The songs include *Let the Sunshine In* and *The Age of Aquarius*. A film version appeared in 1979.

,Brenda 'Hale¹ (1945–) an English lawyer and judge. She taught law at university and worked for a government law commission, before becoming a *High Court judge in 1994. In 2004 she became the first female *Law Lord.

,Nathan 'Hale² /'heɪl/ (1755–76) an American soldier who was hanged by the British during the *American Revolution for being a spy.

> 66 I only regret that I have but one life to lose for my country. 99
> Nathan Hale's words just before he was killed.

,Bill 'Haley /'heɪli/ (1925–81) the US singer who, with his group the Comets, first made *rock and roll popular. They recorded *Shake, Rattle and Roll* and then *Rock Around the Clock*, which Haley wrote. It was used in the film *The Blackboard Jungle* (1955) and became an international hit, with 22.5 million copies sold.

‚half-and-'half *n* [U] (*AmE*) a mixture of milk and cream used especially in coffee: *I like half-and-half in my coffee.*

‚half-'timbered *adj* (of a building) having a visible wooden framework filled in with brick, stone or plaster. Half-timbered buildings were especially popular in England in the *Tudor(2) period, partly because there was already less good wood available for building by this time.

'Halifax¹ /'hælɪfæks/ a large town in *West Yorkshire, in northern England. In the past it was a centre of the wool industry.

the 'Halifax² /'hælɪfæks/ the largest *building society in Britain, established in 1853. In 2001 it joined with the Bank of Scotland to form *HBOS.

‚Edward 'Hall¹ /'hɔːl/ (1967–) an English theatre director who is best known for his modern productions of *Shakespeare plays. He is the son of Peter *Hall.

‚Peter 'Hall² /'hɔːl/ (1930–) an English theatre, opera and film director. He ran the *Royal Shakespeare Company (1960–68) and the *National Theatre (1973–88), and has also been involved with the opera at *Glyndebourne. He was made a *knight in 1977.

the ‚Hallelujah 'Chorus /ˌhælɪluːjə/ a well-known chorus in the *Messiah by George Frederick *Handel. The music expresses great joy. According to tradition, the audience always stands up while the Hallelujah Chorus is being sung, because King *George II did this at the first London performance of the *Messiah in 1743.

the ‚Hallé 'Orchestra /ˌhæleɪ/ a famous orchestra started in *Manchester, England, in 1858 by Sir Charles Hallé (1819–95), a German pianist and conductor. Other famous conductors of the orchestra have included Hamilton Harty and John *Barbirolli.

‚Edmond 'Halley (*also* ‚Edmund 'Halley) /'hæli, 'hɔːli/ (1656–1742) an English astronomer and mathematician who was a close friend of Isaac *Newton. He is best remembered for **Halley's comet**, which was named after him. A comet is a bright object that moves through space round the sun with a tail of burning gas and dust. Halley correctly predicted that this one would return regularly to be seen in the night sky approximately every 76 years. It was last visible in 1986.

'Hallmark™ card *n* any of the *greetings cards made by the US company Hallmark Cards Inc, the biggest company of its kind in the world. It was established in 1910 by Joyce C Hall (a man). Its advertisements include the sentence, 'When you care enough to send the very best.' Hallmark also produces the television show *The *Hallmark Hall of Fame* and owns Hallmark Entertainment, a company that makes television programmes.

*The *Hallmark* 'Hall of 'Fame* the oldest dramatic series on US television, produced by the Hallmark Card company. It has won more *Emmy awards (78 by 2004) than any other series. It began in 1951 with *Amahl and the Night Visitors*, the first opera written for television. It has presented many performances of *Shakespeare, as well as other famous and original plays.

▶ **hallmarks**

Hallmarks are official marks that are stamped into articles made of gold, silver and platinum to prove their quality. Under British law all items made of these metals must be **hallmarked** before they are put on sale. The marks are very small and are usually placed where they will not spoil the appearance of an article.

Hallmarks were introduced in Britain in 1300. They are controlled in Britain by the *Assay Offices. Most modern hallmarks include four symbols: the **sponsor's mark** identifies the company which made the article; the **standard mark** describes the quality of the metal; the **Assay Office mark** indicates the city where the article was tested and marked. A **date letter** which indicates the year in which the article was stamped, may also be added.

The sponsor's mark used to be an emblem such as a bird, but now consists of the initials of the maker. The standard marks consist of a number which indicates the quality of the metal. The number 916, for example, indicates 22 carat (*AmE* karat) gold. Formerly gold items were marked with a crown. Any silver items are marked with a lion, as well as the number 925, to indicate **sterling silver**, which is 92.5% pure. Platinum items may be marked with an orb (= a decorated ball with a cross on top). The Assay Office mark was first added in 1478, when all items had to be tested for quality at Goldsmiths' Hall (hence the name *hallmark*) in London. Britain currently has Assay Offices in four cities: the symbol for London is a leopard, for Birmingham an anchor, for Sheffield a rose and for Edinburgh a castle. Date letters are in different styles of type and set inside a shield. Additional symbols may show that the article was made to celebrate a particular occasion such as a *coronation or the millennium.

In the late 18th and early 19th centuries a system of hallmarks similar to that used in Britain was introduced in the US. Items were stamped with a date letter, **duty mark**, which indicated that tax had been paid, and a lion. The practice did not last long, and instead goldsmiths and silversmiths stamped their work with their initials or full name. Some added a date, but many items have no date, so their age can only be estimated by the style. In 1868 *Baltimore silversmiths were the first to add below their names the **sterling standard** of 925/1000 (i.e. 92.5%). Silversmiths in *Boston and New York City had **guilds** which decided their own standards, and items were often marked with the name of the city in which they were made.

Items made in the US now must have on them the mark of the person or company that made them and a standard mark. Gold items are marked in karats, usually abbreviated to 'K'. Most gold jewellery in the US is 18 karat and marked '18K'. Silver items of sterling standard may be stamped 'silver', 'solid silver', 'sterling silver', 'sterling' or 'ster'.

The idea of a hallmark as a means of identifying the origin and quality of an item has a wider use in English. If something is *the hallmark of* or *has/bears all the hallmarks of* something, it has all the essential features associated with that thing. If somebody *leaves/stamps their hallmark on* something, they have a unique and lasting effect on it.

‚Hall of 'Fame *n* (in the US) a group of people who have been chosen for their special achievements in a particular activity or profession, especially sport or music. New members of such groups are usually honoured at a ceremony after being chosen by special judges or by the public. Some Halls of Fame have their own museums, like the Baseball Hall of Fame and the Rock and Roll Hall of Fame. The original Hall of Fame was a building opened in 1900 in New York to honour famous Americans.

‚Hallo'ween /ˌhæləʊˈiːn; *AmE* ˌhæloʊˈiːn/ (*also* **All Hallows Eve**) the night of 31 October, when people once believed that ghosts could be seen. Now, in Britain and America, it is a time when children have parties, dress up as *witches, make lanterns out of pumpkins (= large round vegetables) from which the inside has been removed, and play *trick or treat.

,William 'Halsey /'hɔːlsi/ (1882–1959) a US admiral who won victories in the South Pacific during *World War II. He commanded the Allied Forces (1942–4) and the US Third Fleet (1944–5) from his ship, the *USS Missouri*. Halsey's popular name was 'Bull'.

,Alexander 'Hamilton¹ /'hæməltən/ (c. 1757–1804) one of America's *Founding Fathers. He fought in the *American Revolution, was one of the writers of *The *Federalist Papers*, and established and led the *Federalist Party. Hamilton was the first US Secretary of the Treasury (1789–95) and established the central Bank of the United States. He died after Vice-President Aaron Burr (1756–1836) wounded him in a duel.

,Lady 'Emma 'Hamilton² /'hæməltən/ (born Amy Lyon 1765–1815) a beautiful English woman from a poor family who became famous as the lover of Lord *Nelson and the mother of his child, although she was married to Sir William Hamilton, the British government's representative at the court of Naples. When her husband and Nelson were dead, Lady Hamilton was put in prison for debt.

,Richard 'Hamilton³ /'hæməltən/ (1922–) an English artist who was one of the first people to introduce *pop art to Britain. His paintings are often about social and political issues in modern society.

'Hamlet /'hæmlət/ the main character in the play of the same name by William *Shakespeare, written in about 1601. Many people consider it Shakespeare's finest play. Hamlet, the Prince of Denmark, becomes very sad when his father, the king, dies and his uncle, Claudius, becomes king. His father's ghost tells Hamlet that Claudius has killed him, and makes Hamlet promise to kill Claudius. Hamlet wants to do this but delays too long. The play is long and complicated, and all the main characters die in the end: Hamlet, his mother Gertrude, Claudius, Ophelia (the woman Hamlet loves), her father Polonius and her brother Laertes. The character of Hamlet has a lot of doubts about himself, and in his most famous speech considers killing himself. See also YORICK.

> 66 To be or not to be: that is the question:
> Whether 'tis nobler in the mind to suffer
> The slings and arrows of outrageous fortune
> Or to take arms against a sea of troubles
> And by opposing end them? 99
> Shakespeare *Hamlet*

'Hamley's /'hæmliz/ the best-known toy shop in Britain. When William Hamley started it in London in 1760, he called it 'Noah's Ark'. It became 'Hamley's's' in 1906 when the shop moved to its present position in *Regent Street.

,Armand 'Hammer¹ /,ɑːmənd 'hæmə(r); AmE ,ɑːrmənd 'hæmər/ (1898–1990) a US businessman who traded with the Soviet Union from 1921 and had influence with Lenin and other Russian leaders. Because of this, he became an informal messenger between the two countries. Hammer was the head of the Occidental Petroleum company and gave money for many good causes. He took doctors to Russia after the Chernobyl disaster.

,Mike 'Hammer² /'hæmə(r)/ the main character in the crime novels by Mickey *Spillane.

,Oscar 'Hammerstein /'hæməstaɪn; AmE 'hæmərstaɪn/ (1895–1960) a US writer of songs. He wrote the words for many famous *Broadway musical plays, most of which were also made into films. With Richard *Rodgers as his partner, his shows included *Oklahoma! and The *Sound of Music. Earlier successes included *The Desert Song* (1926) with Sigmund

*Romberg, *Show Boat* (1927) with Jerome *Kern and *Carmen Jones* (1943).

,Dashiell 'Hammett /,dæʃəl 'hæmɪt/ (1894–1961) a US novelist who wrote tough crime stories of the kind that are sometimes referred to as 'hard-boiled fiction'. He had a great influence on Raymond *Chandler and other writers. Hammett created the character Sam *Spade in The *Maltese Falcon* (1930) and the humorous couple Nick and Nora Charles in The *Thin Man* (1932). These books and many of his others were made into films. Hammett was sent to prison in the 1950s when he refused to say if he was a Communist. See also McCARTHY².

,John 'Hampden /'hæmdən/ (1594–1643) an English politician who opposed King *Charles I by refusing to pay the tax called *ship money. He was one of the *Members of Parliament the king tried to arrest in 1642, an action which started the *English Civil War. Hampden himself was killed in the war.

,Hampden 'Park /,hæmdən/ Scotland's national football ground, in *Glasgow.

'Hampshire /'hæmpʃə(r)/ (abbr Hants) a county on the south coast of England. Its administrative centre is Winchester.

'Hampstead /'hæmpstɪd/ an area of north London, since 1965 part of the *borough of *Camden. It is a fashionable place, with many elegant *Georgian houses, and still has the character of an attractive village, which it once was. Many writers and musicians live there. Hampstead Heath is a large area of open land where people enjoy walking.

,Hampton 'Court /,hæmptən/ a grand palace beside the River *Thames, 15 miles/24 kilometres to the west of London. It was built by Cardinal *Wolsey in 1515 and given by him to King *Henry VIII so that he would remain in favour with the king. The house was made even bigger by King *William III in 1689, the additions being designed by Christopher *Wren. Hampton Court is now open to the public. As well as its fine buildings, it is famous for its gardens and maze (= an area of paths between high hedges designed as a puzzle through which people try to find their way).

Hampton Court Palace

,Herbie 'Hancock¹ /,hɜːbi 'hænkɒk; AmE ,hɜːrbi 'hænkɑːk/ (1940–) a US *jazz musician who plays the piano and writes songs. He performed with the Chicago Symphony Orchestra at the age of 12. He began the Herbie Hancock Sextet in 1968. His successful albums have included *Headhunters* (1973), *Future Shock* (1983) and *The New Standard* (1996). Hancock won an *Oscar in 1986 for his music for the film *Round Midnight*.

,John 'Hancock² /'hænkɒk; AmE 'hænkɑːk/ (1737–93) a leader of the *American Revolution who was President of the *Continental Congress (1775–77). He was the first to sign the *Declaration of Independence and wrote his signature very large so that King *George III could read it. Americans still refer to any signature as a 'John Hancock': *Just put your John Hancock on this cheque.*

,Tony **'Hancock**³ /'hænkɒk; *AmE* 'hænkɑːk/ (1924–68) an English comedian who became famous between 1954 and 1961 in the programme *Hancock's Half Hour*, first on radio and then on television. Hancock played an angry character upset by the little problems of life, such as a missing page in a library book. One of his most famous programmes (on television) was *The Blood Donor*, in which he caused a lot of trouble in a hospital trying to give blood.

'George 'Frederick **'Handel** /'hændl/ (1685–1759) a German composer who came to live in London in 1712 and stayed until his death, becoming a British citizen in 1726. Handel's music has always been especially popular with British people. He wrote 40 operas but his best-known works are his 20 oratorios, musical dramas based on stories from the Bible, especially the *Messiah, about the coming of Jesus Christ. He also wrote music for ceremonies at the court of King *George I, including *Water Music* (1717) and *Music for the Royal Fireworks* (1749). Handel stopped writing music in 1751 because he was going blind. He is buried in *Poets' Corner in *Westminster Abbey.

,W C **'Handy** /'hændi/ (William Christopher Handy 1873–58) a US musician who is often called 'the father of the blues'. He wrote *St Louis Blues* (1914) but failed to sell it, so he began to collect and publish traditional *blues music. His other songs included *Memphis Blues* (1912) and *Beale Street Blues* (1917). He also led a band (1903–21).

'hangman /'hæŋmæn/ *n* [U] a children's game in which one person chooses a word and the others try to guess what it is. They do this by choosing letters which they think may be in the word. Each time they choose wrongly, the first person can draw one part of a man hanging by his neck from a rope on a frame (the way that people used to be officially killed in the past). If the people guessing do not get all the letters of the word before the drawing is complete, they lose and are 'hanged'.

,Tom **'Hanks** /'hæŋks/ (1956–) a US actor who has won *Oscars for his parts in *Philadelphia* (1993) and *Forrest Gump*. He began in comedy films like *Big* (1988), and his other successes have included *Sleepless in Seattle* (1993) and *That Thing You Do* (1996), which he also directed.

,Hanna and Bar'bera /ˌhænə, bɑːˈbeərə; *AmE* bɑːrˈberə/ two US film cartoonists, **Bill Hanna** (1910–2001) and **Joe Barbera** (1911–), who worked together for more than 50 years. They created the film characters of *Tom and Jerry for *MGM. They then set up Hanna-Barbera Productions in 1957 and made the popular television cartoon series *Huckleberry Hound* and *The *Flintstones*. See also SCOOBY DOO, YOGI BEAR.

the ,House of **'Hanover** /'hænəʊvə(r)/ the British royal family between 1714, when George Louis, the leader of the German state of Hanover, became the king of Britain, and 1901, when Queen *Victoria died. George became the king because there was no heir to Queen *Anne, and the leaders of Hanover were related to King *James I through his granddaughter Sophia. Compare SAXE-COBURG-GOTHA.

,Hano'verian /ˌhænəʊˈvɪəriən/ *adj* of or relating to the British kings and queens from *George I to *Victoria (1714–1901): *the Hanoverian succession.*

'Hansard /'hænsɑːd; *AmE* 'hænsɑːrd/ the informal name for the *Official Report* of everything that is said in the British parliament, and in its committees. It is published every day. The name is also used for the reports of

some of the *Commonwealth parliaments. It is probably named after Luke Hansard who first printed the *House of Commons *Journal* in 1774. Since 1909, every word has been printed as it was spoken in the House of Commons: *I looked the debate up in Hansard.*

,Happy 'Birthday to 'You a simple song which is traditionally sung for somebody on their birthday, especially before they blow out the candles on their birthday cake. If the person's name is Peter, the song goes:

> 66 Happy Birthday to you.
> Happy Birthday to you.
> Happy Birthday, dear Peter,
> Happy Birthday to you! 99

,Happy 'Families (in Britain) a children's card game played with a special pack of cards with pictures of members of various families on them. There are four members in each family: a man, his wife, their son and their daughter. The aim of the game is to collect as many complete families as possible. If you have one member of the family already, you can ask somebody if they have another member, e.g. 'Mr Bun, the Baker' or 'Miss Pill, the Doctor's daughter', and if they do, they have to give the card to you.

'hardcore /'hɑːdkɔː(r); *AmE* 'hɑːrdkɔːr/ *n* [U] a type of electronic pop music that became popular in Britain in the early 1990s. It is similar to *techno, with a very fast beat and few words.

,Keir **'Hardie** /ˌkɪə 'hɑːdi; *AmE* ˌkɪər 'hɑːrdi/ (1856–1915) a Scottish miner who became a politician. He started the Scottish Parliamentary Labour Party in 1888, and the *Independent Labour Party in 1893, and then played a major part in creating the British *Labour Party, which he led from 1906 to 1908. He was proud of his *working-class origins, and became known as 'the member for the unemployed'.

,Daniel **'Harding**¹ /'hɑːdɪŋ; *AmE* 'hɑːrdɪŋ/ (1976–) an English conductor. He first conducted the *City of Birmingham Symphony Orchestra in 1994 and worked with the Berlin Philharmonic Orchestra from 1996, the year he became the youngest conductor to perform at a BBC *Promenade concert. He was made principal guest conductor of the *London Symphony Orchestra in 2003.

,Warren G **'Harding**² /'hɑːdɪŋ; *AmE* 'hɑːrdɪŋ/ (Warren Gamaliel Harding 1865–1923) the 29th US *President (1921–3). Some members of his government were involved in illegal activities, including the *Teapot Dome scandal. Harding himself was opposed to the US becoming a member of the League of Nations. He was a member of the *Republican Party and had first been elected to the US Senate (1914–20) from *Ohio.

,hard rock *n* [U] a kind of very loud rock music with a heavy beat which became popular in the late 1960s. Hard rock performers include Deep Purple, *Led Zeppelin and Meatloaf. Compare HEAVY METAL.

,Hard Rock 'Cafe any of a group of *fast food restaurants, started in 1971, with branches all over the world. The restaurants display objects from the history of pop music (e.g. guitars or clothing from famous musicians) on their walls, and are also famous because film actors and pop musicians sometimes go to them.

,Hard 'Times a novel (1845) by Charles *Dickens. It tells how Thomas Gradgrind, a tough businessman, tries to bring up his children according to strict principles, and realizes too late that his very practical character has made their lives unhappy.

,Andy **'Hardy**¹ /'hɑːdi; *AmE* 'hɑːrdi/ a character in 15 *MGM films in the 1930s and 1940s. He was a boy who lived with his family in a small town, and Americans liked the happy, innocent stories. Mickey *Rooney played Andy, and Judy *Garland was his girlfriend. MGM won a special *Oscar in 1942 because the series represented 'the American way of life'.

,Oliver 'Hardy² /'hɑːdi; AmE 'hɑːrdi/ ⇨ LAUREL AND HARDY.

,Thomas 'Hardy³ /'hɑːdi; AmE 'hɑːrdi/ (1840–1928) an English writer of novels and poems. He was born in *Dorset and set most of his stories there, calling it 'Wessex' and its main town 'Casterbridge'. The region is still often called **Hardy country**. Many of his novels show how much of human life is controlled by chance, which can be very cruel. His books often have an unhappy ending. The best-known include *Far from the Madding Crowd (1874), *Tess of the D'Urbervilles (1891) and Jude the Obscure (1895). Many people in Victorian England did not like his books when they were first published, and for this reason Hardy stopped writing novels and wrote mostly poetry for the later part of his life.

the 'Hardy Boys /'hɑːdi; AmE 'hɑːrdi/ two young brothers, Frank and Joe Hardy, who are characters in a US series of mystery adventure books for boys. They were created by Edward Stratemeyer, who also created Nancy *Drew, though the early books were mostly written by Franklin W Dixon. There have been more than 200 Hardy Boys books in all, and several television series.

,David 'Hare /'heə(r); AmE 'her/ (1947–) an English playwright and theatre director whose plays are about moral and political issues, especially in Britain. He has been an Associate Director of the *National Theatre since 1984. His plays include Slag (1970), The Secret Rapture (1988) and Racing Demon (1990). He is married to the fashion designer Nicole Farhi.

,Lord 'Harewood /'hɑːwʊd/ (born George Lascelles 1923–) an English *earl who is a cousin of Queen *Elizabeth II. For much of his life he has been closely involved with music, especially opera, in Britain.

,Harewood 'House /ˌheəwʊd; AmE ˌherwʊd/ a large, grand house to the north of *Leeds in England, built between 1759 and 1771. Much of the inside of the house was designed by Robert *Adam and the park around it was designed by 'Capability' *Brown.

,James 'Hargreaves /'hɑːgriːvz; AmE 'hɑːrgriːvz/ (1720–78) the Englishman who invented the *spinning jenny, a machine for spinning cotton which helped to bring about the *Industrial Revolution in Britain.

'Hark! the 'Herald 'Angels 'Sing the title and first line of a popular *carol sung at *Christmas. It was written by Charles *Wesley in the 18th century.

'Harlech /'hɑːlək; AmE 'hɑːrlək/ a town in *Gwynedd in Wales. It is famous for its castle, on a high rock above the town, built in 1289.

Harlech Castle

'Harlem /'hɑːləm; AmE 'hɑːrləm/ a poor district of north *Manhattan(1) in New York that runs from 110th Street to 162nd Street. It was originally a Dutch village. Many of the people living there now are *African Americans, though there are many Puerto Ricans living in east Harlem, also called Spanish Harlem. Many African Americans moved there from the southern states in the 1920s and made it their cultural centre during the period called the *Harlem Renaissance. See also COTTON CLUB.

the ,Harlem 'Globetrotters /ˌhɑːləm 'gləʊbtrɒtəz; AmE ˌhɑːrləm 'gloʊbtrɑːtərz/ an *African American *basketball team that plays exhibition games in the US and around the world, doing tricks with the balls to music to show their skills and make people laugh. They began in the US in 1927. In 1998 they played their 20 000th game.

the ,Harlem Re'naissance (also 'Renaissance) /ˌhɑːləm rɪ'neɪsns; AmE ˌhɑːrləm 'renəsɑːns/ a movement in *African American culture in the 1920s which began in the New York district of *Harlem. Achievements were made in literature, music, art and the theatre. Among the writers involved were Countee Cullen, Jean Toomer and Zora Neale Hurston, and the musicians included 'Duke' *Ellington. The movement ended with the *Great Depression.

,Harlequin 'Romance™ a US series of romantic fiction books published by Harlequin since the 1960s. The company started by publishing books by the British publisher *Mills & Boon in the US. It publishes several types of romantic fiction including historical novels, romantic comedies and traditional romances.

'Harlequins /'hɑːləkwɪnz; AmE 'hɑːrləkwɪnz/ (also NEC Harlequins; (informal Quins) an English *Rugby Union club based in *Twickenham, south-west London. The team's shirt has many colours and it has been one of the most successful clubs in English Rugby: He plays for Harlequins.

,Harley-'Davidson™ /ˌhɑːli 'deɪvɪdsn; AmE ˌhɑːrli/ n a famous and expensive US motorcycle. Harley-Davidsons are long and heavy, with powerful engines that make a loud sound. William Harley and Arthur Davidson built the first three in 1903 in *Milwaukee, where the company's main office has always been. Popular models have included the 1936 Knucklehead, the 1957 Sportster 'super bike' and the 1990 Fat Boy. Riding a Harley-Davidson on the open road is part of the *American dream for many people: If you're overweight and middle-aged, riding a Harley-Davidson won't change anything.

a Harley-Davidson

'Harley Street /'hɑːli; AmE 'hɑːrli/ a street in central London, England, famous for the many medical specialists who have their surgeries there. See also PRIVATE PATIENTS.

ˌJean **'Harlow** /'hɑːləʊ; AmE 'hɑːrloʊ/ (1911–37) a US actor who was called the 'Blonde Bombshell'. She was a *Hollywood sex symbol in the 1930s, and often played aggressive but cheerful characters in comedy films.

ˌHarriet **'Harman** /'hɑːmən; AmE 'hɑːrmən/ (1950–) a British *barrister and *Labour politician who has been a *Member of Parliament since 1982. She held several important positions in the Labour *Shadow Cabinet before becoming *Secretary of State for Social Security in the Labour government of 1997. In 2001 she became the *Solicitor General.

'Harmsworth /'hɑːmzwɜːθ; AmE 'hɑːrmzwɜːrθ/ ⇨ NORTHCLIFFE, ROTHERMERE.

Harold II /ˌhærəld ðə 'sekənd/ (c. 1019–66) the last *Anglo-Saxon king of England. His army was defeated in 1066 at the Battle of *Hastings on the south coast of England by the *Norman army of *William the Conqueror. Harold died in the battle and William became King of England.

harp n a large upright musical instrument with many strings stretched across a frame that has three corners. There are various types of harp. One is sometimes used as a symbol representing Ireland, e.g. on coins, because it is an important instrument in traditional Irish music.

ˌ**Harpers (and 'Queen)** /ˌhɑːpəz; AmE ˌhɑːrpərz/ a British luxury magazine published once a month. It contains articles about fashion and the social life of the rich and famous. It was first published in 1929 as Harper's Bazaar and changed its name in the 1960s when it merged with the fashion magazine Queen.

ˌ**Harper's Ba'zaar** /ˌhɑːpəz; AmE ˌhɑːrpərz/ a US luxury fashion magazine published once a month. It was first published in 1867.

ˌ**Harpers 'Ferry** /ˌhɑːpəz; AmE ˌhɑːrpərz/ ⇨ BROWN.

ˌ**Harper's Maga'zine** /'hɑːpəz; AmE 'hɑːrpərz/ (also **'Harper's**) an intellectual US magazine known for its news articles, essays and short stories. The oldest US magazine, it was started in 1850 by Harper and Brothers and has been owned since 1980 by the Harper's Magazine Foundation.

'Harrier /'hæriə(r)/ (also ˌ**Harrier 'jump jet**) n a British military aircraft made by Hawker Siddeley, which is the only plane to be able to take off and land with a vertical movement. The plane was first used by the *Royal Air Force in 1969.

a Harrier jump jet

ˌ**Averell 'Harriman**[1] /ˌeɪvrəl 'hærɪmən/ (1891–1986) a US diplomat. He was the US ambassador to the Soviet Union (1943–6) and to Britain (1946). He was also the US Secretary of Commerce (1946–8) and governor of New York (1955–8). Harriman helped to carry out the *Marshall Plan (1949–50) and to establish the Nuclear Test-Ban Treaty (1963). He was the main US representa-

tive at the Vietnam peace talks in Paris in 1968. His wife was Pamela *Harriman.

ˌ**Pamela 'Harriman**[2] /'hærɪmən/ (1920–97) a US ambassador to France (1993–7) who was an important fund-raiser for the *Democratic Party. She was born in Britain as Pamela Beryl Digby, the daughter of an English *Lord, and was regarded as one of the most beautiful women of her time. She was married three times and had many famous lovers. In 1939 she married Randolph Churchill, the son of Winston *Churchill. Her third husband was Averell *Harriman. After her death in France she was given the French Legion of Honour.

'ˌ**Bomber' 'Harris**[1] /ˌbɒmə 'hærɪs; AmE ˌbɑːmər/ (Arthur Harris 1892–1984) a controversial British military leader in charge of the campaign carried out by the 'Bomber Command' (= the part of the air force that drops bombs) during *World War II. He is considered to have been responsible for the success of this campaign, but has also been criticized for the number of civilian deaths it caused, e.g. in the bombing of the German city of Dresden. Before the war he worked to develop bombs that were used against Iraqi tribesmen who were fighting against the British. He was made a *knight in 1942 and a *baronet in 1953.

ˌ**Rolf 'Harris**[2] /ˌrɒlf 'hærɪs; AmE ˌrɑːlf, 'rɔːlf/ (1930–) an Australian entertainer who has been popular in Britain since the 1960s. He appears regularly on television and is especially popular with children. He is known for painting pictures very quickly on television, singing unusual songs and playing unusual musical instruments. He also presents a programme called Animal Hospital.

ˌ**George 'Harrison**[1] /'hærɪsn/ (1943–2001) an English guitar player, singer and song writer who was a member of the *Beatles. He later had a successful solo career, particularly in the 1970s, with records such as My Sweet Lord (1970). He was also involved in film production and supported religious groups whose beliefs are influenced by Indian religions.

ˌ**Tony 'Harrison**[2] /'hærɪsn/ (1937–) an English poet who often performs his poetry in public. He also writes plays, film scripts and translations of plays, all in verse. The two main themes in his work are social class and classical literature. Some of his poems have caused great controversy, especially V about vandalism and A Celebratory Ode on the Abdication of King Charles III.

'Harris Poll™ /'hærɪs/ n any of the studies of public opinion carried out by the US company Harris Interactive.

Harris 'tweed™ /ˌhærɪs/ n [U] a type of thick woollen cloth for making coats, jackets, etc. It is woven by hand on the islands of Harris and Lewis in the Outer *Hebrides. The *Gaelic name is 'Clo Mhor' which means 'the big cloth': a Harris tweed jacket.

'Harrods /'hærədz/ a large, fashionable and expensive department store in the *Knightsbridge area of central London. It claims to be able to supply any article and provide any service. It began in 1861 as a small shop selling food, owned by Henry Harrod, and has been owned since 1985 by Mohamed *Al-Fayed.

Harrods department store

'Harrogate /'hærəgət/ a spa town (= one where there are springs of mineral water considered healthy to drink) in *North Yorkshire, England. Many retired people live there. It has a large conference centre.

'Harrow /'hærəʊ; AmE 'hæroʊ/ (also ,**Harrow 'School**) a well-known British *public school(1) for boys in north-west London, established in 1572. It is considered to be one of the major boys' schools in Britain and many important people were educated there, including Winston *Churchill.

,**Harry 'Potter** ⇨ POTTER.

,**Lorenz 'Hart** /,lɒrənz 'hɑːt; AmE ,lɔːrənz 'hɑːrt/ (1895–1943) a US writer of songs, who with Richard *Rodgers created 29 *Broadway musical plays, many of which became films. Hart wrote the words and Rodgers the music. Their plays included *Babes in Arms* (1937) and *Pal Joey* (1940), and among the songs they wrote were *The Lady is a Tramp* (1937) and *This Can't Be Love* (1938).

the ,**Harvard 'classics** /,hɑːvəd; AmE ,hɑːrvərd/ n [pl] a series of 50 famous works of literature chosen and edited by Charles W Eliot (1834–1926), President of *Harvard University (1869–1909). He said they were 'all the books needed for a real education'. The series was published in 1909–10.

,**Harvard Uni'versity** /,hɑːvəd; AmE ,hɑːrvərd/ the oldest US university and usually considered the best. Harvard is one of the *Ivy League universities. It was established as a college in 1636 in *Cambridge, *Massachusetts. Two years later, it was named after John Harvard, a *Puritan born in England who had given it money and books. Harvard is especially famous for its faculties (= departments) of law and business. Its library is the oldest in the US and one of the largest. Compare YALE.

,**harvest 'festival** n (BrE) a Christian festival held each autumn to celebrate and give thanks for the gathering of crops. Fruit, vegetables, bread, etc. are taken to a church or school to decorate it, and a special service is held. Compare THANKSGIVING.

,**William 'Harvey** /'hɑːvi; AmE 'hɑːrvi/ (1578–1657) an English doctor who first discovered how blood flows around the body.

,**Harvey 'Nichols** /,hɑːvi 'nɪklz; AmE ,hɑːrvi/ a large, expensive department store in *Knightsbridge, London. It was started by Benjamin Harvey in 1813 and is known for selling fashionable clothes and for its Fifth Floor restaurant. It is often referred to by its nickname, Harvey Nicks. There are also Harvey Nichols shops in other British cities including Leeds, Birmingham, Manchester and Edinburgh.

'Harvey's™ /'hɑːviz; AmE 'hɑːrviz/ a British company based in *Bristol, England, which sells various types of sherry. The best known of these is Harvey's Bristol Cream.

,**Harwell La'boratory** /,hɑːwel; AmE ,hɑːrwel/ a British government research centre, near the village of Harwell in *Oxfordshire, England, where research is carried out into atomic energy.

,**hash 'browns** n [pl] (AmE) potatoes that have been cut into small pieces and fried. They are often eaten at breakfast.

the ,**Battle of 'Hastings**[1] /'heɪstɪŋz/ a famous battle (1066) in English history at which *William the Conqueror defeated King *Harold II and became King of England. It was fought near Hastings on the south coast of England.

,**Warren 'Hastings**[2] /'heɪstɪŋz/ (1732–1818) an important figure in the *East India Company who later became the first Governor General of India. When he returned to Britain in 1785, he was accused of corruption but was

found not guilty after a trial lasting seven years. ⇨ note at BRITISH EMPIRE.

'Hatchard's /'hætʃɑːdz; AmE 'hætʃɑːrdz/ a famous bookshop in *Piccadilly in central London, England, It was established in 1797.

,**Anne 'Hathaway** /'hæθəweɪ/ (1556–1623) the wife of William *Shakespeare. Her family home, **Anne Hathaway's Cottage**, is open to the public and is a popular tourist attraction in *Stratford-upon-Avon.

,**Hatton 'Garden** /,hætn/ a street in central London, England, where there are a lot of jewellery companies.

'hat-trick n (in sport) a series of three successes, e.g. scoring three goals in the same game or winning an event three times in a row. The expression was first used in cricket. A bowler who took three wickets in three balls was traditionally given a new hat by his club: *He completed his hat-trick with a wonderful third goal.*

Ha'waii /hə'waɪi/ the 50th and last state to join the US, in 1959, also known as the Aloha State. It consists of eight main islands and other smaller ones in the north Pacific Ocean. Its capital *Honolulu, which is also the largest city, and the port of *Pearl Harbor are on Oahu. The state attracts many tourists and produces sugar, pineapples, flowers, nuts and coffee. Captain James *Cook visited the islands in 1778, and they have been under US control since 1900.

Ha,waiian 'Punch /hə,waɪən/ n [C, U] a US product name for a red fruit juice drink. It is advertised on television by a cartoon character called Punchy. Hawaiian Punch is especially popular with children.

,**Stephen 'Hawking** /'hɔːkɪŋ/ (1942–) a British scientist working in theoretical physics who has greatly influenced people's ideas on the origins of the universe. His books on the subject, *A Brief History of Time* (1988) and *The Universe in a Nutshell* (2001) have sold millions of copies. He suffers from a serious disease which limits his ability to move and speak, so he communicates by means of a specially created computer which 'speaks' for him.

> 66 Someone told me that each equation I included in the book would halve the sales. 99
> Stephen Hawking about *A Brief History of Time*

,**Howard 'Hawks** /'hɔːks/ (1896–1977) an American who directed, produced and wrote films in a *Hollywood career that lasted 52 years. The many famous stars he directed included Cary *Grant and Katharine *Hepburn in *Bringing Up Baby* (1938), Gary *Cooper in *Sergeant York* (1941), Humphrey *Bogart and Lauren *Bacall in *The Big Sleep* (1946), Marilyn *Monroe in *Gentlemen Prefer Blondes* (1953), and John *Wayne in *Rio Bravo* (1959). Hawks received a special *Oscar in 1974.

,**Nicholas 'Hawksmoor** /'hɔːksmɔː(r)/ (1661–1736) an English architect who worked with Sir Christopher *Wren on the building of many churches in London, including *St Paul's Cathedral. He also worked with John *Vanbrugh on the building of *Blenheim Palace and *Castle Howard.

,**Goldie 'Hawn** /,gəʊldi 'hɔːn; AmE ,goʊldi / (1945–) a US actor who has often played innocent and silly characters in comedy films. She first became famous on the comedy television series *Laugh-In* (1968–74). She won an *Oscar for *Cactus Flower* (1969), and her other films include *There's a Girl in My Soup* (1970), *Private Benjamin* (1980) and *First Wives Club* (1996).

'Haworth /'haʊəθ; AmE 'haʊərθ/ a village in *West Yorkshire, England, where the *Brontë sisters lived and wrote their novels. It attracts many visitors, particularly because Emily Brontë's novel *Wuthering Heights* is set in the area.

Na,thaniel 'Hawthorne /'hɔːθɔːn; AmE 'hɔːθəːrn/ (1804–64) a US writer of novels and short stories. He was born in Salem, *Massachusetts, and set his novels in *New England during the time of the *Puritans. The most famous are The *Scarlet Letter (1850) and The House of the Seven Gables (1851) and his best-known collections of short stories are the two volumes of Twice-Told Tales (1837 and 1842). He lived in Europe for seven years and was US consul in Liverpool in 1853.

Joseph 'Haydn /'haɪdn/ (1732–1809) an Austrian composer, known especially for his symphonies and choral music. His music was very popular in Britain and Haydn made two visits to England. His last 12 symphonies are called the London Symphonies because they were first performed in London.

Rutherford B 'Hayes /ˌrʌðəfəd biː 'heɪz; AmE ˌrʌðərfərd/ (Rutherford Birchard Hayes 1822–93) the 19th US *President (1877–81). He was a Republican who ended *Reconstruction in the southern states. He had been a US officer in the *Civil War and a lawyer. Hayes was elected President by one vote of the *Electoral College. He had previously been elected to the US House of Representatives (1865–7) and was governor of Ohio (1868–72 and 1876–7). His wife was called 'Lemonade Lucy' because she would not allow alcohol in the *White House.

the ,Hay 'Festival /ˌheɪ/ a book festival which started in 1988 and is held every year in Hay-on-Wye, a small town in Wales which is famous for having a lot of book-shops that sell second-hand books. Events at the festival include talks by authors, discussions, exhibitions and performances.

'Haymarket /'heɪmɑːkɪt; AmE 'heɪmɑːrkɪt/ **1** a street in the *West End of London, England, in which there are two famous theatres, Her Majesty's and the Theatre Royal, Haymarket. **2** a very old traditional outdoor food market in *Boston, Massachusetts.

The 'Hay Wain /weɪn/ the best-known painting (1821) by the English artist John *Constable. It is in the *National Gallery in London, and shows a typical English countryside scene of the period, in summer. Wain is an old-fashioned word meaning a farm cart.

the 'Hayward ,Gallery /'heɪwəd; AmE 'heɪwərd/ an art gallery on the *South Bank in central London, England. It opened in 1968, mainly for exhibitions of 19th- and 20th-century art. There have also been displays of sculpture in the open air there.

Rita 'Hayworth /'heɪwɜːθ; AmE 'heɪwɜːrθ/ (1918–87) a US actor and dancer famous for her beauty and known as 'The Love Goddess'. She was a major *Hollywood star, especially in the 1940s. She began in musical films, such as Cover Girl (1944), and then made a number of dramatic films, including The Lady from Shanghai (1948), which was directed by Orson *Welles, one of her five husbands.

William 'Hazlitt /'hæzlɪt/ (1778–1830) an English writer and critic, best known for his essays and lectures. He expressed strong, often harsh, opinions, especially about other writers. His best-known works include Characters of Shakespeare's Plays (1817–18), Table Talk (1821) and The Spirit of the Age (1825).

'H-block /'eɪtʃ/ n each of the buildings, built in the shape of an H, in which prisoners were kept (1976–2000) in the *Maze prison near *Belfast in Northern Ireland.

HBO /ˌeɪtʃ biː 'əʊ; AmE 'oʊ/ (in full **Home Box Office**) a US cable television network which is the largest in the world. HBO presents films, sports, special programmes

and series, such as *Six Feet Under, *The Sopranos and *Sex and the City.

HBOS /'eɪtʃ bɒs; AmE bɔːs/ one of the largest banks in Britain. It was formed in 2001 when the *Halifax building society joined with the Bank of Scotland.

Head and 'Shoulders™ n [U] a make of shampoo (= liquid soap for washing the hair) produced by the US company *Procter and Gamble. It is advertised as a treatment for dandruff (= pieces of dead skin in the hair).

'Headingley /'hedɪŋli/ a sports ground established in 1890 in *Leeds, *West Yorkshire, England, where Yorkshire County Cricket and Leeds Rugby League and Rugby Union home matches are played. Headingley is also the name of an area of Leeds.

Heal's /hiːlz/ a fashionable furniture shop in central London, England, known especially for selling modern furniture. It was moved to its present building by Ambrose Heal (1872–1959), whose father had started the business.

the 'Health and 'Safety at 'Work Act a series of laws passed in Britain in 1974 which require employers to make sure that their employees are working in healthy and safe conditions.

the ,Health and 'Safety E,xecutive (abbr **HSE**) a British government organization which recommends action concerning the standards of health and safety at places of work and investigates accidents.

,health 'maintenance organi,zation ⇨ HMO.

,Seamus 'Heaney /'hiːni/ (1939–) a Northern Irish poet who lives in Dublin, Ireland. He won the *Nobel Prize for literature in 1995. His work shows his concern both for the traditions of Irish culture and about the *Troubles in Northern Ireland. His collections of poetry include North (1975), Field Work (1979), The Haw Lantern (1987), and Seeing Things (1991). He won the *Whitbread prize for The Spirit Level (1996) and for his translation of *Beowulf (1999).

,Patty 'Hearst¹ /'hɜːst; AmE 'hɜːrst/ (1954–) the grand-daughter of William Randolph *Hearst, who was kid-napped (= taken away by force) in 1974 by a group called the Symbionese Liberation Army (SLA). They demanded that her father give food to the poor. She then joined the SLA and robbed two banks with them before being arrested. She went to prison and was released in 1979.

'William 'Randolph 'Hearst² /'hɜːst; AmE 'hɜːrst/ (1863–1951) a very rich American who owned news-papers, magazines, radio stations and two film com-panies. He used *yellow journalism in his newspapers to increase their sales. His New York Journal competed fiercely in the 1890s with the New York World, owned by Joseph Pulitzer, and both encouraged the *Spanish-American War as a method to help sales. Hearst built the cas-tle of *San Simeon as his home in *California. Orson *Welles based his film *Citizen Kane on Hearst's life.

The ,Heart of 'Darkness a story by Joseph *Conrad, published in 1902. The story is told by Marlow, a young man who travels up the Congo River in Africa to find Mr Kurtz, who works in the ivory trade. He discovers that Kurtz is worshipped by the local tribe and has fallen into a cruel and immoral way of life.

,Heart of 'Oak a British song written in 1770, with words by the English actor David *Garrick, which cele-brates the qualities and achievements of British sailors. It refers to the fact that the wood of oak trees was used to build ships.

> 66 Heart of oak are our ships,
> Heart of oak are our men,
> We always are ready, steady, boys, steady! 99

Heat a UK magazine published each week containing photographs and articles about famous people and their private lives.

ˌEdward ˈ**Heath** /ˈhiːθ/ (1916–) a British *Conservative politician who became leader of the Conservative Party in 1965 and later *Prime Minister (1970–4). He is mainly remembered for taking Britain into the *European Union in 1973. Faced with economic problems and strikes, he called a general election in 1974, which the Conservatives lost. In 1975 he was replaced as party leader by Margaret *Thatcher. He remains a firm supporter of the European Union. He was made a *knight in 1992.

ˈ**Heathcliff** /ˈhiːθklɪf/ a character in the novel *Wuthering Heights* by Emily *Brontë. He is found as a baby and brought up by the family of Catherine Earnshaw. He develops a strong love for her, but because of his wild nature she will not marry him. He leaves, Catherine marries and he returns three years later to take revenge on the people he blames for ruining his life.

ˈWilliam ˈ**Heath** ˈ**Robinson** /ˈhiːθ ˈrɒbɪnsn; AmE ˈrɑːbɪnsn/ (1872–1944) a cartoonist and illustrator who was known especially for his comic drawings of strange and complicated machines for doing very simple tasks. As a result, any machine that appears ridiculously complicated is now often referred to as 'Heath Robinson': *He had rigged up a Heath Robinson device to help him with the decorating.* Compare GOLDBERG.

Heathˈrow /ˈhiːθˈrəʊ; AmE hiːθˈroʊ/ the largest airport in Britain and the busiest airport for international flights in the world. It is 15 miles/24 kilometres west of London and was opened in 1946. By 1961 it had three terminals (= buildings for arrival and departure) and a fourth opened in 1986. There are plans to open a fifth in 2008, though many people are unhappy about the increased number of flights and passengers this would create. Heathrow is officially known as London Airport.

ˌheavy ˈ**metal** n [U] a kind of rock music which became popular in the 1970s, with very loud guitars, drums and singing. The term is used of groups and performers such as Iron Maiden, Uriah Heep, Black Sabbath, *Metallica and Alice Cooper. Heavy metal groups and their fans often have long hair, wear leather jackets and dance in a way that is known as 'headbanging' (= moving the head backwards and forwards very quickly to the rhythm of the music). The songs are often about violence and the occult (= things connected with magic powers). Compare HARD ROCK.

the ˈ**Hebrides** /ˈhebrɪdiːz/ a group of islands off the west coast of Scotland, consisting of the Inner Hebrides, which include *Skye and *Mull, and the Outer Hebrides, which include Harris and Lewis. All the islands are popular with tourists in the summer.

Uˌriah ˈ**Heep** /jʊˌraɪə ˈhiːp/ a character in the novel *David Copperfield* by Charles *Dickens. He is David's clerk who pretends to be 'humble' and to want to serve him well, but in reality cheats him. His name is sometimes used for a person who pretends to show great respect but is not sincere. An album by a band called Uriah Heep has the title 'Very 'eavy... very 'umble', which refers to Uriah Heep's phrase in the novel, 'Ever so 'umble'.

ˌHugh ˈ**Hefner** /ˈhefnə(r)/ (1926–) the American who began *Playboy* magazine in 1953, and later created a larger company which included the Playboy Clubs. He is known for his 'Playboy Mansion' at which he held extravagant parties and entertained women who appeared in his magazine.

ˈ**Hefty**™ /ˈhefti/ a US make of strong bags for putting rubbish in and for garden work, etc. There are also Hefty One-Zip bags for storing food.

ˈ**Heineken**™ /ˈheɪnəkən/ an international company based in Holland that makes lager (= a type of pale light beer). It became famous in Britain for its humorous advertisements which ended with the words: 'Heineken refreshes the parts other beers cannot reach.'

Heinz™ /haɪnz/ an international company based in the US that makes a large range of food in tins, including *baked beans, soup and baby food. Heinz salad cream and tomato *ketchup (= sauce) are very popular in many countries. At one time the number 57 on Heinz tins was supposed to show the number of varieties of food produced by the company but it was never an accurate figure and the company now sells well over a thousand types of food.

ˌJoseph ˈ**Heller** /ˈhelə(r)/ (1923–99) a US writer of novels, the best known of which is *Catch-22*. His other books include *Something Happened* (1974), *God Knows* (1984), *Picture This* (1988) and *Closing Time* (1994), which is about the characters of *Catch-22* when they are older. Heller also wrote plays and films.

ˌLillian ˈ**Hellman** /ˈhelmən/ (1907–84) a US writer of plays. Her best-known works were *The Children's Hour* (1934), *The Little Foxes* (1939), *Watch on the Rhine* (1941) and *Toys in the Attic* (1960). Her book about her own life, *An Unfinished Woman* (1969), won a *National Book Award. Hellman lived with the writer Dashiell *Hammett for more than 30 years. She had strong socialist opinions, and her career suffered in the 1950s because of *McCarthyism.

He'llo! a popular magazine published each week in Britain which contains photographs of and articles about famous people, and is known for saying only good things about them. It was first published in Britain in 1988 as a British version of the Spanish magazine *¡Hola!*.

ˌHell's ˈ**Angel** n [usually pl] a member of a group of people who ride powerful motorcycles, wear leather clothes and used to have a reputation for wild and violent behaviour. Groups of Hell's Angels are called *chapters*, and they have their own rules which are different from those of the rest of society. The first groups were formed in *California in the 1950s and they now exist in several countries.

ˌHelp the ˈ**Aged** a British charity that provides help for old people both in Britain and abroad. It was established in 1961 and works to reduce poverty, loneliness and prejudice in relation to old people and to improve understanding of old age and standards in the care of old people.

ˌErnest ˈ**Hemingway** /ˈhemɪŋweɪ/ (1899–1961) a US writer of novels and short stories. He created a style of writing using short, simple sentences, and received the *Nobel Prize for literature in 1954. Hemingway drove an ambulance during *World War I and later worked in France and Spain as a journalist reporting on *World War II and the Spanish Civil War. His novels were about the loves and adventures of tough men. They included *The Sun Also Rises* (1926), *A Farewell to Arms* (1929), *For Whom the Bell Tolls* (1940) and *The Old Man and the Sea* (1952). When Hemingway became ill he shot himself at his home in *Idaho.

the ˈ**Hemlock So**ˌ**ciety** a US organization that supports doctors who help people to end their own lives when they want to do so because they have a serious illness that cannot be cured. The organization was established in 1980 and campaigns for changes in the law. It later changed its name to End-of-Life Choices.

ˌJimi ˈ**Hendrix** /ˈhendrɪks/ (1942–70) a US *rock musician who sang, wrote songs and played the guitar. His hit songs include *Hey Joe* and *Purple Haze* (1967). He was left-handed and played with the guitar upside down. He influenced many pop musicians and gave exciting stage performances, sometimes playing his guitar with his teeth or behind his back and ending performances by burning the guitar. He moved to England in 1966 and formed a small band called the Jimi Hendrix Experience. He died there after taking too many sleeping pills.

,Stephen '**Hendry** /'hendri/ (1969–) a Scottish *snooker player, the most successful in the history of the game. He was the youngest winner of the World Professional Championships in 1990 and became world champion for the seventh time in 1999.

'**Henley** /'henli/ a town on the River *Thames in *Oxfordshire, England. It is famous for the rowing races held there during the **Henley Regatta**, an event that began in 1839 and takes place over five days every July. It is a fashionable event, attended by many rich and famous people, and is one of the sports and cultural events held every summer which together are known as the *Season.

the Henley Regatta

,Tim '**Henman** /'henmən/ (1974–) a leading British tennis player who in 1998 became the first to reach the semi-finals at *Wimbledon since the 1970s. He has many fans, whose enthusiasm for watching him play has been called **Henmania**. In the press he is often called 'Tiger Tim'.

,John '**Henry**¹ ⇨ JOHN HENRY.

,Lenny '**Henry**² /'henri/ (1958–) a well-known English comedy actor. His television shows include *The Lenny Henry Show* and *Chef!* and he is well known for his work for *Comic Relief. He is married to the comedy actor Dawn *French.

,O '**Henry**³ /,əʊ 'henri; *AmE* ,oʊ/ (1862–1910) a popular US writer of short stories who was born William Sydney Porter. He began to write in prison after being sent there for stealing money from the bank where he worked. O Henry's stories were simple and often humorous, and they usually ended with a surprise. More than 300 of them were collected in *Cabbages and Kings* (1904), *The Voice of the City* (1908) and other volumes.

,Patrick '**Henry**⁴ /'henri/ (1736–99) a major political leader of the *American Revolution. He was a member of the *Continental Congress (1774–6) and governor of *Virginia (1776–9 and 1784–6). Henry was at first opposed to the US *Constitution because he supported *states' rights, but he later helped to add the *Bill of Rights to it.

> 66 Give me liberty or give me death. 99
> Patrick Henry

,Prince '**Henry**⁵ (1984–) the second child of the *Prince and *Princess of Wales. He is usually called Prince Harry by the British press and public.

Henry I /,henri ðə 'fɜːst; *AmE* 'fɜːrst/ (1068–1135) king of England (1100–35). The youngest of three sons of *William I, he became king when his eldest brother *William II died, because his other brother Robert was

away on a *Crusade. Henry improved the administrative system of the country and established a system by which judges travelled around the country deciding cases.

Henry II /,henri ðə 'sekənd/ (1133–89) king of England (1154–89). He was the grandson of *Henry I, succeeded King *Stephen, and was the first *Plantagenet king. He reduced the power of the *barons and increased the power of the state. He wanted to reduce the power of the Church, which led to his dispute with the *Archbishop of Canterbury, Thomas *Becket, which ended in Becket's murder. During his rule England established control over Ireland. Henry also introduced various systems of justice which can be seen as the beginning of *common law.

Henry III /,henri ðə 'θɜːd; *AmE* 'θɜːrd/ (1207–72) king of England (1216–72) and the son of King *John. He was not popular with the *barons, who disliked his use of foreign people to advise him and criticized him for poor judgement in financial matters. In 1264, Simon de *Montfort led a rebellion of the barons and Henry was defeated and put in prison. He took back power in 1265 after a battle in which the rebels were defeated by an army led by Henry's son (later *Edward I).

Henry IV /,henri ðə 'fɔːθ; *AmE* 'fɔːrθ/ (1366–1413) king of England (1399–1413) after his cousin *Richard II. He was born Henry Bolingbroke, the son of *John of Gaunt, and was a leading opponent of Richard's. In 1398 Richard sent him into exile, but in 1399 he returned to England, defeated Richard and was accepted as king by Parliament. While he was king there were rebellions against him in Wales and the north of England. He was forced to accept the principle that the king should govern through Parliament, and in 1407 Parliament took control of the country's financial affairs.

Henry IV, Parts 1 and 2 /,henri ðə 'fɔːθ; *AmE* 'fɔːrθ/ two plays (c. 1597–8) by *Shakespeare based on the period when *Henry IV was king of England. The play's main characters are Prince Hal (Henry IV's son and later *Henry V) and his friend *Falstaff. In *Part 1* Hal drinks and jokes with Falstaff and others in the Boar's Head, a London tavern (= pub), and his father worries that he is not serious enough to be a king. However, at the end he accepts his responsibilities and fights in a battle to defeat a rebellion against his father. In *Part 2*, Hal is still friendly with Falstaff, but when Henry IV dies and Hal becomes king, he rejects him with the famous line: 'I know thee not, old man'.

Henry V /,henri ðə 'fɪfθ/ (1387–1422) king of England (1413–22) and son of *Henry IV. He is regarded as a symbol of English patriotism (= love of one's own country), especially because of *Shakespeare's play *Henry V*. He took an English army to France during the *Hundred Years War and defeated the French at the Battle of *Agincourt (1415), putting an area of France under English control.

Henry V /,henri ðə 'fɪfθ/ a play (1599) by *Shakespeare which celebrates the military victories in France of King *Henry V. It contains several famous patriotic speeches, including the king's famous speech before the battle of *Agincourt. There have been two film versions of the play, the first in 1944, directed by Laurence *Olivier with himself as Henry, and the second in 1989, directed by Kenneth *Branagh, who also played the title role.

> 66 We few, we happy few, we band of brothers;
> For he today that sheds his blood with me
> Shall be my brother. 99
> *Henry V*

Henry VI /ˌhenri ðə ˈsɪksθ/ (1421–71) king of England (1422–61 and 1470–1) and son of *Henry V. He was not popular, mainly because England finally lost the *Hundred Years War while he was king. Opposition to him led to the *Wars of the Roses, in which the House of *Lancaster was defeated by the House of *York and Henry was put in prison. As a result of this, *Edward became king, but in 1470, with the help of the powerful Earl of Warwick, known as Warwick the Kingmaker, Henry became king again, but he was defeated once more in 1471. He was put in the *Tower of London, where he was murdered, and Edward became king again. Henry VI established *Eton College and *King's College, Cambridge.

Henry VI, Parts 1, 2 and 3 /ˌhenri ðə ˈsɪksθ/ three plays (c. 1590–92) by *Shakespeare, set during the period of the *Wars of the Roses. They are among Shakespeare's earliest plays and some people believe that he may only have written parts of them.

Henry VII /ˌhenri ðə ˈsevnθ/ (1457–1509) king of England (1485–1509), the first *Tudor(1) king. Born Henry Tudor, he was brought up in France. In 1485 he led a rebellion against *Richard III, defeated him at the Battle of *Bosworth Field and became king. In 1486 he married the daughter of *Edward, uniting the House of *Lancaster (to which he belonged) and the House of *York and so bringing the *Wars of the Roses to an end. Although there were rebellions during his rule, including those led by Lambert *Simnel and Perkin *Warbeck, Henry established greater order in the country, introduced a more modern system of government and greatly improved the country's financial position.

Henry VIII /ˌhenri ði ˈeɪtθ/ (1491–1547) king of England (1509–47) and son of *Henry VII. He is one of the most famous of all English kings, partly because he had six wives.

For political reasons, he married *Catherine of Aragon, the wife of his dead brother Arthur, just after he became king. They had a daughter, later *Mary I, but because they did not have a son who could be the future king, Henry decided to divorce her. The Pope refused to give the necessary permission for this, so Henry removed England from the Catholic Church led by the Pope and made himself head of the Church in England. This act, together with others such as the *Dissolution of the Monasteries, was the beginning of the establishment of Protestantism in England.

Henry divorced Catherine of Aragon and married Anne *Boleyn in 1533. They had a daughter, later *Elizabeth I, but Henry had Anne executed for adultery. His third wife was Jane *Seymour, who died giving birth to a son (later *Edward VI). Henry married his fourth wife, *Anne of Cleves, for political reasons, but soon divorced her and in 1540 he married Catherine *Howard. She too was executed for adultery. Henry's sixth and last wife was Catherine Parr, who survived him.

As a young man Henry was known for his love of hunting, sport and music, but he did not rule well and the country was in a weak and uncertain state when he died. See also CROMWELL, GREENSLEEVES, MORE, WOLSEY.

Henry VIII /ˌhenri ði ˈeɪtθ/ a play (1613) by *Shakespeare, possibly the last he wrote. Some people believe he wrote it with somebody else, perhaps John *Fletcher. It is about events surrounding King *Henry VIII's divorce from *Catherine of Aragon.

Jim 'Henson /ˈhensn/ (1936–90) the American who created The *Muppet Show, as well as writing the words and speaking the lines of many of the puppets in it. See also SESAME STREET.

Audrey 'Hepburn[1] /ˈhepbɜːn; AmE ˈhepbɜːrn/ (1929–93) a British actor, born in Belgium. She won an *Oscar for Roman Holiday (1953) and her other films include War and Peace (1956), Funny Face (1957), The Nun's Story (1959), Breakfast at Tiffany's (1961) and *My Fair Lady (1964). After her film career she worked for UNICEF, visiting children in trouble all over the world. In 1992 she received the *Presidential Medal of Freedom.

Katharine 'Hepburn[2] /ˈhepbɜːn; AmE ˈhepbɜːrn/ (1909–2003) a US actor, especially in films, who was best known for playing forceful women, and for her clear, strong voice. She won *Oscars for her performances in Morning Glory (1933), Guess Who's Coming to Dinner (1967), The Lion in Winter (1968) and On Golden Pond (1981). Her other films include The Philadelphia Story (1940) and The African Queen (1951). She had a long love affair with Spencer *Tracy and made several films with him.

George 'Hepplewhite /ˈheplwaɪt/ (died 1786) an English maker of furniture noted for his simple and graceful style. His book The Cabinet-Maker and Upholsterer's Guide (1788) had a great influence, but no piece of furniture that is known to be his work has survived.

Barbara 'Hepworth /ˈhepwəθ; AmE ˈhepwərθ/ (1903–75) an English sculptor. Her work is mainly abstract and marked by strong curving lines. She was married for a time to the painter Ben *Nicholson and from 1939 lived in *St Ives, *Cornwall, a town still known for its many artists. She died in a fire at her home, which is now a museum.

▶ heraldry

Heraldry is the design and study of **coats of arms**. Many British upper-class families, as well as thousands of public institutions such as city councils and universities, have the right to their own coat of arms or shield. This is often printed on notepaper, used as a badge on uniforms and the sides of official vehicles, and put above the door of buildings. The **heraldic devices** (= designs) that can be used on a coat of arms are strictly controlled by the *College of Arms in England, and the **Court of the Lord Lyon** in Scotland.

The origins of heraldry lie in the decorated shields that were carried into battle by *medieval knights. The designs painted on these shields were originally a means of identification. They then became family emblems which have changed little through the centuries. Sometimes the devices have been changed to combine the coats of arms of two families. A husband may **impale** his wife's family arms by dividing the shield vertically down the middle and putting his own arms on the **dexter** (= the wearer's right) side and his wife's on the **sinister** (= left) side.

Heraldry uses many technical terms, mostly derived from Old French. The background of a shield is known as the **field** and its main colour the **tincture**. The heraldic designs on the field are known as **charges**. They may include a simple **pale** (= broad vertical band) or a **fess** (= thin horizontal stripe), or a more elaborate device such as an animal, a cross or a castle. Shields are often **quartered**, with each quarter carrying a different design. On the *royal arms, the quarters represent different countries. The first and fourth **quarters** are **gules** (= red) and each contains three lions **passant** (= walking) shown in **or** (= gold) to represent England. The second quarter contains a red lion **rampant** (= standing upright), the symbol of Scotland, within a **tressure** (= border) on a gold background. The third quarter is **azure** (= blue) and contains a golden *harp with strings of **argent** (= silver) to represent Ireland. Wales is not included because it had its own heraldic device in the arms of the *Prince of Wales before the **quarterings** for Scotland and Ireland were added to the royal arms.

In most coats of arms the shield is surrounded by additional decorations, such as a pair of animal or human **supporters** (for instance, the lion and unicorn on the royal arms), a crown or helmet, and a **motto**. On the royal arms the motto is *Dieu et mon droit*, French for 'God and my right'.

Many Americans whose families came from Europe try to trace their origins and identify their ancestors' coat of arms. They may then use it on objects such as drinking glasses, or hang a drawing of the coat of arms in their house. For many people a coat of arms provides a connection with the past and a way of expressing family pride.

'Herald 'Tribune ⇨ INTERNATIONAL HERALD TRIBUNE.

A P 'Herbert[1] /'hɜːbət; *AmE* 'hɜːrbərt/ (Alan Patrick Herbert 1890–1971) an English writer. He was best known for his articles in the magazine *Punch, many of which made fun of the legal profession. He was made a *knight in 1945.

George 'Herbert[2] /'hɜːbət; *AmE* 'hɜːrbərt/ (1593–1633) an English poet and priest. He was one of the *metaphysical poets and dealt with religious themes such as doubt, suffering and joy, using simple language. The collection *The Temple* was published in 1633 after his death.

James 'Herbert[3] /'hɜːbət; *AmE* 'hɜːrbərt/ (1943–) an English writer of horror stories, which include *The Rats* (1974), *The Fog* (1975), *Shrine* (1983), *The Ghosts of Sleath* (1994) and *Once* (2001). Many of them have been made into films.

Here 'Comes the 'Bride a piece of music which is often played at weddings in church as the bride (= the woman getting married) walks up to join the groom (= the man getting married) just before the marriage ceremony. The music is a chorus from Richard Wagner's opera *Lohengrin*.

he,reditary 'peer *n* (in Britain) a member of the *aristocracy, usually a man, who has received his title from his father and who automatically had the right to vote in the *House of Lords until the reform of 2001. Compare LIFE PEER. note at PEERAGE.

'Hereford /'herɪfəd; *AmE* 'herɪfərd/ **1** a city on the River Wye in the west of England near the border with Wales. Its cathedral contains the *Mappa Mundi, a very old map of the world.
2 *n* a type of cow bred for its meat. Hereford cattle are usually reddish in colour with a white head. They were originally developed around Hereford.

'Herefordshire /'herɪfədʃə(r); *AmE* 'herɪfərdʃər/ an English county, now governed by a *unitary authority. It is famous for its cider and the natural beauty of the *Malverns, the *Wye Valley and the Golden Valley of the river Dore. ⇨ note at COUNTIES. See also KILVERT.

Hereward the 'Wake /,herɪwəd ðə 'weɪk; *AmE* ,herɪwərd/ (11th century) a British military leader who encouraged the *Anglo-Saxons to resist *William the Conqueror and the *Normans in 1070. His military base was the Isle of *Ely in *Cambridgeshire, and after the Normans had defeated him there he is said to have escaped. There are many stories about his adventures although few of them are based on historical fact.

Here We 'Go a song often sung, especially in the past, at British football matches by the supporters when their team is playing well, or by groups of people who have gathered in public, for example to protest against some-thing. The words 'Here we go' are repeated throughout the song.

Heriot-'Watt Uni,versity /,herɪət 'wɒt; *AmE* 'wɑːt/ a university in *Edinburgh, Scotland, established in 1966. It is known especially for teaching scientific subjects.

'heritage ,centre *n* (in Britain) a place like a museum which people visit to learn about life in the past. Heritage centres often contain old buildings, machines, etc. which have been made to look as they did originally: *a railway heritage centre*. See also WORLD HERITAGE SITE.

heritage 'coast *n* [U, C] (in Britain) an attractive area of the coast which is protected by law. There are restrictions on building there and wildlife is preserved, but the public is free to walk there.

Heritage 'Open Days a number of days every year when people can visit places and buildings in Britain which are not normally open to the public. These places are of interest because of their history, architecture or cultural importance.

Robert 'Herrick /'herɪk/ (1591–1674) an English poet and priest. He wrote many short, cheerful poems, including *Gather Ye Rosebuds While Ye May* and *Cherry Ripe*.

James 'Herriot /'herɪət/ (born James Alfred Wight 1916–95) writer, born in Scotland,who is well known for his humorous books about the life of a country vet (= animal doctor) in *Yorkshire. The books were made into a popular television series called *All Creatures Great and Small* (1977–90).

William 'Herschel /'hɜːʃəl; *AmE* 'hɜːrʃəl/ (1738–1822) a British astronomer (= scientist who studies the stars, planets, etc.), born in Germany. He was originally a musician but became an astronomer by studying the sky through telescopes he made himself. He discovered Uranus, the first new planet to be identified since ancient times, and proved the existence of double stars. After becoming the official astronomer to King *George III, he was made a *knight in 1816.

'Hershey bar™ /'hɜːʃi; *AmE* 'hɜːrʃi/ *n* America's oldest chocolate sweet, sometimes called the 'Great American Chocolate Bar'. It was first produced by Milton Hershey in 1894. US soldiers kept Hershey bars to give to children in Europe during and after *World War II when sweets were scarce there. Hershey Foods Corporation in Hershey, Pennsylvania, now also makes many other sweets.

'Hertfordshire /'hɑːtfədʃə(r); *AmE* 'hɑːrtfərdʃər/ (*abbr* **Herts**) a county in southern England, to the north of London. Its administrative centre is the town of Hertford.

Hertz™ /hɜːts; *AmE* hɜːrts/ an international company that hires out cars and other vehicles. Branches of Hertz are often seen at airports.

Charlton 'Heston /,tʃɑːltən 'hestən; *AmE* ,tʃɑːrltən/ (1924–) a US actor famous for playing leading parts in big historical films. He was Moses in The *Ten Commandments* (1956) and received an *Oscar for *Ben-Hur* (1959). He is known for his conservative views (= being opposed to much political and social change), and was President of the *National Rifle Association (1998–2003).

Hever 'Castle /,hiːvə; *AmE* ,hiːvər/ a castle near Edenbridge in *Kent, England, where *Henry VIII is said to have stayed with Anne *Boleyn, his second wife, before they were married. The castle has a fine garden in the Italian style.

HGTV /,eɪtʃ dʒiː tiː 'viː/ (*in full* **Home and Garden television**) a television network in the US and Canada which broadcasts programmes about home decoration and gardening.

the HHS /ˌeɪtʃ eɪtʃ 'es/ ⇨ DEPARTMENT OF HEALTH AND HUMAN SERVICES.

ˌHiaˈwatha /ˌhaɪəˈwɒθə; AmE ˌhaɪəˈwɑːθə/ the main character in The Song of Hiawatha (1855), a long poem by Henry Wadsworth *Longfellow, based on stories about the life of the *Native American leader who established the *Iroquois League, and his marriage to Minnehaha.

ˈWild ˈBill ˈHickok /ˈhɪkɒk; AmE ˈhɪkɑːk/ (1837–76) a famous *frontiersman in the American *Wild West. His real name was James Butler Hickok. He worked as a marshal (= law officer) in several *Kansas towns before joining *Buffalo Bill's *Wild West Show (1872–4). He then moved to Deadwood, *South Dakota, where he was shot in the back and killed while playing cards.

ˈHickory, ˈDickory, ˈDock /ˈhɪkəri ˈdɪkəri ˈdɒk; AmE ˈdɑːk/ the title and first line of an old *nursery rhyme. The full song is:

> 66 Hickory, dickory, dock,
> The mouse ran up the clock.
> The clock struck one,
> The mouse ran down,
> Hickory, dickory, dock. 99

ˈHickstead /ˈhɪkstɪd/ a centre for showjumping (= the sport of riding over difficult barriers) in *Sussex, England. Many national and international competitions are held there.

ˌhide-and-ˈseek (AmE also ˌhide-and-go-ˈseek) n [U] a children's game in which one or more players hide and one or more of the others try to find them. ⇨ note at TOYS AND GAMES.

ˈˌHurricaneˈ ˈHiggins¹ /ˈhɪgɪnz/ (Alex Higgins 1949–) a British *snooker player born in *Belfast, Northern Ireland. He was the youngest ever winner of the world snooker championship in 1972 and went on to win again in 1982. He played his last tournament in 1997. He was given the name 'Hurricane' (= a violent storm) because of the speed at which he played. He was often in trouble with the authorities because of his violent behaviour.

ˌJack ˈHiggins² /ˈhɪgɪnz/ (1929–) an English author of thrillers (= exciting novels). His best-known book is The Eagle has Landed (1975), about an attempt to kill Winston *Churchill during *World War II. He has also written books under several other names, including his real name, Harry Patterson.

ˌHigh ˈChurch n [U] the tradition within the *Church of England that has the closest links with the *Roman Catholic Church. High Church ceremonies are similar to Catholic ones in the emphasis they place on the Virgin Mary, the burning of incense, etc.
▶ **High Church** adj: My family were very High Church. See also ANGLO-CATHOLICISM. Compare LOW CHURCH. ⇨ note at CHURCH OF ENGLAND.

ˌHigh Comˈmissioner n the official representative of one *Commonwealth country in the capital city of another, who is the head of his or her country's **High Commission**.

the ˌHigh Court of ˈJustice (also the **High Court**) the branch of the legal system in England and Wales that deals mainly with serious civil cases (= ones concerned with the private rights of citizens rather than with crimes). It is divided into the *Queen's Bench, the *Chancery Division and the *Family Division. Cases only go to the High Court if they cannot be dealt with in a lower court (e.g. a *county court). Some appeals (= reviews of cases) are dealt with in the *Queen's Bench

Division of the High Court: She's a High Court judge. ⇨ note at LEGAL SYSTEM.

the ˌHigh Court of Juˈsticiary /dʒʌˈstɪʃəri/ (also the **High Court**) the court in Scotland that deals with the most serious criminal cases (e.g. murder). It also deals with appeals (= reviews of cases) from lower courts. Compare SHERIFF COURT.

ˌhigher deˈgree n a degree taken after a first degree, at a more advanced level. Examples are an MA (Master of Arts), an MSc (Master of Science) or a PhD (Doctor of Philosophy). ⇨ note at FURTHER EDUCATION.

▶ **higher education**

In Britain, higher education refers to courses at universities that lead to a degree. British students apply to several universities through *UCAS (Universities and Colleges Admission Service) and receive **offers** of a place on condition they receive certain grades in their *A levels. A **first degree**, which is usually an **honours degree**, generally takes three years. Most courses end with exams called **finals** and results are given as **classes** (= grades): a **first** is the highest class, most students get a **second** which is often divided into upper second, also called a **2.1** (two one), and lower second, called a **2.2** (two two), and below that is a **third**. **Graduates** can add the letters **BA** (Bachelor of Arts), **BSc** (Bachelor of Science), **B Mus** (Bachelor of Music), etc. after their name. Some **graduates** go on to study for a further degree, often a **master's degree (MA)** or a **doctorate (PhD)**. Most students have to pay towards their **tuition fees** and can get **student loans** towards their living expenses.

At most British universities the **academic year** starts in October and is divided into three **terms** or two **semesters**. Students study a main subject throughout their degree course, which is usually a mix of compulsory courses and optional courses, often called **electives**. Most students go to **lectures** and **seminars** (= discussion groups) and there are **practicals** for those doing science subjects. A **professor** is a person in charge of a department or a senior member of staff, and other teaching and research staff are called **lecturers**.

In the US, students talk about 'going to college' even if the institution they attend is a university. Most **colleges** offer classes only for **undergraduate** students studying for a **bachelor's degree**. *Community colleges offer two-year courses leading to an **associate's degree**, and afterwards students transfer to a different college or university to continue their studies. **Universities** are larger and also offer courses for **graduate students** who study in **graduate school**. American *high school students who want to study at a university or college have to take a **standardized test**, such as a *SAT or the *ACT and then apply directly to between three and six colleges in their last year of high school. There are many private colleges and universities but most students choose a public institution because the costs are lower. All universities charge **tuition**, and students pay extra for **room and board**. Students whose families cannot afford the full amount apply for **financial aid** and many students receive a **financial aid package** which may be a combination of **grants** from the government, a **scholarship**, a **student loan** and **work-study** (= a part-time job at college).

The US academic year may be divided into two **semesters** of about 15 weeks or three **quarters** of about 10 weeks. Students take courses in a variety of subjects, regardless of their main subject, as part of a **liberal arts** curriculum. At the end of their **sophomore** (= second) year students choose a **major** (= main subject) and sometimes a **minor** (= additional subject) which they study for the next two years. Students take four or five courses each semester from the **course catalog** which may consist mainly of **lectures** or may include **discussion sections** or **lab sessions**. At the end of each course they are given a **grade** which will be used to calculate a *grade point average (GPA) to check their overall progress. Most people who teach at US colleges or universities and have a doctorate are addressed as 'professor'. **Full professors** are senior to **associate professors**, **assistant professors** and **instructors**.

Highgate 'Cemetery /ˌhaɪgeɪt/ a burial ground in Highgate, a district of north London, England, where many famous people are buried, including Karl *Marx, George *Eliot and Michael *Faraday. Karl Marx's grave is famous for its large sculpture of his head.

Highgrove 'House /ˌhaɪgrəʊv; AmE ˌhaɪgroʊv/ a house owned and lived in by the *Prince of Wales in *Gloucestershire, England.

'Highland a *council area of northern Scotland, to the north of the *Grampians (a range of mountains) and including some of the Inner *Hebrides islands. It is the largest of the council areas and has the lowest population density (= number of people per area of land). Its administrative centre and only city is Inverness.

Highland 'cattle n [pl] a breed of cows and bulls native to the Scottish *Highlands, with long horns and a long hairy brownish coat.

Highland cattle

the ˌHighland 'Clearances the forced removal of farmers from their small rented farms called *crofts in the *Highlands of Scotland during the late 18th century and the 19th century. The owners of the land wanted to use it for sheep and, later, deer. The Clearances caused great poverty and many farmers and their families left Scotland to live in the US.

Highland 'dress n [U] the traditional costume worn by Scottish men on formal occasions or as a military uniform. Its main parts are a *tartan kilt (= a man's skirt with folds, that reaches to the knees), a sporran (= a flat bag made of fur or leather hanging in front of the kilt), and a small knife which is stuck in the top of one of the stockings (= long socks). ⇨ note at CLANS.

Highland 'fling n a lively, traditional Scottish dance for one person, usually a man, in which the dancer dances on the same spot, often with one arm above the head and the other resting on the hip, and makes quick arm and leg movements. It is often performed at *Highland Gatherings.

Highland 'Gathering n (also ˌHighland 'Games) a traditional Scottish outdoor festival which includes music, dancing and sports such as *tossing the caber* (= throwing a long wooden pole). Highland Gatherings are

the Braemar Gathering

held each year in a number of places in Scotland, not only in the *Highlands. The most famous is the Braemar Gathering in north-east Scotland, held in September.

the 'Highlands n [pl] the region of northern Scotland where there are many mountains. Compare LOWLANDS.

the ˌHighlands and 'Islands n [pl] the whole of northern Scotland, including the *Highland *council area and the main island groups (the *Hebrides, the *Orkney Islands and the *Shetland Islands).

ˌHigh 'Noon a US film (1952) which is considered to be one of the best *westerns ever made. It was directed by Fred *Zinnemann. Gary *Cooper won an *Oscar in the role of Marshall Will Kane, who finds out that nobody in the town will help him against four criminals who are coming to kill him. Grace *Kelly played his wife. Many Americans saw the film's story as a criticism of people in the 1950s who failed to oppose *McCarthyism.

'high school n (especially AmE) a secondary school, usually one for the last four years before college. Most US students complete high school at the age of 17 or 18.

ˌHigh 'Sheriff n a representative of the King or Queen in each of the *counties in England, Wales and Northern Ireland. The position is an honorary (= unpaid) one and has existed since the year 995. The High Sheriff is appointed each year from among the local people and the duties include acting as the representative of the Queen or King in matters of law and order.

'high street n (BrE) the main shopping street in the centre of a town or city. It is often used as part of a name: *Cheltenham High Street* ◊ *We met in the high street.* ◊ *high-street banks* ◊ *Marks and Spencer, the UK's most famous high-street brand.* Compare MAIN STREET(1).

ˌhigh 'tea n [U] (BrE) an early evening meal, usually with a cooked dish and bread and butter. It is eaten especially in northern England and Scotland by people who have their main meal in the middle of the day, and is often referred to simply as *tea*. The meal may or may not include a cup of tea. Compare TEA(2). ⇨ note at MEALS.

the ˌHighway 'Code a set of official rules for road users in Britain, published as a small book. Questions about the Highway Code are asked as part of the driving test.

'Hilary term /'hɪləri/ n (in some British universities) the term (= period of study) that begins in January and ends just before *Easter.

ˌBenny 'Hill¹ /'hɪl/ (1925–92) an English comedy actor popular from the mid 1950s to the 1980s. His television series *The Benny Hill Show*, which he wrote himself, consisted mainly of clever visual humour and jokes about sex which some people considered old-fashioned.

ˌGeorge 'Roy 'Hill² /'dʒɔːdʒ 'rɔɪ 'hɪl; AmE 'dʒɔːrdʒ/ (1922–2002) a US film director. His best-known films include *Butch Cassidy and the Sundance Kid* (1969), *The Sting* (1973), for which he won an *Oscar, and *The World According to Garp* (1982).

ˌRowland 'Hill³ /ˌrəʊlənd 'hɪl; AmE ˌroʊlənd/ (1795–1897) a British *Post Office worker who invented the postage stamp, originally costing one penny (the *Penny Black, introduced in 1840). Before this, postage was paid by the person receiving a letter or parcel. Hill was made a *knight in 1860.

'hillbilly /'hɪlbɪli/ n (AmE disapproving) a person who lives in the mountains and is thought to be poor and backward by people living in towns. The word was originally used to describe people living in *Appalachia. **Hillbilly music** is the *folk music of this region which became part of the more commercial *country music.

H

,Nicholas '**Hilliard** /'hɪliəd; *AmE* 'hɪliərd/ (1547–1619) an English painter best known for his miniatures (= very small pictures of people).

'**Hillsborough** /'hɪlzbərə/ a football ground in *Sheffield, England. On 15 April 1989 it was the scene of the **Hillsborough disaster**, in which 96 people died and hundreds more were injured when they were crushed by other fans trying to get into the ground. An official report criticized the police for not doing enough to prevent the disaster.

the '**Hilton** /'hɪltən/ (*also* the ,**Hilton Ho'tel**) any of a large group of modern, comfortable and expensive hotels in many cities around the world. The company that owns them was started by Conrad Hilton (1887–1979), who bought his first hotel in *Texas in 1919. The company now also owns many casinos (= gambling clubs).

'**hip hop** *n* [U] **1** a type of modern music consisting of *rap with an electronic backing, often made by combining and repeating short pieces of recorded music. It was started in the late 1970s by *African American DJs (= people who introduce and play recorded music in clubs) in New York.
2 the popular culture that developed among young *African Americans in the US in the late 1970s. It is associated mainly with *rap music, as well as with 'breakdancing' (= fast dancing on the hands and feet, popular especially in the early 1980s), graffiti art (= painting on the walls of buildings, etc.) and fashion clothing.

'**hippie** (*also* **hippy**) *n* a member of the movement of young people in the 1960s and 1970s who rejected conventional society and social habits. They dressed in unusual clothes, had long hair, often took illegal drugs, and believed in sexual freedom, sometimes living in large groups like families called 'communes'. They were also called 'flower children' because they believed in peace and love. The *Haight-Ashbury district of *San Francisco became their centre, but there were hippies in all parts of the US and Western Europe. See also FLOWER POWER.

the '**Hippodrome** /'hɪpədrəʊm; *AmE* 'hɪpədroʊm/ a name common to many places of public entertainment in Britain, especially theatres, cinemas and concert halls. The Hippodrome in *Leicester Square, London, originally a variety theatre, is a famous nightclub. Several theatres in the US have also had the name. The most famous was the New York Hippodrome (1905–39), where Harry *Houdini performed.

,Damien '**Hirst** /,deɪmiən 'hɜːst; *AmE* 'hɜːrst/ (1965–) an English artist. He became famous in the early 1990s with a series of works consisting of dead animals in glass cases full of formaldehyde (= a special liquid that preserves things). He won the *Turner Prize in 1995 with *Mother and Child Divided (Cow and Calf)*. Some people find his work offensive.

> 66 It's amazing what you can do with an E in A-level Art, twisted imagination and a chainsaw. 99
> Damien Hirst after winning the Turner Prize

,Ian '**Hislop** /'hɪzlɒp; *AmE* 'hɪzlɑːp/ (1960–) an English comic writer, journalist and broadcaster. He has been the editor of *Private Eye* since 1986, and regularly appears on radio and television, including the comedy quiz show *Have I Got News For You?*.

,His '**Master's 'Voice** ⇨ HMV.

Hi'spanic *adj* of or from countries, especially in Latin America, in which Spanish is spoken: *a Hispanic neighbourhood of Los Angeles*.
▶ **Hispanic** *n* a person whose first language is Spanish,

especially one from a Latin American country (or whose ancestors came from such a country) living in the US: *Hispanics are the largest minority group in the United States*. Compare CHICANO, LATINO, TEX-MEX.

,Alfred '**Hitchcock** /'hɪtʃkɒk; *AmE* 'hɪtʃkɑːk/ (1899–1980) an English film director best known for his thrillers (= exciting films with a complicated story) and horror films. Following success with films such as *The Thirty-Nine Steps* (1935) and *The Lady Vanishes* (1938), he moved in 1940 to the US, where his films included *North by Northwest* (1959), *Psycho* (1963) and *The Birds* (1963). Hitchcock often appeared briefly in his own films. He was made a *knight in 1980.

The '**Hitch ,Hiker's 'Guide to the 'Galaxy** a successful radio series (1978–80), book (1979), and television series (1981) written by Douglas *Adams. They are about Arthur Dent's comic adventures in space after the earth is destroyed by the Vogons. There were several further books, including *The Restaurant at the End of the Universe* (1980) and there was a new radio series in 2004.

HMCE /,eɪtʃ em si: 'iː/ ⇨ HM CUSTOMS AND EXCISE.

,HM '**Coastguard** (*in full* Her/His Majesty's **Coastguard**) the British government organization, part of the Maritime and Coastguard Agency (MCA), whose job is to watch the country's coast and help ships and people in trouble at sea.

'HM '**Customs and 'Excise** (*in full* **Her/His Majesty's Customs and Excise**) (*also* **Customs and Excise**) (*abbr* **HMCE**) a British government department that collects tax. Customs duties are the tax collected on certain imports, e.g. alcoholic drinks and cigarettes, and excise is the special tax collected on certain goods produced in Britain, e.g. petrol, beer and cigarettes. When people *go through customs* at an airport or port they must sometimes say whether they are carrying any of these goods, and customs officers are allowed to search them. Her Majesty's Customs and Excise are also responsible for collecting *VAT, preventing illegal imports and providing information about foreign trade.

HMMWV /,eɪtʃ em ,em dʌblju: 'viː/ ⇨ HUMVEE.

HMO /,eɪtʃ em 'əʊ; *AmE* 'oʊ/ (*in full* **health maintenance organization**) a US medical insurance system, with its own hospitals and doctors. Customers make regular payments each month or year and can then receive treatment from HMO doctors and hospitals. Compare PPO, BLUE CROSS(1).

HMSO /,eɪtʃ em es 'əʊ; *AmE* 'oʊ/ ⇨ HM STATIONERY OFFICE.

,HM '**Stationery ,Office** (*in full* **Her/His Majesty's Stationery Office**) (*abbr* **HMSO**) a British government organization responsible for publishing and controlling the copyright (= legal right of ownership) in certain important government documents, including laws. The trading part of HMSO was sold to private owners in 1996 and now trades under the name of The *Stationery Office.

HMT /,eɪtʃ em 'tiː/ ⇨ HM TREASURY.

HM 'Treasury** /'treʒəri/ (*in full* **Her/His Majesty's Treasury**) (*abbr* **HMT**) ⇨ TREASURY.

HMV™ /,eɪtʃ em 'viː/ a British company started in 1921 that sells recordings of music and books. HMV stands for 'His Master's Voice', and the company used to use on its record label a picture of a small dog listening to an old-fashioned gramophone (= a machine for playing records with a large horn to produce the sound). HMV also owns the *Waterstone's bookshops.

,Thomas '**Hobbes** /'hɒbz; *AmE* 'hɑːbz/ (1588–1679) an English philosopher who developed a range of theories about nature, human behaviour and society. He did not believe in God and thought that the only way to hold society together was to have strong social institutions and a powerful ruler. His book *Leviathan* (1651) sets out these views.

The '***Hobbit*** /'hɒbɪt; *AmE* 'hɑːbɪt/ a book (1937) written by J R R *Tolkien. The book is set in the imaginary world of Middle Earth. In the book, hobbits are small, friendly creatures with big feet. The main character, a hobbit called Bilbo Baggins, becomes involved in an adventure involving dragons, dwarves and wizards. Many of the same characters appear again in the book *The Lord of the Rings* (1954–5). *The Hobbit* is popular with both children and adults in many countries around the world.

‚**Hobson's 'choice** /ˌhɒbsənz; *AmE* ˌhɑːbsənz/ *n* [U] a situation in which there is no choice, because only one course of action or result is possible. The expression comes from the name of Thomas Hobson, a 17th–century British horse dealer who would not allow his customers any choice when renting a horse: *It was Hobson's choice: I could resign from the job or wait to be fired.*

▶ **hockey**

In Britain *hockey* refers to **field hockey**. Hockey played on ice is called **ice hockey**. In the US ice hockey is much more common and is called simply *hockey*. Both sports are played by both men and women.

In field hockey there are 11 players in each team, five **forwards**, three **halfbacks**, two **fullbacks** and a **goal-keeper**. A **hockey pitch** (*AmE* **hockey field**) is 100 yards/91 metres long and between 55 and 60 yards/50 and 55 metres wide. There is a **goal** at each end. The aim of the game is to hit a small white ball into the other team's goal with wooden **hockey sticks**. A goal is worth one point. Each game has two halves of 35 minutes. A game begins with a **pass-back**: a forward hits the ball but it is not allowed to cross the centre line until another player from either team has also hit it. There is also an **indoor** game of hockey played with six in each team.

The modern game developed in England in the mid 19th century, and the first hockey club was formed in 1849. English clubs are now organized into three divisions. Each year, the winners of the league competition qualify for the European Club Championship. The Scottish Hockey Union runs leagues in Scotland. The sport is not shown on television as much as *cricket, *Rugby or *football and most people could not name any famous hockey players. Hockey is a game traditionally played at girls' schools. In Britain ice hockey attracts relatively little interest.

An English teacher visiting *Harvard introduced the sport to the US in 1901. At first it was played only by women, and the first men's game was not until 1928. In the US the game is controlled by the USA Field Hockey Association. It is less popular than in Britain.

By contrast, ice hockey, first played in Canada, has long been popular in the US. It is a fast and exciting sport. Each team has six players, a **centre**, two **forwards** and two **wingers**, all of whom try to score, and a **goal-keeper**. Players wear **skates**, and have **helmets**, **gloves** and **pads** for protection. They use small wooden **sticks** to hit the **puck**, a small, hard rubber disc, into the opponent's goal. If they succeed they score one point. The area of the **rink** is up to 67 yards/61 metres long and 33 yards/30 metres wide, and is divided into an attacking zone, a neutral zone and a defending zone. A game has three 20-minute **periods**. Play begins with a **face-off** when the **referee** drops the puck between two opposing players. **Defenders** try to prevent the opposing team from scoring and can **check** (= crash into) another player with their bodies. Professional players often have fights on the ice, and the game has

been criticized for being too violent. A player who commits an illegal action goes to the **penalty box**, informally called the **sin bin**, for a period of between 2 and 10 minutes and the team must continue without him or her.

The US **National Hockey League** has 30 teams, six of which are Canadian. The best teams in the **Eastern Conference** and the **Western Conference** play to decide which two will be in the *Stanley Cup. The Hart Memorial Trophy is given to the best player, and Wayne Gretzky, thought by many to be the greatest ice hockey player ever, won it eight times in the period 1980–7 and in 1989. Among the most successful teams have been the New York Islanders and the Detroit Red Wings. In the northern states college and university teams compete in three *NCAA divisions.

‚**David 'Hockney** /'hɒkni; *AmE* 'hɑːkni/ (1937–) an English artist famous for his paintings, drawings, prints, photographs and stage designs. He has lived mostly in the US since the 1960s, and is perhaps best known for the series of paintings of swimming pools done in *California, e.g. *A Bigger Splash* (1967).

‚**William 'Hodges** /'hɒdʒɪz; *AmE* 'hɑːdʒɪz/ (1744–1797) an English artist who travelled with Captain *Cook on his journey by ship to the Pacific (1772–75), drawing and painting pictures of the landscapes, icebergs (= very large masses of floating ice) and people he saw.

‚**Dorothy 'Hodgkin** /'hɒdʒkɪn; *AmE* 'hɑːdʒkɪn/ (1910–1994) an English scientist who did important work on the structure of crystals. She discovered the structure of penicillin (= a drug used to treat infections), vitamin B12 and insulin (= the substance that controls the sugar in blood). In 1964 she received the *Nobel Prize for chemistry.

‚**Jimmy 'Hoffa** /'hɒfə; *AmE* 'hɑːfə/ (1913–?1975) a US trade union leader. He was President of the International Brotherhood of *Teamsters and greatly increased their power. He was found guilty of trying to bribe a member of a jury and was sent to prison from 1967 to 1971. He disappeared in 1975 and his body has never been found, though people assume he was murdered.

‚**Dustin 'Hoffman** /ˌdʌstɪn 'hɒfmən; *AmE* 'hɑːfmən/ (1937–) a US actor who is known for his close attention to details of character in a wide range of different roles. His first big success was in *The *Graduate*, and he won *Oscars for *Kramer vs Kramer* (1979) and *Rain Man*. His other films have included *Midnight Cowboy*, *All the President's Men* (1976), *Tootsie* (1982) and *Runaway Jury* (2003), based on a novel by John *Grisham.

‚**Gerard 'Hoffnung** /'hɒfnʊŋ; *AmE* ˌdʒerɑːrd 'hɑːfnʊŋ/ (1925–59) a British cartoonist and musician, born in Germany. His humorous drawings, especially of musicians, are still very popular on greetings cards, etc.

‚**Ben 'Hogan** /'həʊgən; *AmE* 'hoʊgən/ (1912–97) a US golf player who won more than 60 major competitions, including the US Open four times (1948, 1950, 1951 and 1953), the *PGA twice (1946 and 1948), the Masters twice (1951 and 1953) and the British Open once (1953). He was called 'Bantam Ben' because of his short height. (A bantam is a small hen.).

‚**William 'Hogarth** /'həʊgɑːθ; *AmE* 'hoʊgɑːrθ/ (1697–1764) an English painter and engraver (= person who cuts or carves designs in metal, stone, etc.), best known for his sets of paintings that tell a moral story, such as *The *Rake's Progress* (1733–5) and *Marriage à la Mode* (1743–5). His house in Chiswick, London, is now a museum.

'**Hogmanay** /'hɒgməneɪ/ the name in Scotland for *New Year's Eve (31 December) and the parties and celebrations traditionally held on that day. These include singing *Auld Lang Syne* at midnight and then going *first-footing.

Hans 'Holbein /ˌhæns 'hɒlbaɪn; AmE 'hɔːlbaɪn/ (also called **Hans Holbein the Younger**) (1497–1543) a German painter who from 1526 lived and worked in England. He was made the official royal painter in 1536 and is best known for his paintings of King *Henry VIII and his court. One of his greatest paintings, *The Ambassadors* (1533), is in the *National Gallery, London.

'Holborn /'həʊbən; AmE 'hoʊbən/ an area of central London, England, between *Westminster(1) and the City. Its important buildings include Lincoln's Inn and Gray's Inn. See also INNS OF COURT.

ˌHolby 'City /ˌhɒlbi, ˌhəʊlbi; AmE ˌhɑːlbi, ˌhoʊlbi/ a popular British *BBC television series about life in a hospital. It is set in the same hospital as the series *Casualty*.

the ˌHole-in-the-'Wall Gang (also **the Wild Bunch**) the group of *Wild West outlaws (= criminals) led by Butch *Cassidy.

ˌBillie 'Holiday /ˌbɪli 'hɒlədeɪ; AmE 'hɑːlədeɪ/ (1915–59) a US singer of *jazz and the *blues whose popular name was 'Lady Day'. She recorded her first record in 1933 with Benny *Goodman, and later sang with 'Count' *Basie and Artie *Shaw. Her best-known songs include *The Very Thought of You* and *These Foolish Things*. She took drugs for most of her life and died young. Her autobiography, *Lady Sings the Blues* (1956), was made into a film (1972) with Diana *Ross.

ˌHoliday 'Inn™ any of the group of hotels owned by the US company Intercontinental Hotels Group, the largest of its kind in the world, with hotels in 70 countries. The first Holiday Inn opened in *Memphis, Tennessee, in 1952. *Holiday Inn* is the title of a 1942 film with music by Irving *Berlin about a hotel that only opens on public holidays. The song *White Christmas* was written for the film.

▶ **holidays and vacations**

Holiday in American English means a day that is special for some reason. Most people do not go to work on an important holiday, but may do so on a minor one. Few people have to work on federal (= national) holidays such as *New Year's Day or *Independence Day, though they may celebrate *St Valentine's Day or *Groundhog Day but still go to work or school. Apart from the main federal holidays each state decides its own holidays. The period from *Thanksgiving to the end of the year when there are several important holidays is called the *holiday season* or simply *the holidays* (e.g. *Stores are getting ready for the holiday season.*). In British English, special days like New Year's Day are called *bank holidays or **public holidays**.

Holiday in British English also means a period of time spent away from work or school, usually of a week or longer. This is called a *vacation* in American English. So, the period of several weeks around Christmas when schools are closed is called the *Christmas holiday* in Britain and the *Christmas vacation* in the US.

Holiday and *vacation* are also used to refer to the period when people go away for a time to a beach resort or to the country, or go travelling. British people have about four weeks' paid **leave** from their jobs. Most take their main holiday in the summer. People without children of school age often **go on holiday** in the **off season** when prices are lower and there are fewer other **holidaymakers**. Some people stay in Britain for their holiday, but many rent a cottage in the country or go to beach resorts in Europe for one or two weeks. Some travel to the US or visit India, the Far East and other parts of the world. Many British people going abroad

buy **package holidays** sold on the Internet or through high-street **travel agents**, which include transport, accommodation and sometimes excursions in the price. Some people see their holidays as an opportunity to relax in the sun, but others prefer **activity holidays** during which they can visit famous buildings or go walking in the countryside. A few go to a holiday centre, often called a **holiday village**, such as *Butlin's or *Center Parcs, which provides entertainment for all the family. People often arrange their holiday a long time in advance and look forward to it through the winter. Many people also have a **short break**, usually three or four days, e.g. at a country cottage in Britain or in a European city.

Americans have less paid vacation, typically two weeks. People with important jobs or who have worked in their company for many years may have longer vacations. People with low-paid jobs in shops, fast food restaurants, etc., often have no paid vacation at all.

The typical family vacation in the US involves driving to a destination within the country. Some people visit relatives or **go sightseeing** in cities like *Washington, DC, or *New York. The *national parks, like *Yellowstone National Park or the *Grand Canyon, are also popular, and people sometimes rent a cabin (*BrE* cottage) in the country. Families often go to **amusement parks** like *Disney World in *Florida. People who do not drive usually fly to a place as air fares are relatively cheap. Package tours are not very common and most Americans arrange their transport and accommodation separately.

Many Americans have not been on vacation outside North America. However, Europe has always been a popular destination for people wanting to travel further, and trips to South America and the Far East are increasingly common, especially with younger travellers. *Cruises* (= journeys by ship, visiting different places) to the Caribbean or Alaska have also become very popular.

ˌJools 'Holland /ˌdʒuːlz 'hɒlənd; AmE 'hɑːlənd/ (1958–) a British musician and television personality. From 1974 to 1980 he played piano with the pop group Squeeze, and he is known for his skill in playing *jazz. He has presented television programmes including *The Tube* (1982–7), *Juke Box Jury* (1989–90) and *Later with Jools Holland* (1992–).

ˌDoc 'Holliday /ˌdɒk 'hɒlədeɪ; AmE ˌdɑːk 'hɑːlədeɪ/ (1852–87) a dentist who gambled and often fought with guns in the American *Wild West. He was born John Henry Holliday in *Georgia and moved west in the 1870s for his health. He helped Wyatt *Earp and his brothers in the famous gunfight at the *OK Corral in *Tombstone, *Arizona, but died six years later of tuberculosis (= a disease of the lungs).

ˌAlan 'Hollinghurst /'hɒlɪŋhɜːst; AmE 'hɑːlɪŋhɜːrst/ (1954–) a British writer whose novel *The Line of Beauty* (2004) won the *Booker Prize. His other books include *The Swimming-Pool Library* (1988) and *The Folding Star* (1994). His work describes the emotional lives of gay men and shows the contemporary gay world.

'Holloway /'hɒləweɪ; AmE 'hɑːləweɪ/ (also **Holloway prison**) a large prison for women in north London, England.

ˌBuddy 'Holly /ˌbʌdi 'hɒli; AmE 'hɑːli/ (1936–59) a US singer in the early years of *rock and roll who played a guitar and wrote songs. He and his group, The Crickets, had a number of hits, including *That'll Be the Day* (1957) and *Peggy Sue* (1957). Although he died at the age of 22 in a plane crash, his music had a strong influence on other pop singers, especially in Britain.

'holly *n* [U] the hard, shiny, pointed, dark green leaves and red berries of the holly tree. It is especially associated with *Christmas, when it is used for decoration in churches and people's homes. A piece of holly is also often used to decorate the top of a Christmas pudding. At Christmas time pictures of holly are used on greetings cards and advertisements. Some people believe it is unlucky to bring holly into a house before Christmas Eve (24 December).

The ,Holly and the 'Ivy the title and first line of a popular *Christmas carol. ⇨ note at CAROLS AND CAROL SINGING.

▶ **Hollywood**

Hollywood, more than any other place in the world, represents the excitement and glamour of the **film industry**. The world's major film companies have studios in Hollywood and many famous **film/movie stars** live in its fashionable and expensive *Beverly Hills district. But Hollywood is also *Tinseltown, where money can buy an expensive lifestyle but the pressure to succeed can ruin lives, as in the case of Marilyn *Monroe and River *Phoenix. Both the British and Americans have mixed feelings about Hollywood: they are fascinated by the excitement of the film world and by the lives of the stars, but also see Hollywood as a symbol of trashy, commercial culture.

Hollywood is now surrounded by *Los Angeles. In 1908, when film companies began moving west from New York, it was a small, unknown community. The companies were attracted to *California by its fine weather, which allowed them to film outside for most of the year, but they also wanted to avoid having to pay money to a group of studios led by Thomas *Edison which were trying to establish a monopoly. Most of the companies were run by people from Jewish families who had come to America from Europe. By the 1920s, companies such as *Universal and *United Artists had set up studios around Hollywood. During this period Mary *Pickford, Douglas *Fairbanks¹, and John *Barrymore became famous in **silent films** (= films without sound). Mack *Sennett, a Canadian, began making comedy films, including those featuring the *Keystone Kops, in which Charlie *Chaplin and 'Fatty' *Arbuckle became stars. D W *Griffith directed expensive 'epic' films like The *Birth of a Nation, and William S *Hart made *westerns popular. Hollywood also created its first sex symbol, Theda Bara (1890–1955).

The 1920s saw big changes. The first film in Technicolor was produced in 1922. *Warner Brothers was formed in 1923 and four years later produced Hollywood's first **talkie** (= film with spoken words), The *Jazz Singer. Huge numbers of Americans were now attracted to the **movies**. Stars like Pickford and Chaplin reached the height of their fame, and new stars were discovered, such as Rudolph *Valentino, *Laurel and Hardy and Buster *Keaton.

The 1930s and 1940s were Hollywood's 'Golden Age' and films became popular around the world. Hollywood even made successes out of America's worst times: *Prohibition led to the gangster films of Edward G *Robinson and James *Cagney, and the *Great Depression to films like The *Grapes of Wrath. *World War II featured in successful films like *Casablanca. The great Hollywood studios, *MGM, Warner Brothers, *20th Century Fox, *Paramount Pictures and *Columbia Pictures, controlled the careers of actors. Famous directors of the time included Orson *Welles and John *Ford and screen stars included Clark *Gable, John *Wayne, Katharine *Hepburn, Errol *Flynn, Henry *Fonda, Humphrey *Bogart, Lauren *Bacall, Bette *Davis, Gregory *Peck, Kirk *Douglas and Robert *Mitchum.

New words were invented to keep up with Hollywood's development: cliffhanger, tear jerker, spine-chiller and western describe types of film. Villains became baddies

or bad guys. As equipment became more sophisticated more people were needed to manage it. New jobs, still seen on lists of film credits today, included gaffer (= chief electrician) and best boy, his chief assistant.

In the 1950s large numbers of people abandoned the movies in order to watch television. The film industry needed something new to attract them back. This led to the development of **Cinerama** and *3-D films, which gave the audience the feeling of being part of the action. These proved too expensive but the wide screen of **CinemaScope** soon became standard throughout the world. The stars of the 1950s, including Marilyn *Monroe, Rock *Hudson, James *Dean and Steve *McQueen, also kept the film industry alive.

In the 1960s many companies began making films in other countries where costs were lower, and people said Hollywood would never again be the centre of the film industry. But the skills, equipment and money were still there, and Hollywood became important again in the 1980s. The old studios were bought by new media companies: 20th Century Fox was bought by Rupert *Murdoch, and Columbia by the Sony Corporation. New energy came from independent directors and producers like Steven *Spielberg, Robert *Redford and Martin *Scorsese. Rising stars included Meryl *Streep, Harrison *Ford, Arnold *Schwarzenegger, Kevin *Costner and Tom *Hanks.

Now, more than ever, Hollywood leads the world's film industry, producing the most expensive and successful films ever made, such as Jurassic Park (1993), *Forrest Gump, Independence Day (1996), *Titanic, Gladiator (2000) and Troy (2004). Companies like MGM own their own **movie theaters** in the US and elsewhere. Studios make extra profits from selling films to television companies and from selling videos and DVDs. The *Oscars, presented by Hollywood's *Academy of Motion Picture Arts and Sciences, are the most valued prizes in the industry.

the ,Hollywood 'Bowl /ˌhɒliwʊd ; AmE ˌhɑːliwʊd/ a large outdoor theatre in the natural curve of a hill in *Hollywood, *California. It was opened in 1919. The Bowl has 17 000 seats and presents concerts, operas, plays and other events.

the Hollywood Bowl

,Kelly 'Holmes¹ /'həʊmz; AmE 'hoʊmz/ (1970–) an English runner who runs in 800 metres and 1500 metres races and won gold medals at both distances at the 2004 Olympics. She was made a *dame(2) in 2005.

'Oliver 'Wendell 'Holmes² /'wendəl 'həʊmz; AmE 'hoʊmz/ (1809–94) a US doctor and writer of stories and poems. In 1857, they began to be published in The *Atlantic Monthly magazine, and his famous 'Breakfast Table' conversations were later collected in several books. His poems include The Chambered Nautilus and Old Ironsides. Holmes also taught medicine at *Harvard University (1847–82).

Holmes's son, **Oliver Wendell Holmes Junior** (1841–1935), became one of the wisest and most respected judges on the US Supreme Court (1902–32). See also FALSELY SHOUTING FIRE IN A CROWDED THEATRE.

,Sherlock 'Holmes³ /ˌʃɜːlɒk 'həʊmz; AmE ˌʃɜːrlɑːk 'hoʊmz/ a private detective in the *detective stories of Arthur *Conan Doyle. Holmes is able to solve crimes and

mysteries using his powers of observation and deduction (= logical thought), sometimes without leaving his flat/apartment in *Baker Street, and often to the amazement of the police and his friend Dr *Watson. People often say, 'Elementary, my dear Watson', when they think that a problem is easy to solve, although Holmes never actually says this in any of the stories. He is often shown wearing a special type of hat called a *deerstalker* and smoking a curved pipe. He also plays the violin and sometimes takes drugs. The Sherlock Holmes stories are still very popular and have been filmed many times.

> 66 It is quite a three-pipe problem, and I beg that you won't speak to me for fifty minutes. 99
> Sherlock Holmes

,Eleanor ,Holmes 'Norton /ˌhəʊmz 'nɔːtən; AmE ˌhoʊmz 'nɔːrtən/ (1937–) a US congresswoman who was known as a leader in the *civil rights movement, a Professor of Law and board member of a number of top companies, before she became a member of *Congress in 1991.

,Gustav 'Holst /ˌɡʊstɑːv 'həʊlst; AmE 'hoʊlst/ (1874–1934) an English composer descended from Swedish and Russian ancestors. His best-known work is The *Planets.

Vic,toria 'Holt /'həʊlt; AmE 'hoʊlt/ a name under which the English author Eleanor Hibbert (1910–93) wrote some of her many historical, romantic or mystery novels. She also used the name Jean Plaidy.

the ,Holy 'Grail (also the Grail) the plate or cup used by Jesus Christ at the Last Supper, in which some of his blood is said to have been collected after his death. There are many old stories about the Holy Grail. In the most famous of these King *Arthur's *Knights of the Round Table go to search for it, and it is finally found by Sir *Galahad, the only *knight who is completely pure. When Galahad dies, his men see the Grail rise into Heaven. The expression *Holy Grail* is sometimes used to mean something very valuable which is very hard to find: *nuclear scientists seeking the holy grail of limitless energy.*

'Holy Island ⇨ LINDISFARNE.

,Holyrood 'House (also Holyroodhouse) /ˌhɒliruːd; AmE ˌhɑːliruːd/ a royal palace in *Edinburgh, used by members of the British royal family when they visit Scotland and open to the public at other times. Most of the original early 16th–century palace burned down in 1544, and the present palace was built for King *Charles II in the 1670s.

Holyrood House

,Home, Sweet 'Home the title of a popular song (1823) by Sir Henry Rowley Bishop (1786–1855), with words by J H Payne (1791–1852), a US writer of plays. People often say 'Home sweet home' when they arrive back in their own house or country again.

> 66 Mid pleasures and palaces though we may roam, Be it ever so humble, there's no place like home … Home! Sweet, sweet home! There's no place like home. 99

,Home A'lone a US film (1990) which became the most successful comedy film ever made. Kevin, played by Macaulay Culkin, is a young boy left at home by mistake when his family flies to Paris. Two further films, Home Alone 2 and Home Alone 3, followed in 1992 and 1997.

'Home and 'Garden 'television ⇨ HGTV.

'homecoming /'həʊmkʌmɪŋ; AmE 'hoʊmkʌmɪŋ/ n (in US high schools, colleges and universities) an event held each year, usually in the autumn, when former students return for special celebrations and social events. These include the homecoming game of football, the homecoming parade (= procession) and the homecoming dance. An attractive and popular girl is elected as the homecoming queen. In some schools, etc. a homecoming king is also chosen.

the ,Home 'Counties n [pl] (in Britain) the counties around London. People living in the Home Counties are generally regarded as being relatively wealthy, especially by those living in other parts of the country: *They enjoyed a comfortable Home Counties lifestyle.*

,Home 'Depot™ any of a large group of shops in the US and Canada that sell building materials for home improvement work, such as wood, paint and tools. The company was established in 1978, and the main office is in *Atlanta, *Georgia.

the ,Home 'Guard an army created during *World War II to defend Britain at home in case the enemy invaded the country. It consisted of men who were too old or young for the armed forces. They were originally called the Local Defence Volunteers. See also DAD'S ARMY.

▶ homelessness

A number of people in Britain and the US are homeless. Many are forced to sleep on the streets (BrE also sleep rough or be a rough sleeper) because they have nowhere else to go. Formerly, people who had no permanent home were called tramps or vagrants. Most were older people. Now, many younger people are homeless. In the US the typical image of a homeless person is of a single man or an older woman. The women are sometimes called bag ladies, because they carry their things around in large bags. But many families with small children are also homeless.

Homeless people sleep in shop doorways, under bridges, or anywhere they can find away from the wind and rain. In Britain, the alternative to sleeping rough is to go to a night shelter or to live in a squat (= live in an empty house or flat without paying rent). Squatters can only be evicted by the owner after a formal court order has been obtained.

Not all homeless people sleep rough or squat. In Britain, a government campaign aims to prevent sleeping rough and begging. Local councils are legally required to find somewhere for homeless families to live, and many families are housed in bed-and-breakfast accommodation. Charities such as *Shelter, *Centre Point and the *Salvation Army run hostels for the homeless. Each winter around Christmas, they also organize campaigns which raise money to provide extra night shelters and soup kitchens (= places giving free hot food).

In the US many towns have laws making it illegal to sleep on the streets, so the police may tell people to move during the night. The US also has shelters but it is not easy to get a bed in one. Many do not have enough space, or have only enough money to stay open for part of the year. They are often away from the centre of town, and people need to have money for the bus fare to get there.

For many people, homelessness begins when they lose their jobs and cannot pay their rent. Some become homeless as a result of family quarrels, broken relationships, violence, and mental illness. Some homeless people survive by **begging**. In Britain homeless people have an opportunity to help themselves by selling The **Big Issue* magazine: they buy copies of the magazine and sell them at a higher, fixed price to members of the public. There are similar publications in the US, but they are less popular.

Many people give to charities, or to the homeless on the streets, but some think homeless people are wasters (= spend money carelessly), or are too lazy to work, and are responsible for their own situation. Americans generally believe that people should work hard to help themselves, instead of taking money from the government. For that reason, many Americans will give money to charities, but are opposed to a system of government benefits. But homeless people who have no address have difficulty getting the limited kinds of help available from the government.

the 'Home ˌOffice the British government department dealing with many matters within the country, including law and order, the control of people entering the country, political elections and broadcasting. The minister responsible for the Home Office is called the *Home Secretary. Compare FOREIGN AND COMMONWEALTH OFFICE.

ˌHome on the 'Range a popular US song about the American West. It was first published in 1873 in the *Smith County Pioneer* newspaper in *Kansas, where it is now the official state song. It begins:

> 66 Oh, give me a home where the buffalo roam,
> Where the deer and the antelope play;
> Where seldom is heard a discouraging word,
> And the skies are not cloudy all day. 99

ˌWinslow 'Homer /ˌwɪnzləʊ ˈhəʊmə(r); AmE ˌwɪnzloʊ ˈhoʊmər/ (1836–1910) a US painter well known especially for his watercolours. They express the strong American spirit and influenced other US painters at the end of the 19th century. He painted scenes of American life, landscapes and scenes of the sea, especially in *New England and *Florida, such as *Cannon Rock* (1895) and *The Gulf Stream* (1899). Early in his career he drew scenes of the *Civil War for the magazine *Harper's Weekly*.

ˌhome 'rule n [U] **1 Home Rule** (in British and Irish history) the government of Ireland by the Irish. There was a strong political movement for this from the 1870s to 1914, when a Home Rule Bill was passed by the British parliament, but because of *World War I nothing was actually done about it. The *IRA was formed and began to use violent methods in order to get a greater degree of independence than the Bill allowed. This led to a change in the situation when in 1920 Ireland was split into Northern Ireland and the *Irish Free State (now the *Republic of Ireland). Many people in Northern Ireland are still today strongly opposed to the idea of being ruled by the government in Dublin. See also PARNELL. **2** the government of any country or region by its own citizens. See also DEVOLUTION.

ˌhome 'run n (in *baseball), the action of a player who hits the ball far enough, often over the fence, to enable him or her to advance around all three bases and return to the 'home base', scoring a 'run' by doing so. See also GRAND SLAM(3).

ˌHomes and 'Gardens a British magazine published every month, which contains articles on house decorating, gardening and other subjects. It first appeared in 1919.

the ˌHome 'Secretary (in Britain) the minister responsible for the *Home Office. The full title is Secretary of State for the Home Department.

the 'Homestead Act a law passed by the US Congress in 1862. It gave 160 acres/65 hectares of government land in the west to anyone who would agree to live on it for five years. A small payment was required. A person who received this land was called a **homesteader**.

'hominy /ˈhɒmɪni; AmE ˈhɑːmɪni/ n [U] (AmE) dry corn that is roughly ground. It is boiled with water or milk to produce a food called **hominy grits**, which is often eaten at breakfast, especially in the southern states. Compare GRITS.

the Hon ⇨ HONOURABLE.

▶ **Hong Kong**

Hong Kong, which means 'Fragrant Harbour' in Chinese, is a former British *Crown Colony off the south-east coast of China. The colony consisted of Hong Kong Island, many smaller islands, and the mainland areas of Kowloon ('Nine Dragons') and the New Territories. British opium traders working for the *East India Company began using Hong Kong Island's harbour in the 1820s. The island was occupied by the British during the first Opium War and was handed over to them by China in 1842 at the end of the war. Kowloon was gained in 1860 following the second Opium War. In 1898 the colony again increased in size when the New Territories were leased to Britain for a period of 99 years. On 30 June 1997 Hong Kong was handed over to China and it is now a Special Administrative Region of China.

Under British rule Hong Kong became a successful manufacturing, business and financial centre. The population of six million people, mostly Chinese, enjoyed a high standard of living and the wealth of Hong Kong attracted people from other countries in the Far East.

British control of Hong Kong became an embarrassment to China, and there were great celebrations in Beijing when the colony was returned to Chinese rule. In 1984 the British and Chinese negotiated an agreement to preserve the existing economic system and way of life for at least 50 years after the handover. As a British dependency, Hong Kong was ruled by a governor appointed by the Queen, but in practice he agreed to all measures passed by the local, democratically elected Legislative Council. A Chinese governor appointed by the authorities in Beijing took over in 1997.

Hong Kong still has its own currency and legal system. A 'Closer Economic Partnership Arrangement' with mainland China was signed in 2003.

ˌHoni ˌsoit qui ˌmal y 'pense /ˌɒni ˌswɑː kiː ˌmæl iː ˈpɒns; AmE ˈɑːni, ˈpɑːns/ ⇨ ORDER OF THE GARTER.

'honky-tonk /ˈhɒŋki tɒŋk; AmE ˈhɑːŋki tɑːŋk/ n (AmE) **1** [U] a type of *African American *ragtime music played on a piano whose wires have been changed to give it a high sound. Honky-tonk music was first played at the beginning of the 20th century in the bars and dance halls of *New Orleans. **2** [C] a cheap bar or dance hall.

ˌHono'lulu /ˌhɒnəˈluːluː; AmE ˌhɑːnəˈluːluː/ the capital city of the US state of *Hawaii. It is a major port on the south-eastern coast of the island of Oahu, and sugar and pineapples are processed there. The University of Hawaii is in Honolulu, and so is *Pearl Harbor, the home of the US Pacific Fleet. The city is very popular with tourists, especially *Waikiki beach.

H

'honor roll *n* (in US schools) a list of students who have achieved high grades in their work in a particular term or year. Compare DEAN'S LIST.

'honor so,ciety *n* (in US schools and colleges) an organization for students who have achieved high grades in their work. There are national and local honor societies, and many have Greek letter names, like the Beta Club. They can be for general academic achievement or for certain specific areas of study.

'Honourable (*AmE* **'Honorable**) **1 the Honourable** (*written abbr* **the Hon**) (in Britain) a title placed before the names of various members of the *peerage, including the children of *barons and *viscounts and the daughters and younger sons of *earls: *the Honourable Mrs Shand Kydd.*

2 (in Britain) used by *Members of Parliament when speaking to or about another member during a debate, even when they are criticizing one another: *I refer you to the answer given earlier by the Honourable Member for Chesterfield.* ◇ *I disagree with my Honourable Friend the member for Bolsover.*

3 (in the US) a title of respect used before the names of certain important officials, but not when speaking to or about them. They include members of *Congress, the US *Attorney General, members of the *Supreme Court, other judges, members of the President's *Cabinet, US ambassadors, state governors and *mayors: *the Honorable Alan Simpson, US Senator.* See also RIGHT HONOURABLE.

the ,Honourable Ar'tillery ,Company the oldest regiment in the British Army, started by King *Henry VIII in 1537. It is now part of the *Territorial Army.

▶ **honours**

Twice a year several hundred British people who have distinguished themselves in some way receive a variety of honours. A few are given **life *peerages**, some are made *knights, and many others are given lesser awards. The **honours lists** are published on *New Year's Day (**the New Year Honours**) and in mid June on the present Queen's official birthday (**the Birthday Honours**). At the end of each parliament before a general election, the *Prime Minister recommends a list of politicians for the **Dissolution Honours**.

For a long time honours were given almost automatically to senior members of the armed forces and the *Civil Service, and to those who had contributed to party political funds. In 1993 John *Major announced a reduction in the number of such honours and said that more awards were to be given to members of the public nominated for honours by colleagues and friends, or by people who admire their achievements. The Ceremonial Secretariat receives nominations and draws up a final list which is approved by the prime minister. As well as the names of politicians and businessmen, it contains charity workers, well-known sports and television personalities, actors, musicians, etc., and many ordinary people. Honours are awarded by the king or queen in a ceremony at *Buckingham Palace.

Many of the honours are associated with one of several **orders of chivalry**. Some of the orders have different grades of membership, e.g. 'knight', 'commander', 'officer' and 'member'. Many people are given awards in the **Order of the British Empire**. Famous people may be given a **CBE** (commander rank) or *OBE (officer rank); people recommended by members of the public are usually given an *MBE (member rank). Some people think the Order of the British Empire should be renamed to get rid of the outdated reference to the Empire, but in 2004 it was decided that the name should not be changed. Most honours allow a person to put the appropriate letters after their name. In addition to these honours there are many *medals and decorations for bravery, for civilians as well as for members of the police and the armed forces.

In the US there is no system of honours like that in Britain, though a number of medals are awarded for outstanding achievement or for bravery. These include the *Presidential Medal of Freedom and the *Congressional Gold Medal.

,Geoff 'Hoon /,dʒef 'huːn/ (1953–) a British *Labour politician. He was a Member of the European Parliament (1984–94) and is well known as a keen supporter of Britain's membership of the *EU. He became a *Member of Parliament in 1992. He was *Secretary of State for Defence (1999–2005).

,Hooray 'Henry *n* (*BrE informal disapproving*) a young *upper-class man with a loud voice and cheerful manner who is regarded as rather stupid. The female equivalent is a **Hooray Henrietta**. Compare SLOANE RANGER.

,Herbert 'Hoover[1] /'huːvə(r)/ (1874–1964) the 31st US *President (1929–33) and a member of the Republican Party. He had earlier been the US Secretary of Commerce (1921–9). A year after he became President, the *Great Depression began and people blamed him because his government failed to stop it. Franklin D *Roosevelt defeated him in the 1932 election. After *World War II Hoover directed the European Food Program. See also HOOVERVILLE.

'J 'Edgar 'Hoover[2] /'huːvə(r)/ (John Edgar Hoover 1895–1972) the head of the *FBI (1924–1972), who made it into a successful and scientific national police organization. He had great power and public support, and no president tried to replace him. He was suspected of keeping illegal personal files on many people and his role during the *McCarthy era has been criticized.

,Hoover 'Dam /,huːvə; *AmE* ,huːvər/ a large dam on the Colorado River on the border of *Nevada and *Arizona. It was completed in 1935 and originally called Boulder Dam. In 1947 the name was changed in honour of the US President Herbert *Hoover. It is 726 feet/221 metres high and 1244 feet/379 metres wide, and it produces electricity for Arizona, Nevada and southern *California.

the Hoover Dam

'Hooverville /'huːvəvɪl; *AmE* 'huːvərvɪl/ *n* any collection of poor houses often made of cardboard or scrap metal, on the edge of a city, that developed in the US during the *Great Depression. They were often temporary places for unemployed people and those without homes, and were named after President *Hoover, who was blamed for the Depression.

,Hopalong 'Cassidy ⇨ CASSIDY.

,Bob 'Hope /,bɒb 'həʊp; *AmE* 'hoʊp/ (1903–2003) a US comedian and comedy actor, born in Britain. He performed for nearly 70 years as a star of *vaudeville, radio, television and films. He was well known for his trips to entertain US soldiers around the world. His many films include the series of seven 'Road movies' (among them *The Road to Zanzibar* and *The Road to Morocco*), in which he appeared with Bing *Crosby and Dorothy Lamour. Hope presented the *Academy Awards television show for many years and received several special *Oscars. He also received the *Presidential Medal of Freedom in 1969 and was made an honorary *knight by the British government in 1998.

HOPE /həʊp; *AmE* hoʊp/ (*in full* **Health Opportunity for People Everywhere**) (*also* ˌProject ˈHOPE) a US charity that provides medical help and training in other countries. Doctors and nurses work without payment for the organization, which receives financial support from individuals, companies and governments. It was started by Dr Bill Walsh in 1958 with the *SS Hope*, a hospital ship that visited different countries from 1960 to 1974. Project HOPE has trained more than a million professional health workers in 70 countries.

ˈHopi /ˈhəʊpi; *AmE* ˈhoʊpi/ *n* (*pl* **Hopis** *or* **Hopi**) a member of a *Pueblo *Native American people living in north-east *Arizona. The Hopis are mostly farmers and very religious. Their god is Kachina, and their religious ceremonies include the snake dance. They have had a long dispute with the *Navajos about land on the border that separates them.

ˌAnthony **ˈHopkins**[1] /ˈhɒpkɪnz; *AmE* ˈhɑːpkɪnz/ (1937–) a Welsh stage and film actor, who became a US citizen in 2000. His theatre successes include *Pravda* (1985) and *King Lear* (1986). He won an *Oscar for his role as the evil Hannibal Lecter in *The **Silence of the Lambs** (1991). He repeated the role in *Hannibal* (2001) and *Red Dragon* (2002). His other films include *Shadowlands* (1993), *Remains of the Day* (1993), *Nixon* (1995), *Surviving Picasso* (1996), *Amistad* (1997) and *Titus* (1999). He was made a *knight in 1993.

ˈGerard ˈManley ˈHopkins[2] /ˈmænli ˈhɒpkɪnz; *AmE* ˈhɑːpkɪnz/ (1844–89) an English Jesuit priest who wrote poems about religious ideas and the beauty of nature, using a form of verse which he called 'sprung rhythm'. His best-known works are *The Wreck of the Deutschland*, *Pied Beauty* and *Windhover*. His poems were first published after his death by his friend Robert *Bridges in 1918 and influenced later poets, including W H *Auden and Dylan *Thomas.

ˌEdward **ˈHopper** /ˈhɒpə(r); *AmE* ˈhɑːpər/ (1882–1967) a US painter and printmaker best known for his pictures of American city scenes and of the countryside and coast of *New England. These often showed people alone in streets or buildings with a strange light. They include *Early Sunday Morning* (1930) and *Nighthawks* (1942), a picture of customers in an all-night diner. His wife, the painter and Hopper's model, Josephine Nivison, left his work to the *Whitney Museum of American Art.

Ho ˈrizon a television documentary series which is broadcast in Britain once a week on *BBC Two. It started in 1964 and includes programmes on different topics in the areas of science, nature, medicine and natural history.

ˈHorlicks™ /ˈhɔːlɪks; *AmE* ˈhɔːrlɪks/ *n* [U] a make of hot drink, usually taken before going to bed to help you sleep better. It is sold as a powder, which is mixed with hot milk or water, and was first made in the US. The expression *make a Horlicks of something* is used in informal British English and means 'make a mess of something'.

ˌHoˌratio **ˈHornblower** /həˌreɪʃiəʊ ˈhɔːnbləʊə(r); *AmE* həˌreɪʃioʊ ˈhɔːrnbloʊər/ the main character in a series of novels by the English writer C S *Forester. Hornblower is an officer in the British Navy during the wars against Napoleon in the early 19th century. A television series of the stories began in 1998.

ˌA S **ˈHornby**[1] /ˈhɔːnbi; *AmE* ˈhɔːrnbi/ (Albert Sidney Hornby 1898–1978) an English teacher and writer of books for foreign learners of English. He is best known for the *Oxford Advanced Learner's Dictionary*, which was first published in Britain by *Oxford University Press in 1948 and is still bought in large numbers by students around the world. New editions of the dictionary are published regularly. He gave money for the Hornby scholarships which pay for teachers from foreign countries to study in Britain.

A S Hornby

ˌNick **ˈHornby**[2] /ˈhɔːnbi; *AmE* ˈhɔːrnbi/ (1957–) a popular English writer who writes books about young men and their interests, such as football and music. His books include *Fever Pitch* (1993), *High Fidelity* (1995) and *About a Boy* (1998). Several of his books have been made into films.

> 66 The natural state of the football fan is bitter disappointment, no matter what the score. 99
> Nick Hornby

ˌ**Horse and ˈHound** a British magazine containing news and information about sporting events involving horses, such as horse racing and *hunting. It first appeared in 1884 and is published every week. Its publishers also publish *Horse*, a magazine for people who ride as a hobby.

the ˈHorse Guards **1** (*also formal* **the Royal Horse Guards**) a group of cavalry soldiers (= soldiers who once fought on horses) in the British Army. They were formed in 1661 and are now part of the Blues and Royals. **2** the building in *Whitehall in London outside which the ceremony of *Changing the Guard takes place.

ˌ**Horse Guards Paˈrade** the open area behind the *Horse Guards(2) building in London, England, where the ceremony of *Trooping the Colour takes place every year on the Queen's *Official Birthday.

the ˌHorse of the ˈYear Show (*abbr* **HOYS**) (in Britain) a contest in showjumping (= the sport of riding horses over barriers) which takes place every year in October at the *National Exhibition Centre Arena in *Birmingham.

the ˈhospice ˌmovement the idea of providing special places where people who are dying can be treated and cared for. The first modern hospice was started by **Dame Cicely Saunders** in London in 1967 and since then many hospices have opened in Britain and the US.

the ˈHospital for ˈSick ˈChildren ⇨ GREAT ORMOND STREET.

ˈhospital ˌtrust *n* an organization that runs a public hospital on behalf of the *National Health Service in Britain. The first hospital trusts were created in 1990 when the British government decided to make hospitals responsible for their own administrative and financial affairs, rather than control them centrally. The idea was that they should be run on a more commercial basis, with less waste of money and resources. In 2004 the government introduced a new type of organization in England called the **foundation trust** or **foundation hospital**. Hospitals that achieve a high level of service can apply for **foundation status**, which gives them the

H

right to raise their own finances, for example by selling assets or borrowing money. The first twenty foundation trusts were created in April and July 2004. Many people are opposed to foundation hospitals because they believe they will create a **two-tier health system** (= a system where some hospitals have a lot of money and others not enough).

the 'hostage ,crisis a dangerous international event in 1979–81, when Iranian students took 66 Americans from the US Embassy in Tehran and kept them as prisoners for more than 14 months. They demanded that the former Shah of Iran should be sent back to Iran from the US for trial. The US President, Jimmy *Carter, ordered a rescue attempt in April 1980, but it failed. The crisis was an important reason for Carter's losing the 1980 election to Ronald *Reagan. The prisoners were released on 20 January 1981, the day on which Reagan became President.

,hot cross 'bun n a small sweet cake containing raisins and spices, and marked with the Christian symbol of the cross on the top. Hot cross buns are traditionally eaten hot, with butter on, on *Good Friday. ⇨ note at EASTER.

'hot dog n a hot sausage served in a soft bread roll, often with onions, mustard, etc. The sausage is sometimes called a *frankfurter*, or, in the US, a *wiener* or *weenie*.

'Hotpoint™ /'hɒtpɔɪnt; AmE 'hɑːtpɔɪnt/ a US company that makes electrical goods for the home: *a Hotpoint washing machine*.

,Harry Hou'dini /huːˈdiːni/ (1874–1926) a US performer of magic, born in Hungary, who became famous for escaping from chains, locked boxes, etc. His name is often used to refer to a person or an animal that seems able to escape from any situation: *It will take a political Houdini escape trick for him to avoid being destroyed by the scandal.*

'hound dog n (AmE) (especially in the southern states) a dog trained to hunt. People in the South joke that hound dogs are often lazy and cannot be relied on.

The ,Hound of the 'Baskervilles /'bæskəvɪlz; AmE 'bæskərvɪlz/ a novel (1902) by Arthur *Conan Doyle in which Sherlock *Holmes investigates crimes involving the Baskerville family and the possible existence of a large, fierce, wild dog living on *Dartmoor near their house. Holmes solves the mystery because he asks himself why it was that the guard dog did not bark. The story is the most famous of the Sherlock Holmes books and has been filmed many times.

the ,Household 'Cavalry a section of the British army consisting of two regiments, the *Life Guards and the Blues and Royals. Among other duties they ride horses to guard the king or queen at official ceremonies.

the Household Cavalry

the ,Household Di'vision (*also the ,Household 'Troops*) the soldiers of the *Household Cavalry of the

British army. With some of the men of the *Guards Division, they carry out special duties for the king or queen.

'house music (*also* **house**) n [U] a style of popular dance music that typically uses electronic drum sounds, a fast beat and a few words repeated many times.

the ,House of 'Commons (*also informal* **the House, the Commons**) the lower house of the British *Parliament, in which elected *Members of Parliament meet to discuss current political issues and vote on *Acts of Parliament. The House of Commons consists of 659 Members of Parliament who each represent an area of the country called a constituency and who are elected in a general election in which everyone over the age of 18 can vote. If an MP dies or resigns, a by-election is held in his or her constituency. Compare HOUSE OF LORDS. See also STATE OPENING OF PARLIAMENT.

the ,House of 'Lords (*also informal* **the Lords**) the upper house of the British *Parliament, whose members are not elected. Its work consists mainly of examining and making changes to *Bills from the *House of Commons and discussing important matters which the House of Commons cannot find time to discuss. It also acts as a final *Court of Appeal. In 1998 the Labour government announced plans to reform the House of Lords and to reduce the number of hereditary peers who have the right to sit in the Lords. In 2003 it also proposed the replacement of the Court of Appeal by a new Supreme Court. ⇨ note at PARLIAMENT, PEERAGE. See also LAW LORDS, LORDS SPIRITUAL, LORDS TEMPORAL.

the House of Lords

the ,House of Repre'sentatives (*also* **the US House of Representatives, the House**) the lower and larger of the two houses of the US *Congress (the other being the *Senate). The *Speaker of the House is its leader. The House has 435 members, who are elected every two years. The states have different numbers of representatives according to the size of their population, so *Delaware has only two members while *California has 52. House members can introduce a proposal for a law and must approve any new law. If no candidate in an election for US President receives a majority of votes in the *Electoral College, the House chooses the President. This has only ever happened twice, in the cases of Thomas *Jefferson and John Quincy *Adams.

the ,House of 'Windsor /'wɪnzə(r)/ the name of the British royal family since 1917 when it was changed from Saxe-Coburg-Gotha.

the ,Houses of 'Parliament 1 the *House of Commons and the *House of Lords.
2 the group of buildings beside the River *Thames in central London where these two assemblies meet. It is also known as the *Palace of Westminster. The original 14th–century palace was badly damaged by fire in 1834. Between 1840 and 1867, new buildings designed by Sir

Charles *Barry and Augustus *Pugin were put up. In 1941 the *House of Commons was destroyed by bombs, but it was built again after the war in exactly the same style. The Houses of Parliament are open to the public at certain times. See also Big Ben.

the Houses of Parliament

The ‚**House that** ‚**Jack Built** a traditional *nursery rhyme in which there are lots of verses, each one adding an extra line to the one before. It begins like this:

> 66 This is the house that Jack built.
> This is the malt
> That lay in the house that Jack built.
> This is the rat,
> That ate the malt
> That lay in the house that Jack built. 99

the ‚**House Un-A**'**merican Ac**'**tivities Com**‚**mittee** (*abbr* **HUAC**) a committee established in 1938 by the US *House of Representatives to investigate activities that might threaten the American government and people. It became famous in the 1950s when, under the influence of Senator Joseph *McCarthy, it accused many innocent people of supporting Communism. It was responsible for several of these being sent to prison. In 1969 the committee changed its name to the House Committee on Internal Security, and in 1975 it was brought to an end.

'**housing associ**‚**ation** *n* (in Britain) a local organization that provides rented homes for poorer families, and especially for old, disabled and single people. It also shares the ownership of houses with people who cannot afford to buy a house on their own. Similar organizations in the US are called **housing authorities** and they receive advice and financial help from the US Department of Housing and Urban Development.

'**housing** ‚**benefit** *n* [U] (in Britain) money given by the government to people who have a low income, to help them pay their rent.

the '**Housing Corpo**‚**ration** a British government organization that provides money for English *housing associations. There are similar organizations in Scotland and Wales.

‚**A E** '**Housman** /'haʊsmən/ (Alfred Edward Housman 1859–1936) an English writer of poetry who taught Latin at *London and *Cambridge universities. His best-known work is *A *Shropshire Lad*, a collection of short poems which have been set to music by at least fifty composers, including George Butterworth, Lennox *Berkeley, Samuel *Barber and John Ireland.

'**Houston**¹ /'hjuːstən; *AmE* 'huːstən/ the fourth largest US city and the largest in *Texas, named after Sam *Houston. It is a financial, commercial, cultural and industrial centre, especially for the oil industry. The city is also a major port connected to the *Gulf of Mexico by the Houston Ship Canal. It has two major universities,

Rice University and the University of Houston, and the *Lyndon B Johnson Space Center is also there.

‚**Sam** '**Houston**² /'hjuːstən; *AmE* 'huːstən/ (1793–1863) a US military and political leader. He helped *Texas gain its independence from Mexico, defeating the Mexican army at the Battle of *San Jacinto. Houston became the first *President of the Republic of Texas, and after Texas became a state he represented it as a US Senator (1846–59). He was also elected Governor of Texas but was forced to leave the job because he did not want Texas to join the *Confederate States.

‚**Whitney** '**Houston**³ /‚wɪtni 'hjuːstən/ (1963–) a US singer of popular music and actor. She has won *Grammy awards for several songs, including *Saving All My Love for You* (1985), *I Wanna Dance with Somebody* (1987) and *I Will Always Love You* (1993). Her films include *The Bodyguard* (1993), *Waiting to Exhale* (1995), *The Preacher's Wife* (1997) and *Cinderella* (1997), a multicultural version of the fairy story that was made for TV.

'**Houyhnhnm** /'huːiːnɪm/ *n* a member of the race of kind and intelligent horses that Gulliver meets in *Gulliver's Travels* by Jonathan *Swift. They are completely different to the *Yahoos, who work for them. The Yahoos look like men but are stupid and cruel. Gulliver later returns to his own land and finds that he now dislikes men, having learned a lot from the Houyhnhnms. (Their name is intended to sound like the sound a horse makes.).

'**Hovis**™ /'həʊvɪs; *AmE* 'hoʊvɪs/ a British make of brown bread. Each loaf has the word HOVIS along its side after baking: *I bought a brown sliced Hovis.*

‚**Catherine** '**Howard**¹ /'haʊəd; *AmE* 'haʊərd/ (*c.* 1521–42) the fifth wife of King *Henry VIII. He had her head cut off after they had been married for two years, when he found that she had had sexual relationships with other men.

‚**Michael** '**Howard**² /'haʊəd; *AmE* 'haʊərd/ (1941–) a British *Conservative politician who held a number of senior government positions, including that of *Home Secretary, in the 1990s. He became leader of the *Conservative Party in 2003.

‚**Howard** '**Johnson's** /‚haʊəd 'dʒɒnsnz; *AmE* ‚haʊərd 'dʒɑːnsnz/ any of a group of US restaurants and hotels. The restaurants became famous for their bright orange roofs and their 28 types of ice cream. The first of these restaurants was opened by Howard Dearing Johnson (1896?–1972) in Quincy, *Massachusetts, in 1929. The company's name is often shortened to Hojo.

the '**Howard** '**League for** '**Penal Re**'**form** /'haʊəd; *AmE* 'haʊərd/ a British organization that since 1866 has worked to improve conditions in prisons, and to help people who are in prison or leaving it. It is named after John Howard (1726–90), a rich Englishman who visited prisons and worked to make the public aware of the terrible conditions in them, until the government was forced to pass laws to improve these.

‚**Howards** '**End** /‚haʊəd; *AmE* ‚haʊərdz/ a novel (1910) by E M *Forster. It describes the relationships between two very different *middle-class families in *Edwardian England. *Howards End* is the name of the house in which one of the families lives. There was a film version by James *Ivory in 1992.

‚**Howard Uni**'**versity** /‚haʊəd; *AmE* ‚haʊərd/ a university in Washington, DC, which was established in 1867 for freed slaves as well as white people, although few of the latter came. It is named after General Oliver O Howard, who helped to establish it and was its president from 1869 to 1873.

‚**Julia** '**Ward** '**Howe** /'wɔːd 'haʊ; *AmE* 'wɔːrd 'haʊ/ (1819–1910) the American who wrote *The *Battle Hymn of*

H

the Republic. She was a supporter of *abolitionism and a writer, mostly of poetry. She also established the New England Woman Suffrage Association (1868) to support women's right to vote, and edited the abolitionist newspaper *Commonwealth* with her husband.

,Frankie 'Howerd /'haʊəd; AmE 'haʊərd/ (1921–92) an English comedian who was famous for his exaggerated way of telling jokes and appearing to be shocked when the audience thought he was being funny in a rude way. He is probably best remembered for his performance in *Up Pompeii!* (1970–71), a television comedy series about the ancient Romans.

'Hoxton /'hɒkstən; AmE 'hɑːkstən/ an area in the *East End of London. The area used to be quite poor but has now become fashionable and has many art galleries and bars.

,Fred 'Hoyle /'hɔɪl/ (1915–2001) an English astrophysicist (= scientist who studies the structure of stars, etc.). He developed theories on the origins of stars and of life itself, and wrote a number of works of popular science. He also wrote science fiction. He was made a *knight in 1972.

HOYS /hɔɪz/ ⇨ HORSE OF THE YEAR SHOW.

,HP 'Sauce™ /,eɪtʃ piː/ n [U] a popular British make of dark brown sauce sold in tall bottles. It is made with vegetables, vinegar and spices and is eaten with various different foods, especially meat, chips, etc. The letters HP stand for *Houses of Parliament(2), and there is a picture of these on the label.

HSBC /,eɪtʃ es biː 'siː/ one of the four big *clearing banks in Britain, with branches in towns and cities all over the country. It was established in China in 1865 as the Hong Kong and Shanghai Banking Corporation. In 1992 it bought the Midland Bank, which was established in *Birmingham in 1836, and it is now one of the largest banks in the world.

HSE /,eɪtʃ es 'iː/ ⇨ HEALTH AND SAFETY EXECUTIVE.

HUAC /'hjuːæk/ ⇨ HOUSE UN-AMERICAN ACTIVITIES COMMITTEE.

'L 'Ron 'Hubbard /'hʌbəd; AmE 'hʌbərd/ (Lafayette Ronald Hubbard 1911–86) a US writer of science fiction who established the Church of *Scientology in 1954. His novels included *Slaves of Sleep* (1939) and a series of ten books with the general title of *Mission Earth* (1985–7).

,Edwin 'Hubble /'hʌbl/ (1889–1953) a US astronomer. He was the first to find evidence that the universe is becoming larger in size. He did this in 1929 when he discovered that galaxies (= very large groups of stars) move away from us in a regular way. This is now called Hubble's Law. In 1923, he had discovered that large galaxies exist beyond our own. His research was done at the Mount Wilson Observatory in *California. The *Hubble Space Telescope is named after him.

the ,Hubble 'Space ,Telescope /,hʌbl/ a large US telescope put into space in 1990 by *NASA. It is named after the US astronomer Edwin *Hubble and provides a much clearer view of the universe than could be obtained from the ground. Three months after it began to operate, it found a 'black hole' with a mass of 300 million suns.

the Hubble Space Telescope

,Huckleberry 'Finn ⇨ FINN.

HUD /hʌd/ ⇨ DEPARTMENT OF HOUSING AND URBAN DEVELOPMENT.

,Henry 'Hudson[1] /'hʌdsn/ (c. 1550–c. 1611) an English explorer who, when he was looking for the *North-west Passage in 1609–10, discovered what are now called the *Hudson River and Hudson Bay, a very large sea in north-eastern Canada connected with the North Atlantic by the Hudson Strait. In 1611 some of his men turned against him there, and put him in a small boat with his 12-year old son. They were never seen again.

,Rock 'Hudson[2] /,rɒk 'hʌdsn; AmE ,rɑːk/ (1925–85) a US actor who became famous playing tough characters but later made several comedies. His films included *Magnificent Obsession* (1954), *Giant* (1956) and *Pillow Talk* (1959). He also made a television series, *McMillan and Wife* (1971–8). Hudson was the first *Hollywood star who said publicly that he had AIDS, from which he died.

the ,Hudson 'River /,hʌdsn/ a river in the US state of New York. It flows 315 miles/510 kilometres from the *Adirondack Mountains to New York City where it joins the Atlantic Ocean. In 1825, it was connected to the *Great Lakes by the *Erie Canal. The river is named after Henry *Hudson who in 1609 was one of the first people to travel along its unknown areas. See also HUDSON RIVER SCHOOL.

the ,Hudson 'River School /,hʌdsn/ a group of 19th-century artists, some of whom were born in Europe, who painted romantic landscapes (= pictures of the countryside) in the US, including in the *Hudson River Valley. The paintings led Americans to see their country in a new way. The founder of the group was Thomas Cole and it also included Asher Durand, Albert Bierstadt and Frederic Church.

> 66 The true province of landscape art is the work of God in the visible creation, independent of man. 99
> Asher Durand

,Hudson's 'Bay ,Company /,hʌdsnz/ a British trading company set up in 1670 to buy and sell the products of northern Canada, such as furs. The company helped to make it easier for people to settle in Canada by establishing trading posts and transport routes all across the country. It owned very large areas of Canada, which it sold to the Canadian government in 1870. The company was run from England until 1931. It now owns department stores throughout Canada.

,Howard 'Hughes[1] /'hjuːz/ (1905–76) a rich American who produced and directed films, and built planes. He owned an oil company and the Hughes Aircraft Company. His films included *Hell's Angels* (1930) and *The Outlaw* (1941). He established several fastest flights (1935–8) and designed the world's largest aircraft (1947). Hughes gained control of *RKO in 1948 and *TWA in 1959, and he helped to develop *Las Vegas in the 1960s. He hid from the public for the last 25 years of his life. A film/movie about Hughes, *The Aviator* (2005) starred Leonardo *DiCaprio.

,Langston 'Hughes[2] /,læŋstən 'hjuːz/ (1902–67) a US poet and writer who was a leading figure of the *Harlem Renaissance. He used African-American rhythms in his poems, most of which are about city life. They include *The Weary Blues* (1926), *Not Without Laughter* (1930) and *One-Way Ticket* (1949). He also wrote novels, plays, children's books and an autobiography.

,Robert 'Hughes[3] /'hjuːz/ (1938–) an Australian art critic, writer and broadcaster. He writes for *Time and has written a number of books about art including *American Visions: The Epic History of Art in America* (1997) which was based on his television series. He is well known in Britain and the US for his television programmes *The Shock of the New* (1981), and *The New Shock of the New* (2004) about modern art. He also speaks for the Australian Republican Movement.

Ted 'Hughes[4] /'hju:z/ (1930–98) an English poet whose work gives a powerful picture of both the beauty and the violence of the natural world. His best-known collections of poetry include *The Hawk in the Rain* (1957) and *Crow* (1970). He also wrote books for children, including *The Iron Man* (1968) (*The Iron Giant* in the US). He was *Poet Laureate from 1984. His first wife was the US poet Sylvia *Plath. In 1998 he published a book of poems about their relationship, *Birthday Letters*.

'Huguenot /'hju:gənəʊ; *AmE* 'hju:gənɑːt/ *n* a French Protestant in the 16th and 17th centuries. After 1685 the Huguenots were attacked by the Catholic majority. Thousands left France for other countries, including Britain and the US, where many became very successful, especially in the silver and textile industries.

Hull /hʌl/ (*also* **Kingston-upon-'Hull**) a port and industrial centre in *Humberside in north-eastern England. It is on the River *Humber.

the ,Human 'Genome ,Project /'dʒiːnəʊm; *AmE* 'dʒiːnoʊm/ a project which was started in 1988 to describe the complete set of genes in humans. Several countries, including Britain and the USA took part in it and it was completed in 2003, earlier than planned.

the 'Humber /'hʌmbə(r)/ a major river in north-eastern England. A suspension bridge (= a bridge hanging from cables supported by towers at each end) across it, called the **Humber Bridge**, has one of the longest spans in the world.

'Humberside /'hʌmbəsaɪd; *AmE* 'hʌmbərsaɪd/ an area of north-eastern England around the River *Humber. It was a county from 1974 to 1996.

'humbug *n* (*BrE*) a type of small, hard sweet, usually flavoured with peppermint, and often with a pattern of stripes on it.

,David 'Hume[1] /'hju:m/ (1711–76) a Scottish philosopher and historian who is regarded as one of the greatest British thinkers. He said that people cannot be certain about anything that is not directly taken in through their senses. Hume was greatly respected during his lifetime, but was unable to get a university teaching job because he was an agnostic (= he could not say that he believed in God). His most important works include *A Treatise of Human Nature* (1739–40) and *History of England* (1754–62).

,John 'Hume[2] /'hju:m/ (1937–) the Northern Irish leader of the *Social Democratic and Labour Party (1979–2001). With David *Trimble he received the *Nobel Prize for peace in 1998.

▶**humour**

A **sense of humour** (*AmE* **humor**), an ability to see the **funny side of life**, is considered essential by most British and American people. Everyone needs to be able to **laugh at themselves** sometimes, and to recognize that the situation they are in may look funny to others. It is considered a serious criticism of somebody to say that they have no sense of humour.

Some people have a **dry** sense of humour, and can **keep a straight face** (= not smile) and let their voice sound as though they are being serious when they are joking. Other people are said to be **witty** (= show a very clever type of humour). A person's sense of humour is influenced by many things, including family and social background and age.

British and American humour on stage have some important differences, although the fact that some **comedy** television programmes are popular in both countries shows that there is some common ground.

American **sitcoms** (= shows in which the humour comes from situations that the characters get into) such as *Frasier, *Friends and *Seinfeld are as popular in Britain, as Britain's own *The *Vicar of Dibley and *The Office*. Sitcoms often have a **laugh track** (= a recording of people laughing) so that the audience at home will laugh in the right places. In many sitcoms gentle fun is made of ordinary life without the risk of causing anyone serious offence.

American stage humour is more direct than British comedy. In the American series *Cheers, for instance, the humour comes from characters like Coach and Woody being more stupid than any real person could possibly be. But in the British comedy *Fawlty Towers Basil Fawlty's funny characteristics are exaggerated versions of those found in the type of Englishman he represents. **Slapstick** comedy, which is based on people falling over, bumping into each other, etc. is now less popular in Britain.

British comedy makes frequent use of **irony**, humour which depends on a writer or performer suggesting the opposite of what is actually expressed. Many novels, films, stage plays, etc. use irony, even when discussing serious subjects such as death. Popular humour may sometimes rely on **double entendre** (= using a phrase that can be understood in two ways, one of which is usually sexual) or on **innuendo** (= making an indirect suggestion of something rude). These were both used a lot in the popular series of *Carry On films that began in the 1960s.

Satire (= making people or institutions appear ridiculous to show how foolish or bad they are) is an important element of popular British political comedy programmes such as *Yes, Minister and *Spitting Image. One of the most successful British comedy series, which also became popular in the US, was *Monty Python's Flying Circus. It had a **zany** (= odd and silly) and **satirical** humour which appealed especially to young people.

*Comic strips and **cartoons**, whether printed in newspapers, shown on television or the Internet or made into films, are popular in both the US and Britain. The most famous include *Peanuts, *Tom and Jerry and The *Simpsons.

Stand-up comedians like Bill *Cosby and Jerry Seinfeld in the US and in Britain Peter Kay, Eddy *Izzard and Jo Brand, perform on television or in clubs, telling **gags** (= jokes) and funny stories which end with a **punch line**, the part where the audience is supposed to laugh. Many comedians **tell jokes** that are funny because of some racial or sexual innuendo, and this may be considered unacceptable for family audiences. In Britain, common targets of comedians include mothers-in-law, foreigners and people from particular parts of Britain, especially Scotsmen (who are supposed to hate spending money) and Irishmen (who are supposed to be stupid). Many people find such jokes offensive, and the new generation of comedians has avoided making fun of people's race. Another form of comedy is for people from minority groups to make fun of their own customs and attitudes.

Many people tell jokes at school, at home and at the office. People may start a speech with a joke or funny story to help **break the ice** (= make people feel more relaxed).

Children tell jokes that involve a play on words, such as *knock-knock jokes or 'What do you call …' jokes e.g. 'What do you call a man with a seagull on his head?' 'Cliff'.

Adults sometimes tell what in the US are called **Polish jokes** because they are about a particular national or racial group. There are also jokes about blondes

H

(= women with fair hair) being stupid, and lawyers having bad characters. For instance, 'Why do they do lab experiments on lawyers?' 'Because there are some things that even a rat won't do.' On the whole this type of humour is considered dated and in bad taste. **Light bulb jokes** make fun of the worst characteristic of any group of people, by suggesting mistakes they would make in trying to change a light bulb: 'How many psychologists does it take to change a light bulb?' 'Just one, but it has to really want to change.'

Practical jokes involve tricking people, and are not usually very popular, but on *April Fool's Day (1 April) people traditionally play practical jokes on each other. Newspapers often include a story that is not true hoping that some readers will believe it and then feel silly.

Barry 'Humphries /'hʌmpfriz/ (1934–) an Australian comedian who is well known in Britain for two characters he has created: 'housewife superstar' Dame Edna *Everage, for which Humphries wears women's clothes, and Sir Les Patterson, a disgusting man who is supposed to be a representative of the Australian government in London.

John 'Humphrys /'hʌmfrɪz/ (1943–) a British journalist and presenter on television and radio. He presents a number of news and political programmes on *BBC television and radio, including the *Today programme on *Radio 4.

Humpty 'Dumpty /ˌhʌmpti 'dʌmpti/ **1** a large egg-shaped character in a popular *nursery rhyme:

> 66 Humpty Dumpty sat on a wall.
> Humpty Dumpty had a great fall.
> All the king's horses,
> And all the king's men,
> Couldn't put Humpty together again. 99

2 a large egg-shaped character in *Through the Looking Glass by Lewis *Carroll who has a strange and clever conversation with Alice.

> 66 When I use a word, it means just what I choose it to mean, neither more nor less. 99
> Humpty Dumpty in *Through the Looking Glass*

'Humvee™ /'hʌmviː/ (High Mobility Multipurpose Wheeled Vehicle) n (abbr **HMMWV**) a large military vehicle made by *General Motors which can be driven in any conditions. It was developed for the US army in 1985 to replace the *Jeep. There is also a non-military version of the vehicle called a **Hummer** which was first made in 1992. It is very expensive and became a popular status symbol.

hundreds and 'thousands (AmE '**sprinkles**) n [pl] tiny pieces of coloured sugar or chocolate, used for decorating cakes, sweets, ice cream, etc.

the ,Hundred Years 'War a war between France and England that lasted, with long periods between battles, from the 1340s to the 1450s. The English were trying to get control of France, and won some major battles, including *Crécy (1346) and *Agincourt (1415), but by the end of the war they had only gained the area around Calais, which they kept until 1558.

Holman 'Hunt¹ /ˌhəʊlmən 'hʌnt; AmE ˌhoʊlmən/ (1827–1910) an English *Pre-Raphaelite painter. His pictures are mostly scenes of the countryside or from the Bible, and many of them contain a moral message. Two of the best-known are The *Light of the World (1854) and The Scapegoat (1855).

Leigh 'Hunt² /'hʌnt/ (1784–1859) an English poet, writer and journalist. He was a close friend of the *Romantic poets, including *Keats and *Shelley. His best-known book was Lord Byron and Some of His Contemporaries (1828), a realistic account of the lives of the great poets he knew.

Holly 'Hunter /ˌhɒli 'hʌntə(r); AmE ˌhɑːli 'hʌntər/ (1958–) a US actor. She won an *Oscar and *Golden Globe Award for her role as a woman who could not speak in The Piano (1993). Her other films include Raising Arizona (1987), The Firm (1993), Crash (1996) and O Brother, Where Art Thou (2000). She has also won two *Emmy awards for television films.

'hunting n [U] ⇨ note at FIELD SPORTS.

The ,Hunting of the 'Snark /'snɑːk; AmE 'snɑːrk/ a nonsense poem (1876) by Lewis *Carroll.

'hurling n [U] an Irish ball game similar to *field hockey, played between two teams of 15 players each. *Shinty is a related form of hurling played in Scotland.

the 'Hurlingham /'hɜːlɪŋəm; AmE 'hɜːrlɪŋəm/ (in full **the Hurlingham Polo Association**) the organization in charge of the sport of *polo in Britain. It was formed in 1886 at the **Hurlingham Club** in London, which is now a club for players of many sports.

,Lake 'Huron /'hjʊərɒn; AmE 'hjʊrɑːn/ the second largest of the *Great Lakes on the border between the US and Canada. It is the fourth largest lake in the world. It covers 23 010 square miles/59 596 square kilometres with a length of 206 miles/332 kilometres and largest width of 183 miles/295 kilometres. Lake Huron separates the US state of *Michigan and the Canadian province of Ontario. Its ports include Alpena and Port Huron.

,Hush-a-bye, 'Baby /ˌhʌʃ ə baɪ/ a popular old lullaby (= song sung to make a young child go to sleep). In the US, the name and first line of the song is Rock-a-bye, baby. The tune is similar to *Lilliburlero

> 66 Hush-a-bye, baby,
> On the tree top.
> When the wind blows,
> The cradle will rock.
> When the bough breaks,
> The cradle will fall,
> And down will come baby,
> Cradle and all. 99

'Hush ,Puppies™ n [pl] a British make of shoes made mostly of soft suede leather with rubber soles in various styles.

'hush ,puppy n (AmE) a food eaten in the southern US, usually with fish. It is a round ball of corn flour that is fried. According to tradition, hush puppies were thrown to hungry dogs to keep them quiet, and this is the origin of their name.

,John 'Huston /'hjuːstən; AmE 'huːstən/ (1906–89) a US film director, actor and writer. He won an *Oscar for The *Treasure of the Sierra Madre, which he directed and wrote. He and his father, the actor Walter Huston, both acted in it. Other films that he directed include The *Maltese Falcon, The African Queen (1952), *Moby-Dick, The Misfits (1960), The Dead (1987) and Prizzi's Honor (1985) for which his daughter, Anjelica Huston, won an Oscar as Best Actress.

'Hutterite /'hʌtəraɪt/ n a member of a Protestant religious group living mainly in the US states of *South Dakota, *North Dakota and *Montana, and also in Alberta in Canada. The Hutterites were established in 1533 in Moravia in Czechoslovakia as a division of the *Anabaptists, and are named after Jacob Hutter. Their way of life is similar to that of the *Mennonites. It includes common ownership of property and a refusal to use violence.

the **'Hutton In,quiry** /'hʌtn/ an inquiry (2003–04) set up by the British government and led by **Lord Hutton**, a retired *Law Lord, to investigate the circumstances surrounding the death of a government scientist, Dr David Kelly, in 2003. After interviewing members of the government, experts and journalists, Lord Hutton's report said it was probable that Dr Kelly had killed himself because of the pressure he was under after talking to a *BBC journalist about the government's reasons for becoming involved in the war in Iraq. The report criticized the government and especially the *BBC for the way the situation was dealt with and, as a result, the Chairman of the *BBC, Gavyn Davies, and the Director-General of the *BBC, Greg Dyke, left their jobs.

'Huxley /'hʌksli/ the name of an English family of scientists and writers. **Thomas Henry Huxley** (1825–95) was a biologist who publicly supported *Darwin's ideas about evolution, and became known as 'Darwin's bulldog'. He also invented the word *agnostic* to describe a person who is not sure whether or not God exists. His son **Leonard Huxley** (1860–1933), a writer, had three famous sons. The first, **Julian Huxley** (1887–1975), was a biologist and writer who was well known for his appearances on the radio and television programme The *Brains Trust* and later became director of UNESCO (1946–8). The second, **Aldous Huxley** (1894–1963), an author, is best known for his novel *Brave New World* (1932), which describes a future society in which people are born in factories and controlled by a continuous supply of drugs and sex. From 1937 Aldous Huxley lived in *California,

where his experiences with drugs became the subject of a later book, *The Doors of Perception* (1954). The third famous son, **Andrew Huxley** (1917–), is a scientist who received the *Nobel Prize in 1963 for his description of how animal muscles work. He was made a *knight in 1974.

Mr 'Hyde /'haɪd/ ⇨ JEKYLL AND HYDE.

Hyde 'Park /,haɪd/ **1** a large public park in central London, England, next to *Kensington Gardens. It is famous for *Speakers' Corner, where people can make public speeches on any topic, *Rotten Row, a riding track for horses, and the *Serpentine lake. In 1851 the *Great Exhibition was held in Hyde Park, and it is now a centre for large public meetings and concerts. At the south-east corner of the park is **Hyde Park Corner**, a place where several busy streets meet.
2 a district to the south of central *Chicago, along the edge of Lake *Michigan. It includes the University of Chicago.

'Hymns 'Ancient and 'Modern a book of hymns (= religious songs) used in *Church of England services. It was first published in 1861 and is still used today in many churches.

Nicholas 'Hytner /'haɪtnə(r)/ (1956–) an English theatre director who has directed musicals, plays and operas in Britain and the US. He also directed a number of films including *The Madness of King George* (1995) and *The Crucible* (1996). He has been the Director of the *National Theatre since 2001.

H

I i

IB ⇨ INCAPACITY BENEFIT.

IBM™ /ˌaɪ biː ˈem/ (*in full* **International Business Machines**) a US company that was the first to develop computers successfully. IBM computers created an international system that most other computers now relate to. The company began in 1911 as the Computing-Tabulating-Recording Company. It developed the first electric typewriter in the 1930s, the first computer in the 1950s and the first IBM personal computer (PC) was introduced in 1981: *an IBM-compatible machine.*

Ibrox 'Stadium /ˌaɪbrɒks; *AmE* ˌaɪbrɑːks/ the football ground, formerly called Ibrox Park, of *Rangers football club in *Glasgow, Scotland.

the ICA /ˌaɪ siː ˈeɪ/ (*in full* **the Institute of Contemporary Arts**) a British institution in The *Mall(1) in central London that exists to promote (= encourage) modern art, dance and film. It was established in 1947 and events held there have sometimes been controversial.

'ice ˌhockey ⇨ note at HOCKEY.

the I'ceni /aɪˈsiːnaɪ/ a tribe of *Celtic people who lived in the area of eastern England which is now *Norfolk and *Suffolk around the first century AD, when England was part of the Roman Empire. Their queen *Boudicca led the Iceni against the Romans around AD 60–62 but was defeated.

Ich 'dien /ˌɪx ˈdiːn/ the words that appear on the Prince of Wales's crest (= the design that represents his title). It was first used in 1346 and is German for 'I serve', indicating the Prince's loyalty to the king or queen.

ICI /ˌaɪ siː ˈaɪ/ (*in full* **Imperial Chemical Industries**) a very large British company, formed in 1926 to make products such as paints, drugs, plastics and industrial chemicals. In 1993 a new company, now called Astra Zeneca, was formed for the drugs business.

the ˌIcknield 'Way /ˌɪkniːld/ an ancient British path first used many thousands of years ago. It leads southwest from the *Wash to Berkshire, often along the tops of hills. Modern roads now follow parts of it and other parts are used by people who enjoy walking in the countryside.

'Idaho /ˈaɪdəhəʊ; *AmE* ˈaɪdəhoʊ/ a state in the northwestern US. Its popular name is the Gem State, because it has many minerals, including silver. It also produces a quarter of all the potatoes grown in the US. It was part of the *Louisiana Purchase and became a state in 1890. Its capital and largest city is Boise. Idaho's attractions include the *Rocky Mountains, Craters of the Moon National Monument and Hell's Canyon, which is the deepest gorge (= valley with steep sides) in North America.

ˌIdeal 'Home a British magazine published every month for people who want to decorate or improve their homes.

the ˌIdeal 'Home Exhiˌbition a popular exhibition of furniture and other products for the home, held every year in *Earl's Court, London, England. It was first held in 1908.

ˌIdylls of the 'King a series of 12 poems by Lord *Tennyson, published between 1842 and 1885. They tell the story of King *Arthur and the *Knights of the Round Table, and were very popular with *Victorian(1) readers.

If a poem published in 1910 by Rudyard *Kipling. It consists of a single long sentence beginning with the word 'if', giving advice to a boy on how to become a man. It is in the *Victorian(2) tradition and now seems rather old-fashioned, but the poem remains extremely popular and is often voted the favourite poem of British readers.

IHT /ˌaɪ eɪtʃ ˈtiː/ ⇨ INTERNATIONAL HERALD TRIBUNE.

IKEA /aɪˈkiːə/ a Swedish company started in 1943 by Ingvar Kampard (1926–) which makes and sells simple, well-designed furniture and other things for the home at low prices. It opened its first store in the US in 1986 and in Britain in 1988, and it now has nearly 200 stores in 31 countries.

'Ilkley /ˈɪlkli/ a town in *West Yorkshire, England. It is known mainly for **Ilkley Moor**, which appears in the popular folk song *On Ilkley Moor Baht 'at* (a local way of saying 'On Ilkley Moor without a hat').

ˌIlli'nois /ˌɪlɪˈnɔɪ/ a state in the US *Midwest, also called the Prairie State. Its largest city is *Chicago and its capital city is Springfield. Manufacturing industry is important and the state produces coal, oil and agricultural products. Illinois became a state in 1818 and is associated with Abraham *Lincoln, who was a lawyer in Springfield.

the ˌIllustrated 'London 'News a British magazine, first published in 1842, which was especially successful in the 19th century with its combination of news stories and pictures, a new idea at the time. It originally appeared every week but is now published twice a year.

ˌI Love 'Lucy a very popular US television comedy series (1951–60) on *CBS with Lucille *Ball as the star. She played Lucy Ricardo and her husband, Desi Arnez, played Lucy's husband Ricky. The shows are still shown regularly around the world.

the ILP /ˌaɪ el ˈpiː/ ⇨ INDEPENDENT LABOUR PARTY.

'I'm A Ce'lebrity ... 'Get Me 'Out Of Here! a British *reality television series in which a group of well-known people go to live together in difficult conditions in the jungle and have to take part in a number of tests. Members of the public vote for who will leave until only one person is left.

IMF /ˌaɪ em ˈef/ ⇨ INTERNATIONAL MONETARY FUND.

im'peachment /ɪmˈpiːtʃmənt/ *n* [U, C] the procedure by which a public official in the US, including the President, is charged with acting illegally and may be forced to leave the job. President Richard *Nixon resigned after the House Judiciary Committee recommended that he should be impeached (= charged) for the crime of *Watergate. Only two presidents have been officially impeached. The first was Andrew Johnson in 1868, who remained as President because the US Senate decided by one vote that he should do so. The second was Bill *Clinton in 1999, who was then judged not guilty of acting illegally.

Imˌperial 'Chemical ˌIndustries ⇨ ICI.

Imˌperial 'College 'London (*also* **Imperial College of Science, Technology and Medicine**) a leading British college for the study of science, in *South Kensington, London. It was established in 1907 as part of *London University and offers courses in such subjects as science, medicine, engineering and business, as well as providing opportunities for scientific research. It also has its own nuclear reactor at its research station at Silwood Park, near Ascot.

▶ the **imperial system**

the traditional system of weights and measures in Britain which is gradually being replaced by the *metric system. **Customary measure** used in the US is similar to the imperial system with a few slight differences. Although most imperial measures have now gone out of use in Britain, many older British people still think of things in terms of the old system. The only imperial measure still widely used officially in the UK is the **mile**, which is used on road signs. In the US, **customary units**, also called **standard units**, are still used and the metric system is only used in scientific research.

Length is measured in **yards**, **feet** and **inches**, and many people know their height in feet and inches. Weight is measured in **pounds** and **ounces**, although many British people say their own weight in **stones** (a stone is 14 pounds) and pounds. Larger quantities are weighed in **hundredweight** and **tons**, the exact sizes of which are slightly different in the UK and US. Volume is measured in **pints** and **gallons**, with a US gallon being slightly smaller than a UK gallon. In Britain, **pints** are still used to measure beer in pubs. The imperial unit of area is the **acre**, an Old English word meaning field, which equals 4 840 square yards and it is still often preferred to the metric **hectare**. Weather forecasters in Britain now describe temperature in degrees **Celsius** or **Centigrade**, but they often convert it to the **Fahrenheit** scale, in which freezing point is 32° and boiling point 212°, for older viewers. Fahrenheit is still used in the US.

the **Im,perial 'War Mu,seum** a large museum in Lambeth, London, founded in 1917. It shows the history of the wars Britain has fought in since 1914 and life during wartime. It also has a reference library of books, maps, photographs and films, and a large collection of work by war artists. Part of the collection is now shown at the **Imperial War Museum North** which opened in 2002 in Manchester and aircraft and military vehicles are displayed at a museum at Duxford, a former air force base in Cambridgeshire.

*The **Im'portance of 'Being 'Earnest** a comedy play by Oscar *Wilde, first performed in 1895. A young man, Jack Worthing, wants to marry the daughter of Lady *Bracknell, but Lady Bracknell disapproves of him because he tells her he does not know his parents as he was found in a handbag at *Victoria Station. The play is often performed in Britain, especially by *amateur dramatics groups, and is much loved for its clever humour and comic situations.

I,naugu'ration Day (in the US) the day every four years when the new *President, elected in November, officially takes power. The Inauguration ceremonies are always on 20 January in *Washington, DC. The President says the Oath of Office, and the Vice-President does the same. The President then gives the **Inaugural Address**, a speech about his plans. This is followed by a long parade along *Pennsylvania Avenue. In the evening there are official Inaugural balls (= formal events at which people dance).

inca'pacity benefit n [U] (abbr **IB**) (in Britain) money that is paid by the government to people who are unable to work because they are ill or disabled. Compare STATUTORY SICK PAY.

In ,Cold 'Blood a US novel (1966) based on fact, written by Truman *Capote. It is about the murder in 1959 of four members of a farming family in *Kansas. Capote talked in prison to the men who killed them, and his book tells their story. It was the first major novel in which specific events were described in a novel in this

way. A film version was made in 1967 and it was also made into a TV series in 1996.

income sup'port n [U] (in Britain) money given by the government to help people with very low incomes, e.g. people without a job or single parents.

'income tax n [U, C] a tax paid according to a person's level of income, with people on higher incomes paying higher rates of tax. It is used by the government to help pay for things like health care and education. It is collected in Britain by the *Inland Revenue and in the US by the *Internal Revenue Service.

*The **In,credible 'Hulk** a US television series (1978–81) on *CBS about a man who sometimes turns into a very powerful creature like a man but with green skin. The character originally appeared in comic books and there is a film/movie Hulk (2003). The Incredible Hulk is Dr David Banner, a scientist who did an experiment that went wrong and who now becomes the creature whenever he gets angry. ⇨ note at COMICS AND COMIC STRIPS.

,Inde'pendence a US city in the state of *Missouri. President Harry S *Truman lived there, and his official library and museum can be visited. The international office of the Reorganized Church of Jesus Christ of Latter Day Saints is also there. In the 1830s and 1840s, people began their journeys west on the *Santa Fe Trail and the *Oregon Trail from Independence.

,Inde'pendence Day ⇨ FOURTH OF JULY.

,Independence 'Hall the building in the US city of *Philadelphia where the *Declaration of Independence was written and signed in 1776 by the *Continental Congress, and where the US Constitution was written and approved in 1787 by the Federal Constitution Convention. It is the most important building in America's history. It was built in 1732 as the Pennsylvania State House. The *Liberty Bell is also

Independence Hall

there. Independence Hall is on Chestnut Street in **Independence National Historic Park**. It was made a *World Heritage Site in 1979.

The ,Inde'pendent a British national daily newspaper, first published in 1986. It aims at political independence (i.e. it does not support any particular political party). Its success led to the publication in 1990 of a related *Sunday paper, *The Independent on Sunday*.

the **,Independent 'Labour ,Party** (abbr the **ILP**) an early British socialist party formed in 1893 by Keir *Hardie. The British *Labour Party later developed from it.

,inde'pendent school n (in Britain) a school that does not receive money from the state and charges fees for teaching and other services. *Public schools and *preparatory schools are independent schools, and the term also applies to other schools including some that offer various types of special education, e.g. for children with learning difficulties.

'India /'ɪndiə/ a country in southern Asia which used to be part of the *British Empire. It became independent and a member of the *Commonwealth in 1947. It is now the world's largest democracy, with a population of approximately one billion. There are 19 official languages including Hindi and English, though over 200 other languages are spoken in different parts of the country. The capital city is New Delhi.

Britain became involved in India in the 17th century, with the *East India Company. The British government took control of India after the *Indian Mutiny, appointing a Viceroy as its ruler. A movement for independence began at this time, when the Indian National Congress Party (later the Congress Party) was formed in 1885. In the early 20th century, the leading figure in the movement for independence was Mahatma Gandhi, who led a campaign of peaceful protest against British rule. This led to India becoming independent in 1947, when it divided into two countries, India and *Pakistan. There are many Indian and Pakistani people who have emigrated to (= left their countries to live in) Britain.
▶ **Indian** adj, n.

,**Indi'ana** /ˌɪndi'ænə/ a US state in the *Middle West which is both agricultural and industrial. It became a state in 1816. Its popular name is the Hoosier State, but nobody knows why. People from Indiana are called Hoosiers, and Americans sometimes joke that they are innocent, old-fashioned farmers. *Indianapolis is the capital city and the largest in the state.

,**Indiana 'Jones** ⇨ JONES³.

,**India'napolis** /ˌɪndiə'næpəlɪs/ the capital and largest city of the US state of *Indiana. It is in an agricultural region in the centre of the state on the White River. The city, which was settled in 1820, is a commercial centre with a large grain and cattle market. Its products include medical and electronic equipment and chemicals. It is known for the *Indianapolis 500 car race.

the **Indianapolis 500** /ˌɪndiə'næpəlɪs faɪv 'hʌndrəd/ (also informal **the Indy 500**) the best-known US car race. The event (500 miles/805 kilometres) is held each year on *Memorial Day in *Indianapolis. It began in 1911 and has always been at the Indianapolis Speedway. The cars that compete are called IndyCars. See also ANDRETTI, FOYT, UNSER.

the ,**Indian 'Mutiny** a serious revolt (1857–8) by the Indian army against British rule in India. It began in the north of India and in some places developed into a general protest. When it was defeated by the British, India was placed under the direct control of the British government, rather than the *East India Company which had previously governed it.

,**Indian reser'vation** n any of the areas of land given to *Native Americans by the US government. The US Bureau of Indian Affairs protects them and provides schools for them. The largest is the *Navajo reservation on land in *Arizona, *New Mexico and *Utah. Most Native Americans on reservations are poor and receive financial help from the government.

,**Indian 'Territory** US land west of the *Mississippi River to which *Native Americans were forced to move in the 19th century. It was originally established for the *Five Civilized Tribes, but other Native Americans were sent there in 1866. The Indian Territory existed from 1834 to 1890, but many white people settled there, and in 1907 most of it became part of the new state of *Oklahoma.

the ,**Indian 'wars** n [pl] the general name given to the various armed conflicts between *Native Americans and people who later settled in America, mostly from Europe, and those who were descended from them. These battles began at *Jamestown in 1622. The great Indian wars in the West were in the 1870s, with the final major battle in 1890 at *Wounded Knee in *South Dakota.

'**indie ,music** (also **indie**) n [U] pop or rock music produced by small, independent record companies. The

expression was first used in the early 1980s, when a number of these companies were established. In Britain, indie music has its own 'chart' (= list of the most popular records), which is published on *BBC Radio 1. There are a number of indie charts in the US, including one published by *Billboard.

,**Indi'vidual Re'tirement Ac,count** ⇨ IRA.

,**individual 'savings account** ⇨ ISA.

the **In,dustrial Revo'lution** the phrase used to describe Britain's progress in the 18th and 19th century from being largely an agricultural country to being an industrial one. Britain was the first country to change in this way. During this time, many important machines were invented. These were mostly made possible by the discovery of steam power from coal and the invention of the steam engine, which allowed one person to do what before had required many workers. As a result, big factories were built which could produce a wide variety of goods in large quantities. New methods of transport, in particular canals and railways, were developed for transporting coal and goods from place to place. During the Industrial Revolution, the populations of cities grew rapidly as people moved from the countryside to work in factories and Britain became known as the 'workshop of the world'. The same kind of development soon began in other countries in Europe and in the US. See also IRONBRIDGE.

in,**dustrial tri'bunal** n (in Britain) a type of court that makes decisions about disputes between employees and employers, particularly when an individual believes he or she have been unfairly or illegally dismissed from a job.

the **Indy 500** /ˌɪndi faɪv 'hʌndrəd/ ⇨ INDIANAPOLIS 500.

'**IndyCar ,racing** /'ɪndikɑː; AmE 'ɪndikɑːr/ n [U] a popular type of car racing in the US. The cars are like those used for the *Indianapolis 500. They are very powerful and can go at more than 230 miles/370 kilometres per hour. Drivers compete in a season of 16 Champcar races between March and September to win the IndyCar World Series. The races are mostly in the US but some are also held in Canada, Australia and Brazil. The Championships were started in 1916 by the American Automobile Association. Compare FORMULA ONE.

'**infant school** n (in Britain) a type of school for children from the age of five (when children are required by law to start school) until the age of seven or eight. Often an infant school forms, together with a *junior school, part of a *primary school.

the **Infor'mation Com'missioner's 'Office** a British government department which helps to make official information available to the public and works to protect people's personal information, especially using the *Data Protection Act.

the **INF ,Treaty** /ˌaɪ en 'ef/ (in full the **Intermediate Nuclear Forces Treaty**) an agreement reached in 1987 between the US and the USSR to destroy all nuclear missiles that could travel between 300 and 3400 miles/ 483 and 5471 kilometres. It was the first reduction in nuclear weapons that had ever taken place. The INF Treaty was signed in Washington, DC, by the US President Ronald *Reagan and the Soviet leader Mikhail Gorbachev. It involved 1752 US missiles and 859 Soviet ones.

in'**heritance tax** n [C, U] **1** (since 1986) a British tax paid to the government if somebody dies and leaves more than a certain amount of property and money. This tax also has to be paid if a person transfers more than a certain amount of wealth to somebody else up to 7 years before they die. People often call the tax **death duties**, the former name for it.

2 (in some US states), a tax that a person pays to the state government on money or property that they receive when somebody dies. Compare ESTATE TAX.

I-9 form /ˌaɪ 'naɪn fɔːm/ *n* (in the US) an official form that a person must complete before beginning a job. An employer must have it as proof that the new employee has the right to work in the US.

INLA /ˌaɪ en el 'eɪ/ ⇨ IRISH NATIONAL LIBERATION ARMY.

the **ˌInland 'Revenue** the government department in charge of the tax system in Britain. It collects *income tax, as well as other taxes including *capital gains tax, *corporation tax, *inheritance tax and *stamp duty. The equivalent in the US is the *Internal Revenue Service.

ˌIn Me'moriam /ˌɪn mə'mɔːriæm/ the most famous poem by Lord *Tennyson, published in 1850. It was written in memory of Tennyson's friend Arthur Henry Hallam, who died at the age of 22. The poem expresses Tennyson's sadness and his fears about life and death.

'Innogy /'ɪnədʒi/ one of the largest of the companies that make the electricity used in Britain. It is now part of RWE, a German company. In 1991 the Central Electricity Generating Board, which was owned by the state, was sold to private owners and there are now many companies making electricity in Britain. See also NATIONAL GRID(1), OFGEM.

the **ˌInns of 'Court** four institutions in the *City of London, established in the Middle Ages, of which all *barristers are members and at which students of law are trained. They consist of Gray's Inn, Lincoln's Inn, the Inner Temple and the Middle Temple. It is thought that they began as hostels for people studying *common law during the Middle Ages, when it was not possible to study the subject at universities. The equivalent institution in Scotland is the Faculty of Advocates.

Lincoln's Inn

the **INS** /ˌaɪ en 'es/ (*in full* the **Immigration and Naturalization Service**) an organization that was part of the US Department of Justice. It was in charge of laws concerning people from other countries who want to move to the US (the process of immigration) and those who then want to become US citizens (naturalization). In 2003 its work was taken over by new government departments, including US Citizenship and Immigration Services, part of the *Department of Homeland Security.

INSET /'ɪnset/ the abbreviation for 'in-service training' used to refer to the system of training given to teachers working in British *state schools.

Inˌspector 'Morse /'mɔːs; *AmE* 'mɔːrs/ a very popular British television series shown during the 1980s and early 1990s, set in and around Oxford. The main character is a police detective, Inspector Morse, who with his assistant, Sergeant Lewis, solves complicated murder cases. The series was originally based on the 13 novels about Inspector Morse by Colin Dexter. See also DETECTIVE STORY.

the **'Institute for Ad'vanced 'Study** a private US centre for research in Princeton, *New Jersey. It was established in 1933 and has four departments: Historical

Studies, Mathematics, Natural Sciences and Social Science. Each department has teachers and 'visiting members' from other research institutions or universities. About 160 financial awards for research work are given each year to members from many countries. Albert *Einstein was one of the first members. The Institute has a close but independent relationship with *Princeton University.

the **'Institute of Con'temporary 'Arts** ⇨ ICA.

the **ˌInstitute of Di'rectors** a British organization, like a club, for business people, especially company directors and senior people in industry. It was established in London in 1903.

'InStyle /'ɪnstaɪl/ a US fashion magazine, started in 1994, which has articles and pictures about famous people, clothes and beauty.

ˌInter'city™ /ˌɪntə'sɪti; *AmE* ˌɪntər'sɪti/ *n* a type of fast train in Britain that travels between major towns and cities, either the **Intercity 225** with a maximum speed of 225km/h (140mph) that runs on the east coast line or the **Intercity 125** (125mph/200km/h).

the **Inˌternal 'Revenue ˌService** ⇨ IRS.

the **ˌInter'national 'Herald 'Tribune** (*abbr* **IHT**) an international US newspaper known for its serious and thorough news items. It is based in Paris and published in more than 180 countries. It began in 1928 as the *Paris Herald*. It is now owned by the *New York Times*.

the **'International 'Monetary Fund** (*abbr* the **IMF**) an independent organization of the *United Nations, created by the *Bretton Woods Conference, which aims to encourage economic stability in countries all over the world. More than 150 countries are members. It was established in 1944 and is based in *Washington, DC.

the **'Internet** (*also informal* **the Net**) *n* [sing] an international computer network available to the public for the exchange of information. It was originally used mainly in the academic and military worlds. Other services, such as the World Wide Web (www), are available through it. Using search engines such as *Google, people have access to a huge amount of information.

'interstate (*also* **ˌinterstate 'highway**) *n* any of the national US roads that cross state borders. They have four lanes (= sections for single lines of traffic) and run for long distances. They are marked with red and blue signs, an 'I' and the road number. Interstates going east to west have even numbers and those going north to south have odd numbers. I-80 goes from New York to *California, and I-95 goes from *Maine to *Florida. They are usually referred to in this way: *They're building a new motel on I-10.*

ˌIn the 'Bleak Mid'winter the title and first line of a popular Christmas *carol (= religious song). The words are by Christina *Rossetti.

▶ **Inuits**

Inuits are a related group of peoples found in *Alaska, and also in *Canada and Greenland. They are thought to have come into North America from Siberia many thousands of years ago. In both the US and Britain they used to be called **Eskimos** but the name *Inuit* which means 'the people' is now usually used and is preferred by many of the people themselves. It is the name always used in Canada. The plural form is *Inuits* or *Inuit*. Although they live in small isolated communities, Inuits have a strong cultural identity and share the Inuit language. Other native peoples of Alaska include **Aleuts**, who come from the *Aleutian Islands to the west of Alaska, the **Tlingits** and the **Haida**.

Many American and British people still think of Inuits as wearing animal skins and furs, living in **igloos** (= houses made of ice), and eating raw fish which they catch from a **kayak** or through a hole in the ice. The traditional life of Inuits involved travelling from place to place, fishing and hunting animals, including seals, whales and caribou (= a type of large deer).

As in the case of *Native American peoples, the traditional way of life of the Inuit has been changed a great deal by the activities of other Americans. In particular, damage to the environment makes it hard for native Alaskans to find enough of their traditional foods. Many now live in permanent settlements which have schools and other facilities. They still live by hunting and fishing but instead of a **sledge** (*AmE* **sled**) pulled by dogs they may use a **snowmobile** (= a special car that can travel over snow) or a motor boat, and have guns and other modern equipment.

an Inuit fishing

In,visible 'Man 1 *The Invisible Man* a novel (1897) by H G *Wells, about a man who cannot be seen. It was later made into a popular film and a television series. **2** a novel (1952) by Ralph *Ellison about an African American's search for identity.

IOM /ˌaɪ əʊ 'em; *AmE* oʊ/ ⇨ ISLE OF MAN.

I'ona /aɪˈəʊnə; *AmE* aɪˈoʊnə/ a small island in the Inner *Hebrides, Scotland. It was a centre of early Christianity and a monastery (= Christian religious community) was established there by St Columba in 563. There are several early Christian monuments there and it is seen as a place of special religious importance, especially by Christian groups who go there in the summer to work and worship.

IOW /ˌaɪ əʊ 'dʌbljuː; *AmE* oʊ/ ⇨ ISLE OF WIGHT.

'Iowa /ˈaɪəʊə; *AmE* ˈaɪoʊə/ a US state in the *Middle West. Its popular name is the Hawkeye State, and people from Iowa are called Hawkeyes, probably after Chief Black Hawk, a Native American leader. Iowa was part of the *Louisiana Purchase and became a state in 1846. Iowa is known for its agriculture, and it is the largest producer of corn, soya beans, and pigs in the US. *Des Moines is the capital and largest city.

iPod™ /ˈaɪppd; *AmE* ˈaɪpɑːd/ a small, portable, digital music player which can store thousands of pieces of music. It is made by *Apple.

'Ipswich /ˈɪpswɪtʃ/ the main town and administrative centre of *Suffolk in eastern England.

IRA¹ /ˌaɪ ɑːr 'eɪ/ (*in full* **Individual Retirement Account**) *n* a US government plan that allows people to put part of their income into special bank accounts. No tax has to be paid on this money until they retire.

the IRA² /ˌaɪ ɑːr 'eɪ/ (*in full* **the Irish Republican Army**) an illegal Irish terrorist organization which believes that Northern Ireland and the Irish Republic should be united under one government. It was formed in 1919, but became more active after 1968, when British soldiers began to be based permanently in Northern Ireland. During this period of 'the *Troubles', the IRA committed many acts of violence in Northern Ireland, England and other countries. In 1994 a ceasefire (= a period during which there is no fighting) was declared, which ended in 1996 but was declared again in 1997. The military part of the IRA is often referred to as the Provisional IRA (also called the *Provisionals or the Provos). *Sinn Fein is often called the 'political wing of the IRA'. See also INLA.

the I,ran-'Contra af,fair /ɪˌrɑːn 'kɒntrə; *AmE* ˈkɑːntrə/ the name given to a series of secret and illegal actions by US government officials under President Ronald *Reagan. In 1985, officials in the *National Security Council sold military weapons to Iran so it would help in freeing US prisoners in Lebanon. The money received for these was then given to the Contras, military groups who wanted to defeat the Sandinista government in Nicaragua. The US Congress had forbidden this type of support. The deal was discovered in 1986 and several officials were charged with acting illegally. See also IRANGATE, NORTH.

I'rangate /ɪˈrɑːngeɪt/ another name, used especially by the media, for the *Iran-Contra affair. The word was invented to be similar to *Watergate.

the ,Irish 'Free State a state consisting of the whole of Ireland except Northern Ireland. It was created by the Anglo-Irish Treaty of 1921. Its name was changed to Eire in 1937 and to the Republic of Ireland in 1949.

the ,Irish 'Guards one of the *Guards regiments of the British army, formed in 1901. The regiment served in the war in Iraq.

the 'Irish 'National Libe'ration ,Army (*abbr* the **INLA**) an Irish terrorist organization which believes that Northern Ireland and the Irish Republic should be united under one government. It was formed in 1974 by former members of the *IRA and was responsible in 1979 for killing the Conservative politician Airey Neave. The INLA declared a ceasefire in 1998.

the 'Irish Re'publican 'Army ⇨ IRA².

the ,Irish 'Sea the area of sea between Britain and Ireland.

,Irish 'whiskey *n* [U, C] a type of *whisky produced in Ireland. (The word is spelt 'whiskey' in Ireland and the US, and 'whisky' in Scotland.) Famous whiskeys include Bushmills, Jameson's and Paddy's.

▶ Iron Age Britain

At the end of the *Bronze Age iron began to be used instead of bronze for making tools and weapons. Iron tools were harder and more efficient, and also cheaper. Bronze came to be used only for decorated items such as bowls or brooches.

In Britain the Iron Age began about 500 BC. Some time before this, *Celts had begun arriving in the British Isles from Europe and had mixed with the people already living there. Some were farmers and grew wheat and beans, and kept animals. The Celts are best known for their metalwork, and there is archaeological evidence of metal workshops in southern England and near Grimsby on the east coast. There was a trading centre at Hengistbury Head near Bournemouth until the middle of the 1st century BC. Metal items such as weapons and jewellery were made near there and sold in Britain and abroad. Iron bars were used as currency before coins were introduced in the 1st century BC. Pieces of pottery indicate that at the same time food and wine were imported from France.

Hill forts such as that at *Maiden Castle in Dorset were the headquarters of local chiefs and centres of administration, craftwork and trade for their tribes, as well as being used for defence. Hill forts covered a large area of land, usually on top of a hill, and were surrounded by ditches and earth ramparts (= banks) with a wooden fence on top. Inside were round thatched houses, workshops and grain stores. Each hill fort also had a shrine or religious building.

The Celtic tribes, now often called the **ancient Britons**, were defeated when the Romans invaded Britain in 43 BC. After peace was established the hill forts were no longer used, though some were later repaired and used for defence against the *Anglo-Saxons in the late 5th century. In the Roman period new artistic influences came to southern Britain and many Celtic chiefs adopted Roman ways. Further north and west, the Celts fought to remain outside the Roman province of *Britannia. The Iron Age ended in England and Wales during Roman times, but little is known of the Celtic regions further north until their culture reached its highest point of achievement in the 7th and 8th centuries.

'Ironbridge /'aɪənbrɪdʒ; AmE 'aɪərnbrɪdʒ/ a town near Telford in *Shropshire, England, in the **Ironbridge Gorge** which was an early centre of the *Industrial Revolution. It has the first major iron bridge in the world (opened in 1779) and several museums related to the history of the Industrial Revolution including a museum of china making.

the ˌIron 'Lady ⇨ THATCHER.

ˌJeremy 'Irons /'aɪənz; AmE 'aɪərnz/ (1948–) an English actor best known for his work in films, including *The French Lieutenant's Woman* (1981), *Reversal of Fortune* (1990), for which he won an *Oscar, and *Lolita* (1997). He first became well known when he played a major part in the 1981 television version of *Brideshead Revisited*.

the 'Iroquois League /'ɪrəkwɔɪ/ (also the ˌIroquois **Con'federacy**) a union of *Native American peoples established about 1570. The groups involved, all in north-eastern America, were the Cayuga, the *Mohawk, the Oneida, the Onondaga and the *Seneca. The League was originally also called the Five Nations. When the Tuscarora joined in 1722, it became known as the Six Nations. Its members were farmers and hunters. They supported the British in the *French and Indian War and, except for the Oneida and Tuscarora, also in the *American Revolution.

the IRS /ˌaɪ ɑːr 'es/ (in full the Internal Revenue **Service**) the US government organization responsible for collecting taxes. These include income tax, company tax and taxes on gifts, goods, services and estates (= money, property and other possessions left by people when they die). The IRS was created by the US Congress in 1789 and is part of the US *Department of the Treasury.

ˌHenry 'Irving[1] /'ɜːvɪŋ; AmE 'ɜːrvɪŋ/ (1838–1905) an English actor who became famous in the late 19th century for his theatre performances of *Shakespeare plays. He often acted with Ellen *Terry. He was made a *knight in 1895, the first actor to receive this honour.

ˌJohn 'Irving[2] /'ɜːvɪŋ; AmE 'ɜːrvɪŋ/ (1942–) a US author of humorous and unusual novels. His best known is *The World According to Garp* (1978), about an author who is killed by one of his readers. It was made into a 1982 film with Robin *Williams. In 1999 he won an *Oscar for the screenplay based on his novel *The Cider House Rules* (1985), and *The Hotel New Hampshire* (1981) was also filmed.

ˌWashington 'Irving[3] /ˌwɒʃɪŋtən 'ɜːvɪŋ; AmE ˌwɑʃɪŋtən 'ɜːrvɪŋ/ (1783–1859) the first US writer to gain an international reputation. He is best known for two short stories, *The Legend of Sleepy Hollow* and *Rip Van Winkle*, which were published in *The Sketch Book of Geoffrey Crayon, Gent* (1820). He also wrote the comic *History of New York* (1809) under the name of Diedrich *Knickerbocker. Irving was later the US ambassador to Spain (1842–6). See also RIP VAN WINKLE.

ISA /'aɪsə/ (in full **individual savings account**) n a type of savings account introduced in Britain in 1999 which allows people to save money each year up to an amount set by the government without paying tax on the interest earned. Most banks and *building societies offer ISAs.

ˌChristopher 'Isherwood /'ɪʃəwʊd; AmE 'ɪʃərwʊd/ (1904–86) an English writer of novels and plays. The musical show *Cabaret* was based on a story in his 1939 collection *Goodbye to Berlin*, and much of his other writing is based on his experiences in Germany before *World War II. He also wrote three plays with W H *Auden. In 1939 he moved with Auden to the US and later became a US citizen.

ˌKazuo Ishi'guro /ˌkæzʊəʊ ɪʃɪ'ɡʊrəʊ; AmE ˌkæzʊoʊ ɪʃɪ'ɡʊroʊ/ (1954–) a writer born in Japan who now lives in London, England. His books include *A Pale View of Hills* (1982), *An Artist of the Floating World* (1986), and *The Remains of the Day* (1989) which won the *Booker Prize and was made into a film. His novels published since then include *When We Were Orphans* (2000) and *Never Let Me Go* (2005).

the 'Isis /'aɪsɪs/ the name given to the River *Thames where it flows through *Oxford, England.

the ˌIsle of 'Dogs an area of London's *Docklands opposite *Greenwich, where the River *Thames surrounds the north bank on three sides. *Canary Wharf tower is in the northern half of the Isle of Dogs.

the ˌIsle of 'Man (abbr **IOM**) a large island in the *Irish Sea which is a possession of the British crown but has its own parliament, the *Tynwald. The ancient language of the island is *Manx and the people are sometimes referred to as Manxmen and Manxwomen. The Manx cat, which has no tail, is native to the island. The Isle of Man is also famous for the TT (Tourist Trophy) races for motorcycles which are held there, and for the fact that *income tax is lower there than in other parts of Britain. The island's main town and administrative centre is *Douglas.

the ˌIsle of 'Wight /'waɪt/ (abbr **IOW**) a large island off the coast of *Hampshire, in southern England. It has a warm climate which attracts tourists and people who enjoy sailing. It is governed by a *unitary authority from the town of Newport. See also COWES.

ˌiso'lationism /ˌaɪsə'leɪʃənɪzəm/ n [U] the policy of not becoming involved in the affairs of other countries. The US has often followed this policy, especially before the mid 20th century. George *Washington, in his *Farewell Address, advised Americans to avoid strong connections with other nations. The US delayed entering both World Wars because of its isolationism.
▸ **isolationist** n, adj.

ˌI-'spy n [U] a children's game in which one player gives the first letter of an object that he or she can see and the others try to guess what it is. For example, if the first letter is 'g', the player says, 'I spy, with my little eye, something beginning with "g".'

ˌAlec Issi'gonis /ˌɪsɪ'ɡəʊnɪs; AmE ɪsɪ'ɡoʊnɪs/ (1906–88) a British car designer, born in Turkey. His two most successful designs were the *Morris Minor (1948) and the *Mini (1959). He was made a *knight in 1969.

I

> 66 A camel is a horse designed by a committee. 99
> Alec Issigonis

It ,Happened One 'Night a US film (1934) which was the first comedy to win an *Oscar for Best Picture. Other Oscars went to Frank *Capra, who directed it, and to the actors Clark *Gable and Claudette Colbert. The story is about a journalist and a rich girl who has left her parents. He helps her hide, because he wants the news story.

,It's a 'Long Way to ,Tippe'rary /,tɪpə'reəri; AmE ,tɪpə'reri/ the title and first line of a *music-hall song popular with British soldiers during *World War I. Tipperary is a town in southern Ireland, and the singer, an Irishman, wants to return there to see 'the sweetest girl I know'. It is still used as a marching song.

,It's a 'Wonderful 'Life a US film (1946) about a man who wishes he had never been born, and the wish becomes real. Frank *Capra directed it, and the star was James *Stewart, who later chose it as his favourite of all the films he made. The story shows how the man's family would live if he had not been born. He realizes the importance of his life and is allowed to live again.

iTunes /'aɪtjuːnz; AmE 'aɪtuːnz/ a website run by *Apple which allows people to download music onto their computer in a digital form legally by paying an amount per song. It is especially aimed at people who want to listen to the music on an *iPod. It started in the US and was launched in Britain and other countries in 2004.

ITV /,aɪ tiː 'viː/ (in full **Independent Television**) (also **ITV1**) a network of 15 regional television channels in Britain which, unlike the *BBC, show advertising. 12 of these channels are owned by **ITV plc** which was formed in 2004 from a number of smaller companies which previously owned the channels. ITV is controlled by *Ofcom.

ITV2 /,aɪ tiː viː 'tuː/ a digital television channel in Britain which started in 1998 and is owned by ITV plc. It makes money by showing advertisements.

ITV3 /,aɪ tiː viː 'θriː/ a digital television channel in Britain that shows drama programmes. It started in 2004 and is owned by ITV plc. It makes money by showing advertisements.

ITV News Channel /,aɪ tiː viː 'njuːz; AmE 'nuːz/ a digital television channel in Britain which broadcasts news 24 hours a day and is owned by ITV plc. It makes money by showing advertisements.

'Ivanhoe /'aɪvənhəʊ; AmE 'aɪvənhoʊ/ a novel (1819) by Sir Walter *Scott. It is set in England after the *Norman Conquest and follows the adventures of Sir Wilfred of Ivanhoe, with appearances by such characters as *Robin Hood, *Friar Tuck and King *Richard I.

,Charles 'Ives /'aɪvz/ (1874–1954) a US composer of modern classical music. His work introduced many new musical ideas but was not much played during his life. One of his best-known pieces is the Concord Piano Sonata (1915).

,James 'Ivory /'aɪvəri/ (1928–) a US film director who has made many successful films with the producer Ismail *Merchant and the writer Ruth Prawer Jhabvala (known as **Merchant-Ivory productions**). These include Shakespeare Wallah (1965), Heat and Dust (1983), A Room with a View (1986), Howards End (1992), The Remains of the Day (1994) and The Golden Bowl (2000).

'Ivory soap /'aɪvəri/ a popular US soap that floats, made by *Procter & Gamble since 1879. It is advertised as being '99 and 44/100ths percent pure' and 'so pure it floats'. Ivory has bubbles mixed into the soap.

▶ **the Ivy League**

US universities and colleges organize themselves into **conferences**, groups of institutions that are near each other and do certain activities, such as sports, together. The most highly respected of these groups is the **Ivy League** in the north-eastern US. Its most famous members are *Harvard and *Yale Universities, whose fierce rivalry in various sports is like that between *Oxford and *Cambridge Universities in Britain. The other members of the Ivy League are Columbia University, Cornell University, Dartmouth College, Brown University, Princeton University, and the University of Pennsylvania. The name Ivy League comes from the ivy that grows on the old buildings of the colleges.

Ivy League institutions have a very high academic reputation, and many more people want to attend them than are able to do so. They are very expensive, with high tuition fees, although **scholarships** are available to help students who cannot pay for themselves. People who are educated in the Ivy League have a good chance of finding a well-paid job, and many political leaders have been to Ivy League universities. Many other colleges and universities in the US offer a high standard of education but none has the status and prestige of the Ivy League institutions. Compare SEVEN SISTERS.

Cornell University

the IWW /,aɪ dʌbljuː 'dʌbljuː/ (in full **the In'dustrial 'Workers of the 'World**) a US trade union of 43 organizations established in 1905 in *Chicago. Its leaders called for a workers' revolution. The IWW was most powerful from 1912 to 1917 when it had nearly 100 000 members (often called Wobblies). During World War I, its violent strikes were considered to be against the country's war effort. The leaders were put into prison, and the IWW soon ended.

,Eddie 'Izzard /'ɪzɑːd; AmE 'ɪzɑːrd/ (1962–) an English actor and comedian. He is best known as a performer on stage rather than on television, and is also known for dressing in women's clothing.

J j

'Jabberwocky /'dʒæbəwɒki; AmE 'dʒæbərwɑːki/ a famous nonsense poem by Lewis *Carroll which first appeared in his book *Through the Looking Glass (1872). It describes the hunt for a monster called the Jabberwock, using humorous invented words. Some of these words, including 'chortle' and 'galumph' are now part of the English language.

Jack and 'Jill a traditional *nursery rhyme. The first verse is:

> 66 Jack and Jill went up the hill
> To fetch a pail of water.
> Jack fell down and broke his crown
> And Jill came tumbling after. 99

Jack and the 'Beanstalk /'biːnstɔːk/ a traditional story often told to children and used as a *pantomime. Jack is a boy who sells a cow for three magic beans. He plants these and they grow into a very tall beanstalk (= bean plant). He climbs up the beanstalk into the clouds where a giant lives, and steals a hen that lays golden eggs, some bags of money and a magic harp (= musical instrument). Jack escapes down the beanstalk and then cuts it down, so that the giant, who is climbing down after him, falls to the ground and is killed.

The details in the story are sometimes mixed with those of another old story, *Jack the Giant Killer*. In it a boy called Jack travels around the country killing giants with his magic sword and wearing a coat that makes him invisible (= unable to be seen). In both stories the giants, trying to find Jack, repeat the rhyme:

> 66 Fee, fi, fo, fum,
> I smell the blood of an Englishman.
> Be he alive or be he dead,
> I'll grind his bones to make my bread. 99

Jack 'Daniels™ /'dænjəlz/ a US 'bourbon' *whisky (= made from maize/corn and rye) which is sold all over the world. It has been produced since 1866 at the Jack Daniels Distillery in Lynchburg, *Tennessee, the oldest in the US. Compare SOUTHERN COMFORT.

Jack 'Russell /'rʌsl/ n a breed of small lively *terrier dog, named after the man who first developed the breed in the 19th century.

Andrew 'Jackson¹ /'dʒæksn/ (1767–1845) the seventh US *President (1829–37), who was also a famous military officer. His popular name was Old Hickory. He won battles against *Native Americans and defeated the British at *New Orleans in the *War of 1812. As President, he began the *spoils system by giving political positions to his own supporters in the *Democratic Party. Jackson believed in the rights of the common man and was especially popular with ordinary people. 'Let the people rule' was a phrase he often used. His policies came to be known as **Jacksonian democracy**.

Glenda 'Jackson² /'dʒæksn/ (1936–) an English actor who worked in theatre, television and films, winning *Oscars for her parts in *Women in Love* (1969) and *A Touch of Class* (1973). She became a *Labour *Member of Parliament in 1992 representing a London constituency.

Janet 'Jackson³ /'dʒæksn/ (1966–) a US singer who is the sister of Michael *Jackson. Her most successful songs have included *When I Think of You* (1986), *That's the Way Love Goes* (1993), which won a *Grammy award, and *All For You* (2001). She has also acted in two television series, *Good Times* and *Diff'rent Strokes*. When she showed a naked breast during a performance at the *Super Bowl in 2004, it was famously described as a 'wardrobe malfunction'.

Jesse 'Jackson⁴ /'dʒæksn/ (The Reverend Jesse Louis Jackson, Sr. 1941–) a US civil rights leader and well-known *Democrat. He failed in his attempts to be chosen as candidate for President in 1984 and 1988. Jackson is also a *Baptist Church leader and is known as an excellent speaker. His son, Jesse L Jackson, Jr, is a member of the *House of Representatives.

Ma'halia 'Jackson⁵ /məˌheɪliə 'dʒæksn/ (1911–72) a US *gospel singer with a strong voice. Her successful songs included *Move On Up a Little Higher* and *Prayer Changes Things*. She was a supporter of the *civil rights movement in the 1960s and sang at the *Inauguration Day ceremony for President John F *Kennedy in 1961.

Michael 'Jackson⁶ /'dʒæksn/ (1958–) a US pop singer, often called Jacko by the British media. As a child he sang as the youngest of five brothers in The Jackson Five. His album *Thriller* (1983) sold more than 30 million copies, and he won eight *Grammy awards in 1984. He was chosen for the Rock and Roll *Hall of Fame in 2001. His first wife was Lisa Marie Presley, the daughter of Elvis *Presley. Despite his great success Jackson is very shy about his private life but it is frequently in the news. It is often said that he has had medical operations to change his appearance and the colour of his skin. In 2003 he was arrested and accused of harming children.

Peter 'Jackson⁷ /'dʒæksn/ (1961–) a New Zealand film writer, director and producer. He is best known for the three *Lord of the Rings films based on the books by J R R *Tolkien: *The Fellowship of the Ring* (2001), *The Two Towers* (2002) and *The Return of the King* (2003), which won three *Oscars.

Samuel L 'Jackson⁸ /'dʒæksn/ (Samuel Leroy Jackson 1948–) a US actor who has appeared in many *Hollywood films and is known for his deep, powerful voice and for playing strong, often violent, characters. His films include *Jungle Fever* (1991), *Pulp Fiction* (1994), *Shaft* (2000) and *Star Wars II: Attack of the Clones* (2002).

'Stonewall' 'Jackson⁹ /ˌstəʊnwɔːl 'dʒæksn; AmE ˌstoʊnwɔːl/ (Thomas Jonathan Jackson 1824–63) an American military leader for the *Confederate States during the *Civil War. He fought at the Battles of *Bull Run and was given the popular name of 'Stonewall' during the first of these, because he stood like a stone wall as the enemy advanced. He was killed during the Battle of *Chancellorsville when his own soldiers shot him accidentally.

Jack,sonian de'mocracy /dʒækˌsəʊniən; AmE dʒækˌsoʊniən/ n [U] ⇨ JACKSON¹.

'Jacksonville /'dʒæksənvɪl/ the largest city in the US state of *Florida, and the US city with the largest area (759 square miles/1966 square kilometres). It is a major port on the St Johns River and has a US Navy base. Jacksonville was first settled in 1816 as Cowford and then named in 1822 after Andrew *Jackson.

,Jack 'Sprat /'spræt/ a traditional *nursery rhyme. The words are:

> 66 Jack Sprat would eat no fat,
> His wife would eat no lean.
> And so between the two of them
> They licked the platter clean. 99

,Jack the 'Giant ,Killer ⇨ JACK AND THE BEANSTALK.

,Jack the 'Ripper /'rɪpə(r)/ the name given to an unknown man who murdered and cut up several prostitutes in *Whitechapel, London, in 1888. The name was used in a letter by someone who claimed to be the killer but may have been a journalist. People have tried ever since to find out who he was, but without success. There have been many novels, plays and films about the murders. See also BOSTON STRANGLER, YORKSHIRE RIPPER.

,Jaco'bean /,dʒækə'biːən/ adj of the period when *James I was king of England (1603–25). This followed the *Elizabethan period (1558–1603) and is noted for its writers (e.g. *Shakespeare, Ben *Jonson and the *metaphysical poets) as well as for its styles of architecture and furniture. The *King James Version of the Bible was also produced during the Jacobean period.

,Derek 'Jacobi /'dʒækəbi/ (1938–) an English actor on stage, in films and on television. He became famous after playing the Roman emperor Claudius in the television series *I, Claudius* (1976) and has since played the title part in the television series *Cadfael* (1994–6), based on books by Ellis Peters (real name Edith Pargeter 1913–95). Cadfael is a *medieval monk who solves crimes. Jacobi has acted in many productions and films of *Shakespeare's plays. He was made a *knight in 1994.

'Jacobite /'dʒækəbaɪt/ (in 17th- and 18th-century Britain) a supporter of King *James II of England (James VII of Scotland) after he lost power to *William III in 1688, or, after James's death, a supporter of his son James Edward *Stuart (the *Old Pretender) or grandson Charles Edward Stuart (*Bonny Prince Charlie). James II and his son and grandson were members of a Scottish family, the House of Stuart, and most Jacobites were Scottish. See also JACOBITE REBELLIONS.

the ,Jacobite re'bellions /,dʒækəbaɪt/ n [pl] a series of three rebellions which took place in Scotland after *James II lost power to *William III in 1688. In them the *Jacobites tried to return the *Stuarts to power in 1689, in 1715 (under the *Old Pretender, James II's son) and in 1745 (under *Bonny Prince Charlie, James II's grandson). After some success under Bonny Prince Charlie the Jacobites were finally defeated at the battle of *Culloden in 1746.

Ja'cuzzi™ /dʒə'kuːzi/ n a type of bath with streams of warm water that come out below the surface. It was developed by an American, Candido Jacuzzi, to help his son, who had arthritis (= a painful disease in the joints of the body). It is now quite common for people to have a Jacuzzi in their home.

'Jaeger™ /'jeɪɡə(r)/ a British chain of shops that sells men's and women's clothing. It has a reputation for high quality. Jaeger shops were started to sell clothes based on the ideas of Dr Gustav Jaeger, who believed that wearing wool next to the skin was healthy.

'Jaffa cake™ /'dʒæfə/ n a small round cake covered on one side with orange jelly and chocolate. Jaffa cakes are made by *McVitie's. They look like biscuits but are called cakes because they are soft and biscuits are crisp.

,Mick 'Jagger /'dʒæɡə(r)/ (1943–) an English pop musician who is the singer for The *Rolling Stones. With Keith *Richard he has written many of the band's songs. He has also acted in films. He was made a *knight in 2003.

'Jaguar™ /'dʒæɡjuə(r)/ a British car company or one of its cars. Jaguar is famous for its sports cars (e.g. the *E-type) and its larger cars of high quality. The company was bought by *Ford in 1989. The informal name often given to a Jaguar car is a **Jag**: *I've always wanted to own a Jag.*

Ja'maica /dʒə'meɪkə/ an island in the *Caribbean Sea that is part of the *West Indies. It has been an independent country and a member of the *Commonwealth since 1962. Its capital city is Kingston and its official language is English. It is popular with tourists. *Rastafarianism and *reggae music have their origins in Jamaica. After *World War II Jamaican people were encouraged by the British government to come to Britain to work, and Britain has a large community of Jamaican origin.
► **Jamaican** *adj, n.*

,Clive 'James¹ /'dʒeɪmz/ (1939–) an Australian television personality and writer who lives in Britain. He is best known for humorous programmes such as *The Clive James Show* (1996 and 1998) and *Monday Night Clive* (1999) in which he discusses news events with guests and introduces comedy acts, etc. He has also written novels, poetry and books about his own life.

,Henry 'James² /'dʒeɪmz/ (1843–1916) a writer, born in the US, whose novels are often about Americans in Europe. They contrast the Americans' innocent ideas with the Europeans' understanding of the world. James settled in London in 1876 and became British in 1915. His novels include *Daisy Miller* (1879), *Portrait of a Lady* (1881), the ghost story *The Turn of the Screw* (1898), *The Wings of a Dove* (1902), *The Ambassadors* (1903) and *The Golden Bowl* (1904). Several of them have been made into films. See also JAMESIAN.

,Jesse 'James³ /'dʒeɪmz/ (1847–82) a US outlaw (= criminal) from the state of *Missouri. With his brother Frank (1843–1915) he led the 'James band', robbing banks and trains between 1866 and 1879. Jesse was finally shot in the back and killed by one of his former friends who wanted to collect the reward for his death that was offered by the state. Frank later lived on a farm. There have been many books and films about the James brothers.

,Naomi 'James⁴ /'dʒeɪmz/ (1949–) an Englishwoman who became the first woman to sail alone around the world, in 1977–8. She was made a *dame(2) in 1979.

,P D 'James⁵ /'dʒeɪmz/ (Phyllis Dorothy James 1920–) an English writer, mainly of *detective stories. Her main characters are the police officer Adam Dalgleish and the private detective Cordelia Gray. Many of her books have been filmed for television, including *An Unsuitable Job for a Woman* (1972), *Devices and Desires* (1989) and *Original Sin* (1997). She was made a *life peer in 1991.

James I /,dʒeɪmz ðə 'fɜːst; *AmE* 'fɜːrst/ (1566–1625) the king of England from 1603 to 1625 and of Scotland (as James VI) from 1567 to 1625. His mother was *Mary Queen of Scots. As a relative of *Elizabeth I he became King of England after she died, uniting Scotland and England under one government. He was not a popular king, however, and Roman Catholic opposition led to the *Gunpowder Plot (1605). His son *Charles I became king after he died. James I is associated with the *Jacobean period in literature and the arts. See also AUTHORIZED VERSION.

James II /,dʒeɪmz ðə 'sekənd/ (1633–1701) the king of England and Scotland from 1685 to 1688. He was the son of *Charles I and the younger brother of *Charles II, becoming king after Charles II died. He faced a lot of opposition because he was a Roman Catholic, and in 1688 he was replaced by the Protestant *William III. James went to Ireland in 1689 to try to win back power, but was defeated at the *Battle of the Boyne. He lived the rest of his life in France.

'Jamesian /'dʒeɪmziən/ adj of a style of writing that is extremely complicated, with long sentences containing many difficult ideas (after the author Henry *James, who wrote in this way, especially in his later novels).

'Jamestown /'dʒeɪmztaʊn/ the first permanent community of English people in North America, in what is now *Virginia. It was established on 14 May 1607 by the London Company and named after King *James I. John *Smith was an early leader. The first tobacco farms were begun here in 1612. The church tower and some graves remain, and are visited by many tourists. Jamestown is now part of Virginia's Colonial National Historic Park.

,Jane 'Doe /'dəʊ; AmE 'doʊ/ a name used in the US to refer to a woman or girl whose identity is unknown or who does not want her real name to be made public. This is usually for cases in court and on legal papers. Compare JOHN DOE.

,Jane 'Eyre /'eə(r); AmE 'er/ a novel (1847) by Charlotte *Brontë. Jane Eyre is an orphan who, after a very unhappy childhood, becomes a private teacher for the daughter of Edward Rochester. Jane and Mr Rochester fall in love and are about to marry when she discovers that he already has a wife, who is mentally ill. Years later the lovers meet again and marry, although Rochester has by this time been badly injured in a fire. The novel is still popular, mainly for the contrast in character between the shy Jane and the mysterious and violent Rochester.

,Derek 'Jarman /'dʒɑːmən; AmE 'dʒɑːrmən/ (1942–94) an English film director, artist and writer who was also known as a campaigner for gay rights. His best-known films include Sebastiane (1976), the *punk film Jubilee (1978), The Tempest (1979), Caravaggio (1986), The Last of England (1987), The Garden (1990), Edward II (1991), Blue (1993) and Wittgenstein (1993). He also directed pop videos and wrote several books, including Dancing Ledge (1991).

'Jarrow /'dʒærəʊ; AmE 'dʒæroʊ/ a town in north-east England where the shipbuilding and steel industries were badly affected by the *Depression in the 1930s, making many workers unemployed. In 1936 about 200 unemployed workers walked 274 miles/441 kilometres from Jarrow to London on a 'hunger march' in an attempt to persuade the government to do something about the problem. See also BEDE.

,David 'Jason /'dʒeɪsn/ (1940–) an English actor, especially on television. He became famous playing the part of *Del Boy Trotter in *Only Fools and Horses and later that of Pop Larkin in The Darling Buds of May. He has also had success with more serious roles, playing the police officer Jack Frost in the crime series A Touch of Frost (1992–2003).

Jaws /dʒɔːz/ a very successful film (1975) about a large shark (= dangerous fish) that attacks people. The film was directed by Stephen *Spielberg and was based on a novel of the same name by Peter Benchley.

'Jaycee /'dʒeɪsiː/ n (AmE informal) a member of a junior *chamber of commerce. The name comes from the first letters of the words 'junior chamber'. The Jaycees are an organization of young business people in several countries involved in projects to support their local communities. The US Junior Chamber of Commerce was established in 1920 and its office is in *Tulsa, *Oklahoma.

▶**jazz**

Jazz is one of the greatest forms of music originating in the US. The names of its stars are known around the world. Most people have heard of stars like Ella *Fitzgerald, 'Count' *Basie, 'Duke' *Ellington and Louis *Armstrong. Wynton *Marsalis, who plays in the traditional style, is one of the best-known jazz musicians today.

Jazz was begun in the *South by African Americans. Many of its rhythms came from the work songs and spirituals (= religious songs) of black slaves. New Orleans street bands first made jazz popular. Early forms of jazz created at the beginning of the 20th century were *ragtime and the *blues. Ragtime musicians included the singer 'Jelly Roll' *Morton and the composer and piano player Scott *Joplin. Famous blues singers included Bessie *Smith and later Billie *Holiday. *Dixieland developed from ragtime and the blues and made a feature of improvisation (= making up the music as it is being played), especially on the trumpet and *saxophone. Dixieland stars included Louis Armstrong and *Sidney Bechet.

In the 1920s many African Americans moved north, taking jazz with them, and *Chicago and New York became centres for the music. This was the beginning of the **big band era**. In the 1930s swing music came into fashion and people danced to jazz. Radio and the new recording industry helped to make it even more popular. The big bands were led by Basie, Ellington, Woody Herman, Glenn *Miller, and 'the King of Swing', Benny *Goodman. In the 1940s there were new styles such as *bebop, developed by 'Dizzy' *Gillespie, Charlie 'Bird' *Parker and Thelonious *Monk. Freer forms like **progressive jazz** and **free jazz** developed in the 1950s with stars including Stan *Getz, John *Coltrane and Dave *Brubeck. **Cool jazz** followed in the 1960s, led by Getz and Miles *Davis. More recent styles have included funky jazz, jazz-rock and hip-hop jazz. Many jazz clubs, like the *Cotton Club, have now closed but others, like Preservation Hall in *New Orleans, and Birdland in *Manhattan, remain.

In Britain jazz attracts a small but enthusiastic audience. The height of its popularity was in the 1940s and 1950s, when large crowds gathered to hear big bands. British jazz has always been heavily influenced by US jazz. In the 1960s pop and rock music replaced jazz as the music of the young generation. There are now few jazz bands, although smaller **combos** (= groups) continue to play a wide range of **trad** (= traditional), bebop, cool and avant-garde jazz. The most famous British jazz musicians have included Johnny *Dankworth and Cleo *Laine, George Melly, Humphrey *Lyttelton and Courtney *Pine. The home of jazz in Britain is Ronnie *Scott's club in London.

the 'Jazz Age a name for the 1920s, when *jazz music was especially popular. The name came from the book Tales of the Jazz Age (1922) by F Scott *Fitzgerald, who was called 'the spokesman of the Jazz Age'. See also ROARING TWENTIES.

,jazz 'funk (also **funk**) n [U] a style of dance music that developed from the *soul music of James *Brown and others during the 1960s and 1970s. Famous jazz funk bands include Parliament and Funkadelic.

The 'Jazz ,Singer the first sound film. It was made in *Hollywood in 1927 by *Warner Brothers and was so successful that other companies soon changed to sound. Al *Jolson was the star and sang six songs, but only 354 words were actually spoken in the film. The story is about the son of a rabbi (= Jewish religious leader) who becomes a singer. Later versions of the film were made in 1953 and 1980.

> 66 'You ain't heard nothing yet.' 99
> Al Johnson in The Jazz Singer

JCB™ /ˌdʒeɪ siː ˈbiː/ n (BrE) a large vehicle for moving earth, etc., with a mechanical shovel at the front and a digging arm at the back. JCBs are made by the British company J C Bamford. In American English they are called 'backhoes'.

J C 'Penney /ˌdʒeɪ siː ˈpeni/ any of a large group of US department stores known for their low prices. The shops/stores were begun in 1902 by James Cash Penney (1875–1971), who called them 'chain stores'.

'J Crew™ any of a group of fashionable US clothes shops. The company began in 1983 by selling clothes through its catalogues (= books sent to people's homes that show items they can buy by post). J Crew is best known for its range of informal sports clothes. Its main office is in *Manhattan(1) in New York City.

▶**jeans**

Jeans were first made in the US. They are now worn all over the world. Jeans were created during the *Gold Rush in the 1840s and 1850s, when many people went to the western US to search for gold. Miners often lived in tents made out of a strong fabric and, because they needed strong clothes, they began to wear trousers made from the same fabric. Many jeans were sold by Levi Strauss, who had a store in California, and today *Levi's are among the most famous jeans.

Traditionally, jeans are blue (and are then also called blue jeans), but the fabric they are made of, denim, comes in many colours. Black jeans, and **stonewashed** jeans that are made from denim which has been washed until it becomes lighter and softer, are also made. Styles include **bell-bottoms**, **flares** and **bootleg cut**, which are halfway between straight and flared, but **straight-leg** is most popular as a universal style and worn by both men and women. **Designer jeans** are sold by top fashion designers.

For a long time jeans were worn only for physical work, but in the 1960s society changed and young people began to question traditional attitudes to dress. Jeans were a symbol of these changes and became very popular. Now, people of any age wear jeans because they are comfortable, practical and relatively cheap. They can be made more or less formal, depending on what is worn with them, but some restaurants and wine bars do not allow in people who are wearing jeans, and some companies do not like their staff to wear jeans for work.

Jeep™ (also **jeep**) n a strong motor vehicle used for driving over rough ground or on mountain roads. The Jeep was first made for the US Army in *World War II. It was called a General Purpose vehicle, the short form of which was 'GP' or 'jeep'. Jeeps are now made by *Chrysler and sold around the world. Popular models include the Cherokee and the Wrangler.

Jeeves /dʒiːvz/ the male servant of Bertie *Wooster in the humorous stories of P G *Wodehouse. Jeeves is the perfect example of an intelligent and efficient servant who remains calm and can solve any problem.

Thomas 'Jefferson /ˈdʒefəsn; AmE ˈdʒefərsn/ (1743–1826) the third US *President (1801–9) and one of the nation's *Founding Fathers. He wrote most of the *Declaration of Independence but was opposed to a strong central government. As president, he supported the *Louisiana Purchase and the *Lewis and Clark Expedition. Jefferson helped design Washington, DC, and was the first president to have his *Inauguration Day there. He was also governor of *Virginia (1779–81) and US Secretary of State (1789–93). He established the University of Virginia (1819) and designed its buildings. He died, like John *Adams, on the 50th anniversary of the Declaration of Independence.

the ˌJefferson Me'morial /ˌdʒefəsn; AmE ˈdʒefərsn/ a building in Washington, DC, in memory of Thomas *Jefferson. It was opened in 1943 in East Potomac Park. John Russell Pope designed it like an ancient Greek building with a round roof, and it is made of white marble. Inside is a statue of Jefferson by Rudolph Evans.

the Jefferson Memorial

ˌJudge 'Jeffreys /ˈdʒefriz/ (George Jeffreys c. 1648–89) a British judge who condemned to death many supporters of the Duke of *Monmouth in the *Bloody Assizes of 1685. He is often given as an example of a cruel and wicked judge. He was made a *baron in 1685 but later fell out of favour and died in prison.

Je,hovah's 'Witness /dʒɪˌhəʊvəz; AmE dʒɪˌhoʊvəz/ n a member of a Christian organization started in the US in the 1870s. Jehovah's Witnesses believe that the end of the world is near and that when it comes everyone except them will be destroyed. They also refuse to do military service, do not celebrate birthdays or *Christmas, and believe in the literal truth of the Bible. Members are encouraged to visit people in their homes and try to persuade them to join and buy the magazine *The Watchtower*. .

ˌGertrude 'Jekyll /ˈdʒiːkɪl/ (1843–1932) an English garden designer. She wanted to create gardens that looked informal and natural and her influence is still strong today. Much of her work was done with the architect Edwin *Lutyens.

ˌJekyll and 'Hyde /ˌdʒekəl, ˈhaɪd/ n a single person with two personalities, one good (Jekyll) and one bad (Hyde). The phrase comes from a character in Robert Louis *Stevenson's story *The Strange Case of Dr Jekyll and Mr Hyde* (1886) who takes a drug which separates the good and bad sides of his personality into two characters: *They soon discovered he was a Jekyll and Hyde.* ◊ *She was leading an almost Jekyll and Hyde existence.*

'jello (also **'Jell-O**™) /ˈdʒeləʊ; AmE ˈdʒeloʊ/ n [U, C] a popular US sweet dish of jelly/gelatin with a fruit flavour. It is eaten as a dessert or with salads. The word is often used in the US to refer to any jelly/gelatin dish.

'jelly ˌbaby n [usually pl] (BrE) a small soft sweet shaped like a baby. Jelly babies are sold in different colours and flavours, and are popular with children.

'jelly bean n a small sweet/candy shaped like a bean. Jelly beans have centres of jelly/gelatin with hard sugar on the outside. They are sold in many different flavours and colours, and in the US they are traditionally put in children's Easter baskets.

ˌRoy 'Jenkins /ˈdʒenkɪnz/ (1920–2003) a British politician and author. He was *Home Secretary (1965–7 and 1974–6) and *Chancellor of the Exchequer (1967–70) in the *Labour governments of Harold *Wilson, and later helped to establish the *Social Democratic Party. From 1977 to 1981 he was President of the *European

Commission. He wrote several books about politics and politicians, and was made a *life peer in 1987.

ˌEdward ˈJenner /ˈdʒenə(r)/ (1749–1823) an English doctor who first used the term vaccination. He found that by deliberately infecting people with cowpox (a disease of cows) he could prevent them from catching smallpox, a serious human disease, and that this was safer than inoculation with smallpox, which had been done previously.

ˌPeter ˈJennings /ˈdʒenɪŋz/ (1938–) the main person presenting the news on *ABC World News Tonight* on US television. Jennings was born in Canada and began at ABC when he was 26, the youngest person ever to present television news in the US.

ˈJeopardy /ˈdʒepədi; *AmE* ˈdʒepərdi/ a popular US television quiz show. The competitors are given answers and have to guess what the questions are for each answer. The programme began in 1964, and Alex Trebek has presented it since 1984.

ˌJerome K ˈJerome /dʒəˈrəʊm; *AmE* dʒəˈroʊm/ (Jerome Klapka Jerome 1859–1927) an English writer, best known for his humorous novel *Three Men in a Boat* (1889).

ˈJersey /ˈdʒɜːzi; *AmE* ˈdʒɜːrzi/ **1** the largest of the *Channel Islands, off the north-west coast of France. The main town is St Helier. Jersey has its own government and tax system but has strong links with Britain, and is popular with British tourists. Both English and French are spoken on the island. It is known for its fruit and vegetables (particularly tomatoes and new potatoes called Jersey Royals). The item of clothing called a *jersey* takes its name from a type of knitted material originally made on the island.
2 *n* a breed of cow originally from the *Channel Islands. Jerseys are light brown in colour and are known for their rich milk.
3 (in the US) another name for the state of *New Jersey.

ˌJersey ˈCity /ˌdʒɜːzi; *AmE* ˌdʒɜːrzi/ an industrial city in the US state of *New Jersey, across the *Hudson River from *Manhattan(1). It is a port with many factories. Many people who live there work in New York. Jersey City was settled in the middle of the 17th century and became a town in 1836.

Jeˈrusalem /dʒəˈruːsələm/ a famous poem (1804) by William *Blake, later set to music by Hubert Parry (1848–1918). It expresses the hope for a future Christian society in 'England's green and pleasant land' to replace the horrors of 'the dark Satanic mills' of the *Industrial Revolution. It is traditionally sung at the *Last Night of the Proms as well as by *Women's Institutes and in churches.

ˈJesus ˈChrist ˈSuperstar a musical stage show about the life and death of Jesus Christ by Andrew *Lloyd Webber and Tim *Rice. It was very successful in Britain and the US in the 1970s and returned to the London stage in 1996. A film version was made in 1973.

The ˌJewel in the ˈCrown a popular British television series, first broadcast in 1983, about the British in India just before it became an independent country. The series was adapted from the *Raj Quartet* novels of Paul *Scott. The phrase 'the jewel in the crown' was formerly used to describe India's place in the British Empire, and is used today to refer to something of great value among other valuable things: *Their new goalkeeper is the jewel in Newcastle's crown.*

JFK /ˌdʒeɪ ef ˈkeɪ/ **1** ⇨ KENNEDY[6].
2 (*also* **Kennedy**) a large international airport in New York, named after President John F *Kennedy. Its former name was Idlewild Airport.

Ruth ˌPrawer Jhabˈvala /ˌprɑːwə dʒæbˈvɑːlə; *AmE* ˌprɑːwər/ (1924–) a novelist and screenwriter who was born in Germany, educated in England and then moved to India. Her novel about India, *Heat and Dust* (1975), won the *Booker Prize and was also made into a film in 1983. She was the writer for many films made by Ismail *Merchant and James *Ivory, including *Howards End* (1993) and *A Room with a View* (1987) for which she won an *Oscar.

ˈJiffy bag™ /ˈdʒɪfi/ *n* a British make of padded envelope for protecting things that are being sent by post.

ˌJim ˈCrow /ˈkrəʊ; *AmE* ˈkroʊ/ (*also* ˌJim ˈCrowism) /ˈkrəʊɪzəm; *AmE* ˈkroʊɪzəm/ *n* [U] (*AmE*) the former policy of *segregation or unfair treatment of *African Americans in hotels, restaurants, businesses, etc. The name came from the title of a song that was sung in musical shows by white entertainers who tried to look and sound like *African Americans: *The South had many Jim Crow laws.*

ˈJingle Bells a popular *Christmas song. It is sung by carol singers or at Christmas celebrations but not usually in church. ⇨ note at CAROLS AND CAROL SINGING.

the ˈjitterbug /ˈdʒɪtəbʌɡ; *AmE* ˈdʒɪtərbʌɡ/ *n* [sing] a fast dance, originally from the US, which was popular in the 1940s. It involved wild movements, with the women being lifted in the air. A version popular with *African Americans was the Lindy or Lindy Hop.

jive *n* [U] **1** a lively style of dance, popular especially in the 1950s, performed to *jazz or *rock and roll music.
2 jive music.
3 (*AmE slang*) talk that is not sincere or is intended to deceive somebody: *Hey, man, don't give me that jive.*
▶ jive *v* [I] to dance jive or play jive music.

ˌJobcentre ˈPlus /ˌdʒɒbsentə(r); *AmE* ˌdʒɑːbsentər/ *n* (in Britain) a government office found in the centre of most towns, where jobs are advertised, the *Jobseeker's Allowance is paid to people without work, and advice is given in order to help people find a job. They are run by the *Department for Work and Pensions. Jobcentre Plus jobs are also advertised on the Internet.

ˌJobseeker's Alˈlowance /ˌdʒɒbsiːkəz; *AmE* ˌdʒɑːbsiːkərz/ *n* [U] (in Britain) money paid by the government to unemployed people. To claim the money, people must be capable of work and must prove that they are trying to find work.

Jock /dʒɒk; *AmE* dʒɑːk/ *n* (*BrE informal or offensive*) a name used especially by English people to refer to a Scotsman.

jock /dʒɒk; *AmE* dʒɑːk/ *n* (*AmE informal disapproving*) a male student in school or college who plays a lot of sport but who is not considered to be very intelligent or good at academic study.

the ˈJockey Club (in Britain) the organization that sets the rules of the sport of horse racing and licenses those who take part in it.

ˌJodrell ˈBank /ˌdʒɒdrəl; *AmE* ˌdʒɑːdrəl/ (*also* **the Nuffield Radio Astronomy Laboratories**) a place in *Cheshire, north-west England, where there are several large radio telescopes (= devices for receiving radio waves from distant objects in the universe). The main one was designed by Sir Bernard *Lovell, and when it began operating in 1957 it was the largest of its kind in the world. Jodrell Bank is part of the University of Manchester.

ˌJoe ˈBloggs /ˈblɒɡz; *AmE* ˈblɑːɡz/ (*AmE* ˌJoe ˈBlow, ˌJoe ˈSchmo; *AmE* ʃmoʊ/) (*informal*) a name used to refer to an average or typical man: *Joe Bloggs is generally more interested in sport than in politics.* Compare JOHN Q PUBLIC.

ˌ**Joe 'Sixpack** /ˈsɪkspæk/ (*AmE informal*) a name given to the typical man who does manual work. A sixpack is a pack of six cans of beer sold together.

John[1] (1167–1216) the king of England from 1199 to 1216. He was the youngest son of *Henry II and became king after the death of his brother *Richard I, having previously tried to take power from him. He was not a popular or successful king. He lost most of the English land in France, quarrelled with the Church, and was forced by his *barons in 1215 to sign the *Magna Carta, which limited his royal powers. He is the subject of *King John*, an early play by *Shakespeare.

Auˌgustus 'John[2] /ɔːˌɡʌstəs ˈdʒɒn; *AmE* ˈdʒɑːn/ (1878–1961) a Welsh painter. He worked as an official war artist during *World War I and later became famous for his pictures of women (especially his wife Dorelia). He also painted many of the leading writers of the time, including George Bernard *Shaw, Thomas *Hardy and W B *Yeats. He was the brother of Gwen *John.

ˌElton 'John[3] /ˌeltən ˈdʒɒn; *AmE* ˈdʒɑːn/ (1947–) an English pop singer and piano player, known for wearing unusual clothes and large colourful glasses. He has been popular since the 1970s and his most successful songs have included *Your Song* (1970), *Rocket Man* (1972), *Don't Go Breaking My Heart* (1976) and *Sacrifice* (1989). He was a friend of *Diana, Princess of Wales, and played and sang a special version of his song *Candle in the Wind* at her funeral service. This immediately became the most successful record of all time, with all the profits going to a special charity set up in memory of Princess Diana. He won an *Oscar in 1994 for the song *Can You Feel the Love Tonight?*, which he wrote for the film *The Lion King*. Elton John was made a *knight in 1998.

ˌGwen 'John[4] /ˈdʒɒn; *AmE* ˈdʒɑːn/ (1876–1939) a Welsh painter who lived in France for most of her life. She began as a pupil of James McNeill *Whistler and often painted single figures (especially girls) in quiet rooms. Augustus *John was her brother, and he is said to have predicted correctly that in the future she would be considered the better painter of the two.

the ˌ**John 'Birch Soˌciety** /ˈbɜːtʃ; *AmE* ˈbɜːrtʃ/ an extreme right-wing US organization, started in 1958 during the *Cold War to oppose Communism. The group has never had great influence. It is named after a US military officer killed by Chinese Communists in 1945.

ˌ**John Brown's 'Body** ⇨ BROWN.

ˌ**John 'Bull** /ˈbʊl/ the name given to an imaginary typical Englishman, representing English people as a whole. He is usually shown in pictures as a fat man with a red face, wearing a top hat, a waistcoat and high boots. He also often has a bulldog, suggesting that he is like the dog in having a brave, fierce and independent character. See also BULLDOG BREED.

John 'Deere™ /ˈdɪə(r); *AmE* ˈdɪr/ a product name of US farm, building and garden vehicles made by Deere and Company and advertised with the slogan 'Nothing runs like a Deere'. The company was established in 1837 and is now the biggest in the world producing agricultural equipment.

ˌ**John 'Doe** /ˈdəʊ; *AmE* ˈdoʊ/ **1** a name used in the US to refer to a man whose identity is unknown or who does not want his real name to be made public. This is usually for cases in court or on legal papers. Compare JANE DOE.
2 a name used in the US to refer to a typical ordinary man: *Any John Doe knows that.* Compare JOE BLOGGS.

ˌ**John 'Hancock** ⇨ HANCOCK.

the ˌ**John 'Hancock ˌBuilding** /ˈhænkɒk; *AmE* ˈhænkɑːk/ a very tall building, 60 floors high, in *Boston, Massachusetts, designed by I M Pei (1917–) and finished in 1976. It has mirror glass on the outside which reflects the city around it.

ˌ**John 'Hancock ˌCenter** /ˈhænkɒk; *AmE* ˈhænkɑːk/ one of the tallest and most impressive buildings in the US, opened in 1969. It is in *Chicago on North Michigan Avenue. The building is of black steel, and the outside has lengths of steel that cross to support it. It is 1 127 feet/344 metres high and has 100 floors. The first five have shops, the next six are for cars, and the rest are offices and apartments with their own supermarket and swimming pool. There is a Skydeck Observatory on the 94th floor.

ˌ*John* 'Henry /ˈhenri/ a US *folk song about a strong *African American who built railway tracks. It was originally sung by African Americans. John Henry was 'a steel-driving man' who could crush more rocks than a machine. Part of the song is:

> 66 John Henry said to his captain,
> 'A man ain't nothin' but a man,
> And before I'd let your steam drill beat me down,
> I'd die with the hammer in my hand, Lord, Lord!
> I'd die with the hammer in my hand.' 99

ˌ**John 'Lewis** /ˈluːɪs/ (*also* **The John Lewis Partnership**) a British company that owns a chain of department stores (= large shops selling many types of goods). Employees are all partners in the company and receive a share of the profits each year. John Lewis also owns the supermarket chain *Waitrose. The original John Lewis started the company with a small shop in *Oxford Street in London in 1864.

ˌ**Johnnie 'Walker™** /ˈwɔːkə(r)/ *n* [U] a make of Scotch *whisky. It is especially popular in the US and is available in several varieties, including Red Label and Black Label.

ˌ**Johnny 'Reb** /ˈreb/ (*also* **Johnny**) (*AmE informal old use*) any soldier in the Confederate Army during the American *Civil War. 'Reb' is short for 'rebel'. See also CONFEDERATE STATES.

ˌ**John of 'Gaunt** /ˈɡɔːnt/ (1340–99) an English prince who was Duke of Lancaster from 1362. He was the son of *Edward II and acted as the head of government before *Richard II was old enough to be king. His son was *Henry IV. His name refers to his place of birth, which was Ghent, now in Belgium.

ˌ**John o'**'Groats** /əˈɡrəʊts; *AmE* əˈɡroʊts/ a village in north-east Scotland, traditionally thought of as the most northern point on the British mainland. The name may come from that of Jan de Groot, a Dutchman who is said to have lived there in the 15th century. Compare LAND'S END, DUNNET HEAD.

ˌ**John Q 'Public** (*AmE informal*) a name used to refer to any average person, especially when seen as representing typical public opinion: *What will John Q Public think of higher taxes?* Compare CLAPHAM OMNIBUS.

ˌ**Jasper 'Johns** /ˈdʒɒnz; *AmE* ˈdʒɑːnz/ (1930–) a US artist, known for his paintings of flags (especially the US flag), numbers and targets, done using thick paint textures. With Robert *Rauschenberg he was partly responsible for the move away from *abstract expressionism to *pop art in the late 1950s.

ˌ**Amy 'Johnson**[1] /ˈdʒɒnsn; *AmE* ˈdʒɑːnsn/ (1903–41) an English pilot who became famous when she flew alone from London to Australia in 1930, winning a £10 000 prize. She then flew alone to Japan in 1931 and to South Africa in 1932. She was killed when her plane crashed off the south-east coast of England.

ˌ**Boris 'Johnson**[2] /ˌbɒrɪs ˈdʒɒnsn; *AmE* ˌbɔːrɪs ˈdʒɑːnsn/ (Alexander Boris de Pfeffel Johnson 1964–)

a British right-wing journalist who has worked for the *Daily Telegraph* newspaper and as editor for *The *Spectator* magazine. He is known for his strong views including his belief that Britain should not have closer links with the *European Union. He became a *Conservative *Member of Parliament in 2001. He became Vice-Chairman of the party in 2003 but was removed from the position in 2004 after there was a lot of publicity about a sexual affair he had.

ˌJack ˈJohnson³ /'dʒɒnsn; AmE 'dʒɑːnsn/ (1878–1946) the first *African-American boxer to become World Heavyweight Champion, when he beat Tommy Burns in 1908 in Sydney, Australia. Johnson was hated by many white people because he married three white women. He was accused of crimes and left America in 1912. He lost his championship to Jess Willard in 1915 in Havana, Cuba. He returned to the US in 1920 and was sent to prison for eight months.

ˌLyndon B ˈJohnson⁴ /ˌlɪndən biː 'dʒɒnsn; AmE 'dʒɑːnsn/ (Lyndon Baines Johnson 1908–73) the 36th US *President (1963–69) and a member of the *Democratic Party, often referred to informally as LBJ. He was a teacher who was elected to the US *Senate in 1948 and became the Senate Majority Leader in 1954. He was elected US Vice-President in 1960 and became President when John F *Kennedy was murdered. Johnson was elected again in 1964. As President, he introduced many social changes with his *Great Society programme, which gave special help to *African Americans and poor people. He decided not to stand again for election after increased protests about the *Vietnam War.

ˌMichael ˈJohnson⁵ /'dʒɒnsn; AmE 'dʒɑːnsn/ (1967–) a US runner who was a star of the 1996 Olympics in *Atlanta. He won gold medals in the 200-metres race (in which he established a new world record) and in the 400-metres race. He won four Olympic gold medals and retired in 2000.

ˌSamuel ˈJohnson⁶ /'dʒɒnsn; AmE 'dʒɑːnsn/ (1709–84) an English writer and critic, often referred to as **Dr Johnson**. He is remembered for his many clever remarks (mostly recorded by his friend James *Boswell, who wrote his life story) and his *Dictionary of the English Language* (1755). Among his other important books are *Rasselas* (1759), which he wrote in a week to pay his mother's funeral expenses, and *The Lives of the Poets* (1779–81). He was an important figure in 18th-century London, and started a club (called simply The Club) with friends such as David *Garrick, Edward *Gibbon and Joshua *Reynolds. He remained poor all his life, but his great reputation as a writer and humorous speaker brought him the honorary title of Doctor from *Oxford University in 1775. His house in Gough Square, London, is now a museum.

> 66 When a man is tired of London, he is tired of life; for there is in London all that life can afford. 99
> Samuel Johnson

ˌJohns ˈHopkins Uniˌversity /ˌdʒɒnz 'hɒpkɪnz; AmE ˌdʒɑːnz 'hɑːpkɪnz/ (also **Johns Hopkins**) a US university in *Baltimore, *Maryland. In 2004, it had about 5400 students. It was established in 1867 with money given by Johns Hopkins, a Baltimore businessman, and opened in 1876. He also gave $4.5 million for Johns Hopkins Hospital, which is part of the university's famous medical school, established in 1893.

ˌJohnson & ˈJohnson /'dʒɒnsn; AmE 'dʒɑːnsn/ a US company which is the world's largest producer of health-care products, with branches in 50 countries. Its many well-known products include *Band-Aid and *Tylenol.

The company was first established in 1886 by Robert Wood Johnson.

ˌJennifer ˈJohnston /'dʒɒnstən; AmE 'dʒɑːnstən/ (1930–) an Irish writer who writes novels about political and cultural problems in Ireland on both sides of the border. Her books include *The Captains and the Kings* (1972), *How Many Miles to Babylon* (1974), *The Old Jest* (1988), for which she won the *Whitbread Book of the Year prize, *The Gingerbread Woman* (2000), *This Is Not a Novel* (2002) and *Grace and Truth* (2005).

ˈJoint ˈChiefs of ˈStaff a US government committee which includes the Chiefs of Staff of the US Army, Navy and Air Force, and the Commandant of the US Marine Corps. It was established in 1942 and advises the US President, the *National Security Council and the Secretary of Defense. In 1989, General Colin *Powell became the first *African American to be the committee's chairperson (= person in charge of meetings).

ˌjoint resoˈlution n (in the US) a decision that has the approval of both the *Senate and the *House of Representatives. It becomes a law when signed by the US President or when Congress passes it if the President refuses to sign.

ˌJolly ˈRoger n [usually sing] (especially in the past) the flag of a pirate ship, showing a white skull and crossed bones on a black background. It is sometimes called the 'skull and crossbones'.

ˌAl ˈJolson /'dʒəʊlsn; AmE 'dʒoʊlsn/ (1886–1950) a US singer and actor, born in Lithuania. He performed on *Broadway in the 1920s and painted his face black to pretend to be an *African American. He was in the first sound film, *The *Jazz Singer*. Jolson sang with great emotion, and his most successful songs included *Swanee*, *Mammy*, *Sonny Boy* and *April Showers*. His story was told in two films, the *Jolson Story* (1946) and *Jolson Sings Again* (1949) with Larry Parks as Jolson.

ˌBobby ˈJones¹ /'dʒəʊnz; AmE 'dʒoʊnz/ (1902–71) a US golf player. He was the most successful amateur player (= one who does not accept money for playing) ever, and never became professional. He won the *US Open four times (1923, 1926 and 1929–30). In 1930 he became the only person ever to win the four major competitions, the Amateur and *Open contests in both the US and Britain. Jones also helped to establish the *US Masters Tournament at Augusta, *Georgia.

ˌBridget ˈJones² /ˌbrɪdʒɪt 'dʒəʊnz; AmE 'dʒoʊnz/ the main character of two best-selling comic novels by Helen Fielding, *Bridget Jones's Diary* (1996) and *Bridget Jones: The Edge of Reason* (1999), which were both made into popular films with Renée *Zellweger as Bridget Jones. She is a young, single woman in her thirties living in London who has problems with men and worries a lot about her appearance, work, lifestyle, etc.

ˌCasey ˈJones³ ⇨ CASEY JONES.

ˌIndiana ˈJones⁴ /ˌɪndiænə 'dʒəʊnz; AmE 'dʒoʊnz/ a character played by Harrison *Ford in three very successful adventure films directed by Steven *Spielberg. They were *Raiders of the Lost Ark* (1981), *Indiana Jones and the Temple of Doom* (1984), and *Indiana Jones and the Last Crusade* (1989). Jones is an archaeologist and regularly gets into exciting, dangerous and sometimes humorous situations.

ˌInigo ˈJones⁵ /ˌɪnɪgəʊ 'dʒəʊnz; AmE ˌɪnɪgoʊ 'dʒoʊnz/ (1573–1652) an English architect and stage designer who introduced *Palladianism (an Italian style) into Britain. Among his buildings are the Queen's House, *Greenwich, and the squares of *Covent Garden and Lincoln's Inn Fields in London. He also worked with Ben *Jonson to produce masques (= plays with music and dancing) for King *James I.

ˌJim **'Jones**[6] /'dʒəʊnz; AmE 'dʒoʊnz/ ⇨ JONESTOWN.

'John 'Paul **'Jones**[7] /'dʒəʊnz; AmE 'dʒoʊnz/ (1747–92) an American navy officer during the *American Revolution, originally from Scotland. He was known for attacking British ships near the English coast. On one occasion in 1799, when his own ship was badly damaged and he was ordered by the British commander to surrender, he replied, 'Sir, I have not yet begun to fight!' He then captured the British ship before his own ship sank. After the war, Jones served in the Russian navy and then lived in Paris until his death. He is buried in the US Navy church in *Annapolis, *Maryland.

ˌTom **'Jones**[8] /'dʒəʊnz; AmE 'dʒoʊnz/ (1940–) a Welsh popular singer with a strong voice. His hits have included *It's Not Unusual* (1966), *Green Green Grass of Home* (1968), *Kiss* (1988) and the album *Reload* (2000). In the 1970s he moved to the US where he performs regularly in clubs, though he remains popular in Britain.

'Jonestown /'dʒəʊnztaʊn; AmE 'dʒoʊnztaʊn/ an agricultural community in *Guyana established in 1977 for a US religious group called the People's Temple of the Disciples of Christ by its leader Jim Jones (1933–78). After US Congressman Leo Ryan and four people with him were murdered while visiting Jonestown in 1978, Jones ordered the members of his community to kill themselves with a drink that contained poison. All 913 died, including more than 240 children, and Jones shot himself.

ˌErica **'Jong** /'jɒŋ; AmE 'jɑːŋ/ (1942–) a US poet and author. She first became well known for her poetry with *Fruits and Vegetables* (1971). She then achieved international success with her novel *Fear of Flying* (1973), about the sexual life of the character Isadora Wing. Jong's more recent novels include *Inventing Memory* (1997) and *Sappho's Leap* (2003). She has also written about real people, including the novelist Henry *Miller in *The Devil at Large* (1993).

ˌBen **'Jonson** /'dʒɒnsn; AmE 'dʒɑːnsn/ (1572–1637) an English writer of plays and poetry. His most famous comedies are *Every Man in his Humour* (1598), *Volpone* (1606), *The *Alchemist* (1610), *Bartholomew Fair* (1614), in which the characters are always trying to trick each other to gain advantage for themselves, and *The Devil is an Ass* (1616). Jonson is regarded as the first English *Poet Laureate. He was a friend of *Shakespeare, who acted in some of his plays.

ˌJanis **'Joplin**[1] /'dʒɒplɪn; AmE 'dʒɑːplɪn/ (1943–70) a US singer popular in the 1960s, especially with *hippies. Her voice was harsh, and she was known for her wild performances on stage. Her best-known songs include *Piece of My Heart* (1968), *Try* (1969) and *Me and Bobby McGee* (1971). She was chosen for the Rock and Roll *Hall of Fame in 1995.

ˌScott **'Joplin**[2] /'dʒɒplɪn; AmE 'dʒɑːplɪn/ (1868–1917) a US piano player who wrote and helped to develop *ragtime music. His most popular tune was *Maple Leaf Rag* (1899). He also wrote the first African-American opera, *Treemonisha* (1911), but it was not successful. His music became popular again when some of his tunes, including *The Entertainer* (1902), were used in the film *The Sting* (1973).

ˌMichael **'Jordan** /'dʒɔːdn; AmE 'dʒɔːrdn/ (1963–) a former US *basketball player with the Chicago Bulls team, thought to be the richest athlete in the world. He was named the *Most Valuable Player of the *National Basketball Association four times (1988, 1991–2 and 1996) and was the only player to have scored the most points in a season eight times (1987–93 and 1996). Jordan was in US Olympic basketball teams that won gold medals in 1984 and 1992. He changed to playing *baseball for two years in the early 1990s, retired in

1999, is president of the Washington Wizards and came out of retirement to play basketball for them in 2001.

ˌChief **'Joseph** /'dʒəʊzɪf; AmE 'dʒoʊzɪf/ (c. 1840–1904) the leader of a group of *Nez Percé Native Americans. When in 1877 they were told to move from *Oregon to a reservation (= land given and protected by the US government) in *Idaho, Chief Joseph's group killed 20 white people and tried to escape to Canada. They travelled over 1000 miles/1600 kilometres, but the US Army caught them 30 miles/48 kilometres from Canada. Chief Joseph lived the rest of his life on a reservation in the state of *Washington.

ˌSt **'Joseph of Arima'thea** /ˌærɪməˈθiːə/ (1st century AD) a rich supporter of Jesus who appears in the Bible. He asks for Jesus's body after he dies and puts it in his own tomb. In traditional English stories he is said to have visited *Glastonbury in Somerset, bringing the *Holy Grail with him, and to have started the first English church. A thorn tree at Glastonbury is said to have grown from the stick that he carried.

'Joshua Fit the 'Battle of 'Jericho /'dʒɒʃʊə, 'dʒerɪkəʊ; AmE 'dʒɑːʃʊə, 'dʒerɪkoʊ/ an old *African-American *spiritual based on the story of Joshua in the Bible. 'Fit' represents a way of saying 'fought'. The song tells how Joshua captured the city of Jericho when he ordered the Israelites to blow trumpets until the walls fell down. It begins:

> 66 Joshua fit the battle of Jericho,
> Jericho, Jericho;
> Joshua fit the battle of Jericho,
> And the walls came tumbling down. 99

ˌTessa **'Jowell** / 'dʒaʊəl/ (1947–) a British *Labour politician. She became a *Member of Parliament in 1992. She was made *Secretary of State for Culture, Media and Sport in 2001 with responsibility for reforming the licensing and gambling laws and for deciding how the BBC is to be paid for in the future.

ˌJames **'Joyce** /ˌdʒeɪmz 'dʒɔɪs/ (1882–1941) an Irish author who is considered to be one of the greatest writers of the 20th century. He left Ireland in 1904 and spent the rest of his life abroad, in Trieste, Zürich and Paris. His novels *Ulysses* (1922) and *Finnegans Wake* (1939) introduced new ways of writing fiction, particularly the 'stream of consciousness' style, which presents a person's rapidly changing thoughts. He also made use of invented words and unusual sentence structures. His work was not well understood during his life and *Ulysses* was banned in Britain and the US until 1936 because it was considered offensive. Earlier books by him include *Dubliners* (1914) (a collection of short stories) and *A Portrait of the Artist as a Young Man* (1914–15), which reflects Joyce's own experiences of growing up in Dublin, and the play *Exiles* (1918).

'Joy Di,vision a British pop group formed in 1977. The group are known for their sad songs about loss and failure, including *Love Will Tear Us Apart* (1980). Their singer, Ian Curtis, killed himself in 1980, and the rest of the group continued under the name New Order.

'Florence 'Griffith **'Joyner** /'grɪfɪθ 'dʒɔɪnə(r)/ (1959–98) a US athlete, also known informally as 'Flo-Jo', who won three gold medals at the 1988 Olympic Games. She ran the fastest time ever in the 200 metres. Joyner was the sister-in-law of Jackie *Joyner-Kersee.

'Jackie **'Joyner-'Kersee** /'dʒɔɪnə 'kɜːsi; AmE 'dʒɔɪnər 'kɜːrsi/ (1962–) a US athlete who won three Olympic gold medals. Two were for the heptathlon (= an event involving seven separate contests) in 1988 (when she scored more points than any other competitor has ever done) and 1992. Her third gold medal was for the long jump in 1988. Her sister-in-law was Florence Griffith *Joyner.

JP /ˌdʒeɪ ˈpiː/ ⇨ JUSTICE OF THE PEACE.

JSC /ˌdʒeɪ es ˈsiː/ ⇨ LYNDON B JOHNSON SPACE CENTER.

Judge 'Dredd™ /ˌdʒʌdʒ ˈdred/ the main character in *2000 AD*, a British *comic first published in 1977. The stories are set in the future in Mega City One, and Judge Dredd is a member of the police who is also a judge of criminals and executes them. The *Hollywood film *Judge Dredd* (1997) was based on the character, which was played by Sylvester *Stallone.

Judge 'Judy /ˈdʒuːdi/ a popular US television programme in which Judy Sheindlin, who was a judge in the *New York family court from 1982 to 1996, gives decisions in cases which are presented to her by members of the public.

ju,dicial 'activism n [U] (in the US legal system) the idea that the *Supreme Court or other courts can approve new laws which do not follow the exact words of the American *Constitution but are based on changes in the nation's values and needs. This is also called a 'broad construction' of the Constitution. Judicial activism is the opposite of *judicial restraint.

the Ju,dicial Com'mittee a committee of the British *Privy Council which acts as the highest court of appeal for the review of cases referred from courts in certain Commonwealth countries and British overseas territories.

ju,dicial re'straint n [U] (in the US legal system) the idea that judges of the Supreme Court or other courts should not try to change laws if they are consistent with the words of the American *Constitution. This is also called a 'narrow construction' of the Constitution. Judicial restraint is the opposite of *judicial activism.

ju,dicial re'view n [U] (in the US legal system) the power of the US Supreme Court to decide if a state or national law or action is consistent with the American *Constitution. If the court states that a law or action is 'unconstitutional', it becomes illegal. See also CHECKS AND BALANCES.

the 'Juilliard 'School of 'Music /ˈdʒuːliɑːd; AmE ˈdʒuːliɑːrd/ a US college established in 1905 for the study of classical music. It is now based at the *Lincoln Center for the Performing Arts, New York.

Julius 'Caesar /ˌdʒuːliəs ˈsiːzə(r)/ (100–44 BC) the best-known of all the ancient Roman leaders, and the first one to land in Britain with an army. He did this twice, in 55 and 54 BC, although Britain did not become part of the Roman Empire until nearly a hundred years later.

Julius 'Caesar /ˌdʒuːliəs ˈsiːzə(r)/ a play written by William *Shakespeare in 1599. It is set mainly in Rome in AD 44, and tells how Brutus, Cassius and other Romans plan to kill Caesar because they think he wants to become king (rather than being the head of the republic). Caesar fails to listen to warnings to 'beware the Ides of March' (= 15 March) and is murdered. Later Mark Antony, in a skilful speech at Caesar's funeral, turns the Roman people against Brutus and Cassius, and a war begins. The army of Antony wins, and Brutus and Cassius kill themselves.

jungle n [U] a style of dance music that developed in London in the early 1990s. It is a form of *house, and relies on very fast electronic drum beats and a strong bass part. See also DRUM 'N' BASS.

The 'Jungle Book a collection of short stories for children by Rudyard *Kipling, published in 1894 and still popular today. They are about Mowgli, a young boy who grows up in the jungle and is taught how to survive by animals such as Mother Wolf, Baloo the bear and Bagheera the panther (= a large member of the cat family). *The Second Jungle Book* followed in 1895. The books have been made into several films, including the Walt *Disney musical cartoon in 1967 and a film with Jason Scott Lee in 1994.

junior 'college n a US college for two years of study instead of the usual four years. Students receive an 'associate degree' when they successfully complete their studies. They can then move on to a four-year college or university for a *bachelor's degree. Junior colleges help many students who could not otherwise go to college, because they are cheaper than other colleges and accept students with fewer qualifications.

junior 'high school (also ,junior 'high) n (in the US) a school between the levels of *elementary school and *high school. A junior high school is linked to a particular high school. If the high school has the usual four years of education, the junior high school will have two years, called seventh and eighth grades. In some systems each of the two offer three years of education, so the junior high school includes a ninth grade.

junior school n [C, U] (in Britain) a *state school for children aged between 7 and 11. Compare ELEMENTARY SCHOOL, INFANT SCHOOL.

junior 'varsity n (abbr **JV**) a sports team at a US school, college or university for players who are younger than the school's regular *varsity(2) team. This is usually in American football and *basketball. The junior varsity competes against similar teams from other schools. ⇨ note at FOOTBALL — AMERICAN STYLE.

▶ juries

Under the *legal system of England and Wales, and also that of Scotland, a person accused of a serious crime who pleads 'not guilty' to the crime will be **tried** by a jury. Juries also hear some civil cases (= disagreements between people about their rights) and decide whether a person is 'liable' (= required by law to do or pay something) or 'not liable'. In the US juries are also used in both criminal and civil cases, though the rules vary from state to state.

In Britain **jurors** (= jury members) are selected at random for each trial from lists of adults who have the right to vote. They must be between the ages of 18 and 70 and have lived in Britain for at least five years. Members of the armed forces, the legal profession and the police force are not allowed to **sit on** juries. Anybody **called for jury service** usually has to attend court for about two weeks, although some cases may go on for much longer. The court pays only their expenses and if they have a job they are paid as normal by their employer. In England and Wales 12 people sit on a jury, in Scotland 15. A larger number of people are asked to attend court and the final jury is selected at random from among them. Lawyers representing either side in a case have the right to object to a particular person being on the jury.

After the jury has heard the evidence presented by both sides, it **retires** to the **jury room**, a private room, to discuss the case. When all members of the jury agree they **return their verdict**, go back into court and say whether the accused is **guilty** or **not guilty**. In Scotland they can also return a verdict of **not proven**, which means that guilt in the case has not been proved and the accused can go free. The verdict is announced by the **foreman** (= the person chosen by the jury as their leader). Sometimes the jury cannot all agree and the judge may accept a **majority verdict**, provided that no more than two members of the jury disagree. If no verdict is reached the trial is abandoned and started again with a different jury. It is not the responsibility of the jury to decide *punishment, though in certain civil cases they may decide how much compensation should be paid.

In the US most juries have 12 members, though some have only six. Otherwise the system is very similar to that in England and Wales. When people are called for **jury duty** they must go, but people who cannot leave their jobs or homes can be excused. Before a trial begins lawyers ask questions to see if jurors are impartial, i.e. do not have strong opinions that would prevent them making a decision based on the facts. Lawyers can **challenge for cause**, if they can give the judge a good reason why somebody should not be a juror. They also have a number of **peremptory challenges** which means they can object to somebody without giving a reason. In some trials it can be difficult to find 12 people who are impartial, especially if a case has received a lot of publicity. Lawyers sometimes do research to find out what kind of person is most likely to support their side, and use challenges to keep other people off the jury. In a criminal trial the jury decides whether the accused person is **guilty** or **innocent**, but does not decide on a punishment. In a civil trial they may decide how much money should be paid in compensation. A majority decision is usually acceptable.

,**Justice of the 'Peace** *n* (*abbr* **JP**) (*pl* **Justices of the Peace**) a person who judges less serious cases in a local court. In England and Wales the title is given to a magistrate, while in Scotland it is given to a judge in a district court. In the US, Justices of the Peace are local judges who deal with minor legal matters, send cases to higher courts of law, and can also perform marriages. ⇨ note at LEGAL SYSTEM.

,**Just Say 'No** a slogan first used in health campaigns against illegal drugs in Britain and the US in the 1980s, which is now common in campaigns against many different things. See also WAR ON DRUGS.

,**Just 'So Stories** a collection of stories and poems for children by Rudyard *Kipling, published in 1902. They give funny explanations for the features of different animals, and have titles such as 'How the Elephant got his Trunk' and 'How the Camel got his Hump'.

'**juvenile ,court** (*BrE also* '**youth court**) *n* a court of law for the trials of young people under the age of 18. It uses special rules which are not as severe as those in adult courts.

JV /,dʒeɪ 'viː/ ⇨ JUNIOR VARSITY.

K k

'kaffeeklatsch /'kæfeɪklætʃ/ *n* (*AmE*) a social event at which people meet for coffee and informal conversation.

Sarah 'Kane /'keɪn/ (1971–1999) a British writer for the theatre whose controversial plays about death, sex, violence and mental illness include *Blasted* (1995), *Phaedra's Love* (1996) and *Cleansed* (1998). Her despairing view of the world led her to kill herself at a young age.

'Kansas /'kænzəs/ a US state in the *Middle West, the most central of all the states. It forms part of the *Great Plains and suffered badly during the *Dust Bowl years. Its popular name is the Sunflower State. The capital city is Topeka, and the largest cities are Wichita, Overland Park and *Kansas City(2). Kansas was part of the *Louisiana Purchase and became a state in 1861. Its main products include wheat, corn, cattle, oil, salt and helium (= a gas used to fill balloons and to freeze things). See also KANSAS-NEBRASKA ACT.

Kansas 'City /,kænzəs/ **1** the largest city in the US state of *Missouri. It is connected to Kansas City, *Kansas and was established at the beginning of the *Santa Fe Trail. It is now a major industrial centre for the production of steel and vehicles. In the late 1920s, Kansas City became a centre for *jazz. 'Count' *Basie and 'Duke' *Ellington both began their careers there. **2** a city in eastern *Kansas. It is connected to Kansas City, *Missouri, but is only one third its large. The two cities are situated where the Missouri River and Kansas River meet. This smaller city was originally formed from eight separate towns.

the Kansas-Ne'braska Act /,kænzəs nə'bræskə/ a law passed by the US Congress in 1854 which was one of the causes of the *Civil War. It replaced the *Missouri Compromise and established the Kansas Territory and the Nebraska Territory as regions which could vote on whether to have slaves or not. This caused people to come from both the South and the North to fight about the issue, until 'bleeding Kansas' had two rival governments.

Kao'pectate™ /,keɪəʊ'pekteɪt; *AmE* ,keɪoʊ'pekteɪt/ a well-known US medicine for the treatment of diarrhoea (= an illness in which waste matter is emptied from the bowels frequently and in liquid form).

'Kaplan /'kæplən/ ⇨ STANLEY KAPLAN.

Boris 'Karloff /'kɑːlɒf; *AmE* 'kɑːrlɑːf/ (1887–1969) an English actor who began his career in silent films but became famous for appearing in many US horror films, especially as the monster in *Frankenstein.

Casey 'Kasem /,keɪsi 'keɪsəm/ (1932–) a US broadcaster who has presented a popular music programme, *Casey's Top 40*, on national radio every week since 1971. He also presents other shows, including *Casey's Countdown* and *Casey's Hot 20*, and has provided the voices for many characters in radio and television advertisements and cartoons, including Shaggy in *Scooby Doo.

Elia Ka'zan /,iːljə kə'zæn/ (1909–2003) a US director of films and plays, born in Turkey of Greek parents. He also wrote and produced films. He helped to start the *Actors' Studio in New York and directed plays there, including *A *Streetcar Named Desire* (1947) and *Death of a Salesman* (1949). He won *Oscars for *Gentleman's Agreement* (1947) and *On the Waterfront* (1954) and

received a special Oscar in 1999. His other films include *A Streetcar Named Desire* (1951) and *East of Eden* (1955).

Edmund 'Kean /'kiːn/ (*c.* 1789–1833) an English actor who was famous for playing the parts of evil characters in *Shakespeare plays, such as *Richard III, *Shylock and Iago in *Othello.

Buster 'Keaton[1] /,bʌstə 'kiːtn; *AmE* ,bʌstər/ (1895–1966) one of the greatest US comic actors in silent films. His popular name was 'the Great Stoneface' because his expression never changed. His best-known films include *The Navigator* (1924) and *The General* (1926). He received a special *Oscar in 1959.

Di,ane 'Keaton[2] /'kiːtn/ (1946–) a US actor, producer and director who won an *Oscar for *Annie Hall* (1977), directed by Woody *Allen. Keaton and Allen made other films together, including *Play It Again, Sam* (1972), *Sleeper* (1973) and *Manhattan* (1979). Among her other films are *The Godfather* (1972), *Looking for Mr Goodbar* (1977), *Reds* (1981) and *Something's Gotta Give* (2003).

John 'Keats /'kiːts/ (1795–1821) an English poet. He is considered to be one of the greatest figures of the *Romantic Movement and was a friend of *Shelley[2], *Hazlitt and *Wordsworth. His best-known poems include *Ode on a Grecian Urn*, *Ode to a Nightingale*, *To Autumn* and La *Belle Dame Sans Merci*, all written in 1819. Common themes in his poems are the beauty of nature and the short time available for human life and happiness. He died in Rome of tuberculosis (= a disease of the lungs), aged only 26. His *Letters* were published in 1848.

Keds™ /kedz/ a popular US make of light, soft shoes with a rubber sole and a top usually made of cotton cloth.

'Keebler™ /'kiːblə(r)/ a US company that makes cookies and crackers (= thin, dry biscuits, typically eaten with cheese). Keebler biscuits were first made in 1853.

'Keep 'Britain 'Tidy a campaign run by the ENCAMS (Environmental Campaigns) charity to persuade people not to leave rubbish in public places. The phrase is widely used on signs, etc. put up around the country.

Garrison 'Keillor /,gærɪsn 'kiːlə(r)/ (1942–) a humorous US writer and broadcaster. His popular weekly radio programme, *A Prairie Home Companion*, which began in 1974, includes *News From Lake Wobegon*, an imaginary town in *Minnesota. It is broadcast in the UK and Ireland as well as in the US. Keillor's books include *Lake Wobegon Days* (1985), *We Are Still Married* (1989), *Home Grown Democrat* (2003) and a book for children, *The Old Man Who Loved Cheese* (1996).

> **66** Welcome to Lake Wobegon, where all the women are strong, all the men are good-looking and all the children are above average. **99**
> *News from Lake Wobegon*

Helen 'Keller /'kelə(r)/ (1880–1968) a US author and public speaker who became blind and deaf at the age of 19 months. Anne Sullivan became her teacher in 1887 and taught her to read, write, use sign language and speak. Keller received a degree from Radcliffe College in 1904 and spent the rest of her life encouraging others with difficulties like hers to overcome them. Her books include *The Story of My Life* (1902) and *Out of the Dark* (1913). She joined the *IWW in 1912 and was one of the first members of the *American Civil Liberties Union. A play about her life, *The Miracle Worker*, was made into a film/movie three times.

the ˌKellogg 'Pact /ˌkelɒg; *AmE* ˌkelɑ:g/ (*also* **the Kellogg-Briand Pact**) /ˌkelɒg ˈbri:ɒnd; *AmE* ˌkelɑ:g ˈbri:ɑ:nd/ an international agreement (1928) that nations would not use war to settle disputes. It was prepared by US Secretary of State Frank B Kellogg (1856–1937) and French Foreign Minister Aristide Briand (1862–1932), and signed in Paris by 15 nations, and then later by 62 others. The agreement failed because it lacked the power to prevent wars.

'Kellogg's™ /ˈkelɒgz; *AmE* ˈkelɑ:gz/ a large US company that sells its many breakfast cereals around the world. They include Kellogg's Corn Flakes, Rice Krispies, All Bran, Apple Jacks, Crunchy Nut Cornflakes and Cocoa Frosted Flakes. Other Kellogg's products include Pop Tarts and Eggo. The company was started in 1906 by Will Keith Kellogg (1860–1951) in Battle Creek, *Michigan, and the main office is still there.

ˌEmmett 'Kelly[1] /ˌemət ˈkeli/ (1898–1979) the best-known US clown (= a person with comic clothes and a painted face who does funny things). Kelly became famous as the character Weary Willie with the Ringling Brothers and Barnum and Bailey Circuses (1942–56). Willie's face was very sad, and everything seemed to defeat him.

ˌGene 'Kelly[2] /ˈkeli/ (1912–96) a US film actor, dancer and singer. He became a star in the *Broadway musical show *Pal Joey* (1940). His film successes included *On the Town* (1949), *An American in Paris* (1951) and *Singin' in the Rain*. Kelly later directed films, including *Hello, Dolly!* (1969). He received a special *Oscar in 1951.

ˌGrace 'Kelly[3] /ˈkeli/ (1928–82) a US film star from a rich Irish-American family in *Philadelphia who became Princess Grace of Monaco when she married in 1956. She received an *Oscar for *The Country Girl* (1954), and her other films included *High Noon*, *Rear Window* (1954) and *High Society* (1956).

ˌRuth 'Kelly[4] /ˈkeli/ (1968–) a British Labour politician who became a *Member of Parliament in 1997. She was Economic Secretary to the *Treasury and then Financial Secretary before becoming *Education Secretary in 2004.

ˌJames 'Kelman /ˈkelmən/ (1946–) a Scottish writer whose books include *Greyhound for Breakfast* (1987), *A Disaffection* (1989) and *How late it was, how late* (1994), for which he won the *Booker Prize.

the ˌKelmscott 'Press /ˌkelmskɒt; *AmE* ˌkelmskɑ:t/ a printing business (1890–98) run by William *Morris at Hammersmith, London, England, which produced fine editions of his own books and other works. *The Kelmscott Chaucer*, an edition of the *Canterbury Tales* with illustrations by *Burne-Jones, is considered to be one of the most beautiful books ever produced. Kelmscott was the name of the manor house in *Gloucestershire where Morris lived for many years.

ˌFanny 'Kemble /ˌfæni ˈkembl/ (1809–93) an English actor who was famous for playing parts in Shakespeare plays. She was also known for her opposition to *slavery in the US, where she lived for a time as the wife of a US farmer. Her aunt was Mrs *Siddons.

ˌKendal 'mint cake /ˌkendl/ *n* [U] a sweet flavoured with mint and sold in hard, flat bars. It is traditional to eat it when walking or climbing in the countryside. It is made in Kendal, *Cumbria.

ˌKenilworth 'Castle /ˌkenɪlwɜ:θ; *AmE* ˌkenɪlwɜ:rθ/ a castle near Coventry, England. It was owned by several kings, and the Earl of *Leicester entertained *Elizabeth I there in 1575. Parts of the castle were pulled down by Oliver *Cromwell's soldiers to sell as building materials.

'Kenmore™ /ˈkenmɔ:(r)/ a US product name for a range of popular household appliances, including refrigerators and washing machines.

'Kennedy[1] /ˈkenədi/ ⇨ JFK(2).

A L Kennedy[2] /ˌeɪ el ˈkenədi/ (Alison Louise Kennedy 1965–) a Scottish writer. Her books include *So I Am Glad* (1995) and *On Bullfighting* (1999).

ˌCharles 'Kennedy[3] /ˈkenədi/ (1959–) a British politician, born in Scotland, who became a *Member of Parliament in 1983 as the youngest person in the House of Commons. He became the leader of the *Liberal Democratic Party in 1999.

ˌEdward 'Kennedy[4] /ˈkenədi/ (1932–) a US Senator from *Massachusetts since 1962, informally called Ted or Teddy, who is the younger brother of John F *Kennedy and Robert *Kennedy. He is a *Democrat with liberal views and for many years has supported a national health programme. His career was damaged when he had an accident in his car which killed his female passenger. In 1980, he tried but failed to be chosen as the Democrats' candidate for US President.

ˌJackie 'Kennedy[5] /ˈkenədi/ (*also* Jackie **Onassis**) (1929–94) the wife of President John F *Kennedy. She was born Jacqueline Bouvier and married him in 1953. She is remembered as an elegant US *First Lady and is admired by Americans for her courage after her husband was murdered. Many, however, did not approve of her marriage to the Greek businessman Aristotle Onassis (1968–75). After his death she lived a very private life in New York, where she worked for a publishing company.

ˌJohn F 'Kennedy[6] /ˈkenədi/ (John Fitzgerald Kennedy 1917–63) the 35th US *President (1961–3). He was the country's youngest president and the first *Roman Catholic ever to be elected. He was also known informally as Jack Kennedy and JFK. His wife was Jackie *Kennedy. He won a medal for courage during *World War I, and was elected to the US House of Representatives (1947–53) and then to the US Senate (1952–60).

  Kennedy's greatest success as President was in dealing with the *Cuban missile crisis and his worst failure was over the *Bay of Pigs incident. He worked with his brother, US Attorney General Robert *Kennedy, to support the *civil rights movement. He was murdered in *Dallas, probably by Lee Harvey *Oswald, in one of the most shocking events in US history. Some people believe that others were responsible for his murder, but nothing has ever been definitely proved. Kennedy's book, *Profiles in Courage* (1956), won a *Pulitzer Prize. See also WARREN[1].

> 66 And so, my fellow Americans: ask not what your country can do for you – ask what you can do for your country. 99
> John F Kennedy

ˌJoseph 'Kennedy[7] /ˈkenədi/ (1888–1969) the father of US President John F *Kennedy. He was a rich businessman who became head of the *Securities and Exchange Commission (1934–5) and later the US Ambassador to Britain (1937–40). He and his wife Rose had nine children. The oldest son, Joe, was killed in *World War II, and Kennedy successfully encouraged his other sons (John, Robert and Edward) to become politicians.

,Ludovic '**Kennedy**[8] /ˌluːdəvɪk ˈkenədi/ (1919–) a Scottish television presenter and author. In the 1960s he presented a number of news and current affairs programmes, including *Panorama and This Week. He is well known for investigating the cases of people thought to have been wrongly put in prison, and also for his support for euthanasia (= allowing people the right to die when they want to do so because of serious illness, etc.). He was made a *knight in 1994.

,Nigel '**Kennedy**[9] /ˈkenədi/ (1959–) an English classical musician who plays the violin. He is well known for his unusual clothes and style of life. His recordings have been very successful, especially one of Vivaldi's *Four Seasons*. In 1992 he announced that he would not perform in public again, but he later changed his mind and is now performing again, preferring to call himself simply Kennedy.

,Robert F '**Kennedy**[10] /ˈkenədi/ (Robert Francis Kennedy 1925–68) a US Attorney General (1961–4) appointed by his elder brother, President John F *Kennedy. He was also informally called Bobby Kennedy or RFK. He strongly supported the *civil rights movement and better conditions for poor people. After his brother was murdered, Kennedy remained Attorney General under President *Johnson[4] until he was elected in 1964 to the US Senate. He wanted to be the Democratic candidate for President in 1968, but was murdered by Sirhan *Sirhan on the day he won the California *primary election.

the '**Kennedy** ˌ**Center** /ˈkenədi/ (*also formal* the **John F Kennedy Center for the Performing Arts**) a US national cultural centre in Washington, DC, on the *Potomac River near the *Lincoln Memorial. It was opened in 1971 as a 'living memorial' to President *Kennedy. The main theatres are the Concert Hall, the Opera House and the Eisenhower Theater. Since 1978, Kennedy Center Honors have been awarded for special artistic achievements.

the '**Kennel Club** an organization in London, England, that holds the official records relating to dog breeding in Britain. The records prove that particular dogs are 'pure' breeds, i.e. have the right features for their breed and are descended from a line of similar animals. The Kennel Club also organizes *Crufts dog show. The *American Kennel Club is a similar organization in the US.

'**Kensington** /ˈkenzɪŋtən/ a district of south-west London, England, part of the *borough of Kensington and *Chelsea. It contains many of London's large museums, including the *Victoria and Albert Museum, the *Natural History Museum and the *Science Museum. It also contains the *Commonwealth Institute and *Imperial College London. Kensington has particular associations with the royal family, and was made a 'royal borough' by Queen *Victoria, who was born in *Kensington Palace. South Kensington is a fashionable and expensive area to live in.

,**Kensington** '**Gardens** /ˌkenzɪŋtən/ a park in south-west London, England, next to *Hyde Park(1). It was formerly the garden of *Kensington Palace, and was opened to the public in the 1830s. It contains the *Albert Memorial and a famous statue of *Peter Pan.

,**Kensington** '**Palace** /ˌkenzɪŋtən/ a 17th-century royal palace next to *Kensington Gardens in south-west London, England, designed partly by Christopher *Wren. Queen *Victoria was born there in 1819 and it has since been the main home for many other members of the royal family including Princess *Diana. Parts of it are open to the public.

Kensington Palace

Kent[1] /kent/ a county in south-east England. Its traditional products are fruit and hops (= plants used in making beer), and it is known as the 'Garden of England'. Its administrative centre is Maidstone. See also MAN OF KENT.

,Clark '**Kent**[2] /ˈkent/ ⇨ SUPERMAN.

the ˌDuke of '**Kent**[3] /ˈkent/ (1935–) a British prince, the grandson of King *George V. His brother is Prince Michael of *Kent and his sister is Princess Alexandra. He is the second Duke of Kent: the first duke was his father George (1902–42), who was killed in a plane crash in *World War II.

Prince ˌ**Michael of** '**Kent**[4] /ˈkent/ (1942–) a British prince, the grandson of King *George V. His brother is the Duke of *Kent and his sister is Princess Alexandra. He married a *Roman Catholic, Marie-Christine Freiin von Reibnitz, who is known as Princess Michael of Kent. Because of his wife's religion Prince Michael lost the right to be one of the people who could become king of England, although their children, Lord Frederick Windsor (1979–) and Lady Gabriella Windsor (1981–), have not.

,William '**Kent**[5] /ˈkent/ (c. 1685–1748) an English painter and architect who also designed gardens and the insides of houses. He studied in Rome and helped to introduce *Palladianism (= an Italian style of architecture) to Britain. Many public buildings in London were designed by him, including the *Treasury building. He is now best remembered for the gardens he designed. In them he introduced a more natural and informal style and has been described as the father of modern gardening. His interior designs can be seen at *Burlington House and at Holkham Hall, near *Norwich. Compare BROWN[2].

'**Kent** '**State Uni**'**versity** /ˈkent/ (*also informal* **Kent State**) a US university in the town of Kent, *Ohio. It is mainly remembered for an incident there on 4 May 1970, when four students were shot and killed and nine wounded by members of the Ohio *National Guard as they protested against the *Vietnam War. As a result many people turned against the *Nixon government and the *Vietnam war.

Ken'**tucky** /kenˈtʌki/ a south-eastern US state, also known as the Bluegrass State. The capital city is Frankfort, and the largest city is Lexington-Fayette. It became a state in 1792. It produces agricultural products, coal and whiskey and is well known for breeding horses for racing. Its tourist attractions include the place where Abraham *Lincoln was born (near the village of Hodgenville) and Mammoth Cave National Park, a *World Heritage Site since 1981.

Kenˌ**tucky** '**Derby** /kenˌtʌki/ the most famous US horse-racing event. It is for three-year-olds and one of the *triple crown races, run every year on the first Saturday in May at Churchill Downs in *Louisville, *Kentucky. The race is 1.25 miles/2 kilometres long. The Kentucky Derby was begun in 1875 by Colonel M Lewis

K

Clark and has become part of a social event that lasts several days. Compare DERBY².

Ken,tucky Fried 'Chicken™ /ken,tʌki/ (*also* **KFC**) any of a group of US 'fast food' restaurants selling pieces of specially fried chicken and other dishes. Their food is advertised as being 'finger lickin' good'. Colonel Harland D Sanders opened the first restaurant in 1952 and the KFC company, which is based in *Louisville, Kentucky, has more than 11000 restaurants in the US and other countries.

,Kenwood 'House /,kenwʊd/ a large 18th-century house in *Hampstead, north-west London, England, designed partly by Robert *Adam. It is open to the public and is known for its fine collection of pictures and its large park, where outdoor concerts are held.

'Kenya /'kenjə/ a country in East Africa which has been described as 'the cradle of humanity' because some of the earliest evidence of human ancestors was found there. Its capital city is Nairobi and its official languages are English and Swahili. It was a British colony between 1895 and 1964 and is now a member of the *Commonwealth. Major exports include tea and coffee, and it is popular with British and American tourists because of its natural beauty and its wildlife.
▶ **'Kenyan** /'kenjən/ *adj, n*.

'Kermit /'kɜːmɪt; *AmE* 'kɜːrmɪt/ (*also* **Kermit the Frog**) one of the main puppet characters in *The *Muppet Show*. Kermit is a green frog who presents the show and is fond of making jokes.

Je,rome 'Kern /'kɜːn; *AmE* 'kɜːrn/ (1885–1945) a US writer of many popular songs, especially for *Broadway musical shows and *Hollywood films. His best-known show was *Show Boat*, which included the song *Ol' Man River*. Kern won an *Oscar for the song *The Last Time I Saw Paris* in the film *Lady Be Good* (1941). His other songs include *Look for the Silver Lining* (1920) and *Smoke Gets in Your Eyes* (1933). Ira Gershwin and Oscar *Hammerstein were among the many people who wrote the words for Kern's songs. See also GERSHWIN.

,Jack 'Kerouac /'keruæk/ (1922–69) a US writer of novels, the son of French-Canadian parents, who has been called 'the spokesman for the *beat generation' of the 1950s. His best-known novel is *On the Road* (1957), about a journey across America by a young person who is opposed to traditional American values. His other novels include *The Town and the City* (1950), *The Subterraneans* (1958) and *Big Sur* (1962). He also wrote poetry.

,John F 'Kerry /'keri/ (John Forbes Kerry 1943–) a US *Senator from *Massachusetts since 1985. He was chosen as the *Democratic Party's candidate in the election for President in 2004. Kerry served in the US Navy from 1966 to 1970 and won medals for courage in the *Vietnam War. He later joined the protests against the war.

'ketchup (*also BrE* **tomato sauce, tomato ketchup,** *especially AmE old-fashioned* **catsup**) *n* [U] a thick red sauce made with tomatoes, used cold to flavour food. People sometimes use the word in a humorous way to refer to artificial blood in films, etc.

,Jack Ke'vorkian /kə'vɔːkiən; *AmE* kə'vɔːrkiən/ (1928–) a US doctor who is famous for his support for people's 'right to die'. Between 1990 and 1998 he helped over 100 people to kill themselves, using one of his 'assisted-suicide machines'. The state of *Michigan put Kevorkian on trial many times without success but in 1999 he was found guilty of murder and was sent to prison.

,Kew 'Gardens /,kjuː/ a park in west London, England, which contains a large collection of plants, trees, etc.

from all over the world and is a major centre for the study of plants. Its official name is the Royal Botanic Gardens and it was opened to the public in 1840 by Queen *Victoria. It is very popular with tourists and local people, and among its famous buildings are the Chinese Pagoda (= a tall tower) and several very large greenhouses, including the Palm House (opened in 1848). Kew Gardens became a *World Heritage Site in 2003. See also BANKS².

'Kewpie doll™ /'kjuːpi/ (*also* **Kewpie**) *n* a US make of child's doll with a fat, happy face, big eyes and a curl of hair on the top of its head. The name comes from Cupid, the god of love. Kewpie dolls were in the past often given as prizes for games of skill at *fairs. They were first sold in 1913.

,Key lime 'pie /,kiː/ *n* [C, U] a light US pie made with the juice and skin of limes (= green fruit like lemons). It also contains sugar, beaten egg whites and sweet condensed (= thick) milk. The pie was first made in *Key West, *Florida, which has a well-known shop called The Key West Key Lime Shoppe.

'John 'Maynard 'Keynes /'meɪnɑːd 'keɪnz; *AmE* 'meɪnɑːrd/ (1883–1946) an English economist whose ideas have had a great influence on modern politics and economics. He argued that governments could deal with the problem of a failing economy by spending more money on public projects such as roads, schools, etc. This was popular until the 1980s when it was argued that such a policy leads to inflation. Keynes also represented Britain in economic conferences after the two World Wars and helped to establish the *International Monetary Fund. He was a leading member of the *Bloomsbury Group and was made a *lord in 1942.
▶ **Keynesian** *n, adj* of or relating to the ideas of Keynes, especially regarding government control of a country's economy through money and taxes: *Keynesian economics*.

the ,Keystone 'Kops /,kiːstəʊn 'kɒps; *AmE* ,kiːstoʊn 'kɑːps/ a team of actors who appeared as a group of comic police officers in a series of US silent films (1912–20) produced by Mack *Sennett and his Keystone Comedy Company. The leader was played by Ford Sterling, and one of the other Kops was Fatty *Arbuckle. They had long and funny scenes in which they chased criminals or wrongly chased innocent citizens, often in cars.

,Key 'West /,kiː 'west/ the last island and town of the *Florida Keys. It is the most southern US town and is closer to Havana, Cuba, than to *Miami. Ernest *Hemingway and John James *Audubon lived there, and President *Truman had a 'summer White House' on Key West for holidays. People who live there are called 'conchs' after the local shellfish. Many artists live there.

KFC /,keɪ ef 'siː/ ⇨ KENTUCKY FRIED CHICKEN.

KG /,keɪ 'dʒiː/ (in Britain) the abbreviation for Knight of the *Order of the Garter: *Sir Thomas Bell KG*.

,Captain 'Kidd /'kɪd/ (William Kidd *c.* 1645–1701) a Scottish sea captain and pirate (= person on a ship who attacks and robs other ships). He was captured and hanged in London after attacking a number of ships in the Indian Ocean. It is said that he hid a large amount of stolen treasure which has never been found.

'Kidderminster /'kɪdəmɪnstə(r); *AmE* 'kɪdərmɪnstər/ a town in the county of *Worcestershire, England. It is famous for producing carpets and used to produce a type of carpet with a pattern in two colours that could be turned over when one side was worn. Today it produces *Axminster and *Wilton carpets.

Ni,cole 'Kidman /nɪ,kəʊl 'kɪdmən; *AmE* nɪ,koʊl/ (1967–) a *Hollywood actor, born in Australia. She received an *Oscar for *The Hours* (2002) and her other films include *Batman Forever* (1995), *Moulin Rouge* (2001) and *Cold Mountain* (2003).

'Kidnapped a novel (1886) by Robert Louis *Stevenson. It is about the adventures of David Balfour, a young man who is kidnapped (= taken away by force) from his home in Scotland and made to work as a slave. He escapes with the help of Alan Breck, a *Jacobite.

'Kilner jar™ /'kɪlnə; *AmE* 'kɪlnər/ *n* (*BrE*) a type of large jar which can be sealed with a rubber ring and is used for preserving fruit, etc. Compare MASON JAR.

'Kilroy was here /'kɪlrɔɪ/ a phrase that people sometimes write on walls, etc. for no obvious reason. It was first used in *World War II, but it is not known who Kilroy was, or even if he was a real person.

kilt /kɪlt/ a form of Scottish dress traditionally worn by men. It is a pleated skirt made of *tartan that reaches to the knees and is now mostly worn only on formal occasions, such as weddings.

Francis 'Kilvert /'kɪlvət; *AmE* 'kɪlvərt/ (1840–79) a Welsh priest known for his diary, which describes country life in Wales in the 1870s.

Kim /kɪm/ a novel (1901) by Rudyard *Kipling. It is about the adventures of a young boy who becomes a spy for the British in India.

the King[1] a popular nickname for the singer Elvis *Presley who was named the King of Rock and Roll in the 1950s.

B B 'King[2] /ˌbiː biː 'kɪŋ/ (Riley B King 1925–) an American *blues singer who plays the guitar. His early hits included *Three O'Clock Blues* (1950). He was an important influence on *rock and roll music. He won *Emmy awards for *The Thrill is Gone* (1970) and the album *Blues 'n' Jazz* (1983). In 1997 he recorded the album *Deuces Wild* with the *Rolling Stones, Eric *Clapton, Willie *Nelson and others and in 2000 made *Riding with the King* with Clapton.

'Billie 'Jean 'King[3] /'kɪŋ/ (1943–) a US tennis player considered as one of the greatest women athletes ever. She won the Women's Singles Championship at *Wimbledon six times (1966–8, 1972–3 and 1975) and 20 Wimbledon championships in all, more than any other player. She also won the *US Open(2) four times (1967, 1971–2 and 1974). King is a strong supporter of women's interests in tennis and other sports.

Larry 'King[4] /'kɪŋ/ (1933–) a US broadcaster who presents *Larry King Live*, a television talk show on *CNN. His guests include important politicians and other well-known people in the news.

'Martin 'Luther 'King[5] /'luːθə 'kɪŋ; *AmE* 'luːθər/ (1929–68) the most important leader of the US *civil rights movement. King was an *African American Baptist minister who led a series of peaceful campaigns against *segregation in the southern states. In 1957 he established the *Southern Christian Leadership Conference. In 1963 he led about 250 000 people on a protest march to Washington, DC, where he made his famous 'I have a dream' speech at the *Lincoln Memorial. He was awarded the *Nobel Prize for peace in 1964. He was murdered four years later in *Memphis, *Tennessee, by Earl Ray. King's wife, Coretta Scott King (1927–) has continued his work. His birthday, 15 January, is an official holiday in many states.

> 66 I have a dream that one day this nation will rise up and live out the true meaning of its creed. We hold these truths to be self-evident: That all men are created equal. 99
> Martin Luther King

Rodney 'King[6] /'kɪŋ/ (1966–) an *African American who was severely beaten in 1991 by *Los Angeles police officers, an incident which led to America's worst race riots. The police stopped King for driving too fast and then hit and kicked him repeatedly. A person on the street made a video of the attack, and four of the police officers were put on trial. When they were judged innocent, African Americans reacted with violence in Los Angeles for four days, during which 52 people were killed and more than 600 buildings were burned. The police officers were later sent to prison. Many Americans are still angry about the way King was treated.

> 66 Can we get along here? Can we all get along? 99
> Rodney King

Stephen 'King[7] /'kɪŋ/ (1947–) a very popular US writer, best known for his horror novels. About 20 of his books have been filmed, including *Carrie* (1974), *The Shining* (1977), *Misery* (1987) and *The Shawshank Redemption* (1994). He writes some of his books under the name Richard Bachman. He has also written original films, directed one and acted in minor roles.

the 'King 'James 'Version ⇨ AUTHORIZED VERSION.

King 'Kong /'kɒŋ; *AmE* 'kɑːŋ/ a famous US film (1933) about a very large ape. In the story, King Kong captures Ann, played by Fay Wray (1907–2004), when she visits his island. She is rescued, and the ape is taken to New York to be put on show. He escapes and climbs to the top of the *Empire State Building, where he is killed by war planes. A second version of the film was made in 1976, with Jessica Lange, and a further film, *King Kong Lives*, appeared in 1986.

King 'Lear /'lɪə(r)/ a play by William *Shakespeare first performed *c.* 1605. It is a tragedy about Lear, a British king who divides his land and possessions among his daughters. Lear foolishly gives a share each to the two older daughters, Regan and Goneril, who are greedy and cruel, but refuses to give anything to the youngest, Cordelia, who is honest and loyal, because she refuses to compete with her sisters in expressing her love for him. Regan and Goneril later treat Lear badly and Cordelia finally comes to rescue him with a French army. In the battle that follows, however, she is captured and killed. Lear dies too and the play ends. It is one of the greatest of Shakespeare's plays and is known for its speeches about the relationship between parents and children.

king of the 'castle a children's game in which one player stands on something and the others try to take his or her place. The traditional rhyme sung by the first player is:

'I'm the king of the castle
And you're the dirty rascal!'

the 'King's 'Bench ⇨ QUEEN'S BENCH.

'King's 'College, 'Cambridge /'keɪmbrɪdʒ/ a college established by King *Henry VI in 1441 as part of *Cambridge University in England. The college chapel is one of the most impressive buildings in Cambridge and known for its stained glass. A famous service of carols (= religious songs) is held there every *Christmas Eve and is broadcast on television and radio.

'King's 'College 'Hospital a large hospital in southeast London, England, which is part of *London University and is used to teach medical students.

'King's 'Counsel ⇨ QUEEN'S COUNSEL.

'King's 'Cross an area of central London, England, that contains two large train stations (King's Cross and St Pancras) and a station on the *London Underground. A fire at the underground station in 1987 killed 31 people

K

Kings and Queens of England and Great Britain

871–99	Alfred (the Great)		1470–71	Henry VI
899–924	Edward (the Elder)		1471–83	Edward IV
924–39	Aethelstan (the Glorious)		1483	Edward V
939–46	Edmund I		1483–85	Richard III (Crookback)
946–55	Eadred		1485–1509	Henry VII
955–59	Eadwig (the Fair)		1509–47	Henry VIII
959–75	Edgar (the Peaceable)		1547–53	Edward VI
975–78	Edward (the Martyr)		1553	Jane
978–1016	Ethelred (the Unready)		1553–58	Mary I
1016	Edmund (Ironside)		1558–1603	Elizabeth I
1016–35	Canute		1603–25	James I (James VI of Scotland)
1035–40	Harold I (Harefoot)		1625–49	Charles I
1040–42	Harthacnut		1653–58	*Oliver Cromwell* (Lord Protector)
1042–66	Edward (the Confessor)		1658–59	*Richard Cromwell* (Lord Protector)
1066	Harold II		1660–85	Charles II
1066–87	William I (the Conqueror)		1685–88	James II
1087–1100	William II (Rufus)		1689–1702	William III
1100–35	Henry I		1689–94	Mary II
1135–54	Stephen		1702–14	Anne
1154–89	Henry II		1714–27	George I
1189–99	Richard I (the Lionheart)		1727–60	George II
1199–1216	John (Lackland)		1760–1820	George III
1216–72	Henry III		1820–30	George IV
1272–1307	Edward I (Longshanks)		1830–37	William IV
1307–27	Edward II		1837–1901	Victoria
1327–77	Edward III		1901–10	Edward VII
1377–99	Richard II		1910–36	George V
1399–1413	Henry IV		1936	Edward VIII
1413–22	Henry V		1936–52	George VI
1422–61	Henry VI		1952–	Elizabeth II
1461–70	Edward IV			

and led to attempts to improve safety generally on the London Underground. A rail link for the Channel Tunnel is planned to open at St Pancras in 2007.

the ˌKing's 'English ⇨ QUEEN'S ENGLISH.

ˌCharles 'Kingsley (1819–75) an English writer and priest. He is best known for the novel *Westward Ho!* (1855), about *Elizabethan England, and the children's book *The *Water-Babies*. He was also the chaplain (= private priest) to Queen *Victoria.

ˌKing's 'Lynn /'lɪn/ a port and market town in the county of *Norfolk, England. It is known for its many fine old buildings and for its Festival of Music and the Arts, held in July every year. The town was given its royal name by King *Henry VIII in 1537.

ˌKing's 'Road (*usually* **the King's Road**) the main street in the district of *Chelsea in central London, England. It is known for its many fashionable and colourful shops and things for the home. In the 1970s it was a centre of *punk fashion.

ˌKingston-upon-'Hull /ˌkɪŋstən əpɑn 'hʌl/ ⇨ HULL.

ˌNeil 'Kinnock /'kɪnək/ (1942–) a British politician who was leader of the *Labour Party and leader of the Opposition from 1983 to 1992. During this period he led the party away from extreme left-wing views and introduced more moderate policies. After he lost the general election to John *Major in 1992, he was replaced as leader by John *Smith. He was a European Commissioner from 1995 to 2004. His wife **Glenys Kinnock** (1944–) has been a Member of the *European Parliament since 1995, representing South Wales. Neil Kinnock was made a *life peer in 2005.

ˌAlfred 'Kinsey /'kɪnzi/ (1894–1956) a US scientist who published the first major scientific studies of human sexual behaviour. The results of his research, which shocked

many people, came from answers to questions given by 10 000 people. His books were *Sexual Behavior in the Human Male* (1948) and *Sexual Behavior in the Human Female* (1953). Together they are called the **Kinsey Reports**. In 1942 he established the Institute for Sex Research at *Indiana University and directed it until his death.

ˌRudyard 'Kipling /ˌrʌdjɑːd 'kɪplɪŋ; *AmE* ˌrʌdjɑːrd/ (1865–1936) an English writer. He was born in India, where many of his books are set (e.g. The *Jungle Book* and *Kim), and worked there as a journalist in the 1880s. He wrote in a wide range of forms, including novels, short stories and poems for adults and children. Many of his poems are still very popular, including *If, *Gunga Din and *Mandalay* (1892). The characters in his work are often soldiers in parts of the British Empire, and he has been accused of taking too much pride in the British Empire and its use of military force. In 1907 Kipling became the first English writer to receive the *Nobel Prize for literature.

'kipper *n* a herring (= type of fish) that has been split open, preserved with salt and then dried or smoked. In Britain kippers are sometimes eaten cooked for breakfast.

ˌKiri'bati /ˌkɪrə'bæs/ a country consisting of a group of 36 islands in the south-west Pacific Ocean. Its capital is Tarawa and its official languages are English and the local Melanesian language. Before 1975 it was part of the British colony of the Gilbert and Ellice Islands. It became fully independent in 1979 and is now a member of the *Commonwealth.

ˌCaptain 'Kirk /'kɜːk; *AmE* 'kɜːrk/ the captain of the *Starship Enterprise in the *Star Trek series.

KISS /kɪs/ a US *heavy metal band which formed in 1972. Members of the band painted their faces, coloured their hair and performed in a wild way on stage. This included destroying guitars, breathing fire and letting false blood come from their mouths. Their albums have included *KISS* (1974), *Unmasked* (1980) and *Carnival of Souls* (1997). See also KISS PRINCIPLE.

Henry **'Kissinger** /'kɪsɪndʒə(r)/ (1923–) a US *Secretary of State (1973–7), born in Germany. He was a special assistant to President *Nixon on National Security Affairs (1969–75). Kissinger's reputation was based on his 'shuttle diplomacy', in which he travelled regularly around the world to improve US relations with other countries and to find solutions to international conflicts and he was given the *Nobel Prize for peace in 1973. Since then his reputation has been damaged by many accusations in relation to his actions concerning the bombing of Cambodia, the Pinochet coup in Chile and the invasion of East Timor.

the **'KISS principle** (*especially AmE*) (in business) the idea that products and advertising should be as simple as possible in order to be successful. KISS is short for 'Keep it simple, stupid'.

Lord **'Kitchener** /'kɪtʃənə(r)/ (Horatio Herbert Kitchener 1850–1916) a British soldier who commanded the army in the Sudan (1883–5), in South Africa during the *Boer War (1900–02) and in India (1902–9). At the beginning of *World War I he became Secretary of State for War and was responsible for encouraging more men to join the army. He appeared on a famous poster telling people 'Your country needs you'. He was made an *earl(1) in 1914 and died at sea during *World War I.

kitchen-sink 'drama *n* [C, U] (*sometimes disapproving*) a type of British play or plays of the 1950s and 1960s which showed the conflicts or unpleasant quality of home life in a realistic way. Typical examples are John *Osborne's *Look Back in Anger and Arnold *Wesker's *Roots*.

'Kit-E-Kat™ /'kɪtikæt/ *n* [U] a well-known British make of cat food. Compare KIT FAT.

'Kitemark™ /'kaɪtmɑːk; *AmE* 'kaɪtmɑːrk/ *n* (*BrE*) an official mark, in the form of a heart shape with an 'S' in the centre, which is put on products that are approved by the *British Standards Institution.

'Kit Kat™ /'kɪt kæt/ *n* the most popular chocolate bar sold in Britain, often eaten as a snack (= quick meal). Each one consists of two or four strips of wafer (= layers of thin crisp biscuit) covered in chocolate. It first appeared in 1937 and for many years it was advertised with the slogan: 'Have a break – have a Kit Kat.'

the **'Kit Kat Club** /'kɪt kæt/ an early 18th-century club whose members included Joseph *Addison, Richard *Steele, William *Congreve and Robert *Walpole. The club was named after Christopher (Kit) Cat, a cook whose house was used as a meeting place. Pictures of the members were painted in a smaller size than usual to fit on the club walls, and pictures this size are still known as 'kit-cat portraits'.

'Kiwanis /'kwɑːnɪs/ (*also* **Kiwanis International**) a social and charitable organization that works to help children. It was started in *Detroit in 1915 and there are now Kiwanis clubs in many countries. The name comes from a *Native American language and means 'we trade' or 'we share our talents'.

the **KKK** /ˌkeɪ keɪ 'keɪ/ ⇨ KU KLUX KLAN.

'Kleenex™ /'kliːneks/ *n* [U, C] (*pl* **Kleenex** *or* **Kleenexes**) a type of soft paper tissue used for wiping the nose, face, etc. or cleaning things. In American English the word is often used to mean any type of paper tissue: *There's a box of Kleenex in the kitchen.* ◇ *Could you pass me a/some Kleenex?*

Calvin **'Klein** /ˌkælvɪn 'klaɪn/ (1942–) a US designer of casual (= informal) clothes. He began his company in

1968 making suits and coats, but changed to 'sportswear' in the 1970s. He is especially known for making fashionable *jeans and for controversial advertisements. In one of these, the actor Brooke Shields wore the jeans and said, 'Nothing comes between me and my Calvins.' There are also Calvin Klein perfumes such as Obsession and CK One.

the **'Klondike** /'klɒndaɪk; *AmE* 'klɑːndaɪk/ an area of the Yukon Territory of north-west Canada where gold was discovered in 1897. This led to the **Klondike gold rush**, in which about 30 000 people, many of them from the US, travelled to the Klondike in the hope of finding gold. Gold worth about $22 million was found in 1900, but the supply did not last long, and many people then moved on to *Alaska. Charlie *Chaplin's film *The Gold Rush* (1925) was based on this event. See also GOLD RUSH.

'Kmart /'keɪmɑːt; *AmE* 'keɪmɑːrt/ any of a group of large US shops that sell a variety of products at reduced prices. The company began in 1899 as the S S Kresge Company and is based in Troy, *Michigan. In 2004 Kmart bought *Sears, Roebuck and Company.

'Knickerbocker /'nɪkəbɒkə(r); *AmE* 'nɪkərbɑːkər/ *n* (*AmE informal*) a person from New York. The word comes from the imaginary Dutch name of Diedrich Knickerbocker used by the writer Washington *Irving as the pretended author of his *History of New York* (1809). **Knickerbockers** (also called **knickers** in the US) are also an old-fashioned type of loose trousers/pants ending just below the knee where they fit closely.

Knickerbocker 'Glory /ˌnɪkəbɒkə; *AmE* ˌnɪkərbɑːkər/ *n* (*BrE*) a dish of ice cream served in a tall glass with other ingredients such as fruit, nuts and cream.

knight (*also* ˌknight **'bachelor**) *n* (*abbr* **Kt**) a man with a rank of honour given to him by the king or queen for his services to the country. He has the title 'Sir' before his first name, used with or without his last name, and his wife has the title 'Lady'. The title cannot be passed on to his children. The equivalent title for women is *dame(2). Other types of knight are men who belong to an *order of chivalry.
▶ **knight** *v* [T] to make sb a knight: *He was knighted in the New Year Honours List.*

Knight Com'mander a *knight who belongs to one of the higher *orders of chivalry. The equivalent title for women is *Dame Commander.

'Knight 'Grand Com'mander a *knight who belongs to one of the higher *orders of chivalry. There is no equivalent title for women.

'Knight 'Grand 'Cross a *knight who belongs to one of the higher *orders of chivalry. The equivalent title for women is *Dame Grand Cross.

'Knightsbridge /'naɪtsbrɪdʒ/ a district of central London, England, between *Kensington and *Westminster(1). It is famous for its expensive shops, such as *Harrods, and its elegant houses.

the **Knights of Co'lumbus** /kə'lʌmbəs/ a US *Roman Catholic organization with branches also in Canada, Mexico and other countries. It was established in 1881 in New Haven, *Connecticut, by Father Michael McGivney, and the main office is still there. Its aim is to help members and their families who are in need, to give to charity and also to create pride in the Catholic religion. The Knights of Columbus is now an important service organization and in 2004 had more than 1.6 million members.

the **Knights of the Round 'Table** (in British legend) the men of high rank who served King *Arthur. They are often shown in pictures wearing heavy armour and riding horses. They sat at a round table so that none of them would appear to have a higher rank than the others. The best-known Knights include Sir *Galahad, Sir Gawain and Sir *Lancelot. See also GAWAIN AND THE GREEN KNIGHT.

the ˌKnights ˈTemplars /ˈtempləz; AmE ˈtemplərz/ (also **the Knights of the Temple of Solomon**) a religious and military organization formed in Jerusalem in 1119 to protect pilgrims (= people travelling to Jerusalem). In the 12th and 13th centuries they fought in the *Crusades.

ˌknock-ˈknock joke n a type of joke that depends on the way in which some words in English sound like other words. The person telling the joke says 'Knock-knock', someone answers 'Who's there?', and the first person says a name which isn't what it seems. A typical example might be: 'Knock-knock.' 'Who's there?' 'Lucy.' 'Lucy who?' 'Lucy Lastic (= loose elastic).'

the ˈKnowledge detailed information about street names, famous buildings, etc. and the shortest routes between places in London, England, which taxi drivers there must have before they can receive a licence for London. Anyone who wants to *do the Knowledge* must pass a series of examinations.

the ˌKnow-ˈNothing ˌParty (also **the ˌKnow-ˈNothings**) the popular name for the American Republican Party, later called the American Party, which was established in 1843 with the aim of restricting immigration and preventing *Roman Catholics from holding public office. They were called Know-Nothings because members of the party were told to say 'I know nothing' when asked about it. They were also called 'nativists' because they believed that foreign-born Americans should not be allowed to hold government posts. They had some success in the 1850s, but were divided over the issue of slaves, and the party soon came to an end. The word *know-nothing* is still sometimes applied in the US to a person with political views which are too fixed and not reasonable.

ˌJohn ˈKnox /ˈnɒks; AmE ˈnɑːks/ (c. 1514–72) a Scottish Protestant leader. He began his career as a *Roman Catholic priest but became a Protestant at the time of the *Reformation. Because of his beliefs he was forced to live abroad for much of his life, and he met John Calvin in Geneva. When he returned to Scotland in 1559 he led the opposition to the Roman Catholic *Mary, Queen of Scots, and spent the rest of his life establishing the *Church of Scotland.

ˈRobin ˈKnox-ˈJohnston /ˈnɒks ˈdʒɒnstən; AmE ˈnɑːks ˈdʒɑːnstən/ (1939–) a British sailor who was the first man to sail alone around the world without stopping. The journey took ten months, from June 1968 to April 1969. He was made a *knight in 1995.

ˈKodak™ /ˈkəʊdæk; AmE ˈkoʊdæk/ a US company which is the world's largest producer of cameras, film and other photographic equipment. It was started in 1892 by George *Eastman, who created the name Kodak because he thought 'K' was a lucky letter. The company first sold its famous Brownie camera in 1900 with the advertising phrase, 'You push the button – we do the rest.' Its other products have included Kodachrome film, the Instamatic Camera and the Panoramic 35 Camera. Kodak's main office is in Rochester, New York.

ˌArthur ˈKoestler /ˈkɜːstlə(r)/ (1905–83) a British author, born in Hungary. His experiences as a Communist in the 1930s and later as a prisoner during the Spanish Civil War influenced his most famous novel, *Darkness at Noon* (1941). He also wrote many books about science, including *The Act of Creation* (1964), about the relationship between science and art.

the ˈKohinoor /ˈkəʊɪnʊə(r); AmE ˈkoʊɪnʊr/ (also **the Kohinoor diamond**) a large diamond given to the British in 1849 by the ruler of the Punjab in India. It is now part of the *Crown Jewels.

ˈKool-Aid™ /ˈkuːl/ n [U, C] a US drink especially popular with children. It is sold as a powder in small paper packets and is available in several flavours.

ˌTed ˈKoppel /ˈkɒpl; AmE ˈkɑːpl/ (1940–) a US television journalist, born in England. Since 1979 he has presented *Nightline*, a news programme on *ABC. He joined ABC in 1963 at the age of 23, the youngest journalist ever to join a national television company.

▶ **the Korean War**

The Korean War began in 1950, during the *Cold War. On 25 June 1950 soldiers from Communist North Korea invaded South Korea, which had links with the US, and the *United Nations (UN) responded by sending soldiers to defend it.

The Soviet Union gave North Korea weapons, and almost certainly encouraged the invasion. The US persuaded the UN to act on behalf of South Korea and supplied many of the soldiers. General *MacArthur, an American, led the UN forces. But the US and the Soviet Union still tried to avoid war, the Soviet Union by denying it was involved, and the US by saying it was only taking part in a UN operation.

The North Koreans were pushed back above the **38th parallel** (= the imaginary line that divided the two Koreas) by the end of October 1950, and then the UN forces tried to take control of the North. At first they were successful, but as the soldiers got close to China's border China attacked and they were pushed back towards the 38th. After this, it seemed that either side could win only by taking control of all Korea, but to do so would have required more effort and resources. Both sides were afraid of **escalating** the situation (= making it more serious) in case that led to nuclear war. Peace talks made slow progress. Finally, on 27 July 1953, an agreement was reached at Panmunjom, ending the war and leaving Korea still divided.

The Korean War was the background for the popular American television programme *M*A*S*H*, short for 'mobile army surgical hospital', which raised questions that many Americans were now asking. For example, why was the US fighting in a place so far away and so little connected with its own interests? Was it right to stop fighting without a clear result? If the US could not or would not use all its strength to win, was it better not to fight at all? And, above all, what was the right role for the country which, after *World War II, was the world's greatest power?.

ˌDavid Koˈresh /kɒˈreʃ; AmE kɔːˈreʃ/ (1959–93) the leader of the religious group called the *Branch Davidians. He was born Vernon Wayne Howell in *Houston and became a member of the Church of *Seventh-Day Adventists but was forced to leave it because he was considered a bad influence. He tried to become a pop singer in *Hollywood but failed. In 1981 he joined the Branch Davidians, later becoming their leader and changing his name. He died with most of the group's members during a battle with US government forces in Waco, *Texas, in 1993.

KP /ˌkeɪ ˈpiː/ (in full **kitchen police**) n [U] (AmE) (in the US armed forces) work done in the military kitchens, in which soldiers help the regular cooks. Such work is often given as punishment. The soldiers doing it can also be called the 'kitchen police' but not the 'KP': *The sergeant assigned Brewster to KP for missing roll-call.*

Kraft™ /krɑːft/ a US company best known for making various types of cheese, including Philadelphia cheese.

Its other products include biscuits, snacks, coffee, sauces and pickles.

Judith 'Krantz /'krænts/ (1928–) a US writer who has been called 'the queen of the glamour novel'. Her stories are about beautiful women and rich, powerful men. Her first and best-known novel was *Scruples* (1978). Others include *Princess Daisy* (1980), *I'll Take Manhattan* (1986), *Till We Meet Again* (1988) and *Spring Collection* (1997). She published her autobiography *Sex and Shopping: The Confessions of a Nice Jewish Girl* in 2000.

'K ,rations /'keɪ/ n [pl] (*AmE*) special meals given to US soldiers during World War II. They were named after Dr Ancel Keys, the leader of the group that created them. The food was supplied in three boxes, one each for breakfast, lunch and dinner, and each contained a healthy number of calories (= units of energy) and vitamins, as well as four cigarettes.

the 'Kray twins /'kreɪ/ two English brothers, **Ronnie Kray** (1934–95) and **Reggie Kray** (1934–2000), who led a group of criminals in the *East End of London in the 1960s. They were found guilty in 1969 of murdering two men and sent to prison for 30 years. Ronnie Kray died in prison.

,Kriss 'Kringle /,krɪs 'krɪŋgl/ a US name for *Father Christmas. It comes from the German word *Christkindl*, meaning Christ child, because German children believe that the baby Jesus brings presents during the Christmas season.

,Ray 'Kroc /'krɒk; *AmE* 'krɑːk/ (1902–84) the American who developed *McDonald's into the biggest *fast food restaurant company in the world. In 1955 he bought the company and its name from two brothers, Richard and Maurice McDonald, who had one restaurant in San Bernardino, *California. Kroc created the gold arches which are the McDonald's symbol, and established a Hamburger University to train the company's employees.

'Kroger /'krəʊgə(r); *AmE* 'kroʊgər/ the largest US group of grocery stores. The company's first shop was opened by Barney Kroger in 1883 in Cincinnati, *Ohio, and its main office is still there.

'Krypton /'krɪptɒn; *AmE* 'krɪptɑːn/ the planet where *Superman was born, according to the original story. The people on Krypton were about to die, so his parents sent the baby Superman away in a spacecraft which later landed on Earth. See also KRYPTONITE.

The 'Krypton ,Factor /'krɪptɒn; *AmE* 'krɪptɑːn/ a popular British television series (1977–95), in which people competed in contests to test their intelligence and physical strength.

'kryptonite /'krɪptənaɪt/ n [U] (in the *Superman stories) a type of green rock from the planet *Krypton. It

is the only thing that can make *Superman weak or even kill him.

Kt /,keɪ 'tiː/ ⇨ KNIGHT.

KT /,keɪ 'tiː/ (in Britain) the abbreviation for Knight of the *Order of the Thistle: *Sir Norman Smith KT*.

K-12 /,keɪ 'twelv/ *adj* (*AmE*) (in the US education system) relating to the years from kindergarten (= school for very young children) to 12th grade: *The state pays for a K-12 education.*

,Kubla 'Khan /,kuːblə 'kɑːn/ a poem by Samuel Taylor *Coleridge written in 1797 but not published until 1816. It was written after the poet dreamed about a palace built by the Mongol ruler Kubla Khan. He was unable to finish the poem, however, because a 'person from Porlock' (a village in *Somerset) interrupted him while he was writing, and he forgot the dream.

,Stanley 'Kubrick /'kuːbrɪk/ (1928–1999) a US film director, known for his great attention to detail. His best-known films include *Spartacus* (1960), *Lolita* (1962), *Dr Strangelove* (1963), *2001: A Space Odyssey* (1968), *A Clockwork Orange* (1971), *Barry Lyndon* (1975), *The Shining* (1980) and *Eyes Wide Shut* (1999).

the ,Ku Klux 'Klan /,kuː klʌks 'klæn/ (*abbr* **the KKK**) a secret US organization opposed to equal rights for *African Americans. The members wear long white robes and tall pointed hats to hide their identity. Their leader is called the Grand Wizard. They sometimes burn the Christian symbol of the cross in front of the houses of African Americans or people who support them. The organization was first formed in *Tennessee in 1866 after the *Civil War and was responsible for lynchings (= hanging people without a trial) and violent attacks on African Americans. It was made illegal in 1871. It began again in 1915, attacking not only African Americans but also Jews, Roman Catholics and people from foreign countries. It had nearly 5 million members in the 1920s, including many outside the South. The Klan became strong again in the 1960s when it opposed the *civil rights movement, often with violence, but today it has less influence.

'Kwanzaa /'kwɑːnzɑː/ a cultural festival celebrated by some *African American groups from 26 December to 1 January. The name comes from a Swahili phrase meaning 'first fruits'.

'Kwik-Fit™ /'kwɪk/ a British company which owns garages where motor vehicles can be repaired or have parts replaced (especially tyres or exhausts).

'Kwik Save™ /'kwɪk/ a British chain of supermarkets selling food and household goods at low prices.

,KY 'jelly™ /,keɪ waɪ/ n [U] a make of soft jelly used to lubricate parts of the body, especially the vagina before having sex.

L l

LA /ˌel ˈeɪ/ ⇨ Los Angeles.

the ˈLaban Centre /ˈlɑːbən/ a dance centre in south London, England which was started by Rudolph Laban (1879–1958) in 1938 and teaches different styles of contemporary dance.

ˈLabor Day /ˈleɪbə deɪ; AmE ˈleɪbər/ a US national holiday to honour workers, established in 1894. Labor Day is the first Monday in September and is the last big holiday before the school year begins.

ˈlabor union /ˈleɪbə juːniən; AmE ˈleɪbər/ ⇨ TRADE UNION.

the ˈLabour ˌParty (also **Labour**) one of the three main parties in British politics, established to represent the interests of workers, and traditionally supported by the *trade unions. It developed from the *Independent Labour Party and formed its first government in 1924 under Ramsay *MacDonald. Other Labour *prime ministers since then have been Clement *Attlee (1945–51), Harold *Wilson (1964–70), James *Callaghan (1974–9) and Tony *Blair (1997–). In the 1980s and 1990s the party moved away from traditional left-wing policies regarding public ownership of industry and giving up nuclear weapons. Because of these changes the party is now also known as *New Labour. It was elected to government in 1997 under Tony Blair, with a large majority in the. Opposition to New Labour policies and to the war in Iraq among traditional Labour Party members has led to a decline in party membership to the lowest level since the 1930s.
▶ **Labour** adj of or supporting the Labour Party: a Labour minister ◇ Her husband is Labour (= supports the Labour Party) .

ˈLabrador (also **ˌLabrador reˈtriever**) n a breed of dog with a smooth black, yellow or brown coat, originally bred in Labrador, part of north-east Canada.

laˈcrosse n [U] a game similar to *field hockey, originally played by Native Americans. It is played on a field with a goal at each end between two teams of 10 or 12 players who use sticks with nets at the end (called crosses) to catch, carry and throw a small rubber ball. In the US it is mainly played by men and is a popular sport in schools. In Britain women's lacrosse is played in some schools.

ˈLadbrokes /ˈlædbrʊks/ a British company best known for its betting shops (= places in towns where people can bet on horse races, football, etc.) and for its online betting and gambling.

ˈLadies' Day 1 (in Britain) the second day of horse racing at *Ascot, when women traditionally wear elegant hats and fashionable clothes.
2 (in the US) a special day at a sports or other event when women are admitted free or for less than the normal price.

ˈLadies ˈHome ˈJournal a US magazine for women, first published in 1883. It is sold in large food shops and in 2004 was bought by more than 4 million people.

ˈLadybird the name of a series of small books started in 1940, which are designed to help children to learn to read. The books have a picture of a ladybird (= a round, red insect with black spots) on the front.

ˌLady ˈBountiful (BrE usually disapproving) a woman, especially an *upper-class woman, who likes to appear generous with her money or time. The name comes from a character in the play The Beaux' Stratagem (1707) by the Irish writer George Farquhar (1678–1707): She likes to help out at the school and play Lady Bountiful.

ˈLady ˈChatterley's ˈLover /ˈtʃætəliz; AmE ˈtʃætərliz/ a novel by D H *Lawrence, first published in Italy in 1928. It is about an *upper-class married woman who has a sexual affair with her gamekeeper (= a person whose job is to take care of animals that are kept on private land in order to be hunted). Lawrence was forbidden to publish the book in Britain until 1960 (1959 in the US) because of its detailed descriptions of sex and use of direct sexual language. However, in a famous British trial the publishers, *Penguin Books, were found not guilty of obscenity (= using offensive sexual language) after publishing the book and it became an immediate success with the public.

ˈladyfinger /ˈleɪdɪfɪŋɡə(r)/ n (AmE) a small, light cake, roughly like a finger in shape, made with eggs, sugar and flour.

The ˌLady of Shaˈlott /ʃəˈlɒt; AmE ʃəˈlɑːt/ a poem by Lord *Tennyson, published in 1833. It tells the story of a mysterious woman living in a castle on an island. She follows Sir *Lancelot in a boat to the city of *Camelot and dies on the way.

the ˌLady of the ˈLake a character in stories about King *Arthur, who gives Arthur the sword *Excalibur by holding it above the surface of the lake in which she lives. The Lady of the Lake (1810) is also the title of a long romantic poem by Sir Walter *Scott.

the ˌLady of the ˈLamp a name given to Florence *Nightingale by wounded soldiers in the *Crimean War, because she carried a lamp with her as she walked around the hospital where she worked.

Marˌquis de Lafayˈette /mɑːˌkiː də læfaɪˈet; AmE mɑːrˌkiː/ (1757–1834) a French soldier and politician who helped the Americans during the *American Revolution and fought at the Battle of *Yorktown. He also persuaded the French king Louis XVI to send more soldiers to America to fight the British. This made him very popular in the US, and towns are named after him in several states, including *Indiana, *Louisiana and *Alabama. He was made an honorary citizen of the US by George W *Bush in 2002.

ˌFioˈrello La ˈGuardia /ˌfiːəˈreləʊ lə ˈɡwɑːdiə; AmE ˌfiːəˈreləʊ lə ˈɡwɑːrdiə/ (1882–1947) a popular *mayor(2) of New York (1933–45). He was known as the 'Little Flower', which is what Fiorello means in Italian. He began his career as a *Republican(1) politician and was elected to the US Congress (1917–19 and 1923–33). As mayor, he introduced measures to deal with problems of health, housing, transport and crime. During a newspaper strike in 1937 he pleased children by reading *comic strips on the radio. *La Guardia Airport is named after him.

La ˌGuardia ˈAirport /lə ˌɡwɑːdiə; AmE lə ˌɡwɑːrdiə/ an airport in New York City used mostly for flights within the country. It is in north *Queens and is the closest to *Manhattan(1) of New York's three airports.

ˌCleo ˈLaine¹ /ˈleɪn/ (1927–) a British singer and actor who has appeared on stage, television and in films. She is married to the *jazz musician John *Dankworth and began her career performing with him, later achieving success with songs such as *You'll Answer to Me* (1961). She was made a *dame(2) in 1997.

Frankie 'Laine² /'leɪn/ (1913–) a US singer, songwriter and actor with a strong voice who was especially popular in the 1950s, when 13 of his records each sold more than a million copies. They included *Jezebel* (1951), *Rawhide* (1952), *High Noon* (1952) and *I Believe* (1953).

the 'Lake ,District (*also* **the Lakes**) a region of lakes and mountains in Cumbria, north-west England. It contains the highest mountain in England, *Scafell Pike, and the largest lake, *Windermere(1). Other lakes include *Ullswater and *Derwentwater. The area is associated with the *Lake Poets, who lived there and wrote about it. It was later the home of the writers John *Ruskin and Beatrix *Potter. Its beautiful scenery is very popular with tourists, and it was made a *national park in 1951.

the Lake District

Lakeland 'terrier /,leɪklənd/ *n* a type of small *terrier dog, originally bred in the *Lake District for use in hunting.

the ,Lake 'Poets (*also* **the Lake School**) a group of English *Romantic poets who lived in the *Lake District. Its best-known members were William *Wordsworth, who was born in the Lake District and lived there for most of his life, and Samuel Taylor *Coleridge, who settled there in 1800. Others included Robert *Southey and Thomas *De Quincey.

Lake 'Pontchartrain 'Causeway /'pɒntʃətreɪn 'kɔːzweɪ; *AmE* 'pɑːntʃɑrtreɪn/ a US *freeway in southeastern *Louisiana which is the world's longest road built over water. It is 25 miles/40 kilometres long and opened in 1957. *New Orleans is at its southern end. The shallow saltwater Lake Pontchartrain is close to the *Gulf of Mexico and has an area of 625 square miles/1619 square kilometres.

the Lakes ⇨ LAKE DISTRICT.

Lake 'Wobegon /'wəʊbɪɡɒn; *AmE* 'woʊbɪɡɔːn/ ⇨ KEILLOR.

'Lallans /'lælənz/ (*also* **Lowland Scots**) *n* [U] a name for the form of English traditionally spoken and written in the *Lowlands of Scotland since the 18th century. It was used by poets such as Robert *Burns and is still used by some Scottish writers today.

Charles 'Lamb¹ /'læm/ (1775–1834) an English writer. His best-known works are *Tales from Shakespeare* (1807), written for children with his sister Mary (1764–1847), and *Essays of Elia*, published in two collections in 1823 and 1833.

Lady 'Caroline 'Lamb² /'læm/ (1785–1828) an English author and the wife of William Lamb, who later became the British *Prime Minister Lord *Melbourne. She is best known for her love affair with the poet Lord *Byron,

whom she described as 'mad, bad and dangerous to know', and who was the model for the main character in her novel *Glenarvon* (1816).

the ,Lambeth 'Conference /,læmbəθ/ a meeting of *Anglican *bishops from around the world. It was first held in 1876 at *Lambeth Palace and is now held every ten years.

,Lambeth 'Palace /,læmbəθ/ the official home of the *Archbishop of Canterbury, the head of the *Church of England, in Lambeth, central London.

the ,Lambeth 'Walk /,læmbəθ/ a dance and a song named after Lambeth Walk, a street in central London, England. The dance involved dancers forming a long line, often in the street, and was popular in the 1930s and 1940s.

LAMDA /'læmdə/ (*in full* **the London Academy of Music and Dramatic Art**) the oldest drama school in London, England, established in 1861. It no longer trains musicians.

,Louis L'A'mour /ləˈmʊə(r); *AmE* ləˈmʊr/ (1908–88) a US author of over a hundred books, most of them *westerns, which sold more than 200 million copies during his life. He is the only US writer to have received a gold medal from Congress (in 1983) and the *Presidential Medal of Freedom (in 1984). His first book, *Hondo* (1953), was made into a *3-D film with John *Wayne. Among his other books which also became films were *The Burning Hills* (1956) and *Heller in Pink Tights* (1960).

'Lancashire /'lænkəʃə(r)/ **1** (*abbr* **Lancs**) a county in north-west England. It was one of the centres of the *Industrial Revolution, and was famous especially for its cotton mills and coal mines. In 1974 the county was reduced in size and it no longer includes the cities of *Liverpool and *Manchester. Its administrative centre is Preston. Compare MERSEYSIDE. **2** (*also* **Lancashire cheese**) *n* [U] a type of mild white cheese that breaks easily into small pieces. It is traditionally made in Lancashire.

,Lancashire 'hotpot /,lænkəʃə; *AmE* ,lænkəʃər/ *n* a dish, originally made in *Lancashire, consisting of lamb and other ingredients covered with slices of potato and baked in the oven.

'Lancaster¹ /'lænkəstə(r)/ a city in *Lancashire, England, on the River Lune. *John of Gaunt became Duke of Lancaster in 1362, and since 1399 the *Duchy of Lancaster has been a possession of the British *Crown. The **Lancastrians** in the *Wars of the Roses were supporters of the royal house descended from John of Gaunt.

Burt 'Lancaster² /,bɜːt 'lænkəstə(r); *AmE* ,bɜːrt 'lænkəstər/ (1913–94) a US actor who was a *Hollywood star in the 1950s and 1960s. He began his career as a circus acrobat. He was known for playing strong characters and for his big smile. Lancaster won an *Oscar for *Elmer Gantry (1960). Among his other films were *From Here to Eternity* (1953), *Trapeze* (1956), *The Birdman of Alcatraz* (1962), *The Leopard* (1963), *Atlantic City* (1980), *Local Hero* (1983) and *Field of Dreams* (1989).

the ,House of 'Lancaster³ /'lænkəstə(r)/ the English royal house (= family) descended from *John of Gaunt, Duke of Lancaster, which ruled England from 1399 to 1461. The three kings of the House of Lancaster were *Henry IV, *Henry V and *Henry VI. During the rule of Henry VI, the *Wars of the Roses began between the **Lancastrians** and the **Yorkists**, which resulted in the creation of a new royal house, the House of *York (1461–85).

,Osbert 'Lancaster⁴ /,ɒzbət 'lænkəstə(r); *AmE* ,ɑːzbərt 'lænkəstər/ (1908–86) an English cartoonist and writer. His 'pocket cartoons' (= small funny drawings) appeared in the *Daily Express* newspaper from 1939 onwards, and were popular for characters such as the *upper-class Lady Maudie Littlehampton. He also wrote books on architecture and did designs for the theatre. He was made a *knight in 1975.

,**Sir 'Lancelot** /'lɑːnsəlɒt; *AmE* 'lɑːnsəlɑːt/ the most famous of King *Arthur's *Knights of the Round Table, sometimes called Lancelot of the Lake. He was Arthur's favourite *knight, but deceived him by becoming the lover of Queen *Guinevere, Arthur's wife. Sir *Galahad was his son by Elaine, the daughter of King Pelles.

The '**Lancet** a British magazine for doctors and other medical workers which first appeared in 1823. It is published every week by the *British Medical Association and contains articles on new medical procedures, drugs, etc. It has many readers in other countries.

'**landlady** *n* **1** a woman who owns a guest house or boarding house and rents rooms to people. In the past British landladies had a reputation for being unfriendly and strict: *seaside landladies*.
2 a woman who rents a building, flat/apartment, etc. to somebody. A man who does this is called a **landlord**.
3 a woman who owns or manages a pub. If the owner or manager is a man, he is called the **landlord**.

the ,**Landmark 'Trust** a British charity started in 1965 which buys and repairs buildings which are of historical interest and then rents them to people to stay in for holidays.

'**Land of 'Hope and 'Glory** the title and first line of a song by Edward *Elgar, originally part of his *Pomp and Circumstance* marches. The words (by A C Benson) are very patriotic (= expressing pride in Britain). The song is traditionally performed at the *Last Night of the Proms with the audience singing the words.

*,**Land of My 'Fathers*** the title of the *national anthem of Wales. The name in Welsh is 'Hen wlad fy nhadau'. It was composed in 1856 with words by Evan James (1809–93) and music by James James (1832–1902).

the '**Land ,Registry** a British government organization that keeps records of the owners of land, and must be informed whenever land is bought or sold.

'**Land ,Rover**™ (*also* **Land-Rover**) /,rəʊvə(r); *AmE* ,rəʊvər/ a strong motor vehicle, first made by *Rover in 1949, and designed for use over rough ground or farm land. Compare JEEP, RANGE ROVER.

,**landscape 'gardening** *n* [U] the art of designing a garden, especially in the land around a large house, palace, etc. British landscape gardening developed in the 18th century under artists such as William *Kent who tried to create landscapes with a natural, informal effect similar to those seen in 17th-century Italian painting. Artificial lakes and buildings such as temples or 'ruins' were specially created for this purpose. The most famous figure in British landscape gardening was Lancelot 'Capability' *Brown, who designed the gardens at *Longleat House and *Blenheim Palace.
  In the US, Frederick Law Olmstead (1822–1903) followed the British style when he created *Central Park in New York City. He was the first person to call himself a 'landscape architect'. Since the early 20th century, gardens and houses have often been designed together, e.g. by Frank Lloyd *Wright.
▶ **landscape gardener** *n* a person whose job is landscape gardening.

,**Edwin 'Landseer** /'lændsɪə(r)/ (1802–73) an English painter and sculptor best known for his paintings of animals. *Monarch of the Glen* (1850), one of his most famous paintings, shows a stag (= male deer) in a Scottish Highland scene. Landseer created the lions at the base of

*Nelson's Column in *Trafalgar Square, and was Queen *Victoria's favourite painter. He was made a *knight in 1850.

,**Land's 'End** the place in England that is furthest to the west, on the coast of *Cornwall. The point furthest to the south is the *Lizard. *John o'Groats is the point furthest to the north in Scotland, and the phrase *from Land's End to John o'Groats* is used to mean 'all over Britain': *He was known from Land's End to John o'Groats*.

Land's End

,**Lois 'Lane** /'leɪn/ ⇨ SUPERMAN.

,**Fritz 'Lang** /ˌfrɪts 'læŋ/ (1890–1976) an Austrian film director who directed many *Hollywood films between 1936 and 1956. He began his film career in Germany, where he directed silent films, including *Metropolis* (1927) and *M* (1933). In America, he became known for his films about violence, including *Fury* (1936), *Hangmen Also Die* (1943) and *The Big Heat* (1953). After returning briefly to Germany, Lang finally settled in *Beverly Hills.

,**Jessica 'Lange** /'læŋ/ (1949–) a US film and stage actor who won *Oscars for her parts in *Tootsie* (1982) and *Blue Sky* (1994). Her other films include *The Postman Always Rings Twice* (1981) and *Sweet Dreams* (1985).

,**William 'Langland** /'læŋlənd/ (*c*. 1330–*c*. 1386) an English poet whose only known work is *Piers Plowman*, a poem describing a man's spiritual journey in search of the truth.

,**Lillie 'Langtry** /ˌlɪli 'læŋtri/ (1853–1929) a British actor born in Jersey and known as the Jersey Lily. She was famous for her beauty and for being the lover of the Prince of Wales, later *Edward VII.

LAPD /ˌel eɪ piː 'diː/ ⇨ LOS ANGELES POLICE DEPARTMENT.

'**lardy cake** /'lɑːdi; *AmE* 'lɑːrdi/ *n* [C, U] a type of sweet cake traditionally made in the south of England. It is similar to bread but also has lard (= pork fat), sugar and dried fruit added.

,**Philip 'Larkin** /'lɑːkɪn; *AmE* 'lɑːrkɪn/ (1922–85) one of the best-known English poets of the second half of the 20th century. His work deals with subjects such as death, love, sex and the natural world, mixing humour with sadness. The poems in collections such as *The Whitsun Weddings* (1964) and *High Windows* (1974) are written in ordinary language but have traditional rhyme, rhythm and verse structure. Larkin also published two novels, *Jill* (1946) and *A Girl in Winter* (1947). He worked as librarian at the University of Hull from 1955 and hundreds of his unpublished poems were found there in 2004.

> 66 Man hands on misery to man.
> It deepens like a coastal shelf.
> Get out as early as you can,
> And don't have any kids yourself. 99
> *This be the Verse*

L

'Lark 'Rise to 'Candleford /'kændəlfəd; *AmE*
'kændəlfərd/ a series of three books, *Lark Rise, Over to
Candleford* and *Candleford Green*, published between
1939 and 1945, by Flora Thompson (1876–1947). They are
about traditional village life in England just before the
changes that happened in the 20th century.

Gary 'Larson /'lɑːsn; *AmE* 'lɑːrsn/ ⇨ FAR SIDE.

'Lassie /'læsi/ a dog that first appeared as a character in
the film *Lassie Come Home* (1943), and went on to appear
in several other films, a radio and television series, and a
television cartoon, all mainly for children. Lassie is an
intelligent dog that often rescues people from danger.

last'minute.com /ˌlɑːst 'mɪnɪt dɒt kɒm; *AmE* ˌlæst
'mɪnɪt dɑːt kɑːm/ a company based in the UK which has
a website through which people can search for and book
holidays, hotels, flights etc. online. It was one of the
most successful British dotcom companies (= companies
that sell goods and services on the Internet) of the 1990s
and one of the few which survived.

the 'Last 'Night of the 'Proms /'prɒmz; *AmE*
'prɑːmz/ the last performance of the *Proms, the series
of concerts of classical music held every summer at the
*Albert Hall in London. The music in the second half
traditionally consists of songs expressing pride in
Britain, such as *Land of Hope and Glory, *Rule,
Britannia!* and *Jerusalem*. It is always a lively occasion,
with the audience singing and waving British flags.

The 'Last of 'England the best-known painting (1855)
by Ford Madox *Brown. It shows a young couple on a
boat leaving England, and was painted at a time when
many people were leaving the country to start a new life
abroad.

The 'Last of the Mo'hicans /məʊ'hiːkənz; *AmE*
moʊ'hiːkənz/ a famous novel (1826) by the US writer
James Fenimore *Cooper. It was one of his
Leatherstocking Tales about 18th-century life on the
American frontier. It tells the story of Hawkeye, who has
grown up with *Native American Mohican people after
his European parents were killed. Film versions were
made in 1936 and in 1992.

Last of the 'Summer 'Wine a *BBC television comedy series about three old men (Compo, Clegg and
Foggy) living in a Yorkshire village. It began in 1974 and
has been running longer than any other comedy series
on British television. See also BATTY.

Las 'Vegas /ˌlæs 'veɪɡəs/ (*also informal* **Vegas**) a US
city where many people go to gamble. It is the largest
city in the state of *Nevada and one of the fastest growing cities in the US. It first became popular in the 1940s.
Criminals once operated many of the hotels, nightclubs
and casinos (= gambling clubs) on Las Vegas Bouvelard,
known as 'the Strip', but this has changed and the city
now offers much more family entertainment. Las Vegas
is also a place where many couples go to get married
quickly.

Las Vegas

Hugh 'Latimer /'lætɪmə; *AmE* 'lætɪmər/ (*c*. 1485–
1555) an English bishop who became one of the leading
figures of the *Reformation in England. When *Mary I
became queen he opposed her Catholic policies and was
executed in Oxford by being burned, together with two
other bishops, Nicholas Ridley (*c*. 1500–55) and Thomas
*Cranmer.

La'tino /læ'tiːnəʊ; *AmE* læ'tiːnoʊ/ *n* (*pl* **-os**) a person
from Latin America or descended from Latin Americans.
Compare CHICANO, HISPANIC, TEX-MEX.

Estée 'Lauder¹ /ˌesteɪ 'lɔːdə(r)/ (1908–2004) a US businesswoman who established an international company
selling beauty products. She began it in 1946, and it
remained a private company until 1996. In 2003 it had
sales of over $5 billion around the world.

Harry 'Lauder² /'lɔːdə(r)/ (1870–1950) a Scottish comic
singer who wore *Highland dress on stage and became
popular with songs such as *I Love a Lassie* and *Roamin' in
the Gloamin'*. He was made a *knight in 1919 for his work
entertaining soldiers during *World War I.

The 'Laughing Cava'lier a well-known painting by
the Dutch painter Frans Hals (*c*. 1580–1666) showing a
smiling man. It was painted in 1624 and became one of
the most popular pictures in Britain. It is now in the
*Wallace Collection.

Charles 'Laughton /'lɔːtn/ (1899–1962) a British actor
who became a US citizen in 1950. His films included *The
Private Life of Henry VIII* (1933), for which he won an
*Oscar, and *The Hunchback of Notre Dame* (1939). He was
not often given romantic parts, and described his own
face as being 'like the behind of an elephant'.

Laura 'Ashley™ /'æʃli/ a company started in 1953 by
the Welsh designer Laura Ashley (1925–85) and her husband Bernard, which owns shops in Britain and abroad.
Its products are well known for their traditional country
designs and soft colours, and include clothes, printed
cotton fabrics and furniture.

Laurel and 'Hardy /ˌlɒrəl, 'hɑːdi; *AmE* 'lɔːrəl,
'hɑːrdi/ a pair of comedy film actors, **Stan Laurel**
(1890–1965) and **Oliver Hardy** (1892–1957), who made
over 100 long and short films together between 1926 and
1940 and formed the most successful comedy team in
the history of *Hollywood. Laurel, born in Britain, was
the thin one and Hardy was the fat one. In their films
Laurel often caused the many accidents that happened
to them both, after which Hardy would get angry and
say, 'This is another fine mess you've gotten me into.'
The Laurel and Hardy Museum is in Harlem, *Georgia,
where Hardy was born.

Ralph 'Lauren /'lɔːrən/ (1939–) a US designer of classic
clothes for men, women and children including a
*preppy range called 'Polo'. He also produces many
other products, such as bed sheets and luggage, and has
designed costumes for films including *The *Great Gatsby*
and **Annie Hall*. There are Ralph Lauren shops in many
countries and the clothes are advertised against a background of luxurious country houses and yachts.

'laver bread /'lɑːvə; *AmE* 'lɑːvər/ *n* [U] a dish that is
eaten mainly in Wales. It is made from laver, a type of
seaweed, which is boiled, mixed with oatmeal (= a type
of rough flour) and fried in flat cakes.

Bonar 'Law¹ /ˌbɒnə 'lɔː; *AmE* ˌbɑːnər/ (1858–1923) a
British *Conservative politician, born in Canada. After a
successful business career he entered *Parliament in
1900, becoming leader of the Conservative Party in 1911.
He was *Prime Minister from 1922 to 1923, but resigned
because of poor health and was replaced by Stanley
*Baldwin.

Jude Law² /ˌdʒuːd 'lɔː/ (1972–) an English film actor
famous for his good looks. His films include *The Talented

L

Mr Ripley (1999), *Artificial Intelligence: AI* (2001) and *Cold Mountain* (2003).

,**Law and 'Order** a US television drama series, started in 1990, about a team of police detectives in New York who investigate serious crimes, especially murder, and a team of lawyers from the *Manhattan *district attorney's office who prosecute (= charge sb with a crime in a court) the criminals.

the '**Law Com,mission** a British government organization formed in 1965 to examine the nation's laws and publish proposals for changing them. There is a separate Law Commission for Scotland.

the '**Law Courts** (*also* the **Royal Courts of Justice**) the building in central London, England, where most *High Court trials are held.

▶ law enforcement

Britain has 52 regional **police forces**, which are responsible for maintaining **law and order** in their own area. London has two police forces, the *Metropolitan Police, often referred to as the **Met**, which covers *Greater London and has its headquarters at *New Scotland Yard, and the smaller *City of London Police.

police constables

Each regional police force is led by a Chief Constable. Police officers wear dark blue uniforms, and **constables** wear tall hard helmets. The British police force is relatively small, with one police officer to every 400 people. Some members of the public are trained as **special constables** and are available to help the police in an emergency.

Each police force has a **Criminal Investigation Department** (**CID**) of detectives. CID officers are chosen from the uniformed police. They do not wear uniforms and have the title Detective before their rank, e.g. Detective Inspector Jones. Individual police forces have other special units for areas such as traffic, child protection, etc. and there are also national police organizations such as **Special Branch**, which works to prevent terrorism. In 2004 the government announced the creation of a new national organization, the **Serious Organised Crime Agency** to replace the National Crime Squad and the National Criminal Intelligence Service.

Attitudes towards the police have changed in Britain over the years. The traditional image of the friendly **bobby on the beat**, a policeman going round his local area on foot or on a bicycle armed only with a whistle and a **truncheon** (= long club), is now out of date. The modern police officer, man or woman, is more likely to be **patrolling** in a **police car** and to have less contact with the public. Police officers generally still carry only truncheons as weapons, and though some are trained to use a gun they only carry one in special circumstances. Dishonesty, racial prejudice and excessive use of force by some officers have damaged the public image of the police and in response the police have tried to get rid of dishonest officers and build better relationships with local communities, a practice called **community policing**. More police do now patrol on foot again, instead of in cars.

In the US, law enforcement is carried out by different organizations at the various levels of government. In all, there are about 17 000 **law enforcement agencies** and

they employ more than 800 000 full-time officers. At national level, the *FBI (**Federal Bureau of Investigation**) has about 11 000 **special agents** who investigate crimes across the US. At state level, **state police departments** are responsible for **highway patrols** and their officers are called *state troopers. Each county within a state has an elected *sheriff and the people who work in the sheriff's office, **deputies**, are responsible for investigating crimes. Cities have their own police departments. They may be very large in cities like New York, but those in small towns have only a few officers. Most colleges and universities have their own small police forces.

The members of the US police force who have most contact with the public are uniformed officers, who patrol in cars and are the first to arrive when a crime is reported. More serious crimes are investigated by detectives, who usually wear **plain clothes** instead of a uniform. In spite of the fact that police officers in the US wear guns, they are seen by many Americans as being honest, helpful people who work hard at a dangerous job. This is the image that has been shown in popular television programmes such as *Columbo and *Hill Street Blues*. But in recent years it has become clear that many police officers are prejudiced against *African Americans and *Hispanics and that in some police forces, such as that in *Los Angeles, prejudice and even violence on the part of the police have been common.

,**Sue 'Lawley** /'lɔːli/ (1946–) a British television and radio broadcaster. She has presented current affairs programmes for television, including *Nationwide* (1972–83) and *Here and Now* (1994–7), and since 1988 she has presented the radio programme *Desert Island Discs*.

the '**Law Lords** the eleven members of the *House of Lords in Britain who, together with the *Lord Chancellor, act as the highest *Court of Appeal in England and Wales. A Law Lord must have been a senior judge or be a former Lord Chancellor.

,**lawn 'tennis** ⇨ TENNIS.

,**D H 'Lawrence**[1] /'lɒrəns; *AmE* 'lɔːrəns/ (David Herbert Lawrence 1885–1930) an English writer of novels, short stories and poetry. His father was a miner and this background is sometimes described in his stories. His novels include *Sons and Lovers* (1913), *The Rainbow* (1915) and *Women in Love* (1920). A common theme in his writing is the importance of free emotional and sexual expression, and many of his books were originally considered to be obscene (= offensive or disgusting). His most famous novel, *Lady Chatterley's Lover*, was not published in full in Britain until 1960. Lawrence was also an important modern poet, and his collected poems were published in 1928.

,**Stephen 'Lawrence**[2] /'lɒrəns; *AmE* 'lɔːrəns/ (1974– 1993) a black British teenager who was murdered in South London in 1993 by a group of teenagers. His death and the way it was dealt with by the police became an important national issue and damaged relations between the black community and the police. Although several men were charged with his murder, two trials were stopped because there was not enough evidence and no one has been convicted. In 1997, there was a public inquiry into the case and, as a result, in 1999 the **Macpherson Report** criticized police for racism (= unfair treatment of people who belong to a different race) in dealing with Stephen's murder and recommended changes to the police in Britain.

,**T E 'Lawrence**[3] /'lɒrəns; *AmE* 'lɔːrəns/ (Thomas Edward Lawrence 1888–1935) an English soldier and writer. He began his career as an archaeologist, but in 1916 went to Saudi Arabia to plan and lead a successful military campaign against Turkish rule in the Middle

East, as a result of which he became known as **Lawrence of Arabia**. He described the campaign in his book *Seven Pillars of Wisdom* (1926). This brought him fame and a romantic reputation, but he disliked publicity and tried to escape it by twice changing his name. He died in a motorcycle accident in *Dorset, England. A film, *Lawrence of Arabia*, about his life appeared in 1962.

'law school n a US college at which people study to become lawyers. It is usually part of a university, and students enter it after they have their first degree: *She's at Harvard Law School*. See also LSAT.

Law School Ad'mission Test ⇨ LSAT.

the **'Law So,ciety** the professional organization to which all *solicitors in England and Wales belong. It holds examinations for those wishing to enter the profession, establishes rules for professional practice and deals with complaints against its members. There is a separate Law Society of Scotland.

,Mark **'Lawson**[1] /'lɔ:sn/ (1962–) an English journalist, broadcaster and writer, the son of Nigel *Lawson. He presents radio and television programmes about the arts including *Front Row* on *Radio 4 and *The Late Review* on *BBC2 and writes a column (= a regular piece of writing in a newspaper) in the *Guardian*. He has also written several books including *Bloody Margaret* (1991) and *Going Out Live* (2001).

,Nigel **'Lawson**[2] /'lɔ:sn/ (1932–) an English *Conservative politician. He became a *Member of Parliament in 1974 and *Chancellor of the Exchequer in 1983. He left his job as Chancellor in 1989 after disagreements with the *Prime Minister, Margaret *Thatcher. He was made a *life peer in 1992.

Ni,gella **'Lawson**[3] /naɪˌdʒelə 'lɔ:sn/ (1960–) an English cookery writer and presenter of television cookery programmes. Her books include *How To Eat* (1999), *How to be a Domestic Goddess* (2000) and *Nigella Bites* (2001) based on her television series with the same name. She is the daughter of Nigel *Lawson and she is married to Charles *Saatchi.

'layaway /'leɪəweɪ/ n [U] (*AmE*) a way of buying goods that is an alternative to using a credit card. A customer can pay a small part of the price of something, and the shop will keep the item for a period of time until the rest is paid. Layaway is commonly used for more expensive items, such as furniture.

'Lays of 'Ancient 'Rome /'rəʊm; *AmE* 'roʊm/ a series of four long poems by Thomas *Macaulay published in 1842. Each tells a story from early Roman history. The best known of these is about how Horatius defended a bridge over the River Tiber against the Tuscan army. A later edition in 1848 added stories from modern times.

LBC /,el bi: 'si:/ (*in full* **London Broadcasting Company**) one of the first two commercial radio stations in London, England, broadcasting from 1973 to 1994 and from 1996. The other was *Capital Radio.

LBJ /,el bi: 'dʒeɪ/ ⇨ JOHNSON[4].

LCY /,el si: 'waɪ/ ⇨ LONDON CITY AIRPORT.

L-driver /'el draɪvə(r)/ (*also* **learner driver**) n (in Britain) a person who is learning to drive and has not yet passed the driving test. L-drivers may not drive without having a qualified driver with them and must display **L-plates**, square signs with a large red letter L on a white background, on the front and rear of the vehicle they are driving. Plates with the letter L or P in green are also available, to show that a driver has recently passed the driving test.

LEA /,el i: 'eɪ/ ⇨ LOCAL EDUCATION AUTHORITY.

,Lea and **'Perrins**™ /,li:, 'perɪnz/ the British company that makes *Worcester sauce.

'Leadbelly' /'ledbeli/ (1888–1949) a US singer of the *blues and *folk music who also played the guitar. His real name was Huddie Ledbetter. He was in prison three times between 1918 and 1939, once for murder, before achieving success as a singer. He had a powerful voice, and his hits included *Rock Island Line*, *How Long Blues* and *Goodnight, Irene*.

the **,Leader of the 'House** n a member of the government who is officially responsible for arranging and announcing the programme of business in the British parliament each week. There is a Leader of the *House of Commons and a separate Leader of the *House of Lords.

the **,Leader of the Oppo'sition** n the leader of the largest political party opposing the government in the British *House of Commons, who is also in charge of the *Shadow Cabinet.

the **'League Against 'Cruel 'Sports** a British organization formed in 1924 which opposes *hunting, shooting and other blood sports, and has campaigned for the government to make them illegal. ⇨ note at PRESSURE GROUPS.

the **'League of 'Women 'Voters** (*abbr* **LWV**) an independent US organization of people interested in politics. It encourages citizens to take part in politics and to vote, and tries to influence the government on important issues. It does not support any particular political parties or candidates but arranges television debates between the candidates for US President and provides information about candidates through its DNet (Democracy Net) website. It was originally called the National American Women Suffrage Association and changed its name in 1920, the year in which American women won the right to vote. Men have been admitted as members since 1974.

,Leamington 'Spa /,lemɪŋtən/ a spa town (= a town where there are springs of mineral water considered to be healthy to drink) in *Warwickshire, England. In the late 18th century it became a fashionable place for *upper-class people to meet, and Queen *Victoria gave it the title of 'Royal Leamington Spa' in 1838.

,David **'Lean** /'li:n/ (1908–91) an English film director. His early films included *Brief Encounter* (1946) and the *Dickens stories *Great Expectations* (1946) and *Oliver Twist* (1948). Lean's later films were on a larger scale, including *The Bridge on the River Kwai* (1957), *Lawrence of Arabia* (1962), *Dr Zhivago* (1965) and *A *Passage to India* (1984). He was made a *knight in 1984.

'leap year n a year which happens every four years and has 366 days instead of 365. On the extra day, 29 February, women can traditionally propose marriage to their boyfriends. Compare SADIE HAWKINS DAY.

,Edward **'Lear** /'lɪə(r)/ (1812–88) an English nonsense writer and painter. He spent his early career drawing and painting animals, and in 1832 began work as a painter for the Earl of Derby. He wrote *A Book of Nonsense* (1846) for the Earl's grandchildren, and it was the first of a series of books of nonsense poetry containing *limericks, drawings and longer poems such as *The *Owl and the Pussy-Cat* and *The *Dong with a Luminous Nose*.

,learner **'driver** ⇨ L-DRIVER.

the **,Learning and 'Skills ,Council** a British government organization which is responsible for planning and providing money for education and training outside universities for people over 16 in England. The **National Council for Education and Training for Wales** has a similar responsibility in Wales.

,Timothy **'Leary** /'lɪəri/ (1920–96) a US psychologist and teacher who supported the use of illegal drugs. He became popular with *hippies in the 1960s when he encouraged people to take the drug LSD. He taught at *Harvard University (1958–63) but was dismissed when he and his students took part in experiments with LSD. He spent three years in prison in the 1970s.

> 66 Turn on, tune in, drop out. 99
> Timothy Leary

the **,Leatherstocking 'Tales** /ˌleðəstɒkɪŋ; AmE ˌleðərstɑːkɪŋ/ a series of five novels by the US writer James Fenimore *Cooper. They follow the life of Natty Bumppo, an 18th-century *frontiersman. He first appears in The Pioneers (1823) and then (called Hawkeye) in The *Last of the Mohicans (1826) and (as the Old Trapper) in The Prairie (1827). The other two novels are The Pathfinder (1840) and The Deerslayer (1841).

,Leaves of 'Grass the best-known collection of poems by the US poet Walt *Whitman. They praise America and the free American man. The collection was first published in 1855 with 12 poems, and then eight more times with poems added each time until there were more than 130. They were not very popular during Whitman's life, but are now considered to have had a great influence on later US poetry.

,F R 'Leavis /ˈliːvɪs/ (Frank Raymond Leavis 1895–1978) an English literary critic. He taught at *Cambridge University from 1936 to 1962 and started the magazine Scrutiny (1932–53). In his books New Bearings on English Poetry (1932) and The Great Tradition (1948) he helped to establish modern ideas on the work of such writers as Gerard Manley *Hopkins, T S *Eliot, Henry *James and D H *Lawrence.

,John Le 'Carré /lə ˈkæreɪ/ (1931–) an English author of novels about spies. His real name is John Cornwell. The character George Smiley appears in many of his books, including The Spy Who Came in from the Cold (1963) and Tinker, Tailor, Soldier, Spy (1974). More recent novels include The Tailor of Panama (1996), The Constant Gardener (2001) and Absolute Friends (2003). Many of Le Carré's books have been made into films or television series.

,Huddie 'Ledbetter /ˌhʌdi ˈledbetə(r)/ ⇨ 'LEADBELLY'.

,Led 'Zeppelin /ˌled ˈzepəlɪn/ a British rock group (1968–80). Their *hard rock style was an important influence on later groups, and they were very popular in both Britain and the US. Their most famous song was Stairway to Heaven (1971).

,Christopher 'Lee¹ /ˈliː/ (1922–) an English actor who has appeared in over 120 films since 1948. He is best known for his parts in horror films such as The Curse of Frankenstein (1956) and Dracula (1958). He played the role of Saruman in The *Lord of the Rings films (2001 and 2002).

'Gypsy 'Rose 'Lee² /ˈliː/ (1914–70) a US striptease artist (= entertainer who takes off her clothes for an audience), known for her elegant stage performances. She was a star of the *Ziegfeld Follies in the 1930s, appeared in several films and became popular on television in the 1960s. Lee's book about her life, Gypsy (1957), became a *Broadway musical show (1959) and later a film (1962).

,Laurie 'Lee³ /ˈliː/ (1914–97) an English writer best known for his three books of autobiography, Cider with Rosie (1959), about his childhood in a *Gloucestershire village, As I Walked Out One Midsummer Morning (1969) and A Moment of War (1991). He also published poetry and travel writing.

,Robert E 'Lee⁴ /ˈliː/ (Robert Edward Lee 1807–70) the leader of the armies of the *Confederate States during the American *Civil War. He was respected for his hon-

our and kindness. General Lee won many battles against the larger Union armies, including the second battle of *Bull Run and *Chancellorsville. He lost at *Gettysburg, however, and soon afterwards surrendered to General *Grant at *Appomattox Court House. Before the Civil War, Lee led US forces to arrest John *Brown at *Harpers Ferry. President *Lincoln asked him to lead the US armies, but Lee was loyal to his state of *Virginia and joined the South. After the war, he became President of Washington College, later named Washington and Lee College.

',Spike' 'Lee⁵ /ˌspaɪk ˈliː/ (Shelton Jackson Lee 1957–) a US writer, producer and director of films. His films are known for their political subject matter and often deal with the lives of African Americans. He also acts in some of them. His films include She's Gotta Have It (1986), Mo' Better Blues (1990), Jungle Fever (1991), Malcolm X (1992), Girl 6 (1996) and Bamboozled (2000).

Leeds /liːdz/ a city in *West Yorkshire, England. In the 16th century it began to be an important centre for the production of woollen cloth, and later became a centre of the *Industrial Revolution. The Leeds and Liverpool Canal was opened in 1816. It remains an important industrial city. Its famous buildings include the Town Hall (1853–8), the City Art Gallery (1888) and Armley Mills, a museum of local industrial history. The Royal Armouries Museum opened there in 1996 and Thackray's Medical Museum in 1997. There are two universities in the city. The Leeds International Pianoforte Competition, open to professional piano players under 30, was started in 1963 and is held in the city every three years.

leek n a vegetable of the onion family with green leaves and a long white bulb. It is a Welsh national *emblem (= symbol for the country), possibly because Welsh soldiers used to wear a leek in their caps to recognize each other in battle. See also DAFFODIL. ⇨ note at EMBLEMS.

the **,Left 'Book Club** a British book club (1936–48). It was started by the publisher Victor Gollancz (1893–1967), and its members received books supporting the left in British politics. It had an important influence on the development of the *Labour Party, publishing books such as George *Orwell's The Road to Wigan Pier (1937).

,legal 'aid n [U] money available from the state to help people pay for legal expenses. Legal aid is only available to people whose income is below a certain level, and may not pay for all the expenses involved in a legal action. In Britain it is the responsibility of the **Legal Services Commission** set up by the government. In the US, the **Legal Services Corporation**, an organization that was set up by *Congress in 1974, gives financial support to local Legal Aid Society offices: They applied for and were granted legal aid.

▶ **the legal system**

In Britain, for historical reasons, the system of law used in Scotland is different from that in England and Wales, with the law in Northern Ireland similar to that in England. When making decisions Scottish courts look for an appropriate general principle and apply it to a particular situation. English law relies on **case law**, a collection of previous decisions, called **precedents**. English courts look at precedents for the **case** being tried and make a similar judgement. A basic principle of law in Britain is that anyone accused is **innocent until proven guilty**, so it is the job of the **prosecution** to **prove beyond reasonable doubt** that the **defendant** (= the person accused) has broken the law as stated in the **charge**. If this cannot be proved the person must be **acquitted** (= allowed to go free, with no blame attached).

British law is divided into **civil law** which concerns disagreements between individuals about matters such as business contracts, and **criminal law** which deals with offences that involve harm to a person resulting from somebody **breaking the law**. In civil cases, the **plaintiff** (= the person who claims to have been wronged) **brings an action** against the **defendant** in the hope of winning **damages** (= a financial payment) or an **injunction** (= a court order preventing the defendant from doing something). Criminal cases are brought against criminals by the state, in England and Wales by the *Director of Public Prosecutions and in Scotland through **procurators fiscal**.

In England and Wales most towns have a *Magistrates' Court where minor cases are judged and more serious cases are passed to higher courts by three magistrates called *Justices of the Peace, specially trained members of the public. The more serious cases are heard in a *Crown Court by a **judge** and a **jury**. Minor civil cases, such as divorce and bankruptcy, are heard in the *county courts and more serious ones in the *High Court of Justice. Appeals against decisions from the Crown Court or the High Court go to the *Court of Appeal and a few cases, where a question of law is in doubt, are passed to the *House of Lords.

In Scotland, criminal cases are heard in **District Courts** by members of the public called **lay justices**. More serious cases go to regional **sheriff courts** and are heard by the sheriff and a jury. Appeals go to the *High Court of Justiciary in Edinburgh. Civil cases begin in the sheriff court and may go on appeal to the *Court of Session.

In the US, the **judicial** system is one of the three branches of the *federal government, but the legal system operates at many levels with state, county and city courts as well as federal courts. The right to **trial by jury** is provided by the *Constitution. Each type of court has its own **jurisdiction**, that is it deals with certain kinds of cases. Both civil and criminal cases are first heard in **trial courts** and there is a right to appeal against the court's decision in a **court of appeals**. Many states have **family courts** where people get divorced and **small claims courts** which deal with small amounts of money. States also have trial courts, which hear a wider range of cases, and courts of appeal called **superior courts** or **district courts**. Most states have a **supreme court** where the most serious appeals are held. States have their own **criminal code**, but some crimes are **federal offences**, i.e. against federal law, and crimes may fall under **federal jurisdiction** if more than one state is involved.

Most courts have only one **judge**, but some higher courts have several. In the US Supreme Court, the nine judges are called **justices**. The people on either side of a case are represented by **lawyers**, also called **attorneys-at-law**. In a criminal trial the defendant is represented by a **defense attorney**, or if he or she is too poor to pay a lawyer, the court will appoint a **public defender**. The **prosecution** is led by an **assistant district attorney** or, in federal cases, by a **federal attorney**.

'Legoland™ /'legəʊlænd; AmE 'legoʊlænd/ a place near Windsor, in Berkshire, England, popular for its displays of **Lego**™, small coloured plastic blocks, etc. that children can fit together to make into models. It was opened in 1996 and has other attractions such as fairground rides and restaurants.

Simon Le'gree ⇨ SIMON LEGREE.

'Leicester¹ /'lestə(r)/ an English city in the county of *Leicestershire, now governed by a *unitary authority. It was one of the largest towns in Roman Britain and parts of the Roman city walls remain, as well as a ruined *medieval castle. Leicester became a centre of the wool

trade in the 15th century and is today an important industrial city. The National Space Science Centre opened there in 2001.

the ‚Earl of 'Leicester² /'lestə(r)/ (born Robert Dudley c. 1532–88) an English nobleman and soldier who was a close friend of Queen *Elizabeth I. He was suspected of murdering his wife Amy Robsart in 1560 in order to be free to marry the queen but he and Elizabeth did not marry. She made him an *earl(1) in 1564. See also KENILWORTH CASTLE.

'Leicestershire /'lestəʃə(r); AmE 'lestərʃər/ (abbr **Leics**) a county in the English *Midlands. Its administrative centre, formerly *Leicester, is now Glenfield.

‚Leicester 'Square /‚lestə; AmE ‚lestər/ a square in central London which is popular with tourists, and best known for its large cinemas. It became a public garden in 1874 and motor vehicles are not allowed in it. In its centre is a statue of William *Shakespeare, and to the north is a statue of Charlie *Chaplin.

‚Mike 'Leigh¹ /'liː/ (1943–) an English film and theatre director. His work is about people's ordinary lives, and is often funny and satirical. His films are often created without a script as he works together with actors. His films for television include *Nuts in May* (1976) and *Abigail's Party* (1977) and his cinema films include *High Hopes* (1988), *Secrets and Lies* (1996), *Topsy Turvy* (1999) about the writing of The *Mikado, *All or Nothing* (2002) and *Vera Drake* (2004).

‚Vivien 'Leigh² /'liː/ (1913–67) an English actor, born in India. She achieved great success in the London theatre in the 1930s. She married Laurence *Olivier in 1940 and they moved to *Hollywood, where she won *Oscars for *Gone with the Wind* (1939) and *A *Streetcar Named Desire* (1951).

‚Jack 'Lemmon /'lemən/ (1925–2001) a US actor, mainly in comic roles. His best-known films include *Some Like It Hot* (1959), *The Apartment* (1960), *The Days of Wine and Roses* (1962) and *The Odd Couple* (1967), in which he appeared with Walter Matthau. Lemmon and Matthau also acted together in *Grumpy Old Men* (1993) and *Grumpier Old Men* (1995).

'Lend-Lease n [U] an arrangement during *World War II following the US Lend-Lease Act (1941). The US lent military and other equipment to countries at war with Germany. The programme cost the US $50 billion and it marked the beginning of war production in the US. Countries paid back the loans (= sums of money lent) in various ways, e.g. by allowing the US to use military bases in Europe, etc.

‚John 'Lennon /'lenən/ (1940–80) an English singer and guitar player with The *Beatles pop group, who with Paul *McCartney wrote most of the group's songs. After the group broke up in 1970 Lennon began a new career with his wife Yoko Ono and the Plastic Ono Band, recording *Give Peace a Chance* in 1970 and the album *Imagine* in 1971. He was murdered in New York in 1980.

‚Annie 'Lennox /'lenəks/ (1954–) a Scottish singer, writer of songs and flute player, formerly with the pop group the *Eurythmics. In 1992 she began a career as a singer on her own with the album *Annie Lennox – Diva*. She won an *Oscar for her song *Into the West* on the soundtrack of the 2003 The *Lord of the Rings* film.

‚Jay 'Leno /‚dʒeɪ 'lenəʊ; AmE 'lenoʊ/ (1950–) a US television personality who has presented The *Tonight Show* since 1992. Leno first appeared on the show in 1977 as a comedian.

Lent /lent/ n [U] (in the Christian year) the 40 days from *Ash Wednesday to *Easter. Traditionally, Christians did not eat meat or rich foods during Lent. Today some

L

people stop doing something they enjoy for Lent, such as eating chocolate or drinking alcohol.

,Elmore 'Leonard [1] /ˌelmɔː 'lenəd; *AmE* ˌelmɔːr 'lenərd/ (1925–) a US writer of crime novels. His books are known for their fast action, tough characters and realistic language. His many novels include *Stick* (1983), *Freaky Deaky* (1988), *Rum Punch* (1992) and *Out of Sight* (1997). Several have been made into films, including *Get Shorty* (1995) with John *Travolta.

"Sugar' 'Ray 'Leonard [2] /ˈʃʊɡə ˈreɪ ˈlenəd; *AmE* ˈʃʊɡər, ˈlenərd/ (1956–) a US boxer, the only one ever to have been world champion at different times in five different weight divisions. He also won a gold medal as the Light-Welterweight Champion at the 1976 Olympics.

,Leopold and 'Loeb /ˌliːəpəʊld, ˈləʊb; *AmE* ˌliːəpoʊld, ˈloʊb/ two young Americans, **Nathan Leopold Junior** (1904–71) and **Richard Loeb** (1905–31), who killed 14-year-old Bobby Franks in 1924. They were from rich *Chicago families and wanted to commit the perfect murder. This 'thrill killing' shocked America. Because of the skill of their lawyer, Clarence *Darrow, they were not condemned to death, but were sent to prison for 'life and 99 years'. Loeb was killed in prison but Leopold was released in 1958 and went to live in *Puerto Rico.

,Lerner and 'Loewe /ˌlɜːnər ənd ˈləʊ; *AmE* ˌlɜːrnər, ˈloʊ/ two Americans who wrote several successful *Broadway musical shows together. **Alan Jay Lerner** (1918–86) wrote the words and stories, and **Frederick Loewe** (1901–88), who was born in Austria, wrote the music. Their shows included *Brigadoon* (1947), *Paint Your Wagon* (1951), *My Fair Lady* (1964) and *Camelot* (1960). All of these were made into films, and Lerner and Loewe also wrote a musical film, *Gigi* (1958).

'Lerwick /ˈlɜːwɪk; *AmE* ˈlɜːrwɪk/ a town in the *Shetland Islands, the islands to the far north of Scotland. It is a fishing port and the administrative centre of the islands. In January every year the festival of *Up-Helly-Aa is held in Lerwick to celebrate the islands' *Viking(1) past.

,Doris 'Lessing /ˈlesɪŋ/ (1919–) a British writer, born in Iran. Her early novels, such as *The Grass is Singing* (1950), used the background of southern Africa, where she lived as a child. Many of her novels, including *The Golden Notebook* (1962), are concerned with social and political issues, especially relating to women. She has also written science fiction novels. Her later novels include *The Fifth Child* (1988), *Love, Again* (1996) and *Ben, in the World* (2000). She has written two books about her life, *Under My Skin* (1994) and *Walking in the Shade* (1997), and a collection of 'views and reviews', *Time Bites* (2004).

,Letter from A'merica a British radio programme, presented every week from 1946 to 2004 on *BBC *Radio 4 by Alistair *Cooke.

,David 'Letterman /ˈletəmən; *AmE* ˈletərmən/ (1947–) a US television personality who presents the chat show *The Late Show with David Letterman* on *CBS. He has won 12 *Emmy awards and is known for his unusual humour, which includes having animals do 'stupid pet tricks'. His show first followed *The Tonight Show* with Johnny *Carson, and when he was not chosen by *NBC to replace Carson he moved to *CBS. Compare LENO.

,Lord 'Leverhulme /ˈliːvəhjuːm; *AmE* ˈliːvərhjuːm/ (*born* William Hesketh Lever 1851–1925) an English businessman. He became rich by making soap, and often gave his money to benefit others. One of his best-known projects was the establishment of a 'model industrial village', *Port Sunlight, near Liverpool. He was made a *viscount(1) in 1922. His company later became *Unilever.

> 66 Half the money I spend on advertising is wasted and the trouble is I don't know which half. 99
> Lord Leverhulme

Le'viathan /ləˈvaɪəθən/ a book published by Thomas *Hobbes in 1651. It discusses human society and the relationship between rulers and people. Its conclusion is that a single powerful authority is necessary to prevent 'a war of every man against every man'. The book also contains the famous phrase describing human life as 'solitary, poor, nasty, brutish and short'.

,James Le'vine /ləˈvaɪn/ (1943–) a US conductor who is the musical and artistic director of the *Metropolitan Opera in New York. He also plays the piano.

'Levi's™ /ˈliːvaɪz/ a type of *jeans produced by Levi Strauss Associates in *San Francisco. They were first made during the *Gold Rush by Levi Strauss (1829–1902), who was born in Germany. He had started a company making tents in 1853 and then began to produce tough work clothes in 1874. Levi's became fashionable in the 1960s and are now sold all over the world.

'Levittown /ˈlevɪt-taʊn/ the name of three US towns designed and built by William Levitt soon after *World War II to meet the need for cheap houses for soldiers returning from the war and their families.

,Carl 'Lewis [1] /ˈluːɪs/ (1961–) a US athlete who won eight Olympic gold medals. He took part in the games in 1988 and 1992.

,C S 'Lewis [2] /ˈluːɪs/ (Clive Staples Lewis 1898–1963) a British author, born in Northern Ireland. He is best remembered for his children's books about *Narnia, but he also wrote serious historical works and science fiction novels. His books on Christian themes are also well known, particularly *The Screwtape Letters*, a humorous collection of letters from a senior to a junior devil. Lewis's life was the subject of the film *Shadowlands* (1993).

'Jerry 'Lee 'Lewis [3] /ˈluːɪs/ (1935–) a US singer of *rock and roll and *country music who plays the piano in a wild way, sometimes using his feet on the keys. He is known as 'the Killer'. His early hits included *Whole Lotta Shakin' Goin' On* (1957) and *Great Balls of Fire* (1957). His career was damaged when he married his cousin when she was only 13, but he returned in the 1960s as a country-music singer. He was one of the first group chosen for the Rock and Roll *Hall of Fame in 1986.

,Jerry 'Lewis [4] /ˈluːɪs/ (1926–) a US comic actor who also directs and produces films. He first became famous in the 1950s with Dean *Martin in a series of 16 comedy films. Lewis was the loud, crazy one and Martin was the calm, romantic one who also sang. Lewis's later films have included *The Nutty Professor* (1963). He became the star of the musical show *Damn Yankees* in which he appeared on *Broadway in 1995 and later in London, England.

,Lennox 'Lewis [5] /ˌlenəks ˈluːɪs/ (1965–) a British heavyweight boxer. He spent his early years in Canada, where he achieved his first successes as a boxer, but returned to Britain to become European champion (1990), British champion (1991) and finally the world champion (1993–4).

,Sinclair 'Lewis [6] /ˌsɪŋkleə ˈluːɪs; *AmE* ˌsɪŋkler/ (1885–1951) a US writer of novels which often show ridiculous aspects of American life. He was the first American to receive the *Nobel Prize (in 1930). His books include *Main Street* (1920), *Babbitt* (1922), *Arrowsmith* (1925) (which won the *Pulitzer Prize though Lewis refused to accept it), *Elmer Gantry* (1927) and *Dodsworth* (1929).

,Wyndham 'Lewis [7] /ˌwɪndəm ˈluːɪs/ (1882–1957) an English artist and writer who led the artistic movement known as *Vorticism. During *World War I he was a soldier and an official war artist, and his later paintings include several portraits of artistic figures of the time, including T S *Eliot and Ezra *Pound. He also wrote several novels.

Lewis and 'Clark /ˌluːɪs, ˈklɑːk; AmE ˈklɑːrk/ two US explorers who made the **Lewis and Clark Expedition** in 1804–5. President Thomas *Jefferson sent Meriwether Lewis (1774–1809) and William Clark (1770–1838) to lead an investigation of America's new *Louisiana Purchase and record what they saw. They left from *St Louis in 1804, reached the Pacific Ocean 18 months later, and then returned in 1806. Their journey encouraged many Americans to move to the West. The story of it was told in the film *The Far Horizons* (1955). See also SACAJAWEA.

the 'Battles of 'Lexington and 'Concord /ˈleksɪŋtən, ˈkɒŋkɔːd; AmE ˈkɑːŋkɔːrd/ the first battles of the *American Revolution. On 19 April 1775, a British armed force of about 700 men marched from Boston to destroy American military weapons at the town of Concord, *Massachusetts. The British were stopped at Lexington by 70 *Minutemen, eight of whom were killed in the battle. They then marched to Concord for another battle in which they lost many more men than the Americans and were forced back. This greatly encouraged American hopes for the war.

Libe'race /ˌlɪbəˈrɑːtʃi/ (Wladziu Valentino Liberace 1919–87) a US piano player who wore expensive and colourful clothes and performed in a very exaggerated style. He won an *Emmy for his popular television show (1952–7) and was a star in *Las Vegas for many years. Liberace played and sometimes sang romantic songs and always had candles on his piano. He died from an illness related to AIDS.

the ˌLiberal Demo'cratic ˌParty (also **the Liberal Democrats**, also informal **the Lib Dems**) the third largest British political party. It was formed in 1988 when the *Liberal Party and the *Social Democratic Party joined together. In recent years it has been particularly successful in local government elections as well as in *by-elections. It argues in favour of *proportional representation and its leader is Charles *Kennedy. See also CONSERVATIVE PARTY, LABOUR PARTY.
▶ **Liberal Democrat** (also informal **Lib Dem**) n a member or supporter of the Liberal Democratic Party.

the 'Liberal ˌParty (also **the Liberals**) a former British political party. It developed in the mid 19th century from the *Whigs, and under William *Gladstone and David *Lloyd George became the party of social and political reform. It lost support after the rise of the *Labour Party in the early 20th century. In the elections of 1983 and 1987 the Liberals achieved some success by joining with the *Social Democratic Party to form the Alliance, and the two parties were officially united in 1988. They are now called the *Liberal Democratic Party.
▶ **Liberal** n a member or supporter of the Liberal Party.

'Liberty 1 an independent organization formed in 1934 to protect the legal rights of British citizens and to argue for greater freedom under the existing law. It has fought campaigns to defend the rights of women, homosexuals and people in prison. Until 1989 it was known as the National Council for Civil Liberties. ⇨ note at PRESSURE GROUPS.
2 (also **Liberty's**) a department store in Regent Street, London, England. It was opened in 1875 and sold goods imported from countries such as India and Japan. It later became well known for its *art nouveau designs in furniture and silver and its range of fabrics and carpets.

the ˌLiberty 'Bell a bell used by Americans during the *American Revolution. It is loved as a symbol of freedom and has these words from the Bible on it: 'Proclaim liberty throughout all the land unto all the inhabitants thereof.' It was made in London and taken to Philadelphia in 1752 where it cracked when it was first used. It was repaired and rung for such events as the *Boston Tea Party and when the *Declaration of Independence was first read to the public. It cracked again in 1835 and 1846. In 1976 it was placed in a special case of glass and steel behind *Independence Hall.

'Liberty ˌBonds n [pl] a special issue of US government bonds (= official papers that are sold with the promise to pay the money back, with interest, on a certain date). Liberty Bonds were sold to raise money for *World War I. *Hollywood stars and other famous people attended large public meetings to encourage citizens to buy them, and John Philip *Sousa wrote a *Liberty Bond March*. The total amount of money raised was about $23 billion.

'Lib-Lab /ˈlɪblæb/ adj of any agreement between the *Liberal Party (or *Liberal Democratic Party) and the *Labour Party in Britain. The **Lib-Lab pact** (1977–8) was an agreement between David *Steel of the Liberal Party and James *Callaghan of the Labour government to work together to oppose the *Conservative Party in the *House of Commons: a Lib-Lab deal/agreement/plan.

▶ **libraries**

Almost every town in Britain and the US has a **public library**. Many older libraries were built with money given by Andrew *Carnegie, a US businessman originally from Scotland.

Public libraries are often open until late evening during the week, part of Saturday, and in the US even on Sunday. **Librarians** manage the libraries and advise people how to find the books or information they need.

Public libraries contain **fiction** (= story books), **non-fiction** (= books containing facts), children's books, and usually magazines, CDs, DVDs and videos and have computers with access to the Internet. Every library has a **catalogue** which shows where books on a particular subject can be found. Many US university libraries use the *Library of Congress system for arranging books in order on the shelves. In Britain and in public libraries in the US the *Dewey decimal classification system is the most used.

Libraries are often divided into a **reference section** and a **lending section**. Books from the reference section, e.g. dictionaries and directories, as well as newspapers and magazines, can only be used in the library. Books from the lending section can be borrowed free of charge for a period of two or three weeks by people who are members of the library. Anyone living in the local area can join a library and obtain a **library card**. If a book is returned late, after the **due date**, the borrower has to pay a **fine**. Public libraries are also a source of local information and a centre for community activities. Many have special programmes for children to help them feel comfortable using a library. In school holidays they organize storytelling and other entertainments.

Travelling libraries (= libraries set up inside large vans) take books round country areas for people who cannot easily get to a town. In the US travelling libraries are called **bookmobiles**. Schools, colleges and universities have their own private libraries for the use of students and teachers.

In both Britain and the US public libraries receive money from local and national government but, increasingly, they do not receive enough for their needs. In Britain some smaller libraries have had to close. In the US people believe strongly that information and educa-

L

tion should be freely available. Libraries are important in achieving this but, as in Britain, they do not get sufficient money and depend on the help of volunteers who work without pay.

The biggest library in Britain is the *British Library in London with over 150 million books, CDs, DVDs, and tape recordings. Other important libraries include the National Libraries of Scotland and Wales, the *Cambridge University Library and the *Bodleian Library in Oxford. These libraries are called *copyright libraries or **legal deposit libraries** and are entitled to receive a free copy of every book that is published in Britain. The largest library in the US is the *Library of Congress in Washington, DC.

the ˌLibrary of ˈCongress the national library of the US. It was established by the US Congress in 1800 and is on Independence Avenue in *Washington, DC. It now has more than 115 million books and other items. The library has the right to receive two copies of every US work published with a copyright (= legal right of ownership).

the Library of Congress

▶ licensing laws

The sale of alcohol in Britain is controlled by licensing laws. These restrict where, when and by whom alcohol may be sold. The Licensing Act of 2003 made changes to the law. In order to open a *pub or wine bar the owner must obtain the approval of the local authority, which must be satisfied that he or she is a suitable person to sell alcohol. If the application is approved the owner obtains a **licence** to sell alcohol and becomes the **licensee**. The name of the licensee is displayed above the front door. The 2003 Act states that many of the restrictions on opening hours will be removed. Worries about the effects of these changes, when drunkenness is already a serious problem in British towns and cities, meant that the introduction of the new law was delayed.

Many pubs are licensed to sell alcohol for drinking **on or off the premises** (= in the pub or somewhere else). However, most people buy alcohol for drinking at home in a supermarket or an **off-licence** (= a shop that sells mainly alcohol). Shops and supermarkets have to get a licence, called an off-licence, before they can sell alcohol. Nobody under 18 is allowed to buy alcohol, either in a pub or in a shop.

Pubs are only allowed to sell alcohol during official **opening hours**. Until all the changes in the new law come into effect, pubs are allowed to remain open all day from 11 a.m. to 11 p.m., though many close in the afternoon, but if they wish to stay open after 11 p.m. they must obtain a special **late licence**. Pubs open for a shorter time on Sundays.

In the US there are local laws about when and where alcohol can be sold. Some towns are **dry**, i.e. no alcohol can be sold there at all. In general, restaurants and bars need a licence to sell beer and wine. In some

states alcohol for drinking at home is sold only in special **liquor stores**; in other places it is sold in any food shop. There are fewer restrictions on when alcohol can be sold than there are in Britain, and bars can stay open very late. The most common restriction is that alcohol may not be sold early on Sunday mornings.

The US has strict laws to try to keep young people from coming into contact with alcohol. The **drinking age** (= the age at which a person can buy alcohol) is 21, and bars and liquor stores often ask customers for proof of age. In many places, people below 21 cannot work in, or even enter, bars or restaurants that serve alcohol. College students, especially, try to drink in bars by pretending to be older than they are. Young people who work in food shops may have to ask an older employee to serve a customer who wants to buy a bottle of wine.

ˌRoy ˈLichtenstein /ˈlɪktənstaɪn/ (1923–97) a US painter who helped to establish *pop art. Many of his pictures, e.g. *Whaam!* (1963), are like large *comic strips, and are seen as comments on popular culture. Lichtenstein sometimes drew other artists' pictures again in his own style, such as his 1992 version of Vincent Van Gogh's *Bedroom at Arles*. He also made plastic and metal sculptures.

Life a US magazine which is known especially for its photographs. It was first published in 1936 by Henry Luce who owned *Time* magazine. His aim was to enable readers 'to see life; to see the world; to witness great events'. After television became popular, *Life* went out of business in 1972, but it was brought back in 1978, appearing every month and then from 2004 every two months.

the ˈLife Guards a regiment of the British royal *Household Cavalry, responsible for protecting the queen or king and appearing at state ceremonies. They also perform the ceremony of the *Changing the Guard. See also HORSE GUARDS(1).

ˌLife on ˈEarth a very successful British television series about the development of life on this planet, written and presented by David *Attenborough and broadcast on the *BBC in 1979. More series on natural history have followed it, all presented by Attenborough: *The Living Planet* (1984), *The Trials of Life* (1990), *The Private Life of Plants* (1995), *The Life of Birds* (1998) and *The Blue Planet* (2001).

ˌlife ˈpeer *n* any of the members of the British *House of Lords who hold their position as a reward for public service but cannot pass their title on to their children. Male life peers are given the title of *baron and are addressed as 'Lord', and female life peers are given the title of *baroness or countess and are addressed as 'Lady', 'Baroness' or 'Countess'. **Life peerages** are given by the government, often to former *Members of Parliament. ⇨ note at PEERAGE.

ˈLife ˌSavers™ small, hard US sweets/candies which are round and have a hole in the middle. They are available in 25 different flavours and sold in tubes. They were invented in 1912 by Clarence Crane and the name refers to the fact that the white rings look like lifebelts/life preservers.

ˌLift ˈEvery ˈVoice and ˈSing a popular song that is often called the 'African-American National Anthem'. It was written in 1900 for *Lincoln's Birthday celebrations by James Weldon Johnson, a writer who was the first *African American to be leader of the *NAACP (1916–30), with music by his brother J Rosamond Johnson. The song begins:

> 66 Lift every voice and sing,
> Till earth and heaven ring,
> Ring with the harmonies of Liberty.
> Let our rejoicing rise
> High as the list'ning skies,
> Let it resound loud as the rolling sea. 99

,light 'ale *n* [U, C] (*BrE*) a type of *bitter beer which is light in colour and usually sold in bottles. ⇨ note at BEER. Compare PALE ALE.

The ,Light of the 'World a very popular painting (1851–3) by Holman *Hunt, who did several versions of it. It shows Jesus Christ holding a lamp and knocking on the door of a house.

,Li'l 'Abner /,lɪl 'æbnə(r)/ a popular US newspaper *comic strip (1934–77), drawn by Al Capp (1909–79). The stories were about *hillbillies who lived in Dogpatch, and the main characters were Li'l (Little) Abner, his beautiful girl friend Daisy Mae and his mother Mammy Yokum. The characters were used for a 1956 *Broadway musical show and later a film, both called *Li'l Abner*. See also SADIE HAWKINS DAY.

,Lili Mar'lene /,lɪli mɑːˈleɪn; *AmE* mɑːrˈleɪn/ a song that became popular with both British and German soldiers during *World War II, especially those fighting in North Africa. It is about a young woman waiting for a soldier outside the gate of the barracks where he is living. The most famous version was sung by Marlene *Dietrich.

,Lillibur'lero (*also* **Lillibulero**) /,lɪlɪbəˈleərəʊ; *AmE* ,lɪlɪbərˈleroʊ, ,lɪlɪbəˈleroʊ/ the signature tune (= tune played to identify a radio station) of the *BBC World Service. The music is by Henry *Purcell and was written for a satirical 17th century song attacking *Roman Catholics. The lullaby (= song sung to make a young child go to sleep) *Hush-a-bye, Baby* has a similar tune.

'Lilliput /'lɪlɪpʊt/ a country visited by Gulliver in *Gulliver's Travels* by Jonathan *Swift. The **Lilliputians** are only six inches tall, and because of this their political disputes and wars with their neighbours are made to look ridiculous. See also BROBDINGNAG, YAHOOS.
  ▶ **Lilli'putian** /,lɪliˈpjuːʃn/ *adj* very small: *Even our largest banks look Lilliputian in comparison with European ones.*

,Rush 'Limbaugh /,rʌʃ 'lɪmbɔː/ (1951–) a US broadcaster. Since 1988 he has had a popular radio talk show on which he expresses his strong right-wing opinions. Limbaugh also appears on television and has written several books.

'limerick *n* a type of short funny poem with five lines, the first two rhyming with the last, and the third with the fourth. They are very popular in Britain and are sometimes quite rude. Limericks first appeared in print in 1820 and were later made famous by Edward *Lear in his *Book of Nonsense* (1846). Lear usually used the same word to end the first and last lines:

> 66 There was an Old Man of the Border,
> Who lived in the utmost disorder;
> He danced with the Cat,
> And made tea in his Hat,
> Which vexed all the folks on the Border. 99

Modern limericks use a different rhyme at the end:

> 66 There was a young lady of Crewe,
> Who dreamed she was eating her shoe.
> She woke in the night,
> In a terrible fright,
> And found it was perfectly true. 99

'Limey /'laɪmi/ *n* (*AmE slang*) a British person. The word was used especially by US military forces during *World War II, often as an insult, to mean a British sailor or soldier. It refers to the old practice in the British navy of drinking the juice of limes (= green fruit like lemons) to avoid getting the disease of scurvy which is caused by the lack of vitamin C.

'Lincoln¹ /'lɪŋkən/ the administrative centre of *Lincolnshire, in the east of England. It was originally a Roman city and has several important Roman remains. It also contains many beautiful *medieval buildings, including a castle, begun in 1068, and a famous cathedral with three spires (= pointed towers), built mainly between the 11th and 14th centuries. The city has one of Britain's newest universities, opened in 1996.

,Abraham 'Lincoln² /'lɪŋkən/ (1809–65) the 16th US *President (1861–5). He is regarded by many people as America's greatest president, because he served during the *American Civil War, preserved the Union and freed the slaves. He is also often referred to as 'Honest Abe'. He was a lawyer who was elected to the US *House of Representatives in 1846 and then elected President as a *Republican(1). Lincoln led the Union in the Civil War and in 1864 appointed Ulysses S *Grant to lead the Union armies. He announced his *Emancipation Proclamation in 1863 to free the slaves in the South. Lincoln was shot and killed by the actor John Wilkes *Booth. See also GETTYSBURG ADDRESS, LINCOLN MEMORIAL.

the 'Lincoln 'Center for the Per'forming 'Arts (*also* the **'Lincoln ,Center**) /'lɪŋkən/ a group of buildings that include theatres and concert halls in New York, west of *Central Park and *Broadway. They were built at various times between 1959 and 1991. The Center is the home of the *Metropolitan Opera, the *New York Philharmonic and the *Juilliard School of Music, as well as other organizations.

,Lincoln 'green /,lɪŋkən/ *n* [U] the colour of a type of green cloth originally made in Lincoln, England, or the cloth itself. It is traditionally said to have been worn by *Robin Hood and his men.

,Lincoln 'Logs™ /,lɪŋkən/ a US make of children's toy which consists of sets of very small wooden logs (= pieces of wood) which can be fitted together to make model buildings. Lincoln Logs were first made in 1916 and are now made by the toy company Hasbro.

the ,Lincoln Me'morial /,lɪŋkən/ a large building in Washington, DC, in memory of President Abraham *Lincoln. It is made of marble and the design by Henry Bacon was based on the Parthenon in Athens, Greece. The Memorial is in West Potomac Park at one end of the *Mall and was completed in 1922. Inside is a large statue of Lincoln sitting in a chair. The words of his

*Gettysburg Address and his speech at his second
*Inauguration Day are cut into stone inside the building.

Lincoln's 'Birthday /ˌlɪŋkənz/ a US holiday on 12
February celebrating the birthday of President Abraham
*Lincoln. It was first celebrated in 1866 in Washington,
DC, and was declared a national holiday in 1892.

'Lincolnshire /'lɪŋkənʃə(r)/ (*abbr* **Lincs**) a county in
the east of England. Its administrative centre is
*Lincoln.

Charles 'Lindbergh /'lɪndbɜːɡ; *AmE* 'lɪndbɜːrɡ/
(1902–74) a US pilot who became the first person to fly
across the Atlantic Ocean alone. His popular name was
Lindy, and he was also known as the 'Lone Eagle'. He
flew from New York on 20 May 1927 and arrived in Paris
33½ hours later. His plane was called *Spirit of St Louis*.
When he returned, he received the largest parade ever
given in New York. In 1932, his baby son was stolen and
killed in a case that shocked America. Lindbergh wrote
the story of his life, called *The Spirit of St Louis*, which
won the 1954 *Pulitzer Prize.

'Lindisfarne /'lɪndɪsfɑːn; *AmE* 'lɪndɪsfɑːrn/ (*also* **Holy
Island**) a small island off the coast of *Northumberland
in north-east England. A monastery (= Christian religious community) was established there in the 7th century, although the ruined buildings that survive are from
the early *Norman period. It also has a 16th-century
castle.

Lindisfarne

the ˌLindisfarne 'Gospels /ˌlɪndɪsfɑːn; *AmE*
ˌlɪndɪsfɑːrn/ a book containing the four Christian
Gospels, produced on the island of *Lindisfarne around
AD 700. It is written by hand, with many beautiful pictures and decorations, and contains early examples of
the northern version of Old English. It is now kept in the
*British Library, London.

'Lindow Man /'lɪndəʊ; *AmE* 'lɪndoʊ/ the body of a man
found in 1984 preserved in Lindow Moss, an area of soft
wet ground in *Cheshire, England. Scientists think that
he was killed in a religious ceremony at some time
between 300 BC and 300 AD, and may have been a local
prince. The body can be seen in the *British Museum,
London. See also PETE MARSH.

'line dancing *n* [U] a style of dancing that became
popular in the US in the early 1990s, and later in Britain.
It involves dancing to *country music, with the dancers
standing in lines and moving together with a series of
steps, turns and kicks. Dancers often wear wide 'cowboy'
hats and other clothing associated with country music.

ˌGary 'Lineker /'lɪnəkə(r)/ (1960–) an English football
player. He began his career with Leicester City (1978–85)
and then played for *Everton and Barcelona before moving to *Tottenham Hotspur (1989–92). His 80 international games for England have included World Cup
matches in 1986 and 1990. He stopped playing seriously

in 1994 and is now a sports presenter on British radio
and television.

'linen a fabric made from flax, used to make high-quality
clothes, sheets, tablecloths, etc. Northern Ireland has
been a centre for the linen industry for hundreds of
years and is an important exporter of **Irish linen** to
countries around the world.

the Lin'nean So,ciety /lɪ'neɪən/ an organization
established in 1788 at *Burlington House, London,
England, for the scientific study of plants and animals. It
was named after Carolus Linnaeus (1707–78), a Swedish
scientist who invented a system for naming living things,
and whose library and scientific collections are kept by
the Society. The Society publishes several scientific
journals.

'Linus /'laɪnəs/ a character in the cartoon *Peanuts. He is
a small boy who is Charlie Brown's friend and is usually
seen holding a blanket for comfort. A **Linus blanket** is
the name sometimes given to the piece of material that a
child uses in this way.

**the ˌlion and the 'uni-
corn** two animals that
appear on the British
*royal arms (= a special
royal symbol). The lion
represents England, and
the unicorn, an imaginary
animal like a horse with a
long horn on its forehead,
represents Scotland. There
is a traditional children's
*nursery rhyme about the
lion and the unicorn,
which may have its origin
in old conflicts between
the two countries:

the lion and the unicorn

> 66 The lion and the unicorn
> Were fighting for the crown;
> The lion beat the unicorn
> All round about the town. 99

the Lions ⇨ BRITISH LIONS.

the 'Lions Club an organization of people who work
together on projects to help their local communities. It
was founded in 1917 in the US and Lions Clubs International, with headquarters in Illinois, has many
thousands of branches around the world.
▶ **Lion** *n* a member of the Lions Club.

ˌWalter 'Lippmann /'lɪpmən/ (1889–1974) a US journalist. He wrote a regular political column called *Today
and Tomorrow*, which appeared in newspapers around
the world. He wrote for the *New York Herald-Tribune*
(1931–62) and then for the *Washington Post (1962–7),
and won the *Pulitzer Prize twice. Lippman also helped
to establish the magazine *New Republic* in 1914.

'Lipton /'lɪptən/ a product name for the many varieties
of tea including iced tea, sold by the Thomas J Lipton
Company, part of *Unilever.

ˌLiquid 'Paper™ *n* [U] a US make of liquid used for
painting over written or typed mistakes on paper. It
dries quickly and the correction can then be written or
typed over it. It is sold in small bottles and is available in
white and other pale colours. Compare TIPP-EX.

ˌliquorice 'allsorts /ˌlɪkərɪʃ 'ɔːlsɔːts; *AmE* 'ɔːlsɔːrts/
n [pl] (*especially BrE*) soft sweets made in a variety of colours and shapes, all containing liquorice (= a black substance obtained from a plant root). They are usually sold
in packets.

listed 'building n (in Britain) a building that is protected by law because it is very old or has some other important feature. It appears on an official list and must not be pulled down or changed without special permission from a government department.

Listen with 'Mother a *BBC radio programme (1950–82) of songs, rhymes and stories for small children. The programme always began with these words: 'Are you sitting comfortably? Then I'll begin.'

Joseph 'Lister /'lɪstə(r)/ (1827–1912) an English doctor who is best known for introducing the antiseptic system (= a way of preventing infection during medical operations by keeping things very clean and using a spray of a special acid). He was President of the *Royal Society (1895–1900) and was made a *baron in 1897.

'Listerine™ /'lɪstəriːn/ n [U] a product name for a liquid for cleaning inside the mouth, sold in bottles. It was first sold in 1895 in the US and is available in different flavours.

the 'Battle of 'Little 'Bighorn /'bɪɡhɔːn; AmE 'bɪɡhɔːrn/ the battle (1876) in which George *Custer was killed with all 259 of his men of the Seventh Cavalry. This became known as Custer's Last Stand. The soldiers were surrounded near the Little Bighorn River in *Montana by a large force of *Cheyenne and *Sioux Native Americans, led by *Crazy Horse and *Sitting Bull.

Little Bo-'Peep /bəʊ 'piːp; AmE boʊ/ a girl in a traditional *nursery rhyme. The first verse is:

> 66 Little Bo-Peep has lost her sheep,
> And doesn't know where to find them;
> Leave them alone, and they'll come home
> Bringing their tails behind them. 99

Little Boy 'Blue a boy in a traditional *nursery rhyme. The full poem is:

> 66 Little Boy Blue, come blow your horn,
> The sheep's in the meadow, the cow's in the corn.
> Where is the boy who looks after the sheep?
> He's under a haycock fast asleep! 99

Little 'Britain a British comedy series on *BBC television which has sketches (= short comic plays) about people and situations which exaggerate different aspects of British life in a funny way. It was a radio programme on *Radio 4 before being made into a television programme.

Little 'Chef any of 350 restaurants on major roads in Britain, selling quick meals for travellers: There's a Little Chef in about five miles.

Little 'Dorrit /'dɒrɪt; AmE 'dɔːrɪt/ a novel (1855–7) by Charles *Dickens. Little Dorrit (whose real name is Amy) is the main character. She is a young woman whose father William Dorrit is in *Marshalsea prison for owing money. She falls in love with Arthur Clennam, a man who tries to help her father. The book is noted for its descriptions of Marshalsea, where Dickens's own father was a prisoner for a time.

Little 'House on the 'Prairie the title of a novel published in 1935 by the US writer Laura Ingalls Wilder (1867–1957), one of the series based on her childhood experiences travelling in the Mid-West. A popular television series (1974–84) was based on the novels.

Little 'Italy /'ɪtəli/ the Italian district of New York City. It is on the *Lower East Side of *Manhattan(1), and Mulberry Street is its lively centre. Little Italy is popular with tourists, especially for its many restaurants. The Feast of San Gennaro is celebrated on the streets in September. In many other US cities, the Italian district is also called Little Italy.

Little Jack 'Horner /'hɔːnə(r); AmE 'hɔːrnər/ a boy in a traditional *nursery rhyme. The poem may refer to a man called Jack Horner who was a servant of King *Henry VIII.

> 66 Little Jack Horner
> Sat in a corner,
> Eating a Christmas pie;
> He put in his thumb
> And pulled out a plum,
> And said, What a good boy am I! 99

Little 'John one of the companions of *Robin Hood. His name was a joke, because he was in fact very tall and strong.

Little Lord 'Fauntleroy /'fɔːntlərɔɪ/ a children's book (1886) by Frances Hodgson *Burnett, about a young American boy who discovers that he is the son of a British *earl(1). He has long fair hair and is always well dressed and polite. The name is now sometimes used to describe a young boy who is dressed in fancy clothes or who is unnaturally polite.

Little Miss 'Muffet /'mʌfɪt/ a girl in a traditional *nursery rhyme. Miss Muffet, it is said, was the daughter of Dr Thomas Muffet, a famous 16th-century scientist who studied insects.

> 66 Little Miss Muffet
> Sat on a tuffet,
> Eating her curds and whey;
> There came a great spider,
> Who sat down beside her,
> And frightened Miss Muffet away. 99

Little 'Nell a character in The Old Curiosity Shop (1841) by Charles *Dickens. The story is about a girl, Nell Trent, who together with her father is forced to leave her home. After many adventures and much suffering Nell finally dies. The scene describing her death is well known, and is sometimes criticized as too sentimental (= full of exaggerated emotion).

Little Orphan 'Annie a popular US newspaper *comic strip. It was begun in 1924 by Harold Gray (1894–1968) and continued until 1979. The main characters are Annie, whose parents are dead, her dog Sandy, and rich 'Daddy' Warbucks who looks after her. They also appeared in a radio series and the *Broadway musical Annie (1977), which became a film (1982).

Little Red 'Riding Hood a traditional story found in many European countries. A girl called Little Red Riding Hood goes to visit her grandmother in the forest, but when she arrives a wolf has eaten her grandmother and put on her clothes. Little Red Riding Hood is surprised at the appearance of her grandmother and says, 'Grandmother, what big eyes you have!' 'All the better to see you with,' replies the wolf. 'Grandmother, what big teeth you have!' says the girl. 'All the better to eat you with,' replies the wolf, and eats her. Little Red Riding Hood and her grandmother are saved when a hunter cuts open the wolf's stomach and they escape.

Little 'Richard (1935–) a US singer of early *rock and roll who also played the piano. He was born Richard Wayne Penniman and was known for his wild, noisy style. His hits included Tutti Frutti (1956), Lucille (1957) and Good Golly, Miss Molly (1957). He stopped singing in 1957 to become a preacher (= religious leader) and said that rock and roll was 'the devil's music'. He began to sing again in 1964, mostly the *blues and *soul music. In

L

1986 he was one of the first people to be chosen for the Rock and Roll *Hall of Fame.

'Little Rock the capital and largest city of the US state of *Arkansas. It is an industrial centre on the Arkansas River. It became known around the world in 1957 when President *Eisenhower sent US Army forces there to protect *African Americans who wanted to attend city schools with white people. This caused a lot of violence. Bill *Clinton later lived in Little Rock as the governor of Arkansas (1978–80 and 1982–90) before he became President.

Little 'Women a very popular US book (1868–9) written mainly for girls by Louisa May *Alcott. The story, based on that of her own family, is about the March family of four sisters, living in *New England in the 19th century. The girls are Meg, Jo, Beth and Amy. Film versions were made in 1933 with Katharine *Hepburn, 1949 with Elizabeth *Taylor, and 1994 with Winona Ryder. Alcott wrote two further books with the same characters: *Little Men* (1871) and *Jo's Boys* (1886).

,Joan 'Littlewood /'lɪtlwʊd/ (1914–2002) an English theatre director. She began her career in the 1930s directing plays for *working-class audiences. She formed a group called Theatre Workshop and developed new ways of presenting plays at the Theatre Royal, Stratford East, in London. Her productions included *A Taste of Honey* (1959) and *Oh What a Lovely War* (1963) both of which were later made into films.

'Littlewoods /'lɪtlwʊdz/ a company that owns department stores with many branches around Britain and a mail order business, selling clothes and household goods.

,Littlewoods 'Pools /ˌlɪtlwʊdz/ a form of gambling on the results of football games run by Littlewoods Gaming. Littlewoods Pools first started in 1923 and there have been many 'pools millionaires'.

'Live Aid two very large pop concerts held at the same time in London, England, and Philadelphia, US, in 1985. The aim of the concerts was to encourage people to give money to help people dying of hunger in Africa and £150 million was given. The concerts were organized by Bob *Geldof and followed the success of *Band Aid. See also COMIC RELIEF. ⇨ note at AID.

Pe,nelope 'Lively /'laɪvli/ (1933–) a British writer, born in Egypt, who has written many novels and stories for adults and children. She won the *Booker Prize in 1987 for *Moon Tiger*, a novel set in Cairo during *World War II.

'liver bird /'laɪvə; AmE 'laɪvər/ n the name of an imaginary bird, from which the name 'Liverpool' is supposed to come. The liver bird is the symbol of Liverpool and can be seen on top of the two towers of the Royal Liver Building in Liverpool. *The Liver Birds* was also the name of a popular *BBC television comedy series (1969–79) about two young women living in Liverpool.

'Liverpool /'lɪvəpuːl; AmE 'lɪvərpuːl/ a large city and port in north-west England, on the River Mersey. It first became important during the *Industrial Revolution, producing and exporting cotton goods. It was also a major port for the slave trade, receiving profits from the sale of slaves in America. In the 20th century the city became famous as the home of the *Beatles and for Liverpool and Everton football clubs. Among its many famous buildings are the Royal Liver Building with its two towers, the Anglican and Roman Catholic cathedrals, and the *Walker Art Gallery. See also MERSEY BEAT.

the 'Liverpool and 'Manchester 'Railway /'lɪvəpuːl ənd 'mæntʃestə 'reɪlweɪ; AmE 'lɪvərpuːl, 'mæntʃestər/ a railway between Liverpool and Manchester in north-west England, opened in 1830. It was the first public railway in the world that used steam trains for its whole length, and was built by George *Stephenson.

'Liverpool Street /'lɪvəpuːl; AmE 'lɪvərpuːl/ a train station in London, England, for trains to and from *East Anglia. It also has a station on the *London Underground.

,Liver'pudlian /ˌlɪvə'pʌdliən; AmE ˌlɪvər'pʌdliən/ n a person who was born in or who lives in *Liverpool (from a humorous use of 'puddle' instead of 'pool' at the end of the word 'Liverpool'). See also SCOUSE.
▶ **Liverpudlian** adj: : a Liverpudlian actor.

'livery ,company n any of the ancient City of London guilds (= associations of business people or skilled workers), each with their own special livery (= uniforms). Guilds of traders selling the same goods or services were once very powerful in London, and modern livery companies are descended from them. There are over a hundred of them, including the Grocers, the Drapers, the Fishmongers and the Goldsmiths. Members of each company meet together for social occasions and for charity work. See also GUILDHALL.

,David 'Livingstone[1] /'lɪvɪŋstən/ (1813–73) a Scottish explorer and missionary (= person sent to teach the Christian religion). He became famous through his travels in Africa, and was the first European to see the Victoria Falls in 1855. In the late 1860s he was thought to be lost while trying to find the source of the River Nile. The journalist Henry Morton *Stanley went to look for him and found him at Ujiji in 1871. Livingstone died in Africa but his body was brought back to England and buried in *Westminster Abbey.

> 66 'Doctor Livingstone, I presume,' 99
> Stanley's words when he met David Livingstone in Africa.

,Ken 'Livingstone[2] /'lɪvɪŋstən/ (1945–) a British *Labour politician. He was leader of the *Greater London Council (1981–6) and was known (especially in the tabloid press) as 'Red Ken' because of his left-wing political views. After the Greater London Council was closed down in 1986 he became a *Member of Parliament. In 2000 he was not chosen as the Labour candidate for *Mayor of London but was elected as an independent candidate. In 2004, he was re-elected, this time as the official Labour Party candidate. He is well known for his unusual hobby of keeping newts (= small animals with long tails that can live in water or on land).

> 66 If voting changed anything, they'd abolish it. 99
> the title of Ken Livingstone's 1987 autobiography

the 'Lizard /'lɪzəd; AmE 'lɪzərd/ a piece of land that sticks out into the sea in southern *Cornwall, England. Its tip, **Lizard Point**, is the place on the British mainland that is furthest to the south. See also LAND'S END.

,Llan'gollen /ˌθlæn'ɡɒθlən; AmE ˌθlæn'ɡɑːθlən/ a town in North Wales where the International Music *Eisteddfod is held every year.

,L L 'Bean /ˌel el 'biːn/ any of a group of US shops selling a large range of equipment for outdoor activities, including boots, jackets, hats, tents, tools and fishing equipment. The company is known for its catalogues (= books sent to people's homes showing items they can order by post). It was established in 1912 by Leon Leonwood Bean in Freeport, *Maine, where the main office still is.

,Harold 'Lloyd[1] /'lɔɪd/ (1893–1971) a US comic actor in over 500 silent films. His typical character was shy and wore glasses, and often got into dangerous situations. The best known of these was a scene in *Safety Last* (1923), in which Lloyd hangs by his hands from a large clock on the outside of a tall building. His other films included *The Freshman* (1925) and *The Kid Brother* (1927). He received a special *Oscar in 1952.

Marie 'Lloyd² /ˌmɑːri ˈlɔɪd/ (1870–1922) one of the most popular of all English *music-hall performers. She was famous for her *cockney humour and for comic songs, such as *A Little of What You Fancy Does You Good* and *Oh, Mr Porter*, which shocked some people because they often referred to sex, though in a humorous way.

'David 'Lloyd 'George /ˈlɔɪd ˈdʒɔːdʒ; AmE ˈdʒɔːrdʒ/ (1863–1945) a British *Liberal politician of Welsh parents, who was *Prime Minister of Britain from 1916 to 1922. As *Chancellor of the Exchequer (1908–15) he introduced *pensions (1908) and *National Insurance (1911), two important elements of the modern *welfare state. He became Prime Minister during *World War I, but after the war *Conservative opposition to his policy of independence for Ireland forced him to resign. He remained in Parliament for the rest of his life, but neither he nor the Liberal Party ever returned to power. He was made an *earl(1) shortly before his death in 1945.

Lloyd's of 'London /ˌlɔɪdz/ (also **Lloyd's**) an association of people in the City of London who provide insurance. These members, known as 'names', share the profits and also the risks involved. The first members used to meet at Edward Lloyd's coffee house in the late 17th century. They were originally concerned with insuring ships, but now deal with insurance of all kinds all over the world. In the early 1990s Lloyd's had to make a number of very large payments to people who were insured with them, with the result that the 'names' lost a lot of money. See also LUTINE BELL.

'Lloyd's 'Register /ˈlɔɪdz/ a society, formed in 1760, which each year publishes **Lloyd's Register Book**, a detailed list of ships, boats, etc., for insurance purposes. The ships are listed according to their size, type and condition.

Lloyds TS'B /ˌlɔɪdz tiː es ˈbiː/ (also **Lloyds**) one of the largest British banks, formed in 1995 when Lloyds Bank, which was established in 1765, joined with the TSB (Trustee Savings Bank). Its symbol is a black horse on a green background.

'Andrew 'Lloyd 'Webber /ˈlɔɪd ˈwebə(r)/ (1948–) a very successful English writer of *musicals. His early shows were 'rock operas' written with Tim Rice, including *Joseph and the Amazing Technicolour Dreamcoat* (1968), *Jesus Christ Superstar* and *Evita* (1976). Later musicals include *Cats*, *The Phantom of the Opera* (1986), *Sunset Boulevard* (1993), *Bombay Dreams* (2002) and *The Woman in White* (2004). He won an *Oscar in 1996 for the song *You Must Love Me* and was chosen for the Songwriters' *Hall of Fame in 1995. He was made a *knight in 1992 and a *life peer in 1997.

the Phantom of the Opera

Ken 'Loach /ˈləʊtʃ/ (1936–) a British film maker who makes film about the lives of ordinary people and the social and economic problems they face. His early work was for television, and included plays such as *Up the Junction* (1965) and *Cathy Come Home* (1966). His later films made for the cinema have included *Kes* (1969), *Raining Stones* (1993), *My Name is Joe* (1998), *Bread and Roses* (2000) and *Sweet Sixteen* (2002).

'Loaded a British magazine published every month since 1994, which is aimed at young men aged around 18 to 30. It contains a lot of pictures and short articles about subjects such as cars, fashion, music and women.

> 66 for men who should know better 99
> slogan of *Loaded* magazine

▶ **lobbying**

Lobbying is the practice of approaching politicians in order to persuade them to support a particular aim or cause, and to speak about it and draw attention to it. In the US this means trying to obtain the support of members of *Congress or a state legislature (= people making laws at state level). In Britain lobbying involves persuading *MPs or members of the *House of Lords to speak in *Parliament and the same is true for members of the Scottish Parliament or Welsh Assembly.

Anyone can write to their MP or a member of Congress, or organize a petition about an issue, but most lobbying is now done by *pressure groups or by professional **lobbyists**. Pressure groups work on behalf of a particular section of society or for a specific issue or cause. Many employ full-time **liaison officers** to develop contacts with politicians who are likely to be sympathetic. In Britain some MPs are employed by pressure groups as **consultants**. They have to give details of such employment in a special **Register of Members' Interests**.

Large companies use professional lobbyists to keep them informed of what is being discussed in Congress or Parliament and to try to persuade politicians to put forward their point of view in debates. In the US lobbyists provide information to politicians, sometimes by testifying (= giving evidence) before Congress. They also try to influence the way members of Congress vote, for example by persuading them that a certain policy will be popular with the people they represent. Lobbyists may try to influence politicians by inviting them to an expensive lunch or dinner in a restaurant, or to a party. There are rules limiting what gifts politicians can accept and any gifts must be reported. Some organizations have many lobbyists who are very active.

In Britain the methods which lobbyists use to influence MPs, and the question of whether MPs should be connected with lobbyists at all, came to public attention in 1996 when two MPs were found guilty of taking money in exchange for asking questions in Parliament. It became known as the *cash for questions affair and led to the setting up of the *Committee on Standards in Public Life and the publishing of the Register of Members' Interests for each new Parliament.

Local Edu'cation Au,thority n (abbr **LEA**) a department of local government in Britain that provides money to run the state schools and colleges in its area. Some of the schools and colleges in the area of any Local Education Authority, however, are given money directly by central government, for example the *City Technology Colleges and *Academies. Compare SCHOOL DISTRICT. See also OPTING OUT.

▶ **local government**

The system of local government is slightly different in England, Scotland, Wales and Northern Ireland. England is divided into **counties** each with a **county council** which is responsible for certain services. Each county is divided again into **districts**, each with a **district council** responsible for a smaller area. Districts are further divided into **parishes** which were originally villages with churches. In some parts of England, there are instead **unitary authorities** which have just one level of local government responsible for an area or city, sometimes called a **metropolitan district**. London has a separate system with an elected **Assembly** and a **mayor**. In Scotland, there are 32 **council areas**. Wales is divided into 22 counties and **county boroughs** and Northern Ireland has 26 districts. All of these are unitary authorities with one level of local government.

Councils consist of **councillors** who are representatives elected by local people for a period of four years. Most councillors belong to a political party and, especially at county level, people often vote for them as representatives of a party, not as individuals. Since the Local Government Act of 2000, councils have been led by a **council leader** and a **cabinet** of councillors, or a **directly elected mayor** and a cabinet. In 2004 there were 12 directly elected mayors in England, including the Mayor of London. Councils meet in a **council chamber** at the local **town hall** or **county hall**.

Councils make policies for their area which are carried out by **local government officers**, who have a similar role to *civil servants. **Local authorities** (= councils and committees) have responsibilities for education, social services, housing, transport, the fire and police services and other local services. Many people are employed by councils, but many services are also now carried out by private companies who are given contracts by the council. Councils receive some money from central government in the form of **grants**, they also collect **council tax** from each household, a locally set tax based on the value of the house.

In the US, local government has three levels, with the **State government**, **County government** and below that, towns and cities. State government is organized in a similar way to the *federal government, with a **state constitution** in most states which explains the powers of the three branches of state government, the executive, the legislative and the judicial. The executive branch is headed by a **governor** and state laws are made by a **legislature**, which usually has two houses, a **Senate** and a **House of Representatives**. The judicial branch usually consists of a state supreme court and several lower courts. States have great influence and organize their own system of courts and set local income tax and sales tax.

States are divided into counties which have a county government located in a town or city called the **county seat**. The structure of county government varies from state to state, but most counties have a **Board of Commissioners**, sometimes called a **Board of Supervisors**, with the Board and other county officials usually being elected. Services provided by a county government depend on the area, whether it is mainly urban or rural. In urban areas, city and county governments may work together to provide services for the area. Counties usually have a **sheriff's department**, a kind of police department, whose officers are called **sheriff's deputies**.

America's cities, towns, villages and other **municipalities** vary greatly from small towns of a few hundred people to cities of millions. For that reason, there is no single system of local government. Most towns and cities have an elected mayor as their head and a council, made up of elected members from different areas of the city, which makes **ordinances** (= local laws). A **municipal government** usually has its own police force and courts, runs local schools, takes care of the roads, and may also provide services like public transport, water and electricity.

ˌlocal 'radio n [U] the radio stations in Britain that broadcast to a local rather than a national audience, within a county or town. Local radio may be run by the *BBC or by a commercial company with a licence from *Ofcom. ⇨ note at RADIO.

ˌLoch 'Lomond /ˌlɒx 'ləʊmənd, ˌlɒk; AmE ˌlɑːx 'loʊmənd, ˌlɑːk/ a traditional Scottish song. Loch Lomond is a lake surrounded by mountains in west Scotland. The song contains the famous lines:

> ❝ Oh, you'll take the high road,
> And I'll take the low road,
> And I'll be in Scotland before you;
> But me and my true love will never meet again,
> On the bonnie, bonnie banks of Loch Lomond. ❞

ˌLoch 'Ness /ˌlɒx 'nes, ˌlɒk; AmE ˌlɑːx, ˌlɑːk/ a long, narrow and deep lake in the *Highlands of Scotland. It is famous for the **Loch Ness monster**, also known informally as **Nessie**. The monster is thought by some people to be a large animal like a dinosaur (= an animal that lived millions of years ago) that spends most of its time underwater. Many people claim to have seen it, and there is a special Loch Ness Monster Exhibition Centre for tourists on the edge of the lake. However several scientific investigations have failed to find any evidence that it exists.

ˌJohn 'Locke /'lɒk; AmE 'lɑːk/ (1632–1704) an English philosopher. In his *Two Treatises of Government* (1690) he opposed the ideas of Thomas *Hobbes, arguing that governments should rule only if they are supported by the people. This was an important influence on the later revolutions in America and France, and on the development of Western democracy. Locke also wrote books on religion, education and economics. His most famous work of philosophy is *An Essay Concerning Human Understanding* (1690), an attempt to show what can and cannot be known.

'Lockerbie /'lɒkəbi; AmE 'lɑːkərbi/ a town in southern Scotland. It became famous in 1988 when a US plane (Pan Am Flight 103) exploded above it, killing all 259 people on board and 11 people on the ground. Authorities in Britain and the US believed the explosion was caused by a bomb placed on the plane by two Libyan men. In January 2001, at the end of their trial, the court decided that one man was guilty and one was not guilty.

ˌLockheed 'Martin /ˌlɒkhiːd 'mɑːtɪn; AmE ˌlɑːkhiːd 'mɑːrtɪn/ a US company, formed in 1994 when the Lockheed Corporation and the Martin Marietta Corporation were joined together. It produces military aircraft, space rockets, satellites (= electronic devices in space) and other electronic equipment. Its F-22 Raptor aircraft for the US Air Force first flew in 1997. The company's main office is in Bethesda, *Maryland.

ˌDavid 'Lodge /'lɒdʒ; AmE 'lɑːdʒ/ (1935–) an English author and critic. He is known especially for his humorous books about life in Britain's universities, such as *Changing Places* (1975), *Small World* (1984) and *Nice Work* (1988), some of which have been made into successful television series. He taught English at *Birmingham University, the model for the 'Rummidge' in his novels. Later works include *Therapy* (1995), *Thinks ...* (2001) and *Author, Author* (2004), a novel about the middle age of Henry *James. He has also written literary criticism.

ˌlog 'cabin n a small, simple house made of logs laid horizontally and joined without nails at the corners. These were common in the frontier parts of America (= at the extreme limits of settled land) from the 17th century. President Abraham *Lincoln was born in one in *Kentucky. Many later politicians also claimed that they had been born in log cabins in order to persuade people that they came from poor, ordinary families and had become successful by hard work.

'logrolling /'lɒgrəʊlɪŋ; AmE 'lɑːgroʊlɪŋ/ n [U] (AmE) the practice among politicians of voting for each other's *bills. By giving support they expect to receive support in turn. The word comes from the early US custom by which friends helped each other to roll logs in order to clear land for farming, etc. Compare PORK BARREL.

Lo'lita /lə'liːtə/ a novel (1958) by Vladimir *Nabokov. The main character, Humbert Humbert, is sexually attracted to a girl called Lolita who is only 12 years old. There have been two film versions of the book (1962 and 1998), the first directed by Stanley *Kubrick. The name 'Lolita' is sometimes used to refer to a young girl who is regarded as sexually desirable.

ˌ**Vince Lom'bardi** /lɒm'bɑːdi; AmE lɑːm'bɑːrdi/ (1913–70) a US professional American football trainer, known for his tough methods. He trained the Green Bay Packers of *Wisconsin from 1959 to 1967, during which time they won 141 games and lost only 39. His teams won the National Football League Championship five times (1961–2 and 1965–8) and the first two *Super Bowls (1967–8). The Vince Lombardi Trophy, given to the team that wins the Super Bowl, is named in memory of him.

> 66 Winning isn't everything. It's the only thing. 99
> Vince Lombardi

'Lombard Street /'lɒmbɑːd; AmE 'lɑːmbɑːrd/ a street in the centre of London, England, which is the city's main financial district, containing branches of many of Britain's major banks. The street's name comes from Lombardy, the area in northern Italy from which many bankers came to settle in London in the late 13th century. Compare THREADNEEDLE STREET.

▶ **London**

The capital city of England and the United Kingdom lies on the River *Thames, which winds through the city. Its many bridges, including *London Bridge, is a famous sight. The most distinctive is *Tower Bridge, which was designed to blend in with the nearby *Tower of London.

The Tower, which is guarded by the *Yeomen Warders, was built in the 11th century. In the medieval period London grew rapidly in size and import-

cafe in the former Covent Garden market

ance. *Westminster Abbey and the *Guildhall date from this time, and the *Palace of Westminster became the meeting place of *Parliament. In 1666 many buildings were destroyed in the *Fire of London. This provided an opportunity for architects like Christopher *Wren to redesign much of the city. As London's population increased, new streets, squares and parks were added, and many public buildings. London was heavily bombed in *World War II, after which a new cycle of rebuilding began.

London is a busy commercial and cultural centre. Many important financial organizations, including the *Bank of England and the London Stock Exchange, are located in the area called the *City. Part of the old port in east London has been redeveloped as a business centre, called *Docklands. In the *West End there are theatres, cinemas, museums and shops. Many people who work in

London commute by train or bus from the suburbs because buying a house or flat near the centre is very expensive. Different parts of the city are linked by the famous red London buses, black taxi cabs and the *London Underground, often called 'the *Tube'.

People from all over the world have been attracted to London and it is now a cosmopolitan, multicultural city. People from other parts of Britain sometimes think that it is very noisy and dirty. Many go there only for the 'bright lights' — the theatres round *Shaftesbury Avenue or the shops of *Oxford Street and *Regent's Street. Others take their children to see the sights, such as *Buckingham Palace, where the Queen lives, and the clock tower from which *Big Ben chimes the hours. Young people are attracted to the bars and comedy clubs of *Covent Garden, to live music concerts, and the stalls of *Camden market and the cafes and pubs of *Notting Hill and similar areas.

ˌ**Jack 'London** /'lʌndən/ (1876–1916) a US writer of adventure novels and short stories. Before starting to write he worked as a sailor and went to the *Klondike to look for gold, experiences which he later used in his books. His novels include *The Call of the Wild* (1903), *The Sea-Wolf* (1904) and *White Fang* (1906). His work influenced Ernest *Hemingway and other US writers.

the ˌ**London As'sembly** /ˌlʌndən/ the group of people who form part of the local government of London, elected by the people of London every four years, at the same time as the *Mayor of London. The Assembly is made up of 25 members. 14 of them are directly elected to represent *constituencies and 11 are elected to represent all of London, using a form of *proportional representation. They examine the Mayor's activities and policies, and question him about his decisions. They are also able to investigate other issues of importance to *Londoners, and make proposals to the Mayor.

ˌ**London 'Bridge** /ˌlʌndən/ a bridge across the River *Thames in London, England, connecting the ancient centre of the city to the district of *Southwark. Until 1750 it was the only bridge crossing the Thames in London. The present bridge, built in 1973, replaced one that was sold to a US businessman and rebuilt in *Arizona.

'**London 'Bridge is 'Falling 'Down** /'lʌndən/ the title and first line of an old children's song. In the song various materials are suggested for rebuilding the bridge, beginning with 'wood and clay' and ending with 'silver and gold'.

ˌ**London 'Broadcasting ˌCompany** /'lʌndən/ ⇨ LBC. ⇨ note at RADIO.

'**London 'Central 'Mosque** /'lʌndən/ a large mosque (= place of worship for Muslims) in *Regent's Park, London, England, completed in 1976 as part of the Islamic Cultural Centre.

ˌ**London City 'Airport** /ˌlʌndən/ (abbr LCY) an airport near *Canary Wharf in east *London. It opened in 1987 and is used mainly for flights to British and European cities. Compare HEATHROW.

'**Londonderry** /'lʌndənderi/ (also 'Derry)
1 ⇨ DERRY.
2 one of the former *Six Counties of Northern Ireland.

the ˌ**Londonderry 'Air** /ˌlʌndənderi/ a traditional tune from Northern Ireland, first published in 1855. Many different words have been set to it, the most famous being those of the Irish song *Danny Boy*.

'**Londoner** /'lʌndənə(r)/ n a person who lives in or comes from London, England.

L

the **London 'Eye**
/ˌlʌndən/ a 135-metre high wheel next to the *Thames in London. It was opened in 2000 and immediately became very popular. The wheel has glass containers which people travel in as it goes slowly round so that they have a view across the whole city.

the London Eye

the **London 'Film Festival** /ˌlʌndən/ a festival held in London every autumn at which new films from around the world are shown to the public. It is organized by the *BFI.

The **London Ga'zette** /ˌlʌndən/ a newspaper that gives British government announcements, including information of interest to people in government departments and the legal profession, as well as lists of recent honours (= awards for services to the country). It first appeared in 1665 and is now published five times a week.

the **London 'Library** /ˌlʌndən/ a large private library in London, England, which members must pay to join. It was established in 1841 and contains over one million books in all European languages. Compare British Library.

London 'Lighthouse /ˌlʌndən/ a British charity formed in 1986 to provide advice, information and medical care for people with the disease AIDS. See also Terrence Higgins Trust.

the **London 'marathon** /ˌlʌndən/ a race for runners held every year in London, England, since 1981. The race is 26 miles/42 kilometres long, starting at *Greenwich and ending at *Westminster Bridge. Thousands of runners take part, many of them to raise money for charity.

the London Marathon

the **London Pal'ladium** /ˌlʌndən pəˈleɪdiəm/ a large theatre in London, England, opened in 1910 and now used mainly for performances of *musicals.

the **London ˌPhilhar'monic 'Orchestra**
/ˈlʌndən/ (abbr the **LPO**) a leading British orchestra established in London in 1932 by Thomas *Beecham. Its main conductor since 2000 is Kurt Masur and past conductors have included Adrian *Boult (1951–7), Bernard Haitink (1967–79) and Georg *Solti (1979–83). It is based at the *Royal Festival Hall and plays at *Glyndebourne every summer.

The **London Re'view of 'Books** /ˈlʌndən/ a British newspaper containing reviews of new books, as well as essays on politics, literature and the arts. It was established in 1979 and appears every two weeks.

the **London 'School of Eco'nomics** /ˈlʌndən/ (abbr the **LSE**) a famous college in London, England, offering courses in economics, politics, law and many other subjects. It was established in 1895 by Sidney *Webb and other members of the *Fabian Society and is part of *London University.

the **London 'Stock Ex,change** /ˌlʌndən/ (abbr **LSE**) an institution in London, England, established in the 18th century, which allows trading in stocks and shares (= parts of the total value of a company). Since *Big Bang in 1986 trading has taken place using computers and telephones, rather than in the offices of the Stock Exchange itself. See also New York Stock Exchange, Stock Exchange Automated Quotations.

the **London 'Symphony ˌOrchestra** /ˌlʌndən/ (abbr the **LSO**) a leading British orchestra established in London in 1904. Famous conductors of the orchestra have included André *Previn (1968–79) and Claudio Abbado (1979–87), and since 1993 its main conductor has been Colin *Davis. It is based at the *Barbican Centre.

the **London to 'Brighton 'Veteran 'Car Run**
/ˈlʌndən, ˈbraɪtn/ a British race for old cars held in November every year. The race starts at *Hyde Park, London, and finishes at *Brighton, and is for cars built before 1905. It is a popular social occasion, with the drivers sometimes dressing in Victorian or Edwardian costumes, and is often shown on television.

London 'Underground /ˌlʌndən/ London's underground train services, which are run by *Transport for London. The first underground railways in London were begun in the 19th century, and were the first of their kind in the world. The 11 lines of the system (usually known as **the Underground** or informally as **the Tube**) are connected to train stations and extend out of the centre of London to surrounding regions. Not all of the lines are in fact underground for the whole of their routes. Additions to the system have included the *Docklands Light Railway, a privately owned railway that provides services to London Docklands.

London Underground

London Uni'versity /ˌlʌndən/ (also **the University of London**) a university in London, England, started in 1836. It consists of a large number of colleges in different parts of the city, including *Imperial College London, the *London School of Economics and *University College. It also includes the *teaching hospitals *Bart's and *Guy's. About one fifth of London University students study abroad and take examinations in their own countries as part of the External Programme.

L

Lord

London 'Zoo /ˌlʌndən/ a zoo in *Regent's Park, London, England. It was established in 1826 by the Zoological Society of London. Today the zoo is an important centre for the study of animals, and breeds animals that are in danger of disappearing in their native environments. Another branch of the zoo is at *Whipsnade.

the ˌLone 'Ranger a character in stories about the American *Wild West who spends his life preserving justice and fighting those who do wrong. He wears a mask and rides a white horse called Silver. His *Native American friend Tonto calls him 'Kemo Sabe' (which means 'trusty scout'). Together they defeat many outlaws (= criminals). Fran Striker created the character for a US radio series (1933–54) and then wrote 17 Lone Ranger novels. *The Lone Ranger* was also a popular television series (1949–57), with Clayton Moore as the Lone Ranger.

Huey 'Long /ˌhjuːi 'lɒŋ; AmE 'lɔːŋ/ (1893–1935) a powerful US politician in the state of *Louisiana, also known as 'Kingfish'. He used emotional speeches and a programme of taxes called Share the Wealth to get money from big businesses and win votes from poor people, while making himself very rich through dishonest deals. He became Governor of Louisiana (1928–31) and a US Senator (1930–35). He had hopes of standing for election as President but was murdered. *All the King's Men*, a novel (1946) by Robert Penn Warren and then a film (1949) was based on Long's life.

'Long Beach 1 a city near *Los Angeles in the US state of *California. It is a popular holiday place and an industrial port that produces oil, aircraft and electronic equipment. The British ship *Queen Mary* was moved there in 1967 as a hotel, museum and tourist attraction. **2** a US town on *Long Island, New York. It has a white beach which has attracted tourists since the 19th century.

'Long Day's 'Journey into 'Night a play by the US writer Eugene *O'Neill, written between 1939 and 1941. It was first performed in 1956 after O'Neill died, and won the *Pulitzer Prize. It is a sad story about the Tyrone family, based on O'Neill's own family. James Tyrone is a cruel father, his wife Mary takes drugs, one son Edmund has tuberculosis (= a disease of the lungs) and the other son Jamie is dependent on alcohol.

ˌlong-distance 'routes a network of paths for walkers and cyclists across Scotland, managed by Scottish Natural Heritage. There are five long-distance routes: the West Highland Way, the Southern Upland Way, which runs from coast to coast across southern Scotland, the Speyside Way, the Great Glen Way and the *Pennine Way which starts in Scotland and continues as a *National Trail in England.

'Henry 'Wadsworth 'Longfellow /'wɒdzwəθ 'lɒŋfeləʊ; AmE 'wɑːdzwərθ 'lɔːŋfeloʊ/ (1807–82) one of the most popular US poets. He wrote long poems which helped to create romantic American legends (= stories from the past which may or may not be true). They include *Evangeline* (1847), *The Song of Hiawatha* (1855), *The *Village Blacksmith* (1841), *The Courtship of Miles Standish* (1858) and *Paul Revere's Ride* (1861). Longfellow also taught modern languages at *Harvard University (1836–54). See also HIAWATHA.

'longhorn /'lɒŋhɔːn; AmE 'lɔːŋhɔːrn/ n a breed of cattle with long horns, originally from Mexico, which was common in the US in the 19th century. The cattle taken along the *Chisholm Trail to Abilene, *Kansas were usually **Texas longhorns**. Longhorns have now mostly been replaced by cows that have more meat.

ˌLong 'Island an island off the southern end of the US state of New York. It is about 118 miles/190 kilometres long and 12–23 miles/19–37 kilometres wide and has an area of 1400 square miles/3627 square kilometres. Its western end includes the New York districts of *Brooklyn and *Queens, and the rest of the island has small towns and holiday places including areas such as the Hamptons where many rich people live. Its beaches are very popular. During the *American Revolution, the army of General George *Washington lost the Battle of Long Island (August 1776) to the British forces of Sir William Howe. See also LONG BEACH(2).

ˌLong John 'Silver /'sɪlvə(r)/ a character in *Treasure Island* by Robert Louis *Stevenson. Long John Silver is a pirate (= a person on a ship who attacks and robs other ships) with one leg and a parrot (= a colourful bird) which sits on his shoulder.

ˌLongleat 'House /ˌlɒŋliːt; AmE ˌlɔːŋliːt/ a large Elizabethan house in *Wiltshire, England, owned by the Marquess of Bath. It was built in the late 16th century. It is now open to the public and has a safari park (= a park where people can drive round and see wild animals, such as lions) and gardens designed by 'Capability' *Brown. ⇨ note at STATELY HOMES.

the ˌLong 'Parliament the English parliament first called to meet by King *Charles I in 1640. Its opposition to the king led to the *English Civil War between the **Parliamentarians** and the **Royalists**. Many of its members were dismissed in 1648 and it became known as the *Rump Parliament. This was itself dismissed in 1653. At the *Restoration in 1660 a new parliament was created.

Studs 'Lonigan /ˌstʌdz 'lɒnɪgən; AmE 'lɑːnɪgən/ a character in three novels by the US writer James *Farrell. They are *Young Lonigan* (1932), *The Young Manhood of Studs Lonigan* (1934) and *Judgement Day* (1935). Lonigan is a good man who struggles to succeed in the 1920s in the poor Irish district of South Side, *Chicago.

ˌLonsdale 'Belt /ˌlɒnzdeɪl; AmE ˌlɑːnzdeɪl/ n a decorated belt given as a prize in British boxing to a boxer of any weight who wins a major professional competition. If a boxer wins such a competition three times in a row he is allowed to keep the belt.

ˌLook 'Back in 'Anger a play (1956) by John *Osborne. Its main character, Jimmy Porter, is an '*angry young man' who directs his anger about British society at his *upper-class wife Alison. The play was a great influence on other writers of the 1950s, and these writers and Osborne himself also became known as 'angry young men'. A film (1959) was later made, with Richard *Burton as Jimmy Porter.

ˌLooney 'Tunes™ /ˌluːni/ the general name for the US film cartoons produced by *Warner Brothers from the 1930s to the 1960s. The film characters included *Bugs Bunny, Porky Pig, *Daffy Duck, *Tweety Pie, Speedy Gonzales and Pepe le Pew. Tex *Avery drew many of them, and Mel Blanc supplied their voices. The characters also appeared in a Warner Brothers' series called *Merrie Melodies*. Every Looney Tunes film ends with the phrase 'That's all, folks' appearing on the screen.

the Loop the central business district of the US city of *Chicago. It gets its name from the loop made by the *El railway/railroad that runs round its edges.

ˌJennifer 'Lopez /'ləʊpez; AmE 'loʊpez/ (also **J Lo**) (1970–) a Puerto Rican-American pop singer and actor whose albums include *On The 6* (1999) and *J Lo* (2001). She has appeared in the films *The Cell* (2000) and *Maid in Manhattan* (2003). She also has her own range of fashion clothing and perfumes.

Lord 1 a title given to all male members of the *House of Lords, including peers and *bishops. (*Dukes, even if they are members of the *House of Lords, are not addressed as 'Lord'.) It is also given as a *courtesy title to

the children of some members of the House of Lords: *Baron Fleming of Rotherham can also be addressed as Lord Fleming.* ◇ *Lord Derby* (= the title of the Earl of Derby) ◇ *Lord Doune, the eldest son of the 5th Earl of Murray.*
2 a title given to certain high officials: *Lord Lieutenant/ Lord Chief Justice/Lord Chancellor.*
3 My Lord a way of addressing judges, *bishops and peers (except *dukes), showing respect. ⇨ note at PEER-AGE.

the ˌLord 'Advocate *n* the senior legal official in Scotland (equivalent to the *Attorney General in England, Wales and Northern Ireland) who is responsible for advising the *Scottish Parliament on the law and who appears on behalf of the state in important cases. ⇨ note at LEGAL SYSTEM.

the ˌLord 'Chamberlain *n* (*in full* the ˌLord 'Chamberlain of the 'Household) (in Britain) the official who is in charge of the royal household and responsible for arranging royal ceremonies.

the ˌLord 'Chancellor (*also* the ˌLord High 'Chancellor) *n* the government minister who is head of the judiciary (= all the judges) in England and Wales. He is also the *Speaker of the *House of Lords, and sits on the *Woolsack. In the Constitutional Reform Bill (2004) it was proposed that the post of Lord Chancellor should be abolished. ⇨ note at LEGAL SYSTEM.

the ˌLord Chief 'Justice *n* (in British law) the President of the *Queen's Bench Division of the *High Court of Justice, who is next highest in rank to the *Lord Chancellor in the legal system of England and Wales. ⇨ note at LEGAL SYSTEM.

the ˌLord High 'Chancellor ⇨ LORD CHANCELLOR.

ˌLord 'Jim a novel (1900) by Joseph *Conrad. It tells the story of a young ship's officer who leaves a ship that appears to be sinking, before all the other passengers on board. He later feels very ashamed of this act and goes to live abroad, where he finally wins back his honour.

the ˌLord Lieu'tenant *n* (in Britain) a representative of the king or queen in a *county, responsible for arranging royal ceremonies there when the king or queen visits. He is also the head of a county's magistrates. Compare HIGH SHERIFF.

the ˌLord 'Mayor *n* the *mayor of certain large cities in England and Wales. He or she is elected every year by the city council, and has mainly ceremonial duties. The *City of London has had a Lord Mayor since 1192, who during his or her period of office lives at the *Mansion House. In Scotland a similar post is held by the *Lord Provost. Compare MAYOR, MAYOR OF LONDON.

the ˌLord Mayor's 'Banquet a large formal meal held every year at the *Guildhall, London, England, to mark the retirement of the previous year's *Lord Mayor of London. It is attended by the *Prime Minister, who traditionally makes a speech.

the ˌLord Mayor's 'Show a public procession held every year in London, England, when the newly elected *Lord Mayor of London rides in a carriage to the *Law Courts to be presented to the *Lord Chief Justice. The carriage is joined by various other vehicles and people in colourful costumes. The ceremony takes place on the second Saturday in November.

the Lord Mayor's carriage

ˌLord of the 'Flies a novel (1954) by William *Golding. It tells the story of a group of boys left on an island after a plane crash. At first they attempt to live together in a peaceful way but later become cruel to each other and worship an invented god, the 'Lord of the Flies' (a pig's head covered in flies). In writing the book Golding used the names of some of the characters of an earlier, very different children's story, *The Coral Island* (1858) by R M Ballantyne.

The ˌLord of the 'Rings a book in three parts (1954–5) by J R R *Tolkien. It features some of the characters from an earlier book, *The *Hobbit* (1937), and tells of their long journey to a place where they can destroy a magic ring. It is set in the imaginary world of Middle Earth. The book is popular with adults and children in many countries around the world. Three films have been made based on the three parts of the book: *The Fellowship of the Ring* (2001), *The Two Towers* (2002) and *The Return of the King* (2003), which won 11 *Oscars.

the ˌLord 'President of the 'Council the title of the British government minister who is President of the *Privy Council (= group of people who advise the king or queen). He or she is also either the *Leader of the House of Commons or the Leader of the House of Lords.

the 'Lord 'Privy 'Seal *n* the British government official who formerly kept the seal (= a piece of metal used to stamp wax to show that documents are genuine) of the king or queen. Today the Lord Privy Seal no longer has this responsibility, but is usually either the *Leader of the House of Commons or the Leader of the House of Lords.

ˌLord Pro'tector (*also* Protector, ˌLord Pro'tector of the 'Commonwealth) the title given to Oliver *Cromwell and later to his son Richard (1626–1712) during the period after the *English Civil War known as the *Protectorate (1653–9). During this time Cromwell and his son claimed greater powers to rule the country, including the power to rule independently of Parliament.

ˌLord 'Provost /ˌlɔːd 'prɒvəst/ *n* the Scottish equivalent of a *Lord Mayor.

Lord's a famous English cricket ground in St John's Wood, north London, where test matches (= international games) are regularly played. It is named after Thomas Lord (1755–1832), who established the ground in 1814. The *MCC and the *England and Wales Cricket Board are both based there, and it is the place where The *Ashes are kept. It is also the ground of Middlesex County Cricket Club. See also OVAL, SEASON.

the ˌLord's 'Prayer (*also* Our Father) the prayer taught by Jesus in the Bible to his followers, beginning 'Our Father'. It is often used in church services and most Christians in Britain and the US know all the words.

the ˌLords 'Spiritual *n* [pl] the 26 senior *bishops of the *Church of England who are members of the British *House of Lords.

the ˌLord's 'Taverners /ˈtævənəz; AmE ˈtævərnərz/ a British cricket team made up of famous actors and entertainers, who play matches to raise money for charity. The team is named after the Tavern, a club at *Lord's cricket ground in London. The **Lady Taverners** was formed in 1987 and organizes fund-raising events.

the ˌLords 'temporal *n* [pl] the members of the British *House of Lords who are not *bishops.

ˌLorna 'Doone /ˈduːn/ a romantic novel (1869) by the English author R D Blackmore (1825–1900). It is set on *Exmoor in the 17th century, and tells the story of a young man who falls in love with a girl called Lorna Doone. Unfortunately she is from the family who murdered his father. Several historical events of the period form part of the story.

Los 'Alamos /ˌlɒs ˈæləmɒs; AmE ˌlɔːs ˈæləmɔːs/ a small US town in northern *New Mexico. The first atomic bomb and hydrogen bomb were developed there at the US government's nuclear research centre established in 1943, and the town grew around the centre. The Los Alamos National Laboratory (LANL) is now operated by the University of California for the US Department of Energy, and its work in education and research includes a Neutron Science Center.

Los 'Angeles /ˌlɒs ˈændʒəliːz; AmE ˌlɔːs/ (also informal **LA** /ˌel ˈeɪ/) the second largest city in the US and the largest in *California, with about 9 million people. Its area covers 34 000 square miles (more than 88 000 square kilometres) in the southern part of the state on the Pacific coast, and is connected by the world's largest road system. The city is famous for *Hollywood and *Beverly Hills and its tourist attractions include *Sunset Boulevard, the *Hollywood Bowl, *Universal Pictures and *Rodeo Drive. Los Angeles is one of the busiest US ports and is an important industrial centre.

The US captured the town from the Mexicans in 1846, and oil was discovered there at the end of the 19th century. Americans think of Los Angeles as an exciting city with many opportunities. But it is also seen as a dangerous place because of its earthquakes, pollution, traffic problems and race riots (= violent conflicts between people of different races). See also KING, UCLA.

the ˌLos ˌAngeles 'Police De,partment /ˌlɒs ˈændʒəliːz; AmE ˌlɔːs/ (abbr **LAPD**) the police department for the US city of *Los Angeles, one of the largest police departments in the world with many divisions for crime and traffic, including the Air Support Division with two planes and 19 helicopters. The department has had problems with the racial prejudice of some of its officers, including the attack on Rodney *King and statements by one officer at the trial of O J *Simpson.

the ˌLos ˌAngeles 'Times /ˌlɒs ˈændʒəliːz; AmE ˌlɔːs/ a newspaper for the US city of *Los Angeles first published in 1881. It has won more than 20 *Pulitzer Prizes and is considered to be one of America's best newspapers. The Los Angeles Times Syndicate supplies special articles to newspapers and magazines in many countries, and the Los Angeles Times-Washington Post News Service sends news to newspapers, magazines, and radio and television stations around the world.

the ˌLost ˌGardens of 'Heligan /'helɪɡən/ gardens in *Cornwall which were originally created by the family who lived at Heligan House from the 16th century until the first half of the 20th century. The family had introduced many plants from around the world and experimented with new methods of growing fruit and vegetables. The gardens were not looked after for many years until **Tim Smit** discovered them in 1991. The gardens have now been restored to their original form and are open to the public.

the ˌlost gene'ration n [sing] **1** a generation (= group of people born at about the same time) with many of its young men killed in war, especially *World War I, or one which has suffered emotional damage by growing up during war. **2** a group of young US writers of the 1920s, among them Ernest *Hemingway, who were opposed to the moral values of US life in the period following *World War I and went to live abroad, especially in Paris.

▶ **lotteries**

Britain did not have a national lottery until 1994 when the government finally approved the project despite strong opposition. The **National Lottery** is run by a pri-

vate company, *Camelot, which was given the franchise (= licence) to run it by the **National Lottery Commission**.

The lottery was an immediate success with the public and its 'crossed fingers' logo, a gesture supposed to bring luck, is familiar throughout Britain. Lottery **tickets** are sold at many shops and supermarkets. For £1 people choose a row of six numbers between 1 and 49, or take a **lucky dip** of random numbers. The **draw** ceremony is broadcast every Saturday and Wednesday night. One of three machines containing 49 numbered balls is switched on and, after the balls have been turned, seven are tipped out. The first six are the winning numbers, the seventh is the **bonus ball**. Anyone who has chosen the six winning numbers wins or shares the **jackpot** (= the main prize), worth several million pounds. People with three, four or five matching numbers, or five plus the bonus ball, can also win prizes. If nobody wins the jackpot there is a **rollover** to the next draw. About 65% of adults play every week. Some also buy **Instants**, cards which show, when the surface is scratched off, if the buyer has won a prize.

Most of the money raised by the lottery is shared out among a variety of **good causes** such as the **Heritage Lottery Fund**, the *Arts Council and **UK Sport**. The lottery is not popular with everyone, and many charities complain that they have received less money from the public since the lottery began.

The US does not have a national lottery but there are lotteries in most states. US lotteries date back to 1776 when the *Continental Congress gave its approval for lottery tickets to be sold to raise money for the *American Revolution. America's strong religious groups have always been against long-running lotteries, and lottery games did not become official until the 1970s.

ˌLough 'Neagh /ˌlɒx ˈneɪ, ˌlɒk; AmE ˌlɑːx, ˌlɑːk/ the largest lake in the British Isles, near Belfast in Northern Ireland.

Lou,isi'ana /luˌiːziˈænə/ a southern US state on the *Gulf of Mexico, also known as the Pelican State. It consists mainly of flat land and is separated from the state of *Mississippi by the *Mississippi River. The largest city is *New Orleans and the capital city is Baton Rouge. It was part of the *Louisiana Purchase, became a state in 1837, and was one of the *Confederate States. Louisiana is known for its *Cajun culture. The state produces oil, gas, salt, rice and sugar.

the Lou,isiana 'Purchase /luˌiːziænə/ an area of US land bought from France in 1803 for $15 million, or less than 3 cents an acre. The area was about 828 000 square miles (more than 2 million square kilometres), and extended from the *Mississippi River to the *Rocky Mountains and from the *Gulf of Mexico to *Canada. It made the US more than twice as large as it had been, and encouraged Americans to move west. The French named the area after King Louis XIV.

'Louisville /'luːiːvɪl/ the second largest city in the US state of *Kentucky, on the *Ohio River. It was settled in 1778 and named after King Louis XVI of France, and the University of Louisville was established in 1798. The US used the town as a military base during the *Civil War. The *Kentucky Derby is held in Louisville, and the city produces bourbon (= whisky made from corn grain), cigarettes, paint and household electrical items.

ˌRichard 'Lovelace /'lʌvleɪs/ (1618–58) an English poet. He was one of the ' *Cavalier poets' who supported King *Charles I during the *English Civil War. He was put in prison during the war and wrote some of his finest works there, including the poem To Althea, from Prison, which contains the famous lines:

L

> 66 Stone walls do not a prison make
> Nor iron bars a cage. 99

,Bernard 'Lovell /'lʌvl/ (1913–) an English astronomer. He helped to develop radar during *World War II and later established the famous radio telescope at *Jodrell Bank to study radio waves sent out by objects in other parts of the universe. He is the author of several books on science and astronomy, and was made a *knight in 1961.

,Love's 'Labour's 'Lost a play (c. 1595) by William *Shakespeare. The story is about a king and three of his lords who decide to keep away from women for three years and spend the time studying. When the Princess of France arrives with three of her ladies, the four men forget their plans and fall in love. The play also contains the character Holofernes, a boring schoolteacher who is described as having been 'at a great feast of languages and stolen the scraps'. ⇨ note at SHAKESPEARE.

'Low Church n [U] a tradition within the *Church of England that gives less importance to religious ceremonies and the authority of *bishops and priests, and more importance to faith and study of the Bible. Compare HIGH CHURCH.
  ► Low Church adj: Many of the social reformers came from a Low Church, dissenting background.

,Robert 'Lowell /'ləʊəl; AmE 'loʊəl/ (1917–77) a US poet who won *Pulitzer Prizes for two books of poems, Lord Weary's Castle (1946) and The Dolphin (1973). His other collections included Life Studies (1959), For the Union Dead (1964) and Day by Day (1977). Lowell used 'confessional poetry' to write about his problems and his unhappy marriages. He also wrote plays and translated the work of European poets.

the ,Lower 'East Side a poor district of New York City in south-east *Manhattan(1). It includes *Little Italy around Mulberry Street, *Chinatown, with Canal Street at its centre, and the Jewish area around Hester Street. Many people from *Puerto Rico have come to live there more recently. Much of the Lower East Side was built again in the 1930s under Mayor Fiorello *La Guardia.

the ,lower middle 'class n [sing + sing/pl v] (also the lower middle classes [pl]) n the class of people in British society, especially in the past, between *working class and *middle class, such as office workers or shopkeepers, but not professional people. Compare WORKING CLASS, MIDDLE CLASS, UPPER MIDDLE CLASS.
  ► lower-middle-class adj: a lower-middle-class suburban neighbourhood.

'lower school n (in Britain) a name sometimes given to the classes for younger students (aged 11 to 14) at a secondary school (for children aged 11 to 18).

the 'Lowlands /'ləʊləndz; AmE 'loʊləndz/ n [pl] the region of Scotland south and east of the *Highlands. It has flatter countryside and a larger population.

,Lowland 'Scots /'skɒts; AmE 'skɑːts/ ⇨ LALLANS.

'L S 'Lowry /'laʊri/ (Laurence Stephen Lowry 1887–1976) an English painter who is famous for his paintings of the industrial north of England, where he lived. They show buildings and factories with simple colours and forms, and crowds of 'matchstick' people represented in a few thin lines.

lox /lɒks; AmE lɔːks/ n [U] (AmE) a type of salty lightly smoked salmon (= a large fish with pink flesh). It is especially popular with Jewish people in New York combined with cream cheese as a filling for bread rolls called bagels.

'Loyalist /'lɔɪəlɪst/ n any of the Protestants in Northern Ireland who want it to stay part of the United Kingdom and not unite with the Irish Republic. Such people are also sometimes known as Unionists. Illegal Loyalist military groups such as the *Ulster Volunteer Force and the *Ulster Freedom Fighters have been responsible for acts of violence in Northern Ireland since the 1960s. Compare REPUBLICAN(2).

the ,loyal 'toast n [usually sing] (in Britain) a toast (= an act of raising your glass and drinking at the same time as other people) at a formal dinner, to show loyalty to the queen or king. People say 'the Queen' or 'the King' and then drink. People are traditionally not allowed to smoke until after the loyal toast.

'loyalty card n a small plastic card given by supermarkets and other shops to their customers in order to persuade them to continue to buy goods from them. Everything the customers buy is recorded, and the customers are given price reductions and other benefits according to the amount they spend.

LPO /,el pi: 'əʊ; AmE 'oʊ/ ⇨ LONDON PHILHARMONIC ORCHESTRA.

LSAT /,el es eɪ 'tiː/ (in full Law School Admission Test) (in US colleges and universities) a test taken by students wanting to be admitted to a *law school. It tests general academic knowledge and can be taken before or after the first degree is received.

LSE /,el es 'iː/ 1 ⇨ LONDON SCHOOL OF ECONOMICS. 2 ⇨ LONDON STOCK EXCHANGE

LSO /,el es 'əʊ; AmE 'oʊ/ ⇨ LONDON SYMPHONY ORCHESTRA.

'Clare 'Booth 'Luce /'buːð 'luːs/ (1903–87) a US politician and journalist who also wrote plays. She was the managing editor of Vanity Fair magazine (1933–4). Her best-known plays include The Women (1936), which became a 1939 film with roles for 135 women and no men, and Kiss the Boys Goodbye (1938). Luce was a *Republican(1) member of the House of Representatives (1943–7), and she later became the US ambassador in Italy (1953–7). Her husband Henry Luce (1898–1967) started *Time magazine.

',Lucky' Luci'ano /lu:si'ɑːnəʊ; AmE lu:si'ɑːnoʊ/ (1897–1962) a US criminal, born in Sicily. He became the head of a powerful criminal organization in New York in the 1920s and probably ordered the murder of his rival, 'Dutch' Schultz in 1935. A year later he was sent to prison and continued to run his illegal activities from prison, but in 1946 he was sent back to Italy.

,Lucky 'Jim a comic novel (1954) by Kingsley *Amis. The main character, Jim Dixon, is a young college teacher who dislikes his job and falls in love with another man's girlfriend. The funniest moments in the book are when Jim gets drunk and behaves badly in front of the senior teachers. The book was made into a film in 1957 by the *Boulting brothers and into a television film in 2003.

,Lucky 'Strike™ a cigarette first sold in the US in 1871 and now made by *BAT. Phrases used to advertise Lucky Strike cigarettes have included 'Reach for a Lucky', 'LS/MFT' (Lucky Strike Means Fine Tobacco) and 'Be Happy, Go Lucky'.

'Lucozade™ /'luːkəzeɪd/ n [U] a sweet orange-coloured drink which is advertised as giving energy to people who take part in sports, etc. or helping people to get well after an illness.

'Luddite /'lʌdaɪt/ n (usually disapproving) a person opposed to change in working methods or the introduction of new machines or technology. The original Luddites were early 19th-century workers, one of whom was called Ned Lud, who destroyed machinery because they thought it would threaten their jobs. Several of them were hanged.
  ► Luddite adj: There was a Luddite terror of new technology.

,Robert **'Ludlum** /'lʌdləm/ (1927–2001) a US author who wrote more than 20 novels which have been translated into 32 languages in 40 countries. The stories are about spies and international crime. Some of his novels have been made into films, including *The Bourne Identity* (1980) and *The Bourne Supremacy* (1986). His other novels include *The Matlock Paper* (1973), *The Icarus Agenda* (1988), *The Bourne Ultimatum* (1990) and *The Matarese Countdown* (1997).

'ludo /'lu:dəʊ/ n [U] (*BrE*) a simple game played with dice and small coloured discs on a special board. A similar game popular in the US is called *Parcheesi.

'Lundy /'lʌndi/ a small island off the coast of *Devon, England, owned by the *National Trust. Its plants and animals are protected by law and it is a breeding ground for puffins (= black and white sea birds with colourful beaks).

the **'Lutheran Church** /'lu:θərən/ a Protestant Church that follows the teachings of Martin Luther (1483–1546). Luther taught the importance of faith and Bible study, and is considered to have started the *Reformation. There are many branches of the Lutheran Church in the US. The largest is the Evangelical Lutheran Church in America (ELCA).

the ,Lutine **'bell** /,lu:ti:n/ n [sing] a bell kept at *Lloyd's of London which is rung when important announcements are made. In former times it was rung to announce good or bad news for the company, such as the loss of a ship insured there, but today it is often rung to mark news of national importance, such as the death of a public figure. The bell was rescued from the *Lutine*, a ship insured at Lloyd's which sank in 1799 carrying a large amount of gold.

,Edwin **'Lutyens** /'lʌtjənz/ (1869–1944) an English architect. His early work on private houses was influenced by a wide range of English architecture, including *medieval styles and those of the *Arts and Crafts Movement. His later designs, as in the *Cenotaph, London, and the government buildings in New Delhi, show the influences of Greek and Roman architecture. He was made a *knight in 1918.

the Deanery, designed by Edwin Lutyens

LWV /,el dʌblju: 'vi:/ ⇨ LEAGUE OF WOMEN VOTERS.

'Lycra™ /'laɪkrə/ n [U] a material that stretches that is used for clothing, especially sports clothing and often mixed with other fibres such as wool and cotton.

Lyme 'Regis /,laɪm 'ri:dʒɪs/ a popular holiday town in *Dorset on the south coast of England. It is famous for the fossils (= animals and plants preserved in rock) that can be found in its cliffs, and for the Cobb, a long stone wall stretching out into the sea that people can walk along.

,David **'Lynch** /'lɪntʃ/ (1946–) a US film director, also known for his unusual television series *Twin Peaks* (1990–01). His films include *Eraserhead* (1977), *The Elephant Man* (1980), *Blue Velvet* (1986), *Lost Highway* (1997) and *Mulholland Drive* (2001).

the **'Lyndon B 'Johnson 'Space ,Center** /'lɪndən bi: 'dʒɒnsn; *AmE* 'dʒɑnsn/ (*abbr* **JSC**) a US space centre at Clear Lake, *Texas, near *Houston. *NASA has its Mission Control there for space flights by astronauts. It was established in 1961 as the Manned Spacecraft Center, but the name was later changed to honour President Lyndon B *Johnson, who was from Texas.

Lo,retta **'Lynn**[1] /lə,retə 'lɪn/ (1935–) a US singer of *country music. Her many hits include *Don't Come Home A Drinkin'* (1966) and, with Conway Twitty, *After the Fire Is Gone* (1971). She wrote the story of her life, *Coal Miner's Daughter* (1976) (the title of one of her songs), and it was made into a 1980 film with Sissy Spacek. Lynn was chosen for the Country Music *Hall of Fame in 1988. Her younger sister, Crystal Gayle (1951–), is also a country music singer, and so are her twin daughters Peggy and Patsy.

,Vera **'Lynn**[2] /'lɪn/ (1917–) an English singer. She was known as the 'Forces' Sweetheart' during *World War II and was very popular for her songs *We'll Meet Again* and *White Cliffs of Dover*. She was made a *dame(2) in 1975.

,**Lyo'nesse** /,laɪə'nes/ an imaginary land between *Cornwall, England, and the *Scilly Isles to the southwest, now said to be covered by sea. It is often connected with stories about King *Arthur.

,**Lyrical 'Ballads** a book of poems (1798) by William *Wordsworth and Samuel Taylor *Coleridge. It was the first major work of *Romantic literature, and contained Wordsworth's *Tintern Abbey* and Coleridge's *The Rime of the *Ancient Mariner*. In the second edition (1800) Wordsworth added a famous introduction saying that poetry should be drawn from ordinary life and written in plain language.

,Humphrey **'Lyttleton** /'lɪtltən/ (1921–) an English *jazz musician, broadcaster and author. He formed his own jazz band in 1948, playing the trumpet, and went on to present a number of jazz programmes on radio. He is also well known for presenting the *Radio 4 comedy show *I'm Sorry I Haven't a Clue*.

L

M m

'Maastricht /'mɑːstrɪkt, 'mɑːstrɪxt/ a city in the Netherlands. The leaders of the 12 countries of the European Community met there in 1992 to sign the **Maastricht Treaty**, an agreement about closer union between European countries. This included plans to have a single currency, a shared defence force and a more powerful *European Parliament. Many people in Britain were opposed to the agreement, and there were disagreements about it within the British *Conservative government. Britain finally signed it in 1993, but the continued disagreements within the government were an important factor in their defeat at the election of 1997. A new version of the Treaty was signed in Amsterdam in 1997 by the British *Labour government. See also EUROSCEPTIC, SOCIAL CHAPTER. ⇨ note at EUROPEAN UNION.

Mac- Some names beginning with **Mac-** are spelt **Mc-** and appear as entries at that form, e.g. **McCarthy**, **McCartney**, etc.

Douglas Ma'cArthur¹ /məˈkɑːθə(r); AmE məˈkɑːrθər/ (1880–1964) a US military officer. In *World War II General MacArthur became Allied Supreme Commander of the Southwest Pacific Area. He left the Philippines when the Japanese were about to capture it, but promised 'I shall return.' He accepted the Japanese surrender in 1945 and was head of the forces that occupied Japan. MacArthur also led the UN forces in Korea in 1950, but was ordered back to the US in 1951 because he wanted to attack China.

Ellen Ma'cArthur² /məˈkɑːθə(r); AmE məˈkɑːrθər/ (1976–) an English yachtswoman who broke the record for sailing alone around the world in 2005 when she completed the journey in just under 71 days and 15 hours. In 2001 she become the youngest person to sail round the world alone when she came second in an around-the-world race. At 18 she sailed alone around Britain and in 2004 she sailed alone across the Atlantic. She was made a *dame(2) in 2005.

Thomas Ma'caulay /məˈkɔːli/ (1800–59) an English writer and politician. His best-known works are his unfinished *History of England*, which was a great influence on later writers of history, and *Lays of Ancient Rome*. He was a *Member of Parliament and Secretary of War (1839–41), and was made a *baron in 1857.

Mac'beth /məkˈbeθ/ a play (1606) by William *Shakespeare telling the story of Macbeth, a figure from Scottish history. At the start he meets three witches who predict that he will one day become king. Lady Macbeth, Macbeth's ambitious wife, encourages him to murder the existing king, Duncan. He does so and takes Duncan's place, but finds he has to murder several more people to remain in power. Lady Macbeth loses her mind, imagining that her hands are covered with blood that cannot be washed off, and kills herself. Finally Macbeth is also killed. The play is one of Shakespeare's most popular works, and contains many famous lines. Actors traditionally consider it an unlucky play, and avoid mentioning it by name, calling it instead 'the Scottish play'.

> **66** Lead on, Macduff. **99**
> a famous misquote for 'Lay on, MacDuff' from
> *Macbeth*

Hugh Mac'Diarmid /məkˈdɜːmɪd; AmE məkˈdɜːrmɪd/ (1892–1978) a Scottish poet. He wrote in the Scottish dialect known as *Lallans and is best known for his poem *A Drunk Man Looks at the Thistle* (1926). He was a Communist and a supporter of Scottish independence, and was one of the first members of the *Scottish National Party.

Flora Mac'donald¹ /məkˈdɒnəld; AmE məkˈdɑːnəld/ (1722–90) a Scottish woman who helped *Bonny Prince Charlie to escape from Scotland in a small boat after his defeat by the English at the Battle of *Culloden.

Ramsay Mac'Donald² /ˌræmzi məkˈdɒnəld; AmE məkˈdɑːnəld/ (1866–1937) a British *prime minister. He was leader of the *Labour Party (1911–14 and 1922–31) and the first Labour prime minister (1924 and 1929–31). His second government failed to deal with economic difficulties, and was replaced by a coalition government (= one supported by all parties). MacDonald continued as prime minister (1931–5), but left the Labour Party, an act which made him unpopular with Labour supporters. In 1935 he resigned and was replaced by Stanley *Baldwin.

Ross Mac'donald³ /ˌrɒs məkˈdɒnəld; AmE ˌrɔːs məkˈdɑːnəld/ (1915–83) a US writer of *detective stories. His real name was Kenneth Millar. The main character in his books is Lew Archer, a tough but sympathetic detective. The books include *The Galton Case* (1959), *The Chill* (1964) and *Sleeping Beauty* (1973).

the mace /meɪs/ n [sing] a rod decorated with silver and gold, kept in the British *House of Commons as a symbol of the authority of the *Speaker. In former times maces were large heavy clubs used as weapons in battle.

Charles 'Macintosh /'mækɪntɒʃ; AmE 'mækɪntɑːʃ/ (1766–1823) a Scottish inventor who developed a material made of rubber to keep out water. A 'mackintosh' or 'mac' is now a word for any coat made of a similar material for keeping off rain.

Compton Mac'kenzie /ˌkɒmptən məˈkenzi; AmE ˌkɑːmptən/ (1883–1972) a British author. He is best known for his novel *Whisky Galore*, about a boat carrying *whisky that gets stuck on the shore of a Scottish island. The people on the island keep the whisky but have to hide it from the authorities. It was made into an *Ealing comedy in 1947. His many other books include *Sinister Street* (1913–14), based on his life in Oxford and London. He was made a *knight in 1952.

Charles Mac'kerras /məˈkerəs/ (1925–) an Australian conductor who was born in America and has lived in Britain since the late 1940s. He has worked for the *English National Opera (1970–77), the *Welsh National Opera (1987–92) and many other groups. He was made a *knight in 1979.

'Charles 'Rennie 'Mackintosh /'reni 'mækɪntɒʃ; AmE 'mækɪntɑːʃ/ (1868–1928) a Scottish architect and designer who produced buildings, furniture and decorative objects in the *art nouveau style. His best-known building is the Glasgow School of Art (opened 1899). He is also known for his watercolour paintings, done mainly in France towards the end of his life.

History and Institutions

The British Isles

the Highlands

Loch Ness

Edinburgh

Shetland
Islands

Fair Isle

Orkney
Islands

John
O'Groats

SCOTLAND

Outer Hebrides

Western
Isles

The Minch

Skye

NORTH-WEST HIGHLANDS

Inverness
Loch
Ness

Moray Firth

Spey

CAIRNGORMS

Dee

Aberdeen

Tiree

Coll

Mull

Inner Hebrides

Jura

Islay

1344m
Ben Nevis

GRAMPIAN MOUNTAINS

Tay

Forth

Dundee

St Andrews

**The
Lowlands**

Loch
Lomond

Stirling

Firth of Forth

**Atlantic
Ocean**

Glasgow

Clyde

Edinburgh

Berwick-up
Tweed

Firth of Clyde

SOUTHERN UPLANDS

Tweed

**NORTHERN
IRELAND**

Ayr

CHEVIOT
HILLS

New
upon

Londonderry

ANTRIM
MOUNTAINS

Lough
Neagh

Belfast

Carlisle

Tyne

Donegal
Bay

Erne

LAKE
DISTRICT

Keswick

Eden

▲978m
Scafell Pike

PENNINES

Durham

Tees

Lough
Conn

MOURNE
MOUNTAINS

▲852m
Slieve
Donard

Isle of
Man

Douglas

Solway Firth

Lough
Mask

Lough
Corrib

Galway

Lough
Ree

Shannon

Boyne

Liffey

Irish Sea

Blackpool

**The
North-
West**

York

Leed

Galway Bay

Barrow

Dublin

Anglesey
Holyhead

Liverpool

Manchester

Bradford

Aire

Ouse

Sheffiel

Mersey

Lough
Derg

CAERNAR MOUNTAINS

Caernarfon

Chester

Stoke-
on-Trent

Derby

Limerick

1085m
Snowdon

Dee

**The
Midlands**

Birmingham

Le

Shrewsbury

Dingle Bay

Blackwater

Severn

WALES

Coventry

Warwick

Saint George's Channel

Worcester

Wye

Hereford

Avon

Stratford-
upon-Avon

Cork

St David's

Usk

Gloucester

COTSWOLD
HILLS

Oxf

BRECON
BEACONS

Swansea

**REPUBLIC
OF IRELAND**

Cardiff

Bristol

Thames

Avon

Bath

Bristol Channel

SALISBURY
PLAIN

EXMOOR

**The
West Country**

DARTMOOR

Taunton

Salisbury

Southampton

Exeter

Bournemouth

Poole

Plymouth

Isles of
Scilly

Land's
End

E n

Camlough Lough, County Down

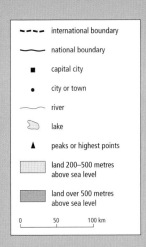

international boundary

national boundary

■ capital city

• city or town

river

lake

▲ peaks or highest points

land 200–500 metres above sea level

land over 500 metres above sea level

0   50   100 km

Liverpool

Cornwall

Caernarfon

St David's

Birmingham

the Brecon Beacons

Brighton

Bath

Lavenham, Suffolk

the Severn Bridge

Lindisfarne

North Sea

ENGLAND

Wensum

Norwich

Anglia

Ipswich

Stour

Colchester

Thames Estuary

Ramsgate

DOWNS Canterbury

Dover

Hastings

Strait of Dover

Eastbourne

BELGIUM

nnel

FRANCE

The British Isles

C3

Timeline of British History

Before 6500 BC Until the English Channel was formed, Britain was linked by land to Europe. Many different peoples lived in Britain as hunter gatherers.

4000−1500 BC By 4000 BC, the land was being farmed and we have evidence of settlements. From about 2500 onwards, the Ancient Britons began constructing huge stone monuments (See Avebury, Skara Brae, Stonehenge.)

Stonehenge

500 BC The Celts arrived in Britain.

55BC−410 AD The Romans invaded Britain. (See Antonine Wall, Bath, Boudicca, Fosse Way, Hadrian's Wall)

From 400 AD Anglo-Saxon invaders settled in Britain and ruled over much of England. The languages of these invaders form the basis of what developed into modern English. (See Anglo-Saxon, Anglo-Saxon Chronicle, Bede , Beowulf, Caedmon, Maiden Castle)

From 800 AD Raids by Vikings from Denmark and Norway were followed in 865 by an invasion of Danes who by 877 controlled the eastern half of England. (See Alfred the Great, Danelaw, Viking, York)

1066 The Norman duke who came to be known as William the Conqueror invaded England and defeated the English king, Harold. For the next few centuries England was ruled by Normans, and French became the language of the court. (See Bayeux Tapestry, Conquest, Harold ii, Hastings, William the Conqueror)

1088 The Domesday Book was completed.

1215 King John signed the Magna Carta. (See King John, Magna Carta, Runnymede)

1283 Wales was conquered by Edward i of England. (See Edward i, Prince of Wales)

1314 The Scots defeated an invading English army at the Battle of Bannockburn. (See Bannockburn, Edward ii, Robert the Bruce)

1534 King Henry viii became the head of the Church in England. (See Boleyn, Catherine of Aragon, Church of England, Dissolution of the Monasteries, Henry viii, Reformation)

1564 The birth of Shakespeare

Shakespeare

1588 The Spanish Armada, a fleet of ships sent to invade England, was defeated. (See Armada, Drake)

1603 King James vi of Scotland became King James i of England, Scotland and Wales.

1605 James i was hated by many Catholics and a group of them attempted to kill him when he was in Parliament. (See Bonfire night, Gunpowder Plot, Guy Fawkes, James i)

1642 The English Civil War began. (See Cavalier, Charles i, Commonwealth, Cromwell, English Civil War, Long Parliament)

1653−1658 Cromwell dismissed Parliament and ruled as Lord Protector of England, Scotland and Ireland. (See Protectorate, Puritan)

1660 The Restoration of the monarchy took place with the return of Charles ii as king. (See Charles ii, Puritan, Restoration)

1689 The Catholic James ii was removed from the throne and the Protestant William of Orange and his wife Mary, James's daughter, were crowned instead .(See Battle of the Boyne, Bill of Rights, James ii, William iii)

1707 The Act of Union joined England, Wales and Scotland as one kingdom called Great Britain.

1721 Sir Robert Walpole became the first Prime Minister in the modern sense.

1783 With the end of the American War of Independence Britain lost her American colonies. (See American Revolution)

1800 The second Act of Union added Ireland to Great Britain to form the United Kingdom of Great Britain and Ireland. (See Act of Union)

1824 The first railway was built, part of the technological development that changed the face of Britain. (See Industrial Revolution, Stephenson, Stockton and Darlington, Watt)

1832 The first Reform Act created more seats in Parliament and gave more men the vote. (See rotten borough)

1880 It became compulsory for children between the ages of five and thirteen to go to school.

1911 The National Insurance Act introduced sickness and unemployment insurance for workers. (See welfare state)

1914–18 World War i (See Armistice Day, Flanders fields, Treaty of Versailles)

1918 Women over 30 were allowed to vote. (See Pankhurst, suffragettes)

1921 Ireland was divided into the Irish Free State and the Protestant counties in the north. (See Home Rule, Parnell)

1926 The General Strike

1928 Women were allowed to vote from the age of 21, the same age as for men.

1939–1945 World War ii. (See Battle of Britain, Blitz, Dunkirk, VE Day, Winston Churchill)

1948 The National Health Service was set up by the Labour government. (See Beveridge, welfare state)

1971 British money changed to a decimal system. (See decimalization, money)

1973 Britain became a member of the European Economic Community. (See European Union)

1998 The first attempt to set up a Northern Ireland Assembly. (See devolution)

1999 The Welsh Assembly and the Scottish Parliament were set up. (See devolution, Scottish Parliament, Welsh Assembly)

the Scottish Parliament

Roman Britain

Britain was a part of the Roman Empire for just under 400 years and the remains of the Roman occupation can still be seen in many places today.

The province of Britannia

Roman influence in Britain began with Julius **Caesar** who came twice, once in 55 BC and again in 54 BC. It was not until 43 AD, however, that the Romans invaded Britain with the intention of making it part of their empire. The invasion was led by the Emperor Claudius who came with about 40 000 soldiers. They quickly took control of southern England and from this time until 410 AD, Britain, or Britannia as it was known to the Romans, was a province of the Roman Empire.

Revolt, expansion and consolidation

The Romans faced several revolts during the years after the conquest. The most important was a rebellion led by Queen **Boudicca** in 60–61 AD during which several towns were burnt to the ground. With the rebellions crushed, the Romans began to expand their area of control and conquered most of Britain including, by 81 AD, the south of Scotland. The Romans eventually left southern Scotland and, in 122 AD, began to build a wall across the north of England as a defence against invading tribes from the north. It was named **Hadrian's Wall**, after the Emperor Hadrian who had ordered it to be built. Later, about 1400 AD, the **Antonine wall** was built further north but was largely abandoned in about 163 AD.

Roman towns

Many towns in Britain were founded or grew considerably in size during the period of Roman rule. The most important were Colchester (*Camulodunum*), Lincoln (*Lindum*), St Albans (*Verulanium*) and London (*Londinium*). Colchester, the original capital of the Roman province was destroyed during Boudicca's revolt, and London became the main administrative and commercial centre. During the third century, York (*Eboracum*) became the main centre for the north.

the Roman baths in Bath

Life in a Roman town

Roman towns had all the amenities that a citizen of Rome would expect such as a market place, a town hall, baths, often supplied by water from an aqueduct, and amphitheatres. The most impressive remains of town life in this period are the Roman baths in the city of Bath where the bathing complex contains hot and cold rooms and systems of drainage and underfloor heating.

Roads

An essential tool for maintaining control was an efficient road system and the Romans were excellent road builders. The word *street* comes from the Latin word *strata*, which originally meant *straight*. The most famous Roman roads in Britain are **Watling Street**, **Ermine Street** and the **Fosse Way**. Today Roman routes are marked on Ordinance Survey maps, and several modern roads follow their course.

Roman villas

The remains of Roman villas such as Fishbourne in Sussex and Chedworth in the Cotswolds demonstrate the wealth of Roman culture. Many of these villas were richly decorated with painting and mosaics showing themes from Roman myths. Some of this decoration can still be seen today.

The end of Roman rule

In the fourth century AD, the Roman Empire itself was under attack from tribes from central and eastern Europe. Britain was being attacked from the west and north by Scottish and Irish tribes and from the east by Germanic tribes such as the Angles and Saxons. Roman soldiers in Britain were called away to defend Rome and eventually, in 410 AD, the Emperor Honorius decided that Britain must defend itself. With the Romans gone, the Germanic tribes gradually took over most of England.

The Celts

Who were the Celts?

The Celts probably came to Britain around 500 BC. Although Stonehenge is often associated with the Celts it had been built many centuries earlier. The Celts came originally from central Europe and settled in Britain, France and Spain.

Celtic society

The Celts were described by Roman and Greek writers as a fierce and warlike people. They were originally ruled by kings, but by the time Julius Caesar came to Britain, around 55 BC, they had broken up into many tribes, each with a different leader. It was possible for women as well as men to hold positions of power, and one of them was **Queen Boudicca**. **Druids** were a powerful group within Celtic society, combining the functions of priest, doctor, and perhaps also lawmaker.

Celtic culture

The Celts were farmers and introduced the iron plough to Britain. They fought using chariots and, when in battle, painted their bodies with a blue dye called **woad**. Although the Celts did not have a written form of their language until after the arrival of the Romans, they had a strong oral tradition of storytelling performed by **bards** (= poets or storytellers). The Celts are described as wearing brightly-coloured clothes and the men usually had long moustaches rather than a beard. Some sources claim that they were very fond of drinking alcohol. In pre-Roman times, the Celts were known to carry out human sacrifice and to cut off and display the heads of their enemies. A possible example of human sacrifice is the preserved body of **Lindow man**.

Celtic carved stones

The Anglo-Saxon invasion and Celtic Christianity

After the invasion of the Anglo-Saxons in the fifth century AD, the Celts were pushed into the western and northern parts of the British Isles, particularly into Cornwall, Wales, the Isle of Man, Scotland, and Ireland. During the next 600 years, a rich Celtic Christian culture developed, centred mainly around monasteries in Scotland and Ireland. One of the most famous of these was the monastery on the island of Iona in Scotland, which was founded by the Irish St Columba in 563 AD. Monks copied texts from the Bible and decorated their work with beautiful patterns and pictures. The best example of these illuminated manuscripts is the **Book of Kells**.

Celtic design

One of the most lasting influences of the Celts is in art and design. Today people buy 'Celtic' jewellery, and Celtic designs were used in the **Arts and Crafts Movement** at the end of the 19th century. Celtic designs are very elaborate, with lines crossing and combining like the branches of a tree or vine. Beautiful brooches, pins, and shields have been found as well as a large number of torcs (= a thin bar of twisted metal worn around the neck). One of the most distinctive Celtic designs, from the Christian period, is the **Celtic cross** which is still used for graves and memorials. It has a circle added to the four bars of the cross and is often elaborately carved.

Celtic languages

Celtic languages are divided into two categories, **Q-Celtic**, which includes Irish, Scottish Gaelic and Manx, and **P-Celtic** including Welsh, Cornish, and Breton (= the language of Brittany in France). Although Celtic languages are official languages as well as English, they are no longer spoken by most people. Welsh is spoken by about 20% of the population of Wales.

Modern Celts

Celtic culture is very much alive, particularly Celtic music using traditional instruments such as the bagpipes. 'Celtic' is often used to describe the people and culture of Scotland, Wales, Ireland and Cornwall, even in the parts where Celtic languages are not spoken.

UK Constitution and Government

The Constitution

There is no single document that forms the **British constitution**. The relationship between the State and the people has developed over time and is based on several elements, including **statutes** (= laws made by Parliament), important court cases, and established practices. Its key principles are the **rule of law**, i.e. everyone is subject to the laws of the land, and the **sovereignty of Parliament**, i.e. there are no restrictions on the laws that Parliament can pass, except that Parliament needs to observe the agreements Britain has made as a member of the **European Union**.

Britain is both a **Parliamentary democracy** and a **constitutional monarchy**. The process of transferring power from the monarch to Parliament began in the 13th century when King John was forced to sign **Magna Carta**. Today, the monarch represents the people as **head of state** but the real power lies with the elected representatives of the people in Parliament.

Parliament

In the UK, national laws are decided by **Parliament**, which is divided into two parts called **houses**. (Laws that affect only part of the United Kingdom are normally made by the **devolved assemblies** in Northern Ireland, Scotland and Wales.) The lower house, the **House of Commons** is elected by the people and has more power. The upper house, the **House of Lords**, is made up of a number of **peers**. Most of these are appointed by the Queen from a list of people chosen by the Prime Minister and the leaders of the other political parties.

the House of Lords

A bill is introduced

Most bills can be introduced in either house. When a bill is first introduced (called the **first reading** of the Bill) no action is taken but a date is set for when it will be discussed (the **second reading**).

The bill is discussed by Parliament

At the second reading the house discusses the general principles behind the bill and there is a vote to decide whether it should be taken further.

The bill goes to a committee

If a bill is approved, it is sent to a committee for detailed discussion. There are different types and sizes of committees. Sometimes a whole house performs the function of a committee (called a **Committee of the House**). This is common in the upper house. The committee considers each paragraph of the bill and makes any **amendments** (= changes) that it thinks necessary.

The house makes changes and votes

The bill then returns to the house where it was introduced for the **report stage** when members of the house consider the committee's amendments and suggest any extra changes. Once all the changes to the bill have been made, the house discusses it briefly during the **third reading** and votes on it.

Changes by the other house

If a bill is approved by one house it is sent to the other to be considered. If the other house wants to make any changes, these must go back to the first house to be approved. This process continues until both houses agree on the content of the bill, or until the House of Commons ends it using the Parliament Act.

The Parliament Act

The Parliament Act was introduced in 1911. It allows the House of Commons to pass a bill finally without the approval of the Lords a year after its second reading.

Royal Assent

Before a bill becomes law it must be signed by the Queen. This is seen as a formal procedure and the last time a bill was rejected was in 1707.

Political Parties

The party system

The British political system is essentially a two-party system in which power is held by one of two main parties. Historically, the main parties were the **Tories** and the **Whigs**, later known as the **Conservative Party** and the **Liberal Party**. Since the 1930s however, the two main parties have been the Conservatives and the **Labour Party**. There are several smaller parties, the most important of which is the **Liberal Democratic Party** (or **LibDems**). Each party has its own emblem and colour: the Conservatives have a blue torch, Labour a red rose, and the Liberal Democrats a yellow bird.

Regional parties

As a result of the process of **devolution**, there are now regional assemblies in Scotland, Wales and Northern Ireland. However, many decisions affecting these areas are still made in the Parliament at Westminster. Wales and Scotland have their own nationalist parties, **Plaid Cymru** (the party of Wales) and the **Scottish Nationalist Party**, both of which want complete political independence. Northern Ireland has several parties, including the **Ulster Unionist Party**, the **Democratic Unionist Party**, the **Social Democratic and Labour Party** and **Sinn Fein**. The Sinn Fein MPs elected to the **House of Commons** are not allowed to take their seats there because they refuse to take the oath of loyalty to the Queen.

The electoral system

The UK has what is often known as a *first-past-the-post* system. The country is divided into 645 **constituencies** or **seats**, which each elect an MP to represent them in Parliament. In an election, the **candidate** who receives the most votes in a particular constituency wins the seat. Generally, Labour wins many seats in the north of England, Wales and Scotland, while the Conservatives do better in the south of England. The Liberal Democrats want to change the system to one of **proportional representation** as they frequently win a far higher percentage of votes than seats in Parliament.

Traditional party policy

For most of its history, Labour has been a left-wing party, representing the interests of the workers and unions, although in recent years it has changed in significant ways. Traditional Labour policies included: public ownership of key industries, regulation of industry to ensure better pay and conditions for workers, and the development of a public health and social security system.

The Conservatives are a right-wing party, seen as representing the interests of professional people and managers in business and industry. They believe in minimum interference by government in industry and the freedom of the individual. Their general policies include: low taxation, encouragement of private rather than state industry, and belief in the free market economy.

The Liberal Democrats are seen as taking a position somewhere in the middle of these two parties.

Party support

In the 1997 general election, for the first time in its history, the Labour party, or **New Labour** as it was called, received more votes from non-manual workers than manual workers. This reflects a major change in British society and politics. Although workers still mainly vote Labour and managers and professional people still prefer the Conservatives, the old class distinctions between parties are no longer so clear. As a result of this, the policies of both of the major parties have moved closer to the centre. New Labour has rejected many socialist policies and adopted some policies traditionally associated with the Conservatives such as the privatization of many public services.

Local Government

Counties

Historically, the UK has been divided into areas called **counties** (e.g. Kent), although in Scotland the divisions are often called **regions**. The old word for a county was a **shire** (e.g. Hampshire, Oxfordshire). Counties and regions are further divided into smaller areas called **districts**.

The structure of local government

There are currently two kinds of local government in the UK: **unitary authorities** and **two-tier authorities**. The former has one level of government so that a single council is directly responsible for all public services. District councils in Scotland and Wales are unitary authorities. In Wales, they are called **county councils** or **county borough councils**. (The word **borough** usually refers to a town rather than a city or rural area.) Unitary authorities in England include all the major cities outside London (e.g. Greater Manchester). They are usually called **metropolitan borough councils** or **city councils**. London is unique in that it is divided into smaller areas called **boroughs** and also has a higher tier of government called the **GLA** (**Greater London Authority**) with a mayor and an assembly. The other system, the two-tier authority has two levels, a **county council** and, at a more local level, a **district council**. For historical reasons district councils in some large towns are called **borough councils**. Sometimes there is a third level, a **local council**, called in England either **town council** or **parish council** and in Wales and Scotland **community council**.

Elections

Elected members of local government are called **councillors**. They usually belong to a particular political party and are elected in a similar way to MPs, apart from in Northern Ireland where there

the London Assembly

the Council House, Birmingham

is a system of **proportional representation**. The local district is divided into smaller areas called **wards** and each ward can elect one councillor. Councillors are usually elected for four years. The council is led by a **chair** or **mayor**, or in Scotland, a **provost**. The leader may be directly elected by local people or chosen by the council.

Local government finance

Local government accounts for 25% of all public spending. About 25% of its money comes from the **council tax**, a tax based on property values. Local councils also receive money from government grants and business taxes.

The role of local government

Local government is responsible for providing public services such as schools, rubbish collection, roads and public transport, libraries, housing, police and fire services, etc. In two-tier authorities the county council is responsible for services that require organization across the county, such as schools, police, social services, roads and transport. District councils are responsible for rubbish collection, local authority housing, etc.

Changes in the role of local government

Since the 1980s local government has changed greatly. Many services are no longer provided directly by councils but are instead bought in from private companies with the aim of improving efficiency. Councils are checked by a government watchdog called the **Audit Commission** which tries to make sure that councils are making the best use of public money.

The Legal System

judges

Sources of law

For historical reasons, the legal system in England and Wales is separate from that in Scotland and in Northern Ireland. In all four parts of the UK, however, the same types of law are applied: **legislation** (= written laws) and **common law**.

   Common law is law developed by judges over time. Judges follow the principles that were applied in similar cases in the past and have the power to adapt these or introduce new ones in new circumstances. England and Wales, Scotland and Northern Ireland have their own sets of cases and principles that they follow.

   The system of **common law** was taken to countries that the British colonized, including the United States.

   Legislation consists of laws decided by the national Parliament in Westminster and the **devolved assemblies** for Scotland, Wales and Northern Ireland. As a member of the European Union, the UK also creates legislation to follow EU laws. An important example of this is **the Human Rights Act of 1998**, which makes the European law on human rights part of British law.

   In general, courts must apply whatever laws Parliament decides. But since the Human Rights Act became law, judges can force Parliament to change legislation that does not follow human rights principles.

The court system

England and Wales, Scotland and Northern Ireland have separate court structures.

   The names of the courts in England and Wales and Northern Ireland are similar. For cases involving minor crimes there are **Magistrates' Courts**. More serious crimes are dealt with in **Crown Courts** by a judge and a jury. Cases involving claims for money, etc. (called **civil cases**) can start in one of the **County Courts**. Where very large sums of money or important legal principles are involved, cases start in the **High Court**. Appeals against decisions made in the Crown Courts or High Court can go to the **Court of Appeal**. A few cases involving important legal principles continue to the highest national court, the **House of Lords**.

   In Scotland, the lowest criminal courts are called **District Courts**. More serious crimes are dealt with in regional **sheriff courts**. Most civil cases start in a sheriff court or, if they are very important or complicated, in the **Court of Session**, which also hears appeals from the sheriff courts. In civil cases, there is an appeal to the House of Lords. The highest court for criminal cases is the **High Court of Justiciary**.

The legal profession

There are two types of lawyers in the UK. Lawyers who provide advice to the public and sometimes appear on behalf of clients in court are called **solicitors**. Lawyers who are specially trained to work in court and provide most of the legal representation in the higher courts are called **barristers**, or in Scotland, **advocates**. Barristers are self-employed and may represent the **prosecution** or the **defence** in a particular case. Senior barristers have the title **Queen's Counsel (QC)**.

   In court, lawyers are expected to present the best evidence for their clients and argue for their client's point of view. Judges are not involved in collecting evidence. They remain neutral during trials and base their decisions on what is presented by the lawyers.

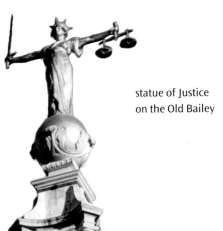

statue of Justice
on the Old Bailey

a barrister

Education

Schools

Under the Education Act of 1944 all children have a right to free school education and education is **compulsory** between the ages of five and sixteen (in Northern Ireland from four). Almost 75% of children stay at school beyond the age of 16 and 44% go on to **higher education**. **Pre-school education** is usually part-time at least until the age of four and is provided partly by the state and partly by private organizations. Schools follow the **National Curriculum** and are regularly inspected by **Ofsted**. Children are tested formally at the ages of 7, 11 and 14 by doing National Curriculum Tests (NCTs) in English, mathematics and science and **league tables** are published so that the results achieved by individual schools can be compared. Children do not have to pass a test, however, in order to be able to move up into the next class at the end of the school year.

Primary school

Primary schools often have two sections, an **infant school** and a **junior school**. Primary schools often have a first class for children younger than five, called a **reception class**. In some areas of the country the last two years of primary school and the first two of secondary school are combined in a **middle school** but it is much more usual for children to go to secondary school at eleven.

Secondary school

Most children move to secondary school at the age of eleven. 94% of children are educated in state secondary schools, the majority of which are **comprehensive schools** where children of all abilities are educated together. In some areas, however, there are also **grammar schools** for which children are selected on the basis of an exam. Usually the state schools in an area are run directly by the **local authority** which is responsible for appointing the teachers and other staff as well as deciding where new schools should be built. This is always the case in Scotland but elsewhere there are alternatives such as **foundation schools** run by a **governing body**, **voluntary schools**, many of which are church schools, and **academies**, which are built with some private money and run as independent schools in the state sector.

The remaining six per cent of children go to **private schools**, also called **independent schools**. Many of the largest and most famous of these are called, rather confusingly, **public** schools, and they are often boarding schools where pupils live as well as study. Children who are going to go to a public school often go at the age of seven to a **preparatory school** (called informally a **prep school**) and stay there until the age of 13 when they sit a **common entrance exam** to get into a public school.

League tables for secondary schools are published on the basis of the results achieved in public **GCSE (General Certificate of Secondary Education)** and **A level (advanced level)** examinations by the pupils in each school. These exams are set and marked by several organizations in a wide range of subjects and schools can choose which organization to use. GCSE subjects include vocational subjects that prepare for specific careers.

Post-secondary education

Further education

After the age of 16 students may stay at school and do A levels or move to a college to do A levels or career-based training. Education between the ages of 16 and 19 is free whether it takes place in schools or colleges (often called **colleges of further education**) and the government provides some financial support in the form of **Educational Maintenance Allowances (EMAs)** to encourage students to stay in education and gain qualifications.

Adults who are already in work have opportunities to continue their education part-time in classes organized by local authorities or other organizations in order to gain further qualifications. People may also attend an evening class as a leisure interest, for example to learn a foreign language which they can use on holiday abroad, to study local history, or to learn to cook.

Oxford University

Higher education

Students who have successfully completed an A-level course may go to university to do a three or four-year course leading to a **first degree** such as **Bachelor of Arts** (**BA**), **Bachelor of Science** (**BSc**), etc. They apply to several universities which then make an offer of a place specifying the minimum grades the student needs to obtain in the A level subjects studied. Higher education is not free. In principle students have to pay a contribution to the cost of teaching (**tuition fees**) and have also to pay their living costs (**maintenance**). The government provides loans to help them pay for university education which have to be paid back from earnings once their income reaches a certain level. In recent years government policy has been to increase the percentage of 18-year olds who go to university, which is now, at 40%, double the 1990 figure, but this growth has been at the expense of the amount of financial support given to individual students.

Universities receive money from the state for each student and are responsible for employing staff and deciding which courses to offer. The head of a university, who is responsible for its management, is called a **vice-chancellor**.

After **graduating** students may choose to study for a **higher degree**, such as a **Master of Arts** (**MA**), **Master of Science** (**MSc**), or a **doctorate** (**PhD**).

One of the largest universities in Britain is the **Open University** (**OU**) where students, who are usually employed, or in some cases retired, study part-time mainly by **distance-learning** and obtain first degrees, higher degrees and professional qualifications by this method.

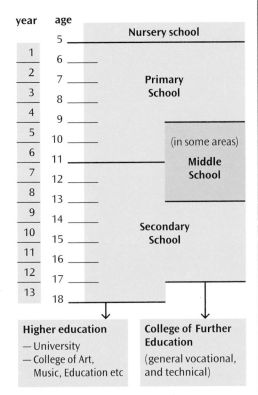

year	age		
	5	Nursery school	
1	6		
2	7	Primary	
3	8	School	
4	9		
5	10		(in some areas)
6	11		Middle
7	12		School
8	13		
9	14	Secondary	
10	15	School	
11	16		
12	17		
13	18		

Higher education	College of Further Education
— University	(general vocational, and technical)
— College of Art, Music, Education etc	

Education and politics

Education is one of the most important topics of political debate in Britain. Governments of both main political parties have recognized the importance of education in helping Britain to adapt to its role as a **post-industrial society**. The loss of millions of manufacturing jobs in the 1980s created an urgent need for an education system that equipped all school-leavers for the demands of a modern economy. Central government now plays a more important role in education policy at the expense of local authorities and individual head teachers, and many people in the teaching profession feel that the many changes introduced by government make their job harder.

The British Empire

By 1920, the British Empire included a quarter of the world and around 600 million people. 40 years later most of these people belonged to independent nations and the British Empire no longer existed.

The building of the Empire

Britain gained its first possessions in 1497 when **John Cabot** claimed **Newfoundland** for King Henry VII. The first British colony in North America was **Virginia**, which was settled in 1585. This was followed by further colonization of the east coast, most famously by the **Pilgrim Fathers** in 1620. Victory over the French during the Seven Years War led to British control of most of Canada. Britain claimed several islands in **the West Indies**, which became Britain's most valuable colonies because of the sugar, tobacco and dye they produced.

An empire of trade

The empire began as a commercial enterprise. The government gave companies the right to trade in certain areas of the world. For example, the **Hudson Bay Company** had a monopoly on the fur trade with Canada. The most famous of these companies was the **East India Company** which gradually took control of India. In the **slave trade** between 1680 and 1807 British merchants transported around three million people from West Africa to the Americas to work on plantations.

The growth of empire

Despite the loss of its US colonies after the American Revolution, the British Empire continued to grow. **Captain Cook** discovered Australia and a penal colony (= a colony for prisoners) was established there in 1788. New Zealand came under British rule in 1840. Victory in the Napoleonic Wars led to other gains, including Trinidad, Malta, Gibraltar, Sri Lanka (called Ceylon) and the Cape of Good Hope in South Africa. **Hong Kong** became a British colony in 1843.

The jewel in the crown

After the **Indian Mutiny** in 1857, the British took direct control, so that India became Britain's most important colony, 'the jewel in the crown' of **Queen Victoria**, who took the title of Empress of India. British rule in India was known as the **Raj**.

Africa

Towards the end of the 19th century, Europeans fought to win control of Africa. The British took large areas of south and east Africa as well as some western states. **Cecil Rhodes** wanted British control to stretch 'from Cairo to the Cape'. However, the **Boer War** ended support for imperial expansion.

In the 20th century, not only did the idea of empire become unpopular but Britain was unable to support the cost of administering it. The two World Wars weakened Britain financially and politically. Many nations in the empire wanted increased independence. In 1931, Canada, Australia, New Zealand and South Africa were officially made 'autonomous communities' within the Empire. Most of the other nations became independent during the 20 years after the Second World War, with India gaining independence in 1947. Hong Kong was restored to China in 1997.

The British Empire in 1914

Northern Ireland

Northern Ireland, with its population of about 1.6 million, is a **province** of the United Kingdom. It is made up of six counties and the capital is Belfast. Once famous for its textile and shipbuilding industries, it is now a popular tourist destination, with its beautiful scenery. Unfortunately, Northern Ireland is still best known for the years of conflict called 'the Troubles', in which more than 3 000 people have died.

The Troubles

Since the late 1960's, **paramilitary groups** (= illegal groups organized like armies) have been fighting each other, the police and the British army. **Republicans** (or **Nationalists**) are mainly Roman Catholic. They do not accept the term 'Northern Ireland', preferring 'the North of Ireland' or 'the Six Counties', and want to be part of the Republic of Ireland. The biggest Republican paramilitary group is the **IRA**. **Loyalists** (or **Unionists**) come from a Protestant background, and want Northern Ireland (which they often call 'Ulster') to remain part of the United Kingdom. Many Loyalists are members of the **Orange Order**. The biggest Loyalist paramilitary groups are the **UVF** and the **UDA**.

members of the Orange Order

History

The relationship between Ireland and Great Britain has been marked by violent conflict for 800 years. During the 17th century, Protestants from England and Scotland took control of **Ulster** (= the northern nine counties of Ireland) by setting up farms on land that had belonged to Irish Roman Catholics. By the late 19th century, Protestants made up approximately two-thirds of the population. They felt strong ties to Britain, and when Ireland won its independence in 1921, six counties voted to remain part of the United Kingdom and be governed by the Parliament of Northern Ireland at **Stormont Castle**.

Stormont Castle

The way Northern Ireland was governed favoured the Protestant majority, and in the late 1960's Catholics campaigned against inequalities in areas such as employment, housing and voting rights. **Civil rights protests** led to violent confrontations between Republicans and Loyalists. The **RUC** (the mostly Protestant police force) intervened which led the Prime Minister to call in the British Army to protect Catholics but the troops soon became the target of IRA attacks.

In 1971 the British government introduced **internment** (= imprisonment without trial) which led to more violence. In 1972, the year of **Bloody Sunday**, **direct rule** from London was introduced and the Stormont parliament abandoned. Paramilitaries became involved in organized crime, and the police and the army were accused of cooperating with Loyalists.

Ceasefires

In 1997, after many attempts to stop the violence, the paramilitaries announced ceasefires. In 1998, after negotiations with the Irish and British governments, the political leaders signed the **Good Friday Agreement**. This created a **Northern Ireland Assembly** based at Stormont.

A Nationalist-Unionist coalition government took power in 1999, but has been suspended several times. According to the Agreement, the IRA had to give up all its weapons but by late 2002 it still had not done so. Many Loyalists believe the IRA will not give up its weapons and will restart its campaign of violence if it does not achieve its goal, the end of British rule in Ireland. Republicans feel that the political system and the police force are still biased against Catholics. They also suspect that Loyalists do not want to share government with them.

Despite the ceasefires, paramilitaries remain active and are involved in organized crime. In other ways, however, the quality of life in Northern Ireland has improved. Companies have begun to invest. New shops, restaurants and bars have opened, and Belfast has become much more cosmopolitan, mainly as a result of the growth in tourism. The province has the youngest population in the UK and the **sectarian divide** is less strong amongst the young.

The USA

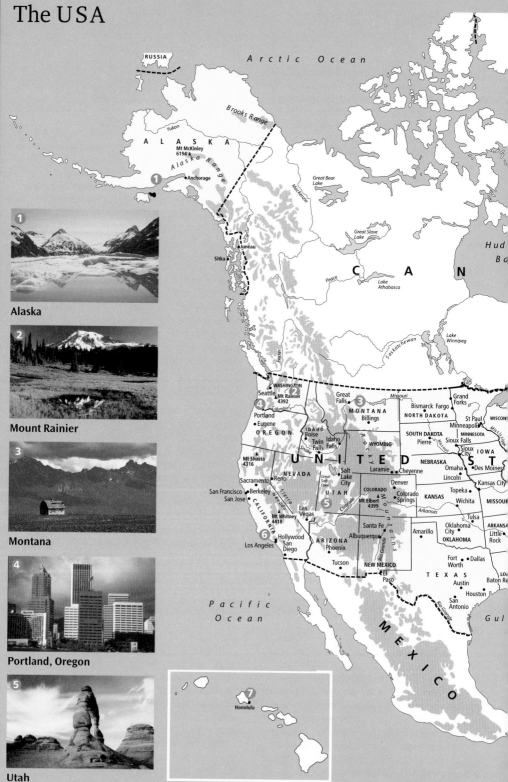

Alaska

Mount Rainier

Montana

Portland, Oregon

Utah

RUSSIA

Arctic Ocean

Brooks Range

A L A S K A
Mt McKinley
6194 ▲
Alaska Range
Yukon
● Anchorage

Great Bear
Lake

Mackenzie

● Juneau
Sitka ●

Peace
Great Slave
Lake

C A N
B a
Hud

Lake
Athabasca

Saskatchewan

Lake
Winnipeg

Fraser

Seattle ● WASHINGTON
Mt Rainier
4392
Portland ●
● Eugene
O R E G O N
Columbia

Great
Falls

Missouri

M O N T A N A
● Billings

Bismarck ● Fargo
NORTH DAKOTA

Grand
Forks

St Paul ●
Minneapolis ●
WISCON

IDAHO
● Boise
Idaho
Falls
Snake
Twin
Falls

WYOMING

SOUTH DAKOTA
Pierre ●

MINNESOTA

Sioux Falls ●
Sioux
City

IOWA

Mt Shasta
4316 ▲

U N I T E D
NEBRASKA

S T

NEVADA
Sacramento ●
Reno
● Berkeley
San Francisco ●
San Jose ●
Great
Salt
Lake
Salt
Lake
City
● Laramie
● Cheyenne

Omaha ●
Lincoln ●

● Des Moines

Kansas City

UTAH
COLORADO
● Denver
Colorado
Springs
Mt Elbert
4399 ▲

Topeka ●
KANSAS
Wichita ●

MISSOURI

Las
Vegas

Santa Fe ●

Arkansas

Tulsa ●

ARKANSAS

C A L I F O R N I A
Sierra Nevada
Mt Whitney
4418 ▲

Oklahoma
City ●
OKLAHOMA

Little
Rock

Hollywood ●
Los Angeles ●
San
Diego
A R I Z O N A
● Phoenix
Albuquerque ●
Amarillo ●

Rocky Mountains

Colorado

Rio Grande

Fort
Worth ●
● Dallas

LO

Baton R

● Tucson
NEW MEXICO
● El
Paso

T E X A S
Austin ●

Houston ●

Gul

Pacific
Ocean

M E X I C O

Rio Grande

San
Antonio ●

● Honolulu

a farm in Wisconsin

Niagara Falls

Washington DC

Daytona beach

Waikiki Beach, Hawaii

Los Angeles

Map labels

ENLAND

Labrador Basin

A

Atlantic Ocean

St. Lawrence

Lakes

Lake Ontario

MAINE
Augusta

NEW HAMPSHIRE
Manchester
VERMONT
Boston
MASSACHUSETTS
Providence
CONNECTICUT
RHODE ISLAND
NEW YORK
Long Island
New York
Newark
PENNSYLVANIA
Philadelphia
Baltimore
NEW JERSEY
Dover
DELAWARE
MARYLAND
Washington DC
Richmond
VIRGINIA
Norfolk

OHIO
olumbus
S
WEST VIRGINIA
Appalachian Mountains
hio

NORTH CAROLINA
Charlotte
Raleigh
Columbia
SOUTH CAROLINA
Charleston
Atlanta
GEORGIA
Savannah
nery
Jacksonville
Tallahassee
FLORIDA
Orlando
Tampa
Miami

THE BAHAMAS

The West Indies

ico

CUBA

HAITI

DOMINICAN REPUBLIC

PUERTO RICO

JAMAICA

HONDURAS
ALA
NICARAGUA
LVADOR
COSTA RICA
PANAMA

Legend

- - - - international boundary
——— state boundary
■ capital city
• city
~~ river
lake
▲ peaks or highest points
land over 1500 metres

0   300 km   600 km

Timeline of US History

Before 4 000 BC Ancestors of modern Native Americans (American Indians and Eskimos) arrived in North America, probably by crossing the Bering Strait from Siberia. (See Inuit, Pre-Columbian North America)

1492 AD Christopher Columbus reached the Bahamas. This led to European exploration and colonization of North and South America.

1607 The first permanent English colony in North America was established at Jamestown, Virginia.

1619 The first African slaves brought to North America landed at Jamestown. (See slavery)

1620 The Pilgrims arrived from England on the *Mayflower* at Massachusetts. (See Native Americans, Pilgrims, Plymouth,Thanksgiving)

1664 The Dutch colony of New Amsterdam was taken by the British and renamed New York.

1754–1763 The French and Indian War gained new land for the American colonists. (See Seven Years War)

1775–1783 The American Revolution led to independence from Britain. The *Declaration of Independence* was signed in 1776. (See John Adams, Boston Tea Party, Continental Congress, Benjamin Franklin, Thomas Jefferson, George Washington)

1787–1791 The US Constitution and Bill of Rights (= first ten amendments) were written and approved. George Washington become the first President of the United States in 1789.

1803 The Louisiana Purchase acquired French lands west of the Mississippi River to the Rocky Mountains and north to Canada for the US.

1804–1806 Lewis and Clark, led by Sacajawea, explored the Louisiana Purchase for the US government and travelled to the Pacific Ocean and back. (See manifest destiny)

1808 Importing slaves was banned but the trade in slaves in the country continued. (See Underground Railroad)

1812–1815 The US fought Britain in the War of 1812.

1848–1849 The California Gold Rush. (See forty-niner)

1861–1865 The Civil War was fought between the Union (= northern states) and the Confederate States (= southern states). The Union won. In 1863 President Abraham Lincoln signed the *Emancipation Proclamation*, abolishing slavery in the US. (See Gettysburg Address, Mason-Dixon Line)

1865	President Lincoln was assassinated. (See Lincoln Memorial)
1865–1867	Reconstruction in the South.
1869	The transcontinental railroad was completed. (See railways, Union Pacific Railroad)
1898	The Spanish-American War. (See Puerto Rico)
1917	The US entered World War I
1919	Prohibition became law, so that it became illegal to produce or sell alcohol in the US until the repeal of the law in 1933. (See Al Capone, Chicago, Mafia, Volstead Act)
1920	Women gained the right to vote. (See Susan B Anthony, suffragettes)
1929–1939	The Great Depression. (See Herbert Hoover)
1941–1945	The US joined World War II after the Japanese attack on Pearl Harbor. Americans fought in both Europe and the Pacific. The war ended after the US dropped atomic bombs on the Japanese cities of Hiroshima and Nagasaki. (See D-Day, Eisenhower)
1950–1953	The Korean War.
1954	The Supreme Court ruled in *Brown v Board of Education* that racial segregation in public schools is illegal.
1961	President John F Kennedy sent advisers to South Vietnam, beginning US military involvement in the Vietnam War.
1963	President Kennedy was assassinated. This event, along with the controversy within the US over its involvement in the Vietnam War and the assassinations of Martin Luther King (1968) and Robert F Kennedy (1968), had a profound effect on American society and optimism.

President Kennedy's grave

| 1964–1965 | The civil rights movement of the 1950s and 1960s led to the Civil Rights Act of 1964 and the Voting Rights Act of 1965, guaranteeing basic rights for African Americans and people of all races. (See Martin Luther King, Malcolm X, Montgomery, Rosa Parks) |
| 1969 | Neil Armstrong became the first person to walk on the moon. (See Buzz Aldrin, the Apollo Program) |

1973	The US military involvement in Vietnam ended.
1973	The Supreme Court decision in *Roe v Wade made abortion legal, a decision that continues to provoke great controversy in US politics.
1974	The Watergate scandal forced President Richard Nixon to resign, making him the first president ever to do so. (See Deep Throat, *Washington Post*)
1991	The first Gulf War.
1991	The collapse of the Soviet Union marked the end of the Cold War.
2001	Terrorists flew planes into the World Trade Center and the Pentagon on September 11.
2003	The Iraq War, followed by the occupation of the country.

The American Revolution

The British colonies in North America

There were British **colonies** in North America from around 1600 and by the 18th century there were thirteen colonies on the east coast of America. By the end of the **Seven Years War** in 1763 the British had taken possession of France's colonies in what is now Canada.

The background to the War

The cost of the Seven Years War had left the British in need of money and they introduced new taxes in America, such as the **Stamp Act**. These were extremely unpopular and led to violent protests and a boycott (=refusal to buy) of British goods. People challenged the right of the British parliament to force taxes on the colonists, using the slogan **no taxation without representation**. They were also angry that the British prevented them trading with other nations and taking more land in the western part of America.

In Boston a group of men calling themselves the **Sons of Liberty** began to organize protests against the British. On 5 March 1770 during an angry protest British soldiers shot and killed five people, which became known as the **Boston Massacre**.

The Boston Tea Party

The British government eventually removed all the taxes except the tax on tea. On 16 December 1773, some of the Sons of Liberty disguised themselves as Native Americans and went on board ships used to transport tea. They threw the tea into the water, an incident that became known as the **Boston Tea Party**. The British government and King George III reacted by passing a series of Acts to increase British control in the colonies. On 5 September 1774, representatives of the colonies met in Philadelphia in the **Continental Congress** and issued a declaration stating that these Acts were not legal.

The outbreak of war

On 18 April 1775, British soldiers marched out of Boston to search for hidden weapons. When the British arrived in the villages of Lexington and Concord both sides began to fire at each other. It is not known who fired the first shot but it marked the start of the war and became known as **the shot heard round the world**. On 17 June 1775, the **Battle of Bunker Hill** was won by the British but almost half their soldiers were killed or wounded.

The Declaration of Independence

In the autumn of 1775, the Continental Congress offered peace to the British but was rejected. In early 1776, Thomas Paine's *Common Sense*, calling for complete independence from Britain, was a great success in America. On 4 July 1776 the **Declaration of Independence** was signed. This document, written by Thomas Jefferson, stated the reasons why America should be independent from Britain and the right of all citizens to **life, liberty and the pursuit of happiness**.

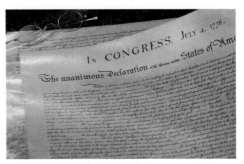

the Declaration of Independence

The War

The Americans chose **George Washington** to lead them. As the British army was larger, he decided to make short, surprise attacks and to avoid major battles. After a series of victories and defeats on both sides, the Americans won a major victory at **Saratoga** on October 17th 1777 and the war turned in the Americans' favour. **Benjamin Franklin** made an agreement with France in February 1778 that the French would help against the British. Soon afterwards the Spanish also joined the war on America's side. In August 1781, the British General, Charles Cornwallis, was forced to move his soldiers to **Yorktown** in Virginia. He was unable to receive supplies as the French navy blocked the harbour. Surrounded by 9 000 Americans and 6 000 French, he surrendered on 19 October 1781.

The Peace Treaty

On 3rd September 1783, the **Peace of Paris** was signed and the United States of America became an independent nation. **The Revolutionary War**, or the **American War of Independence**, as the British call it, is remembered every year on the 4th of July, as one of the principal events in the formation of the American nation.

The Civil War 1861–1865

The causes of the war

One of the main causes of the Civil War was the issue of **slavery**. The northern states were mainly industrial, but the southern states still had an agricultural economy based on cotton and tobacco and depended on slaves for labour. In the north, **abolitionists** wanted to make slavery illegal, particularly in the new states that were being settled in the west. The southern states refused to accept the right of the federal government to interfere in the laws of individual states and many southerners began to believe that southern states should **secede from the Union** (= become independent from the US).

The Confederacy

In 1860, **Abraham Lincoln** was elected president. The **secessionists** believed he would make slavery illegal and so left the Union. In 1860, there were 34 states in the US. Eleven states left to form the **Confederate States of America**, usually called the **Confederacy**. These were: Alabama, Arkansas, Florida, Georgia, Louisiana, Mississippi, North Carolina, South Carolina, Tennessee, Texas, and Virginia. **Jefferson Davis** became their President and, for most of the war, Richmond, Virginia was the capital. The northern states were known as the **Union**.

The beginning of the war

On 12 April 1862, the Confederate army attacked **Fort Sumter** which was occupied by Unionist soldiers. Lincoln did not want war but was determined to keep the Union and so called for 75 000 soldiers to put down the rebellion. So began the Civil War. The Confederate army was brilliantly led by **General Robert E Lee** who managed to keep the larger Union army from taking the South. The battles that followed, such as Shiloh, Antietam, Bull Run and

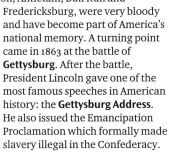

Fredericksburg, were very bloody and have become part of America's national memory. A turning point came in 1863 at the battle of **Gettysburg**. After the battle, President Lincoln gave one of the most famous speeches in American history: the **Gettysburg Address**. He also issued the Emancipation Proclamation which formally made slavery illegal in the Confederacy.

Confederate soldier

The Union victory

After Gettysburg, the Union began to take control. Union soldiers led by Ulysses S Grant won a major victory at Vicksburg and Grant was made Supreme Commander of the Union Army. He attacked the Confederate army on several fronts. The Union navy had control of the sea and prevented all supplies reaching the South. In 1864, General Sherman led 60 000 troops through Georgia, destroying everything in their path including Atlanta, which was set on fire. Finally, on 9 April 1865, when the South could fight no more, General Robert E Lee surrendered to General Grant at **Appomattox Court House** in Virginia. A total of 620 000 people had been killed and many more wounded. Five days later, Lincoln was assassinated by John Wilkes Booth who supported the South.

the Union army

After the war

The long and difficult period that followed was called **Reconstruction**. Although the industrial North had been made rich by the Civil War, the South and the southern way of life had been destroyed. Most of the large plantations were broken up, and the economy remained poor until helped by the New Deal in the 1930s.

The end of slavery

Between 1865 and 1870, the 13th, 14th and 15th Amendments were passed which in theory gave African Americans equal rights. Many southerners, who were now poor as a result of the war, felt angry toward the north and about the freeing of the slaves, and the racist organization the **Ku Klux Klan** was formed. Many Southern states passed **Jim Crow laws** to limit the freedom of African Americans through policies such as **segregation**. It was not until the **civil rights movement** of the 1960s that African Americans saw an end to these racist policies.

The Constitution

The Articles of Confederation

In 1783, at the end of the **American Revolution**, the United States was a group of 13 independent states with a weak central government. The government's powers, agreed in 1781 in the **Articles of Confederation**, did not include powers to collect taxes or enforce laws. The central government was unable to settle disputes between states or develop the economy.

The Constitutional Convention

In May 1787 representatives from the 13 states were called to a **constitutional convention** in Philadelphia to decide on a new, more effective constitution. They included some of most important figures in American history: George Washington, Alexander Hamilton, Benjamin Franklin and James Madison. After much discussion and compromise, the convention approved a new constitution on 17 September 1787 and, by June of 1788, the Constitution had been **ratified** (= accepted) by 9 states and was official.

What is in the Constitution?

The Constitution establishes the **separation of powers** between three different branches of government.

The **legislative branch** consists of **Congress**, a parliament made up of two parts: the **House of Representatives** and the **Senate**. It has a number of specific powers, including the power to collect taxes and control trade between states and with foreign countries, and can make laws to exercise these powers.

The power to run the country is given to the **executive branch**, led by a President and Vice-President.

The **judicial branch** consists of the **Supreme Court** and a number of lower courts created by Congress. It is given power to decide legal disputes, including those involving the Constitution, national laws and differences between the states.

As well as this separation of powers, there is also a system of **checks and balances** so that each branch has some power over the other two in order to stop them becoming too powerful.

The Bill of Rights

Several states refused to ratify (= accept) the Constitution until it was changed to give citizens more protection against the wrong use of power by government. This was done in 10 **amendments** (= changes) to the Constitution in 1791, known as the **Bill of Rights**.

The **First Amendment** gave people the right to freedom of speech and freedom of religion. The **Fifth Amendment** included the right of people accused of crimes to refuse to give evidence against themselves (often called the 'right to remain silent'). The **10th Amendment** made it clear that powers not given to central government by the Constitution remained with the individual states.

A number of further amendments have been made since. Following the **Civil War**, the **13th Amendment** (1865) made slavery illegal. In 1870 the **15th Amendment** extended the right to vote to men of all races and in 1920, the **19th Amendment** guaranteed women's right to vote.

Amending the Constitution

The writers of the Constitution deliberately made it difficult to amend, so that only changes with strong support would be **ratified**. The only method for amending the Constitution that has ever been used works as follows: a bill must pass both houses of Congress with a two-thirds majority in each. Once the bill has passed both houses, it is given to the states. If it passes in three quarters of the states' legislatures the change is ratified. A second method, which allows states to propose an amendment, has never been used.

George Washington

The Federal Government

The federal (= national) government of the US is made up of three branches: the legislative, executive and judicial. The powers and responsibilities of these branches are described in the **Constitution**. The three separate branches, with officials chosen in different ways and for different terms of office, were designed to achieve a **separation of powers** that kept any one branch from becoming too powerful.

The legislative branch

The **legislative** branch consists of the two houses (= parts) of **Congress**: the **Senate** and the **House of Representatives**. Both houses meet in the **Capitol building** in Washington, DC. The main job of Congress is to discuss and decide national laws. Its other responsibilities include establishing federal courts, setting taxes and declaring war. Members of the two houses of Congress are elected separately.

The executive branch

Executive power, or the power to run the country, is given to the **President**. The President works in the **White House**, at 1600 Pennsylvania Avenue, Washington, DC.

The Cabinet

The Constitution does not describe how the President should exercise this power. In practice it is exercised through the **Cabinet**, a committee of advisers whose members are the heads of the **departments of government**. The departments are created by Congress and the President chooses the department heads, although the choice must be approved by the Senate.

the White House

Government departments and agencies

There are 15 federal government departments, each with its own area of activity. The Department of Defense, for example, runs the military services. The Department of Health and Human Services runs programmes such as Social Security, Medicare and Medicaid. The State Department advises the President on relations with foreign countries and runs the embassies. In addition, there are a number of independent agencies within the executive branch, for example the Central Intelligence Agency. Each department has offices in Washington, DC and throughout the country.

The judicial branch

The judicial branch of government has several levels. The Constitution created a **Supreme Court of the United States** and gave Congress the power to create lower federal courts. The lower courts include 13 courts of appeal for different areas in the US and 94 district courts and special courts such as the Court of International Trade.

The nine judges of the Supreme Court are known as **justices**. They meet in the Supreme Court building in Washington, DC.

The federal courts protect people's rights under the Constitution. They have the power to decide that a law is **unconstitutional** (= against the Constitution) and should not be applied.

Checks and balances

The courts' power to declare a law unconstitutional is one example of a concept built into the US Constitution called the system of **checks and balances**. Like the separation of powers, this system gives each branch of government ways to limit the others. For example the process by which a bill becomes law demands that a bill first pass both houses of Congress and then go to the President for approval. In another example, the legislative branch is responsible for conducting trials for the impeachment (= removal from office) of federal officers such as the President and Supreme Court judges.

Law-making

Congress

In the US, national laws are decided by **Congress** a legislative (= law-making) body made up of two parts or 'houses'. The upper house called the **Senate** has two representatives from each of the 50 states The lower house the **House of Representatives** has 435 members who represent individual voting districts from every state in the country

A bill is introduced and sent to a committee

Any member of either the Senate or the House of Representatives can prepare a **bill** (= a suggestion for a new law) and introduce it to their house Once this has been done the bill is referred to a **committee** in order to be discussed

The committee holds **public hearings** at which people representing different groups in society give their opinions about the bill. After the committee has enough information, the members decide on any changes to the bill that need to be made. Sometimes the committee may decide not to take further action to introduce the law, in which case the bill is said to be 'tabled'.

The house makes changes and votes

After the committee has finished with the bill, it is sent back to the house where it was introduced, together with a report that explains its purpose and why it should be accepted. The members of the house discuss the bill and vote on any changes that they want to make. Once all the changes have been decided and any discussion is brought to an end, the members vote to approve or reject the bill.

Virginia state capitol, Richmond

Changes by the other house

When it has been agreed by one house, the law must then be considered by the other house. If the other house decides to makes changes, these must be sent back to the first house for approval. Often a committee of members from both houses (called a **conference committee**) is formed to resolve disagreements and produce a final version of the law

The President's power of veto

Once both houses have agreed to the same version of the bill, it goes to the President to be signed, after which it becomes an official law. The President can decide to **veto** (= reject) the law in which case it returns to the Congress for a final vote. If two thirds of the members of Congress approve the bill it becomes law

Law-making by individual states

At state level laws are passed by the two houses (often called the Senate and the House of Representatives) of the **state legislature** in a similar way and are then sent to the state's **governor** for signature. Law-making by the states, however, is limited by the requirement that state laws should not contradict laws or treaties made by the federal government.

the Capitol, where both houses of Congress meet

The Legal System

The **judicial** system is one of the three branches of the US federal government. In addition to federal courts there are also **state**, **county** and **city courts**.

The courts

Each type of court has its own **jurisdiction** (= the type of cases it can deal with). Some courts **hear** only **criminal cases**. Other courts are for **civil cases**, in which one person **sues** another over a disagreement. Cases are first heard in **trial courts**. A person who is found not guilty in a criminal **trial** can never be **tried** again for the same crime. But a person found guilty in a criminal trial, and both sides involved in a civil trial, have the right to **appeal** against the court's decision. The case then goes to a **court of appeals**.

State courts of appeals are called **superior courts** or **district courts**, and most states have a **supreme court**. This is the highest court in the state and hears only the most serious appeals. There is a separate federal court system, which deals with crimes that are **federal offences** (= against federal law) or crimes that involve two or more states.

The highest court in the US is the **Supreme Court**. It hears appeals of cases that involve important **constitutional** principles and decides if laws are **unconstitutional** (= against the Constitution).

The people in a courtroom

The most powerful person in a courtroom is the **judge**. Most courts have only one judge, but some higher courts have several. State judges are often elected, but federal judges are appointed by the President.

the Supreme Court

The people on either side of a case are represented by **lawyers**, also called **attorneys**. In a criminal trial the **defendant** (= the person accused) is represented by a **defense attorney**, unless he or she is too poor to pay for a lawyer and the court appoints a **public defender**. The **prosecution** is led by a **prosecutor**, who works for the **district attorney**, or, in federal cases, by a **federal attorney**. In a **civil lawsuit** the defendant and the **plaintiff** (= the person who claims to have been wronged) pay for their own attorneys. In cases involving only small amounts of money, people go to **small claims court** and represent themselves.

A group of ordinary citizens called a **jury** listen to most cases and decide the result.

The court process

In a criminal case, the defendant may agree to a **plea bargain** (e.g. agree to plead guilty if the charges are reduced). In a civil case, the two parties may agree to **settle out of court**. If this cannot be done, the case goes to trial.

At the beginning of a trial, both attorneys make **opening statements** to explain their cases. Then each side calls **witnesses** and presents **evidence**. Each witness **takes the stand** (= goes and sits in a special place) and **testifies** (= says what he or she knows about the case). During the trial, the judge decides what information will be **allowed** and also makes sure that the rules of the court are obeyed.

An important principle in a criminal trial is that the defendant is **innocent until proven guilty**. **Jurors** are not allowed to discuss the case with each other or make a decision until both sides have finished. At the end of the trial, both attorneys give **closing arguments** that summarize their cases. The judge may then give special instructions to the jury.

The jury then **deliberate** together. In a criminal trial the jury decide the **verdict** and if the verdict is 'guilty', the judge gives the **sentence**. In a civil trial the jury decide who wins and may also decide the amount of **damages** (= money to be paid as compensation).

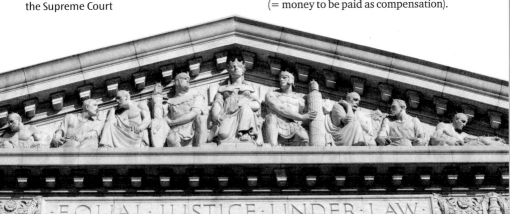

EQUAL JUSTICE UNDER LAW

Political Parties

The two-party system

The US has two main political parties, the **Democratic Party** and the **Republican Party**. There are other smaller parties but they rarely win major elections. The US 'winner-take-all' political system makes it difficult for more than two main parties to exist at one time. The Democratic Party was started in the 1820s growing from an offshoot of the country's first party the **Federalist Party**. The Republican Party began as an anti-slavery party in 1854 with members from the Democratic Party and the **Whigs**.

Party membership and organization

Belonging to a party involves simply choosing that party when you register to vote. There are no membership dues or requirements, and it is not uncommon for people to change membership or vote across party lines. The heads of the national parties do not hold official positions in the government.

campaigning in an election

The role of the parties

Party organizations are less important in the US than in countries that have parliaments. Because of the way the government is structured, the same party does not necessarily control the two houses of Congress or the presidency at the same time. Thus it is often difficult to hold one party responsible for the actions of the government. In addition, citizens vote for individual candidates for each office rather than a **party slate** (= list of candidates) so a candidate's personal qualities are often more important than his or her **party affiliation**.

An important job of the national party is to organize the party **convention** (= meeting), held every four years before the elections for president. The convention officially names the party's candidates for president and vice president and announces the party's **platform**

(= ideas and policies). The national parties also raise money for election campaigns and provide other kinds of help to their candidates. Local branches of the parties work to support local and national candidates, and ordinary people who are active in a party are involved at this level.

In the House of Representatives and the Senate, the **majority party** controls the most powerful committees that make important decisions about which issues and laws are dealt with by Congress. Members of Congress are allowed more independence from their parties than British Members of Parliament. They aim to appear loyal first to the people they represent but also try to be seen as loyal party members so that they will have the chance to sit on important committees and build up support for their own proposals.

Most Americans do not want politicians to appear too **partisan** (= strongly attached to their party) but to show a **bipartisan** (= cooperative) spirit and work together for the good of the country.

What are the parties like?

Compared to many other countries, both US parties are close to the **political centre** but the Democrats are to the **left** and the Republicans are to the **right** of centre. Typically the Democrats support spending on social welfare programmes while the Republicans are against this. The Republicans are usually in favour of spending on the armed forces and believe there should be few laws restricting business. Republicans are sometimes called the **GOP** or **Grand Old Party** and have an **elephant** as their symbol. The Democrats' symbol is a **donkey**.

Democrat donkey

Republican elephant

In recent years the Democratic Party has drawn much of its support from young people, low-paid workers, union members, minorities (especially African Americans) and people in urban areas. People with more money, those with strong conservative religious beliefs and white people who live in the central and southern part of the country have tended to vote for Republicans.

Elections

Elections are held regularly for President, for both houses of Congress and for state and local government offices. Candidates usually **run for office** with the support of one of the two main political parties, the Republicans or the Democrats, but anyone who wants to run as an **independent** can organize a **petition**. If enough signatures are collected, he or she may run. Any citizen over the age of 18 may vote in an election, if he or she registers and meets requirements for residency in a state.

Members of Congress

There are 435 members of the House of Representatives, each serving two-year terms. The number from each state varies according to the size of its population. Some states, such as Montana, with very small populations have only a single representative while California, with the largest population, has 53. The borders of the districts that members of the House represent are changed every ten years after each census (= official counting of the population) so that they include equal numbers of voters.

There are two Senators from every state, each serving six-year terms. Every two years, about one third of the Senate comes up for re-election. The elections take place at the same time as elections for the House of Representatives or for the President.

In both sets of Congressional elections, it is the people in the particular district or state that choose their representative and only the candidate with a **plurality of votes** (= with the most votes) goes to Congress.

In addition to elections on the national level, each state has its own government which, in all but one state, is set up like the federal government with elections held in the same way.

Electing the President

Elections for the President and Vice-President are held every four years and follow a complicated procedure.

Primaries

From January to June in the election year, political parties choose their candidates through a series of **primary elections** in each state. People choose the party whose primary they want to vote in and vote for their choice of candidates.

a polling booth

Congressional convention

In the summer, each party holds a **convention** to make its final choice of candidates. Teams of **delegates** from each state go to the convention to vote for the pair of candidates that won their party's primary. However, the party usually chooses the final candidates informally beforehand, based on who has been most successful in the primaries.

Voting procedure

The presidential election always takes place on the Tuesday following the first Monday in November. A few weeks before the election, registered voters receive a card telling them the address of the **polling station** where they should vote. At the polling station, each voter casts a single presidential vote (for a President plus Vice-President), together with separate votes for a member of the House of Representatives and possibly a senator.

Counting votes in a presidential election

After the votes are counted in an election, each state has a number of **electors** (one for each congressional district and senator) who make up an **electoral college** (= a type of committee). Each elector casts two votes, one for the President and one for the Vice-President, choosing the candidates who received the greatest number of votes in the state. A candidate with the support of at least 270 of the 538 electors becomes President or Vice-President.

Education

The K-12 school system

Although many American children attend **daycare**, **nursery school**, or **preschool**, formal education is usually considered to begin around the age of five when children go to **kindergarten**. Kindergarten, first grade, second grade etc. to twelfth grade are together referred to as **K-12**. Each school system has its own way of organizing and naming schools. Usually, kindergarten to fourth, fifth, or sixth grade is together called **elementary school** or **grade school**. Grades six or seven to twelve are part of **secondary school**, and may be divided in different ways. In some places, fifth or sixth grade to eighth grade is called **middle school**. Other school systems have **junior high school**, which includes seventh, eighth and sometimes ninth grades. **High school** (or **senior high school**) covers three or four years from ninth or tenth grade to twelfth grade.

The K-12 **curriculum** (= subjects studied) includes English, mathematics, social studies, science, and sometimes music, art, and physical education. Foreign languages and other **elective courses** (= subjects that students can choose) are added at different levels depending on the school system. Secondary education is not usually specialized towards training in a specific career. Students who want to go to college often take **college-prep classes**, while other students take courses in practical subjects.

There are no national exams to move from one grade to the next. However, recent federal guidelines require states to monitor students' achievement levels, so that many states now test more frequently. Generally, teachers **grade** students throughout the year on how well they do on tests, on homework and in classroom discussions. At the end of a **semester** or of a year, students who do not have at least a D (= 60%) **grade point average** (**GPA**) have to repeat the class. Students who successfully complete twelfth grade receive a **high school diploma**. Those who do not **graduate** from high school can obtain a **General Equivalency Diploma** (**GED**) by taking an exam.

Public or private education

Most children in the US go to **public schools** run by the government, which are free. But there are many **private schools**, for which parents pay. Private schools generally have a good reputation and parents send children there so that they will have advantages later in life. Some parents choose private religious schools called **parochial schools** for the quality of education or for religious instruction, which is not allowed in public schools. An increasing number of parents choose to **home-school** their children (= teach them at home).

Post-secondary education

Local governments are required to provide free public K-12 education for all children. **Post-secondary** education (= after twelfth grade) is not free, however. Some students attend two-year **community colleges** or **junior colleges**, which have an emphasis on practical career-related courses such as nursing or journalism. These schools are usually subsidized by local governments. There are also many **vocational** and **technical schools** or **institutes** that train students for specific types of work. These institutions are usually private.

Students may choose to attend four-year **universities** and **colleges**, which may be either private or state-run, and earn a **bachelor's degree**. They may do this either immediately after high school or by transferring from community college. State governments subsidize the **tuition** (= cost of teaching) at state-run colleges and universities for students who live in the state, but whether it is public or private, post-secondary education is expensive. Some students receive **scholarships** or **grants** that pay part or all of their tuition. A large percentage of students work, often through **work-study programmes** to help fund their education.

After completing their undergraduate degrees, some students go on to **graduate school** to pursue **master's degrees** or **doctorates** (**PhDs**). Others may choose instead to go to **medical school** or **law school** to become doctors or lawyers.

The funding and hierarchy of the education system

The federal government provides some money and sets some standards for education through the **Department of Education**. But state and local governments have direct control and are responsible for the majority of the cost of students' education from kindergarten to twelfth grade. Individual states have their own **Boards of Education**, which decide the curriculum and what students must have achieved before they can graduate from high school. States also set the general standards of education and qualifications that teachers must have.

School boards have control over how schools in a particular **school district** are run. The boards can be appointed or elected and are usually made up of local people, often parents of children in the schools. A **superintendent**, the person in charge of all the schools in a school district, is sometimes hired by the school board and sometimes elected by local citizens. The board and superintendent have a role in hiring **principals** and **teachers** for each school.

At the elementary and secondary levels, most school districts have a **Parent-Teacher Association** (PTA), which gives all parents a chance to take part in making decisions about how the school is run. Parents regularly visit schools for **parent-teacher conferences** to meet their children's teachers and discuss their progress. Many volunteer (= work without pay) in their children's schools.

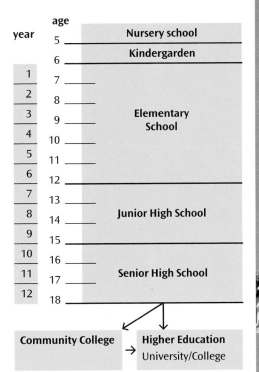

year	age	
	5	Nursery school
	6	Kindergarden
1	7	
2	8	
3	9	Elementary School
4	10	
5	11	
6	12	
7	13	
8	14	Junior High School
9	15	
10	16	
11	17	Senior High School
12	18	

Community College ← → Higher Education University/College →

a graduation ceremony

The quality of education

By many standards, American education is very successful. Although young people must attend school only until they are 16, over 80% continue until they graduate, at around age 18. Over 50% obtain some post-secondary or **further education**, and about 27% graduate from a college or university.

On the other hand, about 20% of adults are said to have very limited reading skills. Since control over education is mostly at the local level, its quality varies greatly from place to place. Money is an important reason for this. Over 40% of the money for elementary and secondary education comes from property taxes paid to the local government, so wealthy areas have better-funded schools than poorer areas. Crime and violence are also serious problems in some schools.

Most Americans agree that a good education gives people the best chance of getting a good job and of improving their social position. **Life-long learning** is an important concept for Americans, and many adults take part in **continuing education**, **adult education**, and **distance-learning** programmes. Adults of all ages return to education to pursue new degrees to further their career or for personal development.

Native Americans

a totem pole

Native Americans are people who were living in North and South America before the arrival of Europeans in the 15th century. In the US the term includes **American Indians** and **Alaska Natives**, i.e. **Eskimos** (= **Inuits** or **Yupik**) and **Aleuts**. The ancestors of today's Native Americans probably arrived from Siberia across the Bering Strait and were in the Americas many thousands of years before the Europeans arrived.

Early contact with Europeans

In **Pre-Columbian North America** there were many tribes of **hunter-gatherers** who lived by hunting, fishing and gathering plants. Most moved around according to the season. When Europeans began settling in what is now the US in the early 1600s, Native Americans were at first happy to have the many new things they brought, such as metal cooking pots, cloth and guns. But the **colonists** also brought diseases that Native Americans had no resistance to and also introduced alcohol, which had a strongly negative impact on Native American society.

The worst problem for Native Americans was that the new settlers wanted land. The idea of land ownership was not part of the Native American culture. They saw themselves as a part of the greater natural world and did not understand that a person might believe a piece of land was theirs and want to keep others from using it. The settlers, on the other hand, believed in **manifest destiny**, meaning that they thought God wanted them to occupy and control the whole continent. They used all means to do this, including signing **treaties** (= making agreements), tricking Native Americans into selling land cheaply, taking it by military force, and killing or enslaving the Indians.

Pueblo Indian ruins

As the settlers began moving west, Native American tribes were moved off their land. Some were forced to go to areas very different from the ones they were used to. The **Trail of Tears** was one terrible example: in the winter of 1838–9, 17 000 Cherokees had to move from their land in the Southeast to what is now Oklahoma and more than 4 000 died. The government promised tribes that, if they agreed to stay in one part of the country, they could keep that land forever, but the promises were seldom kept. Many settlers also believed they should make Native Americans live as they did and teach them Christianity. All this contributed to the destruction of the Native Americans' traditional way of life. White Americans and Native Americans led by chiefs such as Sitting Bull, Tecumseh and Geronimo, often fought when they came into contact.

Native American languages

Before Europeans arrived in North America, there were over 300 Native American languages. Some have now died out and many are spoken by only a few older people. Most Native Americans speak English as their first or second language.

Native American languages have added many words to English, such as **anorak**, **caucus**, **moccasin**, **pecan**, **powwow**, and **totem**. Many American place names, such as Ohio, Mississippi and Yosemite also have their roots in Native American languages.

Native Americans today

There are today more than 550 federally recognized tribes in the US. In 2002, there were about two million American Indians and Alaskan Natives in the US. Of that number, 538 300 lived on **reservations** (= special areas of land set aside for them), about one-third of them on **Navajo** reservations in the US Southwest.

Because state laws regarding gambling do not apply to Indian lands, many tribes have opened casinos and other gambling establishments on their reservations since 1988. This has become a major source of income for the tribes.

Immigration

Apart from Native Americans all Americans are from families who came to America as **immigrants**. People are generally proud to say that their ancestors came to the US with very little and built a better life for themselves.

Museum of Immigration, Ellis Island

The US – a nation of immigrants

Europeans began settling in North America in the late 16th century. The first colonists were Spanish, English, and Dutch, but many German, Irish, Scottish, and French people came to the colonies as well. Many of the early colonists came to escape **religious persecution** at home. From 1619 until 1808, nearly 500 000 Africans came to North America, brought by force as slaves.

The 19th century saw a huge rise in immigration. Between 1820 and 1880, many more people arrived from Germany, Britain, Ireland and the Austro-Hungarian Empire. Large numbers of Chinese also came to California. Between the peak years of 1880 and 1930, when 27 million people entered the country, the main groups were Italians, Austro-Hungarians, Germans, Russians, Canadians, British, Irish and Scandinavians. Many Jews arrived from Germany and Eastern Europe.

Immigration laws passed in the first half of the 20th century limited the number of immigrants according to their country of origin and favoured immigrants from north-west Europe. In 1965 a new law got rid of the **national-origin quotas**. Since then, immigration has increased, with the largest numbers coming from Mexico, the Philippines and other parts of Latin America and Asia. The US continues to accept hundreds of thousands of immigrants each year.

Give me your tired, your poor,
Your huddled masses yearning
    to breathe free,
The wretched refuse of your
    teeming shore.
Send these, the homeless,
    tempest-tost to me,
I lift my lamp beside
    the golden door!

The New Colossus
Emma Lazarus (1849–1887)

carved on the Statue
of Liberty

The immigrant experience

During the 19th and early 20th centuries, many immigrants left home because they were poor and thought they would have better opportunities in the US. Most travelled on crowded ships where diseases spread quickly. Many would-be immigrants died on the journey or arrived weak and ill. The majority arrived in New York and Boston, and **Ellis Island** near New York became famous as a **receiving station**. There the immigrants were examined by a doctor before being allowed to enter the US. But life in the US was not easy. Those who stayed in the cities often had to work in **sweatshops** (= factories where conditions were hard) and live in **tenements**, (= crowded buildings where an entire family often lived in one room). But slowly they improved their lives and many wrote home to encourage others to come.

Today immigrants continue to move to the US for economic and political reasons and to join family members. Immigrants must obtain a **green card** to establish legal permanent residency, a first step towards citizenship.

Attitudes towards immigration

Immigrants have been welcomed during times of economic prosperity but have sometimes been viewed with suspicion during economic hard times. Many people think that immigrants should abandon their original culture and language and join the American **melting pot**, in which people from many cultures form a single new culture.

But Americans continue to be proud of their ethnic backgrounds. From the 1960s the melting pot image was partly replaced by **pluralism**, the idea that a variety of values, traditions and languages was good and that a **multicultural** society made the US stronger. Over time, immigrant families **assimilate**, i.e. change their lifestyle so it becomes more like the **mainstream**. This can be seen in the lifestyles of second- and third-generation Americans.

The English Language

The history of the English language is divided into three periods: **Old English** (c.450 AD–c.1150 AD), **Middle English** (c.1150–c.1500 AD), and **Modern English** (c.1500 to today).

Old English (c. 450 AD–c.1150 AD)

English was originally a West Germanic language brought to England by the **Anglo-Saxons** in the 5th century. The word *English* comes from *englisc* or *ænglisc* (= the language of the Angles) which was spoken by the Germanic invaders of England.

Many of the most basic words in modern English come from Old English e.g.: *child, man, wife, house, good, strong, eat, drink, sleep* and *live*. The grammar was more complicated than modern English as it had a large number of different endings for verbs, nouns and adjectives. It was written using the same alphabet as modern English but included some extra letters such as æ (ash), and Þ (thorn).

At the end of the 8th century, Viking invasions of England began. The language of the invaders was very similar to Anglo-Saxon but they introduced a large number of new words such as: *egg, skin, sky, get, give,* and *take*.

The most famous work of literature in Old English is *Beowulf*, probably composed around 800 AD. **Alfred the Great** (871–899 AD), who wanted to encourage learning, ordered that many books be written in English, including the *Anglo-Saxon Chronicle*.

Middle English (c.1150–1500)

In this period the grammar of English became far simpler. Many words came into the language from French, particularly during the 14th century. The **Normans** invaded England in 1066 and took control of the country. For the next 200 years, the upper classes mainly spoke French while the rest of the people spoke English. This changed slowly and by the 14th century English had become the language used by everyone. Words from French added in the Middle English period include: *art, authority, beauty, biscuit, button, coat, court, cream, judge, jury,* and *parliament*.

People in different parts of the country spoke different dialects of English. By the end of the 15th century, however, the dialect spoken in London was accepted as the standard language, especially after **William Caxton** introduced printing in 1476 and London became the centre of the new printing technology.

Literature

The most famous writer of this period is **Geoffrey Chaucer** (1340–1400) who wrote the *Canterbury Tales*. Other important works include *Piers Plowman* by **William Langland** (c.1330–c.1386) and *Sir Gawain and the Green Knight* by an unknown author.

Modern English (1500–the present)

During the 16th and 17th centuries, English grammar was further simplified. The use of *thou,* a singular and more intimate form of *you,* gradually disappeared. A large number of words came into English from Latin and Greek during the **Renaissance** to express new ideas in science and philosophy. Examples include: *architecture, hypothesis, physics,* and *species*.

This development continued with the growth of science in the 18th and 19th centuries, and many new scientific terms were added. The growth of the British Empire and international trade brought many additions from foreign languages such as *cashmere, china, cocoa, chocolate, gorilla, juggernaut, taboo, tobacco,* and *tomato*.

In the 18th century **Samuel Johnson** produced *A Dictionary of the English Language* (1755), which set a new standard of quality for dictionaries and helped to standardize the spelling system. It was followed in the USA by **Noah Webster's** *A Compendious Dictionary of the English Language* (1806). Webster standardized the spelling system in American English (for example *labour* was changed to *labor*). **James Murray's** *Oxford English Dictionary* was begun in 1858. Its second edition, published in 1989, recorded 615 100 separate word forms.

World English

From the language of a small country on the edge of Europe English has grown into a world language. Varieties of English are spoken in many parts of the world: British English, American English, Canadian English, Caribbean English, Indian English, etc. About 350 million people speak English as their first language and in over 70 countries English is used a second language. Estimates for the number of English speakers in these areas range from 350 million to 2 billion. There are also millions of learners of English as a foreign language. English is now more often spoken as a foreign or second language than as a first language. It is interesting to see how this will affect the development of the language.

room and chair designed by
Charles Rennie Mackintosh

,**Shirley Ma'cLaine** /məˈkleɪn/ (1934–) a US film actor who began her career as a dancer on *Broadway. MacLaine won an *Oscar for *Terms of Endearment* (1983), and her other films include *The Apartment* (1960), *Sweet Charity* (1969) and *Steel Magnolias* (1989). She is the sister of the actor Warren *Beatty.

,**Alistair Ma'clean**[1] /məˈkleɪn/ (1922–87) a Scottish author of adventure novels. They include *The Guns of Navarone* (1957), *Ice Station Zebra* (1963) and *Where Eagles Dare* (1967), which have all been made into successful films. He also wrote books about T E *Lawrence and Captain James *Cook.

,**Donald Ma'clean**[2] /məˈkleɪn/ (1913–83) an English spy. He became a Communist as a young man at the same time as the other British spies Anthony *Blunt, Guy *Burgess and Kim *Philby, and from 1944 worked for the British Foreign Office while acting as a spy for the Russian government. In 1951 he learned of British suspicions against him, and escaped with Burgess to Russia, where he lived until his death. See also FOREIGN AND COMMONWEALTH OFFICE.

,**Harold Mac'millan**[1] /məkˈmɪlən/ (1894–1986) a British *Conservative politician. He entered Parliament in 1924 and was *Foreign Secretary (1955) and *Chancellor of the Exchequer (1955–7) before becoming *Prime Minister (1957–63). After gaining power he concentrated on improving Britain's international relations and encouraging economic growth, becoming known for his phrase 'You've never had it so good' (taken from a US election campaign). Because of his successes he was sometimes called 'Supermac' by the press. The *Profumo affair in 1963 damaged his party and he resigned later that year because of ill health, being replaced by Sir Alec *Douglas-Home. Macmillan was the author of several books, including *Winds of Change* (1966). He was made an *earl(1) in 1984.

> **❝** The wind of change is blowing through this continent, and, whether we like it or not, this growth of national consciousness is a political fact. **❞**
> Harold Macmillan in a 1960 speech on Africa

,**Kenneth Mac'Millan**[2] /məkˈmɪlən/ (1929–92) a Scottish choreographer. He was director of the *Royal Ballet (1970–77), and his work includes *Elite Syncopations* (1974) and *Mayerling* (1978). He was made a *knight in 1983.

,**Louis Mac'Neice** /məkˈniːs/ (1907–63) a Northern Irish poet. His books of verse include *Blind Fireworks* (1929) and *Autumn Journal* (1939), but he is perhaps best known for his radio play *The Dark Tower* (1947) and his friendship with the poet W H *Auden, with whom he wrote *Letters from Iceland* (1937). He also translated ancient Greek poetry.

'**Macy's** /ˈmeɪsiz/ a famous shop in New York City which calls itself 'the world's largest store' and has branches in many other US cities. Each *Thanksgiving, it presents a colourful parade through New York which is shown on television.

MAD /mæd/ (*also **MAD Magazine**) a US humorous magazine, first published in 1952. It is now owned by *Time Warner and appears once a month. It uses an exaggerated cartoon style to make fun of films, advertisements, etc., and to make well-known people look foolish. It has on its cover a picture of the imaginary character Alfred E Neuman, who has a wide face and a stupid smile and says 'What, me worry?'.

,**Madame Tus'saud's** /təˈsɔːdz/ a museum in London, England, started in 1835 by a Frenchwoman, Madame Marie Tussaud (1761–1850). It contains wax figures of famous people from past and present, and the *Chamber of Horrors, an exhibition of famous crimes and punishments.

the Beatles at Madame Tussauds

the ,**Mad 'Hatter** a character in *Alice in Wonderland by Lewis *Carroll. The Mad Hatter, who wears a tall hat, holds a tea party with Alice, the March Hare and the Dormouse. The expression 'as mad as a hatter', meaning completely crazy, was already common when Carroll wrote the book.

James 'Madison /ˈmædɪsn/ (1751–1836) the fourth US *President (1809–17) and one of America's *Founding Fathers. He was called the *Father of the Constitution because of his important work on that document. He was *Secretary of State (1801–8) under President Thomas *Jefferson and was then elected President as a Democratic-Republican. He was in office during the *War of 1812 and when the British burned the *White House(1) in 1814. He later helped to establish the University of Virginia and was the last of the Founding Fathers to die.

,**Madison 'Avenue** /ˌmædɪsn/ a street in New York City where many advertising companies have their offices. The name 'Madison Avenue' has come to mean the US advertising industry itself, and the methods it uses, which many people regard as too aggressive and sometimes dishonest. The street also has several art galleries. In the past a number of rich families owned large houses on Madison Avenue. See p. 282.

'**Madison 'Square 'Garden** /ˈmædɪsn/ (*also **the Garden**) a large building in New York City, opened in 1969, where major sports and cultural events are held. The main area has 20 000 seats.

M

Madison Avenue

Ma'donna /məˈdɒnə; AmE məˈdɑːnə/ (1958–) a US pop singer and actor, born Madonna Louise Veronica Ciccone. She has emphasized sex in her music and stage performances, as well as in the clothes she wears for them. Her films include *Desperately Seeking Susan* (1985) and *Evita* (1996). Her song albums have included *Bedtime Stories* (1994), *Ray of Light* (1998), *Music* (2000) and *American Life* (2003).

'Maestro /ˈmaɪstrəʊ; AmE ˈmaɪstroʊ/ a *debit card service that can be used everywhere in the world. The cards have the Maestro symbol showing a blue and red circle and can be used wherever the symbol is displayed.

'Mafia n **1 the Mafia** [sing+ sing/pl v] a secret organization of criminals, originally in Sicily. It is also sometimes called the Mob, the Syndicate or Cosa Nostra (Italian for 'our thing'). The Italian-American Mafia began in the US in the late 19th century and became organized into powerful 'families'. They controlled the production of illegal alcohol during *Prohibition and only became weaker in the 1980s when several leaders, called 'godfathers', were sent to prison. Well-known members of the Mafia in the US have included Al *Capone and 'Lucky' *Luciano. There have been many books and films about the Mafia, including *The* *Godfather* and *Goodfellas* (1990).
2 mafia [C] (*disapproving or humorous*) a group of people who have, or are thought to have, secret influence in society: *The plans were opposed by a middle-class mafia.*

▶ **magazines**

In Britain and the US there are thousands of weekly and monthly magazines, many of them aimed at particular groups of readers such as teenage girls, new parents, people interested in gardening or professional groups such as doctors. Among the best-sellers are the **television guides**, such as *Radio Times and the *TV Guide in the US. Nearly as popular in both countries is the *Reader's Digest, a collection of articles and short stories. Some magazines have a smaller readership but are considered important because they are respected and have a role in forming opinion. In the US there are several widely-read **news magazines** such as *Time, *Newsweek and *US News and World Report and in Britain *The Economist, *The New Statesman and *The Spectator are read for their political comment. The British satirical magazine *Private Eye is very popular. Literary magazines include *The Times Literary Supplement, *The London Review of Books and *Granta in Britain and *The New York Review of Books in the US.

There are magazines with a **restricted circulation** (= available only to certain people) such as **in-flight magazines** published by airlines for people to read during a flight, and **store magazines** which customers can buy at a supermarket checkout. Special-interest *clubs and societies publish magazines for their members.

General-interest magazines include titles such as *Vanity Fair and *Harper's Magazine, magazines about fashion, of which the most famous is *Vogue, the home, gardens, food and family life. There are also magazines on *DIY, cars, sport, travel, films and music. *Rolling Stone, *Billboard and *New Musical Express are popular music magazines and *Sight and Sound and *Empire are specialist film magazines.

In Britain some football clubs produce a club magazine. **Fanzines** are cheap magazines produced by fans (= supporters) of a singer, group or sports club. **Gossip magazines**, also called **the gossips**, have stories about the rich and famous and these include *Hello!, *Heat and *National Enquirer. which is sold in US supermarkets.

Some magazines are bought mainly for their **listings**, e.g. *Time Out, which gives details of plays, concerts, etc. in London or New York. *Exchange & Mart contains only advertisements of items for sale or wanted. More specialist magazines include *New Scientist, *Scientific American, *Nature and *The Lancet.

Traditionally there were more magazines for women than for men but there are now several fashion magazines for men such as *Esquire, *GQ and *Loaded. *Vogue and *Harpers & Queen are expensive, high-quality fashion magazines for women. Other women's magazines have a more chatty style and contain stories, competitions, articles on fashion, make-up, food and fitness, and an agony (AmE advice) column (= replies to readers' letters on personal problems). One of the most popular magazines is *Cosmopolitan, which also includes film and book reviews and advice on sex and careers. Other women's titles include *Good Housekeeping, *She and *Elle.

Magazines can be bought in supermarkets and bookshops, at bookstalls and news stands, and in Britain at a newsagent's. Some people take out a **subscription** (= make a yearly payment) to a magazine and have it sent by mail because it is cheaper.

Many people do not buy magazines but read **back copies** (= old issues) put out in their doctor's or dentist's waiting room or at the hairdresser's. Libraries have a **periodicals** section containing *newspapers and a selection of more serious magazines which people can read in the library.

Many magazines are also available on the Internet and some, especially academic journals, are available only on the Internet.

the ˌMagic ˈCircle a British association for professional magicians (= people who entertain others with magic tricks) established in 1905. Only the best magicians can join, and members are not allowed to reveal their secrets to the public.

The ˌMagic ˈRoundabout a children's programme shown on *BBC television from 1965 to 1967. It was an English version of *Le Manège Enchanté* (1965) which was written for French television by Serge Danot.The characters were all toys, including a little girl called Florence, a dog called Dougal, a rabbit called Dylan and Ermintrude, a pink cow. Each programme lasted five minutes. A cinema film with the same title and characters appeared in 2005.

> **66** Time for bed. **99**
> the ending of every *Magic Roundabout* programme

'magistrate a person who judges less serious cases in a local court in England or Wales. See also JUSTICE OF THE PEACE.

'magistrates' court n a local court of law in England and Wales where magistrates judge minor criminal cases, and also decide whether more serious cases should be referred to a *Crown Court. Most criminal cases in England and Wales are judged in magistrates' courts. ⇨ note at LEGAL SYSTEM.

Magna 'Carta /ˌmægnə ˈkɑːtə; AmE ˈkɑːrtə/ (also **the Magna Carta**) a document that King *John was forced to sign by the English *barons at *Runnymede in 1215. It restricted the king's power and gave new rights to the barons and the people. Some of these rights are basic to modern British law, e.g. the right to have a trial before being sent to prison. Four of the original copies of the Magna Carta still exist, two in the *British Library and one each in the cathedrals of *Salisbury and *Lincoln.

magna cum 'laude /ˌmægnə kʊm ˈlaʊdeɪ/ (in the US) the Latin expression, meaning 'with great praise', used to indicate a high academic achievement of a college or university student who has completed his or her studies. It is the second of the three highest grades that can be achieved and is shown on the student's final diploma (= document awarded for completing a course of study): *Sally graduated magna cum laude.* Compare CUM LAUDE, SUMMA CUM LAUDE.

The Mag,nificent 'Seven a US *western film (1960) about seven men who are hired by a Mexican village to protect them from bandits. It was based on Akira Kurosawa's Japanese film *The Seven Samurai* (1954). The music for the film was written by Elmer *Bernstein. Three later films used the same characters but different actors.

Magnus 'Magnusson /ˌmægnəs ˈmægnəsən/ (1929–) a British broadcaster, writer and journalist, born of Icelandic parents. He presented the television quiz show *Mastermind* for 25 years (1972–97). He has also presented several other television programmes and written books on historical subjects.

Maiden 'Castle /ˌmeɪdn/ a very large ancient fort on a hill near *Dorchester, *Dorset, England. It was first occupied in about 2000 BC and was attacked and captured by the Romans in AD 43. Today only the impressive earth banks around it remain.

Maid 'Marian /ˈmæriən/ (in old stories) the companion of *Robin Hood. She also appears as a character in *morris dancing and as the *May Queen in the *May Day games.

maid of 'honour (pl **maids of honour**) (AmE **honor**) n **1** (AmE) the chief bridesmaid at a wedding. If she is a married woman she is called a **matron of honor**. **2** a woman who is not married and who is the companion of a princess or queen. **3** (BrE) a type of small cake flavoured with almonds.

the Mail ⇨ DAILY MAIL. See also MAIL ON SUNDAY.

Norman 'Mailer /ˈmeɪlə(r)/ (1923–) a US journalist and author who became famous with his first novel, *The Naked and the Dead*, about *World War II. Many of his books are about real people and events and he won *Pulitzer Prizes for *The Armies of the Night* (1968), about the 1967 peace march to Washington, DC, and *The Executioner's Song* (1979), a novel based on facts about Gary *Gilmore in prison. Mailer's other novels include *An American Dream* (1965), *The Prisoner of Sex* (1971), *Ancient Evenings* (1983) and *Harlot's Ghost* (1991). He has been involved in a number of liberal protest movements, e.g. against the *Vietnam War.

the ,Mail on 'Sunday a British Sunday newspaper published by the same group as the *Daily Mail*. It first appeared in 1982.

Maine /meɪn/ the most northerly of the *New England states in the US. Its popular name is the Pine Tree State, and people from Maine are called Down Easters. The capital city is Augusta and the largest city is Portland. Maine was separated from *Massachusetts in 1820 as a

free state under the *Missouri Compromise. It is a popular area for outdoor holidays and sports, and the northern end of the Appalachian Trail is in Maine. Maine's products include paper, apples, blueberries and canned sardines (= small fish).

a lighthouse in Maine

'main ,street n (especially AmE) **1** [C] the most important street in a small town or city, especially in the business district. It is often called simply Main Street. **2 Main Street** [U] (sometimes disapproving) the attitudes and values thought to be typical of small US towns: *The government's new liberal policies will not go down well on Main Street.* See also LEWIS.

,John 'Major /ˈmeɪdʒə(r)/ (1943–) a British *Conservative politician. He became a *Member of Parliament in 1979 and was *Foreign Secretary and *Chancellor of the Exchequer before replacing Margaret *Thatcher as Prime Minister in 1990. Major was admired by some people for his aim to achieve a 'classless society', but others criticized him for being boring and 'grey' (= dull and ordinary). His period in power was marked by economic problems, and his party was divided over the issue of European union. In spite of this he won the general election of 1992. In 1995 he also won a leadership contest against John *Redwood, but the Conservatives were heavily defeated by the Labour Party in the 1997 general election, and Major was replaced as Conservative leader by William *Hague.

ma,jority 'leader n the leader of the political party that has a majority in the US Senate or US House of Representatives, who organizes the party's members and their programme for new laws. In the House of Representatives, however, the majority leader is under the *Speaker of the House, who is from the same party. Compare MINORITY LEADER, WHIP.

,Major League 'Baseball (abbr **MLB**) the highest level of professional baseball in the US. Major League Baseball is also the organization which operates the two baseball leagues, the *National League and the *American League. ⇨ WORLD SERIES.

,Major League 'Soccer (abbr **MLS**) the highest level football league in the US, which started in 1996 and is run by the **United States Soccer Federation**. The league is divided into Eastern and Western regions and from 2005 will include 12 teams. Soccer is less popular in the US than other sports, but has become more popular since the national team reached the quarter-final stage of the World Cup in 2002.

the 'Majors n [pl] the name given to the four most important tournaments (= sports competitions) in golf. They are the *British Open, the *US Open(1), the *US Masters Tournament and the US *PGA.

,Bernard 'Malamud /ˈmæləmʊd/ (1914–86) a US writer whose novels and short stories were mostly about Jewish life in America. His novels include *The Natural* (1952), about a *baseball player, which was later made into a film (1984) with Robert *Redford. Malamud won a

M

*National Book Award for *The Magic Barrel* (1958), a collection of short stories, and a *Pulitzer Prize for his novel *The Fixer* (1966).

Mrs **'Malaprop** /'mæləprɒp; AmE 'mæləprɑːp/ a character in *The *Rivals*, a comic play by Richard Brinsley *Sheridan. Mrs Malaprop (from the French *mal à propos* meaning 'inappropriate') is the aunt of Lydia Languish, and is noted for the way she confuses words that sound similar, e.g. 'oracular' instead of 'vernacular' and 'epitaph' instead of 'epithet'. Such a wrong use of words is called a **malapropism** after her.

> 66 If I reprehend anything in this world, it is the use of my oracular tongue and a nice derangement of epitaphs. 99
> Mrs Malaprop

Ma'lawi /mə'lɑːwi/ a country in southern central Africa, between Tanzania, Zambia and Mozambique. Its capital city is Lilongwe and its official languages are Chichewa and English. It was formerly a British colony called Nyasaland. It became independent in 1964 and is now a member of the *Commonwealth. Its main exports are tea and tobacco.
▶ **Malawian** *adj*, *n*.

Ma'laysia /mə'leɪʒə, mə'leɪziə/ a country in south-east Asia. It consists of the area to the south of Thailand formerly known as Malaya, and the states of Sarawak and Sabah in the north-west of the island of Borneo. Its capital city is Kuala Lumpur and its official language is Malay. It was formed in 1963 from former British colonies in the area and is now a part of the *Commonwealth. Its main exports are oil, gas, electronic equipment and chemicals. *Singapore was a part of Malaysia until 1965.
▶ **Malaysian** *adj*, *n*.

Malcolm 'X /'eks/ (1925–65) an African American leader, born Malcolm Little. He joined the *Black Muslims in 1952, changed his 'slave name' to Malcolm X and became their leader in 1963. Their aim was to create a separate African-American nation, and he encouraged them to defend themselves in violent ways. In 1964, however, he left the Black Muslims to establish the Organization of Afro-American Unity, declaring that he was in favour of peace between the races. He was murdered, probably by Black Muslims, in *Harlem. He wrote *The Autobiography of Malcolm X* (1964), and 'Spike' *Lee directed a film, *Malcolm X* (1992), with Denzel Washington in the main role.

The 'Maldives /'mɔːldiːvz, 'mɔːldaɪvz/ a country in the Indian Ocean, to the south-west of India, consisting of over 1200 small islands. Its capital is Male and its official language is Divehi. It was formerly a British colony, and became independent in 1965. It is now a member of the *Commonwealth. Its industries include fishing and tourism.
▶ **Mal'divian** *adj*, *n*.

'Malibu /'mælɪbuː/ a fashionable and expensive US town on the Pacific coast of *California, near *Los Angeles. It is known for its beaches, and is the home of several film stars.

The Mall /mæl/ **1** a straight road in central London, England, leading from *Buckingham Palace through *Admiralty Arch to *Trafalgar Square. It was first laid out in the 17th century and is used for royal processions. **2** (*also* **the National Mall**) a long park in *Washington, DC, covering about a mile (1.6 kilometres) between the *Capitol and the *Potomac River. The *White House(1) faces The Mall, which also includes the *Lincoln Memorial, the *Washington Monument and the *Vietnam Veterans Memorial.

mall /mɔːl, mæl/ ⇨ SHOPPING CENTRE.

'Mallard /'mælɑːd; AmE 'mælərd/ the name of a steam engine (= a type of early train) which set an unbeaten world record for a train of its type in 1938 by achieving a speed of 126 miles per hour/203 kilometres per hour. It is now kept at the *National Railway Museum in York.

Mallory and 'Irvine /,mæləri, 'ɜːvɪn; AmE 'ɜːrvɪn/ two English climbers, **George Mallory** (1886–1924) and **Andrew Irvine** (1902–1924), who died while attempting to reach the top of Mount Everest. When Mallory was asked why he wanted to climb Everest, his famous reply was 'Because it is there'. His body was found in May 1999 after being lost on Everest for 75 years.

Thomas 'Malory /'mæləri/ an English author who wrote *Morte d'Arthur*, a collection of stories about King *Arthur and his *Knights of the Round Table. His identity is uncertain but he may have been Sir Thomas Malory, a *Warwickshire *knight who died in prison in 1471.

'Malta /'mɔːltə/ an island and country in the Mediterranean Sea, to the south of Sicily. Malta became a member of the *European Union in 2004. Its capital is Valletta and its official languages are Maltese and English. From 1530 to 1798 it was ruled by the Knights of St John, a military and religious organization. In 1814 it was taken over by Britain and became an important navy base. In *World War II it was given the *George Cross for resisting heavy German air attacks. Together with the nearby islands of Gozo and Comino it became independent in 1964. Malta is a member of the Commonwealth and joined the *European Union in 2004. Tourism is an important part of its economy, and many British people go there on holiday.
▶ **Mal'tese** /mɔːl'tiːz/ *adj* of or from Malta.
Maltese *n* **1** [C] (*pl* **Maltese**) an inhabitant of Malta. **2** [U] the language of Malta.

The ,Maltese 'Falcon /,mɔːltiːz/ a novel (1930) by Dashiell *Hammett, in which he first used the character Sam *Spade, a private detective. The story is about people who commit murder to get a valuable statue called the Maltese Falcon. There have been two film versions, the first in 1931 with Ricardo Cortez as Sam Spade, the second (and more famous) in 1941 with Humphrey *Bogart.

Mal'tesers™ /mɔːl'tiːzəz; AmE mɔːl'tiːzərz/ *n* [pl] a British make of round chocolate sweets with light crisp centres.

Thomas 'Malthus /'mælθəs/ (1766–1834) an English economist and priest. In his *Essay on the Principle of Population* (1798) he suggested that human populations grow faster than the supply of food, and that unless population growth is artificially controlled, this leads to poverty and an increased death rate. His ideas were an important influence on Charles *Darwin.
▶ **Mal'thusian** *adj* of or similar to the ideas of Thomas Malthus: *Malthusian attitudes/ideas/proposals*.

the 'Maltings /'mɔːltɪŋz/ a group of buildings in the village of Snape, near Aldeburgh, *Suffolk, England, that include a concert hall. The concerts that take place there are part of the international *Aldeburgh Festival.

the 'Malverns /'mɔːlvənz; AmE 'mɔːlvərnz/ the name of a group of five villages and a town (Great Malvern) in the **Malvern Hills**, *Worcestershire, England. The hills are famous for their springs of pure water, sold under the name of **Malvern water**. Great Malvern is also famous for its festival of music and theatre, held every summer.

M

the Malverns

,David 'Mamet /'mæmɪt/ (1947–) a US writer and director of plays and films, which are often about human failure and disappointment. Many people have been offended by his use of language. His first successful play was *American Buffalo* (1977). He won the *Pulitzer Prize for *Glengarry Glen Ross* (1984). *Oleanna* (1992), a play about a woman who claims falsely that a man has taken advantage of her sexually, caused a lot of public discussion. Mamet's films include *The House of Games* (1987), which he also directed, *Hoffa* (1992), *The Spanish Prisoner* (1998) and *State and Main* (2000).

the ,Man 'Booker Prize ⇨ BOOKER PRIZE.

'Manchester /'mæntʃəstə(r)/ a large city in north-west England, in the county of *Greater Manchester. It first became important as an industrial city during the 18th century, producing wool and cotton goods for sale in Britain and abroad. It was also a cultural and intellectual centre with a tradition of left-wing politics. Its famous buildings include the Victorian Town Hall (1867–76) and the Bridgewater International Concert Hall (opened in 1996), where the *Hallé Orchestra is based. Since the 1980s Manchester has also had a reputation for its pop groups, including *Oasis and Simply Red.

,Manchester 'City /,mæntʃəstə; AmE ,mæntʃəstər/ (*also informal* **Man City**) a football team from Manchester, England. It was formed in 1894 and has had several wins in the *FA Cup, as well as many other successes in Britain and Europe.

'Manchester 'Evening 'News /'mæntʃəstər/ a newspaper that appears every evening in *Manchester and was first published in 1868. It is owned by the same company that owns the *Guardian.

the ,Manchester 'Ship Ca,nal /,mæntʃəstə; AmE ,mæntʃəstər/ a canal completed in 1894 linking *Manchester with the River *Mersey and the sea. It can take very large ships and allowed Manchester to increase its level of exports in the late 19th and early 20th century.

,Manchester U'nited /'maentʃɪstə(r); AmE ,mæntʃəstər/ (*also informal* **Man United**) a football team from Manchester, England, with a ground at *Old Trafford(1). It was formed in 1902 and has won the *FA Cup more times than any other team, as well as having many other successes in Britain and Europe. In 1958 several of its players were killed in a plane crash in Munich. See also BECKHAM, BUSBY, ROONEY.

,Henry Man'cini /mæn'siːni/ (1924–94) a US composer of music for films and writer of songs. He won *Oscars for *Breakfast at Tiffany's* (1961), which included the song *Moon River*, and for *Victor/Victoria* (1982).

Man'cunian /mæn'kjuːniən/ *n* a person who comes from *Manchester.

,Peter 'Mandelson /'mændlsn/ (1953–) a British *Labour politician. He became a *Member of Parliament in 1992, and was the Labour Party's Director of Campaigns and Communications from 1985 to 1990. He was later made Secretary of State for Trade and Industry and Secretary of State for Northern Ireland in 1999 but he had to resign from both posts because of political scandals. In 2004 he became Britain's European Commissioner.

M&M's™ /,em ənd 'emz/ *n* [pl] small round chocolate sweets, brightly coloured and sometimes with peanuts inside, that are covered with hard sugar to stop them melting in the hand. They were first sold in 1941, and are named after the two Americans who originally made them, Forrest Mars and Bruce Murries.

M & S /,em ənd 'es/ ⇨ MARKS & SPENCER.

,Man 'Friday the name of the faithful servant and companion in Daniel *Defoe's novel *Robinson Crusoe. Crusoe gives him this name after saving his life on a Friday. The phrase **man Friday** is now sometimes used to mean a trusted male assistant or servant and the female equivalent is a **girl Friday**.

Man'hattan /mæn'hætn/ **1** (*also* **Manhattan Island**) the island that forms the main *borough of New York City. It is 14 miles/23.5 kilometres long and 2.3 miles/3.7 kilometres wide, and is between the *Hudson River and the East River. It contains many of New York's most famous buildings, including the *Empire State Building, and its streets include *Broadway and *Fifth Avenue. *Central Park and *Harlem are also in Manhattan. The island is named after a *Native American people who once lived there. **2** *n* a US cocktail (= mixed alcoholic drink). It is made with *whisky, sweet vermouth (= a type of strong wine) and usually bitters, and is served with a preserved cherry.

the **Man'hattan ,Project** /mæn'hæən/ the secret US project to develop the atom bomb, begun in 1942. It involved a team of scientists led by J Robert Oppenheimer, first at Oak Ridge, *Tennessee, and later at *Los Alamos, *New Mexico, where the bomb was built. The first bomb was exploded as a test near Alamogordo, New Mexico, on 16 July 1945.

'Manic 'Street 'Preachers a British pop group formed in 1988, whose best-known albums include *Generation Terrorists* (1992) and *This is My Truth, Tell Me Yours* (1998). Richey Edwards, a guitar player in the group, disappeared in 1995, and it is believed that he may be dead.

,manifest 'destiny *n* [U] a phrase much used in 19th-century America to mean the right of the US to own and occupy land across the continent to the Pacific Ocean. It was first used in 1845 by John L O'Sullivan, editor of the *United States Magazine and Democratic Review*. He wrote that the US should 'overspread the continent allotted by Providence for the free development of our yearly multiplying millions'. The idea of manifest destiny involved taking a lot of land belonging to *Native Americans, especially in *Oregon, and taking *California and *Texas from Mexico, which led to the *Mexican War.

,Barry 'Manilow /'mænələʊ; AmE 'mænəloʊ/ (1946–) a US singer and writer of songs who plays the piano. His music is especially popular with older women. Manilow received a *Grammy for his song *Copacabana* in 1978. His other hits have included *I Write the Songs* (1976) and *Looks Like We Made It* (1977). He has also written music for advertisements, including *You Deserve A Break Today* for *McDonald's.

,Man of 'Kent /'kent/ *n* (*pl* **Men of Kent**) a traditional name for an inhabitant of the eastern half of the English county of *Kent.

M

man of the 'match n [sing] (BrE) a man who is chosen as having given the best performance in a game of football, cricket, etc. If officially chosen, he sometimes receives a prize: *They voted him man of the match.* Compare MOST VALUABLE PLAYER.

Nigel 'Mansell /'mænsl/ (1954–) an English racing driver. After many Grand Prix successes in the 1980s and 1990s he became *Formula One world champion in 1992 in a *Williams car. He later had some success in *IndyCar racing.

Katherine 'Mansfield /'mænsfi:ld/ (1888–1923) a New Zealand writer who lived most of her life in England. Her collections of short stories, including *Bliss* (1920) and *The Garden Party* (1922), are full of intense feeling, often describing only a few hours in a person's life. Her poems and letters were published after her death.

Mansfield 'Park /ˌmænsfi:ld/ a novel (1814) by Jane *Austen. It tells the story of Fanny Price, a young girl who goes to live with her rich uncle and his family at their country house, Mansfield Park. They treat her rather badly, but Edmund, the youngest son, recognizes her true worth and finally marries her.

'Mansion House the official home of the *Lord Mayor of London, in the City of London. The building was completed in 1753 and contains the Egyptian Hall, where official dinners and other events are held.

Charles 'Manson /'mænsn/ (1934–) the leader of a group of *hippies, called his 'family'. In 1969 the group, acting on Manson's orders, murdered seven people including the actor Sharon Tate near *Los Angeles. Manson and four of his followers were sent to prison for life. The murders changed many people's attitude towards hippies.

Manx /mæŋks/ n [U] a *Gaelic language formerly spoken in the *Isle of Man, but now almost completely replaced by English.
▶ **Manx** adj of the *Isle of Man, its people or the language once spoken there.

the Mappa 'Mundi /ˌmæpə 'mʊndi:/ a map of the world painted in the late 13th century and kept in Hereford Cathedral, England. It has a circular shape, with Jerusalem at the centre and the known continents of Europe, Africa and Asia placed around it.

Robert 'Mapplethorpe /'meɪplθɔ:p; AmE 'meɪplθɔ:rp/ (1946–89) a US artist and photographer. Many people are offended by the sexual nature of his images, which often show the naked male body.

Marble 'Arch a large stone arch with three gates, at the north-east corner of *Hyde Park(1) in central London. It was built in 1828 to a design by John *Nash as an entrance to *Buckingham Palace, but was later moved to its present position. Marble Arch is also the name of a nearby *London Underground station.

Marbury v 'Madison /ˌmɑ:bri vɜ:səs 'mædɪsn; AmE ˌmɑ:rbri, vɜ:rsəs/ an important US Supreme Court case in 1803 which established its right to decide if a new law is illegal under the American *Constitution. William Marbury had taken Secretary of State James *Madison to court because he refused to keep an agreement that Marbury would become a judge. The court decided that Marbury was right, and established the principal of *judicial review.

'marching ˌseason n the period in July and August every year when Protestant groups in Northern Ireland, especially the Order of *Orangemen, hold marches through the streets. These celebrate Protestant victories over Catholics in the 17th century, especially the *Battle of the Boyne. The marches are often the cause of conflict with Northern Ireland's Catholic population. In 1998 the Parades Commission was set up to decide where marches should be allowed to go and to make sure they caused no trouble. See also APPRENTICE BOYS' PARADE.

Marching Through 'Georgia /'dʒɔːdʒə; AmE 'dʒɔːrdʒə/ a lively US song about the violent progress of General William Tecumseh *Sherman and his army through *Georgia during the *Civil War in November 1864. The words after each verse are:

> 66 'Hurrah! hurrah! we bring the Jubilee!
> Hurrah! hurrah! the flag that makes you free!'
> So we sang the chorus from Atlanta to the sea,
> While we were marching through Georgia. 99

the ˌMarch of 'Dimes a US charity that works to prevent the deaths of babies and to help young children born with physical problems. Its full name is the March of Dimes Birth Defects Foundation. President Franklin D *Roosevelt, who had polio (= a serious disease of the nervous system), started the charity in 1938 as the National Foundation for Infantile Paralysis. Among other activities it supported the research work which developed the *Salk vaccine. It has had its present name since 1979.

The ˌMarch of 'Time a series of US news films shown in cinemas from 1935 to 1951. They were produced by the company that owned *Time magazine and were one of the main sources of news on film before the days of television. There was a similar series with the same name on US radio.

Mar'coni plc¹ /mɑ:'kəʊni; AmE mɑ:r'koʊni/ a British company which makes radio, telecommunications and *Internet equipment. It was started by Guglielmo *Marconi as the **Wireless Telegraph and Signal Company** in London in 1897, became the **General Electric Company** and then was renamed Marconi plc in 1999.

Guˌglielmo Mar'coni² /guˌljelməʊ mɑ:'kəʊni; AmE guˌljelmoʊ mɑ:r'koʊni/ (1874–1937) an Italian scientist and electrical engineer who lived for most of his life in Britain. Using the work of previous scientists he developed the practical use of radio, sending the first radio signals from England to France in 1898 and from England to America in 1901. He shared the *Nobel Prize for physics in 1909. He was also a successful businessman, establishing the Marconi Wireless Telegraph Company in London in 1899. In 1922 the company was in charge of the first broadcasts of the *BBC.

Herbert Mar'cuse /mɑ:'ku:zə; AmE mɑ:r'ku:zə/ (1898–1979) a US political philosopher, born in Germany. He moved to America in 1934 and taught at several universities, including *Harvard University from 1952 and the University of California at San Diego from 1965. Marcuse's ideas were strongly influenced by those of Marx and Freud. He was especially popular during the 1960s and supported the efforts of young people to change society. His books included *Eros and Civilization* (1955), *Soviet Marxism* (1958) and *One-Dimensional Man* (1964).

Mardi 'Gras /ˌmɑ:di 'grɑ:; AmE ˌmɑ:rdi/ a popular US carnival (= public festival) held in *New Orleans during the week before the first day of *Lent. Mardi Gras is French for 'Fat Tuesday', because it ends on Shrove Tuesday, a day when people traditionally eat a lot before the start of Lent. People come from around the world to see the parades, costumes, parties and decorations and Mardi Gras 'Kings' and 'Queens' are chosen. A few other US cities celebrate Mardi Gras and it is also celebrated in some Catholic countries.

ˌPrincess **'Margaret** (1930–2002) the sister of Queen *Elizabeth II and the younger daughter of King *George VI. In 1960 she married the photographer Tony Armstrong-Jones, who was later given the title of Lord Snowdon, but they were divorced in 1978. Their two children are David, Viscount Linley (1961–), and Lady Sarah Armstrong-Jones (1964–).

Princess Margaret

'Margate /'mɑːgeɪt; *AmE* 'mɑːrgeɪt/ a town on the northern coast of *Kent, England. It is popular for its beaches, and was traditionally a place where people from London went for *bank holidays or family holidays. In Margate in 1835 the Shell Grotto was discovered, an underground chamber and passage decorated with Egyptian and Indian designs using over 50 different kinds of shell. It is not known when it was made.

the ˌMari'anas /ˌmæri'ɑːnəz/ (*also* the ˌMari'ana ˌIslands /ˌmæri'ɑːnə/) a group of islands in the northwest Pacific Ocean. The US got them from Spain in 1898 after the *Spanish-American War. The most southern island is *Guam, where most of the inhabitants live.

Marie '**Claire** the title of magazines for women published every month in Britain and the US. They contain articles on fashion, beauty, travel, the arts and other subjects.

the **Ma'rine Corps** ⇨ UNITED STATES MARINE CORPS.

'Mariner /'mærmə(r)/ the name of a series of flights of *NASA spacecraft that went past or around other planets. *Mariner 1* failed and was destroyed in flight in 1962, but in the same year *Mariner 2* flew past Venus. *Mariner 9* went into orbit around the planet Mars in 1971 and took more than 7000 photographs. *Mariner 10* flew past Venus and Mercury in 1974 and again in 1975.

▶ **markets**

Most people in Britain and the US now buy their fresh food in **supermarkets** rather than traditional markets. But markets are still important to the life of many cities and towns and in recent years **farmers' markets**, where local farmers and others sell **produce** (= fruit, vegetables, etc.) or **home-made** foods directly to the public, have grown in popularity.

In Britain, most markets are held in the open air, in town squares or **market places**. They usually take place only on **market day**, the same day each week, and sometimes on Saturdays, and the stalls are put up for each occasion. Towns where markets have traditionally been held are called **market towns**. Many still have a **market cross**, indicating where the market was originally held, or an old **market hall**, a covered area open at the sides. Today, markets sell flowers, fruit and vegetables, fish and meat, clothes and household goods.

Some towns and cities in Britain and the US have a covered or indoor market. These markets are usually open more days of the week than outdoor markets and operate more like shops. Markets that sell cheap second-hand goods, including clothes, jewellery and books are called **flea markets**. In the US, these are usually in buildings and open during normal shopping hours.

The word *market* is sometimes used in American English to refer to any food shop. A **hypermarket** or **superstore** in both Britain and the US is a very large store or supermarket.

Aˌlicia **Mar'kova** /əˌlɪsiə mɑː'kəʊvə; *AmE* mɑːr'koʊvə/ (1910–2004) an English ballet dancer. She was trained by Anna Pavlova, danced with Sergei Diaghilev's company (1925–9) and took leading parts in the first British productions of many classical ballets. After 1935 she worked mainly with Anton *Dolin, and was famous for her performance of *Giselle*. She retired from dancing in 1962 and became a ballet director for the *Royal Ballet and other companies. She was made a *dame(2) in 1963.

Marks & 'Spencer /ˌmɑːks, 'spensə(r); *AmE* ˌmɑːrks/ (*abbr* **M & S**) a well-known British department store, selling clothes, food and other products. The first shops were started by Michael Marks and Thomas Spencer in the late 19th century, and there are now shops in most British towns. Marks and Spencer's is famous for its well made clothes at fairly low prices, and is traditionally the place where many people go to buy items such as underwear and socks rather than the latest fashions. The company is also known informally as **Marks and Sparks** or simply **Marks**: *I buy all my clothes at Marks.*

'Marlboro™ /'mɔːlbərə/ one of the most popular and heavily advertised US cigarettes. It was first sold by the *Philip Morris company in the 1920s as a woman's cigarette, and advertised as being as 'Mild as May'. Advertisements showing the **Marlboro Man** as a *cowboy began in 1957 with the words 'Come to Marlboro Country.'.

the ˌDuke of **'Marlborough** /'mɔːlbrə/ (*born* John Churchill 1650–1722) one of Britain's greatest soldiers, who won important battles in the War of the *Spanish Succession. These included *Blenheim (1704) and Malplaquet (1709). After his success at Blenheim, Queen *Anne gave him money to build *Blenheim Palace in *Oxfordshire, where his descendant Winston *Churchill was born in 1874. See also MARLBOROUGH HOUSE.

ˌMarlborough **'House** /ˌmɔːlbrə/ a large, grand house in *Pall Mall, London, England. It was designed by Christopher *Wren for the wife of the Duke of *Marlborough and built in 1709–11. After her death it was the home of various members of the royal family until 1962, when it became a centre for meetings of Commonwealth leaders.

ˌBob **'Marley** /'mɑːli; *AmE* 'mɑːrli/ (1945–81) a Jamaican singer and writer of reggae music who also played the guitar. He formed the Wailers group in 1965 and made reggae widely known around the world. His songs were influenced by his religious beliefs as a *Rastafarian and his support of *black power. His albums included *Burnin'* (1973), *Rastaman Vibration* (1976), *Exodus* (1977) and *Uprising* (1980). His early death was caused by cancer.

ˌChristopher **'Marlowe**¹ /'mɑːləʊ; *AmE* 'mɑːrloʊ/ (1564–93) an English writer of plays and poetry. He is considered the greatest English playwright of the period before William *Shakespeare, and was an important influence on Shakespeare's style. His best-known works are *Tamburlaine* (c. 1587), *Doctor Faustus*, *The Jew of Malta* (c. 1590) and *Edward II* (c. 1592). He may also have written parts of the Shakespeare plays *Titus Andronicus* and *Henry VI*. Marlowe led a wild and violent life, was put in prison briefly in 1589 on suspicion of murder, and was himself murdered in a fight at the age of 29.

ˌPhilip **'Marlowe**² /'mɑːləʊ; *AmE* 'mɑːrloʊ/ a character created by the writer Raymond *Chandler. He is a tough but honest private detective and appears in seven Chandler novels, including *The Big Sleep* (1939).

M

'marmalade /'mɑːməleɪd; AmE 'mɑːrməleɪd/ n [U] a type of jam made with oranges or (less often) with lemons. Marmalade on toast is part of a traditional British breakfast.

'Marmite™ /'mɑːmaɪt; AmE 'mɑːrmaɪt/ n [U] a soft black substance usually eaten on bread or toast. Marmite was first produced in 1902 and is made from yeast (= a natural substance used in making beer, wine and most types of bread). Marmite is thought of as a traditional British food, especially as a cheap and healthy filling for sandwiches or as a food for young children.

the ˌBattles of the 'Marne /mɑːn; AmE mɑːrn/ two battles of *World War I around the River Marne in northeast France. In the first battle (1914) a German advance was stopped by British and French forces. In the second (1918) a similar advance was stopped by British, French and US forces, and was the beginning of a series of victories for the *Allies that led to the end of the war.

ˌMiss 'Marple /'mɑːpl; AmE 'mɑːrpl/ a character in several novels by Agatha *Christie. Miss Marple is a gentle, respectable old woman who has a remarkable ability to solve mysteries and crimes. She first appeared in the novel *The Murder in the Vicarage* (1930). There have been many film and television versions of the stories.

'marquess (also **'marquis**) /'mɑːkwɪs; AmE 'mɑːrkwɪs/ n a British peer who is next in rank above an *earl(1) and next below a *duke. The wife of a marquess, or a woman with a similar title, is called a **marchioness.** ⇨ note at ARISTOCRACY.

ˌAndrew 'Marr /'mɑː(r)/ (1959–) a British political journalist who worked for a number of newspapers before becoming political editor for the *BBC in 2000. He has also written a number of books about politics.

ˌNeville 'Marriner /ˌnevl 'mærɪnə(r)/ (1924–) an English conductor, who established the *Academy of St Martin-in-the-Fields in 1959. He has also directed orchestras in the US. He was made a *knight in 1985.

ˌWynton Mar'salis /ˌwɪntən mɑːˈsɑːlɪs; AmE mɑːrˈsælɪs/ (1961–) a US *jazz musician who plays the trumpet. He won a *Pulitzer Prize for Music in 1997 for *Blood on the Fields*. Earlier, he had become the first musician to receive Grammys for both jazz and classical works. He played with the New Orleans Philharmonic Orchestra at the age of 14, before forming his own jazz group in 1981.

'Mars Bar™ /'mɑːz; AmE 'mɑːrz/ (also **Mars**) n a chocolate bar with a soft sweet filling that is very popular in Britain. It was first sold in the 1930s and named after the American who originally made it, Forrest Mars. The advertisements for Mars Bars claim that 'A Mars a day helps you work, rest and play.'

the 'Marsden /'mɑːzdən; AmE 'mɑːrzdən/ (in full **the Royal Marsden Hospital**) a hospital in London, England, established in 1851 by William Marsden (1796–1867). It is a leading hospital for cancer treatment and research.

ˌNgaio 'Marsh [1] /ˌnaɪəʊ 'mɑːʃ; AmE ˌnaɪoʊ 'mɑːrʃ/ (1899–1982) a New Zealand writer of detective stories who lived in Britain from 1928. Her books include *A Man Lay Dead* (1934) and *Hand in Glove* (1962), and her most famous character is Chief Detective Inspector Roderick Alleyn. She was made a *dame(2) in 1948.

ˌPete 'Marsh [2] /'mɑːʃ; AmE 'mɑːrʃ/ a humorous name for *Lindow Man, the very old body of a man found in soft wet ground in *Cheshire, England, in 1984. 'Pete Marsh' is an ordinary English name which also sounds like 'peat marsh' (= an area of soft wet earth formed from decayed plants).

ˌThurgood 'Marshall /ˌθɜːɡʊd 'mɑːʃl; AmE ˌθɜːrɡʊd 'mɑːrʃl/ (1908–93) the first *African American judge of the US Supreme Court (1967–91). He is remembered especially for winning the 1954 case before the Supreme Court which ended *segregation in public schools. He was later US Solicitor General (1965–7).

ˌMarshall 'Field's /ˌmɑːʃl; AmE ˌmɑːrʃl/ a well-known US department store in *Chicago. It was established on State Street in 1868 when Marshall Field moved his small shop there. He increased its size in 1907, and Marshall Field's became a place for social meetings, with a Ladies' Parlour and a Men's Reading and Writing Room. It has seven floors around a large central area which is open to the top of the building. There are now Marshall Field's stores in other US cities.

the 'Marshall Plan /'mɑːʃl; AmE 'mɑːrʃl/ a very large programme of US economic aid to 17 European countries after *World War II (1948–52). Its official title was the European Recovery Program. The plan was named after the person who set it up, US Secretary of State George C Marshall (1880–1959), and it was operated by the Organization for European Economic Cooperation. Marshall received the *Nobel Prize for peace in 1953.

'Marshalsea /'mɑːʃlsiː; AmE 'mɑːrʃlsiː/ a prison in *Southwark, London, England, built around the 14th century and closed in 1842. It was used as a debtors' prison (= one for people who owed money) and is an important part of the story of *Little Dorrit* by Charles *Dickens. Dickens's own father was put in prison there in 1824.

ˌMars 'Rover a small vehicle made by *NASA and sent to explore the surface of the planet Mars. The first Mars Rover, *Sojourner was sent in 1996 and landed successfully in 1997. The second and third Mars Rovers, *Spirit and *Opportunity were sent in 2003 as part of the **Mars Exploration Rover Missions** and landed in 2004, sending back pictures of the planet.

ˌMarston 'Moor /ˌmɑːstən; AmE ˌmɑːrstən/ a place near *York, northern England, where the largest battle of the *English Civil War took place in 1644. The Parliamentarians under Oliver *Cromwell defeated the Royalists under Prince *Rupert and gained control over the north of the country.

Mar,tello 'tower /mɑːˌteləʊ; AmE mɑːrˌteloʊ/ n a type of circular stone tower, about 40 feet/12 metres high, built in Britain in the early 19th century. The purpose of the towers was to defend the south coast of England against possible attack by the French during the *Napoleonic Wars, and each could contain a group of soldiers. About 25 of the towers still exist.

ˌMartha's 'Vineyard an island off the south-east coast of *Massachusetts, just south of *Cape Cod. Many writers and artists live there, and it is popular with tourists in summer. In the 18th and 19th centuries, the island was a centre for people who hunted whales.

ˌChris 'Martin [1] /'mɑːtɪn; AmE 'mɑːrtɪn/ (1977–) an English pop singer; the lead singer with the pop group *Coldplay. He is married to the actor Gwyneth *Paltrow.

ˌDean 'Martin [2] /'mɑːtɪn; AmE 'mɑːrtɪn/ (1917–95) a US singer and actor, well known for his relaxed charm. He and Jerry *Lewis made 16 comedy films together (1949–56). Martin's later films included *Rio Bravo* (1959) and *The Silencers* (1966). His song hits included *That's Amore* (1953) and his theme song *Everybody Loves Somebody* (1964).

ˌSteve 'Martin [3] /'mɑːtɪn; AmE 'mɑːrtɪn/ (1945–) a US comic actor and writer who also produces films. He began his career in 1967 as a writer for *The Smothers Brothers Comedy Hour* and later performed in it. His films include *The Jerk* (1979), which he also wrote, *All of*

Me (1985), *LA Story* (1991), which he also wrote, *Sergeant Bilko* (1996) and *Cheaper by the Dozen* (2003).

ˌJohn 'Martyn (1948–) an English *folk rock singer, songwriter and guitarist. Since his first album, *London Conversation* in 1967, he has made more than 30 albums.

ˌAndrew 'Marvell /'mɑːvl; AmE 'mɑːrvl/ (1621–78) one of the English *metaphysical poets. Among his best-known poems is *To his Coy Mistress*, a clever and entertaining attempt to persuade a young woman to go to bed with him. During his life Marvell was better known as a *Member of Parliament (1659–78) and a supporter of Oliver *Cromwell.

> 66 Had we but world enough, and time,
> Such coyness lady were no crime ...
> But at my back I always hear
> Time's winged chariot hurrying near ...
> The grave's a fine and private place,
> But none, I think, do there embrace. 99
>
> from *To his Coy Mistress*

ˌLee 'Marvin /ˌliː 'mɑːvɪn; AmE 'mɑːrvɪn/ (1924–87) a US actor who played mainly tough characters but won an *Oscar for a comic role in the *western *Cat Ballou* (1965). His other films included *The Killers* (1964), *The Dirty Dozen* (1967) and *Paint Your Wagon* (1969), in which he sang *I Was Born Under A Wandering Star* in a deep and not very musical voice.

ˌKarl 'Marx /ˌkɑːl 'mɑːks; AmE ˌkɑːrl 'mɑːrks/ (1818–83) a German writer on politics and economics. In 1848 he wrote the *Communist Manifesto* with Friedrich Engels (1820–95), and in the following year he came to live in London, England. He spent much of the rest of his life developing his theories, and published the results in *Das Kapital* (1867–95), the major work of Marxist economics. His theories about the need for a workers' socialist revolution had a very great influence on 20th-century history, especially in Russia, China and eastern Europe. Marx died in London and was buried in *Highgate Cemetery.

the 'Marx ˌBrothers /'mɑːks; AmE 'mɑːrks/ a US comedy team of three brothers who made films full of crazy visual humour and quick, clever jokes. They were 'Groucho' (Julius) Marx (1890–1977), 'Chico' (Leonard) Marx (1886–1961) and 'Harpo' (Adolph) Marx (1888–1964). Their films included *Duck Soup* (1933) and *A Day at the Races* (1937). Groucho wore glasses and a large false moustache, walked in a funny way and smoked cigars. Chico played the piano, wore a pointed hat and spoke like an Italian-American. Harpo never spoke, played the harp and chased girls. Groucho later had his own comedy television quiz show, *You Bet Your Life* (1950–61).

> 66 Please accept my resignation. I don't want to belong to any club that will accept me as a member. 99
>
> Groucho Marx

ˌQueen 'Mary (Mary of Teck 1867–1953) a British queen. In 1893 she married George, Duke of York, who in 1910 became King *George V. She was the mother of two kings, *Edward VIII and *George VI, and the grandmother of Queen *Elizabeth II.

Mary I /ˌmeəri ðə 'fɜːst; AmE ˌmeri ðə 'fɜːrst/ (Mary Tudor 1516–58) the queen of England and Ireland from 1553 to 1558. She was the daughter of King *Henry VIII and *Catherine of Aragon, and became queen after the death of King *Edward VI. Among her first acts as queen was the execution of Lady Jane *Grey, who also had a claim to be queen. Mary was determined to bring back *Roman Catholicism to England, and married the

Catholic Philip II of Spain in 1554. Many Protestants opposed this, and she ordered hundreds of them to be burned to death, for which she became known as 'Bloody Mary'. Among those who died in this way were Thomas *Cranmer and Hugh *Latimer. Mary had no children, and after her death she was replaced by her half-sister (= sister by a different mother) *Elizabeth I.

Mary II /ˌmeəri ðə 'sekənd; AmE ˌmeri/ (1662–94) the queen of England, Scotland and Ireland from 1688 to 1694. She was the elder daughter of King *James II, and married William of Orange (later King *William III), her Dutch cousin, in 1677. After James II was removed from power in the *Glorious Revolution of 1688 she and William ruled together until her early death at the age of 32.

the ˌMary Ce'leste /sɪ'lest/ a US ship that was discovered empty in the North Atlantic Ocean in 1872, in perfect condition but with its crew all gone. What happened to them has never been explained: *Where is everyone? It's like the Mary Celeste in here today.*

ˌMary ˌHad a ˌLittle ˌLamb the title and first line of a traditional *nursery rhyme. The first verse is:

> 66 Mary had a little lamb,
> Its fleece was white as snow;
> And everywhere that Mary went
> The lamb was sure to go. 99

Maryland /'meərilənd; AmE 'merilənd/ an eastern state of the US on the Atlantic Ocean. It is also known as the Old Line State and the Free State. The largest city is *Baltimore, and the capital city is *Annapolis. Maryland was one of the original 13 states and gave some of its land to create Washington, DC. Tourists visit the *Harpers Ferry National Historical Park and the Goddard Space Flight Center. Among the state's products are electronic equipment, wood and fish.

Marylebone /'mærələbən/ a district of central London in the *borough of *Westminster(1). It lies south of *Regent's Park and contains famous buildings such as the *Royal Academy of Music, *Madame Tussaud's and the *Wigmore Hall. Marylebone railway station has train services to and from the Midlands, and also has a station on the *London Underground.

ˌMarylebone 'Cricket Club /ˌmærələbən/ (abbr the MCC) a cricket club, established in 1787, which used to be the main administrative organization for all cricket in England and Wales. It owns and has its headquarters at *Lord's in north London. The MCC is still responsible for the rules of cricket, wherever it is played. Many people consider the club and its members to be rather old-fashioned. Membership is limited and there is a long list of people waiting to join. Women members have only been allowed since 1998.

ˌMary, ˌMary, ˌQuite Con'trary the title and first line of a traditional *nursery rhyme, sometimes set to music. The full poem is:

> 66 Mary, Mary, quite contrary,
> How does your garden grow?
> With silver bells and cockle-shells,
> And pretty maids all in a row. 99

ˌMary 'Poppins /'pɒpɪnz; AmE 'pɑːpɪnz/ a popular Walt *Disney film (1964), based on the character created by the Australian writer P L Travers. Mary is a nanny (= a woman who looks after young children) who can fly with an umbrella and do other magic things. Julie *Andrews played the part and won an *Oscar for it. The film's songs include *Chim-Chim-Cheree*, which won an

M

Oscar, and *Supercalifragilisticexpialidocious*. A stage play based on the story opened in London in 2004.

,**Mary, Queen of 'Scots** (Mary Stuart 1542–87) the queen of Scotland from 1542 to 1567. She was the daughter of King James V of Scotland and the cousin of Queen *Elizabeth I, and became queen of Scotland shortly after her birth. She did not rule Scotland until 1561 and was instead brought up in France, where she was queen briefly in 1559. She was a Roman Catholic, and after her return to Scotland became involved in religious disputes with Scottish Protestants. In 1567 she was forced to give up power in favour of her son James VI (later King *James I of England), and moved to England where she was held as a prisoner. In the years that followed there were several attempts by Catholic groups to make her queen of England in place of Elizabeth I, and Elizabeth finally ordered Mary's head to be cut off. Her adventures, love affairs and three marriages have been the subject of many books, plays and films. See also BOTHWELL, DARNLEY.

> 66 In my end is my beginning. 99
> motto of Mary, Queen of Scots

the ,**Mary 'Rose** a ship built for King *Henry VIII in 1509–10 which sank off the south coast of England in 1545 and was brought up from the bottom of the sea in 1982. It can now be seen in a special museum in *Portsmouth.

,**John 'Masefield** /'meɪsfiːld/ (1878–1967) an English poet who often wrote about the sea. His best-known collections of poetry include *Sea Fever* (1902) and *The Everlasting Memory* (1911). He was *Poet Laureate from 1930 until his death. He also wrote children's books, novels and critical works.

M*A*S*H /mæʃ/ a US comic novel, film and television series about military doctors during the *Korean War. M*A*S*H is short for Mobile Army Surgical Hospital. Richard Hooker wrote the novel (1968) as a way of bringing the horrors of the *Vietnam War to people's attention. The film version (1970) was directed by Robert *Altman and won the prize for best film at the Cannes Film Festival. The television series on *CBS (1974–83) won several *Emmy awards, and the final programme was watched by more than 50 million people.

,**Perry 'Mason** /,peri 'meɪsn/ a character created by the US writer Erle Stanley *Gardner. He is a lawyer who appeared in 82 novels about court cases, none of which he ever lost. The first was *The Case of the Velvet Claws* (1933). Raymond Burr played the character in the popular television series *Perry Mason* (1957–66) on *NBC.

the ,**Mason-'Dixon line** /,meɪsn 'dɪksn/ a boundary line between the US states of *Pennsylvania and *Maryland. It came to be seen as a symbol of the division between the free states of the North and those of the South which had slaves. The line was measured and drawn in 1763–7 by Charles Mason and Jeremiah Dixon, two British surveyors, in order to settle a dispute between the two states. Their story was used for the novel *Mason and Dixon* (1997) by Thomas *Pynchon. See also DIXIE.

'**Masonite**™ /'meɪsənaɪt/ n [U] a US make of board or sheet consisting of small pieces of wood that have been pressed and stuck together. It is made to look like smooth sections of wood and is used to build doors, walls, roofs, etc.

'**Mason jar** /'meɪsn/ n (AmE) a glass container used for preserving food such as fruit, especially in the home. It has a wide opening and a metal lid that screws on tightly. It is named after John L Mason, who invented it in 1858. Compare KILNER JAR.

masque /mɑːsk; AmE mæsk/ n [C, U] a type of theatre which was especially popular with kings, queens and the *aristocracy in Britain in the 17th century. It involved actors in elaborate costumes, music and dancing. Many of the most popular masques were written by Ben *Jonson, with costumes and scenery designed by Inigo *Jones . Although masque died out after the *English Civil War, many of its features were used in later forms of theatre, opera and ballet.

,**Massa'chusetts** /,mæsə'tʃuːsɪts/ a north-eastern US state in *New England, also known informally as the Bay State or the Old Colony. The capital and largest city is *Boston. The state was settled in 1620 by the *Pilgrim Fathers. It played an important part in the *American Revolution and was one of the original 13 states. Its main industries include the production of electronic and communication equipment, as well as education and research. It also produces a lot of vegetables and fruit, especially cranberries. Among its historical places visited by tourists are *Independence Hall, *Cape Cod and *Plymouth Rock.

,**Massa'chusetts 'Institute of 'Technology** /,mæsə'tʃuːsɪts/ ⇨ MIT.

,**Massive At'tack** a British pop group, formed in 1988, whose music combines *dub, *rap and other styles. The group's most successful albums include *Blue Lines* (1991), *Mezzanine* (1998) and *100th Window* (2003).

'**Mastermind** a popular British television quiz programme that started in 1972. The four people competing each week take turns to sit in a black chair and answer questions on a subject of their own choice and then general knowledge questions. The person with the most correct answers goes on to the next round until the final winner becomes 'Mastermind' for the series. For many years the questions were asked by Magnus *Magnusson. Two phrases often used on the programme have become widely used by British people in general. They are 'Pass', said when a person is unable to answer a question, and 'I've started, so I'll finish', said if the time for questions ends while the last one is being asked.

'**Master of the 'Queen's 'Music** the title of the musician appointed to write and arrange music for certain British royal occasions, such as weddings. The post first came into existence in the 17th century. When a king is ruling the title is **Master of the King's Music**.

,**Master of the 'Rolls** the most senior civil judge in the legal system in England and Wales. The Master of the Rolls is in charge of the *Court of Appeal and is also a member of the *Privy Council.

,**Masterpiece 'Theater** a US television series on *PBS which shows many of the best British programmes. It began in 1971 and was presented by Alistair *Cooke until 1994. The programmes have included *Upstairs, Downstairs* (1974–7), *The *Jewel in the Crown* (1984) and *The Buccaneers* (1997).

,**Masters and 'Johnson** /,mɑːstəz, 'dʒɒnsn; AmE ,mæstərz, 'dʒɑːnsn/ **William Masters** (1915–2001) and **Virginia Johnson** (1925–), two US doctors who became well known for their study of human sexual behaviour. They discovered that women can enjoy sex as much as men. They wrote several books about their research, including *Human Sexual Response* (1966), and started a programme in *St Louis in 1970 for training experts to help people with their sexual problems. Masters and Johnson were married to each other from 1971 to 1993.

'**master's de,gree** n (also **master's**) a higher degree in British and US universities, usually requiring one year of study. It is between a *bachelor's degree and a *doctorate. Master's degrees include Master of Arts, Master of Science and Master of Business Administration: *She's*

doing her master's in computer studies. See also GRADU-
ATE SCHOOL.

the 'Masters ˌTournament /'mɑːstəz; *AmE*
'mæstərz/ (*also* **the Masters, the US Masters, the US
Masters Tournament**) a major international golf contest held each year in Augusta, *Georgia. It was established in 1934 by Bobby *Jones and is the only one of the
four major golf tournaments (= sports competitions)
that is always held on the same course. The winner
receives a special green jacket as well as money. The
most frequent winner has been Jack *Nicklaus with six
victories.

ˌMatch of the 'Day a British television programme
that shows details of the most important football
matches of a particular day (usually a Saturday). It first
appeared in 1964, and its presenters have included
David *Coleman, Desmond Lynam and Gary *Lineker.

ˌCotton 'Mather /ˌkɒtn 'meɪθə(r); *AmE* ˌkɑːtn/ (1663–
1728) an American Puritan minister (= church leader) in
*Boston. He wrote more than 400 works on religion, his-
tory, science and other subjects. His writings led to an
increased fear of witches and helped to cause the
*Salem witch trials, although Mather himself was
opposed to them. He also helped to establish *Yale
University and was the first person born in America to be
elected to the *Royal Society of London.

Ma'tilda /mə'tɪldə/ (1102–67) the queen of England for
a short time in 1135. She was replaced by King *Stephen.
Her father was *Henry I and her son became *Henry II
in 1154.

The *Matrix* /'meɪtrɪks/ a 1999 science fiction film about
a computer hacker, Neo, played by Keanu *Reeves, who
discovers that the world he is living in is part of a computer program called **The Matrix**. He joins a group of
people who are trying to fight against those controlling
the Matrix. The film uses many new special effects, for
which it won four *Oscars. The most famous is an effect
called **bullet time** in which a camera moves around a
person who is moving in very slow motion. Two more
films continued the story in *The Matrix Reloaded* (2003)
and *The Matrix Revolutions* (2003).

ˌMatrix 'Churchill /ˌmeɪtrɪks 'tʃɜːtʃɪl; *AmE* 'tʃɜːrtʃɪl/
a British engineering company which became well
known in 1992 when three of its directors were accused
of having sold military equipment to Iraq, against official
British government policy. The case against the directors
collapsed when Alan *Clark, who had been the government minister for trade, admitted in court that he had
advised the company not to be completely honest about
what they were exporting. This caused a big political
scandal in Britain. The directors were found not guilty
and the matter became the subject of an official inquiry.

ˌStanley 'Matthews /'mæθjuːz/ (1915–2000) one of the
most famous English football players of all time. He
played on the wing (= as an attacking player along one
side of the field) and was known for his skill at running
past opponents with the ball and then passing it into the
goal area. He is also remembered for having remained a
professional player until the age of 50. He played for
England 54 times and was the first football player to be
made a *knight (in 1965).

the ˌMaudsley 'Hospital /ˌmɔːdzli/ a psychiatric
hospital (= one for the treatment of mental illness) in
south-east London, established in 1916. It is part of
*London University and the main centre for postgradu-
ate education in psychiatry in Britain.

ˌSomerset 'Maugham /ˌsʌməset 'mɔːm; *AmE*
ˌsʌmərset / (1874–1965) an English writer thought to be
one of the best writers of short stories in the English language. He also wrote plays and novels, including *Of*

Human Bondage (1915) and *Cakes and Ale* (1930). Many of
his stories are about human weakness.

'Maundy ˌmoney /'mɔːndi/ *n* [U] specially produced
silver coins given each year by the British king or queen
to a selected group of poor people on **Maundy Thursday**
(the Thursday before *Easter). The ceremony continues a tradition which began in the Middle Ages. At
that time the king or queen washed the feet of the
poor people, in memory of Christ's washing of his disciples' feet.

ˌArmistead 'Maupin /ˌɑːmɪstɪd 'mɔːpɪn; *AmE*
ˌɑːrmɪstɪd/ (1944–) a US writer and author of the popular 'Tales of the City' series of novels. The first of these,
Tales of the City (1978), originally appeared in parts in the
San Francisco *Chronicle* newspaper. Its characters live at
28 Barbary Lane in San Francisco. Like Maupin himself,
several of them are homosexual. A British television series based on the novels caused arguments in the US
when it was shown on *PBS in 1994. Although it had the
largest ever audience for a PBS dramatic programme,
several cities refused to show it.

Mau'ritius /mə'rɪʃəs/ an island in the Indian Ocean
which is a member of the *Commonwealth. Before it
became independent in 1968, it was at various times a
colony of the Netherlands, France, and finally Britain. Its
main industries are sugar and tourism.
 ▶ **Mauritian** *adj, n.*

ˌMax 'Factor™ /ˌmæks 'fæktə(r)/ a company that
makes a range of well-known cosmetics. It is advertised
as 'the make-up of make-up artists'.

'James 'Clerk 'Maxwell¹ /'klɑːk 'mækswel; *AmE*
'klɑːrk/ (1831–79) a Scottish scientist who made important contributions to many areas of physics, including
gases, colour vision (= the power of sight), electricity
and magnetism. His work also influenced the development of telephones and colour photography.

ˌRobert 'Maxwell² /'mækswel/ (1923–91) a British
businessman, publisher and newspaper owner, born in
Czechoslovakia. He came to Britain in 1940 and received
the *Military Cross for his military achievements in
*World War II. He first became rich through his publish-
ing company, the Pergamon Press. However, in 1969, an
official investigation into the company decided that he
was not a suitable person to run a company. He was also
at this time a *Labour Party *Member of Parliament, a
position he held from 1964 to 1970.
  Maxwell built up a large business empire and became
one of the most powerful people in the newspaper
industry. In 1984 he bought *Mirror Group Newspapers
and so became the owner of the *Daily Mirror, the
*Sunday Mirror and The *People, all popular British
newspapers. Maxwell died when he fell from a boat and
drowned. After his death it was discovered that he had
illegally taken money from the *pension funds of
employees. His sons Kevin and Ian were prosecuted for
financial crimes involving his companies but were found
not guilty. Maxwell's reputation, however, was destroyed.

ˌMaxwell 'House™ /ˌmækswel/ a popular make of
instant coffee. It was first made in the US in 1886, and
was often advertised as being 'good to the last drop'.

'May Day the first day of May, which has been marked in
Britain for many centuries by outdoor events held to
celebrate the arrival of spring. In Britain, traditional
events on or near May Day include dancing round the
*maypole and choosing a *May Queen. May Day itself is
not necessarily a holiday in Britain, but since 1978 there
has been a *bank holiday on the Monday closest to 1
May, called the Early May Bank Holiday. In some countries, though not in Britain, May Day has been an occa-

M

sion for socialist celebrations, often involving military parades (= processions).

,**Louis B 'Mayer** /'meɪə(r)/ (Louis Burt Mayer 1885–1957) one of the people who established the US film company *MGM in 1924. As head of the company (until 1951) he became one of the most powerful men in *Hollywood. He also helped to create the *Academy of Motion Picture Arts and Sciences and received a special *Oscar in 1950. Mayer was born in Russia.

'**Mayfair** /'meɪfeə(r); *AmE* 'meɪfer/ a fashionable district in west central London. As well as very expensive houses and flats, it contains many hotels, restaurants, shops and art galleries.

,**Curtis 'Mayfield** /,kɜːtɪs 'meɪfiːld; *AmE* ,kɜːrtɪs/ (1942–1999) a US singer of *soul music who wrote songs, played the guitar, and produced records. He was the main singer for the group The Impressions, and their hit songs included *Gypsy Woman* (1961). After he left the group in 1970, Mayfield wrote the music for the film *Superfly* (1972) and produced several successful albums, including *Honesty* (1981). He was chosen for the Rock and Roll *Hall of Fame in 1999.

The '*Mayflower* /'meɪflaʊə(r)/ the ship in which the *Pilgrim Fathers sailed from *Plymouth in England to what is now the US, in 1620.

the 'Mayo ,Clinic /'meɪəʊ; *AmE* 'meɪoʊ/ one of the largest medical centres in the world. It is in Rochester, Minnesota, and was established in 1889 by William James Mayo (1861–1939) and his brother Charles Horace Mayo (1865–1939). It is famous for the high quality of treatment given there.

mayor *n* **1** (in England and Wales) a man or woman elected every year by other councillors as head of the *council in a town, city or *borough. The mayor performs official duties, such as attending public ceremonies, entertaining visitors to the area or opening new buildings. He or she does not have much political power. The equivalent person in Scotland is called a *provost*. The Mayor of London is elected by the people of London at the same time as the *London Assembly and makes decisions for London as a whole. Compare LORD MAYOR.
2 (in the US) the head of the local government of a town or city, elected by the people living there. US mayors usually belong to one of the two main political parties and often have a lot of political power.

mayo'ress *n* the wife of a *mayor(1) or a woman who acts on behalf of a mayor on public occasions. The word is sometimes used to mean a female mayor.

the ,Mayor of 'London the head of the local government of London, elected by the people of London every four years. The role of the Mayor of London is more like that of a US mayor than a traditional British mayor, with the power to set policies on transport, buildings and land use, culture and the environment. The first Mayor of London was Ken *Livingstone, who was elected in 2000.

'**maypole** *n* a tall decorated pole which people dance around during traditional *May Day celebrations in Britain. The dancers, usually children, hold coloured ribbons attached to the top of the pole, which is fixed upright into the ground. Maypoles used to be common in villages on May Day but are now less often seen.

'**May Queen** (*also* ,**Queen of the 'May**) *n* a pretty girl who is chosen in a town or village to be the central figure of traditional *May Day celebrations in Britain. She wears a crown of flowers and may be driven through the streets on an open vehicle.

the Maze /meɪz/ a prison in Northern Ireland, just outside *Belfast, where people opposed to the government

who were thought to be terrorists were kept without trial (a practice known as 'internment'). It opened in 1971, at a former military base called Long Kesh. The different sections of the prison were known as *H-blocks because each building was shaped like the letter H. When internment ended in 1975, prisoners who had been found guilty of terrorism protested that they should be treated as political prisoners. Some of them went on hunger strike and several died, including Bobby Sands, who had been elected as a *Member of Parliament while in the prison. After the *Good Friday Agreement the prison was gradually emptied and it closed in 2000.

MBE /,em bi: 'iː/ (*in full* **Member of the Order of the British Empire**) an award given to people in Britain for public service. It is given to people twice a year, in the *New Year Honours list and in the *Birthday Honours list. An MBE is the lowest grade of award of this kind.
In 1993, in response to the feeling that awards were not given often enough to ordinary people, the government changed the system so that people who are recommended by members of the public for the service they provide can receive the award.

MC /,em 'siː/ ⇨ MILITARY CROSS.

,**Bernadette Mc'Aliskey** /mək'æləski/ (1947–) a Northern Ireland politician, called Bernadette Devlin before her marriage. She was a leader of the *Roman Catholic *civil rights movement in the late 1960s and became the youngest *MP in the British parliament at *Westminster(2) in 1969. In the same year, she was sent to prison for six months for encouraging violence. She remained an MP until 1974. In 1981 she and her husband were shot and wounded by terrorists.

the MCAT /'emkæt/ (*in full* **the Medical College Admission Test**) (in the US) a standard test that students must normally take in order to be accepted into a medical college.

MCC /,em siː 'siː/ ⇨ MARYLEBONE CRICKET CLUB.

Alexander McCall Smith /mə,kɔːl 'smɪθ/ (1948–) a writer who was born in Rhodesia (now Zimbabwe) and moved to Scotland. He has written a series of humorous books about a female detective in Botswana who solves people's everyday problems. The first book, *The No. 1 Ladies' Detective Agency* was published in 1999. The books have since become popular around the world. He is also a Professor of Medical Law and has written more than 50 books about law and medical ethics.

Cormac McCarthy[1] /,kɔːmæk mə'kɑːθi; *AmE* ,kɔːrmæk mə'kɑːrθi/ (1933–) a US writer who is best known for his novel *All the Pretty Horses* (1992), the first book in *The Border Trilogy*.

,**Joseph Mc'Carthy**[2] /mə'kɑːθi; *AmE* mə'kɑːrθi/ (1908–57) a US politician. As a *Republican(1) *Senator from *Wisconsin he led a campaign against Communists in US society and government in the 1950s, during the Cold War. Important and well-known people were accused of being Communists or sympathetic to Communism, often without evidence, and forced to answer questions from the Senate Permanent Investigations Subcommittee, led by McCarthy. People were also encouraged to give information about their friends and those they worked with. Many people were forced from their jobs and 'blacklisted' (= prevented from getting jobs in future). In 1954 the US Senate officially condemned McCarthy's activities and his influence decreased. Most Americans are now unhappy that the McCarthy trials were allowed to happen, and admire anyone who opposed them or refused to give evidence. Compare HOUSE UN-AMERICAN ACTIVITIES COMMITTEE.
▶ **McCarthyism** *n* [U] extreme opposition to

Communism, as shown by Senator Joseph McCarthy in his campaign against people suspected of being Communists in the US. The word is also used more generally to mean the practice of investigating and accusing people who are thought to be opposed to the government, without sufficient evidence.

,Mary **Mc'Carthy**[3] /məˈkɑːθi; *AmE* məˈkɑːrθi/ (1912–89) a US writer whose intelligent novels made comments about American society. These include *The Groves of Academe* (1952), *The Group* (1963) and *Cannibals and Missionaries* (1979). She also wrote books about literature, travel books and *Memories of a Catholic Girlhood* (1957), about her own early life. She was married to the writer Edmund Wilson (1895–1972).

,Paul **Mc'Cartney** /məˈkɑːtni; *AmE* məˈkɑːrtni/ (1942–) an English musician and writer of songs who was a member of the *Beatles. In the 1960s, together with John *Lennon, he wrote and recorded some of the best-known pop songs of all time. When the Beatles split up in 1970, he formed a new group, Wings, whose successful records include *Mull of Kintyre* (1977).

Although remembered mainly for having been a member of the Beatles, McCartney is still very active as a musician and was chosen for the Rock and Roll *Hall of Fame in 1999. He has composed classical pieces, including *Liverpool Oratorio* (1991) and *Standing Stone* (1997), has established a college for the performing arts in *Liverpool, and continues to make successful pop records. He was made a *knight in 1997.

,Liz **Mc'Colgan** /məˈkɒlgən; *AmE* məˈkɔːlgən/ (1964–) a Scottish runner in long distance races. She won the gold medal for the 10 000 metres at the *Commonwealth Games in 1986 and 1990 and at the World Championships in 1991. She also won the silver medal in the same event at the Olympic Games in 1988. In 1991 she started to compete in marathon races (= ones run over a long distance) and won the first one she entered, the New York marathon. She has also won the *London marathon.

,Jack **Mc'Connell** /məˈkɒnl; *AmE* məˈkɑːnl/ (1960–) a Scottish *Labour politician who is the leader of the party in Scotland. He was elected a Member of the *Scottish Parliament in 1999 and was its Finance Minister and then its Education Minister before becoming *First Minister in 2001.

Tony **McCoy** /məˈkɔɪ/ (1974–) a successful horse racing jockey from Northern Ireland who has won a record number of races, has been a *champion jockey several times and won a record number of races over jumps in one season in 2001–02.

,Carson **Mc'Cullers** /ˌkɑːsn məˈkʌləz; *AmE* ˌkɑːrsn məˈkʌlərz/ (1917–67) a US writer from the state of *Georgia, where most of her novels and short stories were set. She said she wrote about 'spiritual isolation'. The novels included *The Heart is a Lonely Hunter* (1940), *Reflection in a Golden Eye* (1941), and *The Member of the Wedding* (1946), which she wrote again as a play in 1950. Her short stories were collected in *The Ballad of the Sad Cafe* (1951).

Martin **McDonagh** /məkˈdɒnə; *AmE* məkˈdɑːnə/ (1970–) a British playwright whose best-known play *The Beauty Queen of Leenane* (1996), which is set in a remote Irish town, played in Dublin, London and on *Broadway where it won four *Tony awards.

,Trevor **Mc'Donald** /məkˈdɒnld; *AmE* məkˈdɑːnld/ (1939–) a British television newsreader, born in Trinidad. He joined Independent Television News in 1973 and was the main newsreader for *News at Ten* from 1992. He was made a *knight in 1999.

Mc'Donald's™ /məkˈdɒnəldz; *AmE* məkˈdɑːnəldz/ any of a large group of US *fast food restaurants in many countries of the world. The company, established in 1955 by Ray *Kroc, who based it on a restaurant in California run since 1940 by two brothers, Dick and Mac McDonald, has become a symbol of US commercial success.

McDonald's originally sold only hamburgers, such as the Big Mac, but now sells chicken, fish and breakfast foods as well. The restaurants are especially popular with children and are regarded as typical of the American way of life. In 1997 McDonald's won the longest trial in British legal history (over seven years) against two people who handed out leaflets claiming that its food is not healthy and that to get the supply of meat it needs it causes damage to the environment. In 2004 the decision of the British court was declared to be unfair by the European Court of Human Rights in Strasbourg and the British government had to pay compensation to the couple.

,John **'McEnroe** /ˈmækɪnrəʊ; *AmE* ˈmækɪnroʊ/ (1959–) a US tennis player who was especially successful in the early 1980s. He won the men's title at *Wimbledon three times (1981 and 1983–4) and at the *US Open(2) four times (1979–81 and 1984), but he had a reputation for losing his temper and behaving badly during games. He now presents sports programmes in Britain and the US.

> 66 You cannot be serious. 99
> John McEnroe to a Wimbledon umpire

M

,Ian **M'cEwan** /məˈkjuːən/ (1948–) an English writer of short stories and novels, many of which are about the more strange and violent aspects of human nature. He won the *Booker Prize in 1998 for *Amsterdam*. His other novels include *The Child in Time* (1987), *The Innocent* (1990), *Enduring Love* (1997), *Atonement* (2001) and *Saturday* (2005).

,Donald **Mc'Gill** /məˈgɪl/ (1875–1962) an English cartoonist famous for his *seaside postcards. These usually showed fat people in humorous situations saying things that could have a rude meaning.

,William **Mc'Gonagall** /məˈgɒnəgl; *AmE* məˈgɑːnəgl/ (1830–1902) a Scottish poet whose *Poetic Gems* were published in 1890. His poems show no skill or understanding of poetry but are very popular and funny as a result. An example is his *Address to the Rev George Gilfillan*:

> 66 All hail to the Rev George Gilfillan of Dundee,
> He is the greatest preacher I did ever hear or see ...
> He has written the life of Sir Walter Scott,
> And while he lives he will never be forgot,
> Nor when he is dead,
> Because by his admirers it will be often read. 99

Ewan **McGregor** /ˌjuːən məkˈgregə(r)/ (1971–) a Scottish actor who first became known for his part in *Trainspotting* (1996) and later became famous in the *Star Wars* films, *The Phantom Menace* (1999) and *Attack of the Clones* (2002). His other films include *Moulin Rouge!* (2001) and *Big Fish* (2003).

Mc,Guffey's 'Readers /məˌgʌfiz/ a series of six school books (1836–57) designed to teach American children to read. They were created by William McGuffey (1800–73), the President of Cincinnati College, who wrote the first four. He believed that they should also develop good character in children, so he included wise advice and sentences from great British writers such as *Shakespeare and *Shelley[2]. About 122 million copies of the books were sold, and their moral stories influenced Americans for more than a century.

,Mark **Mc'Gwire** /mə'gwaɪə(r)/ (1963–) a US *baseball player who in 1998 hit the most *home runs in a season (70) in the history of the game, beating the record of 61 set by Roger Maris in 1961. McGwire played for the St Louis Cardinals in the *National League.

,Ian **Mc'Kellen** /mə'kelən/ (1939–) a leading English actor known especially for his performances in *Shakespeare plays, although he has appeared in many other plays and in a number of films including the *Lord of the Rings films, in the role of Gandalf. He is also known for his efforts to raise money for the victims of the disease AIDS and for his campaigns in support of equal rights for homosexuals. He was made a *knight in 1991.

,Mount **Mc'Kinley**[1] /mə'kɪnli/ the highest mountain in North America, with a height of 20 320 feet/6 198 metres. It is in *Denali National Park in southern central *Alaska, where it is also called Denali (which means 'the Great One'). The mountain was named after US President William *McKinley, and it was first climbed in 1913.

,William **Mc'Kinley**[2] /mə'kɪnli/ (1843–1901) the 25th US *President (1897–1901). He was a US officer during the *Civil War and a *Republican(1) who served twice in the US House of Representatives (1877–83 and 1885–91) and as governor of *Ohio (1892–6). US power increased greatly during his time as President. He supported the *Spanish-American War and trade with China, and created the highest tariffs (= taxes on imports) in US history. He was murdered by an anarchist (= a person who believes there should be no laws or government).

M'cLaren[1] /mə'klærən/ one of the leading teams in *Formula One motor racing, with its main base in Britain. The company was established by Bruce McLaren (1937–70), a former racing driver from New Zealand. Its most successful period was from the mid 1980s to the early 1990s when its drivers Alain Prost and Ayrton Senna were world champions six times.

a McLaren car

,Malcolm **M'cLaren**[2] /mə'klærən/ (1946–) an English pop group manager and businessman. He is best known for bringing together the *punk(1) group the *Sex Pistols in 1975, and later managing their career. Together with Vivienne *Westwood he also owned the clothes shop 'Sex' in the *King's Road, London, which became a centre of punk fashions.

,Chris **Mc'Manus** /mək'mænəs/ (1951–) a British professor of Psychology who is particularly interested in researching why some people are left-handed (= find it easier to use their left hand than their right hand). His book about the subject, Right Hand, Left Hand (2002), won an *Aventis Prize.

,Robert **McNa'mara** /mæknə'mɑːrə/ (1916–) a US Secretary of Defense (1961–8) under President *Kennedy and President *Johnson. McNamara left this job because he had doubts about the *Vietnam War, and he later said publicly that it was wrong. When his political career ended, he became President of the World Bank (1968–81). In a documentary film about his life, The Fog of War: Eleven Lessons from the Life of Robert S McNamara (2003) he discusses his failures in Vietnam.

,Steve **M'cQueen** /mə'kwiːn/ (1930–80) a US film actor who often played tough but honest characters. He first became well known in a television series, Wanted – Dead or Alive (1958). His films included The *Magnificent Seven, The Great Escape (1963), Bullitt (1968) and The Towering Inferno (1974).

Mc'Vitie's™ /mək'vɪtiz/ a British company that makes biscuits of different types. McVitie's Digestive Biscuits, made with wholemeal flour, are especially popular.

MDT /,em diː 'tiː/ ⇨ MOUNTAIN DAYLIGHT TIME.

,Margaret **'Mead** /'miːd/ (1901–78) a US anthropologist. She studied how children grow up in different cultures, especially in the Pacific islands, and argued that human behaviour is strongly affected by society. Some people criticized her research, but she made anthropology very popular. Her books included Coming of Age in Samoa (1928), Growing Up in New Guinea (1930), Male and Female (1949) and Culture and Commitment (1970).

,Meadowbank **'Stadium** /,medəʊbæŋk; AmE ,medoʊbæŋk/ a sports stadium in *Edinburgh, Scotland, which was opened in 1970 to hold the *Commonwealth Games. The games were held there again in 1986. It has one large outdoor sports ground and several which are indoors.

▶ **meals**

Americans and British people generally eat three meals a day though the names vary according to people's lifestyles and where they live.

The first meal of the day is **breakfast**. The traditional **full English breakfast** served in many British hotels may include fruit juice, cereal, bacon and eggs, often with sausages and tomatoes, toast and marmalade, and tea or coffee. Few people have time to prepare a cooked breakfast at home and most have only cereal and/or toast with tea or coffee. Others buy coffee and a pastry on their way to work.

The traditional **American breakfast** includes eggs, some kind of meat and toast. Eggs may be fried, 'over easy', 'over hard' or 'sunny side up', or boiled, poached or in an omelette (= beaten together and fried). The meat may be bacon or sausage. People who do not have time for a large meal have toast or cereal and coffee. It is common for Americans to eat breakfast in a restaurant. On Saturday and Sunday many people eat **brunch** late in the morning. This consists of both breakfast and lunch dishes, including pancakes and waffles (= types of cooked batter) that are eaten with butter and maple syrup.

Lunch, which is eaten any time after midday, is the main meal of the day for some British people, though people out at work may have only *sandwiches. Some people also refer to the midday meal as **dinner**. Most workers are allowed about an hour off work for it, called the **lunch hour**, and many also go shopping. Many schools offer a cooked lunch (**school lunch** or **school dinner**), though some students take a **packed lunch** of sandwiches, fruit, etc. **Sunday lunch** is special and is, for many families, the biggest meal of the week, consisting traditionally of roast meat and vegetables and a sweet course. In the US lunch is usually a quick meal, eaten around midday. Many workers have a half-hour break for lunch, and buy a sandwich from near their place of work. Business people may sometimes eat a larger lunch and use the time to discuss business.

The main meal of the day for most people is the evening meal, called **supper**, **tea** or **dinner**. It is usually a cooked meal with meat or fish or a salad, followed by a sweet course. In Britain younger children may have tea when they get home from school. *Tea*, meaning a main meal for adults, is the word used in some parts of Britain especially when the evening meal is eaten early. *Dinner* sounds more formal than *supper*, and guests generally receive invitations to 'dinner' rather than to 'supper'. In the US the evening meal is called *dinner* and is usually eaten around 6 or 6.30 p.m. In many families, both in Britain and in the US, family members eat at different times and rarely sit down at the table together.

Many people also eat **snacks** between meals. Most have tea or coffee at mid-morning, often called **coffee time** or the **coffee break**. In Britain in the past this was sometimes also called **elevenses**. In the afternoon many British people have a **tea break**. Some hotels serve **afternoon tea** which consists of tea or coffee and a choice of sandwiches and cakes. When on holiday/vacation people sometimes have a *cream tea of scones, jam and cream. In addition many people eat chocolate bars, biscuits (*AmE* cookies) or crisps (*AmE* chips). Some British people have a snack, sometimes called supper, consisting of a milk drink and a biscuit before they go to bed. In the US children often have milk and cookies after school.

ˌmeals on ˈwheels *n* [U] a service in which meals are taken by car to old or sick people in their own homes. It is provided in Britain by groups such as the *Women's Royal Voluntary Service, and in the US by various charities and service organizations.

ˌMean ˈStreets a US film (1973) that made stars of Martin *Scorsese, who wrote and directed it, and the actor Robert *De Niro. It is about four youths who meet in Tony's Bar in the *Little Italy district of *Manhattan(I). De Niro plays Johnny Boy, a criminal who owes money to many people and creates trouble for others. By 1997 Scorsese and De Niro had made eight more films together.

ˌMeasure for ˈMeasure a play by *Shakespeare, thought to have been written in 1604 and often regarded as one of his comedies. It is about a *duke, Vincentio, who gives his power to his deputy (= assistant), Angelo, and then wears a disguise so that he can watch how Angelo behaves. Angelo behaves in an immoral and cruel way until the duke reveals who he really is and then there is a happy ending.

ˌmeat and two ˈveg (*BrE informal*) a meal consisting of some meat and two different vegetables, one of which is potato. It is a traditional British meal, although now British people enjoy a greater variety of foods, and 'meat and two veg' is sometimes seen as old-fashioned and boring: *He does like his meat and two veg most days.*

ˈMeat Loaf (1951–) a US pop singer, known for his large size, whose real name is Marvin Lee Aday. His first album, *Bat Out of Hell* (1977), sold more than 30 million

Meccano

copies. He won a 1993 *Grammy award for his song *I'd Do Anything for Love (But I Won't Do That)*. He has also appeared in several films.

Mecˈcano™ /məˈkɑːnəʊ; *AmE* məˈkɑːnoʊ/ *n* [U] a toy in the form of a set of metal or plastic parts with which mechanical models can be built. It was invented by Frank Hornby in England in 1893 and has been popular in Britain for many years. Some modern Meccano sets also have electrical parts.

ˌMedal of ˈHonor ⇨ CONGRESSIONAL MEDAL OF HONOR.

▶ **medals**

The highest **decoration** (= award) that can be awarded to a British person is the *Victoria Cross (**VC**), which is given to members of the armed forces 'for conspicuous bravery in the face of the enemy'. It is a bronze cross decorated with a lion and the words 'For Valour', which is hung from a crimson ribbon. The Victoria Cross was introduced by Queen *Victoria in 1856, during the *Crimean War. It is reserved for acts of the greatest courage and is often awarded **posthumously** (= to a person who died as a result of their brave action).

The highest decoration for members of the public is the *George Cross (**GC**), which is also awarded for bravery in great danger. It is a silver cross decorated with St *George and the Dragon and the words 'For Gallantry', and is hung from a dark blue ribbon. It was introduced by *George VI in 1940.

Other highly valued decorations include the Distinguished Service Cross, the Military Cross and the George Medal. There are also medals for acts of bravery by police officers and by members of the fire-fighting, lifeboat and coastguard services.

The US also has many medals for military and civilian achievements. The *Medal of Honor (**MH**), often called the Congressional Medal of Honor, is the highest military award and is given for 'the risk of life, above and beyond the call of duty'. It is a star that hangs from a blue ribbon which is decorated with 13 white stars. It was created in 1862 during the *Civil War, and by 2004 more than 3450 had been awarded. Another well-known military medal is the *Purple Heart (**PH**), which is awarded to Americans wounded in wars. George *Washington introduced it in 1782 as the Badge of Military Merit, and the medal today has a ribbon above a purple heart with Washington's image on it. Other important military awards include the Distinguished Service Cross and the Bronze Star.

The highest US civilian award is the Presidential Medal of Freedom, established in 1945 as the Medal of Freedom. It was originally for military service, but President *Kennedy changed this and also its name. The **Congressional Gold Medal** is also for civilians. The first was awarded in 1776 to George Washington; in 2003 one was awarded to the British Prime Minister, Tony *Blair. The **Carnegie Medal**, another honour for civilians, is given to people who have saved, or tried to save, somebody's life. On the medal is a sentence from the Bible: 'Greater love hath no man than this, that a man lay down his life for his friends.'

ˈMedicaid the US government's medical programme for people under the age of 65 who have low incomes. It helps to pay the cost of doctors, dentists, hospitals, drugs, medicines and other items. Medicaid began in 1965, is operated by the individual states and is paid for by national, state and county governments. Compare MEDICARE.

the ˈMedical ˈCollege Adˈmission Test ⇨ MCAT.

the ˌMedical Reˈsearch ˌCouncil (*abbr* the **MRC**) a British government organization which gives government money to institutions doing medical research, usually universities and hospitals. It was established in 1920.

'**Medicare** the US government's medical programme mainly for people over the age of 65. It began in 1965 and is part of the *social security system. It pays part of the costs of hospitals and offers additional medical insurance to people who pay an amount each month. Medicare costs the government more than was originally expected and its future is the subject of much political debate. Compare MEDICAID.

,**medi'eval** (*also* **mediaeval**) *adj* of the Middle Ages, the period in European history between about 1000 and about 1450. Things which are very old-fashioned, or are not comfortable or convenient, are sometimes described as medieval: *Conditions were pretty medieval – there were no toilets or running water, and no hot food.*

the '**Medway** /'medweɪ/ a river in *Kent in south-east England which starts at the town of Rochester, flows through *Chatham and joins the River *Thames to the east of London.

,**Meet the 'Press** a US television news programme, broadcast every Sunday, in which several journalists ask politicians questions. *Meet the Press* began on radio in 1945 and moved to television in 1947. It has been presented since 1991 by Tim Russert.

the '**me ,generation** *n* [sing+ sing/pl *v*] (*informal disapproving*) the name used to refer to young people in the 1970s and 1980s who were especially interested in money and success and cared more about themselves than about others: *The me generation was one of the legacies of Thatcherism in Britain.*

,**Lord 'Melbourne** /'melbɔːn; *AmE* 'melbɔːrn/ (*born* William Lamb 1779–1848) a British *Whig(1) politician who was twice *Prime Minister (1834 and 1835–41). He is remembered especially for the good relationship he had with Queen *Victoria, who was young when he was in power and welcomed the advice he gave her, and for a very public scandal in 1812 when his wife, Lady Caroline *Lamb, had a love affair with the poet Lord *Byron.

,**Victor 'Meldrew** /'meldruː/ the main character in the popular British television comedy series *One Foot in the Grave* (1990–2000), played by Richard Wilson. He is a retired man who is always bad-tempered, complains all the time, annoys people and often makes terrible mistakes. His name is often used in Britain to refer to somebody who behaves like this and people often quote his favourite phrase, 'I don't believe it!'.

,**Andrew 'Mellon** /'melən/ (1855–1937) a rich US businessman who also served in the US government. He gave large amounts of money to help charities, museums, etc. He was Secretary of the Treasury (1921–31) and then US Ambassador to Britain (1932–3). In 1937 he gave his large art collection to establish the *National Gallery of Art in Washington, DC.

'**Melody ,Maker** a British pop and rock music newspaper published once a week. It first appeared in 1926 and was published until 2000, when it merged with *New Musical Express.

the '**melting pot** *n* a phrase that has been used to describe the US, because it is a country in which people from many different races and cultures are 'melted' together, i.e. mixed, to form the US people. The British writer Israel Zangwill (1864–1926) wrote a play called *The Melting Pot* (1903) about Jewish immigrants in America.

'**Melton 'Mowbray 'pie** /'meltən 'məʊbreɪ; *AmE* 'moʊbreɪ/ a type of pork pie originally made in the town of Melton Mowbray in *Leicestershire, England. It is often eaten cold.

,**Herman 'Melville** /,hɜːmən 'melvɪl; *AmE* ,hɜːrmən/ (1819–91) a US writer of novels whose early life as a sailor provided the material for many of his books, including his best-known novel, *Moby-Dick. His other books include *Typee* (1846), *Omoo* (1847) and the short novel *Billy Budd* (1924), published after he died. Melville's books were not popular during his life, and he died in poverty. His importance as a writer was not recognized until the 1920s.

,**Member of 'Parliament** *n* (*abbr* **MP**) a member of the *House of Commons, elected in a general election or a *by-election. Each MP represents one of the 645 *constituencies into which England, Scotland, Wales and Northern Ireland are divided for these elections. The person elected to be a Member of Parliament in an election is the one who is given the most votes. ⇨ note at ELECTIONS.

'**Member of the 'European 'Parliament** *n* (*abbr* **MEP**) (*also* **Euro-MP**) a person elected as the representative at the *European Parliament of any of the 81 *constituencies into which England, Scotland, Wales and Northern Ireland are divided in elections for this parliament. These elections are separate from general elections for the British *Parliament. They were first held in 1979 and take place every five years.

'**Member of the 'Scottish 'Parliament** (*abbr* **MSP**) a person elected to represent one of the 73 *constituencies or one of the eight regions into which Scotland is divided for this parliament. Each constituency elects one MSP and each region elects seven MSPs. These elections are separate from general elections for the British *Parliament. They were first held in 1999 and take place every four years.

Me'morial Day (*also* ,**Deco'ration Day**) a US holiday to honour Americans killed in all wars. It is the last Monday in May, but a few states have it on 30 May. It began in the South during the *Civil War when flowers were placed on graves, and the North first celebrated it in 1868. Memorial Day traditionally begins the summer holiday from school. Southern states also celebrate **Confederate Memorial Day** on 26 April, 10 May or 3 June.

'**Memphis** /'memfɪs/ the largest city in the US state of *Tennessee. It is on the *Mississippi River in the extreme south-west of the state. Memphis is an agricultural and commercial centre established in 1819 and named after the ancient Egyptian city. It is called the 'home of the *blues' because W C *Handy lived there. Martin Luther *King was murdered in Memphis in 1968, and Elvis *Presley died there in 1977 at his home, *Graceland.

the ,**Menai 'Strait** /,menaɪ/ a channel that separates the island of *Anglesey from the north-west coast of Wales. The **Menai Bridge**, the road bridge that crosses it, was built by Thomas *Telford and was then the biggest suspension bridge (= bridge hanging from cables supported by towers at each end) of its kind in the world.

'**Men Be'having 'Badly** a popular British television comedy series (1992–1998) about two young men sharing a flat/apartment, who get drunk a lot and behave badly, and have unsuccessful relationships with women. A US version of the series, with the same title, was shown between 1996 and 1998.

'**Mencap** /'menkæp/ (*in full* **the Royal Mencap Society**) a British charity which provides help, services and accommodation for people with learning difficulties and campaigns for their rights. It was established in 1946.

,**Sam 'Mendes** /'mendɪz/ (1965–) an English theatre and film director. Among his best known films is *American Beauty* (1999) which won five *Oscars including one for best director. His film *Road to Perdition* (2002) also won an Oscar. He is married to the actor Kate Winslet.

'Mennonite /'menənaɪt/ *n* a member of a Protestant group, mostly in Canada and the US, who have a simple life and religion like the *Amish and the *Hutterites. Their rules come from the Bible, and they only baptize adults. They also refuse to hold public office or serve in the armed forces. The Mennonites came to the US from Switzerland in 1683 and settled mainly in *Pennsylvania and the *Middle West. They named themselves after Menno Simons, a 16th-century Dutch Anabaptist leader.

'Mensa /'mensə/ (*in full* **Mensa International**) a social organization for highly intelligent people. Established in Britain in 1946, it became an international organization in the 1960s. It is based on the idea that intelligence can be accurately measured by tests and only people who achieve very high scores in intelligence tests are allowed to join.

Ye,hudi 'Menuhin /jə,huːdi 'menjuɪn/ (1916–1999) one of the greatest violinists of the 20th century. He was born in the US but settled permanently in England in the 1940s. He first achieved fame as a child violinist, giving his first public performance at the age of seven in *San Francisco. A number of works were later written specially for him by leading composers, including William *Walton.

In 1963 Menuhin started a school for children with special musical ability. He was also a conductor and directed music festivals, as well as writing and broadcasting on humanitarian subjects. He was made a *knight in 1987 and a *life peer in 1993.

MEP /,em iː 'piː/ ⇨ MEMBER OF THE EUROPEAN PARLIAMENT.

MER-A /,em iː ɑːr 'eɪ/ ⇨ SPIRIT.

MER-B /,em iː ɑː 'biː; *AmE* ɑːr/ ⇨ OPPORTUNITY.

,Johnny 'Mercer /'mɜːsə(r)/ (1909–76) an American who wrote the words to more than 1 000 popular songs. They include *Jeepers Creepers* (1938), *That Old Black Magic* (1942), *Laura* (1945), *Come Rain or Come Shine* (1946), *Something's Gotta Give* (1955) and *Moon River* (1961). Mercer won four *Oscars.

,Ismail 'Merchant /,ɪsmaɪl 'mɜːtʃənt; *AmE* 'mɜːrtʃənt/ (1936–) an Indian film producer who, together with James *Ivory and the writer Ruth Prawer Jhabvala, has made a number of successful films, including *Heat and Dust* (1983) and *A Room with a View* (1986), which both won *Oscars. They are particularly associated with making romantic films set in a period of the past, with great attention to historical detail and the attitudes of the characters, such as *The Golden Bowl* (2000) based on the novel by Henry *James.

,merchant 'navy (*also* ,merchant ma'rine) *n* the trading ships of a country and the sailors who work on them. The British merchant navy was very important during both world wars for the continued supply of goods to Britain from abroad, and many of its ships were sunk by enemy submarines. See also BATTLE OF THE ATLANTIC.

The ,Merchant of 'Venice a play by *Shakespeare, thought to have been written in 1596. It is about a merchant, Antonio, who borrows money from a Jew called *Shylock to help Bassanio marry Portia. According to their agreement, if Antonio fails to pay the money back, Shylock can claim a pound of Antonio's flesh. When Antonio is unable to pay the money back, Shylock demands that Antonio keeps to the agreement. However, he is defeated in a court case by Portia, disguised as a lawyer, who makes a powerful speech, wins the case and saves Antonio's life. The play is the origin of

the expression *to demand, want, etc. your pound of flesh*, meaning to want or insist on getting what you have a legal right to, even when it is morally offensive to do so.

'Mercia /'mɜːsiə; *AmE* 'mɜːrsiə/ one of the *Anglo-Saxon regions of England, occupying a large area of central England. It was established in the 6th century and was very powerful during the 8th century, when it was ruled by Offa, who built *Offa's Dyke. Recently, the name Mercia has started to be used again in the names of organizations, buildings and companies in central England.

,Freddie 'Mercury /'mɜːkjəri; *AmE* 'mɜːrkjəri/ (1946–91) the singer with the rock group *Queen. He was known particularly for his energetic performances at live concerts. He died of the disease AIDS.

the 'Mercury program (*also* ,Project 'Mercury) the US space programme (1961–63) to put a man into orbit around the earth. This was achieved when John *Glenn became the first person to go into orbit on 20 February 1962. See also SHEPARD.

the ,Mercury 'Music Prize (*also* the **Nationwide Mercury Prize**) a pop music prize started in 1992 as an alternative to the *Brit Awards because these were seen to be very influenced by the big record companies. The **Mercury prize** is given every year to a band or singer, especially one from a small independent record company, for the best album of the year.

'merit badge any of several badges awarded in the *Boy Scouts of America for different achievements and sewn onto their uniforms. A certain number are needed before a Scout can move to a higher rank. Merit badges are awarded for skills and study in many areas, such as cooking, safety, communications, sports, computers, pets and family life.

'Merlin /'mɜːlɪn; *AmE* 'mɜːrlɪn/ an important character in the stories about King *Arthur. He was a wizard (= a man with magic powers) who gave advice to King Arthur and his father, Uther Pendragon. It was Merlin's idea that the man who could pull *Excalibur out of the stone should be king.

,Merry 'England a phrase used to refer to England in the *Elizabethan period, which is often seen as a great period for the country, when it was powerful and prosperous, the people were happy and there was a lot of singing, dancing and happy music.

,Merry 'Men the group of men who followed *Robin Hood, lived with him in *Sherwood Forest and joined him in his adventures: *the stories of Robin Hood and his Merry Men*.

The ,Merry 'Wives of 'Windsor /'wɪnzə(r)/ a comedy play by *Shakespeare, thought to have been written in 1600. The main character is *Falstaff, who Shakespeare included again because he had been such a popular character in *Henry IV*. In *The Merry Wives of Windsor* Falstaff tries to have affairs with two women at the same time. They realize what he is doing and play cruel tricks on him to cause him embarrassment.

the 'Mersey /'mɜːzi; *AmE* 'mɜːrzi/ a river in north-west England which flows through *Greater Manchester and *Merseyside and into the *Irish Sea. It is usually associated with *Liverpool because it flows through that city and has played an important part in its history. There are three tunnels under it, one for the underground railway and two for roads, and a ferry across it.

the 'Mersey beat /'mɜːzi; *AmE* 'mɜːrzi/ (*also* **the Mersey sound**) the name used to describe a style of pop music which was created and played by a number of groups from *Liverpool in the early and mid 1960s, and which became very popular all over the world. The most famous of these groups was the *Beatles.

'Merseyside /'mɜːzisaɪd; *AmE* 'mɜːrzisaɪd/ a *metro-politan county in north-west England that includes *Liverpool.

'Mesa 'Verde 'National 'Park /'meɪsə 'vɜːdi; *AmE* 'vɜːrdi/ a US *national park in south-west *Colorado. It was established in 1906 and covers 52 122 acres/21 109 hectares. Tourists come to see the cliff houses and the Cliff Palace of the *Anasazi people which are more than 1 000 years old. The park includes mountains and deep valleys. It also has a museum. It was made a *World Heritage Site in 1978.

Mesa Verde Cliff Palace

Mes'siah (*also the Messiah*) /mə'saɪə/ a musical work by *Handel for voices and orchestra, with verses from the Bible. It was first performed in *Dublin in 1742 and has become one of the most popular pieces of classical music among British audiences. It is often sung around Christmas.

Me'tallica /mə'tælɪkə/ a US band whose music combines *punk and *heavy metal. It was formed in 1981 by Lars Ulrich, who was born in Denmark. Their albums have included *Kill 'Em All* (1983), *Metallica* (1991) and *St Anger* (2003).

metaphysical 'poets *n* a group of 17th-century English poets, including John *Donne, George *Herbert and Andrew *Marvell. Their poetry was marked by a clever and complicated mixture of words and ideas, with each poem being based on a central idea, or 'conceit'. They gained a high reputation in the 20th century, mainly because of critical praise from T S *Eliot.

the **Meteoro'logical ,Office** (*also informal* the **'Met ,Office**) a British government organization that collects and provides information on the weather. It was established in 1854 and its headquarters are in the town of Bracknell in Berkshire. Most of the weather forecasts on radio and television are presented by people who work for the Met Office.

'method ,acting *n* [U] a way of acting in which actors try to identify completely with the characters they are playing. It was based on the ideas of the Russian director Constantin Stanislavsky, and developed in the US by Lee *Strasberg at the *Actors' Studio in New York. Famous actors who have used 'the Method' include Marlon *Brando, Dustin *Hoffman and Robert *De Niro.

'Methodist *n* a member of the **Methodist Church**, the largest of the Protestant *Free Churches in Britain and the US. It was established in 1739 by John *Wesley as part of the *Church of England but it became separate from it in 1795. It was introduced into the US in the 18th century and today has members around the world. It emphasizes the importance of moral issues, both personal and social.
▶ **Methodism** *n* [U].

the **'metric ,system** the system of weights and measures used in most countries in the *European Union which is replacing the *imperial system in Britain. The metric system is sometimes also called the **International System** or **Système International** and the units of measurement are called **SI units**. Measurements of length, weight and volume are each derived from a single base unit, the **metre**, the **gram** and the **litre**. Other units of measurement are 10, 100 or 1 000 times smaller or larger than these. Some metric units of measure are spelt differently in British and American English: words ending in -*metre* and -*litre* in British English end in -*meter* and -*liter* in American English.

'Metro-'Goldwyn-'Mayer /'metrəʊ 'gəʊldwɪn 'meɪə(r); *AmE* 'metroʊ 'goʊldwɪn 'meɪər/ ⇨ MGM.

,metro'politan 'county *n* each of six new administrative areas of Britain created in 1974. These were formed from large city areas which were separated from the counties they were formerly in. They are *Greater Manchester, *Merseyside, *Tyne and Wear, *West Midlands, *South Yorkshire and *West Yorkshire. Each one was divided into ten districts and there were two systems of local government, county councils and *district councils. In 1986, this system changed. County councils were abolished, leaving only district councils responsible for each district within the metropolitan counties. See also UNITARY AUTHORITY.

the **,Metro'politan Mu'seum of 'Art** a famous US art museum in New York, first opened in 1880. The building has about 250 rooms and more than 3.5 million works of art from around the world, including the complete Temple of Dendur from Egypt. The museum's American Wing includes, as well as paintings, 25 rooms furnished to show the development of furniture and design from the early colonial period to the 20th century. Much of the *medieval art is at the Cloisters, a separate building in Fort Tryon Park, opened in 1938.

the **,Metro'politan 'Opera** (*also informal* the **Met**) the leading US opera company, and one of the best known in the world, based in New York at the *Lincoln Center for the Performing Arts. It was established in 1838. The company's most famous head was Rudolf Bing, between 1940 and 1972. Its conductors have included Gustav Mahler and Arturo Toscanini, and its singers have included Enrico Caruso, Maria *Callas, Joan Sutherland and Luciano Pavarotti. Since 1940 it has broadcast its Saturday afternoon opera productions live on radio.

the **,Metro'politan 'Police** (*also informal* the **Met**) the police force responsible for *Greater London (except for the *City, where the police force is the City of London Police). It was established in 1827 by Sir Robert *Peel. Its headquarters are at *New Scotland Yard in *Westminster(1). See also CID.

mews /mjuːz/ *n* (*pl* **mews**) (*especially BrE*) a street of buildings where horses used to be kept, but which have since been converted into homes. These homes are usually small but they are considered very fashionable and are therefore expensive to buy or rent, especially in parts of central London such as *Kensington and *Chelsea.

the **,Mexican 'War** /,meksɪkən/ a war (1846–48) fought between the US and Mexico. It began after *Texas became a state in 1845 and there was a dispute about where the border between Texas and Mexico should be. The war was won by the US forces under General Zachary *Taylor, who became President a year later. The Treaty of Guadalupe Hidalgo ended the war, and the US paid Mexico $15 million for land that is now in *California, *Arizona, *Colorado, *Nevada, *New Mexico and *Utah. Many people in the northern states worried that the victory would increase the number of the states with slaves, and this worry was one of the causes of the *Civil War.

MG™ /ˌem ˈdʒiː/ the name given to a series of popular and relatively cheap British sports cars, originally made by the *Morris company (MG is short for 'Morris Garages'). The first were made in the 1920s. MGs were later made by MG *Rover.

MGM /ˌem dʒiː ˈem/ (*in full* **Metro-Goldwyn-Mayer**) a well-known *Hollywood film company established in 1924. In its early days it was especially famous for its musical films, made with great style. The company employed many famous US actors. At the start of every MGM film there is a roaring lion and the words 'More stars than there are in the heavens'. The company has been sold several times since the 1970s. It owns a large group of cinemas and the MGM Grand Hotel and Theme Park, completed in 1993 in *Las Vegas. See also GOLDWYN, MAYER.

MGN /ˌem dʒiː ˈen/ ⇨ MIRROR GROUP NEWSPAPERS.

Mi'ami /maɪˈæmi/ a US city and port in south-eastern *Florida on Biscayne Bay. It is a popular place for holidays because of the warm weather and **Miami Beach**, which is on an island three miles off the coast. The city is also an important financial and industrial centre. It became a town in 1892 and grew rapidly in the 1920s. Many immigrants live in the districts of 'Little Havana' and 'Little Haiti'. More than half of Miami's population are *Hispanic. See also MIAMI HERALD.

Miami Beach

the **Mi,ami 'Herald** /maɪˌæmi/ a newspaper published every day in *Miami, *Florida, which has won 17 *Pulitzer Prizes. The *Herald* is known for its excellent news stories about Latin America.

Mr Mi'cawber /mɪˈkɔːbə(r)/ a character in the novel *David Copperfield* by Charles *Dickens. He is always in financial difficulties, but remains hopeful that 'something will turn up' to solve his problems without his having to make any effort himself. He is usually associated with this attitude to life and with his theory about income: if you spend a bit less than you earn, you will be happy; but if you spend a bit more than you earn, you will be unhappy.

Alun 'Michael[1] /ˌælən ˈmaɪkl/ (1943–) a Welsh *Labour politician who has been a *Member of Parliament for *Cardiff since 1987. He became the leader of the *Labour Party in Wales and the *First Secretary of the *National Assembly for Wales in 1999 but was soon replaced by Rhodri *Morgan who had more local support in Wales. In 2001 he became *Minister of State for Rural Affairs at Westminster.

George 'Michael[2] /ˈmaɪkl/ (1963–) a popular British pop singer and song writer since the early 1980s. He was born in London and has a Greek Cypriot father and an English mother. He first became famous as a member of the group Wham!, and then began a successful career on his own in 1985. His albums have included *Faith* (1987), *Listen Without Prejudice Volume 1* (1990) and *Patience* (2004).

'Michaelmas /ˈmɪklməs/ 29 September, the day celebrated by Christians as the festival of Saint Michael. It is not a *bank holiday in Britain.

'Michaelmas term /ˈmɪkləməs/ the name given to the autumn academic term in some British schools and universities.

James 'Michener /ˈmɪtʃənə(r)/ (1907–97) a US writer who won the *Pulitzer Prize for *Tales of the South Pacific* (1947) based on his experiences there. It was adapted as the musical play and film *South Pacific*. Michener then mainly wrote historical and adventure novels, most of them very long and based on careful research. They include *The Bridges of Toko-Ri* (1953), *Hawaii* (1959), *Centennial* (1974), *Chesapeake* (1978) and *Alaska* (1988). Several of his books were filmed.

'Michigan[1] /ˈmɪʃɪɡən/ a northern US state, also called the Wolverine State and the Great Lakes State, because it is divided into two parts by Lake *Michigan and Lake *Huron, and also has borders with Lake *Superior and Lake *Erie. The largest city is *Detroit, and the capital city is Lansing. Michigan became a state in 1837. Its products include iron and other minerals, cars and cereals (= grains processed as food). Tourists visit the Henry Ford Museum in Dearborn, and Mackinac Island. People who live in the state are called Michiganders.

Lake 'Michigan[2] /ˈmɪʃɪɡən/ one of the *Great Lakes, and the only one completely in the US. It is also the largest lake of fresh water in the US, having an area of 22 300 square miles/57 757 square kilometres. It is linked to Lake *Huron. The states around Lake Michigan are *Michigan, *Wisconsin, *Illinois and *Indiana. Cities on the lake include *Chicago and *Milwaukee. In 1997 oil was discovered under the lake.

Mickey 'Mouse™ a famous cartoon character created by Walt *Disney, who called him 'the mouse that built an empire'. Mickey has become the symbol of the company and his high voice was spoken by Disney himself. He was first seen in *Steamboat Willie* (1928). Mickey's girlfriend is Minnie Mouse and his dog is Pluto. In 1929 Disney began Mickey Mouse Clubs in large shops and cinemas. *The Mickey Mouse Club* was also a popular Disney television programme (1955–59). The children on it wore mouse ears and were called Mouseketeers. In each programme they sang a song that spelled out Mickey's name. Compare DONALD DUCK.

'Microsoft /ˈmaɪkrəsɒft; *AmE* ˈmaɪkrəsɔːft/ the US computer company that produces a large proportion of the computer software in the world. It was established in 1974 by Bill *Gates and Paul Allen. In 1980, the company adapted a system to operate personal computers made by *IBM, and in 1985 it developed the *Windows system.

the **Mid-At'lantic 'states** /ət'læntɪk/ the name given to five eastern US states between *New England and the South. They are *New York, *New Jersey, *Pennsylvania, *Delaware and *Maryland. All are on the Atlantic coast except Pennsylvania.

the **Middle 'Ages** *n* [pl] (in European history) the period between about 1000 and about 1450. It is associated with the *Crusades and *feudalism, and is thought of as a period when the Christian Church was very powerful. Some people also think of it as a period when there was little cultural or social development, but it produced important works of literature such as

M

*Chaucer's *Canterbury Tales*, and many beautiful churches in the *Romanesque and *Gothic styles.

,Middle A'merica /ə'merɪkə/ **1** *middle-class Americans, who usually have traditional values and are politically moderate or conservative. Compare MIDDLE ENGLAND.
2 another name for the *Middle West.
3 the part of North America south of the US, including Mexico, Central America and sometimes the West Indies.

the ,middle 'class *n* [C+sing/pl *v*] the social class between the *working class and the upper class. It consists of people who are generally regarded as having an average status, education, income, etc. in society. In Britain, the middle class is often divided into the upper middle class and the lower middle class.
▶ **middle-class** *adj*.

,Middle 'England *n* [U] British people who have traditional opinions about politics and society, especially *middle-class people living in the south of England: *The government needs to convince Middle England that its policies are working.* Compare MIDDLE AMERICA(1).

▶ **Middle English**

From the 12th century Middle English replaced *Norman French as the most widely spoken language in England but, until the 14th century, French and Latin were used in government and law, and by writers of literature. Middle English developed from *Old English, the language used in England before the Norman Conquest and spoken by the common people throughout the Norman period.

By the time English reappeared as a literary language it had gone through various changes. The grammar was simpler, with fewer inflections, and the vocabulary had gained many French and Latin words. Some Old English words had disappeared, while others remained beside those of French or Latin origin, e.g. *freedom* and *liberty*. Compared with Old English, many more words of Middle English can be understood by speakers of modern English. However, the range of styles and spellings in surviving literature suggest that there was no single way of writing Middle English. The ancient letters, called *runes*, found in Old English soon ceased to be used, with only the thorn (þ) surviving into the 15th century. There were also changes to pronunciation, especially the pronunciation of vowels. Long, stressed vowels were formerly pronounced similarly to those in other European languages, for example the 'i' in *fine* was originally pronounced /i:/ but in late Middle English it became /aɪ/. This change came to be known as the **great vowel shift** and was a significant feature in the development of modern English.

The most important author who wrote in Middle English was Geoffrey *Chaucer. His most famous work, partly in verse and partly in prose, is The *Canterbury Tales* (c. 1387) in which he introduces a varied group of people on a pilgrimage to *Canterbury. The following passage introduces the Miller:

The Miller was a stout carl, for the nones,
Ful big he was of braun, and eek of bones;
That proved wel, for over-al ther he cam,
At wrastling he wolde have alwey the ram.
He was short-sholdred, brood, a thikke knarre,
Ther nas no dore that he nolde heve of harre,
Or breke it, at a renning, with his heed.
(The Miller was a stout ruffian, believe me, very muscular and big-boned. That was well-tested because he towered over all present and in wrestling he would always win the ram. He was a short-necked, broad, thickset fellow and there was no door he couldn't take off its hinge or break with his head at a run.)

Other famous Middle English works include William Langland's *Piers Plowman*, and Sir *Gawain and the Green Knight*, a poem by an unknown author about the adventures of one of King *Arthur's knights.

The first English printing press was set up in London by William *Caxton in 1476. One of the earliest books he printed was *The Canterbury Tales*. Caxton printed over 100 books, many of them by English authors, and so helped spread the literature of the period among a greater number of people.

'Middlemarch /'mɪdlmɑːtʃ; AmE 'mɪdlmɑːrtʃ/ a novel (1871–2) by George *Eliot, widely considered to be one of the greatest English novels. Its subtitle is *A Study of Provincial Life* and it presents a detailed picture of the attitudes and behaviour of a number of people in the imaginary *middle-class town of Middlemarch.

the ,middle 'passage the journey across the Atlantic by ship as part of the slave trade. Ships travelled from Britain to Africa, where the slaves were bought and then taken to be sold in America or the West Indies. Conditions on the journey were terrible and many slaves died during it. ⇨ note at SLAVERY.

'middle school *n* **1** (in England and Wales) a type of state school for children aged 9–13. The name is also given to the classes for children aged 14–15 at a secondary school (for children aged 11–18).
2 (in some places in the US) a type of school for children between finishing *elementary school and starting *high school.

'Middlesex /'mɪdlseks/ a former county to the northwest of London until 1965, when it became part of *Greater London. The name is still used in postal addresses and in the names of some organizations.

the ,Middlesex 'Hospital /,mɪdlseks/ a large *teaching hospital in central London, England. It was established in 1745.

the ,Middle 'West (also the ,Mid'west) the northern central region of the US. It is considered to be between the *Rocky Mountains and the eastern borders of *Illinois or *Ohio, and from the *Great Lakes to the *Ohio River and the southern borders of *Kansas and *Missouri. It is rich farming land. People living in the Middle West are thought to be traditional and conservative. See also MIDDLE AMERICA(2).

the 'Midlands /'mɪdləndz/ the central region of England, consisting of the counties of *Derbyshire, *Leicestershire, *Northamptonshire, *Nottinghamshire, *Staffordshire, *Warwickshire, *Herefordshire, *Worcestershire and the *metropolitan county of *West Midlands. Its biggest cities are *Birmingham and *Coventry. In the 19th and 20th centuries it was an important industrial region.

,Bette 'Midler /,bet 'mɪdlə(r)/ (1945–) a US singer and comic actor. She is small and enthusiastic and makes rude jokes about sex. She is sometimes called the Divine Miss M, which was the title of her first album (1973). Her films have included *Down and Out in Beverly Hills* (1986) and *The First Wives Club* (1996). She won an *Emmy in 1997 for her television programme *Bette Midler: Diva Las Vegas*.

,Midnight 'Cowboy a US film (1969) that won an *Oscar as Best Picture. It was directed by the English director John *Schlesinger, who also received an Oscar. The story is from a novel by James Leo Herlihy. It is about a young man from *Texas, played by John Voight, who goes to New York and becomes a male prostitute.

A ,Midsummer Night's 'Dream a comedy play by William *Shakespeare which takes place in a wood near Athens. The story involves three groups of characters in a mixture of magic and reality. *Oberon, the king of the fairies, is angry with his wife *Titania, and tells his servant *Puck to play a trick on her, so that she falls in love with *Bottom, one of a group of workers who are practising a play they are going to perform for the Athenian court. Bottom's head is changed into that of an ass. Puck also plays magic tricks on a group of young lovers with comic results, until everything is put right and the play ends with wedding celebrations and the performance of the workers' play.

'**Midtown** /'mɪdtaʊn/ the centre or shopping area of a US city. The best-known is Midtown *Manhattan(1) in New York.

the **Mid'west** ⇨ MIDDLE WEST.

'Ludwig '**Mies van der** '**Rohe** /'lʊdvɪg 'miːs væn də 'rəʊə; AmE dər 'rəʊə/ (1886–1969) a US architect, born in Germany, who was known for his glass and steel *skyscrapers (= very tall buildings). He helped to develop modern architecture and is considered one of the major architects of the 20th century. He used simple designs and said 'less is more'. The buildings in the US which he designed include the Lakeshore Drive Apartments in *Chicago (1948–51) and, with Philip Johnson, the Seagram Building in New York (1954–58). He also designed furniture.

MI5 /ˌem aɪ 'faɪv/ the former name (still used, though not officially) of the British government department responsible for state security within Britain. MI5 is short for Military Intelligence section 5. Its main activities used to involve protecting British military secrets and catching foreign spies. Since the early 1990s, it has been mainly responsible for collecting information about and dealing with terrorism.

MI5 was a very secret organization until the early 1990s, when more information about its activities was made known to the public. Its official name is the Security Service. Compare MI6

The **Mi'kado** /mɪ'kɑːdəʊ; AmE mɪ'kɑːdoʊ/ a comic opera (1885) by W S *Gilbert and Arthur *Sullivan, one of their *Savoy Operas. It takes place in a town in Japan called Titipu and contains many well-known songs, including *Three Little Maids from School* and *A Wandering Minstrel, I.* The Mikado himself is the emperor of Japan.

mild *n* [U] a type of English beer, darker and with a milder flavour than *bitter. Mild used to be very popular in pubs but is now less often drunk. ⇨ note at BEER.

ˌ**Milford** '**Haven** /ˌmɪlfəd; AmE ˌmɪlfərd/ a town on the south-west coast of Wales. It has a natural harbour and for many centuries was the place from which English armies crossed the *Irish Sea to Ireland. In the second half of the 20th century it became a port for oil because the deep waters there made it suitable for very large ships transporting oil.

the ˌ**Militant** '**Tendency** an extreme left-wing group within the *Labour Party in Britain, formed in the 1960s with policies based on Trotskyism. It began to gain influence in some *constituencies and *trade unions in the early 1980s, when it also controlled the city council in *Liverpool. The group did a lot of damage to the reputation of the Labour Party, and in the mid 1980s the Labour leader Neil *Kinnock forced its members to leave the party. Since then it has had little real influence.

the ˌ**Military** '**Cross** (abbr **MC**) a medal given to British army officers for brave actions. It was created in 1914.

the ˌ**Military** '**Medal** (abbr **MM**) a medal given to soldiers in the British army below the rank of officers, for brave actions. It was created in 1916.

'**milkman** *n* (pl **milkmen**) a man who goes from house to house every day delivering milk. There are no longer any milkmen in the US and demand for them in Britain has fallen because most people now buy their milk from supermarkets. In Britain, milkmen do their deliveries

early in the morning. In towns and cities they travel in vehicles that use electrical power, called **milk floats**. The milk is usually delivered in glass bottles and left outside the front door of the customer's house. Milkmen are generally thought of as cheerful, friendly people.

ˌ**Milk of Mag'nesia™** /mæg'niːʃə/ *n* [U] a white medicine, in the form of tablets or liquid, for treating stomach problems such as indigestion.

ˌ**Milky** '**Way™** *n* **1** (in Britain) a chocolate bar with a soft, light centre. For many years it was advertised as 'the sweet you can eat between meals without ruining your appetite'.
2 (in the US) a chocolate bar with a soft, light centre and caramel inside it. In Britain it is sold as a *Mars Bar.

'**John** '**Stuart** '**Mill** /'mɪl/ (1806–73) an English philosopher whose ideas had a great influence on modern thought. His best-known works include *On Liberty* (1859), in which he argued that people should be free to do what they want if this does not harm others, and *Utilitarianism* (1863), in which he explained and supported the theory that actions are morally right if they lead to happiness. He criticized the way in which married women were treated at the time.

'**John** '**Everett** '**Millais** /'evərɪt 'mɪleɪ/ (1829–96) one of the original members of the group of British artists known as the *Pre-Raphaelites. His most famous paintings include *Christ in the House of His Parents* (1850), *Ophelia* (1852) and *The Blind Girl* (1856), all of which have the realistic detail characteristic of the Pre-Raphaelites. Later in life, he painted more sentimental pictures, such as *Bubbles*. He was the first painter to be made a *baronet, in 1885.

'**Edna St** '**Vincent** '**Millay** /seɪnt 'vɪnsnt mɪ'leɪ/ (1892–1950) a US poet who wrote romantic poems. Her collections include *The Harp-Weaver and Other Poems* (1922), which won the *Pulitzer Prize, and *Conversation at Midnight* (1937). She also wrote three verse plays.

'**Millbank** /'mɪlbæŋk/ a road in central London along the north bank of the River *Thames. Part of the *Houses of Parliament(2) is at one end of it and *Tate Britain is towards the other end. **Millbank Tower**, a modern office building on Millbank, was the headquarters of the British *Labour Party from 1998 to 2001.

the ˌ**Mil**ˌ**lennium Com'mission** an independent organization set up by the British government to organize events to celebrate the end of the 20th century and the beginning of the 21st century. It was responsible for building the *Millennium Dome. A *millennium* is a period of 1 000 years.

the ˌ**Mil**ˌ**lennium** '**Dome** a very large structure, in the shape of a dome (= a building with a round roof) that was built near *Greenwich, an area of south London. It cost £700 million to build and was designed by Richard *Rogers, a well-known British architect. The Dome is 50 metres high and is the largest structure of its kind in the world. It was open to the public in the year 2000 with an exhibition on various subjects, for

the Millennium Dome

M

example, work, travel, religion, money, the environment and life in Britain. Some people thought that it cost too much and that there were more important projects to spend such a large amount of money on. The Dome is now owned by a private company.

the ‚Mil‚lennium 'Stadium a large sports stadium in *Cardiff which opened in 1999. It is where many important British sporting events, especially football and Rugby matches, are held as well as events such as pop concerts. The stadium has seats for 74 500 people and a roof which can be opened and closed.

‚Arthur 'Miller¹ /'mɪlə(r)/ (1915–2005) a US writer of plays. They include *Death of a Salesman and A View from the Bridge (1955), both of which won the *Pulitzer Prize. In The Crucible (1953) he used the story of the *Salem witch trials as a symbol of *McCarthyism, which he strongly opposed. Miller was married to Marilyn *Monroe from 1955 to 1961 and wrote her last film, The Misfits (1961), which is the subject of Miller's later play Finishing the Picture (2004).

> **66** A good newspaper, I suppose, is a nation talking to itself. **99**
> Arthur Miller

‚Glenn 'Miller² /'mɪlə(r)/ (1904–44) the US leader of a popular *big band which played *swing music in the late 1930s and early 1940s. He also wrote music and played the trombone. His band's successes included his theme tune Moonlight Serenade (1938), which he wrote, and In the Mood (1939), Pennsylvania 6–5000 (1940) and Chattanooga Choo-Choo (1941). Miller joined the US Army Air Force as its band leader during *World War II and was killed when the plane he was travelling in crashed on a flight from England to France.

‚Henry 'Miller³ /'mɪlə(r)/ (1891–1980) a US author whose work had an important influence on the writers of the *beat generation. His early books, Tropic of Cancer (1934) and Tropic of Capricorn (1939), published in Paris, were banned in Britain and the US for many years because of their detailed descriptions of sex. His other books included the series of three, together called The Rosy Crucifixion (1949–60).

‚Jonathan 'Miller⁴ /'mɪlə(r)/ (1934–) a leading figure in the arts in Britain. He is now known mainly for directing plays and operas, but he first became famous as a performer in the satirical comedy show *Beyond the Fringe in the early 1960s. He originally trained as a doctor and used this knowledge to make the popular *BBC television series The Body in Question (1978), in which he explained medical matters in a way that ordinary people could understand.

‚Max 'Miller⁵ /'mɪlə(r)/ (1895–1963) an English comedian who was extremely popular in Britain, especially during the 1940s and 1950s. He was famous for telling rather rude jokes and was widely known by his nickname, 'The Cheeky Chappie'.

‚Kate 'Millett /'mɪlɪt/ (1934–) a US writer and feminist (= person who believes strongly that women should have the same rights and opportunities as men). Her book Sexual Politics (1970) was a major influence on women's campaign for equal rights. Her other books include Flying (1974), The Prostitution Papers (1976) and The Loony Bin Trip (1991), about her mental problems.

‚Spike 'Milligan /‚spaɪk 'mɪlɪgən/ (1918–2002) a British comedian and writer, born in India. He first became famous as one of the stars of The *Goon Show, much of which he also wrote, in the 1950s. He later appeared in a number of television series of his own. Milligan also wrote children's books, poetry, comic novels and humorous books based on his experiences in the British army in

*World War II. His crazy and original style of humour has had a great influence on British comedy.

The ‚Mill on the 'Floss /'flɒs; AmE 'flɔːs/ a novel (1860) by George *Eliot. It is mainly about the relationship between a brother and sister, Tom and Maggie Tulliver, who live in a mill (= a building where grain is ground into flour) on the river Floss. It describes their childhood and a dispute that causes them to separate. The book ends with them happily together again but they are both killed in a flood.

‚Mills & 'Boon™ /‚mɪlz ˌ'buːn/ the best-known British publishing company of romantic fiction, started in 1908. The stories are usually about a young woman who, after many problems, marries the man she considers perfect for her. People sometimes make fun of the books because the stories are very similar and characters in them often seem very innocent, but they are extremely popular and sell in very large quantities: The story of her youthful affair with a Russian prince reads like a Mills and Boon romance.

‚A A 'Milne /‚eɪ eɪ 'mɪln/ (Alan Alexander Milne 1882–1956) an English writer of children's books, known mainly as the person who created *Winnie-the-Pooh. The books in which Pooh appears, Winnie-the-Pooh (1926) and The House at Pooh Corner (1928), came from stories Milne invented for his son Christopher Robin. He also wrote collections of poetry for children, including When We Were Very Young (1924) and Now We Are Six (1927). All of these are still very popular with children today. Milne also wrote plays, including *Toad of Toad Hall (1929), adapted from The *Wind in the Willows by Kenneth *Grahame.

‚John 'Milton /'mɪltən/ (1608–74) one of the most famous of all English poets. He is best known for his great poem *Paradise Lost, which he completed in 1667. This was based on the Old Testament story of the Garden of Eden, and its central character is Satan. It was followed by Paradise Regained and Samson Agonistes, published together in 1671. His earlier works of poetry included L'Allegro and Il Penseroso (both 1631) and Lycidas (1638), and he also wrote political articles supporting Parliament against the king, and the freedom of the press.

‚Milton 'Keynes /‚mɪltən 'kiːnz/ the largest of Britain's *new towns, created in the 1960s in *Buckinghamshire. Many people and businesses were persuaded to move there and it has become a prosperous town. In spite of this, British people sometimes make fun of it as a town that has been artificially created. It also contains the headquarters of the *Open University.

Mil'waukee /mɪl'wɔːki/ the largest city in the US state of *Wisconsin. It is an industrial port on the western shore of Lake *Michigan. Many Germans settled there in the second half of the 19th century, and it is still well

Milwaukee

known for its beer and German foods. It also produces machinery and medical instruments.

MIND /maɪnd/ a British charity that works to help mentally ill people. It collects money for them, gives advice to them and their families, and aims to make people more aware of their problems. It was established in 1946 as the National Association for Mental Health, and changed its name in 1971.

'miners' strikes occasions on which British coal miners have gone on strike, causing major problems for the government. In 1972 the *NUM called a strike for wage increases, after a vote by its members. There were power cuts (= interruptions in the supply of electricity) all over Britain, a state of emergency was announced, and the miners won, gaining a large pay increase. In 1974 the miners again voted for a national strike and the *Conservative *Prime Minister Edward *Heath called a general election on the issue of whether the government or the miners had more power in the country. The Conservatives lost the election, and the new *Labour government gave the miners a big pay increase, ending the strike. In 1984–5 the miners went on strike again because the National Coal Board, which was in charge of all British mines at the time, planned to close several mines, with the loss of over 20 000 jobs. The strike was seen by the Conservative Prime Minister, Margaret *Thatcher, as a test of the new industrial relations laws, which were aimed at reducing the power of trade unions. There was a lot of violence between the miners and the police during the strike, but as it continued more and more miners returned to work, and finally it ended without any agreement being reached. The government therefore won and the National Union of Miners lost. Since then, most of the mines have closed and many miners have lost their jobs. See also SCARGILL.

,Anthony **Min'ghella** /mɪŋ'gelə/ (1954–) an English film director whose films include *The English Patient* (1996), which won nine *Oscars including one for best director, *The Talented Mr Ripley* (1999) and *Cold Mountain* (2003).

,Charles **'Mingus** /'mɪŋgəs/ (1922–79) a US *jazz musician. He played the bass and wrote music for it. His works included *Fables of Faubus* (1959) and *Epitaph* (1962). He was active in the *civil rights movement and wrote the story of his life, *Beneath the Underdog* (1971).

'**Mini**™ *n* the name of a series of small British cars. The Mini, which was designed by Alec Issigonis (1906–88) and first produced in 1959, became the most successful British car of all time. Several versions of a newly designed Mini are now made in *Oxford by the German company BMW.

the ,**Ministry of De'fence** (*abbr* the **MOD**) the British government department in charge of the armed forces. It was established in 1964, when the *Admiralty, the *War Office and the Air Ministry were joined together. It is in *Whitehall and the title of its head is *Secretary of State for Defence.

the ,**Ministry of 'Sound** a well-known nightclub in London, England. It opened in 1991 and is popular with young people for its modern dance music.

the ,**Ministry of 'Transport test** ⇨ MOT.

,**Minne'apolis** /,mɪni'æpəlɪs/ the largest city in the US state of *Minnesota. It is an industrial port near the northern end of the *Mississippi River. The river separates it from *St Paul, Minnesota, and they are together called the 'twin cities'. Minneapolis was settled in 1847 and became a town in 1867. It is an agricultural centre for the northern *Middle West. Other companies there make computers and provide health services.

,Liza **Min'nelli** /,laɪzə mɪ'neli/ (1946–) a US singer, dancer and actor. She was especially popular in the 1970s. She won an *Oscar for her part in the film *Cabaret* (1972), and her other films have included *New York New York* (1977) and *Arthur* (1981). Minnelli is the daughter of Judy *Garland and the director Vincente Minnelli.

,**Minne'sota** /,mɪnɪ'səʊtə; *AmE* ,mɪnɪ'soʊtə/ a state in the northern central US on the Canadian border. It has more than 10 000 lakes, and is also called the North Star State and the Gopher State. The largest city is *Minneapolis and the capital city is *St Paul. It became a

state in 1858. Minnesota produces 75% of the country's iron ore (= rock), as well as agricultural products, machinery and computers. The *Mayo Clinic, a famous medical centre, is in Rochester. Tourists visit Voyageurs National Park and the St Paul Winter Carnival.

'**Minnesota 'Mining and Manu'facturing ,Company** /'mɪnɪsəʊtə; *AmE* 'mɪnɪsoʊtə/ ⇨ 3M.

,**Minnie 'Mouse**™ /,mɪni/ ⇨ MICKEY MOUSE.

,**Kylie Mi'nogue** /,kaɪli mɪ'nəʊg; *AmE* mɪ'noʊg/ (1968–) an Australian singer and actor who lives in Britain. She first became known when she appeared in the Australian *soap opera, *Neighbours*. Her career as a pop singer began in the late 1980s and her first 13 singles reached the top ten in the UK music charts. Her records include *Kylie* (1988), *Light Years* (2000) and *Fever* (2001).

mi,nority 'leader the leader of the political party that has a minority (= fewer members than the largest party) in the US Senate or US House of Representatives. He or she organizes the party's members and their programme of new laws. Compare MAJORITY LEADER.

,**mint 'julep** /'dʒuːlɪp/ (*also* **julep**) *n* an alcoholic drink, especially popular during the summer in the southern states of the US. It usually consists of *bourbon, sugar and crushed ice, served in a tall glass with peppermint leaves on top. A mint julep is the traditional drink at the *Kentucky Derby.

'**Minton**™ /'mɪntən/ *n* [U] high-quality English pottery and china. Until 1992 it was made at the factory in *Stoke-on-Trent established by Thomas Minton (1765–1836). He is thought to have designed the famous *willow pattern.

'**Minuteman** /'mɪnɪtmaen/ *n* (*pl* **-men**) (*AmE*) **1** a member of a group of American citizens during the *American Revolution who fought when they were needed. They said they were ready to fight with only a minute's warning. Minutemen from *Massachusetts fought at the battles of *Lexington and Concord at the start of the war, and similar groups were also formed in *Connecticut, *New Hampshire and *Maryland. **2** a US nuclear missile, developed during the *Cold War.

'**miracle play** (*also* '**mystery play**) *n* any of a number of religious plays from the Middle Ages based on stories from the Bible or on the lives of saints. In Britain these were usually performed by guilds (= associations of skilled workers in Britain in the Middle Ages) in the streets of towns. Miracle plays are still performed today in the towns of *York, *Chester, *Coventry and Wakefield in West Yorkshire.

'**Miramax** /'mɪrəmæks/ a US company that produces films and distributes films to cinemas. It was started by Harvey and Robert Weinstein in 1979 to distribute independent films not considered commercial by the big film companies. The company was bought by the *Walt Disney Company in 1993 but is still run independently.

the **Mi'randa de,cision** /mɪ'rændə/ an important decision affecting police procedures which was reached in 1966 by the US *Supreme Court on the case of *Miranda v Arizona*. It said that people who are arrested for a crime must be informed of their rights under the US Constitution. These are the right not to answer questions and the right to have a lawyer. They must also be told that anything they say can be used against them in court. These rights are often called **Miranda rights**. See also DUE PROCESS OF LAW, FIFTH AMENDMENT.

'**Helen ,Mirren** /'mɪrən/ (1945–) an English theatre, television and film actor who is best known for her role as a female detective in the television series *Prime Suspect*. Her films include *The Madness of King George* (1994), *Gosford Park* (2001) and *Calendar Girls* (2003). She was made a *Dame in 2003.

M

the **'Mirror** one of Britain's national daily newspapers, formerly called the *Daily Mirror*. It was started in 1903 by Alfred *Harmsworth, who later became Lord *Northcliffe, as a newspaper for women. At first it was not a success, but it became very successful when it was made the world's first daily newspaper with pictures. It suffered badly after being bought in 1984 by Robert *Maxwell. It presents political views that are generally left-wing. The paper has a *tabloid format (= size of page), and is considered to be part of the 'popular press', not one of the 'quality papers'. See also SUNDAY MIRROR.

Mirror Group 'Newspapers (abbr **MGN**) a large newspaper company in Britain, part of Trinity Mirror. It publishes the *Mirror, *Sunday Mirror and The *People.

MI6 /,em aɪ 'sɪks/ the former name (still used, though not officially) of the British government department which operates abroad to gather secret information about other countries. MI6 is an abbreviation of Military Intelligence section 6. Like *MI5, its role changed in the early 1990s and its activities became much less secret. It is now called the Secret Intelligence Service.

the **Miss A'merica pageant** /ə'merɪkə/ a US contest held each September in *Atlantic City, *New Jersey, to choose the most beautiful American woman who can also sing, dance, act, etc. It was first held in 1922 and has been a popular television event since 1954. The pageant has sometimes been criticized as an insult to women.

'Mission Con,trol ⇨ LYNDON B JOHNSON SPACE CENTER.

Missis'sippi /,mɪsɪ'sɪpi/ a southern US state, also called the Magnolia State. Jackson is the largest city and also the capital. Mississippi became a state in 1817 and was one of the *Confederate States. It has had conflicts between the races, especially in the 1960s. Its main product is cotton, but other crops include corn, soya beans, peanuts and rice. Tourists can visit the Vicksburg National Military Park and the historical buildings at *Natchez(2).

a boat on the Mississippi

Missis'sippi mud 'pie /,mɪsɪ'sɪpi/ n a sweet dish that is especially popular with *Cajuns in the US. It is made of chocolate ice cream that is frozen on pastry and covered with meringue (= a mixture of egg whites and sugar baked until crisp).

the **Mississippi 'River** /,mɪsɪsɪpi/ a major river of North America that flows from the US state of *Minnesota to the *Gulf of Mexico. It was called the 'Father of Waters' by *Native Americans. It is 2348 miles/3778 kilometres long and passes the cities of *Minneapolis, *St Louis, *Memphis and *New Orleans. The Missouri River is connected to it, and together they form the third largest river system in the world (3741 miles/6019 kilometres long). The Mississippi is an important transport route and is known for its 19th-century river boats. See also OL' MAN RIVER.

Miss 'Lonelyhearts /'ləʊnlihɑːts; AmE 'loʊnlihɑːrts/ a novel (1933) by the US writer Nathanael *West. It was written during the *Great Depression and is about human suffering. It is the story of a journalist who uses the name Miss Lonelyhearts as the writer of a newspaper column giving advice to readers with personal problems. When he becomes too involved with one of his readers, he is killed. The expression *a lonely hearts column* is sometimes used to mean a regular newspaper feature dealing with people's personal problems.

Mis'souri /mɪ'zʊəri; AmE mɪ'zʊri/ a US state in the *Middle West, also called the Show-Me State and, in former times, the Mother of the West. The largest city is *Kansas City(1) and the capital city is Jefferson City. Missouri was part of the *Louisiana Purchase and became a state in 1821 under the *Missouri Compromise. Its products include grain, beer, lead and aerospace equipment. Among places visited by tourists are the Gateway Arch at *St Louis and the homes of President Harry S *Truman at *Independence and Mark *Twain at Hannibal.

the **Mis,souri 'Compromise** /mɪ,zʊəri; AmE mɪ,zʊri/ the general name for several US laws passed in 1820–1 to end disputes between slave states and free states. Both groups wanted new states to follow their systems. According to the Compromise, *Missouri joined the Union as a slave state and *Maine as a free state. It also declared that slaves would not be allowed in the northern part of the *Louisiana Purchase. It was replaced in 1854 by the *Kansas-Nebraska Act.

MIT /,em aɪ 'tiː/ (in full **Massachusetts Institute of Technology**) a US university known especially for its science courses and research. It was established in 1861 in *Boston and moved in 1916 to *Cambridge, *Massachusetts, close to *Harvard University. It is considered to be one of the best science and technology universities in the world.

Warren 'Mitchell /'mɪtʃəl/ (1926–) an English actor best known for playing the role of Alf *Garnett in the television comedy series *Till Death Us Do Part. He has also been successful in the theatre.

Robert 'Mitchum /'mɪtʃəm/ (1917–97) a US actor who often played tough characters. He was noted for his relaxed style and for not taking his work too seriously. He made more than 125 films but once said, 'Movies bore me, especially my own.' His films include *The Story of GI Joe* (1945), *The Night of the Hunter* (1955), *Ryan's Daughter* (1971) and *Farewell My Lovely* (1975), in which he played the character Philip *Marlowe.

'Mitford /'mɪtfəd; AmE 'mɪtfərd/ the family name of six sisters, four of whom became famous for various reasons.

Nancy Mitford (1904–73) wrote humorous novels about girls in *upper-class families, including *The Pursuit of Love* (1945) and *Love in a Cold Climate* (1949). In 1956 she wrote an article in which she used the expressions *U and *non-U to describe language and behaviour that was or was not acceptable to upper-class people, and these expressions became part of the language.

Jessica Mitford (1917–96) also became a writer, well known for her extreme left-wing political views. She wrote *Hons and Rebels* (1960) about the lives of herself and her sisters as children. She later lived in the US, where her books included *The American Way of Death* (1963), about the US funeral industry.

Diana Mitford (1916–2003) and **Unity Mitford** (1914–48) became known for their fascist sympathies. Diana married the English fascist leader Oswald *Mosley in 1936 and Unity became a close friend of Adolf Hitler.

Walter 'Mitty /'mɪti/ the main character in a well-known story by James *Thurber, *The Secret Life of Walter Mitty* (1942). He escapes from his sad, ordinary life by imagining that he is a much more interesting person than he really is and does much more exciting and important things than he actually does. The name is now sometimes used of a person who lives in an imaginary world like this: *He's a real Walter Mitty character, daydreaming the whole time.*

Tom 'Mix /'mɪks/ (1880–1940) a US actor in more than 400 silent *westerns. He was the first 'King of the Cowboys' and was one of *Hollywood's richest actors in the 1920s. He wore white clothes and a white hat, and was an excellent rider. His films included *Riders of the Purple Sage* (1925) and *The Last Trail* (1927). Mix toured the country with his own circus in the 1930s. He died in a car crash.

MLB /ˌem el 'biː/ ⇨ MAJOR LEAGUE BASEBALL.

MLS /ˌem el 'es/ ⇨ MAJOR LEAGUE SOCCER.

M'lud /məˈlʌd/ the way a judge is addressed in a British court of law. It is a form of 'My Lord': *I wish to call another witness, M'lud.*

MM /ˌem 'em/ ⇨ MILITARY MEDAL.

the ˌBattle of Mo'bile 'Bay /məʊˈbiːl; AmE moʊˈbiːl/ a US Navy victory on 5 August 1864 during the *Civil War. The US sent 18 ships against 4 ships of the Confederate Navy in Mobile Bay at Mobile, *Alabama. The bay was also protected by three forts and by containers filled with explosive (called 'torpedoes') that floated in the water. Admiral David Farragut led the successful US attack with the famous remark: 'Damn the torpedoes! Full speed ahead!'.

Moby-'Dick /ˌməʊbi 'dɪk; AmE ˌmoʊbi/ a famous novel about the sea (1851) by the US writer Herman *Melville. It is the story of Captain Ahab's strong desire to find and kill Moby-Dick, a great white whale that had once bitten off his leg. Many people remember the book's first words: 'Call me Ishmael.' Film versions were made in 1926 and 1930, both with John *Barrymore as Ahab, and in 1956, with Gregory *Peck.

'mockingbird *n* a bird that lives mostly in the southern US. It can copy the calls of other birds and even the sounds made by people, dogs and chickens. Many people believe it is morally wrong to kill one, and this idea was used in the novel *To Kill a Mockingbird*. It is also mentioned in several traditional songs and is the official state bird of *Arkansas, *Florida, *Mississippi, *Tennessee and *Texas.

MOD /ˌem əʊ 'diː; AmE oʊ/ ⇨ MINISTRY OF DEFENCE.

mod *n* a young person, especially in Britain in the 1960s, of a group following a fashion of smart modern clothes. Mods had short, neat hair, rode scooters (= small motorcycles) and liked *soul music. Their rivals were the *rockers. Large groups of mods and rockers used to gather at seaside towns on *bank holidays and fight each other.

the ˌModel 'Parliament the name later given to the English parliament set up in 1295 by King *Edward I. It was the first to include not only members of the clergy and the *aristocracy but also elected members to represent ordinary people. In this way it established the pattern for future parliaments.

Model 'T /'tiː/ the first car produced on an assembly line (= a line of workers who build something as it moves along on a belt) and sold at a price that ordinary people could afford. Its popular name was the 'Tin Lizzie' and it was made by the Ford Motor Company

between 1908 and 1927. There is a joke that Henry *Ford told customers they could have the car in any colour as long as it was black. About 15 million Model Ts were produced before it was replaced by the Model A.

'Moderator of the 'Church of 'Scotland /'skɒtlənd; AmE 'skɑːtlənd/ the minister elected to be president for one year of the *General Assembly of the Church of Scotland.

ˌModern 'Times a comedy film (1936) which Charlie *Chaplin wrote and directed as well as acting the main part. It was the last time he used his 'Little Tramp' character. The film is an attack on the use of machines in modern factories and the bad treatment of factory workers.

'Mohawk /'məʊhɔːk; AmE 'moʊhɑːk/ *n* (*pl* **Mohawks** or **Mohawk**) a member of a *Native American people who live mostly in New York State and Ontario, Canada. They were part of the *Iroquois League, and tradition says that *Hiawatha was their leader. They originally lived in New York State in the Mohawk Valley along the Mohawk River, and they helped the British during the *American Revolution. Mohawks are known today as excellent steel workers who help to construct skyscrapers (= very tall buildings).

the Mo'jave 'Desert (*also* **Mohave Desert**) /məʊˌhɑːvi; AmE moʊˌhɑːvi/ a desert in south-eastern *California consisting of low, bare hills and wide, flat valleys. Its area is about 15000 square miles/38850 square kilometres. *Death Valley is at the northern end and the Joshua Tree National Monument at the southern end. The Mojave Desert is part of the Great Basin region that covers parts of *California, *Nevada, *Utah, *Oregon and *Idaho.

ˌAdrian 'Mole /'məʊl; AmE 'moʊl/ the main character in a series of books by the English writer Sue Townsend. He is a teenage boy in the first books and they are in the form of his diary, in which he describes his life, thoughts and problems. They became very popular because they describe in a humorous way the attitudes and worries typical of boys of that age. The books are *The Secret Diary of Adrian Mole – Aged 13¾* (1982), *The Growing Pains of Adrian Mole* (1984), *The Wilderness Years* (1993), *The Cappuccino Years* (1999) and *Adrian Mole and the Weapons of Mass Destruction* (2004). The first book was also made into a stage *musical.

> 66 I have decided to keep a full journal, in the hope that my life will perhaps seem more interesting when it is written down. 99
> Adrian Mole

ˌMoll 'Flanders /mɒl 'flɑːndəz; AmE ˌmɑːl 'flɑːndərz/ a novel (1722) by Daniel *Defoe. The full title is *The Fortunes and Misfortunes of the Famous Moll Flanders*. It takes the form of an autobiography in which Moll Flanders looks back on a life full of adventures, with many marriages and love affairs, as well as time spent in prison for various crimes.

MOMA /'məʊmə; AmE 'moʊmə/ ⇨ MUSEUM OF MODERN ART.

ˌmom-and-'pop *adj* [only before noun] (*AmE old-fashioned informal*) (of a small business, etc.) owned and operated by a small family, often just a married couple: *a mom-and-pop cafe/stand/store.*

The ˌMonarch of the 'Glen (1851) the best-known painting by the English artist Edwin *Landseer. It is of an adult male deer in the Scottish countryside, and is often reproduced on cards and other products.

the 'Monday Club a club formed in 1961 by right-wing members of the British *Conservative Party. Some of its views, especially those concerning immigration into Britain, have been controversial. Its name comes from the fact that its meetings were originally held on Mondays.

,Monday morning 'quarterback /ˈkwɔːtəbæk; AmE ˈkwɔːrtərbæk/ n (AmE rather disapproving) a person who gives opinions and criticism about events, decisions, etc. only after they have happened. The expression comes from the fact that most US professional football games are on a Sunday, and people only get together to discuss them on the following day. A quarterback is the football player who makes decisions for his team during a game.

,Monday Night 'Football a US television programme on *ABC which shows a professional football game each Monday night during the National Football League season. It began in 1970 and is the oldest evening sports programme on US television and the most popular.

M-1 visa /ˌem ˈwʌn ˌviːzə/ a US official government document that gives permission to enter the US to foreign students who want to study on a course which is practical rather than academic, such as one which teaches the skills for a particular job. ⇨ F-1 VISA.

▶ **money**

The US **dollar** is made up of 100 cents. The *Department of the Treasury prints **bills** (= paper money) in various **denominations** (= values): $1, $2, $5, $10, $20, $50 and $100. US bills are all the same size, whatever their value, and measure about 2×6 inches/6.5×15.5 centimetres. All are green and are sometimes called **greenbacks**. On the front, each has a picture of a famous American. The **dollar bill**, for instance, shows George *Washington, the first US president. An informal name for dollars is **bucks**, because in the early period of US history people traded the skins of bucks (= deer) and prices would sometimes be given as a number of buckskins. Buck refers to the dollar itself, and not to the bill. So although you can say 'He earns 500 bucks a week', you have to say 'If I give you four quarters could you give me a dollar bill?'

The Treasury also makes US coins: **pennies** which are worth .01 of a dollar, **nickels** (.05), **dimes** (.10) and **quarters** (.25). There are also **half-dollars** (.50) and **silver dollars** but these are not often seen. Pennies have a dark brown colour; all the other coins have a silver appearance.

When you write an amount in figures the **dollar sign** ($) goes to the left of the amount and a decimal point (.) is placed between the dollars and the **cents** (= hundredths of a dollar). If the amount is less than one dollar, the **cent sign** (¢) is put after the numbers. So you write $5, $5.62 and 62¢.

Britain's currency is the **pound sterling**, written as **£** before a figure. A pound consists of 100 **pence**, written as **p** with figures. Pound coins are round and gold-coloured. They have the Queen's head on one side and one of four designs, English, Scottish, Welsh or Northern Irish, on the other. The £2 coin is silver-coloured with a gold edge. Coins of lower value are the silver-coloured 50p, 20p, 10p and 5p **pieces**, and the copper-coloured 2p and 1p pieces. All are round, except for the 50p and 20p pieces which have seven curved sides. Coins are made at the *Royal Mint. Paper **notes** (not bills), which have the Queen's head on one side and a famous person, e.g. Charles *Dickens, on the other, are worth £5, £10, £20 or £50.

A pound is informally called a **quid**, a £5 note is a **fiver**, a £10 note is a **tenner**. Scottish **banknotes** have their own designs. They can be used anywhere in Britain, though shops can legally refuse to accept them. To pre-

vent people **forging** (= making their own) paper money, designs are complicated and difficult to copy. To check that a note is genuine, a shop assistant may hold it up to the light to see if it has a narrow silver thread running through it.

The **decimal system** now in use in Britain replaced the old **pounds, shilling** and **pence**, or *LSD system in 1971. Formerly British money was in pounds, shillings and pence. There were 12 pence or **pennies** in a **shilling**, and 20 shillings in a pound. The old coins included the **farthing** (= a quarter of a penny) and the **half-crown** (= two shillings and sixpence). There were notes for 10 shillings, £1 and £5.

Gold **guinea** coins were used in the 18th century and were worth 21 shillings. Until 1971 prices were often set in guineas instead of pounds for luxury items, such as antiques and jewellery, for the fees of doctors, lawyers, etc., and at auctions, though the guinea coin had long since gone **out of circulation**. Some racehorses are still auctioned in guineas.

On 1 January 1999 the *euro system was introduced in 11 countries of the *European Union. Britain chose not to be part of this first group and no date was fixed for Britain to start using the euro. However, many British businesses have euro bank accounts so as to be able to pay for goods and be paid in euros and many shops in Britain accept payment in euros.

,Monitor and 'Merrimack two ships during the American *Civil War that fought the first battle in history between 'ironclads' (= ships covered with iron). The battle was on 9 March 1862 at Hampton Roads, a channel of water in *Virginia. There was no clear result, showing that such ships were no longer useful in war.

The,lonious 'Monk /θəˌləʊniəs ˈmʌŋk; AmE θəˌloʊniəs/ (1917–82) a US *jazz musician who played the piano and wrote music. He led a big band in the 1960s and helped to develop modern jazz. His albums include Alone in San Francisco (1959) and Monk's Dream (1962). He was chosen for the Jazz *Hall of Fame in 1963.

The 'Monkees /ˈmʌŋkiːz/ a US television comedy and music series on *NBC (1966–70). The Monkees were a pop group created for television as a copy of the *Beatles. Their most successful records included Last Train to Clarksville, I'm A Believer and Daydream Believer.

the ,Duke of 'Monmouth /ˈmɒnməθ; AmE ˈmɑːnməθ/ (born James Scott 1649–85) an illegitimate son of *Charles II who became a *duke in 1663. Powerful people who were against the idea of a *Catholic becoming king after Charles II supported him because he was a Protestant rather than Charle II's brother, the Catholic Duke of York. Charles, however, wanted his brother to become king after him. A short time after James did become king, in 1685, the Duke of Monmouth started a rebellion but received little support. He was defeated at the Battle of *Sedgemoor and had his head cut off. His supporters were very harshly treated by Judge *Jeffreys at the *Bloody Assizes.

Mo'nopoly™ one of the most popular and successful board games ever produced. Players throw dice and move their pieces round a board, buying and building houses on streets that are marked on it. They then charge the other players rent if they land on the streets that they have bought. Players use artificial money and the winner is the player who has all the money at the end.

The game was invented by Charles Darrow in the US in 1933 and the original version used the names of streets in *Atlantic City, *New Jersey. The British version uses London streets, and there are other versions of the game in other countries.

The expression *Monopoly money* is sometimes used to refer in a humorous way to a sum of money that is considered much too high: *Some football clubs pay Monopoly money for players.*

,**James Mon'roe**[1] /mən'rəʊ; *AmE* mən'roʊ/ (1758–1831) the fifth US *President. He is best remembered for the *Monroe Doctrine, which aimed to keep new European interests out of the Americas. He fought in the *American Revolution and helped to establish the Democratic Republican Party. He was elected as a US Senator (1790–94) and twice as governor of *Virginia (1799–1802 and 1811). His time as President was called the 'Era of Good Feeling'. He bought *Florida from Spain in 1819, settled a dispute with Britain over the US–Canadian border, and signed the *Missouri Compromise. See also DEMOCRATIC PARTY.

,**Marilyn Mon'roe**[2] /ˌmærəlɪn mən'rəʊ; *AmE* mən'roʊ/ (1926–62) a US actor who became *Hollywood's most famous sex symbol, though she was often unhappy. Her films include *Niagara* (1952), *Gentlemen Prefer Blondes* (1953), *The Seven Year Itch* (1954), *Bus Stop* (1956), *The Prince and the Showgirl* (1957), *Some Like It Hot* (1959) and *The Misfits* (1961). Her second and third husbands were the *baseball player Joe *DiMaggio and the writer Arthur *Miller. Many books and films have told her story, and the original version of Elton *John's song *Candle in the Wind* was about her. She died, perhaps accidentally, after taking too much medicine to help her sleep. Many people believe she had love affairs with President *Kennedy[5] and his brother Robert *Kennedy.

> 66 I had the radio on. 99
> Marilyn Monroe when asked if she really had nothing on in a photograph

the **Mon,roe 'Doctrine** /mən,rəʊ; *AmE* mən,roʊ/ a declaration of US foreign policy made in 1823 by President James *Monroe. It is one of the most important policies in US history. Monroe said the US would oppose any new European attempts to control countries in the Americas but it would not interfere with European interests already there. The British, who were well established in the New World, supported this. President Theodore *Roosevelt added in 1904 that the US might have to become involved in problems in other American nations. President Franklin *Roosevelt, however, introduced the *Good Neighbor Policy which said American nations should work together as equal partners. Though the US has been involved in some military and political actions in Latin America, this is still the official US policy.

the ,**Battle of 'Mons** /'mɒnz; *AmE* 'mɑːnz/ (1914) the first big battle of *World War I, fought in August 1914 near the Belgian town of Mons. The British soldiers managed to resist the attacks of much larger German forces for a time before being forced back.

Mon'santo /mɒn'sæntəʊ; *AmE* mɑːn'sæntoʊ/ a large chemical company that was started in *St Louis in 1901 and is now one of the largest producers in the world of chemicals for use in agriculture. The products it has developed include artificial sweeteners for use in food production, *Agent Orange and, in recent years, *genetically modified agricultural products, which have made the company the target of protests by environmental protest groups such as *Greenpeace..

Mon'tana[1] /mɒn'tænə; *AmE* mɑːn'tænə/ a large state in the north-western US, on the Canadian border. The capital city is Helena, and the largest city is Billings. Montana became a state in 1889, and is also called the Treasure State. It produces many minerals, and its mines once supplied half of all US copper. It also produces

grain, potatoes, sheep and cattle. Montana's tourist attractions include the *Rocky Mountains, *Yellowstone National Park, the Glacier National Park and the Little Bighorn Battlefield National Monument.

,**Joe Mon'tana**[2] /mɒn'tænə; *AmE* mɑːn'tænə/ (1956–) a US professional football player with the San Francisco 49ers. He was captain of the team when they won four *Super Bowls (in 1982, 1985, 1989 and 1990). He was also the National Football League's *Most Valuable Player in 1989. After 16 years with San Francisco, Montana played briefly with the Kansas City Chiefs. He was chosen for the Pro Football *Hall of Fame in 2000.

'**Monterey** /'mɒntəreɪ; *AmE* 'mɑːntəreɪ/ a US city on the coast of *California. It is one of the oldest cities in the state and was the Spanish capital of Alta California (1775–1846) until the US Navy captured it. The famous Monterey Jazz Festival has been held there every September since 1958. The Monterey area is popular with artists and attracts many tourists.

,**Simon de 'Montfort** /də 'mɒntfət; *AmE* də 'mɑːntfərt/ (*c.* 1208–65) an English politician and soldier, the leader of the *barons who opposed *Henry III. After being defeated in battle in 1264, he lost the support of the other barons because he wanted to rule the country himself. In 1265, he appointed himself head of government and formed his own parliament in London. The same year he was killed when fighting at the Battle of Evesham against an army led by Henry III's son, who later became *Edward I.

Mont'gomery[1] /mɒnt'gɒməri; *AmE* mɑːnt'gɑːməri/ the capital city of the US state of *Alabama. It is on the Alabama River, and is sometimes called the 'Cradle of the Confederacy' because the city was also the first capital of the *Confederate States. Martin Luther *King began the US *civil rights movement in Montgomery when he led an *African-American refusal to use the buses there. See also PARKS.

'**Field ,Marshal Mont'gomery**[2] /mɒnt'gɒməri; *AmE* mɑːnt'gɑːməri/ (Bernard Law Montgomery 1887–1976) perhaps the best-known British military leader in *World War II, particularly because of his victory when leading the 8th Army against the German forces commanded by Rommel at the Battle of El Alamein in north Africa (1942). The victory at El Alamein was the first major success for the *Allies in the war. It made Montgomery a national hero and did much to make the British forces and people believe that victory in the war as a whole was possible.

In 1944 Montgomery commanded the British forces in northern Europe after the *Normandy landings. However, the Allies at this time were commanded by General *Eisenhower, and Montgomery did not get on well with him or like the fact that Eisenhower was senior to him.

Montgomery was known by his men and the British public as 'Monty' and always recognized because he wore a beret (= military cap) with two badges on it. He had a strong personality and was very popular with his men. He was made a *knight in 1942 and a *viscount(1) in 1946.

,**Monti'cello** /ˌmɒntɪ't ʃeləʊ; *AmE* ˌmɑːntɪ't ʃeloʊ/ the home of US President Thomas *Jefferson, on a hill near Charlottesville, *Virginia. Jefferson himself designed it in the neoclassical style, and it was completed in 1809. He lived there for 56 years and is buried there. It became a National Shrine in 1926 and a *World Heritage Site in 1987. The image of Monticello is on one side of the US nickel (= 5-cent coin) and Jefferson's head is on the other side. See p. 308.

M

Monticello

'Montserrat /'mɒnsəræt; AmE 'mɑːnsəræt/ a small island in the *Caribbean Sea. It became a British colony in 1632 and is now a British *overseas territory. Its main town is Plymouth. The island has a volcano which in 1996–7 sent out clouds of ash and melted rock, forcing many people to leave their homes.

'Monty 'Python's 'Flying 'Circus /'mɒnti 'paɪθənz; AmE 'mɑːnti/ a *BBC television comedy series (1969–74). It was extremely popular with young people, especially students, and its strange, wild and silly humour had a big influence on British comedy. It consisted of sketches (= short comic plays) with no logical connection. Among the most well-known of these are the *dead parrot sketch and the Ministry of Silly Walks. It was written and performed by a team of people who had met at Oxford or Cambridge Universities. Today the most famous of these are John *Cleese and Michael *Palin. After the television series, the team wrote and acted in several successful comedy films.

> 66 And now for something completely different. 99
> Monty Python catchphrase

the 'Monument a stone column in central London set up in memory of the *Great Fire of London in 1666. It was designed by Christopher *Wren and built in 1671–7. Its height (202 feet/61.5 metres) is believed to be the distance from the column to the place where the fire started. There are 311 steps up it, which visitors can climb.

Monument 'Valley an area in north-eastern *Arizona and southern *Utah, west of the *Four Corners, where many films/movies have been made because of the spectacular scenery.

'Helen 'Wills 'Moody /'wɪlz 'muːdi/ (1906–98) a US tennis player in the 1920s and 1930s who was the best woman player of her time. Her popular name was 'Queen Helen'. She won eight *Wimbledon competitions (1927–30, 1932–3, 1935 and 1938), which remained a record for 52 years. Her total of 31 competition victories included the *US Open(2) seven times and the French Open four times. She also won a Gold Medal at the 1924 Olympics. Before she was married in 1929, she played as Helen Wills. She was chosen for the International Tennis *Hall of Fame in 1959.

'Moody's /'muːdiz/ (also **Moody's Investors Service**) a US company started in 1900 which does research into the possible risks of investing money in particular companies and publishes credit ratings for investors.

'Moonie /'muːni/ n (informal) a member of the *Unification Church, a religious group started by the Korean businessman Sun Myung Moon. Many people are worried about the way in which Moonies are persuaded to leave their families to join the Church.

The 'Moonstone /'muːnstəʊn; AmE 'muːnstoʊn/ a novel (1868) by Wilkie *Collins. It is generally regarded as one of the first English *detective novels. The moonstone of the title is a large diamond which disappears. The crime is solved by Sergeant Cuff.

Bobby 'Moore[1] /'mɔː(r)/ (1941–93) one of the most famous English football players of all time, especially because he was captain of the England team which won the World Cup in 1966. For most of his career he played for the London club *West Ham (1958–74). In 1963, at the age of 22, he became the youngest ever England captain. In all he played for England 108 times.

De,mi 'Moore[2] /də,mi 'mɔː(r)/ (1962–) a US actor who became *Hollywood's highest paid female actor when she earned $12 million for Striptease (1996). Her other films include Ghost (1990), Indecent Proposal (1993) and The Scarlet Letter (1995). She was formerly married to the actor Bruce *Willis.

Dudley 'Moore[3] /'mɔː(r)/ (1935–2002) an English comedian, actor and musician, who lived in the US for a long time. He first became known as one of the performers in *Beyond the Fringe and then as the partner of Peter *Cook in several popular television comedy series in the 1960s and 1970s, including Not Only But Also (1965–71). In the late 1970s he became a film star in comedy films such as 10 (1979) and Arthur (1980). He was also well known as a pianist, playing *jazz and classical music in concerts and on television.

Henry 'Moore[4] /'mɔː(r)/ (1898–1986) an English sculptor with an international reputation. He is best known for his very large sculptures, made from stone, wood or bronze (= a mixture of copper and tin) and with smooth curves. In these, the human figure is meant to be seen as part of the surroundings in which the sculpture is placed. Many of his sculptures are in public places.

Julianne Moore[5] /'mɔː(r)/ (1960–) a US actor who first became known in the *soap opera, As the World Turns (1985–88), in which she played twin sisters. She now acts in films and has won *Oscars as Best Actress in Far from Heaven (2002) and Best Supporting Actress in The Hours (2002).

Marianne 'Moore[6] /,mæriæn 'mɔː(r)/ (1887–1972) a US poet, known for her clever and intellectual poetry, who won the *Pulitzer Prize for Collected Poems (1952). Her other collections included Poems (1921), Observations (1924) and Complete Poems (1967).

'Mary 'Tyler 'Moore[7] /'taɪlə(r) 'mɔː(r)/ (1936–) a US comic actor who had her own popular television series, The Mary Tyler Moore Show, on *CBS (1970–77). The show, in which she played a television journalist, won three *Emmy awards (1973–74 and 1976). She was later in the television series Mary (1986), Annie McGuire (1989) and New York News (1995). Moore's films include Ordinary People (1980) and Flirting with Disaster (1996).

Michael Moore[8] /'mɔː(r)/ (1954–) a US documentary film maker and writer whose films and books are about political and social issues in modern America and often use satire (= a way of criticizing someone or something using humour to show their faults and weaknesses). His best-known book is Stupid White Men (2001) and his films include Bowling for Columbine (2002) which won an *Oscar and *Fahrenheit 9/11 (2004).

Patrick 'Moore[9] /'mɔː(r)/ (1923–) an English writer and broadcaster on astronomy He has presented every programme in the television series The *Sky at Night since it began in 1957. Moore is regarded with affection in Britain because of his rather strange manner. He speaks very fast, has untidy hair and often wears a monocle.

'Moorfields /'mɔːfiːldz; *AmE* 'mɔːrfiːldz/ a hospital in central London, England, which specializes in eye treatment. It opened in 1805.

the ,Moors 'murders /,mɔːz; *AmE* ,mɔːrz/ the name given to one of the most famous and terrible crimes in Britain in the 20th century. In the early 1960s Ian Brady and Myra Hindley tortured and murdered several children. They photographed and recorded the children while they were carrying out the crimes. They then buried the bodies on moors near *Manchester. In 1966 they were both sent to prison for life. Hindley died and Brady is still in prison.

The ,Moral 'Maze a weekly radio programme on BBC *Radio 4 presented by Michael Buerk. In each programme, a different moral issue is discussed and a regular panel (= small group of people) ask questions of people, often experts, who have different views on the subject.

,Moral Re-'Armament (*abbr* **MRA**) a Christian movement begun in 1938 by the US *evangelist Frank Buchman (1878–1961). He developed it from his Oxford Group established during a visit to Britain in 1921. The movement, which was especially active in the 1950s and 1960s, aimed to encourage high moral standards of behaviour, based on God's will as interpreted by Buchman. It was strongly opposed to Communism and homosexuality.

,Thomas 'More /'mɔː(r)/ (1478–1535) an English politician, author and scholar. He became a friend of King *Henry VIII, who first employed him as a representative in foreign countries. In 1518 More became a member of the *Privy Council, in 1521 he was made a *knight, and in 1529 he became *Lord Chancellor after Cardinal *Wolsey. However, when the king decided that he, and not the Pope, was the head of the Church in England, More refused to accept this decision. For this he was put in prison and then executed. He was made a saint by Pope Pius XI in 1935. Thomas More was also the author of *Utopia (1516), in which he described his ideas of a perfect society. The book was very successful all over Europe.

,Morecambe and 'Wise /,mɔːkəm, 'waɪz; *AmE* ,mɔːrkəm/ Eric Morecambe (1926–84) and **Ernie Wise** (1925–99), a pair of English television comedians who were very popular in the 1960s and 1970s. Their shows attracted extremely large audiences, particularly on Christmas Day, and they were popular with all sections of the public. Well-known people often appeared on the shows as guests and were made to look ridiculous. Eric made the jokes and Ernie was the serious one and the jokes were often about him. Several of their catchphrases became widely used in Britain and their shows are often repeated on British television.

> 66 The play wot I wrote. 99
> Morecambe and Wise catchphrase

'Morgan™ 1 /'mɔːgən; *AmE* 'mɔːrgən/ a type of sports car made by the small British car company Morgan and first produced in 1935. All models have a wooden frame and each car takes a long time to make. As a result, customers have to wait for as long as 4 years to receive cars they have ordered.

,Henry 'Morgan 2 /'mɔːgən; *AmE* 'mɔːrgən/ (*c.* 1635–88) a Welsh sailor and pirate who operated mainly in the *Caribbean. In 1671 he fought against the Spanish and in 1674 he captured Panama. The same year he was made a *knight.

a Morgan sports car

'J 'Pierpoint 'Morgan 3 /'pɪəpɔɪnt 'mɔːgən; *AmE* 'pɪərpɔɪnt 'mɔːrgən/ (John Pierpoint Morgan 1837–1913) a powerful US industrial leader and financier who established the United States Steel Corporation and had interests in many other areas of business, including railways and shipping. Morgan had become a partner in his father's bank in 1871 and in 1895 he named it J P Morgan and Company. He gave his large art collection to New York's *Museum of Modern Art.

,Rhodri 'Morgan 4 /,rɒdri 'mɔːgən; *AmE* ,rɑːdri 'mɔːrgən/ (1939–) a Welsh *Labour politician who became a *Member of Parliament for *Cardiff in 1997 and *First Minister of the *Welsh Assembly in 2000.

MORI™ /'mɒri; *AmE* 'mɔːri/ (*in full* **Market and Opinion Research International**) a British/US organization that carries out public opinion polls (= asks specially chosen groups of people certain questions, e.g. about political issues). It was established in 1969.

,Professor Mori'arty /mɒri'ɑːti; *AmE* mɔːri'ɑːrti/ a character in the Sherlock *Holmes stories by Arthur *Conan Doyle. He is the clever but evil enemy of Sherlock Holmes. In a story published in 1894 both of them fall to their deaths after a fight on a cliff path, though Conan Doyle later brought Holmes 'back to life' by writing that he had survived the fall. This was because the public was so keen for more Holmes stories.

'Mormon /'mɔːmən; *AmE* 'mɔːrmən/ *n* a member of the Christian religion called the *Church of Jesus Christ of Latter-Day Saints. It was established in the US in New York State in 1830 by Joseph *Smith. Its members later moved west, led by Brigham *Young, to establish *Salt Lake City and the state of *Utah. Their centre is still in Salt Lake City, and most people in Utah are Mormons. Members of the church are well known in many countries for visiting people in their homes to talk about their religion. Mormons have strict moral rules and do not drink alcohol or even coffee. At one time Mormon men were allowed to have more than one wife, but the Church stopped this in 1890.

,Morning 'Edition a US news programme made by *National Public Radio and broadcast on radio stations across America every weekday morning for 2 hours, since 1979. It includes news, interviews and other features and was presented by Bob Edwards (1947–) until 2004.

the ,Morning 'Star a daily newspaper in Britain that expresses socialist views. It started in 1930 as the official newspaper of the *Communist Party of Britain but became independent in 1945. Until 1966 it was called the *Daily Worker*. The newspaper is run as a cooperative society (= it is owned by its readers, who invest in the newspaper by buying shares) and does not allow advertising by commercial companies. See also SOCIALIST WORKER, WEEKLY WORKER.

M

'Morris™ 1 /'mɒrɪs; AmE 'mɔːrɪs/ a British car company started in 1912 near Oxford by William Morris, later Lord *Nuffield. The first car it produced was the Morris Oxford, which was very popular. It also produced *MG cars. In 1949 the company began production of the *Morris Minor, which became one of the most popular cars in Britain for many years. In 1959 it began producing the *Mini, with even greater success. In the 1950s the company combined with *Austin to form the British Motor Corporation, which later became part of *British Leyland.

Desmond 'Morris 2 /'mɒrɪs; AmE 'mɔːrɪs/ (1928–) an English zoologist (= person who studies animals) and anthropologist. He has written several very successful books of popular science, including *The Naked Ape* (1967) and *The Human Zoo* (1968). In these he argues that the behaviour of animals is similar to that of human beings. Some of his more recent work has been about body language (= the way in which people's movements indicate something about their personalities and feelings). Several of his books have been made into television series.

William 'Morris 3 /'mɒrɪs; AmE 'mɔːrɪs/ (1834–96) an English designer, artist, poet, businessman and socialist. As an artist and poet he was influenced by the *Pre-Raphaelites but he is best known as a designer of furniture and decoration for houses. He disliked the mass production methods of his time and wanted the role of the traditional craftsman to continue. He established his own company which produced hand-made furniture and interior decoration using traditional methods. Many of these designs, especially for wallpaper and fabrics, are still used today. His belief in traditional methods led Morris to become much involved in the *Arts and Crafts Movement. He also started the *Kelmscott Press to continue traditional methods of printing.

As one of the early socialists in Britain, Morris was a supporter of social change and formed his own Socialist League in 1884. He led his own campaigns on the streets against what he saw as the terrible effects of the *Industrial Revolution on workers.

'morris dance /'mɒrɪs; AmE 'mɔːrɪs/ n a type of old English dance traditionally performed by men wearing special (usually white) costumes, often with small bells around their legs below the knee. Dances from some parts of Britain involve waving handkerchiefs, and in others the dancers knock sticks together. Morris dances are usually performed outdoors in the summer. Women now also sometimes take part. ⇨ note at FOLK DANCING.

▶ **morris dancer** n
morris dancing n [U].

Morris 'Minor™ /mɒrɪs 'maɪnə(r); AmE 'mɔːrɪs 'maɪnər/ a popular small British car designed by Alec Issigonis (1906–88) and produced by the *Morris company from 1949. The **Morris Minor Traveller** model had a partly wooden frame, an unusual feature in a relatively cheap car. Morris Minors are no longer produced, but old ones are often carefully looked after by their owners and can be valuable.

Herbert 'Morrison 1 /'mɒrɪsn; AmE 'mɔːrɪsn/ (1888–1965) a British *Labour Party politician who held several senior government positions. As Minister of Transport, he established London Transport (now *Transport for London) in 1931. During *World War II, he was *Home Secretary and from 1945 to 1951 he was *Leader of the House of Commons. He was *Foreign Secretary for a short period in 1951 and deputy leader of the Party from 1951 to 1955.

Jim 'Morrison 2 /'mɒrɪsn; AmE 'mɔːrɪsn/ (1943–71) a US singer who led the rock group The *Doors. He led a wild life involving too much sex, drugs and alcohol, and was arrested several times. He left the band in 1971 to live in Paris and died there in his bath, though some people believe he is still alive.

Toni 'Morrison 3 /ˌtəʊni 'mɒrɪsn; AmE ˌtoʊni 'mɔːrɪsn/ (1931–) a US woman writer, the first African American to win a *Nobel Prize (in 1993). She studied at *Harvard University and has taught there as well as at *Princeton and *Yale Universities. Her novels are mostly about African-American life in the southern countryside. They include *The Bluest Eye* (1970), *Song of Solomon* (1977), *Beloved* (1987), which won the *Pulitzer Prize, *Jazz* (1992) and *Paradise* (1998).

Van 'Morrison 4 /ˌvæn 'mɒrɪsn; AmE ˌvæn 'mɔːrɪsn/ (1945–) a Northern Irish singer and writer of songs who has been popular since the 1960s. His first album, *Astral Weeks* (1968), is still regarded as one of the best popular music albums ever produced. His music has used influences from *Celtic culture, *blues, *gospel music, *jazz and *country music and he is considered to have a very individual style.

'Morrissey /'mɒrɪsi; AmE 'mɔːrɪsi/ (Steven Morrissey 1959–) ⇨ SMITHS.

In,spector 'Morse 1 ⇨ INSPECTOR MORSE.

Samuel 'Morse 2 /'mɔːs; AmE 'mɔːrs/ (1791–1872) an American who invented the telegraph (= a device for sending messages on electric wires) and **Morse code**, a special 'alphabet' in which letters are represented by a series of short and long radio signals or flashes of light (*dots* and *dashes*). His first public message, sent in Morse code from *Baltimore to *Washington, DC, on 24 May 1844, was 'What hath God wrought!' His inventions were important to communication during the *American Civil War.

Le ,Morte 'd'Arthur /lə ˌmɔːt 'dɑːθə(r); AmE lə ˌmɔːrt 'dɑːrθər/ stories about the life of King *Arthur, written by Thomas *Malory around 1470 when he was in prison, and printed by *Caxton in 1485. It is considered to be the first great work of English prose.

▶ **mortgages**

Houses are expensive to buy and few people have enough money of their own. Most people have to **take out a mortgage**, a type of loan. In Britain people usually get a mortgage from a **bank** or a *building society; in the US they get one from a bank or a *savings and loan association. People usually **put down a deposit** (= pay a percentage of the price of the property) and borrow the rest, although some lenders will lend up to 100% of the amount needed. Mortgages are paid back in monthly payments over a period ranging from 15 to 30 years. The person borrowing the money has to pay **interest** on the loan, so that the final amount paid is considerably more than the amount of the loan itself. The **security** for the loan is the house itself. If a borrower fails to **keep up payments**, the house may be **repossessed** by the lender and sold so that they can get their money back.

There are different types of mortgages. With a **fixed-rate mortgage**, the amount of interest remains at a particular level and the monthly payments do not change. This type of mortgage is more popular in the US than Britain, where **variable-rate mortgages** (AmE usually **adjustable-rate mortgages**) are more common. With a variable-rate mortgage, the rate of interest can increase or decrease depending on the state of the economy. Another type of mortgage in Britain is the **endowment mortgage**: borrowers pay interest on the loan to the bank or building society and a fixed sum towards an endowment policy, a type of insurance policy which should pay a sum of money that will be used to repay the loan. Many people with endowment mortgages have suffered because the growth of the policy was not enough to repay the loan and they are no longer sold.

For many people, paying back a mortgage is their greatest financial burden. People talk of being 'mortgaged up to the hilt', meaning that their mortgage payments leave them with little money for anything else. It is possible to take out a **second mortgage** on a house. Another practice, called **remortgaging** (AmE **refinancing**) involves changing an existing mortgage to a different type offered by the lender or replacing it with a mortgage from another lender, usually in order to obtain a lower rate of interest.

House prices sometimes rise very fast and then fall again. Some people who buy a house when prices are high can become victims of **negative equity**. Equity means the part of the value of a house that the buyer owns, and negative equity means a situation in which the value of a house falls below the amount borrowed as a mortgage. This makes it impossible to sell the house without being left with debt.

'Jelly Roll' 'Morton /ˌdʒeli rəʊl ˈmɔːtən; AmE roʊl ˈmɔːrtən/ (1885–1941) a US *jazz piano player who is regarded as the first great writer of jazz music. He helped to develop *ragtime into New Orleans jazz. He was born Ferdinand Joseph La Menthe Morton in *New Orleans. He formed a band, the Red Hot Peppers, in 1926 and made many recordings with them. His works include Jelly Roll Blues (1905) and Black Bottom Stomp (1925). In 1998 Morton was chosen for the Rock and Roll *Hall of Fame as a person who had influenced that type of music.

ˌGrandma 'Moses ⇨ GRANDMA MOSES.

ˌOswald 'Mosley /ˈməʊzli; AmE ˈmoʊzli/ (1896–1980) an English politician who joined the *Labour Party in 1931 to form and lead the British Union of Fascists. (He had previously also been a *Conservative and an Independent *Member of Parliament.) The policies of his own party reflected his admiration of the Nazis, and its members became increasingly violent and anti-Semitic. In 1936 Mosley married Diana *Mitford. They were both kept in prison between 1940 and 1943, during *World War II. Mosley himself had become a *baronet in 1928.

ˌKate 'Moss¹ /ˈmɒs; AmE ˈmɔːs/ (1974–) a very successful English fashion model who first worked as a model at the age of 14. She made a very thin, childlike look fashionable in the 1990s. Her personal life is followed closely by the British media.

ˌStirling 'Moss² /ˌstɜːlɪŋ ˈmɒs; AmE ˌstɜːrlɪŋ ˈmɔːs/ (1929–) a very successful English racing driver. Although he never became world champion, he won 16 Grand Prix races before an accident ended his career in 1962. His name is still the one many older British people think of first when asked to mention a famous racing driver.

'Moss Bros™ /ˈmɒs; AmE ˈmɔːs/ a British clothing company that is famous for hiring formal clothes to men for weddings, etc. It started in 1881: I've taken the suit back to Moss Bros.

ˌmost 'valuable 'player (abbr **MVP**) (in some US sports) the award and name given to the best player in a game or series of games or during a particular season. The best known are in *football, *baseball and *basketball. The players given the award are usually chosen by sports journalists: Larry Brown was the MVP for the 1996 Super Bowl. Compare MAN OF THE MATCH.

MOT /ˌem əʊ ˈtiː; AmE oʊ/ n (informal) (in full the **Ministry of Transport test**) (in Britain) an official test carried out on a car to make sure that it is safe to drive. Any car over three years old must have the test once a year. If the car passes the test, a certificate is given; if not, repairs must be carried out. It is illegal to drive a car without a valid certificate. The tests are done by private garages. The abbreviation MOT is used both for the test and for the certificate: I need to take my car in for its MOT. ◊ Make sure you see the MOT before you buy the car.

'Mothercare™ /ˈmʌðəkeə(r); AmE ˈmʌðərker/ any of a group of British shops that sell clothes and equipment for babies and children up to the age of eight, and clothes for women who are pregnant. The first Mothercare shop was opened in 1961.

ˌMother 'Goose an old woman who is supposed to have written *nursery rhymes. She is shown in pictures as a woman with a pointed nose and chin riding on the back of a flying goose. She first appeared in English in two books published in London, Mother Goose's Tales (1768) and Mother Goose's Melody; or Sonnets for the Cradle (1781), some of which was probably written by Oliver *Goldsmith. The name 'Mother Goose' comes from part of a French expression which means 'old wives' tales'.

ˌMother 'Hubbard /ˈhʌbəd; AmE ˈhʌbərd/ ⇨ OLD MOTHER HUBBARD.

'Mother's Day **1** (BrE also **'Mothering ˌSunday**) (in Britain) the fourth Sunday in Lent (around the middle of March), when mothers traditionally receive gifts and cards from their children. It was originally a day when servants were given a holiday to visit their families, taking gifts of flowers or a cake. **2** (in the US) the second Sunday in May, when mothers traditionally receive gifts, etc. from their children and are taken by their family for a meal at a restaurant. A tradition practised by some Americans, though no longer common, is to wear a carnation (= a flower with a pleasant smell) on Mother's Day, a coloured one if their mother is alive and a white one if she is dead. Compare FATHER'S DAY.

the ˌMothers' 'Union an international organization for women, started by the *Church of England in 1876 but now open to women of other Christian groups. It is intended to make family life stronger.

ˌAndrew 'Motion /ˈməʊʃn; AmE ˈmoʊʃn/ (1952–) an English writer of poems who succeeded Ted *Hughes as *Poet Laureate in 1999. His collections of poetry include Love in a Life, Salt Water and The Price of Everything. He has also written novels, and won the *Whitbread prize for biography for his book on Philip *Larkin, A Writer's Life (1994).

'motor inn (also **'motor lodge**, **'motor court**) n (AmE) a motel (= hotel, often near a motorway/freeway, for people driving cars, with space for parking cars near the rooms). Many US companies owning them now use the names motor inn/lodge/court instead of motel.

the 'Motor Show a large international exhibition of new cars, held in October every two years at the *National Exhibition Centre in *Birmingham, England. It started in 1903, in London.

'motorway n (BrE) a major road for fast travel between cities, usually with three lanes (= sections for single lines of traffic) in each direction. The names of British motorways all begin with 'M' – the M1, the M2, etc. Drivers join or leave motorways at **motorway junctions**. People can stop at **motorway service areas** for petrol, food, etc.: We joined the motorway at Junction 7. ◊ I don't like motorway driving. Compare EXPRESSWAY. ⇨ note at ROADS AND ROAD SIGNS.

'Motown /ˈməʊtaʊn; AmE ˈmoʊtaʊn/ **1** the popular US name for *Detroit, *Michigan, because it is the 'motor town', i.e. the centre of the US car industry. **2** a type of *African-American *soul music. Motown Records, established in 1959, became famous for this type of music, sometimes called the **Motown sound**. Its

M

recording stars included the *Supremes and Stevie *Wonder.

the 'Moundbuilders /'maʊndbɪldəz; AmE 'maʊndbɪldərz/ n [pl] early *Native American groups who built mounds (= raised masses of earth). These were used for graves and as the bases for religious temples and other important buildings. Well-known mounds that survive include those at Moundville, *Alabama, and the Serpent Mound in Adams County, *Ohio.

ˌMountain 'Daylight Time (abbr **MDT**) (in the US) the time used between early April and late October in the *Rocky Mountain States. It is one hour later than *Mountain Standard Time.

'mountain man n (pl **mountain men**) (AmE) a man who lives in the mountains, often alone and far from other people. The term was often applied to trappers (= people who catch animals in traps, usually for their fur).

ˌMountain 'Standard Time (abbr **MST**) (also **Mountain Time**) (in the US) the time used between late October and early April in the *Rocky Mountain States. It is seven hours earlier than *Greenwich Mean Time.

the 'Mountain States ⇨ ROCKY MOUNTAIN STATES.

ˌLord Mount'batten /maʊnt'bætn/ (born Louis Mountbatten 1900–79) a British admiral who during *World War II commanded the Allied forces in South-East Asia. He was the last viceroy of India before it became independent, and remained there for a year as its first Governor General. He was killed while sailing off the west coast of Ireland by a bomb put on his boat by the *IRA. Lord Mountbatten was a great-grandson of Queen *Victoria, and the uncle of Prince *Charles. He became an *earl(1) in 1947. See also ALLIES.

ˌMount 'Vernon /'vɜːnən; AmE 'vɜːrnən/ the home of US President George *Washington in *Virginia. It is on the *Potomac River about 15 miles/24 kilometres south of Washington, DC. It was built in 1743 in the *Georgian style. Washington lived at Mount Vernon from 1747 until his death in 1799, and he and his wife Martha are buried there.

Mount Vernon

The 'Mousetrap a mystery play by Agatha *Christie which has been running continuously in the *West End of London since its first performance in 1952. No other play has ever been performed for so long anywhere in the world. The Mousetrap is also the title of the play performed to the court in *Shakespeare's play *Hamlet.

ˌmovie 'rating ⇨ FILM CERTIFICATE.

'Mowgli /'maʊgli; AmE 'moʊgli/ the main human character in The *Jungle Book by Rudyard *Kipling. As a baby, Mowgli is found in the forest by wolves which look after him until he grows up.

ˌMo 'Mowlam /ˌməʊ 'məʊləm; AmE ˌmoʊ 'moʊləm/ (Marjorie Mowlam 1949–) a British *Labour politician. She was a *Member of Parliament from 1987 until 2001 and held several important positions in the Labour *Shadow Cabinet before becoming *Secretary of State for Northern Ireland in the Labour government of 1997. She is well known for her part in the peace talks in Northern Ireland which led to the *Good Friday Agreement of 1998. She was Minister for the Cabinet Office from 1999 to 2001.

'moxie /'mɒksi; AmE 'mɑːksi/ n [U] (AmE informal) courage, energy or an aggressive attitude. The word comes from the name of a former US soft drink (= a drink containing no alcohol) which was advertised with the phrase: 'What this country needs is plenty of Moxie': She had the moxie to ask him to marry her.

MP /ˌem 'piː/ ⇨ MEMBER OF PARLIAMENT.

MRA ⇨ MORAL RE-ARMAMENT.

ˌMr 'Bean /'biːn/ a comedy character played in a British television series by the actor Rowan *Atkinson. The programmes have very few spoken words and show Mr Bean in funny or embarrassing situations: Well, say something! Don't just stand there like Mr Bean.

MRC ⇨ MEDICAL RESEARCH COUNCIL.

ˌMr 'Chad /'tʃæd/ the name of a figure drawn by people on walls and other public places in Britain. He is usually shown as a face appearing above a wall, with a message complaining about a lack of something, such as 'Wot (= What) no sausages?' These drawings began to appear during *World War II when Britain lacked many types of food and other things. They are less commonly seen now.

ˌMr 'Charlie (AmE slang) an informal name used by *African Americans for a white man or for white men in general. It is often meant as an insult.

ˌMr 'Chips /'tʃɪps/ an expression sometimes used to refer to a male teacher, especially one who is loved by his students. It comes from the main character in the novel Goodbye Mr Chips by James Hilton.

ˌMr 'Clean (AmE informal) a man who is considered to be very honest and good. It is used especially in politics for a candidate or elected politician who has done nothing morally wrong in his personal or political life: Many people voted for Jimmy Carter because he was the Mr Clean of US politics.

ˌMr 'Fixit /'fɪksɪt/ (BrE informal) a name for a person who organizes things and solves problems for other people. It is sometimes used to refer to criminals or to show disapproval when referring to other people: He is getting a reputation as the government's Mr Fixit.

ˌMr 'Kipling™ /'kɪplɪŋ/ a British make of cakes of various kinds. They are well known for the advertisements, which say that Mr Kipling makes 'exceedingly good cakes'.

ˌMr Ma'goo /məˈɡuː/ a character in a series of US cartoon films (1949–65). He is old and cannot see very well, so he talks to objects and walks into dangerous situations. A Walt *Disney film, Mr Magoo (1997), used real actors, with Leslie Nielsen as Magoo.

'Mr 'Rogers' 'Neighborhood a popular US television series on *PBS for young children which began in 1966. It was presented by Fred Rogers (1928–2003), who always told children, 'You are special. I like you just the way you are.'

ˌMrs O''Leary's 'cow /əʊ'lɪəriz; AmE oʊ'lɪəriz/ the cow that is traditionally blamed for the great Chicago fire in October 1871. Mrs O'Leary lived in the west part of Chicago on De Koven Street. People there claimed that her cow kicked over an oil lamp, though Mrs O'Leary herself denied it. The fire burned for nearly a week, killing 250 people and destroying 7450 buildings.

MSP /ˌem es 'piː/ ⇨ MEMBER OF THE SCOTTISH PARLIAMENT.

MST /ˌem es 'tiː/ ⇨ MOUNTAIN STANDARD TIME.

MTV /ˌem tiː 'viː/ a US television company that broadcasts music videos and programmes about the music industry all round the world by satellite, 24 hours a day. It began in 1981.

the M25 /ˌem twentiˈfaɪv/ a British motorway that runs in a circle around London. It was completed in 1986, but since then has become quite crowded, and traffic on it often moves very slowly. People often complain or make jokes about the difficulties of driving on the M25.

ˌMuch Aˈdo About ˈNothing a play (c. 1598) by William *Shakespeare. It is a comedy about two love affairs, one between Beatrice and Benedick and the other between Hero and Claudio.

ˈmuckraker /ˈmʌkreɪkə(r)/ n any of a group of US writers in the early 1900s who wrote criticizing aspects of US life, such as dishonest behaviour in business and government, companies making children work long hours, and unfair treatment of black people. President Theodore *Roosevelt gave them the name 'muckrakers' in 1906, suggesting that they were only interested in finding bad things to write about. However, their work increased public knowledge and led to a lot of social changes. One example of a muckraker was Upton *Sinclair, whose book *The Jungle* (1906) led to the US *Pure Food and Drug Act.

ˈmuffin n **1** (*AmE* also **English muffin**) a soft, round, flat cake made with yeast dough and usually eaten hot with butter. **2** a small cake in the shape of a cup, often containing small pieces of fruit. In the US, muffins are usually less sweet than other cakes: *a blueberry muffin*.

blueberry muffins

ˈmugwump /ˈmʌɡwʌmp/ n (*AmE often disapproving*) a person who cannot decide how to vote on a political issue, or who prefers not to become involved in party politics. The word was first applied in US politics to a group of *Republicans who in 1884 supported the *Democrats' candidate Grover *Cleveland for US President. It comes from the *Native American Algonquian language and means 'great man' or 'chief'.

Muˌhammad Aˈli ⇨ ALI.

ˌFrank ˈMuir¹ /ˈmjʊə(r)/; *AmE* ˈmjʊr/ (1920–98) an English broadcaster and writer of comedy who with Denis *Norden wrote several successful comedy series for radio and television, including *Take It From Here* (1947–58). He appeared on a number of popular panel games and quiz shows and was well known for his intelligent humour. He also wrote a novel and children's books.

ˌJean ˈMuir² /ˈmjʊə(r)/; *AmE* ˈmjʊr/ (1933–95) an English fashion designer whose clothes were noted for their elegant, traditional style.

ˌJohn ˈMuir³ /ˈmjʊə(r)/; *AmE* ˈmjʊr/ (1838–1914) an American, born in Scotland, who was one of the first conservationists (= people who work to preserve the natural environment). He helped to establish *Yosemite National Park and Sequoia National Park in *California. Muir Woods National Monument in California and Muir Glacier in *Alaska were named after him. His books include *The Mountains of California* (1894) and *Our

National Parks (1901). The John Muir Trust was established in 1983 to protect land in Britain.

ˈMuirfield /ˈmjʊəfiːld; *AmE* ˈmjʊrfiːld/ a golf course on the east coast of Scotland near *Edinburgh, one of the courses on which the *British Open is regularly played.

the ˌMulberry ˈharbours two very large artificial harbours that were built in Britain and then pulled across the *Channel to the French coast so that supplies could be provided for the Allied soldiers who landed in Normandy on *D-Day in June 1944. See also ALLIES.

Mull /mʌl/ a large island of the Inner *Hebrides in Scotland. It is known for its high cliffs and beautiful scenery, and is popular with tourists. See also STAFFA.

ˈmummer /ˈmʌmə(r)/ n an actor in a traditional English play without words in which the actors wear masks covering their faces. The story involves a fight between St *George and a Turkish *knight. One of them is killed, but a doctor brings him back to life. The idea behind the play, which was performed especially at Christmas, is the earth's death in winter and return to life in the spring. It is occasionally still performed.

ˈMummerset /ˈmʌməset; *AmE* ˈmʌmərset/ n [U] (*humorous*) an invented word meaning the strong accent sometimes used by English actors when they are playing characters from the *West Country, including *Somerset: *It's one of those plays in which everyone speaks broad Mummerset.*

the ˌMunich Aˈgreement /ˌmjuːnɪk/ (*also the ˌMunich ˈPact*) an agreement signed in Munich in September 1938 between Britain, France, Germany and Italy. It allowed Germany to take control of a part of Czechoslovakia. The British Prime Minister, Neville *Chamberlain, said that the agreement represented 'peace in our time', and at the time many people believed that it had saved Europe from war. However, in March 1939 Hitler took all of Czechoslovakia and in September *World War II began. Now people sometimes call an agreement that has no value 'another Munich'. See also APPEASEMENT.

ˌAlfred ˈMunnings /ˈmʌnɪŋz/ (1878–1959) an English painter known especially for his pictures of horses and horse racing, and for criticizing a lot about modern art. He was made a *knight in 1944.

the Munˈros /mʌnˈrəʊz; *AmE* mʌnˈroʊz/ the 277 mountains in Scotland which are all over 3000 feet/913 metres high. In 1891 a man called Hugh Munro published a list of them, and since then people have had the aim of climbing all of them. Munro himself died with only one of them left to climb.

The ˈMuppet™ Show /ˈmʌpɪt/ a popular television comedy series (1976–81) with a range of puppet characters, including *Kermit the frog, Miss Piggy and Fozzy Bear. The Muppets were created in the US in the 1950s by Jim *Henson and Frank Oz, and first became popular in the US children's series *Sesame Street.

ˌMurder, ˈInc /ˈɪŋk/ an informal US name for the *Mafia(1) or other powerful criminal groups. It was first used to refer to a criminal organization run by Albert Anastasia and Louis 'Lepke' Buchalter in *Brooklyn, New York, during the *Great Depression.

ˌIris ˈMurdoch¹ /ˈmɜːdɒk; *AmE* ˈmɜːrdɑːk/ (1919–99) a British writer and philosopher, born in Dublin. Her clever novels explore complicated human and sexual relationships among 20th-century *middle-class people, often with great humour. Among the best-known are *The Sandcastle* (1957), *A Severed Head* (1961) and *The Sea, The Sea* (1978), which won the *Booker Prize. Iris Murdoch suffered from Alzheimer's disease and the film *Iris* (2001) was based on a book about her last years written by her husband, John Bayley. She was made a *dame(2) in 1987.

M

,Rupert '**Murdoch**[2] /'mɜ:dɒk; AmE 'mɜ:rdɑ:k/ (1931–)
a very rich businessman who owns a large share in an
international group of newspaper and broadcasting
companies. He was born in Australia but is now a US citizen. In Britain he owns News International, a group
which includes the *News of the World, the *Sun, The
*Times, and the *Sunday Times, and half of the satellite
television company *BSkyB. In the US Murdoch also
owns the film company *20th Century Fox, the Fox
Television Network and the Los Angeles Dodgers baseball team.

,Eddie '**Murphy** /'mɜ:fi; AmE 'mɜ:rfi/ (1961–) a US
comic actor who usually plays lively, confident characters. He began his career on the television programme
*Saturday Night Live (1981–84). His films include 48
Hours (1982), Trading Places (1983), Beverly Hills Cop
(1984), Coming to America (1988), Harlem Nights (1989),
which he wrote and directed, The Nutty Professor (1996)
and Doctor Dolittle (1998).

,Cardinal ,Cormac ,**Murphy-O''Connor** /,kɔ:mæk
,mɜ:fi əʊ'kɒnə(r); AmE ,kɔ:rmæk ,mɜ:rfi oʊ'kɑ:nə(r)/
(1932–) the *Roman Catholic *Archbishop of
Westminster since 2000. He was made a cardinal (= a
priest of the highest rank) by Pope John Paul II in 2001.

,**Murphy's 'law** /,mɜ:fiz; AmE 'mɜ:rfiz/ the idea that 'if
anything can go wrong in a situation, it will'. People
often talk about Murphy's law in a humorous way when
thinking about possible problems which might happen
in something they are going to do. It is named after an
American scientist **Edward Murphy** who was involved
in experiments for the United States Air Force in 1949.
Compare PARKINSON'S LAW.

,Bill '**Murray**[1] /'mʌri/ (1950–) a US comedian, actor,
film director and producer who first became known
when he appeared regularly on *Saturday Night Live
(1977–80). The well-known films in which he has
appeared include Ghostbusters (1984), Groundhog Day
(1993) and Lost in Translation (2003).

,James '**Murray**[2]
/'mʌri/ (1837–1915) a
Scottish lexicographer
(= writer of dictionaries)
who is mainly remem-
bered as the first editor of
The New Oxford English
Dictionary (later called
The *Oxford English
Dictionary), published
between 1884 and 1933.

'**Murrayfield** /'mʌri-
fi:ld/ the Scottish
national Rugby Union
ground in *Edinburgh,
where all Scotland's
home international   James Murray
matches are played.

,**Edward R 'Murrow** /'mʌrəʊ; AmE 'mʌroʊ/ (Edward
Roscoe Murrow 1908–65) a US radio and television journalist who has been called 'the father of television journalism'. He was head of the *CBS radio European Bureau
during *World War II. In the 1950s, he had two programmes on CBS television, See It Now and Person to
Person. In the first he examined current affairs, and in
the second he talked to famous people in their homes.
Murrow later became head of the *United States
Information Agency (1961–63).

the Mu,seum of '**Childhood** a British museum in
*Bethnal Green, London, which shows what children's
lives were like at different periods in history.

the Mu'seum of ,Modern 'Art (abbr **MOMA**) the
largest museum of modern art and photography in the
world. The collection starts with works from 1880. It
opened in *New York in 1939.

▶ **museums**
Many people have a hobby that involves collecting
things, e.g. stamps, postcards or *antiques. In the 18th
and 19th centuries wealthy people travelled and collected plants, animal skins, historical objects and works
of art. They kept their collection at home until it got too
big or until they died, and then it was given to a
museum. The 80 000 objects collected by Sir Hans
Sloane, for example, formed the core collection of the
*British Museum which opened in 1759.

The parts of a museum open to the public are called
galleries or **rooms**. Often, only a small proportion of
a museum's collection is on display. Most of it is stored
away or used for research. A person in charge of a
department of a museum is called a **keeper**. Museum
staff involved in the care and conservation of items are
sometimes called **curators**.

Many museums are lively places and they attract a lot
of visitors. As well as looking at **exhibits**, visitors can
play with computer simulations and imagine themselves living at a different time in history or walking
through a rainforest. At the Jorvik Centre in *York, the
city's *Viking settlement is recreated, and people
experience the sights, sounds and smells of the old
town. Historical accuracy is important but so also is
entertainment. Museums must compete for people's
leisure time and money with other amusements. Most
museums also welcome school groups and arrange
special activities for children.

In Britain, the largest museums are the *British
Museum, the *Science Museum, the *Natural History
Museum and the *Victoria and Albert Museum. Museums
outside London also cover every subject and period.
Homes of famous people sometimes become museums,
such as the house where *Shakespeare was born in
*Stratford-upon-Avon.

The first public museum in the US was the Charlestown
Museum in South Carolina, founded in 1773. The largest
is the *Smithsonian Institution in Washington, DC, a
group of 14 museums. The most popular of these is the
*National Air and Space Museum. Some US museums
are art museums. Many describe a period of history. In
*Gettysburg, Pennsylvania, for example, a museum
explains the *Civil War and gives details of the battle of
Gettysburg. *Halls of Fame are museums that honour
people who have been outstanding in a certain field,
e.g. baseball or rock music.

National museums receive money from the government but not enough to cover their costs. Museums usually have a shop selling books, postcards and gifts, and
often a cafe. Their profits help to fund the museum.
Some museums have the support of a commercial sponsor. In small museums only a few people have paid jobs,
and the rest are volunteers, called **docents** in the US,
who lead tours and answer visitors' questions.

'**musical** (also **musical comedy**) n an amusing play or
film with songs and usually dancing. Musicals started to
develop in the early 20th century, combining features of
comic opera and the British *music-hall tradition. The
modern *Broadway musical began with *Show Boat,
and others have included *Oklahoma!, *My Fair Lady,
*West Side Story, *Hair and *Sunset Boulevard. Most later
became films. Musicals written originally as films
include *Singin' in the Rain, Gigi (1958) and The
Producers (2001), which is about the making of a
Broadway musical. US writers of musicals have included
Irving *Berlin, George and Ira *Gershwin, Jerome
*Kern, Cole *Porter, Richard *Rodgers, Lorenz *Hart,

Oscar *Hammerstein and *Lerner and Loewe. The best-known British composer of musicals is Andrew *Lloyd Webber, whose work includes *Jesus Christ Superstar and *Cats.

ˌmusical ˈchairs n [U] **1** a game, played e.g. at children's parties, in which people run around a group of chairs while music is played. The number of chairs is always one fewer than the number of people, so that when the music stops the person who cannot find a chair has to leave the game. The winner is the one who manages to sit on the last remaining chair. ⇨ note at TOYS AND GAMES.
2 (figurative often disapproving) a situation in which people or things often change places, or take turns to do something: Government ministers are expected to engage in musical chairs, moving from one department to another.

ˈmusic-hall n **1** [U] a type of popular entertainment in Britain in the late 19th and early 20th centuries. Performers sang cheerful, sometimes rather rude, songs and danced in bright costumes, or performed acts of skill. Some of them, such as Marie *Lloyd and George *Robey, became very famous: the great music-hall entertainers.
2 [C] a theatre in which music-hall was performed. Music-halls were often called 'the Palladium', 'the Palace', 'the Hippodrome', or 'the Empire', names which were kept later when many of them became cinemas. See also GOOD OLD DAYS. Compare VAUDEVILLE.

ˌMutiny on the ˈBounty the name of two films about a famous historical incident which occurred in 1789. The sailors on the British ship HMS Bounty took control of it by force and put the captain and some senior officers in a small boat on the open sea. In the first film (1935), which won an *Oscar as Best Picture, Clark *Gable played Fletcher *Christian, the leader of the mutiny, and Charles *Laughton played Captain *Bligh. In the second (1962), Marlon *Brando took the part of Christian and Trevor Howard that of Bligh. See also PITCAIRN ISLANDS.

ˌEadweard ˈMuybridge /ˌedwəd ˈmaɪbrɪdʒ; AmE ˌedwərd/ (1830–1904) a US photographer, born in England, who used a series of cameras to study the way both animals and humans move. He developed a way of showing series of pictures quickly one after the other to give the impression of continuous movement. He presented these to the public in a theatre in *Chicago, which some people therefore regard as the first cinema.

ˈMuzak™ /ˈmjuːzæk/ n [U] a system that plays continuous recorded light music in public places, e.g. in restaurants, shops and airports. It was first produced in 1922 by the US Muzak Corporation for use in lifts/elevators to help people to stay calm. Many people dislike it and use the name Muzak to refer to music that is boring or that no one listens to.

MVP /ˌem viː ˈpiː/ ⇨ MOST VALUABLE PLAYER.

ˌMy ˈcountry, 'tis of ˈthee the first line of the US patriotic song *America.

ˌMy Fair ˈLady a successful musical version of the play *Pygmalion, by George Bernard *Shaw. It was written by *Lerner and Loewe, and opened on *Broadway in 1956, with Rex *Harrison as Professor Higgins and Julie *Andrews as Eliza Doolittle. Harrison was also in the film version (1964), with Audrey *Hepburn as Eliza. The film won three *Oscars.

the ˌMy Lai ˈmassacre /ˌmiː laɪ/ an incident that occurred during the *Vietnam War on 16 March 1968. A group of US soldiers killed 347 ordinary people, including women and children, in the Vietnamese village of My Lai. In 1971, the officer who ordered the attack, Lieutenant William Calley, was sent to prison for life, but this was later reduced to 10 years and he was in fact released in 1974. Many Americans were shocked by the incident, and as a result protests against the war increased.

ˌMy ˈOld Kenˈtucky ˈHome /kenˈtʌki/ a popular US song written in 1853 by Stephen *Foster. It became the official song of the state of *Kentucky and is played at each *Kentucky Derby when the horses come out. It contains the well-known lines:

66 Oh the sun shines bright on my old Kentucky home,
My old Kentucky home far away. 99

ˈmystery play ⇨ MIRACLE PLAY.

N n

the **NAACP** /ˌen dʌbl ˈeɪ siː ˈpiː/ (*in full* the **National Association for the Advancement of Colored People**) a US organization that supports the rights of *African Americans. It was formed in 1909 and played an important part in the *civil rights movement. One of its major achievements was to bring a legal case which led to the US Supreme Court's decision in 1954 against *segregation in schools. Its main office is in *Baltimore, *Maryland, and it had more than 500 000 members in 2003. See also BROWN V BOARD OF EDUCATION.

the **NAAFI** /ˈnæfi/ (*in full* the **Navy, Army and Air Force Institutes**) a British organization that provides shops and places to eat for members of the armed services in Britain and abroad. Compare PX.

Na'bisco /nəˈbɪskəʊ; *AmE* nəˈbɪskoʊ/ a large US food company. Its products include *Oreo biscuits, *Ritz Crackers and Planters nuts.

ˌVladimir **Na'bokov** /ˌvlædɪmɪə nəˈbəʊkɒf; *AmE* ˌvlædɪmɪr nəˈboʊkɔːf/ (1899–1977) a US writer of novels and short stories, born in Russia, who is much admired for his skilful use of language. He is best known for his novel *Lolita*. His other novels include *Pnin* (1957), *Pale Fire* (1962) and *Ada* (1969). Nabokov taught poetry at Cornell University from 1948 to 1959 before settling in Switzerland.

ˌRalph **'Nader** /ˌrælf ˈneɪdə(r)/ (1934–) a US lawyer who became famous for representing the rights of consumers (= people who buy goods or use services) and led many important campaigns against big companies. In his book *Unsafe at Any Speed* (1965) he attacked the car industry for producing dangerous cars, and this led to new safety laws for cars being passed. The assistants who helped him in his investigations became known as Nader's Raiders. Ralph Nader has strongly opposed recent US foreign policy. He was a *Green Party candidate in the elections for President in 1996 and 2000 and an independent candidate in the 2004 election.

NAFTA /ˈnæftə/ (*in full* the **North American Free Trade Agreement**) an agreement signed in 1989 between the US, Canada and Mexico to allow goods to be transported and sold more easily over their borders. It also makes it easier for business and professional people to move between the three countries. The agreement began to operate in 1994.

ˌ**Naga'saki** /ˌnægəˈsɑːki/ a city and port in south-west Japan. It was, after Hiroshima, the second city to be destroyed by an atom bomb at the end of *World War II. The bomb was dropped from a US plane on 9 August 1945, killing about 75 000 people immediately and another 75 000 who died later.

NAGTY /ˌen eɪ dʒiː tiː ˈwaɪ, ˈnægti/ ⇨ NATIONAL ACADEMY FOR GIFTED AND TALENTED YOUTH.

ˌV S **'Naipaul** /ˈnaɪpɔːl/ (Vidiadhar Surajprasad Naipaul 1932–) a writer of novels, short stories and travel books, born in *Trinidad, who has lived in Britain since 1950. He is perhaps best known for his comic novels, many of them set in the *West Indies, including *A House for Mr Biswas* (1961). He won the *Booker Prize for *In a Free State* (1971). He was made a *knight in 1989 and received the *Nobel Prize for literature in 2001.

Nam /næm/ (*AmE informal*) a short name for Vietnam, first used by US soldiers during the *Vietnam War.

▶**names**

Apart from their *surname or last name, most British and American children are given two personal names by their parents, a **first name** and a **middle name**. These names are sometimes called **Christian** names or **given** names. Some people have only one given name, a few have three or more. Friends and members of a family who are of similar age usually call one another by their first names. In some families young people now also call their aunts and uncles and even their parents by their first names. Outside the family, the expression *be on first name terms* suggests that the people concerned have a friendly, informal relationship

When writing their name Americans commonly give their first name and their **middle initial**, e.g. *George M Cohan*. Both given names are used in full only on formal occasions, e.g. when people get married. In Britain many people **sign their name** on forms etc. using the initials of both their given names and their surname, e.g. *J E Brooks*, but may write *Joanna Brooks* at the end of a letter. The **full name** (= all given names and surname) is usually only required on official forms.

Parents usually decide on given names for their children before they are born. In some families the oldest boy is given the same name as his father. In the US the word **junior** or **senior**, or a number, is added after the name and surname to make it clear which person is being referred to. For example, the son of *William Jones Sr* (Senior) would be called *William Jones Jr* (Junior), and *his* son would be called *William Jones III* ('William Jones the third').

Many popular names come from the Bible, e.g. *Jacob, Joshua, Matthew, Mary, Rebecca* and *Sarah*, though this does not imply that the people who choose them are religious. Other people give their children the name of somebody they admire, such as a famous sports personality, or a film or pop star. In Britain the names *William* and *Harry* became common again after the sons of Prince *Charles were given these names. In the US *Chelsea* was not a common name for a girl until President Bill *Clinton's daughter Chelsea came to public attention.

Names such as *David, Michael, Paul* and *Robert* for boys and *Catherine, Elizabeth* and *Jane* for girls remain popular for many years. Others, e.g. *Darrell, Darren, Wayne, Chloe, Jade* and *Zara*, are fashionable for only a short period. Names such as *Albert, Herbert, Wilfrid, Doris, Gladys* and *Joyce* are now out of fashion and are found mainly among older people. Some older names come back into fashion and there are now many young women called *Amy, Emma, Harriet, Laura* and *Sophie*. The birth announcements columns in newspapers give an indication of the names which are currently popular. In Britain these have included *Jack, Joshua* and *Thomas* for boys and *Emily, Ellie* and *Chloe* for girls and in the US *Jacob, Michael* and *Joshua* for boys and *Emily, Emma* and *Madison* for girls

People from Wales, Scotland or Ireland, or those who have a cultural background from outside Britain, may choose from an additional set of names. In the US Jews, *African Americans or people of Latin American origin may also choose different names.

Na'mibia /nəˈmɪbiə/ a country in south-west Africa which joined the *Commonwealth when it became independent from South Africa in 1990, although it had

never been a British colony. The capital city is Windhoek.
▶ **Namibian** adj, n.

Nancy 'Drew ⇨ DREW.

Nan'tucket /næn'tʌkɪt/ a US island off the south-east coast of *Massachusetts, near *Cape Cod and *Martha's Vineyard. The island is separated from the coast by **Nantucket Sound**. It is 15 miles/24 kilometres long and has a small town also called Nantucket. It attracts summer tourists, and many rich people have homes there.

NAO /ˌen eɪ 'əʊ; AmE 'oʊ/ ⇨ NATIONAL AUDIT OFFICE.

Napa 'Valley /ˌnæpə/ a valley in the US state of *California which is the centre of the US wine industry. It is north of *Oakland, and its largest town is Napa.

the Na,poleonic 'Wars /nəˌpəʊliɒnɪk; AmE nəˌpoʊliɑːnɪk/ a conflict (1802–15) in which the French Emperor Napoleon

Californian vineyards

Bonaparte tried to gain control of the whole of Europe. He had great success against all his enemies except Britain, whose navy under *Nelson defeated the French navy at the Battle of *Trafalgar (1805), and whose army fought the *Peninsular War against him from 1808 to 1814, making him weaker in his other campaigns. In 1812 Napoleon lost half a million men when he invaded Russia in winter, and in 1814 the British, Russians, Prussians and Austrians entered Paris. They sent Napoleon to rule the island of Elba in the Mediterranean, but he collected an army around him and returned to Paris. He was soon defeated again, at the Battle of *Waterloo (1815), and was sent to the island of St Helena in the south Atlantic, where he died in 1821.

Napster /'næpstə(r)/ an *Internet music service started by Shawn Fanning (1980–) in 1999 which allowed people to share MP3 music files and in February 2001 had 13.6 million users. It was shut down in 2001 for breaking copyright laws after legal action by record companies. The service reopened but went bankrupt in 2002. A new service, known as **Napster 2.0**, opened in 2003. It has links to five big record companies and allows people to download music legally.

NARA /'nɑːrə/ ⇨ NATIONAL ARCHIVES AND RECORDS ADMINISTRATION.

Narnia /'nɑːniə; AmE 'nɑːrniə/ an imaginary land of strange people and talking animals in a series of seven children's books (sometimes called the **Narnia Chronicles**) by C S *Lewis. In the first of these, *The Lion, the Witch and the Wardrobe* (1950), four children get into Narnia through an old wardrobe (= a large cupboard for clothes).

NASA /'næsə/ (in full the **National Aeronautics and Space Administration**) the US government organization responsible for research into space and space travel. Its office is in Washington, DC, and the main centres include the John F Kennedy Space Center at *Cape Canaveral, *Florida, the *Lyndon B Johnson Space Center near *Houston, *Texas, and the Jet Propulsion Laboratory at the California Institute of Technology in Pasadena. NASA was established in 1958 by President *Eisenhower to replace the National Advisory Committee for Aeronautics (NACA). See also APOLLO PROGRAM, CHALLENGER, SKYLAB, SPACE SHUTTLE.

NASCAR /'næskɑː(r)/ (in full the **National Association for Stock Car Auto Racing**) the US organization for the sport of racing stock cars

(= ordinary cars fitted with especially powerful engines). It was established in 1948 at Daytona Beach, *Florida, and the NASCAR office is still there. The *Daytona 500 is the most famous of its races. The person with the most victories during a season wins the Winston Cup.

Nasdaq /'næzdæk/ (in full the **National Association of Securities Dealers Automated Quotations**) a US stock exchange which began trading in 1971 as the world's first electronic stock exchange, allowing many people to trade at the same time using its computer system.

the ,Battle of 'Naseby /'neɪzbi/ an important battle (1645) of the *English Civil War, fought in *Northamptonshire. The Parliament's *New Model Army defeated the supporters of the King, and they never became strong again.

,Beau 'Nash[1] /ˌbəʊ 'næʃ; AmE ˌboʊ/ (1674–1762) the name by which Richard Nash is usually known. He was a Welshman who became a leading figure in fashionable English society in the 18th century. He helped to make the English towns of *Bath and *Tunbridge Wells into fashionable holiday centres.

,John 'Nash[2] /'næʃ/ (1752–1835) an English architect. He planned *Regent's Park in London, and the area around it, between 1811 and 1825 for the *Prince Regent, who later became King *George IV. He also designed *Trafalgar Square, *St James's Park and the *Marble Arch in London, and the *Brighton Pavilion on the south coast of England.

Regency terrace, designed by John Nash

,Ogden 'Nash[3] /ˌɒgdən 'næʃ; AmE ˌɑːgdən/ (1902–71) a US writer of humorous verse. Many of his poems were first published in The *New Yorker magazine. He was known especially for his clever rhymes. His 20 collections of verse include *You Can't Get There from Here* (1957) and *Bed Riddence* (1970).

,Paul 'Nash[4] /'næʃ/ (1899–1946) an English painter who did many types of work, including theatre and book design, but who is remembered especially for the pictures he painted as an official war artist in both world wars.

Nashville /'næʃvɪl/ the capital city of the US state of *Tennessee, in the northern central part of the state. It was settled on the Cumberland River in 1779 as Fort Nashborough and its name was changed in 1784. It is the centre of the *country music industry and among its attractions are the *Grand Ole Opry. It is also known as a centre for religious education and for Vanderbilt University.

NASS /næs/ (*in full* **National Asylum Support Service**) a British government office set up in 2000 which provides accommodation and financial help for asylum seekers (= people who have left their country because they were in danger and ask for protection from another country) while their claim is being considered.

the NASUWT /ˌen eɪ es juː dʌbljuː ˈtiː/ (*in full* **the National Association of Schoolmasters/Union of Women Teachers**) a British trade union for teachers, formed in 1975. ⇨ note at TRADE UNION. Compare NUT.

'Natchez /ˈnætʃiz/ **1** *n* (*pl* **Natchez**) a member of a former *Native American agricultural people who lived on the *Mississippi River near the modern city of Natchez, *Mississippi. They spoke the Muskogean language and worshipped the sun. About 400 Natchez were captured by the French in 1729 and sold as slaves in the West Indies. The rest joined the Chickasaw, *Creek and *Cherokee peoples, and some then went to *Oklahoma. **2** a city in the US state of *Mississippi. It is the oldest city on the *Mississippi River and is famous for its beautiful homes built before the *Civil War. Natchez was settled in 1716 by the French who defeated the Natchez people. It was then controlled in turn by Britain, Spain and the US. For a short time (1817–21) it was the state capital. The **Natchez Trace National Parkway** runs from Natchez to *Nashville, *Tennessee.

ˌCarry 'Nation /ˌkæri ˈneɪʃn/ (1846–1911) an American woman who tried to improve society. She is best remembered for her campaign against alcohol during which she often entered bars to destroy bottles and barrels containing alcoholic drink. She was arrested many times, especially in the 1890s. She also destroyed tobacco, foreign food and paintings of naked women. She published a paper called *Smasher's Mail*.

The 'Nation a left-wing US magazine, published each week since 1865. It contains articles on politics, society and the arts.

the 'National (*BrE informal*) **1** the *Grand National horse race. **2** the Royal *National Theatre.

ˌNational 'Academy one of four organizations in the US, the **National Academy of Sciences**, the **National Academy of Engineering** and the **Institute of Medicine**, which support research in these areas, and the **National Research Council** which provides expert advice to the government and *Congress using members of the other three organizations.

the 'National A'cademy for 'Gifted and 'Talented 'Youth (*abbr* **NAGTY**) a centre based at the University of *Warwick in England, set up by the government to provide educational support to children and young people under 19 who have higher than usual academic abilities. It provides help and information for children and teachers and also carries out research.

the 'National 'Air and 'Space Mu,seum a US museum of air and space travel which is part of the *Smithsonian Institution in Washington, DC. Its displays include the Wright Flyer (the first aircraft to fly successfully), Charles *Lindbergh's plane *Spirit of St Louis, *Enola Gay (the US plane that dropped the first atom bomb), the only surviving section of Apollo 11, which made the first space flight to the moon, and a piece of rock brought back from the moon.

ˌNational Air 'Traffic ,Services (*abbr* **NATS**) the organization which controls aircraft travelling to and from the UK. It deals with more than 2 million flights every year from four main centres in England and Scotland.

the National Air and Space Museum

▶ **national anthems**

Britain's official national anthem is *God Save the Queen* (or *God Save the King* if the ruler is a man). It is not known who wrote the words, but it seems that the song, said to be the oldest national anthem in the world, was written many years before it was chosen as an official national song in the 18th century. It was first performed in public in 1745, during the *Jacobite Rebellion, to a musical arrangement by Thomas Arne (1710–78). The first verse is played or sung on formal occasions, especially if the Queen or another member of the *royal family is present:

God save our gracious Queen,
Long live our noble Queen,
God save the Queen.
Send her victorious,
Happy and glorious,
Long to reign over us,
God save the Queen.

Everybody stands while it is being played, as a mark of respect.

Many British people think *God Save the Queen* is too slow and solemn, and would prefer a more lively national song such as *Land of Hope and Glory* or *Rule, Britannia!* Both express pride in Britain's achievements but were perhaps more appropriate in the days when Britain had an empire.

Wales has its own national anthem, *Hen Wlad fy Nhadau* (*Land of My Fathers*). It celebrates the survival of Welsh traditions, language and scenery and is often sung at concerts and at major sports events in which Wales is taking part. Scotland does not have an official national anthem, though *Scotland the Brave* is often sung at public gatherings. The *Flower of Scotland is played and sung as an anthem before international *Rugby games in which the Scottish team is playing.

The national anthem of the US is The *Star-Spangled Banner, referring to the US flag. The words were written in 1814 and set to the music of a popular song. It became the national anthem in 1931. Every American knows the story of how The Star-Spangled Banner was written during a war between the US and Britain. Its author, Francis Scott Key, was a prisoner on a British ship off the coast of *Baltimore. From there he could watch the battle for control of Fort McHenry. The song tells how he watched as the sun went down. He could no longer see the fighting, but since bombs were still exploding he knew that the British had not won. When the morning came he could see the American flag still flying over the fort.

The Star-Spangled Banner is played at official ceremonies and sung at public events. On these occasions everyone present is expected to stand up and sing. Although there are three verses only the first is normally used:

Winners of the National Book Award for Fiction

1950 *The Man with the Golden Arm* Nelson Algren
1951 *The Collected Stories of William Faulkner*
1952 *From Here to Eternity* James Jones
1953 *Invisible Man* Ralph Ellison
1954 *The Adventures of Augie March* Saul Bellow
1955 *A Fable* William Faulkner
1956 *Ten North Frederick* John O'Hara
1957 *The Field of Vision* Wright Morris
1958 *The Wapshot Chronicle* John Cheever
1959 *The Magic Barrel* Bernard Malamud
1960 *Goodbye, Columbus* Philip Roth
1961 *The Waters of Kronos* Conrad Richter
1962 *The Moviegoer* Walker Percy
1963 *Morte D'Urban* J F Powers
1964 *The Centaur* John Updike
1965 *Herzog* Saul Bellow
1966 *The Collected Stories of Katherine Anne Porter*
1967 *The Fixer* Bernard Malamud
1968 *The Eighth Day* Thornton Wilder
1969 *Steps* Jerzy Kosinski
1970 *Them* Joyce Carol Oates
1971 *Mr. Sammler's Planet* Saul Bellow
1972 *The Complete Stories of Flannery O'Connor*
1973 *Chimera* John Barth
1974 *Gravity's Rainbow* Thomas Pynchon
1975 *Dog Soldiers* Robert Stone
       and *The Hair of Harold Roux* Thomas Williams
1976 *Jr* William Gaddis
1977 *The Spectator Bird* Wallace Stegner
1978 *Blood Ties* Mary Lee Settle
1979 *Going After Cacciato* Tim O'Brien

1980 *The World According to Garp* John Irving
       and *Sophie's Choice* William Styron
1981 *The Stories of John Cheever*
       and *Plains Song* Wright Morris
1982 *So Long, See You Tomorrow* William Maxwell
       and *Rabbit is Rich* John Updike
1983 *Collected Stories of Eudora Welty*
       and *The Color Purple* Alice Walker
1984 *Victory Over Japan: A Book of Stories*
       Ellen Gilchrist
1985 *White Noise* Don DeLillo
1986 *World's Fair* E L Doctorow
1987 *Paco's Story* Larry Heinemann
1988 *Paris Trout* Pete Dexter
1989 *Spartina* John Casey
1990 *Middle Passage* Charles Johnson
1991 *Mating* Norman Rush
1992 *All the Pretty Horses* Cormac McCarthy
1993 *The Shipping News* E. Annie Proulx
1994 *A Frolic of His Own* William Gaddis
1995 *Sabbath's Theater* Philip Roth
1996 *Ship Fever and Other Stories* Andrea Barrett
1997 *Cold Mountain* Charles Frazier
1998 *Charming Billy* Alice McDermott
1999 *Waiting* Ha Jin
2000 *In America* Susan Sontag
2001 *The Corrections* Jonathan Franzen
2002 *Three Junes* Julia Glass
2003 *The Great Fire* Shirley Hazzard
2004 *The News from Paraguay* Lily Tuck

N

66 Oh, say, can you see by the dawn's early light,
What so proudly we hailed at the twilight's last gleaming?
Whose broad stripes and bright stars, thro' the perilous fight,
O'er the ramparts we watched were so gallantly streaming?
And the rockets' red glare, the bombs bursting in air,
Gave proof thro' the night that our flag was still there.
Oh, say does that star-spangled banner yet wave
O'er the land of the free and home of the brave? 99 .

the **National 'Archives** the British government organization which is responsible for the collections of official government papers and historical manuscripts, the earliest of which date from the 11th century. It was formed in 2003 when the *Public Records Office and the Historical Manuscripts Commission were combined.

the **'National 'Archives and 'Records Admini'stration** (*abbr* **NARA**) the US government's official collection of historical records, documents, papers, films, maps, etc. They include the original *Declaration of Independence, the American *Constitution and the *Bill of Rights. The National Archives Building is in Washington, DC, on Constitution Avenue.

the **National 'Art Col'lections Fund** a British charity that tries to keep great works of art in museums and galleries in Britain. Since it was started in 1903, it has saved more than 750 000 art objects from being sold abroad or into private collections in Britain.

the **'National As'sembly for 'Wales** /'weɪlz/ ⇨ WELSH ASSEMBLY.

the **'National Associ'ation for the Ad'vancement of 'Colored ,People** ⇨ NAACP.

'National As'sociation of 'Clubs for 'Young 'People (in Britain) an organization of more than 3 000 clubs for young people which provide sports and outdoor activities such as sailing and climbing, usually for people in cities who would not normally be able to take part in such activities.

the **'National A'sylum Sup'port 'Service** ⇨ NASS.

the **,National 'Audit ,Office** (*abbr* **NAO**) an independent organization in Britain which looks carefully at the accounts of government departments and agencies and other public organizations on behalf of *Parliament.

the **,National 'Basketball Associ,ation** ⇨ NBA.

the **,National 'Book A,ward** one of several US awards given each year by the Association of American Publishers. Each winner receives $10 000, and the awards include those for the best works of Fiction, Non-fiction, Poetry and Young People's Literature. They were first presented in 1950.

the **,National 'Book Critics ,Circle** (*abbr* **NBCC**) a US organization for book reviewers. It has about 700 members and was established in 1974. In the same year it started presenting the **National Book Critics Circle Awards**. These are chosen by a group of book reviewers and authors, and given to writers of Fiction, Non-fiction, Biography or Autobiography, Poetry and Criticism.

the **,National 'Broadcasting ,Company** ⇨ NBC.

the **'National 'Childbirth 'Trust** (*abbr* **the NCT**) a British organization that aims to teach people about the process of having babies and about looking after them. People who are having their first child can go to NCT classes, often in the teacher's home. A woman may learn, for example, the best way of breathing to help her to relax when the baby is actually being born.

the **'National Col'legiate Ath'letic Associ,ation** ⇨ NCAA.

the **,National Con'sumer ,Council** an independent organization started by the British government in 1975 to work on behalf of the public who pay for goods and services. It aims to improve companies and products which are not satisfactory, but in a general way. It does not deal with people's individual problems.

,National Con'sumers League (*abbr* **NCL**) a US organization, established in 1899, which tries to persuade the government to pass laws to protect people who buy goods or use services. It is private and does not make a profit. It also informs consumers of their rights, has a National Fraud Information Center and publishes several magazines. Compare WHICH?

▶ the **National Curriculum**

The National Curriculum was introduced in all *state schools in England and Wales in 1988. Children's education from 5 to 16 is divided into four **key stages**. Key stage 1 covers ages 5–7, key stage 2 ages 7–11, key stage 3 ages 11–14 and key stage 4 ages 14–16. At key stages 1 and 2 pupils study English, mathematics, science, technology, history, geography, art, music and physical education. A modern foreign language is added at key stage 3. Pupils at key stage 4 must study English, mathematics, science, physical education, technology and citizenship and may take several other subjects. In Wales the Welsh language is also studied. Detailed guidance about what children should be taught is given in official **programmes of study**. A disadvantage for teachers has been the increase in the number of documents they are expected to read and the reports they have to write. The National Curriculum does not apply in Scotland, where individual schools decide which subjects and topics to teach.

Attainment targets are set within each subject and pupils' progress is checked at the ages of 7, 11 and 14 when they complete *National Curriculum Tests (**NCTs**). Pupils are graded into eight levels for all subjects except art, music and physical education. At the age of 16, at the end of key stage 4, pupils take *GCSE exams, which are also based on material covered in the National Curriculum. Some children struggle to reach the required standard. If they have learning difficulties, their parents may ask for them to be **statemented**, i.e. given an official document saying that they have **special educational needs**.

The NCTs allow education authorities, in theory at least, to compare standards between different schools. Since the National Curriculum was introduced many people have expressed doubts about the publication in the press of **school league tables** showing the relative performance of schools and about the increased competition.

There is no national curriculum in the US. State governments are responsible for deciding the curriculum for primary and secondary schools. The curriculum is often the cause of debate between people who want to emphasize basic skills, such as reading, writing and mathematics, and others who see the curriculum as a political issue and want schools to teach respect for other cultures or history from the point of view of African Americans, or to offer less traditional topics.

,National Cur'riculum Test *n* (*abbr* **NCT**) a test taken by British schoolchildren to check their progress in subjects of the *National Curriculum. Tests are taken at the ages of 7, 11 and 14. They are often referred to by their old name: *SATs (Standard Assessment Tasks).

the **,National 'Cycle ,Network** about 10000 miles/16000 kilometres of cycling and walking routes in Britain which are managed by local organizations and coordinated by the transport charity *Sustrans. A third of the routes are on paths with no motor traffic and the rest are on quiet streets and lanes.

the **,national 'debt** *n* [sing] the total amount of money that has been borrowed by a government to help pay for public spending. In Britain, the amount borrowed every year is known as the *Public Sector Borrowing Requirement, and is added to the National Debt.

the **,National Edu'cation Associ,ation** ⇨ NEA.

The **,National En'quirer** a popular US *tabloid newspaper, first published in 1952. It contains articles which are often difficult to believe about the private lives of famous people, creatures from space, ghosts, etc. It sells about 2.5 million copies a day, mostly in supermarkets and other public places.

the **,National E'xecutive Com,mittee** (*abbr* the **NEC**) a committee elected by the British *Labour Party and *trade unions to make decisions about the policy of the Labour Party. Under the Labour government of Tony *Blair its role in making party policy has been reduced.

the **,National Exhi'bition ,Centre** (*abbr* the **NEC**) a large centre for exhibitions and conferences near *Birmingham in England, opened in 1976. It holds over 100 exhibitions a year. An example is the *Motor Show.

the **'National 'Farmers' 'Union** ⇨ NFU.

the **,National 'Film ,Theatre** (*abbr* the **NFT**) a cinema on the *South Bank in London, run by the *British Film Institute. It shows the best British and foreign films from all periods, and films of special historical interest. The London Film Festival is held there every year.

the **,National 'Football ,Conference** (*abbr* the **NFC**) (in American football) one of two groups of teams in the *National Football League (NFL). The NFC has four divisions with four teams in each division. The other NFL group is the *American Football Conference (AFC).

the **,National 'Football League** (*abbr* the **NFL**) the organization for professional American football teams. It is divided into the *American Football Conference and the *National Football Conference and both have four divisions, with four teams in each. After the regular season, the best six teams in each conference play to decide which two will go to the *Super Bowl. The NFL began in 1933.

,National 'Forest *n* **1** any of 155 forests in the US protected and managed by the *United States Forest Service. Unlike *National Parks, they are used for commercial activities but in a controlled way.
2 a forest which is being created in an area of 200 square miles/520 square kilometres in central England, across *Leicestershire, *Derbyshire and *Staffordshire. The project, which is managed by the National Forest Company, was started in 1990 to encourage planting of more trees by landowners so that one third of the area, much of which was formerly used for mining, will be covered by trees. The National Forest links several ancient forests. By 2004 almost 6 million trees had been planted and the aim of the project is to plant around 20 million trees.

the **,National 'Front** an extreme right-wing political party in Britain. It was formed in 1966 and caused some street violence in the 1970s, mainly because of its campaign against black and Asian people. In 1980 the party

N

split, and some of its members formed the *British National Party. The National Front has put forward many candidates for election to Parliament but none of them has received more than a few hundred votes.

the ˌNational ˈGallery (in Britain) the buildings in *Trafalgar Square, London, which contain the largest collection of paintings belonging to the nation. The paintings represent every period and style in western art from the 14th to the early 20th century. The main building was completed in 1838, and a new building, the Sainsbury Wing, paid for by members of the family that owns *Sainsbury's and designed by the US architect Robert *Venturi, was added in 1991. More modern paintings are held at *Tate Britain and *Tate Modern.

the National Gallery

the ˈNational ˈGallery of ˈArt a US museum of art owned by the nation and supported by the government. It is part of the *Smithsonian Institution in Washington, DC, and was established in 1937, when Andrew *Mellon died and left his collection of art to the nation. The West Building opened in 1941 and contains works by such great artists as Raphael, Reubens, Rembrandt and El Greco. The East Building for 20th-century art was opened in 1978.

the ˈNational ˈGallery of ˈScotland /ˈskɒtlənd; AmE ˈskɑːtlənd/ a building in Edinburgh which contains an important collection of European and Scottish paintings from the 14th to the early 20th century. It was opened in 1859.

ˌNational Geoˈgraphic a US magazine published each month by the National Geographic Society. It has about 9 million readers and is famous for its beautiful photographs and maps as well as its articles about different countries, societies and animals. US readers must join the Society in order to receive the magazine, but in Britain it can be bought in shops. The Society also publishes books and other magazines, and has its own television channel.

the ˌnational ˈgrid n [sing] **1** the network of equipment that supplies electricity all over England, Scotland and Wales.
2 the system of horizontal and vertical lines that is used on British *Ordnance Survey maps to divide the country into squares so that the position of a place on the map can be referred to easily.

the ˈNational ˈGrid for ˈLearning (abbr NGfL) a British government website set up in 1998 which provides information and links to education resources for teachers and students that are available on the *Internet.

the ˌNational ˈGuard a military force of volunteers in each US state. The total force is about 500 000. **National Guardsmen** can be called to service by the nation or by a state, often after destruction caused by violent wea-

ther. They were used by the southern states to oppose the *civil rights movement and by the US government to support it. The Ohio National Guard killed four *Kent State University students during *Vietnam War protests there in 1970. Some National Guard groups took part in the *Gulf War (1990–1) and served in Iraq from 2003.

the ˌNational ˈHealth ˌService (abbr **the NHS**) the British public service providing medical care that is paid for mainly by the government. British people have strong feelings about its importance, and it is always one of the top political issues in Britain. The National Health Service was introduced in 1946 by the *Labour government as part of the *welfare state system recommended in the *Beveridge Report, and it came into operation in 1948. At first it provided free medical, dental and hospital services for everyone, but in the 1960s charges for medicines and dental services were introduced. Since then the cost of the NHS has continued to rise and governments have been forced to find new ways of paying for it. The *Conservative government under Margaret *Thatcher was accused of trying to privatize the NHS (= sell it to private owners) after introducing *hospital trusts and 'fundholding' (= a system allowing doctors to control how they spend their funds), and encouraging the growth of private medical services and private medical insurance. There are now fewer NHS dentists, but treatment by doctors and hospitals is still free of charge to patients. See also PRIVATE PATIENT.

the ˈNational ˈHeritage Meˈmorial Fund a fund (= money for a special purpose) set up by the British parliament in 1980 for buying and preserving buildings, works of art and other objects that are seen as part of Britain's history. The money for the fund comes mainly from the government and, since 1995, from the *National Lottery. It is called a Memorial Fund because it is intended to honour the memory of people who have died for Britain.

the ˌNational ˈHunt the British name for professional horse racing over jumps, also called *steeplechasing*. It comes from the name of the organization that is responsible for the sport in Britain, the National Hunt Committee. Compare JOCKEY CLUB.

ˌNational Inˈsurance n [U] (abbr **NI**) (in Britain) a system of payments, called **National Insurance contributions**, that all working people and employers have to make. The money is used by the government for payments to unemployed people and others in need, and also to help pay for the *National Health Service. National Insurance is therefore an important part of the *welfare state. Every adult has a **National Insurance number** and this number is used by the *Department for Work and Pensions to identify people.

the ˈNational ˈLabor Reˈlations Board (abbr **the NLRB**) an independent US government organization responsible for preventing illegal practices in industrial relations and settling disputes between workers and managers. It was established by the National Labor Relations Act (1935) to direct trade elections and to protect unions from companies that tried to interfere with their organization and members.

the ˌNational ˈLeague (abbr **the NL**) the older of America's two professional *baseball associations. It was established in 1876 as the National League of Professional Baseball Clubs. It now has 16 teams with five in the Eastern Division, five in the Western Division and six in the Central Division. The National League offices are in New York.

the ˌNational ˈLottery (in Britain) a lottery which raises money for the arts, sports, charities, the *National Heritage Memorial Fund, and other projects. The lottery was introduced by the government in 1994. The

National Lottery Commission is in charge of the lottery and was responsible for choosing *Camelot to run it. See also SCRATCH CARD. ⇨ note at LOTTERIES.

the ˌNational ˈMaritime Muˌseum a museum in *Greenwich, London, with a collection of paintings, boats and other historical items connected with the sea.

the ˌNational ˈMotor Muˌseum a museum at *Beaulieu near *Southampton, England, with a large collection of motor vehicles from every period from the late 19th century to the present day. It is one of Britain's most popular tourist attractions.

the ˌNational ˈMotto the official US motto since 1956: 'In God We Trust.' It is based on a line from *The *Star-Spangled Banner*: 'And this be our motto: "In God is our trust",' The motto has appeared on all US paper money and coins since 1955. All US states have their own individual mottoes, often in Latin.

the ˈNational Muˈseum and ˈGallery a museum in *Cardiff, Wales, with exhibitions of archaeology, nature, art, and industrial and social history, mainly, but not only, connected with Wales.

the ˈNational Muˈseum of Phoˈtography, ˈFilm and ˈTelevision a museum in *Bradford, England that opened in 1983. It has historical films and other items connected with the history of photography, film and television, and also has three cinemas.

ˌNational ˈNature Reˌserve n any of several areas of land in Britain that are protected by law in order to preserve the plants and animals that live there, or to preserve other features of the environment. Marine Nature Reserves in Britain also give protection to plants and animals living in areas of water or coastline. ⇨ note at NATIONAL PARKS.

the ˈNational Organiˈzation for ˈWomen (*abbr* **NOW**) a large US organization that works for women's rights. It was established in 1966 by Betty *Friedan, who was its first president. It supported the *Equal Rights Amendment that failed. In 2005 NOW had about 500 000 members.

▶ **national parks and protected areas**

The idea of **national parks** began in the US, which now has 55 of them, covering over 135 000 square miles/ 338 000 square kilometres. The great majority are in western states. The **National Park Service** is responsible for protecting the natural state of the parks for the benefit of the public. America's parks are so popular that they are being harmed by the number of visitors and their cars. To try to stop this, the National Park Service encourages the development of public transport in the parks.

The oldest national park in the world is *Yellowstone National Park, established in 1872. The largest US park is Wrangell St Elias in *Alaska with 13 000 square miles/ 34 000 square kilometres. It has few visitors because it is very remote. The most popular park is the *Great Smoky Mountains. Many parks are well known for some special feature, such as the *Grand Canyon, the *Everglades and the *Petrified Forest.

There are many other sites run by the National Park Service. One of the most visited areas is the Blue Ridge Parkway in *Virginia and *North Carolina which had 21 million visitors in 2002. (Parkways are roads with parkland either side.) **National recreation areas** such as the Golden Gate in *California also receive many visitors. Most have water sports and other activities. **National preserves** are similar to national parks but are not as well protected. Companies can even search for oil and gas on them. Ten of the 17 national preserves are in *Alaska, including the oldest, *Denali, established in 1917.

The US Bureau of Land Management is in charge of many of the **wilderness areas** created by *Congress. Visitors can camp in wilderness areas if they follow the 'leave no trace' policy. *Native Americans are allowed to use them for religious ceremonies.

National parks are also important as recreation areas in Britain. The land is not in national ownership but is mostly owned by farmers and other private landowners. The first two to be established were the *Lake District and the *Peak District in 1951 and there are now 15 national parks, which attract many thousands of visitors each year. The New Forest and the South Downs are the most recent additions to the list. The aim is to keep the National Parks as far as possible in their natural state, while balancing the different needs of agriculture, industry, housing and tourism. Many of the people who live in national parks depend on tourists for their living and are used to crowded roads in summer. A more serious problem is that some visitors who go regularly to a national park buy cottages in the area as second homes. This means there is less property for local people to buy and many are forced to move.

Each park is managed by a National Park Authority. The government provides 75% of the money to run the parks. National Park Authorities control development within each park, look after *public footpaths and run information and study centres. Some of the land in national parks is owned by the *National Trust but a lot is privately owned.

Some other areas, such as the *Gower Peninsula and the *Malverns, are officially protected as **areas of outstanding natural beauty** (**AONBs**). They tend to be less developed than national parks but still attract many visitors. There are 41 AONBs in England and Wales, and another nine in Northern Ireland. Scotland has 40 *national scenic areas, including the *Cairngorms and *Loch Lomond. See also NATURE RESERVES.

ˌNational ˈPark ˌService the US government organization in charge of the National Park System. This includes *national parks and other types of protected area, including national historical parks, national military parks, national monuments, national memorials, national preserves and national recreation areas. The National Park Service was established in 1916 by President Woodrow *Wilson and is part of the US Department of the Interior.

the ˌNational ˈPortrait ˌGallery a building in London containing thousands of paintings and photographs of famous people from British history. It is next to the *National Gallery and was opened in 1896.

ˈNational ˈPublic ˈRadio ⇨ NPR.

the ˌNational ˈRailway Muˌseum a museum in *York which contains a large collection of old railway carriages and steam locomotives, including the world speed record holder for steam engines, the *Mallard. The museum is a branch of the *Science Museum in London and was opened in 1975.

the ˌNational Reˈsearch ˌCouncil one of the four *national academies in the US which carries out research and provides expert advice and information to the government and *Congress.

the ˌNational ˈRifle Associˌation (*abbr* **the NRA**) a US organization, established in 1871, which supports the use of guns for hunting, sport and self-defence. Its 3.4 million members argue that according to the US *Constitution people have a right to own guns, and they form a powerful group trying to prevent *Congress passing new laws restricting the use of guns.

ˌNational ˈSavings (*also* **National Savings and Investments**) (*abbr* **NS&I**) (in Britain) a system that encourages people to save some of their money and enables the government to borrow money from the people. **National Savings** operates mainly through post offices all over Britain and by mail. It offers various ways of saving and investing money, including *National Savings Certificates and *Premium Bonds. About half the people in Britain have some money in National Savings, which raises billions of pounds for the government's *Public Sector Borrowing Requirement.

,National 'Savings Cer,tificate *n* (in Britain) one of the types of investment (= plan for investing money) offered by *National Savings. People buy the Certificates for a fixed period, usually five years, and at the end of the period receive the amount paid plus interest. National Savings Certificates were introduced in 1916 as a way for the government to borrow extra money during *World War I.

'national 'scenic 'area *n* (in Scotland) an area of natural beauty which is protected and preserved, and which people can visit and enjoy. These areas cover about 15% of Scotland. Compare NATIONAL PARKS.

the ,National Se'curity ,Council (*abbr* the **NSC**) a committee responsible for advising the US *President on matters of national security (= the protection of the nation and its interests) and defence policies. It was established by *Congress in 1947. The President leads the committee's meetings, and other NSC members are the Vice-President, the *Secretary of State and the Secretary of Defense. They are advised by the Chairman of the *Joint Chiefs of Staff and the Director of the *CIA.

▶ **national service**

Conscription (= compulsory service in the armed forces) was introduced in Britain in *World War I and again in 1939. It continued long after the end of *World War II under the name **national service**. During wartime, all men between the ages of 18 and 41 were likely to be **called up** to join the armed forces, unless they were medically unfit or were working in a **reserved occupation**. Many women were called up to serve in industry or work on farms as 'land girls'. **Conscientious objectors** (= people who did not want to join the armed forces for moral or religious reasons) were at first the target of public insults, but later established a role for themselves in caring for the wounded.

After 1948 men between the ages of 19 and 25 were expected to serve 21 months (later increased to two years) in the services, and were often based outside Britain. This was very unpopular with most young men, and national service was ended in 1960. Since then, Britain has depended on **volunteers** to join the services and runs recruiting offices in many towns. Some young people join an **Officers' Training Corps** while at school or university, or become members of the *Territorial Army. From time to time politicians and others call for national service to be introduced again, believing that military life is a good way to encourage discipline among young people.

In the US national service is called **selective service** or conscription, but its popular name is **the draft**. It was first introduced during the *Civil War by both the North and the *Confederate States, and was very unpopular. One reason for this was that anyone could avoid service if he paid money ($300 in the North), or hired somebody to replace him. This led to **draft riots** by poor people in New York City, and almost 1 000 African Americans and others were killed.

The US next used conscription during World War I. Some called it 'another name for slavery', but 10 million men put their names on the draft list. America's first conscription in peacetime began in 1940 when Europe was at war. A man could receive an **exemption** if he was in the '4–F' group for physical or mental reasons, or had

an important job. There were also some conscientious objectors who had to take jobs provided by the government.

The draft was stopped in 1947 but begun again a year later, and men aged 18–25 had to serve 21 months. This supplied soldiers for the *Korean War and the *Vietnam War. Many young men were unwilling to fight in Vietnam and some tried to stay in college and university where they could have a '2–S deferment' from the war. **Draft dodgers** sometimes burned their **draft cards** or went abroad. Conscription was finally ended in 1973, and two years later President *Ford offered to forgive draft dodgers, but only 22 000 of the 125 000 accepted. In 1977 President *Carter officially forgave all of them, provided that they had not committed acts of violence. Although the draft has ended, all men must put their names on the draft list when they become 18 in case there is a national emergency.

the 'National So'ciety for the Pre'vention of 'Cruelty to 'Children ⇨ NSPCC.

the 'Royal 'National 'Theatre (*usually* the **National Theatre**, *also informal* the **National**) a modern building containing three theatres on London's *South Bank, and the theatre company that performs there. The National Theatre company was started in 1963. Its home was the *Old Vic until the new National Theatre building was opened in 1976. In 1988 the title *Royal* was officially added to the company's name to mark its 25th anniversary. However, most people call the company and the building by their original name. The three theatres at the National are the Lyttelton, the Olivier (named after the company's first artistic director, Lawrence *Olivier) and the Cottesloe. The directors since Olivier have been Peter *Hall, Richard *Eyre, Trevor *Nunn and Nicholas *Hytner. The theatre presents a wide range of old and new plays and is known for the high quality of its productions.

▶ **National Trails**

The British National Trails form a network of over 2 500 miles/4 000 kilometres of long-distance paths for walkers and cyclists across England and Wales. There are 15 of them managed by the *Countryside Agency in England and the *Countryside Council for Wales.

Keen walkers can spend their holiday/vacation walking a National Trail. Leaflets and books describe the trail and the facilities available nearby. People doing long-distance walks camp out overnight or stay in bed-and-breakfast accommodation in nearby villages.

The first National Trail, the *Pennine Way, which goes from Edale in Derbyshire to the Scottish border, was established in 1965 and was immediately popular. Other routes include the *Pembrokeshire Coast Path, *Offa's Dyke Path, the South-west Coast Path, and the West Highland Way. The use of the paths by many thousands of walkers, and now also people riding mountain bikes, has led to concern about vegetation being damaged or destroyed, and wide scars (= areas of bare rock or soil) being left on hillsides.

In the US there are 19 National Trails. Because they are very long, few people walk their entire length.

The US National Park Service is in charge of the trails and works with local organizations to keep them in good condition. There are 8 **national scenic trails** of which the Appalachian Trail is the best known and most popular. It was completed in 1937 and became an official trail in 1969. It begins at Mount Katahdin in *Maine and ends at Springer Mountain in *Georgia, running more than 2 000 miles/3 218 kilometres and through 12 states over the tops of the *Appalachian Mountains. Other National Trails include the Continental Divide National Scenic Trail running from the Canadian bor-

N

der over the *Rocky Mountains south to the Mexican border, and the *Natchez Trace from *Mississippi through *Alabama to *Tennessee. The Trace is in fact a road for cars and bicycles, but people can walk on some of the old *Native American paths from which it was developed.

There are 11 **national historic trails**, including the Mormon Pioneer National Historic Trail from *Illinois to *Utah which connects places associated with the *American Revolution. The *Trail of Tears runs 2000 miles/3200 kilometres on land and over water following the route used by *Cherokee Native Americans when they were forced to move west.

the ,**National 'Trust** (*abbr* **the NT**) a British organization for preserving old buildings and beautiful *countryside so that people can visit and enjoy them. Its full name is the National Trust for Places of Historic Interest and Natural Beauty. It began as a small private organization in 1895 and was helped in the early years by Beatrix *Potter with gifts of land in the *Lake District. The Trust is now the largest private owner of land in Britain, having bought or been given historic houses, whole villages, *stately homes, gardens and many areas of land and stretches of coastline. It has more than two million members, which makes it one of the most popular membership groups in Britain. Many houses owned by the Trust have a shop and a cafe for visitors. Compare ENGLISH HERITAGE.

the '**National 'Urban 'League** a US organization, established in 1910, which supports the rights of *African Americans and other minority groups. Its main offices are in New York and it has branches in 34 states.

,**National Vo'cational Qualifi,cation** ⇨ NVQ.

the ,**National 'War ,College** (*abbr* **NWC**) the US government's college for training future leaders of the armed forces, the *State Department and other organizations. It was established in 1946 to replace the Army-Navy Staff College and is at Fort Lesley J McNair in Washington, DC.

the ,**National 'Youth ,Orchestra** a British orchestra for musicians under 20 years old. It gives performances during the school holidays, including one every year at the *Proms.

the '**Nationwide** /'neɪʃnwaɪd/ one of Britain's largest *building societies, with branches in many towns and cities.

,**Native A'merican** *n* a member of one of the groups of people who were living in North America before Europeans reached the continent. For a long time white people called them **Indians** because when Christopher *Columbus first arrived in America, he thought he had reached India. Today, many people do not like this name and prefer to use the term Native American or **American Indian**. Before Europeans arrived in North America there were many **tribes** who lived by hunting animals and gathering plants, and who moved from one place to another according to the season. When Europeans first settled after 1607, Native Americans were quite positive about them and were happy to have the many new things they brought. However, the settlers also introduced new diseases that Native Americans had no resistance to, and they wanted to take their land. To Native Americans the idea of owning land was unknown, but the settlers assumed that they would take control of North America and used all means to do this. Gradually the Native Americans were forced to move to new areas very different from the ones they were used to. Before the Europeans arrived there were over 300 Native American languages, some of which have now died out and many of those remaining are only spoken by a few older people. Other languages, like *Cherokee, are more

widely spoken. According to the **Bureau of Indian Affairs**, there are now about 550 tribes including well-known groups like the *Navajo and the *Sioux. In 2000 there were about 1.9 million Native Americans living in the US, some of them on **reservations**, areas of land that the government has allowed them to keep as their own. Away from the reservations many Native Americans find that their culture is very different from that of white people and have difficulty adapting.

,**Native 'Son** a novel (1940) by the *African-American writer Richard *Wright. It is about a young and poor African-American man in *Chicago who is badly treated because of his colour. He kills a white girl and is condemned to death. The book is a strong attack on racism and was a major influence on other writers.

NATO /'neɪtəʊ; *AmE* 'neɪtoʊ/ (*in full* **the North Atlantic Treaty Organization**) an organization originally formed by 12 countries in 1949 to defend Europe and North America against what was seen as the threat of Soviet attack after *World War II. They agreed that an armed attack against one or more of them should be considered an attack against them all, and set up military bases all over Europe to protect themselves against the Communists. After the end of the *Cold War in the late 1980s, and the joining of East and West Germany in 1990, it was suggested that NATO should become a political organization rather than a military one. In 1995 NATO started a major new approach called Partnership for Peace, to make political and military links stronger between NATO and the central and eastern European countries. Its members now include Belgium, Britain, Bulgaria, Canada, the Czech Republic, Denmark, Estonia, France, Germany, Greece, Hungary, Iceland, Italy, Latvia, Lithuania, Luxembourg, the Netherlands, Norway, Poland, Portugal, Romania, Slovakia, Slovenia, Spain, Turkey and the US. Nato's main offices are in Brussels.

NATS /næts/ ⇨ NATIONAL AIR TRAFFIC SERVICES.

the ,**Natural 'History Mu,seum** a big museum in London, England, with displays about plants, animals, insects, fossils (= animals and plants preserved in rock) and minerals. The museum's collections are so large that the discovery of previously unknown insects in the collections is not uncommon. It was originally part of the *British Museum but has been independently run since 1963.

'**Nature** a British magazine containing news and opinions about science and scientific research, and discussion of issues concerning science. It is well respected and important new scientific research is often first published in it. It has been published every week since 1869.

▶ **nature reserves**

Nature **conservation areas** are areas of the countryside which have special protection under law because they have interesting or unusual wild plants or animals in them.

In Britain there are now about 400 **national nature reserves** and 9000 **local nature reserves** and **marine nature reserves**. Many contain species that are protected under the Wildlife and Countryside Act 1981. In addition, some relatively small pieces of land get special protection as **sites of special scientific interest** (**SSSIs**) because rare or **endangered** plants or animals are to be found there, or because they have special geological (= rock) features. There are over 6000 SSSIs in Britain, many of which are not open to the public. In theory, SSSIs are safe from the threat of commercial development, but this is not always the case in fact. Despite protests, several SSSIs have been lost in recent years to make way for new roads.

Nature conservation areas in Britain are managed by English Nature, Scottish Natural Heritage, the Countryside Council for Wales and the Department of the Environment for Northern Ireland, with the help of local naturalists' trusts and natural history societies.

The US also has many **nature preserves**. People can visit them for enjoyment or to do scientific research, but must stay on paths and cannot disturb or remove anything. They are not allowed to drive vehicles, camp, hunt or start fires. *Indiana has 176 nature preserves, more than 23 000 acres (9 300 hectares) in total. A popular type of nature preserve is the **wildlife refuge**, such as Lake Woodruff Natural Wildlife Refuge in Florida, where John James *Audubon once watched and drew birds.

There are also many national forests, rivers and seashores, and scenic trails. Many **national monuments** are also natural areas. They include the Great Sand Dunes in *Colorado, Lava Beds in *California and Organ Pipe Cactus in *Arizona. The US National Park Service is in charge of all of these and cares for the plants, animals and scenery so that they can be enjoyed by the public.

,**Nat'West** /ˌnæt'west/ one of the main *clearing banks in Britain. Since 2000 it has been part of the Royal Bank of Scotland Group.

'**Naugahyde**™ /'nɔːgəhaɪd/ n [U] a type of artificial leather used for covering furniture, etc. and for making gloves. It can be cleaned with soap and water. Some people think that Naugahyde products show bad taste.

'**Nauru** /'naʊruː/ a small island and country in the Pacific Ocean north-east of Australia. It became independent in 1968 and is one of the smallest members of the *Commonwealth, with a population of under 10 000.
▶ **Nauruan** adj, n.

'**Navajo** (also '**Navaho**) /'nævəhəʊ; AmE 'nævəhoʊ/ n (pl **-o** or **-os**) a member of the largest group of *Native American people, related to the *Apache. There are about 100 000 Navajo, and they live mostly in *Arizona, *New Mexico and *Utah on reservations (= lands given and protected by the US government). They work mainly as farmers. They have also earned money from oil and other minerals on their land. The Navajo are known for weaving carpets and blankets and for making pottery and silver jewellery.

Navajo pottery

Mar'tina ,**Navrati'lova** /mɑːˈtiːnə ˌnævrætɪˈləʊvə; AmE mɑːrˈtiːnə ˌnævrætɪˈloʊvə/ (1956–) a US tennis player, born in Czechoslovakia. She was one of the most successful women players in the history of the game, winning *Wimbledon nine times (1978–9, 1982–7 and

1990), more than any other player, and the *US Open(2) four times (1983–4 and 1986–7), as well as many other competitions.

navy ⇨ note at ARMED FORCES.

the NBA /ˌen biː 'eɪ/ (in full **the National Basketball Association**) the US organization in charge of professional *basketball. It was established in 1949, and its office is in New York. There are 30 NBA teams divided between the Eastern Conference (with an Atlantic Division, a Central Division and a Southeast Division) and the Western Conference (with a Northwest Division, a Southwest Division and a Pacific Division). At the end of each season, the best teams play to decide the NBA Champion.

NBC /ˌen biː 'siː/ (in full **the National Broadcasting Company**) the first of the original three US national broadcasting companies. It was established in 1926 by *RCA as two groups of radio stations. The first NBC television channel opened in 1940. Its main offices are at *Rockefeller Center in New York.

NBCC /ˌen biː siː 'siː/ ⇨ NATIONAL BOOK CRITICS CIRCLE.

NBC Uni'versal /ˌen biː siː/ a company created in 2004 by *NBC and Vivendi Universal. It owns a number of important film and broadcasting businesses which include the film production company *Universal Pictures, cable television companies **USA Network** and the Sci-Fi Channel (USA), as well as the Spanish-language broadcaster Telemundo. The USA Network had 86 million subscribers (= homes that pay to receive programmes) in 2003. It shows major sports events, and original and older films and programmes. Series include *Monk, The Dead Zone* and *Traffic*. Series shown by the Sci-Fi Channel (USA) include *Stargate, Farscape* and *Battlestar Galactica*.

the NCAA /ˌen siː dʌbl 'eɪ/ (in full **the National Collegiate Athletic Association**) an organization in charge of US college sports. It establishes rules for sports competitions between colleges and universities. The NCAA was established in 1906, and more than 1 000 colleges and universities are now members. It also publishes information about players, games and seasons. Its offices are in Indianapolis, *Indiana.

NCL /ˌen siː 'el/ ⇨ NATIONAL CONSUMERS LEAGUE.

NCT /ˌen siː 'tiː/ ⇨ NATIONAL CHILDBIRTH TRUST, NATIONAL CURRICULUM TEST.

the NEA /ˌen iː 'eɪ/ (in full **the National Education Association**) a US trade union that aims to improve the school system, conditions for teachers, etc. In 2004 it had more than 2.7 million members, mostly teachers. Its head offices are in *Washington, DC.

,**Lough 'Neagh** ⇨ LOUGH NEAGH.

Ne'braska /nəˈbræskə/ a US state in the western part of the *Middle West, also called the Cornhusker State. The Missouri River forms its eastern border. The largest city is *Omaha, and the capital city is Lincoln. It was part of the *Louisiana Purchase and was explored by *Lewis and Clark. Its agricultural products include corn, wheat, cattle and pigs and it also makes industrial machinery and electronic equipment. Its tourist attractions include Scotts Bluff National Monument and Chimney Rock National Historic Site.

NEC /ˌen iː 'siː/ **1** ⇨ NATIONAL EXHIBITION CENTRE. **2** ⇨ NATIONAL EXECUTIVE COMMITTEE.

the 'Needles /'niːdlz/ three tall pointed rocks sticking out of the sea near the *Isle of Wight. They are among the best-known and most unusual features of the British coast.

N

the Needles

Neighbourhood 'Watch (*AmE* **Neighborhood Watch**) an arrangement by which people who live in a particular street or area watch each other's houses and tell the police if they see anything suspicious. Many people have formed local Neighbourhood Watch groups to try to prevent crime, but others have refused to join them because they do not like the idea of being watched by their neighbours: *It was one of those streets of semi-detached houses with shiny cars parked outside and Neighbourhood Watch stickers in the windows.*

a Neighbourhood Watch sign

'Neighbours an Australian *soap opera that is very popular in Britain. It is about the lives and relationships of the people living on an imaginary street in Melbourne. It has been broadcast five times a week by the *BBC since 1986.

Neiman 'Marcus /ˌniːmən ˈmɑːkəs; *AmE* ˈmɑːrkəs/ (*also* **'Neiman's** /ˈniːmənz/) a very expensive department store with branches in many major US cities. The original shop was opened in *Dallas, *Texas, in 1907 by Carrie Neiman and her brother Herbert Marcus. The company's Christmas Catalog is famous for containing many expensive items which only rich people have enough money to buy.

' 'Baby Face' 'Nelson¹ /ˈnelsn/ (1908–34) a US criminal, born Lester Gillis in *Chicago. He worked for a time with Al Capone and later robbed banks with John *Dillinger and 'Pretty Boy' *Floyd. He was named '*Public Enemy No 1' by the *FBI in 1934 after killing several people. Soon afterwards he was shot dead by FBI men during a gun battle in Barrington, *Illinois.

Lord 'Nelson² /ˈnelsn/ (*born* Horatio Nelson 1758–1805) an English admiral who became famous for winning a number of sea battles against the French in the 1790s. These victories strengthened British military power at sea, and prevented Napoleon's forces attacking Britain. Many people know that Nelson lost his right arm and his right eye in different battles, and there is a famous story that he said 'Kiss me, Hardy' to another officer just before dying at *Trafalgar. He was made a *viscount(1) in 1801.

> **❝** I have only one eye, – I have a right to be blind sometimes … I really do not see the signal! **❞**
> Lord Nelson at the battle of Copenhagen, 1801

Willie 'Nelson³ /ˈnelsn/ (1933–) a US *country music singer and writer of songs. He was very popular in the 1970s and his most successful songs included *On the Road Again* and *Blue Eyes Crying in the Rain*.

Nelson's 'Column /ˌnelsnz/ a tall column in the middle of *Trafalgar Square, London, which was built in memory of Lord *Nelson between 1839 and 1843. It has a statue of Nelson on top, and four bronze lions round its base. It is one of London's most famous tourist sights.

neo'classicism /ˌniːəʊˈklæsɪsɪzəm; *AmE* ˌniːoʊˈklæsɪsɪzəm/ *n* [U] a style of art, architecture and design that is strongly influenced by the styles of ancient Greece and Rome. It became popular in Europe and North America in the second half of the 18th century, when many buildings were designed with geometrical forms, straight lines and Greek columns.
▶ **neoclassical** *adj*.

neocon'servative /ˌniːəʊkənˈsɜːvətɪv; *AmE* ˌniːoʊkənˈsɜːrvətɪv/ (*informal* **neocon** /ˈniːəʊkɒn; *AmE* ˌniːoʊˈkɑːn/) (*often disapproving*) a politician or journalist in the US who supports the idea that the US is the main world power and should promote American values around the world, using force if necessary. Neoconservatives supported George W *Bush's **War on Terror** and the Iraq War and they often show support for Israel. They put less emphasis on social issues than traditional conservatives.

E 'Nesbit /ˈnezbɪt/ (Edith Nesbit 1858–1924) an English writer of children's stories. She wrote several books about the children of the imaginary Bastable family that are still popular with British children today. Her best-known book, *The Railway Children* (1906), was made into a film in 1970 and again, for television, in 2000.

'Nescafé™ /ˈneskæfeɪ/ *n* [U] a popular make of instant coffee. Some people refer to any type of instant coffee as Nescafé: *It'll have to be Nescafé, I'm afraid – we've run out of real coffee.*

Eliot 'Ness /ˌeliət ˈnes/ (1902–57) an officer with the US Justice Department during *Prohibition. With a team of men called the *Untouchables, he led surprise attacks on illegal alcohol operations run by Al *Capone in *Chicago, and helped to end Capone's criminal career. The US television series and film, both called *The Untouchables*, were based on Ness's work.

'Nessie /ˈnesi/ an informal name for the *Loch Ness monster.

'Nestlé /ˈnesl, ˈnesleɪ/ a large international company that produces many types of food and drink, including *Nescafé, powdered milk and many popular makes of chocolate. Since the 1980s many people in Europe and America have refused to buy any Nestlé products as a protest against the way the company sells powdered milk for babies in poor countries.

'netball *n* [U] a game based on *basketball that is played mainly by women and is very popular with British schoolgirls. It is played by two teams who score points by throwing the ball through a net with an open bottom at the opponents' end of the court. The rules are similar to those in basketball except that in netball the player holding the ball is not allowed to bounce it.

Network 'Rail the company responsible for looking after and repairing all the railway tracks, signals and stations, etc. in Britain. Train services are run separately by a number of different companies.

Ne'vada /nə'vɑːdə/ a state in the western US, sometimes called the Silver State because of the large amounts of silver that were discovered there in the 19th century. It consists mostly of desert and mountains. Its capital is Carson City and the largest city is *Las Vegas. Las Vegas and *Reno are popular tourist destinations, especially for gambling. Other tourist attractions include Lake Tahoe and the *Hoover Dam. In the past, Nevada had less strict marriage laws than other states and people travelled to its cities in order to get divorced quickly. The state produces many minerals, including silver, gold and copper. Its most important agricultural product is cattle.

the ˌNever ˈNever Land the imaginary place in *Peter Pan where Peter and the children have adventures with pirates and animals. It is a magic world where children can fly, and never grow up. It is sometimes used to refer to an imaginary perfect place: *He talks about Scotland as if it was the Never Never Land.*

▶ **the New Age**

People have often questioned the accepted philosophies of the modern western **materialist** society, and have looked to much older traditions for an increased spiritual awareness. Since the 1980s this movement, and the ideas behind it, have been given the name *New Age*. The movement started in *California but quickly spread throughout the US and northern Europe. It attracts young people, people who were *hippies in the 1960s and 1970s, and some older people. **New Age people** believe that a more **holistic** approach to life, which takes account of the whole of personal experience and of the cycles of nature, can help to restore the spiritual balance within themselves and harmony in the environment.

The New Age movement has been especially involved in religion, philosophy, medicine, and a broad area of study called **earth mysteries** which includes astrology and people's relationship with the environment. Some people have turned to religions that combine elements of Christianity with the worship of nature, or to eastern religions, such as Buddhism, that emphasize the personal development of the individual. There has also been a fascination with the **occult** and **parapsychology**, including telepathy, the mental communication of thoughts and feelings. In Britain, ancient sites are thought to have special powers. Each year, on Midsummer's Day, large crowds attempt to reach *Stonehenge to celebrate the summer solstice, because they believe that it is one of the most magical places in Britain.

Crystals (= pieces of special kinds of stone) are used for a type of healing. **Meditation** is used as a way to gain greater self-awareness. **New Age music**, which is usually soft and slow, is used to make it easier to meditate. **Incense** helps promote a good atmosphere. Some people use **psychedelic drugs** though they are illegal. New Age food is usually entirely natural. It includes **health foods** and organic products (= fruit, vegetables and meat that have been produced without any chemicals). Many people associated with New Age culture are **vegetarians**.

The New Age interest in nature has led to greater concern for environmental issues among the wider public. New Age people are often involved in protests at the sites of new roads or other projects that threaten to destroy the countryside. They are often prepared to take extreme measures and may be regarded by others as **cranks** (= people obsessed with a particular idea), though they also gain respect for their commitment.

ˌNew Amsterˈdam /ˌæmstəˈdæm; *AmE* ˌæmstərˈdæm/ the name of what is now New York City when it was the Dutch capital of New Netherlands in the 17th century. It was a small town at the southern end of *Manhattan(1). The British captured it in 1664 and named it New York. Dutch forces took it again in 1673 for 15 months and called it New Orange.

ˈNewark /ˈnjuːək; *AmE* ˈnuːərk/ the largest city in the US state of *New Jersey. It is an industrial port on the Passaic River and has one of the three airports used for New York City, which is only 8 miles/13 kilometres away. The city produces chemicals, beer, paint, leather goods and electronic equipment.

the ˈNewbery ˌMedal /ˈnjuːbəri; *AmE* ˈnuːbəri/ a US award presented each year to the author of the best US children's book. It was established in 1922 and is presented by the Association for Library Service to Children, a division of the American Library Association. It is named after John Newbery (1713–67), an Englishman who published children's books.

ˌNewcastle-upon-ˈTyne /ˌnjuːkɑːsl, ˈtaɪn; *AmE* ˌnuːkæsl/ (*also* **Newcastle**) an industrial city and port on the river *Tyne in north-east England. It used to be an important centre for *coal mining and shipbuilding, and many people became unemployed in the region when these industries became less active in the 1980s. It is now an important commercial, cultural and administrative centre. In 2001 the Gateshead Millennium Bridge was opened, which links Newcastle to the south bank of the river.

ˌNew ˈCovent ˈGarden ˈMarket /ˈkɒvənt; *AmE* ˈkɑːvənt/ (*also* **New Covent Garden**) London's main market selling fruit, vegetables and flowers in large quantities to people who then sell them to the public. It has been in *Vauxhall on the south bank of the *Thames since it was moved from *Covent Garden in 1973.

ˌNew ˈDeal 1 the New Deal the programme begun by US President Franklin D *Roosevelt in the 1930s to end the *Great Depression. It introduced new economic and social measures, and made the national government more powerful. New organizations were created to manage it, including the *Securities and Exchange Commission, the *Works Progress Administration and the *Tennessee Valley Authority. Some people criticized the New Deal for being too expensive and for giving too much power to the government. Compare SQUARE DEAL.
2 (in Britain) a government programme that helps people who have been unemployed and claiming benefits (= money from the state) for longer than six months to find employment. It also helps disabled people return to work, as well as the partners of people claiming benefits. The programme provides training, advice and help in starting a business.

ˌNew ˈEngland an area of the north-eastern US which includes the states of *Maine, *New Hampshire, *Vermont, *Massachusetts, *Rhode Island and *Connecticut. It is known for its beautiful small towns which are popular with visitors, especially in the autumn. **New Englanders**, a large number of whom have Irish ancestors, are often called the real Yankees. Other Americans consider them to be very independent, clever, practical and suspicious of people they do not know. The English explorer Captain John Smith named the area in 1614, and the *American Revolution began there.

the ˌNew English ˈBible a version of the Bible that was translated into modern English by a group of British *Protestant writers. It was published in two sections, the Old Testament in 1961 and the New Testament in 1970.

the ˌNew 'Forest an attractive area of countryside in southern England consisting of forest and open wild land covered with rough grass. It has belonged to the *royal family since *William the Conqueror began hunting there in 1079. It is a popular tourist centre, and especially well known for the **New Forest ponies**, a breed of small horses living there in almost wild conditions.

the ˌNew 'Frontier a phrase used by John F *Kennedy to describe his aims and policies. In 1960 he said that the US was on 'the edge of a new frontier', and asked Americans to join together for new achievements in space, science, education and social conditions. This was said during the speech in which he accepted his nomination as the *Democratic Party's candidate for President. Compare NEW DEAL.

'Newgate /'njuːɡeɪt; AmE 'nuːɡeɪt/ (also ˌNewgate 'prison, ˌNewgate 'gaol) a prison in London which was first built in the 12th century on land where the *Old Bailey now stands. It was rebuilt several times before it was finally destroyed in 1902. In the 18th century it became famous for the very bad conditions in which the prisoners were kept. It is mentioned in many 18th– and 19th– century novels.

ˌNew 'Hampshire /'hæmpʃə(r)/ a north-eastern US state in *New England, also called the Granite State. The largest city is Manchester, and the capital city is Concord. New Hampshire was the first independent English colony (from 1776) and one of the original 13 states. It produces electrical goods, stone, clay and paper products, as well as many crops. Popular tourist attractions include the White Mountain National Forest and Lake Winnipesaukee.

ˌNew 'Jersey /'dʒɜːzi; AmE 'dʒɜːrzi/ a north-eastern US state on the Atlantic Ocean. Local people often call it Jersey, and it is also known as the Garden State. The largest city is *Newark, and the capital city is Trenton. New Jersey was settled by the Dutch, became British in 1664, and was one of the original 13 states. It produces vegetables, chemicals, medicines and clothing. *Atlantic City and *Princeton University are both in New Jersey.

ˌNew 'Labour a phrase used by Tony *Blair in the 1990s to refer to his aim of making the British *Labour Party more modern. New Labour moved away from the political left in order to appeal to more people. For example, the party voted to change *Clause 4 and be less influenced by the *trade unions. A phrase used often by Blair in the campaign to win the general election in 1997 was 'New Labour, new Britain!'.

the ˌNew 'Left a group of people who developed left-wing political ideas in many countries, especially the US, in the 1960s. They protested against the conditions of poor people in society, and against the *Vietnam War, but they did not support the Soviet Union. The New Left included many students and writers.

ˌCardinal 'Newman[1] /'njuːmən; AmE 'nuːmən/ (John Henry Newman 1801–90) an English priest and poet. When he was the vicar (= priest) of the Anglican University Church in *Oxford he shocked many people because his opinions seemed closer to those of the *Roman Catholic Church than the *Church of England. He became a Roman Catholic in 1845, and a Catholic priest the next year. In 1879 he was made a cardinal (= a senior Roman Catholic priest). His writing had a wide influence on religious thought, and some of his poems are still sung as hymns.

ˌPaul 'Newman[2] /'njuːmən; AmE 'nuːmən/ (1925–) a US actor who has also produced and directed films. He is perhaps best remembered for his part in *Butch Cassidy and the Sundance Kid* (1969). His other films include *Cat on a Hot Tin Roof* (1958), *The Hustler* (1961), *Cool Hand*

Luke (1967), *The Sting* (1973), *Nobody's Fool* (1994) and *The Road to Perdition* (2002). He received a special *Oscar in 1985 and an Oscar for *The Color of Money* (1986). Newman is married to the actor Joanne Woodward, with whom he has often appeared in films. He has also been a *NASCAR racing driver and he owns a food company called Newman's Own, whose profits are given to charity.

'Newmarket /'njuːmɑːkɪt; AmE 'nuːmɑːrkɪt/ a town in *Suffolk in eastern England, which has been a major horse-racing centre for more than 300 years. It has two famous racecourses where some of Britain's most important races take place each year. It is also the home of the *Jockey Club, the National Stud (= centre for breeding horses) and the National Horseracing Museum.

ˌNew 'Mexico /'meksɪkəʊ; AmE 'meksɪkoʊ/ a south-western US state on the Mexican border, also called the Land of Enchantment. The largest city is Albuquerque, and the capital city is *Santa Fe. It became part of the US in 1848 after the *Mexican War, and a state in 1912. The first atom bomb was exploded at Alamogordo, New Mexico, in 1945. The state produces many minerals, including uranium, gold and silver, as well as oil and gas. Its tourist attractions include *Carlsbad Caverns and White Sands National Monument.

the 'New 'Model 'Army the army organized by Oliver *Cromwell in 1645 to fight the supporters of *Charles I in the *English Civil War. It was Britain's first professional army, and its discipline and training were important factors in winning the war. See also FAIRFAX.

'New 'Musical Ex'press (abbr NME) a British newspaper, published every Saturday, that consists mainly of articles about pop music. It has a reputation for recognizing new groups and musical styles before they become fashionable. It is especially popular with students.

ˌNew Or'leans /ɔː'liənz; AmE ɔːr'liənz/ the largest city in the US state of *Louisiana. It is on the *Mississippi River and the *Gulf of Mexico, and is the second largest US port. Its popular name is the Big Easy. The city is famous for its *French Quarter, *jazz and food, and millions of tourists visit it each year. The French established it in 1718, and it was part of the *Louisiana Purchase. Andrew *Jackson won the Battle of New Orleans against the British, the last battle of the *War of 1812. See also MARDI GRAS.

the French Quarter, New Orleans

'Newport /'njuːpɔːt; AmE 'nuːpɔːrt/ a city in the US state of *Rhode Island. It is on Aquidneck Island on the Atlantic coast. It was famous for the Newport Jazz Festival each year from 1954 until the festival moved to New York in 1972 and the Newport Folk Festival has been held there since 1959. Newport was settled in 1639 and became a place of safety for *Quakers and Jews. It was one of the state's two capitals until 1900. It contains many large houses built by rich people in the 19th century. The *America's Cup races were held there from 1851 to 1953.

The ‚New Re'public a US political and cultural magazine known for its liberal opinions. It was established in 1914 and is published each week. People who have written for the magazine include John *Steinbeck, Thomas *Wolfe and Mary *McCarthy. Its editors have included Walter *Lippmann and Joyce Carol Oates.

the ‚New 'Right a general name for US right-wing politicians since the 1980s who have been in favour of a return to *states' rights and traditional family values, and against abortion and equal rights for homosexuals. Their views have been supported by the Moral Majority of Jerry *Falwell and other religious groups based on *fundamentalism. They helped to elect Presidents Ronald *Reagan, George *Bush, and George W *Bush.

The ‚New 'Scientist a British magazine containing news and opinions about new developments in science and technology and their effects on society and the environment. It has been published every week since 1956.

'News ‚Corp /ˈnjuːz kɔː; AmE ˈnuːz kɔːr/ a large group of companies owned and run by Rupert *Murdoch which includes many newspapers and magazines in Australia, Britain and the US, television channels including *Sky, the *Fox News Channel and *DirecTV, large book publishing companies and the *20th Century Fox film studio.

'New 'Scotland 'Yard /ˈskɒtlənd; AmE ˈskɑːtlənd/ the main offices in London, England, of most departments of the *Metropolitan Police. The original offices were in a street off *Whitehall called Scotland Yard. They moved to a new building near *Victoria Station in 1966, but many people still refer to it as **Scotland Yard** or simply **the Yard**.

'Newsnight /ˈnjuːznaɪt; AmE ˈnuːznaɪt/ a television news programme that is broadcast in Britain on *BBC Two late every evening from Monday to Friday. It usually includes a serious discussion about an important news item. Its aim is 'to make sense of the day's news, to try to explain the detail of current events and hold to account those responsible for them'. Some of its presenters, especially Jeremy *Paxman and Kirsty Wark, are well known for asking politicians difficult questions. On Fridays the programme ends with *Newsnight Review*, a discussion by critics of new films, plays, books and exhibitions.

the ‚News of the 'World a British *tabloid Sunday newspaper, owned by Rupert *Murdoch. It is one of Britain's best-selling newspapers, and consists mainly of news about sport, crime and famous people such as film and television actors or members of the *royal family. It was first published in 1843.

▶ **newspapers**

Many British families buy a **national** or **local** newspaper every day. Some have it delivered to their home by a **paper boy** or **paper girl**; others buy it from a **newsagent** (= a shop that sells newspapers, *magazines, sweets, etc.) or a **bookstall**. Some people read a newspaper **online**. National **dailies** are published each morning except Sunday. Competition between them is fierce. Local daily papers, which are written for people in a particular city or region, are sometimes published in the morning but more often in the early evening.

The US has only one national newspaper, *USA Today*. The rest are local. A few newspapers from large cities, such as the *New York Times* and the *Washington Post*, are read all over the country. The *International Herald-Tribune* is published outside the US and is read by Americans abroad. Many Americans **subscribe** to a newspaper which is delivered to their house. This costs less than buying it in a shop. Papers can also be bought in bookshops and supermarkets and most newspapers have online versions.

In Britain the newspaper industry is often called *Fleet Street, the name of the street in central London where many newspapers used to have their offices. Britain has two kinds of national newspaper: the **quality papers** and the *tabloids. The qualities were also called the *broadsheets because they were printed on large pages, but are now often in tabloid size which is half the size of a broadsheet. They report national and international news and are serious in tone. They have **editorials** which comment on important issues and reflect the political views of the paper's **editor**. They also contain financial and sports news, **features** (= articles), **obituaries** (= life histories of famous people who have just died), **listings** of television and *radio programmes, theatre and cinema shows, a *crossword, *comic strips, *advertisements and the weather forecast.

The main quality dailies are The *Times and the *Daily Telegraph*, which support the political right, The *Guardian*, which is on the political left, The *Independent and The *Financial Times. People choose a paper that reflects their own political opinion. Sunday papers include The *Sunday Times, The *Observer and The *Independent on Sunday. The Sunday and Saturday editions of papers have more pages than the dailies, **supplements** (= extra sections) on, for example, motoring and the arts, and a colour magazine.

The tabloids report news in less depth. They concentrate on **human-interest stories** (= stories about people), and often discuss the personal lives of famous people. People who disapprove of the tabloids call them **the gutter press**. The most popular are The *Sun, The *Mirror, The *Express and The *Daily Mail. The *News of the World, a Sunday tabloid, sells more copies than any other newspaper in Britain.

There are also local papers, many of which are **weeklies** (= published once a week). They contain news of local events and sport, carry advertisements for local businesses, and give details of houses, cars and other items for sale. Some are paid for by the advertisements they contain and are delivered free to people's homes. Some cities also have a daily paper published in the evening, for example, the *Evening Standard* in London.

A daily newspaper from a medium-sized US city has between 50 and 75 pages, divided into different sections. The most important stories are printed on the front page, which usually has the beginnings of four or five articles, and colour photographs. The articles continue inside. The rest of the first section contains news stories, an **opinion page** with editorials, and **letters to the editor**, written by people who read the paper. Another section contains local news. The sport section is near the end of the paper, with the features section. This contains comics and also **advice columns**, such as *Dear Abby. There are advertisements throughout the paper.

Tabloids contain articles about famous people but do not report the news. They are displayed in supermarkets, and many people read them while they are waiting to pay.

On Sundays newspapers are thicker. There are usually fewer news stories but more articles analysing the news of the past week and many more features, including a colour section of comics.

Newspapers get material from several sources. **Staff reporters** write about national or local news. Major newspapers also have their own **foreign correspondents** throughout the world. Others get foreign news from **press agencies** or **wire services**, such as *Associated Press or *Reuters. Some papers have their

N

own **features writers**. In the US features are usually **syndicated**, which means that one newspaper in each area can buy the right to print them. The editor decides what stories to include each day but the **publisher** or owner has control over general policy. Newspaper owners are very powerful and are sometimes called **press barons**. The most famous of these is Rupert *Murdoch.

The ˌNew 'Statesman a British magazine published each week, containing articles about politics, society and the arts, usually written from a left-wing point of view. Established in 1913, it is Britain's oldest and best-known left-wing magazine, and has a reputation for independence and for criticizing the government.

'Newsweek /'nju:zwi:k; *AmE* 'nu:zwi:k/ a US news magazine published each week in New York. It contains articles on politics, science, society, culture and other subjects. It was first published in 1933 and is now owned by the *Washington Post*. In 2003, the magazine had more than 3 million readers in the US.

ˌIsaac **'Newton** /'nju:tən/ (1642–1727) an English scientist. He is well known for discovering **Newton's Laws**, which explained the relationships between force, mass and movement. Many people know the story that he discovered the idea of gravity (= the force that attracts things towards the centre of the planet) when he saw an apple fall from a tree in his garden. He also discovered differential calculus, a branch of mathematics, at the same time as Leibniz discovered it in Germany, and made important discoveries about the nature of light and colour. He was made a *knight in 1705.

'new town n any of the 32 towns that were planned and built in Britain in the second half of the 20th century. They were established by the government to encourage people, businesses and industries to move out of the crowded cities. Some, such as *Milton Keynes and Telford, became large successful towns, but not all of them attracted as many people or businesses as they expected. Many British people think that new towns are ugly, boring places because they do not have many interesting old buildings or streets: *The company is relocating to Glenrothes, a new town to the north of Edinburgh.*

ˌNew 'Year n [U] the first few days of January. In Britain and America many people have parties on **New Year's Eve** (= 31 December). At midnight it is traditional for people to sing *Auld Lang Syne, to wish each other 'Happy New Year', and often to kiss each other. In large cities many people gather in public places on New Year's Eve, such as *Trafalgar Square in London, Princes Street in Edinburgh or George Square in *Glasgow. In Scotland the celebration of the New Year is called *Hogmanay. **New Year's Day** (= 1 January) is a *bank holiday in Britain.

the ˌNew Year 'Honours the aristocratic titles and other awards given to people by the British king or queen on New Year's Day (= 1 January) each year: *She got an OBE in the New Year Honours list.*

▶ **New York**

There is a great sense of excitement in New York and it has a reputation for being 'the city that never sleeps'. The ' *Big Apple', as it is sometimes called, feels alive, fast and at the centre of everything, with cars hooting, yellow taxis weaving through the traffic, brightly lit theatres, and restaurants busy late into the night. The city offers enormous contrasts. Some of the most expensive homes in the world are in New York City, but on the pavements outside are poor people without a home. It is possible to pay hundreds of dollars for a meal in a restaurant, or eat good, filling food for a couple of dollars from a street vendor.

Many Americans have never been to New York, but everyone knows something about the city. They are familiar with the tall *Manhattan skyline, *Times Square with its brightly lit advertisements, *Madison Square Gardens, where many sports events take place, *Wall Street, its financial heart, the *Empire State Building, the *Statue of Liberty, *Ellis Island, where many of their ancestors first arrived in the US and *Ground Zero, where the development of the site is seen as a symbol of New Yorkers' courage and ability to overcome tragedy.

New York was founded in 1624 by the Dutch, who called it *New Amsterdam. Its Dutch origins can be seen in the names of old New York families like Stuyvesant and Vanderbilt, and in place names such as *Brooklyn (originally Breukelen) and *Harlem. In 1664 the English gained control and changed the name to New York. In 1898 several towns were combined to make Greater New York City, which became the second largest city in the world, after London, though at the time part of it consisted of farms. Soon after, many new buildings were constructed, and in 1904 the New York subway was opened.

Many immigrants to the US stayed in New York, giving the city the variety of cultures it has today. During the 1920s, when alcohol was banned, New York had many speakeasies (= bars serving alcohol), which were illegal but very popular. This was also the time of the *Harlem Renaissance, when Harlem became a centre for African-American arts and culture. In the latter half of the 20th century wealthier people began moving out to the suburbs. Today there are about 8 million people in New York City and 19 million in the state.

New Yorkers speak in a very direct way which can seem rude to people from other parts of the US. Some have little patience with visitors who are not used to the fast pace of the city. But for many visitors, meeting real, rude New Yorkers is part of the attraction of going to the city.

'New York 'City 'Police De'partment /'jɔːk; *AmE* 'jɔːrk/ (*abbr* **NYPD**) the large police department for New York City which was created in 1845, based on London's *Metropolitan Police and which was considered to be the first modern style police department in the US. NYPD has around 40 000 police officers and includes the **Transit Bureau**, who are responsible for protecting the subway system.

the ˌNew 'York Daily 'News /'jɔːk; *AmE* 'jɔːrk/ a popular tabloid newspaper published in New York every day. It was established in 1919 and is known for its large headlines, large photographs and short articles.

the ˌNew 'York 'Drama ˌCritics 'Circle A,ward any of several awards given each year by New York theatre critics (= newspaper and magazine writers who give their opinions about plays performed). The awards were first given for the 1935–36 season by members of the New York Drama Critics Circle. Winning plays have included *Three Tall Women* (1993–94) by Edward *Albee and *Arcadia* (1994–95) by Tom *Stoppard.

The ˌNew 'Yorker /'jɔːkə(r); *AmE* 'jɔːrkər/ a famous US magazine published each week in New York. It is known for its long articles, fiction, humour and comic drawings. It was established in 1925 by Harold Ross, and its writers have included Ogden *Nash, Dorothy *Parker, James *Thurber and S J Perelman. The English journalist Tina Brown was the magazine's editor from 1992 to 1998, and some readers complained about the new, more lively style she introduced.

the ˌNew 'York 'Herald-'Tribune /'jɔːk; *AmE* 'jɔːrk/ ⇨ INTERNATIONAL HERALD-TRIBUNE.

the ˌNew 'York Philhar'monic /'jɔːk fɪləˈmɒnɪk; *AmE* 'jɔːrk/ the oldest orchestra in the US, established in

1842. It has more than 100 musicians and performs in the Avery Fisher Hall, completed in 1962 as part of the *Lincoln Center for the Performing Arts. The orchestra's free concert given in *Central Park in 1986 had an audience of about 800 000, the largest ever in the world for a concert of classical music. Musical directors of the Philharmonic have included Gustav Mahler (1909–11), Arturo Toscanini (1928–36), Leonard *Bernstein (1958–69), Zubin Mehta (1978–91), Kurt Masur (1991–2002) and Lorin Maazel (2002–).

the ˌNew ˈYork ˈPublic ˈLibrary /ˈjɔːk; AmE ˈjɔːrk/ the largest research library in the world that lends books to the public. The main building in New York is on *Fifth Avenue and *42nd Street, but it includes 87 other local libraries in Manhattan, the *Bronx and *Staten Island.

The ˌNew ˈYork Reˈview of ˈBooks /ˈjɔːk; AmE ˈjɔːrk/ a US magazine, started in 1963 and published every two weeks, which contains articles about new books and also science, politics, US culture and the arts. It is respected for the high quality of its writing, and had more than 115 000 readers in 2003.

ˌNew York ˈState /jɔːk; AmE jɔːrk/ a north-eastern US state which was one of the 13 original states. It is also known as the Empire State. It has the third largest population of any state, after *California and *Texas. The largest city is *New York, and the capital city is Albany. Henry *Hudson visited the area in 1609, and the first people to settle there permanently were the Dutch in 1624. Tourist attractions include the *Statue of Liberty, *Niagara Falls, the *Adirondack Mountains and the *Catskill Mountains. Important industries include manufacturing, publishing, banking and commerce. See also IROQUOIS LEAGUE.

the ˌNew York ˈStock Exˌchange /jɔːk; AmE jɔːrk/ (abbr **the NYSE**) the largest US stock exchange and one of the largest in the world. It is on *Wall Street in New York City and has about 2800 members. It was first established in 1792.

the *ˌNew York ˈTimes* /jɔːk; AmE jɔːrk/ a famous US newspaper read mainly by people who are well educated. The paper is published each morning in New York and can also be bought all round the world. There is also a large Sunday issue. The *Times* first appeared in 1851 (as the *New York Daily Times*) and has won the most *Pulitzer Prizes of any newspaper, including one for the *Pentagon Papers. The New York Times Company also owns radio and television stations, magazines and other newspapers, including the *International Herald-Tribune* and the *Washington Post*.

> **66** All the News That's Fit to Print **99**
> motto of the *New York Times*

ˌNew ˈYork Uniˈversity /ˈjɔːk; AmE ˈjɔːrk/ (abbr **NYU**) a private university in New York City. Its main buildings are in *Greenwich Village, with some also in the *Bronx. It was established in 1831 and is now one of the largest private universities in the world.

ˌNew ˈZealand /ˈziːlənd/ a country in the southern Pacific Ocean consisting of two large islands and several small islands. The capital city is Wellington. Most of the population is of British origin, people whose ancestors went there to be farmers. There are also many Maoris, who are descended from the original inhabitants of New Zealand and are now demanding some of the rights and areas of land that they believe were unfairly taken from their ancestors in the 19th century. New Zealand became a British colony in 1841, and an independent country in 1907. It is a member of the *Commonwealth. Tourism and agriculture are its main industries. New Zealand lamb, butter and wine are sold in Britain and many other countries.
▶ **New Zealander** *n*.

Next /nekst/ any of a group of *high-street shops in Britain selling fashionable clothes and furnishings.

ˌNez ˈPercé /ˌnez ˈpɜːs; AmE ˈpɜːrs/ *n* (*pl* **Nez Percés** *or* **Nez Percé**) a member of a *Native American people who now live in the state of *Idaho on a reservation (= land given and protected by the US government). Their name means 'pierced nose' in French. They bred excellent horses and originally lived in west Idaho. Although they gave most of their land to the US in 1855, later land disputes led to a war in 1877 in which Chief *Joseph and his people were defeated.

NFC /ˌen ef ˈsiː/ ⇨ NATIONAL FOOTBALL CONFERENCE.

NFL /ˌen ef ˈel/ ⇨ NATIONAL FOOTBALL LEAGUE.

NFT /ˌen ef ˈtiː/ ⇨ NATIONAL FILM THEATRE.

the **NFU** /ˌen ef ˈjuː/ (*in full* the **National Farmers' Union**) an organization for farmers in England and Wales. It is not a *trade union but exists to give practical advice and support to farmers. There is a separate **NFU** Scotland.

NGfL /ˌen dʒiː ef ˈel/ ⇨ NATIONAL GRID FOR LEARNING.

NHS /ˌen eɪtʃ ˈes/ ⇨ NATIONAL HEALTH SERVICE.

NI /ˌen ˈaɪ/ ⇨ NATIONAL INSURANCE.

Niˌagara ˈFalls / naɪˌæɡrə ˈfɔːls/ a famous American waterfall on the Niagara River that joins Lake *Erie to Lake *Ontario on the *border between the USA and Canada. It actually consists of two waterfalls (the American Falls and the Horseshoe Falls), separated by Goat Island. They are a very popular tourist attraction, especially with honeymooners (= people who are just married), and are also used to produce electricity. Both the US and Canada have cities called Niagara Falls, and they are joined by Rainbow Bridge.

Niagara Falls

ˌNicholas ˈNickleby /ˈnɪklbi/ a novel (1839) by Charles *Dickens. Nicholas Nickleby is a young man who has to make enough money to support his mother and sister after his father dies. He first goes to work as a teacher at *Dotheboys Hall, a school run by the evil Wackford Squeers. Nicholas is shocked by the conditions there, and by their cruel treatment of a poor boy called Smike. Nicholas and Smike escape from the school together and later work in a theatre company run by Vincent Crummles. There are many other linked stories in the novel, but its main importance is that it showed *Victorian society how terrible conditions in many of its schools were, and in fact led to a lot of them being closed or improved.

ˌBen ˈNicholson[1] /ˈnɪkəlsn/ (1894–1982) an English artist who was one of the first in Britain to produce abstract paintings (= ones that arrange shapes and colours in a satisfying way instead of showing things in a realistic way). His second wife was Barbara *Hepworth.

ˌJack ˈNicholson[2] /ˈnɪkəlsn/ (1937–) a US actor known for playing attractive but dangerous characters. He won *Oscars for *One Flew Over the Cuckoo's Nest, Terms of Endearment* (1983) and *As Good as it Gets* (1998). He first became internationally known in *Easy Rider*, and his other films include *Five Easy Pieces* (1970), *Chinatown* (1974), *The Shining* (1980), *A Few Good Men* (1993), *About Schmidt* (2002) and *Something's Gotta Give* (2003).

N

Nickel'odeon /ˌnɪklˈəʊdiən; *AmE* ˌnɪklˈoʊdiən/ a US television channel that broadcasts programmes for children during the day. In the evening it changes its name to Nick at Nite and shows old 'television classics'.

Jack 'Nicklaus /ˈnɪkləs/ (1940–) a US golfer who won twenty major tournaments (= competitions) between 1962 and 1986, a world record. These included the British *Open three times, the *US Open(1) four times and the *US Masters Tournament six times, more than any other golfer. The popular name for him is the 'Golden Bear' and in 1988 he was voted the 'Golfer of the Century'.

▶ **nicknames**

Nicknames are informal, sometimes humorous names that are based on a person's real name or on an obvious characteristic or habit. Nicknames were in use before *surnames became widespread in the 13th century and were a means of identifying a person. Some nicknames, such as 'Russell' meaning 'red-haired' and 'Brown' referring to brown hair or skin, later developed into surnames.

Nicknames reduce the level of formality in a relationship and may suggest a close friendship. Many people are given a nickname while they are still children and may keep it throughout their life, whether they like the name or not. Nicknames may also be given to politicians and other public figures, especially by the press, such as the name 'Dubya' often used for George W Bush. This makes famous people seem more ordinary, and also leads to shorter, eye-catching headlines.

There are several kinds of nickname in common use. The most popular are **short forms**, shortened versions of a person's first name. Some common short forms include: Bob or Rob for Robert, Ted or Ed for Edward, Dick or Rick for Richard, Meg or Maggie for Margaret, Beth, Liz or Lizzie for Elizabeth, and Kathy, Kate or Katie for Katherine.

Nicknames may also be derived from surnames. Nicknames for famous people that have been much used by the British media include 'Fergie' for Alex *Ferguson and 'Becks' for David *Beckham. 'Madge' is used for the singer *Madonna.

Other nicknames, like the original ones, reflect a personal characteristic. 'Ginger' is often used for people with red hair. 'Shorty', or even teasingly 'Lofty', is used for short people. Names like 'Fatty', 'Tubby' or 'Skinny' that refer to a person's weight are rude and generally used only as insults. Nicknames based on skin colour are offensive and should not be used. 'Brains' is used for somebody who is very intelligent, and 'Tiger' for someone who is brave or aggressive. The Duke of *Wellington is sometimes called 'The Iron Duke' and Margaret *Thatcher was known as 'The Iron Lady' because of her strength and determination. These more descriptive nicknames are less common in the US.

Nicknames based on a person's race or country can still be heard but are often highly offensive. In England, for instance, men from Scotland used to be addressed as 'Jock' or 'Mac', people from Ireland were 'Paddy' or 'Mick', and people from Wales 'Dai' or 'Taffy'. Members of immigrant groups in both Britain and the US have had to suffer rude names from the native or mainstream population. Nicknames for people in foreign countries are also usually offensive, e.g. 'Yanks' or 'Yankees' for Americans, 'Frogs' for the French, and 'Krauts' for Germans.

The British have nicknames for many other things: a 'Roller' is a Rolls-Royce car and 'Marks and Sparks' is *Marks and Spencers. 'The Hammers' and 'Spurs' are both football teams, West Ham United and *Tottenham Hotspur. In the US all states have nicknames: *California

is 'The Golden State', *Texas is 'The Lone Star State', and *Wyoming is 'The Equality State'.

Harold 'Nicolson /ˈnɪkəlsn/ (1886–1968) a British diplomat and the writer of 125 books, of which his *Diaries and Letters* (1968) is the best known. He was a *Member of Parliament from 1935 to 1945, and was made a *knight in 1953. He married Vita *Sackville-West in 1913, and their marriage survived until her death in 1962 although they both had homosexual affairs.

Nielsen 'ratings /ˌniːlsn/ a service of **Nielsen Media Research**, a US research company which estimates how many people watch television programmes. The information is used by television companies to decide how much to charge for advertising on different programmes.

Ni'geria /naɪˈdʒɪəriə/ a large country on the west coast of Africa. It was a British colony from 1914 and has been a member of the *Commonwealth since becoming independent in 1960, although between 1995 and 1999 its membership was stopped temporarily after a dispute over the execution of nine men. The capital city of Nigeria is Abuja, in the middle of the country, although its biggest city is Lagos, on the coast. The official language is English.
▶ **Nigerian** *adj, n.*

The **Night Before 'Christmas** a poem (1823) by Clement Moore (1779–1863) which is well known to many American children. It presents the traditional image of Santa Claus as a cheerful fat man who travels through the sky at Christmas bringing gifts. It begins:

> **66** T'was the night before Christmas,
> When all through the house
> Not a creature was stirring, – not even a mouse;
> The stockings were hung by the chimney with care,
> In hopes that St. Nicholas soon would be there.
> The children were nestled all snug in their beds,
> While visions of sugar-plums danced in their heads. **99**

Florence 'Nightingale /ˈnaɪtɪŋɡeɪl/ (1820–1910) an English nurse who became famous for her work during the *Crimean War. In spite of a lot of opposition from army officials, she greatly improved the conditions of military hospitals and reduced the numbers of soldiers dying of disease. She used to walk round the hospital beds at night with her lamp, comforting the patients, and so became known as the 'Lady of the Lamp'. Later she ran a campaign to change the British hospital system and improve the training of nurses. In 1907, she became the first woman to receive the *Order of Merit.

▶ **nightlife**

What people do in the evening depends very much on where they live as well as on their tastes. In Britain Friday and Saturday evenings in most city centres are busy, with crowds of mainly young people moving between cinemas, pubs, clubs and wine bars. In the country people often go to the local pub but if they want more choice of entertainment they have to travel to a town. Similarly in the US, people living in New York City have very different possibilities for a good **night out** compared with those living in small towns.

*Pubs in Britain attract a wide range of age groups. Older people tend to choose quieter pubs where conversation is easier than in the pubs popular among younger people, where loud music is played. The main activity is drinking, usually beer or lager. People have to be over 18 to drink alcohol. Some pubs also have live music. **Pub crawls**, in which several pubs are visited in one evening, are popular with younger people. Many pubs close at 11 p.m. and after this people may look for something to eat or go to a **club**.

Wine bars and **cocktail bars** are usually smarter than pubs and more expensive. In the US the **bars** range from those popular with students, where the beer is cheap, to those in hotels where customers must dress smartly. **Bartenders** make hundreds of different drinks by combining various kinds of alcohol. The British custom of buying a round, when each person in a group takes a turn to buy a drink for everyone else, is not always the rule in the US. Sometimes each person pays for his or her own drinks, or a group might **run a tab** (= the bartender writes down what they have) and then everyone pays part of the bill when they leave. Some bars provide free snacks, especially during **happy hour** (= a time around 5 p.m. when drinks cost less). In the US people must be over 21 to drink alcohol. There are special alcohol-free bars for teenagers.

A popular activity among young people is to **go clubbing**, i.e. go to clubs where they can drink and dance. There is a charge for admission and drinks are usually more expensive than in pubs. Cities like New York and London are famous for their clubs. The music is usually modern dance music but some play *soul, *jazz or pop.

People living in or near a city or town can go to the **cinema** (*AmE* **movie theater**) or **theatre** or to a concert. The biggest concert venues in Britain include the *Albert Hall in London and the *National Exhibition Centre in Birmingham. In the US people occasionally go to **dinner theater**: they sit at tables in a theatre for a meal and stay there afterwards to watch a play. Other places to go include comedy clubs, where comedians perform live, and sports events.

Gambling is illegal in some parts of the US but in *Las Vegas and *Atlantic City there are many casinos where people can gamble. Some communities run **bingo** games for low stakes (= bets). In Britain there are casinos and bingo is also popular.

Going out for dinner in a restaurant is a very popular activity. Many people also enjoy entertaining at home. They may have a **dinner party** for a few friends or a **party** with drinks and snacks to which many people are invited.

ˌBill **'Nighy** /'naɪi/ (1948–) a British actor who has been in many television and radio programmes, including *The Men's Room* (1991) and has also appeared in films including *Love Actually* (2003) for which he won a *BAFTA for best supporting actor.

'Nike™ /'naɪki/ a US company that makes sports clothes. Its trainers (= sports shoes) are fashionable among young people, who often wear them when not playing sport. (Nike was the ancient Greek goddess of victory, who had wings.)

> 66 Just do it 99
> Nike advertising slogan

the ˌBattle of the **'Nile** /'naɪl/ a sea battle fought in 1798 between the British and the French near Alexandria in Egypt. The British under *Nelson won an important victory, trapping the army of Napoleon in Egypt and gaining control of the Mediterranean for Britain.

ˌChester **'Nimitz** /ˌtʃestə 'nɪmɪts; *AmE* ˌtʃestər/ (1885–1966) the admiral who commanded the US Pacific Fleet during *World War II.

9/11 /ˌnaɪn ɪ'levn/ an abbreviation for the date *September 11, 2001. It is used to refer to the terrorist attacks that took place on that day in the US and often appears in phrases describing people or things con-

nected with them, e.g. *9/11 families* (= families affected by the attacks), *the 9/11 Commission*, *the post-9/11 world*. People in the US write dates in the form of the month followed by the day, whereas in Britain the month follows the day. But the US form is used in both countries to refer to the day of the attacks.

900 number /ˌnaɪn 'hʌndrəd nʌmbə(r)/ *n* (in the US) a telephone number that begins with 900. A call to it is more expensive than those to ordinary numbers. 900 numbers are used by companies who have 'chat lines', operate competitions, etc., and they usually allow people who call to record messages or answers and their phone numbers and addresses.

ˌNine Inch **'Nails** a US rock band formed by Trent Reznor (1965–), who often performs alone. His style is known as 'industrial music' and his songs are often about sex, suffering and violence. The group's most successful albums have included *The Downward Spiral* (1994) and *And All that Could Have Been* (2002).

999 /ˌnaɪn naɪn 'naɪn/ the telephone number used in Britain for calling the police, fire or ambulance services in an emergency: *Quick! Dial 999!*

the ˌnine o'clock **'watershed** ⇨ WATERSHED.

911 /ˌnaɪn wʌn 'wʌn/ the telephone number used in the US for calling the police, fire or ambulance services in an emergency: *a 911 call*.

ˌNineteen Eighty-**'Four** a novel about the future, written in 1948 by George *Orwell. The main character, Winston Smith, dares to think his own thoughts and fall in love in a society ruled by 'the Party', which tells everyone what they must think and do. The Party is led by Big Brother, who may not even exist, and everywhere there are pictures of him, with the words 'Big Brother is watching you'. The book was very successful, and introduced several new ideas and words into the language, including *Big Brother*, the *Thought Police*, *Newspeak* and *doublethink*. Although 1984 is now in the past, it is still sometimes used to refer to some frightening future world.

the **1922 Committee** /ˌnaɪntiːn twenti'tuː kəmɪti/ (*also* the **Conservative and Unionist Members' Committee**) (in Britain) the group of *Conservative *Members of Parliament that includes all the party's *backbenchers. Its name comes from a meeting of Conservative MPs in the *Carlton Club, London, in October 1922, when the need for an organization through which backbenchers could have more influence was discussed. Members of the Committee now meet regularly and its opinions are passed on to the party leader.

Nir'vana /nɜː'vɑːnə; *AmE* nɜːr'vɑːnə/ a US rock band in the 1980s and 1990s, known for the harsh words of their songs and their wild stage performances. Their main singer was Kurt *Cobain and their albums included *Nevermind* (1991), *Incesticide* (1992) and *In Utero* (1993).

'Nissen hut /'nɪsn/ *n* a large hut shaped like a tunnel, made of curved sheets of metal covering a concrete floor. They were used in Britain, especially during *World War II, to store equipment or as temporary shelters for soldiers. They were named after the man who originally designed them. Compare ANDERSON SHELTER, QUONSET HUT.

ˌDavid **'Niven** /'nɪvən/ (1910–1983) an English film actor well known for playing pleasant, gently comic roles, usually as an elegant English gentleman. His many films included *Wuthering Heights* (1939), *Around the World in Eighty Days* (1956), *The Pink Panther* (1964) and *Death on the Nile* (1978). He also wrote two humorous books about his own life.

ˌRichard **'Nixon** /'nɪksn/ (1913–94) the 37th US *President (1969–74) and the only one to resign. He was

N

elected to the US *House of Representatives in 1946, where he was on the *House Un-American Activities Committee, and then to the US *Senate in 1950. He was Vice-President under President *Eisenhower (1953–61) but was defeated by John F *Kennedy in the 1960 election for President. As President, Nixon was successful in ending the *Vietnam War and establishing a closer relationship between the US and China, but he is mainly remembered for having to leave office because of the *Watergate scandal. He was given the *nickname 'Tricky Dick' because he was often not direct or honest in his dealings with people.

> 66 There can be no whitewash at the White House. 99
> Richard Nixon about Watergate, 1973

the NL /ˌen 'el/ ⇨ NATIONAL LEAGUE.

NLRB /ˌen el ɑː 'biː/; *AmE* ɑːr/ ⇨ NATIONAL LABOR RELATIONS BOARD.

NME /ˌen em 'iː/ ⇨ NEW MUSICAL EXPRESS.

ˌ**Nobel 'Prize** /ˌnəʊbel; *AmE* ˌnoʊbel/ *n* each of six international prizes given each year since 1901 for the highest achievement in physics, chemistry, medicine, literature, economics and work towards world peace. Winners of the prizes are called **Nobel laureates**. The prizes are named after the Swedish scientist Alfred Nobel (1833–96), who invented dynamite: *He won a/the Nobel Prize for his work.*

ˌ**Nob 'Hill** /ˌnɒb; *AmE* ˌnɑːb/ a fashionable district of *San Francisco, *California. It includes Grace Cathedral and two famous hotels, the Fairmont and the Mark Hopkins. Many of the large Victorian houses originally built there by rich people, or 'nobs', were destroyed by the fire that followed the 1906 earthquake.

ˈ**Noddy**™ /ˈnɒdi; *AmE* ˈnɑːdi/ a character in a series of young children's books by Enid *Blyton, the first of which was published in 1949. Noddy is a small boy with a large head on which he wears a long blue cap with a bell on the end of it. He lives in Toytown and drives a small red and yellow car. His best friend is an old man called Big Ears. The local policeman is Mr Plod. The Noddy books have sometimes been criticized by adults for being old-fashioned and even racist but they are still very popular with children.

ˌ**Noncon'formist** *n* (in England and Wales) any member of a Protestant Church which does not follow the beliefs and practices of the *Church of England. For example, members of the *Baptist, *Methodist, and *Presbyterian Churches, or of the *United Reformed Church, are all Nonconformists. Members of independent groups such as the *Quakers, the *Plymouth Brethren, and the *Salvation Army are also referred to as Nonconformists. In Scotland, where the *Presbyterian Church is the official one, members of any other church, including members of the *Church of England, are considered Nonconformists. Compare FREE CHURCH.
▶ **Nonconformist** *adj*.

ˌ**non-'U** /ˌnɒn 'juː; *AmE* ˌnɑːn 'juː/ *adj* (*BrE humorous disapproving*) (of a word or an action) not showing the correct manners that are typical of someone who has been well educated or of an *upper-class person. The terms U (= upper class) and non-U (= not upper class) were first used by an English professor in 1954 to discuss the speaking habits of English people, but they were made popular and their meaning was extended by Nancy *Mitford in her book *Noblesse Oblige* (1956).

NORAD /ˈnɔːræd/ ⇨ NORTH AMERICAN AEROSPACE DEFENSE COMMAND.

ˌ**Denis 'Norden** /ˈnɔːdn; *AmE* ˈnɔːrdn/ (1922–) an English broadcaster and writer of comedy whose clever humour has been popular for many years. With Frank *Muir he wrote many successful radio and television series. Since 1977 he has presented *It'll be Alright on the Night* which shows humorous accidents that have occurred while people were making television programmes.

ˈ**Norfolk** /ˈnɔːfək; *AmE* ˈnɔːrfək/ a county in the east of England, part of *East Anglia. It is known for the Norfolk *Broads and for being very flat. Its administrative centre is *Norwich.

the ˌNorfolk 'Broads /ˌnɔːfək; *AmE* ˌnɔːrfək/ ⇨ BROADS.

ˈ**Norman**[1] /ˈnɔːmən; *AmE* ˈnɔːrmən/ *n* any of the people from Normandy in northern France who settled in England after their leader William defeated the English king at the Battle of *Hastings in 1066. The Normans took control of the country, a process

Norman architecture

known as the **Norman Conquest**. They used many of the existing *Anglo-Saxon methods of government of the state and the church, but added important aspects of their own and made government much more effective. The language of government became first Latin, and then Norman French, and this caused many new words to be added to the existing English language. The name 'Norman' comes from the Old French for 'Northman', as the Normans originally came from Denmark, Norway and Iceland. See also WILLIAM I.
▶ **Norman** *adj* **1** of the Normans: *a Norman castle.* **2** of the style of *Romanesque architecture used in Britain from the Norman Conquest to the early 13th century. Its features included round arches and heavy pillars, and often roofs made of wood. The cathedrals at *Ely, *Norwich, Peterborough and *Durham are in the Norman style.

ˌ**Jessye 'Norman**[2] /ˌdʒesi 'nɔːmən; *AmE* 'nɔːrmən/ (1945–) a US opera singer known for her strong, clear soprano (= highest female) voice. She began her career in Berlin, and first sang in New York with the *Metropolitan Opera in 1973. She is also known for her performances of songs by Wagner and Richard Strauss.

the ˌNorman 'Conquest /ˌnɔːmən; *AmE* ˌnɔːrmən/ ⇨ CONQUEST.

the ˌNormandy 'landings /ˌnɔːməndi; *AmE* ˌnɔːrməndi/ the military operation, beginning on 6 June 1944 (*D-Day) during which large numbers of British, US and Canadian soldiers landed in Normandy in northern France, and began the campaign to drive the Germans out of France.

ˌ**Oliver 'North** /ˈnɔːθ; *AmE* ˈnɔːrθ/ (1943–) a US Marine officer who was a member of the *National Security Council under President Ronald *Reagan. He was charged with being involved in the illegal operations of the *Iran-Contra affair, but the legal case against him was dropped in 1991.

> 66 When I heard the words criminal investigation my mindset changed considerably. 99
> Oliver North

the ˈNorth Aˈmerican ˈAerospace Deˈfense Comˌmand /əˈmerɪkən/ (*abbr* **NORAD**) a military defence organization established in 1957 by the US and Canadian air forces. It has a large underground base in

Cheyenne Mountain near Colorado Springs, *Colorado, to provide early warning of air attacks.

the 'North A'merican 'Free 'Trade A,greement /ə'merɪkən/ ⇨ NAFTA.

,North'ampton /ˌnɔːθ'æmptən; AmE ˌnɔːrθ'æmptən/
a large town in *Northamptonshire, in the area of England known as the *Midlands. The town has a long history of making shoes and there are still shoe factories there today.

,North'amptonshire /ˌnɔːθ'æmptənʃə(r); AmE ˌnɔːrθ'æmptənʃər/ (abbr **Northants**) an English county in the *Midlands. Its administrative centre is *Northampton.

,Northanger 'Abbey /ˌnɔːθæŋgər; AmE ˌnɔːrθæŋgər/ a novel (1818) by Jane *Austen in which a romantic young woman, Catherine Morland, falls in love with a young priest, Henry Tilney. His father believes she is rich and invites her to the family's home, Northanger Abbey. Catherine imagines that the house contains all kinds of terrible secrets. The father discovers that she has no money, and orders her to leave, but she marries Henry in the end. The book was written as a satire on the type of *Gothic novel that was popular at the time.

the 'North At'lantic 'Treaty ,Organization /ət'læntɪk/ ⇨ NATO.

,North Caro'lina /ˌkærə'laɪnə/ a southern US state on the Atlantic Ocean, also called the Tarheel State and the Old North State. The largest city is Charlotte, and the capital city is Raleigh. The state was settled by the English and named after King *Charles I. It was one of the original 13 states and later one of the *Confederate States. Its products include tobacco, corn, furniture, paper and chemicals. Its tourist attractions include the *Great Smoky Mountains, the Blue Ridge National Parkway and the Wright Brothers National Memorial at Kitty Hawk.

the ,North 'Circular a series of roads that join together and pass through many areas of North London. They join the *South Circular at the *Thames, east and west of London. Until the *M25 was built the North Circular formed the main road round London. It still carries a lot of traffic, which often moves very slowly.

,Lord 'Northcliffe /'nɔːθklɪf; AmE 'nɔːrθklɪf/ (born Alfred Charles William Harmsworth 1865–1922) a British newspaper publisher, born in Ireland. He started the *Daily Mail in 1896 and the *Daily Mirror in 1903, introducing a style of journalism that was then new to Britain. Articles were short and lively, with some written specially for women, and more headlines were used. Northcliffe was also the owner of The *Times from 1908 to 1922. He helped the British government with their propaganda (= information published to influence public opinion) during *World War I, and in 1917 was made a *viscount. He was a very strong character who liked power. His younger brother Harold (later Lord *Rothermere) was his partner in his early career.

,North Da'kota /də'kəʊtə; AmE də'koʊtə/ a northern central US state on the Canadian border, also called the Sioux State and the Peace Garden State. The largest city is Fargo, and the capital city is Bismarck. Most of North Dakota was part of the *Louisiana Purchase, and Britain gave the rest in 1818. The state is known for its agriculture: over 90% of its area is used for farming. Its agricultural products include wheat, beans, sunflowers, pigs and cattle. It also produces coal, oil and gas. Tourist attractions include the International Peace Garden on the US–Canadian border, Theodore *Roosevelt National Park and the *badlands.

the ,Northern ,Ireland As'sembly /ˌaɪələnd; AmE ˌaɪərlənd/ the name of a governing body in

Northern Ireland that has existed at various times and then been suspended because of political disagreements between political parties in Northern Ireland and with the British government. From 1921 Northern Ireland was governed by a parliament in *Stormont, in *Belfast, but after the start of the political violence, known as the *Troubles, the **province** was placed under *direct rule from London. The Assembly has been in operation again several times from 1973–75 and again from 1982–86 when the majority party, the *Ulster Unionist Party stopped supporting it because of the *Anglo-Irish Agreement. The assembly was set up again as a separate parliament for Northern Ireland in 1998 as part of the *Good Friday Agreement. It continued until 2003 with David *Trimble as the **First Minister** in charge of the **North Ireland Executive** of 108 elected members which formed the **legislative body** for Northern Ireland with powers **devolved** (= transferred) to it from the *Westminster parliament. The assembly was suspended again in 2003 because of disagreements between political parties about sharing power. Talks are continuing to be held to solve these problems and re-establish the Assembly.

the ,Northern 'Ireland ,Office /'aɪələnd; AmE 'aɪərlənd/ the British government department responsible for Northern Ireland since 1972, when *direct rule was introduced. It is run by the *Secretary of State for Northern Ireland. Its responsibilities changed following the establishment of the *Northern Ireland Assembly, but when the Assembly is suspended it becomes responsible for all areas of government.

the ,North 'Sea a part of the north-eastern Atlantic Ocean. The North Sea has the *Shetland Islands to the north of it, the United Kingdom and the *Orkney Islands to the west, Norway and Denmark to the east, and France, Belgium, Holland and Germany to the south. It covers about 220 000 square miles/570 000 square kilometres, and is relatively shallow, mostly less than 300 feet/90 metres deep. It has less salt in it than the North Atlantic, partly because a lot of fresh water flows into it from the *Thames, the Rhine, the Elbe and other large rivers. There are large amounts of oil and gas under it which are being taken out for commercial use.

,North Sea 'gas (in Britain) natural gas obtained from under the *North Sea, mainly off the east coast of Scotland and the coast of *East Anglia. Britain's gas supply was formerly produced from coal, but since the late 1960s the gas used in Britain is natural gas from the North Sea.

,North Sea 'oil (in Britain) oil obtained from under the *North Sea, mainly from the area around the east coast of Scotland and the north-east coast of England. The oil was discovered in 1969. It was first brought out in 1975 and by 1994 Britain had become the world's eighth largest producer although since 2000 it has been clear that the country needs to plan for the time when the oil runs out. North Sea oil has been a major political issue between the British government and the Scottish people, many of whom feel that Scotland should have benefited more from the great wealth under the sea off its coast.

the ,North-South Di'vide (in Britain) the economic and social differences between the North and the South of England, especially the South-East, shown by things like house prices, employment figures and rates of pay. In the 1980s the North suffered far more from the loss of jobs in industries such as mining but the gap between the North and the South has since become narrower.

Nor'thumberland /nɔː'θʌmbələnd; AmE nɔːr'θʌmbərlənd/ (abbr **Northd**) a county in north-east England, on the Scottish border. It has a number of

N

castles and Roman remains, including *Hadrian's Wall. Its administrative centre is Morpeth.

Nor'thumbria /nɔːˈθʌmbriə; *AmE* nɔːrˈθʌmbriə/ an area of northern Britain ruled by kings from the 7th to the 9th centuries AD. It was famous at that time for its monasteries. The name Northumbria is still sometimes used to mean north-east England and south-east Scotland, especially in books, etc. written for tourists.

the ˌNorthwest 'Ordinance a US law, passed by *Congress in 1787, which established the Northwest Territory, the area from the *Great Lakes south to the *Ohio River. It was the country's first official addition of western lands. The law said that the region could become a state when its population reached 60 000.

the ˌNorth-west 'Passage a sea route along the northern coast of the US between the Atlantic and Pacific Oceans. From the end of the 15th century, many explorers looking for an easy route to Asia tried to find the North-west Passage, including Sir Francis *Drake and Captain *Cook. But it was not until 1906 that the first journey through, taking three years, was made by the Norwegian explorer Roald Amundsen. The Canadian government claims the Northwest Passage as part of Canada, but the US government regards it as an international area of water. For various reasons, including the ice, very few ships have ever used it. See also HUDSON.

ˌNorth 'Yorkshire /ˈjɔːkʃə(r); *AmE* ˈjɔːrkʃər/ (*abbr* **N Yorks**) a county in north-east England, formed in 1974 from parts of the former county of *Yorkshire. Its administrative centre is Northallerton.

'Norwich /ˈnɒrɪdʒ; *AmE* ˈnɑːrɪdʒ/ the administrative centre of the English county of *Norfolk. It has a *Norman castle and cathedral. The University of East Anglia is in Norwich.

the 'Norwich School /ˈnɒrɪdʒ; *AmE* ˈnɑːrɪdʒ/ a group of early 19th-century painters who lived in or near *Norwich, England. They painted scenes of the countryside in *East Anglia. The group included **John Crome** and **John Cotman**.

No 10 ⇨ NUMBER TEN.

the ˌUni'versity of ˌNotre 'Dame /ˌnəʊtrə 'deɪm; *AmE* ˌnoʊtrə 'deɪm/ the most famous Catholic university in the US. It is in South Bend, *Indiana, where it was established in 1842. Notre Dame has America's best-known college football team, sometimes called 'the fighting Irish'.

'Nottingham /ˈnɒtɪŋəm; *AmE* ˈnɑːtɪŋəm/ a large town in the county of *Nottinghamshire, on the River Trent. It is traditionally known for its lace industry. It has a fine *Roman Catholic cathedral and two universities. See also SHERIFF OF NOTTINGHAM.

ˌNottingham 'Forest /ˌnɒtɪŋəm; *AmE* ˌnɑːtɪŋəm/ one of the two football clubs of *Nottingham. The other is *Notts County.

'Nottinghamshire /ˈnɒtɪŋəmʃə(r); *AmE* ˈnɑːtɪŋəmʃər/ (*abbr* **Notts** /nɒts; *AmE* nɑːts/) a county in the *Midlands of England, famous (especially in the past) as a centre of the coal-mining industry. Its administrative centre is *Nottingham.

ˌNotting 'Hill /ˌnɒtɪŋ; *AmE* ˌnɑːtɪŋ/ a fashionable area of west London, England. It is especially famous for the **Notting Hill Carnival**, a colourful street festival held there every year on *Summer Bank Holiday.

ˌNotts 'County /ˌnɒts; *AmE* ˌnɑːts/ one of the two football clubs of *Nottingham. The other is *Nottingham Forest. Notts County is the oldest professional football club in Britain, started in 1864.

'noughth week /ˈnɔːtθ/ the week before the start of a new term (= one of the three periods which the academic year is divided into) at *Oxford University.

ˌIvor No'vello /nəˈveləʊ; *AmE* nəˈveloʊ/ (1893–1951) a Welsh composer, actor and writer of plays. He wrote many successful songs and musical plays, in some of which he also acted. Two of the best-known are *Glamorous Night* (1935) and *King's Rhapsody* (1949), and his songs include *Keep the Home Fires Burning*, which was very popular during *World War I.

NOW /naʊ/ ⇨ NATIONAL ORGANIZATION FOR WOMEN.

NPR /ˌen piː ˈɑː(r)/ (*in full* **National Public Radio**) a network of public radio stations in the US created in 1970. NPR has almost no advertising and receives some money from the government as well as from charities and listeners. It produces news and cultural programmes including its popular morning news programme, *Morning Edition*.

the **NRA** /ˌen ɑːr ˈeɪ/ ⇨ NATIONAL RIFLE ASSOCIATION.

NS&I /ˌen es ˈaɪ/ ⇨ NATIONAL SAVINGS.

NSC /ˌen es ˈsiː/ ⇨ NATIONAL SECURITY COUNCIL.

the **NSPCC** /ˌen es piː siː ˈsiː/ (*in full* the **National Society for the Prevention of Cruelty to Children**) a British charity that has worked to prevent child abuse of all kinds since 1884. It operates a 24-hour national telephone helpline to give help and advice to children and parents, as well as anyone worried about the safety of a child. The NSPCC works closely with social workers, doctors and police officers.

NT /ˌen ˈtiː/ ⇨ NATIONAL TRUST.

ˌLord 'Nuffield /ˈnʌfiːld/ (*born* William Richard Morris 1877–1963) an English businessman who was the first person in Britain to mass-produce cars (= make them in large quantities by mechanical processes). He started his business repairing bicycles in *Oxford, and soon moved into making bicycles and then cars. The *Morris car company was very successful and Morris himself became very rich. He gave a lot of his money to hospitals and charities and also to *Oxford University, where Nuffield College was named after him. See also MG, MORRIS MINOR.

the **NUJ** /ˌen juː ˈdʒeɪ/ (*in full* the **National Union of Journalists**) (in Britain) the main *trade union for people who work in newspaper and magazine journalism, publishing and broadcasting.

the **NUM** /ˌen juː ˈem/ (*in full* the **National Union of Mineworkers**) (in Britain) the main *trade union for people who work in coal mines. For most of the 20th century, the production of coal was very important for Britain's economy, so the NUM was in a powerful position. However, since the 1980s most of Britain's coal mines have been closed down and the power of the unions has been greatly reduced. Compare UDM. ⇨ note at COAL MINING. See also MINERS' STRIKES.

'number plate (*AmE* **license plate**) *n* a metal or plastic plate on the front and back of a vehicle with a series of numbers and letters, the **registration number**, which identifies that vehicle.

In Britain, vehicles have a white plate at the front and a yellow plate at the back. In the past, the year in a which a car was made was shown by the letter at the start or the end of the registration number, so that somebody might describe a car as, for example, 'a T reg Rover'. A new system was introduced in 2001 using seven characters. The first two letters show the area in which the vehicle was first registered, the next two numbers show the year the vehicle was made, for example 04 for the first part of 2004 and 54 for the second part of the same year. The final three letters are chosen randomly. The registration number of each new vehicle is registered with the *DVLA and stays with the vehicle even if it moves to a new area or has a new owner.

In the countries of the *European Union, new number plates include a blue strip on one side which shows the *EU symbol of yellow stars and the country code of the country which the vehicle is from, such as GB for Britain. In the US, license plates are issued by the State government and contain enough letters and numbers for the number of cars in the state, so that small states have shorter **registration numbers**. They often use different colours, symbols and slogans related to the state. If the owner of a vehicle moves to a new state, he or she must get new license plates.

Number 'Ten (also **No 10**) **1** the house at 10 *Downing Street, the official London home of the British *Prime Minister (although Tony *Blair and his family actually live in a flat next door at No 11, the official home of the *Chancellor of the Exchequer): *There has been a stream of visitors to Number Ten today.*. See also CHEQUERS.
2 the British *Prime Minister and the people who advise him or her: *The paper got its story from sources close to Number Ten.*

nu 'metal /ˌnjuː; *AmE* ˌnuː/ *n* [U] a type of *heavy metal music which is influenced by *hip hop and has aggressive songs and a heavy drum beat. Well known nu metal bands include Deftones, Korn and Slipknot.

Trevor 'Nunn /'nʌn/ (1940–) an English theatre director who helped to run the *Royal Shakespeare Company from 1968 to 1987. He has also produced three of Andrew *Lloyd Webber's *musicals in London and some operas at *Glyndebourne. He was director of the *National Theatre from 1996 to 2002. He was made a *knight in 2002.

▶ **nursery rhymes**
Nursery rhymes are short verses and songs for children. Some are more than 200 years old. An early collection of rhymes, *Mother Goose's Melody*, was published in England in about 1780 and in America five years later. *Mother Goose is herself a traditional figure and teller of tales who was later included in *pantomime. Her name is still associated with books of nursery rhymes, especially in America.

Parents sing nursery rhymes to their children while they are still babies, and children soon learn the words themselves. The rhymes are popular because they are short, easy to say, and tell simple, often funny stories. For instance, *The *Queen of Hearts* is about a queen who makes some tarts for the king, but somebody steals them and the king punishes the thief.

Some nursery rhymes may refer to people or events in history. *The *Grand Old Duke of York*, for instance, is supposed to be about the Duke of *Cumberland, a famous army commander, while *Mary, Mary, Quite Contrary* may describe *Mary Queen of Scots. *Ring a Ring o' Roses* may refer to the *Great Plague: the roses are red spots on the skin and the last line, 'We all fall down', refers to people dying. Other rhymes are about country life and farm animals, such as sheep or mice. They include *Baa, Baa, Black Sheep*, *Little Miss Muffet*, *Sing a Song of Sixpence* and *Three Blind Mice*.

Rhymes such as *Hush-a-bye, Baby* are popular **lullabies**, songs that are sung to send children to sleep.

Others are old **riddles**: *Humpty Dumpty, for example, is an oval-shaped figure who breaks after falling off a wall and cannot be mended – the explanation is that Humpty Dumpty is an egg. Some rhymes have simple actions that go with them. Parents say the rhyme *This little pig went to market* while pulling their children's toes. *Pat-a-Cake, Pat-a-Cake, Baker's Man*, *Oranges and Lemons* and *Ring-a-Ring o' Roses* are all associated with simple games. Children use *Eeny Meeny Miney Mo* to choose somebody for a role in a game or to count the seconds to the start of a game.

Most nursery rhymes told in the US come from Britain, though *Mary Had a Little Lamb* was written by an American, Sara Hale. Since rhymes are usually spoken or sung there are often small differences in the words. For example, Americans say *Ring Around the Rosie* and *Pattie Cake, Pattie Cake, Baker's Man*. Nursery rhymes often describe things that are unknown to most American children such as St Ives or *Banbury Cross*. Some rhymes use old or unusual language. For instance, Little Miss Muffet eats 'curds and whey', and few people know that this is a kind of cheese. But none of these things really matter and nursery rhymes continue to be popular with young children everywhere.

'nursery school *n* [C, U] a school for children aged between 2 and 5. Children are not required by law to go to nursery school, and may go instead to other groups such as **playgroups** or **crèches**.

the NUS /ˌen juː 'es/ (*in full* **the National Union of Students**) (in Britain) an organization for students in universities and *colleges of further education, where it organizes entertainments and represents students' interests. It also represents students generally and organizes national campaigns against any threat to their interests.

the NUT /ˌen juː 'tiː/ (*in full* **the National Union of Teachers**) (in England and Wales) the main *trade union for teachers. Most of its members work in *state schools but there are some in *independent schools also.

NVQ /ˌen viː 'kjuː/ (*in full* **National Vocational Qualification**) (in Britain) a system of grades for people in work who acquire technical and other skills through *vocational training. It was started in the late 1980s to establish national standards. The training can be done at people's place of work or at special colleges or schools. See also GNVQ.

NWC /ˌen dʌblju 'siː/ ⇨ NATIONAL WAR COLLEGE.

Michael 'Nyman /'naɪmən/ (1944–) an English composer who is best known for his film music, including that for *The Draughtsman's Contract* (1982) and *The Piano* (1993).

NYPD /ˌen waɪ piː 'diː/ ⇨ NEW YORK CITY POLICE DEPARTMENT.

NYPD 'Blue /ˌen waɪ piː diː/ a US television series on *ABC about police detectives in the imaginary 15th Precinct of New York City. It began in 1993 and won 16 *Emmy awards in its first four years, including Best Drama (1994). Some Americans were offended by its bad language and scenes of naked people. See also DETECTIVE STORY.

NYSE /ˌen waɪ es 'iː/ ⇨ NEW YORK STOCK EXCHANGE.

NYU /ˌen waɪ 'juː/ ⇨ NEW YORK UNIVERSITY.

N

O o

'Oakland /'əʊklənd; *AmE* 'oʊklənd/ an industrial city and port in the US state of *California. It is on the east side of San Francisco Bay and connected to *San Francisco by the Bay Bridge, the largest and busiest bridge in the US. Oakland companies build ships and cars, make electronic equipment and chemicals, and process food and oil.

ˌAnnie 'Oakley /'əʊkli; *AmE* 'oʊkli/ (1860–1926) a famous US sharpshooter (= expert at shooting accurately). Her popular name was 'Little Sure Shot', because she was less than 5 feet/153 centimetres tall. She and her husband Frank Butler, also a sharpshooter, worked as entertainers in *Buffalo Bill's *Wild West Show. The musical play and film *Annie Get Your Gun* was based on her life.

the Oaks /əʊks; *AmE* oʊks/ a major English horse race without jumps run every year at *Epsom. It was first run in 1779.

OAP /ˌəʊ eɪ 'piː; *AmE* oʊ/ ⇨ OLD AGE PENSIONER.

the OAS /ˌəʊ eɪ 'es; *AmE* ˌoʊ/ ⇨ ORGANIZATION OF AMERICAN STATES.

O'asis /əʊ'eɪsɪs; *AmE* oʊ'eɪsɪs/ a British pop group from Manchester, formed in 1991. The best-known members are Noel and Liam Gallagher, two brothers who often argue with each other. Liam is the band's singer, and Noel writes songs and plays the guitar. The group was known for its bad behaviour, often related to drugs and alcohol, but its records have been extremely successful. They include the albums *Definitely Maybe* (1994), *(What's the Story) Morning Glory?* (1995), *Be Here Now* (1997) and *Heathen Chemistry* (2002) and the songs *Live Forever*, *Cigarettes and Alcohol* and *Wonderwall*.

'oast house /'əʊst; *AmE* 'oʊst/ *n* (*especially BrE*) a building containing a special oven for drying hops (= plants used for giving a special flavour to beer). It has an unusual shape, with a round pointed roof. There are a lot of oast houses in the county of *Kent and many of them have been converted into private houses.

converted oast houses

'oater /'əʊtə(r); *AmE* 'oʊtər/ *n* (*AmE slang*) a *western film or television programme. The word comes from the fact that horses, which appear in most *westerns, eat oats (= a type of grain).

ˌCaptain 'Oates¹ /'əʊts; *AmE* 'oʊts/ (Lawrence Oates 1880–1912) an English explorer who went to the South Pole with Captain *Scott. He is remembered for the brave way in which he died on the journey back. He was very ill and walked out of the tent and into the snow to die. People sometimes use his words of farewell as a joke when they leave to do something dangerous or difficult.

> 66 I am just going outside and may be some time 99
> Captain Oates's farewell

ˌTitus 'Oates² /ˌtaɪtʌs 'əʊts; *AmE* 'oʊts/ (1649–1705) an English Protestant priest. He wanted people to turn against the *Roman Catholics, so he invented the *Popish Plot of 1678, a story that the Catholics were planning to kill King *Charles II and make his brother James king. Oates was regarded as a hero, and many people were put to death because of him. Seven years later he was found guilty of lying and sent to prison.

OBE /ˌəʊ biː 'iː; *AmE* ˌoʊ/ (*in full* **Officer of the Order of the British Empire**) a British honour that is given by the queen or king to people who have done something special for their country in any activity, including sport, entertainment, politics and business. People who receive it may put the letters OBE after their name. It is the fourth highest honour within the *Order of the British Empire, above an *MBE but below a CBE (Commander of the British Empire): *Peter Martin OBE* ◊ *She got an OBE in the New Year Honours.* ⇨ note at HONOURS.

'Oberon /'əʊbərɒn; *AmE* 'oʊbəraːn/ the king of the fairies in stories of the Middle Ages. He is best known as a character in *Shakespeare's play *A *Midsummer Night's Dream*, in which he is the husband of *Titania.

'Obie /'əʊbi; *AmE* 'oʊbi/ *n* (*AmE*) any of several US awards given each year for the best plays performed off-Broadway (= not in one of the main *Broadway theatres). They were established in 1955 by *The *Village Voice* newspaper. The name comes from 'OB', the first letters in 'off-Broadway'.

The Ob'server a British Sunday newspaper, regarded as one of the 'quality papers'. First published in 1791, it is the oldest national newspaper in Britain. Its political views are 'left of centre'. It was bought in 1993 by *The *Guardian.

the ˌOccupational 'Safety and 'Health Act a US law which makes sure that employers provide a safe work place for their workers which meets certain standards.

the ˌOccupational 'Safety and 'Health Adminiˌstration (*abbr* **OSHA**) a US government organization that protects the safety and health of workers. Its officers visit work places and can punish companies for bad standards. It also informs the public about possible risks at work, such as the use of dangerous materials. OSHA was set up in 1970 and is part of the US Department of Labor.

O ˌCome, All Ye 'Faithful ⇨ ADESTE FIDELES.

ˌFlannery O''Connor¹ /ˌflænəri əʊ'kɒnə(r); *AmE* oʊ'kaːnər/ (1925–64) a US writer of novels and short stories which combine violence and comedy and are set in the South. Her novels were *Wise Blood* (1952) and *The Violent Bear It Away* (1960) and her collections of short stories include *A Good Man Is Hard to Find* (1955).

'Sandra 'Day O''Connor² /'deɪ əʊ'kɒnə(r); *AmE* oʊ'kaːnər/ (1930–) the first woman to serve on the US

Supreme Court. She was appointed by President Ronald *Reagan in 1981.

'Odeon /'əʊdiən; AmE 'oʊdiən/ n (in Britain) any of a group of cinemas owned for many years by the *Rank Group. Many older Odeons were built in the *art deco style. There is an Odeon in many British towns and cities, usually showing popular *Hollywood films: *They went to see 'The Return of the King' at the Odeon.*

'Ode on a 'Grecian 'Urn /'ɡriːʃn/ a long poem (1820) by John *Keats which describes how perfect art is when compared with natural things that change and grow old. Its most famous lines are:.

66 Beauty is truth, truth beauty, — that is all
Ye know on earth, and all ye need to know. 99

,Ode to a 'Nightingale a long poem (1820) by John *Keats which describes how he feels as he listens to the beautiful song of a nightingale (a small bird).

66 Thou wast not born for death, immortal Bird!
No hungry generations tread thee down;
The voice I hear this passing night was heard
In ancient days by emperor and clown. 99

'Ode to the 'West 'Wind a poem (1820) by *Shelley². The poet describes the violence of the 'wild West Wind' and of nature itself, causing so much destruction in the autumn, but at the same time he finds it good because it prepares the way for new life in the spring.

66 Be through my lips to unawaken'd earth
The trumpet of a prophecy! O Wind,
If Winter comes, can Spring be far behind? 99

,Rosie O''Donnell /,rəʊzi əʊ'dɒnl; AmE ,roʊzi oʊ'dɑːnəl/ (1962–) a US actor, comedian and talk show presenter who has appeared in a number of comedy films and had her own talk show, *The Rosie O'Donnell Show* (1996–2002).

OECD /,əʊ iː siː 'diː; AmE ,oʊ/ ⇨ ORGANIZATION FOR ECONOMIC COOPERATION AND DEVELOPMENT.

OED /,əʊ iː 'diː; AmE ,oʊ/ ⇨ OXFORD ENGLISH DICTIONARY.

Ofcom /'ɒfkɒm; AmE 'ɑːfkɑːm/ (in full **the Office of Communications**) a British government department started in 2004 to control standards in radio and television broadcasting and the telecommunications industry, to see that customers are treated fairly and to encourage new communications networks.

,Offa's 'Dyke /,ɒfəz; AmE ,ɔːfəz/ a large bank of earth along the border between England and Wales. It was built in the 8th century by Offa, a king of *Mercia, as a protection against the *Britons who lived to the west of it. Later, it became the border between the two countries. Today Offa's Dyke is a *National Trail and people enjoy walking along it, or parts of it.

The 'Office a very successful BBC comedy series that began in 2000. It is set in a small office in the town of Slough. The characters are stereotypes of some of the types of people who work in offices, including David Brent, the office manager played by Ricky *Gervais, who tries unsuccessfully to be both friendly and tough with the workers. The series won a *Golden Globe Award in 2004, the first British television series to win this award.

'Office for 'National Sta'tistics (abbr **ONS**) a British government department which researches and publishes social and economic statistics, including trade figures and the *Retail Price Index. It also publishes the results of the census (= an official count of the population) and is responsible for the **General Register Office**

which records all births, marriages and deaths in England and Wales.

the 'Office of 'Fair 'Trading (abbr **OFT**) an organization in Britain which is responsible for protecting consumers by making sure that businesses operate in a fair way and that there is fair competition between them. Compare FTC.

the 'Office of 'Management and 'Budget a US government department that helps the *President prepare each year's national *budget. It also helps to manage government spending. The department was established in 1970 and is part of the Executive Office of the President.

the 'Office of 'Public 'Services Re'form (abbr **OPSR**) a British government department, formed in 2001 to improve public services such as schools, hospitals and the police.

,office 'party n a party, usually just before *Christmas, for the people who work in a particular office or company. Office parties usually take place in the office or in a club or restaurant near it. Most people drink alcohol and behave in a more relaxed way than they usually do at the office. There are many jokes about office parties because people sometimes get drunk or have sex with someone from their office.

the Of,ficial 'Birthday the second Saturday in June, the date on which the birthday of the British king or queen is officially celebrated, though it is not his or her real birthday. It is marked by *Trooping the Colour and the announcement of the *Birthday Honours.

the Official 'Monster 'Raving 'Loony ,Party /'luːni/ a small political party established in Britain in the 1960s by David Sutch (1942–99) who was known as **Screaming Lord Sutch**. It attracted a lot of publicity during elections because of its strange policies and the humorous appearance of its candidates. Before the general election of 1997 it had a candidate in every election and *by-election. Its policies originally concerned rights for young people and some young people voted for it, either as a joke or because they did not support any of the main political parties. Its candidates have in fact won in several local elections.

the Of,ficial 'Secrets Act a British law that aims to prevent important government information from being passed to enemies. People who work for many government departments must 'sign the Official Secrets Act', i.e. sign a document saying that they will not discuss their work with anybody who has not also signed the Act. People who break this rule may be sent to prison.

the Of,ficial 'Unionist ,Party /'juːniənɪst/ a name sometimes used to refer to the *Ulster Unionist Party to distinguish it from the other political parties in Northern Ireland which have the word 'Unionist' in their titles. Compare ULSTER DEMOCRATIC UNIONIST PARTY.

Ofgem /'ɒfdʒem; AmE 'ɑːfdʒem/ (in full **Office of Gas and Electricity Markets**) the British government organization responsible for making sure that gas and electricity companies treat their customers fairly.

Ofsted /'ɒfsted; AmE 'ɔːfsted/ (in full **the Office for Standards in Education**) a British government department, established in 1992, which employs independent inspectors to visit schools and make sure that the standards of education are as high as they should be.

OFT /,əʊ ef 'tiː; AmE ,oʊ/ ⇨ OFFICE OF FAIR TRADING.

'Ofwat /'ɒfwɒt; AmE 'ɑːfwɑːt/ (in full **the Office of Water Services**) the British government organization responsible for making sure that the private water companies treat their customers fairly.

Scarlett O''Hara /ˌskɑːlət əʊˈhɑːrə; *AmE* ˌskɑːrlət oʊˈhɑːrə/ the main female character in the novel *Gone with the Wind* by Margaret Mitchell. Scarlett is a lively woman who uses her charm to get what she wants. She loves Ashley Wilkes, who rejects her because he is already married, so she marries the charming but immoral Rhett *Butler, who finally leaves her. In the 1939 film version of the book, Scarlett was played by the English actor Vivien *Leigh.

O''Hare /əʊˈheə(r); *AmE* oʊˈher/ (*also* **O'Hare International Airport**) the airport for the US city of *Chicago. It is the busiest airport in the world, with about 70 million passengers using it each year.

O'hio /əʊˈhaɪəʊ; *AmE* oʊˈhaɪoʊ/ a north-eastern US state, also called the Buckeye State (and its people Buckeyes). The capital and largest city is Columbus. It is mainly an industrial state and produces steel, motor vehicles and parts, especially in *Cleveland, as well as jet engines, tools and rubber products. Agricultural products include soya beans, corn, milk and grapes. Both the Rock and Roll *Hall of Fame and Pro Football Hall of Fame are in Ohio.

the O,hio 'River /əʊˌhaɪəʊ; *AmE* oʊˌhaɪoʊ/ a major river in the eastern central US. It begins at *Pittsburgh, *Pennsylvania, where the Allegheny River and Monongahela River come together, and flows 981 miles/ 1578 kilometres past Cincinnati and into the *Mississippi River at Cairo, *Illinois. The Ohio was the main route to the West in the late 18th and early 19th centuries.

OHMS /ˌəʊ eɪtʃ em 'es; *AmE* ˌoʊ/ (*in full* **On Her (or His) Majesty's Service**) the abbreviation printed on official documents, envelopes, etc. of British government departments and the armed forces.

,Oh! Su'sanna a well-known US song written in 1848 by Stephen *Foster. It became especially popular with the *forty-niners who sang it on their way to look for gold in *California. It ends:

> 66 Oh! Susanna, oh don't you cry for me;
> For I come from Alabama with my banjo on my knee. 99

O'jibwa /əʊˈdʒɪbwɑː; *AmE* oʊˈdʒɪbwɑː/ (*also* **O'jibway** /əʊˈdʒɪbweɪ; *AmE* oʊˈdʒɪbweɪ/ **'Chippawa** /ˈtʃɪpəwɑː/ **'Chippaway** /ˈtʃɪpəweɪ/) *n* (*pl* **-was/-ways** *or* **-wa/-way**) a member of a *Native American people who speak the Algonquin language. About 100 000 live on reservations (= land given and protected by the government) in the US states of *Michigan, *Wisconsin and *Minnesota, and in Ontario, Canada. They once lived mostly around Lake *Superior and Lake *Huron, where they were farmers who also hunted. The Ojibwas often fought with the *Sioux.

the ,OK Cor'ral /ˌəʊkeɪ; *AmE* ˌoʊkeɪ/ a corral (= place where horses or cows are enclosed within fences) in *Tombstone, *Arizona. It was the scene of a famous fight with guns on 26 October 1881, in which Deputy Marshal Wyatt *Earp, with his brothers Virgil and Morgan and their friend Doc *Holliday, killed three members of the Clanton gang. The Earps were arrested for murder, but then released. The incident has been the subject of many films, including *Gunfight at the OK Corral* (1957) with Burt *Lancaster as Wyatt Earp.

,Georgia O''Keeffe /əʊˈkiːf; *AmE* oʊˈkiːf/ (1887–1986) a US artist known for her colourful abstract images from nature and her pictures of the south-western US countryside. She was married to the photographer Alfred *Stieglitz.

the ,Okefenokee 'Swamp /ˌəʊkəfənəʊki; *AmE* ˌoʊkəfənoʊki/ a large area of land full of water in the US states of *Georgia and *Florida. It covers 600 square

miles/1554 square kilometres and is part of Georgia's **Okefenokee National Wildlife Refuge**. The animals there include alligators, bears, deer, raccoons and many types of birds and fish.

'Okie /ˈəʊki; *AmE* ˈoʊki/ *n* (*AmE informal*) **1** a person who moves from farm to farm looking for work. The original Okies were farmers who had to leave Oklahoma in the 1930s because dry weather had created the *Dust Bowl.
2 (*sometimes offensive*) a person who lives in Oklahoma.

,Okla'homa /ˌəʊkləˈhəʊmə; *AmE* ˌoʊkləˈhoʊmə/ a southern central state of the US. It is also called the Sooner State and people from Oklahoma are called Sooners. The capital and largest city is Oklahoma City. The area was part of the *Louisiana Purchase, and the *Five Civilized Tribes were forced to settle there in the 19th century. Oklahoma became a state in 1907. It produces oil, gas, minerals, wheat and cotton. Its places of interest include the Cherokee Cultural Center at Tahlequah and the National Cowboy *Hall of Fame at Oklahoma City.

,Okla'homa! /ˌəʊkləˈhəʊmə; *AmE* ˌoʊkləˈhoʊmə/ a musical play (1943) by Richard *Rodgers and Oscar *Hammerstein. It ran for 2212 performances on *Broadway and was one of the first modern musical plays to combine a strong story with songs. It is about the love between the *cowboy Curly and the farmer's daughter Laurie. The songs included *Oklahoma!*, which is now the official state song of *Oklahoma state, and *Oh, What a Beautiful Mornin'*. A film version appeared in 1955.

the ,Okla'homa 'City 'bombing /ˌəʊkləˈhəʊmə; *AmE* ˌoʊkləˈhoʊmə/ the occasion on 19 April 1995 when a car bomb exploded in Oklahoma City, *Oklahoma, killing 168 people and injuring more than 400. At the time it was the worst terrorist act ever carried out in the US. The bomb destroyed the city's Federal Building. After investigating the crime, the FBI arrested Timothy McVeigh and Terry Nichols, members of a group who were prepared to use violence to protest against actions by the government. McVeigh was condemned to death. The bombing made Americans aware of new dangerous groups within the country.

▶ **old age**

Society is getting older. In 1990 about 14% of the population of the US was over 60, in 2020 it will be about 20%. In Britain there was a 27% increase in the number of people over 65 between 1971 and 2002. With further developments in medicine more and more people can expect to live a long time. This means that **senior citizens** (= people over about 65) may become a more powerful group, but it also means that services for them will need to improve. As people live longer, the question of how to pay for retirement has become an important social and political issue for governments. Many people may need to work beyond the normal retirement age of 65. For people who have enough money from their *pension and who are in good health, the years of retirement may be an opportunity to do some of the things they did not have time for when they were working. Some people take courses, some go on more holidays/vacations, others do *voluntary work and continue to use the skills they learned for their job. Public transport, theatres, and sometimes restaurants give discounts to retired people to encourage them to go out. In the US especially, senior citizens are expected to be active, if their health permits, and the sight of a 70-year-old lifting weights in a gym is not uncommon. Many elderly people, however, have a more difficult old age. Those who rely on the British state pension or US *social security have to spend most of their money on food and heating and have little left for luxuries (= expensive pleasures). Others have poor health and cannot move around easily. Some are afraid to go out in case they are attacked and robbed. Many are lonely.

Older Americans who can afford a comfortable retirement may move to states like *Florida and *Arizona where the weather is warm all year. Many choose **assisted living** in an apartment in a **retirement community**, where there is somebody nearby to provide help if they need it. If they become ill they may need to move into a **nursing home** where they can get special medical care. Often the patient's husband or wife can live there too. The cost of nursing homes is very high, and while many are excellent, others are not good. A few older people live with their children, but Americans do not usually want to be dependent on their children.

In Britain, too, elderly people like to be independent and to live in their own home for as long as possible. Those who find it difficult to look after themselves may have a **home help** for a few hours each week. Some may use a *meals on wheels service. Some towns have **pensioners' clubs** which serve cheap meals. People who are less able to get about may be taken each day to a **day centre** run by organizations like *Age Concern where they can be with other people. As in the US, some elderly people move into **sheltered accommodation** or **warden housing**. Others go to live with one of their children. Many families, however, do not have room for their elderly relatives or do not want them to live with them. When these people can no longer care for themselves they have to move into a **care home**.

In Britain especially, elderly people get less respect than they do in many other societies. Nicknames such as 'wrinklies', 'crumblies', 'old codgers' and 'old buffers' are sometimes used to describe them in a cruel way. Elderly people are often thought by younger people to have little to contribute to society and to be a burden on the rest of the population. They used to be referred to as **old age pensioners** or **OAPs** but the name 'senior citizens' was introduced as part of a campaign to give the elderly a more positive image.

,old age 'pensioner (also **OAP**) n (BrE old-fashioned) a person who is old enough to receive a *pension from the state. In Britain, men over 65 and women over 60 can receive state pensions. Some people find the phrase 'old age pensioner' offensive, and prefer phrases such as 'senior citizen', 'retired person' or simply 'pensioner'.

the ,Old 'Bailey /'beɪli/ the popular name for the Central Criminal Court in London, England, where serious cases are tried. It is built on the place where *Newgate prison used to be. There have been many famous trials at the Old Bailey. On top of the building is a well-known statue of Justice wearing a blindfold and holding a sword in one hand and a pair of scales (= a weighing instrument) in the other.

,Old 'Blood and Guts ⇨ PATTON.

,Old 'Blue Eyes ⇨ SINATRA.

the ,old 'boy ,network n [sing] (BrE informal often disapproving) (especially in the past) the situation in many British companies, government departments and branches of the armed forces where people give jobs and other privileges to 'old boys' (= former students) of the *public school(1) or university that they went to: Most of the managers were chosen by the old boy network and many of them turned out to be incompetent.

,Claes 'Oldenburg /ˌklɔːs ˈəʊldənbɜːg; AmE ˈoʊldənbɜːrg/ (1929–) a US sculptor, born in Sweden. He was a leading figure in the *pop art movement and used soft materials to make large models of ordinary objects, such as his Soft Telephone (1963) and Lipstick Monument (1969).

▶ **Old English**

Old English, sometimes called *Anglo-Saxon, was the language of the German peoples who settled in England from around 400 AD. It had three main **dialects** : Kentish, Saxon and Anglian. Saxon was the language spoken at the court of King *Alfred the Great, who encouraged people to translate Latin books into English, and so it became the main language of literature. Modern standard English, however, developed from Mercian, a variety of Anglian which was spoken in the Midlands. Relatively few Latin words dating back to the Roman occupation of England survived into Old English. After the arrival of the *Vikings from the 8th century onwards, many Norse words, e.g. dirt, blunder and squeak, were added to the language.

Several written works have survived from the Old English period. Most of these are short religious writings or poems about great heroes. The most famous of these is *Beowulf, composed by an unknown author and written down in the 8th or 9th century. Beowulf is set in 5th-century Scandinavia and tells the story of the hero Beowulf's battles with the monster Grendel and Grendel's mother.

To modern British people Old English looks at first like a foreign language. It was originally written in **runes** or **runic letters**, an ancient alphabet of 24 angular letters, and then in a form of the Roman alphabet that included several of these letters, such as the thorn (þ) for 'th', both voiced /ð/ and voiceless /θ/, and the ash (æ). Some Old English words, such as dead, is, brother and and in the following passage from Beowulf, have survived with little change into modern English. Some words become easier to recognize when they are translated, e.g. yldra meaning 'older' and min for 'my', whereas others are completely foreign to us. Word order is also different from modern English.

Hroðgar maþelode, helm Scyldinga:
'Ne frin þu æfter sælum! Sorh is geniwod
Denigea leodum. Dead is Æschere,
Yrmenlafes yldra broþer,
min runwita and min rædbora,
eaxlgestealla …'
(Hrothgar, protector of the Danes, spoke: 'Do not ask about it! There is more sorrow for the Danish people. Aeschere, Yrmenlaf's older brother, my trusted friend and my adviser, my close companion, is dead …')

Several shorter poems written in Old English have also survived. These include The Seafarer, The Wanderer and The Dream of the Rood, which all have a Christian message. Few authors are known by name, apart from *Caedmon, a 7th-century monk, and the 9th-century Northumbrian or Mercian poet Cynewulf. Other authors of the period, such as Alcuin, wrote in Latin.

The *Anglo-Saxon Chronicle, a history of England beginning with the arrival of Christianity, was probably begun in the court of King Alfred in 891 and was continued in monasteries until 1154. The writers used a wide range of sources for the Chronicle and it is thought to be the first original prose text in English.

Old English was replaced by *Norman French as the official language of England after the Norman Conquest of 1066, but it continued to be spoken by the ordinary people and, influenced by French and Latin, developed into *Middle English, the language of the 12th to the 15th centuries.

,Old ,English 'sheepdog n a breed of very large dog with long thick grey and white hair, often covering its eyes. In former times these dogs were used by farmers in Britain to control sheep. They are now popular as pets. See also DULUX.

,**Old 'Faithful** a famous US geyser (= an underground hot spring that shoots water or steam up into the air) in *Yellowstone National Park. It is a popular tourist attraction. Approximately once an hour it shoots hot water and steam into the air to a height of about 150 feet/46 metres.

Old Faithful

,**Old Folks at 'Home** a popular US song written in 1851 by Stephen *Foster. It is now the official state song of Florida, and it begins:.

66 Way down upon the Swanee River,
Far, far away,
There's where my heart is turning ever,
There's where the old folks stay. 99

,**Old 'Glory** a popular name for the US flag, first used by William Driver, a ship's captain from *Massachusetts, in 1831. See also STARS AND STRIPES, STAR-SPANGLED BANNER.

,**Old 'Ironsides** /'aɪənsaɪdz; AmE 'aɪərnsaɪdz/ the popular name for the famous old American ship the USS *Constitution.

,**Old King 'Cole** /'kəʊl; AmE 'koʊl/ a *nursery rhyme which may refer to a legendary king of England in ancient times, or to an old man who enjoyed drinking, smoking and music. The full rhyme is:

66 Old King Cole was a merry old soul,
And a merry old soul was he.
He called for his pipe
And he called for his bowl
And he called for his fiddlers three. 99

the ,**Old 'Lady of Thread'needle Street**
/θred'niːdl/ a *nickname for the *Bank of England, which is in Threadneedle Street in the *City of London.

,**Old Mac'donald Had a 'Farm** /mək'dɒnəld; AmE mək'dɑːnəld/ an old children's song. Each verse refers to a different animal on Old Macdonald's farm and repeats the sound made by that animal and all the previous ones, so that the verses get longer and longer.

,**Old Moore's 'Almanack** /mɔːz; AmE mʊrz/ a book published once a year in Britain which claims to predict the important events of the next year. It was first published in 1700 by Francis Moore, a London doctor and astrologer. It is a very popular book, and refers to people and events in such a general way that some people believe that it can really predict the future.

,**Old Mother 'Hubbard** /'hʌbəd; AmE 'hʌbərd/ a *nursery rhyme about an old woman trying to feed her dog. Many people in Britain know the first verse:

66 Old Mother Hubbard, she went to the cupboard
To get her poor dog a bone;
But when she got there, the cupboard was bare,
And so the poor dog had none. 99

the ,**Old North 'Church** the popular name for Christ Church, built in *Boston, *Massachusetts, in 1723. On 19 April 1775 Paul *Revere waited for a signal in its tower to tell him the British army had been seen. Henry Wadsworth *Longfellow made the church famous in his poem *Paul Revere's Ride* (1861), which includes the line: 'Hang a lantern in the belfry arch of the North Church tower.' The tower, which has the first bells ever made in America, was blown down by strong winds in 1954 and built again to its former condition.

the ,**Old Pre'tender** a *nickname for James *Stuart, who claimed the right to be the British king. A pretender is a person who claims something, usually the right to be a king or queen, although not everybody agrees that the claim is just. See also FIFTEEN, YOUNG PRETENDER.

,**old school 'tie** n (especially BrE) **1** a tie worn by former students of a particular school, usually a British *public school(1).
2 the school tie used as a symbol of the attitudes considered typical of people who were educated at *public schools. They are usually thought to be old-fashioned, *upper-class, opposed to social or political change, and proud of their country and their old school.
3 another name for the *old boy network.

,**Old 'Trafford** /'træfəd; AmE 'træfərd/ **1** a well-known football stadium in south-west *Manchester. It is the club ground of *Manchester United and is sometimes used for important international matches.
2 a well-known cricket ground in south-west *Manchester, near the football stadium. It is the main ground of *Lancashire County Cricket Club, and test matches (= international matches) take place there when foreign teams tour England.

the ,**Old 'Vic** /'vɪk/ a famous theatre in south London, built in 1818. It was officially named the Royal Victoria Theatre in 1833, and was given the *nickname the 'Old Vic' later in the century. It became well known in the early 20th century when Lilian *Baylis began producing *Shakespeare's plays there. The *National Theatre was based there from 1963 until its own building was completed in 1976.

the ,**Old 'West** a phrase used to refer to the western parts of America in the 19th century when white people first settled there. Compare WILD WEST.

The ,**Old 'Woman Who 'Lived in a 'Shoe** a traditional *nursery rhyme about a poor woman who has many children:

66 There was an old woman who lived in a shoe,
She had so many children she didn't know what to do.
She gave them some broth without any bread;
And whipped them all soundly and put them to bed. 99

O 'Little 'Town of 'Bethlehem /'beθlɪhem/ the title and first line of a popular Christmas *carol.

,**Jamie 'Oliver** /'ɒlɪvə(r); AmE 'ɑːlɪvər/ (1975–) a British cook, broadcaster and writer who is well known for his relaxed, informal style and is often known as **the Naked Chef**, after the title of one of his popular television cookery series and cookery books.

,**Oliver 'Twist** /'twɪst/ a novel (1838) by Charles *Dickens, well known for its realistic descriptions of London's poor districts and criminals. Oliver is a poor orphan (= child whose parents are dead) who runs away

to London. There he joins a group of criminals, including
*Fagin, the *Artful Dodger and Bill Sikes, who try to
turn him into a thief. He is rescued by a good man, Mr
Brownlow, but captured again by the criminals. Nancy,
Sikes's girlfriend, tries to help Oliver and is killed by
Sikes, who dies while trying to escape from the police.
The criminals are all arrested and Oliver goes to live
with Mr Brownlow. It is one of Dickens's most famous
books, and has been made into a successful film (1948)
and a musical show called *Oliver!* (1960).

ˌLaurence **O'livier** /ə'lɪvɪeɪ/ (1907–89) an English
theatre, film and television actor and director. He first
became famous for his Shakespearian roles in the
theatre in the 1930s. He performed many Shakespearian
roles in films, some of them directed by himself, as well
as acting in more modern plays such as *The Entertainer*
(1957) by John *Osborne, and films such as *Sleuth* (1972).
He was the first director of the *National Theatre
(1963–73). He was made a *knight in 1947 and a *life
peer in 1970.

ˌ**Ol' Man 'River** a song about the *Mississippi River
from the musical play *Show Boat. The best-known performance of it was by Paul *Robeson, who joined the
show after it moved to London in 1928. It is sung by the
character Joe and is a sad song about the hard life of
African Americans in the South who are soon forgotten
while the old river goes on.

> 66 Ol' man river, that ol' man river,
> He don't say nothin', but he must know somethin'
> That ol' man river, he just keeps rollin' along. 99

O'lympia /ə'lɪmpɪə/ a group of large buildings in west
London where many conferences, exhibitions and shows
take place.

OM /ˌəʊ 'em; *AmE* ˌoʊ/ ⇨ ORDER OF MERIT.

'**Omaha** /'əʊməhɑː; *AmE* 'oʊməhɑ/ the largest city in
the US state of *Nebraska. It is on the Missouri River on
the border of *Iowa. *Lewis and Clark visited the area in
1804, and it was settled in 1854, being named after a
local *Native American people. It is a centre for insurance companies and companies that process food.

'**ombudsman** *n* (*pl* **-men**) ⇨ PARLIAMENTARY
COMMISSIONER FOR ADMINISTRATION.

'**Omnibus** /'ɒmnɪbəs; *AmE* 'ɑːmnɪbəs/ **1** a British television programme about the arts. It was broadcast by the
*BBC from 1967 to 2003. Each programme was usually
about one particular artist.
2 a US cultural television programme broadcast on *CBS
on Sunday afternoons from 1952 to 1961. It was presented by Alistair *Cooke and offered a mixture of plays,
music, talks with artistic people, and even comedy.

ˌJackie **O'nassis** /əʊ'næsɪs; *AmE* oʊ'næsɪs/
⇨ KENNEDY.

'**Once in 'Royal 'David's 'City** the title and first line
of a Christian hymn about the birth of Christ. It is often
sung as a *carol at *Christmas.

ˌ**one-day 'cricket** *n* [U] a version of *cricket in which
each team bats once, within a limited period, so that the
match finishes in one day. One-day matches were introduced in the 1960s to try to make cricket a more exciting
game for television audiences. There are two popular
one-day competitions for professional teams in Britain,
the Cheltenham and Gloucester Trophy and the ICC
Champions Trophy. There are also many one-day international matches.

'**One Flew 'Over the 'Cuckoo's Nest** a US novel
(1962) by Ken Kesey that became a successful *Broadway
play (1963) and film (1975). It is about a man with mental
problems who tries to resist the harsh discipline of the

hospital where he is a patient. The film, which was directed by Milos *Forman, with Jack *Nicholson in the
main part, won four *Oscars.

ˌ**One 'Foot in the 'Grave** ⇨ MELDREW.

ˌ**Eugene O''Neill** /əʊ'niːl; *AmE* oʊ'niːl/ (1888–1953) a US
writer of plays who received the 1936 *Nobel Prize for
literature. He won *Pulitzer Prizes for his best-known
play, **Long Day's Journey into Night*, and for *Beyond the
Horizon* (1920), *Anna Christie* (1922) and *Strange Interlude*
(1928). O'Neill's other works include *The Emperor Jones*
(1920), *Mourning Becomes Electra* (1931) and *The Iceman
Cometh* (1946). His daughter Oona married Charlie
*Chaplin.

the **1 000 Guineas** ⇨ THOUSAND GUINEAS.

ˌ**On Her 'Majesty's 'Service** ⇨ OHMS.

'**Only 'Fools and 'Horses** a *BBC television comedy
series about two *working-class brothers living in south
London. Most of the humour comes from their attempts
to make money without actually working. In the 1980s it
was one of the most popular series in Britain and programmes are often repeated. See also DEL BOY.

> 66 Rodney, you plonker. 99
> Del Boy to his brother in *Only Fools and Horses*

ONS /ˌəʊ en 'es; *AmE* ˌoʊ/ ⇨ OFFICE FOR NATIONAL
STATISTICS.

ˌ**Lake On'tario** /ɒn'teəriəʊ; *AmE* ɑːn'terioʊ/ the smallest and most eastern of the *Great Lakes. It has an area
of 7 340 square miles/19 011 square kilometres and is
linked to Lake *Erie by the Niagara River. Lake Ontario
separates the state of New York from the Canadian province of Ontario. Cities on it include Toronto, Ontario, and
Rochester, New York.

ˌ**On 'Top of Old 'Smoky** /'sməʊki; *AmE* 'smoʊki/ a
traditional US song which has been recorded by several
performers. It begins:

> 66 On top of old Smoky,
> All covered with snow,
> I lost my true lover,
> By a-courting too slow. 99

'**Onward, 'Christian 'Soldiers** a popular Christian
hymn with a strong rhythm that used to be often sung in
British schools. The music was written by Arthur
*Sullivan.

007 /ˌdʌbl əʊ 'sevn/ the British Secret Service code name
of James *Bond in the novels by Ian *Fleming and in the
films based on them. According to the stories, numbers
beginning 'oo' are given to Secret Service agents who are
'licensed to kill'.

the '**Open** ⇨ BRITISH OPEN.

ˌ**open 'shop** *n* a business, factory, etc. where people can
work without being members of a *trade union. Many
British factories and other places of work used to be
*closed shops, where everybody had to belong to a par-
ticular trade union, until the 1980s when the laws affecting the unions were changed, and they became less
powerful. In the US most companies operate as open
shops though there is no longer a law requiring them to
do so.

the ˌ**Open Uni'versity** (*abbr* the **OU**) a British university providing degree courses that students can take at
home. It started in 1969 and its main office is in *Milton
Keynes. Students can be of any age and, if they do not
have the standard qualifications for entering university,
they take an **access course** before starting their degree.
Teaching is by a mixture of printed materials, and television and radio programmes. Students study at home and

send their work to their tutors. Many go to monthly **tutorials** at **study centres** in a regional centre near their home town, and they may also attend **summer schools**. Most students take part-time degree courses lasting four or five years, though there is no time limit. Postgraduate and professional courses are also offered.

,**Operation 'Drake** /'dreɪk/ a series of scientific and other projects in 16 countries involving 400 young people from 27 countries and a British sailing ship, *Eye of the Wind*, as a floating base. It was started by Prince *Charles and lasted for two years (1978–80), during which the ship sailed completely round the world, as Sir Francis *Drake had done 400 years before. It was followed in 1980 by **Operation Raleigh**, which then developed into a regular international event for young people. The events and the charity that organizes them are now known as *Raleigh International.

'**J 'Robert 'Oppenheimer** /'ɒpənhaɪmə(r); *AmE* 'ɑːpənhaɪmər/ (Julius Robert Oppenheimer 1904–67) the scientist in charge of the US *Manhattan Project (1942–5) which built the first atom bomb. After *World War II, Oppenheimer directed the *Institute for Advanced Study. In the 1950s he opposed the creation of the hydrogen bomb, and because he was thought to hold left-wing opinions he was not allowed to work on government research projects for a time.

,**Oppor'tunity** (*also* **Mars Exploration Rover B**) (*abbr* **MER-B**) the third *Mars Rover vehicle which landed on the planet Mars in 2004 and sent pictures of the planet back to *NASA.

OPSR /ˌəʊ piː es 'ɑː(r); *AmE* ˌoʊ/ ⇨ OFFICE OF PUBLIC SERVICES REFORM.

,**opting 'out** *n* [U] (in Britain) the process of choosing to leave the previous system in order to become more independent. The *Conservative government in the 1990s encouraged many secondary *state schools to 'opt out' of *Local Education Authority control and receive money directly from the central government so that they could be more like independent businesses. Hospitals were also encouraged to opt out by applying to become *hospital trusts.

'**Optrex™** /'ɒptreks; *AmE* 'ɑːptreks/ *n* [U] a liquid for washing sore eyes. A bottle of Optrex can be bought with an eye bath (= a small container for the liquid which is held against the eye to wash it).

'**Oracle** a US company that sells business information database systems to other companies around the world. It was started in 1977 as Software Development Laboratories and is based in *San Francisco. In 2005 it took over a rival company, Peoplesoft, also based in *California.

'**Orange™** /'ɒrɪndʒ; *AmE* 'ɔːrɪndʒ/ a mobile phone company that was started in Britain in 1994 and now operates in many countries. It has a well-known advertising slogan:

66 The future's bright. The future's Orange. 99

'**Orangeman** /'ɒrɪndʒmən; *AmE* 'ɔːrɪndʒmən/ *n* (*pl* **-men**) a member of the Northern Irish **Orange Society** (also known as the **Orange Order**), a political society that aims to preserve *Protestant power in Northern Ireland. The Orangemen march through the streets every year on 12 July to celebrate the victory of the Protestant king *William III of Britain, also known as William of Orange, over the *Roman Catholic *James II at the *Battle of the Boyne in 1690. See also APPRENTICE BOYS' PARADE, MARCHING SEASON.

the '**Orange Prize** /'ɒrɪndʒ; *AmE* 'ɔːrɪndʒ/ *n* a British prize given every year for the best novel written in

English by a woman from any part of the world. The money for this large prize is provided by *Orange, and the competition is organized by Booktrust. The prize was first given in 1996.

Winners of the Orange Prize for Fiction
1996 *A Spell of Winter* Helen Dunmore
1997 *Fugitive Pieces* Anne Michaels
1998 *Larry's Party* Carol Shields
1999 *A Crime in the Neighborhood* Suzanne Berne
2000 *When I Lived in Modern Times* Linda Grant
2001 *The Idea of Perfection* Kate Grenville
2002 *Bel Canto* Ann Patchett
2003 *Property* Valerie Martin
2004 *Small Island* Andrea Levy

,**Oranges and 'Lemons** an old English children's song about the sounds of church bells in various parts of London. It is often part of a game that young children play: two of them form an arch with their arms and the rest take turns to run under the arch until one of them is caught when the arch falls at the end of the song. A similar game is played with *London Bridge is Falling Down. ⇨ note at NURSERY RHYMES.

66 'Oranges and Lemons'
say the bells of St Clements.
'You owe me five farthings'
say the bells of St Martins.
'When will you pay me?'
say the bells of Old Bailey.
'When I grow rich'
say the bells of Shoreditch.
'When will that be?'
say the bells of Stepney.
'I do not know'
says the great bell at Bow.
Here comes a candle to light you to bed.
Here comes a chopper to chop off your head.
Chip, chop, chip, chop; the last man's DEAD! 99

,**Roy 'Orbison** /'ɔːbɪsn; *AmE* 'ɔːrbɪsn/ (1936–88) a US singer and writer of pop songs who was very successful in the early 1960s. He was sometimes called the 'Big O'. His voice had a sad and emotional quality and he always wore dark glasses while performing. His best-known songs include *Only the Lonely* (1960), *Cryin'* (1961) and *Pretty Woman* (1964). Orbison was chosen for the Rock and Roll *Hall of Fame in 1987.

'**Orchard Street** a well-known New York shopping street in the *Lower East Side of *Manhattan(1). There are now many fashionable bars and galleries there but it was originally the home of poor immigrants and one of the houses is now a museum of immigrant life in the early 20th century.

,**order of 'chivalry** *n* (in Britain) any of several special honours given to people as a reward for doing something good or serving the country. They include the *Order of Merit, the *Order of the Bath, the *Order of the British Empire, the *Order of the Garter, the *Order of the Thistle, the *Distinguished Service Order, the Royal Victorian Order and the Order of the *Companions of Honour. ⇨ note at HONOURS.

the ,**Order of 'Merit** (*abbr* **OM**) one of the British *orders of chivalry and the name of the honour that a person receives when appointed to this Order. The Order of Merit, which is limited to 24 British people and one foreigner, was created in 1902 by King *Edward VII for men and women who have achieved great things, especially in the arts, literature and science. Early members included Joseph *Lister and Florence *Nightingale. Current members include Margaret *Thatcher and Lucian *Freud. People who are appointed to this order place the letters OM after their name.

the ˌ**Order of the** ˈ**Bath** (the Most Honourable Order of the Bath) one of the British *orders of chivalry. People who are appointed to this order receive one of three ranks within it: *Knight Grand Cross (or *Dame Grand Cross for a woman), *Knight Commander (or *Dame Commander) or Companion. The full name of the order is the Most Honourable Order of the Bath. It may have been started as early as 1399, but it later disappeared and was started again in 1725. Originally, people receiving the order washed in a bath as part of the ceremony. ⇨ note at ARISTOCRACY, HONOURS.

the ˈ**Order of the** ˈ**British** ˈ**Empire** one of the British *orders of chivalry. People who are appointed to this order receive one of five ranks within it: *Knight Grand Cross (or *Dame Grand Cross for a woman), *Knight Commander (or *Dame Commander), Commander, Officer or Member, and may put the appropriate letters after their name, such as CBE, *OBE or *MBE. The Order was started in 1917. Its full title is the Most Excellent Order of the British Empire. ⇨ note at ARISTOCRACY, HONOURS. .

the ˌ**Order of the** ˈ**Garter** the oldest and highest of the British *orders of chivalry. It includes members of the British and other royal families and a maximum of 24 other people, who receive the rank of Knight Companion when they are appointed to the order, and may put the letters KG after their names. It was probably started in 1348 by King *Edward III. According to tradition, it was named after an occasion when a woman in the presence of the king dropped a garter (= a band worn around the leg to hold up a sock). The king saved her from embarrassment by picking up the garter and fixing it to his own leg, saying 'Honi soit qui mal y pense', French for 'Shame on anyone who thinks badly of this'. This phrase became the motto of the order, whose full name is the Most Noble Order of the Garter. ⇨ note at ARISTOCRACY, HONOURS.

the ˌ**Order of the** ˈ**Thistle** one of the highest British *orders of chivalry. Its full name is the Most Ancient and Most Noble Order of the Thistle. People who are appointed to the order may put the letters KT (meaning *Knight of the Thistle*) after their names. The order was started in 1687 and is mainly for members of the Scottish *peerage. The thistle, a prickly plant, is the national *emblem of Scotland. ⇨ note at ARISTOCRACY, HONOURS.

the ˌ**ordination of** ˈ**women** *n* [U] the process of admitting women as priests in the Church. The *Roman Catholic Church does not allow women to be priests, but the *Church of England and the rest of the *Anglican Communion around the world now does. The first women were ordained in 1974 as priests in the *Episcopal Church in the US, where there has also been a female *bishop since 1989. In Britain, the *Church of England decided at a meeting of the *General Synod in 1985 to allow women to become deacons (= junior priests). Full ordination was allowed from 1992, and the first women became priests in 1994. These decisions were strongly opposed by many people, especially *Anglo-Catholics and *evangelicals.

ˌ**Ordnance** ˈ**Survey** (*abbr* **OS**) the British government organization responsible for making maps of Britain. These are available in a range of different scales, some of which are very detailed. They are especially popular with people who enjoy walking in the countryside. The OS was started in 1791 to make maps for the army. It also produces historical maps. See also NATIONAL GRID(2).

ˈ**Oregon** /ˈɒrɪɡən; *AmE* ˈɔːrɪɡən/ a state in the northwestern US, also called the Beaver State. The largest city is *Portland(1), and the capital city is Salem. Captain James *Cook sailed along its coast in 1778, and *Lewis and Clark visited the area in 1805. Oregon became a state in 1859. Its products include salmon and other fish, wood, paper, berries and nuts. Tourists can visit Crater Lake National Park, the Oregon Dunes National Recreation Area and the John Day Fossil Beds National Monument.

the ˌ**Oregon** ˈ**Trail** /ˌɒrɪɡən; *AmE* ˌɔːrɪɡən/ a US route used in the 19th century by people travelling west to settle new lands. About 10 000 people travelled along it in the 1840s. It was about 2 000 miles/3 218 kilometres long and the journey took about six months in *covered wagons. It went from *Independence, *Missouri, through *Nebraska and *Wyoming and over the *Rocky Mountains to the Columbia River. The route became the **Oregon National Historic Trail** in 1978. Compare OVERLAND TRAIL, SANTA FE TRAIL.

ˈ**Oreo**™ /ˈɔːriəʊ; *AmE* ˈɔːrioʊ/ *n* (*pl* **Oreos**) a popular US cookie. Oreos have two hard, round chocolate sides stuck together by a sweet white filling, and children often open them to eat the white part first.

the ˌ**Organi**ˈ**zation for Eco**ˈ**nomic Coope**ˈ**ration and De**ˈ**velopment** (*abbr* the **OECD**) an international organization set up in 1961 with the aim of helping member countries to work together in areas of economic and social policy. There are 30 members, including Britain and the US. The main offices are in Paris.

the ˌ**Organi**ˈ**zation of A**ˈ**merican** ˈ**States** (*abbr* the **OAS**) an international organization of 35 American nations established in 1948 in Bogotá, Columbia. OAS members work together to settle disputes in a peaceful manner, as well as discussing political, economic, social and cultural issues. Compare MONROE DOCTRINE.

The ˌ**Origin of** ˈ**Species** the short title which many people use to refer to *On the Origin of Species by Means of Natural Selection* (1859) by Charles *Darwin. In it he explained his theory of evolution (= the development of different life forms over millions of years). When it was published, all the copies were sold on the first day. His theory caused a lot of anger at that time, but its main ideas now form the basis of scientific understanding of the subject.

the ˈ**Orkney Islands** /ˈɔːkni; *AmE* ˈɔːrkni/ (*also* **Orkney**, the **Orkneys**) a group of more than 70 islands off the north coast of Scotland. The islands are governed as a single *council area from the town of Kirkwall on the Mainland island. Mainland is the largest of the islands and has a number of prehistoric structures such as *Skara Brae. Orkney and *Shetland belonged to Norway and Denmark until the 15th century, when they were given to Scotland. The inhabitants of Orkney are called **Orcadians**. Fishing and farming are two of the main industries. The islands are popular with tourists.

Orˈ**lando** /ɔːˈlændəʊ; *AmE* ɔːrˈlændoʊ/ a US city in central *Florida, known as an international entertainment centre. It was a quiet farming town until the 1970s but its attractions now include *Disney World, Sea World, Universal Studios and Disney-MGM Studios. Orlando is the centre of an agricultural area which produces a lot of fruit. It also has a US Navy base and industries producing electronic products.

ˌ**Joe** ˈ**Orton** /ˈɔːtn; *AmE* ˈɔːrtn/ (1933–67) an English writer of plays that are full of wild and often shocking humour, including *Entertaining Mr Sloane* (1964), *Loot*

(1965) and *What the Butler Saw* (1967). He was murdered by his jealous lover, who then killed himself.

,George 'Orwell /'ɔːwel; *AmE* 'ɔːrwel/ (1903–50) an English writer of essays and novels. He was born in India and educated at *Eton. His first job was with the British police in Burma (1922–7), but he reacted against his background and spent the next few years living with very little money in Paris and London. He wrote about his experiences among poor people there in *Down and Out in Paris and London* (1933). His next book, *The Road to Wigan Pier* (1937), described *working-class life in Britain during the *Depression. He joined the Republican side in the Spanish Civil War and wrote about this in *Homage to Catalonia* (1938). His two best-known novels, *Animal Farm* and *Nineteen Eighty-Four, were written in the 1940s. In their different ways, they both show his disappointment with the results of socialist revolutions, especially in the Soviet Union.

Or'wellian /ɔː'weliən; *AmE* ɔːr'weliən/ *adj* like something from the writings of George *Orwell, especially the novel *Nineteen Eighty-Four, in which he described a terrible future in which a powerful government controls people's thoughts.

OS /,əʊ 'es; *AmE* ,oʊ/ ⇨ ORDNANCE SURVEY.

O'sage /əʊ'seɪdʒ; *AmE* oʊ'seɪdʒ/ *n* (*pl* Osages *or* Osage) a member of a *Native American people in the US state of *Oklahoma. Many of them have become very rich since oil was discovered on their reservation (= land given and protected by the US government) at the beginning of the 20th century. The Osage had earlier lived in the *Ohio River valley and then along the Osage River in *Missouri. The US government moved them to the Oklahoma reservation in 1872.

,John 'Osborne /'ɒzbɔːn; *AmE* 'ɑːzbɔːrn/ (1929–94) an English writer of realistic plays about *working-class life, including *Look Back in Anger* (1956) and *The Entertainer* (1957). This type of play was new and shocking in the 1950s when they were written, and Osborne and similar writers became known as *angry young men.

66 This is a letter of hate. It is for you my countrymen, I mean those men of my country who have defiled it. The men with manic fingers leading the sightless, feeble, betrayed body of my country to its death … damn you England! 99
John Osborne, 1961

,Osborne 'House /,ɒzbɔːn; *AmE* ,ɑːzbɔːrn/ a house on the *Isle of Wight which was built for Queen *Victoria in 1851 as a quiet and private place for herself and her family. The house has been kept as it was when they lived there. It is open to the public at certain times of the year.

Osborne House

,Ozzy 'Osbourne /,ɒzi 'ɒzbɔːn; *AmE* ,ɑːzi 'ɑːzbɔːrn/ (1948–) a British *heavy metal musician. He was the singer for the group Black Sabbath (1969–79), and later formed his own Ozzy Osbourne group, which achieved success in the 1980s and 1990s with such albums as *Talk of the Devil* (1982). He also appears in *The Osbournes*, a popular US *reality TV show about his family.

'Oscar /'ɒskə(r); *AmE* 'ɑːskər/ *n* another name for a US *Academy Award. The awards, which are in the form of small metal statues, are presented each year at a special ceremony. The ceremony itself is sometimes called the Oscars: *He won the Oscar for Best Supporting Actor.* ◇ *The film won four Oscars*. See also ACADEMY OF MOTION PICTURE ARTS AND SCIENCES.

OSHA /,əʊ es eɪtʃ 'eɪ; *AmE* ,oʊ/ ⇨ OCCUPATIONAL SAFETY AND HEALTH ADMINISTRATION.

the 'Osmonds /'ɒzməndz; *AmE* 'ɑːzməndz/ a US group of popular singers who were all members of the same family. They included six brothers and one sister. The most famous were Donny Osmond (1957–) and Marie Osmond (1959–). The Osmonds were *Mormons and had a reputation for being very religious and morally good. Their hits included *One Bad Apple* (1971). Donny and Marie later had separate careers on their own, as well as recording several songs together, including *I'm Leaving It Up to You* (1974) and other hits. They have had two successful shows on US television, the *Donny and Marie Show* (1976–79) and a talk show *Donny and Marie* (1998–2000).

'Lee 'Harvey 'Oswald /'liː 'hɑːvi 'ɒzwəld; *AmE* 'hɑːrvi 'ɑːzwəld/ (1939–63) the man who was arrested for the murder of US President John F *Kennedy in 1963. He said he was innocent but was never tried, because he was killed by Jack *Ruby two days after being arrested. The official Warren Report stated that Oswald was the only person who shot Kennedy, but many people still believe that others were involved. Oswald was a former US Marine who had lived in the USSR for three years. See also WARREN.

O'thello /ə'θeləʊ; *AmE* ə'θeloʊ/ a play (*c.* 1603) by William *Shakespeare. The story is about a great man who is destroyed by jealousy. Othello is a Moor (= North African) who is a powerful and respected commander in the navy of Venice. He is gradually persuaded by the evil officer Iago that his wife, Desdemona, and another officer, Cassio, are lovers. Othello kills his wife but then discovers that she was innocent and kills himself.

66 O! beware, my lord of jealousy;
It is the green-eyed monster which doth mock
The meat it feeds on. 99
Shakespeare *Othello*

OU /,əʊ 'juː; *AmE* ,oʊ/ ⇨ OPEN UNIVERSITY.

OUP /,əʊ juː 'piː; *AmE* ,oʊ/ ⇨ OXFORD UNIVERSITY PRESS.

,Our 'Father ⇨ LORD'S PRAYER.

,Our 'Mutual 'Friend the last complete novel (1864–5) by Charles *Dickens. Like his previous novel, *Little Dorrit, it is full of comedy and sharp social comment about how wealth can destroy people.

,Our 'Town a play (1938) by the US writer Thornton *Wilder which won a *Pulitzer Prize. It is set in the imaginary small town of Grover's Corners and is about the simple lives of ordinary people. A character called the Stage Manager makes comments on the story directly to the audience. The play is still often performed by amateur groups.

Ouse /uːz/ the name of several English rivers. The longest, the Great Ouse, is in the east of England and flows from *Northamptonshire through the *Fens and out into the *Wash at *King's Lynn. There is another Ouse in the north-east which flows through *York to the *Humber. A third Ouse begins halfway between London and the south coast and flows into the *English Channel at Newhaven.

'OutRage! /'autreɪdʒ/ a British organization that works for the rights of homosexual men and women (= people sexually attracted to others of their own sex) and to encourage public discussion of the issue. OutRage! started in 1990 and quickly became well known for its use of direct action which it often combines with humour, as in the Queer *St Valentine's Day Carnival. One of OutRage's best-known campaigners is the author and political activist Peter Tatchell.

the 'Outward 'Bound™ 'Trust (also **Outward Bound**) an international organization with its base in Britain which arranges outdoor adventure training for young people. Its activities include sailing and rock climbing. The Trust was set up in 1941 by Kurt Hahn, the man who started *Gordonstoun school. Compare DUKE OF EDINBURGH'S AWARD, RALEIGH INTERNATIONAL.

the 'Oval a *cricket ground in south-east London, England. It has been the home of the Surrey County Cricket Club since 1845 and international cricket matches are regularly played there.

the 'Oval 'Office the office of the US *President in the *White House. It has this name because of its shape. The phrase is sometimes also used to mean the President himself and the part of the government that is controlled by him: *Congress is waiting to see how the Oval Office will react.*

'Ovaltine™ /'əʊvltiːn; AmE 'oʊvltiːn/ n [U, C] a hot drink made from a sweet brown powder mixed with water and milk, or the name of the powder itself, which contains dried milk, dried egg and malt (= grain that has been soaked in water and dried). Ovaltine is usually drunk just before going to bed at night. It was first sold in Britain in the early 20th century and is now popular around the world: *Have a nice cup of Ovaltine – it'll help you to sleep.*

the ,Overland 'Trail any of several different routes taken by people travelling to the US West in the 19th century, including the main route to the California goldfields (= areas where gold was found). Compare OREGON TRAIL, SANTA FE TRAIL.

,overseas 'territory (also **dependent territory, Crown Colony**) n any of several small territories (mainly islands or groups of islands) which have a governor appointed by the British government. Examples include the *Falkland Islands, *Gibraltar and *St Helena. Britain is responsible for their defence and some other aspects of their government, e.g. their police and *Civil Service.

,Over 'There a lively song written by George M *Cohan to praise US soldiers serving abroad in *World War I. He wrote it on 6 April 1917, the day on which the US entered the war, and it includes the words: 'The Yanks are coming! And we won't come home 'til it's over over there.' The song was also popular during *World War II.

,David 'Owen[1] /'əʊɪn; AmE 'oʊɪn/ (1938–) a British politician who became *Foreign Secretary in the *Labour government in 1977, but left the Labour Party in 1981 and, with three other politicians, started the *SDP (Social Democratic Party). He was leader of the SDP from 1983 to 1990. In 1992 Owen was made a *life peer, and in the same year he and Cyrus *Vance were appointed to lead the international effort to end the war in the former Yugoslavia.

,Robert 'Owen[2] /'əʊɪn; AmE 'oʊɪn/ (1771–1858) a Welsh industrialist whose ideas on social reform influenced the development of the *Co-operative Movement and *trade unions in Britain. He bought some cotton mills (= factories) in Scotland and created a model industrial community for his workers, providing them with good housing and education. The factories made a good profit and his ideas were admired even among the upper classes, though they were less enthusiastic when he argued that workers should share the ownership of factories. He started several other communities, including New Harmony in the US, but these were less successful.

,Wilfred 'Owen[3] /'əʊɪn; AmE 'oʊɪn/ (1893–1918) an English poet who fought in *World War I and whose poems are about the horrors of war and the waste of life it causes. He was killed a week before the end of the war, and his poems were published two years later by his friend Siegfried *Sassoon. Six of Owen's poems were set to music in Benjamin *Britten's *War Requiem* (1962).

> 66 I am not concerned with Poetry. My subject is War and the pity of War. The Poetry is in the pity. 99
> Wilfred Owen

,Jesse 'Owens /'əʊɪnz; AmE 'oʊɪnz/ (1913–80) a US athlete who won four gold medals (for running and the long jump) at the 1936 Olympic Games in Germany. This annoyed Adolf Hitler, who wanted to show that the white Aryan race was best. Owens later received the *Presidential Medal of Freedom for his achievements.

The ,Owl and the 'Pussy-Cat a well-known nonsense poem (1871) by Edward *Lear. It tells the story of the adventures of an owl and a cat and is very popular with children. Many people know the first few lines:

> 66 The Owl and the Pussy-Cat went to sea
> In a beautiful pea-green boat,
> They took some honey, and plenty of money
> Wrapped up in a five-pound note. 99

▶ Oxbridge

Oxbridge is a word made from the names *Oxford and *Cambridge and is used to refer informally to the universities of Oxford and Cambridge together, especially when they are being distinguished from other universities.

Oxford and Cambridge are the oldest universities in Britain. They are generally also thought to be the best universities to get a place at. An Oxbridge

Oxford dons

degree makes a good impression with many employers, and graduates of these universities may have an advantage when applying for jobs. Although efforts are made to attract more students from state schools, many of the **undergraduates** at each university have been educated at *independent schools. The upper class have traditionally sent their children to Oxbridge, and many *prime ministers and politicians studied there. To many people, Oxford and Cambridge seem very remote places where only the very privileged can study.

Students at Oxford and Cambridge must be accepted at one of around 30 semi-independent **colleges**. Students are chosen after an **interview** in the college they want to go to. The teachers are called **dons**. Each college has

O

its own teaching and research staff, who are **fellows** of the college, and its own buildings, including **hall** (= a dining hall), a library, a chapel, and rooms for students to live in during the term. The buildings are often arranged round a **quad** (= square). Until the 1970s colleges were single-sex, but now almost all are mixed. The universities provide other facilities centrally, including laboratories, lecture rooms and libraries.

The teaching system is different from that at most other universities. Students have **tutorials**, called **supervisions** at Cambridge, at which they read their essays to their **tutor**, a fellow who is a specialist in what they are studying. There are usually no more than one or two students at a tutorial and tutorials are encouraged by the college. Students also go to lectures that are arranged by the university and open to all students. Terms are short, and students are expected to prepare for them in the vacations. Final examinations at Oxford are called **schools**, and at Cambridge **the tripos**. Undergraduates at Oxford and Cambridge study for a BA degree, but after a period of time graduates can convert their BA to an **MA** (**Oxon**) or an **MA** (**Cantab**) without doing any further study. *Oxon* is short for *Oxoniensis*, and *Cantab* for *Cantabrigiensis*, Latin for 'of Oxford' and 'of Cambridge'.

At Oxford students sometimes have to wear **gowns**, at dinner in hall or when they go to see the college principal. When they sit examinations or go to a degree ceremony they have to wear **academic dress**. This consists of **subfusc**, black trousers or skirt, black shoes and socks or tights, a white shirt and a white tie for men and a black tie or ribbon for women. They also wear their gown and a **mortar board** (= a black hat with a flat, square top) and, when they graduate, a **hood** that shows their status. At Cambridge students only have to wear gowns when they **matriculate** (= become members of the university) and at **graduation**.

The two universities are academic rivals, and rivals also in debating and sport. The *Boat Race, held each year around Easter, attracts national attention. *Rugby and *cricket teams play against each other in *varsity matches, as well as against professional teams.

'Oxfam /'ɒksfæm; *AmE* 'ɑːksfæm/ Britain's largest and best-known aid agency (= a charity that helps people in poor countries). It was set up in 1942 (as the Oxford Committee for Famine Relief) to send food to people in other European countries. It now works mainly in developing countries, sending help when there is an emergency, and working with governments on projects to help poor people. Oxfam runs **Oxfam shops** in most British towns and cities, where new and second-hand clothes, books, etc. are sold to raise money for the charity: *My shoes are new but everything else came from Oxfam.*

'Oxford /'ɒksfəd; *AmE* 'ɑːksfərd/ a city in southern England, west of London, and the administrative centre of *Oxfordshire. Oxford is famous for its university, the oldest in Britain, established in the mid 12th century. The buildings of its many colleges are a major feature of the city, which is a tourist centre as well as an important centre of academic research. It is also an industrial city, and was the home for the *Morris car factory. ⇨ note at OXBRIDGE.

Oxford

The 'Oxford 'Book of 'English 'Verse /'ɒksfəd; *AmE* 'ɑːksfərd/ a collection of English poetry that was first published in 1900 and has appeared in several new editions since then. It is one of the most popular books of poetry in Britain, and has had an important influence on which English poems became well known. Compare GOLDEN TREASURY.

the 'Oxford 'English 'Dictionary /'ɒksfəd; *AmE* 'ɑːksfərd/ (*also* **the OED**) a very large historical dictionary of the English language, published by *Oxford University Press. It is one of the most famous dictionaries in the world, well known for including many different meanings of words, and for giving real examples to show how each word was originally used and how its meaning has changed through time. Work on it began in 1858 and the final volume was published in 1928. A second edition, with many new words, was published in 1989. The work of adding to the dictionary continues and *OED Online* is published regularly on the Internet. See also MURRAY[2].

the 'Oxford Group /'ɒksfəd; *AmE* 'ɑːksfərd/ ⇨ MORAL RE-ARMAMENT.

the 'Oxford ˌMovement /'ɒksfəd; *AmE* 'ɑːksfərd/ a group of people based in *Oxford in the 1830s and 1840s who believed that many of the *Roman Catholic ideas and ceremonies should be introduced into the *Church of England. The group included Cardinal *Newman, who became a Catholic, Edward *Pusey and John Keble, and had an important influence on the development of the Church of England, which became more *High Church in the 19th century.

'Oxfordshire /'ɒksfədʃə(r); *AmE* 'ɑːksfərdʃər/ (*abbr* **Oxon**) a county in central southern England. It contains the city of Oxford and some attractive countryside, and the River *Thames runs through it. Its administrative centre is *Oxford.

'Oxford Street /'ɒksfəd; *AmE* 'ɑːksfərd/ a popular shopping street in the *West End of London. It is one of London's best-known streets, containing a number of famous department stores as well as large branches of all the *high-street shops.

ˌOxford Uni'versity /ˌɒksfəd; *AmE* ˌɑːksfərd/ the oldest university in Britain, established in the mid 12th century in the town of Oxford, England. It has a high reputation for academic achievement. The university consists of a number of separate colleges, the earliest of which is University College (established 1249). Other famous colleges include All Souls, Balliol, Christ Church, Magdalen, New College, St John's and Trinity. There is one college for women only. All the rest now take both male and female students. Among the university's famous buildings are the *Bodleian Library and the *Sheldonian Theatre. See also GREATS(1). Compare CAMBRIDGE UNIVERSITY. ⇨ note at OXBRIDGE.

'Oxford Uni'versity 'Press /'ɒksfəd; *AmE* 'ɑːksfərd/ (*abbr* **OUP**) a large publishing company that is part of *Oxford University and has been publishing books since the late 17th century. It is an important publisher of academic and school books, as well as famous dictionaries such as the *Oxford English Dictionary* and the *Oxford Advanced Learner's Dictionary*, and reference books such as the *Oxford Companion to English Literature*.

'Oxo™ /'ɒksəʊ; *AmE* 'ɑːksoʊ/ *n* [U] a popular British make of stock cube (= the dried juices of meat and vegetables). Oxo is used for adding flavour to sauces, soups, etc.: *The gravy was tasteless so he crumbled an Oxo cube into it.*

'Oxon /'ɒksn; *AmE* 'ɑːksn/ **1** an abbreviation for *Oxfordshire, usually written in addresses.

2 an abbreviation for *Oxford University, usually written after a person's degree title: *Peter Smith MA (Oxon)*.

O'xonian /ɒkˈsəʊniən; *AmE* ɑːkˈsəʊniən/ *n* a person who comes from or lives in *Oxford or *Oxfordshire.

'Oxygen a US 24-hour cable television channel, owned by Oxygen Media and started in 1998. It is aimed especially at women.

o'yez! /əʊˈjeɪ ; *AmE* oʊˈjeɪ/ (*old use*) an old word meaning 'listen'. It was traditionally shouted, usually three times, to get people's attention, by officials in courts of law and by town criers (= people whose job is to walk through the streets of towns and shout official announcements and other news).

Oz /ɒz; *AmE* ɑːz/ **1** an informal word for *Australia, used mainly by Australians.
2 the imaginary magic place where Dorothy is carried by a storm in the children's book *The *Wizard of Oz*.

the ˌOzark 'Mountains /ˌəʊzɑːk; *AmE* ˌoʊzɑːrk/ (*also* **the 'Ozarks** /ˈəʊzɑːks; *AmE* 'oʊzɑːrks/) a US area of high land and mountains mostly in southern *Missouri and northern *Arkansas. There are large for-

ests and grand views, and the region is popular with tourists. Parts of it are very remote, and Americans sometimes make jokes about the simple culture of the people who live there.

ˌOzy'mandias /ˌɒzɪˈmændɪæs; *AmE* ˌɑːzɪˈmændɪæs/ a well-known poem (1818) by *Shelley[2]. It describes a broken statue of a legendary king of ancient times, lying forgotten in the desert, with these words carved on its base:

> 66 My name is Ozymandias, king of kings:
> Look on my works, ye Mighty, and despair! 99

ˌOzzie and 'Harriet Ozzie Nelson (1906–75) and his wife Harriet Nelson (1914–94), a popular couple on US radio and television. They used their real names and the names of their sons, Ricky Nelson and David Nelson, as characters in their comedy series about family life, *The Adventures of Ozzie and Harriet* (1952–66). The Nelsons were regarded by many Americans as the perfect family because they appeared so happy and pleasant.

O

P p

the PA /ˌpiː ˈeɪ/ ⇨ PRESS ASSOCIATION.

Pabst ˈBrewing ˌCompany /ˌpæbst/ a US company that makes beer. It was first started in 1844 and is based in *San Antonio, *Texas. It makes a number of different beers in different areas of the US, including **Pabst Blue Ribbon** and **Old Milwaukee**. Its advertising slogan is 'The beer we drink around here'.

PAC /ˌpiː eɪ ˈsiː/ POLITICAL ACTION COMMITTEE.

PACE /peɪs/ ⇨ POLICE AND CRIMINAL EVIDENCE ACT.

Paˌcific ˈDaylight Time /pəˌsɪfɪk/ (*abbr* **PDT**) (in the US) the time used between early April and late October in the far western states, but not *Alaska or *Hawaii. It is an hour earlier than *Pacific Standard Time.

Paˌcific ˈStandard Time /pəˌsɪfɪk/ (*abbr* **PST**) (*also* **Pacific Time**) (in the US) the time used between late October and early April in the far western states, but not *Alaska or *Hawaii. It is eight hours earlier than *Greenwich Mean Time.

Al Paˈcino /pəˈtʃiːnəʊ; *AmE* pəˈtʃiːnoʊ/ (1940–) a US actor who usually plays tough characters. He won an *Oscar for his part in *Scent of a Woman* (1992). He began his career on stage before becoming famous for his performances as Michael Corleone in the three *Godfather* films. His other films have included *Serpico* (1973), *Dog Day Afternoon* (1975), *Scarface* (1983), *Heat* (1992), *Looking for Richard* (1996), which he also produced and directed, and *The Insider* (1999). He also starred in the television series *Angels in America* (2003).

Paddington /ˈpædɪŋtən/ a train station in west London for trains to and from west and south-west England and Wales. It is a large station, built in the 1850s with a glass and iron roof designed by *Brunel. In 1999 thirty-two people died when two trains crashed outside the station. It also has a station on the *London Underground.

Paddington ˈBear /ˌpædɪŋtən/ the main character in a series of children's books by Michael Bond (1926–). Paddington is a toy bear, usually wearing a large hat and coat. He was found at *Paddington station and taken home by an English family. Many of his adventures have been made into children's television programmes.

page-ˈthree girl *n* (*BrE*) a young woman, usually one with large breasts, who appeared naked or partly naked on the third page of some British *tabloid newspapers. The first of these photographs appeared on page three of the *Sun in 1970.

Thomas ˈPaine /ˈpeɪn/ (1737–1809) an English writer and politician who wrote and spoke in favour of freedom and democracy. He moved to America in 1774 and wrote *Common Sense* (1776), a short book proposing American independence from Britain. When he returned to England he wrote The *Rights of Man* in support of the French Revolution, and had to escape to France to avoid being arrested for treason. In France he became a member of the revolutionary government, but was put in prison because he was opposed to killing the king. There he wrote the last of his famous books, *The Age of Reason* (1794–5), which attacked many Christian beliefs and practices.

the ˌPainted ˈDesert a beautiful region in the northern part of the US state of *Arizona, near the *Petrified Forest. It is a tourist attraction east of the Little Colorado River and is about 150 miles/240 kilometres long. It is a high, flat area covered with red, purple, grey and brown rocks whose colours change slightly through the day.

the Painted Desert

ˈpairing /ˈpeərɪŋ; *AmE* ˈperɪŋ/ *n* [U] the practice in the British *Parliament in which two *MPs from opposing parties agree that neither of them will vote on a particular question in parliament, so neither needs to attend the debate on it. MPs who have made such agreements are called **pairs**.

ˈPaisley¹ /ˈpeɪzli/ a town in western Scotland, near *Glasgow, with a long tradition of producing clothes and fabrics in wool and cotton. It became well known in the 19th century when the **paisley pattern** was introduced. It is a design like a feather or teardrop (= a single tear)

paisley

with a curved end which originally came from India and became popular around the world after it was used for cloth and shawls made in Paisley: *a paisley tie*.

ˌIan ˈPaisley² /ˈpeɪzli/ (1926–) a Northern Irish religious and political leader, well known for his strong views against the *IRA, the Republic of Ireland and the *Roman Catholic Church. He was made a *Presbyterian minister (= priest) in 1946 and established his own religious group, the Free Presbyterian Church of Ulster, in 1951. He established the *Ulster Democratic Unionist Party in 1971, and has been its leader since 1974. He has been an *MP since 1970 and an *MEP since 1979. He often appears on British television expressing his opinion that Northern Ireland should remain part of the *United Kingdom.

ˈPaiute /ˈpaɪuːt/ *n* (*pl* **Paiutes** *or* **Paiute**) a member of a *Native American people in the south-western US. There are now only about 4000 of them and they live mostly on reservations (= land given and protected by the US government) in *Nevada, *California, *Utah and *Arizona. They began the *Ghost Dance and its religion. In earlier times the northern Paiutes attacked white people who settled in their areas. The southern Paiutes were called Digger Indians because they ate roots.

Pakiˈstan /ˌpækɪˈstɑːn, ˌpɑːkɪˈstɑːn, ˌpækɪˈstæn/ a country in southern Asia, west of India. During the time

of the *British Empire it was part of India. When India became independent in 1947, Pakistan became a separate state consisting of the two areas where most of India's Muslims lived: West Pakistan to the west, and East Pakistan to the east. In 1971 there was a civil war between the two parts of the country and East Pakistan became *Bangladesh. West Pakistan became Pakistan and left the *Commonwealth in protest against Bangladesh becoming a member. Pakistan joined the Commonwealth again in 1989. Its capital city is Islamabad and its official language is Urdu. There are many Pakistanis living in Britain.
▸ ‚Paki'stani /ˌpækɪ'stɑːni, ˌpɑːkɪ'stɑːni, ˌpækɪ- 'stæni/ adj, n.

Pal™ /pæl/ n [U] a British make of food for dogs. A famous advertisement claimed that Pal 'prolongs active life'.

the 'Palace n **1** (informal) *Buckingham Palace.
2 a way of referring to the British king or queen and his or her advisers: The Palace will not be pleased by the revelations in today's papers.

the ‚Palace of 'Westminster /'westmɪnstə(r)/ the official name of the British *Houses of Parliament(2). Its full name is the **New Palace of Westminster**, since it was built after the **Old Palace of Westminster** was destroyed in a fire in 1834. *Parliament used to meet in the Old Palace, which was first built for *Edward the Confessor in the 11th century. The Palace of Westminster was made a *World Heritage Site in 1987.

‚pale 'ale n [U, C] (BrE) a type of pale *bitter beer, often sold in pubs under the name 'India Pale Ale' or 'IPA'.
⇨ note at BEER.

‚Francis 'Palgrave /'pælgreɪv/ (1824–97) an English writer and teacher. He was professor of poetry at *Oxford University from 1885 to 1895. He is best remembered for his selection of English poems, published as The *Golden Treasury and still often referred to as Palgrave's Treasury. He also wrote several books of his own poetry.

‚Michael 'Palin /'peɪlɪn/ (1943–) an English actor and writer. He first became famous in the 1970s as one of the team of comedy actors and writers of *Monty Python's Flying Circus. He has acted in a wide variety of films and television programmes, and in the 1990s he began presenting programmes for the *BBC in which he travels around the world and gives his own views of the places he visits. He has also written several books including a novel, Hemingway's Chair (1995).

Pal'ladianism /pə'leɪdiənɪzəm/ n [U] a style of architecture based on the work of Andrea Palladio, a 16th-century Italian architect who was influenced by the buildings of ancient Greece and Rome. Buildings in the **Palladian** style often have a pediment (= a large triangle above the entrance) and many columns. The style became fashionable in Britain in the 18th century after it was introduced by Inigo *Jones, and led to the development of *neoclassicism.

the Pal'ladium /pə'leɪdiəm/ (also the **London Palladium**) a well-known theatre in central London. It is used mainly for *musicals, comedies and *music-hall(1) performances.

‚Pall 'Mall /ˌpæl 'mæl/ a street in central London, running west from *Trafalgar Square. It is well known for its many clubs, including the *Athenaeum and the *Reform Club. Pall mall is the name of an old game like *croquet that used to be played there.

Palm 'Beach a city on a long island off the south-east coast of *Florida. It is one of the richest communities in the US, with many large private houses, including the Kennedy family home bought in 1933 by Joseph

*Kennedy. The main shopping street, with many expensive shops, is Worth Avenue.

‚Arnold 'Palmer /'pɑːmə(r)/ (1929–) a US golf player who was especially successful in the 1960s. He was the first person to earn $1 million from golf. He won the *Masters Tournament four times (1958, 1960, 1962 and 1964), a *US Open (1960) and the *British Open twice (1961–2). The many people who came to support him as he played were often referred to as 'Arnie's Army'.

‚Lord 'Palmerston /'pɑːməstən; AmE 'pɑːmərstən/ (Henry John Temple, 3rd Viscount Palmerston 1784–1865) an English *prime minister (1855–58 and 1859–65). He began his career as a *Tory, but in 1830 he became *Foreign Secretary for the *Whig(1) government. He was well known for using the armed forces to protect British interests in other countries. He was Prime Minister during the *Crimean War and the *Indian Mutiny, and nearly involved Britain in the American *Civil War.

‚Palm 'Springs a rich and fashionable city in a desert area of southern *California. It is about 120 miles/193 kilometres east of *Los Angeles and is very popular with *Hollywood stars. Palm Springs has the Betty Ford Center, which helps people with alcohol and drug problems, and there is a large community of homosexuals.

‚Palm 'Sunday (in the Christian Church) the Sunday before *Easter. In many Christian churches people who come to church on Palm Sunday are given a leaf of the palm tree folded in the shape of a cross. This tradition comes from the Bible story that people put palm leaves on the ground in front of Christ as he entered Jerusalem.

‚Mount 'Palomar /'pæləmɑː(r)/ a mountain in southern *California, north-east of *San Diego. It is 6126 feet/1868 metres high. It is the site of the Hale Observatory, which has one of the world's largest telescopes (= instruments for looking at the stars, planets, etc.).

‚palo'mino /ˌpælə'miːnəʊ; AmE ˌpælə'miːnoʊ/ n (pl **-os**) a breed of horse with a yellowish or pale brown colour and a white tail and mane (= hair on the neck). Palominos were first bred in the south-western US, and the name in Spanish means 'young pigeon'. A famous palomino was Trigger, the horse of Roy *Rogers.

‚Gwyneth 'Paltrow /ˌgwɪnɪθ 'pæltrəʊ; AmE 'pæltroʊ/ (1972–) a US actor who won an *Oscar for her performance in Shakespeare in Love (1998). Her other films include Se7en (1995), Sliding Doors (1998) and Sylvia (2003). Her private life has received a lot of media attention, including her relationships with Brad *Pitt and Ben Affleck. She married Chris *Martin in 2003.

66 In Los Angeles everyone has perfect teeth. It's crocodile land. 99
Gwyneth Paltrow

the ‚Panama Ca'nal /ˌpænəmɑː/ a canal through Panama that connects the Atlantic and Pacific Oceans. It was built by the US and completed in 1914. The canal together with the area surrounding it, the **Panama Canal Zone**, was controlled by the US until 1999, when it was returned to Panama. The canal is 51 miles/82 kilometres long and of great importance to world trade.

the ‚Pan 'Am ‚Building /ˌpæn 'æm/ one of the best-known buildings in New York, near *Grand Central Station, built by *Pan American World Airways and completed in 1963. It has the shape of a plane wing. The building was sold to an insurance company in 1991 and is now officially the Met Life Building, though many people still use its original name.

the ‚Pan A'merican 'Games /ˌpæn/ a sports competition between countries of North and South America,

P

held every four years. It began in 1951, and the different sports are similar to those in the Olympic Games.

Pan A'merican 'World 'Airways /pæn/ *(also* **Pan 'Am)** /ˌpæn ˈæm/ a large US company, established in 1927. It was one of the first to use jet passenger planes (in 1958) and the first to use *Boeing 747 'jumbo jets' regularly. One of these crashed in 1988 at *Lockerbie, Scotland, after a bomb on board exploded. Because of this and financial problems, Pan Am went out of business in 1991.

'pancake *n* a type of soft, thin, flat cake made from a mixture of flour, eggs and milk which is quickly fried on both sides in a little hot fat. In Britain, pancakes are traditionally eaten hot, served with lemon and sugar and often rolled up. In the US they are a traditional breakfast food, usually eaten with butter and maple syrup (= a thick, sweet, sticky substance obtained from a type of maple tree). They are also sometimes eaten wrapped round sausages, a dish called 'pigs in a blanket'.

'Pancake Day *(also* **Pancake 'Tuesday)** *(BrE)* another name for *Shrove Tuesday, when many people eat pancakes in Britain. Traditionally, this was the last day when people could enjoy rich food before *Lent.

'pancake race *n* (in Britain) a race in which people carry pancakes in frying pans and repeatedly toss them (= throw them into the air so that they land the other way up in the pan) as they run. Tossing pancakes is the traditional way of cooking them on both sides. Pancake races take place in many parts of Britain on *Shrove Tuesday.

P & O /ˌpiː ənd ˈəʊ/ a British shipping company, well known for its large cruise liners (= ships on which people spend their holidays/vacations, sailing from place to place). The company was established in 1837, when it was called the Peninsular and Oriental Steam Navigation Company, and sailed mainly to Spain and Portugal, but it soon became the most important company sailing between Britain and India and Hong Kong. In the late 20th century it also became one of the largest ferry companies sailing across the *English Channel.

pan'dowdy /pænˈdaʊdi/ *(also* **apple pan'dowdy)** *n* [C, U] *(AmE)* a deep pie or pudding (= a cooked sweet dish) made with apples. Its name may come from an old English word meaning 'custard'.

'panhandle *n* *(AmE)* a narrow piece of land that sticks out from the main part of a state, like the handle of a pan. Two well-known examples are the Florida panhandle and the Oklahoma panhandle, both of which stick out to the north-west of their states.
▶ **panhandle** *v* [I] *(AmE)* to beg for money, especially in the street, e.g. by holding out a pan by its handle. A person who begs is called a **panhandler**.

Emmeline 'Pankhurst /ˌeməliːn ˈpæŋkhɜːst; *AmE* ˈpæŋkhɜːrst/ (1858–1928) an English *suffragette leader. She established a political group, the Women's Social and Political Union, in 1903. Her influence on the campaign for women's right to vote made it more active and determined, and made her the most famous of the British suffragettes. She and her daughters Christabel (1880–1958) and Sylvia (1882–1960) were often put in prison for their actions.

Pano'rama /ˌpænəˈrɑːmə; *AmE* -ˈraema/ a British television documentary programme (= one that presents facts about real life). It has been broadcast by the *BBC once a week since 1957. It usually examines social or political issues that are in the news.

▶ **pantomime**

Pantomimes, also called **pantos**, are traditionally put on in theatres throughout Britain for several weeks before and after *Christmas. Most are intended for children.

They are a British tradition which has developed over several centuries. A pantomime combines a fairy tale with comedy, music and singing, acrobatics and verse. Among the most popular stories are *Aladdin, *Babes in the Wood, *Cinderella, Dick *Whittington and, *Jack and the Beanstalk.

The audience usually takes an active part in a performance: characters on stage speak to the audience directly and they shout back their answer. Sometimes they have noisy arguments, exchanging shouts of 'Oh yes, it is' and 'Oh no, it isn't'. Audiences are often encouraged to join in the singing, and to **boo** loudly whenever a bad character appears. Other pantomime traditions include that of the hero, called the **principal boy**, being played by a young woman, and a comic old woman, called a *dame, being played by a male comedian. Pantomimes often also include several animal characters played by actors in animal costume.

Many of the most successful pantomimes performed in professional theatres have well-known television or sports personalities playing leading roles. Hundreds of amateur pantomimes are also put on each year.

Pantomimes of this kind do not exist in the US where the word *pantomime* means a play or entertainment performed without words. .

Ed,uardo Pao'lozzi /edˌwɑːdəʊ paʊˈlɒtsi; *AmE* edˌwɑːrdoʊ paʊˈlɑːtsi/ (1924–2005) a British artist born in Scotland of Italian parents, who created paintings, sculptures and mosaics (= pictures made out of small pieces of glass), as well as designing fabrics and wallpaper. He was influenced especially by Paul Klee and the Surrealists and had an important influence on the development of *pop art. He was made a *knight in 1989.

Papua New 'Guinea /ˌpæpuə njuː ˈgɪni; *AmE* nuː/ a part of the former country of New Guinea in east Asia. The British and Australian governments had colonial interests there from 1888. Papua New Guinea has been a member of the *Commonwealth since it became fully independent in 1975. Its official language is English and its capital city is Port Moresby.
▶ **Papua New Guinean** *adj, n.*

Papworth 'Hospital /ˌpæpwəθ; *AmE* ˌpæpwərθ/ a hospital near *Cambridge, England, which is especially known for carrying out heart operations.

the 'Parachute ,Regiment *(also informal* **the Paras)** a section of the British army, started in 1940, which is trained in the use of parachutes. They are known for being a very strong and controlled fighting force, and for the red berets (= woollen caps) they wear. See also RED DEVILS.

Paradise 'Lost a very long poem (1667) by John *Milton. It tells the story of Adam and Eve and how they are driven out of the Garden of Eden by God because they do not obey him. In 1671 Milton published *Paradise Regained*, about how Jesus was sent to get Paradise back again for Man.

Paramount 'Pictures /ˌpærəmaʊnt/ a major *Hollywood film company. It originally owned cinemas and began producing films in the 1920s. The company was bought by Gulf & Western Industries in 1966 and by Viacom Inc in 1994.

the 'Paras /ˈpærəz/ ⇨ PARACHUTE REGIMENT.

Par'cheesi™ /pɑːˈtʃiːzi; *AmE* pɑːrˈtʃiːzi/ a US board game played with two dice and coloured plastic pieces which players move around squares on a special board according to the rules of the game, trying to get them to the centre square. Parcheesi was based on an Indian game, Pachisi, and the copyright was first registered in the US in 1867. It is similar to the British game, ludo.

'**parish** n **1** (in Britain) an area with its own church and priest. It is a part of a diocese (= a district for which a *bishop is responsible). People go to their **parish church**, and all the details of local births, marriages and deaths are put down in a special book called the **parish register**. In the US, a parish can mean a church, its administrative area, its members, or the area where they live.
2 (*also* **civil parish**) the smallest unit of *local government in England. Since 1894, a parish of more than a certain size has had to elect a *parish council.
3 (in the US state of *Louisiana) a county.

,**parish 'council** n [C+sing/pl v] (in England) the administrative body of a civil *parish(2). Most of its members are elected by members of the parish.

,**parish 'pump** n (*BrE*) a symbol of local affairs and a restricted attitude to wider issues. In the past, the parish pump was the source of water in a village, and so it became the place where people gathered to discuss problems, exchange news, etc.: *parish pump gossip*.

,**Park 'Avenue** a street in *Manhattan(1), New York, known for its rich, fashionable homes. At one point it runs under *Grand Central Station and the *Pan Am Building, now the Met Life Building. See also WALDORF-ASTORIA.

'**Charlie "Bird" 'Parker**[1] /'bɜːd 'pɑːkə(r); AmE 'bɜːrd 'pɑːrkər/ (1920–55) an American who greatly influenced modern *jazz and helped to create the style of *bebop. He played the saxophone and also wrote music. In the 1940s, he played with such musicians as Miles *Davis, Thelonious *Monk and 'Dizzy' *Gillespie. His problems with drugs and alcohol led to his early death.

,**Dorothy 'Parker**[2] /'pɑːkə(r); AmE 'pɑːrkər/ (1893–1967) a US writer of humorous poems and short stories. She was also a critic for The *New Yorker (1927–33), and a member of the *Algonquin Round Table. Parker's best-known short story was *Big Blonde* (1933).

> 66 Men seldom make passes at girls who wear glasses. 99
> Dorothy Parker

,**Sarah ,Jessica 'Parker**[3] /'pɑːkə(r); AmE 'pɑːrkər/ (1965–) a US actor who is best known for her role as Carrie Bradshaw in the television series *Sex and the City.

Ca'milla 'Parker-'Bowles /kə'mɪlə 'pɑːkə 'bəʊlz; AmE 'pɑːrkər 'boʊlz/ (1947–) an Englishwoman who became the Duchess of Cornwall when she married Prince *Charles in 2005. She had a sexual relationship with the Prince for many years before marrying him.

'**Parkhurst** /'pɑːkhɜːst; AmE 'pɑːrkhɜːrst/ a British prison on the *Isle of Wight for men who have to stay in prison for a long time. It has been a prison since 1838.

,**Michael 'Parkinson** /'pɑːkɪnsn; AmE 'pɑːrkɪnsn/ (1935–) an English journalist and television presenter, best known for the programme *Parkinson* (1971–82 and 1998–), a popular Saturday night chat show. Parkinson often writes and talks about *Yorkshire and especially the town of Barnsley, where he was born. He is sometimes referred to informally as 'Parky'.

'**Parkinson's law** /'pɑːkɪnsnz; AmE 'pɑːrkɪnsnz/ the idea that 'work expands to fill the time available to complete it'. People often mention Parkinson's law when talking humorously about bureaucracy (= a system of official rules and ways of doing things which seem too complicated). The historian Cyril Northcote Parkinson (1909–1993) first wrote about the idea in his book about the British *Civil Service, *Parkinson's Law: The Pursuit of Progress* (1957). Compare MURPHY'S LAW.

,**Park 'Lane** a street in the centre of London, England, along the eastern side of *Hyde Park(1), near *Mayfair. It is known for its very expensive houses and hotels, including the *Dorchester.

,**Rosa 'Parks** /,rəʊzə 'pɑːks; AmE ,roʊzə 'pɑːrks/ (1913–) a woman who is associated with the start of the *civil rights movement in the US. In 1955 she refused to sit in the back of a bus in *Montgomery, *Alabama, as the local law required her to do as an African American. She was arrested, and Martin Luther *King then organized African Americans in a refusal to use the buses. This forced the city to change the law. See also SEGREGATION.

▶ **parks**

British towns and cities have at least one **municipal park**, where people go to relax, lie in the sun, have picnics, walk their dogs and play games. Most US city and town governments also provide parks. They are open to anybody free of charge. The most famous parks in Britain include *Hyde Park and *Regent's Park in London. In the US, New York's *Central Park is the best known. Open-air events, such as plays and concerts, are sometimes held in these parks.

Most British parks were created in the 19th century, when more people moved into the towns. Some still have a rather old-fashioned, formal atmosphere, with paths to walk on, seats or **benches**, tidy **lawns**, flower beds and trees. There are sometimes signs that say: 'Keep off the grass'. A few parks have a **bandstand**, a raised platform on which *brass bands play occasionally during the summer. Most parks are protected by iron railings and gates which are locked by the **park keeper** each evening.

Many parks have a **children's playground** with swings and roundabouts. Larger parks have a sports field, tennis courts and sometimes a boating lake. In the US *softball diamonds are marked on the grass and in Britain there are goalposts for *football. Large parks may have **picnic benches** and, in the US, **barbecues**. In the US it is usually illegal to drink alcohol in a park.

In Britain there are *country parks, large areas of grass and woodland, where people can go for long walks. Some charge an admission fee. Many have **nature trails** where people can see interesting plants, birds or animals. *National parks, such as *Snowdonia in Wales, are areas of great beauty protected by the government. In the US there are both **state parks** and **national parks**. Many provide a safe place for wild animals to live.

Parliament the institution in the UK responsible for making laws, raising taxes and discussing issues which affect the country. It is made up of three parts; the **sovereign** (= the king or queen), the *House of Lords and the *House of Commons. The word 'parliament' was first used in the 13th century, when *Henry III held meetings with his noblemen to raise money from them for government and wars. Several kings found that they did not have enough money, and so they called together representatives from *counties and towns in England to ask them to approve taxes. Over time, the noblemen became the *House of Lords and the representatives became the *House of Commons. The rise of political parties in the 18th century led to less control and involvement of the sovereign, leaving government in the hands of the *cabinet led by the *prime minister. Although the UK is still officially governed by **Her Majesty's Government**, the Queen does not have any real control over what happens in Parliament. Both the *House of Lords and the *House of Commons meet in the *Palace of Westminster, also called the *Houses of Parliament, in **chambers** with sev-

P

eral rows of seats facing each other where members of the government sit on one side and members of the **Opposition** sit on the other. Each period of government, also called a parliament, lasts a maximum of five years and is divided into one-year periods called **sessions**.

the ˌParliaˈmentary Comˈmissioner for Admiˈstration n the official title of the British **Parliamentary Ombudsman**, an important official who examines complaints from members of the public about central government departments and certain government organizations. The Parliamentary Ombudsman is independent of government and has the right to look at any documents or ask any government employee questions. He or she can order the government to pay money to the person making the complaint, or to put things right in some other way. Separate ombudsmen have been established for Scotland and Wales: the **Welsh Administration Ombudsman** and the **Scottish Public Services Ombudsman**. They deal with complaints relating to the *Scottish Parliament, the *Welsh Assembly and various other public authorities and organizations in Scotland and Wales.

ˌParliaˈmentary ˈPrivate ˈSecretary n (abbr **PPS**) (in Britain) a *Member of Parliament who works for a government minister as his or her personal secretary and who also gives the minister advice on political matters. Compare PARLIAMENTARY SECRETARY.

ˌparliamentary ˈprivilege n [U] (in Britain) certain special rights given to *Members of Parliament, especially the right to say something in either of the *Houses of Parliament(1) that attacks somebody else without the fear of being taken to a court of law by that person. The *House of Lords has more such rights than the *House of Commons. Both Houses can, however, punish their own members for 'a breach of privilege' (= unsatisfactory behaviour in Parliament, or behaviour that makes Parliament look bad to the public): *She was accused of hiding behind parliamentary privilege.*

ˌparliamentary ˈsecretary n (in Britain) a *Member of Parliament working in a government job immediately below a minister who is not a *Secretary of State. Compare PARLIAMENTARY PRIVATE SECRETARY, PARLIAMENTARY UNDERSECRETARY OF STATE.

ˌparliaˈmentary underˈsecretary of ˈstate n (in Britain) a *Member of Parliament working in a government job immediately below a minister who is a *Secretary of State. Compare PARLIAMENTARY SECRETARY.

ˈCharles ˈStewart **Parˈnell /pɑːˈnel, ˈpɑːnl; AmE pɑːrˈnel, ˈpɑːrnl/ (1846–91) an Irish politician who led the campaign for *Home Rule in Ireland from 1877 to 1890. He then suddenly lost all his public support because it was revealed that he had been having a sexual relationship with another man's wife for ten years. He was known by his supporters as 'the uncrowned king of Ireland'. Parnell is often mentioned in the books of James *Joyce, who admired him greatly.

paˈrochial ˈchurch ˈcouncil n ⇨ PCC. Compare PARISH COUNCIL.

Louˌella ˈParsons /luːˌelə ˈpɑːsnz; AmE ˈpɑːrsnz/ (1880–1972) a US journalist who wrote about the private life of *Hollywood stars for the newspapers of William Randolph *Hearst. Her great rival was Hedda Hopper.

Parˈtition the division of *India into the independent countries of India and *Pakistan in August 1947 when British rule in India ended. This was one of the conditions of independence, though it led to much violence between Hindus and Muslims.

ˌDolly ˈParton /ˈpɑːtn; AmE ˈpɑːrtn/ (1946–) a US *country music singer and writer of songs who has also

acted in films. She is known for her cheerful personality, large breasts and blonde (= very fair) hair. She has received *Grammy awards for *Here You Come Again* (1978) and *Nine to Five* (1981). In 1987 she opened Dollywood, an entertainment park named after her, in Pigeon Forge, *Tennessee.

> 66 I'm not offended by dumb blonde jokes because I know that I'm not dumb. I also know that I'm not a blonde. 99
> Dolly Parton

ˈparty poˈlitical ˈbroadcast n (in Britain) a short broadcast on radio or television made by a political party to try to persuade people to vote for it, e.g. in a general election. There are special rules to make sure that each party is allowed a fair amount of time for such broadcasts.

Such broadcasts in the US are called **paid political broadcasts**, or, more generally, 'political advertising'. The *FCC requires television companies to give political parties and candidates 'reasonable access' but does not say how many advertisements are allowed.

*A **Passage to ˈIndia** /ˈɪndiə/ a novel (1924) by E M *Forster which examines the cultural differences between the British and the Indians in India when it was under British rule. A film version (1984) was directed by David *Lean.

ˈPasschendaele /ˈpæʃəndeɪl/ a series of *World War I battles (1917) fought near the small town of Passchendaele in Belgium. About 300 000 Allied soldiers and a similar number of Germans died, in terrible conditions. See also ALLIES, YPRES.

ˈPassions a popular US daytime *soap opera shown on *NBC since 1999. It is about the lives and relationships of four families who live in Harmony, an imaginary place in *New England. The characters include a 300-year old witch (= a woman who is believed to have magic powers) called Tabitha.

the ˌPatent and ˈTrademark ˌOffice the US government department that decides who should be given patents (= official documents that give people the right to make, use or sell an invention, and stop other people from copying them).

the ˈPatent ˌOffice the British government department that decides who should be given patents (= official documents that give people the right to make, use or sell an invention, and stop other people from copying them).

ˈPathfinder /ˈpɑːθfaɪndə(r); AmE ˈpæθfaɪndər/ a US spacecraft that landed on the planet Mars in July 1997 and sent back to Earth many pictures of the planet's surface. This was the first trip to Mars since the two *Viking(2) spacecraft landed there in 1976. See also SOJOURNER.

the ˌPatient's ˈCharter a statement of the rights of people who use the *National Health Service in Britain. It was first produced by the government in 1992. Compare CITIZEN'S CHARTER.

ˌSt ˈPatrick (c. 389–c. 461) the national saint of Ireland. He was probably born in Wales, the son of a Roman father. Patrick became a monk in Gaul (= France) and went to Ireland in 432. He converted many people to Christianity, and there are many stories about his great powers, including one which explains why there are no snakes in Ireland. Patrick is said to have tricked them all so that they went into the sea and drowned. He is also said to have used the *shamrock plant to explain the Christian idea of the Trinity, because it has three leaves on one stem. That is why it is traditional for Irish people to wear a shamrock on **St Patrick's Day**, 17 March.

the PATRIOT Act /'peɪtriət/ (the Uniting and Strengthening America by Providing Appropriate Tools Required to Intercept and Obstruct Terrorism Act) a US law passed in 2001 following the *September 11 attacks. It increases the powers of the US government in fighting terrorism, including allowing the government to put non-US citizens in prison for an unlimited period of time without a trial if the *Attorney General considers them to be a threat to national security. It has been strongly criticized by civil liberties organizations. Some parts of the law are due to end in 2005.

Christopher 'Patten /'pætn/ (1944–) a British *Conservative politician who held various important government posts before losing his seat in *Parliament in 1992. He spent five years as the governor of *Hong Kong, before it was returned to Chinese rule in 1997. He became a *European Union Commissioner in 1999. In 2003 he became *Chancellor of the University of Oxford and in 2005 he was made a life peer.

George 'Patton (1885–1945) a senior US Army officer during *World War II. His popular name was 'Old Blood and Guts'. After *D-Day General Patton led the US 3rd Army rapidly through France and into Germany. He was a tough man who demanded strict discipline and was either loved or hated by his soldiers. His story was told in the film *Patton* (1970) with George C Scott, which won three *Oscars.

Linus 'Pauling /ˌlaɪnəs 'pɔːlɪŋ/ (1901–94) a US scientist who won the 1954 *Nobel Prize for his discoveries about how chemicals join together. He was known for his opposition to the testing of nuclear weapons and for his campaigns to have all such weapons destroyed. For this, he won the 1962 Nobel Peace Prize. He also believed that people should take large amounts of vitamin C to prevent colds and other illnesses.

Paul 'Jones /'dʒəʊnz; AmE 'dʒoʊnz/ n [usually sing] a traditional dance in which the dancers change partners repeatedly each time the music stops. It is sometimes used at parties as a way of introducing a lot of guests who do not know each other. It was named after John Paul *Jones.

'Paul Re'vere's 'Ride /rɪ'vɪəz; AmE rɪ'vɪrz/ a poem (1861) by Henry Wadsworth *Longfellow. It was about the ride of Paul *Revere to warn Americans that British soldiers were coming. The poem helped make the ride one of the best-known events in American history. See also OLD NORTH CHURCH.

> 66 For, borne on the night-wind of the Past,
> Through all our history, to the last,
> In the hour of darkness and peril and need,
> The people will waken and listen to hear
> The hurrying hoof-beats of that steed,
> And the midnight message of Paul Revere. 99

'Pawnee /'pɔːniː/ n (pl **Pawnees** or **Pawnee**) a member of a *Native American people of whom only about 2500 survive. Some live in northern *Oklahoma on a reservation (= land given and protected by the US government). They originally lived on the *Great Plains of *Kansas and *Nebraska as farmers who also hunted buffalo. They helped white people who came into their land, and often fought the *Sioux. The Pawnee were moved to the reservation in 1876.

Jeremy 'Paxman /'pæksmən/ (1950–) an English journalist and television presenter. He has presented *Newsnight* since 1989 and is known for his sometimes aggressive questions, especially to politicians. He has presented *University Challenge* since 1994.

PAYE /ˌpiː eɪ waɪ 'iː/ (in Britain) the arrangement by which an employee's *income tax and *National Insurance are taken directly from his or her pay by the employer and sent to the government. The letters PAYE stand for 'pay as you earn'.

the ˌPaymaster 'General the British government minister in charge of the department of the *Treasury which provides bank services for all departments except the *Inland Revenue and *Customs and Excise. Payments of *pensions to civil servants, teachers, the armed forces and workers in the *National Health Service are also made by the Paymaster General's office.

'pay ˌtelevision (also ˌpay-'TV) ⇨ SUBSCRIPTION TELEVISION.

PBS /ˌpiː biː 'es/ (in full the **Public Broadcasting Service**) (in the US) a television system that broadcasts programmes to an association of local stations which use no television advertisements and do not make a profit. It was established by the Public Broadcasting Act (1967) and is supported by money from the US government, large companies and the public. PBS is known for broadcasting programmes of good quality, such as *Sesame Street* and the National Geographic Special series. Many of the best British programmes are shown on *Masterpiece Theater*.

PC /ˌpiː 'siː/ ⇨ POLITICAL CORRECTNESS.

PCC /ˌpiː siː 'siː/ (in full **parochial church council**) n [C+sing/pl v] the administrative body of a *parish(1) church. Its members are usually people who go to church regularly and most of them are elected by members of the parish.

ˌPC 'Plod /ˌpiː siː 'plɒd; AmE 'plɑːd/ (BrE) a name used to refer in a humorous way to a junior police officer. 'PC' stands for 'Police Constable' and to 'plod' means to walk slowly, with heavy steps.

ˌP 'Diddy /ˌpiː 'dɪdi/ (also **Puff Daddy**, **Sean 'Puffy' Combs**) (1969–) a US music producer who has had a big influence on *hip hop music. He started by making his own records, many of which used samples (= pieces of music recorded by someone else), including *I'll be missing you* (1998) which won a *Grammy for best *rap performance. He started the record company **Bad Boy Entertainment** in 1993 which has produced records by artists including Notorious B.I.G, Lil' Kim and Boyz II Men. His other business interests include a range of fashion clothing called *Sean John* and a chain of restaurants called *Justin's*. He is also known for being arrested on various criminal charges connected with disagreements with other musicians.

PDSA /ˌpiː diː es 'eɪ/ ⇨ PEOPLE'S DISPENSARY FOR SICK ANIMALS.

PDT /ˌpiː diː 'tiː/ ⇨ PACIFIC DAYLIGHT TIME.

the 'Peace Corps an independent US government organization that sends Americans, usually young adults, to work without pay in foreign countries. President John F *Kennedy began it in 1961 with the aim of helping other countries in the fields of health, education, farming, etc. and so developing international friendship.

ˌpeace in our 'time a phrase used by the British *Prime Minister Neville *Chamberlain in 1938 after signing the *Munich Agreement by which Britain, France and Italy allowed Hitler to take control of a part of Czechoslovakia. Chamberlain got off the plane from Munich holding up a piece of paper which, he said, represented 'peace in our time' and 'peace with honour'. At the time many people believed that he was right, and that the Munich Agreement had saved Europe from war, but in March 1939 Hitler took all of Czechoslovakia and in September *World War II began when Poland was invaded, so that these phrases are now remembered with rather bitter feelings. See also APPEASEMENT.

'peace pipe n a type of traditional tobacco pipe with a long stem once smoked by most *Native Americans to celebrate a peace discussion or agreement. The pipe was decorated and was respected as a symbol of its owner's power. To 'smoke the peace pipe' is a phrase used in American English meaning to end a dispute or argument: *After much squabbling Linda and Rick finally decided to smoke the peace pipe.*

'Thomas 'Love 'Peacock /'lʌv 'pi:kɒk; *AmE* 'pi:kɑ:k/ (1785–1866) an English writer of novels and poetry. He used satire to attack the attitudes of well-known people of his time. For example, in *Nightmare Abbey* (1818) he makes fun of *Coleridge, *Shelley² and *Byron, among others.

the 'Peak ,District /'pi:k/ an area of hills, valleys, moors (= high land that is not cultivated) and caves, mostly in north *Derbyshire, England. It has been a *national park since 1951 and is very popular with people who enjoy walking and climbing.

'Norman 'Vincent 'Peale /'pi:l/ (1898–1993) a US religious leader who wrote *The Power of Positive Thinking* (1952), one of the most successful 'self-help' books, advising people how to improve the quality of their lives. He also had radio and television programmes, and wrote regularly in newspapers and magazines. He was the leader of the Marble Collegiate Reformed Church in New York (1932–84). His other books include *The Art of Living* (1948) and *Power of the Positive Factor* (1987).

,peanut 'butter n [U] a soft, thick food made from peanuts which in the US is often made sweeter with sugar, and is usually spread on bread or toast. **Creamy** or **smooth** peanut butter is made from finely ground peanuts and **crunchy** peanut butter contains larger pieces of nut. In the US, **peanut butter and jelly sandwiches** (= a sandwich containing peanut butter and fruit jam) are popular, especially with children.

'Peanuts /'pi:nʌts/ a very popular US *comic strip which has also appeared in many newspapers all over the world. It was drawn by Charles *Schulz (1922–2000) and was first published in 1950. It is about children who talk like adults, and the characters include Charlie *Brown, his dog *Snoopy, his aggressive friend Lucy and her nervous little brother *Linus.

,Pearl 'Harbor /,pɜ:l 'hɑ:bə(r); *AmE* ,pɜ:rl 'hɑ:rbər/ a harbour on the island of Oahu in *Hawaii. It is the US Navy's main Pacific base. A surprise attack by the Japanese on the navy ships there on 7 December 1941 brought the US into *World War II. The attack killed 2 403 people, injured 1 178 and destroyed 19 ships and 188 planes. The phrase 'Remember Pearl Harbor' came to be used to encourage Americans to support the war.

,pearly 'king n (*BrE*) (in London) a man who on special occasions wears dark clothes covered in thousands of small shiny buttons. A **pearly queen** is a woman who does the same. This is a tradition among the people who sell fruit and vegetables from carts in the streets, but is now only done for tourists and to collect money for charities.

,pearly 'queen n ⇨ PEARLY KING.

,Peter 'Pears /,pɪəz; *AmE* 'pɪrz/ (1910–86) an English singer with a tenor voice, who worked a lot with Benjamin *Britten. In 1948 they started the *Aldeburgh Festival together. Pears was made a *knight in 1978.

,Robert E 'Peary /'pɪəri; *AmE* 'pɪri/ (Robert Edwin Peary 1856–1920) a US Navy officer and explorer. After two earlier attempts which failed, he became the first man to reach the North Pole, on 6 April 1909.

the ,Peasants' Re'volt an incident in 1381 when the peasants (= poor farmers) of *Kent and *Essex marched to *Canterbury and then to London to protest at their conditions of life and the harsh taxes they had to pay. They occupied several major buildings, including the *Tower of London. The young king, *Richard II, talked to their leader, Wat *Tyler, and promised to help them. Many of them then went home, but Tyler was killed and the Revolt ended in complete failure, gaining nothing for the peasants.

,Gregory 'Peck /'pek/ (1916–2003) a US actor with a pleasant deep voice who usually played honest, good men. He won an *Oscar playing the part of a southern lawyer in *To Kill a Mockingbird. His other films include *Spellbound* (1945), *Duel in the Sun* (1946), *Gentleman's Agreement* (1947), *The Man in the Gray Flannel Suit* (1956), *Moby Dick* (1956), *The Omen* (1976) and *Other People's Money* (1991).

,Sam 'Peckinpah /'pekɪnpɑ:/ (1925–85) a US film director who was sometimes criticized for the amount of realistic violence shown in his films. These include *Major Dundee* (1965), The *Wild Bunch, *Straw Dogs* (1971), *Pat Garrett and Billy the Kid* (1973) and *The Osterman Weekend* (1983).

,Pecos 'Bill /,peɪkəs/ a popular *cowboy character in US legends, about whom many wild stories are told. For example, one says that he dug the *Rio Grande River when he dragged his pickaxe (= heavy tool with a metal point) behind him. Bill's girlfriend was called Slue Foot Sue and his horse was called Widowmaker. Compare BUNYAN.

,John 'Peel¹ /'pi:l/ (1939–2004) an English disc jockey and broadcaster who worked for *Radio 1 from the time it started in 1967. He encouraged good bands which were not well known by playing their records. He also presented the *Radio 4 programme about family life called *Home Truths*.

,John 'Peel² /'pi:l/ ⇨ D'YE KEN JOHN PEEL?.

,Robert 'Peel³ /'pi:l/ (1788–1850) one of the most important British politicians of the early 19th century and one of the people who started the modern *Conservative Party. As *Home Secretary (1822–30), Peel was responsible for giving *Roman Catholics the right to hold jobs in public life and for the organization of the *Metropolitan Police. (British police officers are still sometimes called **bobbies**, from Bobby, the short form of Robert. They were once also called **peelers**.) He was *Prime Minister twice (1834–5 and 1841–6) and his government passed a number of major new laws, especially in relation to British trade. He was made a *baronet in 1830. See also CORN LAWS.

,Peeping 'Tom n a person who likes to watch other people when they are doing something private, for example when they are taking their clothes off or kissing someone. The phrase 'Peeping Tom' comes from the story of Lady *Godiva, who rode through the streets naked. Everyone was told not to look at her, but one man, 'Peeping Tom of Coventry', did and he went blind: *He realized that he was watching the lovers like a common Peeping Tom.*

▶ **the peerage**

Peers of the realm are people who hold the highest ranks in the British *aristocracy. As a group, they are sometimes referred to as **the peerage**. There are two main types of peers: **hereditary peers** hold **titles** that are passed from one generation to the next, while **life peers** have a personal title which lasts for their own lifetime but is not passed on to their children.

The peerage is divided into five main ranks. The most senior rank is that of **duke** (for a man) or **duchess** (for a

Winners of the PEN/Faulkner Award for Fiction

1981	Walter Abish *How German Is It?*	1994	Philip Roth *Operation Shylock*
1982	David Bradley *The Chaneysville Incident*	1995	David Guterson *Snow Falling on Cedars*
1983	Toby Olson *Seaview*	1996	Richard Ford *Independence Day*
1984	John Edgar Wideman *Sent for You Yesterday*	1997	Gina Berriault *Women in Their Beds*
1985	Tobias Wolff *The Barracks Thief*	1998	Rafi Zabor *The Bear Comes Home*
1986	Peter Taylor *The Old Forest*	1999	Michael Cunningham *The Hours*
1987	Richard Wiley *Soldiers in Hiding*	2000	Ha Jin *Waiting*
1988	T. Coraghessan Boyle *World's End*	2001	Philip Roth *The Human Stain*
1989	James Salter *Dusk*	2002	Ann Patchett *Bel Canto*
1990	E. L. Doctorow *Billy Bathgate*	2003	Sabina Murray *The Caprices*
1991	John Edgar Wideman *Philadelphia Fire*	2004	John Updike *The Early Stories*
1992	Don DeLillo *Mao II*	2005	Ha Jin *War Trash*
1993	E. Annie Proulx *Postcards*		

woman), a hereditary title which was created in *Norman times. There are five royal Dukes, including the Duke of *Edinburgh, and 24 other dukes. The second most senior rank is that of **marquess** (man) or **marchioness** (woman), of which there are under 40. The third rank is that of **earl** (man) or **countess** (woman), of which there are nearly 200. This is the oldest title of all. Next in rank is a **viscount** (man) or **viscountess** (woman). The fifth and lowest rank of the peerage is that of **baron** (man) or **baroness** (woman), of which there are around 500 with hereditary titles. At present, about two thirds of all peers hold hereditary titles, many of which were originally given by the reigning king or queen to close friends or in return for some service. Senior titles often include the name of the place where the family comes from, e.g. the Duke of Devonshire, the Marquess of Normanby. A woman may be a duchess, marchioness, etc. in her own right or receive the title when she marries a duke, etc.

Life peers include the **Lords of Appeal in Ordinary**, usually referred to as *Law Lords, who are the most senior judges in the land, the *Lords Spiritual, who are the *archbishops of Canterbury and York and 24 bishops of the *Church of England and, since 1958, many other men and women who have been **given a peerage** in recognition of their public service. Most of these are given the rank of baron or baroness.

There are complicated rules for how to address and refer to members of the peerage. Dukes, for instance, are addressed formally as 'Your Grace', marquesses and earls as 'My Lord', and viscounts and barons as 'Lord X '. There are also rules for addressing members of their families. Most British people know that such complicated forms of address exist but many would not be able to use them correctly, and would probably think that they are rather strange and old-fashioned.

Peers cannot be elected to the *House of Commons as *Members of Parliament unless they have first **disclaimed** their title. Tony *Benn campaigned for members of the peerage to have this right and was himself the first to be able to give up his title and become an MP. Former members of the *House of Commons who have been **elevated to the peerage** as a reward for their service are sometimes said to have been 'kicked upstairs'.

At present, all life peers and some hereditary peers may take part in the government of Britain by **taking their seat** in the *House of Lords, though many do not attend regularly. There has for a long time been talk of changing this right for hereditary peers, which many people consider undemocratic, and even of abolishing the House of Lords. At the end of 1997 there were about 650 hereditary peers compared with 500 life peers. About 500 of the total were *Conservative peers, most of whom were hereditary peers. In 1998 the Labour government announced that it would reform the

House of Lords by introducing laws to abolish the right of hereditary peers to sit in the House of Lords, and creating about 600 new life peers to take their place. The number of hereditary peers in the House of Lords was reduced to 92 but by 2005 the proposed reform was not complete.

,**Nancy Pe'losi** /pəˈləʊsi; *AmE* pəˈloʊsi/ (1940–) a US *Democratic Party politician who was elected to the *House of Representatives in 1987 and became *minority leader of the Democratic Party in the House in 2004, the first woman to lead a main political party in the US *Congress.

'**Pembrokeshire** /ˈpembrʊkʃə; *AmE* ˈpembrʊkʃər/ a county in the south-west of Wales, now governed by a *unitary authority. Part of its coast has been protected as a *national park since 1952.

'**penalty points** *n* [pl] a system used by the government to control the way people drive their cars. If, for example, somebody is stopped by the police for driving too fast or in a dangerous way, they get a number of penalty points on their driving licence. After a certain amount of time, the points are removed from the licence. However, if at any time somebody reaches a particular number of points (12 in Britain) they are not allowed to drive at all for a period of time. A person with points on their licence also pays more for car insurance: *I've still got six penalty points on my licence.* ⇨ note at DRIVING.

the ,**PEN/'Faulkner Foundation** /ˌpen ˈfɔːknə(r)/ an organization originally started by the writer William *Faulkner which gives a prize, **the PEN/Faulkner Award for Fiction**, every year for the best novel by an American writer and also has programmes in schools in certain US cities to encourage young people to become interested in literature.

'**Penguin™** *n* **1** a book published by *Penguin Books: *her collection of battered Penguins.* **2** a British make of chocolate biscuit: *a packet of Penguins.*

,**Penguin 'Books** a British company that publishes paperback books (= books with paper covers). It was started in 1935 and was the first to publish books of good quality in this way at reasonable prices. See also PUFFIN BOOKS.

the **Pe,ninsular 'War** /pəˌnɪnsjələ; *AmE* pəˌnɪnsjələr/ a war (1808–14) fought in Spain and Portugal, in which British, Spanish and Portuguese soldiers defeated the armies of the French Emperor Napoleon Bonaparte. The Peninsular War was one of the *Napoleonic Wars.

,**Sean 'Penn**[1] /ˌʃɔːn ˈpen/ (1960–) a US actor and writer who also directs. He is known for his independent and sometimes violent style of life. In 2002 he paid over $50 000 to publish a letter in the *Washington Post calling on George W *Bush not to start a war with Iraq. His

P

films include *At Close Range* (1985), *The Indian Runner* (1991), which he also wrote and directed, *Dead Man Walking* (1996) and *Mystic River* (2003), for which he won an *Academy Award. He was married to the singer and actor *Madonna from 1985 to 1989.

,William 'Penn² /'pen/ (1644–1718) an English *Quaker who established the American colony of *Pennsylvania on land given to him by King *Charles II. He made it a place of safety for Quakers and all other religious groups, and called this a 'holy experiment'. He also helped to create the city of *Philadelphia.

the 'Pennines /'penaɪnz/ a series of hills in northern England that run from the *Peak District to the Scottish border, a distance of about 250 miles/400 kilometres. They are sometimes called 'the backbone of England'. See also PENNINE WAY.

the ,Pennine 'Way /,penaɪn/ a path along the *Pennines in northern England, used by people who like walking as a hobby. It is about 250 miles/400 kilometres long and passes through three *national parks, including the *Peak District. It was opened in 1965.

,Penn 'Station /,pen/ (also ,Pennsylvania 'Station) /,penslveɪnɪə/ a railway station in New York City. It is under *Madison Square Garden at 34th Street and Eighth Avenue. It is used by trains going to and from *Long Island and *New Jersey, as well as such major cities as *Boston and *Washington, DC.

,Pennsyl'vania /,pensl'veɪnɪə/ a state in the north-eastern US, also called the Keystone State for its central position among the 13 original states. The largest city is *Philadelphia, and the capital city is Harrisburg. The area was established for *Quakers in 1681 by William *Penn, who named it Pennsylvania ('Penn's small forest') for his father. The Battle of *Gettysburg was fought there during the *American Civil War. The state produces chemicals, medicines, electronic equipment and farm products. Tourist attractions include *Valley Forge and the *Pennsylvania Dutch(1) region.

Pennsylvania Avenue

,Pennsylvania 'Avenue /,penslveɪnɪə/ a famous broad street in *Washington, DC. It is 1.3 miles/2 kilometres long and connects the *White House(1) and the *Capitol. Along the way are other government buildings, including the offices of the *FBI, the *FTC, the Commerce Department and the Treasury Department.

,Pennsylvania 'Dutch /,penslveɪnɪə/ n 1 [pl] a group of people who live in the US state of *Pennsylvania, west of *Philadelphia. They are descended from German (not Dutch) *Protestant religious groups who settled there in the 17th and 18th centuries. They include the *Amish, *Mennonites and Moravians. They have a strict, simple way of life, wear plain black clothes and do not use machines, including cars. They are known for making beautiful furniture which is carved or painted with designs of flowers, birds, etc. 2 [U] the language of the Pennsylvania Dutch people. It is a form of German.

,penny 'black n a British stamp first produced in 1840. It cost one penny and had a picture of Queen *Victoria on it. Because it was the first stamp in the world there

was no need to print the word 'Britain' on it, and even today British stamps do not have the country's name on them. Penny blacks are now quite rare and highly valued.

,penny-'farthing n an old type of bicycle, popular in the late 19th century, with a very large wheel at the front and a much smaller one at the back (similar to the old British penny and farthing coins).

▶ **pensions**   a penny-farthing

Pensions are regular payments made to people who have retired. Most people retire and start to receive a pension when they are about 60 or 65. The amount of money they receive depends on how much they have paid into their **pension scheme** and also on the type of scheme.

In Britain, a basic **state pension** has been provided by the government since 1908 for those who paid *National Insurance **contributions** while they were working. Pensions for each generation are paid for out of the contributions of people still working. A problem arising from this arrangement is that more people now live longer but the number of younger people in work has fallen, so that there is less money to pay for pensions.

Some pensioners complain that the state pension does not provide enough money for them to have a reasonable standard of living. People who do not qualify for a state pension, e.g. because they have not paid enough National Insurance, may receive *income support if they have no other source of money. **War pensions** for soldiers injured on duty are also paid by the government.

There are several other kinds of pension which pay larger amounts of money, though people have to pay more towards them. There are many **company pension schemes**, into which both workers and their employers pay certain amounts. A similar scheme, **SERPS**, was started by the government in 1978 for people who could not join a company scheme. Some people, especially those who are self-employed, belong to **private pension schemes** arranged through insurance companies. The money paid into company or private pension schemes is invested in the stock market and the **pension funds**, the organizations that manage this money, are among the most important investors in the *City. In the 1980s the government encouraged people to leave SERPS and company pension schemes and take out private pensions instead and in some cases, where private pension funds have been a poor investment, people have lost money.

In the US there are three main types of pensions. The US government operates a programme called *social security, and people who work have to pay into this programme. The amount of money they get when they retire depends on how much they earned when they were working, but it is never a lot. It would be difficult to live only on social security payments, and so people also arrange to receive a pension from another source.

Many employers and unions operate pension programmes for their workers. As in Britain both employers and workers put money into these private pension funds and the money is invested. By law, pension funds must report to the government and to their members about the way they manage the money. Many people who want to be sure of having enough money when they retire also make their own personal arrangements. One common way of doing this is by opening a special bank account called an *IRA, or **Individual Retirement Account**. With this kind of account people pay less tax than normal, but must agree to leave the money in the bank until they retire.

the **'Pension Service** a British government office, part of the *Department for Work and Pensions, which gives people advice and information about pensions.

the **'Pentagon** 1 the building in Arlington, *Virginia, completed in 1943, which contains the administrative offices of the US *Department of Defense and divisions of the US armed forces. It has five sides and is the largest office building in the world.
2 (*informal*) the military leaders of the US: *The Pentagon says more spy planes are needed.*

the **Pentagon 'Papers** secret papers from the *Pentagon which were printed in the *New York Times* in 1971. The papers had been taken by Daniel Ellsberg, a government employee, and given to the newspaper. They were about a government study of the *Vietnam War, and they revealed military actions about which the public had not been told. The US *Department of Justice tried to stop them being published, but the *Supreme Court decided that the newspaper had the right to publish them under the *First Amendment. The Pentagon Papers helped to turn public opinion against the war and also strengthened the freedom of the press.

Pente'costalist /ˌpentɪˈkɒstəlɪst; AmE ˌpentɪˈkɑːstəlɪst/ n a member of any of the *Protestant **Pentecostal** religious groups or Churches. They believe that illnesses can be healed by faith and in 'baptism in the spirit' in which a person 'speaks in tongues' with unknown words that come from the Holy Spirit. Pentecostalism began in the US at the beginning of the 20th century and now has support in other major Christian Churches. The largest Pentecostal Church in the US is the Church of God in Christ, with more than 5.5 million members.
▸ **Pentecostalism** n [U]
Pentecostalist adj.

'Penthouse a US magazine for men. It is known for its pictures of almost naked women and articles about sex, though it also includes articles on other subjects. It was started by Bob Guccione (1930–), who first published it in London, England, in 1965.

'Pentonville /ˈpentənvɪl/ a large prison for men in north London, England, opened in 1842.

Pen'zance /penˈzæns/ a port in *Cornwall in southwest England, near *Land's End. It is a popular place for holidays/vacations.

'People a popular US magazine published each week. It contains photographs of and articles about film and television stars, as well as news stories. It was begun in 1974 by the Time-Life Company, now *Time Warner.

The 'People one of Britain's national *Sunday papers, started in 1881. It is not regarded as one of the 'quality papers'.

the **'People's Di'spensary for 'Sick 'Animals** (abbr **the PDSA**) a British charity that gives free treatment to sick animals and encourages people to look after their pets properly. It was started in 1917.

Pe'oria /piˈɔːriə/ a small city in the US state of *Illinois. It is considered a typical US city, and people living there are thought to have opinions which in general represent the opinions of the whole country: *Before you go ahead you must ask yourself, will it play in Peoria?*

PEP /pep/ n ⇨ PERSONAL EQUITY PLAN.

'PepsiCo Inc /ˈpepsɪkəʊ; AmE ˈpepsɪkoʊ/ a US company which started in 1965 and is best known for its soft

(= non-alcoholic) drinks, especially *Pepsi-Cola. It also owns *Quaker Oats and *Frito-Lay potato chips.

Pepsi-'Cola™ /ˌpepsi ˈkəʊlə; AmE ˈkoʊlə/ (also **'Pepsi**™) n [U, C] a US sweet dark brown fizzy drink (= one containing many bubbles). It is, after its great rival *Coca-Cola, the second most popular drink of this type in the world.

Pepto-'Bismol™ /ˌpeptəʊ ˈbɪzmɒl; AmE ˌpeptoʊ ˈbɪzmɑːl/ a well-known US make of medicine for stomach problems. It is a thick pink liquid, made by *Proctor & Gamble.

Samuel 'Pepys /ˈpiːps/ (1633–1703) an Englishman known today because of his detailed diaries, written between 1660 and 1669 but not published until the 19th century. He was a senior government officer in the service of two kings, *Charles II and *James II, and he wrote about court and social life in the 17th century, as well as recording major events such as the *Great Fire of London. He also included many private details about his own life. He knew many of the most important figures of his day, including Sir Christopher *Wren and Sir Isaac *Newton. Pepys often ended his writing for the day with the phrase 'And so to bed', which people sometimes use in a humorous way today.

the **Per'forming 'Right So'ciety** (abbr **PRS**) a British organization, started in 1914, that collects money from people and organizations who perform or broadcast music of all kinds and gives it to the people who write music and songs.

The 'Perils of 'Pauline a very popular series of early US silent films telling a continuous story, released in 1914. At the end of each film the main character Pauline, played by Pearl White, was shown in great danger, so people went to see the next one to find out how she escaped. After its success, many other similar series were made.

Carl 'Perkins /ˈpɜːkɪnz; AmE ˈpɜːrkɪnz/ (1932–98) a US singer and writer of *rockabilly songs which combined *country music with *rock and roll. His first hit, *Blue Suede Shoes* (1956), was later recorded by Elvis *Presley. His songs have also been recorded by country music singers like Johnny *Cash and by various pop groups, including the *Beatles. He was chosen for the Rock and Roll *Hall of Fame in 1987.

Permanent 'Secretary n a senior officer in the British *Civil Service who often has the job of advising a government minister: *the Permanent Secretary at the Foreign Office.* Compare PARLIAMENTARY SECRETARY.

the **per'missive so'ciety** n [sing] (*often disapproving*) the social conditions and attitudes in countries such as Britain and the US in the 1960s and 1970s, when there was a new freedom of sexual behaviour and a greater willingness to tolerate different ways of living. These changes were originally made by younger people, and developed from ideas such as *flower power and the *hippie culture. Some people blame the permissive society for modern problems like the use of illegal drugs, lack of respect for authority and low moral standards.

H 'Ross Pe'rot /ˌrɒs pəˈrəʊ; AmE ˌrɔːs pəˈroʊ/ (Henry Ross Perot 1930–) a rich US businessman who stood without success as an independent candidate for US President in the 1992 and 1996 elections. He argued that the government should reduce the amount of money it spends. In the 2000 presidential election he gave his support to George W *Bush. Perot had started the Electronic Data Systems Corporation in 1962 in *Dallas, which made him extremely rich.

P

Perpen'dicular
/ˌpɜːpənˈdɪkjələ(r)/; AmE
ˌpɜːrpənˈdɪkjələr/ n [U] a
style of *Gothic architecture used in England dur-
ing the 14th and 15th centuries. It was marked by
large windows, vertical
lines, and ceiling patterns
in stone called **fan vaulting**. An example of this
style is the chapel of
*King's College,
Cambridge. Compare
DECORATED STYLE,
EARLY ENGLISH.

fan vaulting

Fred 'Perry¹ /ˈperi/
(1909–97) an English tennis player who won the
*Wimbledon men's championship three years in a row
(1934–36). No Englishman has won it since then. Before
his tennis career, Perry had been the men's world champion at *table tennis in 1929. He later started a company
making sports clothes.

Matthew 'Perry² /ˈperi/ (1969–) a US actor who is best
known for playing Chandler in the US comedy series
*Friends.

John 'Pershing /ˈpɜːʃɪŋ; AmE ˈpɜːrʃɪŋ/ (1860–1948)
the army officer who commanded the US Expeditionary
Force in France in *World War I. General Pershing's
popular name was 'Black Jack' because of his tough discipline. He had earlier served in the *Indian wars and
the *Spanish-American War. He received the *Pulitzer
Prize for his book *My Experiences in the World War* (1931).
The US nuclear weapon called the **Pershing missile** is
named after him.

'Persil™ /ˈpɜːsɪl; AmE ˈpɜːrsɪl/ n [U] a British make of
powder or liquid for washing clothes. Its advertisements
claim that 'Persil washes whiter'.

Personal 'Equity Plan n (abbr **PEP**) a savings
scheme in Britain from 1987 to 1999. People who bought
a Personal Equity Plan could invest a limited amount of
money in companies and did not have to pay any tax on
the profits they made. Although the system was replaced
by the *ISA, people still get tax relief on the PEPs they
hold.

▶ **personal space**

Personal space can be imagined as a kind of bubble surrounding a person that protects their *privacy and which
other people may not normally enter. The amount of
space people need to feel around them is different in
every culture, though British and American people have
similar ideas about how much it should be. People from
cultures that like a lot of personal space feel awkward
and embarrassed when somebody comes too close to
them and try to move away; people who need less personal space are often offended when others seem to
want to keep them at a distance.

The amount of personal space people need also
depends on several other factors. People of the same
sex may sit or stand closer to each other than to somebody of the opposite sex. Strangers and casual acquaint-
ances usually need more space than friends and members of the same family who know each other well. But
in a noisy street people may need to stand closer in order
to hear each other, and in underground trains in the rush
hour in London people have to stand squashed together
but they still try to respect each other's space as far as
possible. Some British people avoid sitting next to
strangers on buses and if there are lots of empty seats
they choose one by itself.

For a private conversation Americans need at least a
foot/30 centimetres between each other, and British
people more. Distances as great as 5 feet/1.5 metres may
also seem comfortable. Allowing somebody to get very
close and enter your personal space may be a sign of
trust or love.

British people tend to avoid touching or being physically close to people outside their own family. Americans
are only a little more comfortable about touching each
other. When people meet for the first time they shake
hands and let go quickly and move back. In formal situations they may also shake hands when they say goodbye though they often avoid doing this. Women often
greet members of their family with a hug or kiss on one
cheek, and may also greet friends in this way. They also
hug and kiss each other when saying goodbye. But they
rarely hold hands or link arms with each other when
walking along. Some men are embarrassed about kissing
members of the family or children in public. They may
shake hands but often simply nod and smile. Men rarely
touch their friends unless to shake hands or slap them on
the back in congratulation.

Per'suasion a romantic novel (1818) by Jane *Austen,
the last book she wrote. The main character is Anne
Elliot, who refuses Frederick Wentworth's offer of marriage but regrets doing so and accepts when he asks her
again several years later.

PETA /ˈpetə/ (in full **People for the Ethical
Treatment of Animals**) an international organization
based in *Virginia in the US which campaigns against
cruelty to animals, especially in farming, scientific
research and in entertainments such as circuses. It was
started in 1980. PETA has organized many famous campaigns to persuade people not to eat meat or other animal products, not to wear fur and not to buy things from
firms which it believes treat animals cruelly.

Pete 'Marsh ⇨ MARSH².

Peter 'Jones /ˈdʒəʊnz; AmE ˈdʒoʊnz/ a fashionable
department store in *Sloane Square, London. It is one of
the *John Lewis group of shops.

Peter'loo /ˌpiːtəˈluː; AmE ˌpiːtərˈluː/ (also the
ˌPeterloo 'Massacre) the name given to an incident
that took place in *Manchester, England, in 1819. A
group of people gathered in St Peter's Fields in central
Manchester to demand political change. The crowd was
large, but peaceful and not armed. It was attacked by
the army, who killed eleven people and injured about
500. The name Peterloo is a mixture of St Peter's Fields
and *Waterloo, the battle at which many people had
recently died.

Peter 'Pan /ˈpæn/ a children's play (1904) by J M
*Barrie. Peter Pan is a boy who lives in a magic place
called *Never Never Land and never grows up. One
night he visits three children in London and takes them
to Never Never Land. They have a series of adventures
with Peter, a fairy called Tinkerbell, a group of pirates
and a crocodile. It is a very popular play, and is traditionally performed every *Christmas in London. It was
made into a successful Walt *Disney film in 1953. It is so
well known that a person who seems never to grow any
older is sometimes called a 'Peter Pan': *Still winning
matches at 35, he's the Peter Pan of the tennis world.* See
also CAPTAIN HOOK.

Peter 'Rabbit /ˈræbɪt/ a character in several of Beatrix
*Potter's stories for children, including her first, *The Tale
of Peter Rabbit*. He is a young rabbit who often gets into
trouble.

Ellis 'Peters /ˌelɪs ˈpiːtəz; AmE ˈpiːtərz/ (1913–1995) an
English writer best known for her series of *detective
novels set in the Middle Ages, in which the main character is the monk Brother Cadfael.

the ˌ**Petrified** ˈ**Forest** /ˌpetrɪfaɪd/ a large area in the US state of *Arizona where ancient trees have turned into stone. It has been a *national park since 1962 and includes part of the *Painted Desert.

the Petrified Forest

▶**pets**

Over half of all British and US families keep an animal as a pet. Families with children are most likely to have pets, but other people, especially old people, often keep a pet for company. Some animals belong to a group of people: for example, many British railway stations, old people's homes and even offices have a resident cat.

The most popular pets for children include cats, dogs, birds, fish, rabbits, guinea pigs, hamsters and mice, and children are usually expected to help take care of their pets. Older people are more likely to have a cat or dog, or perhaps a budgerigar. Since dogs and cats have different characters and needs, many people have a strong preference for one or the other. People who say that they are **dog people** like the fact that dogs like to go for walks, enjoy being touched and need lots of attention. **Cat people** like cats because they are independent. Other people prefer **exotic pets**, such as snakes, spiders, iguanas and stick insects. Many pets can be bought at a **pet shop**, though people often buy dogs and cats direct from breeders or from homes for stray (= lost) animals.

Most pets are treated as members of the family. People buy special pet food and biscuits, or sometimes fresh fish or meat. Pets have their own place to sleep, bowls to eat from and toys to play with. There are even clothes for pets, and **salons** where their fur is washed and cut.

Pets are a responsibility which must be taken seriously. Dog owners in the US have to buy a **dog licence** (AmE **dog license**) which allows them to keep a dog. This was formerly also the case in Britain. Pure-bred dogs may also be taken to local and national **shows** where there are prizes for the best of each breed. But many people are not bothered about having a pure-bred dog and are happy with a **mongrel** (AmE **mutt**).

A few dogs are kept outside and sleep in a **kennel** (AmE **doghouse**). Most, however, like cats, are allowed to go where they like inside the house. Most dogs wear a **collar**, with a small metal disc attached giving the dog's name and address. In the US there are laws in most places requiring dogs to be kept on a **leash** (BrE **lead**). People teach their dogs to **walk to heel** (AmE **heeling**) and not to jump up at people. Some also teach them to do tricks like **fetching** or **begging**. Some people take their dog to **obedience school** (BrE **obedience classes**) for training. There is now pressure for dog owners to clear up any mess left by their dog, and people can be fined for not doing so.

Cats are less trouble to look after. They can often enter or leave their house as they please through a **cat flap**. If they are kept inside they are trained to urinate in a litter tray filled with **cat litter** (= a special absorbent

material). Many cat owners give their cats a **flea collar** and a disc with their name and address on it in case they get lost.

Looking after a pet properly can be quite expensive. Many British people pay for their dog to stay at a local **kennels**, or their cat at a **cattery** when they go on holiday. In the US there are **pet motels**. Many people take out insurance to cover medical treatment by a **vet** and animals with emotional problems can be taken to a **pet psychologist**. When a pet dies many people bury it in their garden, but others arrange for it to be buried in a special **pet cemetery**.

If people do not want a pet of their own they can sponsor an animal through a charity and receive regular information about it. Many people also put out bird tables containing food for wild birds.

ˌ**Petticoat** ˈ**Lane** a street in the *East End of London, England, where a famous market takes place every Sunday, selling a wide variety of goods. The name of the street was officially changed to Middlesex Street in the 19th century, but people still refer to the market as Petticoat Lane.

ˌ**Petworth** ˈ**House** /ˌpetwəθ; AmE ˌpetwərθ/ a *stately home near *Chichester in southern England. It was first built in the Middle Ages but most of it was rebuilt in the 17th and 18th centuries. It is well known for its collection of paintings by *Turner[2], who used to stay there as a guest, and for its garden, designed by 'Capability' *Brown.

ˌ**Nikolaus** ˈ**Pevsner** /ˌnɪkələs ˈpevznə(r)/ (1902–83) a British architectural historian, born in Germany. His best-known work, *The Buildings of England* (1941–74), describes every important building in England. It was published in 46 volumes and is often referred to simply as 'Pevsner'. He also wrote *The Englishness of English Art* (1957). He was made a *knight in 1969.

ˌ**Peyton** ˈ**Place** /ˌpeɪtn/ a novel (1956) by the US writer Grace Metalious which shocked many people but still sold millions of copies. It is about the sexual relationships and often dishonest behaviour of people living in a small *New England town. There was a film version in 1957, and it later became the basis for the first evening *soap opera on US television, with the then unknown actors Mia *Farrow and Ryan O'Neal.

P45 /ˌpiː fɔːtiˈfaɪv; AmE ˌpiː fɔːrtiˈfaɪv/ (in Britain) an official form you are given when you leave a job, which shows how much tax you have paid. You give it to your employer when you start a new job.

PG /ˌpiː ˈdʒiː/ a British *film certificate indicating that it is suitable for general viewing but some scenes in the film may not be suitable for children.

the **PGA** /ˌpiː jiː ˈeɪ/ (*in full* the **Professional Golfers' Association**) the US association for men who play or are involved in professional golf, established in 1916. It is in charge of the major tournaments (= competitions) during the golf season and has its own **PGA Tournament** each year. The equivalent women's organization is the **Ladies Professional Golfers' Association** (**LPGA**).

ˌ**Phi** ˈ**Beta** ˈ**Kappa** /ˌfaɪ ˈbiːtə ˈkæpə/ the most famous *honor society for US college and university students in the arts and sciences. It is the oldest organization with Greek letters in the US, having been established in 1776 at the College of William and Mary in *Virginia. Students with high academic grades can be chosen in their third or fourth years.

ˌ**Phila**ˈ**delphia** /ˌfɪləˈdelfiə/ the fifth largest city in the US and the largest in *Pennsylvania. It is a major port on the Delaware River and was established by William *Penn. Philadelphia is one of America's most historic cities. It is the place where the *Declaration of

P

Independence was signed and the American *Constitution was written. *Independence Hall and the *Liberty Bell are also there.

Phila'delphia /ˌfɪlə'delfiə/ the first major US film (1993) about the disease AIDS. Tom *Hanks won an *Oscar as Best Actor, and Bruce *Springsteen received one for his song *Streets of Philadelphia*. In the film Hanks plays a homosexual with AIDS who is dismissed from work and begins a legal case against his employer. The film created a lot of debate in America about equal rights for people with AIDS.

Phila'delphia cream 'cheese /ˌfɪlə'delfiə/ (*informal* **Philly** /'fɪli/) a type of soft white cheese that was first sold in the US in 1880. It is now made by *Kraft and sold in many countries.

Regis 'Philbin /ˌriːdʒɪs 'fɪlbɪn/ (1933–) a US *talk show host who has presented *The Regis Philbin Show*, *Live with Regis and Kathie Lee* and, since 2000, *Live with Regis and Kelly* with Kelly Ripa. He has also presented *Who Wants to be a Millionaire?*.

Kim 'Philby /'fɪlbi/ (1912–88) a British spy who gave British secrets to the Soviet Union. He was a member of a group called the *Cambridge spies, and continued as the 'third man' after Guy *Burgess and Donald *Maclean were discovered. Later, like them, Philby escaped to the USSR and became a Soviet citizen.

the ˌPhilhar'monia /ˌfɪlɑː'məʊniə; *AmE* ˌfɪlɑːr'moʊniə/ (*also* **the ˌPhilhar'monia ˌOrchestra**) a well-known British orchestra which is based in London but regularly performs abroad. It was established in 1945 and has had a number of famous foreign conductors.

Prince 'Philip ⇨ EDINBURGH[2].

Philip 'Morris /'mɒrɪs; *AmE* 'mɔːrɪs/ a large US cigarette company that makes *Marlboro, America's most popular cigarettes, and *Virginia Slims. In 1997, the head of the company became the first leader in the industry to admit that smoking cigarettes has killed many people.

Phillips™ 'screwdriver /ˌfɪlɪps/ *n* a type of screwdriver (= tool that turns a screw) with two small blades on the end shaped like a cross. It is named after the American H F Phillips who invented it, and is used with a **Phillips screw**.

Philly 'cheesesteak /ˌfɪli 'tʃiːzsteɪk/ *n* a sandwich made with a filling of thinly sliced grilled beef, melted cheese and, often, fried onions in a long bread roll. They were first made in *Philadelphia in the 1930s.

Phiz /fɪz/ (1815–82) the name used by Hablot Knight Browne, the artist who drew the illustrations for many of the novels of Charles *Dickens.

'Phoenix[1] /'fiːnɪks/ the capital and largest city in the US state of *Arizona. It is on the Salt River in central Arizona and has a warm, dry climate that attracts tourists. It is a centre for agricultural products and information technology. Phoenix became a city in 1881 and the capital of the Arizona Territory in 1889. It received the Bertelsmann Foundation Award in 1993 as the best managed city in the world.

River 'Phoenix[2] /ˌrɪvə 'fiːnɪks; *AmE* ˌrɪvər/ (1970–93) a US actor who became a cult figure (= a person who is fashionable with a particular group) among young people after he accidentally took too many drugs and died at the age of 23. He played sensitive characters, and his films include *Stand By Me* (1986), *Running on Empty* (1988), *My Own Private Idaho* (1991) and *Sneakers* (1992).

phony 'war (*also* **phoney war**) *n* a situation in which two or more countries have officially declared war but have not yet started to fight. The best-known phony war was the first six months of *World War II. Britain and

France declared war against Germany in September 1939, but did not send any soldiers to fight until Germany attacked Denmark and Norway in April 1940: *The President spoke of the need for a real war, not a phony war, against drugs.*

'Picca'dilly /ˌpɪkə'dɪli/ a famous street in London's *West End, between *Piccadilly Circus and Hyde Park Corner. The origin of the name is not known.

Piccadilly 'Circus /ˌpɪkədɪli/ a place in the *West End of London, England, where several famous streets meet, including *Piccadilly, *Regent Street and *Shaftesbury Avenue. Many tourists go there to see the statue of *Eros and the brightly lit advertisements on the sides of the buildings. There is also a Piccadilly Circus station on the *London Underground. Noisy, crowded places are sometimes compared to Piccadilly Circus: *I can't get any work done, it's like Piccadilly Circus in here.*

Wilson 'Pickett /ˌwɪlsn 'pɪkɪt/ (1941–) a US singer and writer of songs, mostly of *soul music. They include *In the Midnight Hour* (1965), *Mustang Sally* (1966) and *Don't Let the Green Grass Fool You* (1971). He was chosen for the Rock and Roll *Hall of Fame in 1991, and that year appeared in the film *The Commitments*. He still performs on tours.

Mary 'Pickford /ˌpɪkfəd; *AmE* ˌpɪkfərd/ (1893–1979) one of the most famous actors in US silent films, born in Canada, who became known as 'America's Sweetheart'. She had long curls and played innocent characters. In 1919, she joined Douglas *Fairbanks[1] (her husband from 1920 to 1936), Charlie *Chaplin and D W *Griffith to establish the film company *United Artists. Her films included *Rebecca of Sunnybrook Farm* (1917) and *Pollyanna* (1920). In 1976, she received a special *Oscar for her services to the film industry.

'Pickford's /'pɪkfədz; *AmE* 'pɪkfərdz/ a well known British company that transports people's furniture and other possessions in large vans when they move to a new home.

The ˌPickwick 'Papers /ˌpɪkwɪk/ a novel (1837) by Charles *Dickens, the full title of which is *The Posthumous Papers of the Pickwick Club*. It was originally written as a series of stories, published each month, about the amusing adventures of the members of the club established by Samuel Pickwick. Pickwick is a kind, friendly, fat man who often gets into difficult situations caused by misunderstandings or by his own good nature.

Pict /pɪkt/ *n* a member of an ancient British people. They lived in northern Scotland between the 1st and 9th centuries AD, when they became united with the *Scots. Little is known about the Picts, but they are famous for their stone carvings decorated with mysterious symbols.

The 'Pied 'Piper of 'Hamelin /'hæmlɪn/ a poem (1842) by Robert *Browning. It tells the story of an old European legend about a man who gets rid of all the rats in the German town of Hamelin by playing his pipe. The rats follow the music and the piper leads them out of the town. When the people of Hamelin refuse to pay him for getting rid of the rats, he plays his pipe again and leads their children away.

pier *n* a long structure, usually made of wood and iron, built out into the sea or a lake or river. Piers were originally built so that people could walk along them to get onto boats at the end, or load or unload goods, but in the 19th century many British seaside towns built large piers for pleasure, often with theatres, restaurants and entertainments on them and some of them are still popular tourist attractions.

P

a pier

,**Piers** '**Plowman** /ˌpɪəz ˈplaʊmən; AmE ˌpɪrz/ a long poem written in the late 14th century by William Langland. The poem describes a vision (= a religious experience like a dream) in which different objects represent good and evil, and how Piers helps a group of people to search for truth through Christianity. It describes the life of ordinary people in great detail, and criticizes the social and moral evils of the time. See also MIDDLE ENGLISH.

,**Lester** '**Piggott** /ˌlestə ˈpɪgət; AmE ˌlestər/ (1935–) a famous English jockey. He has won more races than anybody in the history of horse racing, including the *Derby nine times. He was *champion jockey eight times. He was sent to prison in 1987 for not paying tax, but started racing again in 1990 and also became a trainer.

'**Piglet** a character in A A *Milne's children's stories about *Winnie-the-Pooh. Piglet, a cheerful young pig, is one of *Pooh's friends.

,**Pike's** '**Peak** /ˌpaɪks/ a US mountain in the *Rocky Mountains near Colorado Springs, *Colorado. 'Pike's Peak or Bust' was the cry of people who rushed to that area when gold was discovered in 1859 and of later people who used the mountain as a place to aim for as they travelled west. It is 14 110 feet/4 304 metres high and named after Zebulon Pike, who discovered it in 1806.

the ,**Pilgrim** '**Fathers** (also the '**Pilgrims**) the 102 English people who sailed to America on the *Mayflower* in 1620. Their group included 35 *Puritans whose aim was to create a safe religious community in the New World. The Pilgrims probably landed at *Plymouth Rock, and they established *Plymouth Colony. Compare FOUNDING FATHERS.

The ,**Pilgrim's** '**Progress** a religious novel written between 1678 and 1684 by John *Bunyan. It is an allegory (= a story in which the characters and events are symbols representing other things, such as truths, fears and human qualities) about a man's journey through life to heaven. The man, whose name is Christian, meets many symbolic difficulties on the way, including the *Slough of Despond, Vanity Fair and Giant Despair. He finally reaches heaven, and his wife and children follow him.

'**Pilkington** /ˈpɪlkɪŋtən/ a British company that makes many different types of glass. The company has produced glass since the early 19th century, but it became well known in 1959 when Alastair Pilkington invented a new way of making flat glass by floating it on metal that has been heated until it becomes liquid.

'**pillar box** n (BrE) a tall iron box in the shape of a pillar for posting letters, etc. Pillar boxes stand in the street and are painted bright red. The letters in them are usually collected several times each day: *I'll post it for you,*

there's a pillar box on the way to the shops. ◇ *She painted her nails pillar-box red.*

'**pillory** n a device used for punishing criminals in Britain from the 13th to the 19th century. It was a wooden framework with holes for the head and hands. Criminals were locked into pillories in public places so that people could laugh at them, insult them and sometimes throw things at them. Compare STOCKS.

'**Pillsbury** /ˈpɪlzbri/ a US company that sells a range of biscuits, bread and other baked products. It is known especially for using the **Pillsbury Doughboy** in its advertisements. He is a small, fat, white boy called Poppin Fresh who is shy and wears a baker's cap.

,**Piltdown** '**man** /ˌpɪltdaʊn/ a type of prehistoric human being that was believed to exist in ancient times. Piltdown man was 'discovered' when some bones were found in 1912 on Piltdown Common in southern England. It was later proved to be a trick, perhaps meant as a joke, when scientific tests showed that they were a mixture of modern human and ape bones that had been treated to look ancient.

'**Pima** /ˈpiːmə/ n (pl **Pimas** or **Pima**) a member of a *Native American people who live in southern *Arizona on two reservations (= lands given and protected by the US government). They are agricultural people known for their beautiful baskets. They fought against the *Apache and were friendly to Europeans who settled in their areas.

Pimm's™ /pɪmz/ n [U, C] a fashionable British alcoholic drink, made with gin. Its full name is **Pimm's Number One Cup** and it is usually drunk mixed with lemonade, ice and pieces of fresh fruit at summer parties and outdoor events: *They were all drinking Pimm's on the lawn.* ◇ *Would you like a Pimm's?*

,**Courtney** '**Pine** /ˌkɔːtni ˈpaɪn; AmE ˌkɔːrtni/ (1964–) an English *jazz musician who plays the saxophone. He became known for mixing jazz with other popular musical forms such as *reggae and *hip hop.

,**Pinewood** '**Studios** /ˌpaɪnwʊd/ a place in *Buckinghamshire, England, where cinema films are made. It was established in 1936.

,**Allan** '**Pinkerton** /ˈpɪŋkətən; AmE ˈpɪŋkərtən/ (1819–84) an American, born in Scotland, who established the first US company of private detectives. He began the Pinkerton National Detective Agency in 1850 in *Chicago. Its advertisements showed a large eye, with the words 'We never sleep'. Pinkerton also established a US organization during the *Civil War which later became the US *Secret Service. The company today operates in 20 countries and provides protection for large companies.

,**Pink** '**Floyd** /ˈflɔɪd/ one of the most popular British *rock music groups, formed in 1965. The group's most successful albums include *The Dark Side of the Moon* (1973) and *The Wall* (1979). The group is particularly well known for its exciting live performances involving lights and screen images.

The ,**Pink** '**Panther** a comedy film (1963) directed by Blake *Edwards in which Peter *Sellers first played the ridiculous French Inspector Clouseau. The Pink Panther is the name of a valuable diamond. There were several later films about Clouseau and the Panther. There was also a series of television *Pink Panther* cartoon films in which the main character is a pink panther (= large member of the cat family).

,**pink** '**slip** n (AmE informal) a letter from an employer that tells someone they must leave their job.

Pi'nocchio /pɪˈnəʊkiəʊ; AmE pɪˈnoʊkioʊ/ a full-length Walt *Disney cartoon film (1940). It is based on an Italian story about a wooden puppet that becomes a real boy.

When the boy tells a lie, his nose grows longer. The story is told by the character Jiminy Cricket, who sings *When You Wish Upon a Star*, a song that won an *Oscar and later became the theme song for a Disney television series: *Cartoons appeared showing the Minister as a long-nosed Pinocchio.*

,Matthew 'Pinsent /'pɪnsnt/ an English sportsman who won gold medals in four Olympic Games (1992, 1996, 2000 and 2004) in the sport of rowing. He was a student at *Oxford and took part in the *Boat Race three times. He won the World Championships with Steve *Redgrave in 1991. He retired from rowing in 2004 and was made a *knight in 2005.

,Harold 'Pinter /'pɪntə(r)/ (1930–) an English writer of plays who has had a major influence on modern British theatre. His characters are often ordinary, unimportant people who find it difficult to communicate properly with each other, and his plays combine humour with an atmosphere of danger and unhappiness. The word **Pinteresque** is sometimes used to describe these qualities. Pinter's best-known plays include *The Birthday Party* (1958), *The Caretaker* (1960), *The Homecoming* (1965), *Old Times* (1971), *No Man's Land* (1975) and *Betrayal* (1978). He has also written many film scripts, including those for *The Go-Between* (1969), *The French Lieutenant's Woman* (1982) and *The Comfort of Strangers* (1983). Pinter has also worked as an actor and director and is a campaigner against war and human rights abuses.

Pip /pɪp/ the central character in the novel *Great Expectations* by Charles *Dickens.

,John 'Piper /'paɪpə(r)/ (1903–92) an English artist and designer. His work includes paintings of buildings, stained glass for church windows (including one in *Coventry Cathedral), and stage designs for the operas of Benjamin *Britten.

,Piper 'Alpha /ˌpaɪpər 'ælfə/ an oil rig (= platform) in the *North Sea which exploded and caught fire in 1988, causing the deaths of 167 people. As a result of this disaster, rules concerning safety on oil rigs were changed.

pipes ⇨ BAGPIPES.

The ,Pirates of Pen'zance /pen'zæns/ a comic opera (1880) by W S *Gilbert and Arthur *Sullivan, one of their *Savoy Operas. It is about a group of pirates who are all in fact of noble birth and a group of policemen who are not very brave. One of the best-known songs in the opera is *A Policeman's Lot is Not a Happy One.*

,Robert M 'Pirsig /'pɜːsɪg; AmE 'pɜːrsɪg/ (Robert Maynard Pirsig 1928–) a US writer best known for his philosophical novel *Zen and the Art of Motorcycle Maintenance* (1974).

,pit bull 'terrier (also 'pit bull) n a fierce breed of dog, originally bred in the US for fighting. In the 1980s a number of people were attacked and badly injured by pit bull terriers and other dogs. As a result a law was passed in Britain in 1991, the Dangerous Dogs Act, requiring owners to register them with a special government department.

the 'Pitcairn ,Islands /'pɪtkeən; AmE 'pɪtkern/ a group of small islands under British rule in the southern Pacific Ocean, only one of which, Pitcairn Island, has people living on it. They are mostly descended from the sailors who took part in the incident shown in the *Mutiny on the Bounty and who then occupied the island in 1789.

,Brad 'Pitt¹ /'pɪt/ (1964–) a US film actor who became a major star in the 1990s. His films include *Thelma and Louise* (1991), *Interview with the Vampire* (1994), *Seven* (1995), *Seven Years in Tibet* (1997) and *Troy* (2004). He is widely considered to be one of the most physically attractive film stars in the world. He married Jennifer Aniston, 'Rachel' in *Friends, in 2000. The couple separated in 2005.

,William 'Pitt² /'pɪt/ (1759–1806) the youngest man ever to become *Prime Minister of Britain (at the age of 24). He was Prime Minister from 1783 to 1801 and again from 1804 to 1806. His achievements included removing much of the corruption from British politics and improving the financial position of the country. He also introduced *income tax and was responsible for the *Act of Union (1800), by which Ireland became part of the United Kingdom. He is often referred to as **Pitt the Younger** and his father, the Earl of *Chatham, as **Pitt the Elder**.

'Pittsburgh /'pɪtsbɜːg; AmE 'pɪtsbɜːrg/ a US industrial city in western *Pennsylvania where the Allegheny and Monongahela rivers come together to form the *Ohio River. It began in 1758 as Fort Pitt, named after William *Pitt. For a century until the 1980s, it was a centre for iron and steel production. Pittsburgh now produces high technology products and leads the world in medical operations for replacing body organs.

'Pizza Hut a US company, owned by *PepsiCo Inc, with a large number of restaurants in the US, Britain and other countries that serve pizzas and other food.

PLA /ˌpi: el 'eɪ/ ⇨ PORT OF LONDON AUTHORITY.

▶ **place names**

Britain and the US have a rich variety of place names. Some names are derived from a feature of the countryside. Others are named after a church or fort. Some honour famous people, while others have been brought from abroad.

Many names reflect the history of an area and of the people who once lived there. Some of the oldest place names in Wales and Scotland date back to the time of the *Celts. Some towns in Southern England have Latin names dating from *Roman times. Other names are of *Anglo-Saxon or *Viking origin and date from the period when these peoples invaded Britain. Later, the *Normans introduced some French names.

In the US many place names are derived from *Native American words: Chicago, for example, means 'place of the onion' in the Algonquian language, Seattle is named after a chief, and Natchez after a tribe. Sometimes the names were translated, sometimes not: the Black Warrior River in Alabama runs through the city of Tuscaloosa, which was named after a Native American whose name means 'Black Warrior'. Names of Spanish origin are found mainly in the South-Western US. They include San Francisco, San Diego, Las Vegas and Los Angeles. A few names are of French origin, e.g. Baton Rouge and La Crosse. Some names are derived from more than one culture: Anaheim combines the Spanish name 'Ana' with the German 'heim' (= home).

Many British towns take their name from a river. In Wales and Scotland many towns have names beginning with *Aber-*, which means 'river mouth', e.g. Aberystwyth, Aberdeen. In England towns close to a river mouth often end with *-mouth*, e.g. Weymouth. The name of the river forms the rest of the name. Names ending in *-ford* (Oxford) suggest a place where a river is shallow enough to cross. A town beside a lake may, in Scotland, contain *loch-* or, in England, *-mere*, e.g. Lochinver, Windermere.

In Scotland, there are several place names beginning with *Dun-*, meaning 'hill', e.g. Dunbar. Any place whose name ends with *-don* (Swindon), *-hurst* (Sandhurst), *-head* (Gateshead) or, in Wales, begins with *pen-* (Penarth), probably stands on or near a hill. Towns near passes may end in *-gate*, e.g. Harrogate, or, in Scotland, begin with *Glen-*, e.g. Glencoe. Names ending with *-coumbe* or *-combe* (Ilfracombe) or *-dale* (Rochdale), or, in

Wales, beginning with *cwm-* (Cwmbran) suggest that the town is in a valley.

American place names based on natural features are easier to recognize. Examples include Two Rivers, River Edge, Mirror Lake, Ocean City, Gulf Breeze, Seven Hills, Shady Valley, Twentynine Palms, Lookout, Little Rock, Round Rock, White Rock and Slippery Rock. French names include La Fontaine and Eau Claire. Some place names describe a product, e.g. Bean City, Copper City.

Many British towns developed around an early fort or castle. This may be indicated by a name ending in *-burgh* (Edinburgh), *-bury* (Salisbury), *-caster* or *-cester* (Doncaster, Gloucester) or *-chester* (Dorchester), or beginning or ending with *castle* (Newcastle). A Welsh variant is *Caer-* (Caernarfon).

Names that include *church-*, *kirk-* or, in Wales *llan-* refer to a church (Offchurch, Kirkby, Llandaff). Towns where there was a monastery may have names ending in *-minster* (Kidderminster).

Names ending with *-ham* (Evesham), *-hampton* (Southampton), *-ington* (Workington), *-stock* or *-stoke* (Woodstock, Basingstoke), *-thorpe* (Scunthorpe), *-wich* or *-wick* (Norwich, Warwick) mean that there was a village or farm there.

In the US place names that refer to buildings include House, Brick Church and High Bridge. Atlanta, Georgia is named after a railway/railroad.

Some British place names refer to ancient tribes. The elements *-ing* and *-ingham* at the end of a name mean 'people of' and 'home of the people of', as in Reading ('Read's people') and Birmingham ('home of Beorma's people'). Places with names ending in *-by* were the homes of Viking invaders, e.g. Grimsby ('Grim's village').

Some towns take their name from Christian saints, particularly if they had local connections. These include St Albans, St Andrews and St David's. Towns named after people who lived in more recent times are rare in Britain. They include Nelson, named after Lord *Nelson and the *new town Telford, named after the engineer Thomas *Telford.

By contrast, many towns in the US honour famous Americans, especially presidents. Abraham *Lincoln is honoured in towns named Lincoln, Lincolnville, Lincolnwood, etc., Andrew *Jackson at Jackson and Jacksonville and Thomas *Jefferson at Jefferson, Jeffersonville and Jefferson City.

Other towns named after famous Americans include Houston, Texas, after Sam *Houston; Cody, Wyoming, after *Buffalo Bill; Boone, Tennessee, after Daniel *Boone; and Custer, Montana, after General George *Custer. Often the person is now little heard of, e.g. H M Shreve, a 19th century boat captain on the *Mississippi River, whose name was used for Shreveport, Louisiana. A few towns are named after companies, e.g. *Hershey, Pennsylvania.

Many American towns are named after a place in Britain or another country from which settlers in the US originally came. British names are used especially in *New England. They include Boston, Cambridge, Gloucester, Manchester-by-the-sea, and Stafford. British names used in other parts of the US include the cities of New York and Birmingham, and Glasgow, a small town in Montana. Like New York (New Amsterdam), Brooklyn (Breukelyn) was originally named by Dutch settlers.

Names from other countries include New Orleans, Moscow, Athens, Paris, Naples and New Holland.

Americans enjoy creating unusual or humorous names, such as Tombstone in Arizona. Truth or Consequences in New Mexico is named after a radio quiz show. Other names include Cannon Ball, Pie Town, Smackover, Humble City, High Lonesome, Cut and Shoot, and Monkey's Eyebrow.

Plaid 'Cymru /ˌplaɪd 'kʌmri/ the Welsh nationalist political party, started in 1925 with the aim of making Wales an independent country, separate from the rest of the United Kingdom. It carries out campaigns to preserve the individual culture of Wales and the *Welsh language. One of its campaigns led to the creation of the television station *S4C, which broadcasts programmes in Welsh. In 1966, a Plaid Cymru candidate was elected as a *Member of Parliament for the first time. Since 2003 the party has had 12 members in the *Welsh Assembly and has formed the main opposition party in the Assembly. The party leader is Ieuan Wyn Jones.

Plain 'English Campaign an organization started in 1979 which encourages the use of clear language in public information so that it can be easily understood. Their symbol, **the Crystal Mark**, can be used on documents to show that they are written in **plain English**. The Campaign gives awards each year for the use of clear English and a **Foot in Mouth Award** for the most nonsensical remark by a public figure.

the ˌPlains 'Indians *n* the traditional name for the *Native American peoples who once lived on the *Great Plains in the western central US. They often fought each other and the white people who settled on their land. They include the *Arapaho, *Blackfoot, *Cheyenne, *Comanche, *Crow and *Sioux. Many now live on western reservations (= land given and protected by the US government).

the ˌPlains 'States the 10 states in the *Great Plains region of the western central US. They are, from north to south, *Montana, *North Dakota, *South Dakota, *Wyoming, *Iowa, *Nebraska, *Colorado, *Kansas, *Oklahoma and *Texas.

Planet 'Hollywood™ /'hɒliwʊd; AmE 'hɑliwʊd/ an international chain of fashionable restaurants, originally partly owned by Demi *Moore, Arnold *Schwarzenegger, Sylvester *Stallone and Bruce *Willis. The first was opened in the US in 1991. The restaurants are decorated with objects connected with films and film stars.

Planet of the 'Apes a US film (1968) about a planet on which apes are the rulers and humans have become like animals. Several later films continued the story. There was also a television series in 1974 and a television cartoon series in 1975. A new film was made in 2001.

The 'Planets a popular piece of music for orchestra by the British composer Gustav *Holst, which had its first complete public performance in 1920. Each of its seven sections has the name of one of the major planets.

'Planned 'Parenthood™ Fede'ration of A'merica (*also* **'Planned ˌParenthood**) a private US organization that gives free information and advice on planning a family. It was established in 1916 and has nearly 850 local branches, with its main office in New York.

Plan'tagenet /plæn'tædʒənət/ the name of the family to which all the kings of England from 1154 to 1485 belonged. The first Plantagenet king was *Henry II and the last was *Richard III. The name came originally from Geoffrey, Count of Anjou in France (1113–51), who was the father of *Henry II. The Anjou family symbol was the *plant à genêt* or broom, a bush with small yellow flowers.

the ˌBattle of 'Plassey /'plæsi/ a battle (1757) fought near Calcutta in north-east India. The British army, led by Robert *Clive, defeated the army of the Indian ruler of Bengal, and the victory established British rule in the region.

ˌSylvia 'Plath /'plæθ/ (1932–63) a US writer who lived in Britain. She is considered one of the most important poets of her generation. Her work is very personal and

P

towards the end of her life she often wrote about death. She was a brilliant student and moved to England to study at *Cambridge University. In 1956 she married the British poet Ted *Hughes. She suffered from depression, and in 1963 she killed herself. After her death, collections of her poems were published, including *Ariel* (1965) and *Collected Poems* (1981), which won the *Pulitzer Prize. She also wrote a novel, *The Bell Jar* (1963) which was based on her own life and personal experiences. In 1998 Ted Hughes published a book of poems, *Birthday Letters*, about their relationship. A film, *Sylvia*, was made about the couple in 2003.

'Playboy a US magazine for men known especially for its pictures of nearly naked women. It was started by Hugh *Hefner in 1953, when it was seen as part of the 'sexual revolution' of that time. The magazine also includes serious articles, short stories, etc., as well as Hefner's own writing on the history and importance of sex. Some people joke that they only buy the magazine for the articles.

'play dough™ (*also* **'Play-Doh™**) *n* [U] a soft substance, similar to clay, which is sold in a range of bright colours for children to play with by shaping it. It was first invented in the US in 1955 by Joseph McVicker.

'PlayStation /'pleɪsteɪʃn/ a small electronic games machine that uses CDs. It is made by Sony and was first sold in 1994. **PlayStation 2**, also known as **PS2**, was launched in 2000 and uses both CDs and DVDs. Popular games include **Tomb Raider** and **Gran Turismo**.

'Playtex™ /'pleɪteks/ the product name of a range of women's underwear, including *Wonderbra.

plc (*also* **PLC**) /ˌpiː el 'siː/ ⇨ PUBLIC LIMITED COMPANY.

the ˌPledge of Al'legiance a promise of loyalty made by Americans to their flag and country. The words are: 'I pledge allegiance to the flag of the United States of America and to the republic for which it stands, one nation under God, indivisible, with liberty and justice for all.' It was first published in 1892 in the magazine *Youth's Companion* and written by the journalist Francis Bellamy. Congress added the words 'under God' in 1954 and this has caused a lot of argument. In 2002, in the case of *Newdow v United States Congress*, a *San Francisco court decided that the added words were unconstitutional (= against the US constitution), but this decision was rejected by the *Supreme Court. Many American children say the Pledge each morning at school as they face the flag and put their right hands over their hearts. Adults also often do this on formal public occasions.

ˌPlessy v 'Ferguson /ˌplesi vɜːsəs 'fɜːgəsn; *AmE* vɜːrsəs 'fɜːrgəsn/ a court case in 1896 which was decided by the US *Supreme Court. It stated that *segregation on trains was legal if black and white people received equal services. Southern states soon also used this idea of *separate but equal in schools, public buildings, etc. The ruling (= decision) was replaced in 1954 by the Supreme Court's decision in the case of *Brown v Board of Education of Topeka*, which stated that segregation in schools was illegal.

'Plexiglas™ /'pleksɪglɑːs; *AmE* 'pleksɪglæs/ *n* [U] a US make of strong transparent plastic that looks like glass. It is used in many products, e.g. car windows.

'Plimsoll line /'plɪmsəl/ *n* [usually sing] a mark on the side of a ship which shows how far down in the water (because of the weight of its cargo) it can legally be. It was named after the English politician Samuel Plimsoll (1824–98), who did a lot to improve the rules about safety at sea.

Plod ⇨ PC PLOD.

ˌploughman's 'lunch (*also informal* **'ploughman's**) *n* (*BrE*) a light meal often served in pubs and usually eaten in the middle of the day. It consists of cheese (or sometimes cold cooked meat), bread and butter, salad and pickles (= a mixture of fruit and vegetables preserved in vinegar). Its name was invented in the early 1970s to suggest the sort of food traditionally eaten by people working the fields: *I'll have a Cheddar ploughman's, please.*

ˌJoan 'Plowright /'plaʊraɪt/ (1929–) an English actor in films and the theatre. She was married to Laurence *Olivier from 1961 and appeared in many plays at the *Old Vic and the *National Theatre.

PLR /ˌpiː el 'ɑː(r)/ ⇨ PUBLIC LENDING RIGHT.

'Plymouth /'plɪməθ/ a city and port on the coast of *Devon in south-west England. It has long been associated with ships and the sea. The *Royal Navy has an important base there. In 1588 English ships waited for the *Spanish Armada at Plymouth, and while they were waiting Sir Francis *Drake is said to have played a game of *bowls on Plymouth Hoe, a piece of flat high ground above the sea. In 1620 the *Pilgrim Fathers sailed from Plymouth across the Atlantic.

the ˌPlymouth 'Brethren /ˌplɪməθ/ (*also* **the Brethren**) *n* [pl] a Christian religious group established in *Plymouth, England, in 1830 by people who did not agree with the ideas and ceremonies of the *High Church. The Brethren have no priests, and live according to a set of strict moral rules that they have taken from the Bible. They believe that Jesus Christ will soon return to judge people.

ˌPlymouth 'Colony /ˌplɪməθ/ the American community in *Massachusetts established in 1620 by the *Pilgrim Fathers. Half of the people died during the first harsh winter, but good crops the next year led to the first *Thanksgiving. Plymouth Colony joined the New England Confederation in 1643 and became part of the colony of Massachusetts in 1691.

ˌPlymouth 'Rock /ˌplɪməθ/ a large rock on the coast of Plymouth, *Massachusetts, where the *Pilgrim Fathers probably landed in 1620, although there is no proof. In 1774, the rock split while it was being dragged into the town of Plymouth as a symbol of freedom from the British. It is now back in its original position, under a protective roof. Next to it is the *Mayflower II*, a copy of the Pilgrims' original ship that was sent as a gift from Britain in 1957. See also MAYFLOWER.

Plymouth Rock

PM /ˌpiː 'em/ ⇨ PRIME MINISTER.

ˌPoca'hontas /ˌpəʊkə'hɒntəs; *AmE* ˌpoʊkə'hɑːntəs/ (*c.* 1595–1617) a *Native American girl who in 1607 saved the life of Captain John *Smith when he was about to be killed by her father, Chief Powhatan. She became a Christian in 1613 and changed her name to Rebecca. A year later, she married the English colonist John Rolfe and in 1616 went to England, where she created a lot of interest. She became ill and died on the way home. Her story was told in the Walt *Disney cartoon film *Pocahontas* (1995).

'Podunk /'pəʊdʌŋk; *AmE* 'poʊdʌŋk/ (*AmE informal disapproving*) any small town that is regarded as dull, remote and not important. There are two actual US towns called Podunk, one in *Connecticut and one in *Massachusetts: *He grew up in Podunk and feels lost in the big city.*

'Edgar 'Allan 'Poe /'pəʊ; *AmE* 'poʊ/ (1809–49) a US writer of short stories and poems. His best remembered works are frightening stories of mystery and death, including *The Fall of the House of Usher* (1839) and *The Pit and the Pendulum* (1843). He is also regarded as having invented the modern *detective story on the basis of such stories as *The Murders in the Rue Morgue* (1841). His poems include *The *Raven* (1845) and *Annabel Lee* (1849). Poe drank too much alcohol and died young. There have been film versions of many of his stories.

Poet 'Laureate /'lɒriət/ *n* (*pl* **Poets Laureate**) (in Britain) a poet officially chosen to write poems on special state occasions such as royal weddings, births and funerals. The first Poet Laureate was Ben *Jonson (from 1616). Others have included *Dryden, *Wordsworth and *Tennyson, and more recently *Masefield, *Day-Lewis, *Betjeman and Ted *Hughes. Since 1999 the Poet Laureate has been Andrew Motion.

The US has had Poets Laureate since 1986 when Robert Penn *Warren became the first. They are appointed by the *Library of Congress but only serve for one or two years.

Poets' 'Corner a part of *Westminster Abbey where many famous English writers are buried or where there are memorials to them. The writers and poets buried there include *Chaucer, *Browning, *Tennyson, *Dickens, *Hardy and *Kipling. There are also memorials to *Shakespeare, *Milton, *Byron, *Shelley[2] and many others.

Poets' Corner

The Pogues /pəʊgz; *AmE* poʊgz/ a British pop group formed in 1983, whose style mixes Irish folk music with *punk. The group's best-known recordings include *Dirty Old Town* (1985), *The Irish Rover* (1987) and *Fairytale of new York* (1988).

Hercule 'Poirot /,eəkju:l 'pwɑ:rəʊ; *AmE* ,erkju:l 'pwɑ:roʊ/ a Belgian detective who appears as a character in many of the mystery novels by Agatha *Christie. He has a very neat appearance and a neat pointed moustache. He often considers English people strange and English people in the books are amused by his accent. He is extremely clever and uses his intelligence, or what he calls his 'little grey cells', to solve every crime. Many of the stories were adapted for a popular British television series called *Poirot* in the 1980s and 1990s. See also DETECTIVE STORY.

,Sidney **'Poitier** (1927–) one of the first *African American actors to play important film roles. He won an *Oscar for his part in *Lilies of the Field* (1963) and received another for lifetime achievement in 2002. His other films have included *Blackboard Jungle* (1955), *Porgie and Bess* (1959), *Guess Who's Coming to Dinner* (1967), *In the Heat of the Night* (1967), *The Wilby Conspiracy* (1975) and *The Day of the Jackal* (1997).

'Polaroid™ /'pəʊlərɔɪd; *AmE* 'poʊlərɔɪd/ *n* a type of camera that produces a print of a photograph immediately after the photograph is taken. It was invented in the US in 1947 by Edwin Land.

po'lice ⇨ LAW ENFORCEMENT.

the 'Police and 'Criminal 'Evidence 'Act (*abbr* **PACE**) a British law passed in 1984 which sets down rules for the behaviour of the police in fighting crime. The rules are about their powers to *stop and search people and to search buildings, about arresting, questioning and keeping people at a police station, and holding information about people and their criminal records.

the 'Police Service of 'Northern 'Ireland (*abbr* **the PSNI**) the police force in Northern Ireland. It was called the *Royal Ulster Constabulary until 2001 when the service was reformed as a result of the *Good Friday Agreement.

po,litical 'action com,mittee *n* (*abbr* **PAC**) (in the US) any group formed to raise money for candidates in elections who support their views and agree to protect their interests.

▶ **political correctness**

Political correctness or being 'politically correct', often called simply **PC**, is concerned with avoiding certain attitudes, actions and, above all, forms of expression which suggest prejudice and are likely to cause offence. This may be against men or women, against older people, or against people with a particular skin colour, racial background or physical disability.

The idea of political correctness developed in the 1980s and 1990s and was based on the belief that the language we use influences the way we think. Later the phrase was often used in a negative way to refer to politically correct expressions that people thought were clumsy or an unnecessary change. Some people doubt whether changing words will remove prejudice in people's minds or in the social system.

In the 1960s and 1970s public debate caused many people to accept the principle that discrimination (= treating some people worse than others) is wrong. Changes of many kinds happened in schools and offices. History has been traditionally taught from the point of view of white people, but now more children learn about the history and culture of other groups in the community. In offices sexual and racial **harassment** (= comments or behaviour intended to worry or upset somebody) are not allowed. The PC movement has also been against **stereotyping** (= having fixed ideas about people), especially of women and black people, and making jokes against minority groups.

A major concern of political correctness has been to avoid racist or sexist language that will offend particular groups. However some language changes are much older than the PC movement. *Ms* has been used for a long time as a title for women who do not wish to identify themselves as being either married (*Mrs*) or single (*Miss*). Other PC phrases, notably *chair* or *chairperson* instead of *chairman*, are also common. Changes in the US include saying *African American* instead of *Black*, *Native American* instead of *Indian* and using the term *people of colour* to refer to people who are not white.

Other changes have been less widely accepted. For example, the words *blind* and *deaf* were felt to suggest something negative, so people began using *visually impaired* and *hearing impaired*, which, they believed, did not carry the same negative associations. Less acceptable PC terms include *vertically challenged* (short), *differently sized* (fat), *physically challenged* (disabled), *economically exploited* (poor), *involuntarily leisured* (unem-ployed), and *domestic operative* (housewife). People who are against the idea of political correctness use such examples to argue against it.

,**James K 'Polk** /'pəʊk; *AmE* 'poʊk/ (James Knox Polk 1795–1849) the 11th US *President (1845–9) and a member of the *Democratic Party. He had earlier been in the US House of Representatives (1825–39), the last four years as the *Speaker of the House, and was then Governor of *Tennessee (1839–41). During his time as President, the US added *Texas to the Union and fought the *Mexican War which also added *California and most of the South-West.

,**Jackson 'Pollock** /,dʒæksn 'pɒlək; *AmE* 'pɑːlək/ (1912–56) a US artist who was a leader of *abstract expressionism. He developed a style of 'action painting', in which paint is dropped or thrown onto a large canvas (= rough cloth) placed on the floor or on a wall. He sometimes used sticks and knives instead of brushes. Pollock drank too much, had severe mental problems and was killed in a car crash. The film *Pollock* (2000) is an account of his life.

'**poll tax** ⇨ COMMUNITY CHARGE.

,**Polly'anna** /,pɒli'ænə; *AmE* ,pɑːli'ænə/ *n* (*AmE*) a girl or woman who is always cheerful and expects good things to happen. The name comes from the character in the novels *Pollyanna* (1913) and *Pollyanna Grows Up* (1915) by the US writer Eleanor H Porter (1868–1920). *Pollyanna* was later a silent film (1920) with Mary *Pickford and a Walt *Disney film (1960) with Hayley Mills.

'**polo** *n* [U] a sport in which two teams of four players each riding on horses try to score by hitting a ball into a goal using a mallet (= a hammer with a long handle and a wooden head). Polo originally came from Asia and in Britain and the US is now popular mainly with rich people, including members of the British *royal family.

a polo player

'**Polo**™ /'pəʊləʊ ; *AmE* 'poʊloʊ/ a popular British peppermint sweet, sold in tubes and made by *Nestlé. Polo mints are round with a hole in the middle. They are advertised as 'the mint with the hole'. Polos are also made with fruit flavours.

,**Pomp and 'Circumstance** a set of five marches by the English composer Edward Elgar, written between 1901 and 1930. A version of one of them later had words written for it and was given the title *Land of Hope and Glory*. This is played every year at the *Last Night of the Proms, with the audience singing the words.

'**Juan 'Ponce de Le'ón** /'hwɑːn 'pɒnθeɪ deɪ leɪ'ɒn, 'pɒnseɪ; *AmE* 'pɑːnθeɪ, 'pɑːnseɪ, leɪ'ɑːn/ (1460–1521) a Spanish explorer who discovered *Florida in 1513 while searching for the *Fountain of Youth. He had captured *Puerto Rico in 1508 and become governor there (1509–12).

Pond's™ /pɒndz; *AmE* pɑːndz/ a product name for a range of creams for cleaning and softening the skin. They are produced by Chesebrough-Pond's. The best

known is Pond's Cold Cream, which is often used to remove make-up from the face.

'**Pontiac** /'pɒntiæk; *AmE* 'pɑːntiæk/ *n* a US car made by *General Motors, named after an 18th–century Native American leader. The company advertises Pontiacs with the phrase 'We are driving excitement', and the models include the Firebird, Bonneville, Grand Am, Grand Prix and Sunfire.

'**Pontin's** /'pɒntɪnz; *AmE* 'pɑːntɪnz/ any of a group of British holiday camps, the first of which was opened by Fred Pontin in 1946. These camps, offering cheap family holidays/vacations, were very popular in the years after *World War II, but became less so towards the end of the 20th century: *We used to go to Pontin's every summer when I was young.* Compare BUTLIN'S.

the '**Pony Club** a British club for children who ride ponies. It was started in 1929 and now has many branches, mainly in country areas, which organize competitions, shows and other activities. It is considered a typically *middle-class organization: *Edward is a prominent member of the local golf club and his daughters are all Pony Club members.*

the ,**Pony Ex'press** a US mail service in the *Old West, using riders and horses (not ponies). It operated from April 1860 to October 1861, between St Joseph, *Missouri, and Sacramento, *California, a distance of 1966 miles/3163 kilometres, which the riders could complete in 10 days by changing horses at regular stations along the way. *Buffalo Bill was one of the riders. The service came to an end when a telegraph line (= a device for sending messages on electric wires) was completed. The **Pony Express National Historic Trail** was established in 1992.

Pooh™ /puː/ (*also* ,**Winnie-the-'Pooh**, ,**Pooh 'Bear**) the main character in A A *Milne's children's stories, *Winnie-the-Pooh* (1926) and *The House at Pooh Corner* (1928). Pooh is a bear who is not very intelligent but very friendly. He enjoys eating, singing songs, and playing with his friends, including *Christopher Robin, *Piglet and *Eeyore.

'**Poohsticks** /'puːstɪks/ *n* [U] a simple children's game, first described in A A *Milne's stories about *Winnie-the-Pooh. A group of people throw sticks off a bridge into a stream, then watch to see whose stick appears first on the other side of the bridge.

pool *n* [U] a game for two people played on a large table with 16 coloured balls. It is often played in *pubs and bars. The players use long sticks (called *cues*) to hit the balls into holes (called *pockets*) at the edge of the table. Compare BAR BILLIARDS, BILLIARDS, SNOOKER.

the **pools** *n* [pl] (*also* '**football pools**) a British gambling competition in which people try to predict the results of football matches. Every week people taking part fill in **pools coupons** (= special documents for marking the results of the matches that will take place on Saturday). Those who predict the results most accurately receive the most prize money. It was the most popular form of gambling in Britain before the *National Lottery was introduced in the 1990s: *I'd buy a big house if I won the pools.*

the '**Poor Laws** *n* [pl] a series of British laws that were concerned with helping poor people. The first Poor Law (1601) stated that the poor were the responsibility of the *parish(1), and that local people should be taxed to provide food for the poor. These taxes became too high when the number of poor people increased in the early 19th century, and in 1834 a new Poor Law stated that the poor should be made to work in *workhouses. This system was very unpopular, but it was not officially

P

changed until the 1930 Poor Law introduced a national system of social welfare.

'Poor 'Richard's 'Almanack a book published each year in the US between 1733 and 1758. It was written by Benjamin *Franklin under the name of Richard Saunders. It contained useful information on important dates, anniversaries, etc., as well as wise advice in the form of short sayings and verses. Many of these are still repeated, such as 'A penny saved is a penny earned,' and:

> 66 Early to bed and early to rise
> Makes a man healthy, wealthy and wise. 99

Mr 'Pooter /'puːtə(r)/ the main character in *The *Diary of a Nobody*. Mr Charles Pooter is a simple and rather boring man who gets into amusing and embarrassing difficulties in his social, family and business life. Awkward social situations, or people who find themselves in them, are sometimes described as **Pooterish**.

pop 'art *n* [U] a style of art that represents objects or people from everyday life, often using materials and techniques from popular culture, such as advertisements and *comics. Pop art was developed in the 1950s by artists such as Eduardo *Paolozzi in Britain and Jasper *Johns in the US. It became well known in the 1960s through the work of **pop artists** such as Andy *Warhol and Roy *Lichtenstein.

Alexander 'Pope /'pəʊp; *AmE* 'poʊp/ (1688–1744) an English poet, well known for his humour and intelligence. He is considered the greatest poet of the *Augustan Age. He gained his reputation as a major writer by translating Homer's *Iliad* (1715–20) and *Odyssey* (1725–6), but is now better known for his satirical poems such as *The *Rape of the Lock* and *An Epistle to Dr Arbuthnot* (1735) which made fun of the writers and fashionable people of the period.

> 66 The proper study of mankind is man. 99
> Alexander Pope

'Popeye™ /'pɒpaɪ; *AmE* 'pɑːpaɪ/ a popular US cartoon character first created for a comic strip in 1929 by E C Segar. Popeye is a sailor who has a kind nature but loves fighting and becomes especially strong when he eats spinach (= a green vegetable). He has a very thin girlfriend called Olive Oyl and his main rival is the big, bad Bluto. A film version of *Popeye* with real actors appeared in 1980, directed by Robert *Altman, with Robin *Williams in the main part.

'Pop Goes the 'Weasel a popular British song in the 19th century, still sung today though mainly by children. Nobody is sure what the title means, and it may be simply a nonsense phrase. The first verse is:

> 66 Half a pound of twopenny rice,
> Half a pound of treacle;
> That's the way the money goes,
> Pop goes the weasel! 99

'Pop ,Idol a very popular British television programme shown on *ITV since 2002 in which young people who want to be pop singers have the chance to perform in front of judges who select a group of the best. In later programmes members of the public can vote by phone for the person they think should win. The show is presented by Ant and Dec (Anthony McPartlin and Declan Donnelly) who have worked together on television since they were children. Compare AMERICAN IDOL.

the ,Popish 'Plot /ˌpəʊpɪʃ; *AmE* ˌpoʊpɪʃ/ ⇨ OATES.

,Karl 'Popper /ˌkɑːl 'pɒpə(r); *AmE* ˌkɑːrl 'pɑːpər/ (1902–94) a British philosopher, born in Austria. He

wrote mainly about science, and argued that scientific ideas cannot be proved to be true, so that the closest thing to a true idea is one that has not been proved false. His books include *The Logic of Scientific Discovery* (1934) and *The Open Society and its Enemies* (1945). He was made a *knight in 1965.

'Poppy Day the popular name for *Remembrance Sunday, when many people in Britain wear plastic or paper poppies (= red flowers) in memory of the people who died in the two world wars. The poppies represent the real flowers that grew in the fields of France and Belgium, where many soldiers died. See also BRITISH LEGION.

'Popsicle™ /'pɒpsɪkl; *AmE* 'pɑːpsɪkl/ *n* a popular US make of sweet flavoured ice on a flat stick, called an *ice lolly* in British English. Children often use the sticks to build things.

▶ population

In 2002 the United Kingdom had a total population of just over 59 million people. About 49.5 million live in England, 5 million in Scotland, 3 million in Wales and 1.7 million in Northern Ireland. Around 4.5 million of the population belong to **ethnic minorities**, of which the largest groups are Indian (1 million), Pakistani (0.7 million) and Caribbean (0.5 million) in origin. Much of the immigration from *Commonwealth countries took place during the 1960s. Since then *immigration regulations have made it much more difficult for people from the Commonwealth to settle in Britain.

In the United States the population in 2003 was about 292 million people, of which about 211 million were white, 34 million were black, 10 million were Asian and 2.4 million were *Native Americans. The US Census Bureau predicts that the nation will have about 323 million people by 2020 and 394 million by 2050. In 2001 immigration was just over a million people of whom the largest group was 206 000 from Mexico.

In 2003 in Britain around 695 000 babies were born. In 2001, the US had more than 4 million births but the birth rate of 14.5 for each 1 000 people was about the same as for 1976, the lowest ever. The birth rate in the US has decreased by 38% since 1960. On average, males born in 2001 in both Britain and the US can expect to live 74 years and females 80 years. The main causes of death are heart disease and cancer.

Around 75% of the population of the UK live in cities, so that although people think of the British Isles as being crowded compared to some other parts of the world, much of the countryside is relatively empty. The most densely populated regions are the south-east, especially London, which has a population of nearly 7 million, and the regions around the industrial cities of *Birmingham, *Liverpool, *Manchester and *Newcastle. Most of the population of Scotland lives in the lowlands, where the cities of *Glasgow and *Edinburgh are.

In the US about 80% of the population live in cities. The largest are *New York with about 8 million people, *Los Angeles and *Chicago. The states with the largest populations are *California with 35 million people, *Texas with more than 21 million and New York with 19 million. Some large states have very few people: *Wyoming has the fewest, 498 000, or about 5 people for every square mile.

,Porgy and 'Bess /ˌpɔːɡi, 'bes; *AmE* ˌpɔːrɡi/ a musical play (1935) by George and Ira *Gershwin which has been called 'America's first folk opera'. It was based on the 1925 novel *Porgy* by Dubose Heyward, and is about poor *African Americans in *Charleston, *South Carolina. The main characters are the lovers Porgy, who lives by begging, and Bess. Its best-known songs are *Summertime*, *I Got Plenty o' Nothing* and *It Ain't*

P

Necessarily So. Sidney *Poitier and Dorothy Dandridge were the stars of the film version (1959).

'pork ,barrel *n* (*AmE informal*) a source of government money for projects which are designed to win votes and not necessarily for the good of the general public: *The new road was a pork barrel that nobody needed.* ◊ *pork-barrel politics*. Compare LOGROLLING.

,Porky 'Pig™ a US film cartoon character. He is a pig that stutters (= speaks with a fault so that he repeats the beginning of some words) and was created by *Warner Brothers for the *Looney Tunes* series. All *Looney Tunes* and *Merry Melodies* cartoons end with Porky saying 'Tha-tha-tha-that's all folks!'.

'porridge *n* [U] a type of soft food made by boiling oats (= grains from a plant that grows in cool countries) in water or milk and eaten hot, usually for breakfast. It is a traditional Scottish food, eaten with salt, but it is now eaten in many countries with sugar. In Britain it is less often eaten for breakfast than it used to be.

'Porridge a British comedy television series set in a prison, broadcast by the *BBC from 1974 to 1977. Ronnie *Barker played the role of an experienced prisoner, and much of the humour came from the clever ways in which he influenced the prison officers and the other prisoners to his advantage. *Porridge* is a British *slang word for time spent in prison.

,Cole 'Porter /ˌkəʊl 'pɔːtə(r); *AmE* ˌkoʊl 'pɔːrtər/ (1892–1964) a US writer of popular songs with clever words for *Broadway musical shows and *Hollywood films. His shows included *Anything Goes* (1934) and *Kiss Me, Kate* (1948), and his films included *High Society* (1956). Among his best-known songs are *Let's Do It* (1928), *I Get A Kick Out of You* (1934), *Night and Day* (1932), *Begin the Beguine* (1935) and *True Love* (1956).

'Portishead /'pɔːtɪshed; *AmE* 'pɔːrtɪshed/ a British pop group formed in 1993. Their songs are particularly slow and sad, dealing with pain and loss, as in their first album, *Dummy* (1994).

'Portland /'pɔːtlənd; *AmE* 'pɔːrtlənd/ **1** the largest city in the US state of *Oregon. It is on the Williamette River. *Lewis and Clark camped there in 1805, and it was settled in 1851. It is an industrial port and a centre for car imports and companies that build ships. The city was named after Portland, *Maine.
2 the largest city in the US state of *Maine. It is on Casco Bay, and many imports for Montreal, Canada, land there. Portland has companies that build ships and sell fish. It was settled about 1632 and was the state capital from 1820 to 1832.

Portland, Oregon

,Portland ce'ment /ˌpɔːtlənd; *AmE* ˌpɔːrtlənd/ *n* [U] the most common type of cement used today, made from chalk and clay. It was invented in England in the early 19th century. When it is hard its colour is like that of **Portland stone**, a type of stone from the Isle of

Portland in *Dorset used to make grand buildings such as *St Paul's Cathedral.

the ,Portobello 'Film ,Festival /ˌpɒtəbeləʊ; *AmE* ˌpɔːrtəbeloʊ/ a film festival which started in 1996 and takes place every year in west *London. It gives free showings of films, especially ones by new film makers, in places such as clubs, pubs and cafes and also outdoors in parks.

,Portobello 'Road /ˌpɒtəbeləʊ; *AmE* ˌpɔːrtəbeloʊ/ a street in the *Notting Hill district of west London. It is well known for its market, which sells food, clothes and second-hand goods. On Saturdays the second-hand area of the market attracts many tourists. In the late 20th century it became a very fashionable street, and many cafes, restaurants and antique shops opened beside the market: *I bought this old lampshade in the Portobello Road.*

the 'Port of 'London Au'thority /'lʌndən/ (*also* **the PLA**) the organization that operates the port of London. It controls all business on the *Thames between west London and the sea, but is mainly concerned with the docks at Tilbury, east of London.

,Porton 'Down /ˌpɔːtn; *AmE* ˌpɔːrtn/ the usual name for the Centre for Applied Microbiology and Research at Porton, near *Salisbury in southern England. It is a British government centre for studying chemical and biological weapons.

'Portsmouth /'pɔːtsməθ; *AmE* 'pɔːrtsməθ/ a city and port on the south coast of England. It is the main base of the *Royal Navy and contains the Royal Naval Museum which has several famous old ships including the *Mary Rose* and the *Victory*.

,Port 'Sunlight a small town near *Liverpool, England, built by Lord *Leverhulme at the end of the 19th century for the people working in his soap factory. It was a 'model village', designed and built to high standards, and meant to be copied by others.

,Posh and Becks /ˌpɒʃ, 'beks; *AmE* ˌpɑːʃ/ a famous British couple, Victoria (1975–) and David Beckham (1975–). 'Posh' refers to Victoria Beckham of the *Spice Girls, and 'Becks' is a *nickname for David *Beckham. They have three sons, Brooklyn, Romeo and Cruz. They moved to Spain in 2003 after David left Manchester United to play for Real Madrid. The catchy name 'Posh and Becks' refers to both of them and is widely used in the media.

,Emily 'Post[1] /'pəʊst; *AmE* 'poʊst/ (1873–1960) a US expert on manners and correct social behaviour. Americans still use her best-known book, *Etiquette* (1922). Post also had a radio programme and wrote a regular newspaper column which was printed each day in more than 200 newspapers.

,Wiley 'Post[2] /ˌwaɪli 'pəʊst; *AmE* 'poʊst/ (1899–1935) a US pilot of early aircraft. He was the first person to fly around the world alone, in 1933. He died with his passenger, Will *Rogers, when their plane crashed near Point Barrow, *Alaska.

'postal ,district *n* a district of a British town or city that has been given a particular code by the *Post Office. Most postal districts have one or two letters for the town, and a number for the district. For example, the districts of Oxford are OX1, OX2, etc. In London, the letters represent an area. N1, for example, is in north London and SW8 is in south-west London.

▶ **postal services**

Most letters and packages posted in Britain are dealt with by the *Royal Mail, which is part of the Royal Mail Group, together with Parcelforce, which delivers larger packages, and the *Post Office, which manages the country's many post offices. As well as selling stamps,

P

post offices take in letters and packages that are to be sent by special delivery. Post offices also sell vehicle and television licences and often greetings cards and stationery. In villages they are often combined with a newsagent's and general store. In recent years, many smaller post offices have been closed because they do not make a profit, though this often led to protests from local people.

Mail (= letters, bills, etc.) is often called **post** in British English. When sending a letter, people can choose between two levels of service, **first class** or the cheaper **second class**. Normally, first-class mail is delivered the day after it is posted and second-class mail within two or three days. Every address in Britain includes a **postcode** of letters and numbers, for example OX1 2PX for an address in Oxford, that makes it possible to sort the post by machine. Letters are posted in red **postboxes**, also called **letter boxes**. Each has a sign giving times of **collections**. Postmen and women deliver mail each morning direct to homes and businesses. They put the mail through a flap in the door, which is also called a **letter box**. In the country they travel round in red vans, but in towns and villages they often ride bicycles.

The system that deals with mail in the US, the **US Postal Service** (**USPS**), is an independent part of the government. Its head is the **Postmaster General**. **Mail carriers**, sometimes called **mailmen** though many are women, deliver mail to homes and businesses once a day. Most homes have **mailboxes** fixed outside, near the door. It is very uncommon for a house to have a letter box in the door for letters. People whose houses are a long way from the road have a special **rural mailbox** by the road. This has a flag which the mail carrier raises so that the people in the house can see when they have mail. To mail (= send) a letter, people leave it on top of their own mailbox or put it in one of the many blue mailboxes in cities and towns. Every address in the US includes an abbreviation for the name of the state and a **ZIP code**, which is used to help sort the mail. Post offices sell stamps and deal with mail that has to be insured. Most cities have one post office which stays open late. Americans complain about the Postal Service, but it usually does an efficient job at a reasonable price.

In the US only Postal Service can deliver mail, though private **couriers**, are allowed to offer **express** services. This competition has hurt the postal services. In Britain Royal Mail lost its monopoly for letter delivery in 2005.

ˌpost exˈchange ⇨ PX.

ˈPost-it™ /ˈpəʊst ɪt; *AmE* ˈpoʊst/ a product name for small pads of paper with a strip of special glue on the back of each piece which allows it to be stuck to something and removed easily. Post-its can have many uses, e.g. for writing notes or marking a place in a book, etc. They are available in different colours and sizes and are made by the *3M Company.

ˌPostman ˈPat™ a character in a series of children's books and *BBC television programmes written by Ivor Wood (1932–2004) and John Cunliffe (1933–). He is a postman (= a person whose job is delivering letters) in a village in the English countryside, who is very friendly to everybody he meets. He also has a black and white cat called Jess.

ˌpostman's ˈknock (*AmE* ˈpost office) *n* [U] a traditional children's game, played e.g. at parties, in which one player pretends to be a postman delivering a letter, knocks on a door, and kisses the player who opens it.

ˌPostmaster ˈGeneral (*pl* Postmasters General) *n* [usually sing] **1** until 1969 the person in charge of the British *Post Office.
2 the person in charge of the US Postal Service.

the ˈPost ˌOffice the organization responsible for post office services in Britain and part of the Royal Mail Group plc. It has more than 16 500 branches, from large post offices in cities to **sub-post offices** in small towns, which are sometimes part of a shop selling other goods. British people use their local post office to send letters and parcels, and also to pay bills and get official documents such as *tax discs and *television licences. ⇨ note at POSTAL SERVICES. See also GPO, ROYAL MAIL.

the poˈtato ˌfamine a disaster that happened in Ireland between 1845 and 1849 when most of the potato crop was destroyed by a plant disease. Potatoes were the main food of the poor in Ireland then, and about a million people died for lack of food. Two million people left Ireland for Britain and America because of the famine and many of them died on the way to America because of disease and hunger in ships known as 'coffin ships'.

ˌPot ˈNoodle™ *n* a type of food, usually sold in plastic cups, which consists of dried noodles (= long thin strips of mixed flour and water that become soft when cooked), meat and vegetables, with different flavours. Pot Noodles are cheap and quick to prepare, simply by adding hot water.

the ˌPotomac ˈRiver /pəˌtəʊmæk; *AmE* pəˌtoʊmæk/ a river in the eastern US. It begins in the *Appalachian Mountains in *West Virginia and flows 285 miles/459 kilometres past *Harpers Ferry, *Mount Vernon and Washington, DC, into Chesapeake Bay on the Atlantic coast.

ˌBeatrix ˈPotter[1] /ˌbɪətrɪks ˈpɒtə(r); *AmE* ˈpɑːtər/ (1866–1943) an English writer of children's books about the adventures of animals, including *Peter Rabbit, Tom Kitten, Benjamin Bunny, Jemima Puddle-Duck, Mrs Tiggywinkle and many others. Because of the quiet wit with which she describes character and social behaviour she has been compared to Jane *Austen. The books have been translated into many languages including Welsh and Latin. Beatrix Potter also painted the watercolour illustrations for the stories, which are still popular in both Britain and America. She was born in London but much preferred the country and spent her later life in the *Lake District. See also NATIONAL TRUST.

ˌDennis ˈPotter[2] /ˈpɒtə(r); *AmE* ˈpɑːtər/ (1935–94) an English writer of television plays, many of them broadcast in several parts. He is well known for his dramatic stories about relationships, often set in the recent past, in which the characters often sing popular songs of the period. He is considered one of the most important television writers of his time. His best-known plays include *Pennies from Heaven* (1978), *The Singing Detective* (1986) and *Lipstick on Your Collar* (1993).

ˌHarry ˈPotter™[3] /ˈpɒtə(r); *AmE* ˈpɑːtər/ the main character in a series of very successful books by British author J K *Rowling (1965–), including *Harry Potter and the Philosopher's Stone*, *Harry Potter and the Goblet of Fire* and *Harry Potter and the Half-Blood Prince*. Harry is a boy with magical powers (a young *wizard*) and the books are about his adventures at his school (*Hogwarts*). Although the books were written for children, they are popular with adults too. There are now three very successful films.

the ˈPotteries the area of the English *Midlands around *Stoke-on-Trent. It has been an important centre of the pottery industry (= making objects such as pots and plates) since the 17th century. See also FIVE TOWNS.

ˈPottery Barn a US group of shops which sell well-designed furniture and other things for the home. The

P

first store opened in *Manhattan in 1949 and there are now shops across the US.

,Ezra **'Pound** /ˌezrə ˈpaʊnd/ (1885–1972) a US poet who had a great influence on other modern poets, including T S *Eliot, Robert *Frost, W B *Yeats and James *Joyce. He moved to Britain in 1907 and then lived in France and Italy. He made broadcasts praising Fascist ideas during *World War II and was accused of helping the enemy. After the war, he was kept in a US mental hospital from 1946 to 1958 and then returned to Italy. Pound's best-known poems are the *Cantos* (1925–60).

,Anthony **'Powell**[1] /ˈpəʊəl; AmE ˈpoʊəl/ (1905–2000) an English writer and critic, best known for his series of twelve novels *A *Dance to the Music of Time* in which a writer, Nicholas Jenkins, describes the lives of a group of upper-class English characters from the 1920s to the 1960s.

,Colin **'Powell**[2] /ˌkəʊlɪn ˈpaʊəl; AmE ˌkoʊlɪn/ (1937–) a senior soldier who became head of the *Joint Chiefs of Staff (1989–93) and directed policy for the Allied Forces during the *Gulf War. General Powell held the highest rank of any African American officer in history. He had earlier fought in the *Vietnam War and been a member of the *National Security Council (1987–9). He was *Secretary of State from 2001 until he resigned from the post after the presidential election in 2004.

,Enoch **'Powell**[3] /ˈpaʊəl/ (1912–98) an English politician. He is mainly remembered for his opposition to the government policy in the late 1960s of allowing people who were not white to come from other countries to live and work in Britain. One of his speeches came to be known as the 'rivers of blood' speech because he predicted violent fights in the streets between different races (though he did not actually use the words 'rivers of blood'). Powell was a *Conservative *Member of Parliament from 1950 to 1974 and an *Ulster Unionist Member of Parliament from 1974 to 1987.

,Michael **'Powell**[4] /ˈpaʊəl/ (1905–90) an English film director. He is best known for the films he made with his partner Emeric Pressburger in the 1940s and 1950s. Films such as *The Life and Death of Colonel Blimp* (1943) and *Black Narcissus* (1946) are considered among the greatest British films of the period.

The ,Power and the 'Glory a novel (1940) by Graham *Greene. It tells the story of a *Roman Catholic priest trying to escape from Mexico at a time when his religion has been made illegal. He is caught and killed when he returns to help a dying man. The novel, considered by many people to be Greene's best, examines his usual themes of religion, moral choices and human weakness.

'Powhatan /ˈpaʊətæn/ (c. 1550–1618) the *Native American leader of the Powhatan people and the Powhatan Confederacy of 30 groups in *Virginia and part of *Maryland. He was the father of *Pocahontas, and after she married an Englishman Powhatan made peace with the *Jamestown community.

'Powys /ˈpaʊɪs/ a large region in central Wales, on the border with England. Since 1996 it has been governed by a *unitary authority. Its administrative centre is the town of Llandrindod Wells.

PPO /ˌpiː piː ˈəʊ; AmE ˈoʊ/ ⇨ PREFERRED PROVIDER ORGANIZATION.

PPS /ˌpiː piː ˈes/ ⇨ PARLIAMENTARY PRIVATE SECRETARY.

'prairie dog n a small animal found mainly in the western US and northern Mexico. It makes a harsh sound like a dog's bark. Large family groups live underground but come out for the sun and to eat. They stand upright on their back legs to look for danger.

A **'Prairie 'Home Com'panion** a live radio show in the US, with an audience of around 4 million who listen each week. It is recorded at the Fitzgerald Theater in St Paul, *Minnesota and presented by Garrison *Keillor. The show includes music and comedy, and stories by Garrison Keillor about the people of the imaginary small town of Lake Wobegon.

'Praise the 'Lord and 'Pass the Ammu'nition a popular US song during *World War II, written in 1942 by Frank Loesser. It was based on words said by a US Navy chaplain (= priest) during the Japanese attack on *Pearl Harbor.

,Terry **'Pratchett** /ˈprætʃɪt/ (1948–) an English author. His best-known books are humorous novels about Discworld, a strange, flat planet inhabited by imaginary beings such as witches and dragons. They include *The Colour of Magic* (1983) and *Small Gods* (1992).

▶ **Pre-Columbian North America**

Pre-Columbian means 'before the time of *Columbus' and refers to the period of North American history before the region was discovered by Christopher Columbus at the end of the 15th century.

bison

The first people to arrive in America crossed over a strip of land, known as Beringia, between America and Eurasia about 40 000 years ago. It is now covered by the *Bering Strait. The people were **nomads** who hunted large animals such as mammoths and bison. They had only basic tools made of stone.

About 6000 BC some groups of people began to rely more on gathering wild fruits, nuts and vegetables for food. They also began to settle in permanent villages. They made a wider range of tools, from stone and animal bone, simple copper items, and baskets and nets from wild plants. This period, which is known as the **archaic period**, lasted from *c.* 6000 to 1000 BC, though in some parts of North America, especially the desert regions of *California, people had a similar lifestyle until the arrival of the first Europeans.

Elsewhere, a major change in society began from about 1000 BC. Although **hunting and gathering** were still the main source of food, agriculture began about this time. Goods were taken long distances across the country to be traded (= exchanged for other goods). Society became much more complex and developed differently in different regions. The people buried their dead in earth mounds, similar to the *barrows of *Stone Age Britain, and often put precious objects in the mounds with them. These developments are known as the **Woodland tradition**.

The period from 800 AD until the arrival of European settlers was one of even greater change. More widespread agriculture, and the growing of crops such as corn, beans and squashes, allowed the development of much larger villages and towns. Cahokia, *Illinois, may have had a population of up to 30 000 people. In these settlements temples were built on top of earth mounds. More than 120 temples were built at Cahokia alone. The style may have been influenced by temples in Central America. Large circles of wooden posts have also been found, which may have acted as a calendar, similar to *Stonehenge in England. Another important site is Moundville, *Alabama, built by people now known as the *Moundbuilders. About 3000 people were buried at this site, many with pottery and copper axes.

In *Colorado and *Arizona people began to live in houses built with adobe (= mud bricks) in the sides of cliffs. The best preserved of these can still be seen at *Mesa Verde. Canals and ditches were dug to take water into the desert so that corn, vegetables and also cotton could be grown there. They made baskets and sandals, and elaborate painted pottery. The Ancestral Puebloans or *Anasazi, the ancestors of the modern *Pueblo people were the most developed people and traded their goods as far away as Mexico for feathers and copper. In the 16th century the Athabaskan tribes moved down from Canada. These were the ancestors of the modern *Navajo and *Apache tribes.

Although Columbus is traditionally believed to have been the first European to discover America there is good evidence that *Vikings had settled in Canada long before. The remains of a Viking settlement have been found at L'Anse aux Meadows, in Newfoundland, Canada. The Viking stories say that while they were in America they met 'Skraelings', probably *Inuit peoples.

The arrival of people from Europe caused serious problems to the pre-Columbian peoples. The Europeans took their land in order to build settlements, and over time they controlled almost all of North America, putting the native peoples on a few **reservations**. In addition, the Europeans brought diseases that the Native Americans could not overcome, and many died.

In the USA today most people know about Native American peoples, or Indians as many still call them, from the time when they came into contact with Europeans but they know little about the Americans of the pre-Columbian period.

pre**ferred pro****vider organi****zation** /prɪˌfɜːd; AmE prɪˌfɜːrd/ n (abbr **PPO**) (in the US) a special type of *health maintenance organization (HMO) which provides health insurance for groups. Companies often pay most of the cost for their employees.

Pre**liminary Scho****lastic ****Aptitude Test** ⇨ PSAT.

the ****Premiership /; AmE / the top 20 teams in English and Welsh football, run by the *Football Association. There are three divisions below it, run by the *Football League. The Premiership, which was formerly Division 1, took the name in 1993. ⇨ note at FOOTBALL – BRITISH STYLE.

Premium Bond (also ****Premium ****Savings Bond**) n (in Britain) a document with a number on it which can be bought from the government and which offers a chance of winning money as a prize every month. Unlike *National Lottery tickets the Premium Bonds can be sold back to the government at any time. They were introduced in 1956 as a way of encouraging people to save money. See also ERNIE.

pre**paratory school** (also ****prep school** /'prep/) n **1** (in Britain) a private school for students aged between 7 and 13, whose parents pay for their education. Preparatory schools prepare their students for the *Common Entrance exam, which allows them (if they pass) to go on to a *public school(1). Most preparatory schools are for either boys or girls, and some students may live at the school rather than at home. **2** (in the US) a private school that prepares students for college.

preppy (also ****preppie**) /'prepi/ n [C] (AmE informal) a person who attends an expensive private school or looks like such a person (e.g. has short hair, dresses neatly, etc.).
▶ **preppy** adj typical of or looking like a preppy; neat and fashionable: the preppy look ◇ preppy clothes.

prep school ⇨ PREPARATORY SCHOOL.

Pre-**Raphaelite** /ˌpriːˈræfəlaɪt/ n any one of a group of late 19th-century British painters who worked in a style influenced by Italian painting of the period before Raphael. The group included John Everett *Millais, Dante Gabriel *Rossetti and Holman *Hunt (who formed what they called the **Pre-Raphaelite Brotherhood**). Other artists associated with the group included William *Morris and Edward *Burne-Jones. Their subjects were usually from literature or the Bible, and were painted in bright colours with realistic detail.
▶ **Pre-****Raphaelite** /ˌpriːˈræfəlaɪt/ adj of or in the style of the Pre-Raphaelites: She had a certain Pre-Raphaelite beauty.

Presby**terian** /ˌprezbɪˈtɪəriən; AmE -ˈtɪriən/ adj (of a *Protestant Church, especially the national Church of Scotland) governed by senior members (**elders** or **presbyters**) who are all equal in rank. The Presbyterian Church in Scotland has been the established Protestant Church since 1690. In England the *United Reformed Church is a Presbyterian Church, and there are other Presbyterian Churches in the US, Ireland, Wales, Switzerland and elsewhere. Compare EPISCOPAL CHURCH.
▶ **Presbyterian** n a member of a Presbyterian Church. **Presbyterianism** n [U] Presbyterian beliefs, or the Presbyterian system of Church government.

John ****Prescott /'preskɒt; AmE 'preskɑːt/ (1938–) a British *Labour politician. He began his career in the *merchant navy before becoming a *Member of Parliament in 1970. From 1994 to 1997 he was deputy leader of the Labour Party under Tony *Blair, and became Deputy *Prime Minister after Labour's victory in the 1997 general election.

pre**scription charge** n [usually pl] (in Britain) money paid (usually to a chemist) for medicine supplied on the *National Health Service. The amount paid is the same for any medicine, and is usually less than its actual cost. Some groups, e.g. old people, children, pregnant women and the unemployed, do not have to pay prescription charges.

▶ **president**

The President is the **head of state** of the US and is part of the *executive branch of government. He (the President has so far always been a man) decides US policy on foreign affairs and is the **commander-in-chief** of the armed forces. He can appoint heads of government *departments and federal judges. *Congress must ask the President to approve new laws, although it is possible to pass a law without the President's approval. Each year, the President gives a *State of the Union Address to Congress. The President works in what may be the most famous office in the world, the *Oval Office in the *White House in Washington, DC.

The *Constitution requires that a president should be at least 35 years old, and have been born in the US. It is often said that the President is **directly elected** by the people, and this is true in comparison with countries like Britain where the *Prime Minister is selected by *Members of Parliament. In fact, although people vote for one of the candidates for President, an *electoral college makes the final choice (⇨ note at ELECTIONS). A president can serve a maximum of two **terms** (four years each).

Americans have a lot of respect for the office of President, and they are shocked when the president is believed to have done something wrong or illegal. In such a case it is possible for Congress to **impeach** the President (= remove him from his job). Congress attempted to impeach President Richard *Nixon during the *Watergate scandal of the 1970s but he decided to resign before the impeachment process was com-

P

Presidents of the United States

1	1789–97	George Washington	*Federalist*	21	1881–85	Chester A Arthur	*Republican*
2	1797–1801	John Adams	*Federalist*	22	1885–89	Grover Cleveland	*Democrat*
3	1801–09	Thomas Jefferson	*Democratic*	23	1889–93	Benjamin Harrison	*Republican*
			Republican	24	1893–97	Grover Cleveland	*Democrat*
4	1809–17	James Madison	*Democratic*	25	1897–1901	William McKinley	*Republican*
			Republican	26	1901–09	Theodore Roosevelt	*Republican*
5	1817–25	James Monroe	*Democratic*	27	1909–13	William H Taft	*Republican*
			Republican	28	1913–21	Woodrow Wilson	*Democrat*
6	1825–29	John Quincy Adams	*Democratic*	29	1921–23	Warren G Harding	*Republican*
			Republican	30	1923–29	Calvin Coolidge	*Republican*
7	1829–37	Andrew Jackson	*Democrat*	31	1929–33	Herbert Hoover	*Republican*
8	1837–41	Martin Van Buren	*Democrat*	32	1933–45	Franklin D Roosevelt	*Democrat*
9	1841	William H Harrison	*Whig*	33	1945–53	Harry S Truman	*Democrat*
10	1841–45	John Tyler	*Whig,*	34	1953–61	Dwight D Eisenhower	*Republican*
			then Democrat	35	1961–63	John F Kennedy	*Democrat*
11	1845–49	James K Polk	*Democrat*	36	1963–69	Lyndon B Johnson	*Democrat*
12	1849–50	Zachary Taylor	*Whig*	37	1969–74	Richard M Nixon	*Republican*
13	1850–53	Millard Fillmore	*Whig*	38	1974–77	Gerald R Ford	*Republican*
14	1853–57	Franklin Pierce	*Democrat*	39	1977–81	James Earl Carter	*Democrat*
15	1857–61	James Buchanan	*Democrat*	40	1981–89	Ronald W Reagan	*Republican*
16	1861–65	Abraham Lincoln	*Republican*	41	1989–93	George Bush	*Republican*
17	1865–69	Andrew Johnson	*Democrat*	42	1993–2001	Bill Clinton	*Democrat*
18	1869–77	Ulysses S Grant	*Republican*	43	2001–	George W Bush	*Republican*
19	1877–81	Rutherford B Hayes	*Republican*				
20	1881	James A Garfield	*Republican*				

pleted. In 1999, President Bill *Clinton was tried by the Senate after admitting that he had had a sexual relationship with Monica Lewinsky, having earlier denied it. Many Americans continued to support him and the Senate decided that he was not guilty of 'high crimes and misdemeanours' (= offences for which a person can be impeached).

the ˌPresiˈdential ˈMedal of ˈFreedom the highest US award given to a person who is not in the armed forces. It was established as the Medal of Freedom in 1945 and was given its new name in 1963 by President *Kennedy⁵. It is given to people who have an important positive effect on US interests, world peace, culture or society. People who have received the award in recent years include Colin *Powell, Thurgood *Marshall and Arthur *Ashe.

ˈPresidents' Day (in the US) a holiday on the third Monday in February. It celebrates the birthdays of both George *Washington (22 February) and Abraham *Lincoln (12 February). Some states celebrate the two birthdays separately.

preˌsiding ˈofficer /prɪˌzaɪdɪŋ/ n (in Britain) an official in charge of a polling station (= place where people go to vote) during an election. ⇨ note at ELECTIONS.

ˌElvis ˈPresley /ˌelvɪs ˈprezli/ (1935–77) a US pop singer and guitar player, sometimes called the 'King of Rock and Roll'. In the late 1950s and the 1960s he was probably the most successful popular singer in the world. He helped to make *African American music popular with young white people and was an influence on many popular singers, including the *Beatles and the *Rolling Stones. He was also known as 'Elvis the Pelvis' because of the way he moved his lower body when he sang. His songs included *Hound Dog* (1956), *All Shook Up* (1957), *It's Now or Never* (1960) and *Good Luck Charm* (1962). He appeared in several films, including *Jailhouse Rock* (1957), *Girls! Girls! Girls!* (1962) and *Viva Las Vegas* (1964). Presley died at his home, *Graceland, after accidentally taking too many drugs, though many people claim or pretend that he is still alive. In 1998 he was chosen for the *Country Music *Hall of Fame.

the ˈPress Associˌation (*abbr* **the PA**) a leading British news organization, established in 1868. Its job is to gather news about Britain and supply it, together with photographs, to newspapers, television stations and radio stations in Britain and abroad.

the ˌPress Comˈplaints Comˌmission a British organization formed in 1991 to deal with complaints about the behaviour of the press, especially its attempts to find out about people's private lives. It replaced a similar organization, the Press Council.

▶ **pressure groups**

Pressure groups work on behalf of a particular section of society, e.g. children or nurses, or for a particular issue or cause, e.g. banning the use of landmines. Groups that work on behalf of a section of society are sometimes called **interest groups**. Those that work for a particular cause are known as **promotional groups** or simply pressure groups. These pressure groups operate in a similar way in Britain and in the US.

There are several types of interest groups. *Trade unions and **labor unions** represent workers in industry and are mostly concerned with their wages and welfare. **Professional bodies** such as the *British Medical Association are similar to trade unions and the *CBI represents the interests of employers. In Britain several *watchdogs have been established by Act of Parliament to monitor (= check the performance of) certain industries, e.g. *Ofgem, which oversees the gas and electricity industries on behalf of users. Many promotional groups are linked to **charities**. Since charities are not allowed to take part in party political activity, many set up a related organization to act as a pressure group. In the US many pressure groups form *political action committees which are allowed to give money to political campaigns. Well-known promotional groups include *Friends of the Earth and *Amnesty International. There are also many smaller groups, usually less permanent, which are formed to protest about local issues.

Pressure groups aim to influence the government to the benefit of their members or the cause they support. They may draw attention to problems by asking people to sign a petition (= a formal request signed by many people), by giving media interviews, or by organizing demonstrations that will attract public and media attention. Groups who demonstrate and are often in the news include animal rights groups such as the *Animal Liberation Front and *PETA, and *Fathers 4 Justice, a group that claims fathers are treated unfairly by the family courts in cases of divorce. Many groups try to get the support of well-known people such as pop stars. They also try to persuade politicians to support their cause and to speak about it in *Parliament or *Congress, a practice known as *lobbying. More established pressure groups may be consulted by a government department or take part in working groups when changes to the law are being considered. There are some groups who are ready to break the law in order to achieve their aims.

the **'Battle of ,Preston'pans** /,prestən'pænz/ a battle fought in 1745 during the *Forty-Five Rebellion, in which the army of *Bonny Prince Charlie defeated the English at Prestonpans, near Edinburgh, Scotland.

'Prestwick /'prestwɪk/ a town on the western coast of Scotland, about 30 miles/50 kilometres south-west of *Glasgow. It has an international airport and port, and is famous for its golf course, where the *Open was held for many years until 1924.

,Pret a 'Manger /,pret æ 'mõʒeɪ; AmE 'mãːʒeɪ/ (also **Pret**) any of a chain of sandwich shops started in London in 1986 by Julian Metcalfe and Sinclair Beecham, which sell sandwiches freshly made in the shops, as well as drinks and other snacks that customers can eat in the shop or take away. There are now Pret shops all over the UK as well as in New York and Hong Kong. The name, meaning 'ready to eat' is an adaptation of the French expression prêt à porter (ready to wear).

the **Pre,vention of 'Terrorism Act** a British *Act of Parliament introduced on a temporary basis in 1984 to prevent terrorism in Northern Ireland. It gives the police power to arrest anyone suspected of terrorist activities (especially members of the *IRA) and to hold them for 48 hours without giving a reason. It was replaced in 2001 by the *Terrorism Act.

,André 'Previn /,ɑːndreɪ 'prevɪn/ (1929–) a US conductor, born in Germany, who also plays the piano and writes music. He has directed orchestras in London, Houston, Los Angeles and Pittsburgh, and has done a lot to make classical music more popular. He has also written film music, winning *Oscars for his work on Gigi (1958), *Porgy and Bess (1959), Irma La Douce (1963) and *My Fair Lady (1964). Previn was formerly married to the actor Mia *Farrow.

,Leontyne 'Price /,liːɒntiːn 'praɪs; AmE ,liːɑːntiːn/ (1927–) an opera singer known for the great range of her voice. She was the first African American to sing with the La Scala Opera Company of Milan (in 1959) and then became a leading singer with the *Metropolitan Opera (1961–85). Price was known especially for her performances in operas by Verdi.

The **,Price is 'Right** a television game show in which competitors try to guess the price of products, and the one with the closest guess wins. It began in the US in 1956 and is now called The New Price is Right, presented on *NBC by Bob Barker. Other countries, including Britain, have had their own versions. The British one, called Bruce's Price is Right (1995–2001), was presented by Bruce *Forsyth.

,Pride and 'Prejudice a novel (1813) by Jane *Austen. Its main characters are the sensible and intelligent Elizabeth Bennet and the rich and handsome Fitzwilliam Darcy. Elizabeth at first dislikes Darcy because of his pride, but they finally recognize each

other's good qualities and fall in love. The book ends with their marriage and that of another couple, Elizabeth's sister Jane and Darcy's friend Charles Bingley. It is one of Austen's most popular books and has been filmed several times.

> 66 It is a truth universally acknowledged, that a single man in possession of a good fortune, must be in want of a wife. 99
> the beginning of Pride and Prejudice

,J B 'Priestley[1] /'priːstli/ (John Boynton Priestley 1894–1984) an English writer. His best-known works are probably the novel The Good Companions (1929), about a small theatre company, and his play An Inspector Calls (1947), but he wrote many other popular novels and plays, often comedies about English life and society. He was also known for his critical writings on English literature and his radio broadcasts during *World War II.

,Joseph 'Priestley[2] /'priːstli/ (1733–1804) an English scientist, priest and writer. His most famous achievement was the discovery of the chemical element oxygen (which he called 'dephlogisticated air'). He attacked the established Church, and was one of the founders of Unitarianism (= a form of Christianity). His support for the American and French Revolutions led to protests in which his house was burned down, and he left England in 1794 to settle in the US.

'primary (pl -ies) (also **,primary e'lection**) n (in the US) an election in a state to appoint representatives of a political party who will attend the party conference, or to select party candidates for a future election. Candidates for US *President are chosen after a long series of state primaries: Bobby Kennedy was assassinated after he won the California primary. ⇨ note at ELECTIONS.

,primary 'care physician (also **primary care doctor**) n (in the US) a general doctor who is the first person a patient visits in the health care system. Primary care physicians treat illnesses and injuries which are not serious or send the patient to a specialist. They also help patients to manage long-term illnesses and provide health education information. Compare GP.

Primary 'Care Trust (in Britain) an organization which is responsible for providing health care such as *GP services to people in a local area, as part of the *National Health Service. They are one of two types of **NHS Trust** which have their own budgets and make decisions about what services are needed in their area.

'primary school n [C, U] (in Britain) a *state school for children aged between 5 and 11. Primary schools often consist of a separate *infant school and *junior school. *First schools are a type of primary school for children aged between 5 and 9.

the **,Primate of All 'England** the official title of the *Archbishop of Canterbury in the *Church of England.

the **,Primate of All 'Ireland** /'aɪələnd; AmE 'aɪərlənd/ the official title of each of the two Archbishops of Armagh in Northern Ireland. One is the *Roman Catholic Archbishop and the other is the Anglican (*Church of England) Archbishop, and each is head of their Church in the whole of Ireland.

the **,Primate of 'England** the official title of the *Archbishop of York in the *Church of England.

▶ **prime minister**

Originally, the king or queen could choose anyone they liked to be chief or 'Prime' Minister, and for a long time the British prime minister could come from either the *House of Lords or the *House of Commons. In recent years the Prime Minister has always come from the

Prime Ministers of Great Britain

1721–42	Sir Robert Walpole	*Whig*
1742–43	Earl of Wilmington	*Whig*
1743–54	Henry Pelham	*Whig*
1754–56	Duke of Newcastle	*Whig*
1756–57	Duke of Devonshire	*Whig*
1757–62	Duke of Newcastle	*Whig*
1762–63	Earl of Bute	*Tory*
1763–65	George Grenville	*Whig*
1765–66	Marquis of Rockingham	*Whig*
1766–68	Earl of Chatham	*Whig*
1768–70	Duke of Grafton	*Whig*
1770–82	Lord North	*Tory*
1782	Marquis of Rockingham	*Whig*
1782–83	Earl of Shelburne	*Whig*
1783	Duke of Portland	*(coalition)*
1783–1801	William Pitt	*Tory*
1801–04	Henry Addington	*Tory*
1804–06	William Pitt	*Tory*
1806–07	Lord William Grenville	*Whig*
1807–09	Duke of Portland	*Tory*
1809–12	Spencer Perceval	*Tory*
1812–27	Earl of Liverpool	*Tory*
1827	George Canning	*Tory*
1827–28	Viscount Goderich	*Tory*
1828–30	Duke of Wellington	*Tory*
1830–34	Earl Grey	*Whig*
1834	Viscount Melbourne	*Whig*
1834	Duke of Wellington	*Tory*
1834–35	Sir Robert Peel	*Conservative*
1835–41	Viscount Melbourne	*Whig*
1841–46	Sir Robert Peel	*Conservative*
1846–52	Lord John Russell	*Whig*
1852	Earl of Derby	*Conservative*
1852–55	Earl of Aberdeen	*(coalition)*
1855–58	Viscount Palmerston	*Liberal*
1858–59	Earl of Derby	*Conservative*
1859–65	Viscount Palmerston	*Liberal*
1865–66	Earl Russell	*Liberal*
1866–68	Earl of Derby	*Conservative*
1868	Benjamin Disraeli	*Conservative*
1868–74	William Ewart Gladstone	*Liberal*
1874–80	Benjamin Disraeli	*Conservative*
1880–85	William Ewart Gladstone	*Liberal*
1885–86	Marquis of Salisbury	*Conservative*
1886	William Ewart Gladstone	*Liberal*
1886–92	Marquis of Salisbury	*Conservative*
1892–94	William Ewart Gladstone	*Liberal*
1894–95	Earl of Rosebery	*Liberal*
1895–1902	Marquis of Salisbury	*Conservative*
1902–05	Arthur James Balfour	*Conservative*
1905–08	Sir Henry Campbell Bannerman	*Liberal*
1908–16	Herbert Henry Asquith	*Liberal*
1916–22	David Lloyd George	*(coalition)*
1922–23	Andrew Bonar Law	*Conservative*
1923–24	Stanley Baldwin	*Conservative*
1924	James Ramsay MacDonald	*Labour*
1924–29	Stanley Baldwin	*Conservative*
1929–35	James Ramsay MacDonald	*(coalition)*
1935–37	Stanley Baldwin	*(coalition)*
1937–40	Neville Chamberlain	*(coalition)*
1940–45	Winston Churchill	*(coalition)*
1945–51	Clement Attlee	*Labour*
1951–55	Sir Winston Churchill	*Conservative*
1955–57	Sir Anthony Eden	*Conservative*
1957–63	Harold Macmillan	*Conservative*
1963–64	Sir Alexander Douglas-Home	*Conservative*
1964–70	Harold Wilson	*Labour*
1970–74	Edward Heath	*Conservative*
1974–76	Harold Wilson	*Labour*
1976–79	James Callaghan	*Labour*
1979–90	Margaret Thatcher	*Conservative*
1990–97	John Major	*Conservative*
1997–	Tony Blair	*Labour*

Commons and the king or queen gives the job to the leader of the party with the largest number of *MPs. Lord Home, who became leader of the Conservative Party in 1963, was the first politician to be allowed to renounce a *peerage (= give up an inherited title and status) to become Prime Minister as Sir Alec *Douglas-Home).

The Prime Minister is by tradition First Lord of the *Treasury and Minister for the Civil Service. He or she chooses and presides over the *Cabinet and heads the government. Unlike an American President, a British prime minister can remain in the job as long as the party he or she represents is in power. Margaret Thatcher, the first woman prime minister, served for eleven and a half years until the Conservative party voted to replace her. The Prime Minister chooses senior ministers and recommends their appointment to the king or queen. While other ministers are responsible for particular government *departments, the prime minister is concerned with policy as a whole. Cabinet committees usually report directly to him or her. The Prime Minister has regular meetings with the sovereign to inform him or her of the activities of the government.

The prime minister lives at 10 *Downing Street, above the offices used by the Cabinet, and is often photographed outside the front door. *Chequers, in the countryside outside London, is also an official home for the prime minister and is used at weekends and for more informal meetings.

Prime 'Minister's 'Questions questions put to the British *Prime Minister in the *House of Commons for half an hour each week, on Wednesday afternoons. The questions are from both government and Opposition *Members of Parliament and are not known by the Prime Minister in advance. The answers often lead to noisy disagreement between members of parliament in different parties. The occasion is broadcast on television.

Prime 'Suspect a successful British series of six television dramas 1990–98, written by Linda La Plante, about murder enquiries led by a police detective, Jane Tennison, played by Helen *Mirren.

Prince /prɪns/ (1958–) a US pop singer and actor. He was born Prince Rogers Nelson in Minneapolis. In 1993 he changed his name into a symbol that nobody could pronounce, so he was called 'the Artist Formerly Known as Prince'. He changed his name back to Prince in 2000. He has shocked a lot of people with his sexual songs and performances on stage. He was the star of the film *Purple Rain* (1984) and won an *Oscar for its music. He also wrote the music for *Batman* (1989).

Prince 'Consort a title sometimes given by a British queen to her husband during her rule. Prince *Albert, the husband of Queen *Victoria, was given the title.

Prince of 'Wales /'weɪlz/ a title given to the eldest son of a British king or queen, who becomes king after them. The title was first used in 1301 and is traditionally given together with the titles of Duke of *Cornwall and Earl of Chester. The present Prince of Wales is Prince *Charles. See also ICH DIEN.

the ˌPrince of ˌWales's ˌPhoenix 'Trust /ˌfiːnɪks/ an organization, started in 1997, whose president is the *Prince of Wales, which repairs and finds new uses for large historic buildings, especially industrial buildings which are no longer used. The projects are designed to create new jobs and encourage business and housing development in an area.

ˌPrince 'Regent the title of George, *Prince of Wales (later King *George IV), who ruled Britain from 1811 to 1820 while his father, King *George III, was mentally ill. *Regent Street and *Regent's Park in London are named after him, and the period 1811–20 is known as the *Regency.

the ˌPrinces in the 'Tower a name given to the two young sons of King *Edward IV, i.e. the boy king *Edward V and his brother Richard, Duke of *York³(3) (1472–83), who went to live in the royal apartments (= private rooms) in the *Tower of London in 1483 after their father died. They disappeared, and some people believe they were murdered either by *Richard III, who had become king, or by *Henry VII. The bones of two young children found in the Tower and tested in 1933 are believed to be theirs. See also WHITE TOWER.

ˌPrincess of 'Wales /'weɪlz/ the title given to the wife of the *Prince of Wales. Until her death in 1997 the title was held by Princess Diana, who married Prince *Charles in 1981.

ˌPrincess 'Royal the title usually given to the eldest daughter of a British king or queen. The present Princess Royal is Princess *Anne.

'Princes Street the main street in *Edinburgh, Scotland, named after the princes who were sons of King *George III. On its north side it has shops and restaurants and on its south side there are large sloping gardens. Also on the south side is the Scott Monument, a very large *Gothic structure built in 1840–4 in memory of Sir Walter *Scott.

the ˌPrince's 'Trust an organization established by Prince *Charles in 1976. It aims to help young people to develop their skills through programmes of training and employment, and gives grants of money to groups and individuals. It includes a number of other organizations doing similar work, such as the Queen's Silver Jubilee Trust and the Prince's Youth Business Trust, and it operates in several countries around the world.

ˌPrinceton Uni'versity /ˌprɪnstən/ one of the oldest and most respected universities in the US. It was established in 1746 and is in Princeton, *New Jersey. Its presidents have included Jonathan *Edwards (1757–8) and Woodrow *Wilson (1902–10). Princeton is known for its studies in international affairs, and it has a special relationship with the *Institute for Advanced Study. See also IVY LEAGUE.

ˌprincipal 'boy n the leading male part in a *pantomime, traditionally played by a young female actor. For example, Prince Charming is the principal boy in the pantomime *Cinderella.

'Pringle /'prɪŋgl/ (also **Pringle of Scotland**) a Scottish clothing company started in 1815 by Robert Pringle, which is best known for its golf clothing and sweaters with a diamond pattern.

'Pringles™ /'prɪŋglz/ a US brand of potato crisps/chips made by *Proctor & Gamble, which are sold in a long tube. They are available in many different flavours.

▶ **prisons**

Britain's system of justice relies heavily on **imprisonment** as a form of *punishment. Until the late 18th century conditions in prisons such as *Newgate were dirty and violent. In the 19th century conditions improved, thanks to the work of reformers like Elizabeth *Fry. New prisons were built, in which most prisoners had their own **cell** facing into a large central area. Many of these prisons, such as *Pentonville and *Strangeways, still exist today, although Strangeways had to be rebuilt after most of the building was destroyed in riots in the 1990s.

The type of prison in which criminals **serve their sentence** depends on their **category**. Category A prisoners are considered dangerous and are held in high-security closed prisons, such as *Wormwood Scrubs. Prisoners may be kept in **solitary confinement** if they are likely to harm others. Category B and C prisoners are also held in closed prisons. Category D prisoners are trusted not to escape and are sent to low-security **open prisons**. Prisoners **on remand** (= waiting for their trial) are held in **remand centres**, but problems of overcrowding have resulted in many of them being kept in prisons or police stations. Young people aged 15–20 are normally sent to *young offender institutions, sometimes called detention centres or youth custody centres. These have replaced the old *Borstals. However, if space is not available young people are sometimes sent to adult prisons. A prison is run by a **governor** who is responsible to the *Home Office, and the prisoners are guarded by **warders**.

There is not enough space available in prisons for the number of people being given **custodial sentences**. In the 1990s there were riots at several prisons because of poor conditions. Cells intended for one person often contain two or three. Despite this, some people think life in Britain's prisons is not hard enough. Some prisons are described as 'universities of crime', where prisoners gain new skills in breaking the law and have access to drugs.

There are many British *slang expressions connected with prison. To *do time* is to serve a prison sentence and to have been *inside* means to have been in prison. Time spent in prison is *porridge*. Prison itself is *the nick, the slammer* or *choky*, warders are *screws*, and the prisoners are *lags*.

In the US the federal and state governments have **prisons**, sometimes called **penitentiaries** or **correctional facilities**. Counties and cities have **jails**. Federal prisons are classified as minimum, low, medium or high security. All **inmates** (= prisoners) who can work must do so. People are sent to a **prison** if their sentence is for several years. If the sentence is a year or less they are sent to **jail**. Some prisoners on **work release** are allowed to leave jail during the day to go to a job. Prisoners often spend the last few months of their sentence in a **halfway house** where they are helped to prepare for life outside prison.

The number of people in prisons and jails in the US is higher as a proportion of the population than in any other country. In 2002 it went above two million for the first time, twice what it was in 1990. Problems include overcrowding and the use of drugs. The fact that over 10% of African American men aged between 25 and 29 are in prison compared to 1% of white men is seen as evidence that African Americans are treated unfairly by the justice system and are more likely to be sent to prison than white Americans.

In the US people who are awaiting trial often do not go to prison but instead **make bail** (= pay money to the court) as a guarantee that they will return for the trial. People sent to prison as punishment rarely serve

P

their full sentence but after some time are released **on parole**, which means they must report regularly to a government official. It is possible that two people who have committed the same crime may receive different punishments. To stop this happening some states have introduced **mandatory sentencing**, which means that the punishment for a crime is fixed by law, not decided by a judge.

V S 'Pritchett /'prɪtʃɪt/ (Victor Sawdon Pritchett 1900–97) an English author. He is best remembered for his short stories, which are full of humorous criticism of British life, and for his writings about literature, e.g. *The Living Novel* (1946). He also wrote the life stories of several authors, including Chekhov, Turgenev and Balzac. He was made a *knight in 1975.

▶ **privacy**

The British value their privacy (= having a part of their life that is not known to other people) and believe that everyone has a right to a **private life**. Many British people like to 'keep themselves to themselves' and do not discuss their private affairs. Things people like to keep private vary but may include personal relationships, family problems, how much they earn, their health, their political opinions, and sometimes what they do in their free time. It is considered rude to ask somebody about their private life, even if you know them well.

In the US the *Constitution protects people's right to privacy. A police officer has no power to stop people and ask them what they are doing unless they have committed a crime. Information about people can be shown to others only under special circumstances, and usually only with their permission. When newspapers print details about the family life of a politician or film actor they are often criticized for **invasion of privacy**. On the other hand, actors and politicians tell the press about their family life for publicity reasons, and ordinary Americans appear on television talk shows where they discuss their bad marriages, health problems and how they cannot control their children. The apparent contradiction in attitudes may be explained by the fact that Americans believe strongly in the right to privacy, but as long as that right is respected, they are happy to give it up. They believe it is better to be open and honest than to have secrets. The British may be less willing than Americans to talk about their own lives but they have an equally strong desire to know about the private lives of famous people. There is a constant argument, for instance, about the extent to which the media should be allowed to report the private lives of members of the *royal family.

Americans don't tell the world everything about their lives. Money and sex are rarely discussed. Husbands and wives usually know how much each other earns, but other family members do not. People may say how much they paid for something, especially if the price was low, but asking somebody else how much they paid is acceptable only for small things, not a house or a car. In general people are happier offering information than being asked for it.

Being given advice can also disturb an American's sense of privacy because it seems to suggest that somebody else can solve your problem better than you can yourself. When offering advice, people use indirect language, and instead of saying, 'You should do this,' they may say, 'I tried doing this, and it worked for me'.

private 'bill *n* a *bill(1) (= the proposal for a new law in the British Parliament) that affects a person or group rather than the whole country. Compare PRIVATE MEMBER'S BILL, PUBLIC BILL.

Private 'Eye a British satirical magazine first published in 1961 and now appearing twice a month. It contains humorous articles and cartoons, but also investigates dishonest behaviour in politics and business. The magazine's editors have appeared many times in British courts of law, charged with falsely accusing people and damaging people's reputations.

private 'limited 'company *n* (in Britain) a type of company, usually small, that does not issue shares to the public. The company's name is usually followed by 'Ltd', short for 'Limited'. Compare PUBLIC LIMITED COMPANY.

private 'member's bill *n* a *bill(1) (= proposal for a new law) presented to the British *House of Commons by a private member (= a *Member of Parliament who is not a minister). Few private member's bills become law because they usually lack support and receive little time for debate. Compare PRIVATE BILL, PUBLIC BILL.

private 'patient *n* (in the British health system) a patient who pays for medical care rather than receiving it free from the *National Health Service. People choose to do this because they believe they will receive better care and will not have to wait. Some private patients make regular insurance payments to companies such as *BUPA, which then provide care when the patient needs it.

private 'road *n* (in Britain) a road that crosses the private property of a person or group of people and is owned by them. Private roads are usually open to the public for them to reach the house or houses that they lead to, but they must be closed at least once a year in order to remain private.

the ˌPrivy 'Council a group of people appointed to advise the British king or queen. It is made up of politicians and other important people in the legal profession, the Church and the Commonwealth, and its head is the *Lord President of the Council. At present it has over 400 members, who are given the position for life. The Privy Council first became powerful in the 14th century, but was replaced in 1688 by the *Cabinet. It now has few functions in government, and is mainly important as a personal honour for its members.

▶ **Privy 'Councillor** (*also* **Privy Counsellor**) *n* a member of the Privy Council. Privy Councillors are formally addressed as 'the Right Honourable Mr/Mrs Smith', etc. and have the letters 'PC' after their name.

the ˌprivy 'purse a payment made every year to the British king or queen from the government, for official expenses and some private expenses. The money comes mainly from the income of the *Duchy of Lancaster. The privy purse is separate from the *Civil List, which pays for other official expenses of the whole royal family.

ˌProcter & 'Gamble /ˌprɒktər, 'gæmbl; AmE ˌprɑːktər/ a large US international company that produces a wide range of household goods. It was established in 1837 by William Procter and James Gamble as a soap and candle business in Cincinnati, *Ohio, where the main offices still are. The company's products include *Ivory soap, *Pringles Biscuits, Sunny Delight drinks, Crest toothpaste, Tide soap for clothes, Mr Clean for bathroom and kitchen surfaces, Oil of Olay cream and Folger's coffee.

The 'Prodigy a British pop group formed in 1991 and known for their fast, aggressive dance music. Their albums include *Music for the Jilted Generation* (1994) and *The Fat of the Land* (1997), and their song *Firestarter* reached Number One in Britain in 1996.

the ˌProfessional 'Golfers' Associˌation ⇨ PGA.

ˌJohn Pro'fumo /prə'fjuːməʊ; AmE prə'fjuːmoʊ/ (1915–) a minister in the *Conservative government of

Harold *Macmillan, who admitted in 1963 that he had had a sexual affair with a prostitute called Christine Keeler. Keeler was also having a sexual relationship with a Russian navy officer, and this was felt to threaten national safety. Profumo resigned, and at the court trial of Christine Keeler shocking details were reported about the behaviour of top government figures, involving prostitutes and criminals. The matter became known as the **Profumo Affair**, and severely damaged public trust in the government. Profumo left politics but later followed a new career in social work and adult education.

pro,gressive edu'cation n [U] an important movement in US education which began at the end of the 19th century, when it was mainly associated with the ideas of John Dewey (1859–1952). It placed emphasis on developing students' practical and social skills in addition to purely academic subjects. Progressive education was popular in US schools in the first half of the 20th century and its influence is still found, though in recent years there has been a return to more basic teaching and learning methods.

the Pro'gressive ,Party the name taken at different times by three separate US political parties in opposition to the two major parties. **Progressivists** wanted social and economic changes to make society fairer, including higher taxes for rich people. Each had a candidate in one election for *President. The first, with the popular name of the Bull Moose Party, chose former President Theodore *Roosevelt as its candidate in 1912, and he gained more than 4 million votes. The second party, established by farm and trade-union leaders, was led by Robert La Follette, who won about 5 million votes. Henry A Wallace was the candidate for the last party in 1948 and received more than 1 million votes.

,Prohi'bition (in the US) the period from 1919 to 1933 when it was illegal by national law to make or sell alcohol and alcoholic drinks. Prohibition was not popular, and it was too expensive to make sure that the law was obeyed. It also produced criminals like Al *Capone who made and sold alcohol. A few states kept prohibition laws for several years, and some counties in certain states still have them.

'Promise ,Keepers a US organization of *evangelical Christian men who promise to worship God, preserve the family and support the nation. They have been criticized by some women who believe they want men to control families. The organization was started in 1990 by Bill McCartney, and holds regular large meetings for men around the US.

the Proms /prɒmz; AmE prɑːmz/ n [pl] a series of concerts started by Henry *Wood in 1895 and now held every year at the *Albert Hall, London. The name is short for 'promenade concerts', i.e. concerts in which there are no seats in parts of the hall and members of the audience stand up or sit on the floor during the performance. The series lasts for eight weeks, and the concerts are broadcast on the *BBC. The *Last Night of the Proms is an occasion for special celebration, when several well-known songs are performed, with the audience joining in. The Proms are particularly popular with young people.

pro,portional represen'tation n [U] a system used in political elections, in which the number of candidates elected for each party is decided according to the number of votes the party receives as a whole. Except for in elections to the *Scottish Parliament and the *Welsh Assembly this system is not used in Britain or the US, which both operate a *first-past-the-post system, in which candidates are elected who receive the most votes in a particular area. Proportional representation is generally thought to benefit smaller parties, and is favoured

by the British *Liberal Democratic Party but not by the larger *Conservative or *Labour Parties.

'Prospero /'prɒspərəʊ; AmE 'prɑːspəroʊ/ the main character in *Shakespeare's play The *Tempest.

the Pro'tectorate the period from 1653 to 1658 when Oliver *Cromwell ruled Britain with the title of *Lord Protector, and from 1658 to 1659 when his son Richard (1626–1712) ruled with the same title. During this time they claimed greater powers, often ruling alone without a parliament. In 1659 the *Long Parliament was established again, which voted for the return of King *Charles II.

'Protestant n a member of any of the Christian groups that separated from the Catholic Church led by the Pope in Rome in the 16th century, or of their branches formed later. Protestant Churches usually have simpler ceremonies than *Roman Catholic Churches, with more emphasis on preaching (= teaching about religion) and the authority of the Bible. Most Christians in the US and Britain are Protestants, and the *Church of England and *Church of Scotland are Protestant Churches. Other Protestant Churches include the *Methodists, the *Baptists, the *Presbyterians and the *Quakers. Disagreements between Protestants and Catholics in Northern Ireland have led to the conflict known as the *Troubles. See also REFORMATION.
▸ **Protestant** adj
Protestantism n [U] the beliefs and teachings of Protestants, or Protestants as a group.

the 'Protestant E'piscopal 'Church ⇨ EPISCOPAL CHURCH.

,E ,Annie Proulx /'pruː/ (1935–) a US writer of novels and short stories whose first novel Postcards (1993) won the *PEN/Faulkner award for Fiction. She won a *Pulitzer prize for The Shipping News (1993) which was made into a film. Her other books include Close Range: Wyoming Stories (1999) and That Old Ace in the Hole (2002).

'Providence /'prɒvɪdəns; AmE 'prɑːvɪdəns/ the capital and largest city of the US state of *Rhode Island. It is on the Providence River and Narragansett Bay. Roger Williams established it in 1636 as a safe place for people of all religions. It is known for its silver products and jewellery. Brown University, an *Ivy League school, was established there in 1764.

'Provident So,ciety ⇨ FRIENDLY SOCIETY.

the Pro'visionals /prə'vɪʒənls/ (also informal the **Provos**) another name for the Provisional *IRA, the part of the IRA that has committed acts of violence for political purposes. Compare SINN FEIN.

'Prozac™ /'prəʊzæk; AmE 'proʊzæk/ n [U] a drug used for treating people who are depressed. It first became available in 1988 and many users claimed it increased their confidence and helped them in their daily lives. It soon became very popular for general use, especially in the US. In recent years some people have become worried about a possible link with suicide and violent behaviour. In 2004 authorities in the US decided that a warning must be given on packets of the drug that it can cause children to become suicidal (= to want to kill themselves).

PRS /,piː ɑːr 'es/ ⇨ PERFORMING RIGHT SOCIETY.

Pru'dential /pruː'denʃl/ (also the **Prudential**, also informal **the Pru** /pruː/) an international company, formed in Britain in 1848, dealing in insurance, property and financial services. It is Britain's second largest insurance company and one of the largest property owners in Britain after the *Crown and the *Church of England.

PSAT /,piː es eɪ 'tiː/ (in full **Preliminary Scholastic Aptitude Test**) (in the US) an examination that *high school students take, mostly to practise for the *SAT examination. It is sometimes called the PSAT/NMSQT (Preliminary Scholastic Aptitude Test/National Merit Scholarship Qualifying Test), because students who do well can receive money from the National Merit Scholarship Corporation to attend a college or university.

PSBR /ˌpiː es biː 'ɑː(r)/ ⇨ Public Sector Borrowing Requirement.

the PSNI /ˌpiː es en 'aɪ/ ⇨ Police Service of Northern Ireland.

PST /ˌpiː es 'tiː/ ⇨ Pacific Standard Time.

'Psycho /'saɪkəʊ; AmE 'saɪkoʊ/ a US film (1960) directed by Alfred *Hitchcock. Anthony Perkins played Norman Bates, a man with mental problems who owns a hotel and kills people who stay there. The scene in which he kills a woman in a shower is considered one of the most frightening ever filmed. Perkins later played Bates in three more films.

PT /ˌpiː 'tiː/ ⇨ Pacific Standard Time.

PT boat /ˌpiː 'tiː/ (in full **patrol torpedo boat**) n a small, fast US Navy boat that carries torpedoes (= tube-shaped bombs that are fired under water). PT boats were used especially during *World War II.

pub (formal ˌpublic 'house) (in Britain) a building where people go to drink and meet their friends which serves a range of alcoholic drinks and soft drinks. Pubs are important in the social life of many people in Britain. People often go to the pub nearest their home, known as their **local**. Pubs have their own character and atmosphere. Some attract young people by playing loud music, others have large television screens so that people can watch sport and there are also traditional village pubs which are often very old and are the centre of village life. Most pubs have more than one **bar** (= a room to drink in) where drinks are sold from a counter, also called a **bar**. Often people in a group will take it in turns to go to the bar to buy a **round** (= a drink for each person in the group). The most popular drinks are *beer and lager. **Tied houses** (= pubs owned by breweries) sell beers made by the company and **guest beers** from other breweries, and **free houses** (= pubs not owned by a brewery) offer beers made by several different companies, often including **real ales** made using traditional methods. Pubs usually sell crisps and nuts and many do simple **pub meals** such as sausage and chips or a *ploughman's lunch. Others, sometimes called **gastro-pubs**, sell a wider range of food and are like restaurants. Under Britain's **licensing laws** alcohol can only be sold to people over 18, and children under 14 are not allowed in pubs unless there is a **family room**, a room without a bar, or an outside area called a **beer garden**. Before 1998 pubs were only allowed to open at lunchtime and in the evening, but since then **opening hours** have become more flexible so that pubs can open all day and even for 24 hours if they have a licence to do so. When **closing time** approaches, the **barman** or **barmaid** rings a bell and calls out 'Last orders!', to give customers time to order one more drink. After the bar person has called 'Time!' customers are allowed ten minutes **drinking-up time** to finish their drinks and leave. Pubs always have a name which is shown on a brightly painted sign hanging outside with a picture on it. Many names are hundreds of years old and may have their roots in legends, such as St *George and the Dragon, some are named after kings and queens or historical figures, and others refer to things in country life, such as The Plough or The Bull.

ˌpublic 'access ˌchannel n (in the US) a cable television channel reserved for broadcasts by people and organizations that do not make a profit. The Cable Act (1984)

requires private cable companies to provide equipment and time for such broadcasts. Compare CATV.

ˌpublic 'bill n a *bill(1) (= a proposal for a new law in the British Parliament) that affects the whole country rather than one person or group. Compare PRIVATE BILL, PRIVATE MEMBER'S BILL.

the ˌPublic 'Broadcasting ˌService ⇨ PBS.

ˌPublic 'Enemy a US *rap music group. They began in 1987 as the Black Panthers of Rap. Their songs often deal with political issues and are known for their aggressive words and ideas. They include Don't Believe the Hype (1988) and Fear of a Black Planet (1990). Among their albums are It Takes a Nation of Millions to Hold Us Back (1988), Give It Up (1994) and Revolverlution (2002).

'Public 'Enemy 'No '1 /'nʌmbə 'wʌn; AmE 'nʌmbər/ the title used by the *FBI in the 1930s to refer to the criminal they considered the most dangerous and the one they most wanted to arrest at any particular time. In 1934 both John *Dillinger and 'Baby Face' *Nelson were named as 'Public Enemy No 1'. The FBI now names the 'Ten Most Wanted Fugitives'.

ˌpublic 'footpath n (BrE) a way or track along which people walk, especially in country areas. In England and Wales public footpaths are marked on *Ordnance Survey maps and are legal rights of way. They are often very old and people have the right to use them even if they cross private land. They allow people to discover the countryside, and organizations like the *Rambler's Association try to make sure that they are kept open and are well looked after.

ˌPublic 'Lending Right (abbr PLR) the system by which authors in Britain receive payment when their books are borrowed from public libraries. It was introduced in 1984 and the money is provided by the British government.

'public 'limited 'company n (abbrs plc, PLC) a type of British company, usually large, that issues shares to the public, and allows the public to examine its accounts. A public limited company must have the letters 'plc' after its name. Compare PRIVATE LIMITED COMPANY. ⇨ note at COMPANIES.

the ˌPublic 'Order Act a British *Act of Parliament which replaced the old *Riot Act in 1986. It was introduced in response to the riots in Toxteth, *Brixton and other places in the early 1980s, and gave the police new powers to control crowds and arrest people who they thought threatened public order. The Act also created several new offences under the law, including 'violent disorder', 'threatening behaviour' and 'disorderly conduct'. Police powers were increased by the Criminal Justice and Public Order Act 1994.

the ˌPublic 'Record ˌOffice the offices in London where government records for England and Wales are kept. These are made available to the public under the Freedom of Information Act (2005) which replaced the earlier *thirty-year rule. Among the important historical documents kept at the Public Record Office is the *Domesday Book of 1086. In 2003 the *National Archives became responsible for the Public Record Office.

ˌpublic 'school n **1** ⇨ note at PUBLIC SCHOOLS. **2** (AmE) a local school paid for by the government and providing free education.

▶ **public schools**

Public schools are, in most of Britain, **independent schools** and, despite their name, are not part of the state education system. Schools run by the state are called *state schools. In Scotland however, which has a separate education system from the rest of Britain, the term *public school* refers to a state school. Only about 10% of children attend independent public schools, and their parents have to pay **fees** that may amount to many thousand pounds a year. A small number of children from less wealthy families win **scholarships**, in which case their fees are paid for them.

public schoolboys

Many of Britain's 200 public schools are very old. They include *Eton, *Harrow, *Winchester and, for girls, *Cheltenham Ladies' College and *Roedean. Most public schools were single-sex schools but many now teach girls and boys together. Public schools were originally *grammar schools which offered free education to the public and were under public management. This was in contrast to private schools which were privately owned by the teachers. Since the 19th century, the term *public school* has been applied to grammar schools that began taking fee-paying pupils as well as children paid for from public funds.

Most pupils go to public school at the age of 13, after attending private *prep schools. Many public schools are **boarding schools** where students live during term-time. Most have a **house system**, with **boarders** living in one of several **houses** under the charge of a **housemaster** or **housemistress**. Older pupils are chosen as **prefects** (= pupils who have authority over younger pupils) and in a few schools younger pupils have to do small jobs for the senior pupils. This is sometimes called *fagging* and was usual in most public schools in the past. At most schools pupils have to wear a school uniform and at some of the oldest schools this is very old fashioned. Sport is an important part of the curriculum and schools compete against each other in *cricket, *Rugby, *football, *hockey, rowing, etc. Many schools have a chapel where pupils attend *Anglican services and there are also a small number of *Roman Catholic public schools.

Public schools aim for high academic standards and to provide pupils with the right social background for top jobs in the *Establishment. A much higher proportion of students from public schools win university places, especially to *Oxford and *Cambridge Universities, than from state schools. Former public school students may also have an advantage when applying for jobs because of the **'old school tie'**, the **old boy network** through which a former public school pupil is more likely to give a job to somebody from a public school, especially his own public school, than to someone from a school in the state system. Some people send their children to public school mainly for this reason; others believe public schools provide a better education than state schools. Public schools have in the past been associated with strict discipline, *bullying and occasionally homosexuality.

In the US a *public school* is a school run by the government. Schools that students have to pay to attend are called **private schools**. There are many private schools in the US, some of which are boarding schools. Some, like Phillips Exeter Academy and the Bath Academy, are very similar to Britain's public schools. They are very expensive, have a high reputation, and many of their students come from rich and well-known families. Children often go to the same school as their parents. Many of the most famous schools of this sort are in *New England.

Some US private schools give special attention to a particular area of study. There are, for example, schools for people who are good at music or art. Military schools are often chosen by parents who are in the armed forces, or who think their children need a lot of discipline. Religious groups also run private schools, although not all of the students who attend practise that religion. Schools run by the Catholic church are called **parochial schools**.

Private schools in the US are often single-sex and their students usually wear a uniform. This is unusual in American public schools. Parents choose a private school for their children for a number of reasons, but in general they believe that the quality of education is higher in private schools, and there is some evidence to support this. Most private schools offer scholarships to students from poorer families, and in some parts of the US the government may under certain circumstances pay for children to attend a private school.

the 'Public 'Sector 'Borrowing Re,quirement (*abbr* **PSBR**) the amount of money the government needs to borrow every year to pay for public spending, if money from taxes is not enough. It is borrowed from the banking system and other sources, and is considered an addition to the *National Debt.

,public 'service ,broadcasting *n* [U] (in Britain) radio or television broadcasting by the *BBC. The aim of public service broadcasting is to make programmes of a high standard that educate, inform and entertain, and the BBC received a *royal charter to do this in 1927. Anyone who owns a television must pay a licence fee, which pays for the service. Compare PUBLIC ACCESS CHANNEL, PUBLIC BROADCASTING SERVICE.

,public 'spending round *n* [usually sing] the arrangement made every year by the British government in which different government departments are given money for the year. The public spending round is announced in the *budget, together with details about how taxes will be collected.

,publish and be 'damned a phrase meaning 'you can publish if you like, I don't care'. It is thought to have been used by the Duke of Wellington when he received threats that private details about him were going to be published. It is now used more often when someone decides to publish something offensive or unpopular even though they know they will face public criticism: *A lot of people will disagree with what I've written – I'll just have to publish and be damned.*

,publish or 'perish a phrase used to express the idea that it is important for teachers in colleges and universities to publish books, etc. about their research, and that if they fail to do so it will have a bad effect on their career. The idea is sometimes criticized because teachers are seen to be spending more time on their writing than on their teaching.

Puck /pʌk/ (*also* **,Robin 'Goodfellow**) (in English legend) a spirit who lives in the English countryside and plays tricks on people. He appears as a character in *Shakespeare's *A Midsummer Night's Dream*.
▸ **puckish** *adj* fond of playing tricks on people; mischievous.

'Pueblo /'pwebləʊ; *AmE* 'pwebloʊ/ *n* (*pl* **Pueblos** *or* **Pueblo**) a member of one of the groups of *Native American people who live in the US states of *Arizona and *New Mexico. The groups include the *Hopi and the Zuñi. They are descended from the *Anasazi people who lived in cliff houses, some of which can be seen in the *Mesa Verde National Park. They now live in communities called *pueblos* and build their houses of dried clay, called *adobe*.

Winners of the Pulitzer Prize for Fiction

1918 *His Family* Ernest Poole
1919 *The Magnificent Ambersons* Booth Tarkington
1921 *The Age of Innocence* Edith Wharton
1922 *Alice Adams* Booth Tarkington
1923 *One of Ours* Willa Cather
1924 *The Able McLaughlins* Margaret Wilson
1925 *So Big* Edna Ferber
1926 *Arrowsmith* Sinclair Lewis
1927 *Early Autumn* Louis Bromfield
1928 *The Bridge of San Luis Rey* Thornton Wilder
1929 *Scarlet Sister Mary* Julia Peterkin
1930 *Laughing Boy* Oliver La Farge
1931 *Years Of Grace* Margaret Ayer Barnes
1932 *The Good Earth* Pearl S Buck
1934 *Lamb in his Bosom* Caroline Miller
1935 *Now in November* Josephine Winslow Johnson
1936 *Honey in the Horn* Harold L Davis
1937 *Gone with the Wind* Margaret Mitchell
1937 *The Late George Apley* John Phillips Marquand
1938 *The Yearling* Marjorie Kinnan Rawlings
1940 *The Grapes of Wrath* John Steinbeck
1942 *In This our Life* Ellen Glasgow
1943 *Dragon's Teeth* Upton Sinclair
1944 *Journey in the Dark* Martin Flavin
1945 *A Bell for Adano* John Hersey
1947 *All The King's Men* Robert Penn Warren
1948 *Tales of the South Pacific* James A. Michener
1949 *Guard of Honor* James Gould Cozzens
1950 *The Way West* A B Guthrie Jr
1951 *The Town* Conrad Richter
1952 *The Conrad Mutiny* Herman Wouk
1953 *The Old Man and the Sea* Ernest Hemingway
1955 *A Fable* William Faulkner
1956 *Andersonville* MacKinley Kantor
1958 *A Death in the Family* James Agee
1959 *The Travels of Jamie McPheeters*
     Robert Lewis Taylor
1960 *Advise and Consent* Allen Drury
1961 *To Kill a Mockingbird* Harper Lee
1962 *The Edge of Sadness* Edwin O'Connor
1963 *The Reivers* William Faulkner
1965 *The Keepers of the House* Shirley Ann Grau

1966 *Collected Stories of Katherine Anne Porter*
1967 *The Fixer* Bernard Malamud
1968 *The Confessions of Nat Turner* William Styron
1969 *House Made of Dawn* N Scott Momaday
1970 *Collected Stories* Jean Stafford
1972 *Angle of Repose* Wallace Stegner
1973 *The Optimist's Daughter* Eudora Welty
1975 *The Killer Angels* Michael Shaara
1976 *Humboldt's Gift* Saul Bellow
1978 *Elbow Room* James Alan McPherson
1979 *The Stories of John Cheever* John Cheever
1980 *The Executioner's Song* Norman Mailer
1981 *A Confederacy of Dunces* John Kennedy Toole
1982 *Rabbit is Rich* John Updike
1983 *The Color Purple* Alice Walker
1984 *Ironweed* William Kennedy
1985 *Foreign Affairs* Alison Lurie
1986 *Lonesome Dove* Larry McMurtry
1987 *A Summons to Memphis* Peter Taylor
1988 *Beloved* Toni Morrison
1989 *Breathing Lessons* Anne Tyler
1990 *The Mambo Kings Play Songs of Love*
     Oscar Hijuelos
1991 *Rabbit at Rest* John Updike
1992 *A Thousand Acres* Jane Smiley
1993 *A Good Scent from a Strange Mountain*
     Robert Olen Butler
1994 *The Shipping News* E Annie Proulx
1995 *The Stone Diaries* Carol Shields
1996 *Independence Day* Richard Ford
1997 *Martin Dressler: The Tale of An American Dreamer*
     Steven Millhauser
1998 *American Pastoral* Philip Roth
1999 *The Hours* Michael Cunningham
2000 *Interpreter of Maladies* Jhumpa Lahiri
2001 *The Amazing Adventures of Cavalier and Clay*
     Michael Chabon
2002 *Empire Falls* Richard Russo
2003 *Middlesex* Jeffrey Eugenides
2004 *The Known World* Edward P Jones
2005 *Gilead* Marilynne Robinson

P

,**Puerto 'Rico** /ˌpwɜːtəʊ ˈriːkəʊ; *AmE* ˌpwɜːrtoʊ
ˈriːkoʊ/ an island in the West Indies, south-east of
*Florida. The capital and largest city is San Juan. **Puerto
Ricans** are US citizens but govern themselves, pay no US
taxes and cannot vote in US elections. The island produces metals, chemicals and sugar and tobacco products. It was discovered by Christopher *Columbus in
1493, captured by Juan *Ponce de León in 1508, passed
to the US in 1898 after the *Spanish-American War, and
became the Commonwealth of Puerto Rico in 1952.
Some Puerto Ricans want it to become a US state, and
many have moved to New York.

,**puffed 'wheat** *n* [U] (*BrE*) grains of wheat which have
been artificially swollen. They are sold in packets and
eaten with milk and sugar as a breakfast food.

,**Puffin 'Books** /ˌpʌfɪn/ a British company that publishes children's paperback books (= books with paper
covers). It was formed in 1941 as part of *Penguin Books.

,**Puffing 'Billy** the name of one of the earliest British
steam trains, first used in 1813 and now kept in the
*Science Museum, London.

,**Puget 'Sound** /ˌpjuːdʒɪt/ a strip of water that extends
into the US state of *Washington from the Pacific Ocean.
*Seattle is on its eastern shore. It has many islands and
is connected to the Pacific by the Strait of Juan de Fuca.

George Vancouver visited it in 1792 and named it after
his assistant, Peter Puget.

Au,gustus 'Pugin /ɔːˌɡʌstəs ˈpjuːdʒɪn/ (1812–52) an
English architect and designer. He was a leading figure
in the English *Gothic Revival, and had an important
influence on the *Arts and Crafts Movement. Pugin was
a *Roman Catholic, and designed several Catholic
churches and cathedrals, but is best remembered for his
work with Charles *Barry on the decoration inside the
*Houses of Parliament(2).

'Pulitzer Prize /ˈpʊlɪtsə; *AmE* ˈpʊlɪtsər/ *n* any of
about 30 awards given in the US each May for achievements in journalism, history, literature, music and other
fields. The Prizes began in 1917 after Joseph Pulitzer
(1847–1911), the owner of the *New York World*, died and
left money to *Columbia University to establish a School
of Journalism and be in charge of the awards.

'Pullman™¹ /ˈpʊlmən/ (*pl* **-mans**) *n* (especially formerly) a comfortable railway carriage, often with beds
for passengers to sleep in during journeys at night. It
was developed by George Pullman (1831–1901) who built
the Pioneer Sleeping Car in 1863 and formed the
Pullman Palace Car Company in 1867. From 1985,
*British Rail applied the name 'Pullman' to its first-class
carriages serving meals, drinks, etc.

Philip **'Pullman**[2] /'pʊlmən/ (1946–) an English writer of fantasy books for children. He is best known for *His Dark Materials*, a trilogy which includes *Northern Lights* (1995), *The Subtle Knife* (1997) and *The Amber Spyglass* (2000) which won the *Whitbread Book of the Year award.

Pulp /pʌlp/ a British pop group formed in 1981 and led by the singer Jarvis Cocker (1962–). The group's songs are often about the experiences and problems of ordinary life, and they include *Do You Remember the First Time?* (1994) and *Common People* (1995).

Pulp 'Fiction a popular US film (1994) directed by Quentin *Tarantino about *Los Angeles criminals. It combines violence and humour. It won the Palme d'Or as the best film at the 1994 Cannes Film Festival. Tarantino and Roger Avary also won *Oscars for the Best Original Screenplay.

Punch /pʌntʃ/ a British humorous magazine, established in 1841, which took its name from the character Punch in *Punch and Judy shows. It became Britain's leading magazine for humorous political and social comment, and included drawings by famous artists such as John *Tenniel. It was originally published every week. In the 1980s it began losing readers to other magazines such as *Private Eye*, and a common joke was that it was only read in dentist's waiting rooms. It stopped appearing in 1992 but appeared again from 1996 to 2002.

Punch and 'Judy the name of a traditional British puppet play, also called a **Punch and Judy show**. Punch (also called **Mr Punch**) is a character with a long curved nose and a big chin who argues with his wife Judy and the other characters (including the policeman and the doctor), shouting in a high voice and hitting them with his stick. He also has a dog called Toby. The characters are glove puppets (= small figures worn over the hand and moved by the fingers) and the show is presented in a special tent, often at the seaside or at parties for children.

a Punch and Judy show

▶ **punctuality**

Most Americans and British people would agree that it is good manners to be **punctual** (= to arrive at the right time) for an appointment. Arriving **on time** for formal events such as a business meeting or an interview is considered important. Many people try to arrive a few minutes early for an appointment to avoid the risk of rushing in at the last minute. Even in less formal situations people are generally expected to think about the person they are meeting and not to keep them waiting unnecessarily.

People are also expected to arrive on time for social events, especially weddings. Traditionally, only the bride is allowed to be late. People are generally more relaxed about the time they arrive for more informal social occasions. When meeting a friend for lunch at a restaurant, people try to arrive at the time arranged, or no more than five minutes late. If they are later than this the person they are meeting will start to think they are not going to come at all. However, when invited to dinner in somebody's home it is actually considered polite to arrive a few minutes late. Under no circumstances should guests arrive early. Some formal invitations to dinner may say 'seven for seven-thirty', meaning that guests should arrive any time after 7 p.m. in order to be ready to eat at 7.30 p.m. At a party, however, people may arrive an hour or more after the start time written on the invitation.

If somebody does arrive late, they are expected to apologize. Depending on the circumstances and how late they are, people may say, 'I'm sorry I'm late' or 'Sorry to keep you waiting'. If they are very late they may feel obliged to give an explanation as well, e.g. 'I'm sorry I'm so late, but the traffic was bad.'

People expect concerts, plays etc. to start at the time advertised, and if they are kept waiting a long time they may start a slow handclap to show that they are impatient. But anyone who arrives late for a show may not be allowed in until there is a convenient break in the performance. People also expect public transport to depart and arrive on time and get very annoyed if delays are frequent. Many people do not like to feel that their time is being wasted and that they are being kept waiting without good reason.

▶ **punishment**

Punishment for people who break the law is decided in a court of law. In the US federal, state and local governments each have their own systems of law and of punishment. The *Constitution forbids 'cruel and unusual punishment', but it is the responsibility of the *Supreme Court to decide whether a punishment is 'cruel and unusual'. In Britain, the Scottish legal system is different from that in England and Wales, but methods of punishment are similar throughout Britain.

When an accused person is found guilty of a crime the judge decides what punishment they should suffer. In both Britain and the US the least serious offences are punished by **fines** which must be paid to the court. Fines (or **fixed penalties** (= fines at a level decided in advance) are often **imposed** for minor traffic offences such as parking illegally and can be paid by post without the need to go to court.

If a fine is not considered adequate, a person may be **sentenced** to do *community service (= work without pay in hospitals, homes for old people, etc.) or be put **on probation** (= required to have regular meetings with a social worker over a set period). When the crime committed is more serious, the **convicted** person is likely to be given a prison sentence. If it is their **first offence** the sentence may be **suspended** (= only carried out if the person is found guilty of another crime) and the person is allowed to remain free on a **conditional discharge**.

If a person is given a prison sentence its length depends on how serious their crime is and on their past **record**. If a person thinks the sentence is too severe they have the right to **appeal** against it in a higher court, which has the power to reduce the sentence. As a reward for good behaviour prisoners are often given **remission** (= are released early). Others get **parole**, which means that they can go free as long as they do not commit any further crimes. In the US the number of people on probation has increased in recent years, as there is not always room in prisons for all those given a prison sentence. A variety of **non-custodial punishments** (= ones not requiring time in prison) have been tried in both Britain and the US, including **electronic tagging**. This punishment requires people to stay in their homes and wear a device that informs the police if they leave.

P

In Britain the maximum sentence that can be **handed down** by a judge is a **life sentence**, which in fact usually means spending about 20–25 years in prison. Convicted murderers are given life sentences. The most serious punishment in the US is the **death penalty**. Not all states allow *capital punishment, and in those that do, before it can be carried out there may be many years of appeals.

punk n **1** [U] a movement in music and fashion that became popular, mainly in Britain, in the late 1970s, with groups such as The *Sex Pistols and the Clash. The music they played, called **punk** or **punk rock**, was usually loud, fast and violent, and expressed anger against society. Punk fashions, introduced by Vivienne *Westwood and others, included torn clothes, safety pins, and brightly coloured hair.
2 (*also* **punk rocker**) [C] a person who dresses in punk fashions and likes punk music.

'punting /ˈpʌntɪŋ/ n [U] the activity of going along a river in a punt (= a long boat with a flat bottom that is moved by pushing against the bottom of the river with a long pole). People go punting for pleasure rather than sport, and punting is especially popular in the British university towns of *Oxford and *Cambridge.

Henry 'Purcell /ˈpɜːsəl, pɜːˈsel; *AmE* pɜːrˈsel/ (1659–95) an English *baroque composer. Many people regard him as the greatest English composer of the period. He wrote many different types of music, including songs, church music and theatre music, and his *Dido and Aeneas* (1689) is considered the first English opera. He was an important influence on later composers, especially *Handel.

the ˌPure Food and 'Drug Act a US law passed in 1906 with the support of President Theodore *Roosevelt. It stated that labels on food and drugs should say exactly what they contain and that no other substances should be added to them. See also MUCK-RAKER.

'Puritan n a member of an English *Protestant group of the 16th and 17th centuries. Puritans believed in simple forms of church ceremony and strict moral behaviour, and were associated with the Parliamentary party during the *Commonwealth of Oliver *Cromwell. Because of this they were treated badly after the *Restoration of King *Charles II, and many left Britain to settle in the US, where their simple way of life and religious discipline became an important influence on American culture.

the ˌPurple 'Heart n a US medal given to members of the armed forces who are wounded in battle. It was established by George *Washington in 1782 as the Badge of Military Merit, but was immediately called the Purple Heart. It is in the form of a purple heart with an image of Washington on it. Compare CONGRESSIONAL MEDAL OF HONOR.

ˌEdward 'Pusey /ˈpjuːzi/ (1800–82) an English *Church of England priest. He was a supporter of *Anglo-Catholicism and became the leader of the *Oxford Movement after John Henry *Newman converted to *Roman Catholicism.

ˌPuss in 'Boots an old children's story that is often used for a *pantomime. It is about a poor young man who owns a cat that can talk and wears boots. By playing a series of tricks on people, the cat makes his owner rich and helps him to marry a princess.

'Pussy Cat, 'Pussy Cat, 'Where Have You 'Been? the title and first line of a traditional children's *nursery rhyme. The full poem is:

> 66 Pussy cat, pussy cat, where have you been?
> I've been up to London to look at the queen.
> Pussy cat, pussy cat, what did you there?
> I frightened a little mouse under her chair. 99

ˌDavid 'Puttnam /ˈpʌtnəm/ (1941–) an English film producer who played a major part in the success of the British film industry in the 1980s. His films include *Midnight Express* (1978), *Chariots of Fire* and *The Killing Fields* (1984). In 1986–88 he was head of the US film company *Columbia Pictures. He was made a *life peer in 1997.

PX /ˌpiː 'eks/ (*pl* **PXs** /ˌpiː 'eksɪz/) (*in full* **post exchange**) n [usually sing] (*AmE*) a general shop on a US army base for members of the armed forces and their families. It sells a wide range of goods, such as clothes, gifts, food, etc. Prices are cheaper than in regular shops because there are no taxes and the PX does not make a profit. Such a shop on a US Air Force base is called a **BX** (base exchange) and on a US Navy base or ship it is called a **commissary**.

Pyg'malion /pɪgˈmeɪliən/ a comic play (1913) by George Bernard *Shaw about a professor, Henry Higgins, who teaches a young *cockney *flower girl, Eliza Doolittle, how to speak in an *upper-class way. She becomes a success in society and falls in love with Higgins. The play was made into a successful musical comedy and a film called *My Fair Lady. Shaw took his title from an ancient Greek story about Pygmalion, an artist who falls in love with a statue he has created. The philologist Henry Sweet (1845–1912) is thought to be the model for Higgins.

ˌJohn 'Pym /ˈpɪm/ (1584–1643) an English politician who led the *Long Parliament against King *Charles I and helped to start the *English Civil War in 1642.

ˌThomas 'Pynchon /ˈpɪntʃən/ (1937–) a US writer of complicated novels. He uses words in humorous ways and often refers to literature and technology. His books include *V* (1963), *The Crying of Lot 49* (1966), *Gravity's Rainbow* (1972), *Vineland* (1990) and *Mason & Dixon* (1997). Pynchon avoids publicity and is rarely seen in public.

Q q

QC /ˌkjuː ˈsiː/ ⇨ QUEEN'S COUNSEL.

the *QE2* /ˌkjuː iː ˈtuː/ a British passenger ship built by *Cunard. The name is an abbreviation for 'Queen Elizabeth II', who launched the ship in 1967. It was the second ship of that name to be built by Cunard, the earlier being the *Queen Elizabeth.

QES /ˌkjuː iː ˈes/ ⇨ QUEEN'S ENGLISH SOCIETY.

QPR /ˌkjuː piː ˈɑː(r)/ ⇨ QUEEN'S PARK RANGERS.

Q-Tip™ n a US make of small plastic stick with a pad of soft cotton on each end. Q-Tips are often used for cleaning the ears but they have many other uses.

'Quaker n any member of the *Society of Friends, a religious group established in England in the 1650s by George *Fox. They were originally called Quakers because members were thought to 'quake' or shake with religious excitement. Quakers worship Christ without any formal ceremony or fixed beliefs, and their meetings often involve silent thought or prayer. They are strongly opposed to violence and war, and are active in education and charity work. There are now Quaker groups in many countries around the world. Many famous businesses in Britain and the US were started by Quakers. They include the Quaker Oats Company, the chocolate firms of Cadbury, Fry and Rowntree, and Barclays and Lloyds banks.

'Quaker 'Oats™ a popular breakfast cereal. The Quaker Oats Company, whose main office is in *Chicago, also makes a range of other food products.

'quango /ˈkwæŋgəʊ; AmE ˈkwæŋgoʊ/ n (pl **-os**) (in Britain) any independent organization established to manage a particular area of public life, with financial support from the government. Examples are the *Arts Councils and the *Equal Opportunities Commission. (The word 'quango' comes from the first letters of 'quasi-autonomous non-governmental organization'.)

ˌMary 'Quant /ˈkwɒnt; AmE ˈkwɑːnt/ (1934–) an English fashion designer. Her shop Bazaar in *King's Road, *Chelsea, London, became famous in the 1960s, and her style included short skirts, short hair and strong make-up.

the 'Quantocks /ˈkwɒntɒks; AmE ˈkwɑːntɑːks/ (also **the ˌQuantock 'hills**) a range of hills in Somerset, England, well known for their attractive scenery.

ˌQuantrill's 'Raiders /ˌkwɒntrɪlz; AmE ˌkwɑːntrɪlz/ n [pl] a small independent military group that fought for the *Confederate States in *Missouri and *Kansas during the *American Civil War. It was led by Captain William Quantrill (1837–65), a former criminal, and included Jesse and Frank *James and the *Younger brothers. The Raiders attacked the town of Lawrence, Kansas, on 21 August 1863, and murdered 150 men and boys who were not soldiers. Quantrill was later killed in a gun fight with US soldiers in *Kentucky.

▶ **quarter days**

In Britain, since the Middle Ages quarter days have marked the beginning of each new **quarter** (= period of three months) of the year. (There are no quarter days in the US.) Rent and interest payments are often made on quarter days, and many contracts, especially concerning property, begin or end then. In former times quarter days were often celebrated with big *fairs. Agricultural workers and servants who wanted to change their jobs went to the fair to try to find a new employer.

The names of quarter days are taken from the calendar of the *medieval Church. In England and Wales the quarter days are: 25 March (**Lady Day**, marking the feast of the Annunciation of the Blessed Virgin Mary), 24 June (**Midsummer Day** or St John the Baptist's Day), 29 September (**Michaelmas Day** or St Michael and All Angels' Day) and 25 December (**Christmas Day**).

In Scotland quarter days are known as **term days**. They formerly followed the Christian calendar and were: 2 February (**Candlemas**), 15 May (***Whit**), 1 August (**Lammas Day**) and 11 November (**Martinmas**). Since 1991 the dates have been changed, although the traditional names have been kept. The dates are now 28 February, 28 May, 28 August and 28 November.

Queen¹ a successful British pop group formed in 1971. Its singer was Freddie *Mercury and the group's albums *A Night at the Opera* (1975), *The Game* (1980) and *Innuendo* (1991) as well as the song *Bohemian Rhapsody* (1975) were all No. 1 in Britain.

ˌEllery 'Queen² /ˌeləri ˈkwiːn/ a detective in many US novels and short stories written between 1929 and 1971 by Frederic Dannay (1905–82) and Manfred B Lee (1905–71) under the same name of Ellery Queen. The first book was *The Roman Hat Mystery* (1929). There were also radio, television and film series, and Dannay and Lee also started *Ellery Queen's Mystery Magazine* in 1941. See also DETECTIVE STORY.

ˌQueen 'Anne **1** a style of architecture and furniture popular in England in the early 18th century, during the rule of Queen *Anne. In furniture its main features were curved legs and simple elegant designs. A later style in architecture, known as Queen Anne or Queen Anne Revival, was popular in England from the 1860s, and used elements such as red brick, high narrow windows and tall chimneys. Its best-known architect was Norman Shaw (1831–1912). **2** ⇨ ANNE².

the ˌQueen E'lizabeth a British passenger ship built by *Cunard, the largest of its type ever built. It was named after Queen Elizabeth, later the *Queen Mother(2), and was launched by her in 1938. It was first used in *World War II to carry soldiers, and after the war carried passengers between England and the US. In 1972 it was destroyed by a fire. See also QE2.

the ˌQueen 'Mary a British passenger ship built by *Cunard and named after Queen *Mary, the wife of King *George V. It was launched by her in 1934 and won the *Blue Riband in 1938, sailing between England and the US in just under four days.

ˌQueen 'Mother **1** a title that may be used by the wife of a British king after his death, if she is the mother of the next king or queen. **2** Queen Elizabeth (1900–2002), the widow (= woman whose husband has died) of King *George VI. She was born Elizabeth Bowes-Lyon, the youngest daughter of the Earl of Strathmore, and married George in 1923, becoming the Duchess of York. He became king in 1936, so she then became known as Queen Elizabeth. When her daughter became Queen *Elizabeth II, she became known as the Queen Mother. She was very popular with the people of Britain.

The ˌQueen of ˈHearts the title and first line of a traditional *nursery rhyme. Characters from the poem appear in *Alice in Wonderland*, where a trial is held at which the knave (= the jack in a pack of cards) is accused of stealing the tarts (= pastries with jam inside) The first verse is:

> 66 The Queen of Hearts
> She made some tarts,
> All on a summer's day;
> The Knave of Hearts
> He stole the tarts,
> And took them clean away. 99

ˌqueen of ˈpuddings (*also* **ˈqueen's ˌpudding**) *n* [U] a traditional English pudding (= cooked sweet dish) made from bread, jam, lemons, sugar and meringue (= a mixture of egg whites and sugar).

Queens /kwiːnz/ the largest of the five *boroughs of New York City. It has a border with *Long Island. It was named after the wife of *Charles II. The area of Queens called Astoria is known for its large Greek community. The John F Kennedy Airport, several racing tracks and the Museum of the Moving Image are all in Queens.

ˈQueen's Aˌward (*also* **Queen's Award for Enterprise**) *n* any of a number of awards given to British companies who have achieved success in any of three areas: International Trade, innovation or sustainable development. Queen's Awards have been given since 1966. Over 100 awards are given each year. A company that wins an award is allowed to display the Queen's Award emblem for five years. The Queen's Award for Enterprise Promotion is a similar award given to individuals.

Queen's Award emblem
© Crown Copyright

the ˌQueen's ˈBench (*also* the ˌQueen's ˈBench Diˌvision) one of the three divisions of the *High Court of Justice in Wales. When a king is ruling it is called the **King's Bench** (**Division**). Its head was formerly the king or queen, but today it is the *Lord Chief Justice. It deals mainly with civil cases, e.g. ones in which money is claimed because of loss or damage, but it may also deal with appeals in criminal cases. See also FAMILY DIVISION, CHANCERY DIVISION. ⇨ note at LEGAL SYSTEM.

the ˈQueensberry Rules /ˈkwiːnzbəri/ *n* [pl] the standard rules for the sport of boxing, named in 1867 in honour of the Marquess of Queensberry (1844–1900). The use of gloves and shorter rounds were among the rules first introduced at that time.

the ˌQueen's ˈBirthday either the real birthday (21 April) or the *Official Birthday of the present British queen, *Elizabeth II.

ˈQueen's Club a sports club in Hammersmith, London, England, established in 1886. It is famous as a centre for *real tennis and *rackets, and the London Grass Court Tennis Championships are held there every year.

ˌQueen's ˈCounsel *n* (*abbr* **QC**) (in Britain) the highest level of *barrister who can speak for the government in court. He or she wears a silk gown (= a long loose piece of clothing worn over other clothes) and is also known as a 'silk'. Other barristers are known as 'juniors'. When a king is ruling the title becomes a **King's Counsel** (**KC**):

Sir Rodney Fisher QC ◇ She was made a QC last year. ⇨ note at LEGAL SYSTEM.

the ˌQueen's ˈEnglish the English language as it is correctly written or spoken in Britain. It is called the **King's English** when a king is ruling.

the ˌQueen's ˈEnglish Soˌciety (*abbr* **QES**) a British charity which aims to encourage the use of good English. It is opposed to many modern developments in the language and encourages traditional teaching methods. The Society publishes a journal, *Quest*, four times a year and organizes talks and conferences about English usage.

ˌQueen's Park ˈRangers (*abbr* **QPR**) an English football club formed in 1885. Its ground is in Loftus Road, near White City, west London.

the ˌQueen's Reguˈlations a set of rules governing the behaviour of the British armed forces, issued as a book. When a king is ruling it becomes the **King's Regulations**.

the ˌQueen's ˈSpeech a speech made by the Queen at the *State Opening of Parliament in the *House of Lords. In it she reads out the government's plans for the coming year. The speech is written for her by members of the government. It is an important occasion and is broadcast on television and radio. When a king is ruling it becomes the **King's Speech**.

ˈQueen's Uniˈversity, ˈBelfast /ˈbelfɑːst; *AmE* ˈbelfæst/ a university in *Belfast, Northern Ireland, established in 1845. It is Northern Ireland's oldest university and was known as Queen's College until 1908.

ˈQueer ˈEye for the ˈStraight ˈGuy a television programme which started in the US and was then also made in Britain. In each programme, five gay (= homosexual) men help a straight (= heterosexual) man to improve his style in areas such as fashion, culture and interior design. The programme was one of the first to show gay life on television.

A ˌQuestion of ˈSport a popular *BBC television quiz show about sport, first shown in 1970, with teams of famous sportspeople. From 1979 to 1997 the questions were asked by David *Coleman and since then they have been asked by Sue *Barker.

ˈQuestion Time (in the British parliament) a period between 2.30 and 3.30 p.m. from Monday to Thursday in which *Members of Parliament can put questions to government ministers in the *House of Commons. See also PRIME MINISTER'S QUESTIONS.

ˈQuestion Time a *BBC television series first shown in 1979 and based on the radio series *Any Questions?* In it a group of four public figures (usually politicians) answer questions on political subjects from an audience. The programme is available on the *Internet and people at home can take part in the debate. The original chairman was Robin Day. It is now David *Dimbleby.

ˈArthur ˈQuiller-ˈCouch /ˈkwɪlə ˈkuːtʃ; *AmE* ˈkwɪlər/ (1863–1944) an English author and professor of English at *Cambridge University (1912–44). He is best known as the editor of the *Oxford Book of English Verse and similar collections, and also wrote novels under the name 'Q'. He was made a *knight in 1910.

Quins /kwɪnz/ ⇨ HARLEQUINS.

ˈQuonset hut™ /ˈkwɒnset; *AmE* ˈkwɑːnset/ *n* a US military shelter. It is a long metal building with a round roof, like a tunnel above ground. The huts are made in sections which can be put together for soldiers to live in. They have also been used for shops, schools, etc. They were first made for the US Navy in 1941 in Quonset Point, *Rhode Island. Compare NISSEN HUT.

the Quorn[1] /kwɔːn; *AmE* kwɔːrn/ one of Britain's best-known fox hunts (= groups of people who hunt foxes), established in *Leicestershire in 1698. In 1991 a film was secretly made showing a fox being torn apart by the Quorn's hounds (= dogs trained to hunt), which shocked many people when it was shown on television. ⇨ note at FIELD SPORTS.

Quorn[™2] /kwɔːn; *AmE* kwɔːrn/ *n* [U] a soft whitish food made from a natural protein, used in cooking as an alternative to meat, especially by vegetarians (= people who do not eat meat).

,**Quote …'Unquote** a British radio quiz show, which has been on *Radio 4 since 1976, in which a number of well-known people try to answer questions about quotations.

Qwest /kwest/ a large US telecommunications company which provides telephone and *Internet services across many states in the western US.

R r

RA /ˌɑːr ˈeɪ/ **1** ⇨ ROYAL ARTILLERY.
2 ⇨ ROYAL ACADEMY.

RAC /ˌɑːr eɪ ˈsiː/ **1** ⇨ ROYAL AUTOMOBILE CLUB.
2 ⇨ ROYAL ARMOURED CORPS.

the ˌRace Reˈlations Acts three British *Acts of
Parliament (1965, 1968 and 1976) together with the Race
Relations Act Amendment (2000) designed to protect the
rights of ethnic minorities living in Britain, and making it
illegal to treat people differently because of their race.
The 1976 Act established the *Commission for Racial
Equality to investigate complaints and improve relations
between the races.

ˌPeter ˈ**Rachman** /ˈrækmən/ (1919–62) a British landlord (= man who owns rented property), who became
widely known for his harsh treatment of his tenants (=
people living in rented property) in London in the 1950s,
charging high rents and sometimes threatening people
with violence. Treating tenants badly is sometimes
called **Rachmanism**.

▶ **racing**

Horse racing has been popular as a **spectator sport**
throughout the British Isles for hundreds of years. It was
also the first sport organized in the American colonies.
This was in 1664 on *Long Island, New York. Four years
later the first American sports trophy, a silver bowl, was
presented there.

There are two main types of horse racing. In **flat racing**
horses run against each other over a set distance. In
*National Hunt racing, also called **steeplechasing**,
horses jump over fences and ditches round a course.
The main **flat races** in Britain each year are the
English Classics, five races for three-year-old horses.
These are the *Derby and the *Oaks (both run at
*Epsom), the Thousand Guineas and the *Two
Thousand Guineas (run at *Newmarket) and the *St
Leger (run at *Doncaster). The four-day *Royal Ascot
meeting is an important social occasion, attended by
members of the *royal family. The most famous
steeplechase is the *Grand National, which was first
run in 1836 and which takes place each spring at
*Aintree. Many people who take no interest in horse
racing have a bet on this race. Racing attracts people
from all levels of British society but only the rich can
afford to own and train a **racehorse**.

In the US flat racing is called **thoroughbred racing** or
just racing; **steeplechasing** is not often seen. The most
famous race is the *Kentucky Derby, which began in
1875 and is run each year at *Louisville, Kentucky. This
is a big event on national television, and informal bets
are made in offices and homes, even in states where
gambling is illegal. Other important races are the
Preakness at *Baltimore, Maryland, and the *Belmont
Stakes at Elmont, New York. The three together are
called the *triple crown. Only 11 horses have won the
triple crown since 1919, and none since 1978. The most
famous was Citation.

Famous British and US jockeys have included Willie
*Carson, Pat *Eddery, Lester *Piggott, Peter
*Scudamore, Willie *Shoemaker, Laffit Pincay, Angel
Cordero, Steve *Cauthen, Kieren Fallon and Frankie
Dettori. Horses famous in Britain have included Arkle,
Desert Orchid, Nijinsky, Red Rum, Best Mate and
*Shergar, and in the US Galant Fox, Secretariat,

Affirmed, Man o' War, Native Dancer and Cigar, which
was chosen **Horse of the Year** in 1995 and 1996.

A type of race popular in America is **harness racing**, in
which a horse pulls a small two-wheeled cart called a
sulky with its driver. The most famous race is the
Hambletonian, popularly called the 'Hambo', at the
Meadowlands Racetrack in *New Jersey. Harness
racing's triple crown is the Hambletonian, the
Kentucky Futurity, and the Yonkers Trot.

Betting on the result of a race is for many British
people an important part of the sport and contributes
to the atmosphere of excitement and tension at a **racecourse**. Before a race starts **bookmakers** take bets, calculate **the odds** and say which horse is the **favourite**.
People can also bet on a race on the *Internet or at a
bookmaker's or **betting shop**. Betting shops show live
television broadcasts of races.

Americans also like to **play the ponies**. People can bet
beside the track or **off-track**. Telephone bets can be
made in some states. Even though many Americans
do not approve of betting, most have accepted horse
racing as an exciting sport and a US tradition. This is
reflected in popular culture. *Camptown Races* is one of
Stephen *Foster's most popular songs. Damon
*Runyon set many of his short stories at race tracks,
the mystery novels of Dick *Francis are set in the
world of racing and *Hollywood has produced popular
films about racing such as *National Velvet* (1945) and *The
Black Stallion* (1980). See also GREYHOUND RACING.

ˈ**rackets** *n* [U] a ball game for two or four people played
with rackets and a small hard ball in an enclosed court.
It first became popular in the 18th century in England,
and is now played mainly at a few boys' *public schools.
*Squash is a similar game that developed from rackets,
and is played in a smaller court with a softer ball.

ˌArthur ˈ**Rackham** /ˈrækəm/ (1867–1939) an English
artist. He is famous for his highly detailed illustrations of
children's books, drawing a world of strange imaginary
creatures such as *Fairy Tales of the Brothers
Grimm* (1900) and *Peter Pan* (1906).

ˈ**racquetball** /ˈrækɪtbɔːl/ *n* [U] a game played by two
or four players using rackets with short handles and a
small ball. The court for play has four walls, and the ball
can be hit against them or the ceiling. The sport began in
the US in the 1960s and is now played in several countries.

RADA /ˈrɑːdə/ ⇨ ROYAL ACADEMY OF DRAMATIC ART.

ˌPaula ˈ**Radcliffe** /ˈrædklɪf/ (1973–) an English long-
distance runner who runs in the 5000 metres, 10000
metres and the marathon. She won the *London marathon in 2002 and in 2003, when she ran it in a world
record time. In 2004 she won the New York Marathon.

▶ **radio**

People in Britain listen to the radio a lot, especially in the
morning and the early evening or while they are in their
cars. Many people rely on the radio to hear the latest
news. Later in the evening television attracts larger audiences. Radio used to be called **the wireless**, but this is
now very old-fashioned.

Around 50% of the British radio audience listen to the
*BBC; the rest listen to independent **commercial
radio**, which has *advertising. There are ten national
BBC **radio stations**. *Radio 1 plays new rock, pop and

dance music, *Radio 2 broadcasts popular music, comedy and documentaries, *Radio 3 offers classical music, *jazz and arts programmes, *Radio 4 broadcasts popular news and current affairs programmes such as *Today, drama and arts programmes, and *Radio 5 Live has sport and news. The other BBC stations,which cater for more specific interests and can be listened to only on **digital radio**, are 1Xtra, Five Live Extra, 6Music, BBC7 and Asian Network. The BBC also operates the *World Service, which broadcasts to most parts of the world. Independent radio stations which broadcast in competition with the BBC and are paid for from advertising include *Classic FM, Virgin Radio, Talk Sport and in London, Capital FM. There are also several commercial digital stations such as Core, Planet Rock and One Word. Programmes broadcast by the BBC and the main independent stations are listed in the *Radio Times and *TV Times and in national newspapers.

Many people also listen to **local radio**. Local radio stations concentrate on local news, traffic reports and pop music. Smaller stations are run by students or by hospitals for their patients. *Ofcom issues licences to commercial broadcasters.

In the US there are more than 13000 radio stations. Many people listen to the radio during **drive time**, the time when they are travelling to or from work. There are no national radio stations, but there are **networks**, groups of stations that are associated with each other. The network **affiliates** (= stations in the group) use some of the same programmes.

The *Federal Communications Commission (FCC), a part of the US government, issues licences to radio stations and says what **frequency** they can use. The FCC also gives a station its **call letters**, the letters that it uses to identify itself. Many stations make their name from their call letters or frequency, e.g. Sunny 95.

Each station has a specific **format** (= style of programmes), which it hopes will be popular with its **listenership** (AmE for 'audience'). Some stations play a particular kind of music, such as 'top 40' (= popular songs) or *country music. Other stations have **talk radio** and **phone-in programmes**, in which radio **presenters** discuss an issue and invite people listening to telephone the station and take part in the discussion. Ethnic radio stations operated by people from particular cultural groups offer programmes in languages other than English. Some stations broadcast religious **programming**. In 2004 *Air America Radio was started as a new network that aims to offer a politically liberal radio to stations nationwide.

Many towns also have a **public radio station**, which is part of the *NPR network. Public radio stations often have public affairs programming and classical music, which is not common on commercial radio. The Broadcasting Board of Governors, an independent agency of the US government, operates the *Voice of America, which brings information about the US, its culture and language to people around the world.

‚Radio 'Caroline a British pirate radio station (= an illegal station), started in 1964, which broadcast pop music from a ship at sea. It was extremely successful and led to the forming of Britain's first official pop music station, *Radio 1, in 1967. Radio Caroline continued broadcasting from a ship until 1990 and can now be heard on *Sky satellite television and the Internet.

'Radio 'City 'Music Hall the largest cinema and theatre in the world, with more than 6000 seats. It is in *Rockefeller Center in New York. It combines films with stage performances by the famous dancers, the *Rockettes. Radio City Music Hall opened in 1932. It was

due to close in 1979 but stayed open because of public demand.

the 'Radio Corpo'ration of A'merica ⇨ RCA.

‚Radio 5 'Live /ˌreɪdiəʊ faɪv 'laɪv; AmE ˌreɪdioʊ/ a British national radio station of the *BBC that broadcasts mainly sport, news and talk programmes. It was established in 1990 and broadcasts 24 hours a day.

Radio 4 /ˌreɪdiəʊ 'fɔː(r); AmE ˌreɪdioʊ 'fɔːr/ a British national radio station of the *BBC. It broadcasts regular news and weather reports as well as plays, comedy shows, live broadcasts of important events, and other programmes. It was established in 1967 and before that was known as the Home Service. It broadcasts from 5.35 a.m. to 1 a.m.

'Radio 'Free 'Europe/‚Radio 'Liberty a private US radio company that broadcasts to central and eastern Europe and the former Soviet Union. It is supported financially by the US government. The main office is in Munich, Germany, and it broadcasts each day in 27 languages to an audience of 20 million. Radio Free Europe was established in 1950 for the European audience, and Radio Liberty began in 1951 for the Soviet one. They joined together in 1976. The programmes have always been about US and world news and topics, including the arts, but they were more political before the end of Communism. Compare VOICE OF AMERICA.

'Radiohead /'reɪdiəʊhed; AmE 'reɪdioʊhed/ a British pop group formed in 1988. Their most successful albums include The Bends (1995) and OK Computer (1997).

Radio 1 /ˌreɪdiəʊ 'wʌn; AmE ˌreɪdioʊ/ a British national radio station of the *BBC that broadcasts pop, rock and dance music and news, and is listened to mainly by young people. It was established in 1967 and broadcasts 24 hours a day.

'Radio Shack™ any of a US group of about 6800 shops that sell a wide range of electrical goods, including computers and video and sound equipment.

Radio 3 /ˌreɪdiəʊ 'θriː; AmE ˌreɪdioʊ/ a British national radio station of the *BBC that broadcasts mainly classical music, but also presents *jazz, plays, talks and readings of short stories and poetry. It was established in 1967 and before that was known as the Third Programme. It broadcasts 24 hours a day.

the ‚Radio 'Times a British magazine published every week by the *BBC. It gives details of the week's radio and television programmes on both BBC and commercial stations, and also contains articles relating to the week's broadcasts. It first appeared in 1923. Compare TV TIMES.

Radio 2 /ˌreɪdiəʊ 'tuː; AmE ˌreɪdioʊ/ a British national radio station of the *BBC that broadcasts popular music, *jazz, news and sport. It was established in 1967 and before that was known as the Light Programme. It broadcasts 24 hours a day.

‚Radley 'College /ˌrædli/ a *public school(1) for boys aged between 13 and 18 near Abingdon, Oxfordshire, England, established in 1847 as St Peter's College, Radley. It is a boarding school (= a school where the pupils live).

‚Henry 'Raeburn /'reɪbɜːn; AmE 'reɪbɜːrn/ (1756–1823) a Scottish painter. He worked in Edinburgh and produced many pictures of important Scottish figures of the time, often in *Highland dress. His best-known painting is probably The Reverend Robert Walker Skating on Duddington Loch (1784). He was made a *knight in 1822.

RAF /ˌɑːr eɪ 'ef; also informal ræf/ the abbreviation for the **Royal Air Force** (= the British air force). ⇨ note at ARMED FORCES.

R

,Stamford '**Raffles** /ˌstæmfəd 'ræflz; AmE ˌstæmfərd/ (1781–1826) an English politician. He is best known for buying *Singapore for the *East India Company in 1819 and for developing the island as a commercial centre. The famous Raffles Hotel there is named after him. He was also the governor of Java (1815–17) and Sumatra (1818–23) and wrote a *History of Java* (1817). In 1826 Raffles became the first President of *London Zoo. He was made a *knight in 1817.

'**ragga** /'rægə/ (also **dancehall reggae**) n [U] a type of pop music that developed from *reggae in *Jamaica in the early 1980s, using fast electronic drum and bass sounds, and a singing style similar to *rap.

The 'Ragged 'Trousered Phi'lanthropists
/'trɑʊzəd; AmE 'trɑʊzərd/ a novel by Robert Tressall (c. 1870–1911) about the harsh lives of working people in the early 20th century. It was published after his death, in 1918, and is still highly regarded for its comments on industrial relations.

'**ragtime** n [U] a style of music developed by *African Americans in the 1890s and played especially on the piano. It led to the development of traditional *jazz. Ragtime is played with a strong rhythm which is 'ragged', i.e. not regular. Pieces of ragtime music are often called **rags**. The most famous ragtime musicians were 'Jelly Roll' *Morton and Scott *Joplin.

'**Railcard** /'reɪlkɑːd; AmE 'reɪlkɑːrd/ n a card that can be bought at train stations in Britain by students, people over 60, disabled people and other groups. It allows them to buy cheaper train tickets for a period of one year.

'**Railtrack** /'reɪltræk/ a company formed in 1994 as part of the privatization of British railways. It owned all of Britain's railways and train stations, and was responsible for signals and train schedules (= times of running). Smaller companies which rented the track and stations from Railtrack and provided the train services. When the company failed in 2001, it was replaced with *Network Rail.

R

▶ **railways and railroads**
The world's first railway along which passengers travelled on trains pulled by **steam locomotives** was opened in 1825 between *Stockton and Darlington in north-east England. By the early 1900s, when railways reached the height of their popularity, there were about 23 000 miles/37 000 kilometres of railway **track**. *Victorian engineers such as Isambard Kingdom *Brunel designed bridges for the railway, and architects designed elaborate station buildings such as *St Pancras in London.

The railways played a vital role in Britain's industrial development during the 19th and early 20th centuries. Later, with the invention of the internal combustion engine (= the type of engine used in cars), *road transport became more popular for both goods and passengers. In 1947 regional railway companies were nationalized and became *British Rail (later BR), but following the Beeching report in 1963 many **lines** (= routes) were closed in order to save money. In 1994 the government decided that BR should be returned to private ownership. Tracks and stations were made the responsibility of a company called *Railtrack, while trains were once again operated by several companies on a regional basis. People have been encouraged to use trains and other forms of public transport to help reduce fuel consumption and pollution.

The railway network connects all the major towns in Britain, and now, via the *Channel Tunnel, links Britain with France and Belgium. Railways are used for both short and long journeys, for *commuting to work each day, and for transporting **freight**. In 2003 more than a

billion journeys were made by rail in Britain and rail travel had increased by 36% in ten years. Some routes are now electrified and have high-speed trains. Others still rely on diesel-powered locomotives. Some trains are old, dirty and overcrowded. They also have a reputation for being late, and jokes are often made about the excuses given for delays. These have included 'leaves on the line' in autumn, and 'the wrong kind of snow'. Tickets are quite expensive, although students and old people can get **railcards** which entitle them to cheaper fares.

Following several major railway accidents and the failure of the Railtrack company in 2002 the government set up *Network Rail to be responsible for the railway system used by the **train operating companies**, private companies which run the trains. These companies provide information about trains to the public through their organization, National Rail.

Most Americans have never been on a train. This is sad because the **railroads**, as they are generally called in the US, were the means by which the *Old West was settled. Passenger trains today mainly serve commuters around large cities. The only major long-distance railway business is done by **freight trains** (BrE also **goods trains**).

The first US rail company was the Baltimore & Ohio Railroad in 1828, but its **cars** (BrE **carriages**) were pulled by horses. Steam power was used by the 1830s, and the *Pullman car was invented in 1856. The *Civil War led to the rapid development of railroads, and the nation was connected from east to west in 1869 when the *Union Pacific Railroad and Central Pacific joined their tracks in *Utah. The 20th century brought more powerful locomotives and huge stations, like *Grand Central in New York. The greatest period of US railroads began in the middle of the 19th century and lasted about 100 years. This time has been celebrated with popular songs like *I've Been Working on the Railroad*, *Freight Train Blues*, *John Henry, *Chattanooga Choo Choo, Orange Blossom Special* and *Casey Jones*. Trains and railroad workers were also the subjects of many films and novels.

After *World War II car ownership greatly increased and people no longer used trains as a means of transport. Union Pacific, once known for its two-level 'dome lounge cars' from which passengers could see the scenery, stopped long-distance passenger services in 1971. *Amtrak, a company controlled by the government, now runs the California Zephyr, the Texas Eagle and other trains but it is not very successful in attracting passengers.

Some Americans are **train buffs** and take special steam locomotive trips. Americans also collect model trains, some of which, including the heavy Lionel sets from the 1940s, are now valuable. In Britain old and young alike visit railway museums at e.g. Didcot and *York. **Trainspotting** (= recording the names and registration numbers of locomotives) used to be a popular hobby, especially for boys, but is less common now.

,Rainbow '**Bridge** the largest natural bridge of rock in the world. It is on Lake Powell in the US state of *Utah, near the border with *Arizona. It is 278 feet/85 metres long, and it curves upward to a height of 309 feet/94 metres. It has always been an important place for the *Navajo people and was made a US national monument in 1916.

,*Rainbow '*Warrior** a ship owned by the organization *Greenpeace, used by them in protests against damage done to the environment at sea. In 1985 it was sunk by French soldiers as it took part in protests against French nuclear testing in the South Pacific Ocean. One member of the crew was killed. A new ship, *Rainbow Warrior II*, replaced it in 1989.

'rain dance *n* a dance performed by many *Native American groups to bring rain. Rain dances sometimes last several days.

ˌMount 'Rainier
/'reɪniə(r)/ the highest mountain in the Cascade Range of the US state of *Washington. It is 14 410 feet/4 395 metres high and is a volcano that is no longer active (= a mountain from the top of which melted rock and gases once exploded with great force). It is in **Mount Rainier National Park**.

Mount Rainier

'Rain Man a US film (1988) which won four *Oscars, directed by Barry Levinson. It is about the relationship between two brothers, one of whom is autistic (= suffering from a serious mental condition which makes him unable to communicate properly). The two brothers are played by Dustin *Hoffman (who won an Oscar) and Tom *Cruise.

the Raj /rɑːdʒ/ (*also* **the ˌBritish 'Raj**) *n* [U] the period of British rule in India. It is often used to refer to the styles of dress, furniture, architecture, etc. and social attitudes of the British in India in the first half of the 20th century: *The food is excellent, and the decor and service are straight out of the Raj.*

The ˌRaj Quar'tet /ˌrɑːdʒ/ a series of four novels (1966–75) by Paul *Scott about the last years of British rule (= the Raj) in India. In 1983 a popular television version of the novels was made under the title The *Jewel in the Crown.

A ˌRake's 'Progress a series of eight paintings (1733–5) by William *Hogarth telling the story of a rake (= a fashionable young man who leads a wild and immoral life) who finally dies in *Bedlam (= a hospital in London for the mentally ill). Hogarth later made the paintings into a popular series of engravings (= cheap printed copies). The phrase 'rake's progress' is still used about somebody ruining their life by wild and immoral behaviour.

'Raleigh¹ /'ræli/ a British bicycle company, established in Nottingham in 1890: *My first bike was a Raleigh.*

ˌWalter 'Raleigh² (*also* **Ralegh**) /'ræli, 'rɑːli, 'rɔːli/ (c. 1552–1618) an English explorer, politician and soldier. He began his career fighting the Spanish and the Irish, and was made a *knight in 1584 by Queen *Elizabeth I. With her support he made several journeys to North America (1584–9) and South America (1595), bringing back tobacco and the potato, but failed to establish a permanent base there. After the death of Elizabeth he was put in prison for treason for 13 years, during which he wrote his *History of the World* (1614). In 1616 he was released by King *James I to look for gold in South America. He was not successful in this, and when he returned he was punished by having his head cut off. One of the most popular stories about Raleigh describes how he spread his coat over a piece of wet ground so that Queen Elizabeth could walk over it.

ˌRaleigh Inter'national /ˌræli/ an international organization based in Britain for young people between 17 and 25. It organizes journeys, usually of 10 weeks, to distant countries for a combination of adventure and useful environmental and community projects. It began

as Operation Raleigh in 1980, following the success of *Operation Drake.

ˌMarie 'Rambert /'rɑːmbeə(r); AmE 'rɑːmber/ (1888–1982) a British ballet dancer and director, born in Poland. After dancing with Sergei Diaghilev's company (1912–13) she opened a ballet school in London (1920) which developed into the *Rambert Dance Company. She was made a *dame(2) in 1962. See also ASHTON.

the ˌRambert 'Dance ˌCompany /ˌrɑːmbeə; AmE ˌrɑːmber/ a British dance company, based in London, which developed out of the ballet school started by Marie *Rambert in 1920. From 1926, the school's students gave regular public performances, and in 1934 a dance company was officially formed, then called the Ballet Rambert. It was directed by Marie Rambert until 1966. It then began to perform mostly modern dance and has performed all over the world. It took its present name in 1987.

the Rambert Dance Company

the 'Ramblers' Associˌation a British association formed in 1935 to keep *public footpaths open for ramblers (= people who enjoy walking in the countryside), and to make sure that the countryside is protected.

'Rambo /'ræmbəʊ; AmE 'ræmboʊ/ a US film character played by Sylvester *Stallone in three popular films based on the novel *First Blood* (1972) by David Morrell. Rambo is a powerful and violent man with big muscles who fights against evil forces threatening the world. The films were *First Blood* (1982), *Rambo: First Blood Part II* (1985) and *Rambo III* (1988). The name Rambo is sometimes used humorously when referring to a tough and aggressive person or way of behaving: *The senator used Rambo methods to get his bill passed.*

ˌRampton 'Hospital /ˌræmptən/ a special hospital near Retford in *Nottinghamshire, England, for men and women who are mentally ill and are considered to be dangerous. Many of them have committed violent crimes and are carefully guarded.

ˌGordon 'Ramsay /'ræmzi/ (1966–) a British chef, writer and broadcaster who owns a number of restaurants. He has written several cookery books and has appeared in television series about working in restaurant kitchens. He is famous for his rudeness and for shouting at people in the kitchen.

ˌAlf 'Ramsey /'ræmzi/ (1920–99) an English football player and manager. He was manager of the England team that won the World Cup in 1966, and was made a *knight in the following year. His career as a player with Southampton and *Tottenham Hotspur was also highly successful, and he played for the England team 32 times.

'ranch house *n* (*AmE*) a type of house on one level with a central room and other rooms connected to it on all sides, sometimes by passages. It copies the style of

R

houses on western ranches (= large farms), and is now common in town suburbs (= outer areas).

,**R and 'B** /ˌɑːr ənd 'biː/ a style of music which originally developed from African American music such as *blues, *jazz and *gospel. It became known as *rhythm and blues in the 1950s and 1960s. Modern R and B includes a wide range of black pop music with influences from *hip-hop, *funk and *soul.

,**R and 'R** /ˌɑːr ən 'ɑː(r)/ **1** an abbreviation for 'rest and recreation' (or 'rest and relaxation' or 'rest and recuperation'). It is now generally used to mean any holiday/vacation, but was originally a US military expression for a time when soldiers were allowed to relax during a war or after very hard work.
2 an abbreviation for *rock and roll.

'**Range ,Rover**™ /ˌrəʊvə(r); AmE ˌroʊvər/ a make of car first produced by *Rover in 1970. It is a large, high vehicle, designed for use over rough ground in the country but is also popular with wealthy people who live in cities. See also LAND ROVER.

'**Rangers** /'reɪndʒəz; AmE 'reɪndʒərz/ a football team from *Glasgow, Scotland, with a ground at *Ibrox Stadium. It was established in 1873 and has had many successes in Scottish football, including several wins in the *Scottish FA Cup. Its traditional rival in Glasgow is *Celtic, which has mainly *Roman Catholic supporters, while Rangers have mainly *Protestant supporters.

,**J Arthur 'Rank** /'ræŋk/ (1882–1972) an English businessman who established two highly successful companies, the *Rank Group and *Rank Hovis McDougall. He was a *Methodist and became involved in films in 1933 as a way of spreading religious ideas. In 1935 Rank helped to establish *Pinewood Studios and in 1941 he gained control of Gaumont and the *Odeon Theatre group, which all became part of the Rank Organization. He was made a *life peer in 1957.

the '**Rank Group** /'ræŋk/ a large British company, established by J Arthur *Rank as the Rank Organization, originally known for making films. Its symbol, often seen at the beginning of films, was a man striking a large gong (= a metal disc that makes a loud noise when struck). The Rank Group owns casinos, *bingo halls and the *Hard Rock Cafe restaurants.

'**Rank 'Hovis Mc'Dougall** /'ræŋk 'həʊvɪs mək'duːgl; AmE 'hoʊvɪs/ ⇨ RHM.

Ian Rankin /'ræŋkɪn/ (1960–) a Scottish crime writer who is best known for his series of novels set in *Edinburgh about the detective **Inspector Rebus**.

,**Arthur 'Ransome** /'rænsəm/ (1884–1967) an English author of children's books. He is best known for his adventure story *Swallows and Amazons, the first of 12 books with the same characters, mostly set in the *Lake District. He also worked as a journalist in Russia during *World War I.

,**Esther 'Rantzen** /ˌestə 'ræntsən; AmE ˌestər/ (1940–) an English television presenter and producer, best known from the programme That's Life! She has also presented programmes about child abuse, including Childwatch (1987), and established the charity *ChildLine. Since 1999 she has presented the discussion show That's Esther.

rap n [U] a style of popular music with a strong beat to which words are spoken rather than sung. It first became popular in the early 1980s and well-known performers include *Snoop (Doggy) Dogg, *50 Cent, the *Beastie Boys and *Eminem. There are many styles of rap and it has had important influence on other types of popular music. Some bands combine aspects of jazz and rap music while others, such as the *Red Hot Chili Peppers mix it with *rock and *funk. It is also important to the music of many *nu metal bands. One style of the music, **gangsta rap**, is often criticized for its violent songs. See also HIP HOP.

▶ **rap** v [I,T] (-**pp**-) to perform rap music or speak in the style of rap.

*The ,**Rape of the 'Lock** a long humorous poem (1712) by Alexander *Pope, about a man who cuts off a small piece of a woman's hair (= a lock). Pope describes this rather unimportant act in grand and elegant language, which gives the poem its humour.

,**Rasta'farian** /ˌræstə'feəriən; AmE ˌræstə'feriən/ (also informal **Rasta**) n a person who believes in **Rastafarianism**, a religion that began in *Jamaica in the 1930s. It is based on the ideas of Marcus *Garvey, who taught that black people around the world would one day return to Africa, and that they should worship the ruler of Ethiopia, Haile Selassie (1892–1975). Rastafarians wear their hair in long twisted pieces, called dreadlocks, sometimes with red, gold, black and green hats. They also often smoke the drug marijuana, which they call ganja. Many *reggae musicians are Rastafarians.

the **rates** /reɪts/ n [pl] a tax which was formerly paid in Britain by owners of houses and businesses and used to provide money for local services. Rates on houses were replaced in 1989–90 by the *community charge, also known as the *poll tax, which taxed everyone registered to vote in a particular area. This was very unpopular and caused widespread protests until it was itself replaced in 1993 by the *council tax, a compromise between the rates and the poll tax. ⇨ note at LOCAL GOVERNMENT.

,**Dan 'Rather** /'ræðə(r)/ (1931–) a US television journalist who presented CBS Evening News from 1981, when he replaced Walter *Cronkite, until 2005. He won many *Emmy awards for his reporting. Compare BROKAW, JENNINGS.

'**rationing** /'ræʃnɪŋ/ n [U] a system of limiting and sharing food, clothing, fuel, etc., especially in times of war. Rationing was introduced in Britain and the US during both world wars, and continued after World War II in Britain for several years. People were given **ration books** which showed how much food, etc. they were allowed to buy each week. Many people grew extra food to feed their families and there was a black market (= illegal trade) in many goods.

,**Terence 'Rattigan** /'rætɪgən/ (1911–77) an English writer of plays, including the comedy French Without Tears (1936) and more serious works such as The Winslow Boy (1946) and The Browning Version (1948). Several of them were made into films. Rattigan was made a *knight in 1971.

,**Simon 'Rattle** /'rætl/ (1955–) an English conductor. He joined the *City of Birmingham Symphony Orchestra in 1980 and became well known for conducting both modern and traditional classical music. He has been a conductor of the Los Angeles Philharmonic. He became Chief Conductor of the Berlin Philharmonic Orchestra in 2002. He was made a *knight in 1994.

,**Robert 'Rauschenberg** /'raʊʃənbɜːg; AmE 'raʊʃənbɜːrg/ (1925–) a US artist who was one of the leading figures of *pop art. He became famous in the 1950s for his 'combine' paintings which include real objects such as bottles, nails and news photographs.

rave n a large party for young people, with dancing to loud, fast electronic music such as *house or *techno. Raves were popular in Britain in the late 1980s and early 1990s, and were often held illegally, in large buildings or outdoors, with the police trying to prevent them. They were especially associated with the use of the drug Ecstasy.

The **'Raven** the best-known poem by Edgar Allan *Poe, first published in 1845. In it a man is visited by a raven (= a large black bird) and asks it when he will see his lost lover again. The bird repeatedly answers 'Nevermore'.

'Rawlplug™ /'rɔːlplʌg/ *n* a British make of small hollow plastic tube that can be placed into a hole to allow a screw to be fixed firmly in position, e.g. in a wall.

'Ray-Bans™ /'reɪ bænz/ *n* [pl] a popular US make of sunglasses (= spectacles with dark glass to protect the eyes from the sun). They were originally developed for US air force pilots but are now regarded as very fashionable.

,Claire **'Rayner** /'reɪnə(r)/ (1931–) an English agony aunt (= journalist who replies to people's letters about their personal problems). She worked for newspapers, radio and television. She has also published many books giving medical and personal advice, and is the author of several novels and an autobiography.

'Raytheon /'reɪθiən/ a large US company started in 1922 and based in Waltham, *Massachusetts. It specializes in areas such as computing, technology and engineering but is particularly known for the advanced weapons it produces, especially missiles (= weapons that are sent through the air and explode when they hit their target). Most of the equipment Raytheon produces is sold to the US government.

RCA /ˌɑː siː 'eɪ; *AmE* ˌɑːr/ (*in full* the **Radio Corporation of America**) a large US company producing electronic equipment, especially for radio, television and music. Started in 1919, it is owned by *General Electric. It began the *RKO film company in 1921, sent the first photographs by radio (from London to New York) in 1924, and established *NBC in 1926.

RE /ˌɑːr 'iː/ ⇨ ROYAL ENGINEERS.

,*Reader's* **'Digest** a US magazine, published each month, which is one of the most popular in the world. It was started in 1922 by DeWitt and Lila Wallace and is now read in 19 languages by more than 100 million people. It originally contained short versions of articles already published, but now has many written by its own journalists. The Reader's Digest Association also sells books, music and other products.

'Reading /'redɪŋ/ a large town in southern England, governed by a *unitary authority. It is famous for its music festivals, especially the Reading Rock Festival. Oscar *Wilde spent two years in Reading prison (1895–7), and he wrote his *Ballad of Reading Gaol there.

,Ronald **'Reagan** /'reɪgən/ (1911–2004) a US film actor and later *Republican(1) politician who became the 40th US *President (1981–9). He was also governor of *California (1966–74). He was a popular president, especially because of his ability to explain the government's plans and problems in a simple way to ordinary people. He reduced taxes and increased government spending on defence. He was strongly opposed to Communism and famously described the Soviet Union as 'the evil empire' but reached agreements with it to reduce the number of nuclear weapons in the two countries. In 1981 Reagan was shot and wounded by a person who was mentally ill. In his last years in power, he was criticized for the *Iran-Contra affair. Some people also said that his wife Nancy had too much power. He was diagnosed as having Alzheimer's disease in 1992. See also INF TREATY, REAGANOMICS.

> 66 You can tell a lot about a fellow's character by his way of eating jelly beans. 99
> Ronald Reagan

,**Reaga'nomics** /ˌreɪgə'nɒmɪks; *AmE* ˌreɪgə'nɑːmɪks/ *n* [U] the economic policies of US President Ronald *Reagan. They involved reducing taxes for companies to help them increase production and create jobs. Government spending was also cut, mainly in the area of social welfare. This made the economy strong but greatly increased the *national debt.

re,**ality T'V** (*in full* **reality television**) a type of television programme which is based on filming ordinary people in 'real' situations instead of actors. The first reality TV shows were documentaries which filmed the lives of ordinary people. These were sometimes called **fly-on-the-wall** documentaries. Later came shows such as *The Real World* on *MTV which films the daily lives of a group of people who have agreed to live together in a house, and *The Osbournes* and *The Anne Nicole Show* which film the lives of famous people. Some reality TV shows use hidden cameras to film the reactions of ordinary people to different, often strange or embarrassing, situations. The best known of these was *Candid Camera and more recent shows include *Trigger Happy TV* in the UK. **Reality game shows** such as *Big Brother* and *Survivor* film a group of people who are put together for a period of time and have to compete to win a prize.

,**real 'tennis** /ˌriːəl/ *n* [U] a very old form of tennis, played by two or four people in a large indoor court with rackets, a hard ball and a net. It was originally played by British kings and noblemen ('real' is an old form of the word *royal*), and lawn *tennis developed from it. Real tennis has complicated rules. There are very few courts, so not many people play the game.

,*Rebel Without a* **'Cause** the US film (1955) which made James *Dean famous. He plays a young person who resists his parents' authority and gets into trouble with the police. Many US parents were shocked by the film because it showed children from good families who were not satisfied with their comfortable and respectable style of life.

'recall *n* [U] (in the US) a system in some states which allows voters to remove an elected official, such as a governor, from office because of corruption or bad management. If enough signatures are collected, a **recall election** takes place in which voters decide whether the official should stay or be replaced.

▶ **Received Pronunciation**

Received Pronunciation, often called **RP**, is the accent that is widely accepted as the standard accent in British English. Although only about 5% of British people speak with an RP accent, it is considered the correct form of speech. Pronunciations given in most dictionaries are RP, or an adapted form of it.

RP is a social accent not linked to any particular region of Britain, though it developed originally from the form of *Middle English spoken around London. At that time London was the economic centre of England and the place where people were trained for professions such as the law. From the 15th century it became a centre for publishing. RP was the accent of upper-class people, and of the most highly educated people. The connection between RP and education was important in establishing the accent.

People became increasingly conscious of accent and by the late 19th century it was considered necessary to adopt RP and lose any trace of a regional accent in order to have a successful career, especially in the army or government. RP was spread among children of the upper and upper middle classes through the *public school system. Others took elocution lessons in order to learn to speak 'properly'. Later, RP was taught in state schools. The *public school accent and the **Oxford accent**, the accent adopted by some members of *Oxford

University, which many former public school pupils attended, are now considered by many to be rather artificial.

The RP spoken by members of the upper class, including the *royal family, is called **advanced RP** or **marked RP**. Many people think that, like the Oxford accent, it sounds affected. It may be described as 'clipped' if it is spoken with a tight mouth, or 'plummy' if it sounds as though the speaker had a plum in his or her mouth. The vowel sounds of marked RP are distinctive, for example the 'a' in *sat* sounds more like the 'e' in *set*, the short 'o' in *cost* sounds like the long 'o' in *for*, and *really* and *rarely* sound the same.

The status of RP was strengthened in the 1920s after the *BBC began radio broadcasts. For a long time announcers spoke with RP accents, and the accent became known as the **BBC accent**. Standard English, the form of English grammar considered correct, is, when spoken with an RP accent, sometimes called **BBC English**, **Oxford English**, or **the Queen's/King's English**.

Today the BBC uses announcers with regional accents although very strong regional accents are avoided because they would be difficult for many listeners to understand. Speakers with slight Scottish or Welsh accents are often chosen because these accents are considered more classless than English regional accents on the one hand or RP on the other. Most educated people now speak a modified form of RP with some regional variation.

,recom'mended re'tail 'price n (abbr **RRP**) (in Britain) a price that a company recommends for one of its products. Shops may then sell the product at this price, but are not legally required to do so.

,Recon'struction n [U] the period of about ten years after the American *Civil War during which the *Confederate States were brought back into the US. US political and military forces controlled and punished the southern states. Laws were passed making *slavery illegal and giving African Americans the right to vote and hold public office. White Southerners were upset by many Reconstruction practices, such as unusual elections that put former slaves in state governments. This was one cause of the growth of the *Ku Klux Klan.

Red a British women's magazine published every month which contains articles and photographs about fashion, beauty, famous people and issues of interest to women.

the ,Red 'Arrows a team of planes from the British *Royal Air Force which is famous for its skilful flying displays. The planes are red, and let out long streams of coloured smoke.

the ,Red 'Berets a popular name for the British Army's *Parachute Regiment. Compare GREEN BERETS, RED DEVILS.

'redcoat /'redkəʊt; AmE 'redkoʊt/ n **1** a name for a British soldier in the 17th, 18th and 19th centuries, when red uniforms were worn.
2 a name for a worker at a *Butlin's holiday camp, who wears a red jacket and whose job is to help and entertain guests.

the ,Red 'Cross the short name used in non-Muslim countries for the International Movement of the Red Cross and the Red Crescent, an international organization formed in 1864 which works to relieve suffering caused by wars and natural disasters. In Muslim countries it is known as the **Red Crescent**. The symbol of the Red Cross is a red cross on a white background. There are Red Cross Societies in many countries around the world, including Britain and the US, which work as part of the international organization and also provide help

locally in cases of need. The American Red Cross organizes the system of blood donation by volunteers.

the ,Red 'Devils a team from the British *Parachute Regiment who are famous for their skilful skydiving displays, in which they jump from planes and let out streams of coloured smoke as they fall.

,Otis 'Redding /,əʊtɪs 'redɪŋ; AmE ,oʊtɪs/ (1941–67) a US singer of *soul music. His successful records included *I've Been Loving You Too Long* (1965) and *My Girl* (1966). The magazine *Melody Maker* chose him as the 'World No 1 Male Singer' in 1967, just before he died in a plane crash. The year after his death, he won a *Grammy award for *The Dock of the Bay*.

,red 'ensign /,red 'ensən/ (also informal **red duster**) n [usually sing] the flag of the British *merchant navy, first used in 1674. It is red with a *Union Jack in the top left quarter: *The ship was flying the red ensign.*

The ,Red 'Flag the official song of the British *Labour Party, written in 1889 by James Connell (1853–1929) and often sung at the end of large party meetings. The red flag is the international symbol of revolution and socialism. The song ends with its best-known line, 'We'll keep the red flag flying here.'

,Robert 'Redford /'redfəd; AmE 'redfərd/ (1936–) a US actor who also directs and produces films. His acting roles include parts in *Butch Cassidy and the Sundance Kid* (1969), *The Sting* (1973), *All the President's Men* (1976), *Out of Africa* (1986), *Indecent Proposal* (1993) and *The Horse Whisperer* (1998). He won an *Oscar as Best Director for *Ordinary People* (1980) and an honorary Oscar, as a Lifetime Achievement Award, in 2002. Redford established the Sundance Film Festival in 1978 at his Sundance Institute in Park City, *Utah. He also leads campaigns for a cleaner environment.

,Michael 'Redgrave¹ /'redgreɪv/ (1908–85) an English actor. He is especially remembered for his stage roles in plays by *Shakespeare and Chekhov, but he also acted in many films, including *The Lady Vanishes* (1938) and *The Browning Version* (1950). He was made a *knight in 1959. He was married to the actor Rachel Kempson and their children Lynn, Corin and Vanessa *Redgrave are also actors.

,Steve 'Redgrave² /'redgreɪv/ (1962–) an English sportsman who won gold medals in five Olympic Games (1984, 1988, 1992, 1996 and 2000) in the sport of rowing, as well as many other international competitions. He retired from rowing in 2000 and was made a *knight in 2001.

Va,nessa 'Redgrave³ /'redgreɪv/ (1937–) an English actor on stage, on television and in films. She began acting with her father, Michael *Redgrave, in 1958, and became well known for her stage performances in *Shakespeare plays. She won an Oscar for the film *Julia* (1977) and her other films include *Blow-Up* (1967), *Howards End* (1991) and *Mrs Dalloway* (1997). She is also known for her involvement in left-wing politics and opposing nuclear weapons. Her daughters Natasha and Joely Richardson, her brother Corin Redgrave and her niece Jemma Redgrave are also actors.

the 'Red 'Hand of 'Ulster /'ʌlstə(r)/ the symbol of *Ulster (= Northern Ireland), shown as a red upright hand cut off at the wrist. It was originally the symbol of one of Ulster's ruling families, the O'Neills.

,Red ,Hot ,Chili 'Peppers a US rock band started in 1983 whose music combines *funk, *hip hop and rock. The band members, especially leader singer Anthony Kiedis (1962–), are particularly known for playing and appearing in videos wearing only a few clothes. Their albums include *Blood Sugar Sex Magik* (1991), *Californication* (1999) and *By the Way* (2002).

R

Red 'Hot Organi,zation (*abbr* **RHO**) a charity set up in 1989 to raise money for the treatment of the disease AIDS around the world. It mostly receives money from the sale of pop music albums.

Red 'Nose Day (in Britain) a day of events and activities organized every two years by *Comic Relief to collect money for charity. Performances by famous comedians are shown on television, and people can also buy and wear red plastic noses, or buy larger noses to put on the fronts of cars, to show their support. The first Red Nose Day was in 1988.

Little Red 'Riding Hood ⇨ LITTLE RED RIDING HOOD.

Red River 'Valley a traditional US song, sung especially by *cowboys. It is about a man who is told that the woman he loves is going to move away. It begins with the line 'From this valley they say you are going' and ends:

> 66 Come and sit by my side, if you love me.
> Do not hasten to bid me adieu.
> Just remember the Red River Valley
> And the cowboy who loved you so true. 99

the 'Red Sox /sɒks; *AmE* sɑːks/ a *Major League Baseball team based in *Boston which was first founded in 1893. The team plays in the *American League, East Division at Fenway Park. They wear red and white and the team logo shows two red socks.

'redwood¹ (*also* **se'quoia**) /sɪˈkwɔɪə/ *n* a very tall tree with reddish wood, found mainly near the US coasts of *California and southern *Oregon. The **giant redwood** (or **giant sequoia**) is the tallest tree in the world. It can grow to more than 300 feet/92 metres tall and live more than 2000 years. Many redwoods grow in the **Redwood National Park**, a *World Heritage Site in north-western California, and in the **Sequoia National Park** in southern central California.

John 'Redwood² /ˈredwʊd/ (1951–) a British *Conservative politician and leading *Euro-sceptic. He was Secretary of State for Wales between 1993 and 1995, when he lost a contest against John *Major for the leadership of the Conservative Party. Redwood again tried without success to become leader after the 1997 election. He has served as a member of the *Shadow Cabinet from 1997 to 2000 and since 2004.

'Reebok /ˈriːbɒk; *AmE* ˈriːbɑːk/ a company that makes sports shoes, usually worn by young people for fashion rather than sport: *a pair of Reeboks*.

Carol 'Reed¹ /riːd/ (1906–76) an English film director best remembered for his film of the Graham *Greene novel *The *Third Man*. His other films include *Our Man in Havana* (1959) and *Oliver!* (1968), a *musical version of *Oliver Twist* by Charles *Dickens, for which Reed won an *Oscar. He was made a *knight in 1952.

Lou 'Reed² /riːd/ (1942–) a US pop singer who plays the guitar and writes songs, many of which have serious or disturbing themes. He began in 1967 with the *Velvet Underground pop group before following a career on his own. His successful albums have included *Transformer* (1972), *New York* (1989), *Songs for Drella* (1990) and *The Raven* (2003).

Martin 'Rees /riːs/ (1942–) an English astronomer whose work has been important for the study of galaxies (= very large groups of stars). He was made a *knight in 1992 and became *Astronomer Royal in 1995.

Christopher 'Reeve /riːv/ (1952–2004) a US actor best known for his role as *Superman in four films. His other films included *The Bostonians* (1984) and *Remains of the Day* (1993). Reeve fell from his horse while riding in 1995 and became paralysed (= unable to move his body). In 1996 he established a charity which has given a lot of money for research into such injuries.

Jim 'Reeves¹ /riːvz/ (1924–64) a US singer of *country music, known for his smooth voice. His popular name was 'Gentleman Jim'. He joined the *Grand Ole Opry in 1955, and his successful records included *Four Walls* (1957), *He'll Have to Go* (1959) and *Distant Drums* (1966). Reeves was killed in a plane crash. In 1967 he was chosen for the Country Music *Hall of Fame.

Keanu 'Reeves² /ˌkiːənuː ˈriːvz/ (1964–) a Canadian stage and film actor who works mainly in the US. He was born in Lebanon of a English mother and Chinese-Hawaiian father. 'Keanu' means 'cool breeze over the mountains' in the Hawaiian language. His most famous films include *Bill and Ted's Excellent Adventure* (1989), *Speed* (1994) and *The *Matrix*.

the Re'form Acts three British *Acts of Parliament passed during the 19th century to change the way *Members of Parliament were elected and to allow more people to vote. The first Reform Act (1832) got rid of the rotten boroughs (= constituencies where very few people were entitled to vote), created more seats in Parliament and increased the number of men able to vote. The second and third Acts (1867 and 1884) created new seats for city and county areas and increased the number able to vote to about 5 million.

the Refor'mation the 16th-century European movement, led by Martin Luther and others, to reform the *Roman Catholic Church. Supporters of the Reformation opposed the political powers of the Pope and argued for a simpler form of religion with less ceremony and more emphasis on the authority of the Bible. In England, King *Henry VIII appointed himself head of a new Protestant *Church of England in 1534, mainly so that he could get divorced from his first wife and marry again. The new Church was supported by bishops such as Thomas *Cranmer and Hugh *Latimer, and became firmly established under Queen *Elizabeth I. In Scotland, the strict Protestant views of John *Knox and others led to the creation in 1690 of the *Presbyterian *Church of Scotland. See also ACT OF SUPREMACY, DISSOLUTION OF THE MONASTERIES. ⇨ note at CHURCH OF ENGLAND.

the Re'form Club a club in *Pall Mall, London, England, established in 1832 by supporters of the first *Reform Act. Its later members were mainly supporters of the *Liberal Party. In modern times it was the first of the traditional London clubs to allow women to become members.

the Refu'gee Council the largest British organization which gives help and support to refugees and asylum seekers. It campaigns for fair treatment for refugees and works directly with people arriving in Britain, giving advice, accommodation and training and also working with smaller community refugee organizations.

the 'Regency the period from 1811 to 1820 when the *Prince of Wales (later King *George IV) ruled Britain as *Prince Regent in place of his father, King *George III, who was mentally ill. The architecture and design of the period is in a simple elegant style based on ancient classical models. The best-known Regency architect is John *Nash, who designed *Regent Street and *Regent's Park.
▶ **Regency** *adj* in the style of the Regency period: *Regency furniture*.

Regent's 'Park a park in central London, England, designed by John *Nash for the *Prince Regent and completed in 1828. It contains an outdoor theatre, flower gardens, sports fields and a large lake, and *London Zoo is on its north side. The park is surrounded by several

R

grand buildings in the *Regency style, known as the Terraces.

'**Regent Street** a main street in central London, England, designed in 1813–23 by John *Nash and named after the *Prince Regent. It joins Oxford Circus to *Piccadilly Circus and contains several famous shops, including *Liberty's and *Hamley's, and restaurants such as the *Café Royal.

'**reggae** n [U] a type of pop music that began in *Jamaica in the 1960s and is now well known in Britain, the US and other countries. Reggae songs often have a *Rastafarian message, and the musicians often wear their hair in long tight curls called *dreadlocks*. Famous reggae groups have included Bob *Marley and the Wailers, Aswad, and Burning Spear.

Re'gina /rɪ'dʒaɪnə/ a Latin word meaning the ruling queen. It is used in official documents or announcements after a queen's name, e.g. *Elizabeth Regina*. In British law it is also used in the titles of court cases involving the government, e.g. *Regina v Jones*, where *Regina* stands for the government. Compare REX.

,**regional 'member** one of the 56 elected members of the *Scottish Parliament who represents one of the eight **Scottish Parliament Regions**, in addition to the 73 *MSPs who represent a *constituency. In elections, voters vote for one constituency MSP and one regional member. All MSPs have equal status in the Parliament.

'**Registered 'General 'Nurse** n (abbr **RGN**) (in Britain) a nurse who is qualified to care for patients in hospitals, schools and elsewhere, after a training period of at least three years.

,**Registered 'Nurse** n (abbr **RN**) (in the US) a person who has a licence to work as a nurse in a particular state. To become registered, a person must first obtain a degree in nursing and then pass the official exam of the state they want to work in.

,**William H 'Rehnquist** /'renkwɪst/ (William Hubbs Rehnquist 1924–) the Chief Justice of the US *Supreme Court since 1986. Before that he was the Chief Legal Counsel for the US Department of Justice (1969–71) and a judge on the Supreme Court (1971–86). He was appointed Chief Justice by Ronald *Reagan, and under his leadership the court has become more conservative.

,**John 'Reid** /'riːd/ (1947–) a British *Labour politician. He became a *Member of Parliament for *Glasgow in 1987. He was Secretary of State for Scotland (1999–2001), Secretary of State for Northern Ireland (2001–02), *Secretary of State for Health (2003–2005) before becoming Secretary of State for Defence in 2005.

,**Lord 'Reith** /'riːθ/ (John Reith 1889–1971) a Scottish broadcaster who became the first general manager of the *BBC. He began his career in industry, but joined the BBC in 1922. During his period as general manager (1927–38) he set high standards in *public service broadcasting, believing that the BBC had a responsibility to inform, educate and entertain the public. He also helped to keep it free from government control. Reith was a government minister during *World War II and was made a *life peer in 1940.

the ,**Reith 'lectures** /,riːθ / a series of talks given each year in Britain on *BBC radio. The talks are on serious subjects, e.g. politics, history or economics, and are given by a leading figure in the subject. They were established in 1948 in honour of Lord *Reith, the first head of the BBC.

Re'late /rɪ'leɪt/ a British organization that gives advice to people who are having difficulties in a relationship, and has a number of centres around the country where couples can talk with trained staff. It was formed in 1938

as the Marriage Guidance Council and changed its name in 1988.

▶ religion in Britain

In the Census of 2001, British people were asked for the first time to answer a question about their religion, although they were not forced to answer the question. 77% replied that they had a religion and 71% of them said that they were Christian, 3% Muslim and 1% Hindu, with smaller groups replying that they were Sikh, Jewish or Buddhist. Although the majority of the population describe themselves as Christian, only a small proportion, about 4%, go to church regularly. British people rarely discuss religion and feel that a person's religious beliefs are a private matter.

The established (= official) church in England is the *Church of England. Members of the Church describe themselves informally as 'C of E'. In Scotland it is the *Presbyterian Church of Scotland, known by Scots as 'the kirk'. There is no established church in Wales and Northern Ireland. In Wales the Church of England is known as the *Church in Wales. The Church is involved in political life as *archbishops and some *bishops are members of the *House of Lords and are chosen by the Queen following the advice of the Prime Minister. The monarch must be a member of the Church of England and is its official head. Christian religious education is provided in state schools but children do not have to take part. About 10% of the population are *Roman Catholic and there are also Catholic schools.

Protestant groups other than the church of England are called *Free or *Nonconformist Churches. The Free Churches include the *United Reformed Church, the *Baptist Church and the *Methodist Church. Nonconformist churches are also sometimes called chapels.

Muslims, Sikhs and Hindus in Britain are mainly from families who came to Britain after *World War II from *India and *Pakistan, although there has been a Muslim community in Britain since the 16th century. Many Jews are from families who came to Britain as refugees from other countries in Europe at various times in the 19th and 20th centuries. Synagogues, mosques, Hindu temples and gurdwaras (= Sikh places of worship) are found in cities and many towns.

▶ religion in the US

In 2002 the largest Christian church in the US was the *Roman Catholic Church with 63 million members, followed by the Southern Baptist Convention with 16 million members. There are many different Christian churches in the US and the majority of religious Americans are *Protestant Christians. In 2001 76% of Americans described themselves as Christian. Although there is no established (= official) religion in the US, religion plays an important part in public life and churches are centres of social events and business activities as well as places of worship. The *Pledge of Allegiance includes the phrase 'one nation under God' and the official US motto is 'In God We Trust'. Since the 1960s some Americans have tried to stop government support of religion. The *Establishment Clause in the Constitution forbids the establishment of a state religion. In 1963 the *Supreme Court decided it was 'unconstitutional' for students to pray or read the Bible in class but many schools ignore this ruling. What is taught about evolution in schools is a subject of much legal debate with some religious people objecting to the teaching of evolution as scientific fact and other Americans arguing that creationism (= the belief that the universe was made by God exactly as described in the Bible) is religion and should not be taught in schools.

The largest Protestant group in the US are the Baptists. Other groups include *Methodists, *Lutherans, *Presbyterians and *Episcopalians, who are part of the *Anglican communion. The Pentecostal Church is a charismatic church, where emotions are freely expressed and spiritual healing is practised. Other Christian religious groups include the *Jehovah's Witnesses, the *Christian Scientists, the *Mormons and the *Seventh-Day Adventists. There are groups who have a special way of life apart from the modern world such as the *Shakers, the *Amish, the *Mennonites and the *Hutterites. There are many *evangelical churches in the US and *evangelists and *televangelists include Billy *Graham, Pat *Robertson and Jerry *Falwell.

Other large religious groups in the US include Jews and Muslims. As in Britain many Jews came to the US as refugees from Europe in the 19th and 20th centuries.

REM /ˌɑːr iː 'em/ a US pop group established in 1980. Their albums have included *Green* (1988), *Out of Time* (1991) and *Automatic for the People* (1992).

Re'membrance ˌSunday the nearest Sunday to 11 November (*Armistice Day), on which ceremonies are held in Britain to remember the people killed during the two world wars and other conflicts. The largest ceremony is held in London, when politicians, Commonwealth figures and members of the royal family lay flowers at the *Cenotaph in *Whitehall. People traditionally wear a paper or plastic poppy (= a red flower) on Remembrance Sunday and the days leading up to it, and the day is also called *Poppy Day. See also VETERANS' DAY, TWO-MINUTE SILENCE.

ˌFrederic 'Remington /'remɪŋtən/ (1861–1909) a US artist and writer, best known for his realistic paintings, drawings and sculptures of the American West. His subjects were usually *cowboys, *Native Americans, and soldiers and horses in scenes of action. His books include *Pony Tracks* (1895).

'Remploy /'remplɔɪ/ a British company formed in 1945 which employs people with physical handicaps (= conditions that affect their ability to walk, see, speak, etc.). It has many factories producing goods such as furniture, textiles and electrical goods. The company receives money from the government.

ˌRen and 'Stimpy /ˌren, 'stɪmpi/ a US television cartoon series that was shown on the *Nickelodeon channel between 1991 and 1996. It was criticized by some people because of the disgusting personal habits of its main characters, the 'asthma-hound' Chihuahua dog Ren Höek and his stupid friend Stimpson J Cat.

ˌRuth 'Rendell /'rendl/ (1930–) an English author of *detective and mystery novels. Her main character is Chief Inspector Wexford, and her books include *Wolf to the Slaughter* (1967), *Shake Hands Forever* (1975), *Road Rage* (1997), *Harm Done* (1999) and *Adam and Eve and Pinch Me* (2002). She also writes under the name of Barbara Vine. Many of her books have been made into successful television series. She was made a *life peer in 1977.

'Reno¹ /'riːnəʊ; *AmE* 'riːnoʊ/ a city in the US state of *Nevada near the border with *California. It is famous for its casinos and in the past its easy laws attracted people who wanted to get married or divorced quickly. Reno is on the Truckee River. It was settled in 1859 and named after General Jesse Reno, a US officer in the *Civil War.

ˌJanet 'Reno² /'riːnəʊ; *AmE* 'riːnoʊ/ (1938–) the first woman to become US Attorney General. She held this position from (1993–2001), the longest period for an Attorney General in the twentieth century. She was criticized for giving approval for the attack in 1993 on the Branch Davidians led by David *Koresh in Waco, *Texas,

and in 2000 she ordered the controversial arrest of the young Elián González so that he could be returned to his father in Cuba. In 2002 she competed, unsuccessfully, to become the Democratic governor of Florida.

the 'Rent Act a British *Act of Parliament of 1977 that established a system of **protected tenancy** in which people living in rented accommodation had a right to a fair rent fixed at a particular amount, and protection from eviction (= removal from a property). It was replaced by the Housing Act 1988.

'Rentokil™ /'rentəkɪl/ a British company that can be employed to kill insects, rats, birds and other animals that cause damage to buildings. Since 1996 the company has been called Rentokil Initial and now also provides other services such as office cleaning and property care.

re'port stage *n* [sing] (*BrE*) one of the stages that a *bill(1) must go through in order to become an *Act of Parliament. It follows the *committee stage, and takes the form of a debate in the *House of Commons. After passing the report stage the bill then goes to the *third reading.

ˌRepre'sentative *n* a member of the US *House of Representatives.

Re'publican *n* **1** (*abbrs* **R, Rep.**) a member or supporter of the US *Republican Party. **2** a person in Northern Ireland who believes that their country should be a part of the Republic of Ireland and not be ruled by Great Britain. Compare LOYALIST.

the Re'publican ˌParty one of the two main political parties in the US, sometimes called the Grand Old Party. It receives more support from rich people and is more conservative than its rival the *Democratic Party. It was established in 1854 by people who wanted to free the slaves. Abraham *Lincoln was the first Republican *President, and others have included Theodore *Roosevelt, Dwight D *Eisenhower, Richard M *Nixon, Ronald *Reagan, George *Bush and George W *Bush. The official symbol of the party is an elephant.

the ˌRepublic of 'Ireland /'aɪələnd; *AmE* 'aɪərlənd/ the official name for Ireland since 1949. See also EIRE, IRISH FREE STATE.

re'search ˌcouncil *n* any of several government organizations in Britain that support and carry out scientific research, and also provide scientific advice and information to the public and to professional groups. Among the largest research councils are the *Medical Research Council, the Natural Environment Research Council and the Particle Physics and Astronomy Research Council.

Re'serve 'Officers' 'Training Corps ⇨ ROTC.

Re'spect - The 'Unity Coaˌlition a British political party started by George *Galloway in 2004 after he was forced to leave the *Labour Party because he criticized Tony *Blair and George W *Bush for invading Iraq. The party is against war and supports traditional socialist ideas.

the ˌResto'ration the return of the British monarchy in 1660, when *Charles II became king after the rule of Oliver *Cromwell. 'The Restoration' refers to this event and the period after it, which is known for its lively developments in the arts, particularly in the theatre. The Earl of Rochester (1648–80) was the period's most famous poet, and other artists included the painter Peter Lely (1618–80) and the playwright William *Wycherley: *a Restoration play*.

ˌRestoration 'comedy *n* [C, U] a type of comedy play written during and after the *Restoration in Britain. Restoration comedies often deal with the sexual adventures of the upper classes, and show characters behaving in a foolish or wicked way. Examples include *The*

R

Country Wife (1675) by William *Wycherley, Love for Love (1695) by William *Congreve and The Beaux' Stratagem (1707) by George Farquhar. They were also the first plays in the British theatre in which women appeared as actors.

the ‚Retail 'Price ‚Index n (abbr **the RPI**) a figure published by the British government every month which shows the change in the overall cost of goods and services bought by an average household. It is used to calculate the rate of inflation. Compare Consumer Price Index, RPIX.

▶ **retirement**

In Britain most people retire in their sixties. The majority of men retire at 65. The **retirement age** for women used to be 60, but now many women retire at 65. Some people **take early retirement** (= choose to retire early) from about 50.

In the US the usual retirement age is also 65. People can choose to retire earlier but may get less money from their *pension. In the US, the phrase early retirement suggests that retirement has been proposed by a person's employer as an alternative to them being made redundant (= unemployed). Companies do this sometimes when they need to reduce the number of people working for them. Since older people are usually paid more than younger ones, the company may ask them to retire and hire younger people to replace them. A few people choose to continue working after the age of 65, though some employers require employees to retire between 65 and 70.

When somebody retired after many years with the same employer they used to be given a present by the company. Traditionally this was a gold watch or a clock. Now, few people work for the same company for all their working lives and do not receive a present from their employer. Instead, their colleagues contribute money for a present and organize a party.

A person's quality of life in retirement depends largely on the amount of money they have. Many receive pensions, some have savings in the bank. In Britain people have at least a basic pension from the state. In the US most people can receive *social security benefits, and can get government help in paying for their medical care. Many retired people have to live on a **fixed income** and find retirement hard.

Now that older people have better health and live longer, people over retirement age are becoming an increasingly important economic and social force. The number of retired people in Britain and the US is growing, and through organizations like the *American Association of Retired Persons and, in Britain, the National Pensioners Convention, they have increased power to demand the services they need and the rights they deserve. This is sometimes referred to as 'grey power'.

re‚turning 'officer n (in Britain) an official who arranges an election in a *constituency and announces the result. Compare presiding officer.

‚Reuben 'sandwich /ˌruːbən/ n (in the US) a popular sandwich made with corned beef (= cow meat preserved in salt), Swiss cheese and sauerkraut (= a type of cabbage) on rye bread, which is then grilled.

'Reuters /'rɔɪtəz; AmE 'rɔɪtərz/ a British company which employs journalists all over the world and sells news to newspapers, television and radio. It also provides stock exchange information and various other business services. The company was formed in 1851 by Paul Julius Reuter (1816–99).

‚HMS Re'venge /ˌeɪtʃ em es/ a ship commanded by Francis *Drake and used in the battle against the *Armada in 1588. It was later commanded by Richard

Grenville (1542–91) and captured by the Spanish in 1591 after a fierce battle. Lord *Tennyson's poem The Revenge (1880) tells the story of the incident, in which Grenville and many of his crew died.

‚Paul Re'vere /rɪ'vɪə(r)/ (1735–1818) a US hero of the *American Revolution. He is remembered for his horse ride at night from *Boston to Lexington on 19 April 1775 to warn people that British armed forces had landed. This is described in *Longfellow's well-known poem *Paul Revere's Ride. Revere had earlier been one of the people involved in the *Boston Tea Party. He was an artist who designed and made silver products, and his illustrations of the *Boston Massacre helped to encourage the *American Revolution. See also Old North Church.

re‚verse discrimi'nation n [U] (in the US) the action of favouring members of minority groups for jobs, entry to college, etc., over other equally or better qualified people, in order to increase their numbers. This was regarded by many people as an unfair aspect of the US government's policy of *affirmative action.

the Re‚vised 'Standard ‚Version (abbr **the RSV**) a modern version of the Bible produced by the British and Foreign Bible Society in 1946–57. It is based on the *Authorized Version. See also American Standard Version.

the Re'vised ‚Version (abbr **the RV**) a version of the Bible produced in Britain in 1881–95, based on the *Authorized Version but using more modern language.

Rex /reks/ a Latin word meaning the ruling king. It is used in official documents or announcements after a king's name, e.g. George Rex. It is also used in British law in the titles of court cases, e.g. Rex v Jones, where Rex stands for the government. Compare Regina.

‚Burt 'Reynolds¹ /ˌbɜːt 'renldz; AmE ˌbɜːrt/ (1936–) a US film actor known especially for appearing in adventure films and romantic comedies. His films have included Deliverance (1972), Smokey and the Bandit (1977), Switching Channels (1988), Striptease (1996), Boogie Nights (1997) and Mystery, Alaska (1999).

‚Debbie 'Reynolds² /'renldz/ (1932–) a US actor, singer and dancer known for her energy and bright personality. Her films include *Singin' in the Rain, Tammy and the Bachelor (1957), The Unsinkable Molly Brown (1964) and Mother (1996). She was formerly married to the singer Eddie Fisher (1928–), and their daughter is the actor Carrie Fisher (1956–).

‚Joshua 'Reynolds³ /ˌdʒɒʃjuə 'renldz; AmE ˌdʒɑː'ʃuə/ (1723–92) an English painter. He was the most successful artist of his time, and painted pictures of many important people, including his friend Samuel *Johnson. He was the first President of the *Royal Academy (1768) and used his lectures, called the Discourses on Art (1769–91), to express his views on the importance of the 'grand manner' in art and the high status of the artist. He was made a *knight in 1769.

RFC /ˌɑːr ef 'siː/ ⇨ Royal Flying Corps.

RFK /ˌɑːr ef 'keɪ/ ⇨ Kennedy⁹.

RGN /ˌɑː dʒiː 'en; AmE ˌɑːr/ ⇨ Registered General Nurse.

‚Rhapsody in 'Blue a popular musical work for piano and orchestra by George *Gershwin. It combines *jazz and classical music, and was first performed in 1924 by the band of Paul *Whiteman, with Gershwin at the piano. The film Rhapsody in Blue (1945) was about Gershwin's life.

RHM /ˌɑːr eɪtʃ 'em/ (in full **Rank Hovis McDougall**) a large British company that makes food products, including bread, cakes and sauces. It was formed by J Arthur *Rank, who bought *Hovis and McDougall in 1962.

RHO /ˌɑːr eɪtʃ ˈəʊ; AmE ˈoʊ/ ⇨ RED HOT ORGANIZATION.

Rhode 'Island /ˌrəʊd; AmE ˌroʊd/ the smallest US state, also called the Ocean State. It is in the north-east of the country on the Atlantic coast. It was named after the Greek island of Rhodes and was one of the original 13 states. *Providence is the capital and largest city. Rhode Island has a fishing and boat-building industry and produces jewellery, electronic products and grapes. Popular tourist attractions include *Newport and Samuel Slater's Mill in Pawtucket.

Cecil 'Rhodes[1] /ˈrəʊdz; AmE ˈroʊdz/ (1853–1902) a British politician and businessman. He went to South Africa in 1870 and made a lot of money from diamond and gold mining, forming the De Beers Mining Company in 1880. His ambition was to bring the whole of Africa under British control, and he took an active part in opposing Britain's rivals in South Africa, the Boers. In 1889 he formed the British South Africa Company, which owned land later known as Rhodesia (now *Zimbabwe and *Zambia), and became the President of Cape Colony in 1890.

Zandra 'Rhodes[2] /ˌzɑːndrə ˈrəʊdz; AmE ˈroʊdz/ (1940–) an English fashion designer. She is known for her unusual and brightly coloured clothes and for dyeing her own hair in a variety of bright colours. The Fashion and Textile Museum which specializes in modern fashion was started by her and opened in London in 2003.

Rhodes 'scholar /ˌrəʊdz; AmE ˌroʊdz/ n a student from the US, Germany or the *Commonwealth who has received an award to study at *Oxford University. The money for these awards was originally provided by Cecil *Rhodes.

the ˌRhondda 'Valley /ˌrɒndə; AmE ˌrɑːndə/ (also the 'Rhondda) an area in south Wales famous for its coal-mining industry in the 19th and early 20th centuries. The last mine closed in 1990, and the area now has a much smaller population.

RHS /ˌɑːr eɪtʃ ˈes/ ⇨ ROYAL HORTICULTURAL SOCIETY.

▶ **rhyming slang**

Rhyming slang is a form of *slang in which a word is replaced by a phrase that **rhymes** with it, and is often humorous. Rhyming slang is closely associated with the *cockney speech of London, though some phrases are more widely heard. It may have developed in the late 18th century as a private language used by thieves or as part of the patter (= talk) of street traders.

Examples of rhyming slang which are familiar to most British people are *apples and pears* (stairs), *trouble and strife* (wife), *plates of meat* (feet) and *dicky dirt* (shirt). Sometimes the rhyming part of the phrase has been dropped. Somebody may say, for instance, that they are going to *take a butcher's* (have a look at something). The original expression was *take a butcher's hook* which rhymed with *look*. Similarly, a person may say *use your loaf* (think about something). Originally the rhyming phrase was *use your loaf of bread*, which rhymed with *head*.

Rhyming slang tends to be thought of as old-fashioned by younger people and phrases like *take a butcher's* and *use your loaf* are now less often heard. But some words that originated in rhyming slang have become part of the regular language. For instance, *raspberry* in the sense of a disapproving sound made with the tongue and lips, comes from *raspberry tart*, the rhyming slang for 'fart'.

Sophie ˌRhys-'Jones /ˌriːs ˈdʒəʊnz; AmE ˈdʒoʊnz/ (1965–) the name before her marriage of the Countess of Wessex, a member of the British *royal family, the wife of Prince *Edward, the Earl of *Wessex.

ˌrhythm and 'blues n (abbr **R and B**) a style of popular music of the 1950s and 1960s played especially by *African Americans. It developed out of the *blues, with added rhythms associated with *jazz and *rock and roll. Leading R and B stars included 'Muddy' *Waters, Joe Turner, B B *King and 'Fats' *Domino.

RIBA /ˌɑːr aɪ biː ˈeɪ/ ⇨ ROYAL INSTITUTE OF BRITISH ARCHITECTS.

Condoleezza Rice[1] /ˌkɒndəliːzə ˈraɪs; AmE ˌkɑːndəliːzə/ (1954–) a US political adviser who was Assistant to the President for National Security Affairs, usually known as **National Security Advisor**, under George W *Bush from 2001 to 2004 and became *Secretary of State in 2004. She is also a Professor of Political Science and has written a number of books about world politics.

ˌTim 'Rice[2] /ˈraɪs/ (1944–) an English writer and performer. He is best known for his work with Andrew *Lloyd Webber, writing words for the *musicals *Joseph and the Amazing Technicolour Dreamcoat* (1968), *Jesus Christ Superstar* and *Evita* (1976). He has also written words for songs in films, including *The Lion King* (1994), and appears regularly on radio and television. He was made a *knight in 1994.

ˌRice 'Krispies™ /ˈkrɪspiz/ n [pl] a well-known breakfast food consisting of small pieces of crisp rice. They are usually eaten with milk and sugar. The famous advertising phrase 'snap, crackle and pop' represents the noise they make when milk is poured onto them.

ˌrice 'pudding n [C, U] a traditional English pudding (= cooked sweet dish) made with rice, sugar and milk. If you say that somebody 'couldn't knock the skin off a rice pudding' you mean that they are very weak or unable to defend themselves in a fight. This is an informal British expression.

ˌCliff 'Richard /ˈrɪtʃəd; AmE ˈrɪtʃərd/ (1940–) an English pop singer. He began his career singing with The Shadows group in 1958, achieving success with *Living Doll* (1959). A series of musical films followed, including *Summer Holiday* (1962). He continues to produce popular records, e.g. *Saviour's Day* (1990), and was made a *knight in 1995. He is well known for his Christian beliefs.

Richard I /ˌrɪtʃəd ðə ˈfɜːst; AmE ˌrɪtʃərd ðə ˈfɜːrst/ (1157–99) the king of England from 1189 to 1199, following his father King *Henry II. He is often called **Richard the Lionheart** or **Richard, Coeur de Lion**, because of his courage in battle. He spent the first part of his rule abroad fighting in the Third *Crusade, at the end of which he reached a peace agreement with Saladin in 1191. On his journey home he was captured and held as a prisoner by the Austrian emperor Henry VI, until a large amount of money was paid for releasing him. He spent his later years fighting against the French, and after his death in battle in 1199 he was replaced as king by his brother *John.

Richard II /ˌrɪtʃəd ðə ˈsekənd; AmE ˌrɪtʃərd/ (1367–1400) the king of England from 1377 to 1399, following his grandfather King *Edward III. He became king at the age of 10, relying on his uncle *John of Gaunt to help rule the country, and was successful in defeating the *Peasants' Revolt of 1381. The rest of his rule was spent trying to control the other powerful men of the country, particularly Henry Bolingbroke, John of Gaunt's son. In 1398 Richard sent Henry abroad, but he returned the following year and seized power, ruling as King *Henry IV. Richard was put in prison, where he died, possibly murdered.

Richard II /ˌrɪtʃəd ðə ˈsekənd; AmE ˌrɪtʃərd/ a play (1595) by William *Shakespeare. It tells the story of the final years of King *Richard II's life, presenting him as a weak man who cannot control the powerful men of the time.

Richard III /ˌrɪtʃəd ðə ˈθɜːd; AmE ˌrɪtʃərd ðə ˈθɜːrd/ (1452–85) the king of England from 1483 to 1485, following his nephew King *Edward V. He is often thought of as a cruel and violent king, who probably ordered the murder of the *Princes in the Tower, but not all historians accept this view. He was killed at the battle of *Bosworth Field by Henry Tudor, who became King *Henry VII.

Richard III /ˌrɪtʃəd ðə ˈθɜːd; AmE ˌrɪtʃərd ðə ˈθɜːrd/ an early play (c. 1592) by William *Shakespeare. It presents King *Richard III of England as a cruel and violent man who murders several people to become king, and is killed at the battle of *Bosworth Field. During the battle Richard is forced to fight on foot, and shouts the famous line: 'A horse! A horse! My kingdom for a horse!' At the start of the play he delivers the famous speech that begins:

> 66 Now is the winter of our discontent
> Made glorious summer by this sun of York. 99

Richard and 'Judy a British television show on *Channel 4 which is a mixture of interviews, competitions and other features. It started in 2001 and is presented by the husband and wife, **Richard Madeley** (1956–) and **Judy Finnigan** (1948–).

Gordon 'Richards¹ /ˈrɪtʃədz; AmE ˈrɪtʃərdz/ (1904–86) an English jockey. He was *champion jockey 26 times during his career (1920–54), winning 4 870 races. He was made a *knight in 1953.

J A 'Richards² /ˈrɪtʃədz; AmE ˈrɪtʃərdz/ (Ivor Armstrong Richards 1893–1979) an English writer and critic of literature. He taught at *Cambridge and *Harvard universities, and with C K Ogden (1889–1957) developed the idea of *basic English. His best-known book is *Principles of Literary Criticism* (1924). He also published several collections of poetry.

Ralph 'Richardson¹ /ˌrælf ˈrɪtʃədsn; AmE ˈrɪtʃərdsn/ (1902–83) an English actor on stage, in films and on television. His early career was spent in the theatre, playing leading parts in plays by Chekhov, Ibsen and *Shakespeare, and he was made a *knight in 1947. Later he appeared in works by modern writers, including J B *Priestley and Harold *Pinter. His many films included *Richard III* (1956), *The Bed Sitting Room* (1969) and *O Lucky Man!* (1973).

Samuel 'Richardson² /ˈrɪtʃədsn; AmE ˈrɪtʃərdsn/ (1689–1761) an English author best known for his novels *Pamela* (1740) and *Clarissa* (1748). They are among the first novels in English literature, and are written in the form of letters between the characters. Both novels contain strong messages about the importance of sexual morals, and were extremely successful when first published.

Lionel 'Richie /ˈrɪtʃi/ (1949–) an American singer and writer of *soul music whose records have sold more than 50 million copies. He helped to form the Commodores group in 1967, and their hits included *Three Times a Lady* (1978). Richie left the group in 1982, the year he won a *Grammy as Best Male Vocal. He won another in 1984 for Album of the Year, *Can't Slow Down*. In 1986 he wrote with Michael *Jackson *We Are the World* for *Live Aid. His later albums have included *Louder than Words* (1996) and *Renaissance* (2001).

'Richmond /ˈrɪtʃmənd/ **1** a town in North Yorkshire, England. It is famous for its castle, built in the late 11th century on a hill above the town, and its theatre, opened in 1788.

2 a town on the River *Thames in the *borough of Richmond-upon-Thames in London, England. It is close to two large parks, *Richmond Great Park and *Kew Gardens. King *Henry VII built a palace at Richmond in the late 15th century, but only a small part of the building now remains.

3 the capital city of the US state of *Virginia. It is a port on the James River. Patrick *Henry made his famous 'liberty or death' speech there. Richmond was the capital city of the *Confederate States during the *Civil War and was destroyed by US soldiers in 1865. Its products include machinery and processed tobacco, food and wood.

Richmond Great 'Park /ˌrɪtʃmənd/ a large public park in *Richmond(2), south-west London, England, created in 1637 for King *Charles I as a place for hunting deer. It is the largest of the royal parks, and still contains large numbers of deer.

Rich 'Tea™ *n* a popular British make of round, thin, sweet biscuits with a yellowish colour. They are made by *McVitie's.

'Alan 'Rickman /ˈrɪkmən/ (1947–) an English actor in theatre, films and television. His film work has included leading parts in *Truly, Madly, Deeply* (1991) and *Michael Collins* (1996). He plays the part of Professor Severus Snape in the series of Harry *Potter films (2001–).

Sally 'Ride /ˈraɪd/ (1951–) the first US woman in space. She went on two flights made by *Challenger* *space shuttles in 1983 and 1984. Ride left *NASA in 1987 to teach and do research. She now directs the California Space Institute.

'Ride a Cock-'horse to 'Banbury 'Cross /ˈbænbri/ a traditional *nursery rhyme, often said by mothers to their babies as they bounce them on their knee. A 'cock-horse' is a child's toy, a horse's head on a stick. The words are:

> 66 Ride a cock-horse to Banbury Cross,
> To see a fine lady upon a white horse;
> Rings on her fingers and bells on her toes,
> And she shall have music wherever she goes. 99

Tom 'Ridge /ˈrɪdʒ/ (1946–) a US *Republican politician who was governor of *Pennsylvania from 1995 until 2001 when he became the first US Secretary of *Homeland Security.

the 'Ridgeway /ˈrɪdʒweɪ/ an ancient path in southern England that leads from *Avebury along the Berkshire Downs to the *Thames at Streatley and then along the Chiltern Hills to Ivinghoe Beacon, a distance of 85 miles/ 137 kilometres. It was once used as a trade route, and passes several places of importance in ancient times, including the Uffington *White Horse. Today the path is popular with ramblers (= people who enjoy walking in the countryside) and looked after as a **National Trail**. ⇨ note at IRON AGE BRITAIN.

'riding /ˈraɪdɪŋ/ *n* each of the three administrative divisions of *Yorkshire, England, until 1974. Their names were **East Riding**, **North Riding** and **West Riding**. The word *riding* comes from an Anglo-Saxon word meaning a third part of something. In 1996 the local government district of **East Riding of Yorkshire** was created, covering most of the original East Riding area. It is governed by a *unitary authority.

Di,ana 'Rigg /ˈrɪg/ (1938–) an English actor who first became well known playing the part of Emma Peel in the television series *The *Avengers* (1965–8). She also worked with the *Royal Shakespeare Company (1959–64) and has appeared in many films. More recent stage work has included *Medea* and *Who's Afraid of Virginia Woolf?* She was made a *dame(2) in 1994.

R

the **Right 'Honourable** (*written abbr* **Rt Hon**) (in Britain) the formal title of *Cabinet ministers, *Privy Councillors, certain members of the *peerage, and others: *the Right Honourable Jack Straw MP* ◇ *the Right Honourable Member for Brent East.* Compare HONOURABLE(2).

the **Right 'Reverend** (*written abbrs* **the Rt Rev**, **the Rt Revd**) the formal title of *bishops in the *Church of England: *the Right Reverend the Lord Bishop of Winchester.*

The **Rights of 'Man** a book (1791–2) by Thomas *Paine. It explained his ideas for a fair society, and supported free education, *pensions for old people, greater rights for women, a fairer tax system, and the right to vote. It also supported the revolutions in America and France, and criticized the British government. Because of this, Paine was accused of treason by the British government, and was forced to leave Britain.

the **right to 'buy** (in Britain) the legal right of people renting *council houses to buy them cheaply, introduced by the *Conservative government in the 1980 Housing Act. Many people bought their homes, which reduced the amount of cheaper property available for rent.

Bridget 'Riley /'raɪli/ (1931–) a leading English painter in the style known as *op art*. Her early paintings featured black, white and grey shapes in repeated patterns, creating effects of movement. She introduced colour into her work from the late 1960s.

Ring a Ring o' 'Roses /ˌrɪŋ ə ˌrɪŋ ə 'rəʊzɪz; *AmE* 'rəʊzɪz/ a traditional children's song and game in which the players join hands and dance in a circle singing, then pretend to sneeze, and fall down on the last line. The words are:

> 66 Ring a ring o' roses,
> A pocket full of posies,
> A-tishoo! A-tishoo!
> We all fall down. 99

'Ringling 'Brothers, 'Barnum and 'Bailey /'rɪŋlɪŋ, 'bɑːnəm, 'beɪli; *AmE* 'bɑːrnəm/ the most famous US circus. It calls itself 'the Greatest Show on Earth' and has three 'ring' areas where people perform at the same time. Two separate circus groups tour around the country and are seen by about 25 million people each year. The five original Ringling brothers started a circus in 1884 and bought their great rival, the *Barnum and Bailey Circus, in 1907. See also KELLY.

Rin Tin 'Tin /ˌrɪn tɪn 'tɪn/ the name of the German shepherd dog that was the popular animal star in many US silent adventure films of the 1920s. His popular name was 'Rinty'. The first Rin Tin Tin was found on the field of battle during *World War I by US Captain Lee Duncan, who made more than $5 million from the dog's *Hollywood career. Compare LASSIE.

the **Rio 'Grande** /ˌriːəʊ 'grænd; *AmE* ˌriːoʊ 'grændi/ the river that forms the border between Mexico and the US state of *Texas. Its Mexican name is the Rio Bravo del Norte. A dispute over this border caused the *Mexican War. The Rio Grande begins in the *Rocky Mountains in south-west *Colorado and flows about 1 885 miles/3 033 kilometres to the *Gulf of Mexico. See also WETBACK.

the **'Riot Act** a British *Act of Parliament, passed in 1715, which allowed the government to use force to control public protest or disorder. During any such disturbance an official could read part of the Act ordering people to leave a place. To *read the riot act* is an expression which means to warn someone forcefully to stop doing something: (*humorous*) *If she comes home late again I'm going to read (her) the riot act.* Compare PUBLIC ORDER ACT.

RIP /ˌɑːr aɪ 'piː/ an abbreviation for the Latin phrase *requiescat/requiescant in pace*, meaning 'may he (or she or they) rest in peace'. It is sometimes seen on people's graves. The letters RIP are often used in cartoons (= humorous drawings) or other jokes to show that somebody has died.

'Ripley's Be'lieve It or 'Not /'rɪpliz/ a US newspaper feature created in 1918 by Robert Ripley (1893–1949) who also drew cartoons (= comic drawings). It brings together strange facts and customs from around the world. It is still published and appears in many different newspapers. Ripley also used the title for a museum of strange things and for a television show. There are now 27 such museums in the US and other countries.

Rip Van 'Winkle /ˌrɪp væn 'wɪŋkl/ a character in a short story by the US writer Washington *Irving. Rip Van Winkle is a man who sleeps for 20 years under a tree and is amazed to wake up and find how much the world has changed.

the **Ritz** /rɪts/ (*also* **the Ritz Hotel**) any of a number of hotels around the world established by or named after the Swiss businessman César Ritz (1850–1918). They are famous for being very comfortable and expensive. The first Ritz Hotel was opened in London, England, in 1906. The word *ritzy*, meaning expensive and elegant, was formed from the name of the Ritz Hotels.

The **'Rivals** a comic play (1775) by Richard Brinsley *Sheridan, in which two young men are rivals for the love of the same young woman, Lydia Languish. The play's most famous character is Mrs *Malaprop, who is known for her tendency to confuse words that sound similar so that examples of this became known as malapropisms.

the **River 'Cafe** a fashionable restaurant by the River *Thames in Hammersmith, London, established in 1987. It is famous for its Italian food and the owners, Ruth Rogers and Rose Gray, have published several River Cafe recipe books.

'Riverdance /'rɪvədɑːns; *AmE* 'rɪvərdæns/ a popular stage show (1994–) based on a type of Irish dancing called 'stepdance', which involves very quick movements of the feet while the arms remain at the side of the body. Its best-known performer is Michael Flatley (1958–), who also appeared in the stage show *Lord of the Dance* (1995–).

Joan 'Rivers /'rɪvəz; *AmE* 'rɪvərz/ (1937–) a US comedian, known especially for her jokes about sex. She has presented several television *talk shows and won an *Emmy award in 1990 as 'Best Host of a Talk Show'.

Brian 'Rix /'rɪks/ (1924–) an English theatre actor and manager. He played in farces at the *Whitehall Theatre for many years, and later became known for his work for the British charity *Mencap, of which he was made director in 1988. Rix was made a *knight in 1986 and a *life peer in 1992.

RKO /ˌɑː keɪ 'əʊ; *AmE* ˌɑːr 'oʊ/ a major *Hollywood film company in the 1930s and 1940s. It was established in 1921 as RKO Radio Pictures. Its successful films include *King Kong, Flying Down to Rio* (1933) and other musical films with Fred *Astaire and Ginger *Rogers, *Citizen Kane* and *Suspicion* (1941). Howard *Hughes took control of the company in 1948, five years before it made its last film.

RLPO /ˌɑːr el piː: 'əʊ; *AmE* 'oʊ/ ⇨ ROYAL LIVERPOOL PHILHARMONIC ORCHESTRA.

the **RMT** /ˌɑːr em 'tiː/ (*in full* **the National Union of Rail, Maritime and Transport Workers**) a British trade union formed in 1990 from the combination of the

National Union of Railwaymen and the National Union of Seamen.

RN /ˌɑːr ˈen/ **1** ⇨ REGISTERED NURSE.
2 ⇨ ROYAL NAVY.

RNA /ˌɑːr en ˈeɪ/ ⇨ ROYAL NEIGHBORS OF AMERICA.

RNLI /ˌɑːr en el ˈaɪ/ ⇨ ROYAL NATIONAL LIFEBOAT INSTITUTION.

ˌHal ˈRoach /ˈrəʊtʃ; AmE ˈroʊtʃ/ (1892–1992) a US director, producer and writer of early films, mostly comedies. He developed the careers of Harold *Lloyd and *Laurel and Hardy, and received a special *Oscar in 1983.

ˈroad fund ˌlicence n (BrE) ⇨ CAR TAX.

ˈroad ˌmovie n (especially AmE) a type of film in which one or more characters travel across the country by road, often to escape the police. The journeys often involve violence. Well-known road movies have included *Easy Rider, Badlands (1973), Smokey and the Bandit (1977), Thelma and Louise (1991) and Natural Born Killers (1994).

▶ **roads and road signs**
The US road system is the largest in the world, mainly because of the long distances between cities. The distance between *Boston and *San Francisco, for instance, is more than 3 000 miles/ 4 827 kilometres. The US began to build the *interstate highway system in 1956. By 2004 it had more than 42 000 miles/(67 578 kilometres of road. The interstate system greatly helped the country's economy, but it also hurt the economies of many small towns not on an interstate. Interstates running north to south have odd numbers and those going from east to west have even numbers. They often have only two or three **lanes** in each direction through the countryside but may have eight or more each way through cities. The New Jersey Turnpike, for instance, has 14 lanes each way near New York City.

Other major roads in the US are called **superhighways**, **freeways**, **expressways**, **thruways** or **parkways**. There are also many county and local roads, called variously **arterial roads**, **feeder roads** or **farm roads**. Some states have **tollways** or **turnpikes**, on which drivers must pay a toll.

Interstate highways are marked with red and blue signs showing an 'I' followed by the road's number. Other US highways have red, white and blue signs. Some state roads, like those in *Louisiana and *Texas, have signs in the shape of the state. Since 1995 states have been able to set their own speed limits. This is usually 65 or 70 mph/105 or 112 kph on interstate roads but lower on other main roads.

In Britain the fastest and most direct routes between major cities are by motorways, which usually have three lanes of traffic in each direction and a speed limit of 70 mph/112 kph. Each motorway is identified by the letter 'M' and a number. Main roads other than motorways are called **A-roads** and are numbered A6, A34, etc. Some A-roads are **dual carriageways** with two or more lanes each way. Most A-roads now follow a **bypass** round towns. Narrower roads which have only one lane in each direction are called **B-roads**. Most roads have **white lines** and **Catseyes**™ (= objects sunk into the ground that reflect a car's lights) down the middle. Only a very few roads have tolls but Britain's first toll motorway, the M6 Toll opened in 2003 as an alternative to the heavily used M6 near Birmingham. Narrow country roads below B-road standard may be known locally by the name of the place they go to, e.g. Orston Lane.

In Britain the *Highway Code describes the many signs placed beside roads. Red circular signs give instructions that must by law be obeyed. These include 'no overtaking' signs and signs about speed limits. Red triangular signs give warnings about possible dangers ahead, e.g. slippery roads. Direction signs to major towns are blue on motorways and green on other roads; signs to smaller places are white. Old-fashioned **signposts** can still be seen in some country areas.

In the US red road signs, like 'Stop', must be obeyed. Signs that indicate danger, as in areas where rocks might fall, have a yellow diamond shape. Arrows indicating bends in the road are shown in green circles on white signs. Many other US road signs are now similar to those in Europe.

In Britain there is pressure from both business and private road users for more and better roads, despite the damage to the environment and increase in pollution that this may cause. People who are against the building of new roads regularly challenge proposed routes of new motorways or bypasses. If they fail, environmentalists set up protest camps along the route of the new road. Recently, experts too have cast doubt on the wisdom of building more roads, saying it simply encourages greater use of cars. In the US there are few protests against road-building. People generally want more roads to make their journeys faster and more convenient.

ˈroad tax ⇨ CAR TAX.

the ˌRoaring ˈTwenties (informal) a name given to the 1920s, when there were exciting new developments in fashion, music and art, and when *Prohibition and *flappers appeared in the US.

ˌrobber ˈbaron n (AmE) a person in business who becomes very rich, often by illegal means and without caring about other people. The term was applied especially to a number of leading US businessmen in the late 19th century, including John D *Rockefeller and Cornelius *Vanderbilt.

ˌHarold ˈRobbins[1] /ˈrɒbɪnz; AmE ˈrɑːbɪnz/ (1916–97) a US author of popular novels that contain a lot of sex and violence. More than 50 million copies of his books were sold and many of them were made into films. The best known is The Carpetbaggers (1961), which sold more than 6 million copies. Others include Never Love a Stranger (1948), A Stone for Danny Fisher (1952), The Betsy (1971), Piranha (1986) and The Stallion (1996).

Jeˌrome ˈRobbins[2] /ˈrɒbɪnz; AmE ˈrɑːbɪnz/ (1918–98) a US dancer and choreographer. He joined the New York City Ballet in 1949 and was later one of its Ballet Masters-in-Chief (1983–9). His ballets included Fancy Free (1944), which he helped to adapt for the film On the Town (1949). He was the choreographer for several *Broadway musical plays, including The King and I (1951), *West Side Story (1957) and Fiddler on the Roof (1964).

Julia ˈRoberts[1] /ˈrɒbəts; AmE ˈrɑːbərts/ (1967–) one of the highest paid US actors. Her films have included Pretty Woman (1990), Sleeping with the Enemy (1991), The Pelican Brief (1993), the successful comedy Notting Hill (1999) and Erin Brockovich (2000), for which she won an *Oscar.

ˌOral ˈRoberts[2] /ˌɔːrəl ˈrɒbəts; AmE ˈrɑːbərts/ (1918–) a US Pentecostal Minister and *televangelist who broadcasts regularly on radio and television. He claims to cure people's illnesses through the power of prayer. In 1963 he established Oral Roberts University in Tulsa, *Oklahoma.

ˌGeorge ˈRobertson[1] /ˈrɒbətsn; AmE ˈrɑːbərtsn/ (1946–) a British *Labour politician. He became a *Member of Parliament in 1978 and held several important positions in the Labour *Shadow Cabinet before becoming *Secretary of State for Defence in the Labour government of 1997. He and served as Secretary General of *NATO from 1999 to 2003. He was made a *life peer in 1999.

,Pat '**Robertson**[2] /'rɒbətsn; AmE 'rɑːbərtsn/ (1930–) a US *televangelist and founder of the Christian Coalition of America. In 1959, he bought a television station in Portsmouth, *Virginia, and a year later began the Christian Broadcasting Network (CBN) which reaches 155 countries in 64 languages. Robertson tried without success to become the *Republican Party candidate for US President in 1988.

'**Robert's** '**Rules of** '**Order** /'rɒbəts; AmE 'rɑːbərts/ a small US book containing rules for running formal meetings, based on the procedures used in the British *Parliament. It was first published in 1876 and has appeared since then in several new versions. It is used by the US *Congress, businesses and even small clubs.

,**Robert the** '**Bruce** /'bruːs/ (also ,**Robert** '**Bruce**, **Robert I**) (1274–1329) the king of Scotland from 1306 until his death. He joined William *Wallace in trying to take power from the English in Scotland, but was defeated several times by the army of King *Edward I. He finally defeated the English at *Bannockburn in 1314, and England recognized Scotland as an independent country in 1328. After his death Robert's son, David II, ruled Scotland from 1329 to 1371. There is a popular story about how Robert the Bruce, when he was hiding in a cave from the English, watched a spider repeatedly trying to attach its web to a rock until it finally succeeded. This made him determined to keep trying to defeat the English.

,**Paul** '**Robeson** /'rəʊbsn; AmE 'roʊbsn/ (1898–1976) a US singer and actor famous for his rich, deep voice. He appeared in the London production of *Show Boat (1928), in which he sang *Ol' Man River. His other stage successes included Emperor Jones (1925) in New York and *Othello in both London (1930) and New York (1943). Because he expressed political views in support of Communism and criticized the US government's treatment of African Americans, his passport was taken away for several years. He later lived in Europe (1958–63) before returning to New York.

,**George** '**Robey** /'rəʊbi; AmE 'roʊbi/ (1869–1954) an English *music-hall(1) performer best known for the song If You Were the Only Girl in the World (1916). He was made a *knight in 1954.

'**robin** n a small brown European bird with a red breast often seen in gardens. In Britain the robin, sometimes called **robin redbreast**, is strongly associated with *Christmas and pictures of robins, especially in snow-covered gardens, are often used on Christmas cards.

,**Robin** '**Goodfellow** /'gʊdfeləʊ; AmE 'gʊdfeloʊ/ ⇨ PUCK.

,**Robin** '**Hood** /'hʊd/ a character in traditional British stories, who is said to have lived in *Sherwood Forest near *Nottingham during the rule of King *Richard I (1189–99). His companions (usually called his *Merry Men) included *Friar Tuck, *Little John and Will Scarlet, and his lover was *Maid Marian. Together they robbed rich people and gave money to poor people, and their enemy was the *Sheriff of Nottingham. There is no evidence that Robin Hood ever existed but there are many stories about him and many films have been made about his adventures. In these he is often shown wearing clothes made of a material called *Lincoln green, and holding a bow.

Anne **Robinson**[1] /'rɒbɪnsn; AmE 'rɑːbɪnsn/ (1944–) an English journalist and broadcaster who is the presenter of the television quiz show The Weakest Link. She behaves in a very critical and unfriendly way towards the people who take part.

'**Bill "Bojangles"** '**Robinson**[2] /'bəʊdʒæŋglz 'rɒbɪnsn; AmE 'boʊdʒæŋglz 'rɑːbɪnsn/ (1878–1949) a US actor and tap-dancer (= a dancer who wears special shoes to beat out the rhythm on the floor). He is best remembered for appearing in films with Shirley *Temple, including The Little Colonel (1935), The Littlest Rebel (1935) and Rebecca of Sunnybrook Farm (1938).

,**Edward G** '**Robinson**[3] /'rɒbɪnsn; AmE 'rɑːbɪnsn/ (1893–1973) a US actor, born in Romania, who was best known for playing tough criminals in films. His films include Little Caesar (1930), The Last Gangster (1938), Double Indemnity (1944), All My Sons (1948), The Cincinnati Kid (1965) and Solvent Green (1973). Robinson received a special *Oscar in 1972.

,**Jackie** '**Robinson**[4] /'rɒbɪnsn; AmE 'rɑːbɪnsn/ (1919–1972) a US baseball player, the first *African-American in either of the two US major leagues (= associations of teams). He played for the Brooklyn Dodgers (1947–56) and was *Most Valuable Player for the *National League in 1949. In 1962 he was chosen for the National Baseball *Hall of Fame.

,**Robert** '**Robinson**[5] /'rɒbɪnsn; AmE 'rɑːbɪnsn/ (1927–) an English radio and television presenter, especially of quiz shows. His programmes for television have included Ask the Family (1967–84) and Call My Bluff (1967–88), and for radio Stop the Week (1974–92) and *Brain of Britain.

',**Smokey**' '**Robinson**[6] /,sməʊki 'rɒbɪnsn; AmE ,smoʊki 'rɑːbɪnsn/ (1940–) a US singer and writer of songs, born William Robinson. His pop group, 'Smokey' Robinson and The Miracles (1957–72), had hits with Shop Around (1960), You've Really Got a Hold of Me (1962) and The Tears of a Clown (1970). He then began singing alone, and had success with Cruisin' (1979), Being with You (1981) and One Heartbeat (1987). Robinson was Vice-President of Motown Records until 1988.

"**Sugar**" '**Ray** '**Robinson**[7] /'ʃʊgə 'reɪ 'rɒbɪnsn; AmE 'ʃʊgər, 'rɑːbɪnsn/ (1920–89) a US boxer who many people regard as the greatest of all time. He was the World Welterweight Champion (1946) and then the only person to become World Middleweight Champion five times. During his career, he lost only 19 of his 202 professional fights.

'**William** '**Heath** '**Robinson**[8] ⇨ HEATH ROBINSON.

,**Robinson** '**Crusoe** /,rɒbɪnsn 'kruːsəʊ; AmE ,rɑːbɪnsn 'kruːsoʊ/ a character in a book of the same name by Daniel *Defoe, published in 1719. Crusoe is left alone on an island after his ship sinks, and uses his few possessions to survive there. He is helped by *Man Friday, a man who becomes Crusoe's faithful servant after Crusoe saves him from death. The book was based on a true story and is often considered to be the first English novel.

,**Rob** '**Roy** (1671–1734) the popular name for Robert MacGregor, a Scottish *Jacobite outlaw (= a person who has broken the law and who must hide to avoid being caught). After his land and property were taken by the English, he lived by stealing cows and forcing people to pay him money for protection. He is the main character in Sir Walter *Scott's romantic novel Rob Roy (1817).

,**Bobby** '**Robson** /'rɒbsn; AmE 'rɑːbsn/ (1933–) an English football player and manager. After playing for Fulham (1950–6 and 1962–7) and West Bromwich Albion (1956–62), he became manager of Ipswich Town (1969–82) and later of England (1982–90). He was made a *knight in 2002.

rock n [U] **1** (also '**rock music**) a type of modern popular music with a strong beat, played with electric guitars, drums, etc. It developed in the 1960s from *rock and roll. Famous rock groups include the *Rolling Stones,

R

*Genesis and *KISS. Rock later developed into forms such as *folk rock and *heavy metal.

2 (*BrE*) a type of hard sugar sweet, usually made in long sticks which are flavoured with peppermint and coloured (usually bright pink) on the outside. In Britain, rock is sold especially in seaside towns, and has the name of the town all through the length of the stick on the inside: *He bought her a stick of Brighton rock as a present.* See also EDINBURGH ROCK.

'rockabilly /'rɒkəbɪli/ *n* [U] a type of US popular music. It combines *rock and roll with *country music, which was originally called ' *hillbilly music'. Rockabilly was especially popular in the mid 1950s, and was sung by Elvis *Presley, Conway *Twitty, Carl *Perkins, Brenda Lee and other early rock and roll stars.

ˌRock-a-bye, 'Baby /ˌrɒk ə baɪ; *AmE* ˌrɑːk ə baɪ/ an alternative to the first line of the children's song *Hush-a-bye, Baby, and the name by which this song is known in the US.

ˌrock and 'roll (*also* **rock 'n' roll**) *n* [U] a type of popular music played with electric guitars, drums, etc., that first appeared in the 1950s. It developed from *jazz and *country music, and was played by such performers as Bill *Haley, Elvis *Presley, Chuck *Berry and Buddy *Holly.

'rock cake *n* a type of small sweet cake traditional in Britain, with a hard rough surface and usually containing currants (= dried grapes).

ˌrock 'candy *n* [U] (*AmE*) a type of sweet/candy, often made by children. It consists of sugar which has been left in water until it forms large, hard crystals that stick together. Artificial flavours and food colours are often added.

ˌJohn D 'Rockefeller[1] /'rɒkəfelə(r); *AmE* 'rɑːkəfelər/ (John Davison Rockefeller 1839–1937) a US businessman who became very rich as the owner and President of the Standard Oil Company. In 1911 he gave the business to his only son, John D Rockefeller Junior (1874–1960) and then gave about $500 million of his own money for good causes. He established the *Rockefeller Foundation and the University of Chicago (1892).

ˌNelson 'Rockefeller[2] /ˌnelsn 'rɒkəfelə(r); *AmE* 'rɑːkəfelər/ (1908–79) the 41st Vice-President of the US (1974–7) and only the second not to be elected. Gerald *Ford chose him after replacing Richard *Nixon as President. Rockefeller had earlier been Governor of New York (1959–73). He tried and failed three times to be the *Republican Party candidate for President. He was the second son of John D Rockefeller Junior.

'Rockefeller ˌCenter /'rɒkəfelə; *AmE* 'rɑːkəfelər/ a group of 19 buildings in *Manhattan(1), New York, used for offices and various kinds of entertainment. They were mostly built between 1931 and 1939, in the *art deco style, by John D Rockefeller Junior, on land owned by *Columbia University. The buildings are connected by underground passages containing shops. They include *Radio City Music Hall and the central General Electric Building (former RCA Building) which contains the offices of *NBC. The center is also famous for its *Christmas tree and lights that are put up each year, as well as its outdoor winter ice-skating rink.

'Rockefeller Founˌdation /'rɒkəfelə; *AmE* 'rɑːkəfelər/ a large US public trust (= organization providing money for projects that help society). It was established in 1913 by John D *Rockefeller and supports research in medical science, agriculture and social issues. These include problems of hunger, education, social equality and the environment.

'rocker *n* a member of a group of young people in Britain, especially in the 1960s, who listened to *rock music, wore leather jackets and rode motorcycles. The rockers were rivals of the *mods and often fought with them.

'Rocket /'rɒkɪt; *AmE* 'rɑːkɪt/ the name of an early steam engine (= vehicle that pulls a train) designed in the 1820s by Robert *Stephenson. It was the first engine to be used regularly on the *Liverpool and Manchester Railway, and the original version of it is now in the *Science Museum, London, England.

the Roc'kettes™ /rɒˈkets; *AmE* rɔːˈkets/ a well-known group of female dancers at the *Radio City Music Hall in New York. They dance in a long line, kicking their legs in the air at the same time and in time to the music. The Rockettes perform all year between the films being shown there, and they also present special shows at Easter and Christmas in cities throughout the US.

'rock music ⇨ ROCK.

ˌRock of 'Ages the title of a well-known Christian hymn first published in 1775. The phrase 'Rock of Ages' refers to Jesus Christ.

the ˌRock of Gi'braltar /dʒɪˈbrɔːltə(r)/ a high cliff in southern Spain, at the south-western edge of the Mediterranean Sea, near the town and port of *Gibraltar. When people say that something is as solid as the Rock of Gibraltar, they mean it is very safe or firm: *I was told the investment was as safe as the Rock of Gibraltar.*

ˌNorman 'Rockwell /'rɒkwel; *AmE* 'rɑːkwel/ (1894–1978) a US magazine artist who drew over 300 covers for the *Saturday Evening Post between 1916 and 1963. His pictures, done in a realistic style, were full of warmth and humour and very popular with most Americans. They showed people in small towns and in the country engaged in ordinary activities at home and at work.

> **66** I paint life as I would like it to be. **99**
> Norman Rockwell

'Rocky /'rɒki; *AmE* 'rɑːki/ a film character created and played by Sylvester *Stallone. He wrote and acted in five successful films about Rocky Balboa, a boxer who overcomes difficulties to defeat strong opponents. The first, *Rocky* (1976), made him famous and won two *Oscars. Stallone himself directed *Rocky II* (1979), *Rocky III* (1981), *Rocky IV* (1985) and *Rocky V* (1990).

The 'Rocky 'Horror 'Picture Show /'rɒki; *AmE* 'rɑːki/ a US comedy musical film (1975) based on a play by Richard O'Brien first performed at the *Royal Court Theatre in 1973. It makes fun of *Hollywood *musicals, horror films and sex. The story is about a nice couple who visit a castle in *Ohio and meet Transylvanians who dress and act in a strange way. It has become a cult film (= one that is fashionable among a particular group).

the Rockefeller Center

People who go to the film often dress as the characters and say or sing the actors' lines.

the ˌRocky ˈMountains /ˌrɒki; AmE ˌrɑːki/ (also **the ˈRockies** /ˈrɒkiz; AmE ˈrɑːkiz/) the largest mountain range in North America. They form the *Continental Divide and were a major barrier for people crossing the country to settle in the *Far West. The range covers more than 3 000 miles/4 800 kilometres, from the Yukon Territory in *Canada through the US *Rocky Mountain States to the Mexican border. The highest mountain is Mount Elbert in *Colorado, which is 14 433 feet/4 402 metres high.

the ˌRocky Mountain ˈStates /ˌrɒki; AmE ˌrɑːki/ the eight US states covered by the *Rocky Mountains. From north to south they are *Montana, *Idaho, *Wyoming, *Colorado, *Utah, *Nevada, *Arizona and *New Mexico.

ˌAndy ˈRoddick[1] /ˈrɒdɪk; AmE ˈrɑːdɪk/ (1982–) a US tennis player who won his first *grand slam competition at the *US Open in 2003 and finished number one in the world rankings in the same year.

ˌAˌnita ˈRoddick[2] /ˈrɒdɪk; AmE ˈrɑːdɪk/ (1942–) an English businesswoman who formed the *Body Shop group in 1976, selling beauty products made from natural materials. She is well known for her campaign to end the testing of these types of products on animals, and for her interest in the environment.

ˈrodeo /ˈrəʊdiəʊ; rəʊˈdeɪəʊ; AmE ˈroʊdioʊ; roʊˈdeɪoʊ/ n (pl **-os**) (in the US and Canada) a popular entertainment in which *cowboys compete for prizes by showing their skills in various events. These include riding dangerous horses and bulls, pulling down young bulls by their horns and catching cows with ropes. The first official rodeo was held in 1888 in Prescott, *Arizona.

cowboys at a rodeo

ˌRoˌdeo ˈDrive /ˌrəʊˌdeɪəʊ; AmE roʊˌdeɪoʊ/ a famous street in *Beverly Hills, *California, which is popular with rich tourists and film stars. It has a lot of expensive shops selling clothes, jewellery, leather goods, etc.

ˌJimmie ˈRodgers[1] /ˌdʒɪmi ˈrɒdʒəz; AmE ˈrɑːdʒərz/ (1897–1933) a US singer who became an early star of *country music, selling over 20 million records between 1928 and 1933. He was sometimes called the 'Blue Yodeler' because of his ability to yodel (= sing in the traditional Swiss manner with sudden changes of note). He was the first person chosen for the Country Music *Hall of Fame, in 1961.

ˌRichard ˈRodgers[2] /ˈrɒdʒəz; AmE ˈrɑːdʒərz/ (1902–79) an American composer who wrote the music for many *Broadway musical shows. He and Lorenz *Hart, who wrote the words, produced 29 such shows, including *Babes in Arms* (1937) and *Pal Joey* (1940). He then joined Oscar *Hammerstein to write many more, including *Oklahoma!*, *Carousel* (1945), **South Pacific*, *The King and I* (1951) and *The **Sound of Music*. Many of these shows became films. Rodgers also wrote the music for the television series **Victory at Sea*.

ˌRoedean ˈSchool /ˌrəʊdiːn; AmE ˌroʊdiːn/ a leading British *public school(1) for girls near *Brighton, *East Sussex. It was established in 1885. ⇨ note at PUBLIC SCHOOLS.

ˌNicolas ˈRoeg /ˈrəʊg; AmE ˈroʊg/ (1928–) an English film director known for his original and imaginative films, including *Performance* (1970), *Walkabout* (1971), *Don't Look Now* (1973), *The Man Who Fell to Earth* (1976) and *Castaway* (1987).

ˌRoe v ˈWade /ˌrəʊ vɜːsəs ˈweɪd; AmE ˌroʊ vɜːrsəs/ a US *Supreme Court case (1973) which ended in a decision making it legal to have an abortion. The judges said that a state must allow any woman, if she wishes, to have an abortion within the first three months after she becomes pregnant. The decision divided US society and caused a lot of discussion all over the country.

Roˈgation Days /rəʊˈgeɪʃn; AmE roʊˈgeɪʃn/ n [pl] the three days before *Ascension Day in the Christian church, during which people traditionally pray for a good harvest. The ceremony of *beating the bounds is sometimes held at this time. The Sunday before Ascension Day is also called **Rogation Sunday**.

Sir ˌRoger de ˈCoverley /də ˈkʌvəli; AmE ˈkʌvərli/ the name of an old English country dance. In early issues of *The *Spectator*(2) magazine, Richard *Steele and Joseph *Addison wrote under the name 'Roger de Coverley', presenting him as a typical English country *gentleman.

ˌBuck ˈRogers[1] /ˌbʌk ˈrɒdʒəz; AmE ˈrɑːdʒərz/ a character in popular US stories. He was a traveller in space in the 25th century and fought criminals, such as Killer Kane. His world capital was Niagra, and he was helped by Wilma Deering, Dr Huer and, from Mars, Black Barney. The Rogers character appeared first in a novel in the 1920s and was then in films, a *comic strip and comic books, and on radio and television. ⇨ note at COMICS AND COMIC STRIPS.

R

ˌGinger ˈRogers[2] /ˌdʒɪndʒə ˈrɒdʒəz; AmE ˌdʒɪndʒər ˈrɑːdʒərz/ (1911–95) a US actor, singer and dancer. She is best remembered as the partner of Fred *Astaire in several musical films, including *Flying Down to Rio* (1933), *Top Hat* (1935) and *Swing Time* (1936). She later appeared on stage in *Hello Dolly* (1966) in New York and *Mame* (1969) in London.

ˌRichard ˈRogers[3] /ˈrɒdʒəz; AmE ˈrɑːdʒərz/ (1933–) a British architect, born in Italy. His buildings include the Pompidou Centre in Paris (1977) with Renzo Piano, the Lloyds Building (1986) in London, both of which are famous for having large tubes for water, air and electricity showing on the outside, and the *Millennium Dome (1999) at *Greenwich. He was made a *knight in 1991 and a *life peer in 1996.

the Lloyds Building by Richard Rogers

‚Roy ˈ**Rogers**[4] /ˈrɒdʒəz; AmE ˈrɑːdʒərz/ (1912–98) a US singer and actor. He was the most popular *Hollywood *cowboy star of the 1940s and was called the 'King of the Cowboys'. He and his famous horse Trigger appeared in about 100 films, including *Under Western Stars* (1938), *The Yellow Rose of Texas* (1944) and *Apache Rose* (1947). His wife, the actor Dale Evans (1912–2001), often acted with him. He made many records and was chosen for the Country Music *Hall of Fame in 1988.

‚Will ˈ**Rogers**[5] /ˈrɒdʒəz; AmE ˈrɑːdʒərz/ (1879–1935) a US entertainer, sometimes called the 'cowboy philosopher'. He was famous for his sharp but humorous comments about politicians and news events. He first became well known in 1916 in the Ziegfeld Follies, a variety show, and later made many films, including *State Fair* (1933) and *Steamboat Round the Bend* (1935). He also wrote a humorous column which appeared in many newspapers.

> 66 All I know is what I read in the papers 99
> Will Rogers

‚*Roget's The*ˈ*saurus* /ˌrəʊʒeɪz; AmE ˌroʊʒeɪz/ (also informal **Roget**) a popular reference book, originally written by Peter Mark Roget (1779–1869) and first published in 1852. Roget was a scientist and inventor who started work on the thesaurus when he retired as Secretary of the *Royal Society in 1848. It contains English words or phrases arranged together in groups according to their meaning, and is still used today by people looking for the most appropriate word or phrase to use in a piece of writing. New editions of *Roget* are published regularly.

Roˈ**hypnol**™ /rəʊˈhɪpnɒl; AmE roʊˈhɪpnɑːl/ the brand name of the drug Flunitrazepam which is used in some countries to treat insomnia (= the condition of being unable to sleep). It has become known as a **date-rape** drug and has been used to commit sexual assaults. The drug makes people relax and causes amnesia (= when someone cannot remember what has happened to them) and is given to victims secretly, for example in a drink. Rohypnol pills have now been changed so that they turn blue when added to liquids but many of the old pills are still available.

the ‚*Rokeby* ˈ*Venus* /ˌrəʊkbi; AmE ˌroʊkbi/ the name used in Britain for a well-known painting (1650) by Diego Velázquez held at the *National Gallery, London. It shows a naked woman lying down and looking in a mirror. In 1914 it was attacked and cut by Mary Richardson, a *suffragette, in order to gain publicity for the campaign to allow women to vote.

ˈ**Rolex**™ /ˈrəʊleks; AmE ˈroʊleks/ a type of expensive watch of high quality, first made in 1908 by the Swiss company Montres-Rolex. Rolex watches are often regarded as a sign of success or wealth: *They beat him up and stole his Rolex.*

‚*Rolling* ˈ*Stone* a US *rock music magazine, known especially for its interviews with famous singers and musicians. It began in 1967 in *San Francisco. Its name came from the words of a Bob *Dylan song.

The ‚**Rolling** ˈ**Stones** (*also informal* **The Stones**) a British pop group formed in 1962. Its original members were Mick *Jagger, Brian Jones (1941–69) and Keith Richard (later Richards) (1943–), who were later joined by Bill Wyman (1936–) and Charlie Watts (1941–). Their music was influenced by US *blues and their most successful early records were (*I Can't Get No) Satisfaction* (1965) and *Jumpin' Jack Flash* (1968), with albums including *Sticky Fingers* (1971) and *Exile on Main Street* (1972). They were known for their noisy and aggressive performances, and they shocked many people by behaving badly in public and taking drugs. Brian Jones died when he accidentally drowned while under the influence of drugs in 1969. His place in the group was taken by Mick Taylor (1948–), who was later replaced by Ron Wood (1942–). The group still play together and make records. Their later albums include *Voodoo Lounge* (1994) and *Bridges to Babylon* (1997).

‚Sonny ˈ**Rollins** /ˌsʌni ˈrɒlɪnz; AmE ˈrɑːlɪnz/ (1930–) a US saxophone player who helped to develop the 'hard-bop' style of *jazz. In his early career he was influenced by Thelonius *Monk. His albums include *Bebop Professors* (1949), *Sonny Meets Hawk* (1963), *Nucleus* (1975) and *Plus 3* (1995). Rollins was chosen for the Jazz *Hall of Fame in 1973.

ˈ**rollmop** /ˈrəʊlmɒp; AmE ˈroʊlmɑːp/ n (*BrE*) a piece of herring (= a type of fish) from which the bones have been removed and which is rolled up and preserved in vinegar.

‚**Rolls-**ˈ**Royce**™ /ˌrəʊlz ˈrɔɪs; AmE ˌroʊlz/ (*also informal* **Rolls**, ˈ**Roller** /ˈrəʊlə(r); AmE ˈroʊlər/) n any of the large, expensive, comfortable cars made by the Rolls-Royce company. Many people recognize them by the small metal statue (representing the 'Spirit of Ecstasy') on the front of every Rolls-Royce car. The company was formed in 1905–6 by Charles Rolls (1877–1910) and Henry Royce (1863–1933) and also produced aircraft engines, e.g. for the *Spitfire during *World War II and later for *Boeing. The motor car business became a separate company in 1973 and the cars are now made in Britain by the German firm BMW. The Rolls-Royce company is a major producer of engines for aeroplanes. The name Rolls-Royce is also used informally to refer to the best product of a particular type: *This is the Rolls-Royce of electric guitars – it costs £5 000.*

▶ **Roman Britain**

The Romans occupied Britain from around 55BC to AD410 and there are many signs of the occupation still visible today at archaeological sites and Roman roads and walls stretching across the countryside.

Julius *Caesar came to Britain in 55BC and 54BC, defeating some of the local *Celtic tribes and introducing taxes and establishing trade. When, in AD43, this was under threat, the emperor Claudius ordered an invasion and southern Britain became **Britannia**, a province of the Roman Empire which was ruled by a Roman **governor**. In AD78 the governor Agricola brought Wales under Roman control, but failed to conquer the *Picts and other Scottish tribes in the north. The emperor Hadrian visited Britain in AD122 and after that *Hadrian's Wall, much of which can still be seen today, was built between *Newcastle-upon-Tyne and Bowness marking the northern frontier of the province.

The Romans founded over 20 large towns called **coloniae**, including *Colchester which was built as the new capital, *Gloucester and *Lincoln. It took many years before a town had all the things expected by a Roman citizen, such as a forum (= meeting place) with shops and a town hall, and baths and theatres, which were all highly decorated. London developed first as a trading centre and became the focus for several roads, soon replacing Colchester as the capital. Many roads were built to transport soldiers to border areas and for travel between towns, the most famous of which are *Watling Street which ran from *Dover to London and then on to St Albans and *Chester, *Ermine Street between London and *York and the *Fosse Way which ran from *Exeter to Lincoln.

By AD410, when Roman officials left Britain, the country had already been attacked by the Picts and invaded by Germanic tribes from northern Europe. More soldiers were sent to defend the province, but when part of the army was moved to deal with trouble elsewhere, the British rebelled against Roman rule and Roman influence declined. Germanic settlers, the Angles, Saxons and Jutes, began arriving in Britain from about AD 430 and took over much of the south and east of the country.

‚Roman 'Catholic (also 'Catholic) n a member of the Christian Church that recognizes the Pope as its head. It was the established Church in Britain until the *Reformation of the 16th century, when it was replaced by the *Protestant *Church of England and *Church of Scotland. After this Roman Catholics were forbidden to hold public positions or receive university education. In the 19th century the *Emancipation Act led to greater religious freedom, but Roman Catholics still cannot be appointed to some high positions in public life, including that of *Lord Chancellor, and the king or queen may not practise the religion or marry a Catholic. The Catholic religion is the main religion in the Republic of Ireland, and there has been violent conflict between Protestants and Catholics in Northern Ireland. The Catholic Church in Britain is led by the *archbishops of *Westminster(1), *Glasgow and *Armagh.
▶ **Roman Catholic** (also **Catholic**) adj
Roman Catholicism (also **Catholicism**) n [U].

‚Roma'nesque adj of the style of architecture that developed in Europe from about 900 to 1200, with round arches, high ceilings and thick walls. English Romanesque architecture, which developed from about 1150, is usually called *Norman architecture, and one of the finest examples is *Durham cathedral. It was replaced by the *Gothic style.
▶ **Romanesque** n [U] the Romanesque style.

Ro'manticism n [U] (also the Ro'mantic ‚Movement) a movement in European literature, art and music that began in the late 18th century. It was partly influenced by the American and French revolutions, and its main themes were the importance of imagination and feeling, the love of nature, and an interest in the past. In Britain, its greatest achievements were in poetry, especially that of *Wordsworth, *Coleridge, *Keats, *Shelley(2), *Blake and *Byron. Romantic novels produced during this period include *Wuthering Heights and *Frankenstein. In painting, Romantic artists included *Constable, *Turner(2) and *Blake.
▶ **Romantic** adj of or relating to the Romantic movement.
Romantic n a person who writes, paints, etc. in the Romantic style.

'Romany /'rɒməni, 'rəʊm-; AmE 'rɑːməni, 'roʊm-/ n (pl -ies) [C] a *Gypsy. Romanies are travelling people, usually living in caravans, who arrived in Britain around 1500 from Asia and now live in both Britain and the US. 2 [U] the language of Romany people.
▶ **Romany** adj of Romanies or their language.

‚Sigmund 'Romberg /,sɪgmənd 'rɒmbɜːg; AmE 'rɑːmbɜːrg/ (1887–1951) a US composer, born in Hungary, who wrote more than 70 *Broadway musical plays and light operas. They included Maytime (1917), The Student Prince (1924) and The Desert Song (1926). Several of his plays where made into films.

‚Romeo and 'Juliet /,rəʊmiəʊ; AmE ,roʊmioʊ/ a play (c. 1595) by *Shakespeare. It is set in Verona in Italy, and tells the story of two young people, Romeo and Juliet, who fall in love although they are from families who are enemies. They marry secretly but are unable to live together and the play ends with their death. It is famous for its beautiful poetry and for the balcony scene, during which Juliet says 'O Romeo, Romeo! Wherefore art thou Romeo?' and 'What's in a name? That which we call a rose/By any other name would smell as sweet.' The bal-

let Romeo and Juliet (1938) by Prokofiev and the musical show *West Side Story were both based on the play.

‚George 'Romney /'rɒmni; AmE 'rɑːmni/ (1734–1802) an English painter. He was one of the most fashionable portrait painters of the late 18th century and was famous for his use of bright colours. He painted many pictures using Lady Emma *Hamilton as his model.

‚Egon 'Ronay /,egɒn 'rəʊneɪ; AmE ,egɑːn 'roʊneɪ also ,iːgɒn; AmE ,iːgɑːn/ (1920–) a British writer about food and restaurants, born in Hungary, who began his career as a professional cook. His books, which include Egon Ronay's Guide to Hotels and Restaurants, give information for travellers and tourists in Britain and abroad.

'Ronseal™ /'rɒnsiːl; AmE 'rɑːnsiːl/ a British brand of paints and other products used to protect wood, especially for use outdoors. It is advertised with the slogan 'Does exactly what it says on the tin'.

‚Room at the 'Top a novel (1957) by John *Braine about Joe Lampton, a young man who leaves the woman he loves and marries another one who has more money. The book, which became very popular, established Braine as one of the *angry young men of the period. It was made into a film in 1958, and Braine later wrote a sequel (= a book continuing the original story), Life at the Top (1962).

‚Mickey 'Rooney[1] /'ruːni/ (1920–) a US actor known for his cheerful personality. He began as a child actor and first became famous in the late 1930s as the film character Andy *Hardy. He then made several films with Judy *Garland. His film successes included Babes in Arms (1939), The Human Comedy (1943) and The Black Stallion (1979). Rooney later had more success in the *Broadway musical play Sugar Babies (1978–81). He received a special *Oscar in 1983.

‚Wayne 'Rooney[2] /'ruːni/ (1985–) an English footballer who has played for *Everton football club and the English national football team. In 2003 he became the youngest player ever to score for England. He moved to *Manchester United in 2004.

‚Eleanor 'Roosevelt[1] /'rəʊzəvelt; AmE 'roʊzəvelt/ (1884–1962) the wife of US President Franklin D *Roosevelt, whom she married in 1905. She was also the niece of President Theodore *Roosevelt. She was known for supporting the rights of women and minority groups. After her husband's death, she became a US representative at the *United Nations and helped to write the Universal Declaration of Human Rights (1948).

‚Franklin D 'Roosevelt[2] /,fræŋklɪn, 'rəʊzəvelt; AmE 'roʊzəvelt/ (Franklin Delano Roosevelt 1882–1945) a *Democratic politician who became the 32nd US *President (1933–45), also known informally as FDR, and the only one to be elected four times. From 1921 he suffered from polio (= a serious disease affecting the nervous system) and could hardly walk without help. Before becoming President he was Governor of New York (1929–33). As President, he introduced his *New Deal(1) programme which helped the US to recover from the *Great Depression. Roosevelt was a cheerful man who gave Americans confidence with his *fireside chats on radio. Before the US entered *World War II, he supported Britain with the *Lend-Lease plan. He died while President just before the war ended. See also FOUR FREEDOMS, MANHATTAN PROJECT, YALTA.

> 66 The only thing we have to fear is fear itself. 99
> FD Roosevelt 1933

‚Theodore 'Roosevelt[3] /'rəʊzəvelt; AmE 'roʊzəvelt/ (1858–1919) the 26th US *President (1901–9) and a member of the *Republican Party. His popular name was

R

Teddy. He led the *Rough Riders in the *Spanish-American War. He became Vice-President in 1900 and replaced William *McKinley as President when McKinley was murdered a year later. As President, Roosevelt introduced his *Square Deal programme, began to build the *Panama Canal, created the *Great White Fleet, and used the *big stick military policy. He won the 1906 *Nobel Prize for peace after helping to end the Russo-Japanese War.

'root beer n [U, C] a sweet fizzy drink (= one containing many bubbles) popular in the US. It is made from the juices of different roots, barks and herbs.

Roots /ru:ts/ a long novel (1976) by the US writer Alex Haley, for which he received a special *Pulitzer Prize. The story, based on Haley's research into his own family's history, is about an African-American family of slaves. A television version (1977) ran for eight nights on *ABC and had an audience of about 100 million, the largest ever. It received nine *Emmy awards.

Ro'seanne /rəʊˈzæn; AmE roʊˈzæn/ the main character in the popular US television comedy series on *ABC of the same name (1988–97). She was played by the US comedy actor Roseanne (originally Roseanne Barr, later Roseanne Arnold). The series is about a *working-class family which is loving but always arguing.

the 'Rose Bowl (in the US) the oldest and best-known of the college football *bowl games. It is played on New Year's Day in Pasadena, *California, in the Rose Bowl stadium which has 102 000 seats. The game follows the **Rose Bowl Parade**, in which many vehicles decorated with flowers take part.

'Rosenberg¹ /'rəʊzənbɜːg; AmE 'roʊzənbɜːrg/ the name of a US married couple, **Julius Rosenberg** (1918–53) and his wife **Ethel Rosenberg** (1915–53), who were executed in 1953 for giving the Soviet Union secret US nuclear information during *World War II. Many people thought they were innocent and there are still doubts about the evidence.

Isaac 'Rosenberg² /'rəʊzənbɜːg; AmE 'roʊzənbɜːrg/ (1890–1918) an English poet and artist who was killed during *World War I. Many of his poems are about the horror of war. His collections of poetry include Night and Day (1912) and Youth (1915).

Rosencrantz and 'Guildenstern /ˌrəʊzənkrænts, 'gɪldənstɜːn; AmE ˌroʊzənkrænts, 'gɪldənstɜːrn/ two minor characters in the play Hamlet by *Shakespeare. They appear as the main characters in Rosencrantz and Guildenstern are Dead (1966), a comedy play by Tom *Stoppard which tells the story of Hamlet from their point of view.

the Wars of the 'Roses ⇨ WARS OF THE ROSES.

the 'Rose 'Theatre a theatre built in 1587 near *Southwark Bridge in the *Bankside area in London, England, where many of *Shakespeare's plays were performed and where Edward *Alleyn acted. It was used until 1603, when all London theatres were closed because of the plague. Surviving parts of the theatre were discovered in 1989 during work on a new office building and were opened to the public in 1999. Compare GLOBE.

the Ro'setta Stone /rəʊˈzetə; AmE roʊˈzetə/ a large, flat, black stone which was discovered in Egypt in 1799 and is now in the *British Museum, London. The same text is written on it three times in three different types of writing, including hieroglyphics (= Egyptian writing). This enabled the French language expert Jean-François Champollion (1790–1832) to read hieroglyphics for the first time.

Rosie the 'Riveter /'rɪvətə(r)/ the name used in the US to refer to any American woman who worked in factories to help the war effort during *World War II. A riveter fixes sheets of metal together with thick metal pins. The name was used as the title of a popular song, and a real riveter, called Rose Monroe, was chosen for a famous poster which showed a woman worker saying, 'We can do it!'.

Betsy 'Ross¹ /'rɒs; AmE 'rɔːs/ (1752–1836) the *Philadelphia woman who, according to tradition, sewed the first US flag in 1776. No evidence for this exists, but she did sew early flags. George *Washington designed the first flag, which had a circle of stars.

Diana 'Ross² /'rɒs; AmE 'rɔːs/ (1944–) a US singer and actor who began her career as the main singer with the *Supremes. She later left the group to sing alone and her hits have included Ain't No Mountain High Enough (1970) and Endless Love (1982). She also played the part of Billie *Holiday in the film Lady Sings the Blues (1970).

Jonathan 'Ross³ /'rɒs; AmE 'rɔːs/ (1960–) an English television personality and presenter. He first became successful as the presenter of The Last Resort (1987–8), a late-night chat show, and now presents Friday Night with Jonathan Ross, a film review show, as well as a show on *Radio 2.

Christina Ros'setti¹ /rəˈzeti/ (1830–94) an English poet, the sister of Dante Gabriel *Rossetti. Her poetry shows her religious faith and a romantic sadness, and she is best known for the collection The Goblin Market and Other Poems (1862). She also wrote poems for children, and the words to the religious song *In the Bleak Midwinter.

'Dante 'Gabriel Ros'setti² /'dænti 'geɪbriəl rəˈzeti/ (1828–82) an English painter and poet. In 1848 he formed the *Pre-Raphaelite Brotherhood with John Everett *Millais and Holman *Hunt. His earliest work includes The Girlhood of Mary Virgin (1849), with his sister Christina *Rossetti as the model. Rossetti's best-known paintings in the period 1850–1862, for example The Daydream (1880), are of tall, thin women with pale skin and sad expressions, and they are now considered to be typical of the Pre-Raphaelite style. For many of them his model was Elizabeth Siddal, whom he married in 1860. From the mid 1860s his model was William *Morris's wife, Jane. Rossetti also published several collections of poetry and translated the work of Dante and other poets.

'Roswell /'rɒzwel; AmE 'rɑːzwel/ a city in *New Mexico which is best known for an incident which happened there in 1947, when something crashed on farmland. At first, people said it was a UFO, but the US military later said that it was a weather balloon (= a piece of equipment used for measuring weather conditions). Many people have claimed that the truth is that it was a 'flying disk' containing an alien body as the first reports stated. They believe that the authorities are trying to conceal the truth. The incident has become the subject of a number of investigations, books, films and a television series, and the area has become popular with tourists.

Ro'tarian /rəʊˈteəriən; AmE roʊˈteriən/ n a member of a *Rotary Club.

'Rotary Club /'rəʊtəri; AmE 'roʊtəri/ n a branch of an international organization of businessmen and -women (called **Rotary International**) who meet for social reasons and to collect money for charity. The first Rotary Club was formed in 1905 by the US lawyer Paul Harris (1878–1947).

ROTC /'rɒtsi; AmE 'rɑːtsi/ (in full **Reserve Officers' Training Corps**) (in the US) a group of students who train to be military officers while at college or university. The army pays for most or all of the education for many ROTC students, who must then spend at least four years in the army. The US Navy and Air Force have similar programmes.

,Philip **'Roth** /'rɒθ; *AmE* 'rɑːθ/ (1933–) a US writer of novels and short stories, many of them about American Jewish life. His best-known early work is *Portnoy's Complaint* (1969). The short novel *Goodbye Columbus* (1959) won a *National Book Award and became a successful film (1969). His other novels include *My Life as a Man* (1974), *Zuckerman Bound* (1985), *Sabbath's Theater* (1995), which won a National Book Award, *The Plot Against America* (2004), and his trilogy of novels about public and private life in post-war America, *American Pastoral* (1997), which won the *Pulitzer Prize, *I Married a Communist* (1998), and *The Human Stain* (2000).

,Lord **'Rothermere** /'rɒðəmɪə(r); *AmE* 'rɑːðərmɪr/ (*also* **the first Lord Rothermere**) (*born* Harold Sydney Harmsworth 1868–1940) an English businessman who owned several newspapers, including the *Daily Mirror* and *Daily Mail*. His brother was Lord *Northcliffe. His grandson, the third Lord Rothermere (born Vere Harold Esmond Harmsworth, 1925–1998), took over the *Daily Mail* from his father in 1971 and also owned the *Mail on Sunday* and *Evening Standard*.

,Mark **'Rothko** /'rɒθkəʊ; *AmE* 'rɑːθkoʊ/ (1903–70) a US painter, born in Russia, who was a leading figure in the *abstract expressionism movement. He was known for producing very large pictures in which bands of strong colour with soft edges are arranged in a vertical format, creating a calm effect.

'**Rothschild** /'rɒθstʃaɪld; *AmE* 'rɑːθstʃaɪld/ the name of a British family of businessmen and politicians, originally from Germany. **Nathan Mayer Rothschild** (1777–1836) opened the bank of N M Rothschild and Sons in London in 1798, and became a British citizen in 1804. His son **Lionel Nathan Rothschild** (1808–79) became the first Jewish *Member of Parliament in 1858 and worked to achieve new legal freedoms for British Jews. Lionel's son **Nathaniel Mayer Rothschild** (1840–1915) became the first Jew to be made a *life peer, in 1885. **Miriam Rothschild** (1908–2005), the granddaughter of Nathaniel, was a famous scientist.

,Rotten **'Row** /,rɒtn 'rəʊ; *AmE* ,rɑːtn 'roʊ/ a wide track for riders of horses that runs along the south side of *Hyde Park(1), London, England.

the '**Rough** ,Riders *n* [pl] the popular name for the First Regiment of US Cavalry Volunteers in the *Spanish-American War. They included many *cowboys and were led by Colonel Leonard Wood and Lieutenant Colonel (later President) Theodore *Roosevelt. They became famous for their part in the victory at San Juan Hill in Cuba (1898), led by Roosevelt on his horse Little Texas.

'**Round 'Britain 'Quiz** a quiz programme on *BBC *Radio 4, in which two teams from different parts of the country are asked difficult questions to test their knowledge. It was first broadcast in 1947. In 1997 the BBC decided to end the programme but so many people protested that the decision was changed.

'**rounders** *n* [U] (*BrE*) a children's game for two teams, played with a bat and a ball, in which players have to run round four **bases**. It has been played in Britain since at least the beginning of the 18th century, and is the origin of modern *baseball.

'**Roundhead** *n* a supporter of *Parliament against King *Charles I in the *English Civil War. Roundheads were given the name because of their short hair. Their opponents were the *Cavaliers.

the ,Round **'Table** **1** the circular table at which the *Knights of the Round Table sat. Its shape meant that none of the knights appeared to be more important than any of the others.

2 an organization for young business and professional people, with clubs in Britain, the US and many other countries, who work together on projects to help their local communities and to improve international understanding. It was started in 1927: *He's a member of the local Round Table.*

'**Routemaster** /'ruːtmɑːstə(r); *AmE* 'ruːtmæstər/ *n* a double-decker bus (= a bus with two levels), designed in 1954, used in *London and popular with tourists. The driver sits in a separate part at the front of the bus and there is an open platform at the back where people get on and off, and money for tickets is collected by a conductor. They have mostly

a Routemaster bus

been replaced by buses where the driver takes the tickets which passengers have to buy before they get on the bus.

Route 128 /,ruːt 'wʌn twenti 'eɪt/ a circular road around *Boston and *Cambridge in the US state of *Massachusetts. Its name has become a symbol for information technology because the technical research done at the local universities of *Harvard and *MIT has created many computer and electronics companies along the Route.

Route 66 /,ruːt sɪksti 'sɪks/ the main road from *Chicago to *Los Angeles from 1926 until the 1960s. Its popular name was the 'Mother Road'. It was 2448 miles/ 3940 kilometres long, passing through eight states, and became a symbol of Americans' freedom of movement. Parts of Route 66 still exist, but it was officially replaced by *interstate motorways/freeways in the 1980s. It gave its name to the *CBS television series *Route 66* (1960–63), whose popular theme song ended: 'Get your kicks on Route 66'.

'**Rover** /'rəʊvə(r); *AmE* 'roʊvər/ a former British company that made cars, especially large, expensive ones. Two of its best-known cars were the *Land Rover and the *Range Rover. It started in Coventry, England, in 1904. It was taken over by the German company BMW in 1994 and sold again in 2000. It became a smaller company called MG Rover which collapsed in 2005.

the ,Rovers Re'**turn** /,rəʊvəz; *AmE* ,roʊvərz/ a pub in the British television *soap opera *Coronation Street* where the characters often meet.

'**Rowan and 'Martin's 'Laugh-In** /'rəʊən, 'mɑːtɪnz; *AmE* 'roʊən, 'mɑːrtɪnz/ (*also informal* **Laugh-In**) a popular US comedy television series (1968–73) on *NBC. It was presented by Dan Rowan (1922–87) and Dick Martin (1923–), with a regular team of actors, and used short, fast jokes and comedy situations, a new idea at the time. Certain phrases were also used regularly each week, such as 'Sock it to me!' and 'Tell it to the judge!'.

,Thomas **'Rowlandson** /'rəʊləndsn; *AmE* 'roʊləndsn/ (1756–1827) an English artist. He is famous for his caricatures (= exaggerated humorous drawings) showing the society and politics of the time, e.g. the series *The English Dance of Death* (1814–16). He also painted portraits and drew illustrations for books by Tobias *Smollett and Laurence *Sterne.

,J 'K **Rowling** /,dʒeɪ ,keɪ 'rəʊlɪŋ; *AmE* 'roʊlɪŋ/ (1965–) a British writer famous for the very successful series of Harry *Potter books. The books include *Harry Potter and the Philosopher's Stone* (1997) (given the title *Harry Potter*

R

and the Sorcerer's Stone in the US in 1998), *Harry Potter and the Chamber of Secrets* (1999), *Harry Potter and the Prisoner of Azkaban* (1999), *Harry Potter and the Goblet of Fire* (2000), *Harry Potter and the Order of the Phoenix* (2003), and *Harry Potter and the Half-Blood Prince* (2005). Although they are written for children, the books are popular with adults too. Rowling has won many awards for her writing and her books have been made into series of films.

,Rowntree 'Mackintosh /ˌraʊntriː ˈmækɪntɒʃ; *AmE* ˈmækɪntɑːʃ/ a British company that makes many well-known types of sweets, including *Kit Kat, *Smarties and *Black Magic. It is now owned by *Nestlé.

the ,Royal A'cademy (*also* the 'Royal A'cademy of 'Arts) (*abbr* the RA) an organization formed in 1768 to encourage the arts of painting, sculpture and architecture in Britain. Its first president was Joshua *Reynolds. The Academy's buildings at *Burlington House, London, contain an art school and a number of galleries, where a popular exhibition is held every summer showing work sent in by the public. Members of the Academy, who are important artists, can put the letters RA after their names. See also ROYAL COLLEGE OF ART, ROYAL SCOTTISH ACADEMY, ROYAL SOCIETY OF ARTS.

the 'Royal A'cademy of Dra'matic 'Art (*abbr* RADA) a college in central London, England, for training professional actors. It was established in 1904 by the actor Sir Herbert Beerbohm Tree, and contains the Vanbrugh Theatre, where students perform plays.

the 'Royal A'cademy of 'Music a college for the study of music in Marylebone, London, England. It was established in 1822 and is London's oldest music college. Compare ROYAL COLLEGE OF MUSIC.

the ,Royal 'Air Force (*abbr* the RAF) ⇨ note at ARMED FORCES.

the 'Royal 'Albert 'Hall ⇨ ALBERT HALL.

the ,Royal and 'Ancient a golf club established in 1754 at St Andrews, Scotland. It is recognized as the world's leading authority on the rules of golf (except in the US). It also organizes The *Open golf competition, which is sometimes played on the course there.

the ,Royal 'Armoured Corps (*abbr* the RAC) a division of the British Army formed in 1939 to combine all the units using armoured vehicles (= tanks or other heavily protected and armed vehicles). It also includes all the old cavalry regiments (= soldiers who fought on horses) except the *Household Cavalry.

the ,royal 'arms n [pl] the personal symbol of the British king or queen, consisting of a *lion and a unicorn holding a shield, on which other symbols represent England, Scotland and Ireland. The words *Honi soit qui mal y pense (the motto of the *Order of the Garter) are written on a belt around the shield. Underneath are the words *Dieu et mon droit (the personal motto of the king or queen). Companies with a *royal warrant to supply goods to members of the *royal family may use the royal arms on their products, etc.

the ,Royal Ar'tillery (*abbr* the RA) a division of the British Army, formed in 1716, whose main weapons are large guns and missiles for shooting at enemy soldiers, aircraft, etc.

,Royal 'Ascot /ˈæskət/ (*also* **Ascot**) a fashionable British horse-racing event held at *Ascot each year in June. Members of the *royal family attend some of the races, and many people go there for social reasons rather than sport. The third day of Royal Ascot is usually *Ladies' Day(1), for which many of the women present wear large and elegant hats. See also ROYAL ENCLOSURE, SEASON.

the ,royal as'sent n [sing] the final stage that a British *Act of Parliament must go through to become law, when it is signed by the king or queen.

the ,Royal 'Automobile Club (*abbr* the RAC) a British club for drivers of motor vehicles. It offers various services to its members, especially help when their vehicles break down. It developed from a club established in London in 1897. Compare AUTOMOBILE ASSOCIATION.

the ,Royal 'Ballet the national ballet company of Britain. It was formed from a company started in 1931 by Ninette *de Valois and became the Royal Ballet in 1956. Its famous dancers in the years before *World War II included Alicia Markova, Anton *Dolin and Robert Helpmann, and after the war Margot *Fonteyn and Rudolf Nureyev. It performs both modern and traditional works. Its main base is the *Royal Opera House, *Covent Garden, London. See also SADLER'S WELLS.

the 'Royal 'Bank of 'Scotland /ˈskɒtlənd; *AmE* ˈskɑːtlənd/ the largest Scottish bank, established in 1727. It is part of the Royal Bank of Scotland Group, which also owns *NatWest.

the 'Royal 'British 'Legion ⇨ BRITISH LEGION.

,royal 'charter n an award given by the British *Privy Council to certain organizations or institutions which are recognized as the leading authorities in their field. Organizations with royal charters include the *BBC, the *British Academy and some British universities.

the 'Royal 'College of 'Art a college for the study of art, in central London, England, established in 1837. Many famous British artists studied there in the 1950s and 1960s, including David *Hockney and Bridget *Riley. It now only offers postgraduate courses (= courses above ordinary degree level). See also ROYAL ACADEMY, ROYAL SOCIETY OF ARTS.

the 'Royal 'College of 'Music a college for the study of music in *Kensington, London, England, established in 1883. The college has a museum of musical instruments. Compare ROYAL ACADEMY OF MUSIC.

the 'Royal 'College of 'Nursing Britain's largest trade union for nurses, which also provides education for its members at the Royal College of Nursing Institute in London.

the 'Royal 'College of Phy'sicians a professional organization for doctors in England, Wales and Northern Ireland, first formed in 1518. Its equivalents in Scotland are the Royal College of Physicians of Edinburgh and the Royal College of Physicians and Surgeons of Glasgow.

,Royal Com'mission n a group of people appointed by the British government to investigate and report on a particular matter. For example, the Royal Commission on Criminal Justice (1993) recommended changes to police and legal procedures after the cases of the *Guildford Four and *Birmingham Six.

the 'Royal 'Courts of 'Justice ⇨ LAW COURTS.

the 'Royal 'Court 'Theatre a theatre in *Sloane Square, established in 1870. It is known for its performances of modern plays, particularly by the *English Stage Company and for the Young Writers Programme it has run since 1966.

the ,Royal 'Crescent a long curved street in the town of *Bath, south-west England, with a continuous row of houses on one side and a large open area on the other. It was designed in 1767–75 by John Wood the younger (1728–81), and is admired as a fine example of *Georgian architecture.

,Royal 'Doulton™ /ˈdəʊltən; *AmE* ˈdoʊltən/ an English company that makes pottery and porcelain (= hard, white, shiny material made by baking a type of fine clay). It was started in London in the early 19th century by John Doulton and his son Henry. The company's factory is now at Burslem near *Stoke-on-Trent, and there is a Doulton museum nearby.

the ˌRoyal En'closure a special area of the grounds at *Royal Ascot, a famous British horse-racing event. People are only allowed in if they have a ticket, and there are strict rules about dress. Men must wear very formal suits and women must wear skirts that reach below the knee.

the ˌRoyal Engi'neers (abbr the RE) a division of the British Army, formed in 1717, which deals with engineering tasks such as building bridges, etc.

the ˌRoyal Ex'change a theatre in *Manchester, England, built in the city's old cotton exchange (= a large circular trading hall). The theatre reopened in 1998 after it was damaged by an *IRA bomb in 1996.

the ˌroyal 'family (in Britain) the term used to refer to the present Queen and her family: her husband, Prince *Philip and their children, Prince *Charles, Princess *Anne, Prince *Andrew and Prince *Edward, together with their wives or husbands and children. The wider family, who gather on ceremonial occasions, includes the Queen's cousins and their children. The present **royal house** (= ruling family) is the House of *Windsor(2) and *Elizabeth II is descended from *William I (1066–97), and before that from Egbert, King of *Wessex 802–39. The **monarch** or **sovereign** (= king or queen) originally had sole power but over time the sovereign's powers have been reduced and, though the present Queen is still **head of state** and **Commander-in-Chief** of the armed forces, she acts on the advice of her ministers and Britain is in practice governed by **Her Majesty's Government**. The Queen has some official duties, such as opening a new session of *Parliament and giving *royal assent to new laws, but her main role is as a representative of Britain and the British people. She is also head of the *Commonwealth and works to strengthen links between member countries. Other members of the royal family also represent Britain, act as patrons of British cultural organizations and support the work of charities. Through most of the 20th century, the royal family were only seen on formal occasions and remained distant and dignified. However, at the end of the 20th century, the younger **royals** began to live more public lives and attracted enormous media attention, and traditional respect for the royal family began to decline. Especially after the death of Princess *Diana, the royal family was criticized and many people began to think that they were out of touch with modern attitudes. Since then they have tried to be more open and to meet a wider range of people. Some people in Britain have no strong feelings about the royal family although they might like some aspects of the **monarchy** to be more modern. Others would not want to see any big changes. There are also people who would prefer not to have a monarchy, to be citizens rather than subjects.

the 'Royal 'Festival 'Hall (also the ˌFestival 'Hall) a large concert hall on the *South Bank of the *Thames in London. It was opened in 1951 as part of the *Festival of Britain. Since then various other concert halls and theatres have been built around it. The *London Philharmonic Orchestra has performed there regularly since 1992.

the ˌRoyal 'Film Per,formance an event held each year in London, England, in which a new film is shown for the first time before an audience including members of the *royal family. Money from the event goes to charity. Its former name was the Royal Command Film Performance. Compare ROYAL VARIETY PERFORMANCE.

the ˌRoyal 'Flying Corps (abbr the RFC) the name of the first British air force, formed in 1912. It became the *Royal Air Force in 1918.

the ˌRoyal 'Free ˌHospital a hospital in *Hampstead, London, England, established in 1828 by William Marsden (1796–1867), who also established London's *Marsden Hospital. It was one of the first hospitals to treat patients free of charge.

the ˌRoyal Geo'graphical So,ciety an organization formed in London, England, in 1830 to provide money and support for journeys of discovery abroad, especially in Africa. Among the first journeys were those of David *Livingstone and Richard *Burton[2]. Its main work today is in scientific publishing and education.

the 'Royal 'Greenwich Ob'servatory /'grenɪtʃ/ ⇨ ROYAL OBSERVATORY.

the ˌRoyal 'Highland ˌRegiment ⇨ BLACK WATCH.

the ˌRoyal Horti'cultural So,ciety (abbr the RHS) a British society of gardeners, started in 1804 by Joseph *Banks and others, which holds the *Chelsea Flower Show each year. The Society owns various gardens around Britain, including the garden at *Wisley where research into horticulture (= growing flowers, fruit and vegetables) is carried out.

the ˌroyal 'household n the staff of a British king or queen. Its senior members include the *Lord Chamberlain, and it also includes representatives of the armed forces and the church, medical staff and various other officials. Other members of the *royal family have their own smaller households.

the 'Royal 'Institute of 'British 'Architects (abbr the RIBA) a British organization, started in 1834, that aims to encourage the understanding, study and practice of architecture. Its members are architects and other people with an interest in architecture, and it arranges various exhibitions, events and talks at its centre in London.

the ˌRoyal Insti'tution a British organization established in 1799 with the aim of teaching science to the public through talks and experiments. Its past directors have included Michael *Faraday and Humphrey *Davy, and Faraday's scientific equipment is kept at the Institution's buildings in London. The most famous of its public talks is the Christmas Lecture for Young People, started in 1826 and now shown every year on British television.

the 'Royal Inter'national Agri'cultural Show (also the **Royal Show**) an exhibition of farming methods, machinery, animals, etc. held every year at Stoneleigh Park, *Warwickshire, England.

the 'Royal Inter'national 'Horse Show an international competition of showjumping (= the sport of riding horses over difficult barriers) held every year at *Hickstead, *Sussex, England.

the 'Royal 'Liverpool Philhar'monic ˌOrchestra /'lɪvəpuːl; AmE 'lɪvərpuːl/ (abbr the RLPO) a leading British orchestra established in Liverpool in 1840. Famous conductors of the orchestra have included Thomas *Beecham and Malcolm *Sargent.

the ˌRoyal 'Mail (in Britain) the organization that collects and delivers letters. It is a part of the Royal Mail Group plc, an independent company that owns the *Post Office and provides a service for delivering parcels, Parcelforce Worldwide. ⇨ note at POSTAL SERVICES.

the ˌRoyal Ma'rines /mə'riːnz/ a branch of the British *Royal Navy that can fight on land as well as at sea. It was formed in 1664 and is best known for its div-

R

isions of *Commandos who are trained to operate in difficult environments (e.g. in extreme cold). Compare UNITED STATES MARINE CORPS.

the **'Royal 'Marsden 'Hospital** /'mɑːzdən; *AmE* 'mɑːrzdən/ ⇨ MARSDEN.

the **'Royal 'Mile** the line of three streets in *Edinburgh, leading down the hill from Edinburgh Castle to *Holyrood House.

the **'Royal 'Military A'cademy** ⇨ SANDHURST.

the **'Royal 'Mint** the British government organization responsible for making all the coins used in Britain. It also makes coins for more than 100 other countries, and produces military and prize medals. Paper money is made by the *Bank of England. Since 1968 the Royal Mint has been based at Llantrisant in South Wales.

the **'Royal 'National Ei'steddfod of 'Wales** /aɪ'steðvɒd, 'weɪlz; *AmE* aɪ'steðvɑːd/ ⇨ EISTEDDFOD.

the **'Royal 'National 'Institute for 'Deaf People** a British organization that helps people who are deaf or cannot hear very well. It was formed in 1911, and provides services such as special employment and housing.

the **'Royal 'National 'Institute of the 'Blind** a British organization that helps people who are blind or cannot see very well. It was formed in 1868. Among its activities it publishes books in Braille (= a system of reading and writing for blind people) and runs schools for blind children.

the **'Royal 'National 'Lifeboat Insti,tution** (*abbr* **the RNLI**) a popular British charity, formed in 1824, which provides boats to rescue people at sea around the coasts of Britain and Ireland. Small models of these boats are found in many shops and pubs, with a hole in the top for people to put money in. The people who work in the rescue service, which is available at all times, do so without pay.

the **'Royal 'National 'Theatre** ⇨ NATIONAL THEATRE.

the **,Royal 'Naval ,College** ⇨ BRITANNIA ROYAL NAVAL COLLEGE.

the **'Royal 'Naval Re'serve** a branch of the British *Volunteer Reserve Forces which works with the *Royal Navy. Its members are volunteers who train in their spare time to do jobs at sea or on land that would be important in time of war or emergency.

the **,Royal 'Navy** (*abbr* **the RN**) ⇨ note at ARMED FORCES.

'Royal 'Neighbors of A'merica (*abbr* **RNA**) a US women's *benefit society started in 1895 which provides life insurance and other financial products for women.

the **,Royal Ob'servatory** (*also* **the Royal Greenwich Observatory**) an observatory (= a building from which to study the stars, weather, etc.) at *Greenwich, London, England. Its original purpose was to study the stars in order to help sailors find their position at sea, and its work led to the widespread use of *Greenwich Mean Time and the Greenwich Meridian, an imaginary line running through Greenwich from north to south around the earth. International time zones are still measured from the Greenwich Meridian. The building is now part of the *National Maritime Museum. See also ASTRONOMER ROYAL.

the **,Royal 'Opera House** a large theatre in London, England, where performances are given by the Royal Opera and the *Royal Ballet. The present building was opened in 1858. The theatre is also known as 'Covent Garden' after the area in London in which it stands.

,royal 'park *n* any of the nine parks in London, England, originally owned by the king or queen and now managed by the government. They include the large central London parks of Green Park, *Regent's Park, *St James's Park, *Kensington Gardens and *Hyde Park(1), as well as *Richmond Great Park, *Hampton Court Park, Bushey Park and Greenwich Park.

the **,Royal Pa'vilion** (*also* **the Brighton Pavilion**) a famous building in *Brighton, England, designed in an Indian style by John *Nash. It was completed in 1820 and was a favourite building of the *Prince Regent, later King *George IV. The rooms are mainly in a Chinese style. It is now kept as a museum.

the **'Royal 'Philharmonic 'Orchestra** a leading British orchestra established in London in 1946 by Thomas *Beecham. Since 1996 its musical director has been Daniele Gatti (1962–).

,royal sa'lute *n* (in Britain) the firing of cannons to mark certain royal or state occasions. These include the *Queen's Birthday, the opening of Parliament, and the visits of foreign heads of state. The guns are normally fired near the *Tower of London or in one of the *royal parks. The number fired varies according to the occasion. For example, 41 guns are fired when a child is born to a member of the *royal family.

the **,Royal 'Scots** /'skɒts; *AmE* 'skɑːts/ the oldest division of the British Army, formed in Scotland in 1633. It is also known as the Royal Regiment.

the **'Royal 'Scottish A'cademy** /'skɒtɪʃ; *AmE* 'skɑːtɪʃ/ an organization formed in 1826 to encourage painting, sculpture and architecture in Scotland, similar to the *Royal Academy in London. Its buildings are in *Princes Street, *Edinburgh.

the **,Royal 'Shakespeare ,Company** /'ʃeɪkspɪə; *AmE* 'ʃeɪkspɪr/ (*abbr* **the RSC**) a leading British theatre company that performs plays by *Shakespeare and other writers. It was formed in 1960 and its first director was Peter *Hall. The company performs regularly at theatres in London, *Stratford-upon-Avon, *Newcastle and *Plymouth, and its present director is Michael Boyd.

the **,Royal 'Shakespeare ,Theatre** /'ʃeɪkspɪə; *AmE* 'ʃeɪkspɪr/ a theatre in *Stratford-upon-Avon, England, where the *Royal Shakespeare Company regularly performs. It began in 1879 as the Shakespeare Memorial Theatre and the present building was opened in 1932.

the **,Royal 'Show** ⇨ ROYAL INTERNATIONAL AGRICULTURAL SHOW.

the **,Royal So'ciety** the oldest and most important scientific organization in Britain, formed in 1660. Among its first members were Robert *Boyle and Christopher *Wren, and its presidents have included Isaac *Newton and Ernest *Rutherford. Its work now includes scientific publishing and giving awards. Being elected as a *fellow* (= member) of the Royal Society is one of the highest honours in British science. The Society's main buildings are at Carlton House Terrace in London.

the **'Royal So'ciety for the Pre'vention of 'Cruelty to 'Animals** (*abbr* **the RSPCA**) a well-known British charity, formed in 1824, which aims to make sure that the laws about protecting animals are being followed. It also tries to get new laws introduced and gives medical care to animals that need it. In the past it has helped to end many forms of cruel treatment, and one of its present concerns is to improve the conditions for the transport of live farm animals.

the **'Royal So'ciety for the Pro'tection of 'Birds** (*abbr* **the RSPB**) a well-known British charity formed in 1889 with the aim of protecting wild birds. It owns over 100 special areas of land in Britain where birds can breed.

the **'Royal So'ciety of 'Arts** (*abbr* **the RSA**) a British organization formed in 1754 by William Shipley to encourage high standards in the arts, industry and business. Its full name is the Royal Society for the Encouragement of Arts, Manufactures and Commerce. It is best known today for holding examinations and giving qualifications in various subjects, including *TEFL (= Teaching English as a Foreign Language): *an RSA Preparatory Certificate in TEFL.*

the **,Royal 'Tournament** an event held every year at *Earl's Court, London, England, in which teams from the British army, navy and air force showed their skill in various physical exercises, displays of motorcycle riding, etc. The last Royal Tournament was held in July 1999.

the **'Royal 'Ulster Con'stabulary** /'ʌlstə; *AmE* 'ʌlstər/ (*abbr* **the RUC**) the police force of Northern Ireland, named in 1922. It worked closely with the British army during the years of political violence in Northern Ireland. After the *Good Friday Agreement a review of policing in Northern Ireland led to its replacement in 2001 by the *Police Service of Northern Ireland.

,Royal U,nited 'Services ,Institute (*abbr* **RUSI**) an organization in *Whitehall, *London started in 1831 which carries out research into defence and security issues, provides advice and information, and has a programme of talks and conferences.

the **,Royal Va'riety Per,formance** a show held every year at a leading theatre in Britain, usually in London, attended by members of the *royal family and shown on television, in which various entertainers perform for charity. Compare ROYAL FILM PERFORMANCE.

,royal 'warrant *n* the right given to some British companies to display the personal symbol of the Queen, the *Duke of Edinburgh, or the *Prince of Wales on their products, etc. The warrant indicates a company that supplies goods or services to these members of the *royal family.

the **,royal 'we** *n* [sing] the use of 'we' instead of 'I' by British kings or queens in former times. Although this is no longer done, people still sometimes make jokes about it.

> **66** We are not amused. **99**
> a famous remark made by Queen Victoria

the **'Royal 'Welsh 'Show** an agricultural show that started in 1904 and takes place over four days every year in July in Builth Wells in Wales. Farmers show their best animals, and there are displays, competitions and other events.

,Royal 'Worcester™ /'wʊstə(r)/ an English company that has been making china of high quality since the 18th century. Its factory is in the city of *Worcester.

,royal 'yacht *n* a ship that was used by members of the British *royal family when making trips abroad. The last royal yacht, *Britannia, was first used in 1953 and was taken out of service in 1997. It is now a tourist attraction in Leith, the port of *Edinburgh.

the **,Royal 'Yacht ,Squadron** a British club for people who own and sail yachts. Its base is at *Cowes on the *Isle of Wight and was established in 1815.

RP /,ɑː 'piː; *AmE* ,ɑːr/ ⇨ RECEIVED PRONUNCIATION.

RPI /,ɑː piː 'aɪ; *AmE* ,ɑːr/ ⇨ RETAIL PRICE INDEX.

RPIX /,ɑː piː aɪ 'eks; *AmE* ,ɑːr/ (*in full* **retail price index excluding mortgage interest payments**) a measurement of inflation which shows the change in the overall cost of goods and services bought by the average household in Britain not including mortgage interest

payments. It is published every month by the *Office for National Statistics. ⇨ RETAIL PRICE INDEX.

RRP /,ɑːr ɑː 'piː; *AmE* ,ɑːr ɑːr/ ⇨ RECOMMENDED RETAIL PRICE.

RSA /,ɑːr es 'eɪ/ ⇨ ROYAL SOCIETY OF ARTS.

RSC /,ɑːr es 'siː/ ⇨ ROYAL SHAKESPEARE COMPANY.

RSPB /,ɑːr es piː 'biː/ ⇨ ROYAL SOCIETY FOR THE PROTECTION OF BIRDS.

RSPCA /,ɑːr es piː siː 'eɪ/ ⇨ ROYAL SOCIETY FOR THE PREVENTION OF CRUELTY TO ANIMALS.

RSV /,ɑːr es 'viː/ ⇨ REVISED STANDARD VERSION.

,Rt 'Hon ⇨ RIGHT HONOURABLE.

,Rt 'Rev (*also* **Rt Revd**) ⇨ RIGHT REVEREND.

,Rube 'Goldberg ⇨ GOLDBERG.

,Rick 'Rubin /'ruːbɪn/ (Frederick Jay Rubin 1963–) a US music producer and record company owner, best known for his work in *rap and *heavy metal. He founded the **Def Jam** record label in 1984 with Russell Simmons and produced records by bands including the Beastie Boys and Run DMC. In 1998 he left Def Jam to form the Def American record label, which later became American Recordings.

,Arthur 'Rubinstein¹ /'ruːbɪnstaɪn/ (1888–1982) a US piano player of classical music, born in Poland. He first played in public at the age of 12, and continued performing until he was 90. He became a US citizen in 1946. Rubinstein made many recordings, including the complete works of Chopin and many by Beethoven and Brahms.

,Helena 'Rubinstein² /,helənə 'ruːbɪnstaɪn/ (1871–1965) a US businesswoman, born in Poland, who created the famous cosmetics company that carries her name. She began her business in 1902 in Australia and later opened salons (= places for beauty treatments) in London, Paris and New York. Her business became a large international company after *World War I. She started the Helena Rubinstein Foundation which gives money for educational projects, especially for women and children in New York.

,Jack 'Ruby /'ruːbi/ (1911–67) the man who shot and killed Lee Harvey *Oswald in 1963. Oswald had been arrested two days before for the murder of President John F *Kennedy and was being taken by the police to a prison in *Dallas. Ruby pushed through the crowd who were watching and shot Oswald at close range in front of television cameras. Some people thought he did this because there had been a secret plan to kill Kennedy and Ruby was told to stop Oswald revealing it, but this was never proved. Ruby was sent to prison and died there.

the **RUC** /,ɑː juː 'siː; *AmE* ,ɑːr/ ⇨ ROYAL ULSTER CONSTABULARY.

'Rudolph, the 'Red-nosed 'Reindeer a children's Christmas song written in 1949 about a reindeer (= type of deer) called Rudolph, who has a shiny red nose, and the other reindeer laugh at him because they think it looks ridiculous. *Santa Claus chooses him to pull his sleigh on Christmas Eve.

▶ Rugby

Rugby is a fast, rough team game that is played throughout the British Isles. The game split off from British *football in the mid 19th century when the *Football Association forbade players to handle the ball. There are two **codes** of Rugby football, **Rugby Union** and **Rugby League**, which have slightly different rules and scoring systems. In Rugby League each team has 13 players, compared with 15 in Rugby Union. Players sometimes change from one code to the other during their careers.

R

In Rugby, teams try to **win possession** of a large oval-shaped ball and carry or kick it towards the opposing team's **goal line**, the line at each end of the **pitch** where the H-shaped **goalposts** are. If the ball is **touched down** (= put down by hand) on the grass beyond the touchline, a **try** (worth five points in Rugby Union, four points in Rugby League) is scored. A further two points are scored if the try is **converted** (= kicked between the goalposts, above the horizontal crossbar). Points can also be obtained from **penalty goals** scored as a result of **free kicks**, and from **drop goals** (= kicks at the goal during play). Players try to stop opponents carrying and passing the ball by **tackling** them. When a minor rule is broken players restart play by forming a **scrum** (= linking together in a group) or by taking a free kick.

Rugby Union, also called **rugger**, is the older of the two Rugby codes. It is said to have begun at *Rugby School in 1823. Rugby Union is played mainly by men, though there are now some women's teams. The most important national competitions include the *county championship, the Pilkington Cup and the Schweppes Welsh Cup.

Rugby League broke away from Rugby Union in the 1890s. Rugby had become popular among adults in northern England and many could not afford to take time off work to play in matches without being paid. The Northern Union, later called the **Rugby League**, was formed in 1895 and soon had many full-time paid professional players. The most important competitions include the Challenge Cup and the League Championship. The two codes may reunite in the future, particularly since in 1995 the International Rugby Board allowed Rugby Union players to become paid professionals.

National Rugby Union teams from England, Wales, Scotland and Ireland play against each other for the *triple crown. The teams also play with France and Italy in the annual *Six Nations' Championship, and against Australia, New Zealand, South Africa and other countries. Major international grounds include *Twickenham and *Murrayfield.

Most Americans have little knowledge of Rugby and in the US it is mostly played by amateur players in colleges and universities. Rugby was first played in the US in 1874 at *Harvard University, but after the development of American football in about 1880 it almost disappeared. It continued to be played in *California, but it was not until 1975 that the USA Rugby Football Union was established in *Denver. By 1998, 1420 clubs were associated with the organization. Competitions include the Saint Patrick's Day Tournament in El Paso, Texas, the Aspen Ruggerfest in *Aspen, Colorado, and, for women, the Mardi Gras Tournament in *New Orleans.

,**Rugby 'School** a leading English *public school(1) in the town of Rugby, *Warwickshire, established in 1567. Its headmaster from 1827 to 1842 was Thomas *Arnold, and it is the school where the book *Tom Brown's Schooldays is set. *Rugby football was first played at the school and is named after it.

,**Rule, Bri'tannia!** /brɪ'tænjə/ a British patriotic song (= one expressing pride in Britain) written in 1740 by Thomas Arne (1710–78) with words by James Thomson (1700–48). It is sung at the *Last Night of the Proms. Its last words, which most British people know, are:

> 66 Rule, Britannia! Britannia, rule the waves! Britons never, never, never shall be slaves. 99

'**Rumpole** /'rʌmpəʊl; AmE 'rʌmpoʊl/ a character who appears in various books and television programmes by the English writer John Mortimer. Rumpole is a bad-tem-

pered old *barrister (= an English lawyer) who helps people with their legal cases, especially difficult ones. He is best known from the television series Rumpole of the Bailey (1978–92), in which the actor Leo McKern played Rumpole.

the ,**Rump 'Parliament** a name given to the parliament that governed Britain from 1648 to 1653 and from 1659 to 1660, after the *Long Parliament had been reduced in size. (The rump of something is a small part left from something that was much bigger.) It voted for the trial and execution of King *Charles I and ended just before the *Restoration.

,**Donald 'Rumsfeld** /'rʌmsfeld/ (1932–) a US politician who is known for his aggressive personality and strong opinions. He was first elected to the *House of Representatives in 1965. He was the US ambassador to *NATO (1973–74) and **US Secretary of Defense** under President Gerald *Ford (1975–77) and again under President George W *Bush from 2001. Rumsfeld is famous for his use of the English language and people like to quote 'the poetry of Donald Rumsfeld'.

> 66 There are known knowns; there are things we know we know. We also know there are known unknowns; that is to say we know there are some things we do not know. But there are also unknown unknowns – the ones we don't know we don't know. 99
> Donald Rumsfeld

'**Runnymede** /'rʌnimiːd/ a field beside the River *Thames near *Windsor¹(1), famous as the place where King *John of England agreed to sign the *Magna Carta.

,**Damon 'Runyon** /,deɪmən 'rʌnjən/ (1884–1946) a US author and sports journalist. He is known for his humorous short stories about unusual and colourful New York characters, including criminals, sports people and actors. They are written in the sort of *slang that is typically used by such people. The *Broadway musical play *Guys and Dolls and its film version were based on Runyon's 1932 collection of stories by that name.

,**Prince 'Rupert** (1619–82) an English soldier. He was the grandson of King *James I and is best remembered for commanding the Royalist cavalry (= soldiers on horses) during the *English Civil War. He was defeated at the battles of *Marston Moor and *Naseby, but escaped abroad, returning to England after the *Restoration. He later helped to form the *Hudson's Bay Company and the *Royal Society.

,**Rupert the 'Bear** (also ,**Rupert 'Bear**) a character in the British children's stories by Mary Tourtel (1874–1948). Rupert is a bear who wears a red top, yellow checked trousers and a yellow checked scarf. He appeared first in 1920 in a regular cartoon strip in the *Daily Express newspaper, and later in several books and television series.

,**Rural 'Rides** ⇒ COBBETT.

Ed Ruscha /,ruː'ʃeɪ/ (Edward Ruscha 1937–) a US artist, a member of the *pop art movement, who became known in the 1960s for his paintings and collages (= a picture made by sticking pieces of paper, photographs etc. onto a surface), especially for his pictures using words and phrases.

,**Greg Ru'sedski** /rʊ'zedski/ (1973–) a British tennis player, born in Canada. He began playing for Britain in 1995 and has won several international competitions.

,**Salman 'Rushdie** /,sælmən 'rʌʃdi/ (1947–) a British writer, born in India. His first successful novel was Midnight's Children (1981), which won the *Booker Prize. It was followed by Shame (1983). A later novel, The

Satanic Verses (1988), was about the religion of Islam, and was thought by some Muslims to be very offensive. The Ayatollah Khomeini of Iran declared that Rushdie should be killed. As a result Rushdie lived under police protection at a secret address for many years. He continues to publish novels, among them *The Moor's Last Sigh* (1995).

,Mount 'Rushmore /ˌrʌʃmɔː(r)/ a high rock cliff in the Black Hills of the US state of *South Dakota. It is famous for the very large heads of four US presidents carved in the rock: George *Washington, Thomas *Jefferson, Abraham *Lincoln and Theodore *Roosevelt. The heads are each about 60 feet/18 metres high and were designed by Gutzon Borglum and carved between 1927 and 1941.

RUSI /ˌɑː juː es 'aɪ; *AmE* ˌɑːr/ ⇨ ROYAL UNITED SERVICES INSTITUTE.

,John 'Ruskin /ˈrʌskɪn/ (1819–1900) an English writer and artist. He supported the work of J M W *Turner and the *Pre-Raphaelites and was a leading figure in the *Gothic Revival. In 1869 he became the first Professor of Art at *Oxford University, and his books about art include *Modern Painters* (1843–60) and *The Stones of Venice* (1851–3). He also wrote about social justice and was in favour of better educational opportunities for working people. Ruskin College, Oxford, is named after him. His house in the *Lake District is kept as a museum.

,Bertrand 'Russell[1] /ˌbɜːtrənd 'rʌsl; *AmE* ˌbɜːrtrənd/ (1872–1970) an English philosopher and writer. He began his career as a writer on mathematics and logic, and his best-known early book is *Principia Mathematica* (1910–13). He also taught philosophy, and in 1912–13 Ludwig *Wittgenstein was one of his students at *Cambridge University. In 1931 he became the 3rd Earl Russell. Among his other works are popular books on philosophy, education and social issues, and his *History of Western Philosophy* (1945) was particularly successful. He won the *Nobel Prize for literature in 1950. In the later years of his life he was famous for his strong political opinions. He became the first president of the *Campaign for Nuclear Disarmament in 1958.

,Jane 'Russell[2] /ˈrʌsl/ (1921–) a US film actor who became a sex symbol. She was discovered by Howard *Hughes, who made her a star in *The Outlaw* (1943). Her other films included *The Paleface* (1948) and *Gentlemen Prefer Blondes* (1953).

,Ken 'Russell[3] /ˈrʌsl/ (1927–) an English film director. He began his career producing films for television about the lives of poets and composers, but is best known for his cinema films. These include *Women in Love* (1969), *The Music Lovers* (1971), *Mahler* (1974) and *Tommy* (1975). He has also made a television version of *Lady Chatterley's Lover* (1993). Some people criticize his films for including too much sex and violence, but others admire his lively and imaginative style.

the 'Rust Belt an informal name for the *Middle West and north-eastern states of the US. This is because many of the large factories in these areas are old or have closed. Some former industries there, such as steel, have now almost gone, and many workers have moved to the *Sunbelt.

,Rutgers Uni'versity /ˌrʌtɡəz; *AmE* ˌrʌtɡərz/ the famous university of the US state of *New Jersey. It was established as Queens College in 1766 at New Brunswick and changed its name in 1825.

' ,Babe 'Ruth /ˌbeɪb 'ruːθ/ (1895–1948) the most famous US *baseball player in the history of the game. He was born George Herman Ruth, and his popular name was the 'Bambino'. He played for the New York *Yankees

(1919–35), and Yankee Stadium is sometimes called 'the house that Ruth built'. He had 60 home runs (= hits that allow the hitter to run around all the bases without stopping) in 1927, the most ever for a baseball season until 1961, and a total of 714 during his career, the most until 1974. He was chosen for the National Baseball *Hall of Fame in 1936.

,Ernest 'Rutherford[1] /ˈrʌðəfəd; *AmE* ˈrʌðərfərd/ (1871–1937) a British scientist, born in New Zealand. His main interest was in the structure of the atom, and he worked for much of his career at the *Cavendish Laboratory at *Cambridge University. In 1902 he explained the process of radioactive decay, in which one chemical element can turn into another, and he received the *Nobel Prize for this work in 1908. Later work identified alpha, beta and gamma rays, and he discovered and named the proton (= part of the atom) in 1919. His work was of great importance in the later development of nuclear technology. He was made a *life peer in 1931.

,Margaret 'Rutherford[2] /ˈrʌðəfəd; *AmE* ˈrʌðərfərd/ (1892–1972) an English comedy actor. She is best remembered for playing rather eccentric older women, e.g. in the film versions of *Blithe Spirit* (1945) and *The *Importance of Being Earnest* (1952). She also played the part of Miss *Marple in several film versions of the novels of Agatha *Christie. She was made a *dame(2) in 1967.

'Rutland /ˈrʌtlənd/ a former county in eastern central England. It was England's smallest county, but became part of *Leicestershire in 1974. Many local people opposed this and in 1996 the people of Rutland chose to have their own separate *unitary authority, Rutland County Council.

RV /ˌɑː 'viː; *AmE* ˌɑːr/ ⇨ REVISED VERSION.

,Nolan 'Ryan /ˌnəʊlən 'raɪən; *AmE* ˌnoʊlən/ (1947–) a US baseball pitcher (= player who throws the ball to be hit). He has made more opponents strike out (= fail to hit the ball three times and be dismissed) than anyone in a single baseball season (383 in 1973) and during a career (5714). He played with the New York Mets (1967–70), the California Angels (1971–8), the Houston Astros (1979–87) and the Texas Rangers (1988–93). He was chosen for the Baseball *Hall of Fame in 1999.

Ryanair /ˌraɪən'eə(r); *AmE* ˌraɪən'er/ an Irish airline started in 1985 by Tony Ryan, which operates low-cost flights across Europe. Ryanair offers flights from many cities in Britain but mainly from *Stansted. The cheap flights it offers have led to a rapid increase in the number of short holidays abroad taken by British people.

,Sue 'Ryder /ˈraɪdə(r)/ (1923–2000) an English charity worker. In 1953 she started the Sue Ryder Foundation, which gives care to sick or disabled people in centres around the world. She had played an important part in *World War II, working with people who resisted the Nazis in Poland. In 1959 she married Leonard *Cheshire, who had done a lot of charity work similar to hers. She was made a *life peer in 1978.

the ,Ryder 'Cup /ˌraɪdə; *AmE* ˌraɪdər/ a professional golf competition for men held every two years between teams of US and European players. From 1927, when it was first held, to 1977 it was played between US and British teams. ⇨ note at GOLF.

,Martin 'Ryle /ˈraɪl/ (1918–84) an English astronomer. His work helped to establish the 'big bang' theory, which argues that all the matter in the universe exploded from a tiny point many millions of years ago. (This was opposed to the 'steady state' theory of Fred *Hoyle and others.) Ryle was made a *knight in 1966 and given the *Nobel Prize in 1974.

R

S s

,Saatchi & 'Saatchi /ˌsɑːtʃi, ˈsɑːtʃi/ a British advertising company started in 1970 by two brothers, **Charles Saatchi** (1943–) and **Maurice Saatchi** (1946–). It was very successful during the 1980s, and was known especially for its work for the British *Conservative Party. Charles Saatchi is now better known for collecting work by British artists including Damien *Hirst and Tracey *Emin which is shown in the Saatchi Gallery in *County Hall, London.

,Sacaja'wea /ˌsækədʒəˈwiːə/ (c. 1784–c. 1884) a *Shoshone *Native American who guided *Lewis and Clark in 1805 when they investigated the *Louisiana Purchase. She was the wife of the French *frontiersman Toussaint Charbonneau, who also travelled with them and interpreted for them. Sacajawea was especially helpful when they reached her home region around the Missouri River.

,Sacco and Van'zetti /ˌsækəʊ, vænˈzeti; AmE ˌsækoʊ/ two Italian-Americans, born in Italy, who were executed in the US in 1927 for the murder of two workers during a robbery at a *Massachusetts factory, although the evidence against them was not very strong. **Nicola Sacco** (1891–1927) and **Bartolomeo Vanzetti** (1888–1927) were anarchists (= people who believe there should be no laws or government). Many people thought that they were found guilty because of their political views and there were strong protests. The city of *Boston decided in 1997 to honour Sacco and Vanzetti with a statue.

,Jonathan 'Sacks¹ /ˈsæks/ (1948–) an English rabbi (= Jewish religious leader) who became Britain's *Chief Rabbi in 1991.

,Oliver 'Sacks² /ˈsæks/ (1933–) an English neurologist (= doctor who studies the nerves and their diseases) who has written many books about unusual mental conditions. He has lived in the US since 1960 and has been Professor of Clinical Neurology at New York's Albert Einstein College of Medicine since 1965. His book *Awakenings* (1973) about a 'sleeping sickness' was made into a 1990 film with Robin *Williams. His other books include *The Man Who Mistook His Wife for a Hat* (1985) and *An Anthropologist on Mars* (1995).

'Vita 'Sackville-'West /ˈviːtə ˈsækvɪl ˈwest/ (1892– 1962) an English writer who published several novels, collections of poetry and other books. She married the writer Harold *Nicolson, but also had sexual affairs with women, including Virginia *Woolf. The gardens she created around her home at Sissinghurst in *Kent are now owned by the *National Trust.

,Sadie 'Hawkins Day /ˌseɪdi ˈhɔːkɪnz/ (in the US) a day when there is a custom that women invite men to a social event, especially a **Sadie Hawkins Day dance** instead of waiting to be invited. This is often done by students in a *high school, college or university. The custom takes its name from a character in the *Li'l Abner *comic strip, who is not married and is very anxious to have affairs with men.

,Sadler's 'Wells /ˌsædləz ˈwelz; AmE ˌsædlərz/ a theatre in north-east London, England. It became famous as the home of three important national companies: the *Royal Ballet, the Sadler's Wells Theatre Ballet (now the Birmingham Royal Ballet) and *English National Opera. All three have since moved to other theatres.

Sadler's Wells was rebuilt in 1998 and presents a variety of theatre, music and dance.

'Safeway /ˈseɪfweɪ/ any of a group of supermarkets in the US and in Britain. The supermarkets in the US and in Britain used to be part of the same American company. Safeway in Britain is now owned by a *Yorkshire firm, Morrisons: *We've got a Safeway just down the road.*

SAG /ˌes eɪ ˈdʒiː/ ⇨ SCREEN ACTORS GUILD.

'Saga /ˈsɑːgə/ a British travel company started in the 1950s which organizes and sells holidays for people aged over 50. The company now also provides financial services for older people, publishes a magazine and runs radio stations in some parts of the UK.

sa'guaro /səˈgwɑːrəʊ; AmE səˈgwɑːroʊ/ n (pl **-os**) a very large US cactus (= plant with thick, usually prickly stems that grows in hot, dry regions). Saguaros are found mainly in the US states of *Arizona and *California and in northern Mexico. They can grow to 50 feet/15 metres tall and live for more than 200 years. The **Saguaro National Park** is in Arizona, and the white flower of the saguaro is Arizona's state flower.

'Sainsbury's /ˈseɪnzbriz/ a large group of British supermarkets. The first Sainsbury's was a small shop in London, opened in 1869 by John James Sainsbury (1844–1928) and Mary Ann Sainsbury (1849–1927). The company developed steadily and opened its first supermarket in *Southampton in 1954. Since then many more have opened all over Britain. The Sainsbury family are also known for supporting the arts and charities in Britain and the Sainsbury Centre for Visual Arts near Norwich has an important collection of art given by the family: *I always buy my food at Sainsbury's.* ◇ *Have you got a Sainsbury's near you?* See also NATIONAL GALLERY.

Saint For entries beginning with the word 'Saint', see **St** (the usual form in written English), e.g. **St Albans**, **St Andrews**, etc. The names of individual saints are shown under the names themselves, not at 'St', e.g. the entry for St George is at **George**.

'Saki /ˈsɑːki/ the name under which the English author Hector Hugh Munro (1870–1916) wrote his short stories. These are often about *upper-class English life, and are humorous in a clever and sometimes cruel way. His collections of short stories include *Beasts and Superbeasts* (1914), and he also wrote three novels. He was killed in *World War I.

the ,Salem 'witch trials /ˌseɪləm/ [pl] a series of trials in 1692 in Salem, *Massachusetts, of people accused of being witches. They began after a group of young girls started behaving in a crazy way and saying that they were 'possessed' (= controlled by an evil spirit). People in the town were quick to accuse each other, and the trials ended with 20 people being executed, on very little evidence. Arthur *Miller used the trials as the basis for his play *The Crucible* (1953).

,J D 'Salinger /ˈsælɪndʒə(r)/ (Jerome David Salinger 1919–) a US writer of novels and short stories which were especially popular with college and university students in the 1950s and 1960s. His best-known novel is *The *Catcher in the Rye.* Many of Salinger's short stories were published in *The *New Yorker.* He is famous for his dislike of appearing in public.

'Salisbury[1] /'sɔːlzbri/ a town in *Wiltshire, southern England, on the River *Avon. It is famous for its cathedral, which has the highest spire (= pointed tower) in Britain, and for the ancient remains at Old Sarum, the original place where the town was built, to the north of the present town. Salisbury and its cathedral appear in many of the paintings of John *Constable.

Lord 'Salisbury[2] /'sɔːlzbri/ (born Robert Gascoyne-Cecil 1830–1903) a British *Conservative *Prime Minister (1885–6, 1886–92 and 1895–1902). He helped to increase the power of the *British Empire, especially in Africa, and supported the activities of Cecil *Rhodes and others. During his final period in power he led Britain in the *Boer Wars.

Salisbury 'Plain /ˌsɔːlzbri/ a large area of open land to the north and west of *Salisbury in southern England. It is used by the British Army as a training ground, and also contains *Stonehenge, an ancient circle of stones.

Salisbury 'steak /ˌsɔːlzbri/ n (AmE) a dish consisting of finely chopped meat mixed with egg and onions and fried, baked or cooked under a strong heat. It was named after J H Salisbury, a 19th-century expert on diet.

the 'Salk ˌvaccine /'sɔːlk/ n [sing] a medicine used to prevent polio (= a serious disease affecting the nervous system), developed in 1954 by the US scientist Jonas Salk (1914–95).

'Salop /'sæləp/ an old name for the English county of *Shropshire, used as its official name from 1974 to 1980.

Sa'lopian /sə'ləʊpiən; AmE sə'loʊpiən/ n **1** a person from the English county of *Shropshire. **2** a person from the town of *Shrewsbury in Shropshire. **3** a pupil or former pupil of *Shrewsbury School. ▸ **Salopian** adj.

'salsa n [U] **1** a type of Latin American dance music popular in Britain and the US. It is played especially by big bands with many brass instruments. **2** a spicy tomato sauce eaten with Mexican food.

SALT /sɔːlt/ ⇨ STRATEGIC ARMS LIMITATION TALKS.

Saltaire /sɔːl'teə(r); AmE sɔːl'ter/ a village near *Bradford in northern England which was built in 1853 as a model village for factory workers by Sir Titus Salt (1803–1876). It is now a UNESCO *World Heritage Site. The old factory building, **Salts Mill**, has been made into an art gallery with a large collection of paintings by David *Hockney and houses have been made into shops and restaurants for visitors.

Salt Lake 'City the capital and largest city of the US state of *Utah, on the Jordan River near the *Great Salt Lake. It was established in 1847 by Brigham *Young for his *Mormon group, and is still the home of that religion and its very large temple. Its original name was Great Salt Lake City and it was also called the 'New Jerusalem'. Local companies now produce processed food, computers and other electronic equipment.

the Sal ˌvation 'Army (also informal the ˌSally 'Army) a Christian organization started by William Booth (1829–1912) in the *East End of London, England, in 1865. Since then it has grown to be a worldwide organization, with branches in over 100 countries. It does a wide range of charity work, and is especially known for providing centres for old people and people without homes. It holds religious services in public with music from *brass bands, and its members wear military uniforms and have military ranks. In Britain, its members are sometimes seen in pubs collecting money for their work. In the US, they are known for singing carols and collecting money outside stores at Christmas time. The organization's magazine, The War Cry, has appeared every week since 1879. ▸ **Sal'vationist** n a member of the Salvation Army.

the Sa'maritans a British charity, started in 1953 by Chad Varah (1911–), which gives free help and advice to people who are very depressed or thinking of killing themselves. People can ring the Samaritans and discuss their problems with someone. The members of staff work without payment. There are now over 200 local branches of the charity and an international organization, Befrienders International, was formed in 1974.

'sambo /'sæmbəʊ; AmE 'sæmboʊ/ (pl **-os**) n [C] (slang offensive) a black man. The children's book The Story of Little Black Sambo (1899) by the English author Helen Bannerman was originally very popular both in Britain and the US but is now regarded as insulting to black people. The US group of Sambo's Restaurants was named after the main character in the book and was criticized for this by African Americans and the *Equal Employment Opportunity Commission.

Sam 'Browne /'braʊn/ (also ˌSam Browne 'belt) n (BrE) a type of leather belt with a strap that passes from the left side over the right shoulder, worn by British army officers, certain police officers, etc.

Pete 'Sampras /'sæmprəs/ (1971–) a US tennis player, thought by many people to be the greatest in the history of the game. By 1999 he had won twelve *grand slam(1) titles, including *Wimbledon six times (1993–5 and 1997–9) and the *US Open four times (1990, 1993, 1995 and 1996).

Samuel 'French /'frentʃ/ a publishing company that produces versions of plays for use by actors. As well as suggesting where and when actors should move on stage, they include information on lighting and sound effects. The company was formed in 1830 and has branches in both Britain and the US.

San An'dreas 'Fault /ˌsæn æn'dreiəs/ a break in the layers of rock forming the earth's surface that runs about 600 miles north to south through the US state of *California. It causes earthquakes, such as those in *San Francisco (1906 and 1989) and *Los Angeles (1994).

San An'tonio /ˌsæn æn'təʊniəʊ; AmE æn'toʊnioʊ/ the second largest city in the US state of *Texas on the San Antonio River. The *Alamo was built there in 1781 and can still be visited. The city attracts many tourists because of its attractive shops and restaurants along the river. It also has five large US military bases.

Carl 'Sandburg /'sændbɜːg; AmE 'sændbɜːrg/ (1878–1967) a US poet, writer and singer of *folk songs. He first worked on farms, and his poems are about ordinary life. He twice won the *Pulitzer Prize, for Complete Poems (1951) and for Abraham Lincoln: The War Years (1939), part of his long biography of Lincoln.

Colonel 'Sanders /'sɑːndəz; AmE 'sɑːndərz/ the man who began the *Kentucky Fried Chicken restaurants.

'Sandhurst /'sændhɜːst; AmE 'sændhɜːrst/ (also formal the **Royal Military Academy**) a training college for British Army officers near the village of Sandhurst, Berkshire, established in 1799. Compare WEST POINT.

San Di'ego /ˌsæn dɪ'eigəʊ; AmE dɪ'eigoʊ/ the second largest city in the US state of *California. It is on San Diego Bay on the Pacific coast near the Mexican border, and has a large US Navy base. Tourists are attracted to its beaches and historical buildings. The city is also known for its electronics and aerospace industries.

S & L /ˌes ənd 'el / (in full **savings and loan association**) ⇨ note at BUILDING SOCIETIES.

Sandringham 'House /ˌsændrɪŋəm/ a country house owned by the British *royal family, near *King's Lynn in *Norfolk. It was built in 1870 for the *Prince of Wales (later King *Edward VII), and is traditionally the place where the royal family spend Christmas. It is open to the public in the summer.

S

'Sandwich /'sændwɪdʒ/ a town on the south coast of *Kent, England, which was one of the original *Cinque Ports. It is now especially famous for its golf course, also called the Royal St George's golf course, where the *Open golf competition is regularly held.

'sandwich (*also BrE informal* **sarnie**) *n* two or more slices of bread and butter with meat, cheese, jam, etc. between, eaten with the hands. Sandwiches are popular as a light midday meal, and are often bought from **sandwich bars**, shops selling a wide range of different sandwiches. The 4th Earl of Sandwich (1718–92) is said to have invented them as a quick and easy meal to eat while gambling: *a lunch of beer and sandwiches* ◇ (*AmE*) *a peanut butter and jelly sandwich*. See also DAGWOOD, REUBEN SANDWICH.

'sandwich board *n* either of a pair of connected boards with advertisements on them which are hung over the front and back of a person (called a **sandwich man**) who walks about the streets to display them. They are no longer very common, but often appear in cartoons etc., especially with the words 'The end is nigh' written on them, because religious people sometimes wore them to warn others that they believed the world was about to end.

San Fran'cisco /ˌsæn frænˈsɪskəʊ; *AmE* frænˈsɪskoʊ/ a city in the US state of California, on **San Francisco Bay**. It is built on hills and is known for its beautiful views and Victorian style houses. It was established by the Spanish in 1776 as Yerba Buena, taken by the US in 1846 and given its present name the following year. It grew rapidly after the *Gold Rush but was badly damaged by an earthquake in 1906. Its many tourist attractions include the cable cars (= public vehicles that carry passengers up and down the steep hills), *Golden Gate Bridge, the restaurants along Fisherman's Wharf, *Nob Hill, *Haight-Ashbury, *Alcatraz and *Chinatown. San Francisco is a financial and communications centre and a centre for trade with Asia.

'San Fran'cisco 'Ballet /'sæn frənˈsɪskəʊ; *AmE* frənˈsɪskoʊ/ a large ballet company based in *San Francisco which was the first professional ballet company in the US when it was started in 1933. The company performs both traditional and modern ballets in the US and around the world. There is also a San Francisco Ballet School for training young dancers.

Frederick 'Sanger /'sæŋə(r)/ (1918–) an English scientist. He is the first scientist to have received two *Nobel Prizes for chemistry (in 1956 and 1980), and his work has been important for the development of genetic engineering (= the deliberate changing of small parts of the cells of plants or animals in order to change the way they grow). He became a member of the *Order of Merit in 1986.

the 'Battle of 'San Ja'cinto /'sæn dʒəˈsɪntəʊ; *AmE* dʒəˈsɪntoʊ/ the battle in 1836 that gained *Texas its independence from Mexico. The US forces led by Sam *Houston defeated a larger Mexican army led by General *Santa Anna. The battle was fought near the San Jacinto River in south-east Texas, and a tall monument was later built there.

'San Joa'quin 'Valley /'sæn wɑːˈkiːn/ a central valley in the US state of *California, around the **San Joaquin River**. It is considered to be one of the best agricultural regions in the US. Farmers there produce such crops as cotton, wheat, nuts, grapes and vegetables.

San Jo'se /ˌsæn həʊˈzeɪ; *AmE* hoʊˈzeɪ/ a city in western *California, in the Santa Clara Valley. Because of the many computer and electronics companies there, the area is often called *Silicon Valley. San Jose also produces fruit and wine. It was the capital of California

from 1849 to 1851. An earthquake in 1989 caused some damage.

'Sanka™ /'sæŋkə/ *n* [U] a make of 'instant' decaffeinated coffee. It was originally made in Germany by Dr Ludwig Roselius but is now produced by *Kraft™.

San 'Quentin /ˌsæn ˈkwentɪn/ a large prison near *San Francisco, *California, established in 1852. It is a 'maximum security' prison, and many of America's most violent criminals are sent there.

San 'Simeon /ˌsæn ˈsɪmiən/ the very expensive 'dream castle' built by the rich US newspaper owner William Randolph *Hearst on the Pacific coast between *San Francisco and *Los Angeles. He began it in 1919 and continued to make additions to it until he died in 1951. It combines Greek, Roman and Gothic architecture and has many original items from the ancient world. More than a million tourists now visit it every year.

An'tonio 'López de Santa 'Anna /æn'təʊniəʊ 'ləʊpez də sæntə 'ænə; *AmE* æn'toʊnioʊ 'loʊpez/ (1794–1876) the Mexican army officer who in 1836 led the attack on the *Alamo. Texas became independent of Mexico when his forces were defeated at the Battle of *San Jacinto in the same year. General Santa Anna later became Mexico's president and lost the *Mexican War in 1848.

▶ **Santa Claus**

Santa Claus, also called simply **Santa** or, in Britain, **Father Christmas**, is a fat, cheerful old man with a long white beard who brings children their presents on *Christmas Eve. Traditionally, he wears a bright red suit, a red hat lined with white fur and shiny black boots. Santa Claus is said to live at the North Pole and to have a workshop there where he and his elves makes toys. Santa Claus is also called **St Nick** and identified with St Nicholas, who lived in the 4th century AD and is the patron saint of children

In the period before Christmas children write letters to Santa telling him what gifts they would like. In Britain these letters are 'posted' up the chimney or sent to local newspapers, which arrange for Santa to send a reply. Children are careful to behave well, because Santa only brings toys to good children.

During this time Santa can also be found visiting many large shops, so that children can sit on his knee and tell him what presents they would like. In Britain children have to pay to enter Santa's **grotto** and in return receive a small gift from him; in America visiting Santa is free.

On 24 December, the night before Christmas, children hang **stockings** (= long socks) at the end of their beds. Santa leaves the North Pole with a **sled** or **sleigh**. Santa's sled is pulled by **reindeer** called Dasher, Dancer, Prancer, Vixen, Comet, Cupid, Donner, Blitzen and Rudolph, who know how to fly. They travel through the air stopping on the roof of every house where a child is sleeping. Santa slides down the chimney and leaves big presents under the Christmas tree and small ones in the stockings. He usually finds that the children have left him a plate of **Christmas cookies** or, in Britain, a **mince pie** (= a small pastry containing dried fruits), and possibly salt or a carrot for his reindeer.

Santa Claus is an important symbol of Christmas, and pictures of him appear on Christmas cards and decorations. He is mentioned in poems and Christmas songs such as *The *Night Before Christmas* and *Rudolph, the Red-nosed Reindeer*. As children get older they realize that Santa Claus cannot be real and stop believing in him.

Santa 'Fe /ˌsæntə ˈfeɪ/ the capital of the US state of *New Mexico. It is in the northern part of the state, close to the Sangre de Cristo Mountains. The Spanish established it in 1610 and built its Palace of Governors, the oldest public building in the US. About 1.5 million tourists visit the city each year.

,**Santa Fe 'Trail** /ˌsæntə feɪ/ an important US trade route in the 19th century. It was about 780 miles/1255 kilometres long and went from *Independence, *Missouri, to *Santa Fe, *New Mexico. Factory products were sent along it from east to west, and furs and gold went in the opposite direction. It stopped being used for trade when the Santa Fe Railroad was opened. Since 1987 it has been the **Sante Fe National Historic Trail**. See also COVERED WAGON.

,**Sara 'Lee™** /ˌseərə 'liː; AmE ˌserə/ a large US food company best known for its frozen sweet dishes. According to its advertisements, 'Everybody doesn't like something, but nobody doesn't like Sara Lee.' It also owns companies that make meat products, frozen fruit and vegetables, and underwear.

Sa'ran Wrap™ /sə'ræn/ n [U] a US make of cling film, thin transparent plastic material used for wrapping food, etc. It is produced by S C Johnson.

,**Sara'toga** /ˌsærə'təʊgə; AmE ˌserə'toʊgə/ the original name of Schuylerville, *New York. The Americans won two important victories over British forces there in October 1777, during the *American Revolution. The battles have been called the 'turning point' of the war, because the French then decided to give military support to the Americans. **Saratoga National Historical Park** was established in 1938.

,**Saratoga 'Springs** /ˌsærətəʊgə; AmE ˌserətoʊgə/ a city in north-eastern New York State which is an international centre for horse racing. It was settled in 1773 around 122 natural mineral springs and became popular as the 'Queen of Spas' during the 19th century. The two battles of *Saratoga were fought not far away.

'**John 'Singer 'Sargent[1]** /'sɪŋə 'sɑːdʒənt; AmE 'sɪŋər 'sɑːrdʒənt/ (1856–1925) a US artist known for painting rich and famous people. They included President Theodore *Roosevelt and the author Robert Louis *Stevenson. Sargent was born in Florence, Italy, of US parents. He studied and painted in Paris (1874–84) but his career in France was damaged when his painting *Madame X* (1884) was considered too sexual. He then settled in London, though he remained a US citizen.

,**Malcolm 'Sargent[2]** /'sɑːdʒənt; AmE 'sɑːrdʒənt/ (1895–1967) an English conductor who is best remembered as a conductor of the *Proms. He was made a *knight in 1947.

Sark /sɑːk; AmE sɑːrk/ a part of the British *Channel Islands, consisting of two islands, Great Sark and Little Sark, which are joined by a narrow strip of land. Sark has its own parliament, and a leader the Seigneur (if a man) or the Dame (if a woman), who passes the title on to his or her children. The islands are popular with tourists.

sarnie /'sɑːni; AmE 'sɑːrnie/ ⇨ SANDWICH.

,**William Sa'royan** /sə'rɔɪən/ (1908–81) a US author of novels, plays and more than 400 short stories. He wrote about ordinary people and refused the *Pulitzer Prize for his play *The Time of Your Life* (1939) because he did not want rich people to support the arts. Saroyan's best-known novel is *The Human Comedy* (1943).

the SAS /ˌes eɪ 'es/ (in full **the Special Air Service**) a branch of the British army consisting of a small group of specially trained soldiers who are used for difficult or secret operations. Members of the SAS are trained in skills such as parachuting, climbing and shooting accurately. They are well known for their ability to surprise groups of terrorists by attacking them very quickly.

'**Sasquatch** /'sæskwɒtʃ; AmE 'sæskwɑːtʃ/ (also '**Bigfoot** /'bɪgfʊt/) n a large hairy creature like a human with big feet and long arms that is believed by some people to live in the north-west mountains of North America. Although reports that such a creature has been seen appear occasionally in popular newspapers, most people regard them as a joke.

,**Siegfried Sas'soon** /ˌsiːgfriːd sə'suːn/ (1886–1967) an English poet and author. He served as a soldier in *World War I and is best known for his poems about the horror of war. He was awarded the *Military Cross for his courage in battle but later rejected it because of his opposition to war. His collections of poetry include *Counterattack* (1918), and he wrote a series of books about his life, including *The Memoirs of a Fox-Hunting Man* (1928).

66 If I were fierce, and bald, and short of breath, I'd live with scarlet Majors at the Base, And speed glum heroes up the line to death. 99
Siegfried Sassoon *Base Details*

SAT **1** /ˌes eɪ 'tiː/ **SAT™** (in full **Scholastic Aptitude Test**) (in the US) a standard test which students must pass in order to be accepted by most colleges and universities. It tests abilities in language and mathematics and is usually taken during the last year of *high school. Compare ACT, PSAT.
2 /sæt/ (in Britain) the abbreviation for a *Standard Assessment Task, the former name for a *National Curriculum Test.

The Sa,tanic 'Verses a novel (1988) by Salman *Rushdie about the religion of Islam. Some Muslims found it very offensive. The Ayatollah Khomeini of Iran declared that Rushdie should be killed, and public protests against the book took place in Britain and many other countries. As a result Rushdie was forced to live for ten years under police protection at a secret address.

'**Satchmo** /'sætʃməʊ; AmE 'sætʃmoʊ/ the popular name of the *jazz musician Louis *Armstrong. It was short for 'satchel mouth', because he had a very large mouth. A satchel is a type of large bag.

The 'Saturday 'Evening 'Post a US magazine established in 1821 and published each week. It became one of America's most popular general magazines from the 1920s to the 1960s and was known especially for its covers painted by Norman *Rockwell and its fiction by such writers as William *Faulkner and Agatha *Christie. It stopped being published in 1969 but began again in 1971 and is now published six times a year.

'**Saturday 'Night 'Live** the longest running US television comedy series, which started in 1975 on *NBC. The careers of many comic actors have begun on the programme. The original group included Chevy Chase, John Belushi and Dan Aykroyd. Later members included Eddie *Murphy, Billy Crystal and Bill Murray. Each show is presented by a different guest, and they have included New York Mayor Ed Koch and the comic actors Robin *Williams and Steve *Martin.

'**Saturn** **1** a US rocket used in the 1960s and 1970s to send spacecraft and satellites into space. The original Saturn was developed in 1958 by Wernher *von Braun, and it had two rockets used in sequence. Saturn 5 had three rockets and carried 12 million US gallons/45.6 million litres of fuel. It was used for the *Apollo program to send men to the moon.
2 a popular make of small US car that is cheap to run, produced by *General Motors since 1990.

,**Jennifer 'Saunders** /'sɔːndəz; AmE 'sɔːndərz/ (1958–) an English comedy actor best known for appearing with Dawn *French in the television comedy series *French *and Saunders* and for playing the part of Edina Monsoon in the television comedy series **Absolutely Fabulous*.

ˌLily ˈSavage /ˈsævɪdʒ/ (1955–) an English comedy performer. Lily Savage is a man who dresses as a woman (real name Paul Grady) and has appeared on television programmes including *The Lily Savage Show* and *Blankety Blank*.

ˌSave the ˈChildren a large international charity that helps children. It was started in London in 1919 and provides services such as education, health care and emergency relief in many of the world's poorer countries. It also works to help children in Britain. Its president is Princess *Anne.

ˌJimmy ˈSavile /ˈsævl/ (1926–) an English radio and television personality and charity worker. He began his career as a disc jockey and later became well known as the presenter of the television series *Jim'll Fix It* (1975–94), in which he arranged for children to do things they specially wanted to do. Savile also works to collect money for British hospitals, and often appears on television wearing heavy gold jewellery and smoking a cigar. He was made a *knight in 1990.

ˌSavile ˈRow /ˌsævl ˈrəʊ; *AmE* ˈroʊ/ a street in London, England, which is famous for its tailors (= people who make clothes for individual customers). It is considered the centre of high-quality men's fashions in Britain: *He was wearing an expensive Savile Row suit.*

ˌsavings and ˈloan associˌation *n* (*abbr* **S & L**) (*AmE*) ⇨ note at BUILDING SOCIETIES.

the Saˌvoy Hoˈtel /səˌvɔɪ/ a very comfortable and expensive hotel in the *Strand, London, England. It was built in 1884–9 by Richard *D'Oyly Carte, who owned the Savoy Theatre nearby, and it has a famous restaurant, the Savoy Grill.

the Saˌvoy ˈOperas /səˌvɔɪ/ a name for the operas of *Gilbert and *Sullivan[1], which were first performed at the Savoy Theatre in London, England. They include *The *Pirates of Penzance*, *The *Mikado* and *The *Gondoliers*.

ˌTom ˈSawyer /ˈsɔːjə(r)/ the main character in *The Adventures of Tom Sawyer* (1876), a novel by Mark *Twain which is especially popular with children. Tom is a lively and clever boy who lives with his Aunt Polly in St Petersburg, *Missouri. He has an exciting life and many adventures on the *Mississippi River with his friends Huckleberry *Finn and Becky Thatcher.

ˌSaxe-ˈCoburg-ˈGotha /ˌsæks ˈkəʊbɜːɡ ˈɡəʊθə; *AmE* ˈkoʊbɜːrɡ ˈɡoʊθə/ the name of the British *royal family from the beginning of the rule of King *Edward VIII in 1901. The name originally belonged to Edward VII's father, the German Prince *Albert. During World War I public feeling against Germany caused King *George V to change it to Windsor in 1917.

ˈSaxon *n* a member of a people from north-west Germany who settled in England in the 5th and 6th centuries. Together with the Angles and the *Jutes they formed the group known as the *Anglo-Saxons. Saxon architecture is Britain's earliest style of architecture, with round arches, small windows and thick stone walls.

a Saxon arch

ˌDorothy L ˈSayers /ˈseɪəz; *AmE* ˈseɪərz/ (1893–1957) an English writer. She is famous for her detective stories, such as

Strong Poison (1930), in which the main character is Lord Peter *Wimsey. She also wrote plays on religious subjects and translated the poetry of Dante into English.

ˌScafell ˈPike /ˌskɔːfel/ the highest mountain in England, in the *Lake District in *Cumbria. It is 3 210 feet/978 metres high.

Pruˌnella ˈScales /pruːˌnelə ˈskeɪlz/ (1932–) an English actor, especially in comedy parts. She is best known for playing the part of Sybil Fawlty in the television comedy series **Fawlty Towers*. She is married to the actor Timothy West.

ˌScapa ˈFlow /ˌskɑːpə ˈfləʊ; *AmE* ˈfloʊ/ an area of the *North Sea surrounded by several of the *Orkney islands and used as a base by the British navy until 1956. Two famous incidents happened there: in 1919 a number of captured German ships were sunk by their own crews, and in 1939 a German submarine sank a British ship, the *Royal Oak*.

ˈScarborough /ˈskɑːbrə; *AmE* skɑːrbrə/ a town on the coast of *North Yorkshire, England. It was popular in the past as a spa town (= one where there are springs of mineral water considered to be healthy to drink) and is now known for its parks, theatres and beaches.

ˈScarface /ˈskɑːfeɪs; *AmE* ˈskɑːrfeɪs/ the *nickname of the famous US criminal Al *Capone. He had a mark on his face where somebody had once cut him with a knife.

ˌArthur ˈScargill /ˈskɑːɡɪl; *AmE* ˈskɑːrɡɪl/ (1938–) an English trade union leader and politician. In 1981 he became the President of the *NUM and in 1984–5 he led the *miners' strike in protest against the *Conservative government's plans to close several mines. In 1996 he formed a new political party, the Socialist Labour Party, which he considered to be closer to the original principles of the Labour Party.

The ˌScarlet ˈLetter a novel (1850) by the US writer Nathaniel *Hawthorne. The story is about *Puritans in 17th-century *New England. Hester Prynne is found guilty of adultery and is made to wear a scarlet (= red) letter A on her dress. There have been three film versions, including one in 1995 with Demi *Moore as Hester.

The ˌScarlet ˈPimpernel /ˈpɪmpənel; *AmE* ˈpɪmpərnel/ a novel (1905) by Baroness Orczy (1865–1947). It is about a group of Englishmen who rescue *upper-class French people from being killed during the French Revolution. The main character is Sir Percy Blakeney, also known as the Scarlet Pimpernel, who dresses in various disguises to avoid being captured by the French. A film of the book was made in 1934 and another in 1994.

ˌscepter'd ˈisle /ˌseptəd; *AmE* ˌseptərd/ a phrase describing England, which appears in *Shakespeare's play **Richard II*, in a speech by the character *John of Gaunt. It is part of a long list of well-known phrases in praise of England, beginning:

> 66 This royal throne of kings, this scepter'd isle,
> This earth of majesty, this seat of Mars,
> This other Eden, demi-paradise
> This fortress built by Nature for herself
> Against infection and the hand of war,
> This happy breed of men, this little world,
> This precious stone set in the silver sea, ...
> This blessed plot, this earth, this realm, this England.
> 99

Simon **Schama** /ˈʃɑːmə/ (1945–) a British historian who has written a number of books about history and art, and is best known for his series of 15 documentary programmes for the *BBC, *A History of Britain* (2000–02). His books include *Landscape and Memory* (1996).

the **'Schengen agreement** /'ʃeŋgən/ an agreement signed in 1985 in the Luxembourg town of Schengen by seven *EU countries (Belgium, the Netherlands, Luxembourg, France, Germany, Portugal and Spain) which came into force in 1995. It removed border controls for people travelling between these countries which made travel easier. More European countries have joined since, and in 2003 15 countries, known as the **Schengen area**, were part of the agreement, with more new *EU countries expected to join in the future. The UK and Ireland have chosen to stay outside the Schengen area.

Schindler's 'List /ˌʃɪndləz; *AmE* ˌʃɪndlərz/ a US film (1993), directed by Stephen *Spielberg, which won seven *Oscars, including Best Picture and Best Director. It was based on the novel *Schindler's Ark* (1982) by the Australian writer Thomas Keneally, which won the *Booker Prize. The story is about a real person, Oskar Schindler, a German who risked his own life during *World War II to save Polish Jews sent to work in his factory.

John **'Schlesinger** /'ʃlesɪndʒə(r)/ (1926–2003) an English film director. His early films examined British *working-class life, and include *A Kind of Loving* (1962) and *Billy Liar* (1963). Later films made in the US include *Midnight Cowboy* and *Marathon Man* (1976). He also worked in theatre, opera and television.

Schlitz™ /ʃlɪts/ n [U, C] a popular US beer, advertised as 'the beer that made Milwaukee famous'. It was produced from 1874 to 1982 by the Joseph Schlitz Brewing Company in *Milwaukee, *Wisconsin, and has since been made by the Pabst Brewing Company of *San Antonio, *Texas.

Scho,lastic 'Aptitude Test™ ⇨ SAT.

school 'district n (in US education) an area containing several *elementary schools and *high schools run by the same administrative **school board**. The board's members are usually elected. A city school district may only cover part of a large city, but one in the countryside may include several towns.

*The **School for 'Scandal*** a comedy play (1777) by Richard Brinsley *Sheridan about two brothers who both want to marry the same young woman.

school 'uniform n [C, U] special clothes worn by pupils at a particular school. Wearing school uniform is a British tradition and is rarely found in the US. In most schools pupils have to wear clothes of a particular colour, often navy blue or dark green, but are free to choose the clothes themselves. Other schools, especially *private schools, require pupils to wear special clothes which have to be bought from a particular shop. School uniform often includes a special striped tie in the school colours for both girls and boys. At very traditional schools, for example old *public schools like *Eton, pupils may have to wear very old-fashioned clothes in a style that dates from the 19th century or even earlier.

Charles **'Schulz** /'ʃʊlts/ (1922–2000) the US artist who created and drew the popular *comic strip *Peanuts*. He based the character of Charlie *Brown on himself.

Arnold **'Schwarzenegger** /'ʃwɔːtsənegə(r); *AmE* 'ʃwɔːrtsənegər/ (1947–) a US actor and politician, known especially for his large muscles and parts in violent action films. He was born in Austria and won several competitions for muscle development, including 'Mr Universe'. His films include *Conan the Barbarian* (1982), the *Terminator* films (1984, 1991 and 2003), *True Lies* (1994) and *Eraser* (1996). In 2003 he became governor of the state of *California.

Schweppes /ʃweps/ ⇨ CADBURY SCHWEPPES.

the **'Science Mu,seum** Britain's largest museum of science and technology, in South *Kensington, London, established in 1909. It contains many objects from the history of science, and has a large number of displays which the public can touch and operate as well as a large cinema.

Scien'tific A'merican a US magazine published each month since 1845 about scientific research and discoveries. The articles are written for the non-specialist reader but are more technical than those in a general magazine. The company owning the magazine also has a television series on *PBS, called *Scientific American Frontiers* which is also available on the Internet. It began in 1990 and is presented by the actor Alan Alda.

Scien'tology /ˌsaɪənˈtɒlədʒi; *AmE* ˌsaɪənˈtɑːlədʒi/ an international religious philosophy established in 1954 by the US writer of science fiction L Ron *Hubbard. It is based on his book *Dianetics* (1950) and officially became the Church of Scientology in 1965. It believes in a 'life energy' and encourages its members to improve themselves in a spiritual way by a greater understanding of themselves. The organization has been criticized for the methods it uses to attract and keep members. They include several well-known actors, including Tom *Cruise and John *Travolta.
▶ **Scientologist** n.

the **'Scilly Isles** /'sɪli/ (*also* the **'Scillies** /'sɪliz/ the **Isles of Scilly**) a group of about 140 small islands about 28 miles off the south-west coast of England. Five of the larger islands have people living on them, and the capital is Hugh Town on the island of St Mary's. The Scillies have a mild climate and are popular for holidays/vacations.

SCLC /ˌes siː el 'siː/ ⇨ SOUTHERN CHRISTIAN LEADERSHIP CONFERENCE.

scone /skɒn, skəʊn; *AmE* skɑːn, skoʊn/ n (*BrE*) a small round cake made of flour, fat and milk, sometimes containing sultanas (= a type of dried fruit). Scones are usually eaten with butter or cream and jam for afternoon tea (= a light meal eaten in the afternoon). Compare DROP SCONE. See also CREAM TEA.

Scooby 'Doo /ˌskuːbi 'duː/ a character in US television cartoons. He is a Great Dane dog who helps to solve mysteries with his human friends Fred, clever Velma, pretty Daphne and the *hippie 'Shaggy'. *Scooby Doo* began on *CBS in 1969.

SCOPE /skəʊp; *AmE* skoʊp/ a British charity which helps people with cerebral palsy (= a condition caused by brain damage before or at birth, which makes people lose control of their movements). It was formed in 1952 as the Spastics Society, and has several schools and other centres in Britain.

the **'Scopes trial** /'skəʊps/ a famous US court case in 1925 in Dayton, *Tennessee. A teacher, John Scopes, was put on trial because he taught Charles *Darwin's theory of evolution, which was illegal under local law. The case was informally called the 'monkey trial'. The *American Civil Liberties Union got Clarence *Darrow to defend Scopes, and William Jennings *Bryan helped to argue the case against him. Scopes was judged guilty but freed for technical reasons. The law was only changed in 1967.

Martin **Scor'sese** /skɔː'seɪzi; *AmE* skɔːr'seɪzi/ (1942–) a US director of films, many of them with the actor Robert *De Niro, including *Mean Streets*, *Taxi Driver*, *Raging Bull* (1980), *GoodFellas* (1990) and *Casino* (1995). Scorsese's other films include *The Last Temptation of Christ* (1988), which was criticized by some religious groups, *The Age of Innocence* (1993), *Kundun* (1997), *Gangs of New York* (2002), and *The Aviator* (2004).

S

Scot /skɒt; *AmE* skɑːt/ *n* [C] **1** a member of a Celtic people from Northern Ireland who moved into and controlled the west coast of Scotland in the 6th century. Their enemies in Scotland were the *Picts.
2 a person who comes from Scotland.

Scotch *n* [U, C] *whisky (= a strong alcoholic drink) produced in Scotland.

The adjective **Scotch** was used in the past to describe the people and things of Scotland, but it is now only used of products like whisky and wool. The adjective **Scottish** is now used to describe the people and things of Scotland, and **Scots** is used to describe its people, its law and its language: *Scotch beef* ◇ *Scottish dancing* ◇ *a Scots accent*.

Scotch 'egg *n* a British snack which consists of a boiled egg, with the shell removed, which is covered with sausage meat (= a mixture of finely chopped meat) and breadcrumbs, fried and eaten cold, for example as part of a salad or picnic.

Scotchgard™ /'skɒtʃgɑːd; *AmE* 'skɑːtʃgɑːrd/ *n* [U] a chemical, produced by the *3M company, which protects cloth and material from water, oil and other substances that make marks. It is often used for carpets.

Scotch 'pancake ⇨ DROP SCONE.

Scotch tape™ *n* [U] (*AmE*) a make of transparent sticky tape used for sticking paper together, mending things, etc.

the Scotland 'Office /ˌskɒtlənd; *AmE* ˌskɑːtlənd/ a British government department responsible for matters outside the control of the *Scottish Parliament, including employment, foreign affairs, defence and social security. It is led by the Secretary of State for Scotland and is part of the *Department of Constitutional Affairs.

Scotland the 'Brave /ˌskɒtlənd; *AmE* ˌskɑːtlənd/ a traditional patriotic Scottish song (= one expressing pride in Scotland), sung (especially formerly) at sports matches. Compare FLOWER OF SCOTLAND.

Scotland 'Yard /ˌskɒtlənd; *AmE* ˌskɑːtlənd/ the main office of the British *Metropolitan Police, now officially called *New Scotland Yard. Its original office was in a building in London that once belonged to the royal family of Scotland: *Scotland Yard detectives have been investigating the crime.*

Scots, wha 'hae /ˌskɒts wæ 'heɪ; *AmE* ˌskɑːts/ the first words of a traditional Scottish song, taken from a poem by Robert *Burns celebrating the victory of the Scots over the English at *Bannockburn. The first line in full is 'Scots, wha hae wi' Wallace bled' (Scots, who have with Wallace bled), referring to the Scottish soldiers who fought with William *Wallace.

the Scots 'Guards /ˌskɒts; *AmE* ˌskɑːts/ one of the *Guards regiments of the British army, established in Scotland in 1660. Compare ROYAL SCOTS.

The 'Scotsman /'skɒtsmən; *AmE* 'skɑːtsmən/ a leading Scottish newspaper, published every day. It first appeared in 1817.

Captain 'Scott[1] /skɒt; *AmE* skɑːt/ (Robert Falcon Scott 1868–1912) an English explorer and navy officer, often referred to as Scott of the Antarctic. He became widely known and admired in Britain as a result of his two journeys to the Antarctic. On the second journey (1910–12) he reached the South Pole a month after the Norwegian explorer Roald Amundsen (1872–1928) had become the first man ever to reach it. Scott and his four companions died of cold on the journey back. His records of the journey were found in 1912 and published in 1913. His son was Peter *Scott. See also OATES[1].

George 'Gilbert 'Scott[2] /skɒt; *AmE* 'skɑːt/ (1811–78) an English architect. He was one of the leading figures of

the *Gothic Revival in England, and designed *St Pancras station and the *Albert Memorial in London, as well as restoring (= repairing) many old churches. He was made a *knight in 1872.

St Pancras Station designed by George Gilbert Scott

Giles 'Gilbert 'Scott[3] /skɒt; *AmE* 'skɑːt/ (1880–1960) an English architect, the grandson of George Gilbert *Scott. His best-known buildings include *Battersea Power Station and the Anglican cathedral at Liverpool (completed in 1978). He was made a *knight in 1924.

Paul 'Scott[4] /skɒt; *AmE* 'skɑːt/ (1920–78) an English author. He served as a soldier in India during *World War II, and is best known for The *Raj Quartet, a series of four novels set in India during the final years of British rule there (= the *Raj). A popular television version of the novels was made under the title The *Jewel in the Crown. A further novel by Scott about India, Staying On, won the *Booker Prize in 1977.

Peter 'Scott[5] /skɒt; *AmE* 'skɑːt/ (1909–89) an English artist and writer, the son of Captain *Scott[1]. He started the Wildfowl Trust at *Slimbridge in 1946 and was made a *knight in 1973 for his work in protecting plants and animals, especially birds.

Ridley Scott[6] /ˌrɪdli 'skɒt; *AmE* 'skɑːt/ (1937–) a British film director and producer who started by making television advertisements and then went on to make many successful *Hollywood films including *Alien* (1979), *Blade Runner* (1982), *Thelma and Louise* (1991), *Gladiator* (2000) and *Black Hawk Down* (2001). He was made a *knight in 2003.

Ronnie 'Scott[7] /'skɒt; *AmE* 'skɑːt/ (1927–96) an English musician and club owner. He played the saxophone in several *jazz bands, starting his own band in 1953, and opened the leading London jazz club, Ronnie Scott's, in 1959.

Sheila 'Scott[8] /'skɒt; *AmE* 'skɑːt/ (1927–88) an English pilot. She flew alone round the world three times, and in 1971 was the first to do this over the North Pole in a light aircraft.

Walter 'Scott[9] /'skɒt; *AmE* 'skɑːt/ (1771–1832) a Scottish author and poet. Most of his poetry and his historical novels are based on the traditions and history of Scotland, especially the border region. His most famous poems include *The Lay of the Last Minstrel* and *The *Lady of the Lake*, and his best-known novels include *Waverley*, *Rob Roy* and *Ivanhoe*. All were extremely popular during his life and influenced writers in Britain and Europe. Scott was made a *baronet in 1820. See also WAVERLEY NOVELS.

'Scottie /'skɒti; AmE 'skɑːti/ (also **'Scottie dog**) ⇨ SCOTTISH TERRIER.

Scottish and 'Newcastle /ˌskɒtɪʃ, 'njuːkɑːsl; AmE ˌskɑːtɪʃ, 'nuːkæsl/ the UK's largest brewery (= company which makes beer) based in *Edinburgh. Its most popular brands include Newcastle Brown Ale, Kronenbourg and Courage.

Scottish 'Borders /ˌskɒtɪʃ 'bɔːdəz; AmE ˌskɑːtɪʃ, 'bɔːrdərz/ a *council area (= administrative region) of south-east Scotland near the border with England. Its name changed from Borders in 1995.

the 'Scottish Cer'tificate of Edu'cation /'skɒtɪʃ; AmE 'skɑːtɪʃ/ n an examination in Scottish schools. The Standard grade of the examination is taken at the age of 16 and is equivalent to *GCSE in England and Wales. The Higher grade is taken at the age of 17.

the ˌScottish 'Colourists /'skɒtɪʃ; AmE 'skɑːtɪʃ/ a group of Scottish artists whose paintings were first shown in the 1920s and 1930s, who used strong colours to paint objects and landscapes. Members of the group include S J Peploe (1871–1935), F C B Cadell (1883–1947), George Leslie Hunter (1877–1931) and J D Fergusson (1874–1961).

'Scottish 'country 'dancing /'skɒtɪʃ; AmE 'skɑːtɪʃ/ a form of *folk dancing originally from Scotland which includes fast lively dances usually for groups of three, four or five couples such as **reels**, **jigs**, **hornpipes** and **strathspeys**.

the ˌScottish E'xecutive /ˌskɒtɪʃ; AmE ˌskɑːtɪʃ/ the government of Scotland for the areas for which the *Scottish Parliament is responsible. It is led by the *First Minister who is chosen by the Parliament and who chooses the other Scottish Ministers who make up the Executive.

the 'Scottish 'FA 'Cup /'skɒtɪʃ 'ef eɪ; AmE 'skɑːtɪʃ/ the series of matches in which Scottish football teams compete to win the Scottish Football Association cup (= a prize in the form of a cup). The first series was held in 1873. The final match, which decides the winner, is played every year at *Hampden Park, Glasgow. Compare FA CUP.

ˌScottish 'law /ˌskɒtɪʃ; AmE ˌskɑːtɪʃ/ ⇨ note at LEGAL SYSTEM.

the ˌScottish 'National ˌParty /ˌskɒtɪʃ; AmE ˌskɑːtɪʃ/ (abbr **the SNP**) a political party formed in 1934 whose aim is to achieve independent government for Scotland (not simply a separate Scottish parliament within the UK). Its leader since 2004 has been Alex Salmond (1954–), who also led the party between 1990 and 2000. Five of its candidates were elected as *Members of Parliament in the 2001 general election in Britain. In 2003 27 of its representatives were elected to the *Scottish Parliament.

the 'Scottish 'National 'Portrait ˌGallery / 'skɒtɪʃ; AmE 'skɑːtɪʃ/ an art gallery in *Edinburgh, established in 1882, which shows paintings and photographs of people. Compare NATIONAL PORTRAIT GALLERY.

ˌScottish 'Opera /ˌskɒtɪʃ; AmE ˌskɑːtɪʃ/ Scotland's national opera company, formed in *Glasgow in 1962 and based at the Theatre Royal, Glasgow. The company has regular tours in Scotland and England.

the ˌScottish 'Parliament /ˌskɒtɪʃ; AmE ˌskɑːtɪʃ/ a separate parliament for Scotland, based in Edinburgh in a new building which opened in 2004. It is made up of 129 *Members of the Scottish Parliament. 73 of them are directly elected to represent *constituencies and 56 are

elected to represent regions of Scotland using a form of *proportional representation. It began work in 1999 and has the power to raise or lower the basic rate of income tax, and to make laws affecting Scotland in areas including education, health, agriculture and justice. It is led by a *First Minister who is chosen by the Parliament and who chooses the other members of the *Scottish Executive.

the 'Scottish play /'skɒtɪʃ; AmE 'skɑːtɪʃ/ ⇨ MACBETH.

the ˌScottish 'Premier League /ˌskɒtɪʃ; AmE ˌskɑːtɪʃ/ (abbr **the SPL**) the top 12 teams in Scottish football. It was formed in 1998 from the Premier Division of the Scottish Football League. ⇨ note at FOOTBALL – BRITISH STYLE.

ˌScottish 'terrier /ˌskɒtɪʃ; AmE ˌskɑːtɪʃ/ (also informal **Scottie**, **Scottie dog**) n a breed of small dog with rough hair and short legs, originally bred in Scotland. See also TERRIER.

Scott v ˌSandford /ˌskɒt vɜːsəs 'sændfəd; AmE ˌskɑːt vɜːrsəs 'sændfərd/ the official legal name for the *Dred Scott Case.

Scouse /skaʊs/ adj (BrE informal) of the people living in and around *Liverpool, north-west England, and their way of speaking, etc.: Scouse humour.
▶ **Scouse** n **1** [U] the way of speaking of the people of *Liverpool: She spoke in broad Scouse.
2 (also **'Scouser** /'skaʊsə(r)/) [C] a person who was born in Liverpool.

the Scouts (also formal **the 'Scout Associ,ation**) an international association formed in Britain in 1908 by Lord Robert *Baden-Powell. It organizes outdoor activities for boys, e.g. camping, and aims to teach them practical skills, discipline and social responsibility. Members wear uniforms, and their motto is 'Be prepared'. The four main groups are *Beaver Scouts (for ages 6–8), *Cub Scouts (8–10½), Scouts (10½-15½) and Venture Scouts (15½-20). Girls were admitted to the Scouts for the first time in Britain in 1990. See also BOY SCOUTS OF AMERICA. Compare GUIDES.

'Scrabble™ /'skræbl/ a popular board game in which players try to build words on a board marked with squares, using letters printed on small square blocks. The words must be arranged to fit together like a *crossword puzzle. Scrabble was invented in the US in the 1930s by Alfred Butts, who first called it 'Criss Cross'. It became very popular in the 1960s, and there are now many Scrabble clubs and national competitions in both Britain and the US.

'scratch card /'skrætʃ kɑːd; AmE 'skrætʃ kɑːrd/ n (in Britain) a small paper card which can be bought from shops as a form of gambling. A covering on parts of the card can be scratched off to reveal whether or not you have won a cash prize. Although scratch cards have been legal in Britain since 1976 they became especially popular in 1995 as part of the *National Lottery. Scratch-card prizes are generally smaller than the major National Lottery prizes. Scratch cards have also been part of state lotteries in the US since the 1980s.

'Screen ˌActors Guild the US trade union for film and television actors, established in 1933.

Scrooge /skruːdʒ/ n (disapproving) a person who is mean with money or does not care about others, similar to the character Ebenezer Scrooge in the book A *Christmas Carol by Charles *Dickens: He's a bit of a Scrooge when it comes to lending money.

the Scrubs /skrʌbz/ ⇨ WORMWOOD SCRUBS.

'scrumpy /'skrʌmpi/ n [U] (BrE) a type of strong cider (= an alcoholic drink made from apples), especially as made in the *West Country of England.

S

,Peter **'Scudamore** /'skuːdəmɔː(r)/ (1958–) an English jockey. He was the *National Hunt *champion jockey every year from 1986 to 1992 and set several records in the sport. His racing career ended in 1993.

,Sean **'Scully** /ˌʃɔːn 'skʌli/ (1945–) a US painter born in Ireland who paints abstract paintings, often of coloured stripes.

SDI /ˌes diː 'aɪ/ ⇨ STRATEGIC DEFENSE INITIATIVE.

the **SDLP** /ˌes diː el 'piː/ (*in full* the **Social Democratic and Labour Party**) a Northern Irish political party, formed in 1970 by a group of *MPs in favour of equal rights for *Roman Catholics. The party, supported mainly by Catholics, would like Northern Ireland and the Republic of Ireland to be united as one country, but does not approve of the violent methods of the *IRA. Its MPs in the *House of Commons vote the same way as the *Labour Party on most issues.

the **SDP** /ˌes diː 'piː/ (*in full* the **Social Democratic Party**) a British political party formed in 1981 by a group of *MPs who left the Labour Party to start a new 'middle party' in British politics. In 1987 it combined with the *Liberal Party to form the *Liberal Democratic Party. A small group led by David *Owen continued to call themselves the SDP until 1990.

SDS /ˌes diː 'es/ ⇨ STUDENTS FOR A DEMOCRATIC SOCIETY.

the **,Sealed 'Knot So,ciety** a British society, formed in 1968, which performs historical scenes, especially from battles of the *English Civil War. Members dress as soldiers of the period and usually perform where the original battles took place. The organization also works as an educational charity in schools.

'Sea Lord *n* either of two senior admirals (the First and Second Sea Lords) who are responsible for the training, equipment, etc. of the British *Royal Navy.

'Sealy™ /'siːli/ a US make of mattress for beds. The advertisements claim that 'Sleeping on a Sealy is like sleeping on a cloud.'

SEAQ /ˌes iː 'kjuː/ (*in full* **Stock Exchange Automated Quotations**) an electronic system for buying and selling shares in companies on the *London Stock Exchange. It was introduced in 1986 as part of the *Big Bang, and allows people to receive information about the Stock Exchange and to buy or sell shares by computer or telephone from anywhere in the world.

,Ronald **'Searle** /'sɜːl; *AmE* 'sɜːrl/ (1920–) an English artist. He is best known for his humorous drawings of the schoolgirls of *St Trinian's, and his work has appeared in many magazines and books. His work as a serious artist includes drawings done while he was a prisoner of the Japanese during *World War II.

,Sears, **'Roebuck and ,Company** /ˌsɪəz 'rəʊbʌk; *AmE* ˌsɪrz 'roʊbʌk/ (*also* **Sears**, **Sears and Roebuck**) any of a very large group of US department stores selling a wide range of products for the family. The company was begun in 1886 in *Minneapolis by Richard Sears. He was then joined by Alvah Roebuck when he moved the company to *Chicago in 1887. In 1891, they began the company's famous mail-order catalogue (= book showing items that can be ordered by post). In 2004 the company was bought by *Kmart. See also SEARS TOWER.

the **,Sears 'Tower** /ˌsɪəz; *AmE* ˌsɪrz/ the tallest building in the US and (from 1974 to 1996) the tallest in the world. It is in *Chicago and was built by *Sears, Roebuck and Company. It is 1454 feet/443 metres high, with 110 floors.

▶ **seaside and beach**

In the 18th century British people started going to the **seaside** for pleasure and for their health. Seaside towns such as *Brighton, *Lyme Regis and *Scarborough became fashionable with the upper class. **Bathing** in the sea became popular and *bathing machines were invented for people to get changed in. Later, towns like *Blackpool, Clacton-on-Sea and Margate, which were close to industrial areas or to London, developed into large **seaside resorts** to which workers went for a day out or for their holiday. Long *piers were built stretching out to sea and soon had a wide range of amusements built on them. **Promenades** were built along the shore for people to walk along. Rows of **beach huts** and **chalets** (= buildings where people could get changed or sit and have tea) took the place of bathing machines, and **deckchairs** were for hire on the beach. There were ice-cream sellers, *whelk stalls, stalls selling buckets and spades for children to build sandcastles, and the occasional *Punch and Judy show. In the early 1900s it became popular to send seaside postcards to friends. Children bought seaside **rock**, a long sugary sweet with the name of the place printed through it.

Most British people like to go to the sea for a day out or for a weekend. Resorts like Blackpool are still popular, but others are run-down and rather quiet. British people now prefer to go on holiday to **beach resorts** in Spain, Greece or the *Caribbean because the weather is more likely to be sunny and warm.

Americans talk of going to the **ocean** or the **beach**, rather than the seaside. Some places, especially on the East coast, have very popular beaches and people travel long distances to go there. *Florida is especially popular and at **spring break** (= a holiday in the spring for high school and college students) it is full of students.

Beach activities include swimming, **surfing** and **windsurfing**, also called sailboarding. Many people go to the beach but never go into the water. They spend their time playing games like **volleyball** (= hitting a large ball backwards and forwards over a net) and **frisbee** (= throwing a flat plastic disc). Other people go to the beach to get a **tan** and spend all their time **sunbathing**. Many people worry about getting skin cancer if they get burnt by the sun and so put on **sun cream** or **sun block** to protect their skin. A day at the beach often also involves a picnic meal or, especially in the US, a **barbecue** (= meat cooked over an open fire).

,seaside **'postcard** *n* a postcard (= a card for sending messages by post without an envelope) traditionally sent while on holiday at a British seaside town. Seaside postcards have brightly coloured comic drawings on one side, often with a mild sexual humour. The best-known artist of postcards of this type is Donald *McGill.

the **'Season** *n* [sing] (*BrE*) the name given to a number of fashionable sports and cultural events held every summer in Britain and attended by many rich, famous or *upper-class people. The main events are *Glyndebourne, *Derby Day, the *Royal Academy Summer Exhibition, *Royal Ascot, *Wimbledon, *Henley Royal Regatta, International Polo Day (held by the Guards Polo Club at *Windsor[1](1)), *Goodwood, *Cowes Week and the *Lord's test match (= international cricket match). Members of the *royal family attend some of the events, and tickets are often expensive and difficult to get.

Se'attle /si'ætl/ the largest city in the north-western US, also known as the 'Emerald City'. It is in the state of *Washington and is a Pacific port on Elliott Bay. It was settled in 1852 and named after a *Native American leader. It is the home of the *Boeing aircraft company and other industries, but tourists are attracted by its clean air and beautiful scenery.

SEC /ˌes iː 'siː/ ⇨ SECURITIES AND EXCHANGE COMMISSION.

,Harry **'Secombe** /'siːkəm/ (1921–2001) a Welsh comic performer and singer. He is best known for appearing in the radio comedy series *The* *Goon Show. He was made a *knight in 1981.

the ,Second A'mendment an amendment (= change) to the American *Constitution, part of the *Bill of Rights, passed in 1791. The Second Amendment gives people **the right to bear arms** (= to own and carry weapons). This has become an issue because of a number of recent tragic events when one armed person has shot a number of people. There is now much disagreement over what this Amendment actually means. Some people believe it only applies to the military and others that it applies to all citizens. It states: 'A well regulated Militia, being necessary to the security of a free State, the right of people to keep and bear Arms, shall not be infringed.'

,secondary **'modern** *n* a type of secondary school for children aged 11–16 that existed in England until the 1970s, providing a general education with an emphasis on practical or technical skills for children who did not go to a *grammar school. Compare COMPREHENSIVE SCHOOL.

,second **'reading** *n* the second stage in presenting a *bill(1) (= proposal for a new law) to the British parliament, usually followed by a debate. ⇨ note at ACT OF PARLIAMENT.

the ,Second ,World 'War ⇨ WORLD WAR II.

the ,Secretary of 'State **1** (in Britain) the head of a major government department.
2 (in the US) the head of the Department of State. The person holding the office is the most important member of the President's *Cabinet and has an important role in the creation of US foreign policy. Well-known Secretaries of State have included John Foster *Dulles, Henry *Kissinger, Madeleine *Albright and Colin *Powell.

the ,Secret In'telligence 'Service the official name for *MI6.

the ,Secret 'Service (*in full* the **United States Secret Service**) a division of the US Treasury Department responsible for protecting the President and his family. It also guards the Vice-President, former Presidents and major political candidates for President. It was originally set up to investigate and arrest people who printed false money. Its present duties began in 1901 after President William *McKinley was murdered. See also PINKERTON.

,Section 'Eight *n* (*AmE*) **1** the action of dismissing somebody from the US armed forces because they are not fit enough physically or mentally. It takes its name from a section of US Army rules in force between 1922 and 1944.
2 a member of the US armed forces who is dismissed under Section Eight: *He said he would never employ a Section Eight.*

the ,Sector ,Skills De'velopment ,Agency (*abbr* **SSDA**) a British government organization started in 2002 under the slogan **Skills for Business** which provides money and support for a network of **Sector Skills Councils** (**SSCs**). They are organizations made up of employers, trade unions and professional groups within an area of business in order to develop the skills needed by businesses, by improving training and working practices among workers.

se,cure 'training ,centre *n* (*abbr* **STC**) a centre in Britain for children up to the age of 17 who repeatedly break the law. The children are kept within the centre and are given education and training. The first centre opened in 1998. Compare YOUNG OFFENDER INSTITUTION.

Se'curicor™ /sɪ'kjʊərɪkɔː(r); *AmE* sɪ'kjʊrɪkɔːr/ a British company best known for guarding and transporting cash or valuable objects, e.g. from shops to banks and for taking prisoners to and from court.

the Se,curities and Ex'change Com,mission (*abbr* the **SEC**) an independent US government organization responsible for controlling the financial markets and making sure that people and companies that deal on the stock exchange do not break the law. It investigates complaints and can take people to court for illegal operations. The SEC was established in 1934 and its five members are appointed by the US President.

the Se'curity 'Service the official name for *MI5.

,Neil Se'daka /sə'dɑːkə/ (1939–) a US pop singer who has written more than 500 songs. He studied at the *Juilliard School of Music. His first hit was *Stupid Cupid* (1958), sung by Connie Francis. He then made several successful records of his own, including *Happy Birthday, Sweet Sixteen* (1961), *Breaking Up Is Hard to Do* (1962) and *Laughter in the Rain* (1974).

the ,Battle of 'Sedgemoor /'sedʒmɔː(r)/ a battle (1685) at Sedgemoor in *Somerset, England, in which a Protestant army led by the Duke of *Monmouth was defeated by an army led by the *Roman Catholic King *James II. See also BLOODY ASSIZES.

,Pete 'Seeger /'siːgə(r)/ (1919–) a US singer who has been called 'the father of the American folk revival'. He plays the guitar and banjo and has written many folk songs (= traditional songs of the people). He first formed and sang with the Weavers (1949–52). Seeger's successful songs of protest have included *If I Had a Hammer* (1949), *Where Have All the Flowers Gone* (1956) and *We Shall Overcome.

,segre'gation *n* [U] the policy of separating certain groups from the rest of the community, especially because of their race. In the US, the policy of segregation, especially in the southern states, denied African Americans their rights and forced them to use separate schools, restaurants, hotels, cinemas, etc. from those used by white people. As a result of the *civil rights movement, laws were passed in the 1950s and 1960s which greatly reduced segregation in US society. This process is called **desegregation** or 'integration'. See also BUSSING, SEPARATE BUT EQUAL.

'*Seinfeld* /'saɪnfeld/ a popular US comedy series (1990–98) on *NBC, in which Jerry Seinfeld played himself, a New York stage comedian. The stories were about humorous situations involving him and his friends Cosmo Kramer, George Costanza and Elaine Benes.

,Hubert ,Selby 'Jr /,hjuːbət ,selbi; *AmE* ,hjuːbərt/ (1928–2004) a US writer best known for his novel *Last Exit to Brooklyn* (1964) which was made into a film in 1989.

se,lect com'mittee *n* a small committee, usually consisting of 10–15 members of the British *Parliament, which is formed to investigate a particular matter or to examine the activities of a particular government department.

the Se,lective 'Service ,System ⇨ DRAFT.

,Monica 'Seles /'seles/ (1973–) a US tennis player, born in Yugoslavia. In 1991 she became the youngest woman ever to hold the position of Number 1 in international tennis. She has won the French Open three times (1990–92), the Australian Open four times (1991–3 and 1996) and the US Open twice (1991–92). Her career was interrupted for two years after she was attacked with a knife by a supporter of the German player Steffi Graf during a match in Hamburg, Germany, in 1993.

S

,Will 'Self /'self/ (1961–) an English writer, journalist, cartoonist and broadcaster. He known for his satirical novels which often include unreal events and situations, including *Cock and Bull* (1992), *Great Apes* (1997) and *Dorian* (2002).

'Selfridges /'selfrɪdʒɪz/ a famous department store on *Oxford Street, London. It was built by an American, Gordon Selfridge in the *art deco style and is one of the oldest and largest department stores in Britain. In recent years new Selfridges stores have opened in other British cities such as *Manchester and *Birmingham.

statue of the Queen of Time, Selfridges

'Sellafield /'seləfi:ld/ a nuclear power station (= a building where electricity is produced) on the coast of north-west Britain, near the *Lake District. It is the only centre in Britain for reprocessing the nuclear waste from other power stations (= making it into a form that can be used again). Most of the waste is converted into nuclear fuel, but some of it is stored at Sellafield. Local people are worried about this, since there are often reports of dangerous nuclear waste being allowed to escape into the environment: *The statistics on childhood leukaemia have put the government under renewed pressure to close the Sellafield plant.*

,Peter 'Sellers /'seləz; *AmE* 'selərz/ (1925–80) an English comedy actor. His skill at copying other people's voices in an amusing way first became well known through the radio programme The *Goon Show. By the 1960s he had become a major comedy film star, best known for playing three different roles in *Dr Strangelove* (1963) and for playing Inspector Clouseau in the *Pink Panther* series of films.

,David O 'Selznick /'selznɪk/ (David Oliver Selznick 1902–65) a successful US film producer. His films included *King Kong for *RKO and *Anna Karenina* (1935) for *MGM. After forming his own company, Selznick International Pictures, in 1936, he produced *A *Star is Born, *Gone with the Wind* and *Rebecca* (1940). The last two won *Oscars as Best Picture.

'Seminole /'semɪnəʊl; *AmE* 'semɪnoʊl/ n (pl **Seminoles** or **Seminole**) a member of the last *Native American people to make peace with the US government. In 1817–18 they defended their land in *Florida against soldiers led by Andrew *Jackson, and then fought another war against white people in 1835–42. They were moved to *Indian Territory in *Oklahoma and became one of the *Five Civilized Tribes. Some who escaped to the *Everglades did not agree to peace until 1934, and many Seminoles are still there today. See also TRAIL OF TEARS.

the 'Senate ⇨ UNITED STATES SENATE.

'Senator n a member of the *United States Senate.

'Seneca /'senəkə/ n (pl **Senecas** or **Seneca**) a member of a *Native American people who formed the largest group in the *Iroquois League. They supported the British during the *American Revolution, which led to their villages being destroyed by US troops. Senecas now live mainly on four reservations (= lands given and protected by the US government) in western New York and eastern *Ohio.

,senior 'citizen n a phrase used to refer to an old person, especially one over the age of 60. Some old people prefer it to the less gentle phrase, *old age pensioner, but others find it patronizing (= treating them as if they were less important or intelligent than other people).

the ,senior 'service n [sing+ sing/pl v] (*BrE*) a name for the *Royal Navy, the oldest of Britain's armed forces.

,Mack 'Sennett /,mæk 'senɪt/ (1880–1960) a US producer and director of silent comedy films, born in Canada. He established the Keystone Company in 1912 and made the first long comedy, *Tilly's Punctured Romance* (1914). Sennett created the *Keystone Kops and brought Charlie *Chaplin to *Hollywood. He received a special *Oscar in 1937.

,Sense and Sensi'bility the first novel (1811) by Jane *Austen, in which she creates a clever comedy about the importance of money and marriage to the English *upper middle class. It is the story of the Dashwood family, in particular two sisters, Elinor, who is very sensible, and Marianne, who is much more emotional. They fall in love with two men but then discover that they are both engaged to be married already. When Edward, the man loved by Elinor, loses both his wealth and the woman he is engaged to marry, he is happy to marry Elinor, the woman he really loves. Willoughby, however, the man loved by Marianne, leaves her to marry a rich woman. She is sad for a time, but finally marries somebody else.

,separate but 'equal the phrase used to support the principle of *segregation in the southern US. It was based on a US *Supreme Court decision in 1896 which said that segregation was legal provided that the separate facilities for black people were equal to those for white people. It was also used as an excuse for segregation in schools, restaurants, etc., where conditions for black people were usually much worse than those for white people. The Supreme Court case of *Brown v Board of Education* in 1954 resulted in a decision which ended the principle of 'separate but equal'.

the ,sepa'ration of 'church and 'state (in the US) the principle that the government must not interfere in matters of religion. This is written into the *First Amendment of the American *Constitution. Since the 1960s, it has been used in court cases to stop prayers in public schools, but many schools continue to allow time for private prayers.

the ,sepa'ration of 'powers a basic principle in the American *Constitution which separates national political power into three 'branches' or divisions of government. They are the executive branch under the *President, the legislative branch (i.e. *Congress) and the judicial branch (i.e. the *Supreme Court). The arrangement is intended to make sure that no one branch has too much power, and this is achieved by a system of *checks and balances.

Sep,tember '11 (*also* **September 11th**) September 11, 2001, the day on which a series of major terrorist attacks took place in New York and other places in the US. The terrorists carried out the attacks using four passenger planes that they hijacked on flights from the east coast of the US. At 8.46 a.m. the first plane crashed into the north tower of the *World Trade Center in New York. At 9.03 a.m. the second plane crashed into the south tower. Less than 90 minutes later both towers fell down. The third plane crashed into the *Pentagon and the fourth into a field in Pennsylvania. Nearly 3 000 people died in the attacks, a greater number than were killed in the attack on *Pearl Harbor in the Second World War. The place where the World Trade Center once stood is now known as *Ground Zero. The attacks were seen as the work of Al Quaeda, a terrorist organization led by Osama Bin Laden. They resulted in strong anti-terrorist laws being passed in many countries and a US-led war in Afghanistan, where Osama Bin Laden was thought to be hiding. See also 9/11.

Se'quoyah (*also* **Se'quoia**) /sɪˈkwɔɪə/ (*c.* 1765–1843) a *Cherokee Native American who created an alphabet of 86 syllables for his people's language in the early 19th century. He is the only person known to have invented a whole alphabet. The Cherokees used it to communicate in writing, and he also recorded their history. Sequoyah had a Cherokee mother and European father. The sequoia tree is named after him. See also REDWOOD.

ˌ**Sergeant 'Pepper** /'pepə(r)/ (*also* ˌ**Sergeant 'Pepper's 'Lonely 'Hearts Club 'Band**) an album (1967) by the *Beatles. Many people consider it to be the record on which the Beatles stopped producing the simple love songs that had made them pop stars, and began to create new themes and new forms of music. It contains some of their most famous songs, including *Lucy in the Sky with Diamonds*. It is one of the Beatles' best-known records, and one of the most successful albums of all time.

the ˌ**Serious 'Fraud ˌOffice** (*abbr* the **SFO**) a British government agency set up in 1987 to investigate cases of fraud (= deceiving people in order to obtain money or goods) which are too large or complicated for the police *Fraud Squad to deal with: *The government confirmed that the Serious Fraud Office was investigating the bank's activities.*

the **Serious Organised Crime Agency** (*abbr* **SOCA**) (in Britain) a police organization of specialists in different areas that was set up to fight organised crime such as drug trafficking (= buying and selling illegal drugs), people smuggling (= bringing people illegally into a country) and money laundering (= moving money made from illegal activities so it can not be found) at a national and international level. It is due to start operating in 2006 and will work together with police forces and other government agencies.

the ˈ**Serpentine** /'sɜːpəntaɪn; *AmE* 'sɜːrpəntaɪn/ the lake in London's *Hyde Park(1). It is mainly used by people sailing small boats, but there is a tradition of swimming in it on *Christmas Day.

ˈ**Sesame Street** /'sesəmi/ a popular US television series for young children on *PBS. The programmes, which combine education and social values with entertainment, began in 1969 and are now shown in more than 50 countries. They include real actors and the *Muppet Show* characters created by Jim *Henson, such as Bert and Ernie, Big Bird, the Cookie Monster, Kermit the Frog and Oscar the Grouch.

ˌ**Vikram 'Seth** /ˌvɪkrəm 'seθ/ (1951–) an Indian writer who has also lived in Britain and the US, whose books include *The Golden Gate* (1986), *A Suitable Boy* (1993) and *An Equal Music* (1999).

the **SETI Institute** /'seti/ (*in full* **the Search for Extraterrestrial Intelligence Institute**) a US organization set up in 1984 to conduct research into whether life exists outside the Earth. It is a private, non-profit organization but often government organizations such as NASA give financial support to some of its projects. It consists of two parts: the **Center for SETI**, which searches for signals from space, and the **Center for the Study of Life in the Universe**, which researches how life began in the universe and how it may have developed.

the ˌ**seven ages of 'man** seven periods into which a human life can be divided, i.e. those of the baby, the child, the lover, the soldier, the middle-aged person, the old person, and second childhood. The seven ages are best known from the description of them in a speech by Jaques in *Shakespeare's *As You Like It* which begins:

> 66 All the world's a stage,
> And all the men and women merely players.
> They have their exits and their entrances;
> And one man in his time plays many parts. 99

7-Eleven /ˌsevn ɪˈlevn/ any of a large number of shops in the US and other countries that sell food, hot drinks, household goods, petrol, etc. and are open from seven o'clock in the morning until eleven at night. The first 7-Eleven opened in *California in 1964.

747 (*also* **Boeing 747**) *n* [C] the largest passenger aircraft in the world, also called informally the 'jumbo jet'. It was first made by the US *Boeing Company in 1969. Each plane can carry more than 400 passengers. The 747–400 model is the longest, at more than 231 feet/70 metres. The safety of 747s was investigated after one exploded and crashed in 1996 off *Long Island, New York, killing all 230 passengers and crew.

The **700 Club** /ˌsevn 'hʌndrəd/ a US Christian television news and talk show presented by Pat *Robertson which presents news stories from a Christian point of view and has interviews with famous people about their Christian beliefs.

ˈ**Seven 'Pillars of 'Wisdom** a book (1926) by T E *Lawrence. It describes his experiences in the Arabian desert during *World War I when he went to help the Arabs in their fight against Turkey.

the ˌ**Seven 'Sisters** **1** the seven oldest and most respected US women's colleges. They are: Barnard in New York City (associated with *Columbia University), Bryn Mawr in Bryn Mawr, *Pennsylvania, Mount Holyoke in South Hadley, *Massachusetts, Radcliffe in *Cambridge, Massachusetts (associated with *Harvard University, forming the Radcliffe Institute for Advanced Study at Harvard in 1999), Smith in Northampton, Massachusetts, Vassar (which now also has male students) in Poughkeepsie, New York, and Wellesley in Wellesley, Massachusetts. Compare IVY LEAGUE. **2** the name of a group of cliffs formed where the *South Downs meet the sea in *East Sussex, England.

ˌ**Seventh-Day 'Adventist** /'ædvəntɪst/ *n* a member of a Christian religious group that was established in 1860. They have their sabbath (= the day of the week when they rest and worship God) on Saturday instead of Sunday, and they believe that Christ will soon return to earth. They are well known for their strict religious rules.

737 (*also* **Boeing 737**) *n* [C] the most widely used passenger aircraft in the world, first made by the US *Boeing Company in 1967.

7UP™ /'sevnʌp/ *n* [C, U] a sweet, clear, fizzy drink (= one containing many bubbles) without alcohol, similar to lemonade and sold in cans or bottles. It was first produced in the US in 1929 and for many years was advertised as 'the Uncola'.

the ˌ**Seven Years 'War** a war (1756–63) between Britain, Prussia and Hanover on one side and Austria, France, Russia, Saxony and Sweden on the other. Its main causes were the struggle between Britain and France to be the most important imperial power (= country in control of an empire), and the struggle between Austria and Prussia to be the most important country in central Europe. The British and Prussian side won, and France had to give most of its land in America,

Canada and India to Britain, while Prussia began to be one of the most powerful countries in Europe.

the 'Severn /'sevən; *AmE* 'sevərn/ the second longest river in Britain. It starts in Wales and flows through western England and into the *Bristol Channel. It is well known for the **Severn Bore**, a tall wave of water that flows up the river from the sea.

the ,Severn 'Bridge /,sevən; *AmE* ,sevərn/ a high suspension bridge (= a bridge that hangs from cables supported by towers at each end) which carries the M4 motorway over the river *Severn between south-west England and south Wales. It was built near *Bristol in the 1960s. A second motorway bridge was built over the Severn in the 1990s.

the ,Severn 'Tunnel /,sevən; *AmE* ,sevərn/ a rail tunnel under the river *Severn between south-west England and south Wales. It was built near *Bristol between 1873 and 1886 and is 4.35 miles/7 kilometres long, the longest tunnel in Britain.

,William H 'Seward /'su:əd; *AmE* 'su:ərd/ (William Henry Seward 1801–72) the US *Secretary of State who persuaded the government to buy *Alaska from Russia in 1867 for $7.2 million. It became known as **Seward's Folly** because many people thought it was foolish to pay so much for such an empty, frozen region. Seward was Secretary of State under Abraham *Lincoln (1861–5) and survived a murder attempt when Lincoln was killed. He then became Secretary of State under Andrew *Jackson (1865–9). A town in Alaska is named after him.

Sex and the 'City a US comedy television series about four female friends in their 30s who are all single and live in New York. The main character, Carrie Bradshaw, played by Sarah Jessica *Parker, writes a newspaper column called *Sex and the City* about the sex lives of people in *Manhattan.

the ,Sex Discrimi'nation Act a British *Act of Parliament which became a law in 1975. Under the Act, people of both sexes have the right to equal opportunities in education and employment, and to be paid the same amount for doing the same work. People who break this law, for example by paying women less than men, can be put on trial and punished in a court of law.

the 'Sex ,Pistols a British *punk(1) group. They were one of the first groups to play punk music in Britain, and became famous in the 1970s for their lack of respect for anybody. Some people were offended by the words of their songs, including *Anarchy in the UK* (1976) and *God Save the Queen* (1977), and others were offended by their behaviour, which included spitting and swearing in public and on television. The best-known members of the group were Johnny Rotten and Sid Vicious.

the Sey'chelles /seɪˈʃelz/ a country in the Indian Ocean consisting of over 100 islands. It was controlled by the French until the late 18th century, when it became part of the *British Empire. It has been an independent republic and a member of the *Commonwealth since 1976. Tourism is an important industry in the Seychelles. In Britain it is thought of as a place where people go for expensive holidays.
  ▶ **,Seychel'lois** /,seɪʃelˈwɑː/ *adj, n (pl **Seychellois**)*.

,Jane 'Seymour /'siːmɔː(r)/ (c. 1509–37) the third wife of King *Henry VIII. She married him in 1536, but died soon after the birth of their son Edward, who became King *Edward VI.

SFO /,es ef 'əʊ; *AmE* 'oʊ/ ⇨ SERIOUS FRAUD OFFICE.

S4C /,es fɔː 'si; *AmE* fɔːr/ (*in full **Sianel Pedwar Cymru**)* the Welsh language television channel. It broadcasts a mixture of programmes in Welsh and *Channel Four programmes seen in the rest of Britain.

SHA /,es eɪtʃ 'eɪ/ ⇨ STRATEGIC HEALTH AUTHORITY.

,Ernest 'Shackleton /'ʃækltən/ (1874–1922) an Irish explorer. He went to the Antarctic as a member of Captain *Scott's group from 1901 to 1904, and later led three more trips to the Antarctic. He died on the fourth journey. He was made a *knight in 1909.

the ,Shadow 'Cabinet the group of British *MPs from the Opposition (= the main party opposing the government) who would probably form the *Cabinet if their party were in power. Each member of the Shadow Cabinet speaks on behalf of his or her party on matters for which he or she would be responsible.

,Peter 'Shaffer /'ʃæfə(r)/ (1926–) an English writer of plays, several of which have been very successful in *West End and *Broadway theatres. His best-known works are *Equus* (1973) and *Amadeus* (1979), both of which were made into films.

,Shaftesbury 'Avenue /,ʃɑːftsbri ; *AmE* ,ʃæftsbri/ a street in central London, running north-east from *Piccadilly Circus. It is famous for the many *West End theatres on it.

the 'Shakers /'ʃeɪkəz; *AmE* 'ʃeɪkərz/ the popular name for the United Society of Believers in Christ's Second Appearing, a Christian religious group that separated from the *Quakers in England and moved to the US in 1774. They were called Shakers because they shook with emotion when they worshipped. Strict Shakers believe people should not have sex, so few children are born, and now only a few Shakers live in *New Hampshire and *Maine. Shakers are well known for the simple, elegant furniture they made.

,William 'Shakespeare /'ʃeɪkspɪə(r); *AmE* 'ʃeɪkspɪr/ (1564–1616) the English poet and playwright (= writer of plays) who is often described as the greatest writer in the English language. He was born in *Stratford-upon-Avon, the son of a wealthy glove maker and merchant. He married Anne *Hathaway in 1582 and they had three children. In 1588 Shakespeare moved to London and joined a leading theatre company called the *Chamberlain's Men. He quickly established a reputation as a writer of plays and appeared in his own dramas at the *Globe Theatre. He wrote 36 plays for the London stage including **comedies** such as *A *Midsummer Night's Dream* and *As You Like It*, **tragedies** such as *Hamlet*, *Othello*, *Macbeth* and *Romeo and Juliet*, **history plays** including *Richard II* and *Henry IV* and two **romances**, *The *Winter's Tale* and *The *Tempest*. The plays are written mainly in verse and are greatly admired for their poetic language, dramatic technique and literary style. He also wrote poems, the best known of which are *The *Sonnets*, famous for their beautiful language and strong emotion. Shakespeare returned to Stratford-upon-Avon in about 1611 and died there in 1616. Today his plays are regularly performed all over the world. In Britain, they are often performed by the *Royal

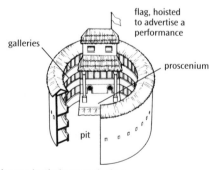

a theatre in Shakespeare's time

(labels: flag, hoisted to advertise a performance; proscenium; galleries; pit)

Shakespeare's plays and their dates

1589–90	Henry VI, Part 1		1599	Julius Caesar
1590–92	Henry VI, Parts 2 and 3			Henry V
1590–94	The Comedy of Errors			As You Like It
	Titus Andronicus		1600–01	Hamlet
	Love's Labour's Lost		1600–02	Twelfth Night
1592	The Taming of the Shrew		1601–02	Troilus and Cressida
1592–93	Richard III		1602–03	All's Well That Ends Well
	The Two Gentlemen of Verona		1604	Othello
1595	A Midsummer Night's Dream		1604–05	Measure for Measure
	Richard II		1605–06	King Lear
1595–96	Romeo and Juliet			Macbeth
1595–97	King John		1605–09	Timon of Athens
1596	Henry IV, Part 1		1606–07	Anthony and Cleopatra
1596–98	The Merchant of Venice		1607–08	Coriolanus
1597	The Merry Wives of Windsor			Pericles, Prince of Tyre
	Henry IV, Part 2		1609–10	Cymbeline
1598	Much Ado About Nothing		1610	The Winter's Tale
			1613	Henry VIII
				The Tempest

Shakespeare Company in Stratford-upon-Avon and around the country, and at the Globe Theatre in London. Every year, during the weekend nearest to 23 April, which is Shakespeare's birthday, there are celebrations in Stratford, and people from all over the world go together to put flowers on Shakespeare's tomb.

ˌTupac Shaˈkur /ˌtuːpæk ʃəˈkʊə(r); AmE ʃəˈkʊr/ (1971–96) a US singer of *rap music, also known as 2Pac. His album All Eyez on Me (1996) sold more than 7 million copies. Shakur led a criminal and violent life which ended when he was murdered in *Las Vegas.

ˈshamrock n [C, U] a plant with three small leaves on each stem. It is well known as the national symbol of Ireland. Many Irish people wear a piece of shamrock attached to their clothes on *St Patrick's Day.

Shane /ʃeɪn/ a US film (1953) which many people consider one of the best *westerns ever made. It was directed by George Stevens, with Alan Ladd in the main role. He plays Shane, a lonely man who visits a farmer and his family and helps them against violent *cowboys who want their land.

the ˌShankhill ˈRoad /ˌʃæŋkɪl/ a street in a *Protestant area of *Belfast, Northern Ireland, where there have been many violent disturbances between *Roman Catholics, *Protestants and British soldiers during the *Troubles.

ˈsharecropper /ˈʃeəkrɒpə(r); AmE ˈʃerkrɑːpər/ n (especially AmE) (in the southern US) a poor farmer who rents land and gives part (i.e. a share) of his crops to the owner as payment. This is usually 50% to pay for his house, equipment, seeds and land. The system, which is widely regarded as unfair, was common after the *Civil War, and many sharecroppers were poor slaves who had been freed.
▶ sharecropping n [U].

ˌHelen ˈSharman /ˈʃɑːmən; AmE ˈʃɑːrmən/ (1963–) an English scientist who became the first British astronaut in 1991 when she spent eight days in space in a Soviet spacecraft.

ˌSharon and ˈTracy (humorous disapproving) (in Britain) two women's names that were used by the writer Keith Waterhouse in a series of newspaper articles in the 1980s to refer to women with poor taste who speak English badly and are not very polite. Sharon and Tracy are also the names of the two sisters in the British television comedy series Birds of a Feather whose husbands are in prison.

Tom Sharpe /ˈʃɑːp; AmE ˈʃɑːrp/ (1928–) a British writer whose books often use satire (= a way of criticizing someone or something using humour to show their faults and weaknesses). His most famous books include Porterhouse Blue (1974), which was also made into a popular television series, and Wilt (1976).

the ˌReverend ˌAl ˈSharpton /ˈʃɑːptən; AmE ˈʃɑːrptən/ (Alfred Charles Sharpton, Jr 1954–) a US politician, Pentecostal preacher and *civil rights activist. He tried, unsuccessfully, to become the candidate for the *Democratic Party in the 2004 election for President.

ˈShavian /ˈʃeɪviən/ adj of or like George Bernard *Shaw or his works.

ˌArtie ˈShaw[1] /ˌɑːti ˈʃɔː; AmE ˌɑːrti/ (1910–2004) a US musician who led *big bands in the 1930s and 1940s. He also played the clarinet and wrote music. One of his best-known tunes is Begin the Beguine (1938). Shaw also led a US Navy band during *World War II. He married eight times and his wives included the actors Lana Turner and Ava *Gardner. He received a *Grammy award in 2004 for lifetime achievement.

ˌGeorge ˌBernard ˈShaw[2] /ˈʃɔː/ (1856–1950) an Irish writer of plays, novels and articles about music and literature who lived in England for much of his life. He is best known for his plays, which are full of intelligent and amusing remarks and criticisms of society. He is also famous for his campaigns for social change. He was one of the earliest members of the *Fabian Society and a supporter of feminism (= women's rights) and vegetarianism (= not eating meat). His best-known works include The Devil's Disciple (1897), Major Barbara (1905) and *Pygmalion (1913). He was given the *Nobel Prize for literature in 1925. When he died he left money for the invention of a new alphabet that would make the English spelling system simpler. See also SHAVIAN.

66 He who can, does. He who cannot, teaches. 99
George Bernard Shaw

ˈShawnee /ˈʃɔːniː/ n (pl Shawnees or Shawnee) a member of a *Native American people living mostly in *Oklahoma. They first settled in the Ohio Valley as farmers who also hunted. *Tecumseh tried to unite them to defend their land against white people but failed. The Shawnees were then moved to the *Indian Territory.

She /ʃiː/ a British magazine for women that contains articles on health, fashion, sex, food and other subjects. It first appeared in 1955 and is published every month.

S

,Alan **'Shearer** /'ʃɪərə(r); AmE 'ʃɪrər/ (1970–) an English football player known for his strength and his ability to score goals. He played for Southampton (1988–92) and Blackburn Rovers (1992–6), and in 1996 he was bought by Newcastle United for £15 million, the largest sum ever paid for a player at the time. He played regularly for the England team from 1992 to 2000.

,George **'Shearing** /'ʃɪərɪŋ; AmE 'ʃɪrɪŋ/ (1919–) an English *jazz pianist and composer who was born blind. He has written many popular pieces of music, including *Lullaby in Birdland* (1952). He moved to the US in 1947.

,Martin **'Sheen** /'ʃiːn/ (1940–) a US actor who was born Ramon Estevez. In 1964 he appeared in the *Broadway play *The Subject of Roses* and later made the 1968 film version. His other films include *Badlands* (1973), *Apocalypse Now* (1979) and *The American President* (1995). He has won several awards for playing the part of the *Democratic president in the television series *The West Wing* (1999–) and is known for his liberal political views in real life. His sons Emilio Estevez (1962–) and Charlie Sheen (1965–) are also actors.

'Sheffield /'ʃefiːld/ a large industrial city in *South Yorkshire, England. It is the historical centre of the British steel industry. There has been an important iron industry there since the 12th century, and by the time of the *Industrial Revolution the high quality of **Sheffield steel** was famous around the world. Many steel items are still produced in Sheffield, particularly cutlery (= knives, forks, etc.) and special tools, but several local factories closed down in the late 20th century, leaving many people unemployed.

,Sheffield **'plate** /,ʃefiːld/ n [U] a type of metal consisting of copper covered with a thin layer of silver. The method of covering copper objects with silver and then heating them to keep it in place was invented by Thomas Boulsover in *Sheffield in the 1740s. It became an important industry because objects could be made of Sheffield plate much more cheaply than if they were made of silver.

,Sheffield **'Wednesday** /,ʃefiːld/ an English football club based at *Hillsborough in north-west *Sheffield. The club was established in 1867 and originally played its matches on Wednesdays. It was in the highest division of English football for much of its history, and had many successes in the *Football League and the *FA Cup in the first part of the 20th century.

,Sidney **'Sheldon** /'ʃeldən/ (1917–) a US writer of books, films, plays and television series. Several of his novels have been made into films, including *The Other Side of Midnight* (1977). His other books include *Windmills of the Gods* (1987) and *Morning, Noon and Night* (1995). He has written six *Broadway plays and won a 1959 *Tony award for *Redhead*. His 23 films include *The Bachelor and the Bobby Soxer* (1947), for which he won an *Oscar, and *Annie Get Your Gun*. Sheldon also wrote the successful television shows *I Dream of Jeannie* (1965) and *Hart to Hart* (1979).

the **Shel,donian 'Theatre** /ʃel,dəʊniən; AmE ʃel,doʊniən/ (also **the Sheldonian**) a large theatre that is part of *Oxford University. It was designed by Christopher *Wren and built in 1663. Graduates of the university are given their degrees there. It is also used for other university ceremonies and for concerts (not plays).

Shell /ʃel/ a large international oil company that was formed when the British company Shell combined with the Dutch company Royal Dutch in the 1890s. It is now involved in producing oil and gas in Asia, the Middle East, the *North Sea and South America. It also owns petrol/gasoline stations in many countries.

,Mary **'Shelley**[1] /'ʃeli/ (1797–1851) an English writer, best known as the author of *Frankenstein*. She was the daughter of Mary *Wollstonecraft, and is also remembered for having run away with the poet *Shelley[2] at the age of 16. She married Shelley after his first wife killed herself in 1816.

'Percy 'Bysshe 'Shelley[2] /'bɪʃ 'ʃeli/ (1792–1822) one of the major poets of the English *Romantic Movement. He is well known for the beauty of his verse. He was an atheist (= a person who believes that there is no God) and an anarchist (= a person who believes there should be no laws or government), whose love of freedom and left-wing political opinions influenced poems such as *Prometheus Unbound* (1820). He ran away twice with young women, and lived the last few years of his life with his second wife Mary in Italy, where he died in an accident at sea. His best-known poems include *Ode to the West Wind* and *To a Skylark*.

'shell game n [C] (AmE) **1** (also **thimblerig** [U]) a game in which one person tries to trick the other players. The first person places a small object under one of three upside-down cups, nut shells, etc. He or she then quickly moves the cups around, and the others try to guess which contains the object, sometimes betting on their choice.
2 any action that is intended to cheat or deceive somebody: *She promised to double my money, but it was just a shell game.*

'Shelter /'ʃeltə(r)/ a British charity established in 1966 to help people who have nowhere to live, either by finding homes for them or by providing places in cities where they can sleep at night. It also acts as a *pressure group to try to influence the government to do more to help people without homes.

,sheltered **'housing** n [U] (in Britain) houses or flats/apartments that are specially designed and built for old or disabled people so that they can live in the local community instead of in hospitals. Sheltered housing is usually arranged in small blocks, with a person in each block whose job is to help the people living there. The term is less often used in the US for this type of housing, though the state of *Maryland has a large Accessory, Shared and Sheltered Housing Program (ACCESS): *The new sheltered housing project will be built close to the shops and main bus routes.* ⇨ note at OLD AGE.

the ,Shenandoah **'Valley** /,ʃenəndəʊə; AmE ,ʃenəndoʊə/ a large, beautiful valley in the northern part of the US state of *Virginia, between the *Allegheny Mountains and the Blue Ridge Mountains. It was used by many Americans when they moved west, and several *Civil War battles were fought there because it supplied food for the Confederate forces. The **Shenandoah River** flows through it and is the subject of the folk song *Shenandoah*, which begins: 'Oh Shenandoah, I long to hear you, Away, you rolling river.' The **Shenandoah National Park** was established in 1926.

,Alan **'Shepard**[1] /'ʃepəd; AmE 'ʃepərd/ (1923–98) the first American in space. He made a short sub-orbital flight (= one that does not go completely round the earth in space) in 1961 as part of the *Mercury programme. He became the fifth man on the moon when he commanded Apollo 14 in 1971.

,E H **'Shepard**[2] /'ʃepəd; AmE 'ʃepərd/ (Ernest Howard Shepard 1879–1976) an English artist, best remembered for his illustrations for *Winnie-the-Pooh and other books and poems by A A *Milne, and for *The Wind in the Willows*. He also drew many cartoons (= amusing drawings) for *Punch magazine.

,Sam **'Shepard**[3] /'ʃepəd; AmE 'ʃepərd/ (1943–) a US actor who also writes and directs plays and films. His play *Buried Child* (1978) won the *Pulitzer Prize, and he wrote such films as *Paris, Texas* (1984) and *Silent Tongue* (1994). His films as an actor include *The Right Stuff* (1983), *Crimes of the Heart* (1986) and *The Pelican Brief* (1993).

,**Shepherd's 'Bush** an area of west London, England, consisting mainly of houses and flats/apartments and a busy market and shopping centre.

,**shepherd's 'pie** (*BrE also* ,**cottage 'pie**) *n* [C, U] a dish consisting of minced meat with mashed potato on top. It is then baked until the top of the potato turns brown. Traditionally, shepherd's pie is made with lamb or mutton (= sheep's meat) and cottage pie is made with beef.

,**Shepperton 'Studios** /ˈʃepətən; *AmE* ˌʃepərtən/ a large film studio near London, England. Since the 1930s it has been one of the two major British centres of film production. Many famous films have been made there, including *The African Queen* (1951) and *The *Third Man*. Compare PINEWOOD STUDIOS.

,**Antony 'Sher** /ˈʃeə(r); *AmE* ˈʃer/ (1949–) a British actor and writer, born in South Africa. He is best known for his theatre performances in plays by *Shakespeare, but he has also worked in films and television. He has written several novels.

'Sheraton[1] /ˈʃerətən/ *n* any of a large international group of US hotels. They include hotels in the major cities and in unusual places, such as The Great Wall Sheraton Hotel in China and the Sheraton Casablanca in Morocco. There are also special Sheraton Four Points Hotels at less expensive prices.

,**Thomas 'Sheraton**[2] /ˈʃerətən/ (1751–1806) an English furniture designer. His book *The Cabinet-Maker and Upholsterer's Drawing Book* (1791–4) was an important influence on the development of neoclassical furniture, and his designs are typically delicate and graceful: *a beautiful Sheraton chair/table*.

'Shergar /ˈʃɜːgɑː(r); *AmE* ˈʃɜːrgɑːr/ a very successful racehorse. It won many important races, including the *Derby in 1981, but in 1983 it was stolen from a farm in Ireland by a group of armed men, and never seen again. Most people believe that it was taken and killed by the *IRA.

'Philip 'Henry 'Sheridan[1] /ˈʃerɪdən/ (1831–1888) a US military leader in the *Civil War. General Sheridan commanded the Army of the Shenandoah Valley in *Virginia and defeated the Confederate army there in 1864. He later forced the army of General Robert E *Lee to surrender near *Appomattox Court House (1865).

'Richard 'Brinsley 'Sheridan[2] /ˈʃerɪdən/ (1751–1816) a British writer of plays, born in Ireland. He wrote a series of popular comedies, including *The *Rivals* and **School for Scandal*, and was well known in London for his quick and intelligent humour. He became a friend of the *Prince of Wales and several important politicians. In 1780 he became a *Whig(1) *Member of Parliament, and held several important government positions. Although he had successful careers in politics and the theatre, he had many debts, and died in poverty.

'sheriff court *n* (in Scotland) a type of court of law where the sheriff (= a Scottish title for a judge) deals with less serious criminal and civil cases. Serious crimes such as murder are dealt with in the *High Court of Justiciary and serious civil cases go to the *Court of Session.

the ,**Sheriff of 'Nottingham** /ˈnɒtɪŋəm; *AmE* ˈnɑːtɪŋəm/ (in old stories) the main enemy of *Robin Hood. He was a cruel and dishonest government official responsible for the town *Nottingham and the area around it.

'William Te'cumseh 'Sherman /təˈkʌmsə ˈʃɜːmən; *AmE* ˈʃɜːrmən/ (1820–91) a US military leader during the *Civil War. General Sherman commanded the US Army in the West (1864–5). He is best remembered for his march through *Georgia with 60 000 soldiers, destroying anything that might be useful to the South in the war, including military equipment, factories, railways, homes and farm animals. After the war, in 1879, he made his famous statement that 'War is hell'.

,**Sherwood 'Forest** /ˌʃɜːwʊd; *AmE* ˌʃɜːrwʊd/ a forest in the English *Midlands, famous in old stories as the place where *Robin Hood's *Merry Men lived and fought against the forces of the *Sheriff of Nottingham. It used to be a very large forest, but only a small part of it still remains. It is preserved as a *country park near *Nottingham.

,**She 'Stoops to 'Conquer** the best-known play (1773) by Oliver *Goldsmith. It is a comedy based on a misunderstanding. Marlow, a shy young man, goes with a friend to visit the Hardcastle family because their parents hope that he and Miss Hardcastle will marry. The friends get lost on the way and look for an inn (= a pub that is also a small hotel) but actually arrive at the Hardcastles' house. Most of the humour comes from the way Marlow treats the family when he thinks that their house is an inn and that Miss Hardcastle is a servant.

the ,**Shetland Islands** /ˈʃetlənd/ (*also* ,**Shetland**, the ,**Shetlands** /ˈʃetləndz/) a group of over 100 islands north of Scotland. The islands are governed as a single *council area from Lerwick, Shetland's only town and main port. The islands' main industries are farming, fishing and making clothes out of the famous **Shetland wool** from local sheep. Since the 1970s the islands have become an important centre of the *North Sea oil industry.

,**Shetland 'pony** /ˌʃetlənd/ *n* a breed of small, strong pony with long, rough hair and a long tail. Shetland ponies were originally bred in the *Shetland Islands and used for work, but they are now popular for children to ride because of their small size.

,**The 'Shield** a US television drama series about a team of four *Los Angeles policemen, led by Vic Mackey, who are shown behaving dishonestly.

,**Carol 'Shields** /ˈʃiːldz/ (1935–2003) a Canadian writer, born in the US. She won the *Pulitzer Prize for *The Stone Diaries* (1993). Her other books include *Swann* (1990), *Larry's Party* (1997) and *Unless* (2002).

the ,**Battle of 'Shiloh** /ˈʃaɪləʊ; *AmE* ˈʃaɪloʊ/ a major battle of the *American Civil War, fought on 6–7 April 1862 at Pittsburgh Landing, *Tennessee. It was won by the US Army, led by General Ulysses S *Grant, after it had been forced back on the first day. More than 10 000 soldiers were killed or wounded on both sides. The victory helped Grant to take control of the *Mississippi River. The battle was named after Shiloh Church, a small Methodist church near where it was fought.

,**Peter 'Shilton** /ˈʃɪltən/ (1949–) an English football player. He was the England national team's main goalkeeper (= player who defends the goal) in the 1970s and 1980s and played for several major English clubs. He has played more *Football League games and appeared more times for England than any other player, and is considered one of England's greatest goalkeepers.

'shinty /ˈʃɪnti/ *n* [U] a traditional Scottish game, similar to *field hockey. The sticks used (also called **shinties**) are shorter and thicker than those used in hockey, and the game is faster, since the ball is often hit when it is in the air. It is mainly played in the Scottish *Highlands. A related form of shinty, called *hurling*, is played in Ireland.

S

,Harold '**Shipman** /ˈʃɪpmən/ (1946–2004) a British doctor who was found guilty of murdering 15 of his patients, mostly older women, by giving them injections of drugs and was sent to prison for life in 2000. A public enquiry into the case found that he had killed at least 200 other patients over a period of 23 years, making him Britain's worst serial killer (= a person who murders several people one after the other). Shipman killed himself in prison.

'**ship ,money** n [U] a tax that English kings and queens traditionally collected from people living on the coast in times of war. In the 1630s *Charles I used the tax to collect money without involving *Parliament, at first on the coast and then all over England, by saying that there was a possibility of war. A group of people led by John *Hampden refused to pay the tax, and in 1640 the *Long Parliament made it illegal.

the '**shipping ,forecast** a detailed report on the weather conditions at sea, prepared by the *Meteorological Office and broadcast four times a day on *BBC *Radio 4. The seas around the British Isles and northern and western Europe are divided into 31 sea areas, and information is given on the speed of the wind and how far it is possible to see in each area.

the **shires** /ʃaɪəz; AmE ʃaɪərz/ n [pl] a traditional name for the counties in the English *Midlands which have names ending in -shire (= an old word for county). Originally they were called this by people from southern counties which did not have -shire in their names. In modern times the shires refer mainly to those counties that were famous for *hunting, especially *Northamptonshire and *Leicestershire, where people had been using dogs to hunt foxes since the 17th century. Many British people think of the shires as country areas where people have old-fashioned attitudes: *For decades the Tories dominated in the shires.*

,**Shirley 'Temple** /ˈtempl/ n a US drink that contains no alcohol but looks like a cocktail (= mixed alcoholic drink). It is usually made with lemon juice and grenadine (= a thick sweet red liquid made from fruit juice). Ice is added and often a cherry on top. It is popular with children and was named after the former child actor Shirley *Temple.

,Willie '**Shoemaker** /ˌwɪli ˈʃuːmeɪkə(r)/ (1931–2003) the most successful US professional jockey ever. His popular name was 'the Shoe'. Between 1949 and 1990 he won 8 833 of his 40 351 races, including victories in four *Kentucky Derby races.

,**shoo-fly 'pie** /ˌʃuː-flaɪ/ n (AmE) an dish of pastry filled with a mixture of brown sugar and molasses (= a dark, sweet, thick liquid obtained from sugar). It takes its name from the fact that people have to shoo (= frighten away) flies that are attracted to it.

'**shopping ,centre** (also especially AmE '**shopping ,mall, mall**) n a large building or covered area containing many different shops. Shopping centres may also have their own car parks, restaurants, banks and other services.

,**shopping days to 'Christmas** a phrase used to explain how many days are left on which the shops will be open between the present time and *Christmas. It is written in the windows of some shops to encourage people to buy their Christmas presents before it is too late: *I can't believe there are only fifteen shopping days to Christmas.*

'**shopping ,precinct** n (BrE) an area of a town or city where cars are not allowed, so that it is easy for people to walk between the many shops, banks, restaurants, etc. in the precinct.

,**Clare 'Short**¹ /ˈʃɔːt; AmE ˈʃɔːrt/ (1946–) a British *Labour politician. She became a *Member of Parliament in 1983 and held several important positions in the *Shadow Cabinet before being appointed International Development Secretary in the Labour government of 1997. She is well known for her support for women's rights and for her opposition to the war in Iraq, which caused her to resign from the *Cabinet in 2003.

,**Nigel 'Short**² /ˈʃɔːt; AmE ˈʃɔːrt/ (1965–) an English chess player. He became a grand master (= a chess player of the highest class) at the age of 19. In 1993 he played at the highest level of chess that a British player had ever reached when he lost the final match of the world championship against Garry Kasparov.

'**shortbread** (also '**shortcake**) n [U] a type of rich sweet biscuit made with flour, sugar and a lot of butter. It is associated especially with Scotland.

'***Shortnin' Bread*** /ˈʃɔːtnɪn; AmE ˈʃɔːrtnɪn/ a traditional African-American children's song about homemade 'shortening bread' (bread made with fat). It includes the lines:

> 66 Two little children lying in bed;
> One turned over, and the other one said,
> 'Mammy's little baby loves shortnin', shortnin',
> Mammy's little baby loves shortnin' bread.' 99

,**short-order 'cook** n (AmE) a professional cook who prepares quick dishes ordered by customers, especially at a *fast food restaurant, cafe, etc.

the '**Short ,Parliament** the first of two parliaments set up by the English king *Charles I in 1640 when he needed the legal power of *Parliament to raise money for a war against Scotland. When the *MPs refused to support the king he dismissed the parliament. It was replaced later in the same year by the *Long Parliament.

Sho'shone /ʃəʊˈʃəʊni; AmE ʃoʊˈʃoʊni/ n (pl **Shoshones** or **Shoshone**) a member of a *Native American people who originally lived as hunters in an area stretching from south-eastern *California to western *Wyoming. About 8 000 still live there on reservations (= lands given and protected by the US government). The *Comanche people separated from the Wyoming group of Shoshone.

'***Show Boat*** a famous *Broadway musical play (1927) by Jerome *Kern and Oscar *Hammerstein. It was based on a novel (1926) by Edna *Ferber about people on the *Cotton Blossom*, a *showboat on the *Mississippi River. It includes the songs *Ol' Man River* and *Only Make Believe*. There have been three film versions (1929, 1936 and 1951).

'**showboat** /ˈʃəʊbəʊt; AmE ˈʃoʊboʊt/ n (AmE) (in the 19th and early 20th centuries) a type of large river boat driven by steam, on which plays and other shows were performed for people living in towns along the rivers, especially the *Mississippi. Well-known showboats included the *Water Queen*, the *Cotton Blossom* and the *Floating Circus Palace*. Ships built to look like showboats now take tourists for rides from *New Orleans.

,**Shredded 'Wheat** /ˌʃredɪd/ n [U] a type of breakfast food consisting of thin crisp strips of wheat shaped into larger pieces. It is eaten with milk and sometimes sugar. It is well known in Britain because of its television advertising, which sometimes shows sports stars giving it to their children, or humorous situations suggesting that it is difficult to eat more than two pieces of Shredded Wheat.

'**Shrewsbury** /ˈʃrəʊzbri; AmE ˈʃroʊzbri/ a town in *Shropshire, England, near the border with Wales. It is the administrative centre for Shropshire and was important in history as a military centre between England and

Wales. It has a *Norman castle and many attractive old churches and other buildings. See also SALOPIAN.

Shrewsbury 'School /ˌʃrəʊzbri; AmE ˈʃroʊzbri/ (also **'Shrewsbury**) a well-known English *public school(1), established in 1552 in the town of *Shrewsbury. See also SALOPIAN.

'Shropshire /ˈʃrɒpʃə(r); AmE ˈʃrɑːpʃər/ a county in the *Midlands of England, on the Welsh border. It consists mainly of agricultural land. Its administrative centre is *Shrewsbury. See also SALOPIAN.

A ˌShropshire 'Lad /ˌʃrɒpʃə; AmE ˌʃrɑːpʃər/ a collection of poems (1896) by A E *Housman. The poems are short and easy to read. They express love for the people and countryside of Housman's home in *Shropshire, and sadness to be away from that home and for lost youth. They became especially popular during *World War I, and are still widely read. Several English composers have set the poems to music.

> 66 Loveliest of trees, the cherry now
> Is hung with bloom along the bough,
> And stands about the woodland ride
> Wearing white for Eastertide. 99
> *A Shropshire Lad*

ˌShrove 'Tuesday /ˌʃrəʊv/ the day before *Ash Wednesday. In the Christian religion it is traditionally the last day on which people can enjoy rich food before *Lent, and it is celebrated in different ways in different countries. In Britain it is often called *Pancake Day and in America it is called *Mardi Gras.

'shuttle ⇨ SPACE SHUTTLE.

M Night Shyamalan /ˌem naɪt ˌʃaɪəmə'lɑːn/ (Manoj Nelliyatu Shyamalan 1970–) a writer and film director who was born in India but grew up in the US. He is famous for the unexpected endings in his work. His films include *The Sixth Sense* (1999), *Unbreakable* (2000), *Signs* (2002) and *The Village* (2004).

'Shylock /ˈʃaɪlɒk; AmE ˈʃaɪlɑːk/ a character in *Shakespeare's play The *Merchant of Venice. He is a Jewish moneylender who demands a pound of flesh from somebody who cannot pay back the money that he borrowed. Although the play shows him as a person who is treated badly as well as a person who treats others badly, his name is sometimes used in a negative way to describe people who lend money at very high rates of interest.

'Sianel 'Pedwar 'Cymru /ˈʃænel ˈpedwɑːr ˈkʌmri/ ⇨ S4C.

ˌWalter 'Sickert /ˈsɪkət; AmE ˈsɪkərt/ (1860–1942) an English artist. He was the most important painter of the *Camden Town Group, and was influenced by the French Impressionists and by *Whistler. He is famous for his paintings of life in the theatre, and for his later paintings of dull rooms, often with a naked model.

ˌMrs 'Siddons /ˈsɪdənz/ (Sarah Siddons 1755–1831) an English actor. She is considered to have been one of the greatest actors in tragedies (= serious plays with sad endings) and was especially famous for playing the role of Lady *Macbeth.

'sidewinder /ˈsaɪdwaɪndə(r)/ n **1** a dangerous North American snake that lives in the desert. It moves sideways by throwing its body in S-shaped curves. **2** (AmE) a hard blow with the closed hand swung from the side. **3 Sidewinder** a US weapon, fired from an aircraft, that can find and destroy enemy aircraft.

ˌPhilip 'Sidney /ˈsɪdni/ (1554–86) an English poet and soldier who is considered one of the greatest Englishmen of the *Elizabethan period. His best-known works are *Arcadia* (1590) and *Astrophel and Stella* (1591). He was made a *knight in 1583 and died of wounds received while fighting the Spanish in the Netherlands. There is a popular story that as he lay dying he refused a drink of water and passed it to another wounded soldier who he said needed it more.

the ˌSidney Street 'siege /ˌsɪdni/ an incident that took place in the *East End of London in 1911. Two anarchists (= people who believe there should be no laws or government) were trapped and finally killed in a house surrounded by police officers and soldiers. It is mainly remembered because Winston *Churchill, who was then *Home Secretary, directed the police operation personally, and was much criticized for it.

the 'Siegfried Line /ˈsiːɡfriːd/ **1** (in *World War I) a line of military defence set up by the Germans in Belgium and France. **2** (in *World War II) the name given by the *Allies to the German line of military defence between France and Germany. A song that was popular with British soldiers at the time began with the line, 'We're gonna (= going to) hang out the washing on the Siegfried Line.'

Siˌerra Le'one /siˌerə li'əʊn; AmE li'oʊn/ a country on the west coast of Africa which is a member of the *Commonwealth. The capital city, Freetown, was established in 1787 by British people who were against the slave trade, as a place where former slaves could start new lives. There have been several conflicts between the descendants of these people and those of the original population. Sierra Leone became part of the *British Empire in the 19th century, and an independent country in 1961. ⇨ note at SLAVERY.
▶ **Sierra Leonean** adj, n.

the Siˌerra Ne'vada /siˌerə nə'vɑːdə/ (also **the Si'erras** /si'erəz/) a mountain range in the US state of *California. It is 420 miles/673 kilometres long, and the highest point is Mount *Whitney. It includes *Yosemite National Park and two other national parks, Sequoia and Kings Canyon.

ˌSilbury 'Hill /ˌsɪlbri/ a prehistoric mound (= raised mass of earth) near *Avebury in south-west England, built before 2000 BC. It is the largest of these mounds in Europe, and, unlike most of the others, has nobody buried in it. Nobody knows what it was built for.

'Silchester /ˈsɪltʃestə(r)/ the site of an ancient Roman town near *Reading in southern England. It was an important regional centre from the second to the fourth century, and contains the remains of many Roman temples.

The ˌSilence of the 'Lambs a US film (1991) in which Anthony *Hopkins plays Hannibal Lecter, a violent murderer who eats the people he kills. Jodie *Foster plays the *FBI agent who needs his help to catch another murderer. Some people were shocked by the violence of the film when it was first shown. In two further films, *Hannibal* (2001) and *Red Dragon* (2002), Anthony Hopkins played Lecter again.

the ˌsilent ma'jority n [pl] the majority of people in a country, who do not have extreme opinions about political or moral matters, and who do not express their opinions in public. Many people think of the silent majority as being old-fashioned and opposed to change: *She claims to speak for the silent majority who have always wanted peace in the province.*

ˌSilent 'Night a popular *Christmas *carol about Christ when he was a baby with his mother.

ˌSilicon 'Valley the popular name given to an area in the Santa Clara Valley of *California where there are many computer and electronics companies. It is near the cities of *San Francisco and *San Jose. Silicon is an

S

important chemical element used in computers and electronic equipment. Compare ROUTE 128.

,Beverly 'Sills /ˌbevəli 'sɪlz; AmE ˌbevərli/ (1929–) a leading US opera singer with a soprano (= highest female) voice. Her first major performance was in 1947 with the Philadelphia Civic Opera. She was later General Director of the New York City Opera (1979–84) and Chairwoman of the *Lincoln Center for the Performing Arts (1994–2000).

,Phil 'Silvers /'sɪlvəz; AmE 'sɪlvərz/ (1912–85) a US comic actor best known as the television character Sergeant Ernie *Bilko. Silvers also won a *Tony award in 1972 for his part in the play *A Funny Thing Happened on the Way to the Forum*.

'Silverstone /'sɪlvəstəun; AmE 'sɪlvərstoun/ Britain's main motor racing track, near *Northampton in southern England. The *British Grand Prix car and motorcycle races take place there every year.

,Victor Sil'vester /sɪl'vestə(r)/ (1900–78) an English popular music band leader in the 1930s and 1940s. He later became famous on radio for playing dance tunes requested by people in countries all round the world. The Victor Silvester Television Dancing Club ran for 17 years and his orchestra appeared in more than 6500 broadcasts for *BBC radio.

'Posy 'Simmonds /'sɪməndz/ (Rosemary Elizabeth Simmonds 1945–) a British cartoonist and a writer and illustrator of children's books. She drew a popular weekly cartoon for the *Guardian newspaper in the 1970s about a middle-class couple called George and Wendy Weber and more recently one called *Literary Life*. She has written novels in picture form including *Gemma Bovery* 1999.

,Lambert 'Simnel /ˌlæmbət 'sɪmnəl; AmE ˌlæmbərt/ (c. 1475–1525) a man who pretended that he had the right to be the king of England during the *Wars of the Roses. He was persuaded by supporters of the House of *York to pretend to be the Earl of Warwick, whose uncle was *Richard III. Simnel was crowned king in 1487 in Ireland, and then invaded England with a small army. It was defeated by the forces of *Henry VII, who pardoned (= decided not to punish) Simnel and gave him a job in the royal kitchen.

'simnel cake /'sɪmnəl/ n [C, U] (BrE) a rich fruit cake with a layer of marzipan (= a soft mixture of sugar, eggs and almond) inside or on top. It is traditionally eaten in Britain at *Easter or on *Mother's Day(1).

,Neil 'Simon /'saɪmən/ (1927–) a US writer of mainly comedy plays, many of which have also appeared as films. He began in the 1950s as a writer for Sid *Caesar, an experience he used for *Laughter on the 23rd Floor* (1993). He has won *Tony awards for *The Odd Couple* (1965), *Biloxi Blues* (1985) and *Lost in Yonkers* (1991), which also won a *Pulitzer Prize. His 30th play, written at the age of 70, was the serious *Proposals* (1997). Simon owns the Eugene O'Neill Theatre in New York.

,Simon and 'Garfunkel /ˌsaɪmən ˌ'gɑːfʌŋkl; AmE ˌgɑːrfʌŋkl/ **Paul Simon** (1942–) and **Art Garfunkel** (1941–), US popular singers who performed together with great success in the 1960s. Their songs included *Sounds of Silence* (1966), *Scarborough Fair* (1966), *Mrs Robinson* and other music for the film *The *Graduate*, and *Bridge Over Troubled Water* (1970), which won three *Emmy awards. They started separate careers in 1970. Simon has since had success with *Mother and Child Reunion* (1972), *Graceland* (1986), which won a Grammy. He was chosen for the Rock and Roll *Hall of Fame in 2001. He produced his first *Broadway musical play, *The Capeman*, in 1998, but it was an expensive failure. Garfunkel continues to tour and perform.

,Nina Si'mone /ˌniːnə sɪ'məun; AmE sɪ'moun/ (1933–2003) an American *jazz singer who also played the piano. Her early hits included *I Loves You Porgy* (1959). Simone's career suffered when she became involved in *black power activities in the 1960s and 1970s. But she later became popular again and her songs were used in the British film *The Crying Game* (1992).

,Simon Le'gree /lə'griː/ n (in the US) a name applied to somebody who forces others to work very hard and is often cruel to them. It comes from the character in the novel *Uncle Tom's Cabin who beats Uncle Tom so badly that he dies: *Charlie said his history teacher was a real Simon Legree.*

,Simon 'Says n [U] a children's game in which a leader gives a series of commands, such as 'Simon says put your hands in the air.' The players must do everything that Simon says, but when the leader gives a command without saying 'Simon says …', they must not do it.

,Simple 'Simon a name used to refer to a foolish man or boy. Originally it was the name of a foolish boy in a long *nursery rhyme which begins:

> **66** Simple Simon met a pieman
> Going to the fair.
> Says Simple Simon to the pieman,
> 'Let me taste your ware.'
>
> Says the pieman to Simple Simon,
> 'Show me first your penny.'
> Says Simple Simon to the pieman,
> 'Indeed I have not any.' **99**

,O J 'Simpson¹ /'sɪmpsn/ (Orenthal James Simpson 1947–) a US football player who was accused of murdering his wife Nicole and her friend Ronald Goldman. Simpson was judged innocent in 1995 after the longest trial ever shown on television. The result divided white and black Americans. He was later accused again in a civil court (= one concerned with private, not criminal, cases) by the families of those killed. He was judged guilty and ordered to pay $8.5 million. During his career as a football player Simpson established many records playing for the University of Southern California and the professional Buffalo Bills. He also acted in films.

,Wallis 'Simpson² /ˌwɒlɪs 'sɪmpsn; AmE ˌwɑːlɪs/ (1896–1986) an American woman who became the Duchess of *Windsor when she married her third husband, Edward, Duke of *Windsor. He had been King *Edward VIII but abdicated (= gave up his position as king) in order to marry her because kings were not allowed to marry divorced women. See also ABDICATION CRISIS.

The 'Simpsons /'sɪmpsnz/ a popular US television humorous cartoon series on the Fox Television Network since 1990. The characters are a family of yellow people with big eyes whose attitudes and language are offensive to some people. Bart Simpson is a boy of ten who hates school and has problems with his stupid father Homer and his sisters Lisa and Maggie.

> **66** D'oh! **99**
> Homer Simpson's usual expression of annoyance

,Frank Si'natra /sɪ'nɑːtrə/ (1915–98) one of the most popular US singers from the 1940s to the 1960s, who continued performing into the 1980s. He also acted in many films. His popular name was 'Old Blue Eyes', and he was known for his romantic voice. He became famous in the 1940s with the big band of Tommy Dorsey. His many successful records included *All the Way* (1957), *Witchcraft* (1958), *Strangers in the Night* (1966) and *My Way* (1968). His films included *On the Town* (1949), **From Here to*

Eternity (1953), in which he won an *Oscar, and *High Society* (1956). Two of his four marriages were to the actors Ava *Gardner and Mia *Farrow.

,**Sinbad the 'Sailor** /ˌsɪnbæd/ (*also* ,**Sindbad** /'sɪnd-bæd/) a character in one of the stories in the *Arabian Nights*. He is a sailor who has unusual and dangerous adventures each time he goes to sea. In the 19th century the story of his seven journeys became a popular subject for *pantomimes in Britain.

,**Clive 'Sinclair**[1] /'sɪŋkleə(r); *AmE* 'sɪŋkler/ (1940–) an English inventor and businessman. He became success-ful in 1972 when he produced Britain's first pocket calcu-lator. He has developed many other successful electronic products including computers, televisions and the Zike (a new type of bicycle), but his most famous invention was his first failure, the **Sinclair C5**, a small electric vehicle with three wheels. It was introduced in 1985 but very few people bought it. Sinclair was made a *knight in 1983.

,**Upton 'Sinclair**[2] /ˌʌptən 'sɪŋkleə(r); *AmE* 'sɪŋkler/ (1878–1968) a US writer of novels and other books intended to improve conditions in society. The first and best-known of these, *The Jungle* (1906), was about the terrible conditions in the *Chicago meat industry, and it resulted in new laws being passed. One of his later novels, *Dragon's Teeth* (1942), won the *Pulitzer Prize.

,**Singa'pore** /ˌsɪŋə'pɔ:(r), ˌsɪŋgə'pɔ:(r)/ a small country in south-east Asia, consisting of the island of Singapore and 54 smaller islands near the end of the Malay Peninsula. It has been a republic and a member of the *Commonwealth since 1965. The first town there was established by Stamford *Raffles in 1819, and it soon became an important port for ships travelling between Europe, India and China. It was part of the *British Empire until it became independent in 1963. Singapore is well known for its political and economic stability. It is still one of the world's most important ports, and has successful banking and high-technology industries.
▶ **Singaporean** /ˌsɪŋə'pɔ:rɪən, ˌsɪŋgə'pɔ:rɪən/ *adj, n.*

'**Sing a 'Song of 'Sixpence** /'sɪkspəns/ an old English children's song, which may refer to the life of *Henry VIII. Some people think that the birds in the song represent the *Roman Catholic choirs after the *Dissolution of the Monasteries. Most people in Britain know the first verse:

> 66 Sing a song of sixpence, a pocket full of rye,
> Four and twenty blackbirds baked in a pie.
> When the pie was opened, the birds began to sing,
> Wasn't that a dainty dish to set before the king? 99

,**Isaac 'Singer**[1] /'sɪŋə(r)/ (1811–75) an American who in 1851 designed and built the first sewing machine to be sold successfully. Today Singer sewing machines are the best-known make in the world.

'**Isaac Ba'shevis 'Singer**[2] /bɑ:'ʃevɪs 'sɪŋə(r)/ (1904–91) a Jewish-American writer, born in Poland, who won the 1978 *Nobel Prize for literature. He is best known for his short stories, in collections which include *Gimpel the Fool* (1957) and *The Death of Methuselah and Other Stories* (1988). His novels include *The Family Moskat* (1950) and *Shosha* (1978).

,**Singin' in the 'Rain** an *MGM film (1952) which many people think is the best musical comedy film ever made. The stars were Gene *Kelly, Debbie *Reynolds and Donald O'Connor. The story is about the troubles that stars of silent films had when sound films began. The songs include *Singin' in the Rain*, *Good Morning* and *Make 'Em Laugh*. In 1983 Tommy *Steele directed and was the star of a stage version in London.

'**Sing Sing** /'sɪŋ sɪŋ/ a US prison for the state of New York. It is in Ossining, New York, and its first building was completed in 1925 by prisoners used as workers. Many of the state's most dangerous criminals have been sent to Sing Sing because of its strong discipline. Its name was officially changed to Ossining State Correctional Facility in 1969, but most people still use the old name.

,**Sinn 'Fein** /ˌʃɪn 'feɪn/ an Irish political party. It was established in 1902 with the aim of making Ireland inde-pendent. Many of its members left to join *Fianna Fáil when it was formed in 1926. Those who stayed in Sinn Fein continued to support the idea that Northern Ireland should become part of the *Republic of Ireland. Sinn Fein has been criticized for being connected to the *IRA, and some of its members were put in prison in Northern Ireland, or refused permission to enter Britain. In the 1990s Sinn Fein was one of the groups responsible for the IRA ceasefire (= a period during which there is no fighting) and the peace discussions between the govern-ments involved. The name means 'we ourselves' in Irish *Gaelic. See also ADAMS[3].

Sioux /su:/ *n* (*pl* **Sioux**) a member of a *Native American people, also called the Dakota people, many of whom live in *South Dakota on reservations (= land given and protected by the US government). The Sioux were originally an association of seven groups on the *Great Plains where, led by *Sitting Bull and *Crazy Horse, they fought the US Army. They defeated General George *Custer at the Battle of *Little Bighorn but lost their final battle at *Wounded Knee.

Sir the title used before the first name of a *knight or *baronet: *Sir Cliff Richard* ◊ *Sir John is in a meeting – would you like to wait?.* ⇨ note at ARISTOCRACY.

Sir,han Sir'han /sɜ:ˌhɑ:n sɜ:'hɑ:n; *AmE* sɜ:rˌhɑ:n sɜ:r'hɑ:n/ (1944–) the man who murdered Robert F *Kennedy on 6 June 1968 in *Los Angeles, as well as shooting and wounding eight other people. Sirhan was a Jordanian who had moved to the US and disliked Kennedy's policy of support for Israel. He was captured immediately and is still in prison.

,**site of 'special scien'tific 'interest** *n* (*abbr* **SSSI**) any of the places or areas of Britain in which the wild animals or plants are considered rare or of scientific importance. There are over 6000 SSSIs in Britain, and they are protected by the government against damage caused by farming or building.

,**Sitting 'Bull** /ˌsɪtɪŋ 'bʊl/ (*c.* 1831–90) a leader of one of the *Sioux peoples. He and *Crazy Horse defeated General George *Custer at the Battle of *Little Bighorn. He then lived for a short time in Canada but agreed in 1881 to settle with his people on the Standing Rock Reservation in *North Dakota, and in 1885 appeared in *Buffalo Bill's *Wild West Show. Because he encouraged the Sioux to keep the *Ghost Dance religion, US soldiers and Native American police tried to arrest him and he was killed.

'**Sitwell** /'sɪtwel/ the name of a sister and two brothers of an aristocratic English family, all three of whom became writers. **Edith Sitwell** (1887–1964) was a poet, best known for writing the series of poems *Façade* (1923). She was also known for her unusual clothes and appear-ance. She was made a *dame(2) in 1954. Her brother **Osbert Sitwell** (1892–1969) wrote poems and novels, but is best known for his autobiography, published in five books. The youngest, **Sacheverell Sitwell** (1897–1988), wrote poetry and books about the history of art.

the ,**Six 'Counties** *n* [*pl*] the six counties that trad-itionally make up Northern Ireland. They are Antrim, *Armagh, Down, *Fermanagh, *Londonderry(1) and Tyrone. Historically, the ancient Irish kingdom of *Ulster was divided into nine counties. Six of these counties remained part of the *United Kingdom in 1921. Because of this, some people, mostly Nationalists (= people who want the whole of Ireland to be one country) refer to Northern Ireland as 'the Six Counties'. In 1973, the six counties were replaced by 26 *local-government areas known as 'districts', each with its own 'district council'.

'Six 'Feet 'Under a popular US television drama series about a family who run a funeral business. It was first shown on *HBO in the US in 2001 and has been broadcast in many other countries. Each episode begins with a death which provides the focus for the events in the lives of the characters.

the 'Six 'Nations 'Tournament a *Rugby Union competition that takes place every year between the national teams of England, France, Ireland, Italy, Scotland and Wales. Each team plays each of the others once, and the winner is the team with the most points at the end.

'sixth form *n* the classes that make up the last two years in British secondary schools, often divided into the **upper sixth** (year 13) and **lower sixth** (year 12) and consisting mainly of students aged between 16 and 18 who are studying for the *A level examination. Some students leave their secondary schools after taking the *GCSE examination and go to a **sixth-form college**, a separate school where students study for A level.

The $64 000 Question /ˌsɪksti fɔː ˌθaʊznd dɒlə ˈkwestʃən; *AmE* fɔːr ˈdɒlə/ a popular US television game show in the 1950s, presented by Hal March. It offered the largest prizes ever given, and even people who lost received cars for competing. It was later copied by other shows.

60 Minutes /ˌsɪksti ˈmɪnɪts/ a US television news programme which has been broadcast each week since 1968 on *CBS. By 2003, it had won 73 *Emmy awards, more than any other news programme, and had been voted one of the ten most popular programmes on US television every year for 22 years.

'Sizewell /ˈsaɪzwel/ a group of nuclear power stations (= buildings where electricity is produced) on the east coast of England, in *Suffolk. The first one, **Sizewell A**, was built in 1966 and **Sizewell B**, a much larger power station, began producing electricity in 1995.

ska /skɑː/ *n* [U] a type of popular music similar to *reggae but with a faster beat, and often using brass instruments. It developed in *Jamaica in the 1960s and was also popular in Britain in the late 1970s and early 1980s. Well-known ska bands included Madness and The Specials.

ˌSkara 'Brae /ˌskærə ˈbreɪ/ a *Stone Age village on Mainland, the largest island of the *Orkney Islands. It is the best preserved village of its period in Europe, because it was covered in sand for almost 3 000 years.

'ˌRed' 'Skelton /ˌred ˈskeltən/ (1913–97) a US comic actor in *vaudeville, in films and on radio and television. *The Red Skelton Show* (1953–64) and *The Red Skelton Hour* (1964–70) were on *CBS. His films included *Whistling in the Dark* (1941) and *Three Little Words* (1950). Skelton was chosen for the Comedy *Hall of Fame in 1993.

'skiffle *n* [U] **1** (in Britain) a style of 1950s pop music. It was a mixture of *jazz and *folk music, and usually played by small groups, sometimes on instruments they had made themselves. One of the most popular British skiffle musicians was Lonnie Donegan (1931–2002). **2** (in the US) a style of 1920s and 1930s jazz which included elements of *blues, *ragtime and folk music. It was played on normal instruments and also on instruments made by the players themselves.

'skinhead *n* a young person, usually a man, with a shaved head and often wearing braces and heavy boots, especially *Doc Martens. Skinheads first appeared in Britain in the 1960s and are known for their violent behaviour and their support for right-wing political groups such as the *British National Party.

ˌB F 'Skinner /ˈskɪnə(r)/ (Burrhus Frederic Skinner 1904–90) a US psychologist who believed that the learning processes in humans and animals were very similar, and that behaviour could be predicted and controlled. He taught at *Harvard University and created the **Skinner Box** to measure how much animals could learn if given rewards. His books included *Science and Human Behavior* (1953) and *About Behaviorism* (1974).

Sky /skaɪ/ Britain's first satellite television company, owned by Rupert *Murdoch. It began broadcasting in 1989 but combined with another company the following year and changed its name to *BSkyB. BSkyB still uses Sky as the name of several television channels broadcast in Europe, which can only be seen by people who have satellite dishes or special cable connections. Most of the channels broadcast one particular type of programme and have names like 'Sky Sports' and 'Sky Movies'.

The ˌSky at 'Night a popular British television programme about the stars and planets, broadcast every month by the *BBC since 1957. It is well known for the way in which its presenter, Patrick *Moore, gives scientific information in an entertaining way.

Skye /skaɪ/ the largest island in the Inner *Hebrides, off the coast of north-west Scotland. Its attractive lakes and mountains make it a popular tourist centre. It is famous as the island to which *Bonny Prince Charlie escaped in a boat after the battle of *Culloden. A bridge, built in the 1990s, now connects Skye to the mainland of Scotland.

the ˌSkye 'Boat Song /ˌskaɪ/ a popular Scottish song about how Flora *Macdonald helped *Bonny Prince Charlie escape to Skye. The sad, slow music is sometimes used to represent Scotland in films and television programmes. Many people in Britain know the first verse:

> 66 Speed, bonnie boat, like a bird on the wing;
> Onward, the sailors cry:
> Carry the lad that's born to be king
> Over the sea to Skye. 99

ˌSkye 'terrier /ˌskaɪ/ *n* a breed of *terrier with short legs and long hair. They were originally bred as working dogs on the island of *Skye.

'Skylab /ˈskaɪlæb/ the first US space station. It was used in the early 1970s for scientific research by three different groups of three astronauts. In 1979 *Skylab* fell to earth in pieces which landed in the Indian Ocean and Australia without causing any damage.

▶ **skyscrapers**

Skyscrapers are very tall buildings that contain offices or places to live. The first were built in *Chicago in the late 1880s but they have since been copied all over the world. After 1913 the top few storeys of skyscrapers were often stepped back (= built gradually narrower, floor by floor) to allow more light to reach street level.

Many of the most famous skyscrapers are in New York City. The *Chrysler Building, at 1 047 feet/319 metres, was by far the tallest building in the world in 1930 when it was built. The taller *Empire State Building, 1 250 feet/381 metres high, was finished the following year. The towers of the *World Trade Center, built in the early 1970s, were about 1 350 feet/412 metres tall. Many visitors to New York took the ferry to *Staten Island so that they could see the **Manhattan skyline**, the outline of all the tallest buildings in New York.

The *Sears Tower in Chicago, built shortly after the World Trade Center, is said to be 1454 feet/443 metres high and is currently the tallest building in the US. The Petronas Towers, built in 1996 in Malaysia, are about 1483 feet/452 metres tall, though some people in Chicago disagree with the way they were measured and say that the Sears Tower is really taller. But in 2004 the Taipei 101 Tower in Taiwan became the world's tallest building at 1660 feet/507 metres high.

By comparison with skyscrapers in the US, those in Britain are rather small. *Canary Wharf, an office building in London's *Docklands, stands only 800 feet/244 metres high but it replaced Tower 42, also in London, as Britain's tallest building in 1986. Other skyscrapers in the *City of London include the Lloyds Building, designed by Richard *Rogers.

Skyscrapers which contain people's homes are, in Britain, usually called **high-rises** or **tower blocks**. They became a common feature of British cities when hundreds of them were built to replace slums in the 1950s and 1960s. Many are 20 or 30 storeys high, and have several flats on each floor. The tallest residential block in Britain is the Shakespeare Tower, part of the *Barbican complex in London, which is 419 feet/128 metres high. At first, high-rises were welcomed because they provided cheap, modern housing but later they were not considered desirable places to live. Many suffered from lack of repair and have been pulled down. People who live in high-rises often complain that they are not private enough, that there is nowhere for children to play, and that they feel cut off from life in the street. Other people argue that the buildings provide housing for large numbers of people and that it is the failure to maintain the buildings that has made them unattractive places to live.

the 'Slade 'School of 'Fine 'Art /'sleɪd/ a famous
art school in London. It is a part of *University College, London and is different from most of London's other art schools because its students study only fine art such as painting and sculpture and not design as well.

▶ slang

Slang words are very informal words. They may be new, or existing words used in a new sense and context. As time goes by, some are used more widely and are no longer thought of as slang. *Clever* and *naughty*, for instance, were both formerly slang words that are now accepted as standard. Many slang words die out after a few years or sooner. The regular introduction of new words to replace them helps keep the language alive.

A lot of slang words are restricted to a particular social group. Use of slang suggests an easy, informal relationship between people and helps reinforce social identity. In the 18th century the word *slang* described the language of criminals, but since then every group in society has developed its own slang terms. The groups that use most slang are still those closest to the edge of society: criminals, prisoners and drug users. Young people also develop slang expressions to distance themselves from older people.

The **street language** of young people changes fast. Street slang includes words relating to young people's attitudes. Young people today may describe something exciting as *cool*, *massive*, *wicked*, or (especially in *AmE*) *bad* or *phat*. If something is old-fashioned or undesirable it is *naff*. Anything bad is *rank* or *minging*. A *geek*, *prat*, *anorak*, *nerd* or (especially in *AmE*) *dweeb* is somebody who seems rather stupid. Going out and having a good time is *chilling*. As people get older they sometimes keep on using the same slang words and in this way slang may indicate a person's age. The parents of today's young people used *great*, *super*, *fab*, *swinging*, *square* or *berk* and *clot*, when they were

young, and many of them still use these words. Some older people try to use current street slang in order not to seem old-fashioned, though in many cases it sounds odd and inappropriate.

A lot of street slang refers to drink, *drugs and sex. Many of these words and phrases are not socially acceptable and are widely considered rude and offensive. The expressions *pissed*, *hammered* and *rat-arsed* relate to being drunk. There are many expressions for vomiting after drinking too much, e.g. *blowing chunks*, *chundering* or (*AmE*) *praying to the porcelain god*. Slang words for drugs include *smack* (heroin) and *crack* (cocaine). Expressions connected with drug-taking include *chasing the dragon* (= smoking heroin in tinfoil) and *jacking/banging up* (= injecting drugs). Some of these terms have become more widely known through films like *Trainspotting. Shagging*, *screwing* and *getting your leg over* all refer to sex. Other common slang expressions refer to the body's waste functions, e.g. *piss*, *take a leak*, *have a shit* and *take a dump*. Some words, such as *fuck* and *shit*, have become frequently used *swear words but they are still likely to offend many people.

Slang words are also widely used for things found in everyday life. The television, for instance, can be called the *box* and the remote control the *flicker* or *zapper*. The *blower* or the *horn* is the telephone. A *dive* or a *hole* is a cheap restaurant, bar or nightclub. Money can be referred to as *dough*, *dosh*, *dollars* (whatever the currency) or *moolah*.

Some slang expressions are **euphemisms**. Many older people use euphemisms for bodily functions, e.g. *spend a penny*, *powder your nose*, and *visit the bathroom*. Some common serious diseases have slang names which are lighter in tone than the formal name, e.g. *the big C* for cancer. Somebody with a bad heart has a *dicky ticker*. People use expressions like *pass away*, *kick the bucket* or *pop your clogs* to refer to dying. In business, some companies, instead of sacking or firing an employee, may speak of *letting them go* or (*AmE*) *dehiring them*.

Some professions and areas of work have their own terms, often called **jargon**, which are different from slang. Many people learn bits of the jargon of other groups through television programmes and films about hospitals, law courts, prisons, etc. Some of the jargon used by people who work with computers has also become well known. Most people know, for instance, that a *hacker* is somebody who gets into other people's computer systems without permission.

▶ slavery

Slavery has been practised in many countries, but played a particularly important role in the history of the US. The first **slaves**, who were considered to be the property of another person and to have no rights of their own, were taken from Africa to North America by the Dutch in 1619 and by the time of the *American Revolution (1775) there were 500000 slaves, mostly in the South. Slaves were taken from Africa in ships in very bad conditions, with many dying during the trip. Once they arrived, they worked mainly on cotton plantations where the quality of their lives depended on the treatment they received from their **master**.

After the Revolution, northern states made slavery illegal, but it continued in the South. It became illegal to bring slaves into the US in 1808, but by then many were being born there, so slave markets continued. In the 1830s opposition to slavery grew from the **abolitionist movement**, whose leaders included William Lloyd Garrison who published an anti-slavery newspaper, *The Liberator* and Harriet Beecher *Stowe who wrote a famous novel about a slave called *Uncle Tom's Cabin*. In 1831 a former slave, Nat *Turner organized an **uprising** of slaves in *Virginia and in 1859 a white man, John *Brown tried to free some slaves. The work of the *Underground Railroad had more effect, trying to help slaves escape to the North, and some people hoped to end slavery by sending slaves back to Africa, creating the new country Liberia in 1822. Laws were made to restrict slavery, but the South wanted it to expand and politicians found it increasingly difficult to agree. In 1820 the *Missouri Compromise said that *Missouri would be admitted to the US as a **slave state** (= one where slavery was allowed) and *Maine as a **free state** (= where slavery was not allowed). However, conflict between the North and South increased and in 1861 the slave states left the US, marking the start of the *Civil War.

After the North won the Civil War and brought southern states back into the US, slavery was ended, but conditions did not improve for many slaves. Some moved to the North, but many of those who stayed in the South continued to work on the plantations where they were paid for their work but didn't get enough money to pay for food and clothes.

The British were also involved in slavery from the 17th century when many slaves were taken from Africa to British colonies in the *Caribbean to work on sugar plantations. Many businessmen made a lot of money from the **triangular trade** between Britain, Africa and the *West Indies. They transported cloth and iron goods to West Africa and exchanged them for slaves which were then taken to the West Indies and exchanged for sugar which was taken back to Bristol and other British ports for sale in Europe. The *Quakers were among the first people to campaign against slavery and it was made illegal in Britain in 1772, but campaigns led by William *Wilberforce and others then grew for the total abolition of the **slave trade**. It was not until 1807 that it was made illegal for British ships to carry slaves and for British colonies to import them, and slavery was not finally abolished in the *British Empire until 1833, when all slaves were set free and their owners were compensated.

'slave state n (in the US) any state that had slaves before and during the *American Civil War. The term was especially important when new states were established as either free states or slave states, as in the *Missouri Compromise. Most slave states were in the South, but several northern states had slaves early in their history.

Wayne 'Sleep /'sliːp/ (1948–) an English dancer. He was a member of the *Royal Ballet before forming his own dance company, Dash, in 1980. He has danced in musicals including *Cats and has often appeared on British television.

The Sleeping 'Beauty a traditional children's story about a princess who falls asleep and cannot wake up because a witch has put a spell (= a condition caused by magic) on her. A hundred years later, a prince finds her and kisses her. The kiss breaks the spell and she wakes up. The story is often used in British *pantomimes.

'Slimbridge /'slɪmbrɪdʒ/ a bird sanctuary (= a place where birds are protected and encouraged to breed) on the river *Severn in south-west England. It has many varieties of birds, and is the main centre of the *Wildfowl and Wetlands Trust.

Sloane 'Ranger /ˌsləʊn; AmE ˌsloʊn/ (also **Sloane**) n (informal humorous) an expression used to refer to a type of *upper-class or *upper-middle-class young person, usually a woman. Sloane Rangers typically live in fashionable areas of London such as *Chelsea, wear expensive clothes (often ones designed to be worn in the country), and have loud voices and old-fashioned ideas about politics and society. The phrase, invented by a journalist in the 1970s, is a mixture of *Sloane Square and the *Lone Ranger. See also GREEN WELLY BRIGADE.

Sloane 'Square /ˌsləʊn; AmE ˌsloʊn/ a square in a fashionable and expensive part of *Chelsea, London. It is connected to *Knightsbridge by **Sloane Street**.

the Slough of De'spond /ˌslaʊ, dɪ'spɒnd; AmE dɪ'spɑːnd/ a place in The *Pilgrim's Progress. It is a slough (= an area of soft, wet ground) that Christian, the main character, has to travel through. It is sometimes used to refer to the mental condition of a person who is depressed or has many doubts and fears: While he was in this slough of despond his agent rang, and suddenly everything seemed all right.

small 'claims court n a type of court of law dealing with cases in which one person has a small claim against another person or a company. This is usually less than £5000 in Britain and $10000 in the US. It is much cheaper to use small claims courts than any other type of court, and they are usually used by customers who feel that they have been treated dishonestly. People often act as their own lawyers. The court can also decide personal disputes that do not involve money, e.g. forcing somebody to return property to its owner.

'Smarties™ /'smɑːtiz; AmE 'smɑːrtiz/ n [pl] small sweets that are hard on the outside with chocolate inside. They are in several different colours and are very popular in Britain, especially with children: She bought a comic and a tube of Smarties.

Samuel 'Smiles /'smaɪlz/ (1812–1904) a Scottish writer and teacher. He believed that people could improve themselves and have better lives, and wrote books about people who had done this, including Lives of the Engineers (1861–2). He also wrote several books explaining how people could improve their lives. The most famous of these was Self-help (1859).

Jane 'Smiley /'smaɪli/ (1949–) a US writer, known for her interest in horses, whose novel A Thousand Acres (1991), which is based on William *Shakespeare's King Lear and is told from the point of view of three daughters on an *Iowa family farm, won the *Pulitzer Prize. Her other books include Barn Blind (1993), Moo (1995), Horse Heaven (2000) and A Year at the Races (2004).

Carol 'Smillie /'smaɪli/ (1961–) a British television presenter, best known for presenting the *BBC home decoration series Changing Rooms in which two couples redecorate a room in each other's houses with the help of an expert.

Smith¹ /smɪθ/ a very common family name in Britain and the US. It is sometimes used by people who do not want their real names to be known: They had registered at the hotel in the names of Mr and Mrs Smith.

Adam 'Smith² /'smɪθ/ (1723–90) a Scottish philosopher and economist. He believed in *free trade and private enterprise (= the idea that business and industry should be controlled by private individuals or companies, not by the state). His book, The *Wealth of Nations, is regarded as the first major work in the modern science of economics. His ideas have influenced several politicians in modern times, including Margaret *Thatcher and Gordon *Brown.

Bessie 'Smith³ /'smɪθ/ (1895–1937) the leading *African-American *blues singer of her time. Her popular name was 'Empress of the Blues'. During her career, she performed with such musicians as Benny *Goodman, Louis *Armstrong and Fletcher Henderson. Her hits included Downhearted Blues (1923). She died after a car crash.

Delia 'Smith⁴ /'smɪθ/ (1941–) an English presenter of popular television programmes on cooking. She is also the author of many cookery books which have sold in their millions.

,Ian **'Smith**[5] /'smɪθ/ (1919–) the last *prime minister of Rhodesia, the country now called *Zimbabwe. In 1965 he declared Rhodesia to be an independent African country ruled by white people. Although very few countries recognized Rhodesia, Smith stayed in charge until the country became Zimbabwe in 1979.

,John **'Smith**[6] /'smɪθ/ (c. 1579–1631) an English colonist (= a person who establishes a colony, an area settled and controlled by people from another country) in America. He was one of the early colonists in Virginia, and was president of the North American colony from 1608 to 1609. In 1614 he explored New England, and gave it its name. He traded goods with Native Americans, and is best known for the story that his life was saved by the Native American princess *Pocahontas.

,John **'Smith**[7] /'smɪθ/ (1938–94) a Scottish *Labour politician. He became *Leader of the Opposition in 1992. In 1993 he was responsible for changing the way decisions are made in the Labour Party by giving each party member and *trade union member one vote. Before that, the unions had always voted on behalf of all their members. When he died Tony *Blair became leader of the *Labour Party.

,Joseph **'Smith**[8] /'smɪθ/ (1805–44) the US religious leader who started the *Mormon Church of Jesus Christ of Latter-Day Saints and published *The Book of Mormon* (1830) containing their basic beliefs. After some of his followers burnt down the offices of a Mormon newspaper that had criticized him, Smith was arrested with his brother Hyrum and taken to a prison at Carthage, *Illinois, where an angry crowd shot and killed them.

,Kate **'Smith**[9] /'smɪθ/ (1909–86) a US singer. She became famous during *World War II for her version of *God Bless America* and for travelling thousands of miles to entertain the military forces. Smith recorded about 3 000 songs including her theme song, *When the Moon Comes Over the Mountain*, which began her radio shows in the 1930s and the 1940s. She later had her own television series, (1950–56).

,Maggie **'Smith**[10] /'smɪθ/ (1934–) an English actor well known for the quality of her many theatre and film performances. She was one of the original members of the *National Theatre company in the 1960s, and in 1969 she won an *Oscar for her part in the film *The Prime of Miss Jean Brodie* (1969). She was made a *dame(2) in 1990.

'Margaret 'Chase **'Smith**[11] /'tʃeɪs 'smɪθ/ (1897–1995) the first US woman elected to both the US House of Representatives (1940–49) and the US Senate (1949–73). She was also, in 1964, the first woman to be named by a major political party as a possible candidate for US President. Smith was a member of the *Republican Party from *Maine.

,Stevie **'Smith**[12] /,sti:vi 'smɪθ/ (1902–71) an English writer of poems and novels. She wrote three novels but is best known for the harsh and intelligent humour of her poetry. Her most famous poem is *Not Waving but Drowning* (1957).

,Sydney **'Smith**[13] /'smɪθ/ (1771–1845) an English writer and *Church of England priest. He played an important role in social and political campaigns such as Catholic emancipation and the abolition of *slavery. He was also famous for making remarks full of clever humour.

,W H **'Smith**[14] /'smɪθ/ (*also informal* **Smith's**) a large group of British shops selling newspapers, magazines, books, cards, etc. Most British *high streets and many train stations and airports have a branch of Smith's.

,Zadie **'Smith**[15] /,zeɪdi 'smɪθ/ (1975–) an English writer who won the **Whitbread First Novel Award** for *White Teeth* (2000), a book about a mixed-race teenager growing up in London, which was made into a television series for *Channel Four. She has also published short stories and two more novels, *The Autograph Man* (2002) and *On Beauty* (2005).

,Smith & **'Wesson** /,smɪθ, 'wesn/ a company that makes guns, and also knives and bicycles. It was established in 1852 in Springfield, *Massachusetts, by Horace Smith and Daniel B Wesson: *He had been shot at close range by a Smith & Wesson handgun.*

,Smithfield **'Market** /,smɪθfi:ld/ London's main meat market. There has been a meat market at Smithfield, on the edge of the *City, since the 12th century. The glass buildings of today's market were built in 1868.

Smith's /smɪθs/ ⇨ Sᴍɪᴛʜ[14].

The Smiths /smɪθs/ a British pop group formed in Manchester in 1982. The group made several successful albums in the 1980s, including *The Smiths* (1984) and *Meat is Murder* (1985). Their best-known songs include *This Charming Man* (1983) and *Shoplifters of the World Unite* (1987). The group's singer Morrissey began a successful solo career in 1987.

the Smith,sonian Insti'tution /smɪθ,səʊniən; *AmE* smɪθ,soʊniən/ (*also* the **Smith'sonian**) a US national institution that consists of several museums and centres for scientific research in Washington, DC. It was established in 1846 by the US *Congress with money given by James Smithson (1765–1829), an English scientist. Its popular name is 'the nation's attic'. The 12 major museums, most of which are situated along the *Mall(2), include the *National Air and Space Museum, the *National Gallery of Art, the National Museum of American Art, the National Portrait Gallery and the National Museum of American History. The *Kennedy Center is an independent part of the Smithsonian.

,Smith **'Square** /,smɪθ/ a square in central London, near the *Houses of Parliament. Until 2004 it was the address of the main offices of the *Conservative Party. People sometimes used 'Smith Square' to refer to the party's central office.

,Smokey the **'Bear** /,sməʊki; *AmE* ,smoʊki/ **1** the symbol used by the US Forest Service to help prevent forest fires. It is a friendly bear wearing a Forest Service hat and is used on posters and television advertisements with the message 'Only you can prevent forest fires.' **2** (*also* **Smokey Bear**, **Smokey**) (*informal*) an informal US name for a member of the highway police, so called because the hats they wear in some states are similar to the one worn by Smokey the Bear.

the ,Smoky **'Mountains** /,sməʊki; *AmE* ,smoʊki/ (*also* the **'Smokies** /'sməʊkiz; *AmE* 'smoʊkiz/) another name for the *Great Smoky Mountains.

To,bias **'Smollett** /tə,baɪəs 'smɒlɪt; *AmE* 'smɑ:lɪt/ (1721–71) a Scottish writer of novels. His early books, *The Adventures of Roderick Random* (1748) and *The Adventures of Peregrine Pickle* (1751) describe the travels and rough adventures of characters who are not always honest but are easy to like. Smollett's other major work, *The Expedition of Humphry Clinker* (1771), is in the form of letters.

the **'Smothers ,Brothers** /'smʌðəz; *AmE* 'smʌðərz/ **Tom Smothers** (1937–) and **Dick Smothers** (1939–), two brothers who entertain with jokes and humorous songs. Tom often reminds Dick, 'Mother always liked you best.' Their television series, *The Smothers Brothers Comedy Hour* (1966–9), was stopped by *CBS because of their jokes about religion, drugs and sex, as well as their songs and comments against the *Vietnam War. They returned with another television series in the late 1980s and they still do tours.

S

,snakes and 'ladders n [U] a popular children's game. It is played with a dice on a board marked with squares, and with pictures of snakes and ladders that go over more than one square. To win the game, a player must reach the top of the board by moving along the squares. A player who arrives on a square where there is the bottom of a ladder can move straight to the top of the ladder, but one arriving at the head of a snake has to move back down to its tail: *a game of snakes and ladders*. Compare CHUTES AND LADDERS.

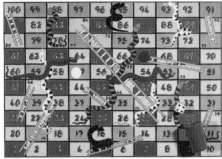

snakes and ladders

snap n [U] (*BrE*) a card game, often played by children, in which players lay down cards at the same time, and shout 'Snap!' when two similar cards are laid down. The player who calls first wins the cards already laid down. The winner of the game is the player who wins all the cards in this way. People sometimes say 'Snap!' when they notice that two things are similar: *Snap! You've got the same shoes as me!*

SNCC /snɪk/ ⇨ STUDENT NONVIOLENT COORDINATING COMMITTEE.

,Sam 'Snead /'sniːd/ (1912–2002) one of the most successful US golf players in the 1940s and 1950s, also known as 'Slammin' Sam' because he hit the ball so far. He won the *PGA Championship three times (1942, 1949 and 1951) and the *Masters Tournament three times (1949, 1952 and 1954).

'snifter n **1** (*especially AmE*) a large glass used for drinking brandy.
2 (*BrE informal*) a rather old-fashioned word used by older people for a small drink of strong alcohol such as whisky or brandy.

a snifter

'snooker n [U] a game for two, played on a large table with fifteen red balls and seven balls of different colours. The players use long sticks (called *cues*) to hit the white ball across the table, trying to make it knock one of the other balls into any of six holes (called *pockets*) round the edge of the table. Points are scored according to the colour of the ball that is hit into a pocket. A red ball, worth one point, must be hit into a pocket first, to allow the player who hit it to try a ball of higher value. Snooker has been popular on British television since the 1970s. Compare BAR BILLIARDS, BILLIARDS, POOL.

'Snoop '(Doggy) 'Dogg /'snuːp 'dɒgi 'dɒg; *AmE* 'dɔːgi 'dɔːg/ (1972–) a US singer of *rap music. He was born Calvin Broadus. His albums include *Doggystyle* (1993), which sold more than 4 million copies, and *Tha*

Doggfather (1996). In 1993, he was accused of a murder but was judged innocent.

'Snoopy /'snuːpi/ the dog owned by Charlie *Brown in the comic strip *Peanuts*. Snoopy sleeps on the roof of his kennel and has human thoughts and ideas. He tries to write novels and has imaginary adventures, such as being a *World War I pilot who has battles with Germany's famous 'Red Baron'.

,C P 'Snow¹ /'snəʊ; *AmE* 'snoʊ/ (Charles Percy Snow 1905–80) an English writer of novels and scientist. He worked as a scientist for the British government during *World War II, and at *Cambridge University. He used these experiences to write his best-known work, *Strangers and Brothers*, a series of novels (1940–70) describing British life in that period, particularly in scientific, academic and government fields. He was also well known for speaking and writing about the lack of communication between the 'two cultures' of scientific and artistic life. He was made a *knight in 1957 and a *life peer in 1964.

,John ,W 'Snow² /'snəʊ; *AmE* 'snoʊ/ (1939–) a US businessman and administrator who became the US Secretary of the Treasury in 2003.

the 'Snow Belt (*also* **the 'Snowbelt**) (*informal*) the north-eastern US states and those in the *Middle West that have cold winters with a lot of snow. Compare RUST BELT, SUNBELT.

'Snowdon /'snəʊdn; *AmE* 'snoʊdn/ a mountain in north-west Wales, in *Snowdonia *national park. It is the highest mountain in England and Wales (1085 metres/3560 feet). There is a railway that goes to the top which was built in the 19th century and is very popular with tourists.

Snow'donia /snəʊ'dəʊniə; *AmE* snoʊ'doʊniə/ a *national park around *Snowdon in north-west Wales. It is an important tourist centre, famous for its attractive mountain scenery.

Snowdonia

The '**Snowman** a children's book (1978) written and illustrated by Raymond *Briggs. It is the story of a small boy's adventures with a snowman (= a figure of a man made with snow). A film version made for television is usually shown on British television each year around Christmas.

Snow '**White** a traditional children's story. Snow White is a beautiful princess. Her stepmother (= the woman who married her father after her mother died) is jealous of her beauty and orders a man to kill her. He takes pity on her and leaves her alive in a forest, where she lives happily with seven dwarfs (= very small people). The stepmother discovers that Snow White is alive, and gives her an apple full of poison. Snow White falls asleep after eating it and does not wake up until a prince kisses her, and all ends happily. The story was made into a successful Walt *Disney film in 1937, and is a popular subject for *pantomimes in Britain. In the film the seven dwarfs are called Dopey, Doc, Sneezy, Bashful, Sleepy, Grumpy and Happy.

SNP /,es en 'pi:/ ⇨ Scottish National Party.

John '**Soane** /'səʊn; AmE 'soʊn/ (1753–1837) an English architect whose work was influenced by *neoclassicism. His best-known buildings are the *Bank of England and his own house in central London, which is now a museum called **Sir John Soane's Museum**, filled with the works of art and other interesting objects that he collected. He was made a *knight in 1831.

the Bank of England by John Soane

▶ **soap operas**

Soap operas, also called **soaps**, are amongst the most popular television programmes. They are stories about the lives of ordinary people that are broadcast, usually in half-hour **episodes**, three times or more each week. Episodes broadcast during the week are often repeated in a single **omnibus** programme at the weekend. They are called *soap operas* because in the US they were first paid for by companies who made soap. Most soap operas have their own website and some people buy books about their favourite soap and visit the places where the stories are supposed to happen.

Most soap operas describe the daily lives of a small group of people who live in the same street or town or who work in the same place such as a hospital. The most successful soaps reflect the worries and hopes of real people, though the central **characters** frequently have exaggerated personal problems in order to make the programmes more exciting. Some **storylines** deal with sensitive social issues, such as alcoholism and racism.

In Britain soap operas are usually broadcast in the early evening. The longest-running soap opera in the world is *The *Archers*, 'an everyday story of country folk', which began on *BBC radio in the 1950s. The most popular of the television soaps is ITV's *Coronation Street*, first broadcast in 1960. Its main rival is the BBC's *EastEnders*. Other popular soaps include ITV's *Emmerdale*. *Neighbours* and *Home and Away*, both from Australia, are aimed at younger audiences. Older US soaps such as *Dallas* and *Dynasty*, are occasionally repeated on satellite television.

In the US, soap operas are also called **daytime dramas**. A few, like *Dynasty* and *Dallas*, have been successful in the evenings, but most soaps are broadcast during the afternoon. Though soaps have a limited audience, the names of many of the long-running ones, e.g. *Days of Our Lives*, *General Hospital* and *The Young and the Restless*, are well known. Many people who watch soaps have one or two favourites which they try never to miss.

SOCA /'sɒkə; AmE 'sɑ:k-/ ⇨ Serious Organised Crime Agency.

the ,**Social** '**Chapter** a section of the *Maastricht Treaty that deals with people's rights. It proposed European laws to protect the rights of employees to be paid fairly and to work in safe conditions, the rights of old people and children to be treated fairly, the rights of men and women to have equal opportunities, and the rights of people to move freely between *European Union countries. It was signed in 1992 by all the member countries of the European Union except Britain, which did not sign until the *Labour government was elected in 1997.

the '**Social Demo**'**cratic and** '**Labour** ,**Party** ⇨ SDLP.

the ,**Social Demo**'**cratic Party** ⇨ SDP.

,Socialist '**Worker** a British newspaper produced by the **Socialist Workers Party**, a left-wing political party. It consists mainly of political articles and is sold on the street in many towns and cities by members of the party.

,**social se**'**curity** n [U] government payments to help people who are unemployed, poor or old, or who cannot work because they are ill or injured. In the US, these payments are made by the government's **Social Security Administration**, established in 1935 as part of the government's *New Deal(1). Money for the payments (called *welfare*) is provided by taxes on employers and workers. In Britain, payments (called *benefits*) are made by the *Department for Work and Pensions, with money from *National Insurance and other taxes. Payments in Britain include the *Jobseeker's Allowance, *income support, *statutory sick pay and *housing benefit. See also Beveridge Report, Medicare, National Health Service, welfare state.

,**Social Se**'**curity** ,**number** n (abbr **SSN**) (in the US) an identity number that everyone must have. It was originally a qualification for work and *social security, but in 1987 the US government decided that children should also be given numbers. The number is now also used in other ways, e.g. on bank cheques and driving licences and as a student's number at college or university. Compare National Insurance.

the So'ciety for Pro'moting 'Christian 'Knowledge ⇨ SPCK.

the So,ciety of '**Friends** the formal name for the *Quakers.

'**softball** n **1** [U] a form of *baseball played on a smaller area with a larger, softer ball and easier to play. Softball is especially popular with children, but many adult com-

petitions are organized, e.g. between company teams.
2 [C] the ball used in the game of softball.

'Soho /'səʊhəʊ; AmE 'soʊhoʊ/ a district in the *West End
of London, between *Oxford Street, *Piccadilly Circus
and *Leicester Square. It is famous for its lively atmosphere and its many cafes, nightclubs, theatres and restaurants. It also has many sex shops, strip clubs (= places
where people pay to watch other people take their
clothes off) and prostitutes. Many film, television, music
and advertising companies have their offices in Soho:
*Before they became famous they used to perform in a tiny
basement club in Soho.* See also WARDOUR STREET.

'SoHo /'səʊhəʊ; AmE 'soʊhoʊ/ a small fashionable area
of *Manhattan(1) in New York City. SoHo is short for
'South of Houston', because it is south of West Houston
Street which separates it from *Greenwich Village.
Many artists live in SoHo in old industrial buildings
which have been made modern. They have iron fronts
and large windows. The buildings were to be destroyed
in the 1960s but were saved when the city made SoHo an
official historical district.

the 'Soil Associ‚ation a British organization, started
in 1946, which encourages organic food and farming. Its
symbol is used on organic products to show that they are
produced and processed to strict standards relating to
the environment and the care of animals.

'Sojourner /'sɒdʒɜːnə(r); AmE 'soʊdʒɜːrnər/ the small
vehicle sent by *NASA on the *Pathfinder* space trip to
Mars in 1997. It weighed 25 pounds/11 kilograms, had six
wheels and was controlled from earth. It moved on the
surface of Mars, taking many photographs and measurements and analysing the rocks, etc. It was named after
Sojourner *Truth.

the 'Solent /'səʊlənt; AmE 'soʊlənt/ the area of sea
between the *Isle of Wight and the south coast of
England, where many sailing events take place.

so'licitor *n* (in Britain) a lawyer who prepares legal
documents, gives people advice on the law and can
speak for them in some courts. Compare BARRISTER.
⇨ note at LEGAL SYSTEM.

so‚licitor 'advocate *n* (in Scotland) a solicitor (= a
lawyer) who can appear in the highest courts instead of
an *advocate.

the So‚licitor 'General *n* (*pl* **Solicitors
General**) **1** (in Britain) a government law officer who
acts as the *Attorney General's main assistant. The
Solicitor General is a lawyer and an *MP belonging to
the ruling party, who advises the government on legal
matters.
2 (in the US) the government law officer who is next in
rank to the US *Attorney General. Some states also have
a Solicitor General as the main assistant to the state
Attorney General.

the 'Solomon ‚Islands /'sɒləmən; AmE 'sɑːləmən/ a
country consisting of a group of islands in the south-
west Pacific. The islands became a British protectorate
(= a country controlled and protected by Britain) in the
1890s, and an independent member of the
*Commonwealth in 1978. The main island, Guadalcanal,
is well known because of the battle that took place there
in *World War II.

‚Georg 'Solti /‚dʒɔːdʒ 'ʃɒlti; AmE ‚dʒɔːrdʒ 'ʃɑːlti/
(1912–97) a British conductor, born in Hungary. He was
in charge of many famous orchestras, including the
Chicago Symphony Orchestra and the orchestra of the
*Royal Opera House, and was considered one of the
leading conductors of his time. He was made a *knight
in 1971.

the ‚Solway 'Firth /‚sɒlweɪ 'fɜːθ; AmE ‚sɑːlweɪ/ the
part of the *Irish Sea that separates north-west England
from south-west Scotland.

'Somerset /'sʌməset; AmE 'sʌmərset/ a county in
south-west England. It consists mainly of agricultural
land, and is well known for its cider (= an alcoholic
drink made from apples). Its administrative centre is
*Taunton.

‚Somerset 'House /‚sʌməset; AmE ‚sʌmərset/ a
large, grand 18th–century building in central London,
between the *Strand and the River *Thames. It is now
an art gallery, but from the 1830s to the 1970s it contained the main offices of the *Inland Revenue and the
General Register Office, where records of all births, marriages and deaths in the country were kept. Some people
still refer to the new General Register Office as Somerset
House.

the ‚Battles of the 'Somme /'sɒm; AmE 'sɔːm/ two
long battles that took place in the valley of the river
Somme in northern France during *World War I. In the
first battle, which lasted from July to November 1916,
more than a million British, French and German soldiers
died. The second battle lasted two weeks in the spring of
1918, and almost half a million soldiers died. Very little
ground or any other advantage was won by either side
in these battles, which are considered among the most
terrible in history.

‚Stephen 'Sondheim /'sɒndhaɪm; AmE 'sɔːndhaɪm/
(1930–) a US writer of *Broadway musical plays, many
of which have been made into films. He wrote the words
for *West Side Story* and *Gypsy* (1959), and the words and
music for *A Funny Thing Happened on the Way to the
Forum* (1962), *Company* (1970), *A Little Night Music* (1973)
and *Sweeney Todd* (1979). *Sunday in the Park with George*
(1984) won the *Pulitzer Prize. His best-known song is
probably *Send in the Clowns* from *A Little Night Music*.

‚Songs of 'Innocence and of Ex'perience a collection of poems (1794) by William *Blake. He had published a group of poems in 1789 called *Songs of
Innocence*, expressing the idea that God's love and sympathy is in everything on earth. Five years later he added
the *Songs of Experience* to the collection. The new poems
express the power of evil as well as the power of love,
and include some of Blake's most famous poems, including *The Tyger*.

‚Songs of 'Praise a regular *BBC television programme in which people sing hymns, usually in a
church, and some of them talk about their faith. It is
broadcast from a different place each Sunday.

The 'Sonnets the sonnets (= poems of 14 lines) of
William *Shakespeare, which were probably written in
the 1590s. Many of them are addressed to a young man,
expressing the poet's affection for him and giving him
advice. Others are written to a beautiful *dark lady. The
sonnets are famous for the beauty of their language, but
also because no one has discovered for sure who the
young man and the dark lady really were. The sonnets
are dedicated to 'Mr *W H', and his identity is also a mystery.

‚Sons and 'Lovers a novel (1913) by D H *Lawrence. It
is one of Lawrence's best-known books and is about a
young man and his relationships with his mother (a
teacher), his father (a coal miner), and the two women
he loves. It is partly based on Lawrence's own life.

the ‚Sons of 'Liberty a number of secret organizations formed in the American colonies in 1765 to protest
against the *Stamp Act. They were strongest in Boston
and New York, where a group of them attacked British
soldiers in 1770, one of the first serious actions that led
to the *American Revolution.

S

ˌSusan **'Sontag** /'sɒntæg; AmE 'sɑːntæg/ (1933–2004) a US writer of novels and short stories who was also well known for her writings on art, culture and politics. These include *Against Interpretation* (1966), *On Photography* (1976), *Illness as Metaphor* (1979) and *AIDS and its Metaphors* (1989).

The **So'pranos** a popular US television drama series on *HBO about a Mafia family (= involved in organized crime) in *New Jersey. It was first shown in 1999 and has since been broadcast in several countries around the world. The show's main character Tony Soprano, played by James Gandolfini (1961–), tries to deal with problems with his family and his criminal associates. The show contains a lot of violence and strong language but is also very amusing.

so'rority n (AmE) a social organization for women students at many US colleges and universities. Members often live together in a **sorority house**. They are called 'Greeks', because each sorority's name consists of two or three Greek letters, such as Chi Omega or Kappa Kappa Gamma. They also help charities and do community work. A few student sororities are academic or professional organizations. Compare FRATERNITY.

SOS pad™ /ˌes əʊ 'es pæd; AmE ˌes oʊ 'es/ n a US product like a rough metal ball for cleaning surfaces and kitchen pans, etc.

'Sotheby's /'sʌðəbiz/ a leading London firm of auctioneers. Sotheby's is famous for dealing in works of art and antiques, and has a particularly strong reputation for selling old books. The company was established in 1744. It also has a branch in New York. Compare CHRISTIE'S.

soul (also **soul music**) n [U] a type of emotional *African-American music that developed out of *gospel and *rhythm and blues in the 1950s and 1960s. The most famous form of soul music was *Motown(2). Well-known soul singers include James *Brown, Marvin *Gaye, The *Supremes, Aretha *Franklin, Otis *Redding, Roberta Flack and Stevie *Wonder.

The ˌSound of '**Music** a *Broadway musical play (1959) by Richard *Rodgers and Oscar *Hammerstein. It is based on the true story of the Austrian Trapp family who sang together and escaped to Switzerland from the Nazis. The film version, in which Julie *Andrews plays Maria Trapp, won six *Oscars. The songs include *The Sound of Music*, *Maria*, *Do Re Mi* and *Climb Every Mountain*.

'**sourdough** n [U] (AmE) dough (= a mixture for making bread, etc.) which is kept from a previous time when something was baked and is later used instead of yeast to make the bread rise. Sourdough breads were first made in the *Old West and are now especially popular in *San Francisco.

'John 'Philip '**Sousa** /'suːzə/ (1854–1932) a US composer, also known as the 'March King'. He wrote about 140 works of music for military marches, including *Semper Fidelis* (1888), *The Washington Post* (1889) and *The Stars and Stripes Forever* (1897). He led the US Marine Band (1880–92) and then formed his own band which made tours of Europe and around the world. The *sousaphone*, a large brass musical instrument, was named after him.

the **South** (also the ˌsouthern '**states**) the south-east and south-central US states, regarded as beginning to the south of the *Mason-Dixon line. Their region is part of the *Sunbelt. The 14 states are *Maryland, *Virginia, *West Virginia, *Kentucky, *Tennessee, *North Carolina, *South Carolina, *Georgia, *Florida, *Alabama, *Mississippi, *Arkansas, *Louisiana and *Texas, especially its eastern part. All were

*Confederate States except Maryland, West Virginia and Kentucky.

The South has sometimes seemed a mysterious region to Americans who live outside it and who associate it with a mixture of romantic charm, traditional family values, dangerous independence and violent prejudice. These ideas have been supported by the works of southern writers such as William *Faulkner and Tennessee *Williams and by the real conflicts of the *civil rights movement. Today, however, a 'New South' has been recognized. *Atlanta and other modern cities have developed, many companies from other parts of the US have moved to the *Sunbelt, and African Americans now serve as *mayors and community leaders. Two recent US Presidents (*Carter and *Clinton) have come from the South, and the US government has even developed the southern idea of *states' rights. In spite of these changes, however, many people still believe that the South is a region that wants to keep its strong separate character. Compare DEEP SOUTH.

ˌSouth '**Africa** /'æfrɪkə/ the country at the southern tip of Africa. Its capital city is Pretoria but Cape Town and Bloemfontein also function as capitals. In the 17th and 18th centuries different areas of the country were settled by the Dutch and the British, who fought each other in the *Boer Wars. South Africa became part of the *British Empire in the late 18th century. In 1909 it became an independent member of the *Commonwealth, but left in 1961 after establishing the policy of apartheid (= trying to keep the races of the country separate, with the white people in control). Most other countries disapproved of this policy, and many countries refused to trade with South Africa or to take part in sporting events with it. In 1994, after years of international pressure, the South African government allowed everybody the same voting rights and Nelson Mandela became the country's first black president. South Africa is the richest country in Africa, and is one of the world's largest producers of diamonds, gold and other valuable metals. Because of the many different peoples and cultures that make up the population and its 11 official languages, South Africa is known as the Rainbow Nation.
▶ **South African** adj, n.

Sou'**thampton** /saʊˈθæmptən/ a city on the south coast of England. It is one of Britain's most important ports. For much of the 20th century it was the main port for passenger ships crossing the Atlantic. Some passenger ships still use the port of Southampton, but it now deals mainly with container ships (= ships that carry goods in large metal boxes).

the ˌSouth '**Bank** an area of the south bank of the River *Thames around Waterloo Bridge which is London's main cultural centre. Most of the centre was built in the 1950s and 1960s. It includes the *Hayward Gallery, the *National Film Theatre, the Purcell Room concert hall, the *Royal Festival Hall and the Royal *National Theatre, as well as gardens and areas where people can walk by the river and see outdoor concerts and exhibitions.

The ˌSouth '**Bank Show** a popular British television programme about the arts. It has been presented by Melvyn *Bragg and broadcast on Sunday evenings by *ITV since 1978. The programmes sometimes include reports and comments on several different artists or artistic events, but usually the show deals with one particular artist or topic.

the ˌSouth '**Beach** ˌDiet a weight loss programme developed by **Arthur Agatsan**, a doctor from *Miami, *Florida to help patients with heart problems. People on the diet restrict the amount of carbohydrates, such as grains and fruits, that they eat.

S

,South Caro'lina /ˌkærəˈlaɪnə/ a south-eastern US state on the Atlantic Ocean, also called the Palmetto State. The capital and largest city is Columbia. The state was named after the English king *Charles I and was one of the original *thirteen colonies. It produces textiles, fruit, tobacco, chickens and cattle. Its tourist attractions include the Fort Sumter National Monument and the Riverbanks Zoo and Garden in Columbia.

the ,South 'Circular a series of roads that join together and pass through many areas of South London. They join the *North Circular at the *Thames, east and west of London, to form a full circle around London. Until the *M25 was built they formed the main road round London. They still carry a lot of traffic, which often moves very slowly.

,South Da'kota /dəˈkəʊtə; AmE dəˈkoʊtə/ a northern central US state, also called the Coyote State and the Mount Rushmore State. The capital city is Pierre and the largest city is Sioux Falls. It was part of the *Louisiana Purchase, and gold was discovered there in 1874. The *Sioux fought white people who settled there, until they were defeated at *Wounded Knee. The state grows wheat, maize/corn and sunflowers, and produces machinery and electronic equipment. Many tourists visit Mount *Rushmore and the *Badlands National Park.

the ,South 'Downs a range of hills across southern *Hampshire and *Sussex near the south coast of England. They are popular with people who enjoy walking.

the ,South-'East the south-eastern region of England that includes London and the *Home Counties. More people live there than in any other part of Britain. Many rich people live there, and most businesses and industries have their main offices in the South-East: *House prices are higher in the South-East than in the rest of the country.*

Sou'thend /saʊˈθend/ (also **Sou,thend-on-'Sea**) a town on the south-east coast of England, east of London. It has the world's longest *pier and was traditionally the place where *Londoners, particularly from the *East End, went for day trips and summer holidays.

,southern 'belle n (AmE old-fashioned) a woman from the southern US who is young and attractive. The term was used especially in the 19th century when it also meant a young woman who belonged to one of the best families. Scarlett *O'Hara was a famous southern belle in literature.

the 'Southern 'Christian 'Leadership ,Conference (abbr the **SCLC**) a US organization started by Martin Luther *King in 1957 at the beginning of the *civil rights movement. Its members were mostly *African-American church leaders. They supported peaceful protests and organized the large 1963 march on Washington, DC. After King was murdered, Ralph Abernathy became the head of SCLC (1968–77). The SCLC Magazine is published five times a year.

,Southern 'Comfort™ n [U, C] a sweet alcoholic drink that tastes of peaches and is made from whisky. It is especially popular in the southern US and is produced by the Brown-Forman Corporation in *Louisville, *Kentucky.

,Robert 'Southey /ˈsaʊði, ˈsʌði/ (1774–1843) an English poet who also wrote histories and biographies. He was a friend of *Coleridge and *Wordsworth and was one of the *Lake Poets. He was made *Poet Laureate in 1813.

,South 'Kensington /ˈkenzɪŋtən/ (also informal ,South 'Ken /ˈken/) a district in west London that contains several museums and foreign embassies (= buildings where people who represent foreign governments work). It is well known for its fashionable and expensive

houses, shops and restaurants. There is a South Kensington station on the *London Underground.

,South Pa'cific /pəˈsɪfɪk/ a *Broadway musical play (1949) and film (1958) by Richard *Rodgers and Oscar *Hammerstein. It was based on Tales of the South Pacific by James *Michener and is a love story about Nellie Forbush, a US Navy nurse working on a Pacific island during *World War II. The songs include Some Enchanted Evening, There Is Nothing Like a Dame and I'm Gonna Wash That Man Right Outa My Hair.

'South Park a US animated television comedy series aimed at both children and adults, about four eight-year-old boys in the small town of South Park. Since it started in 1997, it has used satire and black comedy (= dealing with unpleasant things in a humorous way) to include many current issues in its stories and has often caused controversy. It has also included many well-known actors, musicians, politicians, etc. as characters and sometimes uses the voices of the real people.

'Southwark /ˈsʌðək; AmE ˈsʌðərk/ a *borough of South London, on the opposite side of the *Thames from the *City. Historically it was one of London's main centres for entertainment. It included Shakespeare's *Globe and many other theatres. *Bankside and the *Tate Modern are in Southwark and it has both *Anglican and *Catholic cathedrals.

,Southwest 'Airlines a US airline started in 1971 which operates mainly short flights between US cities at low prices. The flights are often between smaller airports rather than between the cities' main airports and the service is basic, for example no meals are served on the plane.

,South 'Yorkshire /ˈjɔːkʃə(r); AmE ˈjɔːrkʃər/ (abbr **S Yorks**) the southern part of *Yorkshire, in northern England, where there are many industrial towns. It was made into a separate *metropolitan county in 1974. Its administrative centre is *Sheffield.

'sovereignty /ˈsɒvrənti; AmE ˈsɑːv-/ n [U] the condition of being an independent country with the power to govern itself. The British government has always had the authority to make and change laws, but as a member of the *European Union, Britain now has to respect some European laws that cannot be changed by the government. In the 1980s and 1990s some British people thought that this was a serious loss of sovereignty. *Eurosceptics said that there would be more losses of sovereignty, and that Britain should leave the EU, but most people agreed with the idea of 'subsidiarity', i.e. that most local decisions should be made by individual countries or regions, unless there is an important reason for deciding something at a European court.

the 'space race n [sing] the competition between the US and the former USSR to develop spacecraft and send them successfully into space. The USSR was the early leader in 1957 with the Sputnik satellite, but the Americans were ahead by 1969 when the *Apollo program landed men on the moon. The space race was once thought to have military importance, but the US and Russia now work together, e.g. in developing future space stations. See also NASA, STRATEGIC DEFENSE INITIATIVE.

'space ,shuttle (also **shuttle**) n a spacecraft developed by the US to take a crew and cargo into space and then return to the earth for future flights. Space shuttles are part of the US Space Transportation System (STS), and the flights began in 1981. The first four were *Columbia, *Challenger, Discovery and Atlantis. When Challenger exploded in 1986 killing all seven of its crew, all flights were stopped for more than two years. *Endeavor replaced Challenger in 1992. In 2003 Columbia exploded while re-entering the earth's atmosphere and again all flights were stopped. In 2004 the US announced that it will replace the space shuttle with a new type of vehicle by 2010.

,Kevin **'Spacey** /'speɪsi/ (Kevin Spacey Fowler 1959–) a US film and stage actor who won *Oscars for his acting in *The Usual Suspects* (1995) and *American Beauty* (1999) and whose other films include *L A Confidential* (1997) and *The Life of David Gale* (2003). Since 2003 he has been the artistic director of the *Old Vic theatre in London.

,Sam **'Spade** /'speɪd/ a character created in 1930 by the US writer Dashiell *Hammett in his book *The *Maltese Falcon*. Spade is a tough but honest private detective. Hammett also wrote Sam Spade stories for *Black Mask* magazine. Compare MARLOWE.

spa,ghetti 'junction *n* a place where many roads join or pass over or under each other, so that from the air they look a little like spaghetti (= Italian food consisting of many long thin pieces that become soft when cooked). There are many spaghetti junctions in the US, but in Britain the expression is mainly used as the name for a major road link near Birmingham.

spa,ghetti 'western *n* any of the *western films made by Italian film companies in the 1960s and 1970s. They often had complicated stories and contained a lot of violence. The first were directed by Sergio Leone, including *A Fistful of Dollars* (1964). Several US actors, especially Clint *Eastwood, first became famous by appearing in spaghetti westerns.

Spam™ /spæm/ *n* [U] a US make of processed meat, sold in tins and usually eaten cold. It is made mainly from ham and was widely used to feed US soldiers during *World War II, when it also became popular in Britain. It is still popular in the US today but less so in Britain. It is made by the Hormel Foods Corporation of Austin, *Minnesota, and the city is sometimes called **Spamtown**. The word is a shortened form of 'spiced ham'. Because it is a simple and cheap food, people often make jokes about it and a *Monty Python sketch was set in a cafe where every item on the menu included Spam. This may be the origin of the modern use of the word to mean unwanted emails.

'Spanglish /'spæŋglɪʃ/ *n* [U] (*humorous*) language which is a mixture of English and Spanish, used especially in parts of the US with large Hispanic communities, such as those near the Mexican border, in *Florida and in *New York City.

the **'Spanish-A'merican 'War** a war fought between the US and Spain in 1898. The US had promised to recognize the right of Cubans to be independent from Spain. When in 1898 the US warship *Maine* exploded in Havana harbour and sank with 260 deaths, the US blamed Spain and both nations soon declared war. The US won easily, and the Treaty of Paris ended Spanish rule in Cuba, giving the US *Puerto Rico, *Guam and the Philippines. After this victory, the US came to be recognized by other countries as a world power. See also ROUGH RIDERS.

the ,Spanish Ar'mada ⇨ ARMADA.

the ,Spanish 'Main /'meɪn/ a former name for the *Caribbean Sea and the north-east coast of South America. In the 16th and 17th centuries many Spanish ships sailed through this area, carrying gold back to Spain. They were often attacked by pirates and there are many stories and films about the adventures that people had there in this period.

the 'War of the 'Spanish Suc'cession a war (1701–14) between Britain, Austria, the Netherlands, Portugal and Denmark on one side, and France and Spain on the other side. It started when the king of Spain died leaving no children, and Philip, the grandson of the king of

France, became the next king of Spain. The Austrians believed that an Austrian had the right to be the king of Spain, and the British supported them because they did not want France to become too strong. This aim was mainly achieved. At the end of the war, although Britain recognized Philip as the king of Spain, it received large areas of Canada from the French, and *Gibraltar and Minorca from the Spanish.

,Muriel **'Spark** /'spɑːk; *AmE* 'spɑːrk/ (1918–) a Scottish writer whose novels are well known for their intelligent humour. Her best-known work is *The Prime of Miss Jean Brodie* (1961). She has also written poetry and short stories. She was made a *dame(2) in 1993.

the **SPCK** /,es piː siː 'keɪ/ (*in full* the **Society for Promoting Christian Knowledge**) a British organization that was established in 1698 to provide religious education for children in Britain and for people in the *British Empire. Today it is mainly concerned with publishing the Bible and other religious books, and selling them in its own shops in Britain. The SPCK still sends people to some African and Asian countries to teach Christianity.

the **'Speaker** *n* the person who is in charge of debates in the *House of Commons. The Speaker decides who speaks in a debate, calls for a vote at the end, and keeps order. He or she is elected by *MPs of all the political parties, and must treat all parties fairly during debates. When MPs address the Speaker during a debate, they say 'Mr Speaker' or 'Madam Speaker'.

the ,**Speaker of the 'House** *n* the person who is in charge of most of the activities of the *House of Representatives. He or she is responsible for keeping order in debates, for naming the members of committees, and for referring *bills to committees. The Speaker of the House is chosen by the party with the majority in the House and is one of their leaders. He or she is addressed as 'Mr Speaker' or 'Madam Speaker'.

,**Speakers' 'Corner** the north-east corner of *Hyde Park(1) in London, England. Since the 19th century people have been allowed to make speeches to the public there about any subject they choose. At weekends there are usually several people standing on boxes, making speeches about politics, religion or other subjects. Sometimes members of the public argue with them.

the ,**speaking 'clock** *n* [sing] a telephone service in Britain in which a recorded voice gives the correct time to anyone who rings a special number.

,Britney **'Spears** /,brɪtni 'spɪəz; *AmE* 'spɪrz/ (1981–) a US pop singer whose first four albums, including ... *Baby One More Time* (1999) and *Oops! ... I Did It Again* (2000), went to number one in the *Billboard charts.

the ,**Special 'Air ,Service** ⇨ SAS.

the **'Special Branch** the department of the British police force that deals with political crimes. It used to be responsible for fighting terrorist groups such as the *IRA, but *MI5 took over this work in 1992. The Special Branch is now mostly involved in protecting government ministers and foreign politicians in Britain, and investigating people who break the *Official Secrets Act.

,**special 'prosecutor** *n* (in the US) a special official who can be appointed by the US *Attorney General to investigate illegal activities by politicians and government officials. In 1973, *Congress began to consider the *impeachment of President *Nixon after he ordered the Attorney General to dismiss the special prosecutor for *Watergate. In 1998 the special prosecutor Kenneth Starr published the results of his investigation into the relationship between President *Clinton and the junior member of the *White House staff, Monica Lewinsky, which led to the President's impeachment.

the ˌspecial reˈlationship *n* [sing] ⇨ note at BRITAIN AND THE US.

The Specˈtator **1** a British magazine, published each week and containing articles on politics, society and the arts which are usually written from a right-wing point of view. It was first published in 1828.
2 a non-political magazine written by Joseph *Addison and Richard *Steele between 1711 and 1714. It appeared every day, and each issue contained a single long essay.

ˌPhil ˈSpector /ˈspektə(r)/ (1940–) a US pop record producer best known for creating the 'wall of sound' in the 1960s, in which songs were recorded with music played by many instruments. This idea influenced many other recording companies. Spector produced records for such groups as the Righteous Brothers, the Crystals and the Ronettes. In 2003 Spector was arrested for the murder of Lana Clarkson at his home in California.

ˌStanley ˈSpencer /ˈspensə(r)/ (1891–1959) an English artist. He is most famous for his unusual religious paintings, especially the series of pictures of Christ appearing at Cookham, the village on the River *Thames west of London where Spencer was born. His style has been described as 'primitive realism', because many of his paintings look like the work of an artist who has had no formal training and has tried to paint in a realistic style. He was made a *knight in 1958.

ˌStephen ˈSpender /ˈspendə(r)/ (1909–95) an English poet and critic. He was a friend of W H *Auden and Louis *MacNeice, and many of his poems contain left-wing political and social comments, although his style can also be very personal. He was made a *knight in 1983.

ˌEdmund ˈSpenser /ˈspensə(r)/ (*c.* 1552–99) an English poet. His first important work was *The Shepheardes Calendar* (1579), a group of twelve poems about the countryside, one for each month of the year. He is best known for his long poem *The *Faerie Queene*. He invented a new form of verse for this poem, which became known as the **Spenserian stanza** and was used by many later poets. Several important English poets were strongly influenced by Spenser, especially *Milton and *Keats.

the ˈSpey /speɪ/ a river in the *Highlands of Scotland. It flows north-east through the *Grampians (a range of mountains) to the Moray Firth (a narrow area of water stretching from the *North Sea into north-east Scotland), and is famous for its salmon fishing.

the ˈSpice Girls /ˈspaɪs/ an English pop group consisting of young women who sing and dance. The media often distinguish between them by using a different adjective for each, e.g. 'Sporty Spice' and 'Posh Spice'. The group's first five records, released in 1996 and 1997, were all No 1 hits, including *Wannabe*, *Say You'll Be There* and *2 Become 1*. One of the Spice Girls, Geri Halliwell (known as 'Ginger Spice'), left the group in 1998. Their last album, *Forever*, was released in 2000. Since then they have been less active as a band, although each has recorded solo albums. At the height of their popularity they often appeared in the British media, talking about their philosophy of 'girl power', the idea that women should have a strong attitude about their identity, support each other and enjoy themselves. 'Posh Spice' (Victoria Beckham, born Victoria Adams) is married to David *Beckham.

ˈSpider-Man a US cartoon character in Marvel Comics, created in 1962 by Stan Lee and Steve Ditko. He is Peter Parker, a newspaper photographer who changes into Spider-Man to fight criminals. He has great strength and can climb buildings. He has also appeared in films and television cartoons.

ˌSteven ˈSpielberg /ˈspiːlbɜːg; *AmE* ˈspiːlbɜːrg/ (1946–) a US film director and producer. Most of his films

have been very successful financially. They include *Jaws* (1975), *ET*, the *Indiana Jones films, *The Color Purple* (1985), *Jurassic Park* (1993), *Schindler's List* and *Saving Private Ryan* (1998). In 1994 he established his own film company, *DreamWorks SKG, with two partners. He was made an honorary *knight in 2001.

ˌMickey ˈSpilˈlane /spɪˈleɪn/ (1918–) a US writer of crime stories who created the tough private detective Mike Hammer. When the stories first appeared in the late 1940s many people were shocked by the amount of sex and violence in them, but they have been very successful and many have been made into films. They include *I, the Jury* (1947), *My Gun Is Quick* (1950) and *Kiss Me Deadly* (1952).

ˌspinning ˈjenny /ˈdʒeni/ *n* an early machine that could spin many threads of wool at the same time. It was invented by James Hargreaves in *Lancashire(1), England, in the 1760s. It caused a revolution in the wool industry because previously a person could only spin one thread at a time.

ˈSpirit (*also* **Mars Exploration Rover B**) (*abbr* **MER-B**) the second *Mars Rover vehicle which landed on the planet Mars in 2004 and sent pictures of the surface of the planet back to *NASA.

the ˌ*Spirit of St ˈLouis* /snt ˈluːɪs/ the name of the small plane in which Charles *Lindbergh made his famous flight across the Atlantic in 1927. The name was also used for a 1957 *Hollywood film about the flight, in which James *Stewart played Lindbergh.

ˈspiritual *n* a type of religious song traditionally sung by African Americans in the southern US. Spirituals began in the 18th century when American slaves combined African rhythms with Protestant European hymns. Famous spirituals include *Swing Low, Sweet Chariot*, *Steal Away* and *Nobody Knows the Trouble I've Seen*. Well-known singers of spirituals have included Paul *Robeson and Marian *Anderson. See also GOSPEL MUSIC.

ˈSpitalfields /ˈspɪtlfiːldz/ a district of east London, England, east of the *City. It used to be famous for its large fruit and vegetable market, which moved to north-east London in 1991. Spitalfields still has Brick Lane, one of London's largest flea markets (= markets selling old clothes, furniture, etc.). Many groups of immigrants have lived there and it is now the centre of one of the largest *Bangladeshi communities in Britain.

ˈSpitfire /ˈspɪtfaɪə(r)/ *n* a British fighter plane that became famous during *World War II. It was one of the fastest aircraft of its time and Spitfires played an important role in the *Battle of Britain.

ˌ*Spitting ˈImage* a British comedy television series (1984–96) that used large rubber models of famous people to make fun of politicians, film stars and even members of the royal family by making them do and say ridiculous things.

ˌMark ˈSpitz /ˈspɪts/ (1950–) a US swimmer who won seven gold medals at the 1972 Olympic Games, the most ever won by one person on one such occasion. He had also won two gold medals at the 1968 games. During his career, Spitz set 35 world records.

ˌsplit ˈticket *n* (in US elections) a vote in which a person votes for candidates from more than one political party. This happens, for example, when somebody chooses to vote for Congressmen from the party they usually support but votes for a popular candidate for US President from the other party. Compare STRAIGHT TICKET.

ˌBenjamin ˈSpock[1] /ˈspɒk; *AmE* ˈspɑːk/ (*also* ˌDr ˈSpock) (1903–98) a US doctor whose book *The Common Sense Book of Baby and Child Care* (1946) has sold more copies than any book by an American and has had a great influence on parents all over the world. He advised them to use less discipline on children and to understand their needs. Although many people have welcomed his ideas, some think they have led to children being more badly behaved and hard to control. Dr Spock protested against the *Vietnam War and in 1972 was a candidate for US President for the People's Party.

,Mr 'Spock² /'spɒk; AmE 'spɑːk/ a character played by Leonard Nimoy in the US television series *Star Trek. Spock is the First Officer of the *Starship Enterprise* spacecraft. He is from the planet Vulcan (though one of his parents was from Earth) and has large pointed ears. He thinks in a very logical way and does not show or understand normal human emotions.

> 66 highly illogical 99
> Mr Spock's usual comment on humans

Spode /spəʊd; AmE spoʊd/ n [U] pottery and porcelain (= hard white shiny material made by baking a type of fine clay) made at the Spode factory in *Stoke-on-Trent, England. The factory was established by Josiah Spode (1733–97) in 1770 and soon became famous for the quality of its products, which included *willow-pattern plates. The company combined with *Wedgwood in the 1960s but the name Spode is still used for its products.

the 'spoils ,system /'spɔɪlz/ n [sing] (in US politics) the system in which the winner of an election gives government jobs to his or her party workers and supporters. The tradition was begun by President Andrew *Jackson and is followed by each new US president.

,William 'Spooner /'spuːnə(r)/ (1844–1930) an English clergyman and teacher at *Oxford University. He was well known for his habit of accidentally changing round the first sounds of two or more words when he spoke, so that he might say 'the wrong liver' instead of 'the long river'. This type of phrase, which is often humorous, is called a **spoonerism**.

▶ **sport and fitness**

The British are very fond of sport, but many people prefer to watch rather than take part. Many go to watch *football, *cricket, etc. at the ground, but many more sit at home and watch sport on television.

Most people today take relatively little general **exercise**. Over the last 30 or 40 years lifestyles have changed considerably and many people now travel even the shortest distances by car or bus. Lack of exercise combined with eating too many fatty and sugary foods has meant that many people are becoming too fat. Experts are particularly concerned that children spend a lot of their free time watching television or playing computer games instead of being physically active. In recent years, however, there has been a growing interest in fitness among young adults and many belong to a **sports club** or **gym**.

In Britain most towns have an amateur football and cricket team, and people also have opportunities to play sports such as tennis and *golf. Older people may play *bowls. Some people go regularly to a **sports centre** or **leisure centre** where there are facilities for playing badminton and squash, and also a swimming pool. Some sports centres arrange classes in **aerobics**, **step** and **keep-fit**. Some people **work out** (= train hard) regularly at a local gym and do **weight training** and **circuit training**. A few people do judo or other **martial arts**. Others **go running** or **jogging** in their local area. For enthusiastic runners there are opportunities to take part in long-distance runs, such as the *London marathon. Other people keep themselves fit by walking or cycling. Many people go abroad on a skiing

holiday each year and there are several dry slopes and snowdomes in Britain where they can practise.

Membership of a sports club or gym can be expensive and not everyone can afford the subscription. Local sports centres are generally cheaper. **Evening classes** are also cheap and offer a wide variety of fitness activities ranging from yoga to jazz dancing. Some companies now provide sports facilities for their employees or contribute to the cost of joining a gym.

Sports play an important part in American life. Professional *baseball and football games attract large crowds, and many people watch games on television. Although many parents complain about their children being **couch potatoes** (= people who spend a lot of time watching television), there are sports sessions at school for all ages. College students are usually also required to take physical education classes to complete their studies.

Many popular keep-fit activities began in the US. Charles *Atlas, Arnold *Schwarzenegger and others inspired people to take up **body-building** (= strengthening and shaping the muscles). Many women joined the 'fitness craze' as a result of **video workouts** produced by stars such as Jane *Fonda and Cindy Crawford which they could watch and take part in at home. New fitness books are continually being published and these create fashions for new types of exercise, such as **wave aerobics**, which is done in a swimming pool, and **cardio kick-boxing**, a form of aerobics which involves punching and kicking a punchbag. Many richer people employ their own **personal trainer**, either at home or at a **fitness centre**, to direct their exercise programme. Local *YMCAs offer programmes which include aerobics, gym, running, weights, treadmills and rowing machines, as well as steam rooms and swimming. But many people just walk or jog in the local park or play informal games of baseball or football.

The ,Sporting 'Life a British daily newspaper that consists mainly of articles and information about horse racing and other sports that people bet on. It was first published in 1859.

'**Sports ,Council** n each of four British government organizations that aim to encourage sport in England, Northern Ireland, Scotland and Wales. They advise the government on matters relating to sport, give money to sports organizations, local authorities and schools, and run Britain's National Sports Centres, where the highest levels of training and equipment are available to national sports teams.

'**sports day** n (BrE) (AmE '**field day**) one day each year when most of the children at a school take part in outdoor sports competitions. In Britain, it usually takes place in the summer. There are no lessons for the day, and parents are invited to watch the sports and sometimes take part.

,**Sports 'Illustrated** a popular US sports magazine published each week by Time Inc. It first appeared in 1954, and is read mainly by men. The magazine also publishes the *Sports Illustrated Sports Almanac* every year.

,**spotted 'dick** /'dɪk/ (also ,**spotted 'dog**) n [C, U] (BrE) a traditional British sweet dish. It consists of a pudding (= a dish made of flour and fat) in the shape of a roll, with fruit such as currants (= dried grapes) mixed into it.

,**Spring Bank 'Holiday** n [C, U] the *bank holiday that takes place each year on the last Monday in May in England, Northern Ireland and Wales.

,**Jerry 'Springer** /'sprɪŋə(r)/ (1944–) a US entertainer who presents the television *talk show *The Jerry Springer Show* first broadcast in 1991 and now seen in

S

over 30 countries. The programme shows people confessing their guilty secrets and is known for the lively and sometimes violent reactions of the studio audience. Springer was earlier involved in politics, and was made mayor of Cincinnati, *Ohio, in 1977. A very successful British musical show based on the programme, *Jerry Springer – The Opera*, with words by Stewart Lee and music by Richard Thomas, first shown in London in 2002, caused controversy when it was later shown on television because many people were offended by it.

,Bruce 'Springsteen /'sprɪŋstiːn/ (1949–) a US rock singer and writer of songs whose popular name is 'the Boss'. He is known for his powerful live performances. He formed the E Street Band in 1973, and their No. 1 albums have included *Born in the USA* (1984) and *Tunnel of Love* (1987). His song *Streets of Philadelphia* (1994) for the film *Philadelphia* won an *Oscar, a *Golden Globe Award and four *Emmy awards. He was chosen for the Rock and Roll *Hall of Fame in 1999. By 2003, Springsteen had also won 11 *Grammys including three for *The Rising* about the events of *September 11.

Spurs /spɜːz; *AmE* spɜːrz/ the popular name for *Tottenham Hotspur football club.

'*Spycatcher* /'spaɪkætʃə(r)/ a book (1987) by Peter Wright, a former member of *MI5. It describes his life as a spy and reveals many of the secrets of the way MI5 works. It was originally banned in Britain.

'Squanto /'skwɒntəʊ; *AmE* 'skwɑːntoʊ/ (c. 1585–1622) a *Native American who helped the *Pilgrim Fathers to survive when they landed in America in 1621. He taught them to plant corn and to hunt and fish. He had been taken to England by sailors in 1605 and had learned to speak English.

'square dance *n* (*especially AmE*) a dance in which four couples dance together. They usually start in a square, facing inwards. A 'caller' tells them what steps to do. Square dances are popular in all parts of the US, but are especially associated with *Appalachia and the western states.

the ,Square 'Deal the political programme of US President Theodore *Roosevelt. He wanted to give fair treatment to all Americans, and a main part of this was his *antitrust legislation. Compare FAIR DEAL, NEW DEAL(1).

the ,Square 'Mile (*BrE informal*) another name for the *City of London, which covers an area of roughly one square mile. The phrase is often used to refer to the City's financial institutions.

squash (*also formal* 'squash ,rackets) *n* [U] a sport for two players using rackets and a small hollow rubber ball, played in an indoor court with high walls. One player must hit the ball against the front wall, after which it can bounce against other walls and/or the floor before the other player hits it. It is a very fast game, which many people play as a way of keeping fit. It developed from the game of *rackets but is now played by many more people. In the US form of the game, the ball is harder and the regular court smaller than in Britain. There are also larger courts for games of 'doubles' (for four players), which are more popular in the US than in Britain.

,squashed 'fly ,biscuit *n* (*BrE humorous*) ⇨ GARIBALDI.

,Sri ,Guru ,Singh ,Sabha Gur'dwara /,ʃri ,gʊruː ,sɪŋ ,sɑːbə gɜːˈdwɑːrə; *AmE* gɜːr-/ a Sikh temple, or **Gurdwara**, part of the **Singh Sabha Movement**, in Southall in west *London which opened in 2003 and is the biggest Sikh temple outside India.

,Sri 'Lanka /,ʃri 'læŋkə/ an island off the southern tip of *India. Its capital city is Colombo and its official lan-

guage is Sinhalese. When it was part of the *British Empire (1802–1948) it was called **Ceylon**. It is a member of the *Commonwealth and one of the world's most important tea producers. In Britain, many people still refer to **Ceylon tea**.
▶ **Sri Lankan** *adj, n*.

SSDA /,es es di: 'eɪ/ ⇨ SECTOR SKILLS DEVELOPMENT AGENCY.

SSP /,es es 'piː/ ⇨ STATUTORY SICK PAY.

SSRI /,es es ɑːr 'aɪ/ (*in full* **selective serotonin reuptake inhibitor**) any of a group of drugs used mainly to treat depression, including *Prozac™, Seroxat™ and Paxil™, which affect the production of chemicals within the brain. There is some research to suggest that these drugs might be addictive and cause problems for people when they stop taking them.

SSSI /,es es es 'aɪ/ ⇨ SITE OF SPECIAL SCIENTIFIC INTEREST.

St ⇨ SAINT.

St ,Abb's 'Head /,æbz/ a high cliff in south-east Scotland which is well known for the large numbers of sea birds that gather and breed there. It is a *National Nature Reserve.

'Staffa /'stæfə/ an island in the *Hebrides, Scotland, close to *Mull. Nobody lives there but many people visit the island to see *Fingal's Cave and the rocks there, which are well known for their unusual shapes. See also GIANT'S CAUSEWAY.

'Stafford /'stæfəd; *AmE* 'stæfərd/ a town in western central England. It is the administrative centre of *Staffordshire and a traditional centre of the shoe-making industry.

'Staffordshire /'stæfədʃə(r); *AmE* 'stæfərdʃər/ (*abbr* **Staffs**) a county in western central England. It consists mainly of agricultural land and also contains the *Potteries. Its administrative centre is the town of Stafford.

,Staffordshire bull 'terrier /,stæfədʃə; *AmE* ,stæfərdʃər/ *n* a small, strong breed of dog. It was originally bred in *Staffordshire for dog fights (= events in which two dogs fight and people bet on which one will win) and for bull-baiting (= using dogs to annoy a bull) in the early 19th century. In the 1980s it was fashionable in Britain to have these dogs as pets, particularly among people in cities who wanted to appear strong or dangerous. In the 1990s more people bought them after a new law made it difficult to own the larger and more violent American *pit bull terriers.

,Staffordshire 'figure /,stæfədʃə; *AmE* ,stæfərdʃər/ a pottery figure made in *Staffordshire from the 18th century onwards. Many people like to collect the small painted models of animals and people, often of famous or historical figures, and they are often used in people's homes for decoration.

,Staffordshire 'pottery /,stæfədʃə; *AmE* 'stæfərdʃər/ *n* [U] pottery made in *Staffordshire, the traditional centre of the pottery industry in

a 19th-century Staffordshire figure

England. The most famous makes of English pottery, including *Minton, *Spode and *Wedgwood, are all produced in or near *Stoke-on-Trent in Staffordshire.

'stagecoach (also **stage**) n (in former times) a public vehicle pulled by two to six horses along a regular route. Each place where it stopped was called a *stage*. Stagecoaches usually carried up to eight passengers and sometimes also mail, etc. The driver sat outside. In the US West, stagecoaches were sometimes attacked by *Native Americans or robbers. For this reason, a man with a gun often sat next to the driver. This was called 'riding shotgun', and Americans still sometimes call the front passenger's seat in a car the 'shotgun seat'. Compare CONESTOGA WAGON.

'stakeholder ,pension /'steɪkhəʊldə(r); AmE -hoʊldər/ n a type of private pension scheme (= a system where people at work pay money regularly into a fund so that they will receive an income when they retire) introduced in Britain in 2001. Stakeholder pensions must meet certain standards set by the government and a limit is set on the fees the pension companies can charge. They must allow people to pay different amounts at different times, depending on their work situation, and also to keep the same pension scheme if they move jobs.

St 'Albans /'ɔːlbənz/ a town in *Hertfordshire, southern England, built near the old Roman town of Verulamium. Its cathedral (11th–14th centuries) is named in honour of St Alban, a Roman soldier who was the first person in Britain to be killed for his Christian beliefs. Two battles (1455 and 1461) were fought at St Albans during the *Wars of the Roses.

Syl,vester Stal'lone /sɪl,vestə stə'ləʊn; AmE sɪl,vestər stə'loʊn/ (1946–) a US actor who also writes and directs films. His popular name is 'Sly'. He is best known for playing the characters *Rocky and *Rambo. His other films include *Demolition Man* (1993), *Judge Dredd* (1995), *Daylight* (1996), *Cop Land* (1997) and *Get Carter* (2000).

,Stamford 'Bridge /,stæmfəd; AmE ,stæmfərd/
1 a village in north-east England. A famous battle took place there in 1066, when the forces of King *Harold II defeated the invading army of King Harald Hardraade of Norway, three weeks before the Battle of *Hastings.
2 a well-known football stadium in *Fulham(1), west London. It is the home ground of *Chelsea football club.

the 'Stamp Act a British *Act of Parliament in 1765. It stated that all publications and legal documents in British colonies (= parts of the empire) in America must have official stamps, sold by the British government. Many people in America thought that this was an unfair tax. They refused to use the stamps and prevented British ships from entering or leaving their ports. The Stamp Act was removed in 1766 but the tax, and the people's protests against it, are among the important events that led to the *American Revolution.

'stamp ,duty n [U] (BrE) a tax that requires you to pay for a document to receive an official stamp in order to make it valid. In the past, stamp duty was paid on documents used to transfer houses and flats/apartments from one person to another. In December 2003 this was replaced by a **Stamp Duty Land Tax**. The new tax is paid directly to the government rather than by paying for a document to be stamped. The amount depends on the value of the property bought. Homes sold for between £120 000 and £250 000 are taxed at one per cent and the rate increases for more valuable properties. The tax is often still referred to as 'Stamp Duty': *After we'd paid the*

solicitor's fees and the stamp duty we had no money left for furniture.

the 'Standard ⇨ EVENING STANDARD.

,Standard and 'Poor's an international company started in 1941 and based in *New York which publishes information about companies and gives them credit ratings (= a judgement about whether they are able to pay back money that they borrow, and how safe it is to lend money to them).

,Standard As'sessment Task ⇨ SAT(2).

,Standard 'Oil a large US oil company established in 1870 by John D *Rockefeller. In 1911 the US *Supreme Court decided it restricted trade and divided it into 34 individual companies. Rockefeller's original company became Standard Oil (Ohio). It was bought by British Petroleum (*BP) in 1987 and named BP America. The Standard Oil Company (Indiana) became Amoco in 1985. The Amoco Building, opened in 1973 in *Chicago as the Standard Oil Building, is one of the tallest in the world. Compare EXXONMOBIL.

▶ **standards of living**

The British enjoy the high standard of living of an industrialized western country. Most British people tend not to judge **quality of life** by money alone though, and would point out benefits such as a stable political situation, freedom of speech and choice, and relatively little official interference in their lives.

Disposable income (= the amount of money people have to spend after paying taxes) is commonly used to measure the standard of living. This has risen steadily since the 1960s and has more than doubled since 1978. People with low wages or who are unemployed, and people who have retired, have less income and a lower standard of living. Although disposable income has been rising in the country as a whole, the gap between rich and poor grew wider towards the end of the last century after the tax burden on the richest people was reduced in the 1980s. The distribution of wealth as opposed to income is even more uneven. In 2001 the richest 1% owned about 25% of the wealth and the poorer half of the population owned only 5% of total wealth. Standards of living also vary from region to region. The wealthiest region is the *South-East. Figures published for 1999 show that, compared with an average of 15% of the population in the countries of the *European Union living in low-income households, the figure for Britain was 19%. By 2002 it was 17%.

In the 1920s people in the US began to believe in the *American dream, the idea that anyone who worked hard could have material goods as a reward. Having such goods proves that a person is hard-working, so many people try to have everything their neighbours have, a practice called 'keeping up with the Joneses'. As a result, America is often said to be a **consumer society**. The material standard of living is very high and the cost of living relatively low. Many Americans have large **discretionary incomes** (= money which they do not need for food and clothing and can spend as they choose) and can therefore buy many consumer goods but, as in Britain, there is a large and increasing gap between rich and poor as many people in low-paid jobs have not benefited from the general increases in income. In 2003. 12.5% of the population were living below the **poverty line**, the highest figure since 1998.

'standing stone n a large stone placed in an upright position during the *Stone Age or the *Bronze Age. There are many of these stones in Britain, often arranged in circles as at *Stonehenge and *Avebury. Nobody knows exactly why they were put there, though many

S

people think it was for religious reasons, or for the study of the stars and planets.

Castlerigg standing stones, Cumbria

St 'Andrews /'ændruːz/ a town in *Fife, Scotland. It is named after St *Andrew, whose bones are said to have been brought here in the 4th century, and it was an early centre of the Christian Church. Its university, established in 1412, is the oldest in Scotland. The town is also famous for the *Royal and Ancient golf club, which is recognized as an international authority on the rules of golf.

St ,Andrew's 'Cross /,ændruːz/ the national flag of Scotland, consisting of an X-shaped white cross on a blue background. The cross also forms part of the British *Union Jack flag. St *Andrew is Scotland's national saint. Compare ST GEORGE'S CROSS.

St 'Andrew's Day /'ændruːz/ 30 November, the day celebrated as the national day of Scotland (although it is not a public holiday). St *Andrew is Scotland's national saint.

,Stanford-Bi'net test /,stænfəd bɪ'neɪ; AmE ,stænfərd/ n a US test used to measure intelligence, especially in children. It was developed at *Stanford University in 1916.

,Stanford Uni'versity /,stænfəd; AmE ,stænfərd/ a major private university in Stanford, *California, near Palo Alto. It was established in 1885 by Leland Stanford and his wife. In 2003 it had about 14 000 students.

'Henry 'Morton 'Stanley /'mɔːtn 'stænli; AmE 'mɔːrtn/ (1841–1904) a Welsh journalist and explorer. He went to live in the US in 1859, and worked as a journalist for the New York Herald. In 1869 he was sent by his newspaper to find the explorer David *Livingstone, who was thought to have become lost in Africa. Stanley found him at Ujiji in 1871, and is said to have greeted him with the words 'Dr Livingstone, I presume?' Stanley continued to explore Africa until the early 1890s, and returned to live in Britain in 1892. He became a *Member of Parliament (1895–1900) and was made a *knight in 1899.

the ,Stanley 'Cup /,stænli/ a competition to decide the best team in the National Hockey League in America, first held in 1893. It consists of a series of games between the winners of the Eastern Conference and the winners of the Western Conference. The first of the two teams to win four games in the series becomes the Stanley Cup Champion.

,Stanley 'Gibbons /'gɪbənz/ a large British company that sells stamps to people who collect them. It has the world's largest stamp shop in the *Strand, London, and organizes auctions of stamps. It also publishes its well-known stamp catalogues.

,Stanley 'Kaplan /'kæplən/ (also **Kaplan**) a US company that prepares students for examinations which they need to pass in order to enter American colleges or universities. These include the *SAT and *GRE. In 2003 there were more than 3 000 Kaplan Educational Centers in the US and many other countries, including Russia and China. Stanley Kaplan, a teacher from *Brooklyn, began the first one in the 1930s. The centres are now owned by the Washington Post Company, which also publishes Kaplan books.

,Stansted 'Airport /,stænsted/ (also **'Stansted**) an airport in *Essex, north-east of London. It was a very small airport until the 1990s, when it became London's third airport. A new airport building, designed by Norman *Foster, was opened in 1991. With the growth of low-cost airlines such as *Ryanair which use Stansted, the airport expanded to become Britain's fourth busiest airport.

,Barbara 'Stanwyck /'stænwɪk/ (1907–90) a US film actor known for playing strong characters. Her films include Double Indemnity (1944), Sorry, Wrong Number (1948) and Executive Suite (1954). She was also a star of the television *western series The Big Valley (1965–9). Stanwyck received a special *Oscar in 1982.

the Star ⇨ DAILY STAR.

'Starbucks™ /'staːbʌks; AmE 'staːrbʌks/ a US make of coffee sold by the Starbucks Coffee Company in its restaurants and shops around the world. The company's main office is in *Seattle.

the ,Star 'Chamber (also **the Court of Star Chamber**) a British court of law that was first used in the 14th century. It consisted of the members of the *Privy Council, and had no jury. It was often used in the *Tudor(1) and *Stuart periods to deal with cases affecting the state or the *royal family. It already had a reputation for treating people unfairly when *Charles I used it to punish people who refused to do what he wanted. It was closed down by the *Long Parliament in 1641. The phrase is sometimes used to refer to any group of people that makes unfair decisions: This is not a star chamber, you will be given a fair hearing.

A ,Star is 'Born the title of three US films about an old actor who helps a young woman with her career, marries her and then kills himself. The best-known version (1954) was a *musical with Judy *Garland and James *Mason. It was made again in 1976 with Barbra *Streisand and Kris Kristofferson, and its song Evergreen won an *Oscar. The first version of the film was made in 1937.

,Freya 'Stark /,freɪə 'staːk; AmE 'staːrk/ (1893–1993) an English traveller and writer. Her best-known books were about her travels in the Middle East, including The Valley of the Assassins (1934) and The Southern Gates of Arabia (1936). She was made a *dame(2) in 1972.

,Belle 'Starr¹ /,bel 'staː(r)/ (c. 1848–89) a US outlaw (= criminal) in the *Wild West. She was a friend of Jesse and Frank *James and let outlaws stay at her home in *Oklahoma. She was sent to prison for nine months in 1883 for stealing horses. Starr died after being shot by an unknown person.

,Ringo 'Starr² /,rɪŋgəʊ 'staː(r); AmE ,rɪŋgoʊ 'staːr/ (1940–) an English pop musician, best known as the *Beatles' drummer in the 1960s. He now uses his original name, Richard Starkey.

the ,Stars and 'Bars the flag of the *Confederate States during the *American Civil War.

▶ **the Stars and Stripes**

The US flag, usually called the **Stars and Stripes**, is an important symbol to all Americans. It is also known as **Old Glory** or the **Star-Spangled Banner**. During the revolution against Britain, George *Washington asked Betsy *Ross to make a flag as an encouragement for his soldiers. This flag had 13 stripes, seven red and six white, and in one corner 13 white stars on a blue background to represent the 13 states. On 14 June 1777 it became the flag of the independent US. As each new state became part of the US an extra star was added.

Today, the flag is widely seen in the US. Government offices and schools have flags flying from flagpoles, and many people have flags outside their houses, especially on *Independence Day. Children start the school day by saying the *Pledge of Allegiance, a promise to be loyal to the flag and to their country. When somebody important dies, flags are flown at **half mast**/AmE **half staff**. When a soldier dies, his or her coffin is covered with a flag, and after the funeral the flag is given to the family. The flag has also been used as a symbol of protest, especially during the *Vietnam War, when some people burnt the flag to show that they were ashamed of their country's actions.

Each of the US states also has its own flag. State flags may show the state flower or bird, or other emblem.

,**Starship 'Enterprise** /ˌstɑːˈʃɪp; AmE ˌstɑːrˈʃɪp/ ⇨ STAR TREK.

The ,**Star-Spangled 'Banner** /spæŋgld/ the US *national anthem. It was written in 1814 by Francis Scott Key, an American lawyer, as he watched British ships trying without success to capture Fort McHenry in *Maryland during the *War of 1812. He wrote the words and added the music of an old British song. The US *Congress officially made it the country's national anthem in 1931. It ends:

> 66 And the star-spangled banner in triumph shall wave
> O'er the land of the free and the home of the brave! 99

START /stɑːt; AmE stɑːrt/ ⇨ STRATEGIC ARMS REDUCTION TALKS.

'**Star Trek** a US television series first shown on *NBC in the 1960s which later became a cult programme (= very fashionable with a particular group). It is about the spacecraft Starship Enterprise whose crew includes Captain James *Kirk, Mr *Spock, 'Bones' McCoy and 'Scotty' Scott. They made six Star Trek films between 1979 and 1991. A later television series with different actors, Star Trek: the Next Generation, began in 1988, and there have been three further films and various spin-offs such as Voyager and Deep Space 9. See also TREKKIE.

> 66 Beam me up, Scotty. 99
> a famous misquote from Star Trek

,**Start the 'Week** a British radio programme, broadcast on *BBC *Radio 4 every Monday morning. It consists of a discussion between the presenter Andrew *Marr, and guests, who are usually well-known politicians, entertainers, writers or experts on a particular subject in the news.

'**Star Wars** a very successful US film (1977), directed by George Lucas, about a war in space. The story is about Luke Skywalker and Han Solo, who fight the evil *Darth Vader to rescue Princess Leia. The same characters appeared in several further films, including The Empire Strikes Back (1980), Return of the Jedi (1983), and Episode 1 (1999). The term 'Star Wars' was used by President Ronald *Reagan for his *Strategic Defense Initiative, and he also called the USSR 'the evil empire', a phrase taken from the film.

the '**State De,partment** (also the **Department of State**) the US government department responsible for international affairs. It is directed by the *Secretary of State. It advises the president on foreign policy and makes agreements and treaties (= formal agreements) with other countries.

▶ **stately homes**

In Britain there are many large stately homes that belong or used to belong to *upper-class aristocratic families. The houses are called stately homes from the opening lines of a poem by Felicia Hemans (1793–1835). They are sometimes also called **country houses** because most of them are in the countryside. Some are approached through large iron gates down a long drive. Many have formal gardens and are surrounded by a large private **park**, often with a lake.

Stately homes range from small **manor houses** to **palaces**. Manor houses date from the 14th century and are often square stone buildings with a central **courtyard**, and some are entered by crossing a moat which was originally a means of defence. Some larger houses were built in the 16th century, including *Hampton Court in south-west London, *Burghley House near Peterborough and Hardwick Hall near Derby.

Many stately homes date from the 18th century, and are associated with famous architects. *Blenheim Palace near Oxford was designed in the *baroque style by *Vanbrugh and *Hawksmoor. Holkham Hall in Norfolk, designed only a few years later by William *Kent, is in the Palladian style. Kedleston Hall near Derby, the home of the *Curzon family, was mainly the work of Robert *Adam. The large estates attached to stately homes attracted *landscape gardeners such as 'Capability' *Brown, who laid out the gardens at Burghley, Blenheim and *Chatsworth.

Stately homes are very expensive to look after and, in order to get enough money to do this, some owners open their houses to the public. They charge visitors an **admission fee**. Many stately homes have been given by their owners to the *National Trust, an organization which raises the money to look after them from gifts, membership fees and admission charges. In many cases, the former owners continue to live in part of the house. This arrangement means that the house is well cared for, and the family does not have to pay *inheritance tax when the owner dies.

Visitors go to stately homes to admire their architecture, and to walk round the gardens. They also go to see valuable furniture, paintings, tapestries and china that have been collected over a long period. Sometimes, documents about the family or about historical events are also displayed. There is generally a cafe and a shop selling souvenirs. During the summer, concerts or plays may be performed in the house or gardens. Some owners have added other attractions: at *Longleat House, for example, there is a safari park.

> 66 The stately homes of England
> How beautiful they stand!
> Amidst their tall ancestral trees,
> O'er all the pleasant land. 99

> 66 The stately homes of England
> How beautiful they stand!
> To prove the upper classes
> Have still the upper hand. 99
> the first verse of Felicia Hemans' poem followed by Noel Coward's 1938 version

,**Staten 'Island** /ˌstætən/ an island which is one of the *boroughs of New York City. Its former name was Richmond. It is connected to *Brooklyn by the Verrazano-Narrows Bridge. The **Staten Island Ferry** goes to *Battery Park in *Manhattan(1) and provides good views of the city.

S

The states of the United States (with postal abbreviations)

Alabama	AL	Louisiana	LA	Ohio	OH
Alaska	AK	Maine	ME	Oklahoma	OK
Arizona	AZ	Maryland	MD	Oregon	OR
Arkansas	AR	Massachusetts	MA	Pennsylvania	PA
California	CA	Michigan	MI	Rhode Island	RI
Colorado	CO	Minnesota	MN	South Carolina	SC
Connecticut	CT	Mississippi	MS	South Dakota	SD
Delaware	DE	Missouri	MO	Tennessee	TN
Florida	FL	Montana	MT	Texas	TX
Georgia	GA	Nebraska	NE	Utah	UT
Hawaii	HI	Nevada	NV	Vermont	VT
Idaho	ID	New Hampshire	NH	Virginia	VA
Illinois	IL	New Jersey	NJ	Washington	WA
Indiana	IN	New Mexico	NM	West Virginia	WV
Iowa	IA	New York	NY	Wisconsin	WI
Kansas	KS	North Carolina	NC	Wyoming	WY
Kentucky	KY	North Dakota	ND		

the **'State of the 'Union Ad'dress** a speech given each year by the US *President to *Congress. He is required by the American *Constitution to give 'information on the State of the Union', and he also talks about his government's successes, plans and policies. The speech is shown on national television.

the **'State 'Opening of 'Parliament** the official opening of each session (= series of meetings) of the British *Parliament. The ceremony takes place each year in October or November, and after a change of government. The queen or king travels in a special coach to the *Houses of Parliament(2), and makes the *Queen's Speech (or King's Speech) to members of both Houses in the *House of Lords.

'state school n (in Britain) a school that offers free education and receives money from a *Local Education Authority or directly from the government. Most schools in Britain are state schools. Some church schools also receive money from the government and offer free education. Compare PUBLIC SCHOOL(1).

'State ,Second 'Pension ⇨ S2P.

,states' 'rights n [pl] (in the US) the rights held by individual states under the 10th Amendment to the American *Constitution. These include the right to have their own criminal laws, laws regarding commerce and taxes, and laws on education, health and social welfare, and also the right to have their own police force. The principle of states' rights is supported by those who think that the central government should not interfere too much in state affairs. It has been supported especially by the states in the *South, five of which voted for the States' Rights Party in the 1948 election for President. There has been much argument in US history over the division of responsibility between state and national governments. In recent years the national government has given more rights to the states.

,state 'trooper /'tru:pə(r)/ n a US state police officer, especially a member of the highway patrol (= police officers who travel along motorways/freeways to stop dangerous drivers): *He was stopped for speeding by a Mississippi state trooper.*

,state uni'versity n (in the US) a public university run by an individual state and supported by state taxes. Every state has a main university, usually with the state's name, such as the University of Alabama or the University of Colorado. Most states also have other state universities, and all have several state colleges.

the **'State Uni'versity of New 'York** /nju: 'jɔ:k; *AmE* 'jɔ:rk/ (*abbr* **SUNY**) the large *state university system of New York State in the US. It is in the six cities of Albany, Binghamton, Buffalo, New Paltz, Oswego and Stony Brook. There are also SUNY colleges in 11 cities.

the **'Stationery ,Office** a private British organization that publishes and prints official government documents and books. It also has bookshops in London and some other cities. See also HM STATIONERY OFFICE.

the **,Statue of 'Liberty** the famous US statue on Liberty Island in New York harbour. It is a woman holding the torch (= burning light) of liberty (= freedom), and its official name is the 'Statue of Liberty Enlightening the World'. It has become a symbol of freedom and was the first American sight seen by many people who went to the US for a better life. It was designed by Frederic Auguste Bartoldie and given to the US people by France in 1884. The poem by Emma Lazarus on the base of the statue includes the lines: 'Give me your tired, your poor, Your huddled masses yearning to breathe free.' The statue was made a *World Heritage Site in 1984.

,statutory 'sick pay n [U] (*abbr* **SSP**) (in Britain) money that employers must pay their employees when they cannot work because of illness. Employers must pay this, by law, for up to 28 weeks. If the employee is still ill after this time, he or she then receives money from the government, called *incapacity benefit.

St Bar,tholomew's 'Hospital /bɑː,θɒləmjuːz; *AmE* bɑːr,θɑːləmjuːz/ ⇨ BART'S.

STC /,es ti: 'si:/ ⇨ SECURE TRAINING CENTRE.

St ,Clement 'Danes /,clemənt 'deɪmz/ a church in central London, England, designed by Christopher *Wren in 1682 at a place where a group of Danes are thought to have settled in the 9th century. It was partly destroyed by bombs in *World War II and was built again as a special church of the *Royal Air Force. It is probably the church mentioned in the children's song *Oranges and Lemons*, although there is another church called St Clement's in Eastcheap, London.

St 'David's /'deɪvɪdz/ a very small town on the west coast of Wales. It is known as the home of St *David, and its 12th-century cathedral is the largest in Wales.

St 'David's Day /'deɪvɪdz/ 1 March, the day celebrated as the national day of Wales (although it is not a public holiday). St *David is the national saint of Wales. Many Welsh people wear a *daffodil (= a yellow spring flower) on St David's Day.

S

St 'Dunstan's /'dʌnstnz/ a charity providing training and accommodation for blind people who have served in the British or *Commonwealth armed forces. It was started in 1915 by the newspaper owner Arthur Pearson (1866–1921), who was blind himself.

steak and kidney 'pie n [U, C] a traditional British dish made with pieces of beef and kidneys baked in pastry. It is regarded as a typical British dish and is often served in pubs.

steak and kidney 'pudding n [U, C] a traditional British dish made with pieces of beef and kidneys covered in suet pastry (= a mixture of flour and beef fat) and cooked by steaming.

David 'Steel /'sti:l/ (1938–) a Scottish politician and the last leader of the *Liberal Party. He was partly responsible for the Liberal Party combining with the *SDP to form the *Liberal Democratic Party in 1988. He was made a *life peer in 1997.

Richard 'Steele[1] /'sti:l/ (1672–1729) an Irish writer of plays and essays. He moved to London as a young man, and wrote several comedy plays. They contained more social and moral comments than the popular *Restoration comedies, and were not very successful. He is best remembered for starting two magazines, The *Tatler(2) and The *Spectator(2), for which he wrote essays about literature and moral questions. See also ADDISON.

Tommy 'Steele[2] /'sti:l/ (1936–) an English actor and singer, known for his lively and cheerful personality. He began his career as a pop star in the 1950s and appeared in many *West End musical shows (including Half a Sixpence) as well as films and television programmes.

William 'Steig /'staɪg/ (1907–2003) a US cartoonist and writer of children's books who was best known for his cartoons in the *New Yorker magazine, including 117 of its covers. His children's books include Shrek (1990) which was made into a successful animated film in 2001.

Rod 'Steiger /'staɪgə(r)/ (1925–2002) a US actor who often played tough characters. His films include The Pawnbroker (1965), Doctor Zhivago (1965), In the Heat of the Night (1967), for which he won an *Oscar, Waterloo (1970) in which he played Napoleon, The Amityville Horror (1979) and Mars Attacks! (1996).

Gertrude 'Stein /'staɪn/ (1874–1946) a US writer who lived mainly in Paris after 1903. Her home there became a centre for writers, including Ernest *Hemingway and Ford Madox *Ford, and artists such as Picasso and Matisse. She wrote in an unusual style, often repeating words and using no punctuation. Her best-known work is The Autobiography of Alice B Toklas (1933), which is really an account of her own life. She also wrote poetry, including the famous line:

66 A rose is a rose is a rose. 99

Rick Stein /'staɪn/ (1947–) an English chef, cookery writer and television presenter. He owns a popular fish restaurant in Padstow in *Cornwall.

John 'Steinbeck /'staɪnbek/ (1902–68) a US author who received the 1962 *Nobel Prize for literature. He often wrote about poor farmers in California. His best-known books include Of Mice and Men (1937), The *Grapes of Wrath, Cannery Row (1945) and *East of Eden. Many of his books were made into films.

George 'Steinbrenner /'staɪnbrenə(r)/ (1930–) the main owner of the New York Yankees baseball team, known as **The Boss**. He is said to interfere more in the running of the club than owners usually do and is best known for paying high wages to famous players and for changing the team manager very often.

Gloria 'Steinem /'staɪnəm/ (1934–) a US journalist and author who has been a leading figure in the campaign for women's rights since the 1960s. She helped to establish the Women's Action Alliance (1971), the National Women's Political Caucus (1971) and Ms magazine (1972), which she edited until 1987. Her own articles were collected in Outrageous Acts and Everyday Rebellions (1983).

66 A woman without a man is like a fish without a bicycle. 99
Gloria Steinem

Stephen (c. 1097–1154) the king of England from 1135 to 1154. He was the grandson of *William the Conqueror and became king even though he had agreed that his cousin *Matilda had the right to the throne. He spent much of his period as king resisting her attempts to become queen, and finally agreed that her son *Henry II would become king when he died.

George 'Stephenson[1] /'sti:vnsn/ (1781–1848) an English engineer. He designed some of the first steam trains and railways in Britain, including the engines for the first passenger trains for the *Stockton and Darlington Railway in 1825, and the *Liverpool and Manchester Railway in 1826.

Robert 'Stephenson[2] /'sti:vnsn/ (1803–59) an English engineer, the son of George *Stephenson. He helped his father on the *Liverpool and Manchester Railway, for which he designed and built *Rocket, before becoming the engineer on the London and Birmingham Railway. He also designed many important bridges and was a *Conservative *Member of Parliament for the last 12 years of his life.

'Steptoe and Son /'steptəʊ; AmE 'steptoʊ/ a *BBC comedy television series, broadcast between 1964 and 1973. It is about a father and son who are rag-and-bone men (= people who collect old clothes, furniture, etc. to sell again) in London. Much of the humour comes from the characters of the two people, who often argue and trick each other. It is considered one of the best British comedies of all time: Look at all the stuff in this office – it's like Steptoe's back yard!

Isaac 'Stern /'stɜːn; AmE 'stɜːrn/ (1920–2001) a US violin player. He was born in Russia, went to the US as a baby with his family, and first played in public at the age of 11. His many successful world tours began in 1937. In the late 1950s he organized a successful campaign to save *Carnegie Hall from being destroyed.

Laurence 'Sterne /'stɜːn; AmE 'stɜːrn/ (1713–68) a British author, born in Ireland. He spent most of his life as a *Church of England priest in *Yorkshire. He is best known for his novel *Tristram Shandy, one of the most unusual and humorous books in English literature.

'Stetson™ /'stetsn/ n a type of tall hat with a wide brim worn especially by *cowboys and other people in the western US states. It was invented by John B Stetson (1830–1906).

Wallace 'Stevens /ˌwɒlɪs 'sti:vnz/ (1879–1955) a US writer of elegant and imaginative poetry. His Collected Poems (1954) won the *Pulitzer Prize. His other collections included Harmonium (1923), The Man with the Blue Guitar (1937) and Transport to Summer (1947).

Adlai 'Stevenson[1] /ˌædleɪ 'sti:vnsn/ (1900–65) a US *Democratic politician who was defeated by Dwight D *Eisenhower in the 1952 and 1956 elections for US *President. Stevenson was a lawyer known for his clever remarks and fine mind. He was Governor of *Illinois (1949–53) and later US ambassador to the *United Nations (1961–5).

'Robert 'Louis 'Stevenson² /'luːɪs 'stiːvnsn/ (1850–94) a Scottish writer of novels. He is best known for his famous children's adventure stories *Treasure Island* and *Kidnapped*, but he also wrote poetry for children and the well-known adult psychological novel *The Strange Case of Dr Jekyll and Mr Hyde* (1886). Because of poor health Stevenson went to live on the island of Samoa in the Pacific for the last few years of his life. See also JEKYLL AND HYDE.

'Jackie 'Stewart¹ /'stjuːət; *AmE* 'stuːərt/ (1939–) a Scottish racing driver who was very successful in the 1960s and 1970s. He won 27 Grand Prix races and was *Formula One world champion three times. He was made a *knight in 2001.

'James 'Stewart² /'stjuːət; *AmE* 'stuːərt/ (1908–97) a popular US actor who usually played good, honest characters. He was a tall man, known for speaking in a slow and hesitating way. He won an *Oscar for *The Philadelphia Story* (1940) and a special Oscar in 1984 for his contribution to the film industry. His other films include *It's a Wonderful Life*, *Rear Window* (1954), *The Glenn Miller Story* (1954), *The Man from Laramie* (1955), *The Spirit of St Louis* (1957) and *The Shootist* (1986). Stewart was awarded the Distinguished Flying Cross in *World War II and was later a Brigadier General in the US Air Force Reserve.

'Martha 'Stewart³ /'stjuːət; *AmE* 'stuːərt/ (1941–) a US television personality known for cookery, gardening and home decoration. Through the company **Martha Stewart Living Omnimedia** she runs television programmes, magazines and a website and sells several ranges of household products. In 2004 she was sent to prison for several offences related to her business and financial dealings.

'Rod 'Stewart⁴ /'stjuːət; *AmE* 'stuːərt/ (1945–) an English pop singer. He is well known for his rough voice and for his love of Scotland, from where his family originally came. He has recorded many famous songs, including *Maggie May* (1971) and *Sailing* (1975). Since the 1970s he has lived mainly in the US. His songs were made into a *musical called *Tonight's the Night*.

St 'George's 'Cross /ˌdʒɔːdʒɪz; *AmE* ˌdʒɔːrdʒɪz/ the national flag of England, consisting of an upright red cross on a white background. The cross also forms part of the British *Union Jack flag. St *George is England's national saint. Compare ST ANDREW'S CROSS.

St 'George's Day /ˌdʒɔːdʒɪz; *AmE* ˌdʒɔːrdʒɪz/ the saint's day of **St George**, the patron saint of England, which is celebrated on 23 April every year. Although it is the national day of England, it is not a holiday and there are no special celebrations. The **Cross of Saint George** is the flag of England, with a red cross on a white background.

The legend of **St George** says that he was a hero who killed a dragon to save a princess and in many pictures of him, he is shown standing over a dragon with a sword.

The real **St George**, however, is thought to have been a soldier in the Roman army in the first century who was a Christian and was executed because he refused to kill other Christians. .

St He'lena /həˈliːnə/ a small island in the southern Atlantic Ocean. It is famous as the place where Napoleon was kept as a prisoner by the British from 1815 until his death in 1821. It was owned by the British *East India Company from 1659, and became a possession of the British *Crown in 1834. The island's capital is Jamestown. The Governor of Saint Helena is also responsible for *Tristan da Cunha and Ascension Island.

'Mount St 'Helens /'helənz/ a volcano in the Cascade Range of the US state of *Washington. It exploded in 1980 for the first time in 120 years killing about 60 people, and causing damage to the surrounding area. The explosion also reduced the height of the mountain by over 1000 feet/300 metres. There have been several weaker explosions since.

Mount St Helens

'Alfred 'Stieglitz /'stiːglɪts/ (1864–1946) a US photographer who developed photography into a fine art. He managed several New York galleries, where he presented exhibitions of photographs and modern art. He was married to the artist Georgia *O'Keeffe and often photographed her.

'Stilton™ /'stɪltən/ *n* [U] a white English cheese with greenish-blue lines running through it and a strong flavour. It is often eaten at the end of a meal, and traditionally it is eaten with port (= strong sweet wine from Portugal) after large meals on special occasions such as *Christmas. It was originally made in various places in the county of *Leicestershire (though not the village of Stilton, now in *Cambridgeshire, where it was first sold).

'Joseph 'Warren 'Stilwell /'stɪlwel/ (1883–1946) a senior US military officer during *World War II. General Stilwell's popular name was 'Vinegar Joe'. He commanded US forces in China, Burma and India but was sent back to the US in 1944 because of disagreements with Chiang Kai-shek. He later commanded US forces on the Japanese island of Okinawa.

Sting /stɪŋ/ an English pop singer whose real name is Gordon Sumner (1951–). He first became famous in the 1970s as the singer of the group The Police. In 1985 he left the group and began to make pop records with a *jazz influence. He had several successful records in the 1980s and 1990s, including *All This Time* (1991) and *Fields of Gold* (1993). He is also well known for his campaigns to protect the environment, especially in South America.

'Stirling¹ /'stɜːlɪŋ; *AmE* 'stɜːrlɪŋ/ a town in central Scotland. It has an important place in Scottish history. It has a very old castle where the kings and queens of Scotland used to live. Scottish forces defeated the English in two important battles, Stirling Bridge (1297) and *Bannockburn, for control of the castle and the bridge across the *Forth river. It is also the administrative centre of the Stirling *council area, which covers a wider geographical area, including part of the *Grampians.

'James 'Stirling² /'stɜːlɪŋ; *AmE* 'stɜːrlɪŋ/ (1926–92) an English architect. He is well known for designing modern buildings with many straight lines and bright colours. Some people with traditional ideas about architecture do not approve of his work. He has designed buildings for the universities of *Oxford, *Cambridge and *Leicester, and his best-known buildings include a new part of *Tate Britain, the Clore Gallery, and an art gallery in Stuttgart, Germany. He was made a *knight in 1992.

St 'Ives /'aɪvz/ a town on the coast of *Cornwall in south-west England. It is popular with tourists, and several well-known artists have lived there, including Bernard Leach (1887–1979), Barbara *Hepworth, Ben *Nicholson and Patrick Heron (1920–99). A branch of *Tate Britain opened in St Ives in 1993. The town is also mentioned in a traditional nursery rhyme which contains a riddle to which the answer is one, since the man and his wives, etc. were going the other way:

> 66 As I was going to St Ives,
> I met a man with seven wives.
> Each wife had seven sacks,
> Each sack had seven cats,
> Each cat had seven kits;
> Kits, cats, sacks and wives,
> How many were going to Saint Ives? 99

St ˌJames's ˈPalace /ˌdʒeɪmzɪz/ a large, grand house built by King *Henry VIII in 1552 at the edge of *St James's Park in London. It was the main London home of the king or queen from 1697 to 1837. See also COURT OF ST JAMES'S.

St ˌJames's ˈPark /ˌdʒeɪmzɪz/ a park in central London, England, in front of *Buckingham Palace. It is the oldest of London's *royal parks, and contains a long lake with an island where many birds breed.

St ˌJohn ˈAmbulance Briˌgade a British charity. Its staff work without payment to provide medical care at public events, e.g. concerts or football matches. They also run medical centres and homes for sick people. It was started in 1887 and is named after the Order of the Hospital of St John of Jerusalem, an ancient military organization that cared for the sick.

St ˈKilda /ˈkɪldə/ a group of four islands off the west coast of Scotland, at the most western point in Britain. Nobody has lived there since 1930. The islands' high mountains and cliffs are the home of many different sea birds. St Kilda became a *World Heritage Site in 1986.

St ˌKitts-ˈNevis /ˌkɪts ˈniːvɪs/ (*also formal* **St Christopher and Nevis**) a country consisting of two islands in the eastern Caribbean Sea. It was claimed by Britain in 1623, and the island of Anguilla was part of it until 1967. In 1983 it became an independent member of the *Commonwealth. Its capital town is Basseterre.

St ˌLawrence ˈSeaway a major water transport system for the US and Canada. It was built by the two countries and opened in 1959. It connects the St Lawrence River with Lake *Ontario and then, with the *Great Lakes system, forms a channel 2342 miles/3768 kilometres long. Large ships use it to travel between the Atlantic Ocean and the Great Lakes.

the ˌSt ˈLeger /ˈledʒə(r)/ a race held every September at *Doncaster, *South Yorkshire, England, for horses that are three years old. It was first held in 1776.

St ˈLouis /ˈluːɪs, ˈluːi/ a city on the *Mississippi River in the US state of *Missouri. It was established in 1764 by the French, who named it after King Louis IX. It was part of the *Louisiana Purchase and became a major port for steamboats (= river boats driven by steam) in the 19th century. It now produces cars, aircraft, metal and chemicals. The city was known as the 'Gateway to the West', and its Gateway Arch (630 feet/192 metres high) is a symbol of this.

St ˈLucia /ˈluːʃə/ an island in the Caribbean Sea. It was claimed by Britain in 1814 and has been an independent member of the *Commonwealth since 1979. Its capital town is Castries.
▶ **St Lucian** /ˈluːʃən/ *adj, n.*

St ˌMartin-in-the-ˈFields a church in central London, England, designed by James Gibbs and completed in 1726. The *Academy of St Martin-in-the-Fields was originally based there, and performances by other musical groups are still given there. The church also started an art college in 1854, now called the Central St Martin's College of Art and Design in *Bloomsbury.

the Gateway Arch, St Louis

the ˈstockbroker belt *n* [usually sing] (*BrE*) an area outside a city, where rich people live in large expensive houses. Many of them work in the city as highly paid professional people, e.g. stockbrokers (= people who buy and sell shares in companies on behalf of other people). Most people think of the typical stockbroker belt as *Surrey, south-west of London, but the phrase can be used to refer to any expensive area outside a city: *They bought a very large detached house in the heart of the stockbroker belt.*

ˈstock ˌcompany *n* (*AmE*) a US company of actors, usually at one theatre, who present a variety of plays. **Summer stock** is the traditional production of plays by stock companies in small American towns during the summer.

ˈStock Exˌchange ˈAutomated Quoˈtations ⇨ SEAQ.

the stocks /stɒks/ *n* [pl] a device used for punishing criminals in Britain from the 13th century to the 19th century. It was a wooden framework with holes for the feet, and sometimes also for the hands. Criminals were locked into the stocks in public places so that people could laugh at them, insult them and sometimes throw things at them. Compare PILLORY.

the ˈStockton and ˈDarlington ˈRailway /ˈstɒktən, ˈdɑːlɪŋtən; *AmE* ˈstɑːktən, ˈdɑːrlɪŋtən/ the world's first railway on which passengers were carried on steam trains. It was built by George *Stephenson in the 1820s between Stockton, a port on the River *Tees in north-east England, and Darlington, an industrial town ten miles away.

ˌStoke ˈMandeville /ˌstəʊk ˈmændəvɪl; *AmE* ˌstoʊk/ a hospital near the village of Stoke Mandeville in *Buckinghamshire, England. It is well known for its department that deals with injuries and diseases of the spine (= the row of bones along the back). The official name for this department is the National Spinal Injuries Centre.

ˌStoke-on-ˈTrent /ˌstəʊk, ˈtrent; *AmE* ˌstoʊk/ an industrial city on the River Trent in *Staffordshire, England. It was formed in 1910 when the *Five Towns combined, and is the main centre of the *Potteries. Most

S

of the famous *Staffordshire pottery companies have their factories in Stoke-on-Trent.

,Leopold Sto'kowski /ˌliːəpəʊld stəˈkɒfski; AmE ˌliːəpoʊld stəˈkɑːfski/ (1887–1977) a US conductor born in England who did a lot to make classical music more popular in America. He was known for his dramatic style. He directed the Philadelphia Orchestra (1912–36) and they played the music for the Walt *Disney film *Fantasia. Stokowski established the American Symphony Orchestra in 1962.

,Oliver 'Stone¹ /stəʊn; AmE 'stoʊn/ (1946–) a US director, producer and writer of films. His films have been very successful but sometimes criticized for containing too much violence. They include *Platoon* (1986), *Born on the Fourth of July* (1989) for which he won an *Oscar as Best Director, *The *Doors* (1991), *JFK* (1991), *Natural Born Killers* (1994), *Nixon* (1995) and *Alexander* (2004).

,Sharon 'Stone² /stəʊn; AmE 'stoʊn/ (1958–) a US film actor who had her first major success as an attractive but dangerous woman in *Basic Instinct* (1992). Her other films include *Total Recall* (1990), *Casino* (1995), *Diabolique* (1996), *Sphere* (1998) and *Catwoman* (2004).

▶ **Stone Age Britain**

The earliest **archaeological remains** found in Britain are tools thought to have been made before 12000 BC, when Britain was still attached to the rest of Europe. At a site at Boxgrove in *Sussex the earliest human remains, thought to be 500000 years old, were discovered in the 1990s. Before that the earliest human bones found in Britain were those of a woman from Swanscombe, Kent, who lived about 325000 years ago. In 1912 a skull that had characteristics of both humans and apes had been found in a gravel pit in Sussex. This became known as *Piltdown man. From geological evidence it was calculated that the skull belonged to somebody who lived more than two million years ago. Later scientific tests showed that it was not genuine and that the jaw of an ape had been attached with glue to a human skull and then treated to make it look very old.

Most Stone Age remains in Britain are much later and date from after 4000 BC, the Neolithic period. There is evidence of woodland being cleared for farming, and polished stone axes and fragments of pottery have been found. The remains of a Stone Age village built about 3100 BC can be seen at *Skara Brae in the Orkneys. The houses were buried in sand after a storm in about 2000 BC and only found when another storm in 1850 blew the sand away.

Other Stone Age remains include long *barrows, piles of earth up to 300 feet long, found mainly in England and Wales. They were used as burial mounds and sometimes have several rooms inside containing human and animal remains and pottery. **Henges**, circular areas surrounded by a ditch and a bank, may have been built as meeting places. One of the most impressive is at *Avebury. It is large enough to contain the modern village of Avebury. A **stone circle** made of upright **megaliths** (= very large stones) up to 20 feet/6 metres high was added inside the henge in about 2400 BC, at the end of the Stone Age. The henge at Britain's best-known **prehistoric monument**, *Stonehenge on *Salisbury Plain, also dates from the Stone Age, though the circles of huge stones inside it date from about 2100 BC, the beginning of the *Bronze Age.

Stone'henge /stəʊnˈhendʒ; AmE stoʊnˈhendʒ/ Britain's most famous prehistoric monument, on *Salisbury Plain in southern England. It consists of two circles of large *standing stones, one inside the other. The inner circle consisted of arches made by laying one stone across the tops of two others. Some of these have fallen, but some are still in position. Stonehenge was

built between 3000 and 1500 BC. Nobody knows why it was built, but many people think it was to study the stars and planets or to worship the sun, because a line through its centre would point directly to the position of the rising sun on Midsummer's Day or of the setting sun in midwinter. Since the 1980s young people, including many *hippies and New Age Travellers, have been going there for their own midsummer celebrations, but the police usually prevent them from getting near the stones. Stonehenge was made a *World Heritage Site in 1986.

the ,Stone of 'Scone /'skuːn/ a large stone that was the traditional seat on which the ancient kings of Scotland were crowned. It was used until 1296, when *Edward I had it brought to London and made into part of the *Coronation Chair. For many Scottish people it is an important national symbol, and they asked repeatedly for it to be returned. It was removed from *Westminster Abbey several times by Scottish people who thought that it should be kept in Scotland. In 1996 it was returned to Scotland and can be seen in *Edinburgh Castle.

The 'Stones /'stəʊnz; AmE 'stoʊnz/ ⇨ ROLLING STONES.

'Stonewall /'stəʊnwɔːl; AmE 'stoʊnwɔːl/ **1** (also **the Stonewall riots**) fighting between the police and gay people that took place after the *New York police raided a gay bar, the Stonewall Inn in *Greenwich Village in 1969. It was the first time that large numbers of gay people had resisted arrest and the Gay Liberation Front was formed shortly afterwards. The riot is considered as the event that marked the beginning of the gay rights movement.
2 a group formed in 1989 which campaigns for the rights of gay people in Britain. It is involved in political lobbying (= trying to influence the government), carries out research into issues such as discrimination, and fights legal cases to support equal rights for gay people.

,stop and 'search (in Britain) a police power, part of the *Police and Criminal Evidence Act, to stop a person who is suspected of doing something illegal, such as carrying illegal drugs, to question them and to search them.

,Marie 'Stopes /ˌmaːri 'stəʊps; AmE 'stoʊps/ (1880–1958) a Scottish scientist who was one of the first people to write and teach people about sex and contraception (= ways of preventing a woman from becoming pregnant). She wrote two important books on the subject in 1918, *Married Love* and *Wise Parenthood*. They were both extremely popular and successful, although she was criticized at the time by the Church and the medical profession.

,Tom 'Stoppard /'stɒpaːd; AmE 'staːpaːrd/ (1937–) a British writer of plays, born in Czechoslovakia. His plays are noted for discussing philosophical questions in a clever and humorous way. They include *Rosencrantz and Guildenstern are Dead* (1967), *Jumpers* (1972), *Travesties* (1974), *Arcadia* (1993), *The Invention of Love* (1997) and *The Coast of Utopia* (2002). He has also written many film scripts, including *Shakespeare in Love* (1998). Stoppard was made a *knight in 1997.

,storefront 'church /ˌstɔːfrʌnt; AmE ˌstɔːrfrʌnt/ n (AmE) a religious meeting place in a building that is not a church, e.g a shop/store. Storefront churches are associated especially with *evangelical or informal types of worship.

Stork™ /stɔːk; AmE stɔːrk/ n [U] a British make of margarine (= a substance like butter, but usually made from vegetable oil). It became well known in the 1960s and 1970s when many television advertisements claimed that people could not tell the difference between Stork and butter.

'Stormont /'stɔːmɒnt; AmE 'stɔːrmɑːnt/ **1** a district of eastern *Belfast, in which **Stormont Castle** was built. **2** the usual name for **Stormont Castle**, a large administrative building which was built in the 1920s for the Northern Ireland parliament. The parliament met there until 1972, when *direct rule was introduced, and it is now the home of the *Northern Ireland Assembly.

'Stornoway /'stɔːnəweɪ; AmE 'stɔːrnəweɪ/ a port on the east coast of Lewis with Harris, an island in the Outer *Hebrides. It is the administrative centre of the *Western Isles region of Scotland and an important centre of the *Harris tweed industry.

'Stourhead /'staʊəhed; AmE 'staʊərhed/ a *stately home near *Salisbury in southern England. It was one of the first houses in England to be built in the *Palladian style (in 1725), but is more famous now for its *landscape gardening, which includes an artificial lake and several small buildings in the style of ancient Roman and Greek architecture.

stout n [U] a strong, dark type of beer. See also GUINNESS.

Rex 'Stout /'staʊt/ (1896–1975) a US writer of more than 70 popular mystery stories. Most of them were about Nero Wolfe, a fat detective and his assistant Archie Godwin. They include *Malice in Wonderland* (1940), *Royal Flush* (1965) and *Three Aces* (1971). See also DETECTIVE STORY.

'Harriet 'Beecher 'Stowe /'biːtʃə 'stəʊ; AmE 'biːtʃər 'stoʊ/ (1811–96) a US writer whose best-known work, *Uncle Tom's Cabin*, increased support in the northern states for the movement to free the slaves in the South. She wrote 16 books, including several about life in *New England, such as *The Minister's Wooing* (1859) and *Old Town Folks* (1869).

St 'Pancras /'pæŋkrəs/ a large train station in central London, England, for trains to and from the *Midlands. The main part of the station building was originally a hotel, designed in a *Gothic style by George Gilbert *Scott and completed in 1872. St Pancras also has a *London Underground station which it shares with *King's Cross. From 2007 St Pancras will be a terminus for trains using the *Channel Tunnel.

St ,Patrick's Ca'thedral /,pætrɪks/ the largest *Roman Catholic church in the US, on *Fifth Avenue, New York. It was designed by James Renwick (1818–95) in a mixture of French and English *Gothic styles, and completed in 1879.

St 'Patrick's Day /'pætrɪks/ 17 March, the day celebrated as the national day of Ireland. It is named after St *Patrick, and is a public holiday in Ireland. Many Irish people wear a *shamrock on St Patrick's Day. In the US there are St Patrick's Day parades in *Boston, *Chicago and *New York.

St 'Paul the capital city of the US state of *Minnesota. It is on the *Mississippi River which separates it from *Minneapolis, and the two are known as the 'twin cities'. St Paul was first established in 1840, when it was called Pig's Eye Landing. It became the capital of the Minnesota Territory in 1849. Today it produces computers and other electronic equipment and cars. It has a famous Winter Carnival each year.

St ,Paul's Ca'thedral /,pɔːlz/ (also **St 'Paul's**) a large cathedral in London, England. It was designed in the late 17th century by Sir Christopher *Wren to replace a previous cathedral destroyed in the *Fire of London, and was completed in 1710. It has a large dome, inside which is the famous *Whispering Gallery. The cathedral contains the graves of many famous people, including Lord *Nelson, the Duke of *Wellington and Christopher Wren himself.

> 66 Si monumentum requiris, circumspice. (If you seek a monument, look around you.) 99
> words carved in St Paul's Cathedral with reference to Christopher Wren

,Lytton 'Strachey /,lɪtn 'streɪtʃi/ (1880–1932) an English writer and one of the most famous members of the *Bloomsbury Group. He was noted for his intelligent humour, and for creating a new style of biography full of amusing remarks and without too much respect for the subject of the book. His best-known work is *Eminent Victorians*. He also wrote about Queen *Elizabeth I and Queen *Victoria.

'straight glass n a plain glass with no handle that holds one pint of beer. Most pubs in Britain serve beer in these glasses and also in 'pint pots' which have handles and are made of thicker glass, and many beer drinkers prefer their beer in one type of glass or the other: *Would you like a straight glass or a handle?*

a straight glass and a 'pint pot'

,straight 'ticket n (in US elections) a vote in which a person votes for candidates who are all from the same political party. Compare SPLIT TICKET.

the Strand /strænd/ a street in central London, England, between *Charing Cross and *Fleet Street, with famous theatres and hotels, including the *Savoy Hotel.

the 'Strangers' ,Gallery either of two raised areas of seats in the *House of Commons and the *House of Lords where members of the public can sit and watch the debates.

'Strangeways /'streɪndʒweɪz/ a prison in central *Manchester, England. It was in the news in 1990, when many of the prisoners took part in violent protests against the poor conditions there. One person died and the prison was so badly damaged that it had to be rebuilt. A report on the events recommended major improvements to Britain's prisons.

,Lee 'Strasberg /'stræzbɜːg; AmE 'stræzbɜːrg/ (1901–82) a US actor and stage director, born in Austria. He directed the *Actors' Studio in New York City from 1948 to 1982 and is remembered for training actors in *method acting. His many students included Marlon *Brando, James *Dean, Marilyn *Monroe, Al *Pacino, Robert *De Niro, Dustin *Hoffman, Jack *Nicholson and Jane *Fonda.

the Stra'tegic 'Arms Limi'tation Talks (abbr **SALT**) talks between the US and the USSR to limit their nuclear weapons. The first agreement was signed in 1972 by President *Nixon and the Soviet leader Leonid Brezhnev and was known as the SALT I Treaty. In the SALT II talks in 1979, President *Carter[2] and Brezhnev agreed to more limits, but they were not approved by the US Senate because Soviet forces entered Afghanistan.

the Stra'tegic 'Arms Re'duction Talks (abbr **START**) talks between the US and the USSR to reduce the number of their nuclear weapons. Reductions were made after President *Reagan and the Soviet leader

Mikhail Gorbachev signed the *INF Treaty in 1987 and President *Bush and Gorbachev signed the START Treaty in 1991. START II is an agreement made by the US and Russia to halve stocks of nuclear weapons by 2007.

the Stra,tegic De'fense I,nitiative (*abbr* **SDI**) the plan by US President *Reagan to build a defence in space against nuclear weapons. Its popular name was 'Star Wars'. He announced this in 1983, but it was never built because of the expense and the end of the *Cold War. SDI was cancelled in 1993.

Stra,tegic 'Health Au,thority *n* (*abbr* **SHA**) (in Britain) any of 28 local organizations within the *National Health Service responsible for health services in a particular area.

,Stratford-upon-'Avon /ˌstrætfəd; *AmE* ˌstrætfərd/ (*also* **'Stratford**) the town in *Warwickshire where William *Shakespeare was born. Tourists from all over the world come to see plays at the *Royal Shakespeare Theatre and to visit places associated with Shakespeare, including the house where he was born, the church where he is buried, and Anne *Hathaway's Cottage.

,Igor Stra'vinsky /ˌiːɡɔː strə'vɪnski; *AmE* ˌiːɡɔːr/ (1882–1971) a US composer best known for his ballet music. He was born in Russia and studied with Nikolai Rimsky-Korsakov. He settled in France in 1934 and became a US citizen in 1945. Much of his music was not immediately popular but he is now regarded as one of the greatest 20th-century composers. His best-known works include *The Firebird* (1910), *The Rite of Spring* (1913) and the opera *The Rake's Progress* (1951).

,Jack 'Straw /'strɔː/ (1946–) a British *Labour politician. He became a *Member of Parliament in 1979, and held several important positions in the Labour *Shadow Cabinet before becoming *Home Secretary in the Labour government of 1997. He became *Foreign Secretary in 2001.

,Strawberry 'Hill a large house by the River *Thames, west of London, well known for its *Gothic architecture. Horace *Walpole bought the house in 1749 and added several towers and detailed and complicated decorations. It is one of the earliest examples of the *Gothic Revival, and the style of architecture which it influenced is sometimes referred to as 'Strawberry Hill Gothic'.

,Meryl 'Streep /ˌmerəl 'striːp/ (1949–) a US actor known for her ability to play a wide range of different characters. She won *Oscars for her parts in *Kramer versus Kramer* (1979) and *Sophie's Choice* (1982). Her other films include *The French Lieutenant's Woman* (1981), *Out of Africa* (1986), *The Bridges of Madison County* (1995) and *The Hours* (2002).

The Street (*informal*) a popular name for the British television *soap opera *Coronation Street*.

A ,Streetcar Named 'Desire a powerful play (1947) by the US writer Tennessee *Williams which won the *Pulitzer Prize. The main characters are a rough and aggressive man called Stanley Kowalski and his wife's delicate sister Blanche DuBois who is driven mad by Kowalski when he visits them in *New Orleans. A film version (1951) directed by Elia *Kazan, with Marlon *Brando and Vivien *Leigh, won four *Oscars.

▶ **street names**

In Britain, main *roads outside towns and cities are known by numbers rather than names. An exception is the A1 from London to north-eastern England, which is often called the Great North Road. Roads that follow the line of former *Roman roads also have names, e.g. the *Fosse Way. If a main road passes through a town, that part of it usually has a name, often that of the place which the road goes to, e.g. London Road.

The main shopping street in a town is often called High Street, or sometimes Market Street. Many streets take their name from a local feature or building. The most common include Bridge Street, Castle Street, Church Street, Mill Street and Station Road. Some names indicate the trade that was formerly carried on in that area. Examples are Candlemaker's Row, Cornmarket, Petticoat Lane and Sheep Street. Many streets laid out in the 19th century were named after famous people or events. These include Albert Street, Cromwell Road, Shakespeare Street, Wellington Street, Trafalgar Road and Waterloo Street. When housing estates are built, the names of the new roads are usually all on the same theme. Names of birds or animals are popular. Others are based on the old names for the fields that the houses were built on, e.g. Tenacres Road, The Slade and Meadow Walk. The name of a road is written on signs at each end of it, sometimes together with the local postcode.

Some streets have become so closely identified with people of a particular profession that the street name itself is immediately associated with them. In London, *Harley Street is associated with private doctors and *Fleet Street with newspapers.

In the US main roads such as interstates and highways are known by numbers. Most towns and cities are laid out on a **grid** pattern and have long **streets** with **avenues** crossing them. Each has a number, e.g. 7th Avenue, 42nd Street. The roads are often straight and have square **blocks** of buildings between them. This makes it easier to find an address and also helps people to judge distance. In *Manhattan, for example, *Tiffany's is described as being at East 57th Street and Fifth Avenue, i.e. on the corner of those two streets. The distance between West 90th Street and West 60th Street is 30 blocks.

As well as having numbers, many streets are named after people, places, local features, history and nature. In Manhattan there is Washington Street, Lexington Avenue, Liberty Street, Church Street and Cedar Street. Some streets are named after the town to which they lead. The most important street is often called *Main Street. A **suburb** or **subdivision** of a city may have streets with similar names. In a subdivision of Baton Rouge, *Louisiana, all the names end in 'wood', e.g. Balsawood Drive, Limewood Drive and Aspenwood Drive.

Some roads are called boulevards, with *Hollywood's *Sunset Boulevard and *Miami's Biscayne Boulevard among the best known. Avenues usually cross streets, as in New York, but often the word is chosen as part of a name for no particular reason. *Avenue* and *boulevard* once indicated roads with trees along each side, but few have trees today. A *road* in the US is usually found outside cities, though Chicago uses the name for some central streets.

Some street names have particular associations: Grant Avenue in *San Francisco is associated with *Chinatown, *Beale Street in *Memphis with the *blues, and Bourbon Street in New Orleans with *jazz. In New York *Wall Street is associated with the financial world, *Madison Avenue with *advertising and *Broadway with theatres.

'Janet 'Street-'Porter /'striːt 'pɔːtə(r)/ (1946–) an English journalist and television presenter and producer. Until 1996 she was in charge of a wide range of *BBC programmes for young people, often humorously referred to as *yoof programmes, and became well known for her strong *cockney accent and unusual clothes.

,Barbra 'Streisand /'straɪsænd/ (1942–) a US actor and singer known for her clear, strong voice. She became a star in the *Broadway musical play *Funny Girl* (1964) and won an *Oscar for its film version (1968). She won another for *Evergreen*, the song she wrote for her film *A Star is Born* (1976). Her many successful songs include *People* (1964) and *The Way We Were* (1973).

the 'Strip **1** the popular name for part of Las Vegas Boulevard, a long street in the centre of *Las Vegas in the US. It has bright, colourful signs at night. Many of the hotels on the Strip have casinos (= gambling clubs). They include Caesar's Palace, Excalibur, Luxor, Treasure Island, the Tropicana and the MGM Grand Hotel and Theme Park.
2 the popular name for *Sunset Boulevard in *Hollywood.

'strip-,farming *n* [U] a system of farming (sometimes called the **open field system**) which was common in *Anglo-Saxon Britain and lasted until the *common land began to be enclosed by fences in the 13th century. Different fields were divided into long strips in which farmers could grow food for their families. Each farmer had several strips of land in different fields, so that the good and bad areas of soil were shared among the community.

'strip ,mining (*especially AmE*) (*BrE also* **'opencast ,mining**) *n* [U] a method of mining coal that is at or near the earth's surface. The surface is removed and the coal is taken from above, instead of digging a deep mine. People sometimes organize campaigns against this type of mining in their area because it leaves the countryside looking very ugly.

The 'Strokes /'strəʊks; *AmE* 'stroʊks/ a US rock band with five members from New York whose first album *Is This It* was released in 2001 and was followed by *Room on Fire* (2003).

St 'Swithin's Day /'swɪðɪnz/ the Christian church festival of St Swithin, held on 15 July. According to traditional belief in Britain, if it rains on this day it will continue to rain for 40 days afterwards.

St ,Thomas's 'Hospital /,tɒməsɪz/ a large *teaching hospital in central London, England, established in the early 12th century and later named after St Thomas *Becket. It moved to its present buildings opposite the *Houses of Parliament(2) in 1871. Since 1993 it has been managed as part of a *hospital trust with *Guy's Hospital.

St 'Trinian's /'trɪnɪənz/ an imaginary *public school(1) for girls in the humorous drawings of Ronald *Searle. The girls are famous for their bad behaviour, and have appeared in several books and films, e.g. *The Belles of Saint Trinian's* (1954).

'Charles 'Edward 'Stuart¹ /'stjuːət; *AmE* 'stuːərt/ ⇨ BONNY PRINCE CHARLIE.

the ,House of 'Stuart² /'stjuːət; *AmE* 'stuːərt/ the name of the family who were kings and queens of Scotland from 1371 to 1714. When *Elizabeth I of England died without any children in 1603, her relative James VI of Scotland became also *James I of England. The Stuarts continued to be kings and queens of England and Scotland until 1714, when the *Act of Settlement made the House of *Hanover the British royal family. See also JACOBITE.

,James 'Stuart³ /'stjuːət; *AmE* 'stuːərt/ (1688–1766) the son of *James II, also called the *Old Pretender. His supporters, the *Jacobites, referred to him as James VIII of Scotland and III of England. He lived in France and Italy for most of his life, and claimed that he had a right to be the king of Britain. He came to Scotland in 1715 to lead the *Fifteen rebellion, but was defeated by the English.

,George 'Stubbs /'stʌbz/ (1724–1806) an English artist. He is famous for his paintings of horses, which show the animals in realistic detail, often with their owners, and sometimes in imaginary situations.

▶ **student life**

The popular image of student life is of young people with few responsibilities enjoying themselves and doing very little work. This is often not true. Many older people now study at college or university, sometimes on a part-time basis while having a job and looking after a family. Many students are highly motivated and work very hard.

In Britain reduced government support for higher education means that students can no longer rely on having their expenses paid for them. Formerly, students received a **grant** towards their living expenses. Now most can only get a **loan**, which has to be paid back. From 1999 they have had to pay a fixed amount towards **tuition fees** and from 2006 universities will be able to increase the amount up to a maximum of £3000 per year. In the US students already have to pay for **tuition** and **room and board**. Many get a **financial aid package** which may include grants, scholarships and loans. The fear of having large debts places considerable pressure on students and many take part-time jobs during the term and work full-time in the vacations.

Many students in Britain go to a university away from their home town. They usually live in a **hall of residence** for their first year, and then move into a rented room in a private house or share a house with **housemates**. They may go back home during vacations, but after they graduate most leave home for good. In the US too, many students attend colleges some distance from where their parents live. They may live **on campus** in one of the halls, or **off campus** in apartments and houses which they share with **roommates**. Some students, especially at larger universities, join a *fraternity or *sorority, a social group usually with its own house near the campus. Fraternities and sororities often have names which are combinations of two or three letters of the Greek alphabet. Some people do not have a good opinion of them because they think that students who are members spend too much time having parties.

In Britain the interests of students are represented by a **student's union** which liaises with the university on academic matters, arranges social events and provides advice to students. Individual unions are affiliated with (= linked to) the *NUS. The student union building is usually the centre of student life and has a bar and common room, and often a restaurant and shops. British universities have a wide range of societies, clubs and social activities including sports, drama and politics. One of the highlights (= main events) of the year is **rag week**, a week of parties and fund-raising activities in support of various charities.

Especially in their first year, US students spend a lot of time on social activities. One of the most important celebrations, especially at universities which place a lot of emphasis on sports, is *homecoming. Many **alumni** (= former students) return to their **alma mater** (= college) for a weekend in the autumn to watch a *football game. During homecoming weekend there are also parties and dances, and usually a parade.

When social activities take up too much time, students **skip lectures** (= miss them) or **cut class** (*AmE*) and **take incompletes** (*AmE*), which means they have to finish their work after the vacation. In the US this has the effect of lowering their course grades, but most US universities expect this behaviour from students and do little to stop it. Students are thought to be old enough to make their own decisions about how hard

S

they work and to accept the consequences. A few students **drop out** (*AmE* **flunk out**) but the majority try hard to get good grades and a good degree.

'Student Non'violent Co'ordinating Com-,mittee (*abbr* **SNCC**) one of the active *African American organizations during the *civil rights movement. It was begun in 1960 by black and white students in Raleigh, *North Carolina. SNCC was against the use of violence until Stokely *Carmichael became its leader in 1966. It ended three years later.

'Students for a Demo'cratic So'ciety (*abbr* **SDS**) an extreme US student political organization in the 1960s which opposed the *Vietnam War. It was begun in 1960 and spread to many colleges and universities. Its members organized street protests which led to arrests outside the Democratic National Convention in *Chicago in 1968. A year later, it divided into smaller groups.

St 'Valentine's Day /'væləntaɪnz/ (*also* **'Valentine's Day**) 14 February, the day on which lovers traditionally send one another *greetings cards called **Valentine cards** or **Valentines**. The cards usually have designs of hearts, etc. on them and often include a sentimental or funny message. People sending Valentine cards do not usually sign their name. Sometimes people have a similar short message printed in a newspaper or magazine, and may also give each other gifts such as flowers or chocolates. The people who send or receive gifts, etc. in this way are also known as **Valentines**.

the St ,Valentine's Day 'Massacre /,væləntaɪnz/ the murder of seven US criminals in *Chicago on 14 February 1929. The men killed were members of 'Bugs' Moran's 'North Side gang' and were shot by a group of Al *Capone's men dressed as police officers. The murders shocked Americans and caused the Chicago police to increase their efforts against Capone. The incident has been shown in many films.

St ,Vincent and the 'Grenadines /'grenədi:nz/ a country consisting of a group of islands in the Caribbean Sea. It was claimed by Britain in 1783 and became an independent member of the *Commonwealth in 1979. Its capital town is Kingstown.

S2P /,es tu: 'pi:/ (*in full* **State Second Pension**) (in Britain) an extra state pension which people receive in addition to the basic state pension. It is based on their average earnings while they were working. Many people are **contracted out** of the S2P scheme because they have a private or company pension.

'Styrofoam™ /'staɪrəfəʊm; *AmE* 'staɪrəfoʊm/ *n* [U] a type of very light plastic material, also called 'expanded polystyrene', made by the US Dow Chemical Company. It is used as protective material for packing things in, and for making many products, such as coffee cups, which can be thrown away after use.

,William 'Styron /'staɪrən/ (1925–) a US writer of powerful novels. He received the *Pulitzer Prize for *The Confessions of Nat Turner* (1967), which some people criticized for its violent story based on the murders committed by the *African-American slave Nat *Turner. Styron's other novels include *Lie Down in Darkness* (1951) and *Sophie's Choice* (1979), which became a successful film (1982).

sub'scription ,television (*also* **subscription TV**, **pay television**, **pay-TV**) *n* [U] (in the US) a commercial television service that is regularly paid for by people who receive it.

su'burbia *n* [U] (*often disapproving*) the suburbs (= areas of towns and cities that are outside the centre, and consist mainly of houses and flats/apartments). Suburbia is also used to refer to the people who live in

the suburbs and their way of life. They are seen as being typically white, *middle-class and opposed to change. Life in suburbia, both in Britain and in the US, is usually considered rather boring: *The former revolutionary settled for a steady job and a house in suburbia.*

'succotash /'sʌkətæʃ/ *n* [U] (*AmE*) a dish of corn and beans cooked together, often with green and red peppers. See also SYLVESTER.

the 'Suez ,Crisis /'su:ɪz/ a series of events that took place in 1956 after the Egyptian government nationalized the Suez Canal. Britain and France, who had owned shares in the Canal, sent groups of soldiers to attack Egypt. This caused shock throughout the world and many arguments in Britain, where some British people thought that the government was right to use the armed forces and show that Britain was still a strong country, but many others were angry at the use of force. The *United Nations and the US were opposed to the British and French action, and after less than two months the soldiers left Egypt. These events made many people realize that European countries such as Britain and France now had much less influence in the world than in the first half of the 20th century, when they still had large empires. See also EDEN.

'Suffolk /'sʌfək/ a county in *East Anglia, eastern England. It consists mainly of agricultural land. The administrative centre is *Ipswich.

,Suffolk 'Punch /,sʌfək 'pʌntʃ/ *n* a breed of British carthorse (= a large strong horse, bred for pulling heavy carts and farm equipment). It is smaller than other carthorses, and usually a reddish-brown colour.

▶**suffragettes**

The US has had major campaigns to win **suffrage** (= the right to vote in political elections) for two groups of people: women and *African Americans. But the word *suffrage* is more closely associated with women's voting rights, and the women who took part in the movement were often called **suffragettes**. Today, most people in the US use the word **suffragists**, as it also includes the men who supported the movement.

The suffrage movement became important in the US in the second half of the 19th century. As early as 1848 a meeting was held in Seneca Falls, New York, to discuss the issue. But only in 1920 was the US *Constitution changed to give women the right to vote. The **Nineteenth Amendment** to the Constitution is sometimes called the **Anthony Amendment**, after Susan B *Anthony, who was an important suffragist.

In the late 19th and early 20th century women in Britain also began to demand the right to vote. After several bills promising them suffrage were defeated in *Parliament, British suffragettes turned to violent protest. As well as holding noisy public meetings they chained themselves to iron railings and broke windows of government buildings. One suffragette, Emily Davison, threw herself in front of the king's horse during a race at *Epsom and died from her injuries. When suffragettes were put in prison many of them went on hunger strike (= refused to eat anything), so that the authorities had to force food into them to keep them alive. Leaders of the campaign, such as Emmeline *Pankhurst, the head of the Women's Social and Political Union, and her daughters Christabel and Sylvia, were imprisoned on many occasions under the terms of the so-called **Cat and Mouse Act** of 1913, which allowed the women out of prison just long enough for them to get well before they were imprisoned again. The campaign was interrupted in 1914 at the start of *World War I, so that women could contribute to the war effort. When the war ended in 1918 the government at last agreed to give the vote to women over 30, partly in recognition of their role in the war. Finally, in 1928, women won equal voting rights with men and were allowed to vote from the age of 21.

'Sugar Puffs™ n [pl] a well-known breakfast food, made by the Quaker Oats Company. It consists of small pieces of crisp wheat covered in sugar, and is eaten with milk. Its most famous advertising character is a large furry yellow creature called the Honey Monster.

,Arthur **'Sullivan**[1] /'sʌlɪvən/ (1842–1900) an English composer. He is best known for the *Savoy Operas, a series of operettas (= light comic operas) he wrote with W S *Gilbert, which show his skill for writing light, often humorous, music. **Gilbert and Sullivan** wrote 14 popular operettas, including The *Mikado and The *Pirates of Penzance, which are still performed regularly in Britain. He also wrote serious operas and other pieces of classical music, but they are less well known than the Savoy Operas. He was made a *knight in 1883.

,Ed **'Sullivan**[2] /'sʌlɪvən/ (1902–74) a US television personality. He is best remembered as the presenter of Toast of the Town (1948–55), later called The Ed Sullivan Show (1955–71), a popular Sunday variety programme on *CBS.

,John L **'Sullivan**[3] /'sʌlɪvən/ (John Lawrence Sullivan 1858–1918) a US boxer who became the World Heavyweight Champion (1882–92), the last to fight without gloves. His popular name was the 'Boston Strong Boy'. The first time Sullivan wore gloves under the *Queensbury Rules, in 1892, he was beaten by 'Gentleman Jim' *Corbett.

,**Sullom 'Voe** /ˌsʌləm 'vəʊ; AmE 'voʊ/ Britain's largest *North Sea oil terminal (= place where an oil pipeline arrives on land), in the *Shetland Islands. It is also a major port for exporting oil.

,**summa cum 'laude** /ˌsʊmə kʊm 'laʊdeɪ/ (in the US) the Latin phrase, meaning 'with highest praise', used to indicate the highest academic achievement of a college or university student who has completed his or her studies. It is written on the student's diploma (= document awarded for completing a course of study). Compare CUM LAUDE, MAGNA CUM LAUDE.

,**Summer Bank 'Holiday** ⇨ AUGUST BANK HOLIDAY.

'summer camp n (especially in the US) a camp where young people go for sports and other outdoor activities for several weeks in the summer. Summer camps are usually private and expensive. They have been a strong tradition in the US since the early 20th century.

,**summer 'pudding** n [C, U] a traditional British sweet dish. It consists of summer fruit, usually berries such as raspberries and blackcurrants, pressed into a case of bread in a bowl. It is then left so that the fruit juice soaks into and colours the bread, and the pudding becomes the shape of the bowl. Summer pudding is eaten cold, often with cream.

The Sun a British *tabloid newspaper, published every day except Sunday. It is owned by Rupert *Murdoch and is well known for its *page-three girls and its stories about scandals (= things that people have done that are considered wrong and shocking). It has been the best-selling daily newspaper in Britain since the 1970s. The phrase **Sun readers** is sometimes used to refer to British people with little education who hold right-wing opinions and have prejudices about women and people from other countries.

the **'Sunbelt** /'sʌnbelt/ an informal name for the southern and south-western US states, usually from *Virginia to *California. Their economic and political power has grown since the 1960s as more people move

from the *Snow Belt and *Rust Belt to the warm climate and new job opportunities of the Sunbelt.

,**Sun 'City** a community in the US state of *Arizona for people of 55 and older. It organizes special activities for its members and provides them with police protection and medical services. It was established by Del Webb in 1960 because of the dry, warm climate of the area. The Del Webb Corporation now has ten Sun City communities in eight states.

the ,**Sundance 'Film ,Festival** /ˌsʌndɑːns; AmE ,sʌndæns/ a film festival started and organized by the actor and director Robert *Redford. It has been held every year in *Utah since 1978 and shows films by independent film makers.

the ,**Sundance 'Kid** /ˌsʌndɑːns; AmE ,sʌndæns/ (1860–1909) the popular name of the US criminal Harry Longbaugh. He got the name after robbing a bank in Sundance, *Nevada. He was associated for a long time with Butch *Cassidy.

the ,**Sunday Ex'press** a British *Sunday paper, published by the same company as the *Express. Like the Express, it is a *tabloid newspaper that puts forward moderate right-wing opinions. It has a *colour supplement called the Sunday Express Magazine.

the ,**Sunday 'Mirror** a British *Sunday paper, published by the same company as the *Mirror. Like the Mirror, it is a *tabloid newspaper that puts forward moderate left-wing opinions. It has a *colour supplement called the Sunday Mirror Magazine.

the ,**Sunday 'papers** n [pl] (in Britain) newspapers that are sold only on Sundays. Most are published by companies which also publish daily newspapers on the other days of the week, and they usually have the same style, opinions and type of stories as their equivalent daily papers. For example, The Independent on Sunday is similar to The *Independent. Sunday papers have more pages than daily newspapers, and are usually divided into several sections, such as sport, news and the arts. Many of them also have *colour supplements: We spent the whole afternoon in the garden reading the Sunday papers.

the ,**Sunday 'Post** a Scottish *Sunday paper, first published in 1914. It is Scotland's best-selling newspaper and its traditional Scottish opinions and moral values make it popular with many Scottish people living in other countries.

,**Sunday 'roast** (also ,**Sunday 'joint**) n a large piece of meat, usually beef, lamb or pork, cooked in an oven. The Sunday roast/joint is the main part of the traditional lunch that many British families eat on Sundays, usually with potatoes, vegetables and gravy (= sauce made from the juice of cooked meat). See also YORKSHIRE PUDDING.

'Sunday school n [U, C] religious education classes for children held on Sundays. They are usually given in a church building by a priest or an adult member of the church. The first Sunday schools were held in Britain in the 1780s. In the US they are also called **Sabbath schools**.

the ,**Sunday 'Sport** a British *tabloid newspaper sold on Sundays and first published in 1986. It consists mainly of photographs of naked or nearly naked women, sports news and ridiculous 'news' articles that are invented by the writers. Although many people buy it, it is not generally considered a serious newspaper. See also DAILY SPORT.

the ,**Sunday 'Telegraph** a British *Sunday paper, published by the same company as the *Daily Telegraph. Like the Daily Telegraph, it is a *broadsheet newspaper that expresses right-wing opinions and traditional,

S

*Conservative attitudes. It has a *colour supplement and is well known for its detailed news and sports reports. It was first published in 1961.

the ˌ**Sunday** '**Times** a British *Sunday paper, published by the same company as The *Times. It is a *broadsheet newspaper that expresses moderate right-wing opinions. It is Britain's best-selling Sunday paper, and was the first British newspaper to introduce a *colour supplement in the 1960s. The Sunday Times was first published in 1822.

ˌ**Sunday** '**trading** n [U] the practice of opening shops for business on Sundays. Traditionally, most British shops did not open on Sundays except for newsagents and some *corner shops. In the past, even *pubs could only open for a few hours on Sunday afternoon and evening. In the 1980s and 1990s the government made the laws on Sunday trading less strict, allowing pubs and small shops to open all day, and large shops such as supermarkets to open for six hours. Now major shopping centres such as *Oxford Street in London are busy seven days a week. Some religious groups are still opposed to all forms of Sunday trading.

In the US, individual states and sometimes counties make the laws on Sunday trading. Some businesses, such as restaurants and petrol/gasoline stations, have opened on Sunday through most of the 20th century. Many other businesses started to open on Sunday in the 1960s, though religious groups have opposed this. In some parts of the country it is illegal to sell alcohol on Sunday.

'**Sunderland** /'sʌndələnd; AmE 'sʌndərlənd/ a city and port in north-east England. In the *Industrial Revolution it was an important centre for the coal and shipbuilding industries, and many people lost their jobs in the region when these industries became less active in the 1980s. It is now an *assisted area.

ˌ**Sunset** '**Boulevard** a famous street in *Hollywood, also called 'the Strip' or 'Sunset Strip', where many early film companies had their offices. Charlie *Chaplin also lived there. The Boulevard now has shops and restaurants as well as businesses. Sunset Boulevard was the title of a famous film (1950) about an old film star, and of a *musical (1994) based on it by Andrew *Lloyd Webber.

SUNY /'su:ni/ ⇨ STATE UNIVERSITY OF NEW YORK.

the '**Super Bowl** the US football game that decides the *National Football League Championship. It is played each January between the winners of the *American Football Conference and the *National Football Conference. The first Super Bowl was played in 1967.

'**Superglue**™ /'su:pəglu:; AmE 'su:pərglu:/ n [U] a make of very strong liquid glue that sticks things together very quickly. It is sold in small tubes: You can mend it with Superglue but be careful not to get any on your fingers.

'**superhighway** n **1** ⇨ EXPRESSWAY.
2 used to refer to a large electronic network, especially the *Internet.

ˌ**Lake Su**'**perior** /su:'pɪəriə(r); AmE su:'pɪriər; BrE also sju:'pɪəriə(r)/ the largest of the *Great Lakes, and the world's largest lake of fresh water. Its area is 31 820 square miles/82 414 square kilometres. It is the most western of the Great Lakes and is connected to Lake *Huron by the Sault Sainte Marie Canals. It is surrounded by the states of *Michigan, *Wisconsin and *Minnesota and by Ontario in Canada. The main port is Duluth, Minnesota.

'**Superliner** /'su:pəlaɪnə(r); AmE 'su:pərlaɪnər; BrE also 'sju:pəlaɪnə(r)/ n a type of US train run by *Amtrak. It is mainly used over long distances west of *Chicago. Superliner carriages have two levels with large windows for passengers to watch the scenery, and there are also Superliner Sleeping Cars.

'**Superman**™ /'su:pəmæn; AmE 'su:pərmæn; BrE also 'sju:pəmæn/ the best-known hero of US comic books. He was created by the writer Jerry Siegel and the artist Joseph Shuster, and first appeared in 1938 in Action Comics. The character began in newspapers a year later and has been used for novels, radio and television programmes and several films, including four with Christopher *Reeve (the first of them in 1978). Superman has special powers, including great strength and the ability to fly. He uses these powers to fight evil and danger. He only appears when he is needed. For the rest of the time he is Clark Kent, a rather dull and timid journalist. His girlfriend is Lois Lane but she is in love with Superman, not knowing his other identity. One of Superman's regular enemies is Lex Luther. The only thing that can harm Superman is a green mineral called *kryptonite which makes him lose all his powers.
⇨ note at COMICS AND COMIC STRIPS.

▶ **superstitions**

Superstitions are beliefs that certain things or events will bring good or bad **luck**. Many people believe that luck plays an important part in their lives, and they **wish somebody luck** (= say 'good luck') in many situations such as before an exam or an interview for a job. People learn superstitions while they are children, and though few adults will admit to being **superstitious**, many act on superstitions out of habit. Most superstitions are centuries old, and British and American people have many in common.

People are also interested in **fate** (= a power that controls everything) and in knowing what will happen to them in the future. Most people know which **sign of the zodiac** they were born under, and read their **horoscope** or **stars** in *magazines, though only a few take it seriously.

There are many well-known **omens** (= signs) of bad luck, some of which have a religious origin. The number 13 is considered unlucky because there were 13 people (Jesus and the twelve Apostles) at the Last Supper. Tall buildings often do not have a 13th floor; instead the numbers go from 12 to 14. Some people believe they will have a bad day when the 13th day of the month falls on a Friday (**Friday the 13th**) and don't like to travel then. In Britain the **magpie** is widely considered an unlucky bird and has been associated with the Devil. The number of magpies seen is important: 'One for sorrow, two for joy, three for a girl, four for a boy.'

A well-known cause of bad luck is to **walk under a ladder** leaning against a wall. **Treading on cracks** between paving slabs is also bad luck, and it is unwise to **cross on the stairs** (= pass somebody going in the opposite direction). A person who **breaks a mirror** will have seven years' bad luck. It is unlucky to **spill salt**, but bad luck can be avoided by throwing a little of it over the left shoulder with the right hand. People should not **open an umbrella indoors** as this will annoy the sun. Some people think it is bad luck to let a **black cat** cross in front of them; others think black cats bring good luck, and they give paper black cats as tokens at *weddings.

Some people carry a **lucky charm**, such as a rabbit's foot or a special coin. Finding a **four-leaf clover** (= a clover plant with four leaves instead of the usual three) is also lucky. People sometimes place an old **horseshoe** over the front door of their house. It must be hung with both ends pointing upwards; if it is hung upside down the luck will run out through the gap. Sports teams and military regiments often have a lucky

mascot, usually an animal or a model of an animal, which travels with them.

Rituals are actions that people believe are necessary in order to have good luck. When people talk about something that they hope will **come true** (= happen), they may touch something made of wood and say 'touch wood' (*AmE* 'knock on wood'). If something goes badly for somebody on two occasions, people may say 'third time lucky' (*AmE* 'third time's charm'). If people fear that they have **tempted fate** (= assumed too confidently that everything will go well), they may **cross their fingers** to protect their good luck. Actors believe that wishing somebody good luck will bring them the opposite, and often say 'break a leg' instead. They also think it is unlucky to call Shakespeare's play *Macbeth* by its name and prefer to call it 'the Scottish play' instead.

There are many other ways, apart from reading a horoscope, of finding out what will happen in the future. **Fortune-tellers** at fairs use a **crystal ball** or **read a palm** (= look at the lines on a person's hand) to **foretell** the future. Other people use **tarot cards** (= special cards with pictures on) or **read tea leaves** (= look at the size and arrangement of tea leaves left after a cup of tea). Some people take all this seriously but many treat it as fun.

There are superstitions that apply to the weather. A well-known rhyme is 'Red sky at night, shepherd's delight; red sky in the morning, shepherd's warning'. In the US *sailor's* replaces *shepherd's*. (A red sky in the evening means good weather ahead, while a red sky in the morning means storms are coming). British people believe that if it rains on 15 July (*St Swithin's Day) it will rain every day for the next 40 days. On *Groundhog Day, 2 February, Americans look for a groundhog coming out of its hole. If it sees its shadow (i.e. if it is sunny) then winter will last a lot longer, but if it sees no shadow, winter is almost over.

It is common for people to say 'bless you' or 'gesundheit' (German for 'good health') when somebody sneezes. This was originally said in order to prevent a person's soul being sneezed out of their body.

▶ **the Supreme Court**

The **judicial** branch is one of the three branches of US *federal government and operates the system of law courts. The Supreme Court in *Washington, DC is the highest court in the US, and is very powerful. It has nine judges, called **justices**. Traditionally, they are called the **nine old men**, although in 1981 Sandra Day O'Connor became the first woman justice. The head of the court has the title of **Chief Justice of the United States**. Justices are appointed by the *President, although the *Senate must confirm (= give its approval to) the choice.

Some of the power of the Supreme Court was given to it in the *Constitution. In 1803, in a famous case called *Marbury v Madison, the Court gave itself the additional power of **judicial review**. This means that it has the power to decide if a law is constitutional (= follows the principles of the Constitution). If a law is said to be **unconstitutional**, it cannot be put into effect unless it is added to the Constitution, a long and difficult process that has succeeded only 27 times in more than 200 years. In this way the Supreme Court has the power to block laws made by the US government and state as well as local laws.

The Supreme Court is a court of appeal and hears cases on appeal that were first heard in the lower courts. It can hear only a small number of appeals and so tries to choose cases that involve important principles of law. Once the Court has decided a case, lower courts use it as a **precedent**, i.e. they follow the Supreme Court's decision in similar cases.

Many of the Supreme Court's decisions are famous because they changed some aspect of US life. For instance, in the cases *Scott v Sandford (1857), *Plessy v Ferguson (1896) and *Brown v Board of Education (1954) the Court made important decisions about the rights of African Americans. In *Miranda v Arizona (1966) the Court said that police officers must inform the people they arrest of their constitutional rights. In 1978, the decision in *Regents of the University of California v *Bakke upheld (= supported) *affirmative action but made *reverse discrimination illegal. This means that, when trying to give more opportunities to women, African Americans and minority groups, people cannot deny members of other groups fair treatment. The *Roe v Wade decision of 1973 gave women across the US the right to abortion. The decision in *US v Nixon (1974) required President *Nixon to hand over evidence that later led to his having to resign.

the Su,preme Court 'Building /suːˌpriːm kɔːt ˈbɪldɪŋ; *BrE also* sjuː-/ the building in Washington, DC, on *Capitol Hill, where the US *Supreme Court meets. It was built in 1935 and is the last of the national government buildings in the Greek style. Visitors can tour the building when the court is not sitting.

the Supreme Court Building

The Su'premes /suːˈpriːmz; *BrE also* sjuː-/ a US female pop group. They formed in 1959 in *Detroit as The Primettes. The original members were Diana *Ross, Mary Wilson (1944–) and Florence Ballard (1943–76). They joined *Motown(2) Records in 1960, became The Supremes, and had such hits as *Baby Love* (1964) and *Stop! In the Name of Love* (1965). Ross left in 1970 and the group continued with different singers until 1976.

'**surfing** *n* [U] a sport and hobby in which people ride waves in the ocean while standing on a narrow board called a **surfboard**. Surfing is very popular in the US, especially in *Hawaii and *California and also in the UK, in *Cornwall. The culture which often surrounds surfing includes a relaxed, informal style of dress and a relaxed, outdoor lifestyle.

,**Surgeon 'General** the head of the US Public Health Service and the senior medical officer in the US. The Surgeon General is responsible for protecting people's health, and Surgeon General's warnings about the dangers of smoking are printed on every cigarette packet.

▶ **surnames**

In Britain and the US surnames, also called **last names** or **family names**, pass from fathers or, in some cases, mothers to their children. Traditionally, women change their surname when they marry, replacing their **maiden name**, the surname they had from birth, with the surname of their husband. In the US especially, some women keep their maiden name as a middle name. Others choose to keep their maiden name as their surname after they are married. A few create a **double-barrelled** name (*AmE* **hyphenated name**) from the two surnames, such as Johnson-Brown. In a few cases the husband and children may also take this name. In Britain a double-barrelled surname used to suggest an upper-class background, but this is no longer always so.

In the US, laws about changing a last name, whether after marriage or for some other reason, vary from state to state, but it is usually a simple process and in some states people can just begin to use a new name if they want to. In Britain a woman can change her surname automatically after marriage. If people wish to change their name for any other reason they can do so by **deed poll**, a simple legal procedure.

In fact people rarely change their surname except after marriage, and many people are able to research their family history over many centuries. Most families were known by surnames by 1300 and many of the old names are still common. Sometimes the names reflected the place where the family lived, such as the name of their village or a reference to a feature of the local countryside, e.g. *Ford*, *Hill* or *Wood*. Other surnames refer to the original occupation or trade of the family, e.g. *Baker*, *Miller*, *Shepherd* and *Smith*. Sometimes the surname began as a *nickname. For instance, someone with dark hair or dark skin might be called *Black*, *Blake* or *Brown*. Some surnames were taken from personal names, as in *Andrews*, *Martin* and *Roberts*. Others were based on French names that came to Britain during the *Norman Conquest, e.g. *Sinclair* from the French 'Saint-Clair'.

Many surnames occur throughout Britain, but others suggest a particular regional origin. Many Scottish names begin with *Mc-* or *Mac-*, meaning 'son of', e.g. *McDonald* and *MacGregor*. Members of a *clan added this prefix to their father's name. Irish surnames often begin with *O'*, meaning 'descended from', e.g. *O'Brien*. Many Irish surnames are derived from ancient *Celtic names. Common Welsh surnames include *Evans*, *Morgan*, *Price*, *Rees* and *Williams*. The most common surname in England and Scotland is *Smith*, closely followed by *Jones*, a name also widely found in Wales. Other surnames were brought to Britain by families from India, Pakistan, Bangladesh and China. These include *Ahmed*, *Hussain*, *Khan*, *Patel*, *Singh* and *Tsang*.

All the surnames found in Britain are also found in the US, together with many others from all over the world. Some people wanted to sound more American when they arrived in the US and so took English last names. Sometimes government officials could not understand the names of new arrivals and wrote similar English names on their documents. Many Americans of German origin changed their names during the two world wars. *African Americans whose ancestors were slaves do not know what last names their families originally had. Many have English or Irish names, because slaves had to take the names of their owners.

When British and American people introduce themselves they give their **first name** and then their surname, e.g. Michael Johnson, Linda Johnson. The opposite order 'Johnson, Michael' is used only in alphabetical lists. In informal situations people often give only their first name. When people are addressed formally a title is put before their last name, usually **Mr** for men and **Mrs**, **Miss** or **Ms** for women. Married women used always to be called Mrs Johnson, etc. Unmarried women were known as Miss Johnson, etc. Many women now prefer the title *Ms* because, like *Mr*, it does not give any information about whether the person is married. Other titles include **Dr** for medical doctors and people with a doctorate and **General**, **Colonel**, etc. for people holding military ranks. People can be addressed as Dr Jones, Professor Roberts etc. or simply as Doctor (for a medical doctor) and Professor. Men especially may be referred to simply by their last name, e.g. *the previous president*

was Clinton, but addressing somebody in this way can seem old-fashioned or may cause offence.

'Surrey /'sʌri/ a county in south-east England, southwest of London. It consists of some agricultural land and many small towns in the *stockbroker belt for people who work in London. The administrative centre is Kingston upon Thames.

Sur'vival a popular British television series about nature. Each programme described the life of a particular wild animal. It was broadcast on *ITV from the 1960s until the 1990s.

'Sussex /'sʌsɪks/ a former county on the coast of southeast England. In 1974 it was divided into the smaller administrative counties of *East Sussex and *West Sussex, but many people still refer to the whole area as Sussex.

'Sustrans /'sʌstrænz/ (*in full* **Sustainable transport**) a British charity which encourages people to walk, cycle and use public transport rather than private cars in order to reduce motor traffic. Its projects include the *National Cycle Network.

,**Rosemary 'Sutcliff** /'sʌtklɪf/ (1920–92) an English writer of novels. She wrote both adults' and children's literature, mostly set in *Roman Britain, but is best known for her books for older children, including *The Eagle of the Ninth* (1954).

,**Peter 'Sutcliffe** /'sʌtklɪf/ ⇨ YORKSHIRE RIPPER.

,**Graham 'Sutherland** /'sʌðələnd; *AmE* 'sʌðərlənd/ (1903–80) an English artist. He is well known for his portraits, landscapes and religious art. He painted many pictures of *World War II and the Welsh countryside, but his best-known works are a tapestry (= a picture made by sewing coloured threads on a cloth) of Christ in *Coventry Cathedral, and a portrait of Winston *Churchill which was later destroyed by Churchill's wife because he did not like it.

,**Sutton 'Hoo** /,sʌtn 'huː/ an area of *Suffolk, England, where an *Anglo-Saxon ship was found buried in 1939. It was full of treasure and many people think that a 7th–century king was buried in it. The treasure is now in the *British Museum.

Sven'gali /sven'gɑːli/ *n* (*pl* **Svengalis**) a person who controls what another person does in a mysterious way that is hard to resist, usually for dishonest or evil reasons. The original Svengali is a character in *Trilby*, a novel by George *du Maurier: *Her manager, a Svengali figure rarely in the public eye, was the main influence in her life.*

,**Jimmy 'Swaggert** /'swægət; *AmE* 'swægərt/ (1935–) a well-known US *televangelist who lost many supporters in 1988 when it became known that he had visited prostitutes. Swaggert appeared on television asking to be forgiven, and he still broadcasts from his church in Baton Rouge, *Louisiana. He is the cousin of the singer Jerry Lee *Lewis.

,**Swallows and 'Amazons** /,swɒləʊz; ˈæməzənz; *AmE* ,swɑːloʊz/ the first in a series of children's books (1930) by Arthur *Ransome. The series describes the adventures of four children sailing small boats in the *Lake District, and is still popular among British children.

'Swanee /'swɒni; *AmE* 'swɑːni/ a song made popular by Al *Jolson. It was written by George *Gershwin and Irving Caesar for the *Broadway musical play *The Capitol Revue* (1919). Jolson added it later that year to a play he was appearing in, called *Sinbad*.

,**Swanee 'River** ⇨ OLD FOLKS AT HOME.

,**Donald 'Swann** /'swɒn; *AmE* 'swɑːn/ ⇨ FLANDERS AND SWANN.

the **Swan of 'Avon** /ˈeɪvn/ a *nickname for William *Shakespeare. It was invented by Ben *Jonson in a poem he wrote in the *First Folio. The phrase refers to the swans (= large white water birds with long necks) on the River *Avon at *Stratford, where Shakespeare was born, and also to the ancient Greek belief that the souls of poets pass into swans.

'Swansea /ˈswɒnzi; AmE ˈswɑːnzi/ a city and port on the south coast of Wales. It used to be an important port and a major centre of the Welsh coal, metal and ship-building industries. As these industries became less important towards the end of the 20th century the city was developed as a tourist centre. It is the nearest city to the *Gower Peninsula and the *Brecon Beacons. The city and its surrounding area are governed by a unitary authority. See also DVLA.

'Swanson™ /ˈswɒnsn; AmE ˈswɑːnsn/ the name used for a range of frozen food dinners originally produced in 1954 by C A Swanson & Sons. The original 'TV dinners' were frozen on metal trays which could be quickly heated.

Gloria 'Swanson /ˈswɒnsn; AmE ˈswɑːnsn/ (1897–1983) a US actor who was a leading star of silent films in the 1920s. She is best remembered, however, for her part as an old film star in Sunset Boulevard (1950). She was married six times.

the **Swan 'Theatre** a small theatre in *Stratford-upon-Avon which was built in the 1980s for the *Royal Shakespeare Company. It is next to the company's main theatre and was designed to be like the theatres of *Elizabethan and *Jacobean times.

swan-'upping /ˈʌpɪŋ/ n [U] a ceremony that takes place every summer on the River *Thames, in which groups of people in boats mark swans (= large white water birds with long necks) to show who owns them. Most swans in Britain belong to the queen, but in the 15th century a few groups of swans on the Thames were given to two of the *City of London's *livery companies. The young birds descended from these groups are marked each year to distinguish them from the royal swans.

Swar'fega™ /swɔːˈfiːgə; AmE swɔːrˈfiːgə/ n [U] a thick, soft, green substance that is used for cleaning oil, paint and similar materials from the skin.

'Swaziland /ˈswɑːzɪlænd/ a small country in south-east Africa, between *South Africa and Mozambique. It was under the control of the Boers until the *Boer War, when it became a British protectorate (= a country controlled and protected by Britain). It became an independent member of the *Commonwealth in 1968. Swaziland is ruled by a king who chooses the prime minister and the cabinet. It has many cultural and economic links with South Africa. Its capital city is Mbabane and its official languages are Swazi and English.

▶ **swear words**

Many people find **swearing** offensive and it is safest to avoid doing it. Swear words are used mainly in two situations: to relieve feelings of anger and frustration when something bad happens, and to show your anger to somebody who has upset you. The words used often lose their normal meaning and act simply as a way of expressing feelings. Swear words are usually short and have a strong sound that can be spat out. Since many swear words have four letters they are sometimes called **four-letter words**.

Like *slang expressions, swear words come in and out of fashion and over time often lose their power to shock. They are replaced by new, stronger words, though the outdated words may continue to be used by older people. Exclamations such as Drat!, Blow! and Blast!, for instance, are now rarely heard among young people, although the older generation still use them.

Swear words are also called **bad language** and swear words that refer to sex or to bodily functions are called **dirty language** or **obscene language**. Other swear words have a religious origin and are sometimes called **oaths**. Many were used for **cursing** (= asking for the help of a supernatural power to punish somebody). Often, obscene and religious language are combined, as in the expression Fucking hell! A person who is very angry and using a lot of swear words may be said to be **cursing and swearing** or **effing and blinding**.

The most common oaths include Heavens above! and Oh, Lord!, and the stronger Damn!, God! Christ!, Jesus Christ! and For Chrissake! which may cause offence to Christians. Many people are upset when they hear obscene language. The strongest swear words include Fuck! and Shit! Other things people say when they are angry or annoyed are Bugger! (BrE), Dang! (AmE) and Darn! (AmE). Swear words used to insult people include Bastard!, Bitch!, Son of a bitch!, Asshole!, Cunt! and, especially in the US, Motherfucker!

Expressions with 'it' added such as in Damn it! and Fuck it! are used as alternatives to the single word. When 'off' is added, as in Fuck off!, its derivative Eff off!, Piss off! and Bog off!, the expressions take on the meaning of 'Go away!'

The words fucking, frigging, chuffing (BrE) and freaking (AmE) are used as intensifiers (= words that strengthen the meaning of a word) in expressions like Fucking hell! and You're a freaking liar! Damn, and the stronger bloody (BrE), are used before nouns, as in a damn nuisance and You bloody fool!

Some people feel strongly that it is always wrong to swear and do not like to hear others swearing. The angrier the tone of voice, the more unpleasant and frightening it is likely to be. Other people swear only when a situation makes them very upset. But some people use swear words in almost every sentence. People may apologize if they use a swear word in front of somebody who does not approve of swearing, possibly by saying 'Pardon my French'. Some people may use an ordinary word or a mild swear word in place of the stronger one they would really like to say. People may say Sugar!, for example, instead of Shit!, though this is now rather old-fashioned. Children are usually not allowed by their parents to swear, and so often find bad words especially interesting.

When strong swear words are spoken on television they may be **bleeped out** (= replaced by a high-pitched noise) to avoid causing offence. Some words may not be used during times when children might hear them. Film classifications are based partly on the language used in them. Newspapers and books may leave out some of the letters in swear words, for example printing fuck as f***. As a result this is sometimes known as 'the F-word'. See also SLANG.

Sweeney 'Todd /ˌswiːni ˈtɒd; AmE ˈtɑːd/ an imaginary character, also known as the 'demon barber of Fleet Street', who first appeared in 18th–century English cheap magazines and plays. He is a London barber (= a person whose job is to cut men's hair and shave them) who kills his customers by cutting their throats and then sells their bodies to be made into meat pies. Sweeney Todd, a musical show with words and music by Stephen *Sondheim, opened on *Broadway in 1979.

Sweet 'N 'Low™ /ˌswiːt ən ˈləʊ; AmE ˈloʊ/ n [U] a US product name for an artificial sweet substance used instead of sugar in drinks and foods. It is made in *Brooklyn by the Cumberland Packing Corporation.

Graham 'Swift[1] /ˈswɪft/ (1949–) an English writer whose best-known novels include Waterland (1983) and

Last Orders (1996), which won the *Booker Prize and was made into a film in 2001 starring Michael *Caine and Bob Hoskins.

ˌ**Jonathan 'Swift²** /'swɪft/ (1667–1745) an Irish writer, best known as the author of *Gulliver's Travels*. He was the dean (= priest in charge of the other priests) of St Patrick's Cathedral in *Dublin, but also spent much time in London, where he knew many important writers and politicians. He is considered one of the greatest satirists (= writers who use humour to criticize people and things such as the social and political systems) in English literature. He also wrote poetry.

ˌ**Algernon 'Swinburne** /ˌældʒənən 'swɪnbɜːn; *AmE* ˌældʒərnən 'swɪnbɜːrn/ (1837–1909) an English poet and critic. He was a very skilful writer, but his lack of respect for the Christian religion and the sexual themes in his poetry shocked many people in *Victorian(1) Britain. His best-known work includes three plays about *Mary Queen of Scots and the poem *Tristram of Lyonesse* (1882). He was a close friend of Dante Gabriel *Rossetti and the other *Pre-Raphaelites.

swing *n* [U] a type of US *jazz dance music played especially by *big bands in the 1930s and 1940s. The band leader Benny *Goodman was called 'the King of Swing', and other swing bands included those of Glenn *Miller and Jimmy and Tommy *Dorsey. The word *swing* had been used to refer to all *jazz music in the early 1930s.

ˌ**Swing 'Low, ˌSweet 'Chariot** a US *spiritual. It is well known in Britain, where it is often sung at matches by supporters of the English national *Rugby Union team.

ˌ**Tilda 'Swinton** /'swɪntən/ (1960–) an English actor who became famous in 1995 when she appeared as a live exhibit at a *London art gallery, asleep in a glass box. Her films include *Orlando* (1992), *The Beach* (2000), *Vanilla Sky* (2001) and *Young Adam* (2003).

the ˌ**Swiss ˌRe 'Tower** /ˌriː/ a tall office building in the *City of London, the head office of the **Swiss Reinsurance Company**, which opened in 2004. Its unusual round shape which narrows to a point at the top has led to it being called **the Gherkin** (= a small pickled cucumber). It was designed by Norman *Foster and has many features which mean that it uses 50% less energy than a traditional office building.

the ˌ**sword in the 'stone** (in the stories about King *Arthur) the magic sword *Excalibur, which Arthur as a boy is able to pull out of the large stone in which it is fixed. By doing this he shows that he will be the next king of England.

ˌ**Eric 'Sykes** /'saɪks/ (1923–) an English comedian. He is a tall thin man with a funny sad expression who has written and appeared in many films and television programmes. He is best known for his work on television with the comedian Hattie Jacques.

Syl'vester /sɪl'vestə(r)/ a character in *Warner Brothers cartoons from the 1940s to the 1960s. He is a cat who keeps trying to catch a small bird called *Tweety Pie, but never succeeds. He spits when he talks and often says 'Sufferin' succotash!' when he is surprised or angry.

ˌ**J M 'Synge** /'sɪŋ/ (John Millington Synge 1871–1909) an Irish writer of plays. W B *Yeats persuaded him to write about the life of Irish peasants (= poor farmers). His plays use the language of ordinary country people in a dramatic way. His best-known work, *The Playboy of the Western World* (1907), is the story of a man who arrives in a small community and pretends that he has killed his father. Many Irish people were angry at the idea that Irish peasants would welcome a murderer and treat him with respect. There were protests when the play was first performed at the Abbey Theatre in *Dublin, but it is now considered one of the greatest plays in Irish literature.

S

T t

/ˌtiː ˈeɪ/ ⇨ TERRITORIAL ARMY.

Ta'basco™ (*also* **ˌTabasco 'sauce**) *n* [U] a very spicy sauce made from red peppers, vinegar and salt. It is used to flavour food and often *Bloody Mary drinks.

The 'Tablet a British magazine, first published in 1840 which contains articles about issues related to the *Roman Catholic Church. It is published every week and is sold around the English-speaking world.

'table ˌtennis (*also* **'ping-pong**) *n* [U] a game like tennis that is played with small hard bats and a small plastic ball on a table with a net across it. It is a popular children's game, but is also played seriously as an international sport. It was invented in Britain in the mid 19th century.

'tabloid *n* (*sometimes disapproving*) a newspaper with pages that are half the size of those of larger newspapers (called *broadsheets*). Most of Britain's most popular newspapers are tabloids. These include the *Sun, the *Mirror, the *Express and the *Daily Mail. Although some tabloids are serious newspapers and the broadsheets also have tabloid editions, many people talk about **tabloid journalism** or the **tabloid press** to refer to a type of newspaper that contains many articles about sex, sport and famous people, and little serious news, and is often insulting to women and people from other countries. The word *tabloid* is less widely used in the US, where most of the important national newspapers are of a regular size. The best-known US tabloid, which uses short articles and large photographs, is the *New York Daily News. Serious tabloids include the *Chicago Sun-Times*. Compare BROADSHEET.

ˌTaco 'Bell™ /ˌtɑːkəʊ; *AmE* ˌtɑːkoʊ/ any of a large group of US *fast food restaurants serving Mexican food, both in the US and in many other countries. The first was opened in 1962 in Downey, *California.

'William 'Howard 'Taft /ˈtæft/ (1857–1930) the 27th US *President (1909–13). He was a *Republican(1) who had earlier been the US Secretary of War (1904). As President, he created the Department of Labor and continued the foreign policies of President Theodore *Roosevelt. He was later Chief Justice of the *Supreme Court (1921–30), and is the only person to have been the head of two different divisions of the US government.

the ˌTaft-'Hartley Act /ˌtæft 'hɑːtli; *AmE* 'hɑːrtli/ an important US law passed in 1947 to restrict strikes. It gave the US President the power to stop strikes for 80 days if they represented a national emergency. It also set up a special committee to settle labour disputes. The bill, which was opposed by President *Truman, was introduced by Senator Robert A Taft and Representative Fred Hartley.

ˌtake the 'Fifth ⇨ FIFTH AMENDMENT.

A ˌTale of Two 'Cities a novel (1859) by Charles *Dickens, set in London and Paris at the time of the French Revolution. Charles Darnay is a young French aristocrat who disagrees with the cruel way his family has been treating poor people. He moves to London and falls in love with Lucie, the daughter of an old doctor who had been put in prison by Darnay's family. Darnay marries Lucie before going back to France to rescue an old servant, but he is arrested there and condemned to death. He is saved by an Englishman, Sidney Carton,

who is also in love with Lucie. The two men look very similar, and Sidney takes Charles's place on the scaffold (= the structure on which people are killed in public). The book ends with his thoughts as he walks to his death, which form one of the most famous sentences in English literature:

> 66 It is a far, far better thing that I do, than I have ever done; it is a far, far better rest that I go to than I have ever known. 99

ˌTalking 'Heads a US pop group formed in 1975 and known for the unusual words of their songs. David Byrne was the group's singer. Their albums included *Fear of Music* (1979), *Remain in Light* (1980) and *Naked* (1988).

'talk show *n* (*especially AmE*) **1** a television programme in which people, often ordinary members of the public, appear in front of an audience to talk about a particular topic, or about their lives and problems. The audience are encouraged to ask questions and make comments. Talk shows are often broadcast in the morning or afternoon. See also SPRINGER. **2** a *chat show.

ˌThomas 'Tallis /ˈtælɪs/ (*c*. 1505–85) an English composer. He wrote mainly religious music, and was one of the official musicians and composers of the royal family. He is best known now through a piece of his music that was adapted by Ralph *Vaughan Williams: *Fantasia on a Theme by Thomas Tallis* (1910).

the 'Tamar /ˈteɪmɑː(r)/ a river in south-west England. Most of it forms the border between *Cornwall and *Devon. The *Royal Navy keeps ships in the part of the river where it flows into the *English Channel near *Plymouth.

The ˌTaming of the 'Shrew /ˌteɪmɪŋ/ a comedy play (*c*. 1594) by *Shakespeare. It is about Petruchio, a young Italian man who wants to marry Katharina, a rich but unfriendly woman. (*Shrew* is an old-fashioned word for a bad-tempered woman.) She behaves unpleasantly to him but he pretends not to notice. In the end he marries her and 'tames' her by treating her roughly until she becomes as easy to control as wives were expected to be at that time. The musical comedy *Kiss Me Kate* (1948) by Cole *Porter was based on *The Taming of the Shrew*.

ˌTammany 'Hall /ˌtæməni/ the popular name for the powerful but often dishonest Tammany Society, the *Democratic Party organization that ruled New York City from the 1830s to the 1930s. They bought votes and made illegal agreements. The organization was named after the building in which they met. The name Tammany Hall is now used to refer to any dishonest political or other group: *Gloria turned the club's financial committee into Tammany Hall.* See also TWEED.

ˌTam o' 'Shanter /ˌtæm ə ˈʃæntə(r)/ a poem (1790) by Robert *Burns. Tam o' Shanter, a Scottish farmer, gets drunk one night, and when he is riding home he sees three witches and they begin to follow him. He rides away as fast as possible and escapes by crossing a bridge over a river that the witches cannot cross. One of the witches pulls off his horse's tail before it crosses the bridge. The hat which Tam wears in many illustrations of the poem, a traditional round Scottish cap made of wool, is now called a **tam o' shanter**.

T and 'G /ˌtiː ən 'dʒiː/ a short name for the *TGWU.

TANF /ˌtiː eɪ en 'ef/ ⇨ TEMPORARY ASSISTANCE TO NEEDY FAMILIES.

Tanglewood /'tæŋglwʊd/ a music camp in *Massachusetts which started in 1937 and is the summer base for the **Boston Symphony Orchestra** (**BSO**). It also includes the **Tanglewood Music Center** for young musicians and the **Tanglewood Jazz Festival** takes place there every year.

Tanza'nia /ˌtænzə'niːə/ a country in East Africa which is a member of the *Commonwealth. It was formed in 1964 when two other Commonwealth countries, Tanganyika and Zanzibar, combined. Its capital city is Dodoma and its official languages are Swahili and English. It is a mainly agricultural country, with an important tourist industry. Many people visit Tanzania to see the wide variety of wild animals living there.
▶ **Tanzanian** *adj, n.*

the 'Taoiseach /'tiː ʃək/ the title of the *Prime Minister of the Republic of Ireland.

Quentin Taran'tino /ˌtærən'tiːnəʊ; *AmE* ˌtærən'tiːnoʊ/ (1963–) a US film director and actor who also writes films. He has been criticized for the violence in such films as *Reservoir Dogs* (1991) and *Pulp Fiction* (1994), for which he won an *Oscar for Best Original Screenplay. It was also chosen as the best film at the 1994 Cannes Film Festival. Other films written by Tarantino include *True Romance* (1993), *Natural Born Killers* (1994), *Jackie Brown* (1997) and *Kill Bill* (2003).

the 'Tardis /'tɑːdɪs; *AmE* 'tɑːrdɪs/ the vehicle in which *Doctor Who travels through time and space in the British children's television series. Outside, it looks like an old-fashioned British police telephone box. Inside, it is much larger than outside, and looks like a modern spacecraft: *It's not a very big bag, but it's like the Tardis, I can fit everything I need in it.*

'Target™ a chain of stores in the US, first opened in 1962, which sells goods at low prices but which has a reputation for better quality goods and more organized stores than some other discount stores.

Tarka the 'Otter /ˌtɑːkə; *AmE* ˌtɑːrkə/ a novel (1927) by Henry Williamson (1895–1977). It is a very realistic story about an otter (= a small animal with thick brown fur that lives in rivers), which dies after being hunted for a long time by men and dogs.

'Tarmac /'tɑːmæk; *AmE* 'tɑːrmæk/ a large British company that built roads and large buildings. The company was established in the early 20th century by the inventor of **tarmac**™, a material for making road surfaces, and is now owned by Anglo American.

▶ **tartan**

Tartan is a traditional woollen cloth from Scotland that has patterns of squares and lines woven in various colours. Patterns depended originally on dyes available from local plants, so each area developed its own tartan. Tartans were not at first associated with a particular *clan. From the late 18th century, Scottish regiments wore different tartans as an identifying feature, and the design of an individual tartan for each clan followed soon afterwards. The most famous tartans include 'Black Watch', the tartan of the *Royal Highland Regiment, which is black and dark green, and 'Royal Stuart', the mainly red tartan of the *royal family.

Scotsmen may wear a kilt (= a man's skirt with pleats that reaches to the knees) and sometimes a **plaid** (= cloak), or simply a tie, in their clan's tartan. Apart from those who work in the tourist industry, few Scots wear tartan as part of their ordinary clothing. Men wear kilts when taking part in Scottish dancing displays or for formal occasions such as weddings.

Many Scots consider it wrong to wear the tartan of a clan to which they do not belong, but this has not prevented tartan, or tartan-like patterns, becoming fashionable in Britain and abroad. For some people tartan has romantic associations with Scotland's history and its wild and beautiful countryside. Women's kilts, skirts and dresses, as well as scarves, bags, travelling rugs, and many other articles, are made in tartan patterns. Goods sold to tourists, such as tins of *shortbread biscuits, are decorated with tartan patterns to indicate their origin.

'Tarzan /'tɑːzæn; *AmE* 'tɑːrzæn/ a character in a series of novels by Edgar Rice *Burroughs, the first of which was *Tarzan of the Apes* (1914). Tarzan is an English nobleman who has grown up with apes in Africa after his parents died there. He is friendly with the animals and uses his great strength to swing quickly through the trees. There have been many Tarzan films, including several with Johnny *Weissmuller as Tarzan and Maureen O'Sullivan as his partner Jane. Tarzan speaks poor English. Many people know that in one of the films he says 'Me Tarzan, you Jane' to Jane, and make jokes about it. The most recent Tarzan film was *Greystoke* (1984). There have also been radio and television programmes and newspaper *comic strips about him.

TASIS /'tæsɪs/ (*in full* the **American School in England**) a private school in *Surrey, England based on American ideas about education. It prepares students, many of whom come from US families, for the American college and university system.

Tate and 'Lyle /ˌteɪt, 'laɪl/ a large British company that makes sugar. In the 19th century it was one of the first companies to produce sugar in cubes, and became very successful as a result. One of its original owners, Henry Tate (1819–99), gave his collection of paintings to the nation and used some of his wealth to build the Tate Gallery, now *Tate Britain.

Tate 'Britain /teɪt/ an important art gallery on the north bank of the River *Thames in central London. It contains the main national collections of British art from 1500 to the present. It is especially well known for its collection of works by *Turner². Before *Tate Modern opened in 2000, the building and its collection were called the **Tate Gallery** and contained both British and international art.

the Tate 'Collection a large collection of British and international art that is divided between the four Tate galleries. Two of these galleries are in London: *Tate Britain and *Tate Modern, which opened in 2000. Tate *Liverpool opened in 1988 and Tate *St. Ives in Cornwall opened in 1993.

Tate 'Modern an art gallery on the south bank of the River *Thames in London that contains a collection of international modern art from 1900 to the present. It has been extremely popular since it opened in 2000, partly because of the building, which used to be a power station (= a place where electricity is produced). In 2004 there were over 4 million visitors to the gallery.

***The 'Tatler** /'tætlə(r)/ **1** a British magazine, published once a month and containing articles about *upper-class and *upper-middle-class social events, fashion and the arts. It was first published in 1901.
2 a magazine written by Richard *Steele and Joseph *Addison from 1709 to 1711. It was published three times a week and consisted of long articles about a wide range of subjects, written with intelligence and humour, and usually from a *Whig(1) point of view.

Tate Modern

Tattersall's /ˈtætəsɔːlz; AmE ˈtætərsɔːlz/ a well-known British company of racehorse auctioneers. Tattersall's organizes important auctions once a year at *Newmarket.

Art Tatum /ˌɑːt ˈteɪtəm; AmE ˌɑːrt/ (1910–56) a US musician considered one of the greatest *jazz piano players. He was nearly blind all his life.

Taunton /ˈtɔːntən/ a town in south-west England. It is the administrative centre of *Somerset, and is well known for its attractive old buildings, and for the cider (= an alcoholic drink made from apples) produced there.

John Tavener /ˈtævənə(r)/ (1944–) an English composer. He became well known after writing *The Whale* (1968), an unusual piece of music for singers, orchestra, people speaking and recorded sounds. His more recent music has been religious in character. He was made a *knight in 2000.

tax disc n (in Britain) a round piece of paper which must be displayed on the front window of a vehicle to show that the owner has paid the road tax (= a tax on all vehicles that use public roads). People usually pay their road tax and get their tax discs at a post office. They may cover periods of six months or one year.

taxi dancer n (AmE) a woman employed at a dance hall to dance with customers who pay for each dance or a period of time. Taxi dancers are called this because they are hired like a taxi.

Taxi Driver a US film (1976) which was the first big success for Martin *Scorsese, who directed it, and the actor Robert *De Niro. It won the prize for the best film at the Cannes Film Festival. De Niro plays Travis Bickle, an ordinary New York taxi driver who becomes depressed by all the evil and crime he sees and tries to fight it in a violent way. Jodie Foster plays a very young prostitute whom he tries to rescue.

the Tay /teɪ/ the longest river in Scotland, 120 miles/193 kilometres long. From its source in the *Grampians it flows through central Scotland and into the **Firth of Tay**, a narrow strip of sea that runs a long way into the land near Perth.

the Tay Bridge /ˌteɪ/ **1** a rail bridge over the River *Tay near *Dundee in Scotland. It was completed in 1878 and collapsed in 1879 when a train was crossing. It was one of Britain's first serious rail disasters. **2** a second rail bridge over the River *Tay near *Dundee. It was completed in 1888 and is still in use. A road bridge was built near the rail bridge in the 1960s.

A J P Taylor /ˈteɪlə(r)/ (Alan John Percivale Taylor 1906–90) a leading English historian. He wrote many books and newspaper articles about the history of Europe in the 19th and 20th centuries, and became famous in Britain when he appeared on television to explain events such as the Russian Revolution.

Elizabeth Taylor /ˈteɪlə(r)/ (1932–) a US actor, born in England. She began her career as a child star in films that included *National Velvet* (1944). Two of her eight marriages were to Richard *Burton, and their films together included *Cleopatra and *Who's Afraid of Virginia Woolf?*, for which she received an *Oscar. They also acted together in the *Broadway play *The Little Foxes* (1981). Taylor's other films include *Cat on a Hot Tin Roof* (1958) and *Butterfield 8* (1960), for which she won another *Oscar. She was made a *dame(2) in 2000.

Zachary Taylor /ˌzækəri ˈteɪlə(r)/ (1784–1850) the 12th US *President (1849–50). He was an army officer known as 'Old Rough and Ready', who fought in the *War of 1812 and in the *Mexican War, in which he defeated General *Santa Anna. Taylor owned slaves but as President supported *California as a new state without slaves.

Tayside /ˈteɪsaɪd/ until 1996, an administrative region in eastern Scotland. It has been divided into three *council areas: Angus, *Dundee City, and Perth and Kinross.

T-bill /ˈtiː bɪl/ n (AmE) ⇨ TREASURY BILL.

T-Bird /ˈtiː bɜːd; AmE ˈtiː bɜːrd/ n ⇨ THUNDERBIRD.

TBS /ˌtiː biː ˈes/ ⇨ TURNER BROADCASTING SYSTEM.

tea n **1** [U] a drink made by adding hot water to the dried leaves of a plant. It is very popular in Britain, where it is usually drunk hot, with milk, and sometimes sugar. Many British people have a cup of tea in the morning, and several more during the day. Some people stop work for a few minutes to have a **tea break**. Most people in Britain offer a cup of tea to anybody visiting their home or office. Tea also suggests comfort and warmth, and sitting down with a 'nice cup of tea' is a common response to problems and worries: *Mr Lewis will be with you in a minute. Would you like a cup of tea or coffee while you are waiting?* **2** [U, C] (in Britain) a light meal eaten in the late afternoon. It usually consists of tea and cakes, biscuits or sandwiches: *Mary has invited us to tea.* ◇ *The hotel serves afternoon tea.* **3** [U] (in Britain) the word used by some British people to refer to their main evening meal. It is often a hot meal and is usually eaten early in the evening, when the family arrives home from work, school, etc.: *What's for tea tonight, mum?* Compare HIGH TEA. ⇨ note at MEALS.

teaching hospital n a hospital where medical students are taught. Many of Britain's largest and best-known hospitals are teaching hospitals. As well as having medical students, they also have some of the best doctors and equipment in the country. Teaching hospitals in the US are often part of medical schools or associated with them.

the Teamsters /ˈtiːmstəz; AmE ˈtiːmstərz/ (**the Teamsters Union**) the largest US trade union. It was established in 1903 and in 2003 had about 1.4 million members. A teamster is a person who drives a lorry/truck, but the union now includes many other professions. Its full official name is the International Brotherhood of Teamsters. Because of illegal activities within the union, the Teamsters were put out of the *AFL-CIO from 1957 to 1987. See also HOFFA.

Teapot Dome a US political scandal in 1922 in the government of President Warren G *Harding. Secretary of the Interior Albert Fall secretly accepted money from the Mammoth Oil Company to let them develop oil lands at Teapot Dome, *Wyoming, and Elks Hill, *California. The Senate investigated, and Fall left the government in 1923. He was later sent to prison.

Norman Tebbit /ˈtebɪt/ (1931–) an English *Conservative politician who held several important

T

government posts under Margaret *Thatcher. He is known for his right-wing opinions. In the 1980s he was well known for using the phrase 'on your bike' to suggest that unemployed people should look for work, rather than expecting the state to help them. In the 1990s he used the phrase 'the cricket test' to suggest that people in Britain whose families came from other countries could not be regarded as British if they still supported the sports teams of foreign countries. He was made a *life peer in 1992.

'techno /'teknəʊ; AmE 'teknoʊ/ n [U] a type of loud, fast dance music that is a mixture of electronic music and 'samples' (= short pieces of music recorded from other records). It became very popular in Britain and America in the 1990s, especially among young people who go to clubs.

Te'cumseh /tə'kʌmsə/ (c. 1768–1813) a leader of the *Shawnee *Native American people. He tried to unite them to defend their lands against white people. His efforts failed when his brother, Tenskwatawa 'the Prophet', was defeated at the Battle of Tippecanoe (1811). Tecumseh later supported the British in the *War of 1812 and was killed during a battle.

'teddy bear n a soft toy bear. In Britain and America, teddy bears are typically given to babies and very young children. Some older children, and even some adults, still have the teddy bears that they were fond of when they were younger. The first teddy bears were made in the US, where they were named after President Theodore (Teddy) *Roosevelt, because he was thought to have saved a very young bear while hunting one day.

'teddy boy (also **ted**) n (in Britain, especially in the 1950s) a young man following a popular fashion in clothing and music. Teddy boys wore long, loose jackets, called *drape coats*, very narrow trousers, called *drainpipes*, and leather shoes with narrow points at the end, called *winkle-pickers*, or soft shoes with thick rubber soles, called *brothel creepers*. They put special oil on their hair and arranged it so that it stood up at the front. Teddy boys were strongly associated with *rock and roll music. They were seen as being rebellious and were sometimes involved in violence. Their style of clothing was intended to be similar to that of certain fashionable young men in Britain during the *Edwardian period in the early 20th century. (Ted is a short form of Edward.).

Te 'Deum /ˌti: 'di:əm/ an ancient Latin hymn, praising God. It is traditionally sung on special occasions in morning church services, in Latin in the *Catholic church and in English in the *Church of England. In Latin it begins with the words *Te Deum laudamus*, meaning 'We praise you, O God.'

the Tees /ti:z/ a river in north-east England that flows from the *Pennines through the *Teesside region and into the *North Sea at the port of Middlesbrough.

'Teesside /'ti:zsaɪd/ an industrial area in north-east England, consisting mainly of the port of Middlesbrough and its surrounding areas. Its main industries have been steel, chemicals and shipbuilding, although in the last years of the 20th century these industries suffered and many local workers became unemployed.

TEFL /'tefl/ (in full the **Teaching of English as a Foreign Language**) the practice or business of teaching the English language to people for whom English is a foreign language. Both in Britain and in other countries, this often takes place in private language schools and in Britain courses are usually taught completely in English. TEFL began to grow into what is now a major industry in the 1970s.

'Teflon™ n [U] a substance used to form a surface on e.g. cooking implements and pans to stop food, etc. sticking

to them, and so making them easier to clean. It was invented in 1938 by the US company *DuPont. The name is now used to describe politicians and others who make mistakes or act illegally but manage to avoid being blamed or charged. Ronald *Reagan was often called the 'Teflon President'.

the ˌTelecom 'Tower /ˌtelɪkɒm; AmE ˌtelɪkɑːm/ a very tall tower in central London which is one of the city's best-known landmarks. It is 620 feet/189 metres high and was completed in 1966. It is a communications centre for telephone, television and radio communications. It was originally called the Post Office Tower until the *Post Office and British Telecom (now BT) became separate organizations. There was originally a restaurant at the top of the Tower which moved round continuously and gave excellent views over London, but this was closed in 1971 after a bomb attack on the Tower.

the 'Telegraph ⇨ DAILY TELEGRAPH. See also SUNDAY TELEGRAPH.

ˌTele'mundo /ˌtelɪ'mʊndəʊ; AmE ˌtelɪ'mʊndoʊ/ a US television network that broadcasts programmes in Spanish for the *Hispanic population. It is owned by *NBC.

'Teletext a British television information service provided on *ITV and *Channel Four. It offers many different types of information, e.g. weather reports, sports results, financial news and advertisements, and the information is shown without sound. It is available by use of a remote control device on most televisions. Compare CEEFAX.

'Teletubbies /'telitʌbiz/ a popular British television series (1997–) for young children. Its main characters are Tinky Winky, Dipsy, Laa-Laa and Po, four large creatures covered in brightly coloured fur, with television screens on their stomachs, who talk a simple language like that of very young children. In 1997 the characters appeared on a successful pop record, *Teletubbies Say Eh-Oh!*.

ˌtele'vangelist /ˌtelɪ'vændʒəlɪst/ n (especially AmE) an *evangelist who has a series of religious programmes on television. Many have become very rich from money sent in by supporters. Such programmes lost supporters in the 1980s after Jim *Bakker was sent to prison for financial crimes and Jimmy *Swaggert admitted that he had visited prostitutes. In 2001 two well-known US televangelists, Jerry *Falwell and Pat *Robertson, made many people angry by suggesting in a television interview that Americans were partly to blame for the terrorist attacks on the *World Trade Center because of their immoral behaviour.

▶ **televangelism** n [U].

'television ˌlicence (also **TV ˌlicence**) n (in Britain) an official piece of paper giving permission to own a television. The cost of this (the **licence fee**) is decided every year by the government. A licence lasts for one year. The money collected in this way is used to pay for *BBC television and radio programmes.

ˌThomas 'Telford /'telfəd; AmE 'telfərd/ (1757–1834) a Scottish engineer who designed many bridges, canals and roads in Britain. Among his best-known achievements are the *Caledonian Canal in northern Scotland and the *Menai Strait Bridge in north Wales. Many of his bridges are still in use.

ˌEdward 'Teller /'telə(r)/ (1908–2003) a US scientist who has been called the 'father of the hydrogen bomb'. He was born in Hungary and became a US citizen in 1941. He worked on the first atom bomb during the *Manhattan Project and then led the team of scientists who created the first hydrogen bomb, which was exploded in 1952.

the 'temperance ˌmovement a movement involving organized campaigns by various groups in the

US, Britain and other countries in the 19th century to persuade people to drink little or no alcohol. These groups believed that the effects of alcohol were bad both for individual people and for society in general.

The 'Tempest a play by William *Shakespeare, probably written in 1611 and generally thought to be the last play he wrote. In fact the speech by Prospero near the end of the play is often seen as Shakespeare's own farewell to the stage and to life itself. The action of the play takes place on an island and its central character is Prospero, who lives there with his daughter Miranda. Prospero has been replaced as duke of Milan by his brother Antonio and he uses his magic powers to create a storm so that his brother's ship is wrecked and his brother and others come onto the island. With the help of Ariel, a magical creature, Prospero then gets back his position as duke.

> 66 Our revels now are ended. These our actors,
> As I foretold you, were all spirits and
> Are melted into air, into thin air:
> And, like the baseless fabric of this vision,
> The cloud-capp'd towers, the gorgeous palaces,
> The solemn temples, the great globe itself,
> Yea, all which it inherit, shall dissolve
> And, like this insubstantial pageant faded,
> Leave not a rack behind. We are such stuff
> As dreams are made on, and our little life
> Is rounded with a sleep. 99
> Prospero in *The Tempest*

the 'Temple¹ a group of buildings in the *City of London, England, which contain two of the *Inns of Court, the Inner Temple and the Middle Temple. Lawyers work and are trained there.

Shirley 'Temple² /'templ/ (1928–) the most famous and popular child star in the history of *Hollywood. She was known for the curls in her hair and the dimples (= hollow places) in her cheeks. Her many films, in which she also danced and sang, included *Curly Top* (1935), *Heidi* (1937) and *Rebecca of Sunnybrook Farm* (1938). She was later, under her married name of Shirley Temple Black, an active *Republican(1) politician. She was appointed as a US representative to the *United Nations (1969) and as ambassador to Ghana (1974–6) and Czechoslovakia (1989–92).

'Temporary As'sistance to 'Needy 'Families (abbr **TANF**) a US government programme that provides financial help for poor families with children. It is run by the US Department of Health and Human Services, and each state receives a certain amount of money.

The ˌTen Com'mandments a US film (1956) which at the time was the most expensive ever made. It was directed by Cecil B *De Mille, who had made a silent version of it in 1923. It tells the Bible story of Moses and was filmed in Egypt with Charlton *Heston as Moses and Yul Brynner as the Egyptian king Rameses II.

Tender is the 'Night a novel (1934) by the US writer F Scott *Fitzgerald. It is about the unhappy marriage of a rich American couple, Dick and Nicole Diver, living on the French Riviera in the 1920s. The story was based on the Fitzgeralds' own marriage problems. A film version was made in 1962.

1040 form /ten 'fɔːti fɔːm; *AmE* 'fɔːrti fɔːrm/ n (in the US) the main official income tax document that people must complete and send to the *IRS each year by 15 April. It contains questions to show whether a person owes tax or has paid too much. There are shorter versions of the document for people whose income is below a certain amount.

ˌten-gallon 'hat n a tall hat with a wide brim worn, especially by US *cowboys, to protect the face against the bright sun. Compare STETSON.

ˌTen Green 'Bottles a traditional song, sung especially by children. It is about ten bottles falling off a wall one by one and many of the words are repeated many times. The song begins:

> 66 Ten green bottles hanging on the wall.
> Ten green bottles hanging on the wall.
> And if one green bottle should accidentally fall,
> There'll be nine green bottles hanging on the wall.
> Nine green bottles hanging on the wall.
> Nine green bottles … 99

ˌTennes'see /ˌtenə'siː/ a south-eastern US state, also called the Volunteer State. It became a state in 1796 and later joined the *Confederate States. Many *Civil War battles were fought there. The largest city is *Memphis and the capital city is *Nashville. Tourist attractions include the *Great Smoky Mountains, *Graceland and the *Grand Ole Opry. Its products include tobacco, cotton, chemicals, textiles and electrical goods. See also SHILOH, TENNESSEE VALLEY AUTHORITY.

'Tennessee 'Valley Au'thority /'tenəsiː/ (abbr **TVA**) an independent US government organization that provides cheap electricity to seven southern states. TVA was established in 1933 by President Franklin D *Roosevelt, as part of his *New Deal(1), to encourage the economic development of the area around the Tennessee River. As well as providing electricity it builds and operates dams, controls floods and protects the soil.

ˌJohn 'Tenniel /'teniəl/ (1820–1914) an English artist and cartoonist, best known for his illustrations of Lewis *Carroll's books *Alice in Wonderland and *Through the Looking Glass. These still appear in versions of the books produced today and most people associate them closely with the original stories. Tenniel was also for many years a political cartoonist for the magazine *Punch. He was made a *knight in 1893.

'tennis (also ˌlawn 'tennis) n [U] a game for two or four players, who hit a small soft ball backwards and forwards over a low net using rackets. It is often played on a grass court but can also be played on harder surfaces. See also DAVIS CUP, GRAND SLAM(1), REAL TENNIS, US OPEN(2), WIGHTMAN CUP, WIMBLEDON.

ˌLord 'Tennyson /'tenɪsn/ (Alfred Tennyson 1809–92) an English poet known especially for his long narrative poems (= ones that tell a story). He made his reputation with the poem *In Memoriam, which he wrote after the sudden death of his close friend Arthur Hallam and published in 1850. The same year he was made *Poet Laureate. His other well-known poems include The *Lady of Shalott, Maud, *Idylls of the King and The *Charge of the Light Brigade. He was made a *baron in 1884.

1066 /ˌten sɪksti 'sɪks/ the year when the Battle of *Hastings took place, and the *Normans gained control of England. It is one of the few dates that most British people remember, because it was the last time that Britain was successfully invaded by the forces of another country.

1066 And All That /ˌten sɪksti 'sɪks ənd ɔːl 'ðæt/ a humorous book published in 1930 about the history of Britain which also makes fun of the way in which history was taught in schools. The two authors, Walter Sellar and Robert Yeatman, were teachers.

Bryn Terfel /ˌbrɪn 'tervel/ (1965–) a Welsh opera singer, a baritone (= a male singer with a voice between tenor and bass), who has sung with opera companies around the world.

'Studs' 'Terkel /ˌstʌdz 'tɜːkl; *AmE* 'tɜːrkl/ (1912–) a US writer, born Louis Terkel. He is known for his 'oral histories' of Americans in which he records conversations with different groups within US society. His books include *Hard Times: An Oral History of the Great Depression in America* (1970), *The Good War: An Oral History of World War II* (1986), which won a *Pulitzer Prize, and *My American Century* (1997) which marked the end of his 52 years of broadcasting on radio.

the **'Terrence 'Higgins 'Trust** /'hɪgɪnz/ a British charity whose activities are concerned with the disease AIDS. It was established in 1982, when the first cases of AIDS were beginning to appear in Britain, and took its name from one of the first people to die of the disease. It aims to provide care and support for people suffering from AIDS, to give information and advice to prevent the disease from spreading, and to make the public more aware of the problem of AIDS.

'terrier *n* any of several breeds of lively and intelligent dogs. They were originally bred for hunting, during which they were often sent underground to chase out animals being hunted. Common types of terrier include the *Airedale terrier, the *cairn terrier, the *Jack Russell, the *Lakeland terrier, the *Scottie, the *Skye terrier and the *Yorkshire terrier.

the **ˌTerritorial 'Army** (*abbr* the **TA**) a British military force of part-time voluntary soldiers who are trained to join with the professional British Army to defend the country in an emergency. It joined together with the British Army to fight in *World War II. The TA was established in 1908 and now has about 40 000 members as part of the *Volunteer Reserve Forces.

the **'Terrorism Act** a law introduced in Britain in 2000 which made certain groups illegal, gave the police extra powers to investigate terrorists and created some new criminal offences related to terrorism.

ˌEllen 'Terry /'teri/ (1847–1928) an English actor famous for her performances with Henry *Irving in plays by *Shakespeare. She was also known for the clever and amusing letters she and George Bernard *Shaw exchanged in the 1890s, which were published in 1931. She was made a *dame(2) in 1925.

TES /ˌtiː iː 'es/ ⇨ TIMES EDUCATIONAL SUPPLEMENT.

'Tesco /'teskəʊ; *AmE* 'teskoʊ/ (*also* **'Tesco's**) one of Britain's largest chains of supermarkets. It was started by Jack Cohen (1898–1979), a Jewish immigrant who started selling tea in a market in the *East End of London just after *World War I. In 1931 he opened two food shops in London, and by the beginning of *World War II there were about 100 Tesco shops in or near London. In the 1970s, Tesco 'superstores' began to appear and there are now hundreds all over Britain, in or just outside most towns and cities. The largest ones sell not only food but also clothes and household goods, as well as providing other services. In 1997, Tesco started its own bank: *I buy most of my food at Tesco.* ◇ *There's a new Tesco's opening near us.*

TESOL /'tiːsɒl; *AmE* 'tiːsɑːl/ (*in full* **Teaching English to Speakers of Other Languages**) the teaching of English to people whose first language is not English, especially in a country where English is the main language. ⇨ TEFL.

ˌTess of the 'D'Urbervilles /'dɜːbəvɪlz; *AmE* 'dɜːrbərvɪlz/ a novel (1891) by Thomas *Hardy. It tells the sad story of a young woman, Tess, and the troubles she has in her relationships with two men. She marries one and kills the other, for which she is hanged. Many readers were shocked by the book's unhappy ending when it was first published.

the **'Test Act** a law passed in England in 1673 which prevented *Roman Catholics from holding any official public position, including becoming *Members of Parliament, studying at a university or joining military forces. The law stated that people had to be members of the *Church of England to do any of these things. It was not cancelled until 1828.

ˌTest Match 'Special a *BBC radio programme, which provides complete commentary on every cricket test match (= international match) played in England and some test matches involving the England team in other countries. It began in 1957 and has become almost a national institution. It is known for the humorous style of the commentators when describing each game. Listeners regularly send them cakes and other food, which they also describe. The two most famous commentators have been John *Arlott and Brian *Johnston.

'Texaco /'teksəkəʊ; *AmE* 'teksəkoʊ/ a large US oil company that owns petrol/gasoline stations in many countries of the world. It was established in 1902 in Beaumont, *Texas, as The Texas Company.

'Texas /'teksəs/ a large south-western US state, also called the Lone Star State because it was once an independent republic. It has the second largest population of all US states. Its biggest cities are *Houston, *San Antonio and *Dallas, and the capital city is Austin. Texas became independent of Mexico in 1836 and a US state in 1845. It was also one of the *Confederate States. It has been well known for its *cowboys and now produces a lot of oil and gas as well as beef and many agricultural products. Tourists visit the *Alamo, Big Bend National Park and the *Lyndon B Johnson Space Center.

the **ˌTexas 'Rangers** /ˌteksəs/ a division of the Texas state police. They were originally formed in 1823 as a small group of men who offered to protect communities from attacks by *Native Americans and Mexican criminals. The Rangers became a much larger group of law officers during the days of the *Wild West, and in 1935 they became part of the Texas Department of Public Safety.

'Tex-Mex /'teks meks/ *n* [U] (*AmE*) the Texan or other southern US variety of Mexican food, music, architecture, etc.

▶ **Tex-Mex** *adj: Anna took classes in Tex-Mex cooking.*

TfL /ˌtiː ef 'el/ ⇨ TRANSPORT FOR LONDON.

the **TGWU** /ˌtiː dʒiː dʌbljuː 'juː/ (*in full* the **Transport and General Workers' Union**) one of Britain's most important *trade unions, both in size and influence. It represents several different groups of workers, including transport workers, engineers, and factory and office workers. It was established in 1922, when 14 separate trade unions joined together. The TGWU has traditionally had strong links with the *Labour Party.

'William 'Makepeace 'Thackeray /'meɪkpiːs 'θækəri/ (1811–63) an English writer best known for his long historical novel *Vanity Fair(1). He was also a journalist, writing regularly for *Punch and other magazines under many different names. His other successful novels include *The History of Pendennis* (1848–50) and *The Virginians* (1858–9).

ˌIrving 'Thalberg /ˌɜːvɪŋ 'θɔːlbɜːg; *AmE* ˌɜːrvɪŋ 'θɔːlbɜːrg/ (1899–1936) a US businessman who became head of film production at *Universal Pictures at the age of 20 and then at *MGM when he was 25. He was known as the 'boy wonder'. He produced such films as *Ben-Hur, *Mutiny on the Bounty and *The Good Earth* (1937). Thalberg was married to the actor Norma Shearer.

the **Thames** /temz/ the longest and best-known river in Britain. It is 210 miles/338 kilometres long and flows from the *Cotswolds in central England to the *North

Sea after passing through London. Other famous towns on the river include *Oxford, *Windsor[1](1), *Henley and *Greenwich. Well-known bridges across the Thames in London include *London Bridge, *Tower Bridge and *Westminster Bridge. Large ships can sail up the Thames as far as London and smaller ones a further 86 miles/138 kilometres. A large area in the east of London was formerly a major port on the river, but in recent times this *Docklands area has been redeveloped.

the ,Thames 'Barrier /ˌtemz/ a large barrier built across the River *Thames at Woolwich, east of London, to prevent London from being flooded. It was completed in 1982 and officially opened in 1984. It consists of ten gates, which lie on the bottom of the river when the barrier is not required. If there is a danger of flooding, the gates rise to form a solid wall 50 feet/15 metres high.

the Thames Barrier

▶Thanksgiving

Thanksgiving is celebrated in the US on the fourth Thursday in November. For many Americans it is the most important holiday apart from *Christmas. Schools, offices and most businesses close for Thanksgiving, and many people make the whole weekend a vacation.

Thanksgiving is associated with the time when Europeans first came to North America. In 1620 the ship the *Mayflower arrived, bringing about 150 people who today are usually called *Pilgrims. They arrived at the beginning of a very hard winter and could not find enough to eat, so many of them died. But in the following summer *Native Americans showed them what foods were safe to eat, so that they could save food for the next winter. They held a big celebration to thank God and the Native Americans for the fact that they had survived.

Today people celebrate Thanksgiving to remember these early days. The most important part of the celebration is a traditional dinner with foods that come from North America. The meal includes **turkey**, **sweet potatoes** or **yams**, and **cranberries**, which are made into a kind of sauce or jelly. The turkey is filled with **stuffing** or **dressing**, and many families have their own special recipe. Dessert is **pumpkin** made into a pie.

On Thanksgiving there are special television programmes and sports events. In New York there is the *Macy's **Thanksgiving Day Parade**, when a long line of people wearing fancy costumes march through the streets with large balloons in the shape of imaginary characters. Thanksgiving is considered the beginning of the Christmas period, and the next day many people go out to shop for Christmas presents. .

,Twyla 'Tharp /ˌtwaɪlə 'θɑːp; AmE 'θɑːrp/ (1942–) a US dancer and choreographer. She has created more than 80 dances, including *Push Comes to Shove* (1976) for Mikhail Baryshnikov. She also designed the dances for several films, including *Hair* and *Amadeus* (1984). Tharp has worked with the American Ballet Theatre, the Joffrey Ballet, New York City Ballet, the Paris Opera Ballet and the Martha Graham Dance Company.

,Margaret 'Thatcher /ˈθætʃə(r)/ (also ,Mrs 'Thatcher, 'Maggie, now Lady Thatcher) (1925–) a British *Conservative politician who became Britain's first woman *prime minister and was one of the longest serving British prime ministers of the 20th century. She became a *Member of Parliament in 1959 and a member of the *Cabinet in 1970 when she was made *Secretary of State for education and science. In 1975 she defeated Edward *Heath in a party election for leader and became Prime Minister in 1979 when the Conservative Party won the general election.

She believed that the state should not interfere in business, and privatized many industries that were owned by the state. She reduced the power of the *trade unions by a series of laws, and defeated the miners in the *miners' strike in 1985. She wanted people not to rely on the *welfare state, and instead to pay for their own health care, education and pensions.

People were often critical of Mrs Thatcher's policies, and blamed her for the decline of many British industries and high unemployment. However she was seen as a very determined and patriotic prime minister, and she became especially popular after the *Falklands War. Because of this she was often referred to as the 'Iron Lady'.

After winning three general elections, she was forced to resign in 1991 by members of her own party who criticized her attitude to the *European Union. She was succeeded as Prime Minister by John *Major. She was made a *life peer in 1992 . See also POLL TAX, WET.

> 66 There is no such thing as society. 99
> Margaret Thatcher

'Thatcherism /ˈθætʃərɪzəm/ n [U] the political and economic policies of Margaret *Thatcher when she was Britain's *Prime Minister. It is therefore especially associated with the 1980s in Britain. Some British people think that Thatcherism was good for the British economy because of the emphasis it placed on private enterprise (= the idea that business and industry should be controlled by private individuals or companies, not by the state), privatization, a reduction in inflation and government spending, and the idea that people should help themselves rather than relying on the state to help them. An opposite view is that Thatcherism led to the loss of Britain's traditional industries, a greater gap between the rich and the poor, more people without jobs, and a period in which many British people came to care less about each other than about making money.

'Thatcherite /ˈθætʃəraɪt/ n a person, especially a *Conservative Party politician, who agreed completely with the right-wing policies of Margaret *Thatcher and supported them publicly.
   ▶ **Thatcherite** adj associated with or agreeing with the policies of Margaret *Thatcher: *a politician who showed Thatcherite tendencies in his early career.*

'That Was The 'Week That 'Was (also informal **TW3**) a popular satirical programme on British television (1962–3). It was broadcast live late on Saturday nights on *BBC, and was presented by David *Frost. It was the first British television programme to make fun of the *Establishment and to make jokes that were critical of politicians. It caused much public debate and was criticized by several leading politicians. Later satirical programmes were influenced by its style.

the ,Theatre 'Royal a famous theatre in *Drury Lane in central London. It opened in 1812 and is the oldest theatre still in use in London. It is known mostly for presenting *musicals.

Theatr Genedlaethol Cymru (The National Welsh language Touring Theatre Company) a theatre company formed in 2003 which performs plays in the Welsh language at theatres around Wales and at the National *Eisteddfod of Wales.

ˌ**There ˈis a ˈgreen hill ˈfar aˈway** the first line of a well-known Christian hymn traditionally sung at *Easter.

ˌ**There ˈwas an old ˈwoman** ⇨ OLD WOMAN WHO LIVED IN A SHOE.

THES /ˌtiː eɪtʃ iː ˈes/ ⇨ TIMES HIGHER EDUCATIONAL SUPPLEMENT.

The ˌThin ˈMan a crime novel (1932) by the US writer Dashiell *Hammett in which he created the married couple of Nick and Nora Charles. They solved crimes together and often discussed them in a humorous way. It was made into a film (1934) with William Powell and Myrna Loy, which was so successful that five more were made. Although the 'thin man' of the original book title was murdered, most people assumed from the titles of the films that it referred to Nick Charles.

The ˌThird ˈMan a story written by Graham *Greene for a successful film (1949), directed by Carol *Reed, and later published as a short novel. The story takes place in Vienna just after the end of *World War II and is about a US journalist's search for his friend Harry Lime. Lime has made it appear that he died in a road accident but in fact he is involved in selling harmful drugs. The star of the film is Orson *Welles as Lime, although he appears in very few scenes. Many people remember the film's music, which is played on a zither, an instrument with many strings stretched over a flat wooden box, played with the fingers.

ˌ**third ˈreading** n [C] the third and last discussion about a *bill(1) (= a possible new law) in the British parliament. If agreement is reached, the bill later officially becomes a law.

the ˌthird ˈway n [sing] a political position which is seen to offer an alternative to the traditional split between left and right that is neither old-style socialism nor based on a completely free market. The term was used by Bill *Clinton in the early 1990s when he campaigned as a 'New Democrat' and by Tony *Blair about *New Labour.

the ˌthirteen ˈcolonies the original 13 areas controlled by Britain in what is now the eastern US. They joined together to fight the *American Revolution and became the first 13 states. The colonies were, from north to south, *New Hampshire, *Massachusetts, *Rhode Island, *Connecticut, *New York, *New Jersey, *Pennsylvania, *Delaware, *Maryland, *Virginia, *North Carolina, *South Carolina and *Georgia.

ˌ**Thirty ˈdays hath Sepˈtember** the first line of a traditional rhyme which helps people to remember how many days there are in each month. The words are:

> 66 Thirty days hath September,
> April, June and November.
> All the rest have thirty-one
> Excepting February alone. 99

the 38th parallel /ˌθɜːtieɪtθ ˈpærəlel/ the line on the map that marks the border between North Korea and South Korea, established in 1945 after *World War II. When US troops crossed it during the *Korean War in 1950 this caused the Chinese to enter the war. It was again used as the border when peace was signed in 1953.

the ˌThirty-nine ˈArticles the set of religious principles that form the basic beliefs of the *Church of England. They were agreed upon in 1571 and were based on an earlier set produced by Thomas *Cranmer in 1563. Traditionally they are printed at the end of The *Book of Common Prayer and anyone becoming a minister in the Church of England has to agree with them.

the ˌthirty-ˈyear rule n [sing] a British government rule which prevented certain official documents from being made public until a period of thirty years had passed. It was replaced when the *Freedom of Information Act was passed in 2005.

ˌ**This Is Your ˈLife** a popular British television programme, broadcast regularly since 1955. Each programme tells the story of the life of a famous person or one who has helped others. They do not know about it in advance, and the presenter surprises them at the beginning of the programme. They are then taken to a television studio where their friends, family and other people who have been important in their lives appear as guests and tell stories about them. All the details of their life are collected in a big red book, which is given to them at the end of the programme. The programme was presented until 1987 by Eamonn Andrews and by Michael Aspel from 1993 until 2003. A similar programme, with the same title, was broadcast on US television from 1952 to 1961.

ˈ**This little ˈpig went to ˈmarket** the first line of a traditional *nursery rhyme which parents say to small children when counting their toes to amuse them. Each 'pig' is a toe, starting with the biggest. The full rhyme is:

> 66 This little pig went to market,
> This little pig stayed at home,
> This little pig had roast beef,
> This little pig had none,
> And this little pig cried, Wee-wee-wee-wee-wee,
> I can't find my way home. 99

ˈ**thistle** a wild plant with prickly leaves and large purple flowers which is the national flower of Scotland and is seen on many Scottish symbols and the logos of Scottish organizations. ⇨ EMBLEMS.

ˌ**Dylan ˈThomas** /ˌdɪlən ˈtɒməs; AmE ˈtɑːməs/ (1914–53) a Welsh writer. He is known especially for his radio play *Under Milk Wood (1953) and for his poems, the best-known of which were published in two collections, Deaths and Entrances (1946) and Collected Poems (1952). His collection of short stories, Portrait of the Artist as a Young Dog, was published in 1940. Thomas had a reputation for often getting drunk and he died in the US as a result of drinking too much alcohol.

> 66 Somebody's boring me. I think it's me. 99
> Dylan Thomas

the Laugharne Boathouse, home of Dylan Thomas

ˌ**Thomas à ˈBecket** /ə ˈbekɪt/ ⇨ BECKET.
ˌ**Thomas ˈCook** /ˈkʊk/ ⇨ COOK⁵.

,**Thomas, the** '**Tank** ,**Engine** the best-known character in a popular series of British children's stories about railways (1945–72) written by the Rev Wilbert *Awdry and later by his son Christopher. Thomas and the other trains in the books have faces and human characteristics and can speak. The books have been made into television programmes and videos for children.

,**Daley** '**Thompson**[1] /ˌdeɪli ˈtɒmpsn; AmE ˈtɑːmpsn/ (1958–) a British athlete, the son of a Nigerian father and a Scottish mother. He was the greatest athlete of all time in the decathlon, a contest involving ten different events. He won gold medals in the Olympic Games in 1980 and 1984, in the World Championships in 1983, in the European Championships in 1982, and in the *Commonwealth Games in 1978, 1982 and 1986. He also broke the world record four times.

,**Emma** '**Thompson**[2] /ˈtɒmpsn; AmE ˈtɑːmpsn/ (1959–) an English actor. After early work on television she won an *Oscar for her performance in the film *Howards End (1992) and in 1995 directed her own version of Jane *Austen's *Sense and Sensibility. Her other films have included The Remains of the Day (1993), Carrington (1995) and Primary Colors (1998). She has often acted with Kenneth *Branagh, to whom she was formerly married.

,**J J** '**Thomson**[1] /ˈtɒmsn; AmE ˈtɑːmsn/ (Joseph John Thomson 1856–1940) an English physicist who won the *Nobel Prize for physics in 1906 for discovering the electron. He was also responsible for running the *Cavendish Laboratory in Cambridge, England, which became the world's leading centre for research into atomic physics. His son George Thomson (1892–1975) and seven of his assistants all won Nobel Prizes. He was made a *knight in 1908.

,**Roy** '**Thomson**[2] /ˈtɒmsn; AmE ˈtɑːmsn/ (1884–1976) a Canadian newspaper owner who created an international business empire based in Britain. The **Thomson Organization** includes publishing, travel, printing, radio and television companies all over the world. At one time Thomson was the owner of two British national newspapers, the *Sunday Times, which he bought in 1959, and The *Times, which he bought in 1966. He was made a *life peer in 1964.

,**William** '**Thomson**[3] /ˈtɒmsn; AmE ˈtɑːmsn/ (1824–1907) a British physicist and inventor. He did much work on the laws of thermodynamics and in 1848 produced a temperature scale that later became known as the Kelvin Scale. He also did important work in the areas of magnetism and electricity. He invented many scientific instruments, especially for use at sea, and was involved in the laying of the first cable under the Atlantic. He was made a *knight in 1866 and a *baron in 1892.

The ,***Thomson Di***'***rectory*** /ˌtɒmsn; AmE ˌtɑːmsn/ (in Britain) a book containing the names, addresses and telephone numbers of businesses in a particular area. Copies of the book are delivered free to every house and business, and there are different versions for each area of the country.

'**Henry** '**David** '**Thoreau** /ˈθɔːrəʊ; AmE ˈθɔːroʊ/ (1817–62) a US writer and poet who believed strongly in the rights of individual people. As an experiment he lived a simple life for two years (1845–7) in a small wooden house near *Concord, *Massachusetts, and then wrote about this in Walden, or Life in the Woods (1854). He also wrote the essay Civil Disobedience (1849), a work that influenced such leaders as Mahatma Gandhi and Martin Luther *King to protest in a peaceful way. See also TRAN-SCENDENTALISM.

,**Sybil** '**Thorndike** /ˈθɔːndaɪk; AmE ˈθɔːrndaɪk/ (1882–1976) an English actor best-known for her performances in the plays of *Shakespeare, especially at the *Old Vic

theatre in London. She also appeared in several films and continued acting until she was 87 years old. She was made a *dame(2) in 1931.

,**Jeremy** '**Thorpe**[1] /ˈθɔːp; AmE ˈθɔːrp/ (1929–) a British politician who was the leader of the *Liberal Party (now called the *Liberal Democratic Party) from 1967 to 1976. He resigned when a former male model called Norman Scott claimed in public that they had had a homosexual relationship. In 1979 Thorpe and three others were tried and found not guilty of having planned to murder Scott, but the scandal ended his political career. He was a *Member of Parliament from 1959 to 1979.

,**Jim** '**Thorpe**[2] /ˈθɔːp; AmE ˈθɔːrp/ (1888–1953) a US athlete who is widely regarded as the greatest of the 20th century. He was the first to win both the decathlon and pentathlon events at the Olympic Games (in 1912). He later played professional baseball (1913–19) and professional football (1917–29). He was chosen for the Football *Hall of Fame in 1963.

the ,**Thousand** '**Guineas** (also **the 1 000 Guineas** /ˌwʌn θaʊznd ˈɡɪniz/) a horse race that takes place at *Newmarket in eastern England every year in April or May. It is a flat race (= one without jumps) for female horses that are three years old, and the course is 1 mile/1.6 kilometres long. It is one of the most important horse races in Britain and was first run in 1814.

'**Thousand** '**Island** '**dressing** n [U] a US sauce for salads. It is made with mayonnaise, *ketchup, eggs, red peppers, pickles, etc.

Thread'**needle Street** /ˌθredˈniːdl/ a street in the *City of London where the *Bank of England has been situated since 1734. The Bank is sometimes referred to as the *Old Lady of Threadneedle Street.

3-D (also ,**three-**'**D**) n [U] (in films) the quality of appearing to have three dimensions, i.e. depth as well as length and width. Audiences for 3-D films have to wear special glasses to get the proper effect. The process for making such films was invented in 1936 but not used by *Hollywood until the 1950s. Popular 3-D films included House of Wax (1953) and Hondo (1953). Since the middle of the 1990s, many 3-D films have been produced for showing in IMAX cinemas (= a type of cinema that shows films on a very large screen).

the ,**Three** '**As** /ˈeɪz/ the informal name for the *Amateur Athletic Association (AAA), the organization in charge of amateur athletics in Britain, which was established in 1880. It is also the name of the national competition which the AAA organizes every year and which was first held in 1886. Since athletics became a professional sport, both the organization and the event have become less important.

,***Three Blind*** '***Mice*** a well-known *nursery rhyme which tells a rather unpleasant story. The words are:

> 66 Three blind mice, see how they run!
> They all ran after the farmer's wife,
> Who cut off their tails with a carving knife
> Did you ever see such a thing in your life,
> As three blind mice? 99

the ,**Three** '**Choirs** ,**Festival** a British music festival which is held every year in either *Gloucester, *Hereford(1) or *Worcester. The three cities take turns to hold the event. Much of the music is performed by their cathedral choirs, though visiting choirs also take part. Most of the performances also take place in the cathedrals. The festival was first held in 1724.

,**three-day e**'**vent** n a type of horse riding competition that lasts for three days. On the first day there is a dressage contest, in which judges decide how well riders can

control their horses when performing certain movements. On the second day, there is cross-country riding,
when the horses are ridden through the countryside. On
the third day, there is showjumping, when the horses
have to jump over high barriers in a specially constructed area. The riders must ride the same horse on all
three days. The two most important three-day events in
Britain are held at *Badminton and *Burghley every
year. They are less common in the US.

,three-line 'whip *n* a written notice sent by the
*Whips in the main British political parties to tell their
*Members of Parliament that they must attend a particu-
lar debate and vote according to the wishes of their
party leader. The instructions have three lines marked
under them to show that they are very urgent. ⇨ note at
PARLIAMENT.

,Three Little 'Pigs a well-known children's story. It is
about three little pigs and a wolf. The pigs each build
their houses from different materials and the 'big bad
wolf' tries to destroy their houses by blowing on them.
Only the pig whose house is built with bricks remains
safe.

3M /ˌθriː'em/ (*in full* Minnesota Mining and
Manufacturing Company) a large US company best
known for its *Scotch tape, *Scotchgard Fabric
Protection and *Post-it Notes. It actually produces about
50 000 products, including household items, electrical
equipment and chemicals. The company was established
in 1902 and has its main office in *St Paul, *Minnesota.

,Three 'Men in a 'Boat (*full title* Three Men in a
Boat (To Say Nothing of the Dog!)) a humorous
novel (1899) by Jerome K *Jerome. It tells the story of a
journey taken by three men and a dog along the River
*Thames in a rowing boat, and the many accidents that
happen to them and the book is still very popular today.

,Three Mile 'Island a US island south of Harrisburg,
*Pennsylvania, where there was an accident in a nuclear
power station on 28 March 1979. Some radiation got into
the air, causing great fear among local people. This led
to a lot of criticism of the national programme for producing nuclear power.

the ,Three 'Stooges /ˌθriː 'stuːdʒɪz/ a US comedy act
popular from the 1930s to the 1960s made up of three
comedians who appeared in films and on television
using slapstick comedy (= a type of humour based on
people hitting each other, falling over, etc.). The original
characters were called Larry, Moe and Curly, although
the actual comedians who played them changed over
the years.

,three 'strikes law *n* one of a number of laws passed
by states in the US that are known officially as mandatory sentencing laws. The laws make it possible to give
a life sentence to someone who is found guilty of a crime
on three occasions even though the crime itself would
otherwise receive a much shorter sentence. The laws
were first introduced in the 1990s and there have been
many protests against them. The term 'three strikes'
comes from baseball, where a batsman has three
attempts to hit the ball before being 'out'.

'Thriller an album by Michael *Jackson that has sold
more than any other in the history of music. It appeared
in 1982 and by 2003 more than 50 million copies had
been bought. Five of its songs became No 1 hits, including *Beat It* and *Billie Jean*. Jackson later made a short
film, *The Making of Thriller*, which became the best-selling video ever.

,Through the 'Looking Glass a well-known children's book by Lewis *Carroll, first published in 1872
with illustrations by John *Tenniel. It is about the adventures in a strange world of Alice, a little girl who was

also the subject of Carroll's earlier book *Alice in
Wonderland*. Alice dreams that she goes through a looking glass (= mirror) and on the other side meets the red
and white queens, chess pieces who have come to life,
*Tweedledum and Tweedledee, *Humpty Dumpty(2)
and the *lion and the unicorn. See also JABBERWOCKY,
WALRUS AND THE CARPENTER.

> 66 'I don't care for jam.'
> 'It's very good jam,' said the Queen.
> 'Well, I don't want any *to-day*, at any rate.'
> 'You couldn't have it if you *did* want it,' the Queen said.
> 'The rule is jam tomorrow and jam yesterday but never
> jam *to-day*.'
> 'It *must* come sometimes to "jam to-day",' Alice
> objected.
> 'No it can't,' said the Queen. 'It's jam every *other* day;
> to-day isn't any *other* day, you know.'
> 'I don't understand you,' said Alice. 'It's dreadfully
> confusing!' 99
> *Through the Looking Glass*

Thrust SSC /ˌθrʌst es es 'siː/ a British vehicle which in
1997 broke the world land speed record in the Black Rock
Desert, *Nevada. It was driven by Andy Green. SSC
stands for 'supersonic car'.

'Thunderbird /'θʌndəbɜːd; *AmE* 'θʌndərbɜːrd/ (*also
informal* T-Bird) *n* a popular US sports car, first produced in 1954 by the *Ford Motor Company.
Thunderbirds have become a familiar part of American
life.

'Thunderbirds™ /'θʌndəbɜːdz; *AmE* 'θʌndərbɜːrdz/ a
popular British television series for children, first shown
in the 1960s and a film (2004). The puppet characters
included Lady Penelope and the scientist Brains. The
stories were about the Thunderbirds International
Rescue Service which rescues people in space using special aircraft, vehicles and technical inventions.

,James 'Thurber /'θɜːbə(r); *AmE* 'θɜːrbər/ (1894–1961)
a US writer of humorous stories who also drew comic
drawings for them. They are often about men and
women defeated by the ordinary problems of life. From
1927, most of his best work was published in *The *New
Yorker* magazine. His collections of stories include *My
World and Welcome to It* (1942), which contains his best-
known story, *The Secret Life of Walter Mitty*. See also
MITTY.

'J 'Strom 'Thurmond /'strɒm 'θɜːmənd; *AmE* 'strɔːm
'θɜːrmənd/ (James Strom Thurmond 1902–2003) a US
Senator who served longer than any other in the history
of the *Senate. He represented *South Carolina from
1954 until he retired at the age of 100. He was also a candidate for President in 1948 for the States' Rights Party
and was Governor of South Carolina (1947–51).
Thurmond began as a *Democrat but later changed to
the *Republican Party.

'ticker-tape pa,rade *n* a traditional parade in US
cities, especially New York, during which people throw
many small bits of paper from the tall buildings onto the
parade as it passes in the street. Such parades are held to
honour famous people, such as Charles *Lindbergh after
his famous flight. Ticker tape is paper in a thin strip from
a machine used for receiving and recording telegraph
messages, but the paper used in ticker-tape parades
today is usually confetti (= tiny pieces of coloured paper
traditionally thrown at weddings).

'tic-tac man /'tɪk tæk/ *n* (*pl* men) (*BrE*) a bookmaker
(= a man who takes bets) at a horse-racing course, who
communicates betting information to other bookmakers
there by means of tic-tac, a special language of signals
involving movements of the hands and arms.

,**tied 'house** n (BrE) **1** a pub which is owned or controlled by a particular company and sells the beer produced by that company. Compare FREE HOUSE.
2 (also **tied cottage**) a home rented to somebody, especially a farm worker, by their employer, who owns it. The person can only continue to live there if he or she continues to be employed by the owner.

'**Tiffany's** /'tɪfəniz/ a well-known jewellery shop on *Fifth Avenue in New York. It was established in 1839 by Charles Tiffany (1812–1902), and the shop now has branches in London, Paris and other cities.

,**Bill 'Tilden** /'tɪldən/ (1893–1953) a US tennis player who was the leading player in the world during the 1920s. His popular name was 'Big Bill'. In 1920 he became the first American to win at *Wimbledon, and he also won there in 1921 and 1930. He won the *US Open(1) seven times (1920–25 and 1929) and played in 11 *Davis Cup teams.

,**Till 'Death Us Do 'Part** a popular *BBC television comedy series (1965–75). The main character, Alf *Garnett, is not well educated and has extreme right-wing opinions, especially about black people and foreigners living in Britain. He argues all the time with his wife, his daughter and her husband, who all make fun of him. A US television series based on *Till Death Us Do Part*, called *All in the Family*, was broadcast on *CBS in the 1970s and 1980s. See also BUNKER.

,**Vesta 'Tilley** /,vestə 'tɪli/ (1864–1952) a famous male impersonator (= a woman pretending to be a man when performing on stage) in British *music-hall. Her most famous song was *Burlington Bertie*.

Time a popular US news magazine, published every week. It was started in 1923 by Henry Luce, the husband of Clare Booth *Luce, and Briton Hadden. It created offices for its journalists around the world and has developed a particular style of writing which has come to be called 'Timese'. It now has four different international versions. People consider it a great honour to have their picture on the cover of the magazine, and as a special feature every year it chooses a man or woman of the year. Its company, Time Inc, is part of *Time Warner.

,**Time 'Out** a magazine published each week in London, England. It gives details of the entertainment available in London each week (cinema, theatre, music, etc.) and information about exhibitions, museums, sports, special activities, etc. It also contains reviews and other articles. It was first published in 1968.

The Times a British national daily newspaper, the oldest in England. It was first published (as the *Daily Universal Register*) in 1785 and was generally regarded as having a lot of influence on public opinion. Though politically independent, it is seen as representing the attitudes and opinions of the *Establishment, and many of its readers support the *Conservative Party.
The newspaper went through a difficult period in the 1970s, when there were a number of industrial disputes involving *trade unions representing workers in the printing industry. A strike began in 1978 and the paper was not published for nearly a year. In 1981 Rupert *Murdoch became the owner and in 1986 he moved the paper's offices and printing works to a new building in *Wapping, east London.
The Times is known for the extent of its news reporting, for its editorials, in which the paper's own views on issues in the news are given, for the letters from readers, for the announcements of births, deaths and marriages, and for its *crossword. See also SUNDAY TIMES, THOMSON.

the '**Times Edu'cational 'Supplement** (also informal the ,**Times 'Ed**) (abbr the **TES**) a British newspaper published each week by the company that owns *The *Times. It is for teachers and other people involved in education, and contains articles on education issues and advertisements for jobs in the teaching profession. It was first published in 1910.

the '**Times 'Higher Edu'cational 'Supplement** (also informal the ,**Times 'Higher**) (abbr the **THES**) a British newspaper published each week by the company that owns *The *Times. It is similar to the *Times Educational Supplement* but it is for teachers and other people involved in higher education (= education at colleges and universities rather than at schools). It was first published in 1972.

the ,**Times 'Literary ,Supplement** (abbr the **TLS**) a British newspaper published each week by the company that owns *The *Times. It consists mainly of reviews of new books and also includes articles on literature. It was first published in 1902.

,**Times 'Square** a busy square in central *Manhattan, New York City. It is known for its bright lights and many theatres and cinemas. On New Year's Eve, thousands of people gather there to watch a ball move down the side of the No 1 Times Square building as the new year approaches. The square is named after the Times Tower, once the offices of the *New York Times.

,**Time 'Warner** /,taɪm 'wɔːnə(r); AmE 'wɔːrnər/ a very large US media and entertainment company selling magazines, films, television programmes and *Internet services all over the world. It was formed in 1989 when the magazine company Time Inc joined with the film company *Warner Brothers. In 1996 it bought the *Turner Broadcasting System which owns *CNN. Time Warner's magazines include *Time, *Life and *Sports Illustrated. In 2000 it joined with *America Online to form the world's largest media company.

'**Tinker, 'tailor, ...** the first words of an old children's rhyme. It is usually said when counting things, such as the stones from fruit that has just been eaten, in order to see what the child will be when he or she grows up. The full version is:

> **66** Tinker, tailor, soldier, sailor,
> Rich man, poor man, beggar man, thief. **99**

Tinkertoy™ /'tɪŋkətɔɪ; AmE 'tɪŋkərtɔɪ/ a US make of children's toy which consists of a set of small wooden wheels and coloured wooden sticks which fit together to build models. Tinkertoys were first made in 1914 and are now made by the toy company Hasbro.

,**Tin 'Lizzie** (also ,**tin 'lizzie**) /'lɪzi/ n (AmE old-fashioned slang) a popular name for the *Model T car. It is sometimes still used to mean any old or cheap car: *He was very rich but drove a tin lizzie all his life.*

,**Tin Pan 'Alley** (old-fashioned) an informal name for the popular music industry, especially the people who write and publish songs. The name originally referred to an area of New York where such people worked.

'**Tinseltown** /'tɪnsltaʊn/ an informal name for *Hollywood. Tinsel is a collection of bright shiny metal strips often used to decorate Christmas trees. It is cheap and does not last, which led to the comparison with Hollywood's false scenery and most actors' brief fame.

Tin'tagel /tɪn'tædʒəl/ a ruined castle and a village on the north coast of *Cornwall in south-west England. It is supposed to be the place where King *Arthur was born and is very popular with tourists.

,**Tintern 'Abbey** /,tɪntən; AmE ,tɪntərn/ a beautiful ruined abbey by the River *Wye, near the border between England and Wales. It was originally built in the 12th century. It has been painted by many artists, including *Turner[2], and *Wordsworth wrote a romantic

T

poem about the landscape around it in his *Lyrical Ballads*.

> 66 For I have learned
> To look on nature, not as in the hour
> Of thoughtless youth; but hearing oftentimes
> The still, sad music of humanity. 99
> *Lines composed a few miles above Tintern Abbey*

,Tiny 'Tim a character in the story *A *Christmas Carol* by Charles *Dickens. He is a disabled little boy, the son of Bob Cratchit who works for *Scrooge. Tiny Tim speaks the famous last words at the happy ending of the story: 'God bless Us, Every One.'

Di,mitri 'Tiomkin /dɪˌmiːtri 'tjɒmkɪn; *AmE* 'tjɑːmkɪn/ (1894–1979) a US composer of film music. He was born in Russia and moved to the US in 1925. He won *Oscars for *High Noon, *The High and the Mighty* (1954) and *The Old Man and the Sea* (1958). His other films included *It's a Wonderful Life, *Friendly Persuasion* (1956) and *Giant* (1956).

,Michael 'Tippett /'tɪpɪt/ (1905–98) an English composer of classical music, much of which shows his deep concern for the suffering of human beings. He established his reputation in 1941 with the oratorio (= large piece of music for voices and orchestra) *A Child of Our Time*. He also wrote several operas, including *The Midsummer Marriage* (1955) and *The Knot Garden* (1970). His other works include four symphonies and various songs and piano works. During *World War II he was sent to prison for a short time for refusing to fight. He was made a *knight in 1966 and a member of the *Order of Merit in 1983.

'Tipp-Ex™ /'tɪp eks/ *n* [U] a liquid used for painting over written or typed mistakes on paper. It dries quickly and the correction can then be written or typed over it.
▶ tipp-ex *v* [T] to remove a mistake made on paper using Tipp-Ex or a similar product: *You'll have to Tippex the mistakes (out).*

Ti'tania /tɪ'tɑːnɪə/ a character in *Shakespeare's play *A *Midsummer Night's Dream*. She is the queen of the fairies and the wife of *Oberon.

the *Ti'tanic* /taɪ'tænɪk/ a very large British passenger ship which in 1912 sank on its first voyage across the Atlantic after hitting an iceberg (= a large mass of floating ice), although its owners had claimed that it could never sink. There were not enough lifeboats for all the passengers and over 1500 people died. As a result of this disaster, new laws were introduced concerning safety at sea. The wreck of the ship was found at the bottom of the sea in 1985 and there have been several attempts to raise it to the surface, though without success. The disaster has been the subject of several films. The most recent of these, *Titanic* (1997), which won 11 *Oscars, starred Kate Winslet and Leonardo *DiCaprio, and is one of the most financially successful films ever made.

,Alan 'Titchmarsh /'tɪtʃmɑːʃ; *AmE* 'tɪtʃmɑːrʃ/ (1949–) an English expert on gardening who has presented programmes on *BBC television, including *Gardeners' World*, *Ground Force* and *How to be a Gardener*. He has written over 30 books on gardening as well as several novels.

,Titus An'dronicus /ˌtaɪtəs æn'drɒnɪkəs; *AmE* æn'drɑːnɪkəs/ a play by William *Shakespeare and possibly another writer, written about 1591. It is a tragedy that takes place in ancient Rome and there are many murders in it.

'Tlingit /'tlɪŋgɪt/ *n* (*pl* Tlingits *or* Tlingit) a member of the largest group of *Native Americans in *Alaska. There are about 17000 Tlingits, and most live along the coast. They have kept many of their traditional skills and live by catching fish, making baskets, carving wood, and weaving.

TLS /ˌtiː el 'es / ⇨ TIMES LITERARY SUPPLEMENT.

Toad one of the main characters in *The *Wind in the Willows* by Kenneth *Grahame. Toad (an animal like a frog) is a very lively character who owns a big house. He becomes very enthusiastic about cars and is sent to prison for driving in a dangerous way. He escapes dressed as a woman and is then helped by his friends to get back into his home, which has been captured by his enemies.

,toad-in-the-'hole *n* [U] a British dish of sausages cooked in the oven in batter (= a mixture of eggs, milk and flour).

,Toad of Toad 'Hall a play (1929) by A A *Milne, based on the children's story *The *Wind in the Willows* by Kenneth *Grahame. It is still regularly performed in Britain.

,To a 'Skylark one of the best-known short poems by Percy Bysshe *Shelley. It was inspired by the song of a bird he heard when in Italy and begins with the famous lines:

> 66 Hail to thee, blithe Spirit!
> Bird thou never wert. 99

,To 'Autumn a poem (1819) by *Keats that celebrates the autumn season. It is sometimes referred to as *Ode to Autumn*. It is one of Keats's best-known poems, enjoyed by many people for the musical sounds of lines such as the famous opening:

> 66 Season of mists and mellow fruitfulness,
> Close bosom-friend of the maturing sun. 99

'toby jug /'təʊbi; *AmE* 'toʊbi/ *n* a traditional type of large pottery container with a handle, for drinking beer, etc. from. It is usually in the form of a fat old man who is sitting, smoking a pipe and wearing a hat with three corners. Some people collect toby jugs and old ones can be quite valuable.

Toc H /ˌtɒk 'eɪtʃ; *AmE* ˌtɑːk/ a British Christian organization formed after *World War I to encourage friendship and kindness in society. It developed from a club formed by a group of British soldiers in Belgium in 1915, in a building they called Talbot House, after Gordon Talbot, who was killed that year and was the brother of one of the members. The name Toc H comes from the former code in telegraphy for the letters T and H, standing for Talbot House.

To'day 1 a *BBC radio news programme, broadcast on *Radio 4 in the early morning from Monday to Saturday. Many people listen to it while they are getting up and having breakfast. It consists mainly of discussions about important matters in the news, especially politics. It was first broadcast in 1958.
2 a US national television news programme broadcast from Monday to Friday in the early morning on *NBC. It consists of a mixture of news, interviews, special features and informal discussion. People presenting the show have included Dave Garroway, Barbara *Walters, Tom *Brokaw, Jane Pauley and Bryant Gumbel.

,Sweeney 'Todd ⇨ SWEENEY TODD.

TOEFL /'təʊfl; *AmE* 'toʊfl/ (*in full* Test of English as a Foreign Language) an examination for students whose first language is not English and who wish to enter a university in the US.

,Alvin 'Toffler /ˌælvɪn 'tɒflə(r); *AmE* 'tɔːflə(r)/ (1928–) a US writer known for his books about future societies, written with his wife Heidi. *Future Shock* (1970) is about the anxiety felt by people who do not understand new technology. *The Third Wave* (1980) divides history into three periods of great change: the beginning of agriculture, the *Industrial Revolution and the present Information Age. *War and Anti-war* (1993) describes how new technologies will affect the way wars are fought and prevented in the future.

To ˌKill a 'Mockingbird the only novel (1960) by the US writer Harper Lee (1926–). It won the *Pulitzer Prize and is thought by many people to be the best US novel of the 20th century. The story is about Scout Finch, a young girl in *Alabama who learns about prejudice when her father, a lawyer, defends an *African American in a court case. Gregory *Peck won an *Oscar for his performance in the film version (1962).

ˌTokyo 'Rose /ˌtəʊkiəʊ 'rəʊz; *AmE* ˌtoʊkioʊ 'roʊz/ the name given by US soldiers during *World War II to Iva Ikuko Toguri d'Aquino (1916–). She was an American citizen who broadcast on a Japanese radio programme telling US soldiers to refuse to fight. After the war, she was sent to a US prison until 1956, and President *Ford gave her a pardon (= official notice forgiving somebody) in 1977.

ˌJ R R 'Tolkien /'tɒlkiːn; *AmE* 'tɔːlkiːn/ (John Ronald Reuel Tolkien 1882–1973) an English writer, best known as the author of *The Hobbit* (1937) and *The *Lord of the Rings* (1954–5). Tolkien was also a professor at *Oxford University.

ˌtoll-'free *adj* (*AmE*) (of telephone calls) without cost. A person can make a toll-free call by using a company's toll-free number, e.g. one beginning with 1–800. The cost is paid by the company as a service to customers.

ˌtollhouse 'cookie /ˌtəʊlhaʊs; *AmE* ˌtoʊlhaʊs/ *n* (*AmE*) a crisp sweet biscuit that contains small pieces of chocolate and sometimes pieces of nuts. The biscuits were first made in the 1930s at the Toll House restaurant in Whitman, *Massachusetts.

'toll road (*also* **'tollroad** /'təʊlrəʊd; *AmE* 'toʊlroʊd/ (*AmE* **'tollway**, **'turnpike**) *n* a road that drivers must pay to use. In the US such roads are now mostly motorways/freeways. The money may be collected by drivers as they join or leave them.

the ˌTolpuddle 'Martyrs /ˌtɒlpʌdl; *AmE* ˌtɔːlpʌdl/ the name given to six farm workers from the village of Tolpuddle in *Dorset, England, when they were found guilty in 1834 of illegal *trade union activity. They were punished by being sent to Australia for seven years. There were many protests about this, and in 1836 the decision was changed and they were brought back to England as free men.

ˌTom and 'Jerry characters in a popular US series of cartoon films. Tom, the cat, is always trying to catch Jerry, the mouse, but Jerry is too clever for him.

toˌmato 'ketchup ⇨ KETCHUP.

toˌmato 'sauce ⇨ KETCHUP.

the 'Tomb of the ˌUnknown 'Warrior (*also* **the 'Tomb of the ˌUnknown 'Soldier**) ⇨ UNKNOWN WARRIOR.

ˌTom Brown's 'Schooldays /braʊnz/ a novel (1857) by the English author Thomas Hughes (1822–96) about a young boy growing up at *Rugby School, where Hughes himself was a pupil. A real headmaster of Rugby, Dr Thomas *Arnold, appears as a character in the book and has a great influence on Tom, but many of Tom's experiences are unhappy ones and he is often badly treated by a cruel older boy called *Flashman.

'Tombstone /'tuːmstəʊn; *AmE* 'tuːmstoʊn/ a town in the US state of *Arizona known for its violent history. It

was established in 1879 for workers in the local silver mines, and the famous gun fight at the *OK Corral happened there in 1881. It nearly became a ghost town (= a town with no people), but tourists now come to see the OK Corral, *Boot Hill and other *Wild West places of interest.

ˌTom 'Collins /'kɒlɪnz; *AmE* 'kɑːlɪnz/ *n* a drink made with gin, lemon or lime juice, fizzy water (= water containing bubbles of gas) and sugar, with ice added. Other versions can be made with different types of alcohol.

ˌTom 'Jones /'dʒəʊnz; *AmE* 'dʒoʊnz/ a well-known novel (1749) by Henry *Fielding. It describes the complicated adventures of a young man called Tom Jones. Tom is found as a baby and brought up as his own son by Squire Allworthy, a wealthy landowner. He falls in love with Sophie Western, the daughter of another landowner, but is unfairly forced to leave home. Tom then travels around England, often getting into trouble, especially because of his affairs with a number of women. Tom has a good nature but is often not careful in his actions. The novel has many comic scenes and a happy ending, when Tom marries Sophie. The book has been made into a film (1963), with Albert *Finney as Tom, and into a *BBC television series (1997).

Ricky Tomlinson /'tɒmlɪnsn; *AmE* 'tɑːmlɪnsn/ (1939–) an English comedy actor who is best known for his role as a lazy father who swears a lot in the *BBC comedy series *The Royle Family*.

'Tommy /'tɒmi; *AmE* 'tɑːmi/ *n* (*informal, old-fashioned*) a British soldier of the lowest rank. It is short for **Tommy** (Thomas) **Atkins**, the name formerly used as that of a typical soldier on official army documents, to show how these should be completed.

'Tommy /'tɒmi; *AmE* 'tɑːmi/ a rock opera (= a story told through a series of rock music songs), written by Pete Townsend of the group The *Who and originally recorded and performed by the group in 1969. It tells the story of a boy called Tommy who cannot hear, speak or see but who becomes very good at the game of pinball. It was made into a film (1974) directed by Ken *Russell, and later into a stage show.

ˌTom 'Sawyer ⇨ SAWYER.

ˌTom 'Thumb /'θʌm/ a tiny boy (no bigger than a thumb) who appears in many traditional British children's stories, as well as those of other countries.

'Tonga /'tɒŋə; *AmE* 'tɑːŋə/ a country in the south-west Pacific, consisting of over 150 small islands, many of them without inhabitants. Its former name was the Friendly Islands. It was part of the *British Empire from 1900 until 1970, when it became independent and a member of the *Commonwealth. It is ruled by a king or queen. Its capital city is Nuku'alofa and its official language is English.
▶ **Tongan** *adj, n*.

The To'night Show a popular US television *chat show which has been running since 1954. Johnny *Carson presented it for 30 years (1962–92). He was replaced by Jay *Leno who has continued the tradition of telling a few jokes before talking with guests and introducing music by the show's band.

'Tonka™ /'tɒŋkə; *AmE* 'tɑːŋkə/ a product name for a range of toy lorries/trucks produced by the US company Hasbro, Inc. They have been made for more than 50 years, first in metal and later in plastic, and are often collected.

'Tonto /'tɒntəʊ; *AmE* 'tɑːntoʊ/ the *Native American friend of the *Lone Ranger.

'Tony /'təʊni; *AmE* 'toʊni/ *n* (*pl* **Tonys**) any of the awards given in the US each spring by the American Theater

Wing to the best *Broadway plays, actors and other professional theatre people. The Tonys began in 1947 and are named after Antoinette ('Tony') Perry (1888–1946) who produced and directed Broadway plays, and established the American Theater Wing in 1941.

'tooth ,fairy n [usually sing] an imaginary creature that some parents tell their children about. The children are told that, when one of their teeth falls out, the tooth fairy will leave a coin under their pillow if they leave the tooth there while they are asleep.

'Tootsie Roll™ /'tʊtsi/ n a US chocolate candy bar that takes several minutes to chew. It was created in 1896 by Leo Hirshfield, an Austrian who had settled in New York, and named after his daughter. During *World War II, Tootsie Rolls were included in the food boxes of US soldiers. They are now produced by Tootsie Roll Industries in *Chicago, whose other products include Tootsie Roll Pops, Charms and Junior Mints.

'Top Gun the US film (1986) that made Tom *Cruise an international star. He plays the part of an aggressive student pilot at Top Gun, the US Navy Fighter Weapons School at *San Diego, *California. The film contains exciting scenes of air battles, and its song, *Take My Breath Away*, won an *Oscar.

> 66 You can be my wingman any time. 99
> 'Iceman' to 'Maverick' in *Top Gun*

,Top'man a chain of shops in Britain, selling fashionable clothes for boys and young men. They are owned by the company that also owns *Topshop.

,Top of the 'Pops (abbr **TOTP**) a British pop music programme, shown every week on *BBC television. Singers and groups that have made new records perform on the programme and videos are shown. The programme also includes a list of the top 30 most popular records of the week and ends with the No 1 record of the week. *Top of the Pops* was first broadcast in 1964.

'Topshop a chain of shops in Britain selling fashionable clothes for girls and young women. They are owned by the company that also owns *Topman.

'Topsy /'tɒpsi; AmE 'tɑːpsi/ the character of a young black slave girl in the novel *Uncle Tom's Cabin* by Harriet Beecher *Stowe. Topsy has no parents and, when asked to explain this, she answers, 'I 'spect I grow'd (= I expect I grew).' People often mention Topsy when they are talking about something that seems to have grown quickly without being noticed: *Once the arms race began, it just grew, like Topsy.*

Tor'nado /tɔː'neɪdəʊ; AmE tɔːr'neɪdoʊ/ n (pl **-oes**) a British military aircraft, used by the *Royal Air Force. The Tornado is both a fighter and a bomber.

Tor'quay /tɔː'kiː; AmE tɔːr'kiː/ a town by the sea in south *Devon, England. It has an unusually mild climate and this has made it a popular place for holidays since the early 19th century. In 1968 Torquay joined together with the small towns of Paignton and Brixham, which are close to it, to form a district called Torbay. This is advertised as 'The English Riviera' because of its warm weather.

The ,Tortoise and the 'Hare one of the best known of *Aesop's Fables. It tells the story of a race between a tortoise (= a creature that moves very slowly) and a hare. The hare is very confident of winning, so it stops during the race and falls asleep. The tortoise continues to move very slowly but without stopping and finally it wins the race. The moral lesson of the story is that you can be more successful by doing things slowly and steadily than by acting quickly and carelessly.

,Torvill and 'Dean /,tɔːvɪl, 'diːn; AmE ,tɔːrvɪl/ **Jayne Torvill** (1957–) and **Christopher Dean** (1958–), a pair of English ice dancers who together won many international competitions in the 1980s. They were the Olympic champions in 1984 and the world champions every year from 1981 to 1984. They were known for their exciting performances and for the number of times they were given maximum points by judges. Later, they performed in specially created shows on ice.

'Tory n a member of one of the two main political parties in Britain from the 1670s until the 1830s. The Tories were originally a group of politicians who wanted the *Roman Catholic James, Duke of York (later *James II) to be allowed to become king of England. They were powerful for various periods during the 18th and 19th centuries. In the 1830s, the Tories developed into the *Conservative Party and the name is widely used as an informal alternative name for the Conservative Party.

the Tote /təʊt; AmE toʊt/ the informal short name for the Horserace Totalisator Board, a British government organization, established in 1929, which operates a system of betting on all British racecourses and owns a chain of more than 100 betting shops. Its profits are put back into the sport of horse racing. There are plans to turn the Tote into a private company.

TOTP /,tiː əʊ tiː 'piː; AmE oʊ/ ⇨ TOP OF THE POPS.

,Tottenham Court 'Road /,tɒtnəm; AmE ,tɑːtnəm/ one of the main streets in central London. It is known for the large number of shops there selling radio, television and video equipment and home computers. The furniture shop *Heal's is also on Tottenham Court Road.

,Tottenham 'Hotspur /,tɒtnəm; AmE ,tɑːtnəm 'hɑːtspɜːr/ (also informal **Spurs** /spɜːz; AmE spɜːrz/) an English football club whose home ground is at White Hart Lane in the north London district of Tottenham. It was established in 1882 and has had many successes. In 1961 it became the first club in the 20th century to win both the League Championship and the *FA Cup in the same season. It has won the FA Cup eight times and the League Championship twice. Famous players who have played for the club in recent years include Paul *Gascoigne and Gary *Lineker.

the ,Tottenham 'Three /,tɒtnəm; AmE ,tɑːtnəm/ the name given to three young men who in 1987 were sent to prison for life for having taken part in the murder of a policeman during violent events on the Broadwater Farm housing estate in Tottenham, north London. After a campaign of protest, they were officially declared innocent of the crime in 1991, when it was shown that some of the police evidence against them had been false. Together with similar cases at the time, this caused concern in Britain about dishonest behaviour by the police and about whether the legal system was fair. See also BIRMINGHAM SIX, GUILDFORD FOUR.

'tourist ,office (also ,tourist infor'mation ,office) n (in Britain) an office in many towns and cities where tourists can get information on interesting things to see and do in the local area, help with finding somewhere to stay, and advice on travel. Tourist offices often also sell postcards, souvenirs, etc.

the 'Tourist ,Trophy (abbr the **TT**) Britain's most important event for motor cycles, consisting of a series of races held every year on the *Isle of Man. It was first held in 1907 and takes place on ordinary roads. It can be dangerous and a number of riders have been killed taking part in it.

the ,Tour of 'Britain the most important international bicycle race in Britain. It took place every year until 1994 and was first held in 1951. The race lasted for 12 days and took place on roads all over Britain, covering a total distance of approximately 1000 miles/ 600 kilo-metres. From 1987 to 1994 the race was sponsored (= paid for) by *Kellogg's. In previous years when it was sponsored by the Milk Marque, an organization that controlled the supply of milk in Britain, it was often called the Milk Race. The race came to an end in 1994 because of financial problems but returned in 2004 as a shorter five-day race, sponsored by a number of public and private organizations.

,**Tower 'Bridge** a bridge across the River *Thames and one of the most famous structures in London. It was built between 1886 and 1894 and is close to *London Bridge and the *Tower of London. Its towers are in the *Gothic style and the part of the bridge with the road on it can be raised to allow ships to pass through.

Tower Bridge

,**Tower 'Hamlets** /'hæmləts/ a *borough of London, England, on the east side of the city and north of the River *Thames. It includes the *Docklands area.

,**Tower 'Hill** an area of high ground close to the *Tower of London where in former times certain prisoners held in the Tower, especially the most famous and important ones, were executed by having their heads cut off.

the ,**Tower of 'London** /'lʌndən/ one

the Tower of London

of the oldest and most famous buildings in London, England. It is an ancient fortress (= strong castle) on the north bank of the River *Thames to the east of the city, and is a popular tourist attraction. It was made a *World Heritage Site in 1988. The building of the Tower was begun in the 11th century by *William the Conqueror, and completed in the 13th century. At various times it was a royal palace, the last monarch to live there being *James I in the early 17th century. It is best known, however, as a prison in which many famous people accused of crimes against the king or queen were kept. These included Anne *Boleyn and Thomas *More.

The Tower of London has many well-known features. These include the *White Tower, which is the oldest part, the *Bloody Tower, where some prisoners were kept, and *Traitor's Gate, an entrance for prisoners on the bank of the river. The *Crown Jewels have been kept there since 1303 and are on public display. Perhaps the most famous image associated with the Tower is that of the *Yeomen Warders, the official guards, who are also known as *beefeaters. They were established in the 16th century and still wear costume of the *Tudor(1) period.

,**town and 'gown** a phrase used about certain towns and cities where there are universities, especially *Oxford and *Cambridge, to describe the contrast between the two kinds of people who live there. 'Town' refers to the people who live and work there permanently and who are not 'gown', i.e. students or members of the academic staff of the university. The phrase is often used to indicate that there is tension between the two groups because of their different backgrounds and interests: *a town-and-gown incident involving students and local youths*.

,**Townswomen's 'Guild** /,taʊnzwɪmɪnz/ n any of over 1300 branches of a society for women in British towns and cities. The Townswomen's Guilds were established to encourage friendship between women. They hold social events, organize activities to benefit the community and represent the views of women on issues that affect them. They were formed in 1929 and developed from earlier groups which had been involved in trying to change the law so that women could vote. Compare WOMEN'S INSTITUTE.

▶ toys and games

Most young children are given toys for their *birthday or at *Christmas. Many regularly spend their pocket money or allowance on smaller toys. Popular toys include building bricks such as Lego, plastic farm animals, toy cars, model railways and dressing-up costumes. Girls especially have **dolls**, and several sets of clothes to dress them in. *Action Man figures are mainly for boys and *Barbie dolls for girls. Babies are given **rattles**, soft **cuddly toys** and a *teddy bear. **Action figures**, small plastic models of characters from television shows or films, are also popular. Some parents do not allow their children to have guns or other 'violent' toys because they do not want them to think it is fun to kill people.

Among traditional games that are still popular are marbles, which is played with small, coloured glass balls, **board games** such as *snakes and ladders and *ludo, **card games** such as *Happy Families, and **word games** such as *hangman. Board and card games are played with family or friends, but children play alone with computer games or video games.

Many children collect objects, such as shells, model animals, stamps or picture cards. In the US baseball cards, cards with a picture of a baseball player on them, are sold with bubblegum. In Britain picture cards are often given free in packets of breakfast cereal.

Children play outside with skipping ropes, bicycles, skateboards and Rollerblades™. In **playgrounds** there are often swings, a slide, a see-saw and a climbing frame (*AmE* jungle gym) to climb on. Traditional games played outside include hopscotch, a game in which children hop over squares drawn on the ground to try to pick up a stone, and tag, in which one child chases the others until he or she catches one of them and then that child has to chase the rest.

Toys are often expensive and, even if they can afford them, many parents are unwilling to spend a lot of money on something that they know their children will soon get bored with. Children want toys they see advertised on television or in *comics, or toys that their friends already have. There are sometimes crazes for toys connected with characters from a film.

Few people give up toys and games completely when they become adults. Many keep their old teddy bear for sentimental reasons. There are now also **executive toys**, made specially for adults to keep on their desks. Many people play card games like bridge and poker, and board games such as *Scrabble, *Monopoly, backgammon and chess.

T

Toys 'R' Us /ɑːr/ a large company with many shops in the US and other countries that sell children's toys and clothes. The main office is in Paramus, *New Jersey.

Toy Story a US film (1995) by the Walt Disney Company. It was the first film in which all the movements of the cartoon characters were created by computer. It is about a toy *cowboy who becomes jealous when his boy owner gets a toy astronaut.

Dick 'Tracy¹ ⇨ DICK TRACY.

Spencer 'Tracy² /ˌspensə 'treɪsi; AmE ˌspensər/ (1900–67) a US actor, known for playing calm, reliable characters. He won *Oscars for his parts in *Captains Courageous* (1937) and *Boys Town* (1938). He had a long relationship with Katharine *Hepburn, and they made nine films together, including *Adam's Rib* (1949), *Pat and Mike* (1952) and his last, *Guess Who's Coming to Dinner* (1967). His other films include *Father of the Bride* (1950), *Bad Day at Black Rock* (1955), *The Old Man and the Sea* (1958) and *Inherit the Wind* (1960).

the Trade De'scriptions Act a British law, passed in 1968. It states that all goods and services offered to customers must be described in a way that is completely accurate and honest, and that it is illegal to make false claims about goods or services in advertising or in any other attempt to sell them: *They could be charged under the Trade Descriptions Act.*

Trader 'Joe's any of over 200 shops in the US that sell speciality food, much of which is imported from other countries. The first shop opened in *Los Angeles in 1967.

the Trades Union 'Congress ⇨ TUC.

trade 'union (also AmE **labor union**) an organization of workers which exists to protect their interests, improve conditions of work etc. In Britain, the **trade union movement** started in the 19th century after the *Industrial Revolution when workers began to form groups to argue for improved working conditions and pay. Each **trade** (= type of work) formed its own **trade union** but, over the years, some combined to form larger, more powerful groups. In 1900 the Labour Representation Committee was founded to enable the unions to enter politics and it later became the *Labour Party. By 1926 45% of the workforce were members of a union and the *General Strike showed there was wide support for the union movement. After *World War II union membership continued to grow, reaching a peak in 1979 with a total of 13.5 million members. Throughout the 1960s and 1970s **industrial relations** in Britain were bad, with many **strikes**, and in 1979 the *Conservative government introduced a number of changes to the law to control the activities of unions. Unions were not allowed to send members to support strike action by another union (called **secondary picketing**), union leaders could only declare a strike with the support of the majority of their members in a **secret ballot** and the **closed shop** which required all employees in an industry to join a union, was ended. Many trade unions are **affiliated** (= linked) to the *TUC which represents the trade union movement as a whole and in 2004 had 71 affiliated unions and about 7 million members. In the US, the early unions were mainly craft unions, but in 1905 the *IWW united miners and textile workers and became the first **labor union**. Modern labor unions began as a result of Franklin D *Roosevelt's *New Deal and in 1935 the Wagner Act gave workers the right to **collective bargaining** (= negotiation by a group of people) for pay increases, and this led to many new unions being formed. The many strikes after *World War II caused *Congress to pass the *Taft-Hartley Act which restricted the right of workers to strike and also made the closed shop illegal. Most labor unions belong to the *AFL-CIO, which was created in 1955 when the American

Federation of Labor joined the Congress of Industrial Organizations. In 2004 there were 61 unions in the AFL-CIO, representing over 14 million workers.

the Battle of Tra'falgar /trəˈfælɡə(r)/ an important sea battle (1805) in which the English, commanded by Lord *Nelson, defeated both the French and the Spanish. It was fought near Cape Trafalgar, in southwest Spain, during the *Napoleonic Wars. During the battle Nelson was badly wounded on his ship, *HMS Victory*. As he lay dying he made the famous request to one of his senior officers: 'Kiss me, Hardy'. The victory established Britain as the world's leading power at sea for many years. See also ENGLAND EXPECTS.

Tra,falgar 'Square /trəˌfælɡə; AmE trəˌfælɡər/ a large square in central London, England. It was created in 1830–41 and named in honour of Lord *Nelson's victory at the Battle of *Trafalgar. In the centre of the square is *Nelson's Column and on one side of it is the *National Gallery. It is one of London's most popular tourist attractions. It is also a place where political protests and other

Trafalgar Square

demonstrations are often held and very large numbers of people gather there every year to celebrate *New Year. See also ST MARTIN-IN-THE-FIELDS.

'traffic ,warden n (BrE) a person who is employed to make sure that parking laws are obeyed by drivers. Traffic wardens wear special uniforms and each of them is responsible for a particular area in a town, etc. If they find a car parked illegally, they can give a ticket which requires the driver to pay a fine.

the ,Trail of 'Tears the name given to the long journey from *Georgia to *Oklahoma made in 1838 by the *Cherokee and other *Native Americans. They were being forced by the US government to move to the *Indian Territory, and thousands died on the way. ⇨ note at NATIONAL TRAILS.

'Trailways™ one of the two biggest US bus companies which merged with the *Greyhound bus company in the early 1990s. Its buses travelled to all parts of the country. *Continental Trailways Blues* (1983) was a popular song by Steve Earle, a singer of *country music. Compare GREYHOUND BUS.

'trainspotting /ˈtreɪnspɒtɪŋ; AmE ˈtreɪnspɑːtɪŋ/ n [U] (BrE) a hobby in Britain, popular mainly with boys but also with some adult men. It involves going to places where trains can be seen, especially railway stations, and collecting the numbers of railway engines they see by writing them down. People sometimes make fun of this hobby and the people who do it because they think it is a boring and ridiculous thing to do: *Richard goes trainspotting every weekend.*
▶ **trainspotter** n a person whose hobby is trainspotting.

'Trainspotting /ˈtreɪnspɒtɪŋ; AmE ˈtreɪnspɑːtɪŋ/ a British film (1996) about a group of young people living in *Edinburgh who spend their time taking illegal drugs and committing crimes. The film was popular for its humour and realistic scenes, and was based on a novel by Irvine Welsh.

,Traitor's 'Gate the main entrance to the *Tower of London from the River *Thames. It is a wide, low arch through which prisoners accused of crimes against the king or queen were taken on their way to being kept in the Tower.

trance *n* [U] a type of electronic dance music which developed in the 1990s from techno and house music. It has simple repeated tunes and a strong rhythm.

Trans'cash™ /ˈtrænzˈkæʃ/ a service offered by the *Post Office in Britain for people who want to make payments to charity or pay bills. The name Transcash was formerly used for a *Post Office system for sending money to and receiving money from other countries.

transcen'dentalism *n* [U] a philosophy, influenced by the Hindu religion, which emphasizes the spiritual benefits to people of periods of deep thought instead of action. It involves **Transcendental Meditation**, a way of relaxing by sitting quietly and repeating a special phrase over and over again. It was first introduced into Britain by Maharishi Mahesh Yogi and attracted much publicity when the *Beatles practised it for a short period. Many people still practise it today, both in Britain and in the US, especially *California.

'Transit™ (*also* ˌFord 'Transit, 'Transit van) a well-known model of van made by the *Ford Motor Company. It is widely used by companies and individual people such as builders, plumbers and decorators, because it is the right size for transporting the equipment they need in their work.

▶**transport**

Most journeys in Britain and the US are made by *road. Some of these are made on **public transport** (*AmE* **public transportation**) but most are by private car.

In Britain many people rely on their car for daily local activities, e.g. getting to work, doing the shopping, and visiting friends. People living in urban areas may use buses, trains or, in London, the *Underground, to get to city centres, mainly because traffic is often heavy and it is difficult to find anywhere to park a car. Some places in the country may have a bus only two or three times a week so people living there have no choice but to rely on their cars.

In the US large cities have good public transportation systems. The *El railroad in Chicago and the underground systems of New York, *Boston, *San Francisco and *Washington, DC are heavily used. Elsewhere, most Americans prefer to use their cars. In 2000 half of New Yorkers used public transport to get to work. In Los Angeles it was less than 10%. Families often have two cars and, outside major cities, have to drive fairly long distances to schools, offices, shops, banks, etc. Many college and even *high-school students have their own cars.

Long-distance travel in Britain is also mainly by road, though *railways link most towns and cities. Most places are linked by *motorways or other fast roads and many people prefer to drive at their own convenience rather than use a train, even though they may get stuck in a traffic jam. Long-distance **coach/bus** services are usually a cheaper alternative to trains, but they take longer and may be less comfortable. Some long-distance travel, especially that undertaken for business reasons, may be by air. There are regular flights between regional airports, as well as to and from London. A lot of freight is also distributed by road, though heavier items and raw materials often go by rail.

In the US most long-distance travel is by air. America had two main long-distance bus companies, *Greyhound and Trailways which merged in the early 1990s. *Amtrak, which is financially supported by the federal government, provides long-distance rail services for passengers. There are many smaller private companies that operate commuter railways for the cities.

Other private railway companies such as *Union Pacific now carry only freight, though in fact over 70% of freight goes by road.

The main problems associated with road transport in both Britain and the US are **traffic congestion** and **pollution**. It is predicted that the number of cars on British roads will increase by a third within a few years, making both these problems worse. The British government would like more people to use public transport, but so far they have had little success in persuading people to give up their cars or to share rides with neighbours. Nevertheless, in the ten years to 2003 travel by rail increased by almost a third. Most people feel that public transport needs to be improved. Americans have resisted government requests to share cars because it is less convenient and restricts their freedom. Petrol/gasoline is relatively cheap in the US and outside the major cities public transport is bad, so they see no reason to use their cars less.

Despite the widespread use of unleaded petrol/gasoline, exhaust emissions (= gases) from vehicles still cause air pollution which can have serious effects on health. The US was the first nation to require cars to be fitted with catalytic converters (= devices that reduce the amount of dangerous gases given off). Emissions are required to be below a certain level, and devices have been developed to check at the roadside that vehicles meet the requirement. Stricter controls are also being applied to lorries/trucks. Car manufacturers are developing cars that use electricity and other fuels that cause less pollution.

The cheapest and most environmentally-friendly ways to travel are to walk or ride a bicycle. In *Oxford and *Cambridge bicycles are common, and many other cities now have special **cycle routes** or **cycle lanes** beside the main road. Elsewhere, there are so many cars on the roads that cycling can be dangerous. *Sustrans aims to increase travel by bicycle by providing safer routes. In the US bicycles are used mostly for fun or sport.

ˌ**Transport for 'London** (*abbr* **TfL**) the organization responsible for managing the public transport services in London, including bus and underground train services, taxi services and the roads. It is run by a board whose members are appointed by the *Mayor of London.

ˌ**Trans World 'Airlines** ⇨TWA.

T

'Travelcard /ˈtrævlkɑːd; *AmE* ˈtrævlkɑːrd/ *n* (in Britain) a special ticket which allows passengers to travel on underground trains, ordinary trains and buses in Greater London at a reduced cost for a period of one day or one week. Passengers with these tickets can make as many journeys as they want during that period.

'traveller *n* a word used to describe several groups of people including *Gypsies and *New Age travellers, who choose not to live in one place, but travel from one place to another usually living in caravans and often choosing to live separately from the rest of society.

ˌ**Ben 'Travers** /ˈtrævəz; *AmE* ˈtrævərz/ (1886–1980) an English writer of farces (= comedy plays in which characters are often in embarrassing situations and many ridiculous things happen). His plays were especially popular in Britain in the 1920s and 1930s and are still regularly performed. They were originally known as the 'Aldwych farces' because they were first produced at the *Aldwych Theatre in London. They include *A Cuckoo in the Nest* (1925), *Rookery Nook* (1926) and *Thark* (1927).

ˌ**John Tra'volta** /trəˈvɒltə; *AmE* trəˈvɔːltə/ (1954–) a US actor who began on television in the 1970s and became a major star after appearing in two musical films, *Saturday Night Fever* (1977) and *Grease. Other films have included *Pulp Fiction* (1994), *Get Shorty* (1995), *Primary Colors* (1998) and *Swordfish* (2001).

,Treasure 'Island an adventure story by Robert Louis *Stevenson, popular especially with children and published in 1883. The hero of the book is Jim Hawkins, a boy who finds a map of an island where some treasure is buried. He joins a group of sailors on a ship called *Hispaniola* and they set off to search for it. One of the best-known characters in the book is *Long John Silver, a pirate (= a person who robs ships at sea) with one leg, and a parrot (= a colourful bird) that sits on his shoulder. The story has been adapted for the stage and television, and there have been several film versions.

'Treasure of the Si'erra 'Madre /si'erə 'mɑːdreɪ/ a US film (1948) that won three *Oscars. It was directed and written by John *Huston. It is about three American friends who become enemies after finding gold in Mexico. The main actors were Walter Huston, Humphrey *Bogart and Tim Holt.

'treasure trove n [U] valuable objects, such as gold, silver, jewellery, coins and pots, which are found buried in the ground or in a building and have no known owner. According to British *common law, such objects belong to the king or queen and have to be offered first to the *British Museum. The person finding them is given money equal to the full value of the objects if they were sold at their modern value. The *common law term 'treasure trove' was replaced by 'treasure' in the Treasure Act which was passed in 1996.

the 'Treasury the British government department in charge of the country's financial affairs. One of its main responsibilities is deciding how much money should be spent on various aspects of national life, such as education, health care, defence, etc., and providing such money to the appropriate authorities. The department is in *Westminster(1) in central London. Three of its senior officials are also members of the *Cabinet: the First Lord of the Treasury (which is one of the titles of the *Prime Minister), the *Chancellor of the Exchequer, who is really the head of the Treasury, and the *Chief Secretary to the Treasury.

the 'Treasury bench the front row of seats on the government side of the *House of Commons in the British parliament. It is where the most important government ministers sit, including the *Prime Minister and the *Chancellor of the Exchequer.

'treasury bill (also informal **T-bill**) n a type of US government bond (= official paper sold with the promise to pay the money back on a certain date). Treasury bills are sold by the US Department of the Treasury to raise money for the government. They are bought for less money than their value, kept for a fixed time, and then sold back to the government for their full value. No interest is paid.

,Treaty of Amster'dam /,æmstə'dæm; AmE 'æmstər'dæm/ an agreement which was signed in 1997 by *EU leaders and came into force in 1999. It makes some changes to the treaty which established the *European Community and is intended to help European countries deal with such issues as globalization, international crime and environmental problems.

the ,Treaty of U'trecht /juː'trekt/ the agreement in 1713 which marked the end of the War of *Spanish Succession. As part of the agreement, France gave Britain various parts of Canada and accepted Queen *Anne rather than James *Stuart as the British monarch. Britain also received possession of *Gibraltar and Minorca from Spain.

the ,Treaty of Ver'sailles /veə'saɪ; AmE ver'saɪ/ the agreement, made in 1919 between the *Allies and Germany, which officially ended *World War I and established the League of Nations. According to the agreement, Germany was severely punished. It was forced to pay large amounts of money for damage done during the war, tight restrictions were placed on the number of armed forces it was allowed to have, and it lost possession of large areas of territory. This helped to cause poverty and disorder in Germany, and many people believe that the Treaty of Versailles created the circumstances which led to the Nazis coming to power and therefore to *World War II.

'Trekkie /'treki/ n a person who is very keen on following the television science fiction series *Star Trek. Serious Trekkies attend special conferences to share their enthusiasm and discuss the series in great detail.

,Trent 'Bridge /,trent/ a cricket ground in *Nottingham, England, where Nottinghamshire County Cricket Club play and where test matches (= international matches) are regularly held.

,G M Tre'velyan /trɪ'veljən/ (George Macaulay Trevelyan 1876–1962) an English historian best known for his *History of England* (1926) and *English Social History* (1942). His uncle was the historian Thomas *Macaulay. Trevelyan was made a member of the *Order of Merit in 1930.

,Richard Tre'vithick /trɪ'vɪθɪk/ (1771–1833) an English engineer who was the first man to develop steam engines into vehicles carrying passengers. The first of these were for use on roads, but in 1804 he built the first steam engine that moved on rails.

'Tribune /'trɪbjuːn/ an independent British left-wing political magazine which represents the views of some members of the *Labour Party. It was established in 1937 and is published every week. It traditionally supported very left-wing policies but in recent times has become more moderate.

,trick or 'treat a traditional activity at *Halloween, in which children dress in costumes and visit houses. At each house they say 'Trick or treat?' This means that they threaten to play a 'trick', or joke, on the people in the house unless they are given a 'treat', e.g. sweets or money. The practice of 'trick or treat' began in the US in the 1930s but is now common in Britain also.

'Trident /'traɪdnt/ a US missile designed to be fired over long distances from a submarine and able to carry a nuclear bomb. The British *Royal Navy has built several submarines to carry Trident missiles, although many people in Britain are against such weapons and regard them as unnecessary and too expensive.

,Trigger Happy T'V a television programme developed by Dom Joly in which he and actors dressed as animals, etc. are filmed in the street and the reactions of the public are recorded with a hidden camera. It was first shown in Britain and then also became popular in the US.

,David 'Trimble /'trɪmbl/ (1944–) a British politician who was the leader of the *Ulster Unionist Party (1995–2005). In 1998 he became First Minister of the new *Northern Ireland Assembly, and later in the same year he received the *Nobel Peace Prize with John *Hume. In July 2001 he resigned as First Minister because he believed the *IRA had not done enough to decommission (= officially stop using) their weapons. He was re-elected as First Minister in November and kept this position until October 2002 when the Northern Ireland Assembly was suspended.

,Trinidad and To'bago /,trɪnɪdæd, tə'beɪgəʊ; AmE tə'beɪgoʊ/ an independent country consisting of two islands in the *Caribbean near the coast of Venezuela. Trinidad and Tobago was part of the *British Empire until 1962, when it became independent and joined the *Commonwealth. Its capital city is Port of Spain and its official language is English. People from Trinidad are called **Trinidadians** and people from Tobago are called **Tobagans** or **Tobagonians**.

Trinity 'House the British organization responsible for lighthouses, buoys and beacons (= buildings and objects in the sea which warn ships of the danger of rocks) around the coasts of England and Wales. It was established in 1514 and is also a charity, providing homes and financial support for retired sailors and their families.

Trinity 'Sunday the Sunday after *Whit Sunday and an important festival in the Christian year.

'Trinity term the name given to the summer academic term in some British colleges and universities.

triple 'crown n [usually sing] the achievement of winning three important victories in certain sports. It originally meant winning three important horse races: the *Derby[2], the *St Leger and the *Two Thousand Guineas. It is also used in *Rugby Union, where it refers to one of the four countries, England, Ireland, Scotland and Wales, defeating the other three in the same season. In the US, the phrase refers to victories in the country's three most important horse races: the Preakness Stakes, the *Belmont Stakes and the *Kentucky Derby: *win/take the triple crown*.

'tripos /'traɪpɒs; AmE 'traɪpɑːs/ n [usually sing] (pl **triposes** /'traɪpɒsɪz; AmE 'traɪpɑːsɪz/) the examinations for a BA (Bachelor of Arts) degree in certain subjects at *Cambridge University. The name is also given to the course of study for the BA degree in these subjects.

Tristan da 'Cunha /ˌtrɪstən də 'kuːnjə/ the largest of a small group of islands in the south Atlantic which has historical links with Britain. In 1961 the volcano on the island erupted (= exploded, throwing out melted rock and gases) and all the inhabitants were brought to Britain. They returned to the island in 1963.

Tristram 'Shandy /ˌtrɪstrəm 'ʃændi/ a novel (1759–67) by Laurence *Sterne, considered to be one of the first novels in English. Although it sets out to be about the life of Tristram Shandy, there is no clear structure to the way the story is told and the reader is introduced to many other strange and amusing characters.

'Triumph a former British company, established in 1902, which made motor cycles and (later) cars. Triumph motor cycles have been popular both in Britain and abroad since the 1920s. In the 1960s the company went through a period of financial difficulty and closed for a time. The original Triumph company began making cars in 1923. It became part of the Standard Motor Company after *World War II and then part of *British Leyland in 1968. Its most successful models were the TR series of sports cars and the small, relatively cheap, Triumph Herald. These cars are no longer produced.

Trog /trɒg; AmE trɔːg/ the name used by the British cartoonist Wally Fawkes (1924–). He has drawn political cartoons for several newspapers, including the *Observer, but is perhaps best known for creating the humorous cartoon series *Flook*, which appeared for many years in the *Daily Mail newspaper.

Troilus and 'Cressida /ˌtrɔɪləs, 'kresɪdə/ a play by William *Shakespeare, probably written in 1602. It tells the unhappy story of two young lovers in Troy at the time of the Trojan War.

Anthony 'Trollope /'trɒləp; AmE 'trɑːləp/ (1815–82) an English author of many novels, mainly about *middle-class society in *Victorian(1) England. His series of six novels (1855–67) set in the imaginary county of *Barsetshire are mainly about the priests and other church officials connected with a cathedral, and include the novel *Barchester Towers*. Another series of six novels (1864–80) involves the Palliser family and is mainly about politics and society in London. Some of

Trollope's novels were made into popular television series by the *BBC in the 1970s and 1980s and in 2001.

Trooping the 'Colour /ˌtruːpɪŋ/ (also **the 'Trooping of the 'Colour**) a colourful ceremony that takes place every year on *Horse Guards Parade in London on the *Queen's Birthday. Soldiers on foot and on horses parade in front of the queen, carrying the flags that represent their regiments. These include the *Household Cavalry and the *Foot Guards. The ceremony is popular with tourists and is also shown on television.

the 'Trossachs /'trɒsəks; AmE 'trɑːsəks/ an attractive area of countryside in central Scotland, north-east of *Glasgow.

trouble at 't' mill /ˌtrʌbl ət 'tmɪl/ a humorous phrase sometimes used by British people to refer to a problem, especially at home or at work. It is said in the accent of the people of northern England, especially *Yorkshire or *Lancashire(1), where there used to be many mills (= factories where cloth was made), and where the word 'the' is often not fully pronounced. The phrase suggests the idea that there were regular disputes between the workers in the mills and their owners.

the 'Troubles the name given to periods of political and social disturbance in Ireland, especially in the 20th century. The expression is now often used to refer to the period of violence and terrorist activity between Roman Catholics and Protestants in Northern Ireland since 1968, but it has also been applied to events such as the *Easter Rising (1916) and the *Anglo-Irish War (1919–21). Thousands of people have been killed in the Troubles.

True Con'fessions a US magazine containing articles which are supposed to be true stories written by ordinary people about their love and marriage problems. They are written in a very romantic and emotional way and are especially popular with young women.

Fred 'Trueman /'truːmən/ (1931–) a famous English cricket player. He was a fast bowler who played for Yorkshire (1949–68) and for England (1952–65). He was known for his aggressive attitude as a player, as a result of which he was sometimes called 'Fiery Fred' and he was often in trouble with the cricket authorities. He was the first bowler in the history of the game to take 300 wickets in test matches (= international matches). Since he stopped being a player he has appeared regularly on the radio programme *Test Match Special*. He is regarded with both affection and amusement by people who follow cricket in Britain.

Harry S 'Truman /'truːmən/ (1884–1972) the 33rd US *President (1945–53). He was Vice-President under Franklin D *Roosevelt, replaced him when he died in 1945, and then won the 1948 election. He gave permission for the first atom bombs to be dropped on Japan. His government began the *Marshall Plan and helped to establish the *United Nations and *NATO. Truman was strongly opposed to Communism. He began the *Truman Doctrine and involved the US in the *Korean War. He also began the *Fair Deal programme which made him popular with ordinary people. Before becoming President, he represented *Missouri in the US *Senate as a Democrat.

> 66 The buck stops here. 99
> sign on Harry S Truman's desk

the 'Truman ,Doctrine /'truːmən/ a policy announced in 1947 by President Harry *Truman in which he promised American financial and military help for Greece, Turkey and other countries threatened by Communism.

T

,Donald 'Trump /'trʌmp/ (1946–) a very rich US property owner. He built Trump Tower (a large office building) and the Trump International Hotel in New York, and he owns the Trump Castle and Taj Mahal casinos (= gambling clubs) in *Atlantic City, *New Jersey. Trump also bought the famous Plaza Hotel in New York in 1983. His book *The Art of the Comeback* (1997) describes how he became successful again after his businesses failed.

the ,*Trumpet* 'Voluntary a popular piece of music for the trumpet by Henry *Wood which is often played at ceremonies. Wood adapted it from a piece written by Jeremiah Clarke in 1700, called *The Prince of Denmark's March*.

'Truro /'trʊərəʊ; AmE 'trʊroʊ/ the administrative centre of *Cornwall in south-west England. It has a cathedral.

,Lynne 'Truss /'trʌs/ (1955–) an English writer, journalist and broadcaster who has written a number of novels and radio comedy dramas. She is best known for her best-selling book about punctuation, *Eats, Shoots and Leaves* (2003).

,Sojourner 'Truth /,sɒdʒənə 'truːθ; AmE 'sɑdʒərnər/ (c. 1797–1883) an African-American woman who was born a slave but ran away from her master in 1827 and became active in the campaigns to free slaves and to give women the same rights as men. Her name was used for the *NASA *Sojourner vehicle on Mars. See also ABOLITIONISM.

TT /,ti: 'ti:/ ⇨ TOURIST TROPHY.

the Tube /tjuːb/ an informal name for the *London Underground.

,Harriet 'Tubman /'tʌbmən/ (1821–1913) a US woman who was born a slave but escaped in 1849 and became active in the campaign to free slaves. She was given the *nickname Moses because she helped more than 300 slaves to escape by the *Underground Railroad. She also worked as a spy for the US Army during the *Civil War. See also ABOLITIONISM.

the TUC /,ti: ju: 'si:/ (in full the **Trades Union Congress**) the association of English trade unions. It was established in 1868 and its main function is to protect the interests of trade union members in the country as a whole in matters such as pay and conditions of work. The TUC meets every year for four days at the beginning of September, when representatives from all the trade unions gather to discuss various issues that affect them. The head of the TUC is called the General Secretary, and its members elect the General Council every year to represent it. Its headquarters are at *Congress House in central London. The Scottish TUC was established in 1897 and meets in *Glasgow every April.

The TUC established the *Labour Party in 1906 and paid the wages of the first Labour *Members of Parliament. There was traditionally a strong link between the two, with the TUC providing a lot of financial support for the Labour Party and greatly influencing its policies. In recent times this link has become less strong, and the Labour Party has been keen to show that it is not greatly influenced by the TUC.

'Tudor /'tjuːdə(r); AmE 'tuːdər/ adj **1** of or associated with the royal family that ruled England between 1485 and 1603, or this period: *one of the Tudor kings*. **2** of the style of architecture common during the 16th century in England. A characteristic feature of Tudor buildings is the use of black wooden frames surrounding white outer walls. See also HALF-TIMBERED.

,Tudor 'rose /,tjuːdə ; AmE ,tuːdər/ n the symbol of the *Tudor(1) family when its members were the kings and queens of England (1485–1603). It was introduced by *Henry VII when he became the first Tudor monarch,

and was a combination of the white rose (the symbol of the House of *York) and the red rose (the symbol of the House of *Lancaster).

,Jethro 'Tull /,dʒeθrəʊ 'tʌl; AmE ,dʒeθroʊ/ (1674–1741) an English farmer who invented the 'seed drill', a piece of agricultural equipment that made it possible for agricultural production to become mechanical. It was pulled by a horse, sowed (= planted) three rows of seed at the same time and removed weeds. It represented a major advance in agricultural methods, both in England and other countries.

'Tulsa /'tʌlsə/ the second largest city in the US state of *Oklahoma. It is a port on the Arkansas River which connects it to the *Gulf of Mexico. It was settled and named Tulsy in the 1830s by *Native Americans forced to leave *Alabama. Oil was discovered there in 1901, and the city remains a centre for the oil industry. See also ROBERTS.

,Tunbridge 'Wells /,tʌnbrɪdʒ 'welz/ a town in *Kent, southern England, which in the 17th and 18th centuries was an important spa town (= one where there are springs of mineral water considered to be healthy to drink). It has a reputation for being a place where many older, *middle-class, right-wing people live. See also DISGUSTED, TUNBRIDGE WELLS.

,Gene 'Tunney /'tʌni/ (1898–1978) a US boxer who became World Heavyweight Champion when he defeated Jack *Dempsey in 1926. He beat Dempsey again in the famous 'long count' contest (1927) when Tunney was knocked down but got up to win after the referee delayed.

'Tupperware™ /'tʌpəweə(r); AmE 'tʌpərwer/ n [U] a make of plastic containers for storing food in, widely used in Britain. When it was first introduced in the 1960s, the company paid people to hold **Tupperware parties** in their homes, to which they invited friends and offered to sell them Tupperware goods. Tupperware is now sold in many shops.

,Eva 'Turner[1] /'tɜːnə(r); AmE 'tɜːrnər/ (1892–1990) an English opera singer. She was known for her performances of operas by Puccini, Wagner and Verdi, and spent much of her career with the Chicago Opera Company. She retired in 1948 and was made a *dame(2) in 1962.

,J M W 'Turner[2] /'tɜːnə(r); AmE 'tɜːrnər/ (Joseph Mallord William Turner 1775–1851) a major English artist, famous for his landscape and seascape paintings (= scenes of the countryside and of the sea). A characteristic feature of his work is his original treatment of light and weather conditions. His style had a great influence on later artistic movements, especially Impressionism and *abstract expressionism. Turner spent much of his life travelling widely in Britain and Europe, doing drawings for his paintings. His best-known paintings include *The *Fighting Téméraire* (1838) and *Rain, Steam and Speed* (1844), both of which are in the *National Gallery in London. Many of his paintings became the property of the British nation after his death and are in *Tate Britain in London. In 1987 the Clore Gallery was added to the Tate especially to display Turner's works.

,Nat 'Turner[3] /,næt 'tɜːnə(r); AmE 'tɜːrnər/ (1800–1831) a US slave who in 1831 led a group of slaves to murder over 50 white people in Southampton County, *Virginia. This was called the Southampton Insurrection. Turner and 16 other slaves were hanged. The murders almost ended *abolitionism in the South and led to strict new laws to control slaves. See also STYRON.

,Ted 'Turner[4] /'tɜːnə(r); AmE 'tɜːrnər/ (1938–) a successful US businessman who established the *Turner Broadcasting System and *CNN. In 1996 he sold his company to *Time Warner. He also won the 1977 *America's Cup. In 1997, Turner announced that he would give $1 million to the *United Nations. He was married to the actor Jane *Fonda but the marriage ended in 2001.

ˌTina ˈ**Turner**[5] /ˈtɜːnə(r); AmE ˈtɜːrnər/ (1939–) a US singer whose early successes were with her husband Ike. Their records together included *River Deep, Mountain High* (1966) and *Proud Mary* (1972), which won two *Grammy awards. Their marriage ended in 1976. Tina has since then won five more Grammys and is famous for her live performances. She was chosen for the Rock and Roll *Hall of Fame in 1991.

the ˈ**Turner** ˈ**Broadcasting** ˌ**System** /ˈtɜːnə; AmE ˈtɜːrnər/ (abbr **TBS**) the television system created by Ted *Turner from the single station he bought in *Atlanta in 1976. He began *CNN in 1980 as part of TBS, which also now includes the TBS SuperStation, Turner Network Television, the Cartoon Network, the Atlanta Braves *baseball team and the Atlanta Hawks *basketball team. TBS became part of *Time Warner in 1996.

the ˈ**Turner Prize** /ˈtɜːnə; AmE ˈtɜːrnər/ a prize of £25 000 given every year at *Tate Britain to a British artist under the age of 50 for a work of modern art. Winners in the past have included Howard Hodgkin (1985) and Damien *Hirst (1995). The prize is an important cultural event in Britain, and a special exhibition of work by the four leading competitors is held at Tate Britain before the winner is announced.

ˌScott ˈ**Turow** /ˌskɒt ˈtjʊərəʊ; AmE ˌskɑːt ˈtjʊroʊ/ (1949–) a US writer and lawyer who is best known for his thrillers about the legal profession, several of which have been made into films. They include *Presumed Innocent* (1987), *Personal Injuries* (1999) and *Reversible Errors* (2002).

ˌDick ˈ**Turpin** /ˈtɜːpɪn; AmE ˈtɜːrpɪn/ (1706–39) a famous English highwayman (= a criminal who robbed travellers in former times). He was captured and hanged in York, possibly for murder or for stealing horses. After his death many romantic stories were told about him, especially one about his ride from London to York on his horse Black Bess.

ˈ**Turtle Wax**™ /ˈtɜːtl; AmE ˈtɜːrtl/ n [U] a US make of wax polish for cars which is sold in many countries around the world. In 1983, the company also began to sell products to clean shoes and household items.

Tusˌkegee Uniˈversity /tʌsˌkiːɡiː/ a university in Tuskegee, *Alabama, one of the first to provide education for *African Americans. It was first established in 1881 by Booker T *Washington to educate freed slaves. The university has a large library of books on African-American history and a museum.

Maˌrie Tusˈsaud /məˌriː tʊˈsɔːd/ ⇨ MADAME TUSSAUD'S.

ˌTuvaˈlu /ˌtuːˈvɑːluː/ a country consisting of nine islands in the south-west Pacific Ocean. Its capital city is Fongafale and its official languages are Tuvaluan and English. It was formerly a British colony called the Ellice Islands and became an independent member of the *Commonwealth in 1978.
▶ ˌTuvaˈluan n **1** [C] a native or inhabitant of Tuvalu. **2** [U] the language of Tuvalu.
Tuvaluan adj.

TVA /ˌtiː viː ˈeɪ/ ⇨ TENNESSEE VALLEY AUTHORITY.

TV Guide /ˌtiː viː ˈɡaɪd/ the most popular television magazine in the US. It began in 1953 and is published each week. It gives details of the times and channels for programmes but also has stories about stars and shows, and more serious articles about television.

TV licence /ˈtiː viː ˌlaɪsns/ ⇨ TELEVISION LICENCE.

TV Times /ˌtiː viː ˈtaɪmz/ a British magazine that gives details of the week's radio and television programmes,

and also includes articles about television actors, etc. It first appeared in 1968 and is published every week. Compare RADIO TIMES.

TWA /ˌtiː dʌblju: ˈeɪ/ (in full **Trans World Airlines**) a US airline. It was established in 1930, and made its first international flight (to Paris) in 1946. It was the first airline to show films on its planes (in 1961). Since 2001 it has been owned by American Airlines. In 1996 a TWA flight exploded over *Long Island and all 230 people on board were killed. The cause has not been found.

ˌMark ˈ**Twain** /ˈtweɪn/ (1835–1910) the leading US humorous writer of the 19th century. His real name was Samuel Langhorne Clemens. He is best known for the novels *The Adventures of Tom Sawyer* (1876) and *The Adventures of Huckleberry Finn* (1885), but he also wrote travel books and essays, many of them based on his experiences of life on the *Mississippi River. His other books include the historical novels *The Prince and the Pauper* (1882) and *A Connecticut Yankee in King Arthur's Court* (1889), and *Life on the Mississippi* (1889), an account of his early life. See also FINN, SAWYER.

❝ Put all your eggs in one basket and WATCH THAT BASKET. **❞**
Mark Twain

Mark Twain's house

ˈWilliam ˈMarcy ˈ**Tweed** /ˈmɑːsi ˈtwiːd; AmE ˈmɑːrsi/ (1823–78) a New York City political leader, known as 'Boss' Tweed, who became a symbol for dishonest behaviour in city politics. In the 1860s he was the leader of *Tammany Hall and ran the 'Tweed Ring', which accepted millions of dollars illegally from companies wanting to do business with the city authorities. He was finally removed from office and died in prison.

▶**tweed**

Tweed is a rough, thick woollen cloth made with threads of several colours **woven** together to make various patterns. The most common patterns are checks or 'herringbone', which has lines arranged like the bones of a fish. Many tweeds are in shades of grey or brown, and have a few brighter coloured threads woven in. Famous tweeds include **Donegal cloth** from Ireland and *Harris tweed.

Tweed is warm and hard-wearing and is traditionally used for outdoor clothes, such as jackets and coats, and for women's skirts. Men's flat caps are also made of tweed. In Britain tweed clothes are more often worn by older people, and was considered old-fashioned until the 1990s when it became fashionable. Americans think of tweed as something that never goes in or out of fashion. In America tweed is fairly casual, so a tweed jacket could be worn to work by a professor, but probably not by a lawyer.

ˌTweedleˈdum and Tweedleˈdee /ˌtwiːdlˈdʌm ənd twiːdlˈdiː/ two characters in the children's book

Through the Looking Glass by Lewis *Carroll. They are both fat and are dressed in exactly the same way, and their names are sometimes used to describe two people who look or behave like one another: *Two bald politicians in suits appeared, looking exactly like Tweedledum and Tweedledee.*

Tweety Pie /ˈtwiːti paɪ/ a canary (= a small yellow bird) in *Warner Brothers cartoons from the 1940s to the 1960s. He first appeared in 1941 and was joined by his enemy *Sylvester the cat in 1947. Tweety Pie speaks in a high voice rather like a baby, and when Sylvester is near often says, 'I tawt I taw a puddy tat.' ('I thought I saw a pussy cat.').

Twelfth 'Night 1 6 January, the church festival of Epiphany, formerly celebrated as the last night of *Christmas.
2 the evening of 5 January, the day before Epiphany, which traditionally marks the end of Christmas celebrations, so that many people take down the Christmas decorations on 6 January.

Twelfth 'Night a comedy play (c. 1601) by William *Shakespeare. It is set in the court of Orsino, Duke of Illyria, and is a complicated love story. The humour of the play is provided mainly by the characters Malvolio, Sir Toby Belch and Sir Andrew Aguecheek. The play begins with one of Shakespeare's best-known lines: 'If music be the food of love, play on.'

The Twelve Days of Christmas a traditional song often sung at *Christmas. It is about a person who receives a gift for each of the twelve days of Christmas. The song begins: 'On the first day of Christmas, my true love sent to me/A partridge in a pear tree.' Finally, on the 12th and last day, the person receives 'twelve lords a-leaping'.

'20th 'Century 'Fox a major *Hollywood film company. It was established in 1935, with Darryl F *Zanuck as head of production until 1956. Its many successful films have included *The *Grapes of Wrath*, *Cleopatra*, *The *Sound of Music*, *Star Wars*, *Home Alone* and *Independence Day*. The company was bought by Rupert *Murdoch in 1985.

Twickenham /ˈtwɪkənəm/ an area of the *borough of Richmond-upon-Thames in south-west London, England. Twickenham Stadium, also known informally as 'Twickers', is the national ground for *Rugby Union football, where *Six Nations matches and other Rugby Union games are played. It is also the home ground of the *Harlequins club.

Twiggy /ˈtwɪɡi/ (1949–) an English fashion model who became famous in the 1960s. She was known for being very thin, with short hair, and often wore very short skirts. She later became an actor, and appeared in the film of *The Boy Friend*. Her real name is Lesley Hornby.

The 'Twilight Zone a US television series (1959–65) which each week had a different strange story with a surprising ending. There was also a film (1983), and another television series, *The New Twilight Zone* (1985–89). The phrase 'in the twilight zone' is still used in American English to describe something mysterious.

the Twin 'Cities a popular name for *Minneapolis and *St Paul, *Minnesota, because they are next to each other, separated only by the *Mississippi River. They share the Twin Cities International Airport and the Mall of America, the largest shopping area in the US.

Twinings /ˈtwaɪnɪŋz/ a British company that sells tea of high quality. It was started in London by Thomas Twining in 1706.

Twinkie™ /ˈtwɪŋki/ n a small, sweet yellow cake with a soft filling like cream, sold in the US. It is regarded as typical of foods that are very popular but not very good for you.

'Twinkle, 'Twinkle, 'Little 'Star the title and first line of a traditional *nursery rhyme. The words are:

> 66 Twinkle, twinkle, little star,
> How I wonder what you are.
> Up above the world so high,
> Like a diamond in the sky. 99

Oliver 'Twist /ˈtwɪst/ ⇨ OLIVER TWIST.

Conway 'Twitty /ˌkɒnweɪ ˈtwɪti; AmE ˌkɑːnweɪ/ (1933–93) a US singer, mainly of country music. He often sang with Loretta *Lynn and they had five number one hits in a row, including *After the Fire Is Gone* (1971).

the two 'cultures a phrase made popular by the author C P *Snow in 1959. He used it to describe the division between the arts and the sciences in Britain, and argued that people trained in the arts did not understand or appreciate people trained in the sciences.

The Two 'Gentlemen of Ve'rona /vəˈrəʊnə; AmE vəˈroʊnə/ a comedy play (c. 1593) by William *Shakespeare. It is about two friends, Valentine and Proteus, who both fall in love with the same young woman, Silvia. Another young woman, Julia, is in love with Proteus, and a complicated love story follows. It is one of Shakespeare's less well-known plays.

Cy 'Twombly /ˌsaɪ ˈtwɒmbli; AmE ˈtwɑːmbli/ (1928–) a US painter whose works are abstract and often include numbers and letters. He has lived much of his life in Italy.

two-minute 'silence n (in Britain) a silence lasting two minutes, held every year at 11 a.m. on *Remembrance Sunday, in memory of the people who died during the two world wars and other conflicts. The silence is usually held at public ceremonies such as the one at the *Cenotaph in London.

2001: A Space Odyssey /tuː ˌθaʊznd ənd ˌwʌn ə ˌspeɪs ˈɒdəsi/ a film (1968) about future travel in space, written by Arthur C *Clarke and Stanley *Kubrick, who also directed it. The story is about a long trip taken in a spacecraft by two astronauts with an intelligent computer called HAL. It raised interesting questions about the influence of computers and the possibility of life on other planets. The film won an *Oscar for its special visual effects. Clarke later wrote the novel *2010: Odyssey Two* (1982) which was also made into a film (1984).

the Two Thousand 'Guineas (also the 2000 Guineas) /ˌtuː ˈθaʊzənd/ a well-known British horse race run every year at *Newmarket in late April or early May. It was first held in 1809.

Tyburn /ˈtaɪbɜːn; AmE ˈtaɪbɜːrn/ a place in London, England, near the present *Marble Arch, where people were hanged in public between about 1300 and 1783. After this the hangings took place outside *Newgate Prison.

Tylenol™ /ˈtaɪlənɒl; AmE ˈtaɪlənɑːl/ n [U] a US medicine that relieves pain and does not contain aspirin. The drug it contains is called *paracetamol* in Britain.

Anne 'Tyler[1] /ˈtaɪlə(r)/ (1941–) a US writer of popular novels that are intelligent and humorous. She received the *National Book Critics Circle award for *The Accidental Tourist* (1985) and the *Pulitzer Prize for *Breathing Lessons* (1988). Her other books include *If Morning Ever Comes* (1964), *Ladder of Years* (1995), *A Slipping-Down Life* (1997) and *Back When We Were Grownups* (2001).

Wat 'Tyler[2] /ˌwɒt ˈtaɪlə(r); AmE ˌwɑːt/ (died 1381) an English leader of the *Peasants' Revolt of 1381. He brought his army from *Kent to London, where he met and talked with King *Richard II. During the meeting he was injured in a fight, and he was later murdered.

,Kenneth 'Tynan /'taɪnən/ (1927–80) an English journalist and critic. He wrote mainly about the theatre, and was a strong supporter of the work of John *Osborne. Tynan's stage show *Oh, Calcutta!* shocked some people with its sexual humour, and he is also remembered as the first person to say the word 'fuck' on British television (in 1965). From 1963 to 1969 he was literary manager of the *National Theatre.

,William 'Tyndale /'tɪndeɪl/ (c. 1494–1536) an English writer who translated the Bible. His work as a translator was opposed in England and he was forced to live in Germany, where he produced the first English version of the Bible between 1525 and 1531. This later became the basis for the *King James Version of 1611. He was burnt alive in Belgium as a heretic.

the Tyne /taɪn/ a river in north-eastern England which passes through *Newcastle-upon-Tyne and reaches the *North Sea between Tynemouth and South Shields.

,Tyne and 'Wear /,taɪn, 'wɪə(r)/ a small *metropolitan county in north-east England, formed in 1974 from parts of *Durham and *Northumberland.

'Tyneside /'taɪnsaɪd/ an area of north-east England around the River *Tyne, including *Newcastle-upon-Tyne, Gateshead and South Shields. Tyneside was formerly an important centre for the shipbuilding and *coal-mining industries, but the area now has a lot of unemployment. People from Tyneside are informally called *Geordies.

the 'Tynwald /'tɪnwəld/ the parliament of the *Isle of Man, based in the island's capital, *Douglas. It is one of the oldest parliaments in the world, originally formed in the 10th century. In 1881 it became the first parliament to allow women to vote.

,Typhoid 'Mary (1868–1938) the *nickname given to Mary Mallon, the first person known to carry typhoid fever (= a serious disease caused by infected food or water) in the US (though she did not suffer from the disease herself). She was an Irish woman who settled in New York City as a cook and is believed to have infected 25 people in 1906–7. She refused treatment but was kept in New York's Sloane Hospital where she gave more people the disease before dying there. Americans call somebody Typhoid Mary in a humorous way if they think they should be avoided because they bring bad luck or are dangerous in some way.

Ty'phoo™ /taɪ'fu:/ a popular British make of tea.

,Mike 'Tyson /'taɪsn/ (1966–) a US boxer who became the World Heavyweight Champion (1987–90 and 1996). He was sent to prison (1992–5) for rape (= the sex act forced on somebody). In 1996 he was defeated by Evander Holyfield, and when they fought again in 1997, Tyson bit off part of his opponent's ear, and Holyfield was automatically declared the winner.

T

U u

U /juː/ adj (BrE) **1** (humorous) typical of the dress, behaviour, speech, etc. of *upper-class people. Compare NON-U.
2 (BrE) (in full **Universal**) (of films) officially judged to be suitable for anyone, including children; not containing violence, sex or bad language: a U film/certificate.

U3A /juː θriː 'eɪ/ ⇨ UNIVERSITY OF THE THIRD AGE.

UA /juː 'eɪ/ ⇨ UNITED ARTISTS.

UAW /juː eɪ 'dʌbljuː/ (in full **United Automobile Workers**) (also **United Auto Workers**) a large US trade union for workers in the car, aerospace and metal industries. Its full name is the United International Union of the Automobile, Aerospace & Agricultural Implement Workers of America. It was established in 1935 and had 1.2 million members in 2003. It left the *AFL-CIO in 1968.

UCAS /'juːkæs/ ⇨ UNIVERSITIES AND COLLEGES ADMISSIONS SERVICE.

UCATT /'juːkæt/ (in full the **Union of Construction, Allied Trades and Technicians**) a British *trade union for workers in the building trades, formed by joining several other trade unions in 1970.

UCH /juː siː 'eɪtʃ/ ⇨ UNIVERSITY COLLEGE HOSPITAL.

UCL /juː siː 'el/ ⇨ UNIVERSITY COLLEGE, LONDON.

UCLA /juː siː el 'eɪ/ (in full the **University of California at Los Angeles**) the largest of the eight branches of the University of *California. It was established in 1919 and in 2001 had about 37000 students. UCLA is known especially for its film studies. It also has a strong sports programme and has won the *NCAA National Basketball Championship 11 times.

UDA /juː diː 'eɪ/ ⇨ ULSTER DEFENCE ASSOCIATION.

the UDM /juː diː 'em/ (in full the **Union of Democratic Mineworkers**) a British *trade union for coal miners. It was formed in 1985 as a protest against the actions of the *NUM, which had failed to hold an election among its members before the *miners' strike in the previous year.

UDR /juː diː 'ɑː(r)/ ⇨ ULSTER DEFENCE REGIMENT.

UEFA /juːˈeɪfə/ (in full the Union of European Football Associations). UEFA organizes the UEFA Cup and the UEFA Champions League competitions for European football teams.

UFF /juː ef 'ef/ ⇨ ULSTER FREEDOM FIGHTERS.

U'ganda /juːˈgændə/ a country in eastern central Africa. Its capital city is Kampala and its official language is English. The economy is based mainly on farming, and its main exports are cotton and coffee. From 1894 to 1962 Uganda was a British protectorate (= a country controlled and protected by Britain), and it then became an independent member of the *Commonwealth. In the 1970s the country suffered under the violent rule of Idi Amin. One of his acts was to force Ugandan Asians to leave the country, and many of them settled in Britain.
▶ **U'gandan** /juːˈgændən/ adj, n.

the ˌUgly 'Sisters the two older sisters of *Cinderella in the traditional children's story. In *pantomimes the Ugly Sisters are usually played by men dressed as women.

UK /juː 'keɪ/ ⇨ UNITED KINGDOM.

UKAEA /juː keɪ eɪ iː 'eɪ/ ⇨ UNITED KINGDOM ATOMIC ENERGY AUTHORITY.

the ˌUK 'Film ˌCouncil an organization created by the British government in 2000 to develop the film industry in Britain by providing financial support for development and training.

UKIP /'juːkɪp/ (in full the **United Kingdom Independence Party**) a British right-wing political party, created in 1983, which would like Britain to leave the *EU. It has a number of elected members of the *London Assembly and 12 *MEPs. Its leader is Roger Knapman.

'Ullswater /'ʌlzwɔːtə(r)/ one of the largest lakes of the English *Lake District. It is 7.5 miles/12 kilometres long.

'Ulster /'ʌlstə(r)/ another name for Northern Ireland, used especially by *unionists (= people who favour political union between Britain and Northern Ireland). There is also a province of Ulster in the *Republic of Ireland. See also SIX COUNTIES.

the ˌUlster De'fence Associˌation /ˌʌlstə; AmE ˌʌlstər/ (abbr the **UDA**) an illegal *Protestant military group in *Ulster (= Northern Ireland). The group wants Ulster to remain a part of the *United Kingdom, and uses violence to oppose the *IRA. It was formed as a legal political organization in 1971, but was made illegal in 1992 after committing acts of violence against *Roman Catholics. Other similar groups include the *Ulster Freedom Fighters and the *Ulster Volunteer Force.

the ˌUlster De'fence ˌRegiment /ˌʌlstə; AmE ˌʌlstər/ (abbr the **UDR**) a branch of the British Army operating in Northern Ireland. It was formed in 1970 to help to control the violence there. In 1992 it became a part of the Royal Irish Regiment.

the 'Ulster Demo'cratic 'Unionist ˌParty /ˌʌlstə, ˌʌlstər/ (also the **Democratic Unionist Party**) a political party in Northern Ireland. It is supported mainly by *Protestants, and wants Northern Ireland to remain a part of the United Kingdom. It is regarded as having more extreme policies than the *Ulster Unionist Party, and has been led since 1971 by Ian *Paisley. In 2004 it became the largest Northern Ireland party to be represented in the *House of Commons, with six *Members of Parliament.

the ˌUlster 'Freedom ˌFighters /ˌʌlstə; AmE ˌʌlstər/ (abbr the **UFF**) an illegal *Protestant military group in *Ulster (= Northern Ireland), formed in 1973. The group wants Ulster to remain a part of the United Kingdom, and uses violence to oppose the *IRA. Other similar groups include the *Ulster Defence Association and the *Ulster Volunteer Force.

the ˌUlster 'Unionist ˌParty /ˌʌlstə; AmE ˌʌlstər/ (abbr **UUP**) a political party in Northern Ireland, formed in 1905 and led from 1995 to 2005 by David *Trimble. It is one of the main political parties that wants Northern Ireland to remain a part of the *United Kingdom. In 2003 it had six *Members of Parliament in the *House of Commons but three of them resigned in protest at their leader's support of the *Good Friday Agreement.

the ˌUlster Volun'teer Force /ˌʌlstə; AmE ˌʌlstər/ (abbr the **UVF**) a Protestant military group in *Ulster (= Northern Ireland). The group wants Ulster to remain a part of the *United Kingdom, and opposes the *IRA. The present group was formed in 1966, but an earlier group with the same name was formed in 1913. Other similar groups include the *Ulster Freedom Fighters and the *Ulster Defence Association.

Ulysses /'juːlɪsiːz, juːˈlɪsiːz/ a novel (1922) by James *Joyce. It is considered by many people to be one of the greatest novels of the 20th century, although it was not published in Britain and the US until the 1930s because it was thought to be too offensive. It is written in a wide variety of styles, and deals with the events of one day through the experiences of three main characters, Stephen Dedalus, Leopold Bloom and Molly Bloom.

UMIST /'juːmɪst/ (*in full* **the University of Manchester Institute of Science and Technology**) a former university in Manchester, north-west England which was established in 1824 to provide training in engineering and other subjects and became famous for its scientific research. In 2004 it became part of a new combined *University of Manchester.

UN /ˌjuː 'en/ ⇨ UNITED NATIONS.

the 'Unabomber /'juːnəbɒmə(r); *AmE* 'juːnəbɑːmər/ the name used especially by the press and the police to refer to a person in the US who for 17 years (1978–95) sent bombs to people in universities and airline companies who he thought supported modern technology. The bombs killed three people and injured 23. Theodore Kaczynski, a former mathematics teacher at the University of California at *Berkeley, was arrested in 1996 and charged with being the Unabomber. He was found guilty and sent to prison for life in 1998.

ˌUncle 'Ben's™ a US product name for rice produced by the Uncle Ben's Converted Brand Rice Company. The original Uncle Ben was a farmer in *Texas who supplied rice to the Converted Rice Company.

ˌUncle 'Remus /'riːməs/ the character who tells the stories in several books by Joel Chandler Harris (1848–1908). Uncle Remus is a former slave whose stories include Brer (Brother) Rabbit, Brer Fox and Brer Bear. Among the books are *Uncle Remus, His Songs and His Sayings* (1881), *The Tar Baby* (1904) and *Uncle Remus and Brer Rabbit* (1906). He was also the main character in the Walt *Disney film *Song of the South* (1946).

ˌUncle 'Sam the imaginary person who represents the US and its government. He became an official symbol in 1961. Uncle Sam has a white beard and wears red, white and blue clothes, with stars on his tall hat. He was probably named after 'Uncle' Sam Wilson (1766–1854), who examined army supplies for the US government during the *War of 1812. During both world wars, a picture of Uncle Sam appeared on posters telling young men that they should join the armed forces.

ˌUncle Tom 'Cobbleigh /'kɒbli; *AmE* 'kɑːbli/ a character from the traditional English song *Widdicombe Fair*. The song includes a long list of people who go to the *fair, ending with the line 'Old Uncle Tom Cobbleigh and all'. People sometimes use this phrase to mean that a large group of people are present in a place, including everyone that one might expect or imagine: *Everyone turned up at the party – Jack, Ella, Steve, Roger, old Uncle Tom Cobbleigh and all!*

ˌUncle Tom's 'Cabin a novel (1852) by the US writer Harriet Beecher *Stowe which increased support for the movement to free slaves. It is about a kind slave called Tom who is badly treated and finally killed by Simon *Legree. Tom's daughter Little Eva also dies, and another well-known character in the novel is the slave child *Topsy. The name 'Uncle Tom' is sometimes used as an insult to describe an African American who has too much respect for white people.

the 'Underground ⇨ LONDON UNDERGROUND.

the ˌUnderground 'Railroad a secret system used in the US before the *Civil War for helping thousands of slaves to escape to the free northern states or Canada. The slaves were called 'passengers', the people who helped them were 'conductors', and the slaves hid in 'stations' (safe houses) along the way.

ˌUnder Milk 'Wood a play (1953) by Dylan *Thomas about a day in the life of a Welsh village by the sea. It was originally written for radio, and is still very popular because of its rich language and its range of humorous characters.

'unicorn /'juːnɪkɔːn; *AmE* 'juːnɪkɔːrn/ *n* an imaginary animal like a horse with a single straight horn growing from its forehead. It appears in many traditional stories, and can be seen on the *royal arms, where it represents Scotland. See also LION AND THE UNICORN.

the ˌUnifi'cation 'Church a religious organization begun in Korea in 1954 by the businessman Sun Myung Moon (1920–) and now established in many other countries, including the US (where its main offices now are), Britain and Australia. Members of the organization are called *Moonies. Sun Myung Moon was sent to prison in 1984–5 for failing to pay enough US income tax.

'Unilever /'juːnɪliːvə(r)/ a large British and Dutch company that makes food, drink and soap products. It was formed in 1930 by joining two companies, Lever Brothers (established by Lord *Leverhulme) and the Dutch company Margarine Unie. Its best-known products include *Birdseye, *Flora, *Marmite, *Persil and *Wall's.

the 'Union another name for the United States. It was used especially during the *Civil War in which 'the Union' fought the *Confederate States: *The Union forces captured Atlanta in 1864.*

ˌUnion 'Carbide /'kɑːbaɪd; *AmE* 'kɑːrbaɪd/ a large US chemicals company whose main office is in Danbury, *Connecticut. In December 1984, there was a serious accident at the Union Carbide factory in Bhopal, India. Poisonous gases were released into the air, killing more than 2000 people. Many relatives brought legal cases against Union Carbide, and the disaster caused a lot of public discussion about the responsibilities of international companies operating in poorer countries.

'Unionist *n* a person who favours political union between Britain and Northern Ireland, and opposes union between Northern Ireland and the Irish Republic. The main Unionist parties in Northern Ireland are the *Ulster Unionist Party and the *Ulster Democratic Unionist Party. Compare LOYALIST. See also ACT OF UNION, HOME RULE, MARCHING SEASON, ORANGEMEN.

▶ **the Union Jack**

The national flag of the United Kingdom is commonly known as the **Union Jack** and also as the **Union Flag**. It has been used as the British flag since 1603, when Scotland and England were united. The original design combined the red cross of England, *St George's Cross, with the white diagonal cross on a blue background of Scotland, *St Andrew's Cross. The red diagonal cross of Ireland, St Patrick's Cross, was added in 1801, when Ireland became part of the United Kingdom. Wales is not represented on the Union Jack because it is a principality of England. The national flag of Wales with the red dragon of Cadwallader on a green and white background has been recognized since the 1950s as the national flag of Wales.

The Union Jack is most often seen flying from public buildings or at sports events. Children may wave small Union Jacks when a member of the royal family visits their town. During national celebrations strings of small flags are hung across the street as bunting.

The Union Jack is less important to British people than the Stars and Stripes is to Americans. Many people feel a stronger loyalty to the national flags of England, Scotland, Wales or Northern Ireland. The flag of the *European Union, a circle of gold stars on a blue background, is sometimes also seen in Britain, e.g. on car number plates.

'Union Pa'cific 'Railroad /pə'sɪfɪk/ a US rail line built in the 1860s, consisting of 1086 miles/1747 kilometres of track stretching west from *Omaha, *Nebraska. On 10 May 1869, at Promontory Point, *Utah, it met the Central Pacific Railroad, 690 miles/1110 kilometres of track stretching east from Sacramento, *California. There was a special ceremony in which a large gold nail was hit with a silver hammer to mark the first complete railway running all the way from the east to the west of America.

Union 'Square 1 a park in *Manhattan(1), New York City. It is between *Broadway and *Park Avenue and between East 17th Street and East 14th Street. Rich people lived in the area before the *American Civil War. In the 1960s Union Square became associated with illegal drugs and violence but since then the city authorities have made it a more modern and pleasant place. **2** a square in the centre *San Francisco with many hotels and expensive shops.

'Unison /'juːnɪsn/ Britain's largest *trade union, formed in 1993 by combining three existing unions (NALGO, NUPE and COHSE). Its members work mainly in local government, the health service and other industries serving the public.

unitary au'thority /ˌjuːnɪtri; AmE ˌjuːnɪteri/ (also **unitary 'council**) n a type of local *council introduced in some areas of England from 1995 and in all areas of Wales in 1996. Unitary authorities replaced the old system of county and district councils, providing a single level of local government. Some unitary authorities, for example the East *Riding of Yorkshire, govern a wide geographical area, while others control a single large city or town, for example *Portsmouth. There are 46 unitary authorities in England and 22 in Wales. A similar system of local government was introduced in Scotland in 1996 consisting of *council areas. Northern Ireland has had a single-level local government since 1973 made up of 'district councils'.

U'nited an informal name for any British football club with 'United' in its name, e.g. *Manchester United: *United have won all their matches this season.*

U,nited 'Artists (abbr **UA**) a US film company started in 1919 by Mary *Pickford, Douglas *Fairbanks[1], Charlie *Chaplin and D W *Griffith. It was the first *Hollywood company to allow actors to be independent. Its successful films included *The *Gold Rush*, *Scarface* (1932), *The African Queen* (1951), *High Noon* (1953), *Some Like It Hot* (1959), *The *Magnificent Seven* (1960), the James *Bond films of the 1960s, *One Flew Over the Cuckoo's Nest* (1975), *Rocky* (1976) and *Rain Man* (1988). In 1981 the company became part of *MGM.

the U,nited 'Kingdom (abbr **the UK**) (in full **the United Kingdom of Great Britain and Northern Ireland**) a country made up of England, Wales, Scotland and Northern Ireland. It is a member of the *Commonwealth and the *European Union and its capital is *London. The name United Kingdom is found mainly in formal and official use. In more general use the country is referred to as Britain. See also ACT OF UNION. ⇨ note at GREAT BRITAIN.

the U'nited 'Kingdom A'tomic 'Energy Au,thority (abbr **UKAEA**) a British government

organization formed in 1954 to develop Britain's nuclear power programme and produce electricity. Today its main task is to manage the older nuclear power stations and carry out nuclear research.

U,nited 'Kingdom Inde'pendence ,Party ⇨ UKIP.

the U'nited 'Kingdom 'Unionist ,Party a British political party. It is supported mainly by *Protestants in Northern Ireland who want Northern Ireland to remain a part of the United Kingdom.

the U,nited 'Nations (also the ,United 'Nations Organi,zation) (abbrs the **UN**, **UNO**) an international organization, based in New York, which aims to preserve peace around the world and solve international problems. It was formed in 1945, and replaced the League of Nations. Most of the world's independent states are members, and each has one vote in the *General Assembly. The *United Nations Security Council has the power to take military or economic action to settle international disputes. Other branches of the United Nations include the World Bank, the International Court of Justice in The Netherlands, and the United Nations Children's Fund (UNICEF). The Secretary General of the United Nations is Kofi Annan.

the U'nited 'Nations Se'curity ,Council (also the **UN Security Council**) the part of the *United Nations which has the power to take political, economic or military action to settle international disputes and preserve world peace. It has 15 members, of which five are permanent (Britain, China, France, the Russian Federation and the US). Any decisions it makes must be agreed by a majority of its members, including all five of the permanent members.

the U'nited 'Negro 'College Fund a US charity, established in 1944, which raises money to support private colleges and universities with mostly *African American students. It also helps individual students.

U'nited 'Press Inter'national (abbr **UPI**) a US company that collects news items and sells them to newspapers and radio and television stations. It was established in 1958 when United Press and the International News Service joined together. Compare ASSOCIATED PRESS.

the U'nited Re'formed 'Church a Christian Church formed in Britain in 1972 when the *Presbyterian Church in England joined with the *Congregationalists in England and Wales. It has since been joined by two other church groups: the Re-formed Churches of Christ in 1981, and the Congregational Union of Scotland in 2000.

the United States 'Agency for Inter'national De'velopment ⇨ USAID.

the U'nited 'States 'Air Force A,cademy the university that trains officers for the US Air Force. It was established in 1954 in Colorado Springs, *Colorado, and is the newest of the US military colleges. It had about 4000 students in 2003. They receive a *bachelor's degree in science when they complete their four years of studies.

U'nited 'States 'Central Com'mand (abbr **CENTCOM**) a unit of the US military created in 1983 to replace the Rapid Deployment Force under the control of the US Secretary of Defense with its main base in Tampa, *Florida. It includes forces from the army, air force, marines and navy and is involved in military operations in Africa, the Middle East and Asia, such as the war in Afghanistan and the Iraq War.

the U'nited 'States 'Coast Guard the US military service that was controlled by the US *Department of Transportation until 2000 and is now part of the

*Department of Homeland Security. It was established in 1909. The Coast Guard stops ships suspected of carrying drugs and other illegal goods, and can make arrests. It also keeps watch to see that other laws of the sea are obeyed, rescues ships in danger and has a weather service.

the U'nited 'States 'Forest ,Service
⇨ USDA FOREST SERVICE.

the U'nited 'States Infor'mation ,Agency
(*abbr* **the USIA**) a US government organization that was responsible for providing information about the US to other countries of the world, e.g. through libraries and cultural programmes. It also ran the *Fulbright scholarship programme and advised the *National Security Council on what other countries think of US policies. The USIA was established in 1948 and became part of the *State Department in 1999. See also VOICE OF AMERICA.

the U'nited 'States Ma'rine Corps (*also* the
United States Marines) a US armed service that is part of the US Navy. It was established by *Congress in 1798 as the only service trained to fight on the sea, on land and in the air. The Marines became well known during *World War II when they successfully attacked the Pacific islands occupied by the Japanese. They were also active in the *Korean War, the *Vietnam War, the *Gulf War and the war in Iraq.

the U'nited 'States 'Military A,cademy (*also*
,**West 'Point**) the military school that trains officers for the US Army. It is at West Point, New York, and was established by *Congress in 1802. It has about 4 000 students, who are called *cadets*. Famous US generals who were trained there include Robert E *Lee, Ulysses S *Grant, John *Pershing, Dwight D *Eisenhower, George *Patton, Douglas *MacArthur and Norman Schwartzkopf.

the U'nited 'States 'Naval A,cademy (*also*
Annapolis) the military school that trains officers for the US Navy and the US Marine Corps. It was established in 1845 at *Annapolis, *Maryland and has about 4 000 students, called *midshipmen*.

the U'nited 'States 'Senate (*also* the **Senate**) the
upper house of the US *Congress. There are 100 **Senators** (two from each state), and they are elected for periods of six years. Laws must be passed by both houses (i.e. the Senate and the *House of Representatives), but the Senate has special responsibility in matters to do with foreign policy, and it also has the power to 'advise and consent' on appointments made by the President. The Vice-President is the senior officer in the Congress.

the U'nited 'Way of A'merica a large US charity,
established in 1918, with branches in nearly 1 500 cities and towns. It has campaigns once a year to collect money which is then divided among local charities and organizations. The main office is in Alexandria, *Virginia.

,Universal 'Pictures (*also* **Universal**) a *Hollywood
film company, established in 1912. The large area where many of its films are made is called **Universal City** and attracts many tourists. Steven *Spielberg made several of his films there, including *Jaws*, *ET and *Jurassic Park*. The company opened a second Universal City at *Orlando, *Florida, in 1990.

The 'Universe a leading newspaper for *Roman
Catholics in Britain. It appears every week and was first published in 1860.

the ,Uni'versities and 'Colleges Ad'missions
,**Service** (*abbr* **UCAS**) the organization that deals with students wanting to apply to study at British universities and colleges. Students must complete a special form, on paper or on the Internet, and may apply to a maximum of six institutions. Each institution then considers the requests and may offer students places. The organization also publishes *The Big Guide* (*University and College Entrance: The Official Guide*), which lists all the courses available at British universities and colleges, and gives information about them. The only university that does not take part in the UCAS service is the *Open University. ⇨ note at HIGHER EDUCATION.

,Uni'versity 'Challenge a British television quiz
show in which teams of students from different universities compete to answer difficult questions on a wide range of subjects. It was presented from 1962 to 1987 by Bamber Gascoigne and since 1994 it has been presented by Jeremy *Paxman. A phrase often used in the programme is 'Your starter for ten' to introduce a first question worth ten points.

,Uni'versity 'College, 'London /'lʌndən/ (*abbr*
UCL) a college of *London University, established in 1826. It was the first college to be established in England apart from the colleges of *Oxford and *Cambridge, and was originally for students who were *Nonconformists (= Christians who did not belong to the *Church of England).

,Uni'versity 'College 'Hospital (*abbr* **UCH**) a
*teaching hospital in London, England, opened in 1833 as part of *University College, London.

the ,Uni'versity of Cali'fornia at Los 'Angeles
/kælɪˈfɔːniə, lɒs ˈændʒəliːz; *AmE* kælɪˈfɔːrniə, lɔːs/ ⇨ UCLA.

the ,Uni'versity of 'Manchester /'mæntʃəstə(r)/
a university in Manchester, north-west England. In 2004 it was established as the largest university of its kind in Britain when two universities, the Victoria University of Manchester and the University of Manchester Institute of Science and Techchnology (UMIST) combined.

Uni'versity of the 'Third 'Age (*abbr* **U3A**) an inter-
national organization aimed at providing 'lifelong learning for older people'. It organizes courses and other activities for retired people. It started in France in 1968 and the first U3A group started in the UK in *Cambridge after the creation of a charity **The Third Age Trust** in 1983. Most courses in the UK are taught by U3A members themselves using their knowledge and experience.

the 'Tomb of the 'Unknown 'Warrior (*also* the
'**Tomb of the 'Unknown 'Soldier**) a grave inside *Westminster Abbey, London, England, which contains the body of an unknown British soldier who died in *World War I. The grave represents the many other soldiers who died, especially those whose bodies were never identified. There is a similar grave at the *Arlington National Cemetery, Virginia, US, now called officially the **Tomb of the Unknowns**, where unknown US soldiers killed in war are buried.

UNO /ˌjuː en ˈəʊ; *AmE* ˈoʊ/ ⇨ UNITED NATIONS.

'Unser /'ʌnsə(r)/ the name of three successful US racing
car drivers. They are the brothers **Bobby Unser** (1934–) and **Al Unser** (1939–), and Al's son, **Al Unser Junior** (1962–). Bobby won the *Indianapolis 500 race three times (1968, 1975 and 1981), Al won it four times (1970, 1971, 1978 and 1987) and his son has won it twice (1992, 1994).

the Un'touchables the popular name for the team of
US Justice Department officers led by Eliot *Ness. They were given the name because people believed that they were too honest ever to accept illegal payments.

,John 'Updike /'ʌpdaɪk/ (1932–) a US poet and writer of
novels and short stories about the hopes, worries and fears of modern *middle-class Americans. He is best known for his four novels about a former *basketball

U

player, Harry 'Rabbit' Angstrom. They are *Rabbit, Run* (1960), *Rabbit Redux* (1971), *Rabbit is Rich* (1981) and *Rabbit at Rest* (1990). The last two each won the *Pulitzer Prize. His other novels include *The Witches of Eastwick* (1984), *Toward the End of Time* (1997), *Seek my Face* (2002) and *Villages* (2005).

,**Up-Helly-'Aa** /ˌʌp heli 'ɑː/ a festival held every January in *Lerwick, in the *Shetland Islands, to mark the islands' historical links with the *Vikings. In the main ceremony a model of a Viking long ship (= a type of long narrow warship) is burned in the middle of the town.

UPI /ˌjuː piː 'aɪ/ ⇨ UNITED PRESS INTERNATIONAL.

the ,**upper 'class** *n* [sing+ sing/pl *v*] (*also* the **upper classes** [pl]) the people at the top in society. In Britain the upper class are usually from rich families who own land and property. They may have noble titles such as 'Lord' or 'Lady', and they typically send their children to *public schools. Many people also think of them as having a particular way of speaking. Because of their connection with the land and the countryside, they are often associated with country sports such as shooting and horse riding.
▶ **upper-class** *adj*: *an upper-class accent/education/ family.*

the ,**upper middle 'class** *n* [sing+ sing/pl *v*] (*also* the **upper middle classes** [pl]) the class of people in British society between the *middle class and the *upper class. Its members include people such as company directors, professors or *barristers, who have a high social status and may earn a lot of money. In modern Britain, however, it is less common to identify people in this way.
▶ **upper-middle-class** *adj*: *an upper-middle-class lifestyle/background.*

'**upper school** *n* (in Britain) the name given to the classes for older children (aged 14–18) in a secondary school (for children aged 11–18). It may also include a *sixth form.

,**Upstairs, 'Downstairs** a very successful British television series (1971–5) about the life of a rich London family and their servants in the early years of the 20th century. It was common in the houses of such families for the kitchen to be below the ground floor level, i.e. 'downstairs'.

'**Uptown** /'ʌptaʊn/ **1** the part of *Manhattan(1) in New York City which is north of 59th Street. It includes *Central Park and areas on both sides of it. The Upper East Side includes the *Metropolitan Museum of Art, the *Guggenheim Museum and *Bloomingdale's. The Upper West Side has the *Lincoln Center for the Performing Arts and Fordham University. Compare DOWNTOWN.
2 uptown *n* (*AmE*) the outer districts of a city or large town, where its people mostly live.
▶ **uptown** *adj, adv* (*AmE*) to or in the outer districts of a large city or town: *an uptown residential area* ◇ *go/drive uptown.*

,**Urban De'velopment Corpo,ration** any of several organizations started by the British government to develop and improve areas of the *inner cities. The first two were started in 1981 in London's *Docklands and in *Merseyside, and created many new offices, houses and industries. The Corporations especially encouraged businesses from abroad to come to the areas.

the ,**Urban 'League** (*also* the ,**National 'Urban 'League**) a US organization of people who work without pay to help *African Americans and other minority groups to gain equal rights. It was established in 1910 and now has more than 100 local groups that train

minorities for jobs and help them to receive health care and other support.

USAFC /ˌjuː es ˌeɪ ef 'siː/ ⇨ USA FREEDOM CORPS.

,**USA 'Freedom Corps** (*abbr* **USAFC**) a US organization set up by George W *Bush in 2002 to encourage people to work on a voluntary basis for their country. There are three major programmes within the Freedom Corps: firstly, the Citizen Corps, concerned with safety and anti-terrorism measures in the US; secondly, a programme to increase the number of people helping their local communities; thirdly, an expansion of the *Peace Corps programme, particularly in Afghanistan.

USAID /ˌjuː es 'eɪd/ (*in full* the **US Agency for International Development**) an independent US government organization that works to provide help for poor countries. It was established in 1961 by President John F *Kennedy and gives financial, technical and medical assistance.

,**USA 'Network** ⇨ NBC UNIVERSAL.

USA Today /ˌjuː es 'eɪ tə'deɪ/ a national US newspaper read by more people than any other. It sells over two million copies each day. The Gannett Company began *USA Today* in 1979. It has colourful pictures, short news summaries and longer articles.

USCIS (*in full* **US Citizenship and Immigration Services**) the US government department that replaced the *INS in 2003.

the **USDA Forest Service** /ˌjuː es diː 'eɪ/ (*in full* **United States Department of Agriculture Forest Service**) (*also* **United States Forest Service**) the organization controlled by the US Department of Agriculture which protects and manages America's forests. It was established in 1905. It does research and provides educational programmes and advice to individual states and private forest owners. It is also responsible for 39 Special Recreation Areas.

USDAW /'ʌzdɔː/ (*in full* the **Union of Shop, Distributive and Allied Workers**) a British *trade union for people who work in shops, factories, restaurants and other places where they serve the public. It was formed in 1891.

,**used-'car ,salesman** *n* (*pl* **-men**) (*BrE*) a man whose job is selling cars that have already had one or more owners. Used-car salesmen are often presented in jokes, cartoons etc. as not very honest or reliable. The British television character Arthur *Daley is regarded as a typical used-car salesman, i.e. confident and friendly, but dishonest and not very successful. Opponents of US President Richard *Nixon used to show his picture with the words, 'Would you buy a used car from this man?', suggesting that he could not be trusted.

,**US 'English** /ˌjuː es/ a right-wing group in the US started in 1983 which campaigns for English to be the only official language in the US which it sees as a way of forcing immigrants to become more integrated into society. It opposes the use of other languages, such as Spanish, in education, etc.

USIA /ˌjuː es aɪ 'eɪ/ ⇨ UNITED STATES INFORMATION AGENCY.

the ,**US 'Masters ,Tournament** /ˌjuː es/ (*also* the **US Masters**) ⇨ MASTERS TOURNAMENT.

'*US 'News and 'World Re'port* /ˌjuː es/ a popular US news magazine published each week. It is often referred to simply as *US News* and is known for its conservative opinions. It contains many articles on business and economic affairs, and also news about political, social and cultural matters.

the **USO** /ˌjuː es 'əʊ; *AmE* ˌjuː es 'oʊ/ (*in full* the **United Service Organizations**) an organization that provides support for people serving in the US armed forces. It was started in 1941 and most of the people who work for it are volunteers. As well as social clubs and family support, the USO provides entertainment for soldiers serving abroad. Bob *Hope often appeared in USO shows. Compare ENSA.

the ˌUS 'Open /ˌju: es/ **1** a major US golf competition held each year at different places. It was first held in 1895. The most wins by a single player have been four. Four players have achieved this: Willie Anderson, Bobby *Jones, Ben *Hogan and Jack *Nicklaus. Compare BRITISH OPEN, MASTERS TOURNAMENT.
2 a US tennis competition held each year which is one of the sport's *grand slam(1) events. It was first played in 1968 in Forest Hills, New York, and moved in 1978 to Flushing Meadow, New York. Jimmy *Connors has won the men's competition the most times (5), and Chris *Evert has won the most women's events (6). Compare WIMBLEDON.

ˌPeter 'Ustinov /ˈjuːstɪnɒf; AmE ˈjuːstɪnɑːf/ (1921–2004) an English actor, writer and film director. He was best known for playing unusual characters, e.g. in Death on the Nile (1978), in which he played the detective Hercule *Poirot. He was also admired for telling funny stories on stage and television and for his ability to copy many different foreign accents. Ustinov wrote several plays and novels. He was made a *knight in 1990.

USWA /ˌju: es dʌblju: 'eɪ/ (also **USW**) (in full **the United Steelworkers of America**) one of the largest US *trade unions. It was established in 1936 as the Steel Workers' Organizing Committee for steel, iron and tin workers, and took its present name in 1942. It now includes workers in other industries, such as rubber and plastics.

'Utah /ˈjuːtɑː/ a western US state which is one of the *Rocky Mountain States. About two-thirds of the population are *Mormons. It was named after the *Ute *Native American people, and its popular name is the Beehive State. Other Native Americans, such as the *Navajo, lived in the area when the Mormons began to settle there in 1847. It became a state in 1896. Its products include cattle, pigs, copper, gold, silver, oil and medical instruments. Tourist attractions include the *Great Salt Lake, the *Rainbow Bridge and *Zion National Park.

Ute /juːt/ n a member of a *Native American people who mostly live in *Colorado and *Utah on reservations (= land given and protected by the US government). They are farmers and make money from oil and gas on their lands. Their name means 'people of the mountains', and they were originally the same people as the southern *Paiutes. The Utes became excellent fighters after they received Spanish horses in the early 19th century. They were placed on reservations in 1868.

ˌUtili'tarianism /ˌjuːtɪlɪˈteəriənɪzəm; AmE ˌjuːtɪlɪˈterɪənɪzəm/ n [U] a system of ideas based on the work of Jeremy *Bentham and John Stuart *Mill. It argues that actions can be considered good if they produce happiness, and that governments should try to produce 'the greatest happiness for the greatest number' of people.

U'topia (also **u'topia**) /juːˈtəʊpiə; AmE juːˈtoʊpiə/ n [C, U] an imaginary place or state of things in which everything is perfect. The original Utopia was an imaginary island described by Thomas *More in a book of the same name which appeared in 1516. He criticized the political systems of France and England and went on to describe life in Utopia, where everyone shared their possessions and led a happy life.
▶ **U'topian** (also **u'topian**) adj (usually disapproving) having a perfect society or aiming for a perfect society, which may be impossible to achieve: Her political beliefs are just Utopian fantasies.

U2 /ˌju: 'tuː/ an Irish pop group formed in Dublin in 1977. Their successful albums include Boy (1980), The Joshua Tree (1987), Achtung Baby (1991), Pop (1997), All That You Can't Leave Behind (2000) and How to Dismantle an Atomic Bomb (2004). The group's main singer is Bono (real name Paul Hewson).

the U-2 incident /ˌjuː 'tuː ˌɪnsɪdənt/ an incident in May 1960 when a US U-2 spy plane (= aircraft that takes secret photographs of enemy places) was shot down over the USSR. The pilot Gary Powers survived. The Russian leader Nikita Khrushchev ended a meeting in Paris with US President *Eisenhower 11 days later when Eisenhower refused to say he was sorry. Powers was exchanged for the Soviet spy Rudolf Abel in 1962.

UUP /ˌju: ju: 'piː/ ⇨ ULSTER UNIONIST PARTY.

UVF /ˌju: vi: 'ef/ ⇨ ULSTER VOLUNTEER FORCE.

U

V v

VA /ˌviː ˈeɪ/ ⇨ DEPARTMENT OF VETERANS AFFAIRS.

Vail /veɪl/ a town in the US state of *Colorado that is an expensive centre for skiing. It is near the White River National Forest 122 miles/196 kilometres west of *Denver. Its special holiday buildings, opened in 1952, are in the Tyrolean style. Tennis and golf are available in the summer.

valedic'torian /ˌvælɪdɪkˈtɔːriən/ n (AmE) a student in a *high school, college or university who gives the valedictory (= goodbye speech) on the day when degrees are presented. The valedictorian is traditionally the student with the highest grades. Most schools also have a 'salutatorian', who has the next highest grades and gives the salutatory (= speech of welcome to the event).

Rudolph Valen'tino /vælənˈtiːnəʊ; AmE vælənˈtiːnoʊ/ (1895–1926) one of the most successful US stars in silent films. He was born in Italy and went to America in 1913. He played romantic roles and is best remembered for his part in *The Sheik* (1921). His other films included *The Four Horsemen of the Apocalypse* (1921), *Blood and Sand* (1922) and *The Son of the Sheik* (1926). When Valentino died young, over 100 000 people attended his funeral.

Valley 'Forge an area in the US state of *Pennsylvania where General George *Washington and his Continental Army spent the severe winter of 1777–8 during the *American Revolution. Hundreds died of cold and lack of food, but the army remained loyal.

'Valley girl n (AmE) a girl from a rich family who is not very intelligent and only interested in things like shopping, originally one of those living in the San Fernando Valley of *California in the 1980s. Valley girl speech includes the frequent use of 'like' and 'totally'.

Frankie 'Valli /ˈvæli/ (1937–) a US pop singer with a high voice. His group, The Four Seasons, formed in 1956 and still sing together. They were chosen for the Rock and Roll *Hall of Fame in 1990. They had hits in the 1960s with *Sherry* and *Big Girls Don't Cry*. Valli has also had hits singing alone with *Can't Take My Eyes Off You* (1967) and the title song for the film *Grease*.

Value 'Added Tax n [U] (abbr **VAT**) (in Britain) a tax of 17.5% which is added to the price of goods and services when they are sold. The money from the tax is collected by the person selling the goods and must then be paid to the government. Certain types of goods are free

Blenheim Palace designed by John Vanbrugh

from the tax, including food, books and children's clothes. VAT has existed in Britain since 1971 and there are similar taxes in many European countries.

John 'Vanbrugh /ˈvænbrə/ (1664–1726) an English architect and writer of plays. His plays, which are late *Restoration comedies, include *The Relapse* (1696) and *The Provok'd Wife* (1697). In his mid 30s he began a second career as an architect, working with Nicholas *Hawksmoor. Together they designed several grand houses and other buildings, including *Castle Howard and *Blenheim Palace. He was made a *knight in 1714.

Abigail Van 'Buren[1] /væn ˈbjʊərən; AmE ˈbjʊrən/ the writer of the US newspaper column *Dear Abby*, also known as Jeanne Phillips.

Martin Van 'Buren[2] /væn ˈbjʊərən; AmE ˈbjʊrən/ (1782–1862) the eighth US *President (1837–41). His popular name was the 'Little Magician' because of his political skills. He was a lawyer and a *Democrat who first served under Andrew *Jackson as *Secretary of State (1829–31) and Vice-President (1832–6). He is remembered especially for establishing the Independent Treasury System to deal with the country's financial difficulties.

Cyrus 'Vance /ˌsaɪrəs ˈvæns/ (1917–2002) the US *Secretary of State under President *Carter[2] (1977–80). He left the post because he disagreed with Carter's decision to try to rescue the Americans kept as prisoners in Iran during the *hostage crisis. In 1992, Vance and the British politician David *Owen represented the *United Nations and the *European Community in trying to bring peace to Bosnia-Herzegovina.

Van 'Cliburn ⇨ CLIBURN.

the V and A /ˌviː ənd ˈeɪ/ ⇨ VICTORIA AND ALBERT MUSEUM.

Cor,nelius 'Vanderbilt[1] /kɔːˈniːliəs ˈvændəbɪlt; AmE kɔːrˈniːliəs ˈvændərbɪlt/ (1794–1877) a US businessman who became very rich from his shipping and railway companies, and gave a lot of his money to support good causes. He established Vanderbilt University in *Nashville, *Tennessee, in 1873. His sons, especially the oldest, William Henry Vanderbilt (1821–85), increased the family's wealth and continued its financial gifts.

Gloria 'Vanderbilt[2] /ˈvændəbɪlt; AmE ˈvændərbɪlt/ (1924–) a US businesswoman who designs women's products, including *jeans and perfume. Cornelius *Vanderbilt was her father's grandfather. She was called the 'poor little rich girl' after her mother, who had left her, and her aunt had a legal dispute, and a court decided in 1934 that she should live with her aunt. She received $4 million at the age of 21. Leopold *Stokowski was one of her four husbands.

Anthony van 'Dyck ⇨ DYCK.

Dick Van 'Dyke /væn ˈdaɪk/ (1925–) a US comedy actor, singer and dancer. He had his own television series, *The Dick Van Dyke Show* (1961–6), which won three Emmys (1963, 1964 and 1966), and *The New Dick Van Dyke Show* (1971–2). He later played Dr Mark Sloan in the *CBS television series *Diagnosis Murder* (1993–2001). His films include *Bye Bye Birdie* (1963), **Mary Poppins* (1964), *Chitty Chitty Bang Bang* (1968) and *Dick Tracy* (1990).

Vanity 'Fair **1** a novel by William Makepeace *Thackeray. It contrasts the lives of two characters who first meet at school: Becky Sharp, who is intelligent, ambitious and poor, and Amelia Sedley, who is gentle, pretty and rich. The book contains many humorous characters and was published in parts between 1847 and 1848.

2 a magazine published every month both in Britain and the US, with articles about politics, society, culture and other subjects.

Vanu'atu /ˌvænuːˈɑːtuː/ a group of 13 large and about 70 small islands in the south-west Pacific Ocean. Its capital is Port Vila and its official languages are French, English and Bislama. The country was formerly owned by the British and French and known as the New Hebrides, but it became an independent member of the *Commonwealth in 1980.

Va'riety a US newspaper of the entertainment industry, published each week in New York. It includes reviews of plays, films, etc. and special articles about the entertainment world, and is known for its colourful and informal style of language. It was first published in 1905.

the Va'riety Club an international charity that helps children. Its members are famous actors and entertainers who collect money by organizing shows and concerts. The first Variety Club was started in the US in 1927 and the charity now has branches in many countries of the world, including Britain.

'varsity /ˈvɑːsəti; AmE ˈvɑːrsəti/ n **1** [sing, only before noun] (BrE) used to describe sports competitions connected with the universities of *Oxford and *Cambridge: the varsity match.
2 (AmE) a main team representing a university, college or school, especially in sports.

'Vaseline™ /ˈvæsəliːn/ n [U] a thick, soft, yellowish substance used to treat dry skin, or to put on sore parts of the body, etc.

Vassar 'College /ˌvæsə; AmE ˌvæsər/ (also **'Vassar**) a private US college in Poughkeepsie, New York. It had about 2 330 students in 1998. It was established by Matthew Vassar in 1861 as a women's college and became one of America's best. Vassar now accepts some male students.

VAT /ˌviː eɪ ˈtiː/ ⇨ VALUE ADDED TAX.

'vaudeville n [U] (AmE) a type of entertainment on stage, especially popular in the US between the 1840s and the 1930s. A typical vaudeville show included a variety of performers, including singers, dancers, comedians and sometimes animals. The best-known vaudeville theatre was the Palace in New York. US stars who began in vaudeville included Will *Rogers, Al *Jolson, the *Marx Brothers and W C *Fields. Compare MUSIC-HALL(1).

Sarah 'Vaughan /ˈvɔːn/ (1924–90) a US *jazz singer noted for her great range. She sang many songs by 'Duke' *Ellington and George *Gershwin, and she recorded with 'Dizzy' *Gillespie, 'Cannonball' Adderley and many other jazz musicians. Her most successful songs included Mr Wonderful (1956) and Broken-Hearted Melody (1959).

Ralph 'Vaughan 'Williams /ˈreɪf ˈvɔːn ˈwɪljəmz/ (1872–1958) a popular English composer. He was influenced mainly by traditional English music, especially of the *Tudor(1) period, and his work often suggests English life and traditions and the English countryside. His best-known short pieces include Fantasia on a Theme by Thomas Tallis (1910) and The Lark Ascending (1914). He also wrote several works for orchestra, as well as songs, operas and film music. He was made a member of the *Order of Merit in 1935.

'Vauxhall /ˈvɒksɔːl; AmE ˈvɑːksɔːl/ a company that produces cars, mostly of medium price. It was formed in Britain in 1903 and bought by *General Motors in 1925.

VC /ˌviː ˈsiː/ **1** ⇨ VICTORIA CROSS.
2 the VC an informal name used by US soldiers during the *Vietnam War to refer to the enemy Viet Cong soldiers. They also called them Victor Charlie, the communication words for VC, or simply Charlie.

V-chip /ˈviː tʃɪp/ n an electronic device in a television set which parents can use to block programmes they do not want their children to see, e.g. ones containing a lot of sex or violence. According to the 1996 Telecommunications Act all television sets sold in the US must contain a V-chip.

V-E Day /ˌviː ˈiː deɪ/ Victory in Europe Day, 8 May 1945. The day marked the end of fighting in Europe during *World War II, and there were public celebrations in London and many other places.

'Vegas /ˈveɪɡəs/ ⇨ LAS VEGAS.

V8™ /ˌviː ˈeɪt/ n [U, C] a juice made from eight different vegetables. It has been produced by the Campbell Soup Company since 1948, and its advertisements often used the phrase, 'Wow! I could've had a V8!'.

Vel'veeta™ /velˈviːtə/ n [U] a popular US make of processed cheese, made by *Kraft.

the Velvet 'Underground a US rock group that had no big commercial hits but influenced many later groups and singers, including David *Bowie. Their albums included The Velvet Underground and Nico (1967), White Light/White Heat (1967), The Velvet Underground (1969) and Loaded (1970). The group broke up in 1971 and formed again for a short time in the 1990s. See also REED.

'Veni, 'vidi, 'vici /ˈveɪni ˈviːdi ˈviːki/ a Latin phrase meaning 'I came, I saw, I conquered'. It was first said by *Julius Caesar after winning a battle in Asia Minor (now Turkey). Many people, especially in Britain, wrongly think he said it after defeating the *Britons.

Robert Ven'turi /venˈtjʊəri; AmE venˈtʊri/ (1925–) a US architect who developed the Post-Modernist style. Venturi's buildings include the Humanities Classroom Building at the *State University of New York (1973) and the *Sainsbury Wing of the *National Gallery (1991) in London. His books include Complexity and Contradiction in Architecture (1966).

Ver'mont /vɜːˈmɒnt; AmE vɜːrˈmɑːnt/ a *New England state in the US, on the border with Canada. It is also known as the Green Mountain State. The largest city is Burlington and the capital city is Montpelier. The French settled there first in the 17th century, and Vermont became a state in 1791. It produces different types of stone, including granite and marble, and other products include electrical equipment, paper, furniture and maple syrup (= a sweet, sticky sauce produced from a type of maple tree). Tourist attractions in Vermont include the Green Mountain National Forest and the Bennington Battle Monument.

the Verra'zano-'Narrows 'Bridge /ˌvɑːrəˈzɑːnəʊ ˈnærəʊz; AmE ˌvɑːrəˈzɑːnoʊ ˈnæroʊz/ the longest bridge in the US. It is in New York City and connects *Staten Island to *Brooklyn. It is 4 260 feet/1 300 metres long, and one of the world's longest suspension bridges (= bridges that hang from steel cables supported by towers at each end). It is named after Giovanni da Verrazano, an Italian who in 1524 was the first European to land on Staten Island. After the bridge was opened in 1964, many people began to buy homes on the island. Compare GEORGE WASHINGTON BRIDGE, BROOKLYN BRIDGE, GOLDEN GATE BRIDGE.

the Very 'Reverend (written abbrs **the Very Rev**, **the Very Revd**) a title used before the name of certain senior priests, especially a dean or provost of the *Church of England, or a former *Moderator of the

V

Church of Scotland: *the Very Reverend William Wallis.* Compare RIGHT REVEREND.

A‚merigo Ves'pucci /ə‚merɪgəʊ veˈspuːtʃi; *AmE* ə‚merɪgoʊ/ (1454–1512) an Italian sailor and explorer. He made several journeys across the Atlantic and claimed to have been the first to have seen South America (in 1497). The name America is said to have been based on his first name, but other origins of the name have been suggested.

'Veterans Day (in the US and Canada) a holiday on 11 November to honour all men and women who have served in the armed forces. People hang flags outside their homes, and many cities celebrate with parades. It began in 1926 as *Armistice Day in memory of the end of *World War I. Its present name was established in 1954. Compare MEMORIAL DAY.

the 'Veterans of 'Foreign 'Wars (*abbr* **VFW**) a large organization for former members of the US armed forces who fought in wars abroad. It helps those in need, has campaigns to influence the government on military matters, and does community service. It was established in 1899 and has more than 2.8 million members. Compare AMERICAN LEGION.

‚Jack Vettri'ano /vetriˈɑːnəʊ; *AmE* vetriˈɑːnoʊ/ (1951–) a Scottish artist whose paintings of people have become so popular in Britain that he is often described as Britain's favourite artist. More prints of his paintings have been sold in Britain than of those of any other artist.

VFW /‚viː ef ˈdʌbljuː/ ⇨ VETERANS OF FOREIGN WARS.

the ‚Vicar of 'Bray /ˈbreɪ/ a vicar (= a *Church of England priest) in a traditional English song. He changes his religious and political beliefs according to the beliefs of the ruling king or queen, and is concerned only with keeping his job. The name 'Vicar of Bray' is sometimes used to describe somebody who is prepared to change their beliefs to gain some advantage.

The ‚Vicar of 'Dibley /ˈdɪbli/ a British *BBC television sitcom shown since (1994) in which Dawn *French plays the fun-loving vicar (= *Church of England priest) in a small village.

The ‚Vicar of 'Wakefield /ˈweɪkfiːld/ a novel (1766) by Oliver *Goldsmith. It is about a vicar (= a *Church of England priest) who is kind and honest but experiences several disasters in his life, such as his house burning down and his son being put in prison. After many complicated adventures the book ends happily.

le ‚vice an'glais /lə ‚viːs ɒŋˈɡleɪ; *AmE* ɑːŋˈɡleɪ/ *n* [sing] a French phrase meaning 'the English vice'. It sometimes refers to sadomasochism (= gaining sexual pleasure by beating or whipping people), thought to be characteristic of the English, but is often used to mean any typically English fault or weakness.

‚vice 'chancellor *n* (in Britain) the most senior official in a university. The vice chancellor of a British university is responsible for its administration, in contrast to the chancellor, who is given the title as an honour and has only a few formal duties, such as attending ceremonies, etc. In the US, a vice chancellor is the assistant to the chancellor, who is the senior university official, with the most responsibility and power. Many US universities, however, use the titles 'president' and 'vice-president' instead of 'chancellor' and 'vice chancellor'.

'vice squad *n* [C+sing/pl *v*] a police department in Britain or the US that tries to prevent prostitution, gambling, drug dealing and similar offences.

'Vickers /ˈvɪkəz; *AmE* ˈvɪkərz/ a British company known for making military equipment, especially weapons and aircraft. Among the best-known are the Vickers-Maxim machine-gun, the *Spitfire and Wellington planes, the Challenger tank and the *Trident submarine. After the Second World War the company split into different parts. The branches that built ships and aircraft became nationalized industries but now form part of the private company *BAE Systems. The branch building military vehicles continued to operate as an independent company until 2002, when it was bought by Alvis and changed its name to **Alvis Vickers**.

Vicks™ /vɪks/ the name of a range of products for treating coughs produced by the US company Vicks (part of Procter and Gamble) and available without a doctor's written permission. They include Vicks Cough Drops, Vicks 44, Vicks VapoRub and Vicks VapoSteam.

'Vicksburg /ˈvɪksbɜːɡ; *AmE* ˈvɪksbɜːrɡ/ a city on the *Mississippi River in the US state of *Mississippi. During the *Civil War it was captured after the US army of General *Grant had surrounded it for seven months. This gave the *Union control of the river and split the *Confederate States. The **Vicksburg National Military Park** is a popular tourist attraction.

Vic'toria¹ /vɪkˈtɔːriə/ a major train station in London for trains to and from the south of England. It also has a station on the *London Underground.

‚Queen Vic'toria² (1819–1901) a British queen who ruled from 1837 to 1901. She was the granddaughter of King *George III and became queen after the death of King *William IV. Her rule was the longest of any British king or queen, and happened at the same time as Britain's greatest period of world power and industrial development. In 1840 she married her cousin Prince *Albert of *Saxe-Coburg-Gotha. They had nine children. After Albert's death Victoria took no further part in public affairs, but was persuaded to return by her *prime minister Benjamin *Disraeli, who gained for her the title Empress of India. She is often remembered as a bad-tempered old woman. However in her early life she was a happy and enthusiastic queen who was very popular with ordinary people.

the Vic'toria and 'Albert Mu'seum (*abbr* **the V and A**) Britain's national museum of art and design, in *South Kensington, London, established in 1852. It contains over 4 million objects, including important collections of painting, sculpture, textiles, furniture and other objects from around the world, and is one of London's most popular museums.

Vic‚toria 'Cross *n* (*abbr* **VC**) the highest British military award for courage in war. It was first given by Queen *Victoria in 1856, and has the form of a cross with a crown and a lion in the centre and the words 'For Valour': *Leonard Cheshire VC.*

the Vic‚toria Me'morial a large sculpture in front of *Buckingham Palace, London, England. It was made in 1911 in memory of Queen *Victoria, and shows her sitting with several other figures under a gold statue representing Victory.

Vic'torian /vɪkˈtɔːriən/ *adj* **1** of, living in or made during the rule of Queen *Victoria (1837–1901): *The square is dominated by the huge red-brick Victorian town hall.* **2** having the qualities associated with *middle-class people of the 19th century. These qualities are sometimes called **Victorian values**. Some people think they are mainly good, and see them as including loyalty, self-control and the willingness to work hard. Others think they are mainly bad, and see them as including sexual hypocrisy, lack of concern for the poor, and lack of a sense of humour.
▶ **Victorian** *n* a person living during the rule of Queen Victoria (1837–1901): *The programmes are about famous Victorians like Brunel and Disraeli.*

Vic‚tori'ana *n* [U] objects made during the rule of Queen *Victoria (1837–1901), especially when they are for sale or as part of a collection: *She runs a stall selling old dolls, china plates and other Victoriana.*

the 'Victory /'vɪktəri/ Lord *Nelson's ship at the Battle of *Trafalgar. It is now on display at the Royal Dockyard at *Portsmouth in southern England.

,Victory at 'Sea a US television series in 26 parts first shown on *NBC (1952–3). It told the story of the battles fought at sea in the Pacific during *World War II, using real film. The music for the series was written by Richard *Rodgers. The series was later reduced to 97 minutes for a film (1954) shown in cinemas.

,Gore Vi'dal /ˌɡɔː vɪ'dɑːl; *AmE* ˌɡɔːr/ (1925–) a US writer known for his intelligent criticism of American politics and culture. His best-known works are the novel *Myra Breckinridge* (1968) and the play *Suddenly Last Summer* (1958) which was made into a film (1959) with Elizabeth *Taylor. Vidal has acted in a few films, including *The Eighth Day* (1997) and *Gattaca* (1997). He is very critical of people who disagree with him and has had arguments for years with the writer Norman *Mailer.

,Video 'Nation a *BBC project started in 1993 in which ordinary people are given video cameras to film their everyday lives. These films were made into television programmes until 2000, and then from 2001 have been shown on the *Internet as **Video Nation Online**.

the 'Vietnam 'Veterans Me'morial /'viətnæm/ a long wall built in memory of Americans who were killed or lost in the *Vietnam War. It is in Washington, DC, near the *Lincoln Memorial. The wall is V-shaped and made of black polished stone. It has more than 58 000 names on it. The Memorial was designed by Maya Ying Lin, an architecture student at *Yale University, and was dedicated in 1982. It has become an emotional place for former Vietnam soldiers and their families.

the Vietnam Veterans Memorial

▶ **the Vietnam War**

Like the *Korean War, the Vietnam War was a result of US policy during the *Cold War, a period when Americans believed that **Communism**, the political system in the Soviet Union and China, was a threat to their security and power.

Vietnam, a colony of France, wanted to become independent, but the US believed that Communists were behind the independence movement, and so opposed it. The US became involved in Vietnam only gradually. At first, under President *Eisenhower, it provided the French with supplies. In 1954 the **Geneva Accords** divided Vietnam into the Communist North and the anti-Communist South. Under President *Kennedy, in the early 1960s, many US soldiers were sent to the South as advisers. In 1964, after an attack on US ships, *Congress passed the **Gulf of Tonkin Resolution** which gave President *Johnson greater powers to fight a war, and in the spring of 1965 **Marines** were sent to South Vietnam.

It was easy to keep the Communist forces, called the **National Liberation Front** or the **Viet Cong**, out of South Vietnam, but much harder to defeat them. The US used bombs against the Vietnamese troops, and chemicals to destroy crops, which had a terrible effect on people as well as on the land. There were also

reports of atrocities (= acts of extreme violence and cruelty) committed by both sides. In 1968 the *My Lai massacre, in which over 300 civilians were killed by US soldiers, shocked Americans at home. Many US soldiers were not sure why they were fighting the war and became traumatized (= mentally disturbed) by the violence around them. Discipline became a problem, and the use of *drugs was common. Soldiers were accused of committing acts of violence against each other and against Vietnamese civilians.

In 1968 the Viet Cong started a major attack known as the **Tet Offensive**, and the US position in South Vietnam was threatened. As the war **escalated** (= became more intense) it lost support at home and also in other countries. When Richard *Nixon became President he at first tried to attack hard and force the Viet Cong to come to an agreement. The war then spread to Vietnam's neighbour, Cambodia. Finally, in 1972, Nixon got Henry *Kissinger to negotiate a **cease-fire**, and afterwards the US was no longer directly involved in the war, though it continued to provide supplies. In 1975 the government of South Vietnam fell and the country was taken over by the Communist forces.

The Vietnam War divided US society. Opposition to it was led mainly by university students, many of whom were young men facing the *draft (= compulsory service in the armed forces). They said they should not be forced to fight a war that they believed was wrong. As a protest, many burned their **draft cards**. Some became **draft dodgers** by remaining students as long as possible, or by going to Canada. Others took their case to court on the grounds that they were **conscientious objectors** and had moral or religious reasons for not fighting a war. These protests resulted in violent conflicts between police and students. In the summer of 1968, during a protest in *Chicago, people saw on television the violent way in which the police behaved. In 1970, during another protest, the *National Guard shot and killed four American students at Kent State University in *Ohio. After this, many of the *silent majority, people whom Nixon thought supported the government, believed that things had gone too far and began to question government policy and the reasons for US involvement in the war. But others continued to accuse the students of being unpatriotic.

When Vietnam **veterans** returned home they found that, instead of receiving the respect normally given to war veterans, they were the object of public anger. They had to cope with this in addition to the mental stress caused by the violence they had seen and taken part in. In the years since the war, films such as *The *Deer Hunter* (1978), *Born on the Fourth of July* (1989) and *Good Morning, Vietnam* (1987) have shown the war from different angles and helped Americans understand and come to terms with their anger and hurt.

The war in Vietnam taught the US that there are limits to its military strength, and showed that the American people were not willing to pay the high cost in money and in lives for a war away from home. The strong desire to avoid another Vietnam played an important role in deciding US foreign policy in the years that followed.

the ,Vieux Car'ré /ˌvjɜː kə'reɪ/ the old name for the *French Quarter in the US city of *New Orleans. It means 'Old Square' in French.

'Viking /'vaɪkɪŋ/ *n* a member of a people from Scandinavia who attacked parts of northern and western Europe, including Britain and Ireland, in the 8th–11th centuries. In Britain they were also known as Danes or Norsemen. They settled in the Scottish islands and in areas of eastern England, and the Danish king *Canute

V

(often also spelt Cnut) ruled England from 1016. The Vikings were feared as violent and cruel, but they were also noted for their skill in building ships and as sailors. They travelled in their long ships (= long narrow warships) to Iceland, Greenland and North America. They had an important influence on English culture and the English language, and their achievements are still celebrated in festivals such as *Up-Helly-Aa. See also DANEGELD, DANELAW, VINLAND.

'**Viking** /'vaɪkɪŋ/ the name of two *NASA spacecraft that left Earth in 1975 and landed on the planet Mars in the following year. They analysed the surface of the planet for evidence of life but found nothing very important. They also sent the first television pictures of the surface of Mars back to earth.

,**Pancho** '**Villa** /,pæntʃəʊ 'viːə; AmE ,pæntʃoʊ/ (c. 1877–1923) a Mexican soldier who led a revolution against the Mexican government and became very popular with poor people. In 1916, he killed 16 US citizens in Mexico and then attacked Columbus, *New Mexico. The US General John *Pershing took an army to Mexico and hunted for Villa for 11 months without success. Villa later led a peaceful life but was murdered by political rivals.

the '**Village** a short name for *Greenwich Village in New York. See also VILLAGE VOICE.

The ,**Village** '**Blacksmith** a popular poem by the US poet Henry Wadsworth *Longfellow about the simple, healthy life of a country blacksmith (= a person whose job is making things out of iron, especially 'shoes' for horses). American children often have to learn it in school.

,**village** '**green** n (in Britain) an area of grass in the centre of a village. It is one of the traditional centres of village life, used for games, *fêtes and other public events: Traditional English pastimes like cricket on the village green seem to be disappearing.

The ,**Village** '**Voice** (also The Voice) a US newspaper published each week in *Greenwich Village in New York, known especially for its articles on entertainment and the arts. It first appeared in 1955 as a newspaper for *hippies and others with an 'alternative' culture, but is now more traditional. See also OBIE.

,**vinda**'**loo** /,vɪndə'luː/ n [U, C] a type of Indian curry dish, popular in Britain. It contains very hot spices and is usually made with meat or fish: He needed three pints of lager after his prawn vindaloo!

,**Barbara** '**Vine** /'vaɪn/ ⇨ RENDELL.

'**Vinland** /'vɪnlənd/ a *Viking(1) name for an area on the east coast of North America which was visited by the Norwegian explorer Lief Ericsson around the year 1000, and possibly named by him. The exact area is not known, and it may have been named after the grape vines (= climbing plants) found growing there.

,**vintage** '**car** n (BrE) a car made between 1919 and 1930. Owners like to keep their vintage cars in good condition and **vintage car rallies** are held in many parts of the country. Officially a car made before 1919 is called a **veteran car** and an old car made after 1930 is a **classic car** but vintage car rallies often include them as well.

Vi,**rago** '**Press** /vɪˌrɑːgəʊ; AmE vɪˌrɑːgoʊ/ a British company, formed in 1973, that publishes books by and about women. Virago is well known for rediscovering forgotten women writers of the past and for its Modern Classics series.

'**Virgin** /'vɜːdʒɪn; AmE 'vɜːrdʒɪn/ a British company formed in 1970 by Richard *Branson. It began as a record company, producing and selling records through its own shops. In 1984 it introduced an airline service, Virgin Atlantic. The company now offers many other products

and services, and sells music, games and books in its Virgin Megastores. Since 1996 it has also operated some train services in Britain.

Vir'**ginia** /və'dʒɪniə; AmE vər'dʒɪniə/ a US state on the Atlantic coast, also called the Old Dominion. Its largest city is Virginia Beach, and the capital city is *Richmond(3). It was the first permanent English colony in North America and was named after the 'Virgin Queen', *Elizabeth I. It was one of the original *thirteen colonies, and the *American Revolution was ended by the Battle of *Yorktown in Virginia. Richmond became the capital of the *Confederate States and the *Civil War ended at *Appomattox Court House. Eight presidents were born in Virginia, including George *Washington, Thomas *Jefferson and Woodrow *Wilson. Local products include tobacco and electrical equipment. Among the tourist attractions are *Williamsburg, *Mount Vernon and *Monticello.

The Vir'**ginian** /və'dʒɪniən; AmE vər'dʒɪniən/ a US television *western series each week on *NBC (1962–71). The Virginian is a mysterious man with no name who visits the Shiloh Ranch in Medicine Bow, *Wyoming, in the 1880s. The series was based on a 1902 novel of the same name by Owen Wister, the first western novel in American literature, and there had been film versions in 1929 (with Gary *Cooper) and 1946.

Vir,**ginia** '**Slims**™ /və,dʒɪniə; AmE vər,dʒɪniə/ a make of cigarettes produced by *Philip Morris, especially for women. A well-known advertisement for them showed photographs of modern, independent women next to photographs of women in old-fashioned clothes, with the phrase, 'You've Come A Long Way, Baby.'

the '**Virgin** ,**Islands** /'vɜːdʒɪn; AmE 'vɜːrdʒɪn/ a group of over 90 islands in the Caribbean. The western ones have belonged to the US since 1917 and the eastern ones to Britain since 1666. Christopher *Columbus was the first European to visit them, in 1493, and they have long been a popular place for tourists. The **US Virgin Islands** cover 133 square miles/344 square kilometres, with a population of more than 97 000. The capital is Charlotte Amalie. The **British Virgin Islands** cover 59 square miles/153 square kilometres, with a population of more than 13 000. The capital is Road Town.

the ,**Virgin** '**Queen** a name given to the British queen *Elizabeth I, because she did not marry and may never have had sex.

'**viscount** /'vaɪkaʊnt/ n **1** a member of the British *peerage who is next in rank above a *baron and next below an *earl(1). The wife of a viscount, or a female viscount, is called a **viscountess**. A viscount has the title 'Lord' and a viscountess 'Lady'.
2 a *courtesy title given to the eldest son of an *earl(1). ⇨ note at ARISTOCRACY, PEERAGE.

,**Visit**'**Britain** a government organization that works to encourage people from abroad to visit the UK and to encourage British people to visit tourist attractions in England. Separate organizations promote Wales, Scotland and Northern Ireland within the UK and give different symbols to hotels, etc. to show what standard of accommodation they offer.

'**Vitagraph** /'vaɪtəɡrɑːf; AmE 'vaɪtəɡrɑːæf/ the most successful US film company in the early years of the film industry. It was established in 1896 in New York by two men born in Britain, Alfred E Smith and J Stuart Blackton. Its stars included Rudolph *Valentino and Norma Talmadge. Vitagraph moved to *Hollywood in 1911 and was bought by *Warner Brothers in 1925.

Vi'**yella**™ /vaɪ'jelə/ n [U] the name of a mixture of wool and cotton used in knitting, as well as a type of cloth. Both were made for many years by Coats Viyella, a

British clothing and textile company. The company owned the Viyella chain of *high-street clothes shops in Britain. In 2003 the Viyella chain became a separate company: *a Viyella shirt/dress/blouse.*

Viz /vɪz/ a British humorous magazine known for its rude humour. It contains *comic strips with characters like 'The Fat Slags' and 'Billy the Fish', which often show scenes of sex and violence or are funny in a strange, silly way. It first appeared in 1979 and is published ten times a year.

V-J Day /ˌviː ˈdʒeɪ deɪ/ Victory in Japan Day, 15 August 1945, when fighting with Japan ended in *World War II.

VOA /ˌviː əʊ ˈeɪ; *AmE* oʊ/ ⇨ VOICE OF AMERICA.

vo'cational school *n* (in US education) a school, especially a *high school, which teaches students practical skills to prepare them for a particular type of work, such as photography, cooking, etc. **Vocational education** classes are also taught in regular high schools.

▶ **vocational training**

Vocational training is intended to give people the skills and knowledge they need to perform a particular job, and involves practical instruction as well as theory. Most vocational training takes place not in universities but in *colleges of further education and in colleges specializing in art, accountancy, etc. Some secondary schools now also offer an introduction to vocational training.

*NVQs (**National Vocational Qualifications**) are qualifications that can be obtained by people already working in a particular industry. Colleges of further education run courses to provide a theoretical background. NVQs are awarded on the basis of practical work, spoken and written tests, and coursework. There are five levels, from Foundation to Management. Since 1992 many students in schools and colleges have been working for *GNVQs (**General National Vocational Qualifications**), as an alternative to *GCSEs and *A levels. GNVQs cover similar areas to NVQs and are intended as introductions to a particular field of work and the skills required. Students can choose from over 500 subjects. At the lowest of its three levels, Foundation, a GNVQ is equivalent to a GCSE and from 2002 they are being replaced by new vocational GCSEs.

In the US there are no national qualifications like NVQs, though some professional organizations decide on their own qualifications and some of these have become widely accepted. Much vocational training is done by private institutions which are sometimes called **proprietary schools**. Although many of these are good, in general they have a bad reputation. This is partly because there are no controls over who can operate such a school. Some proprietary schools try to get as many students as possible, including some who will probably not be able to complete their training.

Most US secondary schools programmes do not provide a choice between an academic and a practical track (= programme of study), but most do give students an opportunity to take some practical or vocational classes. Large school districts may have **magnet schools**, schools that attract students with certain interests, and some of these may have a larger choice of vocational courses.

Vodafone™ /ˈvəʊdəfəʊn; *AmE* ˈvoʊdəfoʊn/ *n* a large international mobile phone company. It started in 1984 as part of a British company called Racal.

Vogue /vəʊɡ; *AmE* voʊɡ/ a magazine for women published every month in many countries including Britain and the US, which contains articles about fashion,

beauty, the arts and other subjects. It first appeared in the US in 1892 and in Britain in 1916.

the ˌVoice of A'merica (*abbr* **the VOA**) a US government organization that broadcasts news and other programmes to other countries on radio, television and the Internet. It broadcasts from Washington, DC, in 50 languages including Special English, a form of English with simple words and grammar. It was established in 1942 as a radio service to broadcast to Germany during *World War II. Compare RADIO FREE EUROPE/RADIO LIBERTY.

Vol'pone /vɒlˈpəʊneɪ; *AmE* vɔːlˈpoʊneɪ/ a comedy play (1606) by Ben *Jonson. The main character, Volpone, is a rich Italian businessman who pretends that he is dying so that people give him gifts. Finally he is betrayed by his closest friend and punished. All the characters in the play are named after animals, and Volpone means 'fox'.

the 'Volstead Act /ˈvɒlsted; *AmE* ˈvɔːlsted/ the name usually used to refer to the United States National Prohibition Act passed by the US *Congress in 1919 to introduce the laws relating to *Prohibition. It was named after US Congressman Andrew Volstead of *Minnesota who began it. The Act and Prohibition were ended in 1933.

the 'Voluntary Eutha'nasia So'ciety a British organization whose aim is to change the law to make it legal to help very ill people who want to die to do so and to help people to make 'living wills' that make clear their wishes about medical treatment if they become seriously ill. It was started by a group of doctors in 1935.

'voluntary school *n* a type of British school run by a religious group or other independent organization. Voluntary schools receive money from the *Local Education Authority in the same way as other state schools, but may provide the school buildings. Most voluntary schools are run by Christian groups. The first Muslim voluntary school in Britain was created in 1998.

'Voluntary 'Service Over'seas (*abbr* **VSO**) a British charity, established in 1958, which sends doctors, teachers, engineers and other skilled people as well as students, to live and work in other countries. They usually stay and help local people for two years, and are paid only a small amount. Compare PEACE CORPS.

▶ **voluntary work**

Voluntary work is work that you do not get paid for and usually involves doing things to help other people, especially the elderly or the sick, or working on behalf of a **charity** or similar organization. Most charitable organizations rely on unpaid **volunteers**, and thousands of Americans and British people give many hours of their time to doing some form of social work or organizing fund-raising events to support the work. **Volunteering** is especially popular in the US and the reasons for this may be found in basic American values such as the Protestant work ethic, the idea that work improves the person who does it, and the belief that people can change their condition if they try hard enough.

Volunteering is usually enjoyable, as people choose jobs close to their personal interests. For instance, people who like animals may volunteer in an animal shelter, a place for animals which have been treated cruelly. Some voluntary work is short-term, e.g. when people from a community get together to create a park. Other work is longer term, such as that of the US organization Habitat for Humanity which builds houses for poor people. Parents often volunteer at their children's schools, and do things like building a play area or raising money for new equipment. Young people are also encouraged to do voluntary work. Schoolchildren visit old people in hospitals or homes, and students at college often raise money for charities. In the US young people over 18 can

V

take part in **AmeriCorps**, a government programme that encourages them to work as volunteers for a period of time, with the promise of help in paying for their education later. Older Americans who do not work may spend much of their free time volunteering.

In Britain a lot of voluntary work is directed towards supporting the country's social services. The *WRVS and other organizations run a *meals-on-wheels service in many parts of Britain, providing hot food for old people who are unable to cook for themselves. The nationwide *Citizens Advice Bureau, which offers free advice to the public on a wide range of issues, is run mainly by volunteers, and the Blood Transfusion Service relies on voluntary blood donors to give blood for use in hospitals. Political parties use volunteers at election time, and Churches depend on volunteers to keep buildings clean.

Both Britain and the US have organizations dedicated to helping people overseas. Britain's *Voluntary Service Overseas sends people to work in developing countries for up to two years to share their skills with the local population. The US *Peace Corps has similar aims and programmes.

the ˌ**Volunteer Re'serve ˌForces** the branches of the British armed forces that are made up of volunteers (= people who train in their spare time to do various jobs that would be important in times of war or emergency, including fighting). The branches include the *Territorial Army, the *Royal Naval Reserve, the Royal Auxiliary Air Force and the Royal Marines Reserve.

the '**Volvo 'Ocean 'Race** /'vɒlvəʊ; AmE 'vɑːlvoʊ/ a major international race for sailing boats. They start and finish in *Portsmouth or *Southampton, England, and race in stages to different ports around the world. The race takes place every four years and was called the Whitbread Round the World Race until 1988.

ˌ**Wernher von 'Braun** /ˌveənə fɒn 'braʊn, ˌwɜːnə vɒn 'brɔːn; AmE ˌvernər fɑːn, ˌwɜːrnə vɑːn/ (1912–77) a US expert on rockets, born in Germany. He designed Germany's V2 rocket during *World War II. In 1945, von Braun and his German team went to the US where he became head of the Marshall Space Flight Center at Huntsville, *Alabama. He developed the first US satellite, the *Saturn(1) rocket used for the *NASA *Apollo program flights to the moon, and the idea of the *space shuttle.

'**Kurt 'Vonnegut 'Jr** /'kɜːt 'vɒnɪgət; AmE 'kɜːrt 'vɑːnɪgət/ (1922–) a US writer of novels and short stories, known for his dark humour. He was especially popular among American college and university students in the 1960s and 1970s. His best-known novel is *Slaughterhouse Five* (1969), about the bombing of Dresden, Germany, during *World War II, which Vonnegut saw when he was a prisoner of war there. His other books include *Cat's Cradle* (1963), *Galapagos* (1985), *Hocus Pocus* (1990) and *Timequake* (1997).

ˌ**Carol 'Vorderman** /'vɔːdəmən; AmE 'vɔːrdərmən/ (1960–) an English television personality. She has appeared on *Countdown since 1982 and is famous for her skill at mathematics. She has also presented a number of other programmes, including *Tomorrow's World* (1994–5) and *Mysteries* (1997–8).

'**Vorticism** /'vɔːtɪsɪzəm; AmE 'vɔːrtɪsɪzəm/ n [U] a movement in British art and literature that began in 1913 and lasted through the early years of *World War I. Its main figure was Wyndham *Lewis, and other artists associated with the group were Jacob *Epstein and Ezra *Pound. The paintings of the group were influenced by Cubism and Futurism, and dealt with such themes as energy, violence and machines.

the '**Voting Rights 'Act of 1965** /'vəʊtɪŋ raɪts 'ækt əv 'naɪntiːn sɪksti 'faɪv; AmE 'voʊtɪŋ/ a US law passed during the *civil rights movement, signed by President *Johnson. It made illegal a number of restrictions that had been used, mostly in the South, to keep *African Americans from voting. These restrictions included a test of people's ability to read and write.

'**Voyager** /'vɔɪdʒə(r)/ the *NASA programme which in 1977 sent two spacecraft into space to investigate certain planets. *Voyager 1* discovered rings around the planet Jupiter in 1979 and flew past Saturn the following year. It sent back to earth the first close photographs of both planets. *Voyager 2* has had the longest journey in the history of spacecraft. It passed Jupiter in 1979, Saturn in 1981, Uranus in 1986 and Neptune in 1989. Both spacecraft are travelling towards the region beyond the influence of the Sun.

'**V-sign** /'viː/ n the act of holding up the first and second fingers of the hand so they are spread to form a V. With the back of the hand towards the body this expresses 'victory' (as used by Winston *Churchill during *World War II), or peace (as used by *hippies and others during the 1960s). In Britain, however, when it is made with the back of the hand towards another person and an upward movement of the fingers, this sign is very offensive, showing extreme anger and dislike.

VSO /ˌviː es 'əʊ; AmE 'oʊ/ ⇨ VOLUNTARY SERVICE OVERSEAS.

W w

Wac /wæk/ n (AmE) a member of the Women's Army Corps (**WAC**) in the US army.

'wagon train n a long line of *covered wagons used for journeys in the US *Old West. They often carried families going to settle in the West but were also used to move military and other supplies. *Wagon Train* was a popular *NBC television series (1957–65) about people making such a journey. See also CONESTOGA WAGON.

Wai'kiki /waɪˈkiːkiː/ a holiday beach and area of *Honolulu, *Hawaii. Tourists stay in tall hotels on the beach, shop on Kalakaua Avenue and enjoy the area's many entertainments.

Alfred 'Wainwright /ˈweɪnraɪt/ (1907–91) an English author of books that give information to people walking for pleasure in the north of England, e.g. in the *Lake District. The books also contain his own illustrations.

Waiting for 'Godot /ˈɡɒdəʊ; AmE ˈɡɑːdoʊ/ a play (1952) by Samuel *Beckett, originally written in French. It is about two men, Vladimir and Estragon, who are waiting for a third, Godot, to arrive. Very little happens, and during their long wait the men talk about their lives. Godot never comes, and the play suggests that life has no meaning and is full of suffering. It is probably Beckett's best-known play and is often performed in the theatre.

'Waitrose /ˈweɪtrəʊz; AmE ˈweɪtroʊz/ any of a large group of British supermarkets. They were started in 1908 and are now owned by *John Lewis: *I do most of my shopping at Waitrose.* ◇ *They're opening a new Waitrose near the town centre.*

Tom 'Waits /weɪts/ (1949–) a US musician and singer with a rough voice, whose songs are often about the more depressing and violent aspects of life in modern cities. He has written music for films, including *One from the Heart* (1982) and *Night on Earth* (1992), and has also acted in several films. His albums include *Heartattack and Vine* (1980) and *Asylum Years* (1985).

'Walden /ˈwɔːldən/ the best-known book by the US writer Henry David *Thoreau. Its full title is *Walden, or Life in the Woods.*

the Waldorf-A'storia /ˌwɔːldɔːf æˈstɔːriə; AmE ˌwɔːldɔːrf/ a famous New York hotel on *Park Avenue. Every US President has stayed there since Herbert *Hoover in 1931. The Waldorf Hotel and the Astor Hotel, situated where the *Empire State Building now stands, were opened separately by different members of the rich Astor family in the late 19th century. They combined in 1931 in the present building, designed in the *art deco style.

Waldorf 'salad /ˌwɔːldɔːf; AmE ˌwɔːldɔːrf/ n [C, U] a salad made with chopped apples and celery, nuts and mayonnaise (= sauce made from eggs and oil). It was created by a cook at the *Waldorf-Astoria Hotel.

Wales Mil'lennium Centre a large arts centre in *Cardiff opened in 2004 to stage performances of opera, ballet, dance and musicals.

the 'Wales Office a British government department responsible for representing Welsh interests within the British government, and representing the British government in Wales. It is led by the Secretary of State for Wales and is part of the *Department for Constitutional Affairs.

Alice 'Walker /ˈwɔːkə(r)/ (1944–) a US writer. She won the *Pulitzer Prize and the *National Book Award for

The Color Purple (1982). Her other works include the novel *Possessing the Secret of Joy* (1992), a book about her early life, *The Same River Twice* (1996), and several collections of poems.

the Walker 'Art Gallery /ˌwɔːkər/ an art museum in Liverpool, north-west England. It was opened in 1877 and contains one of Britain's largest collections of European painting.

the Walker Art Gallery

the Walker 'Cup /ˌwɔːkə; AmE ˌwɔːkər/ a golf competition for men who are not professional players, held every two years between a US team and a mixed British and Irish team. It was first held in 1922 and named after George Herbert Walker, President of the US Golf Association.

Walkers™ 'crisps /ˈwɔːkəz; AmE ˈwɔːkərz/ the most popular UK brand of potato crisps/chips (= very thin slices of fried potato) eaten cold as a snack and sold in small bags in a range of different flavours including 'ready salted', 'salt and vinegar' and 'cheese and onion'.

▶ walking

Walking, taking long walks in the countryside for pleasure, is a popular hobby in Britain, and many people go walking in *national parks and other country areas at weekends. *Walking* is also called **rambling** (BrE) or **hiking**. Many routes go along *public footpaths. These are **rights of way** (= paths across private land that the public has a legal right to use) which must be kept open and which are marked on *Ordnance Survey maps. Keen walkers may walk one of Britain's many *National Trails during their holiday/vacation.

About half of the land of the US is open to the public, but there is no system equivalent to British public footpaths across private land. There are 19 National Trails as well as many other paths and trails in national parks and other areas of natural beauty including thousands which are the responsibility of the states.

walkers

'David 'Foster 'Wallace[1] /ˌfɒstə ˈwɒlɪs; AmE ˌfɑːstər ˈwɑːlɪs/ (1962–) a US writer who is best known for his novel *Infinite Jest* (1996) which satirizes (= uses humour to criticize) American consumer culture.

,Edgar 'Wallace[2] /'wɒlɪs; *AmE* 'wɑːlɪs/ (1875–1932) an English author. His most popular books are stories about crime and adventure, such as *The Four Just Men* (1905) and *The Ringer* (1926). He was also a successful writer of plays and films, including the film *King Kong* (1933).

,George 'Wallace[3] /'wɒlɪs; *AmE* 'wɑːlɪs/ (1919–98) a US politician. He was governor of the state of *Alabama and tried to keep *segregation in public schools there in the 1960s.

,Lew 'Wallace[4] /,luː 'wɒlɪs; *AmE* 'wɑːlɪs/ (1827–1905) a US writer best known for his novel *Ben-Hur* (1880). He wrote other historical novels, including *The Fair God* (1873) and *Prince of India* (1893). Wallace was also a law-yer, a soldier, governor of the New Mexico Territory (1878–81) and a US government representative in Turkey (1881–5).

,William 'Wallace[5] /'wɒlɪs; *AmE* 'wɑːlɪs/ (c. 1270–1305) a Scottish soldier. He led an army against the English forces of King *Edward I, who had occupied Scotland, and defeated them at Stirling Bridge in 1297. The follow-ing year Wallace was defeated by Edward at Falkirk, and was later captured and hanged. The film *Braveheart* (1995) was made about his life.

,Wallace and 'Gromit™ /,wɒlɪs ənd 'grɒmɪt; *AmE* ,wɑːlɪs, 'grɔːmɪt/ two characters, a man and his dog, who appear in the short animated films made by Nick Park (1958–). In the first film, *A Grand Day Out* (1989), Wallace builds a rocket and takes Gromit to the moon. Two later films, *The Wrong Trousers* (1993) and *A Close Shave* (1995), both won *Oscars.

the 'Wallace Col,lection /'wɒlɪs; *AmE* 'wɑːlɪs/ a museum of art in London, England. It was opened in 1900 and contains a large collection of 18th-century French paintings and furniture, as well as other paint-ings, sculpture, decorative objects and weapons from Europe and around the world.

',Fats' 'Waller /,fæts 'wɒlə(r); *AmE* 'wɑːlər/ (1904–43) a US *jazz musician who sang, played the piano and wrote popular songs. His real name was Thomas Waller. His humorous style influenced many later jazz perform-ers. His hits included *Ain't Misbehavin'* (1928) and *Honeysuckle Rose* (1929), and he wrote the African-American musical shows *Keep Shufflin'* (1928) and *Hot Chocolates* (1929). He later led the group Fats Waller and His Rhythm, whose songs included *The Joint Is Jumpin'* (1937) and *Honey Hush* (1939).

,Barnes 'Wallis /,bɑːnz 'wɒlɪs; *AmE* ,bɑːrnz 'wɑːlɪs/ (1887–1979) an English engineer. He designed some of the most important aircraft and weapons of *World War II, including the Wellington and Wellesley bombers and a 'bouncing' bomb used to destroy dams. After the war he invented the 'swing-wing' aircraft and helped to design *Concorde. He was made a *knight in 1968.

Wall's /wɔːlz/ a British company known for making ice cream. It is owned by *Unilever.

'Wall Street /'wɔːl/ the street which is the centre of New York's financial district, where the *New York Stock Exchange is situated. The street name is often used to refer to the stock exchange itself: *Wall Street has reacted positively to the change in interest rates.*

the New York Stock Exchange, Wall Street

The ,Wall Street 'Journal /,wɔːl/ the leading financial newspaper in the US. It was first pub-lished in 1889 by Charles H Dow and Edward D Jones and is still owned by Dow Jones & Company, which also publishes the *Dow-Jones Average. Although it empha-sizes business and economic news, the *Journal* also has long articles about political and general news. Compare FINANCIAL TIMES.

'Wal-Mart /'wɔːl mɑːt; *AmE* mɑːrt/ any of a very large group of shops in the US and other countries selling a wide range of goods at low prices. The company also owns the *Asda supermarkets in Britain. The first Wal-Mart Discount City was opened in 1962 by Sam Walton, who became one of the richest people in the US.

,Horace 'Walpole[1] /'wɔːlpəʊl; *AmE* 'wɔːlpoʊl/ (1717–97) an English author, the son of Robert *Walpole. His best-known book is *The Castle of Otranto* (1764), an early *Gothic novel set in the 12th–13th centuries. Walpole is also famous for his house, *Strawberry Hill, which he designed as a *Gothic castle.

,Robert 'Walpole[2] /'wɔːlpəʊl; *AmE* 'wɔːlpoʊl/ (1676–1745) a British *Whig(1) politician who was Britain's first *prime minister (1715–17 and 1721–42). He also served the longest time of any prime minister and was the first to live at *Number Ten, *Downing Street. His periods in power were times of peace and economic success for the country, although Walpole himself was accused of dishonest behaviour in government. He was made an *earl(1) in 1742.

The ,Walrus and the 'Carpenter a famous non-sense poem in the children's book *Through the Looking Glass* by Lewis Carroll. It describes how the walrus and the carpenter persuade some young oysters (= a type of shellfish) to come with them, and then they eat them. The poem's best-known lines are:

> 66 'The time has come', the walrus said,
> 'To talk of many things:
> Of shoes – and ships – and sealing-wax –
> Of cabbages – and kings.' 99

,Francis 'Walsingham /'wɔːlsɪŋəm/ (c. 1532–90) an English politician. He was a close adviser to Queen *Elizabeth I and was made a *knight in 1577. By creating an organization of spies he helped to reveal the Babington Plot against the queen, and in 1587 was able to warn the government just before the arrival of the *Spanish Armada.

The ,Walt 'Disney ,Company (*also* Disney) a large US company started in 1923 by Walt *Disney which is best known for its animated children's films. Today it owns a number of film companies including Walt Disney Pictures, Touchstone Pictures and *Miramax, produces toys and children's books, runs *Disneyland theme parks in the US and other countries, and also owns a number of American television networks including *ABC.

'Walter 'Reed 'Army 'Medical ,Center /'riːd/ a large hospital and medical centre in Washington, DC, that provides medical care for members of the US armed forces and their families. The US President often goes there for medical checks. The Center, which also does research, opened as a hospital in 1909 and is named after Major Walter Reed (1851–1902), a US Army doctor who discovered that mosquitoes (= small insects that suck blood) carry the tropical disease yellow fever.

,Barbara 'Walters[1] /'wɔːltəz; *AmE* 'wɔːltərz/ (1931–) a US television journalist known especially for her series *Barbara Walters Special*, in which she has conversations with famous people. She began on *Today(2) and in 1976 became the first woman to present a major news pro-gramme, the *ABC Evening News*, and the first journalist to earn $1 million a year. She won an *Emmy in 1982 for *The Barbara Walters Show* and presented the news programme *20/20* (1984–2004). She was chosen for the Television *Hall of Fame in 1990.

,Julie 'Walters² /'wɔːltəz; *AmE* 'wɔːltərz/ (1950–) an English television, film and stage actor who often appears in comedy roles. Her films include *Educating Rita* (1983), *Billy Elliot* (2000) and *Calendar Girls* (2003) and she won a *BAFTA for best actress for the television drama *My Beautiful Son* (2001).

,William 'Walton /'wɔːltən/ (1902–83) an English composer. His best-known works include *Façade* (1923) and the oratorio (= large piece of music for voices and orchestra) *Belshazzar's Feast* (1931), both of which have words written by members of the *Sitwell family. Walton also wrote operas, pieces for orchestra and music for films, including *Henry V* (1944) and *Hamlet* (1948). He was made a *knight in 1951.

The 'Waltons /'wɔːltənz/ a US television series (1972– 81) about a large family in the Blue Ridge Mountains of *Virginia during the *Great Depression. It was very popular, but some people made jokes about the simple stories of honesty, love and family values. Compare LITTLE HOUSE ON THE PRAIRIE.

,Sam 'Wanamaker /'wɒnəmeɪkə(r); *AmE* 'wɑːnəmeɪkər/ (1919–93) a US actor who also directed films and plays. He settled in England in 1951 and worked for many years on a plan to build a copy of the *Globe theatre in London. It was completed after his death. His daughter is the actor Zoe Wanamaker.

'Wapping /'wɒpɪŋ; *AmE* 'wɑːpɪŋ/ an area of *Docklands in London, England. It is known especially as the British base of News International, the newspaper company owned by Rupert *Murdoch. When the company moved there in 1986 there was a conflict with trade union members about the introduction of the new computer technology.

,Perkin 'Warbeck /,pɜːkɪn 'wɔːbek ; *AmE* ,pɜːrkɪn 'wɔːrbek / (c. 1474–99) a man who claimed that he should be made the king of England because he was really Richard, Duke of York, brother of *Edward V and the younger of the two *Princes in the Tower. He was supported against the king at the time, *Henry VII, by the House of *York and by the king of France. He made several attempts to start rebellions against Henry VII but in 1497 he was captured before being kept for a time in the *Tower of London and later executed.

'Wardour Street /'wɔːdə; *AmE* 'wɔːrdər/ a street in the *Soho district of central London, England, known mainly as the place where a lot of film companies have their offices. The name Wardour Street is sometimes used to refer to the British film industry in general.

the 'War Graves Com,mission an organization, started in 1917, that cares for the graves of members of the British and *Commonwealth armed forces who died in both world wars. It looks after over a million graves and other monuments around the world. Its full name is the Commonwealth War Graves Commission.

,Andy 'Warhol /'wɔːhɒl; *AmE* 'wɔːrhoʊl/ (1928–87) a US artist who was a leading figure in the *pop art movement in the 1960s. He painted such familiar objects as *Campbell's soup cans and dollar bills. Another famous picture consisted of several similar images of Marilyn *Monroe. Warhol made a number of long films in which very little happened, including *Chelsea Girls* (1966). The Andy Warhol Museum in *Pittsburgh, where he was born, is said to be the largest museum in the world containing the work of a single artist.

> 66 In the future everyone will be world-famous for fifteen minutes. 99
> Andy Warhol

'Warner ,Brothers /'wɔːnə; *AmE* 'wɔːrnər/ a major *Hollywood film company established in 1923 by four brothers, **Harry Warner** (1881–1958), **Albert Warner** (1884–1967), **Sam Warner** (1888–1927) and **Jack Warner** (1892–1978). It produced the first sound film, *The *Jazz Singer*, in 1927. Other Warner Brothers films have included *Casablanca*, *Yankee Doodle Dandy*, *My Fair Lady*, *The Exorcist* (1973), *Superman*, *Driving Miss Daisy* (1989), *Batman*, *Unforgiven* (1992), *The *Fugitive*, *Fallen* (1998), and the *Harry Potter films (2001–). The company also makes the television series *ER and *Friends. Warner Brothers Records produces music by such singers as *Madonna and Rod *Stewart. Warner Brothers combined with Time, Inc in 1989 to form *Time Warner.

the **War of 1812** /'wɔːr əv 'eɪtiːn 'twelv/ a war (1812– 15) fought between Britain and the US. One of the main causes was the British action of forcing American sailors to serve on British ships. During the war, US soldiers attacked Canada, but without success. The British captured Washington, DC, in 1814 and burned the *Capitol and the *White House(1). American successes, however, led to the Treaty of Ghent (1814) which ended the war. General Andrew *Jackson, not aware of the Treaty, defeated the British three weeks later at the battle of *New Orleans (1815). The war made Americans more united and less willing to become involved in European affairs. See also ISOLATIONISM, STAR-SPANGLED BANNER.

the 'War Office the former name of the British government department in charge of the Army, established during the *Crimean War. In 1964 it became the army department of the *Ministry of Defence.

,War of the 'Worlds a science fiction novel (1898) by H G *Wells. It is about an attack on Earth by creatures from the planet Mars. The creatures have powerful weapons and technology, but are finally killed by Earth's bacteria. A famous US radio version of the story, broadcast in 1938 by Orson *Welles, caused great fear because people thought that the attack was actually happening.

the ,War on 'Drugs the name given to the US government programme started by Ronald *Reagan in the 1980s to try to stop the use of illegal drugs. It has continued ever since and includes public information campaigns and attempts to stop the trade of drugs into the US from other countries.

,War on 'Want a British organization, established in 1951, which campaigns against the causes of poverty throughout the world.

the 'War Powers Act a US law passed in 1973 which allows *Congress to limit the President's use of military forces. It states that the President must tell Congress within 48 hours if he sends armed forces anywhere, and Congress must give approval for them to stay there for more than 90 days. The Act was passed in spite of a veto (= refusal to sign a law) by President Richard *Nixon.

,Earl 'Warren¹ /,ɜːl 'wɒrən; *AmE* ,ɜːrl 'wɔːrən/ (1891– 1974) a Chief Justice of the US *Supreme Court (1953– 69). He was a strong supporter of the *civil rights movement and his court decided against *segregation in public schools in the famous *Brown v Board of Education case (1954). Warren led the **Warren Commission**, a committee formed to investigate the murder of President *Kennedy. It published the **Warren Report** (1964) which said that Kennedy had been killed by Lee Harvey *Oswald, acting alone.

W

'Robert 'Penn 'Warren² /'pen 'wɒrən; *AmE* 'wɔːrən/ (1905–89) a US writer who was the country's first *Poet Laureate and the only American to receive the *Pulitzer Prize for both fiction and poetry. He wrote mostly about the *South. His Pulitzer Prizes were for the novel *All the King's Men* (1946) and his poetry collections *Promises* (1957) and *Now and Then* (1979). Warren was also a well-known critic.

the ˌWars of the 'Roses the name now used for the period of fighting (1455–85) in England between the supporters of the two most powerful families in the country at the time, the House of *Lancaster, whose symbol was a red rose, and the House of *York, whose symbol was a white rose. The aim of each side was to make a member of their family the king of England. Each side was successful at different times and the wars only ended when Henry *Tudor (House of Lancaster) defeated *Richard III (House of York) and became King *Henry VII. His marriage to Elizabeth of York united the two sides and ended the fighting. See also BOSWORTH FIELD, TUDOR ROSE.

'Warwick /'wɒrɪk; *AmE* 'wɔːrɪk/ an ancient town on the River *Avon in central England. It is the administrative centre of the county of *Warwickshire. It contains **Warwick Castle**, a very popular tourist attraction, the earliest parts of which were built in the 14th century. The town also has other buildings from the Middle Ages, although many of these were destroyed in a fire in 1694.

'Warwickshire /'wɒrɪkʃə(r); *AmE* 'wɔːrɪkʃər/ (*abbr written* **Warks**) a county in central England, with the town of *Warwick as its administrative centre. It was reduced in size when part of it, including the city of *Coventry, became part of the *West Midlands, one of the *metropolitan counties created in 1974. *Stratford-upon-Avon is in Warwickshire.

the Wash /wɒʃ; *AmE* wɑːʃ/ a large, shallow bay on the east coast of England, where the *North Sea separates the *counties of *Norfolk to the south and *Lincolnshire to the north. Many English people know the story of how in 1216 King *John lost his luggage and some of his men when they tried to cross the Wash where the water was shallow, during a military campaign.

'Washington¹ /'wɒʃɪŋtən; *AmE* 'wɑːʃɪŋtən/ a north-western state of the US, also called the Evergreen State. The largest city is *Seattle and the capital city is Olympia. Both Britain and the US occupied the land in the first half of the 19th century. Washington became part of the Oregon Territory in 1848 and a state in 1889. Its products include wood, paper, apples and fish, and it has a large aerospace industry. Tourist attractions include Mount *Rainier, Mount *St Helens and Seattle's Pacific Science Center and Space Museum.

ˌBooker T 'Washington² /ˌbʊkə tiː 'wɒʃɪŋtən; *AmE* ˌbʊkər, 'wɑːʃɪŋtən/ (Booker Taliaferro Washington 1856–1915) a US teacher, born into a slave family in *Virginia. In 1881 he started Tuskegee Institute (now *Tuskegee University) for black students. He encouraged African Americans to achieve economic independence before fighting for equal rights, and for this he was sometimes criticized. The best known of his many books is *Up from Slavery* (1901), the story of his own life.

Denzel Washington³ /ˌdenzl 'wɒʃɪŋtən; *AmE* 'wɑːʃɪŋtən/ (1954–) a US actor who first became known in the television hospital drama series *St Elsewhere* (1982–88). He won *Oscars for the films *Glory* (1989) and *Training Day* (2001). His other films include *Cry Freedom* (1987), *Malcolm X* (1992) and *Courage Under Fire* (1996).

ˌGeorge 'Washington⁴ /'wɒʃɪŋtən; *AmE* 'wɑːʃɪŋtən/ (1732–99) the first US *President (1789–97), who had led its army to success in the *American Revolution. He is called 'the Father of His Country'. The *Continental Congress placed him in charge of the American forces in 1775. Although his army had a difficult and dangerous winter at *Valley Forge, General Washington led them to several victories, including the final Battle of *Yorktown. He later gave his important approval for the American *Constitution and was elected in 1789 as the country's first president. He supported a strong central government but disliked political party arguments. He was elected a second time, but refused to stand as a candidate for a third time and returned to his home at *Mount Vernon.

Americans have always admired Washington as one of their best and most moral presidents. He is considered by many to have been the country's greatest leader and perhaps the only one who could have united the colonists during the American Revolution. Most people know the story of how as a boy he cut down his father's cherry tree and then admitted what he had done, saying, 'I cannot tell a lie.' The story may not be true but it is seen as a symbol of his honesty. Washington's fine personal qualities and fair politics were recognized during his life, and they seem even more impressive today. His memory is honoured by the *Washington Monument and the names of the country's capital city, a state, many counties, government buildings, schools, streets, mountains, etc., and his image appears on the dollar note and the 25-cent coin.

ˌWashington, DC /ˌwɒʃɪŋtən diː 'siː; *AmE* ˌwɑːʃɪŋtən/ (Washington, District of Columbia) the capital city of the US, whose area covers the *District of Columbia. The place was chosen by George *Washington in 1790, and since 1800 the main departments of the US government have been there. It is known for its historical monuments and important buildings, including the *Capitol, the *White House(1), the *Supreme Court, the *National Archives, the *Library of Congress, the *Smithsonian Institution, the *National Gallery of Art and the *Kennedy Center. See also ARLINGTON NATIONAL CEMETERY, JEFFERSON MEMORIAL, LINCOLN MEMORIAL, PENTAGON(1), VIETNAM VETERANS MEMORIAL, WASHINGTON MONUMENT.

the ˌWashington 'Monument /ˌwɒʃɪŋtən; *AmE* ˌwɑːʃɪŋtən/ a tall, thin monument on The *Mall(2) in *Washington, DC, built to honour the memory of George *Washington. It is 555 feet/169 metres high and made of white marble. Tourists can climb the 898 steps to the top, from which there are fine views of the city. The Monument took 40 years to build and was completed in 1888.

The ˌWashington 'Post /ˌwɒʃɪŋtən; *AmE* ˌwɑːʃɪŋtən/ (*also informal* **The Post**) a US national newspaper, published in Washington, DC, and known for its liberal opinions. It was the first newspaper to investigate the full *Watergate story, and for this it won a *Pulitzer Prize (1973). It was first published in 1877, and now owns other newspapers, magazines and several television stations.

Wasp (*also* **WASP**) /wɒsp; *AmE* wɑːsp/ (*in full* **white Anglo-Saxon Protestant**) *n* (*AmE sometimes disapproving*) a white person in the US whose family came originally from Britain or northern Europe and whose religion is *Protestant. Wasps are considered to have the best social status and the most political power. People in all social classes who are white have sometimes been called Wasps, especially if they have prejudices against other races.
▶ **Waspy** (*also* **WASPy**) *adj*.

The ˈWaste Land a poem (1922) by T S *Eliot, which has been seen as an expression of the depressed mood and sense of disorder after *World War I. Many of its lines refer to other works of literature and to cultural matters, and these are explained in notes at the end of the poem. The style of the poem, involving short sections that do not at first seem to be closely connected, has had a great influence on modern poetry.

> 66 April is the cruellest month. 99
> *The Waste Land*

'**watchdog** *n* a person or organization that exists to protect people's rights and to check on the behaviour of others, especially that of big companies and institutions. In Britain the word is often used of organizations set up by the government to make sure that the actions of former public companies and institutions which became privately owned in the 1980s and 1990s are both legal and fair. Such organizations include the *National Lottery Commission, *Ofgem, *Ofcom and *Ofwat.

The '**Watchtower** /'wɒtʃtaʊə(r); *AmE* 'wɑːtʃtaʊər/ the magazine produced by the religious group the *Jehovah's Witnesses. Members often try to interest people in it and in their beliefs by going from house to house offering it to them and trying to discuss matters in it.

The '**Water-**,**Babies** a children's book (1863) by Charles *Kingsley. It is about a small boy who works cleaning chimneys, escapes from his cruel employer and falls into a stream, where he meets the little creatures who live there, the water-babies. It is a moral story about good and evil. Many people remember the names of two of its characters especially: Mrs Bedonebyasyoudid, who is fierce, and Mrs Doasyouwouldbedoneby, who is very kind.

'**Watergate** /'wɔːtəgeɪt; *AmE* 'wɔːtərgeɪt/ the US political scandal that forced President Richard *Nixon to leave office in 1974. It involved *Republican Party members who in 1972 tried to steal information from the offices of the *Democratic Party in the Watergate building in Washington, DC. Nixon said he did not know about this, but *The* *Washington Post and tapes of his telephone conversations proved he did. He resigned as *Congress was about to begin *impeachment, and several important government officials were sent to prison for illegally trying to keep the affair secret. The Watergate incident made the role of the President weaker for several years and many people were shocked that people in power had behaved so badly. The word ending *-gate* has since been used to create names for other scandals, e.g. *Irangate.

,**Water'loo**[1] /,wɔːtə'luː; *AmE* ,wɔːtər'luː/ one of London's main train stations, for trains to and from the south, south-east and south-west of England. In 1993 a new part was added to the building for trains travelling to and from the rest of Europe through the *Channel Tunnel. Waterloo also has a station on the *London Underground, and it is one end of the **Waterloo and City Link**, a special underground railway service that transports people who arrive from outside London to the *City for work each day.

the ,**Battle of Water'loo**[2] /wɔːtə'luː; *AmE* wɔːtər'luː/ a battle fought on 18 June 1815 in which the British, led by the Duke of *Wellington, and the Prussians defeated the French army of Napoleon. It was the last battle of the *Napoleonic Wars and took place near the village of Waterloo, not far from Brussels in Belgium. It is seen as one of the most important victories in British history and it made Wellington a national hero. The phrase *to meet one's Waterloo* means to suffer a serious defeat.

'**Water** ,**Music** a popular piece of music for orchestra by the composer George Frederick *Handel. It was written

and first performed in 1717, probably for a party held by King *George I on a boat on the River *Thames.

',**Muddy**' '**Waters**[1] /,mʌdi 'wɔːtəz; *AmE* 'wɔːtərz/ (1915–83) a US *blues singer who played the guitar and wrote songs, often with a sexual theme. His powerful style influenced many other rock musicians. He first became famous with his song *Rollin' Stone* (1950), a name later taken by the *Rolling Stones group and the music magazine *Rolling Stone*. Waters formed a band in 1950, and his later hits included *I'm Your Hoochie Coochie Man* (1954) and *Got My Mojo Working* (1957).

,**Sarah** '**Waters**[2] /'wɔːtəz; *AmE* 'wɔːtərz/ (1966–) a Welsh writer of historical novels. Her first novel *Tipping the Velvet* (1998), deals with lesbian relationships in the 1890s. It was adapted as a BBC television drama in 2002. Her second novel, *Affinity* (1999) won the Somerset Maugham prize in 2000 and her third novel, *Fingersmith* won the Crime Writers' Association Historical Dagger Award in 2002 and was also made into a television drama.

the '**watershed** /'wɔːtəʃed; *AmE* 'wɔːtərʃed/ (*also* **the nine o'clock watershed**) *n* [sing] (in Britain) 9.00 p.m, the time before which the main television stations agree not to broadcast programmes that are not suitable for children, e.g. because they include too much sex, violence or bad language. If this rule is broken, complaints can be made to an official organization, *Ofcom.

,**Watership** '**Down** /,wɔːtəʃɪp; *AmE* ,wɔːtərʃɪp/ a very successful novel for children (1972) by Richard Adams. It tells the story of a group of rabbits who are forced to leave the place where they live and go to live in an area called Watership Down. The book was also very popular with adults and was made into a cartoon film.

'**Waterstone's** /'wɔːtəstəʊnz; *AmE* 'wɔːtərstoʊnz/ a chain of bookshops in Britain which opened its first shop in London in 1982 and now has over 200 shops in the UK, Ireland and Europe, including the biggest bookshop in Europe in *Piccadilly in *London. It also works with Amazon to sell its books over the Internet.

'**Watford** /'wɒtfəd; *AmE* 'wɑːtfərd/ a town in *Hertfordshire, just to the north of London. The phrase 'north of Watford' is sometimes used in a humorous way to mean the parts of England that are north of the London area and the south and south-east of England: *He seems to think that everywhere north of Watford is uncivilized.*

'**Watling Street** /'wɒtlɪŋ; *AmE* 'wɑːtlɪŋ/ a road in England, originally built by the Romans and still in use today under various different names. It runs from Dover, on the south-east coast of England, through London and *St Albans to Wroxeter, a small town in *Shropshire. Its name comes from the *Anglo-Saxon name for St Albans.

,**Dr** '**Watson**[1] /'wɒtsn; *AmE* 'wɑːtsn/ the companion of Sherlock *Holmes in the stories by Arthur *Conan Doyle. He is the narrator of most of the stories and his simple, pleasant attitude to life and events contrasts with the complicated thought processes of Sherlock Holmes. In the stories, he lives with Holmes at 221B *Baker Street.

,**James D** '**Watson**[2] /'wɒtsn; *AmE* 'wɑːtsn/ (James Dewey Watson 1928–) a US scientist who did important work on DNA (= the substance in the human body that passes from parents to children and makes it possible to identify every individual human being). He worked mainly at the *Cavendish Laboratory in Cambridge, England, and in 1962, with Francis *Crick and Maurice Wilkins, he won the *Nobel Prize for medicine for his work.

,**James** '**Watt** /'wɒt; *AmE* 'wɑːt/ (1736–1819) a Scottish inventor whose work played an important part in the

W

development of the steam engine. His designs for engines improved on those in existence at the time because they used much less fuel. Watt's engines were the first to be suitable for use in factories and were therefore one of the major advances in industry that led to the *Industrial Revolution.

,Evelyn 'Waugh /ˌiːvlɪn 'wɔː/ (1903–66) an English writer of novels which are greatly admired for their elegant style and humour. In novels such as *Decline and Fall* (1928) and *A Handful of Dust* (1934), he made fun of the upper class and *upper middle class in England in the 1920s and 1930s. His travels in Africa provided the ideas for novels such as *Black Mischief* (1932) and *Scoop* (1938). In 1930 he became a *Roman Catholic and his interest in Catholic beliefs is shown in the more serious novel *Brideshead Revisited* (1945), about an upper-class English Roman Catholic family. Waugh's other books include a series of three with the title *Sword of Honour* (1952–61), based on his experiences as a soldier in *World War II. He had a reputation as a rude, bad-tempered man with fixed, rather right-wing views.

,Lord 'Wavell /'weɪvəl/ (born Archibald Percival Wavell 1883–1950) a senior military officer in charge of British forces in the Middle East from 1939 to 1941, during *World War II. He later commanded British forces in India and from 1943 to 1947 he was Viceroy of India (= the representative of the British government ruling India when it was part of the *British Empire). He was made an *earl(I) in 1947.

'Waverley /'weɪvəli; AmE 'weɪvərli/ the main railway station in *Edinburgh, Scotland, at the eastern end of *Princes Street. It was opened in 1846, when it was called the General Station, but in 1854 it was named after the *Waverley novels by Sir Walter *Scott.

the 'Waverley ,novels /'weɪvəli; AmE 'weɪvərli/ the name given to the novels of Sir Walter *Scott because he said at the beginning of them that they were written 'by the author of Waverley' and did not give his name. The first of them (itself called *Waverley*) was published in 1814, and it was not until 1827 that Scott announced publicly that he was in fact the author of the novels.

,Ruby 'Wax /ˌruːbi 'wæks/ (1953–) a US television presenter who appears mainly on British television. She is known for programmes such as *The Full Wax* (1991–4) and *Ruby Wax Meets …* (1996–8), in which she meets famous people and asks them questions in a funny and energetic way. She has also been a guest actor in the comedy series *Absolutely Fabulous* and worked on its scripts.

,John 'Wayne /'weɪn/ (1907–79) a US actor who made more than 200 films, many of which were *westerns. His popular name was 'the Duke' or 'Duke', and he came to represent the image of the strong, independent American character. John *Ford[6] directed many of his films, including *Stagecoach* (1939), which made him famous. His other films included *Fort Apache* (1948), *The Searchers* (1956), *The Alamo* (1960), which he also directed and produced, and *True Grit* (1969), for which he won an *Oscar.

the ,Ways and 'Means Com,mittee a permanent committee of members of the US *House of Representatives which makes suggestions about laws for raising money for the US government. It suggests new laws or changes to existing ones affecting things such as taxes and trade agreements with other countries.

The ,Weakest 'Link a television quiz show which first appeared in Britain on the *BBC in 2000 and now has versions in countries around the world. A team of nine contestants answer general knowledge questions in a **chain** (= one after the other), building up an amount of money for each correct answer. When someone **breaks the chain**, by answering incorrectly, all the money is

lost. At the end of each round, the contestants vote for the **weakest link**, the contestant who is least useful to the team, and that person then leaves the team. This continues until only one person is left, who is the winner. The winner is given all the money which has been won. The British and American versions of the show are presented by Anne *Robinson who has a very hard image and strongly criticizes the contestants.

the 'Weald /wiːld/ an area of attractive countryside in south-east England which includes parts of the counties of *Kent, *Surrey and *Sussex. It is known especially as an area where many fruit and vegetables are grown. It was formerly covered by woods, and *weald* is an old-fashioned word meaning wild, i.e. not cultivated.

The ,Wealth of 'Nations an important work of economic and social theory by Adam *Smith, published in 1776. Its full title was *Inquiry into the Nature and Causes of the Wealth of Nations*. In it he analysed the relationship between work and the production of a nation's wealth. His conclusion was that the best economic situation results from encouraging free enterprise (= an economic system in which there is open competition in business and trade, and no government control). This idea has had a great influence on economic theories since and it formed the basis of the economic policies of the *Conservative government in Britain in the 1980s.

▶**weather**

The popular view of the British weather is that it rains all the time. This is not true and Britain gets no more rain in an average year than several other European countries. In some summers the country goes for weeks with nothing more than a **shower**. Perhaps the main characteristic of Britain's weather is that it is hard to predict. This is probably why people regularly listen to **weather forecasts** on radio and television. However, the **weather-forecasters** are sometimes wrong.

The British are not used to extremes. In summer the temperature rarely goes higher than 30°C (86° F). **Heatwaves** are greeted with newspaper headlines such as 'Phew! What a scorcher!' In winter the south and west are fairly **mild**. The east and north get much colder, with **hard frosts** and snow. A **cold snap** (= period of very cold weather) or heavy falls of snow can bring transport to a halt.

Samuel *Johnson observed that 'when two Englishmen meet their first talk is of the weather', and this is still true. The weather is a safe, polite and impersonal topic of conversation. Most British people would agree that bright sunny weather, not too hot and with enough rain to water their gardens, is good. Bad weather usually means dull days with a lot of cloud and rain or, in winter, fog or snow. The British tend to expect the worst as far as the weather is concerned and it is part of national folklore that summer *bank holidays will be wet. It may be *pouring with rain, teeming down, bucketing*, or even just *drizzling* or *spitting*, but it will be wet.

The US is large enough to have several different **climates**, and so the weather varies between regions. In winter the temperature in *New York state is often −8° C (17° F) or lower; in the summer in *Arizona it is often above 40° C (104° F). Arizona gets less than an inch/2.5 centimetres of rain most months; the state of *Washington, DC can get 6 inches/15 centimetres. The Northeast and Midwest have cold winters with a lot of snow, and summers that are very hot and humid. The South has hot, humid summers but moderate winters. The Southwest, including Arizona and *New Mexico, is dry and warm in the winter and very hot in the summer. Some parts of the US suffer tornadoes (= strong circular winds) and hurricanes.

In autumn people put **storm doors and windows** on their houses, an extra layer of glass to keep out the cold wind. Cities in the **snow belt** have several **snow days** each winter, days when people do not go to school or work. But then **snow ploughs** clear the roads and life goes on, even when the weather is bad.

In the US it is considered boring to talk about the weather, but some phrases are often heard. In the summer people ask, 'Is it hot enough for you?' or say that the street is 'hot enough to fry an egg'. When it rains they say 'Nice day if you're a duck', or that they do not mind the rain because 'the farmers need it'.

Many people in Britain and the US, as elsewhere, are worried about **global warming** due to emissions from vehicles and factories of **greenhouse gases** such as carbon dioxide (CO_2) and nitrous oxide (NO_2) and any **climatic changes** this may cause.

Webb /web/ the name of a married couple who were important figures in socialist politics in Britain during the late 19th and early 20th century. **Sidney Webb** (1859–1947) and his wife **Beatrice Webb** (1858–1943) wrote several books together which had a great influence on political thought at the time. These included *The History of Trade Unionism* (1894) and *Industrial Democracy* (1897). Together they helped to establish the *London School of Economics and the *New Statesman* magazine. Sidney was made a *baron in 1929.

John **'Webster**[1] /'webstə(r)/ (c. 1578–c. 1632) an English writer of plays. The best known of these are *The White Devil* (c. 1608) and *The Duchess of Malfi* (c. 1614), which are full of violence and strong emotions. Little is known about his life, but he is now considered to be one of the greatest *Jacobean writers.

Noah **'Webster**[2] /,nəʊə 'webstə(r); AmE ,noʊə/ (1758–1843) a US teacher and author, best known for his *American Dictionary of the English Language* (1828). He also helped to establish a standard American spelling of English with *The Elementary Spelling Book* (1783). His name is now used on many dictionaries published by different US companies.

'wedding march *n* a piece of music traditionally played at wedding ceremonies in church in Britain, either when the bride enters the church or while the couple who have just been married walk down the aisle before leaving the church. The most popular piece for the entry of the bride is from Wagner's opera *Lohengrin*, and the most popular piece for the end of the ceremony is from Mendelssohn's music for *A Midsummer Night's Dream*.

▶ **weddings**

A *wedding* is the occasion when people **get married**. *Marriage* is the state of being married, though the word can also mean the wedding ceremony.

Before getting married a couple **get engaged**. It is traditional for the man to **propose** (= ask his girlfriend to marry him) and, if she accepts, to give his new **fiancée** an **engagement ring**, which she wears on the third finger of her left hand. Today many couples decide together to get married.

The couple then **set a date** and decide who will perform the marriage ceremony and where it will be held. In the US judges and religious leaders can perform weddings. Religious weddings are often held in a *church or chapel, but the ceremony can take place anywhere and couples often choose somewhere that is special to them. In Britain many couples still prefer to be married in church, even if they are not religious. Others choose a **civil ceremony** conducted by a **registrar** at a **registry office**, or, since 1994 when the law was changed, at one of the many hotels and historic buildings which are licensed for weddings.

Traditionally, the family of the **bride** (= the woman who is to be married) paid for the wedding, but today the couple usually pay part of the cost. Many people choose a traditional wedding with a hundred or more **guests**. Before the wedding, the couple send out printed **invitations** and guests buy a gift for them, usually something for their home. In the US couples **register** at a store by leaving there a list of presents they would like. Guests go to the store to look at the list and buy a present. In Britain couples send a **wedding list** to guests or, as in America, open a **bride's book** in a large store.

Before a wedding can take place in a church it must be announced there on three occasions. This is called **the reading of the banns**. Some religious groups refuse to allow a couple to marry in church if either of them has been divorced, but they may agree to **bless** the marriage after a civil ceremony.

Before the wedding the bride and **bride groom** or **groom** (= her future husband) often go to separate parties given for them by friends. At the groom's **stag party** guests drink alcohol and joke about how the groom is going to lose his freedom. For the bride there is a **hen party**, called in the US a **bachelorette party**. Sometimes these parties take the form of a weekend trip to a foreign city.

At the wedding the groom's closest male friend acts as the **best man** and stands next to him during the ceremony. Other friends act as **ushers** and show guests where to sit. The bride's closest woman friend is **chief bridesmaid** (*AmE* **maid of honour**), or **matron of honour** if she is married, and other friends are **bridesmaids** if they are girls or **pages** if they are boys. Many women choose to have a **white wedding**, and wear a long white **wedding dress**, with a **veil** (= a piece of thin white material) covering the face. The bride's wedding clothes should include 'something old, something new, something borrowed, something blue', to bring luck. The bridesmaids wear matching dresses specially made for the occasion and, like the bride, carry **bouquets** of flowers. The bridegroom, the best man and other men may wear **morning dress** (= a long-tailed jacket, dark trousers and a top hat) or, in the US, a **tuxedo** (= a black suit with a white shirt). Women guests dress smartly and often wear hats. Men often hire the clothes for a wedding but women often use a wedding as an opportunity to buy something new.

The bride traditionally arrives at the church a few minutes late and enters with her father who will **give her away** to her husband. The bride and groom **exchange vows** (= promise to stay together and support each other). The groom places a **wedding ring** on the third finger of the bride's left hand, and sometimes the bride gives him a ring too. The couple are then declared **man and wife**. They **sign the register** (= the official record of marriages) and as they leave the church guests throw rice or **confetti** (= small pieces of coloured paper in lucky shapes, such as horseshoes and bells) over them.

The '**happy couple**' and their guests then go to the **wedding reception** at the bride's home, a hotel or the place where the ceremony took place if it was not a church or registry office. There are often speeches by the best man, the bride's father and the bridegroom. The bride and groom together cut a **wedding cake**, which usually has several tiers (= layers), each covered with white icing (*AmE* frosting), with figures of a bride and groom on the top one. Before the **newly-weds** leave for their **honeymoon** (= a holiday to celebrate their marriage) the bride throws her bouquet in the air: there is a belief that the woman who catches it will soon be married herself. The car the couple leave in has usually been decorated by their friends with the words '**just married**' and with old tin cans or shoes tied to the back.

W

'Wedgwood™ /'wedʒ-wʊd/ n [U] fine English pottery and china made by the company established in 1759 by Josiah Wedgwood (1730–95) near *Stoke-on-Trent in *Staffordshire. Its most characteristic design, called Jasper, uses raised white patterns or figures on a blue background.

Wedgwood Jasperware

This design was influenced by *neoclassicism and became very fashionable when first produced. It is still made today.

▶ **weekends**

The weekend lasts from the end of working hours or school hours on Friday until Monday morning. For most people it is a chance to be at home with their family, spend time on a sport or hobby or go out somewhere. Both adults and children look forward to the freedom of the weekend and to having time to please themselves. On Friday people with jobs may say **TGIF** (Thank God it's Friday) and may go to a bar together after work. People who work in factories, shops and restaurants and on buses often have to work at weekends and instead get time off during the week. Sometimes people take an extra day off on Friday or Monday to make a **long weekend**, especially if they want to have a short holiday/vacation. Several holidays, such as *Memorial Day in the US and *Spring Bank Holiday in Britain, are on a Monday in order to create a long weekend.

At the weekend (*AmE* **On the weekend**) people may do jobs around the house, look after their garden, wash the car, play sport or watch television. On Saturday mornings many US television channels show cartoons. The weekend is also the busiest time of the week for shopping. Shops are open on both Saturday and Sunday. For a long time many British people opposed **Sunday trading** and wanted to 'keep Sunday special', but there was pressure from some of the larger stores and *DIY shops to be allowed to open, and now many people like shopping on a Sunday.

Friday and Saturday nights are popular, especially among young people, for parties and visits to clubs and *pubs. People also go to the theatre or cinema, eat out at a restaurant, or invite friends to their house for dinner or a barbecue.

On Sundays many people have a **lie-in** (= stay in bed longer than usual). Some people go to church on Sunday morning. In the US many adults enjoy reading the newspaper while eating **brunch**, a combination of breakfast and lunch that includes dishes from both. Brunch is eaten between about 10 and 12 in the morning and is enjoyed in a relaxed atmosphere. In Britain some people sit around and read the Sunday papers. They may have other members of the family round for **Sunday lunch**. Many people go out for a walk or visit a theme park, *stately home or other attraction, depending on their interests. In summer many families go out for the day to the countryside.

In general people are very busy at the weekend and often finish it more tired than they began it, so for many Monday morning is the least pleasant part of the week.

the ¸Weekly 'Worker a weekly newspaper published by the *Communist Party of Britain since 1993. The party's original newspaper was The *Daily Worker (1930–1945). See also MORNING STAR, SOCIALIST WORKER.

'Weetabix™ /'wiːtəbɪks/ n [U, C] (pl **Weetabix**) a popular breakfast cereal made from processed wheat

formed into blocks. These are usually eaten with milk and sugar: Would you like some Weetabix? ◊ I always have a couple of Weetabix for breakfast.

¸Wee Willie 'Winkie /¸wiː wɪlɪ 'wɪŋki/ a character in a traditional *nursery rhyme. The words are:

> 66 Wee Willie Winkie runs through the town,
> Upstairs and downstairs in his nightgown,
> Rapping at the window, crying through the lock,
> Are the children all in bed, it's past eight o'clock? 99

'Weight ¸Watchers™ an organization in both Britain and the US that gives advice and special classes for people who are worried that they are too fat and want to lose weight. It advises customers on what foods to eat and produces a range of its own foods.

¸Kurt 'Weill /¸kɑːt 'vaɪl; *AmE* ¸kɜːrt 'waɪl/ (1900–50) a US composer, born in Germany. He is best known for Die Dreigroschenoper (in English The Threepenny Opera) (1928). He moved to the US in 1935 to escape from the Nazis, and wrote the music for several *Broadway musical plays, including Knickerbocker Holiday (1938), Lady in the Dark (1941) and Street Scene (1947). His music was used by Woody *Allen in Shadows and Fog (1992).

¸Johnny 'Weissmuller /'waɪsmʊlə(r)/ (1909–84) a US swimmer who later became a film actor. As a swimmer, he established 28 world records in various events and won a total of five gold medals at the Olympic Games of 1924 and 1928. He then played the role of *Tarzan in several popular films of the 1930s and 1940s.

¸Jack 'Welch /'weltʃ/ (1935–) a well-known US businessman who was in charge of *General Electric from 1981 to 2001 and was known for his strong policies to make the business more competitive, such as regularly getting rid of the company's least successful managers.

¸Fay 'Weldon /'weldən/ (1931–) an English writer known especially for the feminist themes of her novels. These have included The Life and Loves of a She-Devil (1983), which was made into a British television series and later a film. She caused controversy by accepting payment from a jewellery company to write a novel in which their products are mentioned (The Bulgari Connection 2001).

the ¸welfare 'state n [sing] the system by which the government of a country cares for its citizens through a range of services provided and paid for by the State, including medical care, financial help for poor people and homes for old people. In Britain the term applies mainly to the *National Health Service, *National Insurance and *social security. The US does not consider itself a true welfare state, but Americans use the terms 'welfare' and 'welfare programmes' for the various ways the national, state and local governments help people who are poor, sick, old, unemployed, etc. The national programmes include *Medicare, *Medicaid and *Temporary Assistance to Needy Families. See also BEVERIDGE REPORT.

¸Welfare to 'Work a phrase used in Britain and the US for government programmes that are aimed at reducing the number of people who are unemployed and receiving money from the State, by creating jobs for them or training them for work.

the 'Wellcome Trust /'welkəm trʌst/ a British charity that provides money for medical research projects. It was originally financed from the profits of a company producing drugs and other medicines started in Britain by two US chemists, Henry Wellcome (1853–1936) and Silas Burroughs (1846–95).

'well-¸dressing n [U] a traditional English custom, especially in the towns and villages of *Derbyshire. It involves decorating wells (= places where water can be taken from under the ground) with pictures made from flowers, leaves and other natural materials in early summer, especially around the time of *Whit.

,Orson 'Welles /ˌɔːsən ˈwelz; AmE ˌɔːrsən/ (1915–85) a US actor who also wrote, directed and produced films and plays. He became famous in 1938 when his radio production of H G *Wells's *The War of the Worlds* frightened many people who thought it was describing a real attack by Martians. Welles's most famous film was his first, *Citizen Kane* (1941). Others included *Jane Eyre* (1944), *The Lady from Shanghai* (1948) with his wife Rita *Hayworth, *The *Third Man*, *Othello* (1952) and *Touch of Evil* (1958).

the ,Duke of 'Wellington /ˈwelɪŋtən/ (born Arthur Wellesley 1769–1852) an English soldier and politician, sometimes called the Iron Duke. He was made a *duke in 1814 as a reward for his victories against the French general Napoleon in the *Peninsular War. The next year Wellington's army, with the Prussians, completely defeated Napoleon at the Battle of *Waterloo. The Duke then began an active political career and in 1828 became leader of the *Tories and *Prime Minister of Britain. He made a lot of enemies in only two years. First he supported the *Emancipation Act, giving *Roman Catholics the right to vote. This was unpopular in his own party. Then he opposed the *Reform Act, which was popular in the country. In 1830 he was forced to resign, although he returned to the government in 1834. He is buried in *St Paul's Cathedral, beside *Nelson. See also APSLEY HOUSE.

,We'll Meet A'gain one of the best-known songs in Britain during *World War II, originally sung by Vera *Lynn and still popular today. The sentimental words express hope for the future at a time of trouble.

Wells¹ /welz/ a town in *Somerset in the west of England. It is famous for its fine cathedral, built in the 13th and 14th centuries, and its many other old buildings.

,H G 'Wells² /ˈwelz/ (Herbert George Wells 1866–1946) an English author known especially as a writer of early science fiction novels. These include *The Time Machine* (1895), *The Invisible Man* (1897) and *The War of the Worlds* (1898). He also wrote successful comic novels about life in Britain, including *Kipps* (1905) and *The History of Mr Polly* (1910). Wells believed strongly in the importance of science and the need for social change and world peace.

,Kitty 'Wells³ /ˈwelz/ (1919–) an American *country music singer known as **The Queen of Country Music.** Her best-known songs include *It Wasn't God Who Made Honky Tonk Angels* (1952), *Make Believe* (1955) and *I Can't Stop Loving You* (1958).

,Wells 'Fargo /ˌwelz ˈfɑːɡəʊ; AmE ˈfɑːrɡoʊ/ a US company that became famous in the *Old West for carrying goods and passengers between *San Francisco and New York. Their *stagecoaches also carried gold, money and mail and were often attacked by thieves. The company was established as a bank in 1852 by Henry Wells and William G Fargo. In 1861 they bought the *Pony Express. In 1918 Wells Fargo combined with several other companies to form the American Railway Express Company.

Welsh¹ /welʃ/ n [U] the ancient Celtic language of Wales. Welsh is spoken as a first language by about 16% of the population of Wales, mainly in the north and west of the country. Groups like the Welsh Language Society and the *Welsh Language Board encourage its use. Welsh and English are the official languages of the *Welsh Assembly and its laws are written in both languages. Welsh is taught as a first or second language in all schools in Wales and other subjects are taught in Welsh in about 500 schools. Road signs, etc. in Wales are

in both Welsh and English. There are also programmes in Welsh on the Welsh radio station, Radio Cymru, and on the television station *S4C.

Irvine Welsh² /ˌɜːvɪn ˈwelʃ; AmE ˌɜːrvɪn/ (1961–) a Scottish writer best known for his novel *Trainspotting* (1993) written in the *Edinburgh dialect about a group of heroin addicts. It was made into a film (1996) with Ewan *McGregor. His other books include *The Acid House* (1993), *Filth* (1998) and *Porno* (2002).

> ❝ I don't give a toss about writing really. It's a bit ironic that the things I'm really into are music and football and I have never been really good at either. ❞
> Irvine Welsh

the ,Welsh As'sembly /ˌwelʃ/ (also formal the **National Assembly for Wales**) the people who are elected as a government for Wales with limited independence from the British Parliament in *Westminster. The Assembly meets in *Cardiff and is made up of 60 *Assembly Members. 40 of them are directly elected to represent *constituencies and 20 are elected to represent regions of Wales using a form of *proportional representation. The Welsh Assembly began work in 1999. It has the power to develop and carry out policies affecting Wales in areas including education, culture, health, agriculture, the environment, tourism and the Welsh language but cannot raise taxes. It is led by a *First Minister who is chosen by the Assembly and who chooses the other Assembly Ministers to make up a *cabinet. Compare NORTHERN IRELAND ASSEMBLY, SCOTTISH PARLIAMENT. ⇨ note at DEVOLUTION.

the ,Welsh 'dragon /ˌwelʃ/ a red dragon which is the official symbol of Wales.

the ,Welsh 'Guards /ˌwelʃ/ a regiment in the British Army. It is one of the *Guards regiments and was established in 1915 from a group of Welshmen in the *Grenadier Guards.

the Welsh dragon

the ,Welsh 'Language ,Board /ˌwelʃ/ an organization started by the *Welsh Assembly to encourage the use of *Welsh in Wales.

'Welsh 'National 'Opera /ˈwelʃ/ an opera company based in *Cardiff. It first performed in Cardiff in 1946 and became fully professional in the 1970s. The company makes regular tours in Wales and parts of England. See also SCOTTISH OPERA.

,Welsh 'rabbit /ˌwelʃ/ (also **Welsh rarebit** /ˈreəbɪt; AmE ˈrerbɪt/) a dish eaten as a small meal or as part of a meal, consisting of bread with cheese on it cooked under heat until the cheese melts. The origin of its name is not clear, and it is often simply called 'cheese on toast'.

the ,Welsh 'valleys /ˌwelʃ/ (also informal the **valleys**) the industrial region of south Wales, for example the *Rhondda Valley. The main industries there were coal and steel, and coal mines were first established there in the early 19th century. For many years these industries employed most of the men in the region but the coal industry has now disappeared and the steel industry has become much smaller.

Eu,dora 'Welty /juːˌdɔːrə ˈwelti/ (1909–2001) a US writer of novels and short stories about her home state of *Mississippi and the US *South. She won the *Pulitzer Prize for her novel *The Optimist's Daughter* (1972) and her collections of stories include *The Golden Apples* (1949).

W

Wembley /'wembli/ (*also* ,Wembley 'Stadium) a famous sports stadium in the district of north-west London of the same name. It first opened in 1923 and was considered to be England's national sports stadium. It closed in 2000 to allow for a new **Wembley National Stadium** to be built on the same site. It will be ready in 2006. The most important sporting event held at Wembley is the football *FA *Cup Final, which takes place every year. The Olympic Games were held there in 1948 and England's national football team plays its home games there. Important *Rugby League and *hockey matches are also played at Wembley. Next to the stadium, a separate building, the **Wembley Arena** is used for rock concerts, shows (especially on ice) and sports events, especially competitions in showjumping (= the sport of riding horses over difficult barriers). The original name for the Wembley Arena was the Empire Pool as it contained a big swimming pool. Close to the Arena and Wembley Stadium site is the large Wembley Conference Centre, which opened in 1977.

Wendy /'wendi/ a character in the children's story *Peter Pan* by J M *Barrie. She is one of the children of the Darling family who are taken by Peter Pan to the *Never Never Land, where they have many adventures. Barrie invented the name Wendy, which has since become a popular name for girls.

Wendy's™ /'wendiz/ any of a group of US *fast-food restaurants that serve mostly hamburgers. The company has over 6000 restaurants around the world. It was established in 1969 by Dave Thomas who named it after one of his daughters.

Wensleydale /'wenzlɪdeɪl/ *n* [U] a type of English cheese which is mild and white and easily breaks into pieces. It was originally made in the valley of Wensleydale in *Yorkshire.

Wentworth /'wentwəθ; *AmE* 'wentwərθ/ a famous golf course in *Surrey in southern England. A number of important competitions are held there, including the World Match Play Championship, which has taken place there every year since it began in 1964.

Timberlake 'Wertenbaker /,tɪmbəleɪk 'wɜːtnbeɪkə(r); *AmE* ,tɪmbərleɪk 'wɜːrtnbeɪkər/ (1951–) an American writer of plays who works mainly in Britain. Her plays include *The Grace of Mary Traverse* (1985), *Our Country's Good* (1988), *Three Birds Alighting on a Field* (1992) and *Credible Witness* (2001).

We Shall Over'come a song used during the *civil rights movement by *African Americans and their supporters to show that they intended to overcome prejudice and *segregation. Mahalia *Jackson often sang it at their meetings. It was originally a *gospel song, and includes the lines:

> 66 Deep in my heart, I do believe
> We shall overcome some day. 99

Arnold 'Wesker /'weskə(r)/ (1932–) an English writer of plays. He grew up in a left-wing Jewish family in London and many of his plays reflect this background and the problems created by class divisions in Britain. They include *Chicken Soup with Barley* (1957), *Roots* (1959), *I'm Talking about Jerusalem* (1960), *Chips with Everything* (1962) and *Annie Wobbler* (1983).

Charles 'Wesley¹ /'wezli/ (1707–88) one of the people who helped to establish the *Methodist Church in Britain, with his brother John *Wesley. He is mainly known as the writer of over 7000 hymns, many of which are still popular today. These include *Love Divine, All Loves Excelling* and the Christmas *carol *Hark! the Herald Angels Sing*.

John 'Wesley² /'wezli/ (1703–91) the person mainly responsible for establishing the *Methodist Church in Britain. He became a priest in the *Church of England in 1725 and in 1729 joined a religious group started by his brother Charles *Wesley in *Oxford. People called the group 'Methodists' because of their fixed methods of praying and studying. They were known for the very personal and intense style of their preaching (= speaking about religion) during church services and for the highly emotional response of those who heard them. When the Church of England decided not to allow the Methodists to continue preaching in its churches, John Wesley spent the next 50 years travelling around Britain on a horse preaching to people, mostly outdoors. As a result, the number of people following his religious beliefs greatly increased. The Methodist Church remained part of the Church of England until after Wesley's death, when it became a separate Church following a disagreement with the Church of England.

Wessex /'wesɪks/ a region of southern England in *Anglo-Saxon times. Originally part of what is now *Hampshire and *Oxfordshire, it grew to include most of southern England by the 9th century. The name Wessex was used by Thomas *Hardy for the area of south-west England (especially *Dorset) where his novels are set. It is also used today in the names of certain local authorities and companies in the region.

the ,Earl of 'Wessex /'wesɪks/ (1964–) Prince Edward, the fourth child of Queen *Elizabeth II. He was educated at *Gordonstoun in Scotland and at *Cambridge University, where he studied history. He joined the *Royal Marines in 1986, but left the next year to begin a career producing plays for the theatre and films for television. In 1999 he married Sophie *Rhys-Jones, who became the Countess of Wessex on her marriage. Their daughter, Lady Louise Windsor, was born in 2003.

Frederick and 'Rosemary West¹ /'west / a married couple at the centre of one of the most famous and terrible criminal cases in Britain in the 20th century. Over a number of years they together murdered a number of young women and buried them in the garden and cellar of their house in Cromwell Street in *Gloucester. The bodies were discovered in 1994 and the house became known as the 'House of Horror'.

Mae 'West² /,meɪ 'west/ (1892–1980) a US actor who became a sex symbol in the 1930s and was famous for her humorous remarks suggesting sex. Her films include *My Little Chickadee* (1940) and *Myra Breckinridge* (1970).

> 66 Why don't you come up sometime 'n see me? 99
> Mae West in *She Done Him Wrong*.

Na,thanael 'West³ /nə,θænjəl 'west/ (1903–40) a US author. His novels, which did not become well known until after his death, were strongly critical of American society. They include *Miss Lonelyhearts* and *The Day of the Locust* (1939), based on his experiences as a *Hollywood writer. West was killed in a car crash.

Re,becca 'West⁴ /'west/ (1892–1983) an English writer and journalist. She wrote many novels, including *The Thinking Reed* (1936), *The Fountain Overflows* (1956) and *The Birds Fall Down* (1966), but is best remembered for the books she wrote as a result of her work as a journalist. These include *The Meaning of Treason* (1949), about the spies *Burgess² and *Maclean², and *A Train of Powder* (1955) about the Nuremberg trials. West had a long love affair with the writer H G *Wells. She was made a *dame(2) in 1959.

the ,West 'Coast the name commonly used for the states on the west coast of the US, especially *California. To many people the West Coast suggests a place that has sunny weather most of the time, where the people have a relaxed way of life and often invent or follow new fashions, particularly those involving physical fitness or psychology.

the **'West ‚Country** the name often used to refer to the south-west of Britain, particularly the *counties of *Cornwall, *Devon, *Somerset and *Dorset.

the ‚**West 'End** the area of west central London that contains the city's most famous streets for shopping, theatres and cinemas, as well as many restaurants and other forms of entertainment. It includes such places as *Soho, *Oxford Street, *Shaftesbury Avenue, *Chinatown, *Leicester Square, *Regent Street and *Piccadilly Circus.

'**western** n a book or film that tells a story about *cowboys in the *Wild West. Westerns involve guns, horses and often Indians (*Native Americans). They are popular because they represent the traditional struggle between good and bad, often in a simple but exciting way. Famous western films include *High Noon and *Shane. Western television series have included *Gunsmoke and *Bonanza. See also COWBOYS AND INDIANS, L'AMOUR, SPAGHETTI WESTERN.

the ‚**Western 'Isles** a *council area of north-west Scotland, often called by its official *Gaelic name 'Eilean Siar'. It consists of the islands of the Outer *Hebrides: Lewis with Harris, North Uist, South Uist and Barra. Its administrative centre is *Stornoway. The term Western Isles is also sometimes used to mean all the islands in the Hebrides.

‚**Western Sa'moa** /sə'məʊə; AmE sə'moʊə/ a group of islands in the southern Pacific which has been an independent country since 1962 and a full member of the *Commonwealth since 1970. Its official languages are English and Samoan. The main exports are copra (= the dried inner part of coconuts), coconut oil and fish.
▶ **Samoan** adj, n.

‚**Western 'Union** a US telegraph company (= one offering a service of sending people's messages by the use of electric current along wires). It was established in 1851 and used during the *American Civil War. Since it could deliver written messages quickly in an emergency, people often feared it was bad news when one arrived. The company now offers ways of sending money to other countries.

‚**West 'Ham** /'hæm/ (also ‚**West 'Ham United**) an English football club whose home ground is Upton Park in the West Ham area of east London. Its most successful period was in the 1960s when players such as Bobby *Moore and Geoff Hurst played for it. It was established in 1900 and its informal name is the Hammers. It has won the *FA Cup three times. It has not had any major success in recent years.

the ‚**West 'Indies** /'ɪndiz/ several groups of islands between the south coast of the US and the north coast of South America, forming a line which encloses the *Caribbean Sea. There are about 1200 islands in all. They include Cuba, *Jamaica, Hispaniola, *Puerto Rico, *Dominica, *St Lucia, *Barbados, *Grenada, and *Trinidad and Tobago. Many of the islands in the West Indies formerly belonged to Britain and are now members of the *Commonwealth.
▶ **West Indian** adj, n.

'**Westinghouse** /'westɪŋhaʊs/ a large US company which supplies goods and services to the nuclear power industry in many countries. It was established in 1886 by George Westinghouse as the Westinghouse Electric Company and was mostly responsible for the US decision to use AC (= alternating current) instead of DC (= direct current) electricity.

the ‚**West 'Lothian Question** /'ləʊðiən; AmE 'loʊðiən/ a question originally asked by *Labour MP Tam Dalyell, whose *constituency in Scotland used to be called West Lothian. Before *devolution, he asked how it could be right that a Scottish MP in the British parliament in London would be able to vote upon matters affecting English constituencies but that same MP could not vote on matters affecting his or her own constituency because they would be the responsibility of the *Scottish Parliament. Today, most people think that the question refers to the fact that Scottish MPs in London can still vote on English matters, while MPs from England have lost the power to influence Scottish affairs. Many politicians continue to disagree about the answer to this question, but some think that the best way to resolve it would be to reduce the number of Scottish MPs in the British parliament.

the ‚**West 'Midlands** /'mɪdləndz/ a *metropolitan county in central England, created in 1974 and consisting of seven districts which were previously parts of the counties of *Warwickshire, *Worcestershire and *Staffordshire, including the cities of *Birmingham and *Coventry.

'**Westminster** /'westmɪnstə(r)/ **1** a *borough of central London which contains many important government buildings, including the *Houses of Parliament, the offices in *Whitehall and *Downing Street, and the royal palaces, *Buckingham Palace and *St James's Palace. Other well-known places there include *Westminster Abbey, *St James's Park, The *Mall(1) and *Victoria station. The River *Thames flows on one side of it.
2 the British Houses of Parliament and British government and politics in general: *There was a heated debate at Westminster today.*

‚**Westminster 'Abbey** /‚westmɪnstər/ a very big church in *Westminster(1), London, which is one of the most famous buildings in Britain. Most of the present building, which replaced an earlier one, was built in the 13th and 14th centuries, in the *Gothic style. Every English king and queen has been crowned there since *William the Conqueror in 1066. Many famous English people are

Westminster Abbey

buried in the Abbey or have memorials in it, and it contains *Poets' Corner and the *Tomb of the Unknown Soldier. The Abbey was made a *World Heritage Site in 1987. See also CORONATION CHAIR.

‚**Westminster 'Bridge** /‚westmɪnstə; AmE ‚westmɪnstər/ one of the best-known bridges over the River *Thames in central London. The Houses of Parliament are close to the north end of the bridge, and the south side leads to County Hall and the *South Bank. It is popular with tourists, who like to take photographs of each other with the *Houses of Parliament(2) in the background. See also WORDSWORTH.

‚**Westminster 'Cathedral** /‚westmɪnstə; AmE ‚westmɪnstər/ the main *Roman Catholic church in England. It was built in neo-Byzantine style (= like the architecture of the Byzantine Empire) at the end of the 19th century, and the inside of the building is still being decorated. It is near *Victoria Station in central London.

W

the 'Westminster 'Kennel Club 'Dog Show
/'westmɪnstə; AmE 'westmɪnstər/ the oldest and most important dog show in the US. It began in 1877 and is now held every February in *Madison Square Garden with more than 150 breeds of dogs competing. Compare CRUFTS.

‚Westminster 'School
/ˌwestmɪnstə; AmE ˌwestmɪnstər/ a well-known British *public school near *Westminster Abbey. It began as a *Roman Catholic school in the 12th century, and became a *Church of England school at the *Reformation. Traditionally it only accepted boys as students, but in the late 20th century it began to take girls in the *sixth form.

'Westmorland
/'westmələnd; AmE 'westmərlənd/ a former county in north-west England. In 1974 it was combined with *Cumberland and part of *Lancashire(1) to form *Cumbria.

West 'Point ⇨ UNITED STATES MILITARY ACADEMY.

the 'West Side
the western part of *Manhattan(1) in New York City, from *Fifth Avenue to the *Hudson River. It contains *Rockefeller Center, *Times Square, *Madison Square Garden, *Macy's, *Carnegie Hall and the theatre district. The Upper West Side has the *Lincoln Center for the Performing Arts and *Columbia University.

‚West Side 'Story
a *Broadway musical play (1957) with music by Leonard *Bernstein and words by Stephen *Sondheim. The film version (1961) won several *Oscars, including Best Picture. The story is a modern version of Shakespeare's play *Romeo and Juliet set in the tough 1950s West Side of New York's *Manhattan(1). The songs include Maria, Tonight and There's a Place for Us.

‚West 'Sussex
/'sʌsɪks/ a county in southern England created when the former county of *Sussex was divided into two separate counties in 1974. Its administrative centre is the town of *Chichester.

‚West Vir'ginia
/vəˈdʒɪniə; AmE vərˈdʒɪniə/ a central eastern state of the US, also called the Mountain State. The capital and largest city is Charleston. West Virginia separated from *Virginia in 1861 because its people did not want to join the *Confederate States, and became a US state two years later. It produces apples, milk products, coal, steel, glass and chemicals. Tourist attractions include *Harpers Ferry National Historical Park and Monongahela National Forest. Nearly 75% of the state is covered by forests.

The 'West ‚Wing
a popular US television drama series on *NBC which started in 1999 about a US President, played by Martin *Sheen, and his staff. It often deals with current political issues and has won a number of *Emmys.

‚Vivienne 'Westwood
/ˌvɪviən 'westwʊd/ (1941–) an English fashion designer, well known for her unusual clothes based on historical themes. She first became famous in the 1970s by selling her *punk(1) designs in a shop on *King's Road, London, with her partner Malcolm *McLaren.

‚West 'Yorkshire
/'jɔːkʃə(r); AmE 'jɔːrkʃər/ (written abbr **W Yorks**) a *metropolitan county in the north of England, created in 1974 and consisting of five districts which were previously part of the West *Riding of *Yorkshire.

wet
n (in Britain) a politician who believes in moderate rather than extreme policies. The word was used by Margaret *Thatcher in the 1980s to insult the members of her own party who did not agree with some of her more right-wing policies. Later, moderate members of the *Conservative Party began to refer to themselves as wets.

'wetback
/'wetbæk/ n (AmE informal, disapproving, often offensive) a Mexican worker who enters the US illegally, often by swimming across the *Rio Grande river.

Mr W H
/ˌmɪstə 'dʌbljuː 'eɪtʃ/ an unknown man for whom William *Shakespeare said he had written his *Sonnets at the beginning of the first published version of the poems. Shakespeare was in love with a young man when he wrote them and this has led many people to think that Mr W H and the young man were the same person, but nobody knows this for certain. There have been many different theories about the true identity of Mr W H.

Wham!
/wæm/ a British pop group formed in 1982, which was very successful in the 1980s, with songs including Wake Me Up Before You Go-Go (1984) and I'm Your Man (1985). Its main singer was George *Michael, who left the group to begin a career on his own in 1986.

‚Edith 'Wharton
/ˌiːdɪθ 'wɔːtn; AmE 'wɔːrtn/ (1862–1937) a US writer of novels and short stories, many of which are about high society in New York. Her best-known novel is The Age of Innocence (1920), which won a *Pulitzer Prize and was made into a film in 1993, directed by Martin *Scorsese. Wharton's other novels include The House of Mirth (1905) and Ethan Frome (1911). She lived in France after 1913.

‚What the 'Papers Say
a British television programme that examined the different ways in which the news was reported in different newspapers. It was first broadcast in 1956 and continued until the 1990s. The name is now frequently used for a summary of newspaper reports.

the 'Wheat Belt
the western central region of the US, where most of the country's wheat is grown. It includes the *Great Plains.

'Wheaties™
/'wiːtiːz/ n [pl] a popular US breakfast cereal made of wheat. It is advertised as 'The Breakfast of Champions'. The packets carry pictures of successful sports people and teams, which young people save and exchange. Wheaties were first produced in 1924 and are made by the General Mills company.

‚Charles 'Wheatstone
/'wiːtstəʊn; AmE 'wiːtstoʊn/ (1802–75) an English scientist and inventor. He invented many things, including the kaleidoscope (= a toy consisting of a tube containing pieces of coloured glass and mirrors which reflect these so that changing patterns are formed when the tube is turned), the electric clock and the **Wheatstone bridge**, a device for measuring electrical resistance. He taught physics at *London University, and was made a *knight in 1868.

‚Wheel of 'Fortune
a popular US television game show, first broadcast in the 1970s. It has been presented for many years by Pat Sajak and his assistant Vanna White, and is watched regularly by millions of people around the world. The game involves competitors trying to guess popular expressions. Other countries, including Britain, have their own versions of the show.

'whelk stall
n (in Britain) a small covered stand from which whelks (= small sea animals in shells) and other types of cheap seafood are sold. Whelk stalls were traditionally found on the streets of the *East End of London, and in British seaside towns.

‚When 'Johnny Comes 'Marching 'Home
a song from the American *Civil War which was popular with people on both sides. It was written in 1863 by Patrick Gilmore (1829–92) who was born in Ireland. The first verse is:

> 66 When Johnny comes marching home again,
> hurrah! Hurrah!
> We'll give him a hearty welcome then, hurrah! Hurrah!
> The men will cheer, the boys will shout,
> The ladies, they will all turn out,
> And we'll all feel gay, when Johnny comes marching
> home. 99

,**When the 'Saints Go 'Marching 'In** one of the best-known traditional *Dixieland songs in the US. It is played every day in the *French Quarter of *New Orleans. The first verse is:

> 66 Oh, when the saints go marching in,
> Oh, when the saints go marching in,
> Oh, Lord, I want to be in that number,
> When the saints go marching in. 99

Which? a British organization that tests the quality of products and publishes the results each month in its magazine *Which?*. This helps people to choose the best products and also gives the organization influence, which it uses to protect the interests of consumers (= people who buy goods or use services). The organization was formed in 1956 as the Consumers' Association and changed its name in 2004. It has over 700 000 members. It also publishes books, including The *Good Food Guide.

Whig /wɪg/ n **1** a member of a British political party established in the late 17th century. The Whigs believed that *Parliament should have more power than the king or queen, and supported the *Hanoverian kings against the *Stuarts. They believed in religious freedom and political reforms. The Whigs, who were mainly rich businessmen and people who owned land in the country, were in power for the first half of the 18th century. In the 19th century they changed into the *Liberal Party. Compare TORY.
2 a member of an American political party established in 1834 to oppose the *Democrats. In the 1850s the party broke up and many of its members joined the new *Republican Party.

,**While 'Shepherds 'Watched Their 'Flocks by 'Night** a popular *carol often sung at Christmas.

Whip n (in Britain) any of several *MPs who are responsible for keeping discipline among the MPs belonging to their party, making sure that they go to debates and advising them how to vote. In the US *Congress there are also Whips for each party. The *House of Representatives has a Democratic Whip and a Republican Whip, and each has many assistants. The *Senate Whips are called Assistant Majority Leader and Assistant Minority Leader, and each is assisted by four *senators.

'**Whipsnade** /'wɪpsneɪd/ a zoo in southern England, north-west of London. When it opened in 1931 it was one of the first zoos in the world to breed animals that were in danger of dying out, and to allow them to live freely in natural surroundings, rather than in cages.

'**whisky** (also '**whiskey**) n [U] a strong alcoholic drink made from cereals. Whisky made in Scotland, often called 'Scotch', is made mostly from *barley and is usually sold as a **blend** (= mixture) of several types. A more expensive type of Scotch whisky is **single malt**, made in the *Highlands from a single type of grain. Many people drink whisky mixed with water, soda water or soft drinks (= drinks containing no alcohol) such as ginger ale or cola, while others prefer to drink it with nothing added, or with ice (called **on the rocks**). **Whiskey** is the usual spelling for the drink made in Ireland and the US. See also BOURBON.

,**whisky 'mac** (AmE ,**whiskey 'mac**) /'mæk/ n a drink that is an equal mixture of *whisky and ginger wine (= a

type of wine made with ginger, a hot-tasting plant). Its name comes from 'Mac-', the beginning of many Scottish names.

the '**Whispering ,Gallery** the famous gallery (= a raised platform along the inner wall of a building) that goes all the way round the inside of the dome of *St Paul's Cathedral in London. It is well known for the way it carries sounds: if a person whispers close to the wall on one side of the gallery, they can be heard by another person close to the wall on the other side of the gallery, 107 feet/32 metres away.

'**James Mc'Neill 'Whistler** /mək'niːl 'wɪslə(r)/ (1834–1903) a US artist who was educated in France and lived mostly in London, England, after 1859. His best-known painting is usually called *Whistler's Mother. In a famous legal case he took John *Ruskin to court for publicly criticizing his painting Nocturne in Black and Gold: The Falling Rocket. Whistler won the case but was awarded only a quarter of one penny.

,**Whistler's 'Mother** /,wɪsləz; AmE ,wɪslərz/ the popular title of the painting Arrangement in Grey and Black (1872) by the US artist James *Whistler. It is a picture of his mother, Mrs George Washington Whistler, sitting in an upright chair and painted from the side. It is now in the Musée d'Orsay in Paris.

,**whistle-stop cam'paign** n a political campaign in which a politician makes short stops at many different towns. The expression was first used in the US, where small American towns were called 'whistle-stops' because trains only stopped at them if a whistle signal was given. President *Truman was well known for his whistle-stop campaigns, during which he made speeches in many small towns from the platform on the end of a train.

Whit /wɪt/ (also '**Whitsun**) the seventh Sunday after Easter (also called **Whit Sunday**) and the days close to it. Whit Sunday is an important Christian religious festival which celebrates the Holy Ghost coming down from Heaven to the apostles (= the twelve people sent out by Christ to spread his teaching). See also WHIT MONDAY.

,**Whitaker's 'Almanack** /,wɪtɪkəz; AmE ,wɪtɪkərz/ a well-known British reference book that was first published in 1868. It is published in December every year and consists of a wide range of information about Britain and other countries, including lists of organizations and officials, details of important events in the previous year, and information about the positions of the planets and stars.

'**Whitbread** /'wɪtbred/ a large British company that owns hotels, pubs and restaurants. In the past it made several types of beer, but its beer business was sold to Interbrew in 2000.

'**Whitbread 'Book of the 'Year** /'wɪtbred/ a major British literary prize, organized and paid for by *Whitbread. At the beginning of January each year, five new British or Irish books are chosen as the best book of their type: best novel, best first novel, best book of poems, best biography and best children's book. At the end of the month, one of the five is chosen as the book of the year. See p. 516.

,**E B 'White¹** /'waɪt/ (Elwyn Brooks White 1899–1985) a US author known for his humorous pieces about American society in The *New Yorker magazine. He received a special *Pulitzer Prize in 1978. His books included Is Sex Necessary? (1929), written with James *Thurber, and the children's book Charlotte's Web (1952). His introduction to the art of writing, The Elements of Style, first published in 1959, is a standard book in US schools.

W

Winners of the Whitbread Book of the Year Award (until 1984 winners of the Whitbread Novel Award)

1971	*The Destiny Waltz* Gerda Charles	1989	*The Chymical Wedding* Lindsay Clarke
1972	*The Bird of Night* Susan Hill	1990	*Hopeful Monsters* Nicholas Mosley
1973	*The Chip-Chip Gatherers* Shiva Naipaul	1991	*A Life of Picasso* John Richardson
1974	*The Sacred and Profane Love Machine* Iris Murdoch	1992	*Swing Hammer Swing!* Jeff Torrington
		1993	*Theory of War* Joan Brady
1975	*Docherty* William McIlvanney	1994	*Felicia's Journey* William Trevor
1976	*The Children of Dynmouth* William Trevor	1995	*Behind the Scenes at the Museum* Kate Atkinson
1977	*Injury Time* Beryl Bainbridge	1996	*The Spirit Level* Seamus Heaney
1978	*Picture Palace* Paul Theroux	1997	*Tales from Ovid* Ted Hughes
1979	*The Old Jest* Jennifer Johnston	1998	*Birthday Letters* Ted Hughes
1980	*How Far Can You Go?* David Lodge	1999	*Beowulf* Seamus Heaney
1981	*Silver's City* Maurice Leitch	2000	*The Amber Spyglass* Philip Pullman
1982	*Young Shoulders* John Wain	2001	*Twelve Bar Blues* Patrick Neate
1983	*Fools of Fortune* William Trevor	2002	*Spies* Michael Frayn
1984	*Kruger's Alp* Christopher Hope	2003	*The Curious Incident of the Dog in the Night-Time* Mark Haddon
1985	*Elegies* Douglas Dunn		
1986	*An Artist of the Floating World* Kazuo Ishiguro	2004	*Small Island* Andrea Levy
1987	*Under the Eye of the Clock* Christopher Nolan		
1988	*Coleridge* Richard Holmes		

ˌGilbert ˈWhite² /waɪt/ (1720–93) an English naturalist (= a person who studies animals, birds, plants, etc.). He spent most of his life working as an assistant to a *Church of England priest in Selborne, a village near *Winchester(1) in southern England, and wrote in great detail about the natural life of the countryside there. His best-known work is *The Natural History and Antiquities of Selborne* (1789).

ˈWhitechapel /ˈwaɪt-tʃæpl/ a district in the *East End of London. It once had a reputation as one of the poorest areas of central London, and many immigrants settled there. In the late 19th and early 20th centuries many Jewish people came to live in Whitechapel, and it still has many Jewish shops and businesses. It is also well known as the area where *Jack the Ripper committed his murders.

the ˌWhitechapel ˈArt ˌGallery /ˌwaɪt-tʃæpl/ A building in *Whitechapel, London, where art exhibitions are held. It was opened in 1901 as the East End Art Gallery. The Whitechapel Open is an exhibition of work by artists in East London shown there every two years.

ˌWhite ˈChristmas a song by Irving *Berlin. It has become a traditional song for Christmas, when many people hope that there will be snow. The song was first written for the film *Holiday Inn* (1942) and won an *Oscar. Bing *Crosby sang it in the film and his recording has sold more than 40 million copies, the most for any recording until recent years. He was also in a second version of the film, made in 1954 with the new title *White Christmas*.

ˌWhite ˈCity an area of north-west London, England, where there used to be a famous sports stadium. The Olympic Games took place there in 1908, and for most of the 20th century it was a well-known stadium for *greyhound racing. It was destroyed in the 1980s.

the ˌwhite cliffs of ˈDover /ˈdəʊvə(r); AmE ˈdoʊvər/ n [pl] the tall chalk cliffs on the south-eastern coast of England, around the port of *Dover. They can be seen from several miles away at sea, so they are the first part of England that people see as they approach Dover by ship. To many British people in other countries, they represent the idea of going home. One of the most popular songs of *World War II, sung by Vera *Lynn, begins with the lines:

> 66 There'll be bluebirds over
> The white cliffs of Dover
> Tomorrow, just you wait and see. 99

ˌwhite ˈensign /ˈensən/ n a flag used only by ships of the British *Royal Navy and members of the *Royal Yacht Squadron. It is white with an upright red cross and a small British flag in the top left quarter. Compare BLUE ENSIGN, RED ENSIGN.

ˌwhite ˈflight n [U] (AmE) (in the US) the movement of *middle-class white people away from the centre of cities into the suburbs (= outer areas). It began in the 1950s and was caused by worries about the increase in crime in city centres.

ˈWhitehall /ˈwaɪtɔːl/ a street in central London, between *Trafalgar Square and the *Houses of Parliament(1). Most of the buildings in it are government offices, so that 'Whitehall' is often used to refer to the government: *Whitehall is extremely embarrassed about the leaked memo.*

the ˌWhitehall ˈTheatre /ˌwaɪtɔːl/ a theatre on *Whitehall, London, in the *art deco style. It is famous for the farces (= light comedy plays based on ridiculous situations) which were performed there and were known as the Whitehall farces. See also RIX.

ˌWhite Hart ˈLane a well-known football ground in north London. It is the home of *Tottenham Hotspur football club.

ˌwhite ˈhorse n any of several large figures of white horses in the English countryside, mainly in southern England. Most of them were made in prehistoric times, by cutting the grass away from the surface of chalk hills and probably had a religious meaning for the people who made them. Others are believed to be more recent. The best-known white horses are at Uffington in *Oxfordshire and at Westbury in *Wiltshire.

ˌMary ˈWhitehouse /ˈwaɪthaʊs/ (1910–2001) an Englishwoman who became famous in the 1960s and 1970s for her campaigns against sex, violence and bad language on British television and radio and in the theatre and cinema.

the ˈWhite House the home and office of the US President, at 1600 *Pennsylvania Avenue in Washington, DC. It is built of stone painted white and was designed in 1800 by James Hoban, who was born in Ireland. The building was burned by British troops during the *War of 1812 and later built again. The 'White House' is often used to mean the President and his advisers: *The White House has refused to comment on the allegations.* See also OVAL OFFICE.

the White House

᷉**Paul 'Whiteman** /'waɪtmən/ (1890–1967) a US musician, also known as the 'King of Jazz', who led bands and orchestras playing 'symphonic jazz', a mixture of *jazz and classical music. George *Gershwin wrote *Rhapsody in Blue* for Whiteman's orchestra, and they were the first to play it in 1924. The orchestra made a European tour in 1926 and played at the *Albert Hall in London.

the ᷉**white man's 'burden** (*old use rather offensive*) a phrase that was used mainly in the 19th century to express the idea that European countries had a duty to run the countries and organizations of people in other parts of the world with less money, education or technology than the Europeans. The phrase was first used in a poem by Rudyard *Kipling.

᷉**White 'Paper** *n* (in Britain) an official report presenting the government's policy on a particular question to be discussed in *Parliament.

the ᷉**White 'Rabbit** a character in Lewis *Carroll's *Alice in Wonderland*. He is the white rabbit that Alice follows down a hole at the beginning of the story. He is worried that he is late for something and keeps looking at his watch.

White's /waɪts/ the oldest and one of the most famous of London's clubs. It first opened in 1693 as a place where famous and fashionable people went to drink chocolate and gamble. In the late 18th century it began to be connected with the *Tory Party. ⇨ note at GENTLE-MEN'S CLUBS.

the ᷉**White 'Tower** the oldest part of the *Tower of London. It is a large *Norman keep (= an ancient castle, built to be very strong) made of white stone at the centre of the group of buildings. In the 17th century the bones of two children were found there, and many people believe that they are the bones of the *Princes in the Tower.

the ᷉**Whitewater af‚fair** /'waɪtwɔːtər/ the name used by the press, etc. to refer to the illegal sale of property in *Arkansas by the Whitewater Development Corporation, a company that had connections with US President Bill *Clinton and his wife Hillary. Investigations into the affair, which were begun in 1994 by *Congress and the Independent Counsel Kenneth Starr led to a trial of Clinton by the *United States Senate in 1999 in which he was acquitted. The investigation was finally closed in 2001 when Clinton left office.

᷉**Walt 'Whitman** /‚wɔːlt 'wɪtmən/ (1819–92) a major US poet who wrote about individual freedom, equal rights and sexual love, as well as about his love for America. Though many readers thought his poems were immoral, he had a strong influence on later American poets, especially the *beat generation. He used the new form of 'free verse', in which lines do not rhyme. His best-known works are *Leaves of Grass*, *Drum Taps* (1865) and a collection of writings, *Democratic Vistas* (1871).

> ❝ I think I could turn and live with animals, they are so placid and self-contain'd,
> I stand and look at them long and long.
>
> They do not sweat and whine about their condition, ...
> Not one is dissatisfied, not one is demented with the mania of owning things,
> Not one kneels to another, nor to his kind that lived thousands of years ago,
> Not one is respectable or unhappy over the whole earth. ❞
> *Leaves of Grass*

᷉**Whit 'Monday** the day after *Whit Sunday. It used to be a *bank holiday in Britain. In the 1960s it was replaced by the *Spring Bank Holiday, which some people still call Whit Monday.

᷉**Eli 'Whitney**[1] /‚iːlaɪ 'wɪtni/ (1765–1825) an American who in 1793 invented the cotton gin, a machine for separating cotton from its seeds which greatly helped the development of the cotton industry in the *South. He was also the first person to produce large numbers of small parts for guns which could be changed without replacing the whole gun.

᷉**Mount 'Whitney**[2] /'wɪtni/ a mountain in the *Sierra Nevada range in central *California. It is 14 494 feet/4 421 metres high and was named after Josiah Whitney (1819–96), the first head of the California State Geological Service, who measured it in 1864.

the ᷉**Whitney 'Museum of A‚merican 'Art**
/'wɪtni/ a museum in *New York which contains art from the beginning of the 20th century. The original museum was opened by the American artist and art collector **Gertrude Vanderbilt Whitney** (1875–1942) in 1931. It moved to its present building on *Madison Avenue in 1966.

᷉**John 'Greenleaf 'Whittier** /'griːnliːf 'wɪtiə(r)/ (1807–92) a US poet and journalist who supported the campaign to free American slaves. Whittier's work, most of which is about *New England, includes *Legends of New England* (1831) and *In War Time and Other Poems* (1864). Among his best-known poems is *Snow-bound* (1866).

᷉**Dick 'Whittington** /'wɪtɪŋtən/ (*died* 1423) *Lord Mayor of London three times (1397–98, 1406–7 and 1419–20). Most British people know the stories about him: that he was running away from London when he was a boy, but thought he heard the church bells telling him to 'Turn again, Whittington, Lord Mayor of London', and that he became rich by selling his cat to a foreign king. The story of his life is a popular subject for *pantomimes.

᷉**Frank 'Whittle** /'wɪtl/ (1907–96) an English engineer, best known for inventing the jet engine, the type of engine now used in most aircraft, which gives forward movement by releasing a stream of gases at high speed behind it. He was made a *knight in 1948.

The 'Who a British pop group. It began as a *mod group in the 1960s, and by the early 1970s was one of the most popular *rock groups in the world. The members of the group were known for behaving wildly and sometimes destroying their equipment during their performances. The Who's best-known records include *My Generation* (1965) and two rock operas (= stories told through a series of *rock music songs), *Tommy* (1969) and *Quadrophenia* (1973).

᷉*Who Killed Cock 'Robin?* an old English *nursery rhyme in which a group of animals talk about the death of a robin (= a small bird) and offer to help at his funeral. It may refer to the loss of political power of Robert *Walpole in 1742.

Whoppers

'Whoppers™ /'wɒpəz; *AmE* 'wɑːpərz/ *n* [pl] a US make of round chocolate sweets with light crisp centres made by Hershey Foods. Compare MALTESERS.

'Who's A'fraid of Vir'ginia 'Woolf? /'wʊlf/ the best-known play (1962) by the US writer Edward *Albee. It is about a college teacher and his wife who constantly argue and play cruel games with each other and a younger couple who visit them. In the film version (1966) the older couple were played by Elizabeth *Taylor and Richard *Burton[3].

Who's 'Who a British book, published every year, which gives the personal details of important, rich or famous people. The details are written by the people themselves, and some of them write amusing things about their hobbies and interests. It was first published in 1849.

'Who 'Wants to 'be a Millio'naire? a television game show which was first shown in Britain in 1998, presented by Chris Tarrant (1946–). It has since been produced in different versions in many countries around the world. Contestants have to answer a series of general knowledge questions, for which they are given four possible answers, and, if they answer all the questions correctly, they can become a millionaire.

WI /ˌdʌblju: 'aɪ/ ⇨ WOMEN'S INSTITUTE.

Widdicombe 'Fair /ˌwɪdɪkəm/ a popular old English song about a group of people who borrow a horse to go to a horse *fair in Widdicombe, a village in *Devon. Each verse of the song ends with the names of the people in the group: Bill Brewer, Jan Stewer, Peter Gurney, Peter Davy, Dan'l (Daniel) Whiddon, Harry Hawk and old *Uncle Tom Cobbleigh.

the 'Wife of 'Bath /'bɑːθ; *AmE* 'bæθ/ one of the best-known characters in *Chaucer's *Canterbury Tales. She is a lively woman who has been married five times and makes many humorous remarks about sex. The story she tells, the **Wife of Bath's Tale**, is about one of King *Arthur's *knights. He has to find the answer to the question 'What do women love most?' to avoid being killed. An ugly old woman says that she will tell him the answer, but only if he marries her. He agrees, and she becomes a beautiful young woman.

'Wigan /'wɪgən/ an industrial town in *Greater Manchester, England. In the *Industrial Revolution it had important coal-mining and cotton industries. It is famous today for its *Rugby League club, one of the oldest in England and the most successful in the history of the sport. George *Orwell's book *The Road to Wigan Pier* describes the life of poor people, especially the unemployed miners in the north of England during the 1930s.

Wigan 'Pier /ˌwɪgən/ an area of factories and warehouses next to the *Leeds and *Liverpool canal in *Wigan. It was a centre for industry in the 19th century when goods were transported by canal and has now become a popular tourist attraction. It was also made famous by George *Orwell's book *The Road to Wigan Pier* about the difficult conditions of working-class life in the 1930s.

the Wightman 'Cup /ˌwaɪtmən/ a women's tennis competition between British and US players which took place every year from 1923 to 1989. It was then stopped because the British players were not good enough to compete with the US players, who almost always won easily.

the Wigmore 'Hall /ˌwɪgmɔː; *AmE* ˌwɪgmɔːr/ a hall for concerts in the *West End of London. It is used mainly for the performance of classical songs and chamber music (= music written for a small orchestra).

William 'Wilberforce /'wɪlbəfɔːs; *AmE* 'wɪlbərfɔːrs/ (1759–1833) an English politician, best known for his successful campaigns to stop the slave trade and to make *slavery illegal in the *British Empire.

the 'Wild Bunch ⇨ HOLE-IN-THE-WALL GANG.

The 'Wild Bunch a violent *western film (1969), directed by Sam *Peckinpah, about a group of outlaws (= criminals) who become involved in the Mexican Revolution. Some people consider it to be one of the best *westerns ever made.

Oscar 'Wilde /'waɪld/ (1854–1900) an Irish writer of plays, poetry and one novel, *The Picture of Dorian Gray* (1891). He became famous after moving to London, where he wrote his most successful comedy plays, including *Lady Windermere's Fan* (1892) and *The *Importance of Being Earnest*. He is also well known for his humorous and intelligent remarks, and for being homosexual. In 1895 he was sent to prison for his homosexuality, which was illegal at the time. He described his prison experience in the poem *The *Ballad of Reading Gaol*. After he was released he lived the rest of his life in France and Italy. Many of his clever and amusing remarks are still repeated today and his type of wit is called Wildean.

> 66 I have nothing to declare except my genius. 99
> Oscar Wilde to a customs officer

Billy 'Wilder[1] /'waɪldə(r)/ (1906–2002) a US writer, director and producer of films, born in Austria. His many successful films, some of which he also wrote or helped to write, include *Double Indemnity* (1944), *The Lost Weekend* (1945), *Sunset Boulevard*, *The Seven Year Itch* (1955), *Some Like It Hot* (1959) and *The Apartment* (1960). He won a total of six *Oscars.

Thornton 'Wilder[2] /ˌθɔːntən 'waɪldə(r); *AmE* ˌθɔːrntən 'waɪldər/ (1897–1975) a US writer of novels and plays. He won *Pulitzer Prizes for the novel *The Bridge of San Luis Rey* (1927) and the plays *Our Town* and *The Skin of Our Teeth* (1942). His comedy play *The Matchmaker* (1954) was used as the basis for the *Broadway musical play *Hello, Dolly!* (1964).

the 'Wildfowl and 'Wetlands 'Trust a British organization, set up in 1946 by Peter *Scott to study and protect wildfowl (= wild birds that live on or near water, such as ducks and geese). See also SLIMBRIDGE.

the Wild 'West the western US during the later part of the 19th century, when communities were settled but there was not much law and order. This is the period shown in *westerns, though the picture they present of the Wild West is not often very accurate. Towns that were known for their outlaws (= criminals) and violence included *Tombstone, *Arizona, and *Dodge City, *Kansas. Famous outlaws included Jesse and Frank *James, *Billy the Kid and the *Younger brothers. Compare OLD WEST.

Wild 'West show *n* (in the US) a show in which performers create the atmosphere and characters of the *Wild West, with *cowboys and *Native Americans. They ride horses, shoot at objects and demonstrate other western skills. Such shows were especially popular at the end of the 19th century, when they were often performed in large tents. The most famous was *Buffalo Bill's Wild West Show, which he took to many US cities and also to Europe. See also OAKLEY.

'William[1] the main character in a series of stories by Richmal *Crompton. He is a *middle-class English schoolboy and the leader of the Outlaws, a group of children who have amusing adventures and often get into trouble.

ˌPrince 'William² (1982–) the first child of the *Prince and *Princess of Wales. He is sometimes called Wills in the press.

William I /ˌwɪljəm ðə 'fɜːst; AmE 'fɜːrst/ (also ˌWilliam the 'Conqueror) (c. 1027–87) the king of England from 1066 to 1087. He was the Duke of Normandy, in northern France, when the English king *Edward the Confessor died. William claimed that Edward had promised him the right to be the next king of England. He invaded England and defeated King *Harold II at the Battle of *Hastings in 1066. Later that year he became king. He gave power and land in England to other *Normans, and built many castles to control the English people.

William II /ˌwɪljəm ðə 'sekənd/ (also ˌWilliam 'Rufus) (c. 1056–1100) the king of England from 1087 to 1100. He became king when his father *William I died. He was a skilful leader but his attempts to take money from his *barons and the Church made him unpopular. He died in an accident while hunting, but many people think he was murdered so that his brother *Henry I could be king. He was called Rufus, meaning red, because of the colour of his hair.

William III /ˌwɪljəm ðə 'θɜːd; AmE 'θɜːrd/ (also ˌWilliam of 'Orange /'ɒrɪndʒ; AmE 'ɔːrɪndʒ/) (1650–1702) the king of Great Britain and Ireland from 1688 to 1702. He was a Dutch prince, married to Mary, the daughter of *James II. They were invited by British *Protestants to be the king and queen of Britain in order to prevent the *Roman Catholic James II from being king. William became king in the *Bloodless Revolution and defeated the forces of James II in Ireland at the *Battle of the Boyne. He is remembered by a group of Protestants in Northern Ireland who are opposed to Ireland becoming one republic, and call themselves *Orangemen. See also WILLIAM AND MARY.

William IV /ˌwɪljəm ðə 'fɔːθ; AmE 'fɔːrθ/ (1765–1837) the king of Great Britain and Ireland from 1830 to 1837. He was the son of *George III and spent many years in the *Royal Navy. He is also remembered for having had ten illegitimate children (= children born outside marriage) with a female actor. His most important action was to create 50 new *Whig(1) peers to vote for the *Reform Act against the *Tories in *Parliament who were opposed to it.

ˌWilliam and 'Mary n [U] a style of furniture that was popular in Britain at the end of the 17th century, during the reign of King *William III and Queen *Mary. Elegant tables, chairs and cupboards with designs carved into the wood are typical of the style.

ˌWilliam of 'Ockham (also Occam) ⇨ OCKHAM.

ˌWilliam of 'Wykeham /'wɪkəm/ (1324–1404) the *bishop of *Winchester(1) from 1367 to 1404. He is best remembered for establishing *Winchester(2) College, whose pupils are still called Wykehamists.

ˌWill and 'Grace /ˌwɪl ənd 'ɡreɪs/ a popular US television comedy series, which started in 1998, about Grace and her male best friend, Will, who is gay (= homosexual).

'Williams¹ /'wɪljəmz/ the common name for WilliamsF1 ('Williams Formula One'), a British company that makes racing cars and organizes teams of drivers, mechanics (= people skilled in working on engines), etc. to enter competitions. It was established in 1977 by Frank Williams (1942–) and Patrick Head (1946–), and has been one of the most successful teams in motor racing.

ˌAndy 'Williams² /'wɪljəmz/ (1930–) a US popular singer. His hits include Moon River (1963) and Born Free (1967). He had his own television series, The Andy Williams Show (1970–1), on which the *Osmonds first became famous.

ˌHank 'Williams³ /ˌhæŋk 'wɪljəmz/ (1923–53) the most important early singer and writer of US *country music. His sad voice and simple songs influenced many later singers. His best-known songs include Lovesick Blues (1949), Your Cheatin' Heart (1953) and Take These Chains from My Heart (1953). Williams drank too much alcohol and died young. He was chosen for the Country Music *Hall of Fame in 1961. In a film about his life, Your Cheatin' Heart (1964), his songs were sung by his son Hank Williams, Junior (1949–).

ˌJ P R 'Williams⁴ /'wɪljəmz/ (John Peter Rhys Williams 1949–) a famous Welsh *Rugby Union player. He was a skilful defensive player, and played 55 times for Wales between 1969 and 1981. He also played eight times for the *British Lions.

ˌKenneth 'Williams⁵ /'wɪljəmz/ (1926–88) an English actor, well known for his funny, exaggerated way of speaking. He appeared in several popular radio comedy programmes, but is perhaps best remembered for acting in the *Carry On films.

ˌRobbie 'Williams⁶ /'wɪljəmz/ (1974–) a British pop singer. He began his career as a member of the group Take That but left them in 1995 to perform on his own. His successful records have included Angels (1997) and Rock DJ (2000), and the albums Life Thru a Lens (1997), Sing When You're Winning (2000) and Escapology (2002).

ˌRobin 'Williams⁷ /'wɪljəmz/ (1952–) a US actor known for his energy and wild humour. He began his career on the television comedy series Mork and Mindy (1978–82). He has won an *Oscar for Good Will Hunting (1998) and *Golden Globe Awards for Good Morning, Vietnam (1987), The Fisher King (1991) and Mrs Doubtfire (1993). His other films include Dead Poets Society (1989), The Bird Cage (1996), Flubber (1997) and Insomnia (2002).

ˌRowan 'Williams⁸ /ˌrəʊən 'wɪljəmz; AmE ˌroʊən/ (1950–) the *Archbishop of Canterbury since 2003. He was born in Wales and was Archbishop of Wales before becoming leader of the *Anglican Communion.

Seˌrena 'Williams⁹ /səˌriːnə 'wɪljəmz/ (1981–) a US tennis player who has won several singles *grand slam titles and a number of doubles titles with her sister, Venus *Williams.

ˌShirley 'Williams¹⁰ /'wɪljəmz/ (1930–) an English politician. She began her career in the *Labour Party and was a member of the *Cabinet in the 1970s. In 1981 she left Labour to help set up the *SDP. She was made a *life peer in 1993.

ˌTennessee 'Williams¹¹ /ˌtenəsiː 'wɪljəmz/ (1914–83) a major US writer of plays. These were often set in the *South and about people with emotional and sexual problems, which many people found shocking when the plays were first performed. Two of his 24 plays, A *Streetcar Named Desire and Cat on a Hot Tin Roof (1955), won *Pulitzer Prizes. Others included The Glass Menagerie (1945), Sweet Bird of Youth (1959) and Night of the Iguana (1961). There have been film versions of many of them.

ˌVenus 'Williams¹² /ˌviːnəs 'wɪljəmz/ (1980–) a US tennis player, the older of the Williams Sisters, who has won several singles *grand slam titles, as well as a number of doubles titles with her sister, Serena *Williams.

'Williamsburg /'wɪljəmzbɜːɡ; AmE 'wɪljəmzbɜːrɡ/ a historic US town in south-eastern *Virginia. It was settled in 1633 as Middle Plantation but soon named after the English king *William III. It was the capital of the colony from 1699 to 1779. The College of William and Mary was established there in 1693. The 18th-century town

W

was built again in the 1930s as Colonial Williamsburg and is now very popular with tourists.

William the 'Conqueror ⇨ WILLIAM I.

Bruce 'Willis /'wɪlɪs/ (1955–) a US actor, especially in action films. His career began with the television series *Moonlighting* (1985–9). His films include four *Die Hard* films, 1988, 1990, 1995 and 2004, *Pulp Fiction* (1994), *Day of the Jackal* (1997) and *Armageddon* (1998). Willis was formerly married to the actor Demi *Moore.

'willow ,pattern *n* [U] a design that is often seen on English pottery. It consists of a blue and white picture, in traditional Chinese style, which usually includes people on a bridge over a river, near a willow (= a tree with long thin branches that grows near water). It was first used in *Staffordshire pottery in the late 18th century, and is still popular today.

Helen 'Wills ⇨ MOODY.

Angus 'Wilson[1] /'wɪlsn/ (1913–91) a British writer of novels and short stories, born in South Africa. His books, including *Hemlock and After* (1952) and *Anglo-Saxon Attitudes* (1956), are known for their humorous descriptions of unusual characters in the different social classes. He was made a *knight in 1980.

Harold 'Wilson[2] /'wɪlsn/ (1916–95) an English *Labour politician who was twice *Prime Minister (1964–70 and 1974–6). His government aimed to make Britain a more modern country, encouraging more people to be involved in science and technology, but had to face serious economic problems. Many people were surprised when he resigned in 1976. It was later discovered that *MI5 had been dishonestly trying to bring down Wilson's government during the 1960s and 1970s. He was made a *knight in 1976 and a *life peer in 1983.

> **66** A week is a long time in politics. **99**
> Harold Wilson

Jacqueline 'Wilson[3] /'wɪlsn/ (1945–) an English writer and journalist who wrote for the girls' magazine *Jackie*, which was named after her, for many years and has written many popular children's books including *The Story of Tracy Beaker* (1992), *Double Act* (1996), *Bad Girls* (1997), *The Illustrated Mum* (1999) and *How to Survive Summer Camp* (2002). She is one of Britain's favourite children's authors and in 2003 and 2004 more of her books were borrowed from public libraries than those of any other author.

Woodrow 'Wilson[4] /ˌwʊdrəʊ 'wɪlsn; AmE ˌwʊdroʊ/ (1856–1924) the 28th US *President (1913–21). He was a Democrat and is remembered as an honest man who worked hard for world peace. Earlier in his career he had been President of *Princeton University (1902–10) and Governor of *New Jersey (1911–3). As US President, he tried to keep the US out of *World War I, but he finally sent US soldiers to join the Allied forces in 1917, saying that 'the world must be made safe for democracy'. After the war Wilson's *Fourteen Points were used as the basis for the peace agreement, and he was given the *Nobel Prize for peace in 1919. He also created the idea for the *League of Nations and was greatly disappointed when *Congress decided that the US should not join it. Wilson's government also established the *Federal Reserve System and the *Federal Trade Commission.

'Wilton /'wɪltn/ *n* [C, U] a type of carpet made of loops of wool which are cut to produce a thick, even surface. Wilton carpets are usually plain, but some have patterns of different colours. They were first made in Wilton, a town in *Wiltshire, England.

'Wiltshire /'wɪltʃə(r)/ (*abbr* **Wilts**) a county in south-west England. It consists mainly of agricultural land. Its administrative centre is Trowbridge.

'Wimbledon /'wɪmbldən/ a district of south-west London, consisting mainly of houses. It is well known around the world as the home of the *All England Club. Many people refer to the major international tennis competition which takes place there each summer simply as Wimbledon. It was first held in 1877: *She became Wimbledon champion for the fourth time.*

'Lord 'Peter 'Wimsey /'wɪmzi/ a character in several crime novels by Dorothy *Sayers. He is an English *lord who is a very good amateur detective.

Walter 'Winchell /'wɪntʃəl/ (1897–1972) a popular US radio and newspaper journalist in the 1930s and 1940s. He began his radio broadcasts with the phrase 'Good evening, Mr and Mrs America and all the ships at sea'. His style of reading the news was very dramatic and he was one of the first journalists to add his own comments to news stories. From 1929 to 1969 he wrote a regular column about politicians and entertainers for *The Mirror* in New York.

'Winchester[1] /'wɪntʃestə(r)/ **1** a city in southern England. It is the administrative centre of *Hampshire and until *Norman times was the capital of England. It is well known for its cathedral, which was begun in the 11th century, and other very old buildings.
2 (*also* **Winchester College**) a well-known *public school(1) in Winchester. It was established by *William of Wykeham in 1382 and was the first of its kind.
3 (*also* **Winchester rifle**) *n* a type of rifle developed in the US by Oliver F Winchester and first produced in 1860 by the Volcanic Repeating Arms Company. It was especially successful because it could be fired repeatedly without the need to put bullets in each time. Winchesters were widely used in the *American Civil War and are often seen in *western films.

Simon 'Winchester[2] /'wɪntʃestə(r)/ a British journalist and writer who writes about travel and history. He was the foreign correspondent for The *Guardian newspaper for 20 years and has also written for magazines such as *National Geographic. His books include *The Surgeon of Crowthorne* (1998) (published in the US as *The Professor and the Madman*), *The Map That Changed The World* (2001), *The Meaning of Everything* (2003) and *Krakatoa* (2003).

'Windermere /'wɪndəmɪə(r); AmE 'wɪndərmɪr/
1 the largest lake in England (10.5 miles/17 kilometres long), in the *Lake District. It is known for the natural beauty of its scenery, and for water sports such as sailing and fishing.
2 a town on the eastern edge of Lake Windermere, in the county of *Cumbria. It is one of the main tourist centres in the *Lake District.

The ,Wind in the 'Willows a children's novel (1908) by Kenneth *Grahame. It describes the adventures and relationships of a group of small animals, including a mole, a rat, a toad and a badger, who live by a river. It was one of the most popular British children's books of the 20th century. A version of it for the stage, called *Toad of Toad Hall*, written in 1929 by A A *Milne, is still often performed.

the ,Windmill 'Theatre a former small theatre in the *West End of London (1931–1964). It was well known for its shows of dancing by naked or almost naked women. Comedians used to tell jokes between the dancing shows, and many famous performers (including Tony *Hancock and Peter *Sellers) started their careers there. It was the only theatre that stayed open when bombs were being dropped on London during *World War II.

'Windows™ /ˈwɪndəʊz; *AmE* ˈwɪndoʊz/ a system developed by the US company *Microsoft to operate computer programs. Each program has its own window on the screen. There have been several versions of the system since it was first produced in 1990. Microsoft have also produced Windows NT for large computers and Windows CE for small computers.

'window tax *n* [U] a historical tax that British people had to pay according to how many windows they had in their houses. It was in use between 1675 and 1851. It is still possible to see old houses in Britain that had their windows filled in with bricks, etc. in order to save tax.

'Windsor¹ /ˈwɪnzə(r)/ **1** a town in southern England on the River *Thames, west of London. It is famous for its castle.
2 the family name of the British *royal family since 1917. It was changed from the German *Saxe-Coburg-Gotha by *George V because of the strong feelings in Britain against Germany during *World War I.

the ,Duke of 'Windsor² /ˈwɪnzə(r)/ the title given to *Edward VIII after he abdicated (= gave up his right to be king). His wife was given the title of the **Duchess of Windsor**. See also ABDICATION CRISIS.

,Windsor 'Castle /ˌwɪnzə; *AmE* ˌwɪnzər/ a castle in *Windsor¹(1). It is one of the official homes of the British king or queen. It was started by *William I in the 11th century, and parts were added to it by several later kings and queens. Most of the present castle was either built or decorated in the early 19th century. Some of the rooms are open to the public when the king or queen is not staying there. In 1992 some parts of the castle were badly damaged by a fire, but these have now been repaired.

the ,Windy 'City a popular name for the city of *Chicago in the US, because of the strong winds that blow there from across Lake *Michigan.

,Oprah 'Winfrey /ˌəʊprə ˈwɪnfri; *AmE* ˌoʊprə/ (1954–) a US entertainer who presents *The Oprah Winfrey Show*, the most popular US television *chat show. She won the 'Lifetime Achievement Award' from the National Academy of Television Arts and Sciences in 1998, by which stage she had already won seven *Emmy awards as 'Outstanding Talk Show Host'. The show began in 1986 and includes ordinary people talking about their personal problems, often in a very emotional way. A part of the show from 1996 to 2002 was 'Oprah's Book Club', in which she recommended and discussed books. Books chosen for the show became best-sellers. In 1996 Winfrey was paid more than any other US entertainer and in 1998 she was named one of the '100 Most Influential People of the 20th Century' by *Time maga-zine. Winfrey has her own magazine called 'O'.

,Winne'bago™ /ˌwɪnɪˈbeɪgəʊ; *AmE* ˌwɪnɪˈbeɪgoʊ/ *n* (*pl* **-gos**) a popular US make of motor home (= a large motor vehicle fitted as a home and used for holidays, etc.). The first Winnebago was made in 1966 at Forest City, *Iowa, where Winnebago Industries still is. The company is named after a *Native American people.

,Winnie-the-'Pooh /ˌwɪni ðə ˈpuː/ ⇨ POOH.

,winter of discon'tent a phrase first used by some British newspapers and politicians to describe the winter of 1978–9 in Britain, when there were many strikes and economic problems. The phrase was taken from the opening lines of *Shakespeare's play *Richard III*. It was used to suggest that people were not happy with the way the *Labour government was running the country. The same phrase is now used to refer to any difficult political situation that occurs during the months of winter: *The problems in the power industry led to another winter of discontent.*

The ,Winter's 'Tale a play (c. 1610) by William *Shakespeare. It begins sadly and ends happily. Leontes, king of Sicilia, thinks that his wife is not faithful. He puts her in prison and orders his baby daughter to be left on a 'desert shore'. He believes that they are both dead, and feels very sorry for what he has done. His daughter, however, is found by a shepherd (= a person whose job is to look after sheep), and grows up to become a shepherd herself. When she falls in love with a prince they run away together to Sicilia. There, Leontes recognizes his daughter and finds out that his wife is also alive. The young lovers are married and the king and queen are united again.

Wired a US magazine published every month in print and online containing news and opinions about computer technology. It reports on how technology and the Internet affect culture, the economy and politics. It is published in *San Francisco and was started in 1993.

the 'Wirrall /ˈwɪrəl/ the large area of land between the River *Mersey and the River Dee, south of *Liverpool in north-west England.

Wis'consin /wɪsˈkɒnsɪn; *AmE* wɪsˈkɑːnsɪn/ a northern US state which has borders with Lake *Michigan and Lake *Superior. Its popular name is the Badger State. The largest city is *Milwaukee and the capital city is Madison. The US won the land from Britain in the *American Revolution, but the British did not leave until after the *War of 1812. Wisconsin became a state in 1848. Its farm products include cheese, milk and corn, and it also produces paper, beer, cars and machinery. The state has more than 14 000 lakes, many of which are popular with tourists.

farms in Wisconsin

'Wisden /ˈwɪzdən/ (*full title* , **'Wisden 'Cricketers' 'Almanack** /ˈwɪzdən/) a British book of information about cricket. It has been published each year since 1864 and contains details such as the results of all the previous year's matches and the achievements of individual players. It also contains a lot of historical information and essays on various aspects of the game. Many lovers of cricket collect copies of *Wisden* from different years. The publisher also has a website called Cricinfo.

,Ernie 'Wise /ˌɜːni ˈwaɪz; *AmE* ˌɜːrni/ ⇨ MORECAMBE AND WISE.

'Wisley /ˈwɪzli/ the main public garden of the *Royal Horticultural Society in *Surrey, south of London. It consists of a large and attractive garden and several smaller areas which are designed to show people how to grow different types of plant or arrange different types of garden.

witch *n* a person, usually a woman, who is believed to have or use magic powers. Witches are often shown in pictures and described in old stories as ugly old women with black clothes and pointed hats who are able to fly on broomsticks. In the past, women who were con-

W

sidered to be witches were burnt alive or hanged. In the late 20th century many young people began to call themselves witches as part of the *New Age interest in ancient beliefs and cultures: *The witch made her sleep for many years but she woke up when the handsome prince kissed her.* See also SALEM WITCH TRIALS.

,Withnail and 'I /ˌwɪðneɪl/ a British comedy film (1986) about two young actors in the 1960s. They have no work, and spend most of their money on drink and drugs. When they leave London to spend some time in a small house in the *Lake District, much of the humour comes from the difference between their attitudes and behaviour and those of the people they meet in the countryside.

,Ludwig 'Wittgenstein /ˌlʊdvɪg 'vɪtɡənstaɪn/ (1889–1951) an Austrian philosopher. He studied in Britain under Bertrand *Russell before *World War I. After the war he moved back to Britain, becoming a British citizen in 1938. He worked on theories of language and philosophy. In his *Tractatus Logico-Philosophicus* (1922) he suggested the theory that language represents pictures of things according to established conventions (= general agreement). Later, he decided that this was wrong, and worked on the theory that usage was more important.

The ,Wizard of 'Oz /'ɒz; AmE 'ɑːz/ a very popular US film (1939) based on the children's book *The Wonderful Wizard of Oz* (1900) by Frank Baum (1856–1919). In the film a little girl called Dorothy, played by Judy *Garland, is blown by a strong wind from her home in *Kansas to the strange land of Oz in order to defeat the Wicked Witch of the West in order to return home, and she does this with the help of the Scarecrow, the Tin Woodman, the Cowardly Lion and the Wizard of Oz himself. The film's best-known songs include *Over the Rainbow*, *We're Off to See the Wizard* and *Follow the Yellow Brick Road.*

the 'Wobblies /'wɒbliz; AmE 'wɑːbliz/ n [pl] an informal name for the members of the US trade union *IWW.

,Lake 'Wobegon /'wəʊbɪgɒn; AmE 'woʊbɪgɑːn/ ⇨ KEILLOR.

,Woburn 'Abbey /ˌwəʊbɜːn; AmE ˌwoʊbɜːrn/ a *stately home near the town of Bedford in southern England. It was built in the 18th century on land where an abbey had once been. It is open to the public, who come to see the many works of art in the house, and the deer and birds in the attractive gardens.

,P G 'Wodehouse /'wʊdhaʊs/ (Pelham Grenville Wodehouse 1881–1975) an English writer of humorous novels and short stories. He is best known for his books about *Jeeves and Bertie *Wooster, but he wrote many other stories of life among the English *aristocracy. He also wrote the words for several successful American musical comedies. He became a US citizen in 1955, and was made a *knight in 1975.

,Terry 'Wogan /'wəʊgən; AmE 'woʊgən/ (1938–) an Irish radio and television presenter. He was one of the first disc jockeys on *Radio 1 when it opened in 1967, and later had his own *chat show on *BBC television (1984–92). He has a morning show on BBC Radio 2, *Wake Up to Wogan*, and is now perhaps best known as the presenter on British television of the *Eurovision Song Contest, in which he gently makes fun of the whole event.

the 'Wolds /wəʊldz; AmE woʊldz/ n [pl] two ranges of hills in north-east England. The range to the north of the River *Humber used to be called the **Yorkshire Wolds**, and is now simply called the Wolds. The range to the south of the Humber is known as the **Lincolnshire Wolds**.

'General 'James 'Wolfe[1] /'wʊlf/ (1726–59) an English soldier. He is remembered in history for leading the

attack on Quebec, Canada, in 1759, and for dying during the battle. His victory there led to France giving up Canada to Britain at the end of the *Seven Years War.

,Nero 'Wolfe[2] /ˌnɪərəʊ 'wʊlf; AmE ˌnɪroʊ/ the detective created by the US writer Rex *Stout. See also DETECTIVE STORY.

,Thomas 'Wolfe[3] /'wʊlf/ (1900–38) a US writer whose four long and powerful novels are set in the *South and are based on his own life. They are *Look Homeward Angel* (1929), *Of Time and the River* (1935), and two published after he died, *The Web and the Rock* (1939) and *You Can't Go Home Again* (1940). Wolfe also wrote short stories.

,Tom 'Wolfe[4] /'wʊlf/ (1931–) a US writer, many of whose books are about US popular culture and social life. They include *The Electric Kool-Aid Acid Test* (1968) and the novels *The Bonfire of the Vanities* (1988), *A Man in Full* (1998) and *I am Charlotte Simmons* (2004). In the 1960s, Wolfe was a leading figure in the 'New Journalism' movement, in which facts were written about in the style of fiction. He was a journalist for *The *Washington Post* (1959–62) and *The New York Herald-Tribune* (1962–6).

the 'Wolfenden Re,port /'wʊlfəndən/ a British government report, completed in 1957, on homosexuality. It was responsible for homosexual acts between consenting (= agreeing) adults becoming legal in Britain. All homosexual acts had been illegal until then.

,Paul 'Wolfowitz /'wʊlfəwɪts/ (1943–) the US Deputy Secretary of Defense under George W *Bush since 2001. He is known for his *neoconservative views.

,Mary 'Wollstonecraft /'wʊlstənkrɑːft; AmE 'wʊlstənkræft/ (1759–97) an English writer and feminist (= person who believes strongly that women should have the same rights and opportunities as men). She led a campaign for equal opportunities in education for women, and wrote books on the subject, including *A Vindication of the Rights of Woman* (1792). Her daughter was Mary *Shelley.

,Cardinal 'Wolsey /'wʊlzi/ (Thomas Wolsey c. 1474–1530) an English *cardinal (= very senior Roman Catholic priest), who was *Henry VIII's most important political adviser in the first half of his reign. Wolsey became very powerful, but was dismissed by Henry when he failed to get the Pope's permission for the king to divorce *Catherine of Aragon.

WOMAD /'waʊmæd; AmE 'woʊmæd/ (in full **World of Music, Arts and Dance**) an organization started by Peter *Gabriel in 1982 which organizes festivals which include music, art and dance from around the world. The outdoor festivals usually last for several days and take place in a number of different countries including Britain, Spain and Australia.

,Woman and 'Home a British women's magazine. It has been published once a month since 1926 and contains articles on subjects such as fashion, homes, cooking and travel. It is read mainly by older women.

'Woman's 'Hour a British radio programme consisting of a wide range of reports, talks and fiction by, for and about women. It has been broadcast every weekday on *Radio 4 since 1946.

,Woman's 'Own a popular British women's magazine. It has been published once a week since 1932 and contains short stories, usually about love, as well as articles on subjects like fashion and cooking. It is read mainly by older women.

,Woman's 'Realm a British women's magazine. It has been published once a week since 1958 and contains a wide range of true and fictional stories. It is read mainly by older women.

‚**Woman's** '**Weekly** a popular British women's magazine. It has been published once a week since 1911 and consists of a mixture of true stories about people's lives, fictional love stories, articles about famous people such as film stars, and articles about practical subjects such as homes and cooking. It is read mainly by older women.

'**Womble** /'wɒmbl; *AmE* 'wɑːmbl/ *n* any of a group of imaginary animals with long fur and long noses. They live underground in a large London park and at night they come out to collect the rubbish that people have left behind. They were invented by the children's writer Elizabeth Beresford in her book *The Wombles* (1968), and became very popular when the children's television series *The Wombles* was broadcast in the 1970s.

the ‚**Women's** '**Army Corps** ⇨ WAC.

‚**Women's** '**Institute** *n* (*abbr* **WI**) (in Britain) any of the local branches of the **National Federation of Women's Institutes** (itself sometimes referred to as the Women's Institute). This organization was started in 1915 with the aim of improving and developing the lives of women living in country areas. Each branch organizes social, cultural and charity events, and holds meetings where members can learn skills connected with the home, such as cooking. Most small towns and country areas have a Women's Institute. People generally associate the organization with older *middle-class women. The film *Calendar Girls* (2003) was based on a true story about the members of a Women's Institute in Yorkshire.

‚**women's** '**lib** /'lɪb/ (*in full* ‚**women's libe**'**ration**) *n* [U] (*becoming old-fashioned*) the name that most people used to refer to feminism in the 1960s. At that time, many women in Britain and America began to demand the same rights and opportunities as men. They were sometimes called **women's libbers**.

the '**Women's** '**Royal** '**Air Force** ⇨ WRAF.

the '**Women's** '**Royal** '**Army Corps** (*abbr* the **WRAC**) the women's section of the British Army for most of the 20th century. In 1992 it combined with the rest of the army.

the '**Women's** '**Royal** '**Voluntary** ‚**Service** ⇨ WRVS.

‚**Stevie** '**Wonder** /‚stiːvi 'wʌndə(r)/ (1950–) a US singer and writer of *soul and *rock music who also plays the piano. Wonder, who was born blind, has won 17 *Grammy awards, including ones for *You Are the Sunshine of My Life* (1973) and *For Your Love* (1995). His other hits have included *For Once in My Life* (1968), *Yester-me, Yester-you, Yester-day* (1969), *Superstition* (1973) and *Happy Birthday* (1981). His albums include *Innervisions* (1973) and *Songs in the Key of Life* (1976).

'**Wonderbra**™ /'wʌndəbrɑː; *AmE* 'wʌndərbrɑː/ *n* a popular make of bra (= an item of underwear that women wear to support their breasts). Wonderbras, which were introduced in 1968, make the breasts appear larger. They became very well known in Britain in the 1990s after a major advertising campaign showing attractive women wearing them.

'**Wonder Bread**™ *n* [U] a popular US make of soft white bread produced by the Interstate Bakeries Corporation, the largest company of its kind in the US.

‚**Henry** '**Wood**[1] /'wʊd/ (1869–1944) an English conductor, best known for establishing the *Proms. He was one of the greatest conductors of his time, and did much to improve the standard of music in Britain. He introduced the work of many new foreign composers, and allowed women to play in orchestras for the first time. He was made a *knight in 1911.

‚**Vic**‚**toria** '**Wood**[2] /'wʊd/ (1953–) an English comedy entertainer and writer. She has written and appeared in many British television programmes, and is well known for her intelligent humour and clever songs.

'**Woodcraft Folk** /'wʊdkrɑːft; *AmE* 'wʊdkræft/ a British organization for children and young people started in 1925 with groups around the country at which children take part in activities such as games, drama, crafts, singing and dancing.

‚**John** '**Wooden** /'wuːdn/ (1910–) a successful US university *basketball manager at *UCLA (1948–75). His teams were US National Champions 10 times (1964–5, 1967–73 and 1975), and he was chosen Coach of the Year seven times. The US Basketball Writers Association each year presents the John R Wooden Award to the best US college or university basketball player.

‚**Parson** '**Woodforde** /'wʊdfəd; *AmE* 'wʊdfərd/ (James Woodforde 1740–1803) an English parson (= a priest of the *Church of England). He wrote a diary that describes his life over many years in a village in *Norfolk. It was published later (1924–31) as *The *Diary of a Country Parson*.

‚**Tiger** '**Woods** /‚taɪgə 'wʊdz; *AmE* ‚taɪgər/ (Eldrick Tiger Woods 1975–) one of the most successful US golf players of all time. Before he became a professional, he was the US Junior Amateur Champion for three years running (1991–3), followed by the US Amateur Champion for a further three years (1994–6). Woods won six of his first 21 *PGA competitions, including the *US Masters Tournament. At 21 he was the youngest winner ever of the Masters and achieved the lowest score (270) in its history. He won again in 2001 and 2002. He has also won the *US Open (2000, 2002), the Open Championship (2000) and the PGA Championship (1999 and 2000).

'**Woodstock** /'wʊdstɒk; *AmE* 'wʊdstɑːk/ a very large *rock music festival held in August 1969 near Bethel, New York, 60 miles/97 kilometres south-west of Woodstock, the place originally planned for it. Many famous singers and groups performed, including Jimi *Hendrix and Jefferson Airplane. The festival was attended by hundreds of thousands of young people, many of whom took drugs, but there was no violence. It became a symbol of the new youth culture of the *hippies.

‚**Wookey** '**Hole** /‚wʊki / a group of caves in south-west England. In prehistoric times people lived in the caves, and there is a local story that a *witch used to live there. The caves are now a tourist attraction.

‚**Vir**‚**ginia** '**Woolf** /'wʊlf/ (1882–1941) an English writer of novels. She is well known for the experimental style of many of her books. She was one of the first writers to use the 'stream of consciousness', a way of describing a person's thoughts and feelings as a flow of ideas as the person would have experienced them, without using the usual methods of description. She was a member of the *Bloomsbury Group and is considered an important early writer about feminism (= the idea that women should have the same rights and opportunities as men). Her best-known novels include *Mrs Dalloway* (1925), *To the Lighthouse* (1927) and *Orlando* (1928).

> 66 A woman must have money and a room of her own if she is to write fiction. 99
> Virginia Woolf

'**Woolite**™ /'wʊlaɪt/ *n* [U] a US make of soap for washing delicate clothes and fabrics.

the '**Woolsack** /'wʊlsæk/ the seat on which the *Lord Chancellor sits in the *House of Lords in the British parliament. It is a large square cushion filled with wool and covered with red cloth, and it has no back, arms or legs.

W

,F W 'Woolworth /'wʊlwəθ; AmE 'wʊlwərθ/ (Frank Winfield Woolworth 1852–1919) a US businessman, the son of a poor farmer, who began the group of *five-and-ten shops/stores named after him. The first was opened in 1879 in Lancaster, *Pennsylvania, and when he died, there were more than 1000. See also WOOLWORTH BUILDING.

the 'Woolworth ,Building /'wʊlwəθ; AmE 'wʊlwərθ/ a New York building which was the tallest in the world when it was completed in 1913. It is on *Broadway and is 792 feet/242 metres high. It cost $13.5 million and was built by F W *Woolworth for his company. The *Chrysler Building replaced it in 1930 as the world's tallest.

'Woolworth's /'wʊlwəθs; AmE 'wʊlwərθs/ a chain of large shops in Britain and other countries, selling a wide variety of goods at low prices. It has branches in many British towns and cities and for many years was Britain's leading chain of retail shops. The first shop was established in the US in 1879 by F W *Woolworth (1852–1919) and the first British shop opened in *Liverpool in 1909. In Britain Woolworth's is sometimes called 'Woolie's'.

,Bertie 'Wooster /,bɜːti 'wʊstə(r); AmE ,bɜːrti 'wʊstər/ one of the main characters in many humorous stories by P G *Wodehouse. He is a young *upper-class man who often gets into difficult situations because he is rather foolish, and relies on his servant *Jeeves to solve all his problems for him. Wooster and his friends are members of the Drones Club in London, England.

'Worcester[1] /'wʊstə(r)/ a city in west central England, on the River *Severn. It is the administrative centre of the county of *Worcestershire. It was an *Anglo-Saxon town and has a famous cathedral, which was mostly built in the 14th century. The city is known as the place where Royal Worcester porcelain is produced and it is also one of the cities where the *Three Choirs Festival is held.

the ,Battle of 'Worcester[2] /'wʊstə(r)/ a battle (1651) in which *Charles II was defeated by Oliver *Cromwell. Charles was trying to establish himself as the king of England after the execution of his father *Charles I. His attempt failed and the *Commonwealth, led by Cromwell, continued. Charles escaped by hiding in a tree when the battle was lost.

,Worcester 'sauce /,wʊstə; AmE ,wʊstər/ (AmE **Worcestershire Sauce**) n [U] a very popular dark sauce with a strong flavour made in *Worcester by the *Lea and Perrins company. It was originally created in 1835 by two chemists, Lea and Perrins, in Worcester and they began commercial production of it in 1837. How it is made and exactly what it contains has always been kept a secret but it is known to contain vinegar and spices. It is widely used in cooking and often added to tomato juice as a drink. See also BLOODY MARY.

'Worcestershire /'wʊstəʃə(r); AmE 'wʊstərʃər/ a county in west central England. Its administrative centre is *Worcester. The *Malvern Hills are on its western border and the *Cotswolds on its southern border.

,William 'Wordsworth /'wɜːdzwəθ; AmE 'wɜːrdzwərθ/ (1770–1850) one of the most popular of all English poets who, together with Samuel Taylor *Coleridge, started the *Romantic Movement in English poetry. His poems are mainly about the beauty of nature and its relationship with all human beings. Many of them describe the countryside of the *Lake District in north-west England, where he was born and spent most of his life. His best-known works include *Lyrical Ballads (1798), a collection of poems by himself and Coleridge, Poems (1807), which includes the poems *Daffodils and Intimations of Mortality, and The Prelude, a long poem about his early life and his intense experiences of nature

then, which was published in 1850 after his death. For much of his life he lived in the Lake District with his sister Dorothy (1771–1855), who had a great influence on him and kept a journal (= written record) about their life together. He wrote many of his best-known poems while they were living in *Dove Cottage in *Grasmere. The house is now a museum and a popular tourist attraction.

> **66** Earth has not anything to show more fair;
> Dull would he be of soul who could pass by
> A sight so touching in its majesty.
> This city now doth like a garment wear
> The beauty of the morning: silent, bare,
> Ships, towers, domes, theatres, and temples lie
> Open unto the fields, and to the sky,
> All bright and glittering in the smokeless air. **99**
> Wordsworth *Upon Westminster Bridge*

the 'Work Foun,dation a British organization, known as **The Industrial Society** until 2002, which aims to improve the quality of people's working lives by carrying out research and providing advice to businesses about issues such as the work-life balance (= the balance between a person's work and the rest of their life).

'workhouse n [C] (often **the workhouse** [sing]) (in Britain in the 19th century) a place where very poor people were sent by the authorities to live and work. Conditions in these places were very bad and the people living there had to work very hard and obey strict rules. As a result, poor people were frightened of being sent there. Life in the workhouse is described in some of the novels of Charles *Dickens.

the ,working 'class n [C+sing/pl v] the social class consisting mainly of people who do physical work, and their families. It is regarded as below the *middle class in education, background and culture, but many people from working-class families, including those who are well educated and rich, are proud of their family background.

,working men's 'club n (in Britain, especially in the industrial areas of the *Midlands and northern England) a club where people go after work to meet each other, drink in the bar, play games such as *darts, cards and *bingo, and watch entertainments including singing, dancing and comedy. Since the 1960s, many famous British entertainers have started their careers performing in these clubs. They were established in the 1850s by the church and grew in number after a central organization, the Working Men's Club and Institute Union (WMCIU), was established in 1862.

,workmen's compen'sation (also informal **,workmen's 'comp** /'kɒmp; AmE 'kɑːmp/) n [U] (in the US) payments made to a person who is injured while at work or who becomes ill because of their work. To protect their workers, employers are required by law to pay money into a workmen's compensation insurance scheme run by the US government. The system began in 1908: Sam had to spend a week in bed, but workmen's comp covered it.

the ,Works 'Progress Admini,stration (abbr the **WPA**) a US government programme (1935–43) established by President Franklin D *Roosevelt as part of his *New Deal(1). Its name was later changed to the Works Projects Administration. It created millions of jobs for unemployed people during the *Great Depression, mainly in building and the arts.

The ,World 'Almanac the oldest US almanac (= book of facts on many subjects) still published. The New York World newspaper began it in 1868. It is now published regularly by World Almanac Books, which also publishes The World Almanac for Kids.

W

The ,World at 'One a well-known British national radio news programme, broadcast on *Radio 4 every day from Monday to Friday at 1 p.m. It contains reports and comments on the important news events of the day. It was first broadcast in 1965.

▶ World English

English is the most widely spoken language in the world. It is the **first language**, or **mother tongue**, of over 300 million people living in countries such as Britain, Ireland, the US, Australia, New Zealand, Canada and South Africa, and it is spoken as a **second language** by many millions in countries where English is an official language. English is learned by many more people worldwide as a **foreign language**. English has many regional varieties such as South African English and Indian English and has also developed as a **global language** or **international language**, used as a **lingua franca** (= shared language), sometimes called **ELF** (English as a Lingua Franca) between people for whom it is not a first language. It is estimated that now only one out of every four users of the language is a native speaker of English.

English has achieved the status of a world language over a long period of time, and for various historical and cultural reasons. In the 17th century English was spread by settlers going from Britain to America, and in the 18th and 19th centuries by the expansion of the *British Empire. Many countries which were part of the empire kept English as their official language after independence because there were several local languages. As an official language, English is generally used in government, public administration and the law, and children may be taught in English. Since the middle of the 20th century, English has been an official language of international organizations such as the *United Nations.

Economic factors are also important. Britain and the US are both major business and financial centres, and many multinational corporations started in these countries. Elsewhere, a knowledge of English is often seen as necessary for success in business, and in countries which have become tourist destinations.

Advances in technology and telecommunications have also helped to establish English as a global language. Many inventions important to modern life, e.g. electricity, radio, the car and the telephone, were developed in Britain or the US. English became the language for international communications in air traffic control and shipping. Now, major computer systems and software developers are based in the US, and English is one of the main languages used on the Internet.

Britain and the US have invested in the development of **English Language Teaching (ELT)**. The *British Council has offices worldwide which promote British culture and support the teaching of English. The United States also has libraries and cultural programmes in many countries. The English language broadcasts of the *BBC World Service, *Voice of America and other services are widely popular, and many people listen to the news broadcasts in order to get news about events in their own country. The BBC and Voice of America also broadcast programmes for learners of English.

As an international language, English continues to develop. People who speak English as a first or second language have their own variety of the language, each of which is changing independently of other varieties. There are many differences, for instance, between British English and American English, and between Australian, South African, Indian, African and Jamaican English, though all can be understood, more or less, by speakers of other varieties. Foreign learners of English learn one of the major varieties, usually British or American English, or some sort of international English.

As a global language, English can no longer be thought of as belonging only to British or American people, or to anyone else. This loss of ownership is often uncomfortable, especially in Britain. As the number of people using English as a second or foreign language is increasing faster than the number who speak it as a first language, further drifts away from a British or American standard are likely.

The status of English as a global language has unfortunately tended to mean that British and American people assume everyone speaks English, so they do not need to learn foreign languages. The numbers of students who study foreign languages have decreased.

World 'Heritage Site *n* a place or structure included on an official list produced by the World Heritage Committee of UNESCO. Places are chosen for the list because they are considered to be 'of outstanding universal value', often for historical reasons, and are therefore preserved. There are several in Britain, including *Hadrian's Wall, *Stonehenge, the *Tower of London and *Westminster Abbey. World Heritage Sites in the US include *Grand Canyon National Park, *Independence Hall and the *Statue of Liberty.

World in 'Action a well-known television programme shown on British independent television, in which situations and problems of interest to the British public were investigated. It was broadcast from 1963 to 2000.

the ,World 'Series a series of games each year to decide the best US professional *baseball team. It began in 1903 and is between the *American League and *National League. The four best teams in each have a short series, and the two winners then play in the World Series. The first team to win four World Series games becomes World Champion.

the ,World 'Service ⇨ BBC WORLD SERVICE.

the ,World 'Trade ,Center (*also* **the Twin Towers**) two very tall office buildings in *Manhattan(1), New York City, built by the Port Authority of New York and New Jersey in 1972–3. For a short time they were the tallest buildings in the world. Each was 1350 feet/412 metres high and had 110 floors. A terrorist bomb exploded in the Center in 1993 killing six people and injuring more than a thousand. On September 11th 2001 the Twin Towers were both destroyed in another terrorist attack. Two planes crashed into the towers, and a short time later both towers collapsed. The area where the building used to be is now called *Ground Zero. A memorial to the victims of the attack is planned for the site. See also SEPTEMBER 11.

W

World War I /ˌwɜːld wɔː ˈwʌn; *AmE* ˌwɜːrld wɔːr/ (*also* **the First World War**, *also old-fashioned* **the Great War**) a war (1914–18) between the Central Powers (Germany, Austria-Hungary and Turkey) and the *Allies (Britain, France, Russia, Italy and the US). Most of the fighting took place in Europe, around the borders of Eastern Germany, Poland and Russia, and in north-east France and Belgium, where millions of soldiers died in long battles between armies in trenches (= long narrow holes dug in the ground). For many people these battles represent the essential horror and waste of war. The Germans agreed to stop fighting in 1918, after more than 10 million people had been killed.

World War II /ˌwɜːld wɔː ˈtuː; *AmE* ˌwɜːrld wɔːr/ (*also* **the Second World War**) a war (1939–45) between the Axis powers (Germany, Italy and Japan) and the *Allies (Britain and the countries in the *British Empire, France, and later the USSR and the US). Many other countries were also involved both directly and indirectly.

The war started when Germany, under Adolf Hitler and the Nazis, invaded and took control of other countries and the Allies wanted to prevent German power growing in this way. Britain declared war on Germany in September 1939 when German troops entered Poland, and soon afterwards Winston *Churchill, who in Britain is closely associated with the Allies' victory in the war, became the British *prime minister.

In 1940 Germany attacked Britain but was not successful, mainly because of the British victory in the *Battle of Britain. In 1941 Germany invaded Russia and Japan attacked *Pearl Harbor, an action which brought the US into the war. In 1942 Japan increased its control over several countries in Asia but was checked by US forces in the Pacific. In the same year, at the Battle of El Alamein, Allied forces began to defeat Germany and Italy in northern Africa. In 1943 the Allies took Italy and Russian forces began to advance on Germany from the east. In 1944 the Allies invaded northern Europe with the *Normandy landings and began to defeat Germany in Europe. The war ended in 1945 when the Allies took control of Germany, Hitler killed himself, and Japan was defeated as a result of atom bombs being dropped on the cities of *Hiroshima and *Nagasaki. Germany and Japan surrendered separately in 1945.

Over 50 million people were killed in the war, more than 20 million of them Russians. World War II is also remembered for the very large number of Jewish and other people killed in German concentration camps and the harsh treatment of prisoners of war captured by the Japanese. See also D-DAY, DUNKIRK.

Wormwood 'Scrubs /ˌwɜːmwʊd ˈskrʌbz; AmE ˌwɜːrmwʊd/ (also informal **the Scrubs**) a prison for male prisoners in west London. It was built in 1874–90, partly by prisoners who were being kept there.

'Worship /ˈwɜːʃɪp; AmE ˈwɜːrʃɪp/ **Your/His/Her Worship** (in Britain) the title used when speaking or referring to certain important officials, particularly *magistrates and *mayors: May I say something, Your Worship?

Wounded 'Knee /ˌwuːndɪd ˈniː/ a small river in the US state of *South Dakota where US soldiers killed more than 200 *Native American men, women and children of the *Sioux people on 29 December 1890. This was the final major battle of the *Indian wars. In 1973 members of the American Indian Movement occupied the village there for over two months, demanding that the US Senate take action to help Native Americans.

WPA /ˌdʌblju: pi: ˈeɪ/ ⇨ WORKS PROGRESS ADMINISTRATION.

WRAC /ræk/ ⇨ WOMEN'S ROYAL ARMY CORPS.

the WRAF /ræf/ (in full the **Women's Royal Air Force**) the women's section of the *RAF for most of the 20th century. In 1992 it combined with the RAF.

'Wranglers™ /ˈræŋgləz; AmE ˈræŋglərz/ a make of *jeans which is popular in Britain and the US, made by the Wrangler company.

The ˌWreck of the 'Hesperus /ˈhespərəs/ a poem by the US poet Henry Wadsworth *Longfellow. It was in his collection Ballads and Other Poems (1841), which also included The *Village Blacksmith. It tells the story of a father and his small daughter who die when their ship hits rocks during a storm. The phrase like the wreck of the Hesperus may be used to mean 'very untidy' or 'in a ruined state'. The poem includes these lines:

> 66 'O father! I see a gleaming light.
> Oh, say, what may it be?'
> But the father answered never a word,
> A frozen corpse was he. 99

Wren¹ /ren/ n a member of the *WRNS.

ˌChristopher 'Wren² /ˈren/ (1632–1723) one of the most famous English architects, known especially for designing the present *St Paul's Cathedral (where he is buried) and other churches in London that replaced those destroyed in the *Great Fire of London. Among other buildings he designed are *Chelsea Hospital, *Marlborough House, the *Royal Naval College and parts of *Hampton Court. His buildings combined the *baroque style with the classical style. He was also a scientist and astronomer and one of the group of people who established the *Royal Society. He was made a *knight in 1673.

St Paul's Cathedral, designed by Christopher Wren

'wrestling n [U] a sport in which two people (usually men) fight, each trying to force the other onto the ground, using a variety of holds. The popular variety of it is more of an entertainment than a serious sport, with the competitors wearing colourful costumes and crowds being encouraged to cheer or insult them. Many people think that the fights are merely a performance, with the results arranged before they start.

ˌFrank ˌLloyd 'Wright¹ /ˈlɔɪd ˈraɪt/ (1869–1959) a leading US architect who helped to develop modern architecture. His 'prairie-style' houses used long, low lines and open spaces inside, and his 'organic' buildings were designed to match their natural surroundings and often used their materials. One of Wright's best-known buildings is the *Guggenheim Museum.

ˌRichard 'Wright² /ˈraɪt/ (1908–60) a US writer whose best-known books are the novel *Native Son and his own life story, Black Boy (1945). He also wrote a collection of stories, Uncle Tom's Children (1938). Wright was a Communist for many years. He lived in Paris after *World War II and died there.

the 'Wright ˌbrothers /ˈraɪt/ Wilbur Wright (1867–1912) and Orville Wright (1871–1948), US engineers who built the first successful aircraft that used an engine and was heavier than air. They first flew their aircraft, called Flyer, on four successful flights on 17 December 1903 near Kitty Hawk, *North Carolina. Their longest flight was 852 feet/260 metres, and lasted 59 seconds.

'Wrigley's™ /ˈrɪgliz/ n [U] chewing gum made by the US William Wrigley Jr Company of *Chicago. It is available in several different flavours, including Wrigley's Spearmint and Juicy Fruit, as well as Hubba Bubba bubble gum.

'write-in ˌcandidate n (AmE) a candidate in an election for public office whose name is not printed on the official list of candidates, usually because he or she has not been selected by a political party. People voting for such a candidate must therefore write his or her name

W

on the voting paper. Some use this **write-in vote**, or **write-in**, as a form of protest by writing ridiculous names on the voting paper.

the WRNS /ˌdʌbljuː ɑːr en 'es/ (*in full* **the Women's Royal Naval Service**) (*also* **the Wrens**) the female section of the British *Royal Navy. It was established in 1917 and until 1990 its members could not serve on ships. In 1993 the WRNS became officially part of the Royal Navy and ceased to exist as a separate section.

WRVS /ˌdʌbljuː ɑː viː 'es; *AmE* ɑːr/ (*in full* **the Women's Royal Voluntary Service**) a large organization of British people, both men and women, who do voluntary work (= without pay) in their communities. For example, they deliver *meals on wheels and visit people in hospitals and prisons.

W-2 form /ˌdʌbljuː 'tuː fɔːm; *AmE* fɔːrm/ *n* (in the US) an official document prepared each year by employers for their employees, for tax purposes. It shows how much an employee has earned and how much tax the employer has taken from his or her pay to send to the government. When employees send in their *1040 forms or other tax documents, the W-2 form must be included.

Wuthering 'Heights /ˌwʌðərɪŋ/ the only novel (1847) by Emily *Brontë. The story is set on the *Yorkshire Moors and is about the intense relationship between Catherine Earnshaw and *Heathcliff, which leads to many problems and sad events. Laurence *Olivier played Heathcliff in the 1939 film version, directed by William *Wyler. In 1978 the book was the subject of a successful pop song by Kate Bush, and in the 1990s it was made into a musical show, with Cliff *Richard as Heathcliff.

William 'Wycherley /'wɪtʃəli; *AmE* 'wɪtʃərli/ (1640–1716) an English writer of *Restoration comedy plays. His best-known play is *The Country Wife* (1675), which is still performed today and which has as its theme the immoral behaviour of a section of the society of his time.

John 'Wycliffe /'wɪklɪf/ (c. 1330–84) an English writer on religion who criticized various bad practices that were common in the Church at that time. He said that the Bible, not the Church, was the most important religious authority, and was involved in translating the Bible into English. The group who supported his beliefs were called Lollards.

the Wye /waɪ/ a river that flows from *Powys in central Wales, passes through the city of *Hereford(1) in England and forms, in one section, the border between Wales and England. It is 130 miles/210 kilometres long and flows into the sea in the *Bristol Channel.

Andrew 'Wyeth /'waɪəθ/ (1917–) a US painter whose realistic pictures often show the people or lonely countryside of *Pennsylvania and *Maine. His best-known work is probably *Christina's World* (1948).

'Wykehamist /'wɪkəmɪst/ *n* a pupil or former pupil at *Winchester(2) College school. Wykehamists are named after the man who established the school, *William of Wykeham.

William 'Wyler /'waɪlə(r)/ (1902–81) a US film director, born in Germany and known for his great attention to detail. He won *Oscars for directing *Mrs Miniver* (1942), *The Best Years of Our Lives* (1946) and *Ben-Hur* (1959). His other films include *Wuthering Heights* (1939), *Roman Holiday* (1953), *The Big Country* (1958) and *Funny Girl* (1968).

John 'Wyndham /'wɪndəm/ (1903–69) an English writer of science fiction novels, including *The Day of the Triffids* (1951), *The Chrysalids* (1955) and *The Midwich Cuckoos* (1957). His books are often about how people deal with disasters, both natural ones and those created by humans.

Tammy Wy'nette /ˌtæmi wɪ'net/ (1942–98) a popular US *country music singer with a strong, sad voice. Her best-known song was *Stand By Your Man* (1968). She was married for a time to the singer George Jones, and they often sang songs together about their difficult marriage, including *D-I-V-O-R-C-E* (1969), *We're Gonna Hold On* (1973) and *Golden Rings* (1976). Wynette was chosen for the Country Music *Hall of Fame in 1998.

Wy'oming /waɪ'əʊmɪŋ; *AmE* waɪ'oʊmɪŋ/ one of the *Rocky Mountain States in the western central US. It is also called the Equality State because it was the first state to give women the right to vote (in 1869). Although it is the 10th largest state it has the smallest population (about 501 000 in 2003). The capital and largest city is Cheyenne. Wyoming was part of the *Louisiana Purchase and became a state in 1890. Its products include wheat, wool, oil, gas and minerals and wood. Tourist attractions include *Yellowstone National Park, Grand Teton National Park, Fort Laramie National Historic Site and the Cheyenne Frontier Days celebration.

Grand Teton National Park, Wyoming

W

X x

X-Acto™ /ɪgˈzæktəʊ; *AmE* ɪgˈzæktoʊ/ *n* (*pl* **-os**) a US make of knife with thin steel blades which can be changed. It is used for delicate work, e.g. by artists to cut paper accurately and by people building model aircraft.

ˈX certificate /ˈeks/ a label formerly given to certain cinema films in Britain by the British Board of Film Censors (now called the *British Board of Film Classification). Films were given an X certificate if they were considered to be not suitable for people under 18, usually because they contained violence, sex or bad language. In 1982, the label 'X certificate' was changed to '18', but people still sometimes use the old name informally.

ˈXerox™ /ˈzɪərɒks; *AmE* ˈzɪrɑːks/ a large US company that produces copying and printing machines, as well as scanners (= devices that copy documents, etc. onto a computer screen) and faxes. Its name is based on the process of 'xerography' (meaning 'dry writing') which the company developed. In Asia and Australia Xerox works with the Fuji company as Fuji Xerox. People sometimes use the word 'xerox' as a noun meaning any photographic copy and the verb 'to xerox' meaning 'to make a photographic copy of something'.

The ˈX-Files /ˈeks/ a popular US television series that began in 1993 and is widely shown in other countries. It is about two members of the FBI, Agent Mulder (David Duchovny) and Agent Scully (Gillian Anderson), who investigate mysterious events suggesting other forms of life in space. There has also been a film, *The X-Files* (1998).

Y y

the Y /waɪ/ (*AmE*) an informal short form for the *YMCA(1) or the *YWCA(1).

Yaˈhoo¹ /jɑːˈhuː/ *n* any of an imaginary race of creatures in *Gulliver's Travels* by Jonathan *Swift. The Yahoos are animals with human form who behave in a rude, aggressive manner. The word *yahoo* is now used to mean a rude, violent and aggressive person.

ˈYahoo!™² /ˈjɑːhuː/ a popular website that provides a number of services, including a search engine (= a way of finding information on the Internet), a list of websites arranged in categories and email. It was founded in California in 1994 by David Filo (1967–) and Jerry Yang (1968–). The name Yahoo! comes from the first letters of the words 'Yet Another Hierarchical Officious Oracle'. The founders also chose the name because they liked the concept of the *Yahoo described in *Gulliver's Travels*.

ˌYale Uniˈversity /ˌjeɪl/ a major US university, often seen as a rival of *Harvard University. It is in New Haven, *Connecticut, and is known for its large library, the Yale Art Gallery and the Peabody Museum of Natural History. Yale was established (originally as Yale College) in 1701 and was named after Elihu Yale (1649–1721) who gave it books and other items. See also IVY LEAGUE.

ˈYalta /ˈjæltə/ a holiday town by the sea in the Ukraine in the former USSR, where the **Yalta Conference** took place in February 1945. The leaders of the *Allies, Winston *Churchill, Franklin D *Roosevelt and Joseph Stalin, met to agree on plans to defeat Germany in *World War II, to decide on what the borders of various countries in Europe would be after the war ended, and to make plans for setting up the *United Nations.

ˈYankee /ˈjæŋki/ *n* **1** (*also* **Yank**) (*BrE informal sometimes disapproving*) a person from the US; an American. **2** (*often disapproving*) (in the southern US) a person from the northern states. US soldiers and people from the North were called Yankees during the *Civil War.

3 (in the US, especially the northern states) a person from *New England. See also YANKEE DOODLE.

ˌYankee ˈDoodle /ˌjæŋki ˈduːdl/ an 18th-century marching song which has become almost a national song in the US. It was first sung by British soldiers to make fun of Americans during the *American Revolution, but then became popular with George *Washington's soldiers. 'Yankee' probably comes from 'Janke', the Dutch for 'Johnny' and a common name in early New York. 'Doodle' is an old-fashioned English word meaning a stupid person. The song begins:

> 66 Yankee Doodle came to town:
> Riding on a pony;
> He stuck a feather in his cap
> And called it macaroni. 99

ˌYankee Doodle ˈDandy /ˌjæŋki ˌduːdl ˈdændi/ a lively song written by George M *Cohan for his *Broadway musical play *Little Johnny Jones* (1904). It became a favourite American song for *Independence Day and during the world wars. The *Hollywood film about Cohan's life was also called *Yankee Doodle Dandy* (1942). The song begins:

> 66 I'm a Yankee Doodle Dandy,
> A Yankee Doodle, do or die,
> A real live nephew of my Uncle Sam,
> Born on the Fourth of July. 99

the ˈYankees /ˈjæŋkiz/ the New York City professional baseball team. It has won 26 *World Series, more than any other team. Famous Yankee players have included 'Babe' *Ruth, Lou *Gehrig and Joe *DiMaggio. The team plays its home games in the famous **Yankee Stadium** in the *Bronx.

The Yard an informal name for *Scotland Yard or *New Scotland Yard, referring both to the *Metropolitan Police and to its head offices in central London.

,**W B 'Yeats** /'jeɪts/ (William Butler Yeats 1865–1939) a leading Irish writer of poetry, plays and stories. His best-known works of poetry include *The Wild Swans at Coole* (1917), *The Winding Stair* (1933) and *Collected Poems* (1933). His plays include *The Land of Heart's Desire* (1894) and *The Green Helmet* (1910), and several were written to be performed at the Abbey Theatre in Dublin, which he helped to establish. His book of stories, *The Celtic Twilight*, created a lot of interest in traditional Irish stories. Yeats was also much involved in politics as a nationalist and became a *Senator in the Irish parliament (1922–8). He received the *Nobel Prize for literature in 1923.

the ,**Yellow Brick 'Road** a course of action that a person takes believing that it will lead to good things. It comes from the Yellow Brick Road in *The *Wizard of Oz* which Dorothy and her friends follow to the Emerald City.

'**yellow 'journalism** *n* [U] a type of journalism that exaggerates news stories and deliberately includes exciting or shocking material in order to attract readers. The name comes from the *Yellow Kid* *comic strip which began in the New York *World* in 1895 and used yellow ink to attract readers' attention. Newspapers that include yellow journalism are often called the **yellow press**.

the ,**Yellow 'Pages**™ a book (or in the US sometimes part of a book) printed on yellow paper and containing the telephone numbers and addresses of companies, arranged in alphabetical order according to the kind of business they are involved in. There are different versions for each area of the country. In Britain the company that publishes the *Yellow Pages*, Yell Limited, also provides business telephone numbers and addresses through its *Yell* website. In the US, the same company publishes the *Yellow Book*™, a popular type of Yellow Pages, and operates an Internet service by the same name. A well-known advertisement for the Yellow Pages uses the phrase 'Let your fingers do the walking': *If you need a local builder, try looking in the Yellow Pages.*

,**yellow 'ribbon** *n* (in the US) a piece of yellow ribbon used as a sign to show that people, especially those in the armed forces, are not forgotten while they are away from home. It comes from a story about a man coming out of prison who asked his wife to tie a yellow ribbon round a tree if she wanted him back. Yellow ribbons were used during the *Vietnam War and were later used during the Iranian *hostage crisis, the *Gulf War, and the war in Iraq. *Tie A Yellow Ribbon Round the Ole Oak Tree* was a very popular song in 1973.

> **66** Whoa, tie a yellow ribbon 'round the ole oak tree
> It's been three long years, do ya still want me?
> If I don't see a ribbon 'round the ole oak tree
> I'll stay on the bus, forget about us, put the blame on me
> If I don't see a yellow ribbon 'round the ole oak tree …
> Now the whole darn bus is cheerin' and I can't believe I see
> A hundred yellow ribbons 'round the ole oak tree. **99**

'**Yellowstone 'National 'Park** /'jeləʊstəʊn; *AmE* 'jeloʊstoʊn/ the first US national park, established in 1872, and one of the largest. It covers about 3 500 square miles/9 065 square kilometres in north-west *Wyoming and parts of *Idaho and *Montana. It has many wild animals, including bears and buffalo, and is famous for its fine scenery, hot springs and geysers (= underground hot springs that shoot hot water or steam up into the air). The park was made a *World Heritage Site in 1978. See also OLD FAITHFUL.

ye 'olde /ji: 'əʊld; *AmE* 'oʊld/ a phrase meaning 'the old' in an old form of English. (The old letter 'y' was sometimes used to represent what is now written as 'th'.) The phrase is now sometimes used in the names of restaurants, shops, pubs or hotels in Britain to show or pretend that they are very old: *Ye Olde Tea Shoppe.*

,**Yeoman 'Warder** *n* (*pl* ,**Yeomen 'Warders**) any of the group of men who guard the *Tower of London. They are thought to have existed since the *White Tower was built in the 11th century. They wear a red uniform from the *Tudor(1) period similar to that worn by the *Yeomen of the Guard and are also called *beefeaters. For visitors to London, they are often seen as one of the symbols of the city.

the ,**Yeomen of the 'Guard** *n* [pl] a military unit of men who traditionally guard the British king or queen at certain ceremonies. It was created in 1485 for the ceremony in which *Henry VII became king. Its members still wear a red uniform in the *Tudor(1) style of that period, similar to that worn by *Yeomen Warders, though the two groups are quite separate.

The ,**Yeomen of the 'Guard** one of the operas by *Gilbert and *Sullivan[1]. It is about a man who gets married just before he is to be executed in the *Tower of London and is then told that he has been forgiven and will not be executed after all.

,**Yerkes Ob'servatory** /,jɜːks; *AmE* ,jɜːrks/ the observatory (= a building from which to study the stars, weather, etc.) of the University of Chicago in the US. It was built in 1892 at Lake Geneva, *Wisconsin, with money given by Charles Yerkes. It contains the world's largest refracting telescope (= an instrument that uses light rays to make distant objects appear much larger).

'**Yes, ,Minister** a very popular and successful *BBC television comedy series (1980–5), which made fun of those involved in politics. The main characters are a government minister who is often not sure how to solve problems affecting his work and career, and a senior member of the *Civil Service, Sir Humphrey Appleby, whose job is to advise him and who creates complicated plans for solving these problems and protecting his own position. In a later series, *Yes, Prime Minister* (1986–7), the minister had become *prime minister.

YHA /,waɪ eɪtʃ 'eɪ/ ⇨ YOUTH HOSTELS ASSOCIATION.

the **YMCA** /,waɪ em si: 'eɪ/ **1** (*in full* the **Young Men's Christian Association**) a Christian organization that offers a wide range of religious, educational, sports and social activities to young men of all races, religions and social backgrounds. It was established in Britain in 1844 and now operates in many countries around the world. It is known especially for its hostels (= places offering cheap food and accommodation). See also Y. **2** *n* a building owned and run by the YMCA: *I stayed in a YMCA in London for two weeks.*

,**Yogi 'Bear** /,jəʊgi; *AmE* ,joʊgi/ a US television cartoon character created in 1958 by *Hanna and Barbera. Yogi is a cheerful bear who wears a flat hat and white collar and lives in Jellystone National Park with his small bear friend Boo Boo. He is always trying to steal food. See also BERRA.

yoof /ju:f/ *n* [U] (*BrE informal, humorous*) young people in general, especially when seen as a group for whom a particular product or type of entertainment is designed. The word was invented in the 1980s as a deliberate wrong spelling of *youth*. It implies that much of what is produced for young people assumes that they are not very intelligent: *I find the whole notion of yoof culture pretty depressing.*

'Yorick /'jɒrɪk; *AmE* 'jɔːrɪk/ a former court jester (= a man employed to amuse the king in the Middle Ages) whose skull is found by the men digging Ophelia's grave in *Shakespeare's play *Hamlet*. Hamlet picks up the skull and makes a famous speech, which begins:

> 66 Alas, poor Yorick. I knew him, Horatio;
> A fellow of infinite jest … 99

York[1] /jɔːk; *AmE* jɔːrk/ a city in north-east England on the River *Ouse. It it in the county of *North Yorkshire, but has its own *unitary authority. It is known especially for its ancient buildings, including *York Minster. It was an important city in Roman times and in the Middle Ages, and it was the most important city in the *Anglo-Saxon region of *Northumbria. The city has many visitors and its attractions include the *National Railway Museum and the Jorvik Viking Centre, which has exhibitions about the period when people from Scandinavia invaded Britain.

the ,Duchess of 'York[2] /'jɔːk; *AmE* 'jɔːrk/ (1959–) the title given to Sarah *Ferguson after her marriage in 1986 to Prince *Andrew, Duke of *York. The couple have two children, Princess Beatrice and Princess Eugenie. They divorced in 1996. The Duchess is often referred to informally as 'Fergie'.

the ,Duke of 'York[3] /jɔːk; *AmE* 'jɔːrk/ **1** (1960–) Andrew, the third child of Queen *Elizabeth II. He was educated at *Gordonstoun in Scotland, a college in Ontario, Canada, and the *Royal Naval College, Dartmouth. He became a helicopter pilot in the *Royal Navy, and took part in the *Falklands War. He used to be known as 'Prince Andrew', but in 1986 the Queen made him the Duke of York. He married Sarah *Ferguson in

Prince Andrew

that year, and she therefore became the Duchess of York. They have two daughters, Princess Beatrice, born in 1988, and Princess Eugenie, born in 1990. In 1996 the Duke and Duchess divorced. ⇨ note at ROYAL FAMILY. **2** a title given to various second sons of kings and queens of Britain since 1474, when King *Edward IV gave it to his son Richard. King *Henry VIII held the title of Duke of York before he became king. **3** (1763–1827) the second son of King *George III, who was a soldier. See also GRAND OLD DUKE OF YORK.

the ,House of 'York[4] /'jɔːk; *AmE* 'jɔːrk/ the English royal house (= family) to which the kings of England between 1461 and 1485 belonged. They were *Edward IV, *Edward V and *Richard III, and were descended from the first Duke of York, Edmund of Langley (1341–1402). See also WARS OF THE ROSES.

'Yorkist /'jɔːkɪst; *AmE* 'jɔːrkɪst/ *n* a member or supporter of the House of *York.
▶ **Yorkist** *adj*.

,York 'Minster /,jɔːk; *AmE* ,jɔːrk/ the cathedral in the city of *York[1], one of the largest and best known in Britain. It was built during the 13th, 14th and 15th centuries and is famous for its beautiful stained glass windows.

'Yorkshire /'jɔːkʃə(r); *AmE* 'jɔːrkʃər/ a former county in north-east England. In 1974 it was divided into two new counties, *North Yorkshire and *Humberside, and

two *metropolitan counties, *West Yorkshire and *South Yorkshire. See also RIDING.

the ,Yorkshire 'Dales /,jɔːkʃə; *AmE* ,jɔːrkʃər/ *n* [pl] an area of countryside, valleys and villages in the north of England. They are mainly in the county of *North Yorkshire but also partly in *Cumbria. The area became a *national park in 1954. It is considered one of the most beautiful areas in England and is especially popular with British people on walking holidays or making tours around it by car.

the Yorkshire Dales

the ,Yorkshire 'Moors /,jɔːkʃə; *AmE* ,jɔːrkʃər/ *n* [pl] areas of high, open land with few trees in *North Yorkshire, England. They include the area known as the North York Moors, which has been a *national park since 1952.

,Yorkshire 'pudding /,jɔːkʃə; *AmE* ,jɔːrkʃər/ *n* [C, U] a British dish made by baking a mixture of flour, eggs and milk in fat, usually in separate pieces like small cakes. Yorkshire pudding is usually eaten with roast beef as part of a traditional Sunday lunch. See also SUNDAY ROAST.

the ,Yorkshire 'Ripper /,jɔːkʃə 'rɪpə(r); *AmE* ,jɔːrkʃər/ the name given by the press to Peter *Sutcliffe, an Englishman who murdered thirteen women and tried to kill several more in the north of England in the 1970s, before he was caught in 1981. The name was meant to suggest that his crimes were similar to those of *Jack the Ripper.

,Yorkshire 'terrier /,jɔːkʃə; *AmE* ,jɔːrkʃər/ *n* a breed of small *terrier dog with long, straight, shiny hair that is dark grey or brown. It was originally bred in *Yorkshire.

'Yorktown /'jɔːktaʊn; *AmE* 'jɔːrktaʊn/ the town in south-east *Virginia where the final military campaign of the *American Revolution took place. The British Army, led by General Charles *Cornwallis, was surrounded there in 1781 by 16 000 American and French soldiers. The surrender of Cornwallis to General George *Washington ended the war.

Yo'semite 'National 'Park /jəʊ'seməti; *AmE* joʊ'seməti/ a US *national park in the *Sierra Nevada mountains of eastern *California. It was established in 1890 and covers 1 189 square miles/3 080 square kilometres. It was named after the **Yosemite River** that runs through it and contains **Yosemite Falls**, the highest waterfall in the US (2 425 feet/740 metres).

Yosemite Falls

The park is also famous for its many giant sequoia trees. It was made a *World Heritage Site in 1984. See also REDWOOD.

Yo,semite 'Sam /jəʊ,seməti; *AmE* jəʊ,seməti/ a US cartoon character created for *Warner Brothers in 1948. He is a very short *cowboy with guns, a long red moustache and a bad temper. His regular opponent is *Bugs Bunny.

Andrew 'Young¹ /'jʌŋ/ (1932–) a leader in the US *civil rights movement. He was a member of the US House of Representatives (1973–7) and the first African-American representative to the *United Nations (1977–9) where he was known for his strong, open comments. He later became *mayor of Atlanta (1982–9).

Brigham 'Young² /,brɪgəm 'jʌŋ/ (1801–77) the US leader of the *Mormons who brought them to *Utah in 1846–7 and established *Salt Lake City. He became the first Governor of the Utah Territory in 1850. He is believed to have had 27 wives. See also SMITH.

',Cy' 'Young³ /,saɪ 'jʌŋ/ (1867–1955) a famous US *baseball player (1890–1911). He was a pitcher (= player who throws the ball to be hit) who played in more games (906) and had more wins (511) than any other player in the history of the game. His real name was Denton True Young. His nickname 'Cy' was a short form of 'Cyclone', a wind storm. He played for the Cleveland Indians, the St Louis Cardinals, the Boston Red Sox and the Boston Braves. He was chosen for the National Baseball *Hall of Fame in 1937.

Jimmy 'Young⁴ /'jʌŋ/ (1923–) a popular British radio broadcaster who had his own programme every morning from Monday to Friday on *Radio 2 (1973–2002). It combined popular music and other entertainment with discussion of news items and interviews with politicians. Young began his career as a singer and he was also one of the original disc jockeys on *Radio 1 when it was established in 1967. He was made a *knight in 2002.

Whitney 'Young⁵ /,wɪtni 'jʌŋ/ (1921–71) an African-American leader during the *civil rights movement. He was head of the *National Urban League (1961–70). Young was criticized by some African Americans because he made compromises with white political leaders, but he had great influence.

The ,Young and the 'Restless a very popular US television *soap opera on *CBS. It began in 1973 and has won many *Emmy awards, including five as the 'Best Daytime Drama Series'.

the 'Younger ,brothers /'jʌŋgə; *AmE* 'jʌŋgər/ four US outlaws (= criminals) in the *Wild West. The best-known of the four brothers were **Cole Younger** (1844–1916) and **Jim Younger** (1848–1902). They were cousins of Jesse and Frank *James, and the group was sometimes called the James-Younger Gang. Three of the brothers were captured and sent to prison after trying to rob a bank in Northfield, *Minnesota, in 1876. There have been several films about them, including *The Long Riders* (1980) and *American Outlaws* (2001). See also QUANTRILL'S RAIDERS.

the ,Young Men's 'Christian Associ,ation ⇨ YMCA.

,young of'fender insti,tution *n* a type of prison in Britain for young people who have committed crimes.

Young offender institutions contain people aged 15–17 who have been found guilty in *youth courts and people aged 18–20 who have been found guilty in ordinary courts for adults. They were called *Borstals until 1983.

the ,Young Pre'tender a *nickname of Charles Edward *Stuart (1720–88), also known as *Bonny Prince Charlie. A pretender is a person who claims something, usually the right to be a king or queen, although not everyone agrees that the claim is just. See also FORTY-FIVE, JACOBITE, OLD PRETENDER.

,Young Women's 'Christian Associ,ation ⇨ YWCA.

'youth court *n* (in England and Wales) a court of law for young people aged 10–17 accused of committing crimes. Three magistrates (at least one of whom is always a woman) decide whether the accused person is guilty or not. The cases are held privately and the names of those accused are usually not published. Young people aged 10–14 can only be found guilty if it is proved that they knew that what they were doing was legally and morally wrong. Youth courts were formerly known as *juvenile courts. See also ATTENDANCE CENTRE, COMMUNITY SERVICE, YOUNG OFFENDER INSTITUTION.

the 'Youth Hostels Associ,ation (*abbr* the **YHA**) an organization that provides cheap accommodation (called **youth hostels**) for people who are travelling from place to place, usually on holiday, and who are members of the organization. It was established in Britain in 1930 and is part of the International Youth Hostel Federation which operates in more than 50 countries around the world. Although mostly young people stay in youth hostels, people of any age can become members.

'Ypres /'iːprə/ a town in Belgium near which three separate battles (1914, 1915 and 1917) were fought in *World War I. In the first, the *British Expeditionary Force suffered terrible losses, the second involved the first use of poisonous gas as a weapon by the Germans, and the third resulted in the deaths of over half a million men.

'yuppie (*also* **yuppy**) *n* (*pl* **-ies**) (*informal, often disapproving*) a young person with a high income who is considered to be mainly interested in impressing others with the things that they can buy, such as expensive cars and homes. The word was widely used in the 1980s when such people were thought to be too ambitious and to care only about themselves and not the rest of society. The word was formed from the first letters of 'young urban professional person' or 'young upwardly-mobile professional person'. Compare DINKIE.

the YWCA /,waɪ dʌblju: si: 'eɪ/ **1** (*in full* the **Young Women's Christian Association**) a Christian organization, similar to but separate from the *YMCA(1). Its main role used to be providing safe and cheap accommodation for young women living away from home, but in Britain and the US this has now mostly been replaced by a service giving support and advice to girls and young women who are experiencing problems. It was established in Britain in 1855 and now operates in many countries around the world. See also Y.
2 *n* a building owned and run by the YWCA.

Z z

Za'gat ˌSurvey™ /zæˈgæt/ a US publisher of guides to restaurants and hotels, started in 1979 by Tim and Nina Zagat, which are based on the opinions of customers. The guides give information and opinions about restaurants and hotels in cities or areas in the US and around the world.

''Babe'' Didrikson Za'harias /ˈbeɪb ˈdɪdrɪksn zəˈhæriəs/ ⇨ DIDRIKSON.

'Zambia /ˈzæmbiə/ a country in southern central Africa. As Northern Rhodesia it was formerly part of the *British Empire and became independent and a member of the *Commonwealth in 1964. Zambia has many minerals and produces a large amount of the world's copper. Its official language is English and its capital city is Lusaka.
▶ **Zambian** adj, n.

ˌDarryl F 'Zanuck /ˌdærəl, ˈzænək/ (Darryl Francis Zanuck 1902–79) a US film producer. After working for *Warner Brothers he formed his own company, which became *20th Century Fox. Darryl Zanuck's successful films included The *Grapes of Wrath, The Longest Day (1962), How Green Was My Valley (1941), The *Sound of Music and Patton (1970). He won a special *Oscar in 1937.

ˌFrank 'Zappa /ˈzæpə/ (1940–93) a US singer and writer of *rock music who was especially popular with *hippies. He joined the Soul Giants group in 1964 and a year later changed their name to the Mothers of Invention. They were known for 'psychedelic rock', wild stage performances and songs which were deliberately shocking. Their albums included Freak Out (1966). Zappa later made the album Hot Rats (1970) without the group.

'Z Cars /ˈzed/ a popular *BBC television series (1960–78) about a group of fictional police officers in *Liverpool. It dealt with the problems of ordinary police work in a realistic way and strongly influenced later programmes of this type.

ˌzebra 'crossing n (BrE) (in Britain) an area of road with broad white lines painted on it, at which vehicles must stop if people on foot wish to walk across. Zebra crossings are indicated by *Belisha beacons on each side of the road to warn approaching drivers. The name comes from the zebra, a wild animal similar to a horse with black and white lines on its body.

Reˌnée 'Zellweger /rəˌneɪ ˈzelwegə(r)/ (1969–) a US actor. She won an *Oscar for her part in Cold Mountain (2003) and her other films include Bridget Jones's Diary (2001) and Chicago (2002).

ˌRobert Ze'meckis /zəˈmekɪs/ (1952–) a US director and writer of films. He won an *Oscar as 'Best Director' for *Forrest Gump. His other films include Romancing the Stone (1984), Back to the Future (1985), which he also wrote, Who Framed Roger Rabbit (1988), Death Becomes Her (1992) and The Polar Express (2004).

'Zenith /ˈzenɪθ; AmE ˈziːnɪθ/ a leading US company in the production of radio and television equipment, first established in 1918. Its full name is the Zenith Electronics Corporation. For many years it has used the advertising phrase, 'the quality goes in before the name goes on'. It made the world's first portable radio (= one that is easy to carry), the first practical television remote control device (= one that operates a television from a distance,

using electronic signals), and the first digital high-definition television system.

ˌBenjamin Zepha'niah /zefəˈnaɪə/ (1958–) a British *Rastafarian writer and poet whose poetry is influenced by *reggae music. His books of poetry include Pen Rhythm (1980) and Too Black, Too Strong (2001).

ˌCatherine ˌZeta-'Jones /ˌziːtə ˈdʒəʊnz; AmE ˈdʒoʊnz/ (1969–) a Welsh actress whose appearances include the British television drama The Darling Buds of May (1991) and the films Chicago (2002) for which she won an *Oscar, and Intolerable Cruelty (2003). She is married to the actor Michael *Douglas.

ˌFlorenz 'Ziegfeld /ˌflɒrəns ˈziːgfeld; AmE ˌflɔːrəns/ (1869–1932) a US theatre manager who produced *Broadway shows. He is remembered especially for the **Ziegfeld Follies**, variety shows which he put on each year from 1907 until his death. They included the beautiful 'Ziegfeld Girls' who danced in a long line. Ziegfeld helped the early careers of many performers, including Fred *Astaire, Will *Rogers and W C *Fields. He also produced *Show Boat.

Zim'babwe /zɪmˈbɑːbwi/ a country in southern Africa, formerly called Rhodesia and earlier Southern Rhodesia. It was part of the *British Empire and became independent and a member of the *Commonwealth in 1980. From 1964 until it became independent, Zimbabwe was ruled by a white minority government led by Ian *Smith, who announced a Unilateral Declaration of Independence (UDI) from Britain. After many discussions with the British government, the country became fully independent, with a black majority government led by Robert Mugabe. In 2002 Zimbabwe was suspended from the Commonwealth and this led to a decision by Robert Mugabe to leave the Commonwealth in 2003. The capital city is Harare and the official language is English.
▶ **Zimbabwean** adj, n.

ˌFred 'Zinnemann /ˈzɪnəmən/ (1907–97) a US film director who won *Oscars for *From Here to Eternity (1953) and A Man for All Seasons (1966) but not for his best-known film, *High Noon (1952). He was born in Austria and went to *Hollywood in 1929. His other films include *Oklahoma! (1955), The Nun's Story (1959) and The Day of the Jackal (1973).

'Zion 'National 'Park /ˈzaɪən/ a US *national park in the state of *Utah, established in 1919. It is known for its canyons (= deep, narrow valleys) with rocks of many beautiful colours and unusual shapes.

'ZIP code /ˈzɪp/ n (AmE) a string of numbers following the name of a state at the end of a postal address in the US. 'ZIP' is an abbreviation for the Zone Improvement Plan, a system introduced by the US Postal Service in 1963. The word 'zip' also suggests speed, because the numbers help mail to be delivered quickly. ZIP codes have five numbers, and ZIP+4 Codes have five numbers and another four numbers separated by a hyphen, e.g. NY 10016–4314. Compare POSTAL DISTRICT.

'Ziploc™ /ˈzɪplɒk; AmE ˈzɪplɑːk/ a US product name for a make of plastic bags with edges that close tightly. Ziploc bags are mostly used for storing food and are made by SC Johnson.

'zoning /'zəʊnɪŋ; *AmE* 'zoʊnɪŋ/ *n* [U] (in US town planning) the process of dividing parts of a town or city into **zones**, areas reserved for houses, businesses or industries.

'Zorro /'zɒrəʊ; *AmE* 'zɔːroʊ/ a character in US *westerns who first appeared in a *comic strip in 1919. Zorro (which means 'the Fox' in Spanish) wears a black mask to hide his real identity when fighting evil. He fights with a sword and sometimes makes a sign like the letter 'Z' with it in the air or even on an enemy's shirt. There have been many Zorro films as well as a Walt *Disney television series.

,Adolph 'Zukor /,ædɒlf 'zuːkə(r); *AmE* ,ædɑːlf 'zuːkər/ (1873–1976) a US film producer. He was born in Hungary and moved to the US in 1888. In 1912 he began the Famous Players film company which later became *Paramount Pictures. He received a special *Oscar in 1949 for his services to the film industry.

the ,Zulu 'War /,zuːluː/ a war in South Africa (1879) between Zulu tribes and British armed forces. After several battles the Zulus were finally defeated at Ulundi.

'Zuni /'zuːni/ *n* (*pl* **Zunis** *or* **Zuni**) a member of a *Native American *Pueblo people in western *New Mexico. Nearly 6 000 live in the town of Zuni Pueblo, which was established about 1695. The Zunis are now mostly farmers. They are known for making jewellery and for their religious dance ceremonies and colourful costumes.

'zwieback /'zwiːbæk/ *n* [U] (*AmE*) a type of dry, hard biscuit or sweet cake that is cut into slices and baked. The word means 'twice baked' in German. Zwieback is often given to babies to chew when their teeth are starting to appear.

Z

Suggestions for further reading

USA

Stephen Ambrose, Bernard DeVoto (editors)
The Journals of Lewis and Clark 1997

Black Elk and John G Neihardt
*Black Elk Speaks: Being the Life Story of
a Holy Man of the Oglala Sioux* 2000

Daniel Boorstin *The Americans:
The Democratic Experience* 1974

Borgna Brunner (editor) *Time Almanac* 2005

Dee Alexander Brown *Bury My Heart at
Wounded Knee* 1970

Bill Bryson *The Lost Continent: Travels in Small-
Town America* 1989

Bill Bryson *Made in America: An Informal History
of the American Language in the United States*
1994

Alistair Cooke *Alistair Cooke's America* 2002

Wayne Craven *American Art: History and Culture*
2002

Alexander Hamilton, John Jay, James Madison
The Federalist Papers 1788

John Hartley and Roberta E Pearson
American Cultural Studies 2000

Barbara Haskell, Lisa Phillips
*The American Century: Art and Culture
1900–1950, The American Century:
Art and Culture 1950–2000* 1999

E D Hirsch, Joseph F Kett, James Trefil
*The New Dictionary of Cultural Literacy:
What Every American Needs to Know* 2002

Robert Hughes *American Visions:
The Epic History of Art in America* 1997

Les Krantz, Jim McCormick (editors)
Peoplepedia 1996

James McPherson *Battle Cry of Freedom:
The Civil War Era* 1988

Joyce Carol Oates (editor)
The Oxford Book of American Short Stories 1994

Thomas C Reeves *Twentieth-Century America:
A Brief History* 2000

Sam Roberts *Who We Are Now: The Changing Face
of America in the Twenty-First Century* 2004

Alexis de Tocqueville *Democracy in America* 1835

Britain

Peter Ackroyd *Illustrated London* 2003

Asa Briggs *A Social History of England* 1999

Bill Bryson *Notes from a Small Island* 1996

Ian Buruma *Voltaire's Coconuts: or Anglomania
in Europe* 1999

David Daiches (editor) *The New Companion to
Scottish Culture* 1993

Niall Ferguson *Empire: How Britain Made the
Modern World* 2003

Kate Fox *Watching the English: The Hidden Rules
of English Behaviour* 2004

Eric Hobsbawm *Industry and Empire:
From 1750 to the Present Day* 1999

Will Hutton *The State We're In* 1996

Philip Jenkins *A History of Modern Wales
1536–1990* 1991

Robert Kee *Ireland: A History* 2003

Michael Lynch *Scotland: A New History* 1992

David Morley and Kevin Robins (editors)
*British Cultural Studies: Geography,
Nationality and Identity* 2001

Office for National Statistics *UK 2005*

Jeremy Paxman *The English:
A Portrait of a People* 1999

Anthony Sampson *Who Runs this Place?:
The Anatomy of Britain in the 21st Century* 2004

Nikolaus Pevsner *The Englishness of English Art*
1956

Simon Schama *A History of Britain, Volumes I–III*
2002

Ben Weinreb and Christopher Hibbert
The London Encyclopedia 1993

Pronunciation and phonetic symbols

Stress

The mark /ˈ/ shows a strong (primary) stress. For example, in the word ˈOxford the first syllable has a primary stress and the second syllable is unstressed. Unstressed syllables are shown without a mark. A stressed syllable is relatively loud, long in duration, said clearly and distinctly, and made noticeable by the pitch of the voice.

The mark /ˌ/ shows a secondary stress, which is felt to be weaker than a strong stress nearby. For example, in ˌOxford Uniˈversity there are two stresses, but the stress on **University** seems stronger because that word carries the main change of pitch (this will generally be a falling pitch when the phrase is said on its own). Many examples with two important words (including names of people such as ˌJohn ˈBrown, ˌJane ˈAusten) have the same secondary-plus-primary stress pattern.

Sometimes the main stress is not on the last word of a phrase. In this case you must look for the last (or only) primary stress mark earlier in the phrase. For example, in ˈOxford Street the main stress (pitch change) is on **Oxford**, with **Street** said on a low-level pitch. Where they are necessary to show the rhythm, secondary stress marks are put after the main stress as in ˈOxford ˌMovement but they do not affect the position of the main stress – again, the main stress is on **Oxford**.

Longer phrases, with more than two important words, are generally shown with several primary stresses. Here the last one should always be made the main stress. For example, in ˈOxford Uniˈversity ˈPress there are three fairly equal beats in the rhythm, but the main fall in pitch should come on **Press**.

Pronunciation

Phonetic symbols are used in the dictionary to show pronunciations (both British and American) for uncommon or difficult words. The pronunciations include stress marks which match those shown on the entry words themselves. If there is a difference between British and American pronunciations, the British one is given first, with *AmE* before the American pronunciation. For example, ˈOxford /ˈɒksfəd; *AmE* ˈɑːksfərd/. Pronunciations are not shown for everyday words (such as **university**, **street**, **movement**) or for common first names (such as **John** or **Jane**). The British pronunciations given are those of younger speakers of General British, which includes RP (Received Pronunciation) and a range of similar accents which are not strongly regional. The American pronunciations chosen are also as far as possible the most general (not associated with any particular region).

Many British speakers use /ɔː/ instead of the diphthong /ʊə/, especially in common words, so that **pure** becomes /pjɔː(r)/, etc. (r) indicates that British pronunciation will have /r/ only if a vowel sound follows directly at the beginning of the next word as in **far away**; otherwise the /r/ is omitted. For American English, all the /r/ sounds should be pronounced.

The mark /~/ over a vowel indicates a nasal quality. Nasalized vowels are often retained in certain words or names taken from French.

Consonants

p	pen	/pen/
b	bad	/bæd/
t	tea	/tiː/
d	did	/dɪd/
k	cat	/kæt/
g	get	/get/
tʃ	chin	/tʃɪn/
dʒ	jam	/dʒæm/
f	fall	/fɔːl/
v	van	/væn/
θ	thin	/θɪn/
ð	this	/ðɪs/
s	see	/siː/
z	zoo	/zuː/
ʃ	shoe	/ʃuː/
ʒ	vision	/ˈvɪʒn/
h	hat	/hæt/
m	man	/mæn/
n	now	/naʊ/
ŋ	sing	/sɪŋ/
l	leg	/leg/
r	red	/red/
j	yes	/jes/
w	wet	/wet/
x	loch	/lɒx/

Vowels and diphthongs

iː	see	/siː/
i	happy	/ˈhæpi/
ɪ	sit	/sɪt/
e	ten	/ten/
æ	cat	/kæt/
ɑː	father	/ˈfɑːðə(r)/
ɒ	hot	/hɒt/ (*BrE*)
ɔː	saw	/sɔː/
ʊ	put	/pʊt/
u	actual	/ˈæktʃuəl/
uː	too	/tuː/
ʌ	cup	/kʌp/
ɜː	fur	/fɜː(r)/
ə	about	/əˈbaʊt/
eɪ	say	/seɪ/
əʊ	go	/gəʊ/ (*BrE*)
oʊ	go	/goʊ/ (*AmE*)
aɪ	five	/faɪv/
aʊ	now	/naʊ/
ɔɪ	boy	/bɔɪ/
ɪə	near	/nɪə(r)/ (*BrE*)
eə	hair	/heə(r)/ (*BrE*)
ʊə	pure	/pjʊə(r)/ (*BrE*)